Interventions for Achievement and Behavior Problems

Edited by

Gary Stoner **Mark R. Shinn** **Hill M. Walker**

University of Oregon

National Association of School Psychologists

First Printing: 1991

Published by The National Association of School Psychologists
8455 Colesville Road, Suite 1000
Silver Spring, MD 20910

ISBN 0-932955-15-0

Printed in the United States of America

Acknowledgments

This Monograph is a product of the contributions and support of many persons whom we wish to thank. First and foremost, we thank all of the contributors who generously donated their valuable knowledge, skills, and time. Next, we thank Lawrence Moran for his thoughtful copy-editing, and Judy Fulwider for her skillful typesetting. Thanks to Karen Bilter, who served as the Editorial Assistant on the project, and helped to keep us organized and on track. We thank NASP Publications Committee members Tom Fagan, Cathy Telzrow, and Alex Thomas who guided the fiscal and production aspects of the project. Finally, we thank all of the University of Oregon School Psychology Program graduate students who donated their careful proofreading services to the project.

Gary Stoner
Mark R. Shinn
Hill M. Walker

From NASP Publications Policy Handbook

The content of this document reflects the ideas and positions of the authors. The responsibility lies solely with the authors and does not necessarily reflect the position or ideas of the National Association of School Psychologists.

List of Contributors

Richard W. Albin, PhD
Assistant Professor
Specialized Training Program
University of Oregon
Eugene, OR 97403

Anita Archer, PhD
Special Education
San Diego State University
San Diego, CA 98182-0144

Andrea S. Canter, PhD
School Psychology Staff
Minneapolis Public Schools
254 Upton Ave., So.
Minneapolis, MN 55405

Douglas Carnine, PhD
Professor of Education
Teacher Education
University of Oregon
Eugene, OR 97403

Judith J. Carta, PhD
Juniper Garden's Children's Project
1614 Washington Blvd.
Kansas City, KS 66102

Ann Casey, PhD, NCSP
Coordinator
Anwhatin Junior High S/MS Program
Minneapolis Public Schools
256 Upton Ave., So.
Minneapolis, MN 55405

John Cawley, PhD
Professor of Education
Department of Learning and Instruction
State University off New York–Buffalo
553 Christopher Baldy Hall
Buffalo, NY 14260

Lynette Chandler, PhD
Assistant Professor
Department of Special Education
Southern Illinois University at Carbondale
Carbondale, IL 62901

Elaine Clark, PhD
Educational Psychology
University of Utah
1251 E600S
Salt Lake City, UT 84102-3273

Geoff Colvin, PhD
Lane County Educational Service District
1200 Highway 99
P.O. Box 2680
Eugene, OH 97402

Stanley L. Deno, PhD
Special Education
University of Minnesota
178 Pillsbury Dr., SE
Minneapolis, MN 55455

Donald D. Deshler, PhD
Director
University of Kansas Institute for
    Research in Learning Disabilities
223 Carruth-O'Leary Hall
Lawrence, KS 66045

George DuPaul, PhD
Department of Psychiatry
University of Massachusetts
    Medical Center
Worchester, MA 01655

Stephen N. Elliott, PhD
Department of Educational Psychology
University of Wisconsin–Madison
1025 West Johnson St.
Madison, WI 53706

Christine A. Espin
Special Education
University of Minnesota
178 Pillsbury Dr., SE
Minneapolis, MN 55455

Kathleen Fad, PhD
Special Education
University of Texas at Austin
Education Building 306
Austin, TX 78712

Steve Forness, PhD
Professor, Inpatient School
    Principal, and UAP Director
Mental Retardation and Child
    Psychiatry Program
University of California, Los Angeles
760 Westwood Plaza
Los Angeles, CA 90024

Douglas Fuchs, PhD
Associate Professor of Special Education
Box 328, Peabody College
Vanderbilt University
Nashville, TN 37203

Kimberly Galant, MS, CCC–S/LP
Program Director
Child Development Center
United Cerebral Palsy of Tampa Bay, Inc.
10891 102nd Ave., N
Seminole, FL 34648

Ralph Gardner III, PhD
Department of Educational Services
    and Research
The Ohio State University
1945 North High St.
Columbus, OH 43201-1172

Gary Germann, MS
Director of Special Education
Pine County Special Education
    Cooperative
P.O. Box 228
Sandstone, MN 55072

James Gilliam, PhD
Special Education
University of Texas at Austin
Education Building 306
Austin, TX 78712

Mary Gleason, PhD
Assistant Professor
Teacher Education
University of Oregon
Eugene, OR 97403

Charles Greenwood, PhD
Juniper Garden's Children's Project
1614 Washington Blvd.
Kansas City, KS 66102

Bonnie Grossen, PhD
Teacher Education
University of Oregon
Eugene, OR 97403

David Guevremont, PhD
Department of Psychiatry
55 Lake Avenue, North
University of Massachusetts Medical
    Center
Worchester, MA 01655

Daniel P. Hallahan, PhD
Curry School of Education
University of Virginia
Charlotesville, VA 22903-2495

Michelle Hecht
School Psychology Program
Department of Educational Psychology
N548 Elliott Hall
University of Minnesota
Minneapolis, MN 5455

Timothy E. Heron, EdD
Department of Educational Services
    and Research
The Ohio State University
1945 North High St.
Columbus, OH 43201-1172

William L. Heward, EdD
Department of Educational Services
    and Research
The Ohio State University
1945 North High St.
Columbus, OH 43201-1172

Robert H. Horner, PhD
Director
Specialized Training Program
University of Oregon
Eugene, OR 97403

Steven V. Horton, PhD
Assistant Professor
Special Education
College of Education
Wichita State University
Wichita, KS 67208

William Jenson, PhD
Educational Psychology
University of Utah
327 Milton Bennion Hall
Salt Lake City, UT 84112

Kenneth Kavale, PhD
Professor
Special Education Division
College of Education
N 259 Lindquist Center
University of Iowa
Iowa City, IA 52244

Thomas Kehle, PhD
Department of Educational Psychology
U-64
University of Connecticut
249 Glenbrook Road
Storrs, CT 06269

Thomas R. Kratochwill, PhD
Department of Educational Psychology
University of Wisconsin–Madison
1025 West Johnson St.
Madison, WI 53706

Timothy J. Landrum
Curry School of Education
University of Virginia
Charlottesville, VA 22903-2495

John Wills Lloyd, PhD
Curry School of Education
University of Virginia
Charlottesville, VA 22903-2495

Thomas C. Lovitt, EdD
Professor of Special Education
Experimental Education Unit
College of Education
University of Washington
Seattle, WA 98195

Larry Maheady, PhD
Department of Education
State University of New York at Fredonia
Fredonia, NY 14063

G. Roy Mayer, EdD
Professor
Division of Administration and Counseling
School of Education
California State University, Los Angeles
Los Angeles, CA 90032

Scott McConnell, PhD
Associate Professor
School Psychology Program
Department of Educational Psychology
N548 Elliott Hall
University of Minnesota
Minneapolis, MN 55455

Philip C. McKnight, PhD
Professor
Department of Curriculum & Instruction
406 Bailey Hall
University of Kansas
Lawrence, KS 66045

Gloria Miller, PhD
Barnwell College Bldg.
Department of Psychology
University of South Carolina
Columbia, SC 29208

Victor Nolet
Teacher Education
University of Oregon
Eugene, OR 97403

Beatrice A. Okyere, PhD
Department of Educational
    Services and Research
The Ohio State University
1945 North High St.
Columbus, OH 43201-1172

Robert E. O'Neill, PhD
Research Associate
Specialized Training Program
University of Oregon
Eugene, OR 97403

Pamela G. Osnes, MA
Assistant Professor
The Florida Mental Health Institute
Department of Child and Family Services
University of South Florida
13301 Bruce B. Downs Blvd.
Tampa, FL 33612-3899

Kathleen Paget, PhD
Department of Psychology
University of South Carolina
Columbia, SC 29208

Renee Parmar, PhD
Assistant Professor
Department of Learning and Instruction
State University of New York–Buffalo
553 Christopher Baldy Hall
Buffalo, NY 14260

Gerald Patterson, PhD
Oregon Social Learning Center
207 E. 5th Street, Suite 202
Eugene, OR 97401

David Peterson, NCSP
Director of Support Services
Northern Suburban Special Education
  District
760 Red Oak Lane
Highland Park, IL 60035

Rene Prayzer, MA
Upper Arlington Schools
Columbus, OH 43220

Ronald Prinz
Barnwell College Bldg.
Department of Psychology
University of South Carolina
Columbia, SC 29208

David Putnam, Jr., PhD
Staff Psychologist
Charter Lake Hospital
3500 Riverside Dr.
Macon, GA 31210

John Reid, PhD
Oregon Social Learning Center
207 E. 5th Ave., Suite 202
Eugene, OR 97401

William M. Reynolds, PhD
Professor
Department of Educational Psychology
University of Wisconsin–Madison
1025 West Johnson Street
Madison, WI 53706

Herbert Rieth, EdD
Professor and Chair
Special Education
Peabody College
Vanderbilt University
Box 328
Nashville, TN 37203

Ed Sabornie, PhD
College of Education and Psychology
Department of Curriculum and
  Instruction
North Carolina State University
402 Poe Hall, Box 7801
Raleigh, NC 27695-7801

Jean B. Schumaker, PhD
Coordinator of Research
University of Kansas Institute for
  Research in Learning Disabilities
223 Carruth-O'Leary Hall
Lawrence, KS 66045

Melvyn Semmel, EdD
Professor and Director
Special Education Research Laboratory
Special Education
University of California at Santa Barbara
Santa Barbara, CA 93106

Herbert Severson, PhD
Oregon Research Institute
1899 Willamette St.
Eugene, OR 97401

Paul Sindelar, PhD
Professor and Chair
College of Education
Department of Special Education
University of Florida
G 315 Norman Hall
Gainesville, FL 32611

Randy Sprick, PhD
Teaching Strategies, Inc.
P.O. Box 5205
Eugene, OR 97405

Kim Stoddard, PhD
Assistant Professor
College of Education
Department of Special Education
University of Louisville
Louisville, KY 40222

Trevor F. Stokes, PhD
Professor
The Florida Mental Health Institute
Department of Child and Family Services
University of South Florida
13301 Bruce B. Downs Blvd.
Tampa, FL 33612-3899

Gary Stoner, PhD
Assistant Professor
School Psychology Program
Division of Special Education
   and Rehabilitation
University of Oregon
Eugene, OR 97403

Laura Stough, MA
Special Education
University of Texas at Austin
Education Building 306
Austin, TX 78712

Beth Sulzer-Azaroff, PhD
Professor
Department of Psychology
University of Massachusetts
Amherst, MA 01003

W. D. Tilly III, MS
School Psychology Program
Division of Special Education
   and Rehabilitation
University of Oregon
Eugene, OR 97403

Gerald Tindal, PhD
Assistant Professor
Teacher Education
University of Oregon
Eugene, OR 97403

Hill Walker, PhD
Associate Dean
College of Education
University of Oregon
Eugene, OR 97403

Joseph C. Witt, PhD
Psychology Department
Louisiana State University
Baton Rouge, LA 70803-5501

Leslie Zoref, PhD
Oregon Research Institute
1899 Willamette St.
Eugene, OR 97401

Preface

This monograph is organized around several major themes, namely: the changing context for the professional practice of school psychology, classroom- and school-based prevention and intervention programs, and professional training issues specific to intervention-oriented school psychology. We concur with the leadership of NASP that the profession of school psychology is moving toward an emphasis on solving educationally relevant problems, in contrast to identifying problems and serving as gate-keepers (i.e., into special education classes). This movement is consistent with current debates and rhetoric surrounding the restructuring of regular and special education, as well as more broad-based school reform. Chapters 1, 2, and 3 address numerous reform and restructuring issues, and their relationship to interventions in schools and classrooms. It is important to note that assessment issues are not neglected herein. Rather, consistent with the recent professional school psychology and special education literatures, the need to carefully link assessment and intervention has been emphasized throughout the monograph.

Within the changing context of educational service delivery, professional functioning for school psychologists will require proficiency in designing, implementing, and evaluating interventions for achievement and behavior problems. These skills are emphasized throughout this book, along with a focus on teaching and learning of skills and knowledge by children, parents, and professionals. Also emphasized is the *prevention* of problems via re-arranging instructional environments, teaching prerequisite skills and knowledge, and designing instruction aimed at the mastery of skills needed for competent, independent learning. Chapters are organized by the following general topics: Evaluation Issues (Chapters 4 and 5); General Intervention Strategies that cut across age and grade levels (Chapters 6 through 12); Interventions at the Preschool Level (Chapters 13 and 14), Elementary Level (Chapters 15 through 19), and Secondary Level (Chapters 20 through 23); and, Interventions for Specific Problems (Chapters 24 through 32). The monograph closes with two chapters regarding specific professional training issues that focus on the knowledge and skills needed by pre-service and inservice professionals to function effectively as instructional and behavioral interventionists.

It is our hope that professionals will find the contents of this volume to constitute a comprehensive set of ideas and procedures that contribute significantly to the education of *all* children.

Gary Stoner
Mark R. Shinn
Hill M. Walker

Table of Contents

Part 1: Introduction

Part 2: Evaluation Issues

Part 6:
Training Intervention Oriented School Psychologists

Foreword

Wesley C. Becker
University of Oregon

In February of 1971, nearly 20 years ago, I wrote what is quoted below as an introduction to a paper presented at the Florida State University Conference on "New Roles for School Psychologists." Many of the problems described in that paper are still present in the practice of school psychology today. In the edited collection which is the body of this book, I finally see a hope that school psychologists may be trained in and apply the intervention skills needed to be the "teacher's best friend" when it comes to solving classroom problems.

I stated at that time: "Many current problems in education can be traced to practices, presumably derived from psychological research, which have had the effect of encouraging teachers to get rid of their teaching failures rather than learning to deal with them. Many of these doubtful practices center around the use of tests by school psychologists to 'diagnose problems' and make recommendations on placement in special classes, treatment programs, the grouping of slow and fast learners, or grouping on the basis of readiness tests. Historically, many of these practices were generated from the application of a medical model to problems in clinical psychology which was subsequently transferred to educational problems. The basic idea was that if a child is failing to learn or behave appropriately in school, there is something wrong with the child. . . ."

I then proceeded to describe in the paper some of the ways children with problems were characerized then. "Some children have low IQs and it is assumed that they learn at slower rates and should be taught less. [This assumption has been clearly contradicted by recent research (Gersten, Becker, Heiry, & White, 1984)]. . . . Another kind of practice which actively leads to not trying to solve problems is diagnosing the failure as due to a lack of readiness. Often readiness is assumed to come with maturation, so that there is little the teacher can do but wait. In the meantime, valuable instructional time is lost and the not-ready children get further behind their peers. . . . However, more enlightened educators today (1971) see this 'lack of readiness' as an absence of certain preskills which can be taught. In the area of reading, however, the diagnosis of what needs to be taught often misses the mark. Chidlren are given much practice in visual discriminations ('picture reading') and training in motor skills (walking a balance beam), little of which involves the skills needed in discriminating letters or tying 'saying sounds' to the letter symbols. That current readiness tests (remember, 1971) miss the mark is illustrated by findings in one of our Follow Through sites. The kindergarten children pretested at the 50th percentile on the Metropolitan Reading Readiness Test (and could not read). They posttested six months later at only the 52nd percentile but now they all could read."

I went on to describe problems of

poorly motivated students. "Some children are difficult to manage and motivate using traditional methods and curricula. School psychologists in the past have often supported the teacher's inclination to blame the child (or his family), by labelling the child as emotionally disturbed and recommending treatment outside of the classroom — treatment which usually was not available or which had little effect on classroom progress when it was available. Much current research (see Becker, Thomas, & Carnine, 1969) supports the conclusion that most such problems can be handled in the classroom if the teacher is trained to use effective reinforcers to motivate learning and to provide instructional programs that do in fact teach the skills the child needs to succeed in that class."

We found in our work in the Follow Through Program that "economically disadvantaged children had commonly been given all of the above labels and more. . . . New labels were also coming into vogue. Psychologists came to the 'aid' of teachers with a new diagnosis for children with normal IQs who do not learn. They are said to have specific learning disabilities, again requiring special treatment by experts. . . . For the most part, the children so labelled had not been taught to read (cf., Haring & Bateman, 1977). . . . It is hard for us to believe that 25% of middle-class children have caught this disease. . . "

In our view then and now: "There is a need for new roles for school psychologists. . . . Most psychologists working in schools have not been trained to apply the knowledge of learning processes to classroom problems. They have been taught to stay out of the classroom and pretend they know nothing about instructional processes. In fact, it has only been recently that the Division of School Psychology of the APA has even suggested that the training of school psychologists include training in curriculum and instruction."

"There is an obvious need for a drastic change in the orientation and use of psychologists in the schools. . . . They need to be trained to provide teachers with information and procedures that we know can produce effective learning conditions. . . . They need to use curriculum relevant tests . . . to find out what students know and what they need to learn . . . and to help teachers to apply the best instructional technology available. The new school psychologist needs to be an expert in instruction and curricula, bringing to bear in the classroom knowledge derived from research on what it takes to make learning happen."

While the problems I described in 1971 have not gone away, the collection of intervention practices for school psychologists in this volume suggest that things are changing. They constitute first, a "proclamation" that school psychology is changing its focus to one of problem solving in the schools: second, they constitute clear evidence that many of the leaders in the field are working hard for that change; and third, they provide me with new hope for the viability and educational relevance of the field. This collection is potentially a valuable resource for both the trainers of school psychologists and those already "out there" desiring to upgrade their practices.

REFERENCES

Gersten, R. M., Becker, W. C., & White, W. A. T. (1984). Entry IQ and yearly academic growth of children in Direct Instruction programs: A longitudinal study of low SES children. *Educational Evaluation and Policy Analysis, 6,* 109–121.

Becker, W. C., Thomas, D. R., & Carnine, D. (1969). *Reducing behavior problems: An operant conditioning guide for teachers.* ERIC. Urbana, IL: Clearinghouse in Early Childhood.

Haring, N. G., & Bateman, B. (1977). *Teaching the learning disabled child.* Englewood Cliffs, NJ: Prentice-Hall.

School Psychologists' Roles and Functions: Integration Into the Regular Classroom

Steven R. Forness
University of California, Los Angeles

Kenneth A. Kavale
University of Iowa

The school psychologist has long been the professional most allied with children with school learning and behavior problems. Long before the advent of mandatory special education programs, the school psychologist was the primary consultant to teachers and parents of such children, often filling a service vacuum in the absence of any systematic special help or services. Prior to the last two decades, such programs, especially for children with relatively less noticeable problems such as mild mental retardation, learning disabilities, or behavior disorders, were not universally available; the school psychologist often represented the only source of potential assistance to such youngsters. With rapid growth of special education services in the past decade, however, the role of the school psychologist has been transformed remarkably. Both school psychology and special education are just beginning to come to terms with this transformation, and the present chapter is an attempt to capture the thrust of these changes and what they might portend for both disciplines.

Special education itself has been in transition and turmoil for the past decade or more. Its programs generally are determined not by empirical evidence or professional experience but by legal action or legislative fiat (Forness, 1981; Gerber 1984; Lambert, 1988). It depends largely on whims of regular education teachers as its initial referral source (Stainback & Stainback, 1984). It relies on psychoeducational assessment instruments of dubious reliability (Berk, 1984) that seem capricious in classifying special education pupils (Ysseldyke, Algozzine, & Epps, 1983). It focuses on mainstreaming with little compelling evidence for the efficacy of such an approach (Forness & Kavale, 1984; Reynolds, 1988). Its service delivery system places both regular and special education teachers in a position of quite limited influence or prestige in that placement decisions are often made by ancillary professionals not working in classroom settings (Forness, Sinclair, & Russell, 1984). Finally, its research base provides relatively few answers about effective classroom intervention (Iano, 1987; Stainback & Stainback, 1984). Although it is hazardous to ascribe responsibility for such a parlous state of affairs, this chapter will supply evidence that the field of psychology, school psychology in particular, must share a major part of the blame because of its failure to recognize that its principal role, determining eligibility for special education, is no longer appropriate and that other critical school psychology roles are being neglected.

Before making this case, however, it is important to note the interdependency between school psychology and special education. Special education indeed has its very beginnings in the field of psychology. The origin of special education is the prototypic teaching experiment of a special child in 1800 by a physician who was essentially functioning as a psychologist, or at least in the psychological tradition (Shattuck, 1980). This early legacy of psychology continues largely unbroken into this country's modern special education era (Forness & Kavale, 1984). The founders of modern-day special education, such as Kirk, Dunn, Cruickshank, and others, were initially trained as psychologists. It is, in fact, only the *current* generation of special educators, largely trained by these psychologists, who were the first to receive doctorates in special education departments as special educators.

The case to be made against psychology, however, rests largely on certain outmoded psychological traditions — outmoded in the sense that, although they may apparently still serve psychologists well *as psychologists*, they have long outlived their usefulness in special education. The discipline of psychology itself faces many fundamental conceptual difficulties (Meehl, 1978; Sarason, 1981; Staats, 1983; Valentine, 1982). The need for the field of special education, therefore, is to "de-psychologize" and thus disabuse itself of certain psychological practices and procedures that perpetuate the state of affairs described earlier.

HOW SCHOOL PSYCHOLOGY CONTINUES TO SHAPE SPECIAL EDUCATION

More than 15 years ago, an article entitled "Educational Prescription for the School Psychologist" began with the following statement:

> The psychologist is not a well man. His malady, while not particularly acute, is nonetheless a chronic one, endemic to his profession. The patient often presents such symptoms as distension of the referral . . . rupture of the arteries of communication . . . atrophied recommendations . . . and accumulation of jargon

deposits in the report. . . . The syndrome might best be described as a "paralysis of the analysis" and a discussion of its pathology forms the basis for this paper. (Forness, 1970, p. 96).

The paper went on to make the case against the relevance of school psychology in special education and to support a prescription for this malady. However, the syndrome has since gotten worse; and even stronger medicine, if not radical surgery, is called for.

Lest anyone doubt that the practice of psychology still persists in special education, both indirectly as an influence and even more directly in the functioning of school psychologists, consider the following. A number of studies have examined outcomes of individual education planning (IEP) meetings with regard to types of professionals who seem to exert the most influence upon critical special education decisions made in these meetings (Frankenberger & Harper, 1986; Gilliam, 1979; Gilliam & Coleman, 1981; Smith & Knoff, 1981; Turnbull, Strickland, & Brantley, 1982; Yoshida, 1983; Ysseldyke, Algozzine, & Epps, 1983; Ysseldyke, Thurlow, et al., 1983). Note that IEP meetings have largely become the primary forum in which special education decisions are made in regard to diagnosis, eligibility, classroom placement, educational goals, and assignment of staff responsibility for each child entering special education (Forness, 1979). The IEP is essentially the cornerstone of the special education referral process.

Who has the most influence in these meetings? Is it the parent, who has raised a child with suspected learning or behavior problems from birth and therefore has a wealth of developmental experience that bears on issues at hand? Is it the child's current teacher, who has spent weeks or even months in daily contact with this child, most of them in pursuit of answers on how best to teach or manage the child in the classroom? Is it even the school principal, who is responsible for the welfare of all teachers and children in the school and who may have already been involved, indirectly or even directly, in seeking solutions for this child's schooling?

It is, of course, none of these. The professional with the most influence on IEP decisions is the person who probably has spent the *least* time with the child, both directly *and* indirectly. It is the professional who has spent this limited time evaluating the child with relatively unreliable measures, in a context usually far removed from the ecological validity of the classroom, and who consequently is most likely to determine a diagnosis that is, at best, often irrelevant to classroom functioning and, at worst, occasionally compromising to the child's future school progress. It is, of course, the school psychologist.

The studies cited earlier seem to suggest, rather convincingly, that school psychologists and/or test evaluation results almost inevitably bear the greatest influence on outcome of special education decisions. Such influence occurs in those instances when expectations, prior to IEP meetings, suggest that parents, teachers, or others *should* be the most influential on outcome of special education decisions. Such influence occurs in those instances when expectations, prior to IEP meetings, suggest that parents, teachers, or others *should* be the most influential. It also has been found that school psychologists are not generally active in preparing parents or others to participate more fully in such meetings (Vaughn, Bos, & Laskey, 1988). It should be noted, however, that the school psychologist is essentially an "uninvited guest" at such meetings. The only persons actually *required* to be present at an IEP meeting, as stated in Public Law 94-142, are the parent, the child's teacher, and a representative of special education. The school psychologist, indeed, is not even mentioned in the entire text of PL 94-142. The question then arises as to exactly how helpful the school psychologist actually is in this process currently.

PSYCHOLOGICAL EVALUATION: DOES IT HELP?

The reason the school psychologist was not mentioned in PL 94-142 is open to speculation. It is clear that many procedures introduced by this legislation were aimed quite directly at limiting certain abuses of psychological testing in special education. Most readers are familiar with these abuses, some of which were most clearly brought to public attention in the state of California in a series of class-action lawsuits, such as *Covarrubias, Diana,* and *Larry P.* (Forness, 1985). These cases involved not only misuse of IQ tests in determining educational placement but misdiagnosis of educational needs as well. These and related problems in psychological testing have been reviewed extensively by Swanson and Watson (1982), and continuing adverse influence of testing in the area of mental retardation has been discussed by Zucker and Polloway (1987). Many strictures in PL 94-142 were therefore directly or indirectly targeted at school psychology (e.g., inclusion of more than one criterion test in classification, classroom observation of learning-disabled children prior to diagnosis, use of multidisciplinary teams, due process, and several others).

While many issues in testing center on the use of IQ in placing children in special classes for the mentally retarded, other psychological evaluation problems with other exceptionalities continue to be apparent. For example, in the area of learning disabilities, IQ results frequently are misused in other ways. Recategorization of IQ subtests to denote underlying types of learning disabilities, for example, continues as a common practice, even though extensive empirical analyses show little, if any, support for such procedures (Kavale & Forness, 1984). Furthermore, the use of discrepancy criteria between IQ and achievement test results to establish the diagnosis of learning disability also persists, despite the fact that one can affect the determination of severity simply by choosing from among a variety of available formulae (Algozzine & Ysseldyke, 1987; Forness, Sinclair, & Guthrie, 1983; Sinclair & Alexson, 1986). Indeed, the entire battery of tests used in diagnosing learning disabilities has been under

TABLE 1
Technical Adequacy of Selected Tests

Type of Test: Test Name	Norms	Validity	Reliability
Intellectual			
WISC–R	+	+	+
Stanford-Binet	+	–	–
PPVT	–	+	+
Achievement			
PIAT	+	+	+
Woodcock Reading	+	+	+
WRAT	–	–	–
Psychologic Processes			
Bender	–	–	–
ITPA	–	–	–
VMI	–	–	–

Adapted from tabular data appearing in Berk (1984, p. 58–59). Plus (+) indicates minumum standards have been met in the area; minus (–) indicates standards not met.

consistently serious attack (Coles, 1978, 1987).

Consider Table 1, for example, in which reliability, validity, and adequacy of normative data are rated for three of the more commonly used measures in each of the three areas currently used for assessment and determination of learning disabilities. The data in Table 1 have been adapted from a review in which the latest edition of the joint *Standards for Educational and Psychological Tests* were applied to these instruments (Berk, 1984). Note that a number of instruments common in the armamentarium of most school psychologists fail to meet acceptable standards in at least one, and often in all three, criterion areas (Bennett, 1983; Forness, 1982; Fuchs, Fuchs, Benowitz, & Barringer, 1987). Even achievement tests, arguably the most defensible of such instruments, have been soundly criticized for their lack of relevance to curricular considerations (Shapiro & Derr, 1987). Learning disability specialists, who operate under a psychologically oriented model, use the worst of the three types of tests, the process ones (e.g., Bender, Wepman, Detroit Tests of Learning Aptitude, etc.), a great deal; but remedial reading specialists, who operate under a pedagogically oriented model, use them relatively infrequently, if at all (German, Johnson, & Schneider, 1985).

In the area of behavioral or emotional disorders, the situation may be even worse. We need look no further for problems inherent in this area than to some telling prevalence figures. The reported percentage, for example, of handicapped children served who are seriously emotionally disturbed is 27.3 in Utah and 2.5 in California (U.S. Department of Education, 1988). That one state serves, proportionately, more than 10 times as many of its handicapped children in a single category than a state in a neighboring region suggests the capriciousness of our identification and diagnostic systems in this area. Consider yet another example, from a single state, in which children in the seriously emotionally disturbed category decreased by nearly 60% in 5 years, while children in a related category, learning disabilities, increased over 150% in the same period (Forness, 1985). There do not seem to be obvious programmatic variables that would tend to explain these discrepancies (Center & Obringer, 1987). Instead, these results seem more the result of diagnostic inconsistencies.

Smith, Wood, and Grimes (1988) have reviewed available research and current practice comprehensively in the category of emotionally disturbed/behavior-disordered in special education. Their conclusions suggest as dismal a picture as in the fields of mental retardation or learning disabilities. Lack of adequate diagnostic measures, inconsistencies in their interpretation, capriciousness in identification, and diminished relevance of diagnostic batteries to intervention are but a few of the problems they document in considerable detail. The profile of these programs has indeed not changed appreciably in terms of identification procedures in the past two decades (Grosenick, George, & George, 1987).

Given such difficulty in this admittedly complex area of special education, school psychologists have begun to cast about for new ways to determine a diagnosis of behavioral or emotional disorders. In at least one state, for example, they have proposed to borrow from yet another discipline, psychiatry (California Association for School Psychologists, 1984). In this proposal, selected *DSM III* psychiatric diagnoses have been equated with certain of the five criteria currently used to define serious emotional disturbance under PL 94-142. The intent was thus to use psychiatric diagnoses to determine special education eligibility and even to exclude certain children from the category of serious emotional disturbance (SED), such as those with a diagnosis of conduct disorders. The problem of exclusion of socially maladjusted children from the SED category has long been a matter of some concern (Peterson, 1986). The diagnosis of conduct disorders, in many such *DSM III* proposals, has been equated by school psychologists with "social maladjustment."

The folly of such an approach is apparent not only in the demonstrated lack of concordance between *DSM III* and standard psychoeducational test criteria (Barnes & Forness, 1982; Sinclair & Forness, 1988) but also in the wide variability of special education classroom placements within each *DSM III* diagnostic group. In regard to the latter, Table 2 is a summary of data on 120 children admitted to the UCLA Neuropsychiatric Hospital for behavior disorders who were later returned to schools in the community (Sinclair & Forness, 1983). It depicts their post-discharge special education classroom levels by major psychiatric diagnostic category, according to *DSM III*.

Note that subjects in each diagnostic group range across nearly every level of regular and special education classroom placement, indicating little or no pattern of relationship between a child's psychiatric diagnosis and his or her need for special education. These findings have essentially been replicated with another sample of 350 outpatient children in the same hospital, using even more refined diagnostic groups (Sinclair, Forness, & Alexson, 1985) as well as with a sample of 160 youngsters in a psychiatric hospital in Iowa (McGinnis & Forness, 1988). There were additional findings that counterindicated the school psychology proposal to equate mental health diagnoses to special education eligibility. For example, in a subsample of 12 "psychotic" children in the former study, not one returned to an SED classroom; and in the latter study most of the conduct-disordered children *did* return to SED programs. Furthermore, that psychologists might use such techniques as projective testing to assist in *DSM III* differentiation has also been soundly criticized (Gittelman, 1980).

This "calibration fantasy" (i.e., that critical intellectual or behavioral characteristics can be measured in a way that determines treatment) has compromised the eligibility decisions of almost every subspecialty of education of the handicapped. In relation to special education, then, psychological evaluation has been shown to be not only of limited validity for diagnosis but also of questionable relevance to intervention.

MISGUIDED PSYCHOLOGY AND SPECIAL EDUCATION INTERVENTION

It is exactly the question of relevance to intervention that has characterized the

TABLE 2
Classroom Placement by Psychiatric Diagnosis

Diagnostic Disorders	Special Education Level[a]					
	1	2	3	4	5	Total
Mental Retardation	2	1	5	4	1	13
Schizophremia/Autism	0	2	8	8	4	22
Somatic	6	3	1	1	0	11
Anxiety/Affective	4	2	4	0	0	10
Personality	2	1	4	0	1	8
Conduct, Aggressive	1	7	4	4	0	16
Conduct, Nonaggressive	0	1	4	3	3	11
Adjustment	3	1	6	2	2	14
Attention Deficit	1	4	8	1	1	15
Total	**19**	**22**	**44**	**23**	**12**	**120**

[a] 1, regular class; 2, resource room; 3, self-contained class for mild handicaps; 4, self-contained class for severe handicaps; 5, residential class.

Adapted from data in Sinclair and Forness (1983).

principal difficulty with school psychology's influence on special education. The modern-era founders of special education, referred to earlier, were developmental or clinical psychologists. Quite fortunately for special education, they were co-opted into the field because they clearly saw the need for more systematic intervention with groups of handicapped children who were not being adequately served by educators. They brought with them, however, the practice of careful differential diagnosis prior to treatment that still characterizes the field of psychology today. This approach is implicitly involved in problems, just described, with the school psychologist's quintessential role in individual educational planning.

Related to this approach, however, is yet another difficulty. At least until the past two decades, intervention by training or education in groups, as opposed to intervention by therapy with individuals, seemed *not* to characterize psychology. Almost all special education interventions, on the other hand, are conducted with groups of children in the classroom, unlike interventions in the tradition of psychology, which are more likely to take place in individual therapy sessions, the more recent tendency in psychology toward

group therapies notwithstanding. Thus the type of intervention clearly called for, in most special education situations, did *not* place these early "special education" psychologists on familiar ground. Special education intervention thus tended not to evolve as completely as it should because its founders came from a psychology background that did not emphasize group approaches.

That the field of special education, as developed by these early psychologists, continues to put less of a premium on intervention than diagnosis may be rather obvious from a survey of recent special education literature. Classification of articles published over a recent 3-year period in journals of the three major divisions of the Council for Exceptional Children are presented in Table 3 (note however that *Learning Disability Quarterly* removed itself from division sponsorship during this 3-year period).

The data in Table 3 were obtained by independent classification of total articles published over a 3-year period from mid-1982 to mid-1985 in these journals. Classification of articles, excluding book reviews and editorials but including all review and research articles, was made on the basis of whether the article dealt

TABLE 3
Classification of Articles in Selected Special Education Journals from 1982 to 1985

Journal	Number of Articles by Primary Topic			Percent of Articles on Intervention
	Characteristics	Intervention	Total	
Behavioral Disorders	53	24	77	31.2%
Education and Training of Mentally Retarded	101	47	148	31.7%
Learning Disability Quarterly	120	42	162	25.9%
All Journals	274	113	387	29.2%

primarily with special education intervention or primarily with characteristics or related matters pertaining to exceptional children (e.g., diagnosis, attitudes, social interaction not involving intervention, and the like). Classification was determined by independent agreement of at least two of three judges (special education teachers) that the article belonged in either the "intervention" or "characteristics" category. As the data in Table 3 suggest, classification articles outnumber intervention articles by a factor of more than two to one. These data are similar to the findings reported by Scruggs and Mastropierri (1985) and by Swanson and Trahan (1986).

A related issue is whether even this relatively small body of scholarship or scientific inquiry has led to productive outcomes for special education intervention. Such a question cannot be answered completely in this limited space, of course, but there can be some indication through examining research syntheses of various areas of special education intervention. Research synthesis has been attempted empirically in a number of critical education areas only recently, through meta-analytic findings. An illustrative sample of nine available meta-analyses is presented in Table 4. These results are derived from both secondary and original data reported in Kavale and Forness (1985, 1987), with one exception as noted.

Presented in Table 4 are the overall mean effect sizes (*ES*) and standard deviations (*SD*) for nine areas of special

education intervention studies. These constitute a relatively comprehensive sample of critical special education approaches. They are further arranged in Table 4 somewhat in the temporal order in which they might be attempted in the course of a child's progress through the special education system (i.e., finding a smaller regular classroom, placing a child in a special class if regular class placement is not sufficient, devising special language or perceptual approaches if direct behavioral approaches fail to work, using medical intervention such as psychopharmacology or diet restriction as a last resort, etc.)

In Table 4, most effect sizes are well below .5. This finding suggests that the aggregate *ES* across available empirical studies for each intervention represents less than half a standard deviation advantage for the treated groups, as compared to placebos or controls. Exceptions are special education placement, in which the negative *ES* implies a disadvantage, and somewhat larger *ES*s for both behavioral interventions and stimulant drugs. Note, however, that standard deviations of *ES*s are typically as great in magnitude as mean *ES*s themselves, if not quite a bit larger. This result implies a great deal of unexplained variation across studies, unfortunately suggesting no clear resolution as to differential effectiveness of various special education interventions as a result of this research. There are a number of reasons for such a disappointing outcome. In relation to the issue at

TABLE 4
Summary of Meta-Analyses in Special Education Research

Intervention	Number of Studies	ES	SD
Reducing class size	77	.31	.70
Special class placement	50	-.12	.65
Behavior modificaton	41	.93	1.16
Psycholinguistic training	34	.39	.54
Perceptual motor training	180	.08	.27
Modality instruction	39	.15	.28
Stimulant drugs	135	.58	.61
Psychotropic drugs	70	.30	.75
Diet intervention	23	.12	.42

Adapted from data in Kavale and Forness (1985) with the exception of the Modality instruction data from Kavale and Forness (1987); Behavior modification from Skiba and Casey (1985).

hand, however, it has been discussed at length elsewhere (Kavale & Forness, 1985) how the legacy of psychology appears to have resulted in a research model that relies far too heavily on atheoretical accumulation of empirical data obscured by methods of statistical significance testing that result in minimal scientific progress in special education. In addition we have shown how complex interactions among learner, instructional, and environmental variables have not been captured sufficiently through research approaches in psychology, especially in relation to classroom instruction.

GETTING ALONG WITHOUT SCHOOL PSYCHOLOGISTS IN SPECIAL EDUCATION

Given that the role of the school psychologist, or at least the most problematic aspect of it, involves identification and diagnosis, could special education survive without school psychologists as they function now? The answer is that, at least in several reported instances, it has. Moreover, it has done so quite well.

For example, it has been shown that, for most children initially referred for special education, teachers or parents usually initiate the referral and that the role of school psychologist has been mainly to confirm the diagnosis (Adelman, 1978; Ysseldyke & Algozzine, 1981). Other studies have shown that few of the data in traditional assessment reports are actually useful for determining the needs of children with behavior disorders and learning disabilities (McGinnis, Kiraly, & Smith, 1984; Ysseldyke, 1986; Ysseldyke & Algozzine, 1981; Ysseldyke, Algozzine, & Epps, 1983; Zabel, Peterson, Smith, & White, 1981). These reports apparently lead to diagnosis for eligibility but not diagnosis for instructional purposes (Howell, Kaplan, & O'Connell, 1979). A number of additional studies have shown that time-series monitoring of data supplied by teachers in the regular classroom has been quite effective as an alternative to traditional assessment for determining referrals and types of intervention (Bergquist, 1982; Fuchs, Deno, & Mirkin, 1983; Hasselbring & Hamlett, 1983; Marston, 1988; Marston, Mirkin, & Deno, 1984; Shinn & Marston, 1985; Shinn, Tindal, & Spira, 1987; Shinn, Ysseldyke, Deno, & Tindal, 1986). Tucker (1985), Galagan (1985), and Deno (1987; Deno & Fuchs, 1987) provide an introduction to this general area of assessment based on data supplied by teachers, which is referred to generally in the literature as curriculum-based assessment.

In addition to substituting assessment procedures based on teachers' observations in place of psychological or psychoeducational testing, special education also has begun to emphasize screening by teachers, through prereferral intervention. In regard to intervention, putting emphasis on teacher consultation *prior* to referral, rather than wasting similar levels of resources on testing and placing children, has been demonstrated to be an effective alternative to the traditional methods of the school psychologist. Graden, for example (Graden, Casey, & Christenson, 1985; Graden, Casey & Bonstrom, 1985) has demonstrated a complex, yet relatively effective, school psychologist–*regular* teacher consultation service that generally has been able to handle more than half the cases referred for potential special education. Chalfant and Pysh (1979) likewise demonstrated how a small group of regular teachers can, with special training, serve as a first-line consultation and intervention team for classrooms in their school. Such teacher-based teams were effectively able to handle nearly two-thirds of the children referred for learning and behavior problems. Such approaches have tried to avoid certain previous problems associated with resource or teacher consultation approaches, by which resource rooms became miniature special class placements or regular teachers were not provided realistic alternative interventions (Friend, 1984; Friend & McNutt, 1984). The advantages of such consultation teams would seem vastly to outweigh their disadvantages (Hayek, 1987; Huefner, 1988; Idol & West, 1987; West & Idol, 1987).

Describing such advantages of curriculum-based assessment and prereferral intervention is not meant to imply that teacher-based referral, diagnosis, and intervention is altogether an entirely adequate method. The point has been made, however, that we should put our effort into refining these service delivery processes and perfecting teacher-based systems rather than continuing to rely on outmoded systems inherited from psychology (Gerber & Semmel, 1984; Stainback, Stainback, Courtnage, & Jaben, 1985).

To do so is to restore the primacy of the teacher in what has essentially been a teacher-based system all along. That the school psychologist in particular and the discipline of psychology in general has managed to exert inordinate influence on this system has been due largely to issues of professional status. Having a PhD and periodically conducting evaluations or therapies with individuals in separate rooms with arcane procedures largely unfamiliar to all but the initiate is obviously seen, even by teachers, as more prestigious than having a BA and daily teaching an entire roomful of children with methods familiar to almost everyone. Although it is one thing to be somewhat intimidated by status, it is quite another to perpetuate an entirely wrongful state of affairs because of it.

How primacy of the teacher is to be restored to special education has been detailed elsewhere (Forness, 1981, 1983; Forness, Sinclair, & Russell, 1984; Forness & Kavale, 1984; Hewett & Forness, 1984). A capsule picture of this system is one of a highly trained teacher operating from a learning center within the regular school. He or she has direct responsibility for perhaps two or more times the number of children ordinarily assigned to a special class teacher, plus at least some responsibility for training and supervising a teacher consultation team, composed of regular classroom teachers, as the first line of referral and intervention. In the learning center are a number of paraprofessionals or assistant teachers, who are given far more responsibility than is ordinarily assigned to classroom aides (Forness, 1974). They do most of the hands-on daily teaching, while the master special education teacher makes daily rounds and sees children only for brief sessions, much like a chief of service in a teaching hospital. The concept of such a learning center is depicted in Figure 1, which is a combination of the floor plan for such a center and a listing of the six major roles such a master special education teacher might be expected to play. Within the learning center are depicted the range of curriculum materials and technologies that would be needed to serve such a disparate special education population, with perhaps separate teaching areas for children with multiple handicapping conditions. Although curriculum-based assessment, specialized teaching, and supervision of routine hands-on teaching would be ongoing roles for the master teacher *within* the learning center, periodic outside responsibilities would also involve consulting with regular class teachers, and perhaps even coordinating services with outside agencies (depicted as "doors" on the floor plan in Figure 1 leading from the learning center to the rest of the outside school and community).

While such an approach may seem overly idealistic, given current special education legal guidelines and reimbursement procedures, it should be noted that several of the studies and programs cited above have demonstrated, and continue to demonstrate realistically, not only the various components of such a plan but their cost effectiveness. The approach, moreover, is only one example that could be used to demonstrate a growing trend towards systems of service delivery completely provided by teachers, without school psychologists, IQ and other psychologic testing, or categorical diagnoses. It should also be stressed that the authors are decidedly *not* advocating for such a program within the context of the so-called regular education initiative (REI). REI purports to deliver the bulk of special education services through improved instruction in the regular classroom and has been criticized from several perspectives as unrealistic and lacking empirical support (Hallahan, Kauffman, Lloyd, & McKinney, 1988; Anderegg & Vergason, 1988; Kauffman, 1988). However, the learning center concept described above, with its emphasis on *teacher* identification and delivery of service, should thus free school psychologists from current identification and diagnostic preoccupations to provide other, more relevant services more in keeping with their *psychological* training and tradition.

SCHOOL PSYCHOLOGISTS AND THE NEW SERVICE DELIVERY SYSTEM

What would become of school psychologists in a system in which highly trained special education teachers handle most of the referral interventions, perform most of the tasks of identification and diagnosis previously reserved for school psychologists, consult with regular classroom teachers on routine learning and behavioral disorders, and operate a generally more responsive and specialized program for a wide variety of children with handicaps? The new role of the school psychologist might well involve two distinct types of efforts. We have termed these as *front-loading* and as *back-loading.*

In front-loaded effort, school psychologists would become more involved in early identification and prevention. In other words, long before problem children come to the attention of special educators, school psychologists might focus their efforts, up front, to prevent minor problems from becoming worse or to identify potentially more serious problems early in their initial stages. A good example of such an early identification system is that proposed and developed by Walker and his associates (Walker et al., 1988). In this system, teachers are asked to identify and rank children with potential disorders and then, in a step-by-step fashion, prioritize those who might require intervention. The role of the school psychologist is to organize this system, to check teachers' judgments according to normative standards, and finally to confirm or disconfirm teacher judgments by brief but systematic classroom and playground observations. At any point in the system, the school psychologist could intervene directly or indirectly through consultation, direct treatment, or referral to special education, mental health services, and the like.

Front-loading could also involve a variety of other direct and indirect methods in which routine classroom problems might be handled by the school psychologist either through direct consultation with regular teachers in ongoing classrooms or through organizing periodic staff development activities. Numerous examples are provided in the chapters that follow in such areas as social skills training, academic or study skills interventions, peer tutoring, and a variety of

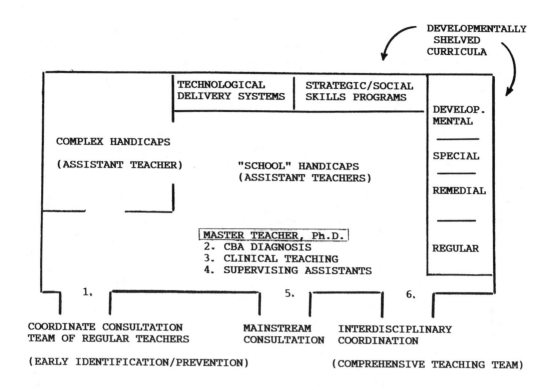

FIGURE 1. Conceptual depiction of master special education teacher's role in conjunction with proposed learning center (20 children).

interventions for specific problem behaviors. Also important are school- or district-wide programs developed by school psychologists in such areas such as substance abuse, health enhancement, and the like. All these efforts call for the particular expertise of the school psychologist, who may, in some instances, choose to work in concert with guidance counselors, special educators, or curriculum supervisors. A number of authors have indeed suggested that school psychologists intervene in this way with the entire educational environment (Bergan, 1985; Elliott & Witt, 1986; Lambert, 1986; Reschly, 1988; Ysseldyke, 1986).

Back-loading, on the other hand, would involve intervention with children already identified and currently in the service delivery system. For example, only *after* a child has failed to respond to appropriate remedial and special interventions in the learning center or other special education programs might the school psychologist be called upon. At that point, he or she might examine the child's record of progress and previous interventions with a view toward performing those functions for which psychologists are not only best trained but for which they also seem to complain they never have sufficient time (Meyers, Martin, & Hyman, 1977).

Such functions could indeed include individual and group psychotherapy, parent training, family therapy, and liaison with medical or psychiatric services. It is clear that at least some of these activities are beginning to be seen as essential to the related services mandate of Public Laws 94-142 and 99-457 (Osborne, 1984). It would seem that, rather than referring children to agencies outside the school, at least some of these services could and should be delivered within the school system by school psychologists to ensure closer cooperation and coordination with ongoing educational programs. A good example of such therapeutic interventions is a recent study by Reynolds and Coats (1986) in which school psychologists provided effective brief-term, school-based group therapy to adolescents with depression.

There are also a variety of complex problems that may indeed need to be treated in other service delivery systems such as mental health, vocational rehabilitation, public health, developmental services, and the like. For this reason, proposed regulations under PL 99-457 (early childhood amendments to PL 94-142: Education of the Handicapped Act) have provided for a "case manager" to ensure that there is effective coordination and transition among agencies serving very young children needing special services. It is not unrealistic to expect that not only infants and young children but also older children with handicaps might begin to require a case manager as well. The school psychologist would seem to be the ideal professional to fulfill such a role.

Other back-loaded roles are certainly possible in the general area of cooperation and coordination with other professional disciplines treating children outside the school setting. It is quite probable, for example, that the school psychologist might coordinate treatments between schools and child or adolescent psychiatrists. It is now becoming clear that psychopharmacotherapy is an increasingly important adjunct in treatment of a variety of school learning and behavioral problems and that *combinations* of psychopharmacology and behavioral treatments may be more effective than either medication or behavior modification used alone (Forness & Kavale, 1988). The process of effective feedback to psychiatrists on both the therapeutic and the side effects of psychoactive drugs in the classroom, especially during the titration phase, is quite complex (Gadow, 1986 a, b). The training of school psychologists in observation and behavioral analysis would seem to make them the ideal professionals to assist in such feedback, to coordinate or monitor treatments, and generally to serve as liaison in this important area among teachers, parents, and psychiatrists.

Similar roles may begin to occur in other areas. School psychologists may well be called upon, for example, to coordinate transition to vocational rehabilitation programs (Rusch & Phelps, 1987) or to assist in monitoring the technology needed for increasing numbers of medically fragile or "treatment-assisted" children who are being placed in both regular and special classroom settings (Sirvis, 1988). These and other such efforts may eventually become even more important than front-loading, in that special education teachers may ultimately be better trained for most tasks involving instructional interventions in both regular and special classrooms, whereas back-loading calls upon skills or expertise that only the school psychologist may possess.

CONCLUSION

The psychologist has an absolutely vital contribution to make. Both special education and psychology might be better served, however, if this contribution took place largely alongside rather than *within* the special education enterprise and if such contribution placed more emphasis on the school psychologist as *psychologist* rather than on his or her largely outmoded role as psychometrist, diagnostician, or special education gatekeeper. Such a role would bring the school psychologist into an alliance with special educators not only to provide *noneducational* (i.e., psychological) services to selected handicapped children, but also to serve regular education by means that special educators are neither trained nor inclined to use.

REFERENCES

Adelman H. S. (1978). Diagnostic classification of learning problems: Some data. *American Journal of Orthopsychiatry, 48*, 717-726.

Algozzine, B., & Ysseldyke, E. (1987). Questioning discrepancies: Retaking the first step 20 years later. *Learning Disability Quarterly, 10*, 301-312.

Anderegg, M. L., & Vergason, G. A. (1988). An analysis of one of the cornerstones of the regular education initiative. *Focus on Exceptional Children, 20*(8), 1-8.

Barnes, T., & Forness, S. (1982). Learning characteristics of children and adolescents with various psychiatric diagnoses. *Monographs in Behavioral Disorders, 5*, 32-41.

Bennett, R. E. (1983). Research and evaluation priorities for special education assessment. *Exceptional Children, 50*, 110-117.

Bergan, J. C. (1985). The future of school psychology. In J. C. Bergan, (Ed.), *School psychology in contemporary society* (pp. 421-437). Columbus, OH: Merrill.

Bergquist, C. C. (1982). A methodology for validating placement of children in exceptional child programs. *Exceptional Children, 49*, 269-270.

Berk, R. (1984). *Screening and diagnosis of children with learning disabilities.* Springfield, IL: Charles C. Thomas.

California Association of School Psychologists. (1984). Educational and Diagnostic Manual for the SED Student: The background and participants. *CASP Today* (September issue).

Center, D. B., & Obringer, J. (1987). A search for variables affecting underidentification of behaviorally disordered students. *Behavioral Disorders, 12*, 169-174.

Chalfant, J. C., & Pysh, M. V. (1979). Teacher assistance teams: A model for within building problem solving. *Learning Disability Quarterly, 2*, 85-96.

Coles, G. S. (1978). The Learning-Disabilities Test Battery. Empirical and social issues. *Harvard Educational Review, 48*, 313-340.

Coles, G. S. (1987). *The learning mystique: A critical look at "learning disabilities."* New York: Pantheon Books.

Deno, S. L. (1987). Curriculum-based measurement. *Teaching Exceptional Children, 20*, 41-47.

Deno, S. L., & Fuchs, L. S. (1987). Developing curriculum-based measurement systems for data-based special education problem solving. *Focus on Exceptional Children, 19*(8) 1-16.

Elliott, S., & Witt, J. (1986). Fundamental questions and dimensions of psychological service delivery in schools. In S. Elliott and J. Witt (Eds.), *The delivery of psychological services in schools: Concepts, processes, and issues* (pp. 1-26). Hillsdale, NJ: Erlbaum.

Forness, S. R. (1970). Educational prescription for the school psychologist. *Journal of School Psychology, 8*, 96-98.

Forness, S. R. (1974). *Teacher aides in special education.* Paper presented at American Association on Mental Deficiency, Toronto.

Forness, S. R. (1979). Developing the individual educational plan: Process and perspectives. *Education and Treatment of Children, 2*, 43-54.

Forness, S. R. (1981). Concepts of school learning and behavior disorders: Implications for research and practice. *Exceptional Children, 48*, 56-64.

Forness, S. R. (1982). Diagnosing dyslexia: A note on the need for ecologic assessment. *American Journal of Diseases of Children, 136*, 794-799.

Forness, S. R. (1983). Diagnostic schooling for children or adolescents with behavior disorders. *Behavioral Disorders, 8*, 176-190.

Forness, S. R. (1985). Effects of public policy at the state level: California's impact on MR, LD, and ED categories. *Remedial and Special education, 6*(3), 36-43.

Forness, S. R., & Kavale, K. (1984). Education of the mentally retarded: A note on policy. *Education and Training of the Mentally Retarded, 19*, 222-227.

Forness, S., & Kavale, K. (1988). Psychopharmacologic treatment: A note on classroom effects. *Journal of Learning Disabilities, 21*, 144-147.

Forness, S. R., Sinclair, E., & Guthrie, D. (1983). Learning disability discrepancy formulas: Their use in actual practice. *Learning Disability Quarterly, 6*, 107-114.

Forness, S. R., Sinclair, E., & Russell, A. (1984). Serving children with emotional or behavioral disorders: Implications for educational policy. *American Journal of Orthopsychiatry, 54*, 22-32.

Frankenberger, W., & Harper, J. (1986). Variations in multidisciplinary team composition for identifying children with mental retardation. *Mental Retardation, 24*, 203-207.

Friend, M. (1984). Consultation skills for resource teachers. *Learning Disability Quarterly, 7*, 246-250.

Friend, M., & McNutt, G. (1984). Resource room programs: Where are we now? *Exceptional Children, 51*, 150-155.

Fuchs, L. S., Deno, S. L., & Mirkin, P. K. (1983). Data-based program modification: A continuous evaluation system with computer software to facilitate implementation. *Journal of Special Education Technology, 6*, 50-57.

Fuchs, D., Fuchs, L., Benowitz, S., & Barringer, K. (1987). Norm-referenced tests: Are they valid for use with handicapped students? *Exceptional Children, 54*, 263-271.

Gadow, K. D. (1986a). *Children on medication, Vol. 1: Hyperactivity, learning disabilities, and mental retardation.* San Diego, CA: College-Hill.

Gadow, K. D. (1986b). *Children on medication, Vol. 2: Epilepsy, emotional disturbance, and adolescent disorders.* San Diego, CA: College-Hill.

Galagan, J. E. (1985). Psychoeducational testing: Turn out the lights, the party's over. *Exceptional Children, 52,* 288-299.

Gerber, M. (1984). The Department of Education's Sixth Annual Report to Congress on PL94-142: Is Congress getting the full story? *Exceptional Children, 51,* 209-224.

Gerber, M. M., & Semmel, M. I. (1984). Teacher as imperfect test: Reconceptualizing the referral process. *Educational Psychologist, 19,* 137-148.

German, D., Johnson, B., & Schneider, M. (1985). Learning disability vs. reading disability: A survey of practitioners, diagnostic populations and test instruments. *Learning Disability Quarterly, 8,* 141-157.

Gilliam, J. E. (1979). Contributions and status rankings of educational planning committee participants. *Exceptional Children, 45,* 466-468.

Gilliam, J. E., & Coleman, M. C. (1981). Who influences IEP committee decisions? *Exceptional Children, 47,* 642-644.

Gittelman, R. (1980). The role of psychological tests for differential diagnosis in child psychiatry. *Journal of the American Academy of Child Psychiatry, 19,* 413-438.

Graden, J. L., Casey, A., & Bonstrom, O. (1985). Implementing a prereferral intervention system: Part II. The data. *Exceptional Children, 51,* 487-496.

Graden, J. L., Casey, A., & Christenson, S. L. (1985). Implementing a prereferral intervention system: Part I. The model. *Exceptional Children, 51,* 377-384.

Grosenick, J. K., George, M. P., & George, N. L. (1987). A profile of school programs for the behaviorally disordered: Twenty years after Morse, Cutler, and Fink. *Behavioral Disorders, 12,* 159-168.

Guetzole, E. (1989). *Youth Suicide: What the educator should know.* Reston, VA: Council for Exceptional Children.

Hallahan, D. P., Kauffman, J. M., Lloyd, J. W., & McKinney, J. D. (1988). Questions about the regular education initiative. *Journal of Learning Disabilities, 21*(1), 3-5.

Hasselbring, T. S., & Hamlett, C. L. (1983). *AIMSTAR: Charting and graphing individualized student data in the classroom.* Portland, OR: Applied Systems of Instructional Evaluation Publishing.

Hayek, R. A. (1987). The teacher assistance team: A prereferral support system. *Focus on Exceptional Children, 20*(1), 1-8.

Hewett, F., & Forness, S. (1984). *Education of exceptional learners* (3rd ed.). Newton, MA: Allyn & Bacon.

Howell, K., Kaplan, J., & O'Connell, C. (1979). *Evaluating exceptional children.* Columbus, OH: Merrill.

Huefner, D. S. (1988). The consulting teacher model: Risks and opportunities. *Exceptional Children, 54,* 403-414.

Iano, R. (1987). The study and development of teaching: With implications for the advancement of special education. *Remedial and Special Education, 7*(5) 50-61.

Idol, L., & West, J. F. (1987). Consultation in special education (Part II): Training and practice. *Journal of Learning Disabilities, 20,* 474-493.

Kauffman, J. (1988). A revolution can also mean returning to the starting point: Will school psychology help special education complete the circuit? *School Psychology Review, 17,* 490-494.

Iano, R. (198). The study and development of teaching: With implications for the advancement of special education. *Remedial and Special Education, 7*(5), 50-61.

Kauffman, J. (1988). A revolution can also mean returning to the starting point: Will school psychology help special education complete the circuit? *School Psychology Review, 17,* 490-494.

Kavale, K. (1983). Fragile findings, complex conclusions, and meta-analysis in special education. *Exceptional Education Quarterly, 4,* 97-106.

Kavale, K. & Forness, S. (1984). A meta-analysis assessing the validity of Wechsler Scale profiles and recategorization: Patterns or parodies? *Learning Disabilities Quarterly, 7,* 136-156.

Kavale, K., & Forness, S. (1985). *The science of learning disabilities.* San Diego: College-Hill.

Kavale, K., & Forness, S. (1987). Substance over style: Assessing the efficacy of modality testing and teaching. *Exceptional Children, 54,* 228-234.

Lambert, N. M. (1986). Engineering new designs for school psychological service delivery: A commentary on *School psychology: A Blueprint for Training and Practice. Professional School Psychology, 1,* 295-302.

Lambert, N. M. (1988). Perspectives on eligibility for and placement in special education programs. *Exceptional Children, 54,* 297-301.

Marston, D. (1988). The effectiveness of special education: A time series analysis of reading performance in regular and special education settings. *Journal of Special Education, 21*, 13-26.

Marston, D., Mirkin, P., & Deno, S. (1984). Curriculum-based measurement: An alternative to traditional screening, referral, and identification. *Journal of Special Education, 18*, 109-117.

McGinnis, E., & Forness, S. (1988). Psychiatric diagnosis: A further test of the special education eligibility hypothesis. *Monographs in Behavioral Disorders, 11*, 3-10.

McGinnis, E., Kiraly, J., & Smith, C. R. (1984). The types of data used in identifying public school students as behaviorally disordered. *Behavioral Disorders, 9*, 239-246.

Meehl, P. E. (1978). Theoretical risks and tabular asterisks: Sir Karl, Sir Ronald, and the slow progress of soft psychology. *Journal of Consulting and Clinical Psychology, 46*, 806-834.

Meyers, J., Martin, R., & Hyman, I. (1977). *School consultation: Preventative techniques for pupil personnel workers.* Springfield, IL: Thomas.

Osborne, A. G., Jr. (1984). How the courts have interpreted the related services mandate. *Exceptional Children, 51*, 249-252.

Peterson, R. (1986). Inclusion of socially maladjusted children and youth in the legal definition of the behaviorally disordered population: A debate. *Behavioral Disorders, 11*, 213-222.

Reschly, D. (1988). Special education reform: School psychology resolution. *School Psychology Review, 17*, 459-475.

Reynolds, M. C. (1988). A reaction to the *JLD* special series on the regular education initiative. *Journal of Learning Disabilities, 31*, 352-356.

Reynolds, W. M., & Coats, K. I. (1986). A comparison of cognitive-behavioral therapy and relaxation training for the treatment of depression in adolescents. *Journal of Consulting and Clinical Psychology, 54*, 1-8.

Rusch, F. R., & Phelps, L. A. (1987). Secondary special education and transition from school to work: A national priority. *Exceptional Children, 53*, 487-492.

Sarason, S. B. (1981). *Psychology misdirected.* New York: Free Press.

Scruggs, T. E., & Mastropieri, M. A. (1985). The first decade of the journal. *Behavioral Disorders: A quantitative evaluation. Behavioral Disorders, 11*, 52-59.

Shapiro, E. S., & Derr, T. F. (1987). An examination of overlap between reading curricula and standardized achievement tests. *Journal of Special Education, 21*, 89-68.

Shattuck, R. (1980). *The forbidden experiment: The story of the wild boy of Averyon.* New York: Farrar, Strauss, Giroux.

Shinn, M., & Marston, D. (1985). Differentiating mildly handicapped, low-achieving, and regular education students: A curriculum-based approached. *Remedial and Special Education, 6*, 31-38.

Shinn, M. R., Tindal, G. A., & Spira, D. A. (1987). Special education referrals as an index of teacher tolerance: Are teachers imperfects tests? *Exceptional Children, 54*, 32-40.

Shinn, M. R., Ysseldyke, J. E., Deno, S. L., & Tindal, G. A. (1986). A comparison of differences between students labeled learning disabled and low achieving on measures of classroom performance. *Journal of Learning Disabilities, 19*, 545-553.

Sinclair, E., & Alexson, J. (1986). Learning disability discrepancy formulas: Similarities and differences among them. *Learning Disabilities Research, 1*(2), 112-118.

Sinclair, E., & Forness, S. (1983). *Concordance between* DSM III *and special education placement.* Paper presented at Annual Meeting of American Academy of Child Psychiatry, San Francisco.

Sinclair, E., & Forness, S. (1988). Special education classification and its relationship to DSM III. In T. Kratochwill & E. S. Shapiro (Eds.), *Behavioral Assessment in Schools* (pp. 494-521). New York: Guilford.

Sinclair, E., Forness, S., & Alexson, J. (1985). Psychiatric diagnosis: A study of its relationship to school needs. *Journal of Special Education, 19*, 333-344.

Sirvis, B. (1988). Students with special health care needs. *Teaching Exceptional Children, 20*,(4) 40-45.

Skiba, R., & Casey, A. (1985). Interventions for behavior disordered students: A quantitative review and methodological critique. *Behavioral Disorders, 10*, 239-252.

Smith, C. R., & Knoff, H. M. (1981). School psychology and special education students' placement decisions: IQ still tips the scale. *Journal of Special Education, 15*, 55-64.

Smith, C., Wood, F., & Grimes, J. (1988). Issues in identification and placement of emotionally disturbed/behavior disordered students. In M. C. Wang, M. C. Reynolds, & H. Walberg (Eds.), *Handbook of special education: Research and practice* (Volume 2, pp. 95-124). New York: Pergamon.

Staats, A. W. (1983). *Psychology's crisis of disunity: Philosophy and method for a unified science.* New York: Praeger.

Stainback, S. & Stainback, W. (1984). Broadening the research perspective in special education. *Exceptional Children, 50,* 400-408.

Stainback, W., & Stainback, S. (1984). A rationale for the merger of special and regular education. *Exceptional Children, 51,* 102-111.

Stainback, W., Stainback, S., Courtnage, L., & Javen, T. (1985). Facilitating mainstreaming by modifying the mainstream. *Exceptional Children, 52,* 144-152.

Swanson, L., & Watson, B. (1982). *Educational and psychological assessment of exceptional children: Theories, strategies, and applications.* St. Louis: Mosby.

Swanson, H. L., & Trahan, M. (1986). Characteristics of frequently cited articles in learning disabilities. *Journal of Special Education, 20,* 167-182.

Tucker, J. A. (1985). Curriculum-based assessment: An introduction. *Exceptional Children, 52,* 199-204.

Turnbull, A. P., Strickland, B., & Brantley, J. C. (1982). *Developing and implementing individualized education programs* (2nd ed.). Columbus, OH: Merrill.

U.S. Department of Education. (1988). *Tenth annual report to Congress on implementation of the Education of the Handicapped Act.* Washington, DC: U.S. Government Printing Office.

Valentine, E. R. (1982). *Conceptual issues in psychology.* London: George Allen & Unwin.

Vaughn, S., Bos, C. S., Harrell, J. E., & Lasky, B. A. (1988). Parent participation in the initial placement/IEP conference ten years after mandated involvement. *Journal of Learning Disabilities, 21,* 82-89.

Walker, H. M., Severson, H., Stiller, B., Williams, G., Haring, N., Shinn, M., & Todis, B. (1988). Systematic screening of pupils in the elementary age range at risk for behavior disorders: Development and trial testing. *Remedial and Special Education, 9*(3), 8-20.

West, J. F., & Idol, L. (1987). School consultation (part I): An interdisciplinary perspective on theory, models, and research. *Journal of Learning Disabilities, 20,* 388-408.

Yoshida, R., (1983). Are multidisciplinary teams worth the investment? *School Psychology Review, 12,* 137-143.

Ysseldyke, J. E., (1986). Current practice in school psychology. In S. Elliott & J. Witt (Eds.), *The delivery of psychological services in school: Concepts, processes, and issues* (pp. 27-51). Hillsdale, NJ: Erlbaum.

Ysseldyke, J. E., & Algozzine, B. (1981). Diagnostic classification decisions as a function of referral information. *Journal of Special Education, 15,* 429-435.

Ysseldyke, J., Algozzine, B., & Epps, S. (1983). A logical and empirical analysis of current practice in classifying students as handicapped. *Exceptional Children, 50,* 160-166.

Ysseldyke, J. E., Thurlow, M., Graden, J., Wesson, C., Algozzine, B., & Deno, S. (1983). Generalizations from five years of research on assessment and decision making: The University of Minnesota Institute. *Exceptional Education Quarterly, 4,* 75-93.

Zabel, R. H., Peterson, R. L., Smith, C. R., & White, M. A. (1981). Placement and reintegration information for emotionally disabled students. In F. Wood (Ed.), *Perspectives for a new decade* (pp. 41-53). Reston, VA: Council for Exceptional Children.

Zucker, S. H., & Polloway, E. A. (1987). Issues in identification and assessment in mental retardation. *Education and Training in Mental Retardation, 22,* 69-76.

A previous version of this chapter was published as an article in *Monographs in Behavioral Disorders,* 1987, *9,* 2-14.

It should be noted, in relation to the authors' credentials to criticize practices in school psychology as they have done herein, that Dr. Forness is Chief Educational Psychologist in the UCLA Neuropsychiatric Institute Child Outpatient Department, serves as an oral commissioner on educational psychology licensing examinations for the State of California Department of Behavioral Sciences, and has published widely in school psychology journals. Dr. Kavale likewise has a degree in psychology and has both taught and published widely in the area of psychoeducational diagnosis. Their primary professional identity, however, is in special education.

School Psychology and the Regular Education Initiative: Meaningful Change or Lost Opportunities?

David W. Peterson
Northern Suburban Special Education District
(Highland Park, Illinois)

Ann Casey
Minneapolis Public Schools

The profession of school psychology can make important contributions to the implementation of what has become known as the Regular Education Initiative (REI) (Will, 1986). How much these contributions will be realized will depend upon whether practitioners and university trainers can successfully implement reforms and develop new roles so that school psychologists begin to spend more of their time designing, implementing, and evaluating substantive educational interventions and less time assessing students' deficits and assigning negative school labels. We will first address some simultaneously converging forces in both the education community and the profession of school psychology that are contributing to an evolving change process. Next, the opportunities and corresponding roles and competencies necessary for school psychologists to participate in this change process will be reviewed. Finally, we will examine strategies for creating needed changes at the school building and systems level.

School psychologists are approaching a crossroads in regard to the role they will play in the nation's schools. A number of reform initiatives in both regular and special education have converged with long standing calls for change from within the profession to create the potential for school psychologists to embrace roles fundamentally different from those they have traditionally fulfilled. Underlying our discussion of these opportunities for change is the assumption that school psychology can contribute to the establishment of more responsive educational environments for all students.

FORCES CREATING CHANGE

Forces for Change Within School Psychology

A good deal of the impetus for change in the scope and practice of school psychology has emerged from within the profession. The Springhill Symposium, a planning conference conducted in 1981, attempted to capture the consensus views of a representative group of practitioners and university trainers in order to develop a visionary plan for the profession of school psychology. Among the themes that resulted from this conference was the belief that school psychologists must look beyond norm-referenced tests and seek more useful ways to enhance the process of schooling. Moreover, the participants suggested that school psychologists would need new and expanded skills to fulfill such functions (Peterson, 1981). Training programs would need to focus on classroom management and evaluation and improvement of instruction, in the hope that school psychology could have broader impact in education.

In 1984, the National School Psychology Inservice Network published a paper entitled *School Psychology: A Blueprint for Training and Practice*. While significantly predating the Regular Education Initiative, this document cited a number of flaws in the system of educating students with special needs, characterizing the current array of compensatory services as an "emerging non-system." These deficiencies included (a) unrelated categorical programs delivered to specific populations of students who must be removed from the mainstream of regular education in order to receive these services; (b) the use of categorical classification systems that do not relate to instruction in any meaningful way; and (c) dysfunctional funding systems that provide monetary incentives for removing students from regular education programs.

In a review of these problems and other aspects of the system, which it found to be characterized by "disjointed incrementation," the *Blueprint* called for a transformation of services for students with special needs. The *Blueprint* also criticized the existing role of the school psychologist, calling for an end to the narrowly prescribed evaluation and gatekeeping function that most school psychologists have in the categorical system of service delivery. The authors of the *Blueprint* further prescribed a new role for school psychology that would support the development and maintenance of educational services designed to respond to students' instructional needs within the regular classroom. These roles would encompass skills in classroom management and organization, instructional consultation, social skills training, staff development, and systems planning, among others.

Other calls for change both in the educational practices to be used to serve students with special needs and in the corollary role of the school psychologist have come from within the profession. The National Association of School Psycholo-

gists (NASP) has taken an aggressive role in promoting modification of the educational system. The "Advocacy for Appropriate Educational Services for All Children" position statement (NASP/NCAS, 1985) criticized arbitrarily defined categories for classification of low-achieving students, their accompanying labels, and assessment practices that are focused on determining eligibility at the cost of obtaining information useful to instruction. Perhaps most important, the position paper suggests that regular education is "bordering on abdication of responsibility," and criticizes the system's ability to meet the needs of students whose skills are not convergent with the norm. In its recommendations for change, this statement called for a national effort to develop viable alternatives to categorical special education systems. Alternatives suggested include reevaluation of funding mechanisms, regulatory waivers to promote pilot programs, and massive retraining of educational personnel.

Furthermore, "Rights Without Labels" (National Coalition of Advocates for Students, 1987) was endorsed by NASP and identifies a variety of problems associated with classifying and labeling students with special needs. This position paper cites the stigmas associated with negative school labels (Blackman, 1989) and the removal of students from regular classrooms, as well as difficulties associated with returning students to the regular classroom. Moreover, this position statement calls for prereferral intervention, curriculum-based assessment that is relevant to effective instruction, and the provision of special services to the student within the regular classroom.

Forces for Change in Other Parts of the Educational Community

Calls for change in the way our educational system responds to atypical students also have come from other parts of the educational community. Several researchers have begun to question how extensively basic elements of Public Law 94-142 have been applied to all students. For example, the provision of educational services in least restrictive environment, one of the key provisions of the act, appears to be more a function of the student's area of residence than any single aspect of their disability (Blackman, 1989). Other special educators have cited flaws similar to those discussed earlier and have urged combining the resources of special and regular education into a single, more fully integrated system (Stainback & Stainback, 1984). Gartner and Lipsky (1989) reviewed a variety of frequently cited problems and also questioned the overall effectiveness of full-time special education programs, citing a number of studies that show that there is "no compelling body of evidence that segregated special education programs offer significant benefits" (p. 13).

Furthermore, an increasing number of educators concerned with the education of persons with severe disabilities are calling for the full inclusion of such students in regular education programs with all programs and services being provided to these students in their neighborhood schools (Macdonald & York, 1989; Brown et al., 1989). Their position is that such inclusion promotes normalization and eventually more complete participation in the community. This point of view is vigorously supported by The Association for Persons with Severe Handicaps (1986). As a result, a number of schools have initiated special education programs that do not require the removal of students from regular education in order to receive educational and supportive services.

The Regular Education Initiative and the Ensuing Controversy

The aforementioned problems with the existing system of services to students with special needs served as an impetus for the publication of *Educating Students With Learning Problems — A Shared Responsibility* (Will, 1986), the U.S. Department of Education report often credited with establishing the Regular Education Initiative (REI). Like the previously cited papers, Will (1986) depicted the current system of special

services as characterized by fragmented and parallel systems of services that inhibit communication and collaboration among special and regular educators. In outlining possible remedies, the paper advocates the expansion of support systems for regular class teachers, increasing instructional time and individualization, focusing the responsibility for services at the building level, and developing new instructional approaches. The paper was intended to serve as a basis for discussion and to promote a "search for ways to serve as many of these children as possible in the regular classroom by encouraging special education and other special programs to form a partnership with regular education" (p. 20).

The REI is currently the most controversial issue being debated in the special education literature (Davis, 1989). Will (1986) has promoted the REI as a means of sharing the responsibility of educating students with learning problems. One of the major tenets of Public Law 94-142 is to provide services to students in the least restrictive environment (LRE). Interpreted broadly, this means that students with disabilities should be educated to the greatest extent possible within the regular education environment. Given that this significant component of the law has been in effect for more than 12 years now, it is difficult to understand the current controversy surrounding the REI. If LRE is still accepted as an important value, then REI should seem to be a logical extension of the mandate. If students have a right to an education in the least restrictive environment, then energy should be focused on identifying the most effective ways to ensure that this occurs. Instead, a heated debate has ensued in which a number of professionals question the efficacy of REI.

Certain model projects have been touted as examplary demonstrations of the effectiveness of REI. At the same time, others have suggested that the research evidence does not support the claims being made and therefore that REI should not be so heartily embraced. It may be that the wrong questions are being debated and that misspent energy is being poured into this debate. If it is agreed that students are better educated in the least restrictive environment, then our efforts should be directed toward developing the most effective means to accomplish this. Rather than asking the question "What's wrong with REI?" perhaps we should ask "How do we provide effective education with as much access as possible to regular education?"

There are several issues that complicate development of solution to the problem. First, even though PL 94-142 requires education in the least restrictive environment, there are many interpretations of what is meant by LRE. Not everyone is convinced that handicapped students can be better educated in integrated environments. This point of view is often the result of deeply held beliefs or values that may not be easily changed, even by research evidence that another way is better. Perhaps an even larger issue is that at the same time that PL 94-142 advocated LRE, it also created a large second layer of bureaucracy in the educational system: special education. In essence, a two-tiered educational system developed: a special, and often separate, system for students with special needs and the existing regular education system for the remaining, and increasingly homogeneous students with more typical needs. With this dual education system, teachers became used to the idea that students who had learning difficulties had to be referred to special education. Special educators became known for taking care of all students who had learning or behavioral difficulties. The unintended effect has been that regular educators have less need to individualize instruction, and they are not used to planning programs for students with diverse educational needs. This has led some to suggest that we have created a continually expanding, but often ineffectual system with the proliferation of special education over the last 10 years (Gartner & Lipsky, 1989).

There is at least one more issue contributing to the current controversy over the regular education initiative. For years, numerous studies have questioned the various methods of identifying and placing handicapped students in special education classrooms (Ysseldyke et al., 1983), particularly in the areas of mild retardation and learning disabilities (Reschly, 1987). With few valid models for identifying students as needing special education services, it was only a matter of time before policy analysts suggested that some special education students were never really handicapped in the first place and, thus, should be returned to regular education.

To summarize these concerns, some professionals are questioning the efficacy of separate delivery systems for special education, and others believe that some students currently receiving special education services were never really appropriately selected for these services in the first place. Additionally, there are some who think the intent of REI is to return all handicapped students to the regular classroom, regardless of the degree of handicapping condition. Given these factors, it is easy to see why the debate regarding REI has become so vocal.

OPPORTUNITIES FOR SCHOOL PSYCHOLOGISTS TO EFFECT CHANGE IN THE EDUCATIONAL SYSTEM

Some school psychologists may view REI as a threat to current practices; others will see opportunities to change and improve the services that are provided. Those who are unwilling or unable to change may find themselves facing a declining need for the traditional services they offer. REI offers the opportunity to put into use nontraditional school psychology services that heretofore have been displaced because too much time has been spent in traditional assessment. Those who do not have the skills that underlie REI will need to set out on a planned effort in continuing professional development to upgrade their skills.

Regardless of one's position on these issues, no convincing empirical rationale for educating mildly handicapped students in segregated settings remains. In fact, Nevin and Thousand (1987) suggest that as general educators improve their instructional delivery system, referrals for special assistance will diminish. With this premise, it is logical to assume that regular education teachers will require some assistance in improving instruction and adapting curriculum for mildly handicapped students, providing an excellent opportunity for school psychologists to perfect the consultation role. As more handicapped students are returned to the mainstream and fewer are found eligible for special education services, the role of school psychologists will have to change. These changes will require considerably less emphasis on traditional assessment, since classification issues will become less prominent.

While school psychologists have long maintained they can offer skills beyond assessment, the fact remains that the majority of their time is spent in classification and placement activities (Reschly, Genshaft, & Binder, 1987). In fact, most school personnel see assessment as school psychologists' only role. REI offers the opportunity to demonstrate otherwise and bring about the needed change. In the course of such change, it seems likely that the environments in which school psychology services are provided and the ways in which services are delivered will undergo significant transformation. The remainder of this discussion will examine some of these changes and the skills that school psychologists will need in order to effect them.

COMPETENCIES AND ROLES NEEDED TO SUPPORT REI

If school psychologists are to become effective change agents, efforts should be directed toward two primary areas: making assessment more relevant to instruction and designing classroom interventions. Assessment will always be important in education, and the school psychologist should remain an expert in this area. However, assessment activities should focus on gathering information for instructional intervention rather than on classification. The second major focus should be to assist teachers in developing

interventions within the regular classroom. Research has demonstrated that special education placement can be avoided by direct support to regular teachers in developing effective interventions (Nevin & Thousand, 1987). Each of these areas requires a unique set of skills and competencies that need to be addressed in preservice training and inservice personnel development.

Changes in Assessment Practices

Assessment for intervention differs dramatically from assessment for classification on one dimension: The focus is no longer on making normative comparisons, but rather on identification of deficiencies in skills, error analysis, and monitoring the progress of a particular child. If assistance is to be provided to teachers in developing instructional interventions for students who are not making the desired progress, school psychologists can no longer rely on assessment instruments that provide normative scores such as percentile ranks and standard scores. These scores are not useful in planning intervention strategies for a particular student. Typically, norm-referenced measures have too few items in any given area to provide specific, helpful information, and they are not sensitive enough to measure growth in the curriculum. Information is needed about the student's strengths and weaknesses in the curriculum, the pattern of errors he or she makes, the cognitive strategies (or lack thereof) the student employs, the student's ability to attend to task, and other relevant variables. To be successful in this new assessment realm, school psychologists must develop competencies in curriculum-based assessment, in task analysis, and in assessing the learning environment.

Curriculum-based assessment (CBA) is a general term used to describe a number of systems currently in use. Shinn, Rosenfield, and Knutson (1989) described four such models. They are similar in that each is a measurement device that requires observation of performance in the student's curriculum, but they differ on a number of variables. CBA has been used as an alternative to standardized norm-referenced assessment for placement purposes and also has been successfully used as a means of monitoring student progress in the curriculum. Other uses include identifying the appropriate place to begin instruction, determining the types of errors a student makes, and evaluating programs. Finally, task analysis is an essential part of CBA. A particular skill that is presenting a student with difficulty can be broken down into its component parts so that the student can be tested on each of the components to determine where remediation should be focused.

To assess the instructional environment, school psychologists must be able to use observation skills to view the classroom ecology. Stated simply, this means that the observation must include what the teacher is doing, what the student is doing, and the interactions between the teacher and student. It can be equally important to determine if certain variables are absent in the classroom environment. The Instructional Environment Scale (Ysseldyke & Christenson, 1987) and the Classroom Observations Keyed for Effectiveness Research (Coker & Coker, 1982) are examples of published scales used to conduct this type of assessment. Informal devices, however, can be developed.

If a student is referred for lack of progress in reading, one might investigate the problem by asking, for example, does the teacher provide an adequate amount of time for both skill development and individual practice of a skill? provide prompt feedback for error correction? reinforce correct responses? provide cues or prompts to assist the student who is uncertain of the correct response? These are just a few teacher variables that might be relevant to the identified problem. In addition, it is important to observe student performance. Does the student attend to teacher instruction? use practice (seatwork) time wisely? ask for assistance when it is needed? Is there a pattern to the errors the student is making? Is the student able to ignore normal classroom disruptions? A general

instructional variable that is important to observe is the amount of time students are actually engaged in reading; intervention might appropriately focus on increasing the amount of time set aside for reading.

These are but a few variables that could be investigated for a student who is not making adequate progress in reading; any of them might shed light on the difficulty and lead to the development of a variety of interventions.

Changes in Intervention Practices

The previous section has described needed changes in assessment practices if students are to be served effectively within regular education. Reschly (1987) suggested that school psychology will change rapidly in the 1990s and that school psychologists will need to broaden their skills to provide prereferral interventions, behavioral consultation, instructional design, and behavioral interventions to develop academic survival skills, among others. This section will describe some of the competencies that school psychologists must have to effectively assist regular educators to meet the needs of the more diverse groups of learners that they will encounter.

Instructional intervention and adaptation. If REI is to bring the school psychologist into the classroom, he or she must not only be adept at CBA but also at linking the results of such assessments to practical academic interventions that will meet the needs of discrepant students and promote the overall achievement of all students. If school psychologists are going to communicate meaningfully with classroom teachers, they must understand the scope and sequence of the local curricula and clearly understand the essential skills required for success with those curricula.

School psychologists must also become knowledgeable about instructional techniques that have proven effective with students with special needs. For example, peer tutoring and cooperative learning (Johnson & Johnson, 1986) have proven to be effective ways to increase academic engaged time and are effective with a wide range of learners in regular classrooms (Peterson & Miller, 1990). Additionally, practitioners will need to be aware of proven instructional technologies like learning strategies (Deshler & Schumaker, 1986), the elements of effective teaching (Rosenshine, 1983), and Direct Instruction (Carnine, Granzin, & Becker, 1988), among others. These and other instructional alternatives must be incorporated into a broad array of options that can be made available to students with academic deficiencies.

Finally, if the movement to include students with moderate and severe disabilities in regular classrooms (Brown et al., 1989) continues, there will be a new and important role for school psychologists in finding ways to modify the regular curriculum and adapt regular classrooms to ensure that these students can participate meaningfully and continue to learn functional, age-appropriate skills. Macdonald and York (1989) discuss some of the ways in which appropriate instructional opportunities can be addressed in regular classrooms.

Behavioral and social/emotional interventions. Knoff (1988) points out the need to promote positive social interactions among students in regular classrooms. While the mental health needs of students has always been within the realm of school psychologists, their role has largely been limited to the diagnosis and classification of students with behavioral and emotional disorders. REI creates the need for school psychologists to become active not only in providing direct services to these students, but also in consulting with regular class teachers to develop in-class interventions. Knoff (1988) recommends a number of areas in which the practitioner should be competent, including social skills training, environmental interventions, applied behavioral interventions, cognitive-behavioral interventions, and self-control techniques. Although by no means exhaustive, these interventions include a variety of techniques that can assist in meeting the needs of students with behavioral problems within regular classrooms. From a preventive perspective, it is also important that the practitioner be well versed in general classroom management strategies.

Collaborative consultation. While content knowledge in the areas outlined above is important, school psychologists must possess the skills necessary to work effectively with classroom teachers and other educators in such a way that their expertise will be put to use and, most importantly, that teachers will implement real changes in the classroom. Gutkin and Curtis (1982) describe a process of collaborative consultation that has proven effective in diverse settings. While a variety of models for consultation exist, Curtis and Meyers (1988) describe a general framework for consultation that provides for collaborative and mutual interactions between the consultant and consultee. Further elaboration of the importance of consultative skills is beyond the scope of this chapter, but the importance of effective skills in this area cannot be overemphasized.

Other roles. The preceding discussion has centered on the school psychologist's role in academic and behavioral interventions. In addition there are various other school psychology roles that are consistent with REI. These include the development of systemwide preventive programs (e.g., suicide prevention programs), systems development and organizational planning, and staff training. Once the decision is made to develop alternative approaches for serving students with special needs and to create more inclusive school communities, opportunities and needs for role expansion are almost limitless.

EFFECTING CHANGE TO SUPPORT REI

Strategies to Facilitate Change

If school psychologists are to be active contributors to the implementation of REI, it is imperative that they collaborate with other educators to improve service delivery systems. The process of change can take place at a variety of levels within a given system. Three levels of system change will be discussed: macrosystems, microsystems, and individual change strategies. School psychologists who want to participate in the change process should first determine on which levels they can have the greatest impact, given their particular situation and individual strengths.

Macrosystems are large, usually bureaucratic, entities such as federal and state governments. Change at this level can have far-reaching effects, yet the process for change is more complex and time-consuming. In some cases, there may be state laws or regulations that hinder or restrict REI. Although there are strategies one can develop to circumvent some regulatory restrictions, the best long-term solution is to work for change in these laws or regulations. This can be done on an individual basis by discussing the issues with the legislators and congressional representatives, or by writing to the state and federal agencies responsible for developing educational regulations. While it is possible for an individual to have an impact at this level, perhaps a more effective strategy is to work with professional groups that lobby for change at this macro level. Professional associations, such as the National Association of School Psychologists (NASP) or state school psychological associations, have a louder voice because of the sheer numbers of members. As a member of such associations, the individual can participate in lobbying efforts as part of a structured strategy to effect change.

In contrast, microsystems may be more accessible or have more immediate meaning for an individual interested in working toward change. Microsystems include entities such as local school systems or school buildings. Each school system has its own rules and policies governing the ways in which special services are provided to students. If there are barriers at this level that impair movement toward collaboration between regular and special education, then efforts should begin there. For example, there may be a policy statement that specifically dictates the role and function of school psychologists and that prescribes duties that are no longer conducive to providing exemplary services (e.g., a policy dictating a minimum number of psychological evaluations per year). Changing such restrictive local rules is a good example of how microsystem change can promote the provision of services by school psychologists that will support REI program initiatives.

One may encounter resistance in working toward change at this level. Simply pointing out that a particular school district policy is not in keeping with best practices may not be enough to change the policy. In such a circumstance, it can be helpful to enlist the support of colleagues and continue to raise the issue in a variety of contexts. It may also be helpful to distribute applicable professional articles supporting REI and alternative service delivery models to those who are in a position to influence policy making at the district level. If one's immediate superior is a stumbling block, consider lobbying administrators at a higher level. This may be a risky undertaking depending upon a particular district's line and staff relationships, but it is worth considering if change is possible at another level.

The last level of systems change to be addressed involves actions that can be taken as an individual. Change does not have to occur from the top down. In fact, change at the grassroots level can ultimately have an impact on district, state, and federal policies. Individual school psychologists can have an enormous impact on the services they provide. A school psychologist who has the necessary skills to support REI initiatives but has been constrained by traditional roles and demands may be in an excellent position to begin the change process. Consider the following hypothetical example. John Jones, a school psychologist at Lincoln Elementary, wanted to begin to develop an alternate model of services incorporating prereferral interventions and curriculum-based assessment. A teacher with whom he had a history of positive relations (and who also happened to be influential in the building) asked that he test a child because of poor progress in reading. He reviewed the referral with the teacher, suggesting that they try a new approach. John interviewed the teacher to determine what types of interventions had already been attempted and observed the student in the classroom during reading to collect information about instructional variables and the student's responses to instruction. He next conducted a curriculum-based assessment of the student's reading skills to determine if the student was being assigned appropriate reading materials and to assess the types of reading mistakes the student was making. He then formed several hypotheses about the student's lack of progress and began to meet with the teacher to collaboratively develop an intervention plan. In this case, not only was an intervention plan developed for this student, but the school psychologist and teacher also began to develop a classwide peer tutoring program to increase academic engaged time in reading. If this referral had been handled in a traditional fashion, the student may or may not have been eligible for special education services in a pull-out resource or self-contained special education program. In this case, John Jones is well on his way to changing his role at Lincoln.

Obstacles to Change

As has been discussed, change can occur at a variety of levels, and each school psychologist must decide at what point the change should occur. Unfortunately, there seem to be a great many school psychologists who feel rather powerless to effect change. Many feel that the demands on their time are too great and that a change in role would only create more work than they can handle. Others suggest that they work for administrators who will not let them engage in alternative services. Other excuses involve complaints of teachers who will not cooperate with classroom interventions or who simply want students removed from their class. While any of these may be substantive

obstacles in a given situation, they can all be classified as professional resistance or as attributions that one's destiny is controlled solely by external factors. As professionals, school psychologists must accept that they can make a difference. School psychologists cannot accept role demands that are not in keeping with best practices despite the fact that it is easy to become discouraged in the face of resistance.

Another obstacle in this change process is the lack of effective demonstration models. There are too few school districts that have embraced the philosophy underlying REI. For those school psychologists for whom "seeing is believing" or for those who need to observe alternative service models in order to adapt them to their own work environments, there are a shortage of sites to visit. This is particularly problematic in the training of new school psychologists. Even if one's training has focused on classroom interventions, university personnel may have difficulty finding appropriate field placements that will reinforce the training provided. Internships in particular are very important in the development of professional skills, and well-trained interns placed in mediocre work environments do not have the opportunity to refine skills acquired during their training.

Equally likely is the problem of entry-level school psychologists who do not have the necessary training to embrace the kind of role outlined in this chapter. Moreover, there are many practicing school psychologists who do not have the necessary competencies. Training at both the preservice and staff development levels will have to change to meet the needs of schools that are seeking to educate all of their students in the least restrictive environment, regardless of handicap. Unfortunately, not all professionals see the need to develop these kinds of skills and thus, even when afforded the opportunity to develop them, resist profiting from additional training. Our experience suggests that this group cannot be forced to change, and will either leave the field if the pressure to change is great enough or will continue in current roles with diminishing impact.

Kovaleski (1988) suggests that neither the Regular Education Initiative or reform movement will succeed without a major paradigmatic shift in education. He states that the predominant paradigm currently in education is the medical model: Children with learning problems are thought to have something innately wrong with them. The problem is within the child; thus, the focus is on "fixing" the child. Sarason and Doris (1979) have also referred to this model as the "search for pathology." For the reform movement to be successful, a new model for viewing student learning problems must come into use. Several key principals would undergird this model: (a) adults responsible for education would have to believe that all students can learn; (b) prevention would be promoted through mental health services to all students; and (c) there is no single intervention that can be assumed to be effective (Kovaleski, 1988). Under this model, when a student has learning difficulties, school psychologists would not assume that the child has a learning disability or behavior disorder, but instead, would observe the student in relevant environments and look for interactional variables to determine how peers and the teacher respond to the student. After identifying potential antecedent, situational, and consequent events, the teacher and school psychologist could develop hypotheses about the problem and design interventions to test those hypotheses. This experimental teaching approach suggests that there is no a priori solution for a problem, and that the only way to determine if an intervention will be effective is to implement it and measure the effect (Casey, Deno, Marston, & Skiba, 1988).

Kovaleski (1988) may be correct in predicting that this paradigm shift must occur before the Regular Education Initiative can become a reality. It seems, though, that school psychologists can have a major influence in beginning this shift in thinking. Given that the school psychologist fulfills a major role as "gatekeeper" in the current categorical system, changes

in that model can have visible impact. As stated previously, these changes can be implemented at a variety of levels within a given system. Practicing school psychologists should develop a personal set of objectives for change and develop a system for measuring progress toward these objectives. In the example given above, having the teacher carry out a classroom intervention would be a measure of success on such an objective. Although such changes may be small, they can provide the practitioner with measurable evidence of positive progress toward a more functional system of providing services to students with special needs.

CONCLUSION: MEANINGFUL CHANGE OR LOST OPPORTUNITIES?

Whether the Regular Education Initiative will become a reality and enable school psychologists to become full collaborators in the development of educational programs that promote competence for *all* students remains to be seen. The themes in this chapter have not varied from a number of other works calling for change in education and school psychology (National School Psychology Inservice Network, 1984; NASP/NCAS, 1985).

Simply put, it is our premise that school psychology must change to better meet the needs of the students we serve just as schools must change to respond to the changing needs of our nation's student population.

This chapter has outlined some of the conditions creating the need for this change in the ways in which we serve students with special needs and has also suggested the ways in which school psychologists can support the regular education initiative and pursue some long-desired professional roles, particularly those roles involving intervention and consultation. If the professionals who advocate REI and its underlying components are successful, we may be witness to a revision of the educational system that will empower schools to support and educate students with disabilities without segregating them in separate schools and classrooms.

School psychology, as it is currently practiced in most school districts, is not prepared to support such a system. If school psychology is to contribute to this process, practitioners must begin to develop a role in which the school psychologist is an intervention specialist and instructional consultant who can assist teachers and other school staff members in adapting educational materials and modifying instruction so that all students gain maximum benefit from our schools. Whether REI becomes a lost opportunity depends on the extent to which school psychologists develop new skills and assist in changing a long-entrenched system of compensatory education that seems to have outlived its usefulness.

ACKNOWLEDGMENT

The authors express sincere appreciation to Colleen B. Wilcox who made valuable editorial suggestions to an earlier draft of this chapter.

REFERENCES

Blackman, H. (1989). Special education placement: Is it what you know or where you live? *Exceptional Children, 55,* 459–462.

Brown, L., Long, E., Udvari-Solner, A., Schwartz, P., Ahigren, C., Johnson, F., Gruenewald, L., & Jorgensen, J. (1989). Should students with severe intellectual disabilities be based in regular or in special education classrooms in home schools? *Journal of the Association for Persons with Severe Handicaps, 14,* 8–12.

Carnine, D., Granzin, A., & Becker, W. (1988). Direct instruction. In J. L. Graden, J. E. Zins, & M. J. Curtis (Eds.), *Alternative Educational Delivery Systems: Enhancing Instructional Options for All Students* (pp. 327–349). Washington, DC: National Association of School Psychologists.

Casey, A., Deno, S., Marston, D., & Skiba, R. (1988). Experimental teaching: Changing beliefs about effective instructional practices. *Teacher Education and Special Education, 11*(3), 123–131.

Coker, J. G., & Coker, H. (1982). *Classroom observations keyed for effectiveness research.* Atlanta: Georgia State University.

Curtis, M. J., & Meyers, J. (1988). Consultation: A foundation for alternative services in the schools. In J. L. Graden, J. E. Zins, & M. J. Curtis (Eds.), *Alternative Educational Delivery Systems: Enhancing Instructional Options for All Students* (00. 35–48). Washington, DC: National Association of School Psychologists.

Davis, W. E. (1989). The regular education initiative debate: Its promises and problems. *Exceptional Children, 55,* 440–446.

Deshler, D., & Schumaker, J. (1986). Learning strategies: An instructional alternative for low-achieving adolescents. *Exceptional Children, 52,* 583–589.

Gartner, A., & Lipsky, D. (1989). *The yoke of special education: How to break it.* New York: National Center on Education and the Economy.

Gutkin, T. B., & Curtis, M. J. (1982). School-based consultation: Theory and techniques. In C. R. Reynolds & T. B. Gutkin (Eds.), *The handbook of school psychology* (pp. 796–828). New York: Wiley.

Johnson, D. W., & Johnson, R. T. (1986). Mainstreaming and cooperative learning strategies. *Exceptional Children, 52,* 553–561.

Knoff, H. M. (1988). Effective social interventions. In J. L. Graden, J. E. Zins, & M. J. Curtis (Eds.), *Alternative Educational Delivery Systems: Enhancing Instructional Options for All Students* (pp. 431–453). Washington, DC: National Association of School Psychologists.

Kovaleski, J. F. (1988). Paradigmatic obstacles to reform in school psychology. *School Psychology Review, 17,* 479–484.

Macdonald, C., & York, J. (1989). Instruction in regular classes for students with severe disabilities: Assessment, objectives, and instructional programs. In J. York, T. Vandercook, C. Macdonald, & S. Wolff (Eds.), *Strategies for full inclusion* (pp. 83–99). Minneapolis: University of Minnesota, Institute on Community Integration.

National Association of School Psychologists/ National Coalition of Advocates for Students. (1985). *Advocacy for appropriate educational services for all children.* Washington, DC: Author.

National Coalition of Advocates for Students. (1987). *Rights without labels.* Washington, DC: Author.

National School Psychology Inservice Training Network. (1984). *School psychology: A blueprint for training and practice.* Minneapolis, MN: Author.

Nevin, A., & Thousand, J. (1987). Avoiding or limiting special education referrals: Changes and challenges. In M. C. Wang, M. C. Reynolds, & H. J. Walberg (Eds.), *The handbook of special education: Research and practice* (pp. 273–286). Oxford, England: Pergamon.

Peterson, D. R. (1981). Overall synthesis of the Spring Hill Symposium on the Future of Psychology in the Schools. *School Psychology Review, 10,* 307–314.

Peterson, D. W., & Miller, J. (1990). Best practices in peer-mediated learning. In A. Thomas & J. Grimes (Eds.), *Best practices in school psychology* (pp. 531–546). Washington, DC: National Association of School Psychologists.

Reschly, D. J. (1987). Learning characteristics of mildly handicapped students: Implications for classification, placement, and programming. In M. C. Wang, M. C. Reynolds, & H. J. Walberg (Eds.), *The handbook of special education: Research and practice* (pp. 35–58). Oxford, England: Pergamon Press.

Reschly, D. J., Genshaft, J., & Binder, M. S. (1987). *The 1986 NASP survey: Comparisons of practitioners, NASP leadership, and university faculty on key issues.* Washington, DC: National Association of School Psychologists.

Rosenshine, B. V. (1983). Teaching functions in instructional programs. *Elementary School Journal, 83,* 335–352.

Sarason, S., & Doris, J. (1979). *Educational handicap, public policy, and social history.* New York: Free Press.

Shinn, M. R., Rosenfield, S., & Knutson, N. (1989). Curriculum-based assessment: A comparison of models. *School Psychology Review, 18,* 299–316.

Stainback, W., & Stainback, S. (1984). A rationale for the merger of special and regular education. *Exceptional Children, 51,* 102–111.

The Association for Persons with Severe Handicaps. (1986). *Resolution on the redefinition of the continuum of services.* Seattle: Author.

Will, M. (1986). *Educating students with learning problems: A shared responsibility.* Washington, DC: U.S. Department of Education.

Ysseldyke, J. E., & Christenson, S. (1987). *The Instructional Environment Scale.* Austin, TX: Pro-Ed.

Ysseldyke, J. E., Thurlow, M., Graden, J., Wesson, C., Algozzine, B., & Deno, S. (1983). Generalizations from five years of research on assessment and decision-making: The University of Minnesota Institute. *Exceptional Child Quarterly, 4,* 75–93.

Effective Psychological Services for All Students: A Data-Based Model of Service Delivery

Andrea S. Canter
Minneapolis Public Schools

The desire to change or expand roles is hardly a new trend among school psychologists. Each generation of trainers and practitioners has sought to better meld the disciplines of psychology and education, to address the needs of students at risk within regular education as well as those who fall within the political and economic boundaries of "retarded," "learning disabled," or "emotionally disturbed." Yet, to implement such change, the profession must overcome some of its basic historical underpinnings.

Contemporary school psychology is haunted by its traditional ties to medical and special education models. The early clinics of Lightner Witmer gave birth to the first mental health centers in the public schools, often very appropriately termed child study units. Children suspected of retardation or emotional pathology were referred for diagnostic evaluations and treatment prescriptions. Consulting psychiatrists, clinical psychologists, and welfare specialists were among the early providers of mental health services to schoolchildren. In most cases, little changed until the special education movement of the 1960s and 1970s culminated in the implementation of Public Law 94-142. While one might view this change in service delivery as a shift from a medically-rooted orientation to an educational model, it might be more appropriately described as a simple transition from one model of pathology to another, or the "transfer of old wine into new bottles"

(Christenson, Abery, & Weinberg, 1986, p. 358). Rather than concentrating on mental health ailments, psychologists began to address educational health ailments. Clinical consultants were no longer necessary, and child study units were replaced by "student support teams," "multidisciplinary teams," or even "child study teams." With new mandates and allocations for support services from federal and state legislatures, the future of the school psychologist as gatekeeper seemed assured.

Despite the increased opportunities for employment that accompanied the special education mandates of PL 94-142, school psychologists have been frustrated by the discrepancies between their professional skills and assigned roles (e.g., Hyman, 1988). A recent national survey indicated much dissatisfaction among school psychologists with current categorical models of service delivery (Reschly, Genshaft, & Binder, 1987). At the same time, the evidence of the need for alternatives to typical special education placements easily overwhelms any findings supporting the current system (Graden, Zins, Curtis, & Cobb, 1988). Overemphasis upon the identification of handicapping conditions deflects resources from prevention and intervention services, and may in fact lead to inappropriate labeling and placement by perpetuating rather than addressing the lack of educational alternatives. With the majority of their time allocated to gatekeeping evaluations, school psychologists typically have been frozen in the traditional search for pathology, unavailable, unable, or even unwilling to address issues of prevention, instruction, behavior management, classroom ecology, school organization, or cultural differences.

Certain trends suggest that the profession of school psychology is ready for large-scale change. A current theme in the literature, training, and daily practice of school psychology is the need to extend services to nonhandicapped students. As the Regular Education Initiative (Will, 1986) gains momentum, school psychologists can expect more support for their efforts to serve the at-risk student, to provide prevention as well as intervention programs, and to serve the broader educational system (Reschly, 1988). The growing interest in prereferral or "intervention assistance" consultation, curriculum-based assessment, and instructional effectiveness research, along with such documents as the *Blueprint for Training and Practice* (Ysseldyke, Reynolds, & Weinberg, 1984) and *Advocacy for the Education of All Children* (National Association of School Psychologists, 1985), reflect concern for providing a broader range of services to a broader range of student and system needs. Particularly, the increasing emphasis on consultation in both training and practice suggests that school psychology is moving away from problem-finding and toward problem-solving services. Indeed, consultation is viewed as the basic foundation for the implementation of alternative service delivery models (Curtis & Meyers, 1988).

Given this apparent shift in the conceptualization of school psychological services and the desirability of role change, what prevents implementation of new models? While role expansion is often possible on an individual basis, efforts to expand service delivery systems beyond the traditional special education sphere are often hindered by funding restrictions, rigid organizational structures, training limitations, personnel attitudes, the failure to demonstrate effectiveness, and the lack of appropriate models.

To promote system-wide change, professionals must address these problems: (a) the presumed limitations of special education funding on the allocation and functioning of support personnel; (b) traditional structures of support services that promote segregation of students for assessment and intervention (Stainback & Stainback, 1988); (c) the limited training of school psychologists in consultation, functional assessment, and classroom intervention skills (Curtis & Meyers, 1988); (d) the reluctance of school personnel to embrace new models of assessment and service delivery (Stainback & Stainback, 1988; Reynolds, 1988); (e) the failure to demonstrate the need for change or the effectiveness of alternative models of psychological services (Zins & Fairchild, 1986; Bennett, 1988); and (f) the limited dissemination of models of system-wide change in service delivery.

This chapter explores one model of school psychological service delivery that addresses these problems, the Psychological Services program in the Minneapolis Public Schools. There was no formal plan to create what currently may be considered an alternative service delivery system. Rather, the development of a model that emphasizes indirect services to the total school system was more the product of a gradual convergence of multiple influences and long-term planning than of any single event or policy. This model evolved slowly in the context of theoretical, political, and professional forces, particularly: (a) a tradition of concern for child development and individual differences; (b) a statewide system of special education renowned for innovation; (c) the specific implementation of a curriculum-based measurement approach to special education placement, exit, and progress monitoring; and (d) a staff commitment to program evaluation as the basis for decision making and professional development. These foundations are examined as a means of understanding the gradual shift from a problem-finding to a problem-solving system. Two data-based approaches, program evaluation and curriculum-based measurement, are described as significant contributors to the current practice of school psychology. Finally, specific examples of alternative practices are presented.

FOUNDATIONS OF CURRENT PRACTICE

While the delivery of both special education and psychological services in Minneapolis Schools has traditional roots, Minneapolis and, more broadly, Minnesota have deviated significantly from national trends. This pattern is apparent in all major factors influencing service delivery: (a) theoretical foundations, (b) special education policies, (c) administrative organization, and (d) personnel variables.

Historical and Theoretical Context

Initially established as the nation's first school-based psychiatric child guidance clinic in 1924, the Minneapolis Child Study Department was reorganized in 1933 as a diagnostic program reflecting the child welfare agendas of the era (Martens, 1939). Psychiatrists, clinical psychologists, and "visiting teachers" (e.g., psychometrists) formed a unit much like a hospital outpatient clinic. With funding and direction provided by the state's Bureau of Child Welfare, and undoubtedly influenced by the Child Welfare Station at the University of Minnesota, Child Study Department assessments frequently focused upon the identification of retarded children who subsequently were referred for special programming in both state and public school facilities (Thomson, 1963). Through the 1960s, the Child Study "visiting teachers" (later, school psychologists) were somewhat unusual, as their training reflected not only clinical psychology but also child development and teacher education. The melding of psychology and education was perhaps less a struggle than was typical in the early years of school psychology.

Despite this relatively unique blend of clinical, developmental, and educational influences, provision of psychological services continued as a Child Study model through the 1960s, diagnostic evaluations (not necessarily "eligibility" assessments)

being the key activity. Academic failure and behavioral disorder exhibited in the regular education classroom prompted referral for psychological assessment, leading to some type of treatment rendered within or outside of the public school system.

A nearly complete turnover in personnel occurred between the late 1960s and mid-1970s as many staff simultaneously reached retirement age. The next generation of school psychologists reflected the transition from the clinical and developmental orientations of traditional training to the more empirical, behavioral, and ecological orientations promoted today. Some of the new staff had been trained and had worked as child clinicians in mental health centers and hospitals. Some were recent graduates of the cross-disciplinary school psychology training program at the University of Minnesota. Additionally, a behavioral consultant trained in clinical psychology and behavioral analysis was added to the staff. Child Study became Psychological Services, a name change that would soon reflect substantive functional as well as semantic differences.

Special Education

The focus on child development and individual differences was apparent in the initial stages of special education in Minnesota. In 1957, Minnesota enacted special education legislation to assure educational opportunities to a broad range of students who were not successful in the regular classroom, and to provide state funds to reimburse a broad range of special education personnel (Lindborg, 1988). Mental health service providers fell under the definition of "other essential personnel," a forerunner of "related services." At the time, this recognition of support personnel was a radical departure from prevailing practice.

Minnesota's implementation of special education services has deviated in some significant ways from typical practices; these deviations have had important implications for school psychologists. It is very important to note that Minnesota has not mandated special education eligibility criteria, but has instead (through the Department of Education) established *guidelines* for eligibility and assessment that are revised periodically and, at least legally, are open to local interpretation.[1] Basic to the current state of regulation is the longstanding principle that individual differences transcend categorical labels. This concept is apparent in the state's publication, *Guidelines for Reimbursable Services of School Psychologists* (Minnesota Department of Education, 1982), which promotes activities geared to prevention and early intervention with nonhandicapped students at risk.

While state categorical aids financed special education programs and personnel, the staff of the Minneapolis Schools' Psychological Services Department were never the primary gatekeepers. Special education services in the district were comprehensive in scope and personnel long before PL 94-142 mandated such programs. To require psychological assessments to determine eligibility for such a potentially large referral population was unrealistic, both in terms of costs and available staff. Psychologists, no longer "visiting teachers," nevertheless were considered important contributors to the well-being of students, serving as liaisons between child, family, and school (Lindborg, 1988).

Owing to Minnesota's history of progressive special education services, the implementation of regulations tied to PL 94-142 had little effect on school psychology practice in Minneapolis, compared to the dramatic changes observed in many service units. The declining public school enrollment and subsequent budget crises that shortly followed federal special education mandates negated the possibility of increased staffing; rather, there actually was some reduction in staff during this period. Thus, it continued to be unrealistic to establish district eligibility criteria that would require that all students be evaluated by the school psychologist prior to special education placement. As they had done for many years prior to 1975, school psychologists

continued to provide consultation to school personnel regarding placements, frequent assessments for a variety of referral concerns (e.g., poor achievement, disruptive behavior), classroom and school-wide behavior management plans (e.g., time-out procedures), and staff development training (e.g., normal child development).

With the rapid increase in student referrals that accompanied the expansion of special education services through PL 94-142, the need for an indirect model of psychological services delivery could not be denied. While *eligibility* assessments were not routine services, a greater number and variety of student problems were now regarded as legitimate concerns to be addressed by support personnel; this typically involved some type of diagnostic evaluation by the school psychologist. Fortunately, the administrative pressures for school psychologists to assume or maintain gatekeeping roles, common elsewhere, were largely absent in Minneapolis Schools. Local policies and practices were historically open to innovation, and by the early 1980s these organizational patterns were very compatible with school psychologists' desires to implement alternatives to traditional psychological services.

Administration of Services

Paralleling the professional's own identity crises (e.g., Bardon, 1983; Goldwasser, 1982; Trachtman, 1971), Minneapolis Schools historically has been uncertain as to the ideal organizational alignment of Psychological Services. Funding for school psychologists has long been tied to state special education reimbursements, as the school psychology credential is a Board of Teaching "special education" license. However, at times, the program has been part of the regular education system, even as recently as the late 1970s when it was administered under Student Support Services together with guidance, social work, and health staff. There also have been several tenures as a program within Special Education, where the administrative responsibility currently resides. This pattern of administrative shifts has undoubtedly fostered collaboration among a wide range of school personnel (e.g., social workers, counselors, chemical dependency staff, nurses, Chapter One teachers, speech clinicians); such broad alliances appear to promote the delivery of effective psychological services (Henning-Stout & Conoley, 1988).

Within Psychological Services, centralized administrative supervision has been provided by a Chief Psychologist. In Minnesota, and perhaps in many parts of the country, school psychologists typically are assigned as building staff to specific schools and are responsible directly to principals. Consequently, a decentralized staff is supervised by an administrator who is physically (and often professionally) removed from school psychology practice. Despite the size of the Minneapolis district (from a peak enrollment of 85,000 students in 1927 to a low of 38,000 in 1983), there have never been more than 15 positions in Psychological Services; centralization of staff has permitted flexible allocation of services based upon student needs, staff skills, and service priorities.

EMERGENCE OF A NEW MODEL

The Need for Change

The initial expansion of school psychological services was implemented through a "differentiated staffing" model in the late 1960s (Holbrook, 1969), when several consultants were hired to provide specific services not ordinarily within the role of the staff psychologists (e.g., behavioral and psychiatric consultation, direct treatment). However, within a few years this effort was clearly inadequate, as the consultants could address only a very small segment of the referral population and could do so only in a time-limited fashion.

A growing awareness of the importance of indirect services was stimulated by several trends: (a) the changing character of the student population, (b) the loss of revenue from declining enroll-

ment, and (c) the interests and allocation of staff. During the 1960s and 1970s, the Minneapolis Schools reflected the patterns in enrollment and demographics typical of other urban areas, with enrollment decline, budget retrenchment, and a shift from a largely white middle class population to a racially, culturally, and economically diverse clientele. The non-white population (largely black with significant groups of Native Americans, Southeast Asians, and Latinos) was fast approaching a majority. With "white flight" to the suburbs and court-ordered desegregation, a variety of alternative school programs (e.g., open classrooms, science and arts magnets, programs for the gifted and talented) were initiated to foster integration across the district and to attract more affluent families to the inner city schools.

By the 1980s, family stresses seldom observed in the 1950s and 1960s were becoming tragically commonplace; nearly half of the district's families received some type of social assistance, and about one-third were headed by single parents. Responding to the needs of this population was increasingly difficult in the face of some reductions in staff due to declining budgets; the staff–student ratio in 1980 was approximately 1:3,000.

Thus in the late 1970s the shift toward indirect services was a logical response to the increased need for more diverse services, particularly teacher training, group and classroom intervention, and involvement in systems change within both special and regular education (e.g., district policies, program development, and curriculum). An internal reexamination of priorities indicated that reduction of direct services to individual students with a concomitant increase in systems-level services was the most appropriate option for school psychologists.

During the next decade, Psychological Services in Minneapolis became an increasingly consultation-based system providing services directed to the teacher and administrator at least as often as those directly provided to the student. Figure 1 illustrates this change from a

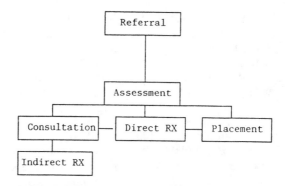

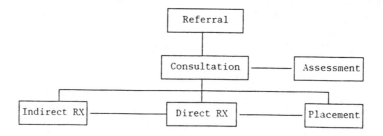

FIGURE 1. Comparison of the traditional and the Minneapolis psychological services models.

model that is largely assessment-driven to one primarily consultation-driven. Assessment practices that had emphasized clinical and diagnostic issues became increasingly functional, more directly addressing classroom issues of instruction and behavior management. The student clientele, never limited to special education populations, included students at risk for school failure due to problems such as limited social skills, poor learning strategies, dysfunctional families, chemical dependency, and truancy. Organizing and training the school psychology staff to effectively deliver indirect services to this diverse population became the major challenges of the 1980s.

Allocation of Personnel

Centralized professional management of Psychological Services, decentral-

ized deployment of staff (e.g., specific building assignments), and a combination of specialized and general service staffing form a unique administrative model that overcomes at least some of the "logistical hurdles" inherent in the urban school systems (Jackson, 1986). Because the administrator (Chief Psychologist) has considerable autonomy in the allocation of resources, different approaches to staff organization have been attempted in an effort to provide more broadly based services.

During the Child Study era, service delivery was completely centralized, with no specific school assignments; psychologists traveled throughout the district in response to referrals. With the hiring of consultants and some new staff in 1970, an experimental team model was established in one set of schools to encourage consultation with teachers as an alternative to testing. Geographically organized units of school psychologists were implemented during the late 1970s, with teams of four or five psychologists serving groups of approximately 15–20 schools. Referrals and service requests were distributed among team members on the basis of staff skills and interests. An immediate outcome of this model was the dramatic increase in staff development, program consultation, and other systems-level interventions sparked by collaboration among psychologists. However, school administrators and student support teams often reported that the assignment of several psychologists impeded communication and limited any single psychologist's familiarity with a school's specific problems.

In the 1980s this lack of service continuity in a school system experiencing increased mobility and school closings and reopenings, as well as a growth in alternative school organizations (e.g., open schools), led to the current model. Each staff psychologist is assigned to a set of four to six schools as the primary service provider; they continue to offer some services as teams (e.g., inservice training, group intervention) and use each other as consultants and collaborators.

Another change in the past 10 years, reflecting the increased emphasis on indirect services and the growing multicultural character of the district, has been the creation of "special assignment" positions. One school psychology position is allocated 50% time to research and program evaluation projects; another position is allocated 50% time to serving students from foreign cultures, including students in the Limited English Proficiency (LEP) and bilingual education programs. One position, jointly funded with the University of Minnesota, primarily is allocated to graduate student training and field supervision. The Chief Psychologist has retained his initial role as a district-wide behavioral consultant.

The creation of additional positions for school psychologists has resulted in further specialization and opportunities for professional collaboration across district programs. For example, school psychologists have been hired directly by the preschool special education program and the secondary program for emotionally and behaviorally disordered students. Psychologists also have been hired by the special education resource (instruction) programs to serve as behavioral consultants to special education teachers throughout the district. In addition, two school psychology positions have been created to manage externally and internally funded research and evaluation projects for the Special Education Department. While not administratively assigned to the Psychological Services program, these school psychologists have had considerable impact on the delivery of services to both regular and special education. They represent a new generation of school psychologists, well versed in research and instructional methodologies.

Staff Development

While the need to move toward indirect services for the total school population was recognized by staff and administration, changing psychologists' roles from direct service providers to consultants was initially difficult because of (a) staff resistance in the schools and among psychologists and (b) school psychologists' lack of confidence in their consultation skills. All had been trained prior to 1976, well before the term "alternative service delivery" entered our professional jargon; none of the staff psychologists had received specific training in consultation as part of their graduate programs. The notion of reducing direct activity with students created a great deal of ambivalence and anxiety in professionals who entered the field, in part, because of the high degree of satisfaction gained from working with children. Consultation and systems intervention were somewhat nebulous concepts, hard to define and difficult to imagine in a system that was accustomed to viewing psychologists primarily as diagnosticians.

Thus, implementation of new roles required a continuing professional development program specifically designed to meet local staff concerns about alternative service delivery activities. Internal staff development became a regular component of Psychological Services, initially emphasizing behavioral consultation to teachers and involvement with parents of minority students. More recently, training has stressed instructional consultation, criterion-referenced assessment, observation, and measurement of intervention effectiveness. Staff attendance at continuing professional development conferences and workshops has been encouraged and supported by special education administration, as has peer collaboration in developing interventions aimed at the building and system level (e.g., school-wide programs for self-esteem enhancement and reducing truancy). Recent reports of research and practice published in the school psychology literature have been circulated for consideration and discussion. Such ongoing staff development and internal peer support are considered keys to effective implementation of consultation-based services (e.g., Lennox, Hyman, & Hughes, 1988). During the 1988-1989 school year, a voluntary staff support group met regularly with a University of Minnesota trainer to discuss issues, share experiences, and brainstorm strategies. In essence, such peer consultation serves to enhance school consultation services.

As the preceding discussion indicates, no single political, economic, or professional factor led to the development of the current model of psychological services in Minneapolis. Two specific practices, however, can be identified as playing critical roles in the implementation of the present service delivery system: (a) the development of a proactive approach to evaluating school psychological services and (b) the implementation of curriculum-based measurement procedures in special education. Each of these practices provides a database for decision making, enhancing opportunities for services directed toward improving the school experience of all students.

A PROACTIVE SYSTEM OF ACCOUNTABILITY

The need for accountability procedures — methods of documenting services and measuring effectiveness — has been apparent among school psychologists for many years. A variety of approaches have been described and disseminated (e.g., Zins, 1985; Zins et al., 1982); yet many school psychologists have no systematic process of gathering data that describe practices, justify costs, or measure outcome (Zins & Fairchild, 1986). With the rapid change in student population and subsequent increased demand for services in the early 1970s, it became apparent that Minneapolis school psychologists needed not only a new model of service delivery, but a systematic process of documenting and evaluating that model. Thus, procedures were developed that enabled psychologists to monitor their roles in service delivery, examine referral issues, document staff development needs, and measure effectiveness of interventions, as well as to track changes in these areas over time. All staff psychologists have participated in accountability activities since 1971, using procedures initiated by Jerry Tomlinson, now Chief Psychologist (Tomlinson, 1973, 1974). Over the years, this evaluation system has undergone numerous revisions and expansion to reflect changes in the district, professional concerns, and program goals. Descriptive frequency tallies of professional activities and direct outcome data are collected throughout the school year; specific studies of time allocation are conducted at 3- to 4-year intervals.

Procedures: Services to Individual Students

Using a data record for each student served, Minneapolis psychologists continuously collect data describing referred students in terms of gender, ethnicity, age, referral concerns, services provided, and outcome of interventions. When specific academic or behavioral intervention strategies are implemented (e.g., time-out, social skills training), target behaviors,

Minneapolls Publlc Schools
Speclal Educatlons Servlces Traller
PSYCHOLOGICAL SERVICES

Staff___CANTER, Andrea_____ Employee #___12416_____ Date_____

STUDENT_____ SIN:_____ School_____Sch #_____

Grade_____ DOB _____ Retentlon _____1 _____2+

Sex _____M _____F   Ethnlc _____Mj _____Blk _____NA _____As _____Hs _____Other

---

| Referral | Service Type | Outcome |

Referral

____ Sp Ed Re-eval:
_____ MR
_____ LD
_____ EBD

____ Academlc:
_____Skllls
_____Task compl

____ Behavlor:
_____Act out/dlsrupt
_____Aggress
_____Anx/depr
_____Chem
_____Crlsls
_____Dlstract/atten
_____Noncompllance
_____Soclal
_____Truant

Service Type

____ INDIRECT DX:
_____Observe
_____Record Rev
_____Behav Data
_____Envlron.
_____Rate/Chklst

____ Consult:
_____Staff
_____Parent
_____Agency/other

____ DIRECT DX:
_____Intell. Test
_____Soc/Em Test
_____Intervlew
_____Academlc
_____Other

____Treatment/Interv*:
_____ Indlv _____Group

Outcome

_____Informatlon

_____Plan*
_____IEP-Psy

_____Placement:
_____Sp Ed
_____SERCC
_____Refer out
_____Other

---

* Consultation/intervention plan and evaluation

Focus/target behavlor:
_____ Act out/dlsrupt _____Aggress _____Anx/depr _____Noncomply _____Soclal _____Truant
_____ Ac skllls _____Task _____Study Skllls
_____ Other:

Intervention type: _____Behav mgt (Indlrect)   _____behav mgt (dlrect)
_____group   _____ Indlv cslg   _____sklll tralnlng
_____Instruc modlflcatlon
_____other (Describe):

RATING 1: _____A _____B _____C _____N/Alt   RATING 2: _____A _____B _____C _____N/Alt

FIGURE 2. Minneapolis Schools individual student data entry form.

---

baseline data, intervention plans, and performance goals are coded. Outcome data, such as direct observation or teachers' records of performance, are collected with respect to goal attainment, as described later. The most recent version of this record is presented in Figure 2.

In conjunction with these descriptive procedures, psychologists formerly rated outcomes of interventions primarily on the basis of teachers' reports ("no problem," "improved," or "no improvement"), rather than direct performance data (Tomlinson, 1974). Although this provided fairly reliable data about teachers' willing-ness to implement recommendations and their perceptions of change in students' behavior, there were no means of obtain-ing objective information about actual change in the target behavior. Nor was this an acceptable means of evaluating the psychologist's role in any observed change. More recently, psychologists have used a structured monitoring procedure to obtain more objective outcome data, using direct measures of student performance and/or more systematic staff ratings of perceived change (Figure 2).

Goals are set for each intervention at two levels of improvement (i.e., Level A = *desired* level of improvement; Level B = *acceptable* level of improvement; Level C = no significant improvement), using modifications of goal attainment scaling procedures described by Maher (1983). Thus, outcome ratings are derived in a uniform manner across all psychologists, regardless of the type of intervention approach or nature of the target behavior. Documentation of behavior change in-cludes direct observation over time, classroom performance data (e.g., test scores, completion rates, curriculum-based measurement), or pre- and post-intervention ratings of target behaviors or attitudes by staff and/or students.

Procedures: Services to Classrooms and the Larger System

In addition to the record of services directed to individual students, a parallel data-recording procedure documents direct and indirect services at the class-room, building, or system level. These last two levels correspond to Level 3 and Level 4 consultation as described by Lennox, Hyman, and Hughes (1988). Data also are collected regarding staff training and research. For each of these broad-based activities, psychologists record the type of service (e.g., staff development, classroom management, or group intervention), type and number of participants (teachers, administrators), and the hours spent planning and providing the service (Figure 3). An additional code regarding the level of staff development (awareness, knowl-edge, skill-building, or applied skills) has been included to be consistent with such data collected statewide. A recent addi-tion to this data record is outcome evaluation. A description of the evaluation plan and service outcome for the target individuals or programs is recorded on the reverse side of the data form. Data are analyzed descriptively as a means of monitoring service delivery in relation to department goals, particularly as systems-directed services relate to individual student-directed services.

Systems-level interventions (e.g., staff training, program consultation, research) have posed specific problems in evaluating effectiveness. Staff training, for example, presents logistical problems in obtaining follow-up data, as well as difficulties related to nebulous goals and lack of objective measures (Davis, 1986). Efforts to evaluate the effects of inservice training have yielded ambiguous results. Imme-diate feedback, such as participants' ratings of presentations, tends to be unrelated to the ultimate application of the information or skills taught, although such ratings can be helpful in examining the organization and pacing of a presen-tation. Responses from teachers to specific questions about their application of new skills several months following training have provided more useful information regarding the degree to which inservice promotes change in teachers' behavior. However, this type of feedback tends to yield information regarding the frequency or nature of their application of the new skills, rather than data regarding the direct impact of the teachers' training on their students' performance.

Depending upon the focus of inservice training, it has been possible in specific instances to obtain direct teacher and student performance data in a pre- and post-training format. For example, before and after a 6-week program to train teachers in assertive classroom manage-ment techniques, target students and participating teachers were observed in their classrooms, and teachers' attitudes toward management issues were exam-ined using questionnaires. Unfortunately, the vast majority of staff development

SPECIAL SCHOOL DISTRICT NO 1-MINNEAPOLIS, MINNESOTA

PSYCHOLOGICAL SERVICES

SCH/ORG	SCHOOL/ORGANIZATION	TARGET:	T	S/SP	ADM	PSY	PAR	STU	PARA	O
1 2 3	DESCRIPTION:		14	15	16	17	18	19	20	21
TOTAL N		FROM:	SCH	MPS	DIS	ORG	AGY	UNI	O	
5 6 7			23	24	25	26	27	28	29	
N PSY		TYPE:	INS	TRG	MGT	PRO	GRP	RES	COM	ADM
9 10			31	32	33	34	35	36	37	38
	PSYCHOLOGIST:	LEVEL:	AW	KN	SK	AP				
*EVAL 12	OTHER PSY:		40	41	42	43				

TOTAL HOURS

HOURS LOG

SYSTEMS INTERVENTION FORM

45 46 47

*EVALUATION PLAN

Goals of Intervention:

Eval Procedure: _____ post rating _____ pre/post rating _____ follow-up _____ direct meas _____ other

Describe:

Outcome: _____ surpassed goals _____ met goals _____ met some goals _____ ineffective _____ no action

Describe:

FIGURE 3. Minneapolis Schools systems intervention data record.

activities are single presentations of information rather than intensive training in specific skills that can be directly evaluated.

Other consultation and intervention activities at the classroom, building, or systems level prompt a variety of evaluation efforts. Classroom management and group interventions (such as social skills groups) typically have specific goals and observable target behaviors that are appropriate to pre- and post-treatment designs. Consultations regarding program development, curriculum, or district policy are evaluated most easily in terms of implementation (e.g., Bennett, 1988): Were the intended activities carried out,

timelines addressed, target students served, policies written? Research activities similarly are evaluated most easily in terms of implementation, adherence to timelines, or ultimate application of findings. There has been no staff-wide effort to systematize evaluation of research or program-level consultation services.

Procedures: Evaluating Consultation

The evaluation of consultation activities has been of particular concern in the past few years as consultation-based services have been emphasized in Psychological Services. Student outcomes are evaluated as indicated earlier, in terms of intervention effectiveness based upon performance data. However, student outcome evaluation assumes that *implementation* has actually occurred (Bennett, 1988), and tends to address the effectiveness of intervention strategies rather than the *process* of consultation or the application of a consultation model of service delivery. Furthermore, a considerable amount of staff time is spent in consultation activities that may not be tied directly to a specific intervention plan. For example, psychologists provide information, suggestions, interpretations, and collaborative brainstorming with teachers and administrators regarding a variety of issues that are not always specific to an individual student problem. Thus, it became necessary to develop evaluation procedures that addressed consultation implementation, consumer satisfaction, and specific consultant skills in order to better understand the consultation process and its acceptance as a viable approach to serving schools.

In 1987, a multi-method approach to evaluating consultation processes was initiated, first with a sample of district schools, and later with all schools in the district. Consumer (e.g., teacher, support staff, administrator) satisfaction was evaluated at the end of the school year with a questionnaire based on the Psychological Services Assessment Questionnaire (PSAQ) developed by Zins (1981). The questionnaire included ratings on a 5-point Likert scale regarding the consultant's interactions and the effectiveness of the consultation process. Although this type of evaluation seems most appropriate for use by staff who have frequent interaction with the psychologist (i.e., administrators, special education team members, and social workers), individual classroom teachers often have only one or two experiences with any given psychologist during the year. During the 1988–1989 school year, a sample of classroom teachers was asked to complete a questionnaire regarding a specific consultation service shortly after the service was provided. This process was facilitated by asking all psychologists to provide, throughout the school year, the names of at least two classroom teachers with whom they had consulted in the past month. Thus, periodic feedback from classroom teachers was focused on consultation regarding specific issues, whereas year-end feedback from support and administrative staff emphasized perceived overall effectiveness of consultation services provided to the school.

Another evaluation approach initiated in 1987 concerns the implementation of consultation-based services as perceived by the psychologist. To obtain information about the ongoing efforts and experiences of consulting with school staff, each psychologist was interviewed by the Chief Psychologist or Research Psychologist at approximately 8-week intervals during the 1987–1988 school year. The structured interview questions addressed the specific activities of "marketing" consultation, perceived barriers to implementation, examples of consultations, estimates of time spent, and ratings of effectiveness and staff acceptance. At the end of the school year, a final self-administered questionnaire was given to the psychologists that was very similar in content and format to the interview. While the psychologists considered the information to be very useful, the logistics of scheduling staff interviews were such that a periodic self-administered questionnaire replaced the interviews the following year. The content was very similar to that of the interview, and each psychologist completed the questionnaire three times during the school year. Extensive evaluation of consultation services will be conducted at 2- to 3-year intervals.

Allocation of Staff Time

Further understanding of current practice and priorities can be facilitated by determining how professional time is allocated. Although time spent on each systems-level service is recorded continuously by Minneapolis psychologists (Figure 3), time spent on services directed at individual students has been studied periodically. Five systematic data-gathering activities have been implemented since

1978 in order to obtain information about changes in the allocation of time across all professional school psychology activities (Canter & Tomlinson, 1987). In 1978, 1981, 1986, and 1988, each staff member coded the amount of time spent in professional activities (e.g., testing, reviewing records, consulting, report writing, counseling, staff training) during five consecutive work days. A work log was used to record activity at 15-minute intervals and a systematic coding of defined service categories was completed following data collection. In a fifth study of time allocation conducted in 1985, each staff member recorded the amount of time spent specifically in assessment, consultation, and treatment (direct intervention) activities for five referred students, again using a work log and 15-minute-interval recording.

Applications of Program Evaluation

Accountability data, to be useful, must be accessible to relevant personnel and be applied to problems of service delivery (Zins & Fairchild, 1986). Psychological Services staff receive monthly caseload reports, with a more detailed analysis at midyear and at the beginning of the new school year. Data analysis in recent years has been enhanced greatly by the use of microcomputers and database software. An annual staff review of the previous year's data often generates modifications in the procedures and goals of data collection as well as discussion of school psychologists' service delivery issues. Accountability projects are managed by the Research and Evaluation Psychologist, who is responsible for coordinating accountability activities, summarizing data, and reporting to staff. However, all psychologists have input into decisions regarding data collection procedures and changes in service delivery. Staff thus are invested sufficiently in the evaluation system to comply with data collection requirements and regard the system as useful.

Modifications in school psychology practice have been direct and indirect outcomes of the accountability system in Minneapolis. Analyzing the frequency and type of professional activities (e.g., testing, consultation, direct treatment, record review) allows psychologists to describe their current roles, practices, and clientele. For example, for any given time period, psychologists can easily note the percentage of students receiving intellectual assessment in contrast to individual counseling, the number of males and females referred, and the distribution of referrals by student age. While the collection of such data has been criticized for providing only quantitative rather than qualitative information (Bennet, 1980; Sandoval & Lambert, 1977), access to such data over time enables psychologists to better understand the nature of the referral population and to identify, monitor, and anticipate trends in service needs.

These longitudinal data have suggested activities to address the needs of a wide range of students, particularly those in regular education who are at risk for special education referral and poor achievement. For example, when data over 10 years consistently indicated that boys are referred two to three times as often as girls, discussion and reviews of the research literature generated concerns regarding the underreferral of girls for problems such as anxiety and depression. Further literature review, internal staff development, inservice programs for schools, and consultation with community professionals helped heighten awareness of less visible problems that could be addressed by early prevention and intervention activities. The disproportionate referral of minority students and the interaction between gender and ethnicity relative to referral problems (Tomlinson, Acker, Canter, & Lindborg, 1977) similarly led to staff development and inservice training regarding cultural issues relevant to school performance and referral rates. Alternatives to both traditional assessment and intervention strategies were explored and subsequently received greater emphasis in daily practice.

Time allocation data have provided the basis for further study of service delivery and the development of improved practices. When time-sampling data indicated that each psychological assessment involved an average of 7 hours of professional time (Canter & Tomlinson, 1987), concern was expressed regarding the relevance as well as efficiency of these assessments. The form and function of psychological reports were discussed and appropriate literature was reviewed. A study of the relevance of assessments to referral questions and subsequent intervention was completed (Canter, 1987b), the results suggesting the need to better link assessment and intervention. Consequently, recent staff development topics have emphasized alternative assessment approaches (criterion-referenced, curriculum-based, ecological, and observational); and different psychological report formats have been explored. In order to encourage attention to specific intervention strategies in report writing, an interactive computer program, "Supplemental Report," was developed by two staff members (Acker & Tomlinson, 1988). A follow-up of the 1987 study of assessment reports is planned to examine the degree of change in actual practice following these internal interventions.

The distribution of school psychological services and time spent in each can only describe, not evaluate, the effectiveness of a service delivery program. While program outcomes are difficult to assess because of the lack of control over many confounding variables (Zins & Fairchild, 1986), the measurement of effectiveness may be the most crucial component of program evaluation. Effectiveness data have been particularly useful in improving professional practices: The *documentation* of student outcomes alone has been helpful in encouraging systematic planning of behavioral interventions, setting specific goals, and monitoring student performance. Analysis of aggregated data also has suggested specific student problems, intervention strategies, and demographic variables that must be addressed to improve student performance. For example, when a specific issue or concern is identified through staff review of outcome data, such as intervention with aggressive minority boys, appropriate staff

development, literature review, and community consultation can take place in efforts to modify current practice.

An examination of all data specific to consultation has permitted an integrated analysis of actual services provided, student outcomes, consultant and consultee perceptions, and implementation issues. Comparing rates of consultation to rates of other professional activities also has permitted the evaluating of consultation implementation rates across the district and an understanding of the differential results of varying approaches to service. As one would anticipate, data regarding the implementation of consultation indicate considerable variation in both psychologists' consultation strategies and the response of school personnel to these services. Most important, some effective means of implementing consultation in the district have been identified and incorporated into subsequent consultation efforts. For example, factors associated with high consumer ratings and successful implementation include regular scheduling of time spent by the psychologist in the school, high rates of contact with classroom teachers *in* the classroom, participation on building prereferral or special education teams, a willingness to modify strategies to encourage consultation requests, and documentation of intervention plans and outcomes.

Ultimately, consultation appears to affect a greater number of students and staff than do traditional direct services. However, the data clearly have indicated that effective consultation is also very time-consuming. Given present assignments of four to six schools per psychologist, it seems unrealistic to expect that consultation can be implemented with equal effectiveness in every building. Potentially, the consultation data may be used to support requests for increased staffing. Meanwhile, these data have enabled psychologists to make better decisions in setting priorities for implementation activities at each school based upon other factors influencing effectiveness, such as building communication systems, acceptance of consultation by teachers and administrators, the efficacy

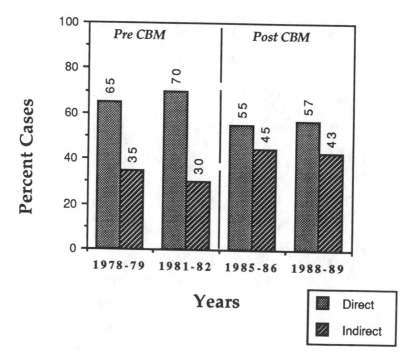

FIGURE 4. Direct and indirect services to students. Direct services include direct assessment (testing, interviewing) and direct treatment (counseling, group treatment, skill training). Indirect services include consultation, intervention planning, and observation. Students who received *only* indirect services are counted as "indirect"; all others are included as "direct" in these data.

of school teams, and individual psychologists' skills and interests.

Summary: Documenting Role Change through Accountability Procedures

The documentation of role change has been an important application of the accountability system. Descriptive data regarding professional functions and time allocation have reflected a gradual shift from traditional services (direct services, diagnostic emphasis) to more indirect, consultation-based services. For example, through the middle to the late 1970s, staff development programs were occasionally offered to schools by a few staff members; likewise, most staff participated only marginally in interventions aimed at the system of the school or district. With the initiation of new priorities that placed less emphasis on direct individual student services in favor of more indirect and

systems services, considerable change was documented in the following 10 years. More psychologists provided systems intervention services, spent greater portions of time in staff training, research, and program consultation activities, and at the same time provided assessment service to fewer students (Figures 4 and 5).

Time allocation and professional function data also have documented a change in the distribution of services to individual students. Consultation is provided more frequently, while the relative number of students receiving assessment services has decreased. This shift has been particularly dramatic since the implementation of curriculum-based measurement (CBM) as the primary approach to special education assessment and progress monitoring (Figures 4 and 5). While district needs and deliberate efforts to expand roles already accounted for some change,

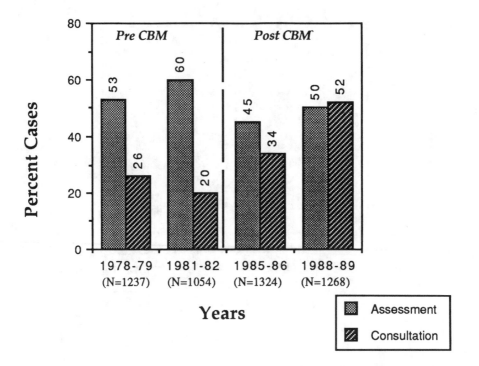

FIGURE 5. Direct assessment versus consultation. *Direct assessment* includes testing and interviews. *Consultation* is defined as problem-solving activities, often in conjunction with the development of specific intervention plans, and includes school, agency, and parent consultation. These services are not mutually exclusive; some students receive both assessment and consultation services. Other services not accounted for here include direct treatment, record review, and classroom observation.

the development of the local CBM model had far-reaching effects on the delivery of psychological services to all students.

IMPACT OF CURRICULUM-BASED MEASUREMENT

While PL 94-142 had little apparent effect on school psychology practice in Minneapolis, the implementation of a curriculum-based measurement (CBM) system for determining special education eligibility and measuring student progress created both new opportunities and new concerns regarding professional roles.

The CBM Model

The CBM model was developed to address many of the shortcomings of traditional assessment, including technical adequacy, the mismatch between curriculum and assessment, instructional relevance, and sensitivity to student progress. Measurement is based upon direct and repeated observation of academic performance and behavior in the student's curriculum. Time-series graphic analyses are applied to performance data to determine the effectiveness of academic and behavioral interventions (Deno & Mirkin, 1977). In Minneapolis this approach has been standardized locally, with prescribed materials drawn from the district curriculum in reading, math, spelling, and written language; norms have been established for fall, winter, and spring periods of the school year (Marston & Magnusson, 1985, 1988).

The assessment materials and procedures have been researched extensively and described in detail elsewhere (e.g., Deno, 1985; Marston & Magnusson, 1985, 1988). Briefly, students are asked to read passages from the district's reading curriculum, to compute arithmetic problems, to spell words dictated from the district spelling program, and to write endings for "story starters." At kindergarten and first grade, students are administered readiness measures, including naming and copying letters and numbers. Typically, these CBM procedures are administered by a special education teacher following the classroom teacher's referral as part of the screening process. Students who fall below specified criteria on screening are referred for additional assessment which includes more extensive application of CBM procedures, graphing of student progress in the mainstream program, diagnostic instruction over 6 weeks, classroom observation, and other measures of performance. Nationally standardized achievement measures might also be included in the assessment phase. If mental retardation or emotional/behavior disorder is suspected, the school psychologist provides further assessment as appropriate. Although achievement data are collected primarily by special education teachers, psychologists are available to participate in assessment planning and interpretation of data prior to team decisions regarding placement, and they may directly participate in assessment activities.

Eligibility for special education resource services (e.g., pullout tutoring in a resource room) is determined by comparing the student's progress in the curriculum with his or her expected level of progress, generally assumed to be within the normal range of instruction at that grade level. Based upon rate of progress, goals are established in reference to an "aim line," a graphic portrayal of the student's expected progress. Progress is monitored continuously by frequent assessment with the same CBM procedures. The student's actual rate of progress (the trend line) can thus indicate the need for modification of instruction or individual education plan (IEP) objectives, or readiness to exit from the special education program. Five years of extensive and ongoing research have demonstrated the efficacy of this approach as

an identification system, as well as its utility for making data-based decisions about instruction (e.g., Marston & Magnusson, 1985, 1988; Shinn, 1988; Shinn, Tindal, & Stein, 1988).

CBM and Psychological Services

Like all new tools that challenge tradition, CBM has not been free of critics and skeptics (e.g., Lombard, 1988). While questions of technical adequacy have been well addressed by recent research (e.g., Allen & Marston, 1988; Marston & Magnusson, 1985; Shinn, 1988; Shinn, Tindal, & Stein, 1988), anxiety among school psychologists (locally and nationally) surfaces whenever CBM is suggested as an alternative to traditional psychometric methods. Some administrators have suggested that school psychologists will no longer be necessary if CBM is implemented to determine special education eligibility (Canter, 1987a), implying that the gatekeeping function is indeed the only role to which school psychologists are well suited and essential. Although there appears to be no evidence of the validity of this fear, concern for self-preservation among school psychologists might nevertheless prevent an objective evaluation of the model's merits. Similar concern was expressed in the last decade with the publication of the Woodcock-Johnson Psycho-educational Battery, which was not specifically limited to administration by psychologists and, in some areas, was embraced by special education teachers as *their* tool (McGrew, 1987).

In fact, it has been primarily through the efforts of school psychologists that CBM has been implemented in local school districts (Canter & Allen, 1989; Germann & Tindal, 1985; Marston & Magnusson, 1985). Not only have school psychology positions continued in these districts, but the implementation of CBM has enabled psychologists to assume new roles as direct and indirect service providers to address multifaceted problems of students. Furthermore, CBM has provided an ongoing database from which to develop effective interventions, particularly as alternatives to special education placement. As Shinn (1988) notes, CBM can not prescribe new roles nor direct alternative practices; it does, however, relieve psychologists of gatekeeping duties, which consume so much of their professional time.

Psychologists in Minneapolis never were required to individually assess all students prior to special education placement in the pre-CBM era. However, they did spend considerable time reviewing other evaluations, observations, and performance data that often varied from school to school or that lacked definable relationships to classroom instruction. Individual psychological evaluations, including intelligence tests, were often requested when existing data provided little indication of a student's academic aptitude. Time spent on such tasks did restrict time available to help design prevention and intervention activities, regardless of the psychologists' motivation to expand services.

The implementation of CBM provided opportunities for such services by systematizing the special education assessment process in a manner directly linked to instruction, eliminating the majority of requests for psychological assessments of learning disabilities. The CBM model itself opened doors to new positions for psychologists as teacher trainers, facilitators, and researchers regarding CBM procedures. Because psychologists are typically the most appropriate school professionals to develop, implement, and evaluate any new measurement system, it was argued convincingly that this new district-wide program required psychologists' expertise to insure sound application of assessment procedures to instruction.

The implementation of CBM procedures to monitor student progress has enhanced psychological consultation by providing an easily accessible database for students receiving or referred for special education services. Both instructional and behavioral data are collected as part of the special education eligibility assessment and as part of ongoing performance monitoring of mildly handicapped students. These data reduce the need for psychologists to design separate (and

often cumbersome) intervention evaluation plans. CBM procedures also have provided a formative model of evaluation of student progress in regular education, in which the psychologist, classroom teacher, or paraprofessional can assume responsibility for data collection. With access to such a database, the psychologist can truly serve as an "experimenter who tests educational reforms" (Deno, 1986, p. 373). By avoiding imposition of a new monitoring system on the classroom teacher, psychologists also are more likely to find acceptance of their own consultation and recommendations, and thus greatly increase the probability of success.

CBM also promotes more functional approaches to assessment among psychologists as well as special education personnel, with assessment frequently linked to intervention. When assessments were geared toward identifying within-child deficits to diagnose learning or emotional handicaps (e.g., searching for a verbal-performance discrepancy), there seemed to be little relationship between testing and teaching. Research associated with CBM models has heightened psychologists' awareness of the failure of traditional diagnostic procedures to help identify relevant classroom interventions. Today, Minneapolis school psychologists are more likely to use measures that directly address instructional and ecological variables, and thus are linked more readily to classroom interventions. Furthermore, the CBM data provide a systematic and (locally) normative base from which to develop some hypotheses about a student's instructional needs, usually eliminating the need to obtain other normative achievement data to determine current levels of performance.

CBM and Role Change

While the Psychological Services program evaluation system has documented gradual changes in service delivery over the past 15 years, of particular interest are the changes that followed implementation of CBM in the fall of 1983. A review of accountability data collected between 1978 (before CBM) and 1988

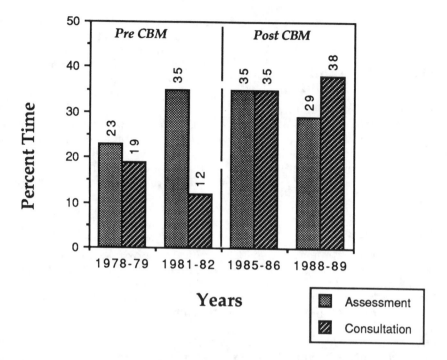

FIGURE 6. Assessment versus consultation time. Assessment includes all diagnostic activities — observation, interview, testing, scoring, report writing. Consultation includes consultation with teachers, parents, agencies, administrators, and building teams. Other services not accounted for as assessment or consultation include direct treatment, teacher or parent training, research, supervision, administrative tasks, policy development, professional development, travel between buildings, school and district committee activity, and attending school conferences.

indicates that psychologists now provide proportionately more consultation regarding individual students (from 12% to 52% of caseload), more direct intervention services (from 1.5% to 10%), and fewer assessment services (from 66% to 49%) in the "CBM era." While half of all students served by Minneapolis psychologists received some type of assessment service in 1988–1989, only half of these assessments included evaluation of intellectual functioning. These figures compare to 66% assessments, of which about two-thirds included intelligence evaluation, prior to CBM implementation in 1982–1983 (see Figure 5). Data also suggest that assessments are *qualitatively* different as well, as more time is spent per assessment since the introduction of CBM (see Figure 6).

While acknowledging that more comprehensive assessments require more time, it is also important to note that Minneapolis school psychologists only spend about 29% of their time engaged in assessment activity (Canter & Tomlinson, 1987; Canter, 1989) compared to a statewide average of 44% (Minnesota Department of Education, 1983), and national estimates of 47% (Lacayo, Morris, & Sherwood, 1981). There is no doubt that the implementation of an alternative assessment and eligibility system has had a positive impact on the school psychologist's role in Minneapolis, and there is potential for even further change in service delivery. As the CBM system undergoes expansion and refinement, and as school-based research yields a greater understanding of the variables affecting student learning and behavior, there should be an even greater demand for the professional roles of school psychologists as classroom and systems-level problem solvers.

PSYCHOLOGICAL SERVICES FOR ALL CHILDREN

The remainder of this chapter will be devoted to a series of examples of services provided to the total school population by Minneapolis Schools psychologists — to handicapped, at-risk, and even nonreferred students, to school staff and parents, and to the larger system.

Functional Assessment

As noted earlier, Minneapolis school psychologists continue to spend a significant portion of time (29%) in assessment-related activities. However, these activities tend to be *qualitatively* different, as well as more time-consuming, than traditional assessment activities. Typically, evaluation follows consultation with the classroom teacher regarding referral concerns. Problem-centered consultation drives decision making regarding assessment, rather than assessment driving decision making regarding consultation or intervention. Consultation and subsequent intervention planning are often sufficient to address referral concerns without any formal evaluation procedure.

Furthermore, assessments are typically directed toward the development of instructional or behavioral interventions (formative evaluation) rather than toward eligibility and placement issues. Assessments of regular education students might *precede* special education referral, or *follow* special education assessments when students' difficulties do not meet placement criteria but continue to be of significant concern to teachers or parents. Examples of current assessment approaches include ecological and criterion-referenced assessments, informal measures of academic performance, a variety of behavioral observation systems, review of CBM and other direct performance data, informal interviews with the student, and published norm-referenced procedures. Again, the explicit goal of the school psychologist's assessment is to provide the classroom teacher with specific information about current skills and recommendations regarding materials, instructional approaches, progress monitoring, and ecological factors affecting performance. The Instructional Environment Scale (Ysseldyke & Christenson, 1987) has proven to be an invaluable tool for directing classroom observations and teacher consultation, not only because of the structure it provides, but also as a means of increasing sensitivity to factors related to instructional effectiveness and student performance.

Task-related behaviors such as work completion, following directions, and organizing work, collectively labeled "academic survival skills" (Cobb & Hops, 1973), are a frequent focus of assessment and intervention planning in the mainstream classroom. Rating scales, behavioral observations, and direct performance data, such as task completion rates, are typical evaluation approaches. The development of a locally normed *Mainstream Survival Skills Assessment* is one outcome of psychologists' concern for instructionally relevant assessment procedures (Canter & Heistad, 1988).

Finally, with both handicapped and nonhandicapped students, assessments tend to emphasize *response* to intervention at least as much as the *need* for intervention. Reschly (1988) predicts that future applications of tests such as the WISC-R will be limited to students "who have severe persistent achievement problems which have been unresponsive to a variety of remedial programs, including the kind of instruction now provided in special education" (p. 464); such is the *current* state of school psychologists' practice in Minneapolis Schools. Students already placed in special education services might be referred for evaluation of limited progress or even possible readiness for less restrictive placements. Evaluation includes a careful review of current performance data relative to IEP goals, objectives, and changes in instruction. Modifications in instructional strategies might be suggested, implemented, and monitored over time to determine their effectiveness. Observations of the student in different school environments might provide additional data to support changes in programming.

For students placed in minimally or partially integrated categorical programs, formal reevaluation by the school psychologist is required every 3 years. However, in Minneapolis readministration of formal tests is not routine; reevaluation focuses upon the student's progress in the current setting and his or her instructional needs rather than test scores relative to categorical criteria. Emphasis is given to functional academic skills, social skills, and adaptive behaviors that relate to success in mainstream settings, and to the appropriateness of opportunities for interaction with nonhandicapped peers.

In the regular education setting, psychologists may perform some type of evaluative service to determine the effectiveness of consultation and prereferral intervention. Observation prior to, during, and following intervention provides a database from which to modify and evaluate change strategies. Reviewing students' performance data (CBM, task completion, task accuracy) similarly enables the psychologist to evaluate their progress and the need for additional services.

Consultation with Special Education Staff

While not serving as gatekeepers for special education, psychologists are part of the special education team at each school and participate at varying levels in the full special education decision-making process from prereferral to placement to programming. Most frequently, they function as consultants to other team members and the classroom teacher. There are variations in the degree and nature of the psychologist's involvement in the special education process, depending upon professional preferences and building needs. As students move through the special education assessment sequence, the psychologist may offer assistance in determining appropriate areas and personnel for assessment, help to integrate data as necessary to make placement decisions, and may directly evaluate students, particularly if mental retardation or severe emotional disturbance is suspected. As noted earlier, the availability of CBM data (both assessment and progress-monitoring information) enhances consultation with special education staff, often providing a basis for recommendations regarding instructional modifications as well as for judging the effectiveness of such modifications.

Consultation with Regular Education Teachers

Minneapolis school psychologists increasingly regard regular education teachers as the preferred focus of their consultation efforts. As national, state, and local policies place more emphasis on prereferral intervention, involvement with regular education staff will become an even greater part of the service delivery system (Reschly, 1988). At the present time, classroom teachers are required to document two or more interventions prior to special education referral; however, no systematic guidelines exist to facilitate implementation. School psychologists often have been the organizers of prereferral ("intervention assistance") teams, small groups of support staff who respond to teachers' concerns by providing consultation regarding classroom intervention strategies (e.g., Zins & Ponti, 1987). On a less formal basis, school psychologists encourage regular education teachers to seek assistance in dealing with instructional or behavior problems at an early stage, before difficulties have accelerated to the point that special education referral seems to be the only option for support.

The biggest hurdle in providing such consultation is not the severity of the problems or the paucity of options available for intervention, but the initial steps in implementing the service — encouraging teachers to request assistance and dealing with teachers' resistance. Successful implementation seems to depend upon a number of factors including organizational structure, school climate, and staff attitudes (e.g., Gutkin, Clark, & Ajchenbaum, 1985), as well as consultant skills.

Each psychologist deals with implementation issues somewhat differently, depending upon personal style, experience, and school characteristics. Tactics such as direct invitations to meet (as at a school staff meeting), "office hours," classroom visits (observation with no specific referral issue), and offers of staff development programs have typically been successful approaches to initiating consultation services at the elementary school level. The nature and structure of secondary schools create additional problems in serving classroom teachers, who typically feel isolated from support services. Participation on regular education teams (e.g., grade-level representatives or subject matter groupings) has increased psychologists' visibility and accessibility; leading support groups for secondary teachers has been another avenue.

In addition to individual student behavior and achievement problems, ecological issues are receiving more attention as targets of consultation, with intervention strategies directed at teacher–student interaction and the principles of effective instruction. Consultation also is frequently directed at the classroom as a whole, particularly regarding behavior management or classroom organization issues.

Consultation with Parents

Parent consultation is an important component of services to children and the larger community. It often occurs in conjunction with direct assessment or treatment services in the course of obtaining background information or seeking outside resources for a student and family. Parents also directly *request* consultation regarding both school and home problems, often leading to the development of specific behavioral plans around issues such as homework, compliance, and tantrums. Parent consultation sometimes is provided more proactively through parent groups and workshops. One of the most productive features of parent consultation services is the opportunity to link home, school, and community interventions by coordinating information and planning among parents, teachers, and agency professionals. The school psychologist is often in the best position to serve as this liaison, as the professional bridging mental health and educational issues.

Direct Intervention Services

An outgrowth of classroom consultation may be direct intervention with an individual or group of students experiencing common difficulties. Among the direct psychological services provided to regular education students are group training in social or study skills and individual interventions to teach cognitive-behavioral strategies to improve problem-solving, organization, or social skills. Group training and treatment programs also have been developed to address specific needs, such as preparing sixth-grade students for the transition to junior high school, improving the social adjustment of students from foreign cultures, supporting the emotional needs of children from alcohol- or drug-abusing families, and helping students to deal with death or illness. Typically, these are short-term interventions, often conducted in collaboration with a building staff member who is trained to continue such support services without the psychologist's direct involvement. Because of the number of community agencies offering group services in schools, there are also many opportunities for psychologists to team with agency staff.

Sometimes an entire class will be the focus of direct service. Recently, psychology staff have developed and implemented programs concerning social skills, acceptance of individual differences, interracial relations, and even principles of psychology and child development for classroom groups.

Crisis Prevention/Intervention

One of the most vital services provided by school psychologists in Minneapolis is crisis prevention and intervention. In the early to middle 1980s, it became apparent that a systematic program to respond to suicide threats, abuse, sudden death, and other crises was essential. Primarily through the efforts of one psychologist and one social worker, a city-wide crisis model was developed, a crisis team and hotline established, and an extensive program of staff training initiated (Minneapolis Schools, 1988). While the two-person crisis team oversees activities and responds directly to most initial requests for assistance, typically the full psychology staff is responsible for follow-up and monitoring of crisis situations in assigned buildings. Unfortunately, the need for these services has been extensive and growing.

Depending upon the crisis situation, reactive services (e.g., following an incident, threat) may be handled by one or more professionals. After obtaining relevant information and recommending immediate actions, the psychologist may work with appropriate staff, students, and family members, as well as community resources, to develop a support plan. In the case of completed suicide, typically there is an immediate need for support that often involves two or more psychologists and members of the crisis team on call at the school to meet individually with any staff or student as needed. Also, under these circumstances, it has been most appropriate to meet with groups of students and/or faculty, and with parent groups as well. Students identified as particularly at risk for suicide or depression are monitored and their families may be contacted regarding staff concerns, warning signals, and available resources.

Similar steps have been taken to provide support following the sudden death of a staff member or student, child abuse, homicide, accident, or serious illness. As times change, so do the crisis issues confronting psychologists in the schools. While suicide and sudden death continue to be major concerns, recent charges of sexual abuse by teachers and police raids of "crack houses" have prompted intervention with victims, their classmates, and teachers.

Proactive services (e.g., staff training, prevention, support for at-risk students) are central to the crisis intervention and support model; furthermore, they have provided a foundation from which to address a broader range of mental health issues. Psychologists have participated in the development of workshops for teachers and parents, and in the development of curriculum for students regarding drug awareness, depression, anxiety, and finding support (e.g., Minneapolis Schools, 1987). Developing positive working relationships with community agencies (e.g., hospital crisis units, child protection services, police department) has also been a focus, as has community education. Even the media, which locally have often reacted to school crises in a sensational manner, have been the target of psychologists' interventions to minimize the types of public responses that tend to further the crisis.

SERVING THE TOTAL SYSTEM

Intervention and consultation services directed at the level of the individual school, district, or even larger educational system have become increasingly important as a means of affecting policy and practice. Within this framework of indirect services, staff psychologists participate in a variety of activities related to staff training, research, curriculum planning, and development of educational programs and policy.

Staff Training

Inservice programs have been provided to teachers, administrators, special educators, community professionals, paraprofessionals, parents, and university trainees on a variety of issues that pertain to school psychology. Specific topics have included behavior management, child development, crisis management, assessment, and self-esteem. Often such programs consist of single presentations, although staff training in behavior management has typically involved more intensive levels of skills development over several sessions, often provided in a small-group context. Psychologists, sometimes working with other district consultants, have offered presentations on classroom management to large groups of teachers, followed by ongoing small-group sessions to share experiences and ideas, or to engage in problem-solving regarding specific classroom situations.

The recent emphasis of state and federal regulations on adaptive behavior criteria for mental retardation eligibility has stimulated professional interest in both assessment and intervention issues. To address this area, psychologists have been responsible for districtwide training of appropriate personnel in the use of adaptive behavior scales, leading to a number of workshops and presentations within special and regular education. In some areas, particularly crisis management, psychologists have extended their training sphere far beyond district boundaries, offering training and presentations to neighboring districts and to professionals at state and national conferences.

Research

Research is a relatively new focus of Minneapolis Schools' Psychological Services, although the department has a history of empirically based decision making. The creation of the Research and Evaluation Psychologist position solidified this commitment to research as a basis of practice, and enabled the staff to move beyond internal program evaluation activities and into areas of applied research appropriate to local school district needs. Obviously, with responsibility residing primarily with one staff member, research efforts are not extensive. However, in conjunction with research conducted in other programs, particularly special education, psychologists are able to make significant contributions to the knowledge base regarding practices that are applicable to the total student population.

For example, the lack of appropriate measures of school-based adaptive behavior was the impetus for a recent research project, "Mainstream Survival Skills Assessment," funded by grants from the Minnesota Department of Education (1987–1990) and National Association of School Psychologists (1988–1990). This project involved development of a teacher rating scale, student interview and observation procedures, local and statewide norms, and investigation of consultation and intervention strategies related to identified deficits in school-based adaptive behaviors (Canter & Heistad, 1988, 1989).

Another topic, early entry to kindergarten, has been an ongoing concern in Minneapolis as in many districts. In 1980 psychologists developed and locally normed an early-entry inventory for administration by teachers or principals. This inventory was designed to yield both developmental and readiness information relevant to the local kindergarten curriculum, such as expressive language and fine-motor tasks, knowledge of the alphabet, counting objects, etc. The Research and Evaluation Psychologist also manages a longitudinal study of early entrants, providing a database from which to recommend revisions in district policy.

As noted in the discussion of accountability procedures, findings from internal program evaluation often prompt other investigations, such as the study of the utility and relevance of psychological assessment reports. Other such offshoots have included an analysis of race and gender as variables influencing referral and service (Tomlinson et al., 1977), a study of risk factors contributing to referral for service (e.g., family histories of abuse, handicap, welfare services, etc.), and surveys of local attitudes and practices regarding grade retention.

Curriculum and Program Development

Staff psychologists frequently provide consultation regarding program development through participation in formally organized building and district committees and task forces. Behavior management is often a focus, such as development of classroom- and building-level management systems, and consultation about school or district policy regarding the use of time-out and other procedures. The efforts of school psychologists in Minneapolis have significantly contributed to the development of alternative programs and policies, including crisis intervention teams, teacher assistance teams, gifted education programs, Limited English Proficiency (LEP) services, employee assistance programs, drug awareness and preventive mental health curricula, interventions to promote self-esteem, preschool screening procedures, criteria for special education placements, retention and truancy policies, parent involvement, and guidelines for best practices in special education assessment.

In addition to their participation on district committees and task forces, Minneapolis school psychologists have also served on statewide task forces regarding special education and LEP issues and have provided testimony to legislators regarding corporal punishment, special education reimbursements, and mental health funding. To further influence state policies, several Minneapolis psychologists have worked with district administrators to develop informational presentations and recommendations to the state's Department of Education officials and to state legislators regarding special education regulations and guidelines (e.g., learning disabilities criteria, CBM).

Promoting Alternative Roles

The district-wide implementation of alternative psychological services has been perhaps the most difficult but most important intervention at the systems level. As noted earlier, staff have used a variety of strategies to implement consultation-based services with individual teachers. At the building level, psychologists often offer to participate on school committees or teams regarding curriculum issues, human relations, and grade retention as a means of influencing school-wide issues. Changing the perceptions of the psychologist's role at the larger systems level is a greater challenge. The absence of a "marketing orientation" is regarded as one of the major barriers to change in school psychology, in part reflecting limited professional attention to consumer needs and attitudes (Illback, 1988). It is important that school psychol-

ogists model new roles both for colleagues and for consumers (e.g., teachers, parents, administrators), to "establish a system that will reinforce desirable school psychology practices" (Kovaleski, 1988, p. 482).

Professional visibility is a key variable, particularly with a very small staff in a large school system. Selective efforts to participate in district and state level reform can potentially alter teachers' and administrators' perceptions of the school psychologist's role as a change agent. In addition to specific systems-level services already noted, Minneapolis school psychologists have developed several activities to promote both their professional image and student mental health, including a department newsletter, a district emergency line, a computerized mental health resource directory, and a slide presentation of local efforts to build student self-esteem. Members of the psychology staff also have taken active roles in a series of wellness activities within Special Education to promote professionals' physical and mental health. Public awareness beyond district boundaries has been enhanced through presentations and workshops for other school districts, professional organizations, and community agencies.

CURRENT DILEMMAS AND FUTURE DIRECTIONS

The model of service delivery presented in this chapter is not a static system but a continuing evolution of theory and practice, constantly modified in response to internal and external needs and changes. While today the service delivery system can generally be described as a data-based consultation model promoting services to all students and to all facets of the larger educational organization, there is also no single set of beliefs and practices that characterize the staff as a whole. Perhaps the most unifying concept is the belief in, and acceptance of, individual differences, not only among children but among professional colleagues. While these differences have allowed the development of a wide range of service options to address a wide range of student and district needs, such diversity also creates dilemmas in service delivery. These dilemmas within Minneapolis Schools' Psychological Services unit reflect the basic dilemmas of the profession today:

1. Are services delivered *to children* or *on behalf of children?* While psychologists generally are promoting indirect service delivery as an effective and efficient model, there are differences in the confidence with which they provide such services. For many psychologists, consultation and systems intervention skills were virtually absent from their training. For some psychologists, providing service *indirectly* to students without first obtaining direct assessment data is professionally discomforting. While the proportion of referred students receiving direct assessment services has certainly declined, there is considerable variation across the staff. At times, such professional differences can confuse consumers and thus hinder implementation of services.

2. Are we providers of *mental health* services or are we specialists in *educational intervention?* Old identity crises continue to haunt us to some degree as we observe vast needs in both areas. This dilemma is further compounded by differences in staff training: clinical and developmental orientations versus educational and behavioral orientations. To some extent, this diversity in background enables Minneapolis school psychologists to integrate the *school* and the *psychology* in school psychology; yet this diversity also invariably leads to questions regarding the appropriate focus of our services.

3. Are we *problem identifiers* or *problem solvers?* While this has probably been the most successfully resolved of our dilemmas in Minneapolis, the relative importance of diagnosis to intervention or prevention services is not universally accepted, internally or externally. We continue to find our credibility questioned by other professionals when we cannot refer to test scores, personality profiles, or labels of pathology; the temptation to retreat to such practices "just to get a foot in the door" is sometimes overwhelming. Furthermore, we were largely trained as problem identifiers and consequently have more confidence in our diagnostic skills. Problem solving for many school psychologists requires a greater understanding of the nature of instruction, classroom organization, curriculum, and systems analysis.

Responding to these dilemmas is obviously part of the ongoing development of the service delivery system. A rigorous plan of staff development is addressing issues of skills building. Fortunately, the accessibility of the University of Minnesota's training program and its highly respected cadre of consultants and researchers enhances professional growth at many levels. The development of mindsets that incorporate clinical, developmental, behavioral, and educational perspectives, however, will require ongoing discussion, consideration of current research regarding service delivery and student outcomes, and careful attention to our own evaluation of service effectiveness.

A variety of issues, in the following framework, will likely become priorities of future practice for Minneapolis (if not all) school psychologists:

1. *Prevention:* Primary prevention is regarded as a significant means of expanding psychological services to the regular education population (Zins, Conyne, & Ponti, 1988). Preventing special education labeling and placement for many students currently regarded as at-risk or mildly handicapped is often addressed through prereferral intervention. On a larger scale, however, we need to begin to address the antecedents of our most disturbing problems — drug abuse, family violence, teen pregnancy, illiteracy, and poverty. These certainly are not just school problems, and prevention efforts will require collaboration with community agencies and political leaders. Psychologists will be needed to develop staff and parent awareness programs, curricula at all levels of instruction, and preventive mental health services that are available

to every student and appropriate to a culturally diverse population.

2. *School organization:* We were largely trained before the era of school alternatives and educational reform. The typical school of our own childhood was the school for which we were trained to serve. Today we must serve a diversity of programs with vastly different methods of grouping students, scheduling, and providing instruction. Beyond the individual building is an increasingly complex system of district administration and policy-making bodies. To effectively address the process of schooling for the total student population, we will need to better understand the dynamics and management of systems, and have in our intervention repertoire a variety of strategies to address administrative and personnel issues.

3. *Linking research and practice:* The body of knowledge related to effective instruction and, more broadly, to effective schools is growing much faster than we can assimilate it. We may need to literally take time to consume and digest key findings and then work to translate data into meaningful daily practice and promotion of appropriate school policies.

4. *Lifespan services:* Special education regulations have prompted interest in the earliest and the postsecondary years of life, but the nonhandicapped population has largely been left out of this developmental linkage in school programs. As we become increasingly concerned with the prevention of disability and maladjustment, we must consider the role of public schools in early and postsecondary services. Interventions that promote school and adult adjustment for the handicapped are no less important for the at-risk population. Psychologists, through research and program development, can apply their lifespan view of development to appropriate prevention and intervention efforts.

5. *Community collaboration:* The provision of services described will require far more resources than are likely to be available within one school district. The funding, expertise, and political clout of many community agencies have been largely untapped by the public school system; yet many of our most pressing problems reflect broad social concerns and ultimately affect the community far beyond the school walls. Due to the nature of their multidisciplinary training and frequent roles as liaison with other mental health agencies, school psychologists are ideally suited to the task of encouraging collaborative efforts in the larger professional community. Cooperative clinics, training programs, and interdisciplinary curricula could evolve through the efforts of school psychologists and their colleagues.

SUMMARY

This chapter has presented a model of delivering psychological services to the total school population. In Minneapolis, a unique blend of direct and indirect services has evolved from the convergence of a number of factors — the historical tradition of the "child study" model; staff preparation in educational, developmental, and clinical psychology; special education reform, including an emphasis on curriculum-based measurement; and ongoing program evaluation. In a special education system emphasizing alternative practices, Minneapolis school psychologists have been able to avoid the "retreat from excellence" so common among the many school psychologists faced with discrepancies between professional skills and professional responsibilities (Hyman, 1988). The model has as many variations as there are staff to implement it, a diversity that is both a strength and a source of professional ambiguity. However, overall, this diversity and a tradition of innovation have sparked a variety of services to address the needs of a culturally and economically diverse student population in both regular and special education.

The future of service delivery to all children holds much promise as we move to address the prevention of the conditions that contribute to school failure and dysfunctional adult adjustment, as we establish practical links between research and instruction, and as we learn to collaborate more effectively with community resources. Through these efforts, "alternative service delivery" will truly describe the daily practice of school psychology.

ACKNOWLEDGMENTS

The author wishes to thank the staff of Psychological Services, Minneapolis Schools, for their continual participation in data collection. Appreciation is also expressed to Drs. Jerry Tomlinson, Sherrie Lindborg, and Sandra Christenson for their suggestions during the preparation of this chapter, and to Arthur and Miriam Canter for their editorial assistance and support. Finally, the author wishes to acknowledge Dr. Keith Kromer, Director of Special Education (Minneapolis Schools), for his ongoing support of our efforts to improve delivery of psychological services.

FOOTNOTE

[1]While eligibility criteria had not been mandated as of January 1, 1990, the Minnesota Department of Education has proposed that guidelines become rule. It is ironic that at a time when many state and federal policy units are considering special education reforms and moves *away* from categorical services, Minnesota may finally seek to enforce traditional standards.

REFERENCES

Allen, D., & Marston, D. (1988). A response to Tom Lombard's review of curriculum based measurement. *School Psychology Minnesota, 19*(4), 33-38.

Acker, N. A., & Tomlinson, J. R. (1988). *The supplemental report* [computer program]. Minneapolis: ATM.

Bardon, J. I. (1983). Psychology applied to education: A specialty in search of an identity. *American Psychologist, 38,* 185-196.

Bennett, R. E. (1980). Methods for evaluating the performance of school psychologists. *School Psychology Monograph, 4,* 45-59.

Bennett, R. E. (1988). Evaluating the effectiveness of alternative service delivery systems. In J. Graden, J. Zins, & M. Curtis (Eds.), *Alternative educational delivery systems: Enhancing instructional options for all students* (pp. 513-524). Washington: National Association of School Psychologists.

Canter, A. S. (1987a). LD: Is the great debate regressing? *School Psychology Minnesota, 19*(4), 9-10.

Canter, A. S. (1987b). *Psychological services assessment reports study.* Minneapolis: Minneapolis Public Schools.

Canter, A. S. (1989). Unpublished raw data.

Canter, A. S., & Allen, D. (1989, March). *Curriculum-based measurement: Impact on the delivery of school psychological services.* Paper presented at the annual convention of the National Association of School Psychologists, Boston.

Canter, A. S., & Heistad, D. (1988). *Mainstream survival skills assessment: Scale development and standardization* (Project Report No. 031-088). St. Paul: Minnesota Department of Education.

Canter, A. S., & Heistad, D. (1989). *Validation of the Mainstream Survival Skills Assessment* (Project Report No. 051-089). St. Paul: Minnesota Department of Education.

Canter, A. S., & Tomlinson, J. R. (1987). Change and effectiveness: Applications of accountability procedures [Summary]. In *Proceedings of the 19th Annual Convention of the National Association of School Psychologists* (pp. 99-100). Washington, DC: National Association of School Psychologists.

Christenson, S., Abery, B., & Weinberg, R. A. (1986). An alternative model for the delivery of psychological services in the school community. In S. N. Elliott & J. C. Witt (Eds.), *The delivery of psychological services in schools* (pp. 349-392). Hillsdale, NJ: Erlbaum.

Cobb, J. A., & Hops, H. (1973). Effects of academic survival skills training on low achieving first graders. *Journal of Educational Research, 67,* 108-113.

Curtis, M. J., & Meyers, J. (1988). Consultation: A foundation for alternative services in the schools. In J. L. Graden, J. E. Zins, & M. J. Curtis (Eds.), *Alternative educational delivery systems: Enhancing instructional options for all students* (pp. 35-48). Washington, DC: National Association of School Psychologists.

Davis, T. (1986). *Inservice training, professional development, and school system change.* Unpublished doctoral dissertation, University of Minnesota.

Deno, S. L. (1985). Curriculum-based measurement: The emerging alternative. *Exceptional Children, 52,* 219-232.

Deno, S. L. (1986). Formative evaluation of individual student programs: A new role for school psychologists. *School Psychology Review, 15,* 358-374.

Deno, S. L., & Mirkin, P. K. (1977). *Data-based program modification: A manual.* Minneapolis: University of Minnesota, Leadership Training Institute/Special Education.

Germann, G., & Tindal, G. (1985). An application of curriculum-based assessment: The use of direct and repeated measurement. *Exceptional Children, 52,* 244-265.

Goldwasser, E. B. (1982). The emperor's used clothes. *Professional Psychology, 13,* 969-976.

Graden, J. L., Zins, J. E., Curtis, M. J., & Cobb, C. T. (1988). The need for alternatives in educational services. In J. L. Graden, J. E. Zins, & M. J. Curtis (Eds.), *Alternative educational delivery systems: Enhancing instructional options for all students* (pp. 3-16). Washington, DC: National Association of School Psychologists.

Gutkin, T., Clark, J., & Ajchenbaum, M. (1985). Impact of organizational variables on the delivery of school-based consultation services: A comparative case study approach. *School Psychology Review, 14,* 230-235.

Henning-Stout, M., & Conoley, J. (1988). Influencing program change at the district level. In J. L. Graden, J. E. Zins, & M. J. Curtis (Eds.), *Alternative educational delivery systems: Enhancing instructional options for all students* (pp. 471-490). Washington, DC: National Association of School Psychologists.

Holbrook, S. F. (1969, September). A plan for utilizing differentiation of functions in delivery of psychological services. In M. D. Hall (Chair), *Psychology and education: Discussion about a partnership.* Symposium conducted at the meeting of the American Psychological Association (Division 16). Washington, DC.

Hyman, I. (1988, September 21). School psychology: A retreat from excellence. *Education Week,* pp. 40, 33.

Illback, R. (1988). Improving school psychological services through strategic marketing and planned change. In J. L. Graden, J. E. Zins, & M. J. Curtis (Eds.), *Alternative educational delivery systems: Enhancing instructional options for all students* (pp. 457-470). Washington, DC: National Association of School Psychologists.

Jackson, J. H. (1986). Conceptual and logistical hurdles: Service delivery to urban schools. In S. N. Elliott & J. C. Witt (Eds.), *The delivery of psychological services in schools* (pp. 171-202). Hillsdale, NJ: Erlbaum.

Kovaleski, J. (1988). Paradigmatic obstacles to reform in school psychology. *School Psychology Review, 17,* 479-484.

Lacayo, N., Morris, J., & Sherwood, G. (1981). Daily activities of school psychologists: A national survey. *Psychology in the Schools, 18,* 184-190.

Lennox, N., Hyman, I., & Hughes, C. (1988). Institutionalization of a consultation-based delivery system. In J. L. Graden, J. E. Zins, & M. J. Curtis (Eds.), *Alternative educational delivery systems: Enhancing instructional options for all students* (pp. 71-90). Washington, DC: National Association of School Psychologists.

Lindborg, S. (1988). Special education in Minnesota: An interview with Evelyn Deno. *School Psychology Minnesota, 20*(2), 21-24.

Lombard, T. J. (1988). Curriculum based measurement: Megatesting or McTesting? *School Psychology Minnesota, 19*(3), 27-32.

Maher, C. (1983). Goal attainment scaling: A method for evaluating special education services. *Exceptional Children, 49,* 529-536.

Martens, E. H. (1939). *Clinical organizations for child guidance within the schools* (Offices of Education, Bull. No. 15.) Washington, DC: Government Printing Office.

Marston, D., & Magnusson, D. (1985). Implementing curriculum-based measurement in special and regular education settings. *Exceptional Children, 52,* 266-276.

Marston, D., & Magnusson, D. (1988). Curriculum-based measurement: District level implementation. In J. L. Graden, J. E. Zins, & M. J. Curtis (Eds.), *Alternative educational delivery systems: Enhancing instructional options for all students* (pp. 137-172). Washington, DC: National Association of School Psychologists.

McGrew, K. S. (1987). School psychologists' acceptance of the Woodcock–Johnson Tests of Cognitive Ability. *Trainers Forum, 7*(2), 1-4.

Minneapolis Schools. (1987). *The elementary curriculum guide for chemical awareness and personal development.* Minneapolis: Author.

Minneapolis Schools. (1988). *Responding to an urgent student crisis: Minneapolis Public Schools guidelines for student suicide prevention.* Minneapolis: Author.

Minnesota Department of Education. (1982). *Guidelines for reimbursable activities of special education personnel.* St. Paul: Author.

Minnesota Department of Education. (1983). *Time study of special education reimbursable activities of school psychologists and social workers.* St. Paul: Author.

National Association of School Psychologists. (1985). *Advocacy for appropriate educational services for all children.* Washington, DC: Author.

Reschly, D. J. (1988). Special education reform: School psychology revolution. *School Psychology Review, 17,* 459-475.

Reschly, D., Genshaft, J., & Binder, L. (1987). *The 1986 NASP survey: Comparison of practitioners, NASP leadership, and university faculty on key issues.* Washington, DC: National Association of School Psychologists.

Reynolds, M. (1988). Alternative educational delivery approaches: Implications for school psychology. In J. L. Graden, J. E. Zins, & M. J. Curtis (Eds.), *Alternative educational delivery systems: Enhancing instructional options for all students* (pp. 555–562). Washington, DC: National Association of School Psychologists.

Sandoval, J., & Lambert, N. (1977). Instruments for evaluating school psychologists' functioning and services. *Psychology in the Schools, 14,* 172–179.

Shinn, M. R. (1988). Development of curriculum-based local norms for use in special education decision-making. *School Psychology Review, 17,* 61–80.

Shinn, M. R., Tindal, G., & Stein, S. (1988). Curriculum-based measurement and the identification of mildly handicapped students: A research review. *Professional School Psychology, 3,* 69–86.

Stainback, S., & Stainback, W. (1988). Changes needed to strengthen regular education. In J. L. Graden, J. E. Zins, & M. J. Curtis (Eds.), *Alternative educational delivery systems: Enhancing instructional options for all students* (pp. 17–34). Washington, DC: National Association of School Psychologists.

Thomson, M. (1963). *Prologue.* Minneapolis: Gilbert.

Tomlinson, J. (1973). Accountability procedures for psychological services. *Psychology in the Schools, 10,* 42–47.

Tomlinson, J. R. (1974). Functional analysis and accountability of psychological services. *Psychology in the Schools, 11,* 291–295.

Tomlinson, J. R., Acker, N. E., Canter, A. S., Lindborg, S. L. (1977). Minority status, sex, and school psychological services. *Psychology in the Schools, 14,* 456–460.

Trachtman, G. (1971). Doing your thing in school psychology. *Professional Psychology, 2,* 377–382.

Will, M. (1986). *Educating students with learning problems: A shared responsibility.* Washington, DC: United States Department of Education.

Ysseldyke, J., & Christenson, S. (1987). Evaluating students' instructional environments. *Remedial and Special Education (RASE), 8*(3), 17–24.

Ysseldyke, J., Reynolds, M., & Weinberg, R. A. (1984). *School psychology: A blueprint for training and practice.* Minneapolis: National School Psychology Inservice Training Network.

Zins, J. E. (1981). Using data-based evaluation in developing school consultation services. In M. J. Curtis & J. E. Zins (Eds.), *The theory and practice of school consultation* (pp. 261–268). Springfield, IL: Thomas.

Zins, J. E. (1985). Best practices in accountability. In A. Thomas & J. Grimes (Eds.), *Best practices in school psychology* (pp. 493–504). Washington, DC: National Association of School Psychologists.

Zins, J. E., & Fairchild, T. (1986). An investigation of the accountability practices of school psychologists. *Professional School Psychology, 1,* 193–204.

Zins, J. E., Grimes, J., Illback, R., Barnett, D., Ponti, C., MacEvoy, M., & Wright, C. (1982). *Accountability for School Psychologists: Developing Trends.* Washington, DC: National Association of School Psychologists.

Zins, J. E., & Ponti, C. R. (1987). Pre-referral consultation: A system to decrease special education referral and placement. *Community Psychologist, 20*(2), 10–12.

Evaluation Strategies for Preventing and Remediating Basic Skills Deficits

Stanley L. Deno
Christine A. Espin
University of Minnesota

Effective teaching requires ongoing evaluation of student performance. Even the dialogue between Socrates and the slave boy Meno — our early exemplar of teaching and learning — illustrates the close connection between the questions asked by Socrates and the previous answers given by Meno. Likewise, contemporary instructional design models specify the close connection between student performance data and adjustments in various components of the instructional model. Current books on teaching disabled learners begin with the assertion that "good teaching requires assessment" (Zigmond, Vallecorsa, & Silverman, 1983, p. 1). And, finally, the landmark *Education for All Handicapped Children's Act* (Public Law 94-142) includes the requirement that each student's individual educational plan (IEP) specify procedures for evaluating the effectiveness of the program provided for that student. In this chapter, our purpose is to provide school psychologists with simple evaluation strategies that they can use not only to comply with rules and regulations regarding intervention accountability, but also to increase the likelihood that their efforts to intervene will be more successful. We begin with a conceptual and empirical rationale for evaluating academic interventions, follow with illustration and analyses of alternative evaluation models applied in special and compensatory education programs, and close with a case

presentation of the school psychologist applying a data-based evaluation model informed by curriculum-based measurement (CBM).

To say that CBM data inform evaluation is to clarify that measurement and evaluation are different activities. Measurement is quantitative description, while evaluation is decision making. The distinction is important because it emphasizes that data are relatively inert and must be acted upon by decision makers whose values and cost-benefit analyses will influence evaluation outcomes as much as the measurement data. Thus, CBM is an approach to quantitative description. In this discussion, we go beyond description to consider evaluation of academic interventions.

RATIONALE

The rationale for evaluating instruction and interventions derives from the idea that humans modify their performance as a result of environmental experience. Whether the conceptual and analytical model used to account for those performance changes is behavioral or cognitive is unimportant to this discussion. More important is the fact that both cognitive and behavioral models emphasize the key role that the environmental effects of actions play in altering subsequent actions. In the behavioral paradigm, the mechanisms that account for this change are reinforcing and punishing consequences (Skinner, 1954). In the cognitive model, that mechanism is the feedback loop (Miller, Galanter, & Pribram, 1960). By invoking consequences and feedback, both approaches are attempting to account for the fact that most changes in our behavior are related in an orderly way to the results of our previous actions.

When considering behavioral change, in general, a wide variety of different environmental events might be identified as important influences on subsequent performance. For example, a child's experience in touching a hot stove might be used to account for decreases in reaching for objects on the stove. In the case of instruction, however, the range or variety of events crucial in influencing the teacher's performance is, or should be, limited primarily to the performance of that teacher's students. Thus, in the best of all instructional worlds, we should see teachers making changes in their instruction in response to observations of how well (or how poorly) their students are learning in response to that instruction.

Not surprisingly, instructional evaluation models explicitly provide for the use of student performance data to correct or adjust instructional programs (Bloom, Madaus, & Hastings, 1981; Gagne, Briggs, & Wager, 1988). In these models, a distinction is made between using student performance data in *summative* and *formative* evaluation. Summative evaluation is retrospective. Data are aggregated *after* the completion of instruction and used to determine whether a program was successful. In contrast, formative evaluation involves use of student performance data *during* the course of instruction as a basis for altering that instruction in ways that ultimately will increase program effectiveness. Thus, formative evaluation is both contemporaneous and prospective, rather than retrospective. Since the focus of this chapter is on using evaluation to improve the effectiveness of interventions, the emphasis of our discussion will be on evaluating formatively, rather than summatively.

A key feature of formative evaluation is that the data important to improving program effectiveness are those collected *during* rather than before or after program implementation. The reason why data collected after program implementation do not benefit the student is, of course, obvious. After a program has been completed (e.g., the end of a school year, or even a grading period) it is too late to make a change that will benefit the student. While data collected upon completion of a program are useful in evaluating the effectiveness of the program, the opportunity to benefit from that program has passed for that student.

Less obvious may be the reason why data collected *prior* to instruction may not suffice to improve program effectiveness. After all, the purpose of collecting data during an initial assessment includes diagnosis of problems and prescription of those instructional and intervention techniques that are most likely to benefit the student. Our problem is that, despite their hallowed place in the traditions of psychology and special education, diagnostic-prescriptive approaches to instruction have not been demonstrably successful (Lloyd, 1984). In fact, the data on the validity of the diagnostic-prescriptive approach is so thin that Ysseldyke and Salvia (1974) described it as experimentation without consent.

The question that must be answered, then, is whether data on students' performance collected during implementation of a program improves instructional effectiveness. In a meta-analysis of 21 studies, Fuchs and Fuchs (1986b) found that students gained approximately .70 standard deviations, or about 25 percentile points, in basic skills when their teachers used individual student performance data to evaluate instruction formatively. A key finding in their meta-analysis and in subsequent research (Fuchs, Fuchs, & Hamlett, 1989) is that collecting student performance data during an instructional program produces greater effects if teachers systematically use the data. For example, in their 1989 article, they reported that teachers who raised student performance goals when the data indicated that higher goals were attainable produced higher levels of achievement than teachers who did not revise goals upward when the data indicated that such a revision was warranted. The important distinction to be made here is between measurement and evaluation. Measuring during program implementation can produce a reliable and valid quantitative picture of a student's performance, but the data will not be dynamic in their function unless they are used to evaluate and modify programs.

The rationale for using evaluation to improve academic interventions is clear. Theoretical models of human behavior include environmental consequences (e.g., reinforcement, punishment, response cost) as a key construct controlling behavior change. Instructional design models prescribe the use of student performance data to provide feedback to both student and teacher. Finally, the available research evidence indicates that real gains are made when individual student programs are evaluated continuously and the data are used to evaluate those programs formatively. The conclusions seems inescapable. We *can* increase the success of academic interventions if we evaluate the student performance effects of our interventions. Despite a lack of history in this area, we must learn to bring our intervention behavior under the control of student performance outcomes. The procedures outlined in this chapter are a step toward helping those of us who create academic intervention programs to use student performance data to modify our intervention behavior in response to the data effects produced by the students' performance. Our assumption is that academic programs improve to the extent that we regulate our behavior (Watson & Tharp, 1989). Several approaches to regulating our interventions through evaluation are available. In the next section of this chapter we consider three of those alternatives.

ALTERNATIVE EVALUATION MODELS

Traditional methods of evaluation have not proved to be a useful means of formative evaluation. The most widely used method, published norm-referenced measures, differentially sample curriculum content (Armbruster, Stevens, & Rosenshine, 1977; Jenkins & Pany, 1978; Shriner & Salvia, 1988), are technically inadequate for making decisions regarding individual students (Salvia & Ysseldyke, 1988), and are not useful in making instructional decisions (Salmon-Cox, 1981). As a result, school personnel are left to design their own formative evaluation procedures and tests if they are to engage in instructional program design and evaluation.

Practitioners are faced with numerous questions when deciding to evaluate academic interventions. The first is to define the problem, that is, to determine exactly what skill deficiency needs to be overcome. This question guides the specification of what behavior is measured, and its answer depends on the values that society holds for educational success. Students can successfully progress on an infinite number of tasks. The ultimate question is whether these skills will enable the student to function successfully in society upon leaving school.

The second issue is to determine what measurement procedures can be used to evaluate the specified behavior. Specific considerations in this area include what schedule of measurement will be undertaken, who will conduct the measurement, and when measurement will take place. As will be illustrated in the case presentation, school personnel other than the teacher (especially the school psychologist) will need to be involved in the organization and monitoring of student progress.

The final question concerns the evaluation of the data or the decision rules for using the measurement information. Evaluation involves decisions to act and also incorporates value judgments such as how often and to what degree the student's instructional program should be changed, what resources are available for the student and how many of these should be allocated to this student's instruction, whether there is a better placement for this student, and so forth.

Several formative evaluation models have been designed to evaluate students' instructional programs. In each, an attempt is made to address the traditional problems of assessment by measuring students' performance on tasks directly related to the curriculum and to generate information useful for instructional decision making.

Three of these alternative evaluation models are (a) Mastery Monitoring, (b) Precision Teaching, and (c) Data-Based Program Modification. Each model addresses the issues that face the practitioner in a different manner. The following three components will be described for each of the evaluation models: (a) specification of goals or objectives (i.e., what to measure), (b) procedures for measurement (i.e., how to measure), and (c) rules for data utilization (i.e., how to use data to make instructional decisions).

In the following sections, the models will be described in terms of the assumptions underlying each model and these basic components. A case study then will be presented to illustrate the use of the Data-Based Program Modification model for evaluating educational programming for children with learning difficulties.

Mastery Monitoring

Mastery Monitoring (MM) is monitoring student progress through a series of *different tasks* over time (Deno & Mirkin, 1977). In the Mastery Monitoring approach, objectives for a particular curriculum area are clearly defined and arranged hierarchically from simple to more difficult. A criterion for mastery is then determined for each objective. Objectives can refer to the actual skill that the student is expected to learn (e.g., reading words with short vowel sounds) or the amount of material the student is expected to cover (e.g., one page in a basal reading series). In either case, competence in the curriculum is judged by evaluating the student's progress through the hierarchy of subskills contained within the curriculum.

Mastery Monitoring itself is a generic method of evaluating student progress.

The major components of the system, specification of objectives, establishment of criteria for those objectives, and frequent assessment of progress toward those criteria, are illustrated in the Mastery Learning Model (Block, 1971, 1984; Bloom, 1976; Bloom et al., 1981), Resource/Consulting Teacher Model (Idol-Maestas, 1981, 1983; Idol-Maestas, Lloyd, & Ritter, 1982), the Vermont Consulting Teacher Model (Christie, McKenzie, & Burdett, 1972), and Directive Teaching (Stephens, 1976; Stephens, Blackhurst, & Magliocca, 1988; Stephens, Hartman, & Lucas, 1982).

Assumptions. Mastery Monitoring rests on the assumption that students acquire general curriculum competence through attainment of specific subordinate skills in a hierarchical sequence. Knowledge and skill, then, are viewed as the results of learning isolated skills that are ultimately integrated and retained as the larger goals of the curriculum. For example, knowledge and skill in reading is a product of learning skills in comprehension, oral reading, phonetic analysis, structural analysis, sight word recognition, and so forth. Even further, knowledge and skill in phonetic analysis is a product of learning skills related to long vowels sounds, short vowels sounds, initial consonant sounds, final consonant sounds, blends, diagraphs, etc.

Implicit in this assumption is the belief that a definite hierarchy of subskills can be identified that will maximize (optimize) learning in a given curriculum. Also, the Mastery Monitoring approach assumes that all students can learn the curricular skills given the appropriate amount of time and quality of instruction, an assumption based on Carroll's (1963) model of school learning.

What to measure. The primary focus of Mastery Monitoring is on the analysis and sequencing of skills to be measured. Specification of the hierarchical skills sequence is crucial, since that is the sequence that will serve as the basis for all teaching and measurement decisions. Task analysis (i.e., breaking a complex skill down into subcomponents or subskills) usually serves as the tool for specifying the sequence of skills to be mastered and, once that is established, students typically do not progress to a new skill until all prior skills have been learned or mastered. Test material, then, is directly tied to instructional content. If the task to be mastered is decoding words with short *a* vowel sounds (e.g., "bat," "mat," "ran"), test items are produced to evaluate student proficiency on that task. Once the student meets the mastery criterion for decoding short vowel *a* sounds, both instruction and testing change. If the next skill in the hierarchy is decoding words with short *i* vowel sound, both the instruction and test probes focus on words with short *i* vowel sound (e.g., "sit," "fit," "win"). Because the skill sequence is hierarchical, the measurement tasks increase in difficulty as the student progresses through the curriculum.

How to measure. How to measure a student's proficiency at a given skill is not always specified in a Mastery Monitoring approach to evaluation. Often an arbitrary measurement system is simply overlaid upon the sequence of skills (Deno, 1986). What is consistent in mastery measurement procedures, however, is a focus on accuracy. A general criterion for proficiency (most often, 80–90% accuracy) is usually adopted; however, the individual instructor is often free to establish procedures for determining whether a student has reached this criterion.

In general, the measurement procedures involve generating a series of probes to sample a particular objective or skill. As in the previous example, if the instructional objective is to read words with short vowel sounds, procedures for presenting words containing the short vowel sounds are designed. The procedures might involve reading of words presented in isolation or in context, with varying constraints on number of words to be read and amount of time available. Once students reach the minimal criterion for proficiency (e.g., reading 9 of 10 words correctly 3 days in a row), they move on to the next task, for which new measures have been generated.

If the mastery objective is stated in terms of content coverage rather than skill mastery, then the objective is the amount of material to be covered. For example, if the objective is successful completion of Unit 1 in spelling, the student is tested on words from Unit 1, and if the established criterion is met, she or he progresses to the next unit.

How to use the data collected. The data collected through Mastery Monitoring lead to one basic instructional decision: Move the student on to a new skill (when the mastery criterion is attained), or reteach and retest the student on the current skill (when the mastery criterion is not attained). This decision does not require graphic display of the data, but rather that a data record be generated for each task.

It is possible, however, to incorporate a graphing system with Mastery Monitoring that can illustrate the student's rate of progress through the curriculum. This rate can be compared to the rate of progress for peers of average achievement. A sample mastery graph designed by Deno and Mirkin (1977) is presented in Figure 1. To the far left of the vertical axis are the objectives the student is expected to master, in this case, the units the student will cover in the math series. Beside each unit, the date on which the objectives are expected to be achieved are listed. On the horizontal axis, the time that the student is actually working on the objectives is indicated.

When the student has mastered the objective, a point is plotted at the intersection of the objective (on the vertical axis), and the date on which test data established actual mastery (on the horizontal axis). The diagonal line cutting the graph in half illustrates the desired rate of progress for average students. The line represents the expected time at which each task will be mastered. To achieve this straight, desired progress line, estimates must be made of the amount of time typically required for mastery of the task. The open circle indicates the actual level of mastery for a low-achieving student

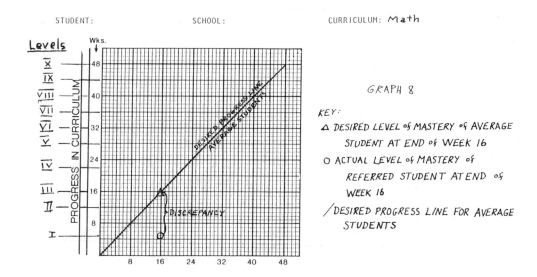

FIGURE 1. Progress monitoring graph for Mastery Monitoring.

referred for special education services during week 16 of the school year. The discrepancy between this student's actual performance and the desired level of progress can be obtained by comparing the student's level of performance at any point in time to the level of the line at the time of testing. As the student is given remedial instruction, his or her rate of progress through the curriculum can be compared continuously with the desired, predetermined rate of progress. In this manner, the teacher can judge whether the math instruction is serving to decrease the gap between the level at which the student is performing and the level specified for his/her average peers.

Precision Teaching

Precision Teaching (PT) is a data-based instructional system that was developed by Ogden R. Lindsley at the University of Kansas in the mid 1960s (McGreevy, 1984) and thoroughly described by White and Haring in *Exceptional Teaching* (1976, 1980). Like Mastery Monitoring, Precision Teaching typically employs a task analysis model in which a hierarchy of subskills is specified for instruction and measurement. In Preci-

sion Teaching, however, the procedures for measurement produce data on both accuracy and fluency of performance, since time is controlled. Additionally, more elaborate rules have been devised to guide the instructor in using the measurement data to make program decisions.

Assumptions. As is the case with Mastery Monitoring, the measures used in Precision Teaching are based on the assumption that curriculum content is defined in terms of a hierarchy of subskills and that a student's acquisition of proficiency in the subject matter is determined by demonstration of competency on those skills. Furthermore, competence is defined in terms of *frequency* of behavior. The rationale for this emphasis on the frequency is that the usefulness of behavior is often determined by speed as well as accuracy (White, 1986).

An implicit assumption of Precision Teaching is that important growth in proficiency is curvilinear or proportional rather than linear or additive. Thus, an increase in correct responses from 2 to 4 (100% change) is depicted as larger than an increase in correct responses from 20 to 30 (50% change) in the evaluation of teaching effectiveness. We will clarify this later when discussing the Standard Behavior Chart.

What to measure. Precision Teaching consists of four basic steps: (a) pinpoint the behavior to be changed; (b) count and chart the occurrences of behavior within a specified period of time; (c) change/teach something; and (d) evaluate the data to determine the need for program modification (White, 1986).

To pinpoint the target behavior, that is, identify the behavior to be measured, two aspects of behavior are taken into account: movement and repeatability. For the target behavior to be observed and measured, it must entail some physical movement such as talking, writing, or pointing. Sitting quietly does not involve physical movement, and would be a less desirable target behavior than one involving movement such as answering questions. It is also important that the behavior be repeated often enough during instruction to allow for collection of data that reflect growth. For example, it may be more practical to count *words* read than count *pages* read because words read would indicate finer gradations of growth than would pages read.

How to measure. Once the target behavior is pinpointed, students' progress is monitored by counting the occurrences of target behavior, called movement cycles, within a specified period of time. The number of movement cycles are charted on a Standard Behavior Chart (see Figure 2), which uses a semilogarithmic scale to allow equal proportional changes in student behavior to be depicted as equidistant on the chart. Along the vertical axis, the number of movements per minute are indicated, while the horizontal axis represents days. The scale on the vertical axis has been adjusted to show proportional changes in behavior. The proportional change in performance on each successive probe is charted on the day on which the probe was taken. If the performance changes from 13 letters spelled correctly in one minute to 26, two movement cycles are indicated on the graph because this represents a two times change in performance.

How to use the data collected. In Precision Teaching, data are utilized to evaluate the effectiveness of the instructional program. There are two basic rules for evaluating the data: (a) If the student has met the aim, move to a new skill; (b) If the student is not making progress, change the instructional program (White, 1986).

More formal guidelines are often implemented, such as those suggested by White and Haring in *Exceptional Teaching* (1976). In this case, the discrepancy between the student's current level and the desired level of performance is used to determine the minimum rate of change required of the student for successful progress. An aim line, representing the minimum rate of change is drawn on the graph, and the student's performance is compared with this value. If performance falls below the line 3 days in a row, a change is made in the student's instructional program and a new aim line is calculated and drawn. Performance subsequently is evaluated against this new aim. When the student reaches the aim (the final goal), the program is terminated, and instruction on a new skill begins.

Data-Based Program Modification

Data-Based Program Modification (DBPM) is a measurement and evaluation system designed to allow teachers to make continuous decisions regarding when and how to modify a student's instruction (Deno & Mirkin, 1977). Like Precision Teaching, DBPM is designed to evaluate the successfulness of an instructional program for improving student performance. Unlike Precision Teaching, DBPM attempts to obtain a generalized index of student growth in the complex skill itself, rather than to track progress on a specified hierarchy of subtasks for that skill. The student is measured in materials other than that used for instruction.

The measurement procedures currently used in DBPM are based on research conducted at the Institute for Research

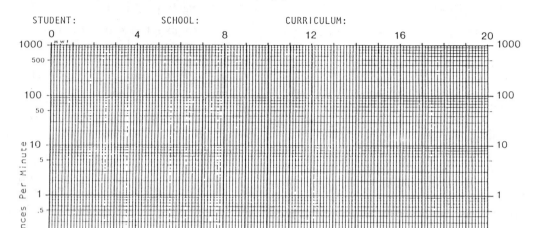

FIGURE 2. Progress monitoring graph for Precision Teaching.

on Learning Disabilities at the University of Minnesota (Deno, 1985). These procedures are referred to as curriculum-based measurement (CBM) (Deno, 1985). While CBM has been used to make a variety of programming decisions, from identification of students as academically at risk, or eligible for special education, to termination of students from programs, our focus here is on using CBM to improve intervention effectiveness — the program improvement phase of DBPM.

Assumptions. Data-Based Program Modification is similar to Precision Teaching in that both emphasize frequent measurement on curriculum tasks, and include time-based as well as accuracy-based procedures for quantifying task performance. In contrast to Precision

Teaching, a limited number of alternatives for what and how to measure are prescribed, and the measurement procedures used in Data-Based Program Modification do not require specification of a progression through any given skills sequence. Rather, *all* components of a student's instructional program, including the curriculum content, are viewed as the *independent variables* that, when modified, constitute operational hypotheses that should be empirically tested (Deno, 1986). In DBPM, the effectiveness of any instructional intervention for a student is viewed as potentially idiosyncratic, and it can be judged only by the data obtained through repeated measurement of the student's performance.

It follows, then, that DBPM does not assume a direct connection between the method of measurement and the content of instruction. A clear differentiation is made between deciding how and what to teach and deciding how and what to measure (Mirkin, Deno, Fuchs, Wesson, Tindal, Marston, & Kuehnle, 1981). Even though the complex act of reading can be described in terms of a variety of word recognition and comprehension skills, and lessons may include direct teaching of these skills, the assumption in DBPM is that teaching these particular skills constitutes a testable hypothesis about what might help a student learn to read. While we may measure to determine whether the student is learning the skills we are teaching, such measurement represents a check on the fidelity of our treatment rather than a measure of the effectiveness of our program in teaching this student to read. Thus, we must still measure our desired outcome of teaching these skills. In DBPM, measurement produces an index of overall growth in reading, such as the number of words read correctly in one minute of reading aloud from text. This global indicator, then, is the *dependent variable* used to evaluate instructional effectiveness. The choice of what specific behaviors are measured in DBPM is addressed in the following section.

What to measure. When using the CBM procedures in DBPM, options exist for choosing what to measure. For each option the behavior that is measured is representative or indicative of general proficiency in a complex academic skill, such as reading. Each option is also (a) reliable and valid with respect to student achievement, (b) simple and efficient for teachers to use, (c) easily understood by parents, teachers, and students, and (d) inexpensive (Deno, 1985). Several types of options in the areas of reading, spelling, and written expression meet the criteria or standards that have been established. The CBM procedures in arithmetic are not as well developed and, while reliable, do not meet the same high validity standards as in the other basic skills.

How to measure. In DBPM, students complete short (1- to 3-minute) CBM probes in an academic area one to three times a week. Each probe can be scored easily by counting the number of correct responses. For example, in reading, the most common method of data collection is to count the number of words the student reads in 1 minute. It is also possible to use a cloze procedure, in which every seventh word is deleted from a reading passage, and the students are required to fill in the correct word. In this case, the number of words filled in correctly are counted and charted. Several variations for measurement procedures are possible (for further explanation, see Fuchs, 1989).

How to use data. As in Precision Teaching, the data collected in DBPM are represented on a time-based graph and a student's progress is compared to a desired rate of growth. When the student is not making adequate progress, an instructional change is made.

Unlike Precision Teaching, the data in Data-Based Program Modification are plotted on an equal-interval graph. The vertical dimension on the graph displays the number of behaviors that occur within the time allotted for measurement (e.g., 1 minute of reading aloud from text, 2 minutes of spelling from dictation, 3 minutes of writing). The horizontal dimension of the graph indicates school days. Students' scores from assessment are graphed at the intersection of the day and number of correct responses (see Figure 3).

There are two data utilization strategies that can be implemented for deciding when to change (Fuchs, 1989). The first is the "goal-oriented" approach: The student's progress is evaluated in comparison with an aim line, or goal line, that is drawn on the graph. The goal line indicates the student's expected level of performance in a given period of time, usually the next annual review of the IEP. Teachers using the goal-oriented approach would change the student's instructional program any time a certain number of data points fell below the goal line.

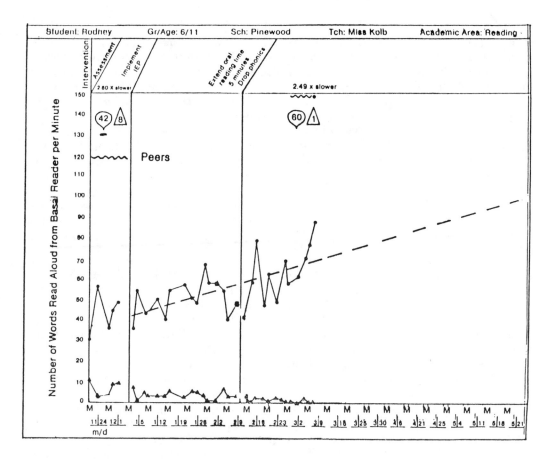

FIGURE 3. Progress monitoring graph for Data-Based Program Modification.

In the "treatment-oriented" approach, the student data are collected for a specified period of time (usually 7–10 data points), and a slope line or line of best fit is drawn through the data. Progress is evaluated by comparing the student's rate of growth after an instructional change with the rate of growth prior to the change. Comparisons of the rate of growth are made on the basis of the median (score that falls at the 50th percentile), the trend of the data (indicating how rapidly and in what direction student performance is changing), the shift up or down of the data on the first day of a new intervention, and the variability of the data with respect to the trend line (Deno & Fuchs, 1987). The goal-oriented approach is used when the primary concern is whether the long-range goal is being met; the treatment-oriented approach is used to determine which instructional methods work better for a student.

SIMILARITIES AND DIFFERENCES AMONG MODELS

Mastery Monitoring, Precision Teaching, and Data-Based Program Modification bear many similarities. All three use curriculum-based assessment procedures as defined by Tucker (1985) because the data typically used in evaluation are obtained from the local school curriculum. Subtle yet important differences distinguish the three approaches (see Table 1).

What to Measure

Both Mastery Monitoring and Precision Teaching incorporate a task-analysis

TABLE 1
Similarities and Differences Among Mastery Monitoring,
Precision Teaching, and Data-Based Program Modification

	Key Assumptions Regarding Learning	What to Measure	How to Measure	How to Use Data
Mastery Monitoring	Learning is an accumulation of proficiency on a hierarchy of subskills.	Behaviors logically determined from the hierarchical skill sequence — changing with successive task mastery.	Different measurement procedures created for different behaviors in the skill sequence yielding accuracy/percentage data.	Data used: Mastery or nonmastery of current skill. Decision: Move to new skill or reteach current skill.
Precision Teaching	Same as Mastery Monitoring, but fluency building also is essential.	Behaviors logically determined from the hierarchical skill sequence — changing with successive task mastery.	Different measurement procedures created for different behaviors in the skill sequence yielding data on number correct behaviors per minute.	Data used: (a) Mastery or nonmastery of current skill; (b) rate of change in performance on successive tasks. Decision: (a) move to new skill; (b) change program.
Data-Based Program Modification	Variables determining learning differ for different students.	Behaviors empirically determined to be global indicators of proficiency — measurement tests remain constant.	Consistent standardized measurement procedures yielding data on number correct in fixed time periods.	Data used: Rate of change in performance on standard task. Decision: Change or continue student's current instructional program.

approach to measurement and establish a direct connection between what is tested and what is taught. The advantage of this close connection is the ease with which teachers can interpret the data and communicate its meaning to parents, students, and other professionals (Deno & Fuchs, 1987). The disadvantage is that this close alliance between teaching and testing precludes examination of the external validity of the curriculum itself. With Mastery Monitoring and Precision Teaching, it is difficult to use the data to determine whether a given scope and sequence of curriculum skills and their associated mastery standards are an efficient and effective approach for teaching any given student.

The efficiency of the task-analysis approach as employed in Mastery Monitoring and Precision Teaching depends on the accuracy with which the sequence of skills adequately reflects the optimal sequence of learning for the individual student. It is possible that a given sequence is not representative of the most efficient learning sequence for a particular student (Cox & Dunn, 1979; Mueller, 1976). For example, for some students, it may be most efficient to learn vowel sounds before consonant sounds, whereas for other students, the opposite may be true.

More important than the question of efficiency is the question of effectiveness: Will learning *these* skills improve *this* student's performance in a given academic area (e.g., reading, spelling, arithmetic)? In task analysis, objectives are formed by expert opinion on what should constitute the curriculum. Because the measurement systems of Mastery Monitoring and Precision Teaching are based on the short-term objectives within the given instructional curriculum, it is difficult to evaluate the validity of mastering that sequence of objectives on moving the student closer to the desired goals of the school and society (Deno, 1986; Jenkins, Deno, & Mirkin, 1979). For some students, mastery of a particular set of phonic skills may not be a necessary prerequisite for learning to read.

A meta-analysis conducted by Fuchs and Fuchs (1986a) addressed the question of external validity for the measures we are discussing. In this investigation, the differential effects of short-term and long-term goal setting on student achievement were compared. The short-term goal approach is synonymous with the task-analysis approach of Mastery Monitoring and Precision Teaching, in which a series of objectives are created to correspond to steps in a hierarchical curriculum and a pool of items are created for each objective. The long-term approach is that employed in DBPM: An annual goal is specified and a large pool of measurement items are generated. The testing format and difficulty level of the test probes remained constant (e.g., counting the number of words read aloud in 1 minute from Level IV basal passages).

Student achievement was measured both with global achievement tests (e.g., subtests from the Stanford Diagnostic Reading Test) and probe-like measures (measures similar to the monitoring probes). The results of the study showed an interaction between goal setting and achievement measure: When student progress was measured against short-term goals, the effect size was .40 times higher on probe-like outcomes than on global achievement measures. When progress was monitored against long-term goals, the effect size was .51 times higher on the global achievement measures than on the probe-like measures. These results indicate that students in a mastery approach scored better on tests directly related to the instructional items, but the amount of transfer to the general task domain itself, as indicated by performance on standardized achievement tests, was less. In the long-term goal condition, student performance in the global domain

was greater than performance on task-related probes.

It is probably the case that both short-term and long-term goal approaches are useful in instruction. Fuchs and Fuchs (1986a) suggested that both short-term and long-term systems should be employed. The short-term approach is effective in guiding the instructional program and holding teachers to a set of instructional objectives. The long-term system can be used to assess the global effects of the curriculum on student achievement.

How to Measure

Both accuracy and time are integral to the measurement procedures of Precision Teaching and Data-Based Program Modification. In Mastery Monitoring, accuracy is typically the prime concern. Time-based measures possess several advantages over monitoring accuracy alone. First, adding the time dimension to the measurement of performance produces data on fluency. Completing 20 of 20 multiplication problems correctly in 2 minutes is more proficient than completing 20 of 20 correctly in 30 minutes.

Second, including time in measurement produces a scale with fine gradations and without a ceiling. Use of accuracy alone imposes a ceiling on the level of performance at 100% correct. Counting the number of correct responses the student makes within a given time period removes the measurement-produced ceiling.

Finally, since accuracy is expressed as percentage, important performance information is obscured. It is not necessarily the case that a student who scores 80% correct on addition probes by answering 4 of 5 correctly is at the same level of proficiency as the student who answers 80 of 100 problems correctly.

Accuracy alone gives useful but limited information. Time-based measures provide additional information that is critical to evaluating a student's level of proficiency on academic tasks.

How to Use Data

The three evaluation systems differ on the prescribed manner of data utilization. Mastery Monitoring does not dictate that data be graphed, nor that specific rules be followed with regard to use of data. Both DBPM and PT involve the use of graphing and provide specific data utilization strategies. The data that are graphed and the type of graph differentiate DBPM and PT.

Graphing may be more advantageous for bringing about change in students' achievement. In their meta-analysis of systematic formative evaluation studies, Fuchs and Fuchs (1986b) found that graphing the data had a significant effect on student achievement. The effect size for recording and graphing data was .70, substantially greater than the effect size for recording only (without graphing). Fuchs and Fuchs offer two possible reasons for the positive effects of graphing. First, graphing may make it easier for teachers to analyze performance trends more accurately and frequently. Second, it may facilitate evaluating students' performance. In either case, it would seem advantageous to include graphing as a part of Mastery Monitoring.

Although both Precision Teaching and Data-Based Program Modification include graphing as a part of their systems, the method of graphing differentiates the two. Precision Teaching employs semilogarithmic graph paper, which utilizes a ratio scale. Proponents of Precision Teaching recommend the semilogarithmic paper because they believe it better represents actual growth in academic areas and because it allows more than one behavior to be charted on the same graph (White & Haring, 1980). DBPM uses equal-interval paper. The users of DBPM believe that equal-interval paper is easier for teachers to use and understand (Fuchs, 1989; Mirkin, Fuchs, & Deno, 1982).

Fuchs and Fuchs (1987) conducted a meta-analysis to investigate the relation between methods of graphing student performance data and achievement. The authors examined 15 studies that employed a system of data-based program development in which data collection occurred at least two times a week, and decisions regarding program modifications were formulated on an individual rather than a group basis. The results showed no significant differences between the graphing method and student achievement. The authors concluded that the type of graphing method does not affect achievement reliably, although they caution that there is need for direct investigation of data-based program components in controlled experimental investigations.

Marston (1988) conducted an analysis of the accuracy of predicting future student performance by using equal-interval and semilogarithmic charting. Using data collected in reading and math over a period of 7 weeks, he compared predictions for future performance by the two charting methods with actual performance during weeks 8, 9, and 10. He found that slopes based on equal-interval charts predicted future student performance more accurately than slopes derived from semilogarithmic charts. Although this investigation addressed the question of representation of actual growth on both semilogarithmic and equal-interval graphs, it did not address the use of the same graph for different behaviors.

Given that neither type of graphic scale represents a distinct advantage, and that the use of either graphic method affects student achievement, logistical rather than technical considerations might better influence the choice of graph. For many practitioners, use of equal-interval charting may be easier to implement and understand. If, however, more than one behavior is to be charted on the same graph, it may be desirable to use semilogarithmic paper.

A final factor differentiating the three methods of evaluation is the use of systematic data utilization rules. Both Precision Teaching and DBPM prescribe specific data evaluation rules that are designed to guide the teacher in using the data to systematically make changes in the student's instructional program. Fuchs and Fuchs (1986b) found a significant effect on student achievement when teachers used explicit, systematic rules to evaluate the data they collected. They defined data evaluation rules as analyzing the data at regular intervals, and implementing instructional changes when patterns in the data suggested it be done. This condition was contrasted with the use of teachers' judgments, as to when to analyze data and when to make changes. The effect size for the use of evaluation rules was .91, but for teacher judgment it was only .42.

The positive effects for graphing and the use of data evaluation rules imply that to improve academic interventions *measurement* alone is not enough. Measuring student behavior is only a means to an end. In order to enhance a student's achievement, it is necessary to *evaluate;* that is, it is important to use the data systematically to make decisions regarding the effectiveness of the student's instructional program.

Summary

Each of the three measurement systems described in this chapter can be useful in instruction. A combination of approaches may, in fact, prove most useful. A task-analysis approach like Mastery Monitoring or Precision Teaching could be used to guide instruction, and Data-Based Program Modification could be used to evaluate that instruction.

The use of Data-Based Program Modification for designing and evaluating students' educational programs prior to and following referral into special education is illustrated in the following section.

APPLYING EVALUATION STRATEGIES: CASE EXAMPLE

Each of the three models just described involves the collection of data for purposes of making instructional decisions for all students. Students who are not succeeding in the regular classroom present a special set of problems involving instructional decisions of a more complex nature, that is, decisions regarding placement in special education and the need for additional or differentiated instruc-

tion. Data-Based Program Modification is applicable in all steps in the decision-making process for students in danger of failing in the regular education program and for students with disabilities. Because the focus of this chapter is intervention, only the use of DBPM for monitoring students' progress in regular and special education will be examined.

In the hypothetical example that follows, we illustrate the use of evaluation procedures to improve the effectiveness of prereferral and special program interventions.

Classroom Evaluation of Prereferral Interventions

The students in Central Elementary School are screened during the first month of school. The classroom teachers, paraprofessionals, Chapter 1 teachers, and school psychologists participate in the screening procedures. All students are screened on three consecutive days using standard grade-level passages chosen from the Holt curriculum (a curriculum that is *not* used for instruction in Central Elementary). Students read three passages each day. The number of words read aloud in 1 minute for each student is recorded. The median score for each day is noted, and at the end of the three days the student is assigned a score based on the median score across the three days. The school psychologist rank-orders student scores within each grade level and identifies the lowest 15% of the students as those who are at risk for failure in the regular education reading program. Teachers are asked to monitor the progress of the students identified as high risk, as well as any other students they believe might experience difficulty in the regular education classroom.

Patrick J. is in the fourth grade and is in the lowest reading group in his class. Patrick is identified as being at risk for failure in regular education. His progress is monitored weekly by his regular education reading teacher.

Expected rate of growth. Prior to the first week of monitoring, the classroom

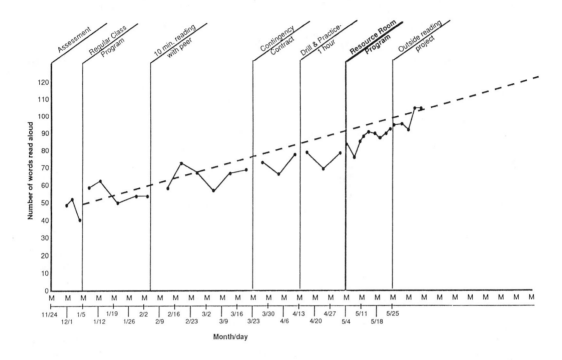

FIGURE 4. Performance chart for Patrick J.

teacher and school psychologist determine an expected rate of growth for Patrick and the other students being monitored in the classroom. The data collected from the schoolwide screening indicate that the average median score for fourth graders on the Holt screening passages was 104 words read correctly in 1 minute. Patrick's median score for the three days of screening was 47. His teacher and the school psychologist want to move Patrick closer to his peers in reading performance, so they set an annual goal for Patrick of 107 words read correctly in 1 minute, or an increase of 2 words per week. Data from previous monitoring at Central indicate that the average fourth grader increases at the rate of 2.0 words per week. Patrick's teacher believes he will succeed in the regular education class if he can progress at a rate equal to his peers, that is, a gain of 2 words per week. This expected rate of growth is drawn on the graph for Patrick from his median baseline score (47) to his expected score in 30 weeks (Figure 4).

Monitoring. Patrick is monitored on Wednesday of each week. He reads a sample passage from the grade-appropriate Holt series. His teacher records the number of words he reads in 1 minute and draws it on the graph each day.

Data utilization. Two data utilization rules have been established at Central Elementary: (a) If a student's score falls below expected rate of growth on three consecutive weeks, a change in the reading program is made; (b) if after three interventions (a minimum of 9–10 weeks) the student's progress is still not equal to or above the expected rate of growth, and the student is experiencing difficulty in the regular education reading program, referral to special education is considered.

Once a month, Patrick's teacher and

the school psychologist meet to discuss the progress of the students who are being monitored. Patrick's progress is illustrated in the graph in Figure 4. On weeks 3, 4, and 5, Patrick's performance falls below the expected rate of growth, as indicated by the goal line, necessitating a modification of his reading program. Because his scores are only slightly below his goal line, Patrick's teacher and the school psychologist feel that a minor intervention will be appropriate. Since Patrick arrives at school early in the morning, they decide to have him read with a sixth-grade peer for 10 minutes each morning. Patrick has an interest in many of the books in the classroom but is not skilled enough to read them independently.

Evaluation of first program modification. Immediately following this first program modification, Patrick's performance improves, and it seems as though the program change is effective. During weeks 9, 10, and 11, however, Patrick's performance falls below his goal line once again. A second program modification is implemented in Patrick's reading program.

Patrick's teacher has observed that he has not been completing his work in class, even though he seems able to do it. The psychologist suggests establishing a contingency contract with Patrick, allowing him to earn points for completion of tasks, the points to be exchanged for computer time.

Evaluation of the second program modification. Following the second modification, Patrick's performance improves slightly, but not enough to indicate that he will achieve his goal. His data remain below the goal line, and his teacher notices that he is experiencing increasing difficulty in reading in class. At this time, the teacher and school psychologist discuss the possibility that Patrick may need a more intensive reading program, but are convinced that it is worthwhile to try one more modification in his regular program before making a referral. Because Patrick seems to be falling further and further behind his peers, they decide an intensive intervention is warranted. Each day after

school, Patrick is given an hour of additional drill and practice on the material covered that day during reading class.

Evaluation of third program modification. Following this third modification, Patrick's performance increases slightly, but not enough to bring him up to a level commensurate with his expected rate of growth. Patrick's teacher and the school psychologist decide to refer Patrick for assessment and possible placement in special education.

On the basis of the prereferral monitoring data, Patrick is referred for possible special education services in reading. Patrick's teacher has observed, however, that he also has been experiencing difficulty in spelling. Although Patrick has not been monitored in spelling, the teacher maintains that his problems are severe enough to warrant further assessment. The psychologist conducts the assessment, and determines that Patrick is eligible for special education services in both reading and spelling. He will receive 1 hour of service in reading in the resource room in addition to the reading instruction he currently receives in the regular education classroom. His deficit in spelling performance is not as severe as that in reading. Patrick's progress in spelling in the regular classroom will be monitored, and he will receive additional time in spelling instruction in the regular education classroom.

Evaluating Interventions Following Placement in Special Education

Formulation of the individual education plan (IEP). An IEP is developed for Patrick in reading and spelling, and long-range goals are developed. In reading, the long-range goal initially developed for Patrick in the regular classroom is maintained, that of 107 words correctly read in 1 minute. The special education teacher, regular education teacher, and school psychologist feel that with special instruction in reading, it is possible to move Patrick toward that goal.

In spelling, peer-normative data are utilized to determine the long-range goal for Patrick. It is hoped that the additional service provided in spelling will move him toward a level comparable with peer performance. The long range goal for Patrick is to correctly spell 70 letter sequences in 2 minutes of dictation of words taken from the basal curriculum in which Patrick is being monitored for reading.

Program planning. The special education resource teacher plans a reading program for Patrick. She will work on his phonics skills using the DISTAR program for half an hour daily. For a second half-hour of instruction each day, she will use direct-instruction methods to teach the material in the basal reading book that is used for instruction in the regular classroom. The resource teacher will also implement the same program of tasks that Patrick is using in the regular classroom. The resource teacher monitors Patrick 3 days a week using the same monitoring material (Holt) as that used by the regular classroom teacher for monitoring. Patrick's performance improves with the addition of the special education resource services. At the end of 5 weeks, Patrick's progress indicates that he will achieve his long-range goal. The resource teacher feels that Patrick's performance could increase at an even greater rate with additional modifications in the program. She adds an outside reading project to his program. Patrick chooses a book to read and records the number of pages he reads each day. He receives a sticker each day he reaches a goal that he and the teacher have set.

Examination of the initial data collected by the teacher indicates that this intervention improves Patrick's reading performance, bringing him up to a level slightly above his goal line. His teacher will need to collect additional data before making a decision regarding the need for additional modifications in Patrick's reading program.

In spelling, Patrick's performance is monitored, and his progress toward his goal is evaluated. By procedure similar to that applied in the prereferral monitoring for reading, if interventions in the regular

classroom do not prove effective for Patrick, consideration will be given to more intensive services in spelling.

SUMMARY

In this chapter, three alternative evaluation procedures that are utilized in education were described and compared. Each approach involves monitoring of students' progress on basic skills taught in the curriculum. Each approach also involves utilization of the data in program planning and modification.

The curriculum-based measures used in Data-Based Program Modification provide general indicators of a student's progress in basic academic skills. A case study was presented to illustrate the use of Data-Based Program Modification in prevention and intervention, and the possible roles of the school psychologist in these educational processes was highlighted.

An advantage of using a systematic evaluation model is the continuity of monitoring and programming from the regular classroom services into special education services, as illustrated with the reading procedures utilized with a hypothetical case study of a student with reading deficits. Another advantage is the use of data in making decisions regarding the level of service, as illustrated with the spelling program. Finally, the use of an evaluation model rooted in student performance data can provide a team approach that involves the regular classroom teacher, the school psychologist, and the special education resource teacher. Thus, evaluation strategies become key components of a model for preventing and remediating problems as well as evaluating outcomes.

REFERENCES

Armbruster, B. B., Stevens, R. G., & Rosenshine, B. (1977). *Analyzing content coverage and emphasis: A study of three curricula and two tests (Technical Representative N26)*. Urbana, IL: University of Illinois, Center for Study of Reading.

Block, J. H. (Ed.). (1971). *Mastery learning.* New York: Holt, Rinehart & Winston.

Block, J. H. (1984). Making school learning activities more play like: Flow and mastery learning. *Elementary School Journal, 85*(1), 65-75.

Bloom, B. (1976). *Human characteristics and school learning.* New York: McGraw-Hill.

Bloom, B. S., Madaus, G. F., & Hastings, J. T. (1981). *Evaluation to improve learning.* New York: McGraw-Hill.

Carroll, J. B. (1963). A model of school learning. *Teachers College Record, 64,* 723-733.

Christie, L., McKenzie, J., & Burdett, C. (1972). The consulting teacher approach to special education: Inservice training for regular classroom teachers. *Focus on Exceptional Children, 4*(5), 1-10.

Cox, W. F., Jr., & Dunn, T. G. (1979). Mastery learning: A psychological trap? *Educational Psychologist, 14,* 24-29.

Deno, S. L. (1985). Curriculum-based measurement: The emerging alternative. *Exceptional Children, 52,* 219-232.

Deno, S. L. (1986). Formative evaluation of individual student programs: A new role for school psychologists. *School Psychology Review, 15*(3), 358-374.

Deno, S. L., & Fuchs, L. S. (1987). Developing curriculum-based measurement systems for data-based special education problem solving. *Focus on Exceptional Children, 19,* 1-15.

Deno, S. L., & Mirkin, P. K. (1977). *Data-based program modification: A manual.* Arlington, VA: Council for Exceptional Children.

Education of All Handicapped Children Act of 1975, Public Law 94-142, 20 U.S.C. §1401 (1975).

Fuchs, L. S. (1989). Evaluating solutions: Monitoring progress and revising intervention plans. In M. Shinn (Ed.), *Curriculum-based measurement: Assessing special children* (pp. 153-181). New York: Guilford.

Fuchs, L. S., & Fuchs, D. (1986a). Curriculum-based assessment of progress toward long-term and short-term goals. *Journal of Special Education, 20*(1), 69-82.

Fuchs, L. S., & Fuchs, D. (1986b). Effects of systematic formative evaluation: A meta-analysis. *Exceptional Children, 53,* 199-208.

Fuchs, L. S., & Fuchs, D. (1987). The relation between methods of graphing student performance data and achievement: A meta-analysis. *Journal of Educational Technology, 8*(3), 5-13.

Fuchs, L., Fuchs, D., & Hamlett, C. (1989). Effects of alternative goal structures within curriculum-based measurement. *Exceptional Children, 55,* 429-439.

Gagne, R., Briggs, L., & Wager, W. (1988). *Principles of instructional design.* New York: Holt, Rinehart & Winston.

Idol-Maestas, L. (1981). A teacher training model: The resource consulting teacher. *Behavior Disorders, 6*(2), 108-121.

Idol-Maestas, L. (1983). *Special educator's consultation handbook.* Rockville, MD: Aspen.

Idol-Maestas, L., Lloyd, S., & Ritter, S. (1982). *A model for direct, data based reading instruction.* Champaign, IL: Department of Special Education. (ERIC Reproduction Service No. ED 219738)

Jenkins, J. R., Deno, S. L., & Mirkin, P. K. (1979). Measuring pupil progress toward the least restrictive alternative. *Learning Disability Quarterly, 2*(4), 81-91.

Jenkins, J., & Pany, D. (1978). Standardized achievement tests: How useful for special education? *Exceptional Children, 44,* 448-453.

Lloyd, J. W. (1984). How should we individualize instruction - or should we? *Remedial & Special Education, 5*(1), 7-16.

Marston, D. (1988). Measuring academic progress of students with learning difficulties: A comparison of the semilogarithmic chart and equal interval paper. *Exceptional Children, 55,* 38-44.

McGreevy, P. (1984). Frequency and the standard celeration chart: Necessary components of Precision Teaching. *Journal of Precision Teaching, 5*(2), 28-36.

Miller, G. A., Galanter, E., & Pribram, K. (1960). *Plans and the structure of behavior.* New York: Holt.

Mirkin, P. K., Deno, S. L., Fuchs, L. S., Wesson, C., Tindal, G., Marston, D., & Kuehnle, K. (1981). *Procedures to develop and monitor progress on IEP goals.* Minneapolis: University of Minnesota, Institute for Research on Learning Disabilities.

Mirkin, P. K. Fuchs, L. S., & Deno, S. L. (1982). *Consideration for designing a continuous evaluation system: An integrative review* (Monograph No. 20). Minneapolis: University of Minnesota, Institute for Research on Learning Disabilities.

Mueller, D. J. (1976). Mastery learning: Partly boon, partly boondoggle. *Teachers College Record, 78,* 41-52.

Salmon-Cox, L. (1981). Teachers and standardized achievement tests: What's really happening? *Phi Delta Kappan, 62,* 631-634.

Salvia, J., & Ysseldyke, J. (1988). *Assessment in special and remedial education* (4th ed.). Boston: Houghton Mifflin.

Shriner, J., & Salvia, J. (1988). Chronic non-correspondence between elementary math curriculum and arithmetic tests. *Exceptional Children, 55*, 240-248.

Skinner, B. F. (1954). *Science and human behavior.* New York: MacMillan.

Stephens, T. (1976). *Directive teaching of children with learning and behavioral handicaps* (2nd ed.). Columbus, OH: Merrill.

Stephens, T., Hartman, A. C., & Lucas, V. H. (1982). *Teaching children basic skills: A curriculum handbook* (2nd ed.). Columbus, OH: Merrill.

Stephens, T. M., Blackhurst, A. E., & Magliocca, L. A. (1988). *Teaching mainstreamed students* (2nd ed.). Elmsford, NY: Pergamon.

Tucker, J. A. (1985). Curriculum-based assessment: An introduction. *Exceptional Children, 52,* 199-204.

Watson, D., & Tharp, R. (1989). *Self-directed behavior* (5th ed.). Monterey, CA: Brooks/Cole.

White, O. R. (1986). Precision Teaching — Precision learning. *Exceptional Children, 52,* 522-534.

White, O. R., & Haring, N. G. (1976). *Exceptional teaching.* Columbus, OH: Merrill.

White, O. R., & Haring, N. G. (1980). *Exceptional teaching* (2nd ed.). Columbus, OH: Merrill.

Ysseldyke, J., & Salvia, J. (1974). Diagnostic prescriptive teaching: Two models. *Exceptional Children, 41,* 181-185.

Zigmond, N., Vallecorsa, A., & Silverman, R. (1983). *Assessment for instructional planning in special education.* Englewood Cliffs, NJ: Prentice-Hall.

FOOTNOTE

[1]The use of DBPM in any of these three ways assumes nothing about the need for additional testing that may be required by the law, regulations, or local district policy. Data-Based Program Modification can be used as a part of the process, but it does not have to be the sole source of data used for referral. In some districts that implement Data-Based Program Modification, referral decisions are made on the basis of the data collected prior to referral and during the referral process. In others, DBPM is only a portion of the data used in making referral decisions.

Selecting, Implementing, and Evaluating Classroom Interventions

Stephen N. Elliott
University of Wisconsin–Madison

Joseph C. Witt
Louisiana State University

Thomas R. Kratochwill
University of Wisconsin–Madison

INTRODUCTION

Significant challenges confront psychologists involved in selecting, implementing, and evaluating treatments for children with learning and behavior problems. The major challenge, in most cases, is not the result of a lack of potentially effective treatments. Rather, it is the result of a combination of factors emanating in part from a limited relationship with the child and/or teachers and parents, a lack of a technology that clearly links assessment results to treatments, and a narrow conceptualization of treatment targets. The purposes of this chapter are to provide (a) an overview of the problem-solving process involved in treatment selection and evaluation and (b) a review of three constructs (treatment acceptability, teacher empowerment, and treatment integrity) that are critical to the effective use of classroom interventions. In addition to these two major goals, we discuss treatment evaluation briefly so that a context for effectiveness is established. Readers interested in the mechanics and effects of actual treatments for children will find excellent summaries in many of the remaining chapters in this volume and in comprehensive volumes such as *The Handbook of Behavior Therapy in Education* (Witt, Elliott, & Gresham, 1988) and *The Practice of Child Therapy* (Kratochwill & Morris, 1990; Morris & Kratochwill, 1983). Readers desiring more information on the therapeutic relationship than is covered in this chapter, are referred to *Interviewing Techniques for Helpers* (Cormier & Cormier, 1985).

The Problem-Solving Process and Models of Treatment

Although this chapter focuses on treatment, it is premised on the assumption that treatments follow from an adequate assessment of the problem and conceptually are consistent with a *model of psychopathology*. Loosely defined, a model of psychopathology is a collection of assumptions regarding the role of biological, psychological, social, environmental, and other factors thought to contribute to the development of a person's problem(s). Numerous models for conceptualizing deviant behavior exist: the medical or biological model, the psychodynamic model, and the behavioral model have a long history (Johnson, Rasbury, & Siegel, 1986). More recent models include the family model, the limited-capacities model, and the cognitive model (Levine & Sandeen, 1985). These models range from those that emphasize the individual to those that focus on the entire family, and from those that emphasize biological factors to those that focus on social and environment causes of problem behavior. Models also vary as to whether the child's problem behavior is viewed as an overt symptom of some inferred underlying process or whether the overt symptom(s) are considered to be the problem.

Each model provides a conceptual framework to organize information about a child's problem behavior and to identify potential treatment targets or impact points. Let us examine the attributes of a behavioral model in understanding a child's problem and planning treatment strategies.

Various nuances of the behavioral model have been developed; however, Kanfer's (1973) S-O-R-K-C- formula serves as a working approach (Figure 1). In this characterization of behavior, the S stands for stimulus, the O for the biological state of the organism, the R for response, the K for the ratio of consequence frequency to response, and the C for consequence. The formula describes the smallest unit of analysis for a behavior episode and summarizes the major components acting at the time of a response that affect the probability of the occurrence of the response. Target problems in a behavioral model generally are characterized as either a deficit or excess in the client's behavior, inappropriate environmental stimulus control, inappropriate client-generated stimulus control, and/or inappropriate reinforcement contingencies. A behavioral model offers a rather substantial array of environmental (S, K, and C) and personal (O and R) components that are hypothesized to influence behavior and could become the focus of intervention. Thus, the psychologist's goal in the problem-solving process is to assess and functionally analyze these several components *and* to select one or more components to change, with the prediction that the target problem behavior will also change.

To reiterate, the value of any model, whether it be the S-O-R-K-C behavioral model or one of the several others listed earlier, is its information-organizing role. Assuming psychologists and educators collectively have the ability and methods to assess the critical components in the model accurately, they are well on their way to generating a number of treatment alternatives if they are given reasonable resources and staff time.

Four Factors That Influence Treatment Selection and Use

Given our previous discussion about the various models of psychopathology, the multicomponent nature of problem behavior, and the variety of potential treatment impact points, it logically follows that for the overwhelming majority of problems, there are many treatments (or more likely treatment packages) available. Thus, as noted at the outset of this chapter, the major problems confronting applied psychologists are the *selection* and appropriate *use* of treatments, rather than a lack of appropriate treatments.

Issues of selection and use are magnified when a psychologist works in a consultative or indirect service arrangement in which a consultee, most likely a teacher and/or a parent, actually implements the treatment with the target child. Under such indirect service conditions, treatments must meet with the approval of significant adults (i.e., parents, teachers, other school officials) and be sufficiently easy to implement by nonpsychologists with varying degrees of treatment knowledge and skills. In sum, psychologists are charged with the primary responsibility of selecting a treatment for a given problem. The primary factor driving this decision is that the selected treatment must be, first and foremost, likely to be effective. *Effectiveness* alone, however, is not enough. Treatments also must be socially valid, capable of being delivered as prescribed, and ideally within the resources and skills of the treatment agent. These factors, supplemental yet important to the overall

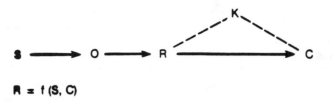

FIGURE 1. Kanfer's S-O-R-K-C formula of behavior.

effectiveness of a treatment are referred to as *treatment acceptability, teacher/ parent empowerment,* and *treatment integrity.* In the remainder of this chapter, we examine each of these selection and use factors. A brief overview and discussion of the relative importance of each of these four factors serves as an advance organizer to a detailed review of research and practical guidelines underlying them.

Treatment effectiveness. The topic of treatment effectiveness has engendered much discussion and nearly as much research (e.g., see the special series, "Psychotherapy Outcomes," in the *Journal of Consulting and Clinical Psychology* [1986, Vol. 54-1], and the *American Psychologist* [1986, Vol. 41-2]). Whether one is primarily a researcher or a practitioner, the first question about a treatment usually is "Does it work?" The reason for addressing this concern was captured over 20 years ago by Baer, Wolf, and Risley (1968): "If the application of behavioral techniques does not produce large enough effects for practical value, then application has failed. . . . Its practical value, specifically its powers in altering behavior enough to be socially important, is the essential criterion" (p. 96). This social importance criterion that Baer et al. referred to essentially amounts to a difference in performance that results in a constructive difference as perceived by significant others, measured by comparison to an objective standard, and maintained over time.

Although much has been written about treatment effectiveness, many questions and issues remain to be examined. For example, How much change in behavior is enough? What are the side

effects of our treatments? Should a clinical judgment model, a statistical model, or both be used to make decisions about outcome effectiveness? These questions are beyond the central focus of this chapter, but currently are influencing both research and practice. Interested readers are referred to conceptual works by Jacobson, Follette, and Revenstorf (1984) on clinical versus statistical criteria for outcome effectiveness; Yeaton (1988) and Yeaton and Sechrest (1981) on treatment-effect norms and treatment strength; and to a special issue of *Behavioral Assessment* (Jacobson, 1988) for further information.

Treatment acceptability. Concern about the acceptability and use of treatments has been a persistent theme in behavioral psychology (O'Leary, 1984; Reppucci & Saunders, 1974). The causes of this concern about acceptance have ranged from the real possibility that a treatment will restrict an individual's rights (U.S. Congress, 1974a, 1974b) to negative reaction to the use of nonhumanistic jargon (Witt, Moe, Gutkin, & Andrews, 1984). Consequently, behavioral researchers have invested substantial energy and resources to identify the features of treatments that consumers (i.e., teachers, parents, children) like and dislike. Kazdin (1981a) gave this work on the likes and dislikes of consumers of psychological services the label *treatment acceptability,* and defined it as "judgments by laypersons, clients, and others of whether treatment procedures are appropriate, fair, and reasonable for the problem or client" (p. 493). This line of research has been the central focus of the larger domain of work on the social validity of treatments (Kazdin, 1977; Wolf, 1978) and is now also gaining considerable interest among researchers and practitioners interested in the treatment selection and implementation phase of behavioral consultation (Elliott, 1988; Gresham & Kendell, 1987).

In addition to a scientific interest in treatment acceptability, there are strong pragmatic and legal/ethical reasons for assessing consumers' acceptance of treatments. Courts, for example, have ruled out certain procedures that might be unacceptable because they infringe on client rights (Budd & Baer, 1976). Institutional review committees, which are standard elements of practice today, routinely are used to decide whether a treatment is acceptable for a given problem. Ethics codes and research on children's involvement in treatment decisions support the involvement of children in selecting treatment procedures (Melton, 1983). Finally, perhaps the most compelling rationale for being concerned about the acceptability of a treatment was cited by Wolf (1978):

> If the participants don't like the treatment they may avoid it, or run away, or complain loudly. And thus, society will be less likely to use our technology [behavior modification], no matter how potentially effective and efficient it might be. (p. 206)

Treatment resistance and empowerment. The fact that some apparently effective treatments are never tried or are rejected after only a day or two of use often is a sign that the treatment agent dislikes or has some objection to the treatment. Recent research on help-giving (Dunst & Trivette, 1988) and problem-solving consultation (Witt & Martens, 1988) has focused on the fact that many "installed" interventions simply don't fit into the routines and environments of help givers (i.e., teachers). This work has called for a reorientation to a philosophy of empowerment as a means of avoiding resistance from help givers. A philosophy of empowerment assumes (a) that the help giver already possess many competencies to change a problem and (b) that the failure to use these competencies is the result of the existing social structure and lack of resources available within that structure. Given this orientation, the role of a consultant becomes one of helping a teacher identify needs and locate resources for meeting the needs, and of linking the teacher to these resources. In the development of many interventions, it seems that school psychologists do a good job of helping identify needs. Resistance from teachers, however, often occurs when psychologists simply try to install treatment packages without consideration of the teachers' skills and the resources indigenous to their classrooms. Thus, recognizing resistance and utilizing a philosophy of empowerment in developing interventions are critical components of the implementation and continued use of a treatment.

Treatment integrity. Treatment integrity is the degree to which an intervention plan is implemented as intended. Many intervention failures probably can be attributed to the fact that intervention plans were not implemented as intended (Gresham, 1989). The reasons for poor treatment integrity are multifaceted; for example, the treatment may be too complicated, the treatment agent may lack time or skills to implement it, or the target child may resist and deter application of the treatment. Surprisingly, few studies in the behavioral literature have assessed the integrity of interventions. A review of all empirical reports of research in the *Journal of Applied Behavior Analysis* from 1968 through 1980 indicated that only 16% of the researchers reported on the integrity of their interventions (Peterson, Hommer, & Wonderlich, 1982). In sum, most research published in one of the most rigorous journals failed to demonstrate that changes in dependent or outcome variables were due to intentional changes in independent or treatment variables. Establishing that a treatment was implemented as prescribed remains an important challenge to researchers and practitioners alike.

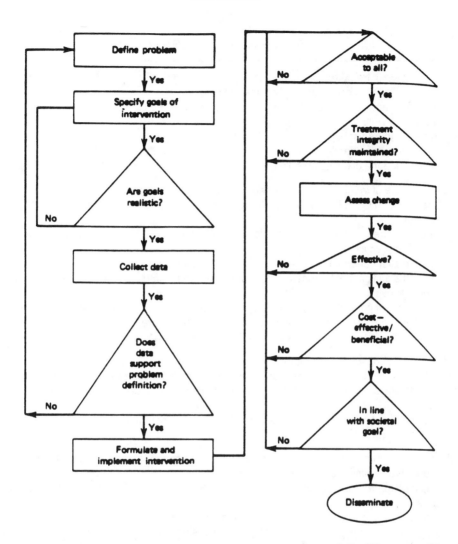

FIGURE 2. Intervention flowchart. From *School Psychology: Essentials of Theory and Practice*, by C. R. Reynolds, T. Gutkin, S. N. Elliott, and J. C. Witt, 1984, New York: John Wiley. Copyright 1984 by John Wiley. Reprinted by permission.

Guiding the Treatment Process

Clearly, we believe, the information and actions associated with treatment acceptability, intervention agent empowerment, and treatment integrity are critical but often ignored in the day-to-day handling of classroom interventions. Securing information and eliciting cooperation on these issues, however, are only a few of the many features that define a successful treatment plan. As illustrated in Figure 2, the typical treatment conceptually consists of at least 13 steps driven

by a series of questions, such as: Are the treatment goals realistic? Do the data support the problem definition? Is the treatment acceptable to all parties involved? Is the integrity of the treatment maintained? Is the treatment effective? Is it cost-effective and beneficial? And finally: Is the treatment in line with societal goals? Most of these questions can be contextualized as ethical concerns in human services. In fact, as illustrated in Table 1, the Association for the Advancement of Behavior Therapy has published a similar

TABLE 1
Ethical Issues for Human Services

A. Have the goals of treatment been adequately considered?
1. To insure that the goals are explicit, are they written?
2. Has the client's[a] understanding of the goals been assured by having the client restate them orally or in writing?
3. Have the therapist and client agreed on the goals of therapy?
4. Will serving the client's interests be contrary to the interests of other persons?
5. Will serving the client's immediate interests be contrary to the client's long-term interest?

B. Has the choice of treatment methods been adequately considered?
1. Does the published literature show the procedure to be the best one available for that problem?
2. If no literature exists regarding the treatment method, is the method consistent with generally accepted practice?
3. Has the client been told of alternative procedures that might be preferred by the client on the basis of significant differences in discomfort, treatment time, cost, or degree of demonstrated effectiveness?
4. If a treatment procedure is publicly, legally, or professionally controversial, has formal professional consultation been obtained, adequately considered, and have the alternative treatment methods been more closely reexamined and reconsidered?

C. Is the client's participation voluntary?
1. Have possible sources of coercion of the client's participation been considered?
2. If treatment is legally mandated, has the available range of treatments and therapists been offered?
3. Can the client withdraw from treatment without a penalty or financial loss that exceeds actual clinical costs?

D. When another person or an agency is empowered to arrange for therapy, have the interests of the subordinated client been sufficiently considered?
1. Has the subordinated client been informed of the treatment objectives and participated in the choice of treatment procedures?
2. Where the subordinated client's competence to decide is limited, have the client as well as the guardian participated in the treatment discussions to the extent that the client's abilities permit?
3. If the interests of the subordinated person and the superordinate persons or agency conflict, have attempts been made to reduce the conflict by dealing with both interests?

E. Has the adequacy of treatment been evaluated?
1. Have quantitative measures of the problem and its progress been obtained?
2. Have the measures of the problem and its progress been made available to the client during treatment?

F. Has the confidentiality of the treatment relationship been protected?
1. Has the client been told who has access to the records?
2. Are records available only to authorized persons?

G. Does the therapist refer the clients to other therapists when necessary?
1. If treatment is unsuccessful, is the client referred to other therapists?
2. Has the client been told that if dissatisfied with the treatment, a referral will be made?

H. Is the therapist qualified to provide treatment?
1. Has the therapist had training or experience in treating problems like the client's?
2. If deficits exist in the therapist's qualifications, has the client been informed?

(Table 1, continued)

3. If the therapist is not adequately qualified, is the client referred to other therapists, or has supervision by a qualified therapist been provided? Is the client informed of the supervisory relation?
4. If the treatment is administered by mediators, have the mediators been adequately supervised by a qualified therapist?

Note. The questions related to each issue have deliberately been cast in a general manner that applies to all types of interventions and not solely or specifically to the practice of behavior therapy. Issues directed specifically to behavior therapists might imply erroneously that behavior therapy was in some way more in need of ethical concern than therapies not based on behavior therapy.

[a]In the list of issues, the term *client* is used to describe the person whose behavior is to be changed, *therapist* is used to describe the professional in charge of the intervention; *treatment* and *problem,* although used in the singular, refer to any and all treatments and problems being formulated with this checklist. The issues are formulated so as to be relevant across as many settings and populations as possible. Thus, they need to be qualified when someone other than the person whose behavior is to be changed is paying the therapist, or when that person's competence or the voluntary nature of that person's consent is questioned. For example, if the therapist has found that the client does not understand the goals or methods being considered, the therapist should substitute the client's guardian or other responsible person for *client,* as each of the issues is reviewed.

Note. From "Ethical Issues for Human Services" by the Association for Advancement of Behavior Therapy, 1977, *Behavior Therapy, 8,* pp. v–vi. Copyright 1977 by AABT. Reprinted by permission.

list of questions in their "Ethical Issues for Human Services" document.

In summary, guiding the treatment process, whether in a consultative arrangement or directly with the client, ideally requires an array of technical skills that encompass both assessment and treatment domains, a conceptual model of psychopathology, and communication skills that demonstrate sensitivity and respect for others. In the following discussion, we review applied research and practical guidelines about acceptability, empowerment, integrity, and evaluation of effectiveness. We believe knowledge of these can advance one's role in guiding the treatment process.

TREATMENT ACCEPTABILITY: UNDERSTANDING AND IMPROVING TREATMENT SELECTION

Although no theory of acceptability is well established, several factors have been demonstrated empirically to influence people's judgments of treatment acceptability. These factors have been incorporated into conceptual models by Witt and Elliott (1985) and Reimers, Wacker, and Koeppl (1987).

Models of Treatment Acceptability

Witt and Elliott (1985) developed a "working" model of treatment acceptability that stressed the interrelations among four elements: treatment acceptability, treatment use, treatment integrity, and treatment effectiveness. The hypothesized relationships among these four elements can be characterized as sequential and reciprocal. That is, *acceptability* is ultimately the initial issue in the sequence of treatment selection and use. Once a treatment is deemed generally acceptable, the probability of *using* the treatment is high, relative to treatments of lower rated acceptability. A central element hypothesized to link use and effectiveness is treatment *integrity.* If integrity is high, the probability of effecting a behavioral change is enhanced. Finally, if the *effectiveness* of the treatment meets or exceeds the expectations of the service provider, the probability of judging the treatment acceptable is enhanced. The reaction of a recipient of the treatment toward the service provider also should influence the service provider's evaluation of the treatment. To date, empirical evidence has not been amassed in a single investigation to support or refute this model; however, researchers have provided evidence about several of the interrelationships among the four elements.

Stimulated by the Witt and Elliott model, Reimers et al. (1987) developed a more complex model of treatment acceptability (Figure 3). These authors assumed that a treatment must be well understood before acceptability is assessed, and they therefore incorporated a treatment knowledge component into their decision-making flowchart concerning acceptability. According to the Reimers et al. model, when a proposed treatment is perceived to be low in acceptability, it is likely that low compliance will follow, thus decreasing the probability of the treatment being effective. In this model, compliance represents a teacher's or parent's attempt to implement a treatment. Once a treatment has been attempted, maintenance (continued use of the treatment) is the major issue. If a treatment is rated high in acceptability, it is likely that compliance with the recommendations will be high. However, the effects of treatment can still range from ineffective to highly effective. If the treatment is ineffective, there will not be maintenance of treatment, and reassessment of the problem behavior, the recommended procedure, or the treatment integrity is probably warranted. If the problem behavior was identified correctly, and if the recommended treatment was implemented as prescribed, some modifications of the treatment may be warranted or another treatment might be proposed. At this point, then, the cycle would repeat itself. When a treatment is highly effective, it is assumed that maintenance of treatment effects will also be high, provided that a family or school routine was not significantly disrupted either by the resulting change in behavior, or by the changes brought about by implementing the procedure. Disruption can occur, for example, when unusual resources or amounts of time are needed to continue a treatment.

Neither the Witt and Elliott (1985) model nor the Reimers et al. model fully characterizes the complex array of variables that potentially interact to influence the selection and implementation of behavioral treatments. Although imperfect, these models have been heuristic guides to stimulating research questions. Major research questions center around (a) the measurement of treatment acceptability, (b) the influence of child variables (e.g., type of behavior problem, severity of problem, age, sex, race) on teachers' ratings of acceptability, (c) the influence of teacher variables (e.g., years of teaching experience, knowledge of behavioral treatments) on the evaluation of different types of treatments, and (d) the relationship between consumers' and clients' pretreatment acceptability evaluations and posttreatment effectiveness.

Research Methods and Findings

With the publication of two treatment acceptability studies in 1980, Kazdin (1980a, 1980b) provided a paradigm that subsequent researchers have worked within. The essential elements of this paradigm have been a pencil-and-paper problem treatment vignette followed by objective evaluative ratings about the treatment. Within this paradigm, the primary independent variables manipulated have been severity of the target problem and type of treatment used. Other independent variables of interest have included an array of demographic characteristics of the rater of the treatments. For example, when teachers have been the treatment evaluators, information about years of teaching experience, type of training, and knowledge of behavioral principles and methods have been measured. In addition, some acceptability researchers (e.g., Elliott, Turco, & Gresham, 1987; Kazdin, French, & Sherick, 1981) have investigated how different consumers (i.e., parents, teachers, children, and hospital staff) evaluate treatments, thus involving rater as an independent variable. The primary dependent variable of interest in treatment acceptability research has been consumers' evaluative reactions to treatments as operationalized by one of several rating scales, namely the Behavior Intervention Rating Scale (BIRS); Children's Intervention Rating Profile (CIRP); Intervention

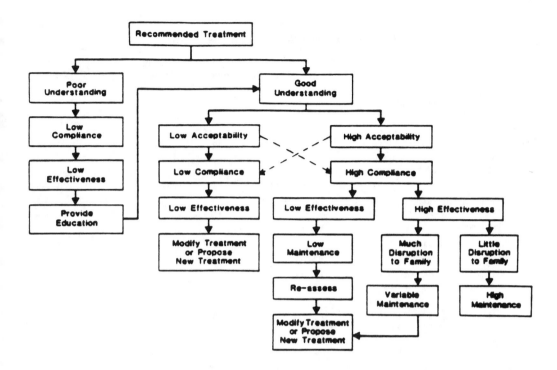

FIGURE 3. Reimers, Wacker, and Koeppl's (1987) proposed model of treatment acceptability. From "Acceptability of Behavioral Treatments: A Review of the Literature" by T. M. Reimers, D. P. Wacker, and G. Koeppl, 1987, *School Psychology Review, 16,* p. 225. Copyright 1987 by *School Psychology Review.* **Reprinted by permission.**

Rating Profile-20 (IRP-20); Intervention Rating Profile-15 (IRP-15); and Treatment Evaluation Inventory (TEI). We discuss only the BIRS and CIRP here. Interested readers are referred to Elliott (1988) for a review of all the treatment acceptability rating scales.

Von Brock (1985) and Von Brock and Elliott (1987) expanded the IRP-15 to create a new 24-question scale, the Behavioral Intervention Rating Scale (BIRS). Structurally, the BIRS has three factors: (a) the IRP-15 (15 questions and 63% of the variance), (b) effectiveness (7 questions and 6% of the variance), and (c) rate of change (2 questions and 4.3% of the variance). The total BIRS (24 items) yielded a Cronbach's alpha of .97. The BIRS appears as Table 2.

To date, only one objective scale has been published that has been specifically designed to measure the treatment acceptability judgments of children, the

Children's Intervention Rating Profile (CIRP) (Witt & Elliott, 1985). The CIRP is a seven-question, six-point Likert scale of children's social acceptability ratings ranging from *I agree* to *I do not agree.* The CIRP represents an objective instrument that has been validated on over 1000 students in Grades 5-10 and found to have an average coefficient alpha of .86 (Turco & Elliott, 1986). Several published studies have used the CIRP to assess the acceptability ratings of children (Elliott, Witt, Galvin, & Moe, 1986; Shapiro & Goldberg, 1986; Turco & Elliott, 1986). The CIRP appears as Table 3.

Before examining specific studies, it is important to highlight that the majority of published research on treatment acceptability has been *analogue* studies and, with the exception of a few studies (e.g., McMahon & Forehand, 1983; Shapiro & Goldberg, 1986), has been concerned predominantly with *pretreatment* judg-

TABLE 2
Behavior Intervention Rating Scale (BIRS)

	Strongly Disagree	Disagree	Slightly Disagree	Slightly Agree	Agree	Strongly Agree
1. This would be an acceptable intervention for the child's problem behavior.	1	2	3	4	5	6
2. Most teachers would find this intervention appropriate for behavior problems in addition to the one described.	1	2	3	4	5	6
3. The intervention should prove effective in changing the child's problem behavior.	1	2	3	4	5	6
4. I would suggest the use of this intervention to other teachers.	1	2	3	4	5	6
5. The child's behavior problem is severe enough to warrant use of this intervention.	1	2	3	4	5	6
6. Most teachers would find this intervention suitable for the behavior problem described.	1	2	3	4	5	6
7. I would be willing to use this intervention in the classroom setting.	1	2	3	4	5	6
8. The intervention would *not* result in negative side-effects for the child.	1	2	3	4	5	6
9. The intervention would be appropriate for a variety of children.	1	2	3	4	5	6
10. The intervention is consistent with those I have used in classroom settings.	1	2	3	4	5	6
11. The intervention is a fair way to handle the child's problem behavior.	1	2	3	4	5	6
12. The intervention is reasonable for the behavior problem described.	1	2	3	4	5	6
13. I like the procedures used in the intervention.	1	2	3	4	5	6
14. The intervention is a good way to handle this child's behavior problem.	1	2	3	4	5	6
15. Overall, the intervention would be beneficial for the child.	1	2	3	4	5	6
16. The intervention would quickly improve the child's behavior.	1	2	3	4	5	6
17. The intervention would produce a lasting improvement in the child's behavior.	1	2	3	4	5	6
18. The intervention would improve the child's behavior to the point that it would not noticeably deviate from other classmates' behavior.	1	2	3	4	5	6
19. Soon after using the intervention, the teacher would notice a positive change in the problem behavior.	1	2	3	4	5	6

(Table 2, continued)

20. The child's behavior will remain at an improved level even after the intervention is discontinued.	1	2	3	4	5	6
21. Using the intervention should not only improve the child's behavior in the classroom, but also in other settings (e.g., other classrooms, home).	1	2	3	4	5	6
22. When comparing this child with a well-behaved peer before and after use of the intervention, the child's and the peer's behavior would be more alike after using the intervention.	1	2	3	4	5	6
23. The intervention should produce enough improvement in the child's behavior so the behavior no longer is a problem.	1	2	3	4	5	6
24. Other behaviors related to the problem behavior also are likely to be improved by the intervention.	1	2	3	4	5	6

Note. The BIRS was developed by Von Brock and Elliott (1987).

TABLE 3
The Children's Intervention Rating Profile (CIRP)

	I agree	I do not agree
1. The method used to deal with the behavior problem was fair	+ - - - + - - - + - - - + - - - + - - - +	
2. This child's teacher was too harsh on him	+ - - - + - - - + - - - + - - - + - - - +	
3. The method used to deal with the behavior may cause problems with this child's friends	+ - - - + - - - + - - - + - - - + - - - +	
4. There are better ways to handle this child's problem than the one described here	+ - - - + - - - + - - - + - - - + - - - +	
5. The method used by this teacher would be a good one to use with other children	+ - - - + - - - + - - - + - - - + - - - +	
6. I like the method used for this child's behavior problem	+ - - - + - - - + - - - + - - - + - - - +	
7. I think that the method used for this problem would help this child do better in school	+ - - - + - - - + - - - + - - - + - - - +	

Note. The CIRP was developed by Witt and Elliott (1985).

ments of consultees (treatment agents) rather than clients. This emphasis on analogue, pretreatment acceptability research is warranted during the development phase of a research paradigm. At the time of this writing, scientist-practitioners are beginning to transfer the methods and knowledge base from analogue research to naturalistic investigations and their practice in schools. In the next section, we examine specific studies and their major findings.

An Examination of Variables That Influence Teachers' Treatment Selections

A rather long list of variables can be generated that can influence a teacher's selection of a treatment for a misbehaving child. In the context of a consultation service delivery model, within which a psychologist interacts with a teacher to assess and treat a child, Table 4 was developed to characterize the variables that have been investigated by researchers interested in understanding pretreatment acceptability and the effects on treatment outcomes.

Psychologist-associated variables that affect treatment acceptability. Two variables, jargon used in describing treatments and involvement in treatments, are the only psychologist-associated variables that have been studied within the treatment acceptability paradigm.

Several researchers have demonstrated that people's evaluations of psychological treatments vary as a function of what the treatment is called and how it is described. For example, Woolfolk and her associates (Woolfolk & Woolfolk, 1979; Woolfolk, Woolfolk, & Wilson, 1977) presented preservice teachers a videotape of a teacher who reinforced appropriate behavior, ignored inappropriate behavior, and used a backup token economy during an elementary school class. For one group of preservice teachers, the videotape was described as illustrative of "behavior modification" and for the other group it was called "humanistic education." These

investigators found that the personal qualities of the teacher and the effectiveness of the teaching method were perceived more positively when the method was labeled humanistic education as opposed to behavior modification.

As an extension of his acceptability research, Witt and several colleagues (Witt, Moe, Gutkin, & Andrews, 1984) investigated the effects that the type of language used to describe interventions had on teachers' rating of the intervention's acceptability. Specifically, these researchers manipulated three types of jargon (behavioral, pragmatic, and humanistic) used to describe an intervention that required a target child to stay in at recess for his misbehavior. The major finding with regard to the jargon variable was that the intervention described in pragmatic terms was rated significantly more acceptable than the same intervention described in either humanistic or behavioral terms.

To date, there have not been any published studies in which researchers have directly manipulated the amount or type of treatment involvement on the part of a psychologist. Intelligent inferences about the influence of psychologists' involvement in treatment can be gleaned, however, from two investigations (Algozzine, Ysseldyke, Christenson, & Thurlow, 1983; Martens, Peterson, Witt, & Cirone, 1986). Using a case description methodology, Algozzine et al. investigated teachers' preferences among 40 treatment alternatives applied to three types of classroom problems. These researchers concluded that teachers preferred interventions that they could implement directly rather than depend on consultation with a psychologist and/or place the child outside the classroom.

In a follow-up study to the work of Algozzine and his associates, Martens et al. (1986) investigated the treatment preferences of 2,493 teachers, both regular and special education, from Iowa and Nebraska. Using the Classroom Intervention Profile, a 65-item questionnaire that requires the rating of 49 classroom interventions on three scales (i.e., Effectiveness, Ease of Use, and Frequency of

TABLE 4
Variables in a Consultative Framework That Can Influence
Teachers' Evaluations of Treatment Acceptability

Consultant (psychologist)	→	Consultee (teacher)	→	Treatment	→	Client (child)
Jargon		Years of experience		Time required		Severity of problem
Involvement		Knowledge of behavior principles		Type of treatment		Type of problem
		Type of training		Reported effectiveness		
		Class management techniques used				

Note. The variables in this table have been investigated empirically. Many more variables, such as the race and sex of the consultant, consultee, and client could be investigated. Most analogue research to date has been with female teachers and hypothetical male problem children because this is most representative of reality. The arrows in this table indicate direction of influence.

From "Acceptability of Behavioral Treatments: A Review of Variables that Influence Treatment Selection" by S. N. Elliott, 1988, *Professional Psychology: Research and Practice, 19,* p. 70. Copyright 1988 by the American Psychological Association. Reprinted by permission.

Use), these researchers were able to deduce several significant tendencies with regard to teachers' treatment preferences. Of interest here is their finding that consultation with other personnel was rated relatively low as to effectiveness and ease of use. By comparison, interventions involving verbal redirection, manipulation of a material reward, and in-class time-out were rated consistently higher than consultation with a specialist such as a psychologist. Martens et al. attributed this poor acceptance of consultation to the relatively large time involvement required. The variable of amount of time required for an intervention has been found consistently to influence teachers' acceptability ratings of interventions (Witt, Elliott, & Martens, 1984).

This time variable, as it relates to a psychologists' involvement in treatment, requires more detailed examination and clarification. At present, we know, from self-reports, that teachers generally prefer to use treatments that can be conducted in their own classrooms and that require little time in consultation (indirect service) with specialists such as psychologists. It has yet to be established empirically, however, that teachers do not want psychologists to be highly involved in *direct* treatment of students within their classrooms.

It is logical to assume that psychologists will suggest treatments they find acceptable to teachers who are requesting assistance with a misbehaving student. Surprisingly, very few data exist that document psychologists' acceptability of treatments. In fact, within the scope of the present research only one investigation has been published in which psychologists' pretreatment acceptability ratings have been collected and also compared with teachers' and children's ratings. Elliott, Turco, and Gresham (1987) investigated fifth graders', teachers', and school psychologists' acceptability evaluations of three types of group contingencies (dependent, interdependent, and independent) with a consequence of positive reinforcement for appropriate behavior.

The major conclusion of this study was that although the children, psychologists, and teachers found the use of group contingencies generally acceptable for treating disruptive classroom behavior, they preferred forms of group contingencies when the consequences for an individual were based upon either the individual himself or herself (independent group contingency) or the entire group (interdependent group contingency). Letting a subset of a group (dependent group contingency) determine the consequences for the entire group was least acceptable for the fifth-grade children and teacher samples, and unacceptable for the psychologist respondents.

Teachers' treatment preferences and variables that influence these preferences. Unlike the acceptability research with psychologist-associated variables, the research investigations with teachers are numerous and provide insights about the variables that impact on treatment selection and use. In this section we review research that covers child variables (e.g., severity of problem, type of problem), treatment characteristics (e.g., time involved, punishment vs. reinforcement, group vs. individual contingencies, strong vs. weak treatment effects), and teacher background variables (e.g., years of experience, special vs. regular education training, knowledge of behavioral principles).

The severity of a child's problem has appeared as an independent variable in many studies (Elliott, Turco, & Gresham, 1987; Elliott, Witt, Galvin, & Peterson, 1984; Frentz & Kelley, 1986; Kazdin, 1980a; Martens, Witt, Elliott, & Darveaux, 1985; Van Brock & Elliott, 1987; Witt, Elliott, & Martens, 1984; Witt, Martens, & Elliott, 1984; Witt, Moe, Gutkin, & Andrews, 1984). This severity variable has been operationalized by changes in the *degree* to which a target child behaves inappropriately or by the *number* of children who are behaving inappropriately. In general, the collective results of these studies have demonstrated that the more severe a child's problem, the more acceptable any given treatment. Several specific studies

concerning the problem severity variable are of interest.

It appears that the severity of a target problem influences how complex an acceptable treatment can be. For example, in a two-experiment study, Elliott, Witt, Galvin, and Peterson (1984) investigated experienced teachers' acceptability ratings for behavioral interventions. In the first part of the study, regular and special education teachers were asked to read one of three case descriptions of an elementary school student whose misbehaviors were of a low (daydreaming), moderate (obscene language), or severe (destruction of others' property) nature and to rate the acceptability of one of three positively oriented intervention methods that were either low in complexity (praise), of moderate complexity (home reinforcement), or highly complex (token economy). The results indicated that the least complex intervention (praise) was the most acceptable treatment for the least severe problem behavior (daydreaming). The most complex treatment (token economy) was rated the most acceptable intervention for the most severe behavior problem (destroying property) (Elliott et al., 1984).

In the second part of the Elliott et al. (1984) study, all of the variables remained the same except that teachers were asked to evaluate the acceptability of one of three reductive intervention methods that were either low (ignoring), medium (response cost lottery), or high (seclusion time-out) in complexity. The results indicated that the least complex intervention (ignoring) was the most acceptable treatment for the least severe behavior problem (daydreaming).

An investigation by Frentz and Kelley (1986) of parents' acceptability ratings of reductive treatments provides support and generalizable evidence for the conclusion that treatment acceptability is affected significantly by the severity of the target problem. Frentz and Kelley asked 82 mothers to rate, by the Treatment Evaluation Inventory (TEI), five treatment procedures (i.e., differential attention, response cost, time-out, spanking alone, time-out with spanking) as methods for resolving a mild or a severe child behavior problem. The results indicated that the sampled parents rated all treatments as being more acceptable when applied to the severe problem.

The type of treatments assessed on acceptability studies generally have been characterized as either positive (e.g., praise, DRO, DRL, token economy) or reductive (e.g., response cost, time-out, overcorrection). In the child clinical literature, treatments involving medication and electroshock also have been assessed with regard to acceptability. In general, researchers have found that the acceptability ratings of all varieties of consumers (teachers, parents, children) consistently have been higher for constructive than reductive treatment procedures (Elliott, Witt, Galvin, & Peterson, 1984; Kazdin, 1980a, 1980b, 1981a; Martens, Peterson, Witt, & Cirone, 1986; Witt, Elliott, & Martens, 1984; Witt & Robbins, 1985). For example, in the first investigation with educators as subjects, Witt, Elliott, and Martens assessed 180 preservice teachers' acceptance of six treatments, three positive (praise, home reinforcement, token economy) and three negative (ignoring, response cost, seclusion time-out) for changing target behaviors of daydreaming, obscene language, and destroying others' property. These researchers found significant main and interaction effects for both the treatment and problem severity variables, but of interest here is the fact that the positive treatments were evaluated consistently more acceptable on the IRP-20 than were the negative treatments for the same problems.

In a replication and extension of the Witt, Elliott, and Martens (1984) investigation, Elliott, Witt, Galvin, and Peterson (1984) provided empirical support for the assertion that acceptability varies as a function of treatment type. They assessed experienced teachers' acceptance for the same six interventions as Witt, Elliott, and Martens (1984). Again they found that the average acceptability ratings for the positive treatments were significantly more favorable than for the reductive

treatments. In addition, there was a clear interaction between the variables of problem severity and treatment type, the least complex positive and negative treatments (i.e., praise and ignoring) being rated most acceptable for the mild problem (i.e., daydreaming) and the most complex treatments (i.e., token economy and seclusion time-out) being rated the most acceptable for the severe problem (i.e., destroying others' property).

Time is a valuable asset to teachers, who often are responsible for educating 25 or more children at once. Thus, it should not be surprising to find that when teachers evaluate a behavior change procedure prior to use, they are time-conscious. The research on treatment acceptability has indicated that time consumption is a very salient factor in teachers' pretreatment acceptability ratings of treatment procedures (Elliott, Witt, Galvin, & Peterson, 1984; Kazdin, 1982; Witt, Elliott, & Martens, 1984; Witt & Martens, 1983; Witt, Martens, & Elliott, 1984).

As a means of illustrating the relationship between acceptability and time consumption, we will review one study in detail. Witt, Martens, and Elliott (1984) directly manipulated the variables of teacher time involvement, intervention type, and behavior problem severity in a factorial design to assess how 180 teachers would evaluate treatments on the IRP-20. Descriptions of the treatments included estimates of the amount of time required to implement the treatment. A treatment was classified as requiring *low* amounts of teacher time if it required less than 30 minutes per day, as requiring *moderate* amounts of teacher time if it required 1–2 hours to prepare and 30–60 minutes to maintain, and as requiring *high* amounts of teacher time if it necessitated more than 2 hours of start-up and approximately 1 hour per day to maintain. The results of the study indicated that time in itself affected acceptability ratings, and, more importantly, time interacted significantly with both problem severity and treatment type. In summary, all other things being equal, teachers preferred treatments that were more time-efficient; however, when confronted with a severe problem, they seemed to adjust their expectations upward about the strength of treatment and consequently the time involved to change the problem behavior. Based on this and other analogue studies, it seems that teachers are time-conscious but not time-obsessed when selecting treatments.

After a treatment has been implemented, the ultimate criterion for evaluating it is effectiveness: Did the prescribed treatment change the target behavior in the desired direction and to the desired extent? In the preceding argument, however, we have hypothesized that prior to selection and implementation of a treatment, acceptability is an important evaluation criterion. Given the existence of these two important treatment evaluation criteria, the relationship between them requires attention. Several researchers, in fact, have investigated the effect of treatment outcome, or effectiveness information, on consumers' ratings of treatment acceptability (Clark & Elliott, 1988; Kazdin, 1981a; Von Brock & Elliott, 1987).

The impact of outcome information on teachers' ratings of treatment acceptability has been examined by Von Brock and Elliott (1987). They had 216 experienced teachers rate one of three treatments (token economy, response cost, or time-out) for changing a mild or severe classroom behavior problem. One of three types of effectiveness information accompanied each problem treatment scenario. Teachers received either no effectiveness information, teacher-satisfaction effectiveness information, or researcher-supplied effectiveness information. The results suggested that effectiveness information did influence ratings when the problem severity was taken into consideration. The milder the problem, the greater the influence of information from research sources about an intervention's effectiveness on effectiveness and acceptability ratings compared with a no-information condition. This was a surprising finding. One possible explanation for this finding is that with mild problems, teachers consider what researchers have to say about interventions, but with severe

problems they rely more on their own judgments. This finding suggests that teachers may be more amenable to information about interventions before a problem becomes too severe. Catching problems early may give psychologists greater freedom in choice of treatment with their consultees. Another explanation may be that teachers have preconceived notions about interventions. When presented with a mild problem, they feel there is more room for decision making about how to handle the problem, and therefore they are willing to experiment with different treatments. In such a circumstance, they are more influenced by information concerning these treatments. In contrast, with severe problems, teachers may not be as comfortable about experimenting with interventions and may rely more on past experience or judgment.

In a follow-up investigation to the Von Brock and Elliott (1987) study, Clark and Elliott (1988) examined the effects of treatment effectiveness information on teachers' pretreatment acceptability ratings of overcorrection and modeling-coaching procedures for social behavior deficits. The variable of treatment effectiveness had two levels, strong and weak, and was presented in a treatment description narrative accompanied by a graph illustrating the target child's and a "normal" comparison of peers' behavior over a 12-week period. The results confirmed the hypothesis that treatment effectiveness information does affect teachers' pretreatment ratings of acceptability. When given a treatment that was described as strong and successful, teachers rated it higher than if it had been described as weak and relatively unsuccessful.

There have been numerous studies examining the influence of treatment effectiveness information on ratings of acceptability. Prior to the Clark and Elliott study, two investigators specifically studied this relationship (Kazdin, 1981a; Von Brock, 1985). In the Kazdin study, no relationship was found between the strength of therapeutic effects and ratings of pretreatment acceptability. Some researchers (McMahon & Forehand, 1983; Witt, Elliott, & Martens, 1984) have questioned Kazdin's methodology and believe that his treatment strength variable had a restricted range and his sample of college students was unrepresentative of the persons usually involved in treatment decisions. The results from the Clark and Elliott study suggest that when classroom teachers clearly understand what is being presented to them, treatment effectiveness information does affect their perceptions of acceptability of a treatment.

In addition to the three pretreatment analogue investigations of the effectiveness → acceptability relationship we have reviewed, there has been one treatment study (Shapiro & Goldberg, 1986) in which the posttreatment acceptability and effectiveness relationship has been examined. Briefly, these researchers were interested in children's reactions to three types of group interventions that had been used to influence their spelling achievement. Using the CIRP to operationalize treatment acceptability, Shapiro and Goldberg reported that although no differences in effectiveness in promoting spelling were found among the three different group contingencies, the sixth graders rated the independent contingency more acceptable than either the interdependent contingency or the dependent group contingency. This naturalistic, posttreatment rating of group contingencies by children is consistent with the findings of Elliott, Turco, and Gresham's (1987) analogue investigation of pretreatment acceptability.

In the continuing search for explanations for differential acceptance of treatments, investigators have begun intentionally to measure, control, or manipulate rater variables such as technical knowledge of treatments, past experience with treatments, and type of education. To date, however, only four published studies have systematically considered teachers' background information and its effect on treatment acceptability ratings.

Several research teams (e.g., Jeger & McClure, 1979; McMahon, Forehand, & Griest, 1981) have suggested that more positive attitudes toward behavioral techniques follow increases in knowledge of such techniques. On the basis of this premise, McKee (1984) set out essentially to replicate Kazdin's (1980a) investigation of the acceptability of reinforcement of incompatible behavior, positive practice, time-out from reinforcement, and medication with a group of teachers who varied in their knowledge of behavioral principles. McKee measured teachers' knowledge with a modified 16-item version of the Knowledge of Behavioral Principles as Applied to Children test (KBPAC) (O'Dell, Tarler-Benlolo, & Flynn, 1979) and was able to assign teachers to a high- or low-knowledge group by using a median-split technique. Specifically, McKee found that the teachers in the high-knowledge group generally rated all treatments more acceptable on the TEI than did the teachers in the low-knowledge group. These data are supportive of the understanding component in the Reimers et al. model of treatment acceptability in that it suggests that improved acceptability and potentially increased use of treatments may be facilitated through increased familiarity with basic behavioral intervention principles.

Another teacher background variable of interest to some researchers has been teaching experience (Witt, Moe, Gutkin, & Andrews, 1984; Witt & Robbins, 1985). Witt and his associates reported finding an inverse relation between years of teaching experience and treatment acceptability. Specifically, in the Witt, Moe, Gutkin, and Andrews (1984) study, which was reviewed earlier when we examined the jargon variable, years of teaching experience was found to be a significant covariate with teachers' acceptability evaluations of behavioral, pragmatic, and humanistic treatments. In general, teachers with more experience in the field seem to find all treatments less acceptable.

Children's treatment preferences and variables that influence these preferences. Few researchers have investigated the acceptability of interventions from a child's perspective. Notable exceptions include treatment studies by Foxx and Jones (1978), by Ollendick, Matson, Esveldt-Dawson, and Shapiro (1980), and by Kirigin, Braukmann, Atwater, and Wolf (1982) in which anecdotal information was collected about clients' satisfaction with a treatment. Kazdin, French, and Sherick (1981) have assessed children's acceptability of psychological treatments more directly using the TEI. The Kazdin et al. (1981) investigation was an analogue study of how child psychiatric inpatients, their parents, and the institutional staff rated the acceptability of four treatments (positive reinforcement of incompatible behavior, positive practice, medication, and time-out from reinforcement) for children with severe behavior problems. The relative ratings of acceptability for the four treatments were identical for children, parents, and staff, although children rated all treatments as less acceptable than did parents or staff members. Specifically, reinforcement of incompatible behavior was evaluated as the most acceptable treatment for a child displaying a severe behavior problem. Positive practice, medication, and time-out from reinforcement successively received lower ratings than reinforcement of incompatible behavior.

Elliott, Witt, Galvin, and Moe (1986) investigated normal sixth-grade children's reactions to 12 interventions for classroom misbehaviors involving a male student who either destroyed another student's property or frequently talked out of turn. The students' acceptability ratings were documented by the CIRP (Witt & Elliott, 1985). The alternative treatments that were rated by 79 sixth graders were private reprimand by teacher, public reprimand by teacher, private praise by teacher, public praise by teacher, individual loses recess, individual gains extra recess, whole class loses recess, whole class gains extra recess, individual stays in for recess, individual goes to a quiet room, individual goes to principal's office, and individual earns rewards via a point system. These 12 treatments were classified by the investigators either as a verbal, a reinforcement, or a traditional intervention and were designed to vary on dimensions of individual-group and positive reinforcement-negative reinforcement. Elliott and his associates found that sixth graders rated the acceptability of the 12 interventions variously. Specifically, interventions that emphasized individual teacher-student interactions, or group reinforcement, or punitive sanctions for the misbehaving child were rated the most acceptable. Public reprimands of an individual and punitive contingencies for a group when only one child misbehaved were rated as unacceptable interventions by sixth graders. The four traditional interventions (i.e., principal's office, point system, staying in during recess, quiet room) as a group were rated the most acceptable methods when compared with the group of behavioral interventions. A final finding by Elliott et al. (1986) was that severity of the behavior problem did not significantly affect sixth-grade students' ratings of interventions except for the traditional interventions.

Given the perceived popularity of group contingency interventions among teachers' and children's differential acceptability responses to group contingency methods (Elliott, Witt, Galvin, & Moe, 1986; Turco & Elliott, 1986), a more detailed investigation of various types of group contingency methods was undertaken by Elliott, Turco, Evans, and Gresham (1984). A sample of 660 black and white, male and female, fifth graders responded on the CIRP to one of three problem severities (two children being disruptive, half a class being disruptive, a whole class being disruptive) and one of the three group contingency methods. Significant results were observed for interactions between rater's gender and problem behavior severity and between rater's race and problem behavior severity. The major new findings of this study of treatment acceptability were the following: (a) Female students rated the three forms of group contingency interventions less acceptable than did the males, the disparity increasing as the severity of the problem increased; (b) black students, in general, rated group contingency interventions significantly more acceptable than did white students, and (c) the three forms of group contingency interventions were rated acceptable in an *absolute* sense and were not rated significantly different. These findings highlight the impact of two basic individual differences, race and gender, on children's acceptability judgments of interventions, and they reinforce a common perception that group contingency interventions generally are acceptable to children.

Summary of Research Findings with Recommendations for Practice

The majority of the research on treatment acceptability has been published in the last 6 years. Much of this research has been concerned with simply measuring the construct of treatment acceptability and cataloging consumers' acceptance of an array of treatments for children exhibiting inappropriate behavior.

Based on the studies reviewed, the following four general conclusions seem warranted. First, a meaningful methodology exists for quantifying consumers' and clients' evaluations of descriptions of treatments. Second, treatment acceptability is a complex construct that is influenced by several salient child, teacher, and psychologist variables. Third, under most conditions, typical educational consumers evaluate constructive treatments relatively more acceptable than reductive treatments. Fourth, a moderate to strong positive relation exists between pretreatment acceptability and perceived treatment effectiveness.

Research on consumers' acceptability of treatment procedures is relevant to successful consultation and treatment in educational settings. Although the findings do not provide a direct prescription for selecting a treatment, they do provide a conceptual organizer and sensitize a consultant and consultee to a list of variables that require consideration prior to the implementation of a treatment. At a very basic level, treatments can be evaluated on two dimensions: acceptability and effectiveness. Ideally, only treatments with a history of documented effectiveness should be considered, thus narrowing pretreatment discussion to issues of acceptability. At this point a consultant can begin to assess the consultee's philosophy about treatments (e.g., reinforcement vs. punishment; teacher-initiated vs. psychologist- or parent-initiated; individual vs. group) his or her treatment knowledge and skills, time and material resources, and past experience with treatments.

Most researchers have taken a "majority" approach (Garfield, 1983) to the study of treatment acceptability. With this approach, although we learn what treatments the majority of the consumers prefer, we risk overlooking a significant minority of consumers' evaluations. We have learned that consumers who vary in their knowledge of behavioral principles differentially rate the acceptability of treatments. This finding argues for much more attention to subjects' background information in our research and also for more single-subject investigations.

TEACHER EMPOWERMENT: INCREASING THE LIKELIHOOD THAT TEACHERS WILL IMPLEMENT TREATMENTS

It would be very convenient for school psychologists to be able to function unobstructed in the following way: A teacher has a student with a problem; from a review of the treatment literature, an intervention is developed by the school psychologist for *the* problem, whereupon the teacher conducts the intervention successfully. This process is attractive to many school psychologists because it requires very little of their time and it allows them to feel good about their expertise and a job well done.

The application of *an intervention* to *the problem* is a common process. As it typically occurs in schools, this process largely is reactive (i.e., it occurs in response to an acute need), it is problem-focused (i.e., it results in the application of an intervention for a particular child), it is time-limited (i.e., it does not continue for more than two or three sessions because of time constraints on all parties), and its evaluation is short-term, child-focused, and subjective (e.g., a consultant may ask a teacher "How have things been going with Susan the past couple of weeks?"). Researchers who have examined this process have provided evidence that suggests that many discrete behaviors that teachers consider intolerable, when clearly defined and thoroughly operationalized, can be reduced or eliminated over short periods of time (Lentz, 1988; Witt et al., 1988).

The goals of consultative interventions typically have two characteristics in common. First, there is a recognition that something is not functioning properly (usually having to do with the child and/or the consultee) and that this something should be "fixed." Second, emphasis is usually placed upon only a small part of the ecological system, usually with little recognition of the reciprocal interactions that can occur between the many elements of a system. In a typical case, a teacher reports to a consultant that a child is performing below expectations. After a thorough analysis, the consultant determines that the child has a performance deficit and suggests that the teacher implement an intervention, such as a point system, to reinforce performance. Even though attempts usually are made to involve the teacher in the design and implementation of an intervention, the focus of such consultation is both molecular and child-centered in that only one element of the system is singled out for treatment, that one element typically being the child. Simply stated, the primary goal of this type of problem-centered consultation is to provide the teacher with a solution to a well-defined problem. This solution is usually something that will address a particular behavior the child is exhibiting.

We advocate a systems orientation in determining desired outcomes (Bergan, 1977; Bergan & Kratochwill, 1990). This perspective can help in three ways. First, it makes it possible to enter the multivariate world of the teacher. If the teacher had only to focus on and "fix" the problem under consideration in a consultative interaction, she or he could probably do a pretty good job; but the teacher has to

solve the particular problem and simultaneously consider and act upon all the other problems that are occurring. Second, a systems orientation reminds us that "we can never do just one thing" (Willems, 1974, p. 162), and changes in one behavior of one child can have strong ramifications for other elements within the system (Petrie et al., 1980). Third, when one moves away from "fixing" a problem as the sole objective in a consultative intervention, other outcomes become important, including engendering in teachers and students the perception that they exist in a supportive environment that is conducive to their well-being and to optimal functioning. We elaborate on each of these issues in the following sections in the context of collaboration with teachers to establish interventions.

Some Assumptions About Working with Teachers in Classroom Management

Assumption 1. *Most referrals for intervention are due to inappropriately arranged antecedents rather than inappropriately arranged consequences* (Gresham & Witt, 1987).

Corollary A: It is always easier to prevent behavior problems than to remediate them (i.e., it is easier to control antecedents than to control consequences).

Corollary B: Most consultative interventions ignore the complexity of the environmental context of behavior (i.e., they may fix the problem, but not help the system).

The strongest evidence we can provide in support of this overall assumption is that effective and ineffective teachers do *not* differ much with respect to how they handle discipline problems. Instead, they differ with respect to the number of discipline problems they encounter, the effective teachers having fewer problems (Duke, 1982). In behavioral terms, effective teachers are likely to focus on antecedent control and establish a structure such that problems are less likely to occur. The interested reader is referred to Duke (1982) for an extensive list of skills displayed by effective teachers.

Suffice it so say, effective teachers do a lot. The things they do prevent many discipline problems. If we approach a problem, the cause of which is some teacher or environmental antecedent, with a view to addressing and directly fixing the difficulty, as defined by the teachers, then the fix (which typically involves the application of consequences to student behavior) will probably be short-term. In conceptualizing the teacher's behavior as a set of antecedent conditions that can prevent misbehavior, it is useful to move from the abstract to the concrete. Witt and Martens (1988), for example, have used the problem of the time-efficient transitioning of students from one activity to another as a way to examine the issue of antecedent control. The literature on effective teaching is very clear that transitions in the classroom are periods when there is a high probability that students will engage in misbehavior and when valuable academic learning time is lost (Gettinger, 1988). Effective teachers set extremely high standards for student behavior during transitions; they take all the time necessary at the beginning of the year to teach children how to make the transitions, and they have well-established consequences for violations of established standards.

In general, good teachers establish routines and procedures that prevent most problems. Contrast this with the practice of a teacher who simply assumes children will know what to do during transitions, will not waste time, and will not get into trouble. There is an extremely high probability that this teacher will have problems. He or she will want these problems fixed either through the advice of a consultant or, more likely, through referral of the disturbing children to special education. It seems unwise, in the case of an ineffective teacher, to engage in case-centered consultation with the goal of reducing the amount of time wasting, talking without permission, and bothering of other children by developing techniques for applying individual consequences to children who engage in high

rates of inappropriate behavior during transitions. Instead, our efforts might be more appropriately focused upon establishing antecedent conditions that involve displaying what we call good teaching behaviors, expecting appropriate behavior on the part of the children. A list of activities designed for antecedent control of behavior is presented in Table 5. According to Ysseldyke and Christenson (1987), these antecedent-oriented interventions are synonymous with the effective teaching behaviors.

Assumption 2. *Consultative activities directed toward child behaviors may not lead to decreases in teachers' complaints.* Except in rare cases, consultation does not occur proactively. The antecedent event that occasions consultation is not a system-level demand that we work to prevent problems. Because most school psychologists have more to handle than time permits, they seldom say proactively: "Teacher, I noticed you were having some difficulty with Joshua today and I would like to help you." Instead, consultation intervention most frequently is reactive, rather than proactive.

If it is correct to assume that consultation is mostly reactive, then to what stimulus events is consultation a reaction? Consultation occurs in response to problems that prove frustrating or aversive to teachers. However, to say that consultative behavior is occasioned chiefly by problems of this nature is not completely correct. A problem is a necessary but not sufficient condition for consultation to occur. Teachers encounter dozens of problems in a single day that are not brought to consultants. Thus, a problem situation is but the first step in a chain of circumstances that leads to consultation and intervention activities.

The critical element linking a problem with consultative intervention is a *complaint* or referral (Baer, 1987, 1988). Consultation typically originates when a problem is present and after a complaint or referral. Other factors, such as system-level expectations for consultation to occur, round out the necessary and sufficient antecedent conditions.

TABLE 5
Teacher-Related Antecedent Behaviors Designed to
Control Inappropriate Student Behavior

- Teacher reminds students of the classroom rules.
- Teacher maintains eye contact with students.
- Teacher reminds students about expected behaviors that are critical to an activity before beginning the activity.
- Teacher uses nonverbal signals to redirect a student while teaching other students.
- Instructional routines for academic and nonacademic activities are understood by students.
- Pace of instructional lessons is brisk and directed by the teacher.
- Transitions from one task to another are short and organized.
- Expectations about the use of class time are communicated clearly and frequently.

On the consequent side of the functional analysis equation for consultative behavior there are pleasant and unpleasant events that maintain consultative behavior. Certainly there are positively reinforcing events that accrue to consultants assisting teachers with problems (e.g., admiration, knowledge of a job well done); however, negative reinforcement is probably the most potent of the consequences that influence the rate of consultative behavior. Consultants are motivated to avoid or reduce pain and the most common form of pain for school-based professionals is the complaint. Teachers are likewise motivated to reduce their frustration and the irritability associated with the problem(s) through the consultation process.

It is generally assumed that consultants and teachers want to solve the problem(s) being complained about. Furthermore, one would suppose that if the problem(s) that have motivated a complaint are resolved, then so will the complaint. Baer (1987) suggested that we have virtually no data to support a hypothesis that solving a given problem will reduce complaining. On the other hand, there is considerable evidence to suggest that the solutions generated in consultative interventions provide teachers with *additional* problems about which to complain (Witt, 1986; Witt & Elliott, 1985). Teachers complain about the solutions generated by problem

solving, saying that such solutions (e.g., a point system) take too much time, are not realistic in a classroom of 25 children, have negative effects on other children, or will not work. When a teacher initiates an intervention through consultation, the intervention may bring with it side effects and possibly more complaining. Reaction could take the form of complaints from other children, who also want a contract because they too would like to be rewarded for their work. If the teacher spends too much time on an intervention for a particular child and neglects other areas of responsibility, there will be complaints about the neglected areas and the teacher may complain to the consultant about these problems.

The proposition that we consult mostly in reaction to complaints also implies that the quieting of a complaint is a desired outcome of the consultation process. The quieting of a complaint remains an implicit goal because consultants are reluctant (if they ever think about it) to aspire toward the goal of reducing teachers' complaints. Instead, what is talked about during consultation is the more explicit goals of solving the stated problems; and we assume that solving the problem that has prompted the teacher's complaining will reduce frequency or intensity of complaining.

Teachers have a difficult job because, in addition to teaching large numbers of children, they often have many forms to complete, playground duty, after-school activities, and so forth. They perform these activities with very minimal technical, clerical, or even social support and often receive a considerable amount of negative feedback (e.g., criticism and complaining) in the process. The demand characteristics of the system in which they function, including institutionalized methods for handling problems in schools (e.g., referral to special education), have the effect of limiting the kinds of problems about which teachers can legitimately complain. If they want to get raises and move up in the system, then it is difficult for them to complain (except possibly to other teachers) about too much paperwork or other manifestations of "stupidity" within a school's administration. The system does, however, establish methods by which they can complain about the worst children in their classes. These formal complaints are called referrals to special education and at a more informal level are called requests for consultation.

This context suggests a recipe for failure. Take one marginally effective teacher who is not well trained in classroom management, is overburdened with responsibilities, is feeling undervalued and perhaps even victimized by the system, and give this teacher a classroom with several unruly children. Allow this teacher only a limited number of issues about which to complain. For example, allow the teacher to complain only about children who may be "behaviorally handicapped" and in need of special services. Add to this a consultant interested only in reducing the frequency of behavior problems in the teacher's classroom and who is mostly unaware of the complexities and other demands under which the teacher must operate. The consultant attempts to "fix" problems identified by the teacher by asking this overburdened and ineffective teacher to do even more than he or she currently is doing. The teacher responds passively by either haphazardly doing what was asked or not doing it at all and continues to complain about the same problems as before; in addition taking issue with the solutions offered by the consultant. Introduction by a consultant

of a new intervention in a system that is not working properly is relatively common, and it frequently leads to frustration and failure for both consultant and teacher. Some relatively circumscribed problems may even be resolved along the way, but complaining may remain unchanged or even increase.

If the complaint plays such a powerful role in the consultative process, then school-based consultants may want to consider its importance as an initiator of consultative activities and as an outcome of the consultation process. Viewing the reduction of complaining as a legitimate outcome will influence how we work with teachers and will cause us to monitor teacher complaints. In the next section we will discuss an empowerment philosophy of teacher consultation in which the focus of consultative intervention may be more appropriately directed toward helping teachers be more effective in making the total system work and doing this in a way that simplifies rather than complicates their lives and allows for the development of a strong sense of self-efficacy.

Assumption 3. *School-based consultants tend to interact with a teacher in ways that imply that the teacher is a subordinate junior partner; this can lead some teachers to become resistant and others to become dependent, and it does not serve to empower and enable the teachers to provide a sustained high level of service to children.* The provision of assistance is not as simple as it may appear. Even the most benevolent of help providers can do more harm than good if advice or assistance is of the wrong type or if it is provided in the wrong way. Under certain conditions, interventions can have negative consequences and can lead to decreased competency and self-efficacy. Help, such as that provided by a school-based consultant, can adversely affect the recipient in four ways:

> First of all, the help may be so overwhelming that it directly reduces the control that recipients have over their own lives. . . . [Second], even the little acts of kindness we perform for one another can

be killing by directly undermining the acquisition of new skills or the maintenance of old ones. . . . [Third], even when help does not directly reduce control or impair the development of certain abilities, it can directly undermine the perceived self-efficacy of recipients [when] help carries with it the implication that recipients are relatively inferior and incapable of solving problems on their own. . . . Finally, help can undermine competence and control by creating confusion as to who should get the credit or blame for the way things turn out. If the help is successful in resolving or lessening the problem, the recipients may attribute this outcome to the helper, with the result that they feel no more capable of dealing with the problem on their own. (Coats, Renzaglia, & Embree, 1983, pp. 253–255)

The "fixing" of problems in problem-solving consultation can lead to successful outcomes as to change in the client children's behavior but constitute failure as to building teachers' competency and increasing teachers' feelings of self-efficacy. Thus, a potentially more enduring and satisfying outcome of the consultation process is to empower a teacher to function more effectively. This is a more broadly construed goal than simply assisting teachers to handle similar problems in the future, which, in addition to solving the referral problem, has been advanced for many years as a goal of consultation. Rather, an empowerment philosophy assumes that consultees basically are skilled professionals who can become more capable of solving their own problems by knowing what resources are available and how to gain access to them (Dunst & Trivette, 1988). From this perspective, it is the social or administrative structure of the situation that is presumed to prevent fully independent functioning:

Empowerment implies that many competencies are already present or at least possible. . . . Empowerment implies that what you see as poor functioning is a result of social structure and lack of resources which make it impossible for the existing competencies to operate. It implies that in those cases where new

competencies need to be learned, they are best learned in a context of living life rather than in artificial programs where everyone, including the person learning, knows that it is really the expert who is in charge. (Rappaport, 1981, p. 16)

The role of a consultant then becomes one of helping consultees to identify needs, to locate the formal and informal resources necessary for meeting those needs, and to help link the consultee with identified resources (Bergan, 1977; Bergan & Kratochwill, 1990; Hobbs et al., 1984).

Thus, in consultation there is often an assumption that the problem is at least partially attributable to the lack of skill on the part of the teacher, whereas from an empowerment philosophy the cause of the problem is a social structure that prevents or has not enabled the teacher to acquire and/or display effective teaching behaviors. Both the teacher's skill and the social structure may be factors in a teacher's functioning. Yet, placing more emphasis on the system than the teacher may represent a big difference in respect to the teacher's ability and willingness to change, the teacher's self-efficacy, and the school psychologist's success in making significant and enduring changes.

In their work with families, Dunst and Trivette (1988) developed recommendations to increase the probability that help will have positive, and only positive effects. These recommendations for working with families are also of value for consultants working with teachers and groups of children. Here are the summaries of four recommendations of Dunst and Trivette (1988):

1. To increase the probability of family responsiveness and commitment to early intervention efforts, base such efforts on family identified needs (personal projects, agendas, priorities, goals, etc.).

2. To increase the probability of acquisition of self-sustaining behavior, use existing family functioning styles (strengths and capabilities) as a basis for developing and implementing interventions to meet needs.

3. To increase the probability of the effectiveness of intervention efforts, promote the family's acquisition of the skills necessary to acquire resources and support that match family identified needs and priorities.

4. To increase the probability that there will be positive results from efforts to provide or mediate resources and support, use helping behaviors that are positive, enabling and empowering.

In summary, we have advanced some propositions about working with teachers in implementing classroom interventions. Specifically, it has been argued that for some children who exhibit difficulties in the classroom, the problem can be traced to inappropriately arranged antecedents. When teachers complain about children, the usual strategy is to develop an intervention that applies stronger or more direct consequences. The tacit assumptions are that the teacher only lacks the skill to develop such an intervention independently, that the intervention will reduce the behavior problem, and as a result of the improvement in the child's behavior, the teacher will stop complaining. None of these assumptions have adequate empirical support.

In contrast, the empowerment literature has suggested working with teachers so they have the support and the capability to do the job they are intended to do. Here school psychologists can play an instrumental role in finding out what teachers need and in working with the system to provide it. It is likely they need and want to learn new skills and to be treated with respect, and they especially need the opportunity to interact with colleagues. Hence, in-service activities that occur at the beginning of the year, which help teachers identify and recruit resources, and which encourage teachers to talk with teachers, are likely to be well received and to have a continuing effect within a system.

TREATMENT INTEGRITY: IMPROVING IMPLEMENTATION AND EVALUATION

Standardization or procedural specification of treatment refers to the development of formal guidelines, response protocols, and training manuals when the treatment is implemented (Luborsky & DeRubeis, 1984). Use of a standardized format for treatment has several advantages for research (Kratochwill, 1985a; Kratochwill, Van Someren, & Sheridan, 1989; Kratochwill & Van Someren, 1985). First, standardization of treatment will allow *replication* of treatment procedures in research and eventually dissemination in practice. Replication is important to develop the empirical efficacy of various treatments and to generalize the techniques in research and practice across problem behaviors, settings, and therapists.

A second reason for recommending standardization of treatment in research and practice is to facilitate *training* in specific treatment skills. A major shortcoming of some treatment techniques is the lack of specific procedures for training individuals in their use (Matarazzo & Patterson, 1986). Some empirical work has suggested that a standardized approach focused on competency-based criteria can be used to train school psychologists in behavioral consultation (Kratochwill & Bergan, 1978; Kratochwill, Bergan, & Mace, 1981). Competency-based training approaches have been used to train school psychology students in consultation skills (e.g., Brown, Kratochwill, & Bergan, 1982; Kratochwill et al., 1989) and for preservice and in-service preparation of classroom and special education teachers (West, Idol, & Cannon, 1987). The use of standardized formats in consultation training and practice would appear to be essential in the empirical development of effective techniques that are disseminated in practice to assist consultees and clients (Kazdin, Kratochwill, & VandenBos, 1986).

Third, the development of standardized treatments may also enhance development of appropriate *psychometric characteristics.* The issue of appropriate psychometric properties in the behavioral field may be subject to debate. However, it is quite possible that the issues surrounding the appropriate choice of psychometric models (i.e., traditional vs. behavioral) cannot be resolved unless a standardized format is developed and used in research. In this way, the efficacy of traditional (e.g., classical test theory, domain-sampling model, multitrait–multimethod matrix, and latent trait theory) versus behavioral measurement formats in "treatment validity" can be developed (Hayes, Nelson, & Jarrett, 1986; Nelson, 1983).

Once treatment procedures have been specified or standardized, a major issue that must be addressed is implementation *integrity* — the degree to which treatment is being implemented as intended. Psychotherapy researchers recently have emphasized the evaluation of treatment programs to insure their integrity (Kazdin, 1986; 1988). Integrity is evaluated by comparison of a treatment as it is actually implemented with how it is intended to be implemented. Researchers have stressed that when a treatment is implemented, it must be carried out as originally intended (Peterson et al., 1982; Yeaton & Sechrest, 1981). Assessment of treatment integrity in behavioral consultation is important for several reasons. Investigators must assess the implementation of the *consultation process* to insure that consultation actually is being practiced, that the consultant is following the four stages of behavioral consultation, and that the consultee is implementing the intervention program as discussed during the problem analysis phase. In fact, some research has recently supported the notion that the entire consultation *process* is necessary in reducing problem behaviors of students (Fuchs & Fuchs, 1989). Failure to monitor the integrity of consultation can threaten the reliability and validity of a study.

Integrity can be evaluated at several levels (Kratochwill, Sheridan, & Van Someren, 1988). First, integrity of the *consultation process* must be assessed. It must be demonstrated that the professional consultant is following a specific consultation model or format. Typically, the integrity of this process can be checked by direct assessment of consultation video or audiotapes. Usually, objective coding procedures of these products will be necessary. For example, a verbal coding strategy called the Consultation Analysis Record (CAR) has been developed in behavioral consultation (Bergan & Tombari, 1975); it provides information regarding the source, content, and process of verbalizations of the consultant and consultee. Figure 4 displays the CAR.

Demonstrating the integrity of the consultation process in the Problem Identification Interview (PII), Problem Analysis Interview (PAI), and Problem Evaluation Interview (PEI) is only the first step. At the next level, it must be demonstrated that the *consultee* is implementing the intervention program as intended. This is the level at which treatment integrity usually has been assessed. Integrity at this level can be evaluated through assessment of the consultee and through data on the client's responsiveness to the treatment. Data on consultee integrity can be obtained from the CAR and coded to examine topics discussed during the consultation interviews. In addition, direct observational assessment data can be gathered to determine if the consultee is implementing the intervention program as intended. Gresham (1989) also presented examples of a self-report integrity assessment (see Table 6) and a rating scale that can be completed by the consultee or consultant, or by an independent observer (see Table 7). Both examples refer to a response cost lottery program implemented in a classroom.

Finally, if a child is involved in implementing an intervention (e.g., a self-control strategy), program implementation and its integrity must be monitored at the client level. In addition to direct observational assessment of the child, self-monitoring strategies can be used to monitor intervention integrity (Gardner & Cole, 1988). Piersel and Kratochwill

CONSULTANT _____ CASE NUMBER _____

CONSULTEE _____ INTERVIEW TYPE _____

PAGE _____

CONSULTATION-ANALYSIS RECORD

	Message Source		Message Content								Message Process								Message Control	
	Consultee	Consultant	Background Environment	Behavior Setting	Behavior	Individual Characteristics	Observation	Plan	Other	Negative Evaluation	Positive Evaluation	Inference	Specification	Summarization	Negative Validation	Positive Validation	Elicitor	Emitter
1																		
2																		
3																		
4																		
5																		
6																		
7																		
8																		
9																		
10																		
11																		
12																		
13																		
14																		
15																		
16																		
17																		
18																		
19																		
20																		
21																		
22																		
23																		
24																		
25																		

FIGURE 4. Consultation-analysis record form. From "The Analysis of Verbal Interactions Occurring During Consultation" by J. R. Bergan and M. L. Tombari, 1975, *Journal of School Psychology, 13,* p. 212. Copyright 1975 by Human Sciences Press. Reprinted by permission.

TABLE 6
Example of a Self-Report Integrity Assessment

Date: _____ Teacher _____ Day: M   T   W   Th   F

Response Cost Lottery

Directions: Please complete this form each day *after* the period in which the intervention has been implemented in your classroom.

	Strongly Disagree				Strongly Agree
1. I described the response cost lottery system to the class.	1	2	3	4	5
2. I displayed and described the rewards which students could receive in the lottery.	1	2	3	4	5
3. I placed a 3 × 5 inch card on top of each student's desk.	1	2	3	4	5
4. I taped the card on 3 sides with one side open.	1	2	3	4	5
5. I inserted 4 slips of colored paper inside each card using different colors for each student.	1	2	3	4	5
6. I left the lottery in effect for ½ hour today.	1	2	3	4	5
7. I removed slips from each card whenever a student violated a class rule.	1	2	3	4	5
8. I restated the class rule whenever a student violated a class rule.	1	2	3	4	5
9. I placed the remaining tickets in the lottery box after lottery time concluded today.	1	2	3	4	5
10. I conducted the drawing for the winner today (Friday only).	1	2	3	4	5
11. The winner was allowed to select a reward (Friday only).	1	2	3	4	5

Note. From "Assessment of Treatment Integrity in School Consultation and Prereferral Intervention" by F. M. Gresham, 1989, *School Psychology Review, 18.* Copyright 1989 by *School Psychology Review.* Reprinted by permission.

(1979) provided an example of a format that involves self-monitoring of academic and social behaviors.

In determining the degree to which behavioral consultation integrity is maintained in research and practice, it is important to identify elements that enter into the process *in addition* to the usual components of treatment (Kazdin, 1986). These variables include, for example, such factors as the number of therapeutic contacts, duration of contacts, and time between visits. Such information may have a bearing on successful programs and outcomes for the client.

In summary, we strongly encourage more attention be paid to the integrity of interventions. This attention does not require new technology: Methods such as component checklists or rating scales, or direct observation of the treatment implementation, may provide the necessary information to decide whether a treatment has been implemented as designed. Without such information, efforts to modify or refine apparently ineffective interventions may be misguided.

TABLE 7
Example of a Behavior Rating Scale for Treatment Integrity

Consultee: _____ Date: _____ Consultant: _____

Response Cost Lottery

	High Integrity				Low Integrity
1. Described system to students	1	2	3	4	5
2. Displayed and described reinforcers	1	2	3	4	5
3. Placed 3 × 5 card on students' desks	1	2	3	4	5
4. Card taped on 3 sides	1	2	3	4	5
5. 4 slips of colored paper inserted (different colors for each student)	1	2	3	4	5
6. Lottery in effect for ½ hour	1	2	3	4	5
7. Slips removed contingent on rule violations	1	2	3	4	5
8. Teacher restates rule contingent on violation	1	2	3	4	5
9. Remaining tickets placed in box	1	2	3	4	5
10. Drawing occurs on Friday	1	2	3	4	5
11. Winner selects reinforcer on Friday	1	2	3	4	5

Note. From "Assessment of Treatment Integrity in School Consultation and Prereferral Intervention;; by F. M. Gresham, 1989, *School Psychology Review, 18.* Copyright 1989 by *School Psychology Review.* Reprinted by permission.

Assessing Treatment Process and Outcomes

Questions about treatment effectiveness are relevant before, during, and after the implementation of a given treatment. Prior to selecting a specific treatment, one identifies a treatment procedure that is theoretically consistent with the intended approach to change, then focuses on what target problems and populations the treatment has been used with, and finally examines the relative effectiveness of the treatment in comparison with several other treatments. The effectiveness information available before a given treatment is to be put to use may come in the form of a case study, a single-case data-based report, a group (mean) comparison study, and/or meta-analytic review of effect sizes, or more likely by way of testimonial from an "expert" source. Generally, the more sources of information about the effectiveness of a given treatment the better. Yet prior to using any treatment in a "new" problem area or situation, past effectiveness information is imperfect. Thus, psychologists and other treatment agents ethically are bound to monitor the effects (both intended and unintended) of their treatment procedures during treatment and after termination of the treatment. Some basics of treatment evaluation are worth reviewing because of their influence on planning treatment procedures and on the establishment of accountable practices. Specifically, case study and single-subject design methodologies are emphasized. Readers interested in a more comprehensive examination of treatment evaluation are referred to Barlow, Hayes, and Nelson's (1984) book on the scientist-practitioner and to the insightful article of Jacobson et al.

(1984) on reporting variability and evaluating clinical significance.

A discussion of the dimensions of behavior change and of outcome expectations provides a context for treatment evaluation before the specific methods of case study and single-subject designs are examined. Change in some aspect of a client's functioning, whether it be directly observable or not, is always a central goal of treatment. The dimensions of behavior of primary interest can be characterized as frequency, duration, intensity, and latency. These dimensions of behavior usually can be measured effectively through direct methods (e.g., observation or self-monitoring). However, numerous other assessment methods are often used, including rating scales completed by teachers or parents; functioning; role-play; and self-report inventories (Kratochwill & Sheridan, 1990). It is desirable to use several methods of assessment and several sources of information (Kazdin, 1988). Ideally, the client's functioning should be measured several times within four time frames: before treatment (baseline), during treatment, immediately after treatment, and several months following termination of the treatment. By definition, at least two assessments, one pretreatment and the other posttreatment, of a client's functioning are essential to determine the trend and magnitude of change. The more data points available during treatment, the more information about variability of change, from which more accurate inferences can be made about the process of change about treatment components.

Decisions about treatment outcomes should involve information from many sources (e.g., parents, teachers, peers, self-report) about changes in the client's targeted problem behavior and related behavior. Information about the trend and the magnitude of change is difficult to interpret without some comparative standard or criterion. However, in academic domains, outcome criteria are readily available in the form of curriculum mastery tests, lists of essential grade skills, or assigned learning objectives. In contrast, outcome criteria in behavioral domains are less standardized and more variable across settings. Therefore, comparisons with "normal" peers, with treatment goals established a priori, and with behavior standards established by "significant" adults are the primary criteria by which behavioral changes are interpreted. Additional criteria for a successful treatment are maintenance of the change over time and generalization of the behavior across settings.

A strong case for treatment effectiveness requires repeated measurements over time of a well-defined problem and the comparison of the measurement results with an "appropriate" standard of functioning. Procedures for accomplishing such a goal vary largely depending on the cooperation of others involved in delivering the treatment and the setting in which the client is treated. We now examine two procedures for evaluating school-based, individualized treatments.

Case Study Methods

Case studies have been a popular method for describing and documenting treatment effectiveness. There are three basic types of case studies (Kratochwill, 1985): the nontherapeutic case study, the assessment/diagnosis case study, and the therapeutic/intervention case study. Of particular interest here is the therapeutic/intervention case study, which is further subdivided into uncontrolled, preexperimental, and clinical replication cases. In all three subtypes of intervention case studies, a treatment agent is interested in evaluating the efficacy of some treatment for a single client or small group of clients. Usually, case studies are conducted in the absence of experimental controls; hence, various sources of internal validity may not be addressed. As a result, many rival interpretations to account for any client changes in behavior may not be ruled out.

Advocates of the case study approach (e.g., Kazdin, 1981b; Kratochwill, 1985) acknowledge its limitations for reaching valid decisions about outcome effectiveness, but they also recognize that in many situations case studies provide a method for enhancing best professional practices. Kazdin (1981b) and Kratochwill (1985) identified several means by which intervention case studies can be improved: (a) collecting direct measures of behavior change to supplement traditional anecdotal descriptions of clients; (b) increasing the number of assessments of client behavior over the course of treatment in addition to the traditional pre- and post-intervention assessments; (c) involving control over some important independent treatment variables to decrease inference levels about which variables affect behavior; and (d) using relatively standardized assessment and treatment procedures so that appropriate replication by other practitioners or researchers is possible. Information about the projected performance of the stipulated behaviors (with and without treatment) in view of the severity of the clients' problems, the number and diversity of clients, the addition of social validity measures of the behavior change, the integrity of the treatment, and reports of maintenance and generalization also are enhancements of case study methods (Kratochwill, 1985). A good example of intervention case studies that is worthy of inspection is a published report by Kazdin, Esveldt-Dawson, French, and Unis (1987) on the treatment of antisocial child behavior.

Single-Case Designs

Single-case strategies are constructed from basic design elements and are classified as within-, between-, or combined-series designs.

Within-series designs: Simple and complex phase changes. In a simple phase-change single-case design, the dependent measures are evaluated within a time series. At the point of phase change or treatment implementation, differences in levels and trends in the data series are evaluated. Several phases of the design are structured so that there is a replication of the treatment effect. A variety of single-case studies have used the simple phase-change structure in applied research. For example, Wagner and Winett (1988) used a simple within-series design structure to evaluate a program designed to promote selection of items from a low-fat, high-fiber menu (salads) in a fast food restaurant. Specifically, the authors use an A/B/A/B/ design, the baseline of which involved an analysis of the percentage of sales of salads by total sales for a period of 3 weeks. Following this phase, the intervention consisted of placing prompts at the entrance and near the cash register and placing 10 cards on tables for approximately 3 weeks. The authors found that the diners in the fast food restaurant in fact increased their consumption of salads during the intervention period. This effect was replicated in the second B (salad-promoting) phase, in the replication component of the design.

This common design can be extended to more complex phase changes. Basically, complex phase changes can be designed by using the same logic as the simple phase-change strategies and allowing comparison of the effects of adding or subtracting various treatment components across phases of the investigation. For example, an investigator may be interested in evaluating the effects of a component package in which the B treatment has several specific components added to it (e.g., B+C+D). A design would be developed in which the investigator uses the logic of the simple phase-change strategy to evaluate the intervention effect. This strategy would consist of the design paradigm A/B+C+D/A/B+C+D/A/B+C+D. Indeed, one of the more common applications of the complex phase-change designs is to examine interventions that consist of multicomponent programs. Various single components could also be evaluated in this design strategy by systematically dropping out various components across replication series. In this way, the researcher can determine whether the intervention effects are additive or which optimal combinations of treatment components are contributing to the outcome.

Between-series designs: Alternating treatment designs. Researchers using a between-series format for single-case research essentially have the option of using an alternating treatment design (ATD) or a simultaneous treatment design (STD).

The STD is used in rather rare instances where the researcher is interested in comparing reinforcement contingencies that are presented simultaneously. Although current applications of this design are rather limited, the procedure would have some application to assessing clients' preference among alternative interventions that have been presented during the same session or interval. Therefore, it is not discussed here. The researcher using ATD compares different interventions with the same client, and two or more data series are compared across time, the analysis taking into account trend and variability in the dependent variable. The client is exposed to different treatments for equal periods of time, and the treatment phases are alternated within a very short period of time, such as from one session to the other or from one part of the day to the other. The researcher sequences these treatments randomly or through a counterbalancing procedure, but the client receives equal exposure to the treatments while setting and time variables are controlled across phases of the experiment.

Stern, Fowler, and Kohler (1988) used an alternating treatment design in a study in which they compared two interventions in which the clients were assigned two different roles: peer monitor and point earner. In the study, two fifth-grade students' off-task and disruptive behaviors were decreased during an intervention in which they were appointed as either peer monitors or point earners. Children in the study worked in dyads in which one child served as a peer monitor and the other earned points for his or her monitor for performing good behavior. The points were accumulated as part of a group contingency program. The researchers introduced the two appointments in an independent math period in which they alternated these appointments across days. Specifically, the peer monitor and point earner roles were alternated every other day. The researchers found that the peer monitor and point earner roles were equally effective in reducing each student's inappropriate behavior. Moreover, the frequency of the students' target behavior declined during the intervention to a level within the range of inappropriate behavior levels exhibited by normative peers. The researchers also monitored the speed with which the students completed math problems. They found that although their speed increased during both treatments, their accuracy varied.

As can be seen from this study, the major advantage of the ATD is that the scientist-practitioner can compare two or more interventions in a relatively short period of time. Moreover, it is not always necessary to withdraw the intervention completely in this type of design to establish an intervention's effects. The ATD unfortunately is greatly influenced by many treatment interference problems and requires rather careful monitoring during implementation.

Combined-series (multiple-baseline) designs. Combined-series designs, as the name implies, involve an integration of within- and between-series elements in a single study. Usually, combined-series designs involve straightforward application of the multiple-baseline procedure and its associated variations. In these designs, a single within-series element (e.g., A/B phase) is replicated across clients, settings, or behaviors. Various threats to validity are controlled by the staggered implementation across data series. Basically, this procedure is structured so that as each intervention is implemented the changes involved affect only the series in which the treatment is introduced, the other series remaining stable across phases. Although the multiple-baseline design requires a minimum of two series, it is recommended that four or more series by structured, depending on practical constraints in the setting.

In one example of a multiple-baseline design, McEvoy et al. (1988) used group affection activities to increase the interaction of three young autistic children with nonhandicapped peers. The authors found that peer interaction increased during free play when the affection activities were conducted, but not when similar activities were used without the affection treatment package. This interaction included initiations by both autistic and nonhandicapped children. Reciprocal interactions occurred more frequently with nonhandicapped peers who had participated in the affection activities. This application of the multiple-baseline design essentially involved the application of the affection activities across three subjects and the percentage of peer interaction served as the dependent variable.

Considerations

One major challenge confronting school psychologists involved in implementing interventions in applied settings is designing an evaluation scheme to determine if services are effective. We have placed special emphasis on case study and single-case designs because these procedures have a history of application to the evaluation of clinical problems in applied settings. Moreover, these procedures have often been recommended as the "best choice" for empirical evaluation (Barlow et al., 1984). Although there is debate about whether these procedures can be implemented in the usual routine practice of a clinician (Kratochwill & Piersel, 1983), case study and single-case research designs have been used extensively in psychology and education to evaluate *research* projects (Kazdin, 1982). Our perspective is that for most practitioners, the methodology of *case studies* will be most helpful and compatible with the demands of practice, recognizing there will be many compromises necessary in the evaluation process.

CONCLUSIONS

We have focused on an array of interrelated intervention issues in this chapter, beginning with a discussion of problem-solving and treatment models and then focusing on aspects of treatment selection, implementation, and finally

evaluation. Our opening premise was that the major challenge facing school psychologists who are involved in treating students' classroom problems is the identification of acceptable and effective interventions that a teacher can implement with integrity. We believe that many such interventions exist, as evidenced in the content of several other chapters in this volume. In designing interventions for implementation in the regular classroom, the major task in identifying such interventions requires knowledge of and respect for many variables associated with the teachers, such as skill, knowledge, time, and the availability of resources. This review of the treatment acceptability research and analyses of treatment integrity and teacher empowerment is intended to provide a foundation for improving the effectiveness of classroom interventions.

REFERENCES

Algozzine, B., Ysseldyke, J. E., Christenson, S., & Thurlow, M. (1983). *Teachers' intervention choices for children exhibiting different behaviors in school.* Minneapolis: University of Minnesota, Institute for research on Learning Disabilities.

Baer, D. M. (1987). The difference between basic and applied behavior analysis is one behavior. *Behavior Analysis, 22,* 101-106.

Baer, D. M. (1988). If you know why you're changing a behavior, you'll know when you've changed it enough. *Behavioral Assessment, 10,* 219-223.

Baer, D. M., Wolf, M., & Risley, T. (1968). Some current dimensions of applied behavior analysis. *Journal of Applied Behavior Analysis, 1,* 91-97.

Barlow, D. H., Hayes, S. C., & Nelson, R. O. (1984). *The scientist-practitioner: Research and accountability in clinical and educational settings.* New York: Pergamon.

Bergan, J. R. (1977). *Behavioral consultation.* Columbus, OH: Merrill.

Bergan, J. R., & Kratochwill, T. R. (1990). *Behavioral consultation and therapy.* New York: Plenum.

Bergan, J. R., & Tombari, M. L. (1975). The analysis of verbal interactions occurring during consultation. *Journal of School Psychology, 13,* 209-226.

Brown, D. K., Kratochwill, T. R., & Bergan, J. R. (1982). Teaching interview skills for problem identification: An analogue study. *Behavioral Assessment, 4,* 63-73.

Budd, K. S., & Baer, D. M. (1976). Behavior modification and the law: Implications of recent judicial decisions. *Journal of Psychiatry and Law, 4*, 171-244.

Clark, L., & Elliott, S. N. (1988). The influence of treatment strength information of knowledgeable teachers' pretreatment evaluations of social skills training methods. *Professional School Psychology, 3*, 241-251.

Coats, D., Renzaglia, G. J., & Embree, M. C. (1983). When helping backfires: Help and helplessness. In J. D. Fishner, A. Nadler, & B. M. DePaulo (Eds.), *New directions in helping: Vol. 1. Recipient reactions to aid* (pp. 251-275). New York: Academic.

Cormier, W. H., & Cormier, L. S. (1985). *Interviewing strategies for helpers* (2nd ed.). Monterey, CA: Brooks/Cole.

Duke, D. L. (1982). *Helping teachers manage classrooms*. Alexandria, VA: Association for Supervision of Curriculum and instruction.

Dunst, C. J., & Trivette, C. M. (1988). Helping, helplessness, and harm. In J. C. Witt, S. N. Elliott, & F. M. Gresham (Eds.), *Handbook of behavior therapy in education* (pp. 343-376). New York: Plenum.

Elliott, S. N. (1988). Acceptability of behavioral treatments in educational settings. In J. C. Witt, S. N. Elliott, & F. M. Gresham (Eds.), *Handbook of behavior therapy in education* (pp. 121-150). New York: Plenum.

Elliott, S. N., Turco, T. L., & Gresham, F. M. (1987). Consumers' and clients' pretreatment acceptability ratings of classroom-based group contingencies. *Journal of School Psychology, 25*, 145-154.

Elliott, S. N., Witt, J. C., Galvin, G. A., & Moe, G. L. (1986). Children's involvement in intervention selection: Acceptability of interventions for misbehaving peers. *Professional Psychology: Research and Practice, 17*, 235-241.

Elliott, S. N., Witt, J. C., Galvin, G., & Peterson, R. (1984). Acceptability of positive and reductive interventions: Factors that influence teachers' decisions. *Journal of School Psychology, 22*, 353-360.

Foxx, R. M., & Jones, J. R. (1978). A remediation program for increasing the spelling achievement of elementary and junior high school students. *Behavior Modification, 2*, 211-230.

Frentz, C., & Kelley, M. L. (1986). Parents' acceptance of reductive treatment methods: The influence of problem severity and perception of child behavior. *Behavior Therapy, 17*, 75-81.

Fuchs, D., & Fuchs, L. S. (1989). Exploring effective and efficient prereferral interventions: A component analysis of behavioral consultation. *School Psychology Review, 18*, 260-279.

Gardner, W. I., & Cole, C. L. (1988). Self-monitoring procedures. In E. S. Shapiro & T. R. Kratochwill (Eds.), *Behavioral assessment in schools: Conceptual foundations and practical applications* (pp. 206-246). New York: Guilford.

Garfield, S. (1983). Some comments on consumer satisfaction in behavior therapy. *Behavior Therapy, 14*, 237-241.

Gettinger, M. (1988). Methods of proactive classroom management. *School Psychology Review, 17*, 227-242.

Gresham, F. M. (1989). Assessment of treatment integrity in school consultation and prereferral intervention. *School Psychology Review, 18*, 37-50.

Gresham, F. M., & Kendall, G. K. (1987). School consultation research: Methodological critique and future research directions. *School Psychology Review, 16*, 306-316.

Gresham, F. M., & Witt, J. C. (1987, October). *Practical considerations in the implementation of classroom interventions*. Paper presented at the annual meeting of the Oregon School Psychological Association, Eugene, Oregon.

Hayes, S. C., Nelson, R. O., & Jarrett, R. B. (1986). Evaluating the quality of behavioral assessment. In R. O. Nelson, & S. C. Hayes (Eds.), *conceptual foundations of behavioral assessment* (pp. 463-503). New York: Guilford.

Jacobson, N. S. (1988). Defining clinically significant change: An introduction. *Behavioral Assessment, 10*, 131-132.

Jacobson, N. S., Follette, W. C., & Revenstorf, D. (1984). Psychotherapy outcome research: Methods for reporting variability and evaluating clinical significance. *Behavior Therapy, 15*, 336-352.

Jeger, A. M., & McClure, G. (1979). Attitudinal effects of undergraduate behavioral training. *Policy Studies Review, 23*, 147-186.

Johnson, J. H., Rasbury, W. D., & Siegel, J. L. (1986). *Approaches to child treatment: Introduction to therapy, research, and practice*. New York: Pergamon.

Kanfer, F. H. (1973). Behavior modification — An overview. In C. Thoresen (Ed.), *Behavior modification in education* (pp. 10-47). Chicago: University of Chicago Press.

Kazdin, A. E. (1977). Assessing the clinical or applied significance of behavior change through social validation. *Behavior Modification, 1*, 427-452.

Kazdin, A. E. (1980a). Acceptability of alternative treatments for deviant child behavior. *Journal of Applied Behavior Analysis, 13*, 259-273.

Kazdin, A. E. (1980b). Acceptability of time-out from reinforcement procedures for disruptive child behavior. *Behavior Therapy, 11*, 329-344.

Kazdin, A. E. (1981a). Acceptability of child treatment techniques: The influence of treatment efficacy and adverse side effects. *Behavior Therapy, 12*, 493-506.

Kazdin, A. E. (1981b). Drawing valid references from case studies. *Journal of Consulting and Clinical Psychology, 49*, 183-192.

Kazdin, A. E. (1982). *Single case research designs: Methods for clinical and applied settings.* New York: Oxford University Press.

Kazdin, A. E. (1986). Comparative outcome studies of psychotherapy: Methodological issues and strategies. *Journal of Consulting and Clinical Psychology, 54*, 95-105.

Kazdin, A. E. (1988). *Child psychotherapy: Developing and identifying effective treatments.* New York: Pergamon.

Kazdin, A. E., Esveldt-Dawson, L., French, N. H., & Unis, A. S. (1987). Problem-solving skills training and relationship therapy in the treatment of antisocial child behavior. *Journal of Consulting and Clinic Psychology, 55*, 76-85.

Kazdin, A. E., French, N. H., & Sherick, R. B. (1981). Acceptability of alternative treatments for children: Evaluating of inpatient children, parents, and staff. *Journal of Consulting and Clinical Psychology, 49*, 900-907.

Kazdin, A. E., Kratochwill, T. R., & VadenBos, G. R. (1986). Beyond clinical trials: Generalizing from research to practice. *Professional Psychology: Research and Practice, 17*, 391-398.

Kirigin, K. A., Braukmann, C. J., Atwater, J. D., & Wolf, M. M. (1982). An evaluation of teaching-family (Achievement Place) group homes for juvenile offenders. *Journal of Applied Behavior Analysis, 15*, 1-16.

Kratochwill, T. R. (1985). Case study research in school psychology. *School Psychology Review, 14*, 204-215.

Kratochwill, T. R., & Bergan, J. R. (1978). Evaluating programs in applied settings through behavioral consultation. *Journal of School Psychology, 16*, 375-386.

Kratochwill, T. R., & Bergan, J. R. (1990). *Behavioral consultation in applied settings: An individual guide.* New York: Plenum.

Kratochwill, T. R., Bergan, J. R., & Mace, F. C. (1981). Practitioner competencies needed for implementation of behavioral psychology in the schools: Issues in supervision. *School Psychology Review, 10*, 434-444.

Kratochwill, T. R., & Morris, R. J. (Eds.). (1990). *The practice of child therapy* (2nd ed). New York: Pergamon.

Kratochwill, T. R., & Piersel, W. C. (1983). Time-series research: Contributions to empirical clinical practice. *Behavioral Assessment, 5*, 165-176.

Kratochwill, T. R., & Van Someren, K. R. (1985). Barriers to treatment success in behavioral consultation: Current limitations and future directions. *Journal of School Psychology, 23*, 225-239.

Kratochwill, T. R., Sheridan, S. M., & Van Someren, K. R. (1988). Research in behavioral consultation: Current status and future directions. In F. J. West (Ed.), *School consultation: Interdisciplinary perspectives on theory, research, training, and practice* (pp. 77-102). Austin, TX: Association of Educational and Psychological Consultants.

Kratochwill, T. R., Van Someren, K. R., & Sheridan, S. M. (1989). Training behavioral consultants: A competency-based model to teach interview skills. *Professional School Psychology, 4*, 41-58.

Lentz, F. E. (1988). Reductive procedures. In J. C. Witt, S. N. Elliott, & F. M. Gresham (Eds.), *Handbook of behavior therapy in education.* New York: Plenum.

Levine, F. M., & Sandeen, E. (1985). *Conceptualization in psychotherapy: The models approach.* New York: Erlbaum.

Luborsky, L., & DeRubeis, R. J. (1984). The use of psychotherapy treatment manuals: A small revolution in psychotherapy research style. *Clerical Psychology Review, 4*, 5-14.

Martens, B. K., Peterson, R. L., Witt, J. C., & Cirone, S. (1986). Teacher perceptions of school-based intervention: Ratings of intervention effectiveness, ease of use, and frequency of use. *Exceptional Children, 53*, 213-223.

Martens, B. K., Witt, J. C., Elliott, S. N., & Darveaux, D. X. (1985). Teacher judgements concerning the acceptability of school-based interventions. *Professional Psychology: Research and Practice, 16*, 78-88.

Matarazzo, R. G., & Patterson, D. (1986). Research on the teaching and learning of psychotherapeutic skills. In S. L. Garfield & A. E. Bergan (Eds.), *Handbook of psychotherapy and behavior approach* (3rd ed.; pp. 821-843). New York: Wiley.

McEvoy, M. A., Nordquist, V. M., Twardosz, S., Heckaman, K. A., Wehby, J. H., & Denny, R. K. (1988). Promoting autistic children's peer interaction in an integrated early childhood setting using affection activities. *Journal of Applied Behavior Analysis, 21,* 193-200.

McKee, W. T. (1984). *Acceptability of alternative classroom treatment strategies and factors affecting teachers' ratings.* Unpublished master's thesis, University of British Columbia, Vancouver.

McMahon, R. J., & Forehand, R. L. (1983). Consumer satisfaction in behavioral treatment for children: Types, issues, and recommendations. *Behavior Therapy, 14,* 209-225.

McMahon, R. J., Forehand, R., & Griest, D. L. (1981). Effects of knowledge of social learning principles on enhancing treatment outcome and generalization in a parent training program. *Journal of Consulting and Clinical Psychology, 49,* 526-532.

Melton, G. B. (1983). Decision making by children: Psychological risks and benefits. In G. B. Melton, G. P. Koocher, & M. J. Saks (Eds.), *Children's competence to consent* (pp. 137-159). New York: Plenum.

Morris, R. J., & Kratochwill, T. R. (Eds.). (1983). *The practice of child therapy.* New York: Pergamon.

Nelson, R. O. (1983). Behavioral assessment: Past, present, and future. *Behavioral Assessment, 1,* 1-16.

O'Dell, S. L., Tarler-Benlolo, L., & Flynn, J. M. (1979). An instrument to measure knowledge of behavioral principles as applied to children. *Journal of Behavior Therapy and Experimental Psychology, 10,* 29-34.

O'Leary, K. D. (1984). The image of behavior therapy: It is time to take a stand. *Behavior Therapy, 15,* 219-233.

Ollendick, T. H., Matson, J. L., Esveldt-Dawson, K., & Shapiro, E. S. (1980). Increasing spelling achievement: An analysis of treatment procedures utilizing an alternative treatments design. *Journal of Applied Behavior Analysis, 13,* 645-654.

Peterson, L., Hommer, A. L., & Wonderlich, S. A. (1982). The integrity of independent variables in behavior analysis. *Journal of Applied Behavior Analysis, 15,* 477-492.

Petrie, P., Brown, K. D., Piersel, W. C., Frinfrock, S. R., Schelble, M., Lablanc, C. P., & Kratochwill, T. R. (1980). The school psychologist as behavioral ecologist. *Journal of School Psychology, 18,* 222-233.

Piersel, W. C., & Kratochwill, T. R. (1979). Self observation and behavior change: Applications to academic and adjustment problems to behavioral consultation. *Journal of School Psychology, 17,* 151-161.

Rappaport, J. (1981). In praise of paradox: A social policy of empowerment over prevention. *American Journal of Community Psychology, 9,* 1-25.

Reimers, T. M., Wacker, D. P., & Koeppl, G. (1987). Acceptability of behavioral treatments: A review of the literature. *School Psychology Review, 16,* 212-227.

Reppucci, N. D., & Saunders, J. T. (1974). The social psychology of behavior modification: Problems of implementation in natural settings. *American Psychologist, 29,* 649-660.

Shapiro, E. S., & Goldberg, R. (1986). A comparison of group contingencies for increasing spelling performance among sixth grade students. *School Psychology Review, 15,* 546-667.

Stern, G. W., Fowler, S. A., & Kohler, F. W. (1988). A comparison of two intervention roles: Peer monitor and point earner. *Journal of Applied Behavior Analysis, 21,* 103-109.

Turco, T. L., & Elliott, S. N. (1986). Assessment of students' acceptability of teacher-initiated interventions for classroom misbehavior. *Journal of School Psychology, 24,* 307-313.

U.S. Congress, House Committee on the Judiciary, Subcommittee on Courts, Civil Liberties, and the Administration of Justice. (1974a). *Oversight hearing: Behavior modification programs in the Federal Bureau of Prisons.* 93rd Cong., 2nd sess., February 27, 1974 (Serial No. 26). Washington, DC: U.S. Government Printing Office.

U.S. Congress, Senate Committee on the Judiciary, Subcommittee on Constitutional Rights. (1974b). *Individual rights and the federal role in behavior modification.* 93rd Cong., 2nd sess., November 1974. Washington, DC: U.S. Government Printing Office.

Von Brock, M. B. (1985). *The influence of effectiveness information on teachers' ratings of acceptability.* Unpublished master's thesis, Louisiana State University, Baton Rouge.

Von Brock, M. B., & Elliott, S. N. (1987). The influence of treatment effectiveness information on the acceptability of classroom interventions. *Journal of School Psychology, 25,* 131-144.

Wagner, J. L., & Winett, R. A. (1988). Prompting one low-fat, high-fiber selection in a fast-food restaurant. *Journal of Applied Behavior Analysis, 21,* 179-185.

West, J. G., Idol, L., & Cannon, G. (1987). *A curriculum for preservice and inservice preparation of classroom and special education teachers in collaborative consultation*. Austin: The University of Texas at Austin, Research & Training Project on School Consultation.

Willems, E. P. (1974). Behavioral technology and behavioral ecology. *Journal of Applied Behavior Analysis, 7*, 151-165.

Witt, J. C. (1986). Teachers' resistance to the use of school-based intervention. *Journal of School Psychology, 24*, 37-44.

Witt, J. C., & Elliott, S. N. (1985). Acceptability of classroom management strategies. In T. R. Kratochwill (Ed.), *Advances in school psychology* (Vol. 4, pp. 251-288). Hillsdale, NJ: Erlbaum.

Witt, J. C., Elliott, S. N., & Gresham, F. M. (Eds.). (1988). *Handbook of behavior therapy in education*. New York: Plenum.

Witt, J. C., Elliott, S. N., & Martens, B. K. (1984). Acceptability of behavioral interventions used in classrooms: The influence of teacher time, severity of behavior problem, and type of intervention. *Behavioral Disorders, 10*, 95-104.

Witt, J. C., & Martens, B. K. (1983). Assessing the acceptability of behavioral interventions used in classrooms. *Psychology in the Schools, 20*, 510-517.

Witt, J. C., & Martens, B. K. (1988). Problems with problem-solving consultation: A re-analysis of assumptions, methods, and goals. *School Psychology Review, 17*, 211-226.

Witt, J. C., Martens, B. K., & Elliott, S. N. (1984). Factors affecting teachers' judgments of the acceptability of behavioral interventions: Time involvement, behavior problem severity, and type of intervention. *Behavior Therapy, 15*, 204-209.

Witt, J. C., & Robbins, J. R. (1985). Acceptability of reductive interventions for the control of inappropriate child behavior. *Journal of Abnormal Child Psychology, 13*, 59-67

Wolf, M. M. (1978). Social validity: The case of subjective measurement or how applied behavior analysis is finding its heart. *Journal of Applied Behavior Analysis, 11*, 203-214.

Woolfolk, R. C., & Woolfolk, A. E. (1979). Modifying the effect of the behavior modification label. *Behavior Therapy, 10*, 575-578.

Woolfolk, A. E., Woolfolk, R. C., & Wilson, G. T. (1977). A rose by any other name . . . : Labeling bias and attitudes toward behavior modification. *Journal Consulting and Clinical Psychology, 45*, 184-191.

Yeaton, W. H. (1988). Acceptability of behavioral treatments in educational settings. In J. C. Witt, S. N. Elliott, & F. M. Gresham (Eds.), *Handbook of behavior therapy in education* (pp. 171-188). New York: Plenum.

Yeaton, W. H., & Sechrest, L. (1981). Critical dimensions in the choice and maintenance of successful treatments: Strength, integrity, and effectiveness. *Journal of Consulting and Clinical Psychology, 49*, 156-167.

Ysseldyke, J. E., & Christenson, S. (1987). *The Instructional Environment Scale*. Austin, TX: Pro-Ed.

Interventions for Improving Study Skills

Mary M. Gleason
University of Oregon

Geoff Colvin
Lane County Educational Service District

Anita L. Archer
San Diego State University

Currently, more than 4 million students receive remedial services for academic deficits in classrooms for the mildly handicapped. The academic difficulties experienced by these students could be ameliorated with a variety of approaches including (a) teaching these students basic skills such as reading, writing, and mathematics; (b) modifying instructional delivery to make it easier for those students to learn, thus lessening the instructional demands; and (c) teaching students how to learn better. Many suggestions are presented elsewhere in this monograph for ways that the regular classroom teacher can teach basic skills effectively and/or modify the instructional demands presented to mildly handicapped students. Both are critical interventions for students faced with academic challenges. However, as mildly handicapped students progress and become more proficient with basic skills, they need more help in meeting academic demands. In order to be successful in mainstream classes, these students need to learn specific study strategies that will assist them to meet the demands of the complex tasks required in content area classes, which include (a) skimming through textbook material to find information

needed for answering a particular question, (b) reading textbook material and deciding which information is important and which is not, and (c) using the identified relevant information to take notes and study the material.

In this chapter, we will focus on how teachers can assist students to establish new behaviors that would help them achieve more success in the regular classroom. This chapter will address (a) the kinds of problems encountered by mildly handicapped students who are expected to meet the demands of the regular classroom, and (b) study skills interventions that school psychologists must be aware of to improve student achievement at both prereferral and referral levels.

DEFINITION OF STUDY SKILLS

The systematic procedures that students initiate to complete such complex tasks as skimming, determining relevant information, taking notes, and studying material for a test are called interchangeably *study skills, study strategies*, or *learning strategies*. We will use the terms study skills and study strategies in this chapter because they are the terms most used by teachers and school psychologists and in the professional literature. Study skills are not necessarily related to specific academic content (e.g., history), but are used across content areas. Devine (1987) describes study skills as "competencies associated with acquiring, recording, organizing, synthesizing, remembering, and using information and ideas found in school" (p. 5). Others describe learning strategies as systematic techniques involving use of cognitive and megacognitive elements to respond independently to specific classroom tasks (Deshler & Schumaker, 1986; Ellis, Lenz, & Sabornie, 1987a; 1987b). Whether they are called study skills, study strategies, or learning strategies, these techniques are taught to students to empower them to respond successfully to academic demands and to increase their potential for learning independently. For the purposes of this chapter, we will focus on three major study skill goals: (a) to gain information, (b) to respond to information, and (c) to organize information. To accomplish the goal of *gaining information*, students must be taught study strategies that allow them to extract information from lectures, discussions, demonstrations, textbooks, and reference materials. To accomplish the goal of *responding to information*, students must be able to study for and take tests, complete written assignments and papers, write answers to questions, and participate in discussions. To accomplish the goal of *organizing information*, students must be taught to organize notebooks, keep assignment calendars, and organize content on papers.

RATIONALE FOR STUDY SKILLS INTERVENTIONS

Student Needs

A great deal of evidence exists that mildly handicapped students lack the organizational and study skills needed to respond to the task demands of the regular classroom and that they experience difficulty in acquiring those skills. For example, several studies have found that mildly handicapped students are not actively involved in learning and show deficiencies in spontaneous use of study skill strategies (Torgeson, 1977). Other studies have found that these students do not improve recall through minimal study skill instruction (Gelzheiser, Cort, & Shepherd, 1987; Newman & Hagen, 1981). In other words, many mildly handicapped students do not possess or self-generate effective study strategies, and they frequently do not use those strategies that have been taught. Mildly handicapped students appear to need extensive practice after a strategy has been taught. Even then, they often do not recognize the need for, or know how to perform, a learned skill in a novel situation (Chan & Cole, 1986; Ringel & Springer, 1980). Consequently, many mildly handicapped students fail in mainstream settings and fail to graduate.

Teachers' Expectations

While many mildly handicapped students do not possess successful study strategies, or fail to activate known strategies at the appropriate time, regular education teachers do *expect* students to employ these study skills. In fact, regular classroom teachers usually expect these study skills without providing explicit instruction in the skills or in the many ways in which the skills can be used. A large percentage of mildly handicapped students receive special education only a small part of the day and are in the mainstream the remaining part of the day. Because mildly handicapped students spend a great deal of time in the regular classroom, special education teachers and regular classroom teachers alike must be concerned with the teaching of study skills. The reality of the regular classroom teacher's expectation suggests three implications for teaching study skills to mildly handicapped students:

1. If students are still in the regular classroom, teachers must work to maintain their participation and success there.

2. If students are still in the regular classroom, teachers must intervene if students are experiencing failure.
3. If students are in a special education setting, teachers must prepare students for eventual mainstreaming and success in the regular classroom.

To determine teachers' perceptions about students' needs, Gleason and Archer (1989) conducted a survey of 217 junior high content area teachers in the San Diego School District on current practices in respect to information sources, responses used by students, and grading tools. At the junior high level, students gain most information through lectures, respond most frequently through tests, and receive their grades from test scores (Table 1). When asked to rate 36 behaviors on a scale of 1 to 5, indicating how critical each behavior was to classroom success, teachers indicated that many behaviors were critical to classroom success beyond listening to lectures and performing well on tests. These behaviors and the ratings are listed in Table 2.

On the last section of the questionnaire, teachers were asked to choose three school or study behaviors from the previous list of 36 that they believed students were least able to perform. Although their responses varied, more than 21% of the teachers selected the following critical behaviors as one of four that students were least able to perform: (a) utilizes independent work time in class effectively, (b) listens during lectures/discussions, (c) reads and follows written directions independently, and (d) prepares for tests. In Table 2, these four behaviors were rated by over 75% of the teachers as critical to classroom achievement (e.g., ratings of 4 or 5 on a 1–5 scale of increasing importance), yet teachers are saying that these behaviors are among those that mildly handicapped students are least able to perform. Utilizing work time, listening, following directions, and preparing for tests all require active engagement and the use of effective study strategies on the part of the students.

The simple argument is that if teachers use certain common methods to deliver and assess instruction and are expecting students to use certain behaviors for success in class, then the students need to have a set of skills to learn from these methods. For example, because teachers almost always (97%) use lectures to present information, then students *must* know how to listen, take notes, identify key points, and follow directions if they are to learn from the lecture. Similarly, given that 87% of teachers reported the use of written tests as the most common method to grade students, students need to have test-taking skills to succeed. Even the student who "knows" the information may not obtain good grades because of problems with test taking.

In effect, the commonly used methods of instruction imply a common set of study skills for students. If these skills are adequate, the student will succeed; if the skills are not adequate, the student will have problems. Some students will fail, some students will drop out, and other students will be referred for special education. That students learn from teaching is predicated on the assumption that students have adequate study skills.

Responses by School Psychologists

Despite the need for mildly handicapped students to use study skills in regular and special education, Colvin and Gleason (1989) found that study skill objectives usually are not addressed during the formation of Individualized Educational Programs (IEPs) or in a student's day-to-day instructional program. They conducted a survey among members of the Oregon School Psychologists Association to examine the perceived relationship between deficits in study skills and referrals to special education in the areas of learning disabilities (LD) and behavior disorders (BD) and the extent to which study skills are taught or used in evaluation and interventions. The results from 56 survey respondents are presented in Table 3.

The following conclusions can be drawn from the results. The percentages indicated reflect the combined scores of

TABLE 1
Survey Results: Current Practices

A. Information sources most often used in class
   Lectures given in class — 97%
   Classroom discussion — 93%
   Reading from textbook — 86%

B. Responses most often used in classes
   Taking tests — 55%
   Participating in class discussion — 54%
   Completing written worksheets — 51%

C. Grading tools most often used in classes
   Written tests — 87%
   Written worksheets — 41%
   Participating in discussion — 40%

the scales ratings of *frequently* and *occasionally*, as reported by the Oregon school psychologists.

1. School psychologists (92%) in Oregon perceive that deficits in study skills significantly contribute to problems of LD or BD students.

2. According to school psychologists, teachers in general education classrooms (60%) do not teach study skills directly as a rule, but special education teachers (79%) do.

3. While most school psychologists identify deficits in study skills as a factor contributing to school problems of LD and BD students (92%), the number of school psychologists who address study skills as part of an evaluation or as part of an IEP or remediation process is considerably less: evaluation (59%), interventions (67%), IEPs (61%), multidisciplinary teams (MDT) and IEP meetings (79%).

4. School psychologists indicated that if they had more training in study skills, they would utilize the information to evaluate student deficiencies and write IEPs (91%).

Overall, most school psychologists in the survey perceived that study skills were a factor significantly contributing to referrals to special education for LD and BD students. Yet in practice, a disparity appears to exist between what is believed to be a significant factor in student needs and what is in place to address those needs. The school psychologists who were surveyed believed that this gap could be minimized through training in the area of study skills.

SUCCESSFUL STUDY STRATEGIES

Many mildly handicapped students are passive in their approach to classroom tasks (Torgesen, 1982). Teachers face the challenge of transforming passive learners into learners who are involved more actively and who are more successful in meeting classroom expectations. We will accomplish this task by teaching students effective study strategies for gaining information, responding to information, and organizing information.

Most work in the area of improving study strategies has been conducted at junior high school, high school, or college levels, most notably by Schumaker, Deshler, and their colleagues at the University of Kansas (see Chapter 22 in this monograph). For the past 8 years, Archer and Gleason (1989) have been field-testing and revising strategies that could be introduced at the elementary level (Grades 3-6) so that the behaviors might be firmly established by the time students reach the challenges of junior high or high school.

To determine the effectiveness of teaching study skills at the elementary level, a four-level curriculum was designed and implemented in the regular class-

TABLE 2
Study and School Behaviors Needed in Classes

Study or School Behavior[a,b]	Percentage Responding[c]					
	Not Critical			Critical		Combined
	1	2	3	4	5	4 and 5
Asks for help when needed.	0	1	5	33	60	93
Listens during lectures/ discussions.	0	1	6	25	67	92
Attends class regularly.	0	2	7	33	58	91
Comes to class with proper materials.	0	2	8	27	63	90
Utilizes independent work time in class effectively.	1	2	6	33	57	90
Is ready to work at beginning of class sessions	0	3	9	37	51	88
Turns work in on time.	0	4	7	31	57	88
Socializes only at appropriate times.	2	2	9	32	54	86
Prepares for tests.	3	1	11	27	58	85
Reads and follows written directions independently.	0	3	19	36	41	77
Answers written questions independently.	3	4	21	38	34	72
Is punctual to class.	0	9	18	32	40	72
Works well with other students.	3	4	32	36	25	61
Reads textbook independently	8	11	20	30	30	60
Determines meaning of words in context.	4	8	28	28	32	60
Utilizes effective test-taking strategies.	10	8	26	32	24	56
Volunteers pertinent information in class discussions.	3	7	34	34	20	54
Writes complete sentences.	15	11	23	22	30	52
Scans materials for specific information.	9	9	30	29	23	52
Writes legibly.	5	11	33	35	16	51
Skims written material for main ideas.	15	10	27	34	14	48
Turns in neat papers.	5	10	40	29	15	44
Takes notes from lectures/discussions.	13	14	32	23	17	40
Writes clear paragraphs.	21	14	27	22	16	38
Proofs papers for punctuation and spelling errors.	21	17	25	21	15	36
Maintains a neat and organized notebook.	23	16	27	23	10	33

(Table 2, continued)

Study or School Behavior[a,b]	Percentage Responding[c]					
	Not Critical			Critical		Combined
	1	2	3	4	5	4 and 5
Decodes longer words (multi-syllabic words).	23	14	30	19	12	31
Utilizes reference materials (e.g., dictionary, encyclopedia).	27	17	26	18	12	30
Takes notes from written materials.	19	20	33	17	11	28
Utilizes library resources (e.g., card catalogue).	32	10	31	19	8	27

[a]Remaining school and study skills were rated 4 or 5 by fewer than 25% of the teachers. Thus, they were omitted from this table.

[b]Study School behaviors have been reordered in descending order of percentage of teachers judging the behaviors critical to classroom success by marking 4 or 5.

[c]Percentages were rounded and as a result do always add to 100%.

rooms of elementary schools in a large school district in Arizona. Throughout each year, feedback was collected from the teachers and the students on the teaching formats and on perceived student performance. In addition, at the end of each year, a posttest was administered. On the basis of each year's results, the program underwent extensive revision and the revised program was field-tested in the subsequent year. At the same time, a large-scale evaluation study was conducted in two school districts that served similar populations of students in a large city in the state of Washington. One district served as the experimental group, while the other served as the control group. Preliminary analysis of the data shows that students at all grade levels scored significantly higher on the posttests than students in the control district. The strategies that were successful are featured in this chapter.

Gaining Information from Content Area Textbooks

A major goal in content area classes is that of gaining information from content area textbooks. Using study skills to gain information from textbooks can be diffi-

cult if students are left to devise their own strategies. Chan and Cole (1986) found that self-questioning only, underlining only, and self-questioning combined with underlining were equally effective in teaching LD students to attend to and remember what they read and that comprehension scores of students in all three conditions were significantly different from scores of control group students.

During their field-testing, Archer and Gleason determined that for students to gain information from textbooks, they must be taught directly the following strategies: (a) surveying the chapter and forming a general impression of the important information to be emphasized in the chapter, (b) reading the text and attending to the main ideas and important details, (c) attending to the content of maps and graphics that accompany the text, and (d) verbally rehearsing the main ideas and details and/or completing written notes on the main ideas and details. Archer and Gleason (1989) used teacher-directed instruction to teach all four component strategies. In addition, other researchers have studied one or more of the strategies in isolation. Each strategy will be described with enough detail that a school psychologist could

TABLE 3
School Psychologist Survey: Study Skills

Question	Never	Seldom	Occasionally	Frequently
1. To what extent do deficits in study skills contribute to referrals for learning disabilities?	—	4 (4%)	2 (28%)	65 (67%)
2. To what extent do deficits in study skills contribute to referrals for behavior disorders/emotional disturbance?	1 (1%)	5 (16%)	45 (47%)	36 (37%)
3. Do teachers in regular education teach study skills directly as a program or lesson?	6 (6%)	54 (54%)	32 (33%)	6 (6%)
4. Do teachers in special education teach study skills directly as a program or lesson?	3 (3%)	18 (8%)	51 (53%)	25 (26%)
5. Do school psychologists assess study skills as a part of student evaluations?	10 (10%)	29 (30%)	37 (39%)	19 (20%)
6. Do teachers report deficits in study skills as part of referral information?	3 (3%)	27 (28%)	33 (34%)	30 (31%)
7. Do school psychologists design study skills as an intervention for students who need these skills?	4 (4%)	32 (32%)	46 (48%)	18 (19%)
8. Are study skills used as an intervention in student/s IEP?	5 (5%)	35 (36%)	40 (48%)	18 (19%)
9. Given school psychologists were well trained in the area of study skills, would they utilize this information in evaluations and IEPs?	1 (1%)	4 (4%)	34 (35%)	57 (59%)
10. Are study skills addressed in MDT or IEP meetings?	2 (2%)	21 (22%)	45 (47%)	31 (32%)

implement the strategy or facilitate implementation with a classroom teacher.

Surveying the chapter. In a strategy called *Warm-up*, Archer and Gleason (1989) taught students to preview a content area chapter to determine the important information to be emphasized and to develop an organizational framework for the information. The Warm-up strategy suggests specific items to preview in the chapter, and the students are guided through the procedure with several different chapters in different kinds of content area textbooks.

In discussing the rationale for the strategy, students are told that they must warm up for reading just like they warm up for an athletic event. They warm up for reading by finding out what the chapter is about and making guesses about what is to be learned from the chapter. Through a series of questions, the teacher guides students through the warm-up strategy by asking students to read the title of the chapter and the introduction, headings and subheadings, the chapter summary, and the questions at the end of the chapter. As students examine different parts of the chapter, they make predictions about what is to be learned from the chapter. The steps for warming up are written out on a poster for all to see, and the teacher covers the poster and provides students an opportunity for verbal rehearsal of the steps in the Warm-up strategy. Students then practice the Warm-up strategy with several textbook chapters, verbally reporting their predictions to the teacher or to a peer. Students then complete a written worksheet that demonstrates their predictions about the chapter content and share the content with the teacher.

Another survey strategy was suggested by Aukerman (1972) but without the preview of the questions at the end of the chapter or the ongoing predictions about the chapter content. The Aukerman strategy also differed from the Archer and Gleason (1989) strategy in the written response required of the students. His survey technique consisted of the following steps: (a) analyzing the chapter title, (b) analyzing the subtitles, (c) analyzing the visual aids, (d) reading the introductory paragraph, (e) reading the concluding paragraph, and (f) deriving the main idea. A whole-group discussion would follow in which students would share their main ideas and organize one main idea statement "owned" by the whole class, then read the chapter to gain further information.

Reading the text. After students have previewed the chapter sufficiently, they must read the chapter and attend to the main ideas and important details that are worth remembering and that will assist students in answering questions at the end of the chapter. The strategy that will work best for a particular group of students depends on their reading level and their experience with reading content area material. Many study strategies for reading expository materials have been developed and tested with elementary and secondary students (e.g., Adams, Carnine, & Gleason, 1982; Archer & Gleason, 1989; Chan & Cole, 1986; Schumaker, Denton, & Deshler, 1984; Schumaker, Deshler, Alley, Warner, & Denton, 1982; Wong, Wong, Perry, & Sawatsky, 1986). These strategies have several similarities (Archer & Gleason, 1990). First, they all attempt to engage students more actively in the reading process. Students are asked to formulate questions, take notes on content, or verbally paraphrase the critical information. Second, all strategies attempt to direct students' attention to the *most important* ideas and details.

Third, the strategies engage the students in rehearsal by asking them to recite or write down critical information. Three strategies that appear to exemplify these key steps are outlined here.

The *self-questioning summarization strategy* developed by Wong et al., 1986 teaches students to ask themselves a series of six questions as they proceed paragraph by paragraph and section by section to read and summarize a chapter.

1. In this paragraph, is there anything I don't understand?
2. In this paragraph, what's the most important sentence (main idea sentence)? Let me underline it.
3. Let me summarize the paragraph. To summarize, I rewrite the main idea sentence and add important details.
4. Now, does my summary sentence link up with the subheading?
5. When I have written summary statements for a whole subsection:
   a. Let me review my summary statements for the whole subsection. (A subsection is one with several paragraphs under the same subheading.)
   b. Do my summary statements link up with one another?
   c. Do they all link up with the subheading?
6. At the end of an assigned reading section: Can I see all the themes here? If yes, let me predict the teacher's test question on this section. If no, let me go back to Step 4. (Wong et al., 1986, pp. 24–26).

The *verbal rehearsal strategy* developed by Archer and Gleason (1989) is called Active Reading. Before learning the Active Reading strategy, students first are taught some component preparatory skills. Using several short paragraphs, the teacher demonstrates *naming the topic of the paragraph*, then asks students to practice naming the topics of several paragraphs. Once students can say a word or phrase to name the topic of a paragraph, students are taught to *identify critical details in the paragraph* and to *retell the topic and details* in their own words. During additional practice, with either the teacher or peers, students practice saying and checking off on a checklist that they have said the topic, have noted the important details, and have used their own words.

When students can retell paragraph content fluently, the Active Reading strategy is modeled, guided practice is provided, and then independent practice is expected. The Active Reading strategy is based on a strategy, learned earlier in the curriculum material for memorizing material, called RCRC (Archer & Gleason, 1989). First, the teacher discusses the rationale for the strategy. Students are told that using this strategy will help them remember more information from a chapter. Then, students read (R) a paragraph and tell themselves the topic and details. They cover (C) the paragraph and recite (R) the important information in their own words. Then they uncover the paragraph and check (C) their recitation by examining the paragraph again. Students verbally rehearse the RCRC steps used in the Active Reading strategy and practice the Active Reading strategy with several paragraphs, verbally reporting their topics and details to a teacher or peer. Finally, they complete a written worksheet in which the peer checks on a checklist whether the recital included topic and details, and was in the student's own words (Figure 1).

Another way to engage students actively in reading content area textbooks is to enlist them in *taking notes on the important information*. The notes then can be used in studying for tests, writing summaries of what was read, answering chapter questions, or writing a report.

A system of note taking appropriate for upper elementary students and lower-performing junior high or high school students was developed by Archer and Gleason (1989). As with the Active Reading strategy, the note taking depends on the single paragraph as the unit for reading and writing notes and requires students to attend to the topic and important details. Students should demonstrate mastery of the Active Reading strategy before attempting the note-taking strategy. As with all teacher-directed

strategies, the teacher provides a rationale, demonstrates use of the strategy, and guides students through the steps. Students are told that taking notes will help them concentrate better on what the author is saying and that their notes can be used for other purposes, such as studying for tests. The teacher tells students why notes should be written briefly and in their own words. Students record headings or subheadings in the center of the paper followed by the corresponding page numbers. Then they take notes on each paragraph, using an indenting style (Figure 2).

To achieve notes such as those in Figure 2, students first record the topic. Then they indent and record the important details, using abbreviations and symbols when possible and indenting again when recording subordinate details. When notes have been completed, the students check them for clarity. Next to each paragraph section of notes, the students write a question in the left-hand margin that could be asked about those notes.

Note taking will benefit students only if they are provided with opportunities to use the notes. If students take notes but do not look at them again, they will likely remember less information than if they review the notes to remember the information for class discussions or for written tests. To remember the information contained in the notes, students can use a verbal rehearsal strategy such as RCRC (read the question, cover, recite the answer, check the answer). They can participate in a class study session, in which the teacher asks questions about the content and the students answer the questions, then quickly show where the information can be located in their notes. Students also can conduct similar sessions with their peers, thus giving them practice in the use of their notes, feedback on the adequacy of their notes, and participation in study teams.

Attending to content of maps and graphics that accompany text. The strategies described so far have concentrated on reading the text portion of

4.   Humans, as you know, have an endoskeleton. The human skeleton is made of 206 separate bones. These bones make up only 18 percent of a person's weight. Though bones are hard, they are a small percentage of your weight because most bones are hollow inside.

This paragraph talks about _____ .

5.   Many bones in your body protect important organs. For example, your skull protects your brain. Your breastbone and ribs protect your heart and lungs. Your backbone protects your spinal cord. Bones that protect organs are very strong and solid.

Did your partner
a. Say the topic?   yes   no
b. Say the important details?   yes   no
c. Say it in his or her own words?   yes   no

6.   Bones not only protect organs but also support your body. Your upper body and head are supported by your backbone. Leg bones help support your body also.

Did your partner
a. Say the topic?   yes   no
b. Say the important details?   yes   no
c. Say it in his or her own words?   yes   no

7.   Some parts of your skeleton can move because of the way that bones are joined together. The place where two bones meet is called a *joint*. Bones are held together at the joint with tough strands of tissue called *ligaments*. Ligaments allow the bones joined at a joint to move freely. Where in your body do you have joints?

Did your partner
a. Say the topic?   yes   no
b. Say the important details?   yes   no
c. Say it in his or her own words?   yes   no

8.   Some joints allow you to move back and forth only in one direction. These movable joints are called *hinge joints*. Like a door hung on hinges, your knees and elbows can swing back and forth only in one direction.

Did your partner
a. Say the topic?   yes   no
b. Say the important details?   yes   no
c. Say it in his or her own words?   yes   no

FIGURE 1. Checklist for determining a student's fulfillment of the requirements of the Active Reading Strategy. From *Skills for school success: Book five* (p. 38), by A. Archer and M. Gleason, 1989, North Billerica, MA: Curriculum Associates. Copyright 1989 by Curriculum Associates. Reprinted by permission.

content area textbooks. In addition, students must be taught to attend to the graphics, pictures, and maps that accompany the text. The information contained in these visual aids is not necessarily repeated in the text itself. Frequently, the questions at the end of a social studies chapter or the questions on tests require answers that can be found only in the aids. Students begin to encounter these visual aids as early as third grade. However, explicit instruction in the interpretation of these aids typically is lacking. For example, a perusal of basal and content

C. Jessica's social studies notes

Jessica Tomasi
October 15, 1992
Social Studies

The Federal Government (p. 87)

Division of govt. powers
- divided among executive, legislative &
  judicial branches
- some but not all powers

Legislative Branch (p. 87)

Congress
- makes laws
- two bodies
  - Senate
  - House of Representatives
Senate
- 2 senators from each state
- elected every 6 years
- can be reelected
House of Representatives
- # of reps. depends on # people in state
- elected every 2 years
- can be reelected
Powers of Congress
- makes laws
- passes tax laws
- can declare war
- decides how much money to print
- borrows money
- controls trade between states
How a bill becomes a law
- Senate & House must vote for bill
- President signs

FIGURE 2. Example of notes taken by following the prescription of the Archer and Gleason (1989) procedure. From *Skills for school success: Book five* (p. 41), by A. Archer and M. Gleason, 1989, North Billerica, MA: Curriculum Associates. Copyright 1989 by Curriculum Associates. Reprinted by permission.

area textbooks shows that the use of graphs and tables usually is taught in the math basal, but not in the content area textbooks.

When a student is experiencing difficulty in a content area class, the school psychologist should examine that student's textbooks and determine the types of visual aids that student is failing to use and interpret correctly. Archer and Gleason (1989) found direct teaching of interpretation of tables and graphics, such as pie graphs, pictographs, bar graphs, and line graphs, to be particularly efficient. In a few short days, a student could answer questions above a 90% level. They taught their strategy by demonstrating and guiding students through a series of steps. First, the teacher and students determined the topic of the graphic material by interpreting the title or caption. Then they looked at the numbers or words across the bottom or top and up and down the left side to understand the organization of the graphic. The students located information in the graphic and answered literal questions about the information. Comparisons were made by using the nonnumerical information in the graph (e.g., size of the pie pieces, height of the bars, etc.) as well as the numerical information. The teacher guided the students in calculating answers to questions by adding, subtracting, or multiplying information in the graphs. Finally, students made inferences based on the information.

In some lessons, students learned to compare information from two graphs. The teacher provided relevant information, demonstrated how the comparison of two graphs works, and asked a set of structured questions about a particular set of graphs (Figure 3). The series of questions might sound like this: What are the titles of the two graphs we're going to compare? Notice how the numbers of miners in Virginia and Utah have declined over the years. Why might the number of miners have declined? What do the numbers across the bottom of each graph refer to? What do the numbers on the left side of each graph refer to? In which year were the most miners employed in Vir-

ginia? In which year were the fewest number of miners employed in Virginia? How many more miners worked in Utah than in Virginia in 1925? Figure out the difference between the number of miners in the two states in 1945. What was the total number of people employed in the mines for the two highest employment years in Virginia?

Students also must be taught when to refer to the visual aids and how to move from reading the text to the aid and back again. Typically, various cues are embedded in text to let the reader know when to refer to a visual aid. Some cues may take the form of explicit directions (such as "see diagram") but text often has cues that are only implicit, such as a general discussion of a subject that is supplemented with a visual aid but includes no explicit reference to the visual. Readers should be taught to read in the text to the point where discussion covers information that might correspond to that illustrated in a proximate visual aid, place a finger at that place in the text, refer to the visual aid, examine the information, then resume reading where the finger was keeping the place. Teachers must emphasize to students that they must not skip the visual aids while reading a content area textbook.

Responding to Information Learned from Content Area Textbooks

The previous section presented strategies that students could use to gain information from content area textbooks. A second major goal in content area classes is to lead students to respond to information learned from content area textbooks. Using study skills to respond is difficult for students who must create their own strategies without direct help from the teacher. It is possible for students to design their own strategies, but they are frequently time-consuming and ineffective. For example, a student might decide, in order to do well on content area tests, to memorize every sentence of an assigned chapter. Clearly, the student must be introduced to a more efficient strategy. Students need strategies that will

C. Comparing two line graphs

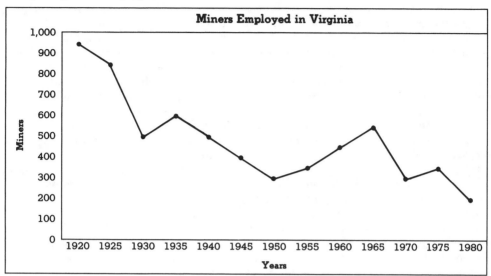

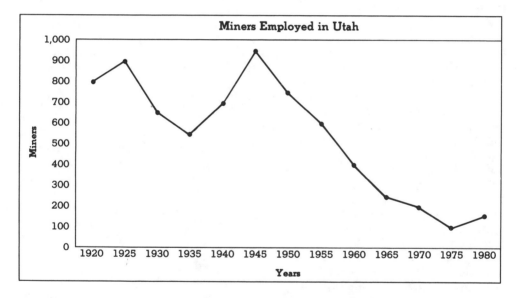

FIGURE 3. Pair of graphs appropriate for demonstrating how information can be derived from comparison of graphs.. From *Skills for school success: Book five* (p. 102), by A. Archer and M. Gleason, 1989, North Billerica, MA: Curriculum Associates. Copyright 1989 by Curriculum Associates. Reprinted by permission.

assist them in (a) answering questions at the end of a chapter or on worksheets, (b) performing well on tests and quizzes, (c) writing summaries of what they read, (d) writing papers or reports, and (e) participating in discussions. Only the first three will be discussed here because Archer and Gleason have not finished designing and field-testing strategies for the latter two.

Answering questions about assigned chapter. To respond to information learned from their reading, students typically must answer questions at the end of chapters in texts or on worksheets prepared by teachers. To be able to accomplish these activities successfully, students must be taught directly to turn the question into part of the answer, find the answer in the text material, write the complete answer to the question, and proofread their answers. Archer and Gleason (1989) teach all four components in two strategies called *Answering Chapter Questions* and *Proofreading Your Assignments.*

Before learning the Answering Chapter Questions strategy, students must be taught to read the question carefully, turn the question into part of the answer, then write that part down. This initial step is beneficial to students because it gives them a way to focus on the content of the question and a written referent while they are looking back in the chapter for the answer. It also helps the students write a complete sentence for the answer and ensures that they will answer the question that was asked. Working on the preparatory skill of turning the question into part of the answer may take many practice sessions before students are ready to learn the Answering Chapter Questions strategy. When they have mastered this skill, the teacher demonstrates and guides the students through the whole strategy. The teacher begins by having the students preview, then read a chapter or part of a chapter. Then the students on their own read a question carefully, and change the question into part of the answer and write that part down (see the model in Part A of Figure 4). After writing down part of the answer, students locate headings or subheadings in the section of the chapter that treats the topic indicated by the question. They read that section of the chapter until they find the answer, then write the rest of the answer so that they have a complete sentence that answers the question. After repeated practice with the teacher, students use this strategy independently.

Writing summaries of materials read. Writing a summary of what has been read can help students remember and comprehend text material (Murrell & Surber, 1987), as well as provide the type of writing practice that will be needed for writing reports or research papers. Despite its benefits, summarizing is a difficult skill to develop to proficiency (Brown & Day, 1983; Hare & Borchardt, 1984). Students must determine what information should be included and excluded and how the information should be reorganized and reworded into a concise summary.

The most explicit strategy found in the literature was one developed by Sheinker and Sheinker (1989). Their strategy guided students in summarizing content area material by teaching students to first skim a passage and list key points, then to combine related points into single statements, cross out the least important points, reread the list, and combine and cross out some statements to condense the points. Finally, the remaining points are numbered in a logical order and written into a paragraph in numbered order (p. 135).

Taking tests. When studying for and taking tests, students must be taught a strategy for anticipating what will be on the test, a strategy for studying and memorizing the necessary information, and a strategy for responding to specific test formats (e.g., multiple-choice, true-false, etc.). The first strategy can be taught through the self-questioning summarization strategy developed by Wong et al. (9186) and in the note-taking strategy designed by Archer and Gleason (1989), which have been described above.

The second part of test taking — studying and memorizing the necessary information — can be accomplished with the RCRC strategy also described earlier (Archer & Gleason, 1989) or with any number of mnemonic strategies reported in the literature (e.g., Mastropieri, Scruggs, & Levin, 1985; Schumaker, Deshler, Alley, & Warner, 1983). The third part of the test-taking strategy, responding to specific formats (e.g., multiple-choice, true–false, etc.), should be taught in several forms. Students should be taught one form for each testing format that they will be faced

Lesson 27 Changing a Question into Part of the Answer

A. Listen to your teacher change a question into part of the answer.

    1. What is the study of fossils called? <u>The study of fossils is called</u>. . .
    2. Why must an organism be buried quickly in order to form a fossil?
       <u>An organism must be buried quickly in order to form a fossil because</u>. . .
    3. How does a fossil form? <u>A fossil forms</u>. . .

B. Work with your teacher to change each question into part of the answer.

    1. Where are most fossils found?

    _____

    2. What parts of animals are preserved?

    _____

    3. How do the remains of living things become petrified?

    _____

    4. What happens when a living thing becomes petrified?

    _____

C. Read each question carefully. Then change the question into part of the answer. Do not complete the answer.

    1. How does a fossil in sedimentary rock form?

    _____

    2. What do index fossils tell scientists?

    _____

    3. How old would a rock containing trilobites be?

    _____

    4. Why are most fossils found in bodies of water?

    _____

    5. How is a mold formed?

    _____

    6. How does wood become petrified?

    _____

FIGURE 4. Worksheet for training students in following the Answering Chapter Questions strategy. From *Skills for school success: Book five* (p. 50), by A. Archer and M. Gleason, 1989, North Billerica, MA: Curriculum Associates. Copyright 1989 by Curriculum Associates. Reprinted by permission.

with. The following is an example of a teaching procedure for teaching students how to take a multiple-choice test (Archer & Gleason, 1989).

The teacher explains the test-taking steps to the students, then guides students in use of the strategy. Students begin by reading the first test item carefully, reading the choices while noting the presence of *all of the above* and *none of the above*, and crossing out the obviously wrong choices. Then, the students pick the best answer from the remaining choices. If they can't answer a question, they learn to put a mark next to it and come back to it later. Finally, students learn to check their answers. They also learn the rule that they should change an answer only for a very good reason, because their first answer is usually the best.

The teacher guides the students in applying the test-taking steps to several multiple-choice items, some with *all of the above* and some with *none of the above* as one of the choices. Students complete some items independently, then check answers with the teacher. The teacher provides several opportunities for practice and students use the strategy each time they complete a multiple-choice test.

Scruggs, Mastropieri, and Tolfa-Veit (1986) found that mildly handicapped (MH) fourth- fifth- and sixth-grade students who received training on test-taking skills like those required for the Stanford Achievement Test (SAT) scored significantly higher on tests of reading decoding and math concepts. They concluded that the results of this and previous investigations suggest that MH students know more than they are able to demonstrate on published tests. Furthermore, training in test-taking skills should be undertaken not only to add to the strategy repertoire of these students but also to promote generalization and transfer of learned information.

Organizing Information

Managing the use of time for school tasks and managing materials used in completion of school tasks are important parts of being successful students. These management skills become more critical to students' success around Grade 3 and continue to increase in importance as students move from one grade level to the next. Mildly handicapped students, in particular, have difficulty locating homework, coming to class with materials, and tracking when assignments are due.

Three major organizational skills must be modeled directly by teachers, practiced by the students, and reinforced on a daily basis. The first skill is the organization of materials in a notebook or set of folders for easy retrieval and for study. The second skill is the organization of time through the use of an assignment calendar so that students can record assignments, determine nightly homework activities, and remember important events. The third skill is the completion of neat, well-organized papers so that the appearance meets the standards usually expected of successful students.

Notebook organization. Students must be taught to build an organizational system that allows them to store papers, retrieve necessary materials, and transport materials between classroom and home (Archer & Gleason, 1989). Intermediate and secondary students can use a three-ring notebook that contains a pen and pencil pouch, pocket dividers for each subject area, and notebook paper. Younger students might be taught to use two folders: one for in-class use and one for taking things home. The pockets of the in-class folder might be labeled "Paper" and "Work" and the take-home folder "Leave at Home" and "Bring Back to School." Students with notebooks should label each divider with the name of a subject area, then label one divider "Extra Paper" for blank notebook paper and one divider with the word "Take Home" for finished work or notices to parents to take home. The pen and pencil pouch is placed at the front of the notebook.

Regardless of the system used, notebook or folders, the teacher must demonstrate how to use the system, then provide daily opportunities for students to *practice* storing and retrieving materials and keeping materials organized, or reorganizing materials if they have become unorganized. Teachers can encourage maintenance of organization systems through a variety of activities. They can tell students how organized materials will help them be better students, just as remembering their work materials would help them be a good employee. They might assist students in placing papers behind the correct pocket divider in the notebook each time a paper is handed back. Frequent feedback regarding notebook organization can be given and students can learn to use a checklist to give themselves feedback about their organization. Teachers can praise students who remember to take notebooks home, bring them back, and take them to other classes, and they can invite students to show their organized notebooks to significant school personnel (e.g., the principal). The teacher can use any activity that promotes the notebook as integral to the daily successes of students.

Assignment calendars. As students begin to assume responsibility for longer assignments and for bringing various materials home (Grades 3 and above), they must be taught basic time management skills. One of these skills involves keeping a monthly assignment calendar on which students record when assignments are due or when special events will occur (Archer & Gleason, 1989). Students also can learn to use their calendars to determine nightly study activities, such as reading several pages in their content area textbook, studying notes for a test on Friday, or beginning to collect samples of objects that demonstrate earth science principles.

Teaching the assignment calendar skills requires teaching a number of component skills first. Students must learn to locate today's date on a monthly calendar, locate a due date given a variety of directions, write abbreviations for subject areas and for assignments, and record appropriate calendar entries. Once they have learned those component skills, they begin to plan for nightly activities by breaking homework assignments into small parts and using calendar entries to determine homework assignments that should be completed. The teacher should teach each of these components separately and provide many opportunities for practice.

After the preskills have been demonstrated and practiced, the teacher can give assignments and ask students to record them on their calendars, then follow through by asking students to turn in their assignments on the date due. Teaching students to maintain the use of the assignment calendars throughout the school year is a challenging task. A large class calendar located in front of the room can be made each month, on which are recorded the assignments that should have been included in individual calendars. The teacher can assist students in daily use of the calendars by providing time each day for them to consult their calendars and prepare materials to take home that will help them with their homework. Students can also be encouraged to show their assignment calendars to their parents and tell them about homework assignments and special events.

Neat papers. A third organizational skill is that of organizing the written papers that students complete. Students frequently hear teachers ask them to make their papers neater but most students *do not know* the attributes of a neat, well-organized paper. These features include use of a heading, organized appearance, and neat writing. In a strategy called HOW, Archer & Gleason (1989) introduced students to the standards outlined in Figure 5.

The standards for neat and well-organized papers are taught also through demonstration and guided practice. The teacher should present positive examples that show what is wanted in a neat paper and negative examples that illustrate what is not desired in a student paper. The purpose for showing both positive and negative examples is to demonstrate the difference to the students, so that they can determine for themselves when their papers have achieved a neat appearance and when they do not look acceptable.

HOW Should Your Papers Look?

H = Heading

1. First and last name
2. Date
3. Subject
4. Page number if needed

O = Organized

1. On the front side of the paper
2. Left margin
3. Right margin
4. At least one blank line at the top
5. At least one blank line at the bottom
6. Good spacing

W = Written neatly

1. Words and numbers on the lines
2. Words and numbers written neatly
3. Neat erasing or crossing out

FIGURE 5. Checklist indicating the standards to be applied in the HOW strategy. From *Skills for school success: Teacher's manual* (p. 166), by A. Archer and M. Gleason, 1989, North Billerica, MA: Curriculum Associates. Copyright 1989 by Curriculum Associates. Reprinted by permission.

Students should practice evaluating other people's papers until they understand what makes a paper attractive; then they should begin evaluating their own papers.

Teachers can assist students in maintaining use of this skill by following up with a number of activities. For example, teachers might make a large poster that states the standards and one that shows an example of an attractive paper, posting them in the front of the room. They might provide a checklist to students so they can evaluate their papers' appearance. Papers that are well done can be displayed publicly on a bulletin board or in the hallway. Or, excellent papers can be shared with parents at conference time. To encourage constant attention to producing neat papers, teachers can ask students to redo papers if they do not meet the standards.

GENERAL PROCEDURES FOR TEACHING STRATEGIES

For each study strategy to be learned, students must receive teacher-directed instruction on separate components of the strategy before incorporating them into an entire strategy. For example, for writing answers to questions at the end of a textbook chapter, students must be taught separate strategies for turning the question into part of the answer, for finding the answer in the text material, for writing the complete answer to the question, and for proofreading their answers. Likewise, when studying for and taking tests, students must be taught a strategy for anticipating what will be on the test, a strategy for studying and memorizing the necessary information, and a strategy for responding to specific formats (e.g., multiple-choice, true–false, etc.). Learning to perform each step in the strategy before attempting to use the entire strategy will provide students with more immediate success and will result in more efficient learning of the strategy.

To achieve the goal of enabling mildly handicapped learners actively and independently to use study strategies, the teacher must systematically follow several steps (Gleason, 1988). When teaching a new strategy, the rationale for the strategy first should be discussed with the students. In part, this rationale should center around how the new strategy will contribute to success in school and how it will assist the student to become a more active participant in class. Next, the teacher should use all the design principles that would be used to teach any new cognitive routine, for example, long division (Engelmann & Carnine, 1982). The teacher would demonstrate or model the strategy, prompt or guide students in use of the strategy, and finally, check the students' use of the strategy without the teacher's assistance. The model, guide, and check series of steps will be explained as they apply to instruction in study strategies.

Modeling the Strategy

Teaching any strategy requires teachers to present an initial demonstration of it. While they are demonstrating, they should exaggerate the critical steps in the strategy and, at the same time, describe exactly what they are doing. Stating explicitly what they are thinking is an important part of their instruction. For example, when teaching students how to use an index, the instructors should open a book to the index and demonstrate how to run a finger down the page until the correct letter of the alphabet is located and then until the desired topic is located. At the same time, they should talk about what they are doing and what they are looking for. Then they demonstrate and talk about how to determine the pages to look at within the textbook to find the desired information.

Guiding Students through the Strategy

Using a novel situation or different materials, the student is guided through the strategy by the teacher, who asks questions ad listens for correct answers from the students. Several opportunities (at least three) are provided for practice. For each practice opportunity, a novel situation or new set of materials is used. By providing novel situations and materials, the teacher is showing the students that the steps in the strategy remain the same across a wide range of situations and materials. For example, when teaching students to use an index for locating particular information, the teacher provides several different textbooks, each with an index that looks different, and is organized a little differently, from the others. Students are shown that the purpose for, and the way they use, an index remains the same. As the guided practice continues, the teacher, by cueing or prompting the next step less and less, allows the students to employ more and more of the strategy on their own.

Checking Student Performance of the Strategy

After two or three sessions of guided practice, students should practice the strategy independently. The teacher can show students how to become independent users of the strategy by teaching them to use verbal rehearsal (Dawson, Hallahan, Reeve, & Ball, 1980) and/or self-monitoring (Gelzheiser, Sheperd, & Wozniak, 1986; Wong & Jones, 1982). Once the students are independent users of the strategy in a particular context or content area, they must learn to generalize the strategy to other settings.

GENERALIZATION AND TRANSFER

One of the major assumptions underlying special education services for mildly handicapped students at all grade levels is that eventually students will be able to *use* the skills and behaviors they learn in special education in other settings. The transfer setting might be a regular classroom, a social situation, or an employment situation. However, transfer cannot be taken for granted. In most cases, mildly handicapped students do not automatically transfer the skills they learn from one setting to another (Anderson-Inman, Walker, & Purcell, 1984; Brown, Bransford, Ferrara, & Campione, 1983; Ellis, Lenz, & Sabornie, 1987a). These students typically lack the organizational and study skills needed to approach a new situation and meet its demands.

For example, suppose students are taught to identify the key idea in a paragraph. The examples used are from worksheets and are composed of three or four sentences. The students are then presented with a textbook to identify the main idea in a second paragraph, which happens to be seven sentences long. It would not be surprising to find that many of the students were not able to complete the task, for the very particular reason that they were not taught to work from paragraphs in a textbook and they were not taught to identify the key idea for paragraphs with more than three or four sentences.

This kind of problem is called a generalization problem. A skill has been *generalized* when the student can reliably perform the skill with untrained examples in a variety of settings. For example, suppose that a student who has learned to apply the paragraph rule (identify the key idea) with examples taken in the course of instruction from worksheets, textbooks, and journals, is asked to identify the key idea in a paragraph from a newspaper. If the student is successful, we can conclude that he or she has learned a generalized skill on the basis that a newspaper was not presented as an example during the lessons.

Teachers frequently do not attend to generalization techniques until after instruction has been completed. However, to ensure generalization and transfer of study strategies to other settings and other sets of materials, teachers must systematically plan for that to occur. Teachers can organize generalization planning around three time frames: before, during, and after strategy instruction. Not all suggestions in the following section need to be utilized for each strategy taught, but the listing can serve as an outline for teachers' planning.

Generalization Planning Before Instruction

Two major procedures used before instruction will increase the probability that students will generalize skills to other settings and environments. Teachers must carefully select relevant study skills to teach to their students and then must follow at least two basic rules in choosing the examples to be used for instruction.

Carefully select relevant study skills. Because the major purpose for teaching study skills is to empower students for success and promote independent learning, the strategies taught must be of particular relevance to the students. For example, if students attend three classes in which the teacher lectures, learning a strategy for taking notes from lectures would meet an immediate need. In addition, teachers must select skills that can be applied in a variety of settings, have proven effectiveness, and have a specific outcome that can be observed by the teacher. If the study skills taught are relevant to the students' success in school, students are more likely to use the skills.

Basic rules. To promote generalization, teachers should apply the following two rules in choosing examples for instruction.

First rule. Select teaching examples that sample the range of examples likely to be encountered. When a particular skill is targeted for instruction, the teachers should examine the contexts in which that particular skill is likely to be needed or applied. For example, suppose the teacher decides to teach the students comprehension and specifically to teach the rule that a paragraph has one key idea. The first step would be to identify the various contexts in which the students are likely to be required to read paragraphs at school. These contexts could include worksheets, overheads, workbooks, textbooks, novels, periodicals, newspapers, letters, and magazines. Teaching examples should then be selected to adequately represent the range of examples included in these contexts (Horner, Bellamy, & Colvin, 1984).

Instruction is more likely to be effective if the teaching examples are sequenced so that successive examples are maximally different and cover a range of examples that communicate a breadth of application to students. The assumption is that by teaching the paragraph using these *representative* examples the student would be able to apply the skill to *all* examples. For example, the first example used in teaching the paragraph rule could be an overhead. The successive examples could be paragraphs from a textbook, a worksheet, and a newspaper. Similarly, examples could be sequenced on the basis of print variation (overhead, handwriting; textbook, offset printing; worksheet, computer dot matrix printing). In addition the length of the paragraph should vary (overhead, three sentences; textbook, six sentences, worksheet, two sentences; newspaper, five sentences). In effect these successive examples are sequenced to show maximum variation across the possible variables.

Second rule. Since students may not be able to apply skills taught to mastery to examples not used in instruction, examples should be introduced that were not part of the initial teaching set, in order to test acquisition of the generalized skill. Let us suppose that a student has met criteria on the skill of identifying the key idea in a paragraph (it is assumed that the teaching examples were representative of the contexts likely to be encountered by the student and the examples were sequenced so that successive examples were maximally different). Test examples, for example, a periodical and/or a letter, should now be introduced that were not used in teaching. Other variations that were not used in initial training could also be introduced, such as a periodical that utilizes three columns of print (given that the training examples had one or two columns of print).

Generalization Planning During Instruction

While the teacher is demonstrating and guiding students through a new study strategy, several steps can be taken to promote generalization and transfer.

Provide rationale for use of the strategy. As discussed earlier in the chapter, the teacher can assist students in understanding the relevance of learning a particular strategy by explaining what is to be gained by its use. In particular, emphasize the increased success that students likely will experience after learning a new study skill.

Discuss when and where the strategy can be used. In addition to discussing why students should learn the strategy, teachers should discuss when and where students might use the strategy. Teachers also might ask students to name other settings and other sets of materials in which they could use their new study strategy.

Ensure that students achieve mastery of the new strategy. In all cases, systematic instruction must be provided that ensures that students become proficient in the use of a particular study skill. If students cannot perform the skill at a high level of success in the training setting, they probably will not generalize use of the skill to another setting.

Teach students effective self-monitoring or self-evaluation procedures. While receiving instruction on using a strategy independently, students will benefit from learning self-management skills such as self-questioning, self-monitoring, self-evaluation, or self-recording skills (Gelzheiser et al., 1986; Wong & Jones, 1982). Later, students can use these skills to monitor their progress in other settings.

Generalization Planning After Instruction

While it is important to address generalization before and during instruction, teachers also must attend to it after instruction. Typically, mildly handicapped students forget what they have learned if it is no longer reviewed or maintained.

Inform others of new strategies. While it would be ideal if all teachers encountered by a group of students would teach and require use of study strategies, occasionally study strategies are taught in one setting (e.g., resource room) with the expectation of generalization to another setting (e.g., regular classroom). In this case, regular classroom teachers should be encouraged to review a new strategy in their classes, display a poster listing the steps in the strategy, and reinforce use of the strategy on a consistent basis. Teachers might teach the steps in the strategy to everyone in the regular class, and then pair more successful students with less successful students until they are independently using the new strategy in the transfer setting.

Tell students to use the strategy in other settings. While this procedure may seem obvious, many teachers do not routinely tell students to use new skills in other settings. At the end of a lesson or at the end of a school day, teachers should remind students that new strategies are to be used in other classes throughout the school day.

Ask students to verbalize their success with strategies in other settings. Many mildly handicapped students experience difficulty in associating their skills and knowledge with their successes in school. To strengthen this association, teachers should encourage students to report their use of new strategies in other settings. Teachers should show particular interest in students' reports of increased

success in other settings that can be attributed directly to the use of study strategies.

Discuss cues in other settings that signal use of the strategy. Generalization of study skills is particularly difficult because they are content-free and not associated with certain subjects or classroom tasks. For this reason, it is important to discuss the similarities and differences between the response demands and cues of the training setting and those of the transfer setting. For example, the cue for taking notes in the training setting may be the teachers' announcing that students should take out notebook paper and begin taking notes. The cue for taking notes in the transfer setting may be the same, but it might be the teacher's announcement that students are going to have a test on Friday or the teacher's writing an outline on the blackboard while talking about a particular topic.

Use role-playing to practice transfer to other settings. Assisting students in role-playing transfer of skills to other settings is especially beneficial if the response demands and cues of the other settings are considerably different from those used during the training. For example, students could practice responding to various cues that indicate that it is time to listen to the teacher and take notes. The teacher who is presenting study strategies to the students might mix up a variety of cues to see if the students can choose which study strategy to use. Students need many opportunities to practice and review all the strategies they've learned.

ROLE OF THE SCHOOL PSYCHOLOGIST WITH REGARD TO STUDY SKILLS

While direct service in the area of study skills would not be practical, a number of clear-cut functions could be served by the school psychologist in relation to the implementation of study skills.

School psychologists can create an awareness of the need for study skills interventions at a prereferral level. In the Colvin and Gleason (1989) survey, school psychologists were in strong agreement that deficits in study skills contributed to referrals for learning disabilities and behavior disorders. It would seem appropriate that school psychologists advocate or simply raise the possibility of testing for and teaching study skills at a prereferral level.

The Colvin & Gleason survey indicated that school psychologists typically do not test for deficits in study skills. School psychologists might be interested in developing tests to assess a student's level of proficiency in study skills. Some level of testing in the area of study skills should become a routine part of the battery of tests that are typically administered following a referral.

The IEP should be used for establishing study skills interventions as procedures for meeting students' individualized needs. If the testing reveals weaknesses in the area of study skills, the school psychologist should advocate that the IEP reflect study skills as an intervention or strategy.

School psychologists identified in the survey the need for systematic in-service in the area of study skills. It would seem appropriate for presentations to be offered in study skills at national and state conferences for school psychologists. In addition, articles in the area of study skills could be solicited for the school psychology journals such as *School Psychology Review*.

REFERENCES

Adams, A., Carnine, D., & Gersten, R. (1982). Instructional strategies for studying content area texts in the intermediate grades. *Reading Research Quarterly, 13*(1), 27-55.

Anderson-Inman, L., Walker, H., & Purcell, J. (1984). Promoting the transfer of skills across handicapped students in the mainstream. In W. L. Heward, T. E. Heron, D. S. Hill, & J. Trap-Porter (Eds.), *Focus on behavior analysis in education*. Columbus, OH: Merrill.

Archer, A., & Gleason, M. (1989). *Skills for school success (grades 3-6)*. North Billerica, MA: Curriculum Associates.

Archer, A., & Gleason, M. (1990). Direct instruction in content area reading. In D. Carnine, J. Silbert, & E. Kameenui (Eds.), *Direct instruction reading* (rev. ed.). Columbus, OH: Merrill.

Aukerman, R. C. (1972). *Reading in the secondary school*. New York: McGraw-Hill.

Brown, A. L., Bransford, J. D., Ferrara, R. A., & Campione, J. C. (1983). Learning, remembering, and understanding. In J. H. Flavell & E. M. Markman (Eds.), *Handbook of child psychology* (4th ed., Vol. 3, pp. 77-166). New York: Wiley.

Brown, A. L., & Day, J. D. (1983). Macro-rules for summarizing texts: The development of expertise. *Journal of Verbal Learning and Verbal Behavior, 22*, 1-14.

Chan, L. K., & Cole, P. G. (1986). The effects of comprehension monitoring training on the reading competence of learning disabled and regular class students. *Remedial and Special Education, 7*(4), 33-40.

Colvin, G., & Gleason, M. (1989). School psychologist survey: Study skills. Unpublished data, University of Oregon.

Dawson, M. M., Hallahan, D. D., Reeve, R. E., & Ball, D. W. (1980). The effect of reinforcement and verbal rehearsal on selective attention in learning disabled children. *Journal of Abnormal Child Psychology 8*, 133-144.

Deshler, D. D., & Schumaker, J. B. (1986). Learning strategies: An instructional alternative for low-achieving adolescents. *Exceptional Children, 52*(6), 583-590.

Devine, T. G. (1987). *Teaching study skills: A guide for teachers* (2nd ed.). Boston: Allyn & Bacon.

Ellis, E. S., Lenz, B. K., & Sabornie, E. J. (1987a). Generalization and adaptation of learning strategies to natural environments: Part 1: Critical agents. *Remedial and Special Education, 8*(1), 6-20.

Ellis, E. S., Lenz, B. K., & Sabornie, E. J. (1987b). Generalization and adaptation of learning strategies to natural environments: Part 2: Research into practice. *Remedial and Special Education, 8*(2), 6-23.

Engelmann, S., & Carnine, D. (1982). *Theory of instruction: Principles and applications*. New York: Irvington.

Gelzheiser, L. M., Cort, R., & Shepherd, M. J. (1987). Is minimal strategy instruction sufficient for LD children? — Testing the production deficiency hypothesis. *Learning Disability Quarterly, 10*, 267-275.

Gelzheiser, L. M., Sheperd, M. J., & Wozniak, R. H. (1986). The development of instruction to induce skill transfer. *Exceptional Children, 53,* 125-129.

Gleason, M. M. (1988). Teaching study strategies. *Teaching Exceptional Children, 20*(3), 52-53.

Gleason, M., & Archer, A. (1989). *Critical school behaviors and study skills needed in junior high school content area classes.* Unpublished manuscript, University of Oregon.

Hare, V. C., & Borchardt, K. M. (1984). Direct instruction of summarization skills. *Reading Research Quarterly, 21,* 62-78.

Horner, R. H., Bellamy, G. T., & Colvin, G. T. (1984). Responding in the presence of nontrained stimuli: Implications of generalization error patterns. *Journal of the Association for Persons with Severe Handicaps, 9*(4), 287-295.

Mastropieri, M. A., Scruggs, T. E., & Levin, J. R. (1985). Maximizing what exceptional students can learn: A review of research on the keyword method and related mnemonic techniques. *Remedial and Special Education, 6*(2), 39-45.

Murrell, P. C., Jr., & Surber, J. R. (1987, April). *The effect of generative summarization on the comprehension of main ideas from lengthy expository text.* Paper presented at the annual meeting of the American Educational Research Association, Washington, DC.

Newman, R. S., & Hagen, J. W. (1981). Memory strategies in children with learning disabilities. *Journal of Applied Developmental Psychology, 1,* 297-312.

Ringel, B. A., & Springer, C. J. (1980). On knowing how well one is remembering: The persistence of strategy during transfer. *Journal of Experimental Child Psychology, 29,* 322-333.

Schumaker, J. B., Denton, P. H., & Deshler, D. D. (1984). *The paraphrasing strategy.* Lawrence, KS: The University of Kansas.

Schumaker, J. B., Deshler, D. D., Alley, G. R., & Warner, M. M. (1983). Toward the development of an intervention model for learning disabled adolescents. *Exceptional Education Quarterly, 3*(4), 45-50.

Schumaker, J. B., Deshler, D. D., Alley, G. R., Warner, M. M., & Denton, P. H. (1982). Multipass: A learning strategy for improving reading comprehension. *Learning Disability Quarterly, 5,* 295-304.

Scruggs, T. E., Mastropieri, M. A., & Tolfa-Veit, D. (1986). The effects of coaching on the standardized test performance of learning disabled and behaviorally disordered students. *Remedial and Special Education, 7*(5), 37-41.

Sheinker, J., & Sheinker, A. (1989). *Metacognitive approach to study strategies.* Rockville, MD: Aspen.

Torgesen, J. K. (1977). Memorization processes in reading disabled children. *Journal of Educational Psychology, 69,* 571-578.

Torgesen, J. K. (1982). The learning-disabled child as an inactive learner: Educational implications. *Topics in Learning and Learning Disabilities, 2,* 45-52.

Wong, B. Y. L., & Jones, W. (1982). Increasing metacomprehension in learning disabled and normally achieving students through self-questioning training. *Learning Disability Quarterly, 5,* 228-240.

Wong, B. Y. L., Wong, R., Perry, N., & Sawatsky, D. (1986). The efficacy of a self-questioning summarization strategy for use by underachievers and learning disabled adolescents in social studies. *Learning Disabilities Focus, 2,* 20-35.

Measuring and Teaching Social Skills in the Mainstream

Edward J. Sabornie
North Carolina State University

The social competence of students with mild handicapping conditions — that is, learning disabilities (LD), mild mental retardation (MMR), or behavior disorders (BD) — as an assessment and intervention domain is of interest to school psychologists for a number of reasons. Some of these are the difficulties that these students can have when attempting to fit in with mainstream classrooms, make and keep friends, get along with coworkers on the job, and adjust to various interpersonal demands of everyday life. Four decades ago, Johnson and Kirk (1950) found that handicapped students were socially rejected by nonhandicapped classmates because

> "he teases me," "he cheats in games," "he pulls my hair," "he hits me over the head with his lunch bucket," "he says bad things," "he takes my jumping rope," "he steals my bicycles," "he stinks." (p. 87)

No doubt many of these same concerns hold true today.

Research has shown that students with mild handicaps of all ages evince a vast array of social problems. Mildly handicapped pupils, in comparison to those without handicaps, often are rejected socially in mainstream classrooms (Bruininks, Rynders, & Gross, 1974; Bryan, 1974, 1976; Gottlieb, Gottlieb, Berkell, & Levy, 1986; Rucker, Howe, & Snider, 1969; Vacc, 1968, 1972). Likewise, some mildly handicapped adolescents and youth reject their nonhandicapped classmates (Sabor-

nie, 1987; Sabornie & Kauffman, 1987). Other research has demonstrated that mildly handicapped students have social cognition deficiencies (i.e., lack ability to comprehend others' nonverbal behaviors, or intentions, motives, and emotions; see Bachara, 1976; Bryan, 1977; Maheady, Maitland, & Sainato, 1984; Pearl & Cosden, 1982; Wiig & Harris, 1974). Furthermore, students with mild handicaps attract fewer friendships than nonhandicapped comparison students (Zetlin & Murtaugh, 1988); mildly handicapped adolescents express dissatisfaction with their social lives (White, Schumaker, Warner, Alley, & Deshler, 1980); and low participation rates in school-related and out-of-school group activities characterize certain mildly handicapped pupils (Deshler & Schumaker, 1983; Sabornie, Thomas, & Coffman, 1989). Finally, loneliness is typical in students identified as mildly handicapped (Luftig, 1988; Sabornie et al., 1989). It appears, therefore, that more than sufficient data exist to validate the inclusion of social skills instruction as an important component of educational treatment for students with mild handicaps.

Additional justification for targeting the social competence of mildly handicapped students is found in the psychological risk literature. For example, Kupersmidt (1983) demonstrated a relationship between student social rejection of students and their risk of repeating a grade in school, dropping out, and becoming involved in juvenile delinquency. Other studies, although somewhat dated, have demonstrated that (a) socially rejected elementary school students face later psychological adjustment problems (Cowen, Pederson, Babigian, Izzo, & Trost, 1973); (b) students with social skills deficits are at risk for psychiatric hospitalization (Goldsmith & McFall, 1975); and (c) social status problems are correlated with juvenile delinquency (Roff, Sells, & Golden, 1972). Citing the above risk research has become a "perfunctory necessity" (Putallaz & Gottman, 1983) in similar research discussions of poor peer status. It should be noted that these studies did not include students identified as mildly handicapped; however, collectively they indicate that social competence deficits should be viewed as more than simply an inability to make friends or become accepted in a group.

Presented in this chapter are a discussion of valid methods that are used to assess the social domain of students with mild handicaps, and an outline of social skills instruction strategies that have been shown to be effective with students who spend time in mainstream environments. Specific foci address measurement of social capabilities by sociometric techniques and teachers' ratings. These two types of assessment were chosen for their ease of administration and the fidelity of their results. School psychologists, who suffer from ever-increasing demands on their time, should be able to conduct such assessment with few problems. The discussion of interventions features effective techniques to employ with pupils found to be lacking in the basic necessities for social success in the mainstream. For the purpose of social skills treatment presented here, school psychologists can serve as consultants to teachers who implement such instruction in various settings.

ASSESSMENT

Measuring the social characteristics of students in the mainstream is a task that has many technically adequate methodologies. Data from only one type

of social skills assessment should never serve as the *sine qua non* for identification or treatment purposes. The power of social competence assessment is enhanced when multiple measures are included, when perspective is gained from different sources, and when behavior is examined in various settings (Hops, 1983). Furthermore, social skills assessment results are dependent on the measurement devices employed, and they are best viewed in relation to the purpose of assessment: typically identification/classification or intervention/therapy (Gresham, 1986; Hops & Greenwood, 1981). Thus, multifactored social skills measurement results can contribute to an overall sketch of the social problems and strengths of a student.

Sociometry

Sociometric assessment is an example of measurement used for identification of students with peer relationship problems. According to McConnell and Odom (1986), sociometric assessment has three valid concerns: (a) identifying an individual's social position in a group, (b) documenting change in group social position following intervention, and (c) highlighting behavioral characteristics that are related to differential social standing. Below is a description of the different types of sociometric assessment used for the purposes cited by McConnell and Odom.

Peer nomination. Peer nomination is the sociometric assessment method with the longest history of use in classrooms. Administration of this type of sociometry is relatively uncomplicated; examiners simply ask respondents to list a specific number of classmates (usually 3-5, but the number can be unrestricted) whom they wish to work or play with, or sit next to, and so on. Also, participants can be asked to list the classmates they like best or those who are their best friends in the same room. The specific style of question asked and its wording should be chosen with caution, for nominations can change when students are asked to name workmates versus playmates or best friends. The relative number of positive nominations determines the level of popularity or friendship among group members.

Negative nominations also can be used to determine a different category of sociometric status (i.e., dislike or rejection). Nominations of this type ask participants to name peers whom they like least, those with whom they do not like to play, and so on. Although sociometric choices described with negative statements have been used less frequently than choices with only positive criteria, negative nominations are necessary for comprehensive screening of children who may need social skills intervention. Ethical concerns often have prevented sociometric practitioners from including negative nominations in their efforts to determine social standing of target children. Some have assumed, for example, that having students name others they do not like may serve as a catalyst for additional negative perceptions and rejection in social interactions. Some experts (e.g., Havyren & Hymel, 1983; Hops & Lewin, 1984), however, have questioned the notion that use of negative criteria in peer nomination is unethical. Additional research is necessary to verify or reject the belief that negatively oriented sociometric choices among classmates lead to questionable research methodologies.

Combining information from both positive and negative classroom nominations leads to identification of children who may be candidates for interventions aimed at improving their social standing among peers. Contemporary methods of treatment of data from peer nominations were first proposed by Peery (1979) and later refined by Coie, Dodge, and Coppotelli (1982), and they require a systematic approach to tabulation. Summing a student's number of positive and negative nominations yields what is called *social impact*. This is viewed as the overall social profile of a target pupil. *Social preference* is derived when the number of negative nominations is subtracted from a student's total of positive sociometric choices. Social preference is viewed as the relative extent to which a person is either liked or rejected in coterie. A positive social preference score indicates that more students are accepting than rejecting a peer. A negative social preference score indicates the opposite. At the classroom level, when social impact and social preference indices are combined and standardized by Z scores, five distinct subgroups of social status are identified (see Coie et al., 1982, for group cut-off scores):

- *Popular:* students very high in social preference, above average in acceptance, and below average in rejection

- *Rejected:* those very low in social preference, above average in rejection, and below average in acceptance

- *Neglected:* pupils with very low social impact scores and zero positive nominations

- *Controversial:* children with very high social impact scores and above average in negative and positive nominations

- *Average:* those near the mean in social preference

Sociometrically rejected students have been described as "at risk" and worthy of attention with regard to social skills treatment. Researchers such as Coie (1985) and Putallaz and Gottman (1983) characterized rejected students as aggressive, unhappy, easily provoked to anger, frequently off-task and disruptive in the classroom, lacking in socially facilitative behavior, uncooperative, tending to seek help often, and disposed to engage in high levels of inappropriate behavior, such as initiating activities that exclude classmates, hitting peers, engaging in aversive verbal and physical behavior, and reacting aggressively to aversive behaviors. Thus, the rejected group are eminently appropriate candidates for the attention of psychologists who are concerned with the social adjustment and competence of students in mainstream classrooms.

Peer nomination techniques have found mildly handicapped students to be sociometrically rejected in mainstream classrooms (e.g., Bryan, 1974, 1976; Bryan & Bryan, 1978; Gresham & Reschly, 1986;

Hutton & Polo, 1976; Iano, Ayers, Heller, McGettigan, & Walker, 1974; Johnson, 1950; Lapp, 1957; Prillaman, 1981; Scranton & Ryckman, 1979; Siperstein, Bopp, & Bak, 1978); however, the Coie et al. (1982) procedures for treatment of nomination data have been applied only recently, as specified here, with these pupils in integrated settings (Kistner & Gatlin, 1989; Stone & La Greca, 1990). There is a clear need for additional research, given concerns about the behavior of rejected children in general.

Sociometric rating scale. An alternative method of sociometric assessment involves the use of rating scales. These instruments also have been applied extensively with mildly handicapped students in regular classrooms (e.g., Baldwin, 1958; Bruininks, 1978a, 1978b; Bruininks et al., 1974; Coben & Zigmond, 1986; Gottlieb & Budoff, 1973; Monroe & Howe, 1971; Rucker et al., 1969; Sabornie, 1987; Sabornie & Kauffman, 1985, 1986, 1987; Sabornie, Kauffman, Ellis, Marshall, & Elksnin, 1987–1988; Sabornie, Marshall, & Ellis, 1988, 1990).

Rating scales ask student respondents to judge classmates listed on a class roster, and a numerical or pictorial (i.e., faces, stick figures) classification is usually associated with each type of rating. Such instruments typically include ratings such as positive (e.g., best friends, other friends), neutral (e.g., not friends but alright), familiarity (e.g., do not know the person), and negative (e.g., do not care for them, dislike them). Participants simply read classmates' names prepared on a class roster and rate each peer with one of the choices. Descriptive paragraphs, which usually include situations such as working with, playing with, and sitting next to a peer, are used to explain and highlight the numerical or other code associated with each rating type.

Three different sociometric rating scales have been used frequently with handicapped students in mainstream classrooms. The *Peer Acceptance Scale* (PAS; Bruininks et al., 1974), a three-category instrument intended for use with elementary-level students, includes stick figures to illustrate ratings of acceptance, neutrality or tolerance, and rejection. Raters choose one of these three categories following each roster name, to best fit each of their classmates. The illustrations used in the PAS appear in Figure 1.

The *How I Feel Toward Others* rating scale (HIFTO; Agard, Veldman, Kaufman, & Semmel, 1978) was developed as part of Project PRIME, a research project that focused on elementary-level students characterized as LD and MMR in various educational environments. The HIFTO is similar to the PAS in that it includes the three rating categories of acceptance, tolerance, and rejection, but also included is a rating of familiarity. The HIFTO's inclusion of a "don't know them" rating is an improvement over the PAS, for peer familiarity exists outside the boundaries of acceptance and rejection and should not be included in overall social status (Sabornie, 1985). The technical adequacy of the HIFTO is particularly robust in light of its standardization for use with mildly handicapped elementary-level students in integrated classrooms. Respondents refer to the HIFTO's illustrations (shown in Figure 2) to rate classmates listed on a roster.

Research using the HIFTO with mildly handicapped students in the mainstream (e.g., Coben & Zigmond, 1986; Sabornie et al., 1988) separated students' ratings into four different types of sociometric status: acceptance (the smiling face), tolerance or neutrality (the straight-mouth face), rejection (the frowning face), and familiarity (the question mark). Similar to the use of positive and negative nominations, this data treatment method, in comparison with using *average* rating scale sociometric status for each target student, results in status that also depicts different types of social standing (e.g., acceptance vs. rejection vs. tolerance). Students having high percentages of total classroom ratings in a negative rating category with few positive ratings, therefore, would be analogous to the group found by the Coie et al. (1982) peer nomination methodology to be rejected. Sabornie, Marshall, and Ellis (1990) used the HIFTO with main-

FIGURE 1. Illustrations used in the *Peer Acceptance Scale*. From "Social acceptance of mildly retarded pupils in resource rooms and regular classes" by R. H. Bruininks, J. E. Ryners, and J. C. Gross, 1974. *American Journal of Mental Deficiency, 78,* pp. 377-383. Copyright 1974 by the American Association on Mental Retardation. Reprinted by permission.

streamed LD students and applied Peery's (1979) data treatment paradigm, which was originally meant for peer nomination data. They found 40% of the LD sample in the popular subgroup (vs. 36% of the nonhandicapped students), 26% of the LD sample in the "amiable" or accepted subgroup (vs. 44% of the nonhandicapped pupils), 14% of the LD sample in the isolated or neglected category (vs. 8% of nonhandicapped students), and 16% of the LD sample in the rejected group (vs. 8% of the nonhandicapped cohorts). Applying methods of treating peer nomination data to rating scale sociometric status, however, awaits further testing with regard to its efficacy for identifying students at risk or in need of improved status among peers. Of equal importance is work aimed at assessing the reliability and validity of these unconventional data treatment procedures.

The *Ohio Social Acceptance Scale* (OSAS; Fordyce, Yauck, & Raths, 1946) is a multiple-category rating scale intended for use with secondary-level respondents. Ratings are numbered 1-6 (found after roster names) and denote the following: 1 = "my very, very best friends"; 2 = "my other friends"; 3 = "not friends, but okay"; 4 = "don't know them"; 5 = "don't care for them"; and 6 = "dislike them." Research using the OSAS with mildly handicapped students in integrated educational settings consistently has shown such pupils to be low in acceptance and high in rejection. For example, Sabornie, Kaufman, and Cullinan (in press) used OSAS rating scale data to determine the mainstream social standing of MMR, LD, and BD adolescents. In that study, the researchers applied the Coie et al. (1982) peer nomination data treatment technique to rating scale scores and found more MMR and more BD students than LD or than nonhandicapped adolescents in the rejected sociometric category. Although replication of this study will determine whether such results are typical of others similarly labeled, the initial results indicate that BD and MMR students may be more socially incompetent among peers than those identified as LD. However, the same limitations dis-

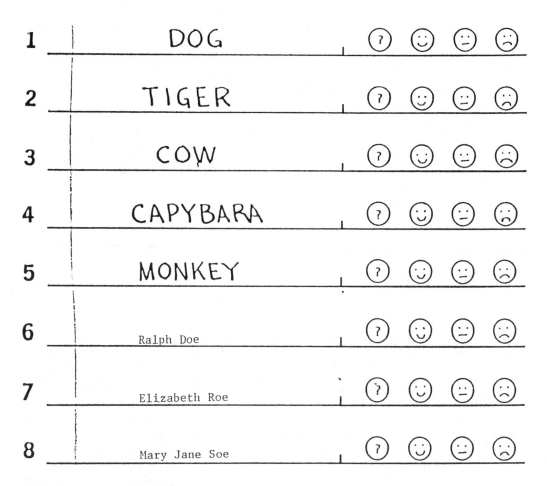

FIGURE 2. Illustrations used in the *How I Feel Toward Others* instrument. From How I Feel Toward Others: An Instrument of the PRIME Instrument Battery, by J. A. Agard, S. M. Veldman, M. J. Kaufman, and M. I. Semmel, 1978. Baltimore: University Park Press. Copyright 1978 by University Park Press. Reprinted by permission.

cussed above (i.e., with regard to reliability, validity, and efficacy for identification of students in need of intervention) also apply to the Sabornie, Kauffman, and Cullinan (in press) data treatment methods.

Sociometric assessment considerations. Several issues should be kept in mind when considering which type of sociometric measurement to employ in mainstream classrooms. Hops and Lewin (1984), for example, stated that peer nomination questions such as "play with" and "work with" are assessing two distinct types of social acceptance. In other words, a playmate may not necessarily be chosen as a workmate. Students have been known to positively nominate a peer but spend very, very little time interacting with him or her in a group (Greenwood, Walker, Todd, & Hops, 1979). There is also some agreement that rating scales measure acceptance or likeability, and peer nomination methods tap friendship (Asher, 1985; Asher & Taylor, 1981; Gresham, 1981; Gresham & Elliott, 1989). Acceptance and friendship, therefore, are not necessarily the same. With mildly handicapped students who have peer relationship problems in the mainstream, perhaps enhancing acceptance is more easily attained than developing friendships (Sabornie & Ellis, 1987).

The sociometric literature also supports the technical adequacy of peer nomination and rating scales. Rating scales tend to have higher test–retest reliability than the peer nomination technique (Asher & Taylor, 1981; Hops & Lewin, 1984). Moreover, because of the many shades of sociometric status that are used (e.g., acceptance, tolerance, rejection), rating scales are more sensitive to change in status over time. The exact role that sociometric tolerance plays in correlations with overt behaviors and adjustment, however, awaits further testing. The validity of sociometric assessment techniques has also been documented in research, although it is important to note here that mainstreamed mildly handicapped students were not featured in the samples studied. Criterion-related validity is shown in the close association between teachers' ratings of peer popularity and acceptance status (Connolly & Doyle, 1981; Greenwood et al., 1979). Sociometrically rejected children simultaneously demonstrate increased aggression and an inability to make friends (Dodge, Coie, & Brakke, 1982; Gottman, Gonso, & Rasmussen, 1975), which indicates concurrent validity strength.

Another consideration involved in sociometry with mildly handicapped students is the relationship between acceptance and rejection. One study (Hartup, Glazer, & Charlesworth, 1967) showed that *peer nomination* acceptance and rejection were correlated only moderately. This finding leads to the conclusion that acceptance and rejection are not opposites of the same continuum, but rather two distinct phenomena on separate continua. However, Sabornie et al. (1988) in research using the HIFTO with LD, BD, and nonhandicapped students, showed that acceptance was significantly — and strongly — correlated with rejection across all three groups (LD: $r = -.91$; BD: $r = -.62$; nonhandicapped: $r = -.66$). Perhaps it is time to reconsider the conclusions drawn by Hartup et al. (1967), especially with mildly handicapped students, when considering the bipolarity of *rating scale* sociometric acceptance and rejection.

Lastly, Parker and Asher (1987) raised another issue that school psychologists should keep in mind when using sociometry with mainstream mildly handicapped children. These authors concluded that sociometrically rejected children may experience such status in only one classroom, but not in other environments outside school. In Parker and Asher's words, such children would become "six-hour unpopular children." Therefore, psychologists need to consider the global (i.e., outside school) peer relationships of children rejected in the classroom.

Teachers' Ratings

The use of teachers' ratings to identify children who lack specific social skills is one of the easiest ways for child study teams to engage in assessment for screening, identification, and intervention. Recent advances in this measurement domain provide strong data with regard to exceptional students in the mainstream. In conjunction with sociometrics, teachers' ratings of social competence provide an accurate depiction of those who may need comprehensive educational treatment that includes instruction in appropriate social behavior. Three instruments that have been developed for use with mildly handicapped pupils, in various educational settings, are reviewed below.

The Walker–McConnell Scale of Social Competence and School Adjustment (WMC). A recently developed social skills teacher rating scale with superb technical adequacy is the Walker–McConnell instrument (Walker & McConnell, 1988). Normed on over 1,800 cases from the four major U.S. census zones, the WMC is one of the best instruments for assessment of the social competence of mildly handicapped students in the mainstream.

The WMC measures school-related interpersonal competence and adaptive behavior of elementary-level students (i.e., K–6). The test consists of 43 items divided into three subscales: Teacher-Preferred Social Behavior (Subscale 1; 16 items), Peer-Preferred Social Behavior (Subscale 2; 17 items), and School Adjustment

Behavior (Subscale 3; 10 items). Respondents reply to the items using a 5-point Likert scale ranging from *never* to *frequently*, and the items are written such that they can be included as objectives on target students' individual education plans.

The internal consistency of the WMC reaches coefficients well over .90, test-retest reliability (from several studies) ranges from .61 to over .90, and total score interrater reliability correlations range from .53 to .77. The manual also presents impressive data with regard to item, factorial, discriminant, criterion-related, and construct validity. Sabornie et al. (1989) showed that the WMC, administered to regular classroom teachers serving BD students, could discriminate between preidentified BD and nonhandicapped students with 89% accuracy. Sabornie and Thomas (1989) found the discriminant accuracy of the WMC to be 75% with LD, BD, and nonhandicapped youths when rated by regular educators in mainstream settings. Special education teachers of LD students, however, rated the social competence of their students in resource rooms significantly higher than did regular teachers of the same students. The WMC is strongly supported for assessment of social competence of mainstream students. The WMC's relative ease of completion (i.e., usually less than 15 minutes) is another positive benefit of its use, especially with teachers who are already overburdened with paperwork.

Social Behavior Assessment (SBA; Stephens, 1981). The SBA is one of the first social skills assessment instruments created for use with elementary level (i.e., K-6) handicapped students in the schools. The SBA provides for the assessment of 136 social skills, divided into 30 different subcategories (e.g., greeting others, helping others, making conversation, accepting consequences), and further separated into the domains of self-related, task-related, interpersonal, and environmental behaviors. Teachers judge the criterion-referenced social behavior of students by rating *acceptable, less than acceptable,* or *never* on the 136 items. A unique feature

of the SBA is that it includes measurement of behaviors in the classroom that are not entirely of a social nature. Categories such as on-task behavior, quality of work, and ethical behavior, for example, are behaviors that teachers perceive as important in a classroom, but are not solely socially oriented.

The technical adequacy of the SBA is more than sufficient, its internal consistency and its test-retest and interrater reliability being well into the .80s and .90s. The manual also reports adequate content and construct validity information, but predictive validity is limited to only identified groups of handicapped children. Gresham and Reschly (1986) used the SBA to assess the teacher-perceived social behavior of 200 LD and nonhandicapped students and found extreme differences between the two groups. Behavior-disordered and nonhandicapped students were also found to differ significantly on SBA teacher ratings (Stumme, Gresham, & Scott, 1982). Although a considerable amount of time is needed to complete the SBA for a single student (approximately 45 minutes), it does provide a comprehensive picture of pupils' social skills. The SBA can be easily used by school psychologists interested in assessing a wide spectrum of classroom-related social skills. Such assessment results can also contribute to choosing target students and behaviors for social skills intervention.

Social Skills Rating System (SSRS; Gresham & Elliott, 1990). The teacher rating scale of the SSRS is composed of 55 items divided into the domains of self-control, interfering behaviors, assertion, and cooperation. This instrument is intended for use with children and youths aged 3-18. Teachers rate students' social behaviors on a frequency metric ranging from *never* to *often true.* Also included for teacher respondents are additional criteria related to perceived importance of the individual behaviors being rated. Teachers rate whether individual student behaviors are *critical, important,* or *unimportant* to social success in the classroom. The authors state that the additional criteria used for teachers' ratings contribute to enhanced social validity and identification of social skills for intervention (see also Gresham & Elliott, 1989).

The SSRS demonstrates more than adequate discriminant ability among mildly handicapped and nonhandicapped students in mainstream classrooms (Gresham, Elliott, & Black, 1987). The internal consistency coefficients of the SSRS are quite robust (i.e., in the .90s). Test–retest (.90s), and interrater (.70s) reliability data are also strong. Its content, concurrent, and predictive validity data are more than sufficient. The SSRS was standardized on 4,700 children of representative national and racial groups that included exceptional and nonhandicapped pupils. Also available in the SSRS package are parent and self-rating scales — features not found in the rating scales reviewed above. The scope of the SSRS, therefore, is very comprehensive. It is highly recommended for use by psychologists concerned with assessing the social skills of mildly handicapped students.

Although sociometry and teachers' ratings of social behaviors are highly recommended for implementation by school psychologists, several notes of caution must be added to fully understand how each method contributes to functional treatment schemes. Sociometric assessment does not involve the measurement of specific student behaviors — only the consequences (i.e., acceptance, rejection) of such overt manifestations in classrooms. For this reason, sociometry should be viewed as an initial screening device in spite of its correlation with specific student behaviors. Sociometrics should also be used to determine whether target students are in need of additional assessment that focuses on distinct social behaviors, and to judge the efficacy of intervention in pre- and posttesting fashion. If social skills training is effective, there should be minimal correlation between target students' sociometric status before and after treatment. The scope of this chapter does not include emphasis on direct observation of student interaction in the classroom, but it, too, could be considered as an adjunct assessment procedure for students who may need treatment (see Gresham, 1986; Gresham & Elliott, 1989; La Greca & Stark, 1986; Hazel & Schumaker, 1987, for reviews). Direct observation of social behavior in natural settings (not contrived ones) does not measure the same constructs as sociometrics, but rather specific behaviors that may hinder or enhance acceptance and rejection. Teachers' ratings, on the other hand, enable psychologists to express students' social skills in the manner of how closely they approximate norms. As to intervention, teacher rating scales show how badly a particular student may need social skills training. Psychologists who use the assessment procedures reviewed here, with their limitations and foci in mind, will find the results of social skills training easier to interpret.

INTERVENTION

The global objective of any social skills training procedure is to enhance the social competence of those who receive treatment. Those responsible for instruction in this area should choose target skills that (a) are acquired expeditiously, (b) can be used readily in encounters with other persons within and outside the instructional setting, and (c) will be powerful enough to elicit positive responses from others. This last point, concerning social reciprocity, is one that is often neglected in training regimens that target social competence of students (Strain, Odom, & McConnell, 1984; Walker, Greenwood, Hops, & Todd, 1979). Instructional programs aimed at enhanced social relationships of mildly handicapped pupils in the mainstream, therefore, must consider procedures that shape the behavior of both the handicapped children and their peers. Schumaker, Pederson, Hazel, and Meyen (1983) also recommended that effective social skills training curricula for mildly handicapped students should address the following:

- Does the curriculum promote social competence (i.e., ability to perform social tasks at an acceptable level)?

- Does the curriculum accommodate the learning characteristics of mildly handicapped individuals?

- Does the curriculum target the social skills deficits of those with mild handicaps?

- Does the curriculum provide training in situations as well as skills?

- Does the curriculum incorporate instructional methodologies found to be effective with mildly handicapped students?

This section will discuss social skills training "packages" that are designed for mildly handicapped students who spend time in the mainstream. Specific social skills interventions that have been shown to be effective with such students in single empirical reports (see Gresham, 1981, 1982, 1985; Schloss, Schloss, Wood, & Kiehl, 1986; Schumaker & Hazel, 1984a, 1984b, for reviews) will not be presented. The intent of the following discussion is to present effective instructional procedures to school psychologists who may be responsible for intervention, consultation with teachers, and service delivery coordination for students who are diagnosed as mildly handicapped.

Walker Programs

The *ACCEPTS* program (Walker, McConnell, Holmes et al., 1983) is one of the most widely used curricular approaches to teaching prosocial skills to both mildly handicapped and nonhandicapped elementary-level pupils. The materials are designed for use in both regular and special education environments. The complete package includes lesson scripts for instructors, behavioral management techniques, and multistep instructional procedures based on effective teaching behaviors with mildly handicapped students (i.e., direct instruction). Instructors using *ACCEPTS* define skills

to be learned, provide examples and counterexamples of prosocial behaviors, witness students' active practice, offer performance feedback, and contract with participants for enhanced generalization.

The *ACCEPTS* program concentrates on over 25 different social skills subdivided into classroom rules (e.g., listening to the teacher), basic interaction skills (e.g., eye contact), getting along skills (e.g., sharing), making friends skills (e.g., smiling), and coping skills (e.g., appropriate behavior when someone says no). An instructional videotape that accompanies the program shows students actually performing the skills to be learned. The package can be used with small-group, large-group, or in one-to-one teaching situations, and it is ideally suited for use with mildly handicapped and nonhandicapped pupils in mainstream classrooms (see Walker, McConnell, Walker et al., 1983, for research validation).

The *ACCESS* program (Walker, Todis, Holmes, & Horton, 1988) is designed for use with middle and high school students in special and regular classrooms. This program emphasizes the teaching of peer-to-peer social skills (e.g., having conversations), self-management skills (e.g., being organized), and direct-instruction teaching that includes provisions for reinforcement and performance feedback, contracting for generalization, and role-play practice activities, as well as suggestions for grouping students. The program manual also provides keys to behavior management, and enhancing students' motivation — a particularly important component in working with adolescents. The comprehensiveness of *ACCESS* is impressive, and in view of its scope, cost ($68), appropriateness for use in regular classrooms, and focus on generalization, psychologists should consider use of this program for youths in middle schools and high schools.

Goldstein Programs

A social skills training package designed for the purpose of teaching prosocial alternatives to antisocial outbursts is *Skillstreaming the Elementary School*

Child (McGinnis & Goldstein, 1984). This program was developed with young, mildly handicapped and aggressive students in mind. The program is built around the components of "structured learning," a psychoeducational and behavioral approach to instruction. *Skillstreaming the Elementary School Child* supports the teaching of prosocial behaviors through (a) modeling, (b) role-playing, (c) performance feedback, and (d) transfer of training. Each individual social skill is task-analyzed, and subcomponent skill parts are taught to mastery levels. Students observe models performing the exact skill to be learned, they rehearse individual behaviors, and they receive feedback from other students and trainers; procedures are selected that increase the likelihood of demonstrating the social skill in real-life situations. Methods of teaching a specific social skill and a transcript of an actual lesson are given in the manual, but instructional scripts are not provided.

The teaching of 60 prosocial skills is included in the elementary-level *Skillstreaming* package. These skills are divided into five domains: (a) classroom survival skills (e.g., following instructions); (b) friendship-making skills (e.g., beginning and ending a conversation), (c) skills for dealing with feelings (e.g., expressing affection appropriately), (d) skill alternatives to aggression (e.g., appropriate responding to teasing), and (e) skills for dealing with stress (e.g., in reaction to failure). The elementary-level *Skillstreaming* program can be used in either regular or special education, but ideally it should be used in both settings for maximum effectiveness (see program manual for research validation).

Skillstreaming the Adolescent (Goldstein, Sprafkin, Gershaw, & Klein, 1980) is the original structured learning package developed for teaching prosocial behaviors to withdrawn, immature, and aggressive older pupils. Instructional techniques of modeling, role-playing, feedback, and transfer of training, similar to the elements of the *Skillstreaming* package for elementary-level students, are also used in the adolescent program. There are 50

structured-learning social skills included in the Goldstein et al. program for adolescents, which are divided into six groups: (a) beginning social skills (e.g., asking a question), (b) advanced social skills (e.g., giving instructions), (c) skills for dealing with feelings (e.g., understanding the feelings of others), (d) skill alternatives to aggression (e.g., using self-control), (e) skills for dealing with stress (e.g., sportsmanship after a game), and (f) planning skills (e.g., deciding on something to do). The manual describes trainer behaviors to be used while teaching behavioral steps, techniques for managing problem behaviors, procedures that facilitate skills training (e.g., making instructions clear), and ways in which to model prosocial behaviors; however, scripts are not included for use by the social skills instructor. Both *Skillstreaming* packages include many proven strategies for teaching social skills to handicapped pupils through a multifactored approach (see program manual for research validation).

Stephens's Program

Another social skills training package that has been used with mildly handicapped elementary-level students is *Social Skills in the Classroom* (Stephens, 1978). Although this program is recommended for use with special populations (Cartledge & Milburn, 1986), it has little research validation to demonstrate its efficacy. For this reason, school psychologists should use caution when determining whether to choose this approach. This program was developed with the "directive teaching" instructional model as its foundation. Social skills instructors using the Stephens curricula first model the behavior to be acquired, specify the exact movements that are needed, and stress the conditions under which the specific target behavior is to occur. Skills levels are subsequently assessed and, based on this measurement (using Stephens's SBA is recommended), corrective teaching strategies are developed. Guidelines for writing social skills instructional strategies are presented in the manual. The last step in the instructional sequence is evaluation of the strategy's effectiveness. Stephens recommends the use of reinforcement strategies, contingency contracting, and token economy systems to motivate students to perform the newly learned behaviors.

The sheer number of social skills that are taught by the Stephens curriculum is noteworthy. The same 136 social skills that are assessed with the SBA can be taught to target students through *Social Skills in the Classroom.* Particularly useful to school psychologists are its suggestions for a consultant's use of the program (e.g., helping teachers maintain special needs students in regular classes by showing them how to change disruptive behaviors) (pp. 12-22). Specific weaknesses of the Stephens program include scant research validation, lack of attention to skills generalization, and lack of scripts for lesson presentations. The effectiveness of this program, therefore, is unknown and is likely to be limited if social skills are taught to target students in only one environment (i.e., in special education but not in mainstream classes).

Camp and Bash's Program

Designed for mainstream students with social skills problems (e.g., aggressive behaviors) in Grades 1-6, *Think Aloud* (Camp & Bash, 1981) is a social-problem-solving skills curriculum. The program has a cognitive self-control focus and combines the work of Meichenbaum and Goodman (1971) and of Spivack and Shure (1974) to teach appropriate social responses. *Think Aloud* instructs students to ask themselves the following questions when faced with social situations: (a) "What is my problem?" (b) "What is my plan?" (c) "How is my plan working?" and (d) "How did I do?"

Training in this social skills program consists of cognitive modeling (i.e., covert verbalizations that guide appropriate social response thought processes), overt external practice of self-questioning and appropriate responding in social situations, faded self-questioning with correct problem-solving responses, and covert self-questioning. The 1981 version of the package consisted of 23 guided lessons (with scripts) directed toward social problem-solving behaviors of a preventive, educational, or therapeutic nature. The 1985 editions of *Think Aloud* are subdivided according to grade (Grades 1-2, 3-4, and 5-6), with different social problem-solving skills highlighted according to grade level. The version for Grades 1 and 2, for example, includes scripted lessons that range from identifying emotions to predicting consequences of behavior. Generalization of skills is addressed by providing students with problem-solving tools that can be applied in a variety of situations. The efficacy of *Think Aloud* is supported by many mainstreaming studies (see program manuals for research validation), and psychologists with experience and interest in cognitive training should find this program interesting.

ASSET

One of the most widely used programs for teaching social skills to at-risk adolescents is *ASSET* (Hazel, Schumaker, Sherman, & Sheldon-Wildgen, 1981a). One drawback of this package is its cost ($1,400), but that has not prevented *ASSET* from attaining repute (e.g., it is being used in middle schools across the entire state of South Carolina) and acceptance that surpasses that of nearly all other social skills training regimens. This program features videocassettes that are used to teach the following social skills: giving positive and negative feedback, accepting negative feedback, resisting peer pressure, problem solving, negotiation, following instructions, and conversation. The leader's guide of *ASSET* includes over 150 pages of scripted lessons, instructional procedures, and objectives for each filmed lesson. The films, which keep required reading by participants to a minimum, show adolescents modeling appropriate and inappropriate social skills in interactions with peers, teachers, parents, and adults.

ASSET is a skills approach to the teaching of prosocial behaviors. Specific behaviors to be learned are practiced by participants in structured role-plays, with instructor feedback, until criterion performance levels are attained. Lessons are introduced by providing the rationale for learning the specific skill. Program evaluation includes parents who judge their child's newly acquired skills. Research has established the efficacy of *ASSET* (see Hazel, Schumaker, Sherman, & Sheldon-Wildgen, 1981b, 1982, for research validation). This program is also very appropriate in school psychologists' work with mildly handicapped adolescents with behavior problems.

SUMMARY

Social skills assessment and training by means of packaged approaches are interrelated in that intervention should not be made without systematic assessment to determine the effectiveness of the training. Sociometric measurement and teachers' ratings (and behavioral observation, if necessary) should serve as the basis for judging specific outcomes of social skills training regimens. With consistent assessment of changes (or lack thereof) in target students' prosocial behaviors, psychologists can assist with or engage in efficient intervention by using the data to decide which skills need more emphasis, reteaching, or no therapeutic concentration. Furthermore, sociometric research has documented that not all mildly handicapped students are equally deficient in social standing in mainstream classes (Sabornie & Kauffman, 1986; Sabornie, Kauffman, & Cullinan, in press). Concentrating on only those mildly handicapped students who are truly in need of social skills training, determined through assessment, is likely to make a psychologist's role somewhat easier.

Ideally, social skills intervention should include many qualified trainers, in different educational settings (i.e., special and regular classes), to help ensure success. Moreover, without attention to generalization of learned prosocial skills, much of the effort to change students' behavior will be lost. Teaching appropriate social response repertoires should not be considered a short-term undertaking; that is, follow-up checks and programming for maintenance of skills are also necessary. Improving the social skills of students who are lacking in this area should become part of a systematic daily instructional regimen, rather than an informal or unstructured activity. In order to avoid past problems with mainstreaming, psychologists must view appropriate social skills as a basic necessity — and not a burden — in working with mildly handicapped and other target students.

REFERENCES

Agard, J. A., Veldman, S. M., Kaufman, M. J., & Semmel, M. I. (1978). *How I feel toward others: An instrument of the PRIME instrument battery.* Baltimore: University Park Press.

Asher, S. R. (1985). An evolving paradigm in social skill training research with children. In B. H. Schneider, K. H. Rubin, & J. E. Ledingham (Eds.), *Children's peer relations: Issues in assessment and intervention* (pp. 157-171). New York: Springer-Verlag.

Asher, S. R., & Taylor, A. R. (1981). Social outcomes of mainstreaming: Sociometric assessment and beyond. *Exceptional Education Quarterly, 1*(4), 13-30.

Bachara, G. H. (1976). Empathy in learning disabled children. *Perceptual and Motor Skills, 43,* 541-542.

Baldwin, W. K. (1958). The educable mentally retarded child in the regular grades. *Exceptional Children, 25,* 106-108.

Bruininks, V. L. (1978a). Actual and perceived peer status of learning disabled students in mainstream programs. *Journal of Special Education, 12,* 51-58.

Bruininks, V. L. (1978b). Peer status and personality characteristics of learning disabled students. *Journal of Learning Disabilities, 11,* 484-489.

Bruininks, R. H., Rynders, J. E., & Gross, J. C. (1974). Social acceptance of mildly retarded pupils in resource rooms and regular classes. *American Journal of Mental Deficiency, 78,* 377-383.

Bryan, T. (1974). Peer popularity of learning disabled children. *Journal of Learning Disabilities, 7,* 621-625.

Bryan, T. (1976). Peer popularity of learning disabled children: A replication. *Journal of Learning Disabilities, 9,* 307-311.

Bryan, T. (1977). Learning disabled children's comprehension of nonverbal communication. *Journal of Learning Disabilities, 10,* 501-506.

Bryan, T., & Bryan, J. H. (1978). Social interactions of learning disabled children. *Learning Disability Quarterly, 1*, 35-38.

Camp, B. W., & Bash, M. A. (1981). *Think aloud.* Champaign, IL: Research Press.

Cartledge, G., & Milburn, J. F. (1986). *Teaching social skills to children* (2nd ed.). New York: Pergamon.

Coben, S. C., & Zigmond, N. (1986). The social integration of learning disabled students from self-contained to mainstream elementary school settings. *Journal of Learning Disabilities, 19*, 614-618.

Coie, J. D. (1985). Fitting social skills intervention to the target group. In B. H. Schneider, K. H. Rubin, & J. E. Ledingham (Eds.), *Children's peer relations: Issues in assessment and intervention* (pp. 141-156). New York: Springer-Verlag.

Coie, J. D., Dodge, K. A., & Coppotelli, H. (1982). Dimensions and types of social status: A cross-age perspective. *Developmental Psychology, 18*, 557-570.

Connolly, J., & Doyle, A. (1981). Assessment of social competence in preschoolers: Teachers versus peers. *Developmental Psychology, 17*, 454-462.

Cowen, E. L., Pederson, A., Babigian, H., Izzo, L. D., & Trost, M. A. (1973). Long-term follow-up of early detected vulnerable children. *Journal of Consulting and Clinical Psychology, 41*, 438-446.

Deshler, D. D., & Schumaker, J. B. (1983). Social skills of learning disabled adolescents: Characteristics and intervention. *Topics in Learning and Learning Disabilities, 3*(2), 15-23.

Dodge, K. A., Coie, J. D., & Brakke, N. P. (1982). Behavior patterns of socially rejected and neglected preadolescents: The roles of social approach and aggression. *Journal of Abnormal Child Psychology, 10*, 389-410.

Fordyce, W. G., Yauck, W. A., & Raths, L. (1946). *A manual for the Ohio guidance tests for the elementary grades.* Columbus, OH: State Department of Education.

Goldsmith, J. B., & McFall, R. M. (1975). Development and evaluation of an interpersonal skill-training program for psychiatric inpatients. *Journal of Abnormal Psychology, 84*, 51-58.

Goldstein, A. P. Sprafkin, R. P., Gershaw, N. J., & Klein, P. (1980). *Skillstreaming the adolescent.* Champaign, IL: Research Press.

Gottlieb, B. W., Gottlieb, J., Berkell, D., & Levy, L. (1986). Sociometric status and solitary play of LD boys and girls. *Journal of Learning Disabilities, 19*, 619-622.

Gottlieb, J., & Budoff, M. (1973). Social acceptability of retarded children in nongrades schools differing in architecture. *American Journal of Mental Deficiency, 78*, 15-19.

Gottman, J. M., Gonso, J., & Rasmussen, B. (1975). Social interaction, social competence, and friendship in children. *Child Development, 46*, 709-718.

Greenwood, C. R., Walker, H. M., Todd, N. M., & Hops, H. (1979). Selecting a cost-effective screening device for the assessment of preschool social withdrawal. *Journal of Applied Behavior Analysis, 12*, 639-652.

Gresham, F. M. (1981). Social skills training with handicapped children: A review. *Review of Educational Research, 51*, 139-176.

Gresham, F. M. (1982). Misguided mainstreaming: The case for social skills training with handicapped children. *Exceptional Children, 48*, 422-433.

Gresham, F. M. (1985). Strategies for enhancing the social outcomes of mainstreaming: A necessary ingredient for success. In J. Meisel (Ed.), *Mainstreaming handicapped children: Outcomes, controversies, and new directions* (pp. 193-218). Hillsdale, NJ: Erlbaum.

Gresham, F. M. (1986). Conceptual and definitional issues in the assessment of children's social skills: Implications for classification and training. *Journal of Clinical Child Psychology, 15*, 3-15.

Gresham, F. M., & Elliott, S. N. (1989). Social skills assessment technology for LD students. *Learning Disability Quarterly, 12*, 141-152.

Gresham, F. M., & Elliott, S. N. (1990). *Social skills rating system.* Circle Pines, MN: American Guidance Service.

Gresham, F. M., Elliott, S. N., & Black, F. L. (1987). Teacher-rated social skills of mainstreamed mildly handicapped and nonhandicapped children. *School Psychology Review, 16*, 78-88.

Gresham, F. M., & Reschly, D. J. (1986). Social skills and low peer acceptance of mainstreamed learning disabled children. *Learning Disability Quarterly, 9*, 23-32.

Hartup, W. W., Glazer, J. A., & Charlesworth, R. (1967). Peer reinforcement and sociometric status. *Child Development, 38*, 1017-1024.

Havyren, M., & Hymel, S. (1983). Ethical issues in sociometric testing: the impact of sociometric measures on interactive behavior. *Developmental Psychology, 20*, 844-849.

Hazel, J. S., & Schumaker, J. B. (1987). *Social skills and learning disability.* Paper presented at the National Conference on Learning Disabilities, Bethesda, MD.

Hazel, J. S., Schumaker, J. B., Sherman, J. A., & Sheldon-Wildgen, J. (1981a). *ASSET: A social skills program for adolescents.* Champaign, IL: Research Press.

Hazel, J. S., Schumaker, J. B., Sherman, J. A., & Sheldon-Wildgen, J. (1981b). The development and evaluation of a group skills training program for court-adjudicated youth. In D. Upper & S. Ross (Eds.), *Behavioral group therapy: An annual review* (pp. 113-152). Champaign, IL: Research Press.

Hazel, J. S., Schumaker, J. B., Sherman, J. A., & Sheldon-Wildgen, J. (1982). Application of a group training program in social skills and problem solving to learning disabled and non-learning-disabled youth. *Learning Disability Quarterly, 5,* 398-408.

Hops, H. (1983). Children's social competence and skill: Current research practices and future directions. *Behavior Therapy, 14,* 3-18.

Hops, H., & Greenwood, C. (1981). Social skills deficits. In E. J. Marsh & L. G. Terdal (Eds.), *Behavioral assessment of childhood disorders* (pp. 347-396). New York: Guilford.

Hops, H., & Lewin, L. (1984). Peer sociometric forms. In T. H. Ollendick & M. Hersen (Eds.), *child behavioral assessment: Principles and procedures* (pp. 124-147). New York: Pergamon.

Hutton, J. B., & Polo, L. (1976). A sociometric study of learning disability children and type of teaching strategy. *Group Psychology and Psychodrama, 29,* 113-120.

Iano, R. P., Ayers, D., Heller, H. B., McGettigan, J. F., & Walker, V. S. (1974). Sociometric status of retarded children in an integrative program. *Exceptional Children, 40,* 267-271.

Johnson, G. O. (1950). A study of the social position of mentally handicapped children in the regular grades. *American Journal of Mental Deficiency, 55,* 60-89.

Johnson, G. O., & Kirk, S. A. (1950). Are mentally handicapped children segregated in the regular grades? *Exceptional Children, 17,* 65-68, 87-88.

Kistner, J. A., & Gatlin, D. (1989). Correlates of peer rejection among children with learning disabilities. *Learning Disability Quarterly, 12,* 133-140.

Kupersmidt, J. B. (1983). Predicting delinquency and academic problems from childhood peer status. In J. D. Coie (Chair), *Strategies for identifying children at social risk: Longitudinal correlates and consequences.* Symposium conducted at the biennial meeting of the Society for Research in Child Development, Detroit, MI.

La Greca, A., & Stark, P. (1986). Naturalistic observations of children's social behavior. In P. S. Strain, M. Guralnick, & H. M. Walker (Eds.), *Children's social behavior: Development, assessment, and modification* (pp. 181-214). Orlando, FL: Academic.

Lapp, E. R. (1957). A study of the social adjustment of slow learning children who were assigned part-time to regular classes. *American Journal of Mental Deficiency, 62,* 254-262.

Luftig, R. L. (1988). Assessment of the perceived school loneliness and isolation of mentally retarded and nonretarded students. *American Journal of Mental Retardation, 92,* 472-475.

Maheady, L., Maitland, G., & Sainato, D. (1984). The interpretation of social interactions by mildly handicapped and nondisabled children. *Journal of Special Education, 18,* 151-159.

McConnell, S., & Odom, S. L. (1986). Sociometrics: Peer referenced measures and the assessment of social competence. In P. Strain, M. Guralnick, & H. M. Walker (Eds.), *Children's social behavior: Development, assessment, and modification* (pp. 215-284). Orlando, FL: Academic.

McGinnis, E., & Goldstein, A. P. (1984). *Skillstreaming the elementary school child.* Champaign, IL: Research Press.

Meichenbaum, D., & Goodman, J. (1971). Training impulsive children to talk to themselves: A means of developing self-control. *Journal of Abnormal Psychology, 77,* 115-126.

Monroe, J. D., & Howe, C. E. (1971). The effects of integration and social class on the acceptance of retarded adolescents. *Education and Training of the Mentally Retarded, 6,* 20-24.

Parker, J. G., & Asher, S. R. (1987). Peer relations and later personal adjustment: Are low-accepted children at risk? *Psychological Bulletin, 102,* 357-389.

Pearl, R., & Cosden, M. (1982). Sizing up a situation: LD children's understanding of social interactions. *Learning Disability Quarterly, 5,* 371-373.

Peery, J. C. (1979). Popular, amiable, isolated, rejected: A reconceptualization of sociometric status in preschool children. *Child Development, 50,* 1231-1234.

Prillaman, D. (1981). Acceptance of learning disabled students in a mainstream environment: A failure to replicate. *Journal of Learning Disabilities, 14,* 344-352.

Putallaz, M., & Gottman, J. M. (1983). Social relationship problems in children: An approach to intervention. In B. B. Lahey & A. E. Kazdin (Eds.), *Advances in clinical child psychology* (Vol. 6, pp. 1-39). New York: Plenum.

Roff, M., Sells, S. B., & Golden, M. M. (1972). *Social adjustment and personality development in children.* Minneapolis: University of Minnesota Press.

Rucker, C. N., Howe, C. E., & Snider, B. (1969). Participation of retarded children in junior high academic and nonacademic regular classes. *Exceptional Children, 35,* 679-680.

Sabornie, E. J. (1985). Social mainstreaming of handicapped students: Facing an unpleasant reality. *Remedial and Special Education, 6*(2), 12-16.

Sabornie, E. J. (1987). Bi-directional social status of behaviorally disordered and nonhandicapped elementary school pupils. *Behavioral Disorders, 13,* 47-57.

Sabornie, E. J., & Ellis, E. S. (1987). Sociometry for teachers of behaviorally disordered students. In R. B. Rutherford, C. M. Nelson, & S. R. Forness (Eds.), *Severe behavior disorders of children and youth* (pp. 28-40). San Diego: College-Hill.

Sabornie, E. J., & Kauffman, J. M. (1985). Regular classroom sociometric status of behaviorally disordered students. *Behavioral Disorders, 10,* 268-274.

Sabornie, E. J., & Kauffman, J. M. (1986). Social acceptance of learning disabled adolescents. *Learning Disability Quarterly, 9,* 55-60.

Sabornie, E. J., & Kauffman, J. M. (1987). Assigned, received, and reciprocal social status of adolescents with and without mild mental retardation. *Education and Training in Mental Retardation, 22,* 139-149.

Sabornie, E. J., Kauffman, J. M., & Cullinan, D. A. (in press). Extended sociometric status of adolescents with mild handicaps: A cross-categorical perspective. *Exceptionality.*

Sabornie, E. J., Kauffman, J. M., Ellis, E. S., Marshall, K. J., & Elksnin, L. K. (1987-1988). Bi-directional and cross-categorical social status of LD, BD, and nonhandicapped adolescents. *Journal of Special Education, 21*(4), 39-56.

Sabornie, E. J., Marshall, K. J., & Ellis, E. S. (1988). Behaviorally disordered, learning disabled, and nonhandicapped students' social status in mainstream classes. *Monograph in Behavioral Disorders: Severe Behavior Disorders of Children and Youth, 11,* 32-45.

Sabornie, E. J., Marshall, K. J., & Ellis, E. S. (1990). Restructuring of mainstream sociometry with learning disabled and nonhandicapped students. *Exceptional Children, 56,* 314-323.

Sabornie, E. J., & Thomas, V. (1989). *Social/affective adjustment of mildly handicapped and nonhandicapped early adolescents.* Paper presented at the annual meeting of the American Educational Research Association, San Francisco, CA.

Sabornie, E. J., Thomas, V., & Coffman, R. M. (1989). Assessment of social/affective measures to discriminate between BD and nonhandicapped early adolescents. *Monograph in Behavior Disorders: Severe behavior Disorders of Children and Youth, 12,* 21-32.

Schloss, P. J., Schloss, C. N., Wood, C. E., & Kiehl, W. S. (1986). A critical review of social skills research with behaviorally disordered students. *Behavioral Disorders, 12,* 1-14.

Schumaker, J. B., & Hazel, J. S. (1984a). Social skills assessment and training for the learning disabled: Who's on first and what's on second? Part I. *Journal of Learning Disabilities, 17,* 422-431.

Schumaker, J. B., & Hazel, J. S. (1984b). Social skills assessment and training for the learning disabled: Who's on first and what's on second? Part II. *Journal of Learning Disabilities, 17,* 492-499.

Schumaker, J. B., Pederson, C. S., Hazel, J. S., & Meyen, E. L. (1983). Social skills curricula for mildly handicapped adolescents: A review. *Focus on Exceptional Children, 16*(4), 1-16.

Scranton, T., & Ryckman, D. (1979). Sociometric status of learning disabled children in an integrative program. *Journal of Learning Disabilities, 12,* 49-54.

Siperstein, G. N., Bopp, M. J., & Bak, J. J. (1978). Social status of learning disabled children. *Journal of Learning Disabilities, 11,* 49-53.

Spivack, G., & Shure, M. B. (1974). *Social adjustment of young children: A cognitive approach to solving real-life problems.* San Francisco: Jossey-Bass.

Stephens, T. M. (1978). *Social skills in the classroom.* Columbus, OH: Cedars Press.

Stephens, T. M. (1981). *Social Behavior Assessment (SBA).* Columbus, OH: Cedars Press.

Stone, W. L., & LaGreca, A. M. (1990). The social status of children with learning disabilities: A reexamination. *Journal of Learning Disabilities, 23,* 32-37.

Strain, P. S., Odom, S. L., & McConnell, S. (1984). Promoting social reciprocity of exceptional children: Identification, target behavior selection, and intervention. *Remedial and Special Education, 5*(1), 21-28.

Stumme, V., Gresham, F. M., & Scott, N. (1982). Validity of *Social Behavior Assessment* in discriminating emotionally disabled from nonhandicapped students. *Journal of Behavioral Assessment, 4,* 327-342.

Vacc, N. A. (1968). A study of emotionally disturbed children in regular and special classes. *Exceptional Children, 35*, 197-204.

Vacc, N. A. (9172). Long term effects of special class intervention for emotionally disturbed children. *Exceptional Children, 39*, 15-22.

Walker, H. M., Greenwood, C. R., Hops, H., & Todd, N. M. (1979). Differential effects of reinforcing topographic components of social interaction. *Behavior Modification, 3*, 291-321.

Walker, H. M., & McConnell, S. R. (1988). *The Walker–McConnell Scale of Social Competence and School Adjustment: A social skills rating scale for teachers.* Austin, TX: Pro-Ed.

Walker, H. M., McConnell, S. R., Holmes, D., Todis, B., Walker, J., & Golden, H. (1983). *The Walker social skills curriculum: The ACCEPTS program.* Austin, TX: Pro-Ed.

Walker, H. M., & McConnell, S. R., Walker, J., Clarke, J., Todis, B., Cohen, G., & Rankin, R. (1983). Initial analysis of the *ACCEPTS* curriculum: Efficacy of instructional and behavioral management procedures for improving the social adjustment of handicapped children. *Analysis and intervention in Developmental Disabilities, 3*, 105-127.

Walker, H. M., Todis, B., Holmes, D., & Horton, G. (1988). *The Walker social skills curriculum. The ACCESS program.* Austin, TX: Pro-Ed.

White, W. J., Schumaker, J. B., Warner, M. M., Alley, G. R., & Deshler, D. D. (1980). *The current status of young adults identified as learning disabled during their school career* (Research Report No. 21). Lawrence, KS: University of Kansas Institute for Research in Learning Disabilities.

Wiig, E. H., & Harris, S. P. (1974). Perception and interpretation of nonverbally expressed emotions by adolescents with learning disabilities. *Perceptual and Motor Skills, 38*, 239-245.

Zetlin, A. G., & Murtaugh, M. (1988). Friendship patterns of mildly learning handicapped and nonhandicapped high school students. *American Journal of Mental Retardation, 92*, 447-454.

Peer Tutoring Programs in the Regular Education Classroom

Charles R. Greenwood
Judith J. Carta
University of Kansas

Larry Maheady
Michigan State University

INTRODUCTION

Research has revealed a number of components of effective instruction in recent years. First, students must have the opportunity to learn in order for learning to take place. Thus, the allocation of instruction time is of basic importance in respect to what actually may be learned in school. Second, teaching and the design of instruction makes a difference in the rate of learning. Third, students learn more when (a) more time is devoted to a particular subject matter and when (b) they are provided well-designed learning tasks that actively engages them.

Findings from research on teaching indicate that (a) students need repeated practice on material to the point of overlearning (Rosenshine & Stevens, 1986); (b) they need to perform these tasks successfully, that is with 80-90% correct results (Brophy, 1986); (c) they need to receive new content when mastery criteria are reached (Keller, 1968); and (d) the rate or pacing of instruction needs to be relatively high to maintain student engagement (Carnine, 1976).

Yet researchers have documented clearly that students' engagement levels vary widely in the same classroom and within the same instructional groups during lessons (Greenwood, Delquadri, & Hall, 1984; Ysseldyke, Thurlow, Christenson, & Weiss, 1987). In each classroom this variation across students can be viewed in terms of the typical normal curve with the majority of students demonstrating levels of engagement during lessons near the class mean and small percentages performing well above and well below the mean. The "normal curve of student engagement" is a rather new and unfamiliar concept for those who serve low performing students. It becomes important when one considers that various alterable factors can powerfully influence positively or negatively the levels of individual student engagement and hence the shape of the curve of classwide performance.

The effective use of instruction time for any student may be threatened by variables that reduce or interrupt either the opportunity to learn or student engagement. Interruptions of the opportunity to learn may result from frequent or prolonged absences from school, school schedules that allocate inordinate amounts of time to nonacademic subjects, frequent "pullout" sessions, and long duration transitions between classroom instructional activities. Reductions in student engagement result primarily from the sustained use of instructional procedures that establish low levels of student engagement and that also facilitate high rates of acting-out and/or off-task student behaviors.

For example, Stallings (1977) reported that direct instruction produced significantly greater levels of engagement than did alternative instructional models in the follow-through evaluation in the 1970s. Classwide peer tutoring methods have also been demonstrated to produce significantly more engagement than many conventional teacher-designed and teacher-mediated procedures of instruction used in spelling and reading (Greenwood, Dinwiddie et al., 1984).

Clearly then, the rate at which students learn academic skills will be accelerated or decelerated by how the school and classroom teachers organize and deploy procedures to manage the use of instruction time (Greenwood, Delquadri et al., 1981; Rosenshine & Stevens, 1986).

EDUCATIONAL REFORM

Nationally, there is an increased interest in educational reforms that potentially affect all students' opportunity to learn. Of particular concern is the rigidity of the current dual system of regular versus special education. At the center of concern is redefinition of the relationship between regular and special education (e.g., Gartner & Lipsky, 1987; Reynolds, Wang, & Walberg, 1987; Stainback & Stainback, 1984). We currently have a system of public education in which regular, compensatory, and special education programs are defined by separate legislative mandates, supported by separate sources of funding, characterized by separate practices, and perpetuated by separate teacher training programs. Because we have separated programs of service delivery, not all students are eligible for and not all students may receive optimal educational services (e.g., Reynolds et al., 1987). Consequently, some children are at risk of not receiving an appropriate education.

In response to these issues, the National Association of School Psychologists (NASP) has taken the position that all children can learn, that increased instructional options within general education are needed, and that nonbiased assessment related to the services actually provided students are needed (NASP, 1987). The NASP policy statement also asserts that the current rigid system of special education requires a new direction so that all children can receive an appropriate education. The NASP statement supports development of systems and the retaining of school personnel to work with children with special needs in general education programs. It is felt that a system of education is needed in which all students may have a greater independence to function in the broadest possible learning environment.

In the 1990s, we must develop the capacity to educate students with wide-ranging abilities within the regular classroom. The principle of integration requires first and foremost a school organizational structure that freely enables children with disabilities to be present in the regular classroom (Skrtic, 1988). It means that district and building level school personnel must be empowered legislatively, administratively, and technologically to provide service delivery to all students (e.g., Will, 1986). Thus, we will require a technology of instruction that can deliver effective learning for all students in the regular classroom. The characteristics of this technology at this time, however, are not entirely clear, and procedures, models, and delivery systems for carrying out integration are not developed and validated. However, several methods have been employed in recent years in an effort to accommodate heterogeneous groups of students, including students with mild handicaps. Because of this ability to accommodate heterogeneous abilities, they have been frequently used as exemplars of the types of instructional technology that will be required for integration (e.g., Hallahan, Kaufmann, Lloyd, & McKinney, 1988; Lloyd, Crowley, Kohler, & Strain, 1988). These methods include among others (a) cooperative learning

(Slavin, 1984; Johnson, Johnson, Warring, & Maruyama, 1986), (b) direct instruction (Becker, 1977; 1986), (c) peer tutoring (Greenwood, Carta, & Hall, 1988), and (d) the Adaptive Learning Environments Model (Wang, Peverly, & Randolph, 1984).

PURPOSE OF THIS CHAPTER

In this chapter, we review the use of peer tutoring in the regular classroom as an *instructional option* for accommodating students with *diverse instructional needs*. Peer tutoring is a *class of procedures* by which the elements of effective instruction just discussed can be orchestrated in the classroom. In this chapter, we have restricted our review to procedures in which the goal is to use peers directly to teach each other academic content. Thus, we are excluding many of the peer-mediation and peer-influence strategies in the literature that support classroom behavior management and that facilitate peer social interaction (Greenwood & Hops, 1981; Greenwood et al., 1988). We also are excluding cooperative learning procedures that are based solely on the use of a group-oriented reinforcement contingency and in which peers assist one another only spontaneously. In this chapter, our focus is on direct peer teaching.

First, we provide a background perspective on our own interest in peer teaching methods. Because of the number of procedures that exist that can be described as "peer tutoring," we discuss procedural issues and how they relate to integration in general (e.g., Allen, 1976; Ehly & Larsen, 1980; Osguthorpe & Scruggs, 1986). This discussion is followed by consideration of the recent development and validation of classwide peer tutoring (CWPT) as a specific case in point. We then review data supporting the effectiveness of CWPT. This discussion is followed by consideration of the role and training of the school psychologist in reference to tutoring programs and CWPT in particular. We conclude with a discussion of the implications of tutoring procedures.

PEER TUTORING AS AN INSTRUCTIONAL OPTION FOR THE REGULAR CLASSROOM

Since, 1977, research at the Juniper Gardens Children's Project has focused on the development of instructional procedures to improve the learning of children in urban school classrooms. Urban schools and classrooms contain students with widely diverse academic and behavioral ability levels that most likely are influenced by poverty, the stresses of urban life, and minority group/ethnic cultural differences (e.g., Carta & Greenwood, 1988; Edmonds, 1979; Tucker, 1980).

The work at the Project reported after 1977 (see reviews in Greenwood, Delquadri, & Hall, 1984; Hall, Delquadri, Greenwood, & Thurston, 1982) sought to address the persistent problem of academic delay and failure in this population. Both naturalistic and experimental studies of the instruction provided to these students indicated that the opportunity to learn in urban school classrooms was not uniform, and in fact, frequently discriminated most against students at greatest risk for academic failure.

For example, we reported (Greenwood, Delquadri, & Hall, 1984; Hall, Delquadri, Greenwood, & Thurston, 1982) the following:

1. Instruction that was scheduled was not actually implemented or that only a portion of it was implemented.

2. Frequently, students engaged in low levels of academic responding and high levels of task management and off-task behavior.

3. The lowest level reading group actually met for less time per day than did higher-ability groups.

4. Teachers rarely taught to mastery, but instead were required by district policies to cover standard amounts of material by particular times in the school year regardless of students' performance and/or preparation for new material.

We also reported that fourth graders in urban schools engaged in academic behaviors 5% *less* (i.e., 12 minutes per day) than did their suburban counterparts (Stanley & Greenwood, 1983). These dramatic daily differences in student engagement indicated that students in urban schools needed to attend school for 10.5 months to accumulate the same amount of engaged time as their suburban counterparts did in 9 months. Such differences provided an operational explanation for the delayed academic development of this vulnerable group of students.

To address this problem, we sought an instructional approach that *at minimum* would increase the daily engagement levels for urban students to equal those of suburban students. Included were procedures that potentially would affect the opportunity to learn and that also could be widely implemented in urban school classrooms with students of heterogeneous abilities. We also sought procedures that were acceptable to teachers and were likely to be implemented by them.

Previously we had been impressed with the effects produced by training teachers in applied behavior analysis procedures (e.g., Hall, Copeland, & Clark, 1975) and strategies that employ classroom rules combined with group-oriented contingencies (e.g., Greenwood, Hops, Delquadri, & Guild, 1974; Greenwood, Hops, & Walker, 1977; Greenwood, Hops, et al., 1979). However, these procedures, although effective, were largely teacher dependent, required considerable teacher effort, and oftentimes resulted in low quality implementations. Also impressive had been the effects of one-on-one tutoring (Delquadri, 1978). For example, students' engagement in academic tasks during tutoring conditions was consistently and dramatically higher than when they were taught in the conventional manner. We also were impressed with the amount students learned in short tutoring sessions, as evidenced by substantial gains on curriculum-based measures and teacher-prepared tests. Furthermore, tutoring was a procedure teachers appeared to use "naturally" in their efforts to individualize instruction. It was also a

procedure broadly accepted by school administrators and parents.

Others have recognized tutoring as an effective instructional procedure as well (e.g., Bennett, 1986; Bloom, 1984). Bloom (1984), for example, reported that one-on-one peer tutoring by a fully skilled tutor was more effective than both conventional (i.e., teachers' lecturing) and mastery learning methods of teaching. Across several replications of academic content and age of students, Bloom (1984) reported that peer tutoring produced effect sizes on the order of 2.0 standard deviations above the mean of the control group (i.e., students receiving conventional lecture-based teaching), compared with 1.3 standard deviations for mastery learning.[1]

Tutoring had previously been reported to be cost-effective. For example, Levin, Glass, and Meister (1984) noted that peer tutoring produced the greatest gain in achievement per dollar spent on the program than did either increased learning time or use of computer-assisted instruction.

In the late 1970s, however, tutoring was viewed by most teachers as strictly a remedial procedure and not appropriate for general classwide instruction. To many teachers, peer tutoring seemed to have neither wide-scale nor long-term applicability. In order to reap the academic and social benefits of tutoring, we and others (e.g., Heward, Heron, & Cooke, 1982) sought to develop acceptable, functional applications of peer tutoring to the *entire classroom* and the *entire school* (e.g., see review by Greenwood, Carta, & Hall, 1988).

PEER TUTORING AND INTEGRATION IN GENERAL EDUCATION

In this section, we discuss peer tutoring procedures and how they can support the principle of regular classroom integration. Ideally, peer tutoring procedures support integration by enabling lower-skill and handicapped students to participate directly (a) in at-level instruction, and (b) in interactions with students of heterogeneous abilities. However, because tutoring procedures vary, so does the extent to which they support integration. Frequently the tutoring arrangement, as defined by how peers are assigned to work together and the instructional procedures they use, determines the actual extent of integration support.

Logically, schoolwide and classwide peer tutoring programs in which tutors are taught to implement structured teaching practices offer the greatest support for integration because (a) *all* students can play a role in the program, and (b) effective instructional practices are employed by all tutors. In contrast, single-pair, cross-age or cross-ability tutoring, based on teaching approaches determined by the tutor (naturalistic procedures), provide the least support for integration. The latter approach is the traditional remedial model of tutoring in which a limited number of students actually participate, tutoring is considered to be a temporary arrangement, and optimally effective instructional practices are rarely employed by tutors.

PROCEDURAL DIFFERENCES IN PEER TUTORING

Peer tutoring programs vary across a number of procedural factors that offer differential supports to integration. Among these factors are (a) the way the program addresses the problem of tutor obsolescence, (b) the program's use of naturalistic versus structured instructional procedures, (c) the content and tasks employed (d) the procedure the program employs for training tutors, (e) secondary or side effects of the program, (f) pairing stategies used for tutoring, (g) the arrangement of students in tutoring pairs or on teams, (h) the use of contingencies and consequences, (i) the evaluation measures employed to improve program performance, and (j) the extent of administrative support for the program.

Tutor Obsolescence

Integration is most supported by wide-scale and long-term tutoring procedures. A problem in the use of tutoring is the fact that any single tutor–tutee pairing may become obsolete as soon as the tutee has mastered the skill(s) the tutor originally was assigned to teach (Gerber & Kauffman, 1981; Young, 1981). This problem is particularly true in the absence of procedures that prevent obsolescence. Because of this obsolescence problem, tutoring has been used traditionally for short durations, usually until a student was capable of being instructed by conventional methods.

Obsolescence can be avoided in tutoring programs that include consistent input of new material to be learned (e.g., Maheady & Harper, 1987) and that employ procedures for introducing both tutors and tutees to new material prior to tutoring sessions. Systematic error correction procedures also enable tutors to detect errors and provide corrective feedback, such that tutoring interactions may continue to be productive as new content is added and old content is reviewed.

Naturalistic versus Structured Teaching Procedures

Integration is supported by tutors' sustained use of structured peer teaching procedures. Tutoring programs differ in the extent to which tutors' teaching strategies are left to the discretion of the tutor or conform to accepted principles of effective instruction. Conventional tutoring methods have not sought to equip tutors with teaching procedures. Instead, tutors have been given substantial responsibility for determining how to work with their tutees. Unfortunately, teachers are seldom in a position to turn over the responsibility of selecting teaching procedures to more than a few tutors and then for only limited periods of time. Consequently, to employ wide-scale and long-term tutoring, tutors require training in effective instructional procedures.

As early as 1970, Niedermeyer (1970) reported that training tutors in specific instructional techniques (e.g., task presentation and feedback) resulted in better achievement outcomes than no training at all. Thus, most tutoring programs provide varying types of peer teaching structure (e.g., sequences and routines for task presentation, error correction, and provision of feedback and reinforcement).

One benefit of structured tutoring procedures is that the accuracy or fidelity of implementation by tutors can be assessed, monitored, and shaped on an ongoing basis. The assessment of implementation is particularly important because researchers have reported considerable variation in the accuracy with which tutors have followed specific procedures (e.g., Johnson & Bailey, 1974; Kohler, 1986). Oftentimes, contingencies have been employed to maintain tutors' performance at a high level (Greenwood, Delquadri, & Carta, in press). In this regard, structured tutoring programs fit models of accountability better than do naturalistic tutoring programs.

Content and Tasks

Integration is supported by most procedures that provide instructionally relevant subject matter and at-level content and tasks for *all* students. The learning tasks used in tutoring, compared to those in conventional teacher-mediated instruction, often require specialized properties. For example, if tutoring is based on a mastery learning approach (as is often the case) learning tasks need to be organized into short, daily units that are sequenced hierarchically by difficulty level. If based on a cooperative learning approach in which students are assigned to develop a product, task individuization can be accomplished by differentiating students' contributions on the basis of their ability levels. For example, when painting a mural depicting the western movement in the 1870s, the tutee with fine motor deficits might paint the sky and the nonhandicapped tutor might sketch in the covered wagons.

Rather than the open-ended study tasks or the worksheets often used during independent study or seatwork activities, tutoring materials may need to be designed so that they fit an *interactive, discrete trials format* of tutor presentation and tutee response (e.g., Heron,

Heward, Cook, & Hill, 1983). For example, from a list of spelling words the tutor asks the tutee to spell the word cat. The tutee then attempts to write the word, spelling it orally while also writing it on a work sheet. When complete, the tutor checks the word against the list and awards points or provides a correction.

In some tutoring applications, conventional curriculum materials can be employed directly but in a nontraditional design of instruction. An example is the use of basal textbook stories that are divided into several shorter 100-word passages for use each day during tutoring sessions. Rather than assigning an entire story, shorter passages that can be read repeatedly during tutoring are employed (e.g., Greenwood, Delquadri, & Hall, 1989).

Materials and procedure that enable correction of tutee responses frequently are required in peer tutoring (e.g., answer lists, words spelled phonetically to prompt correct pronunciation by tutors, correction routines, etc.). Additionally, procedures that make it possible to chart tutees' performance trends frequently are employed. Thus, sheets for recording points earned or graphing the number of correctly spelled words are typical.

Tutor Training

Integration is most supported by procedures that enable tutors to be optimally effective teachers. The amount of training provided tutors and their tutees may vary widely, depending on the complexity of the program and the skills of the tutors. If tutors need to learn specific methods of task presentation and error correction and the uses of consequences (e.g., points, tokens, praise), tutor training requires advance planning. Additionally, several sessions are often needed to implement tutor training and to monitor the acquisition of tutoring skills.

In applications in which tutors will be working with children with special needs, it also may be desirable that tutors learn about the nature of disability, what to reasonably expect, and how to deal effectively with responses that may fall outside of the usual range of conventional classroom behavior (e.g., Whorton, Rotholz, Walker, McGrale, & Locke, 1987).

In some tutoring programs with very young and/or handicapped students, it also may be necessary to teach tutors the academic responses that they then must teach to their tutees. For example, Kohler (1987) reported that tutors of preschoolers had to be trained first in color names prior to tutoring their peers in the same skills. A similar preteaching procedure was employed by Brown, Fenrick, and Klemme (1971) with trainable-level students.

Secondary or Side Effects

Integration is most supported by programs that produce largely positive side effects. Research has demonstrated that an often observed side effect of tutoring programs is that tutors benefit academically as much or more than their tutees (e.g., Greer & Polirstok, 1982; Polirstok & Greer, 1986). However, this outcome has not always been the case. It may be that tutors who are required to teach skills that they have mastered only recently may have the opportunity of firming up these skills as a result of tutoring other students. In other circumstances, tutors may have opportunities to maintain and generalize uses of academic skills acquired in other situations (e.g., as a result of direct teacher instruction).

Tutoring programs implemented primarily to improve students' academic skills also have been linked to increases in the sociometric status of tutored students (e.g., Maheady & Sainato, 1985), increases in peer social interactions between handicapped and nonhandicapped students (e.g., Johnson, Johnson, Warring, & Maruyama, 1986), improved relationships between minority group and majority group students (Sharan, 1980), and improved social adjustment for both tutor and tutee (Maheady & Sainato, 1985).

On of the negative side, however, being a tutor may mean time away from the conventional classroom program. The trade-off between time away and time

tutoring others is a consideration that must be made relative to the potential benefits for both tutor and tutee (e.g., Greenwood, 1981).

Tutoring programs in which one person is always the tutee also may create additional problems for some teachers and students. Such programs indirectly may stigmatize tutees as low achievers or as slow learners. Tutees who never have the opportunity to serve as tutors may have a higher risk of becoming reluctant participants, sometimes even refusing to engage in tutoring activities (e.g., Greenwood, Carta, & Hall, 1988).

Who May Tutor Whom

Integration is supported best by those systems that enable a wide variety of students to serve as tutors. Traditionally, the "ideal" tutor has been considered to be the student who has both the social and academic skills necessary to instruct a tutee with a minimum of training, teacher planning, and teacher assistance. Consequently, selection of ideal tutors most frequently has been made on the basis of a teacher's judgment alone or aided by academic test information (Jenkins, Mayhall, Peschka, & Jenkins, 1974). Thus, in many tutoring applications, tutors have been upper-grade and/ or higher-ability students who spend a portion of the day working one-on-one in a lower-grade or special education classroom (e.g., Jenkins & Jenkins, 1981; 1985).

Unfortunately, tutor selection based on the ideal tutor concept produces only a limited number of tutors that meet ideal criteria, and higher-skilled tutors are always in short supply. Short of the ideal, however, peers of equal or even less academic ability (e.g., Osguthorpe & Scruggs, 1986) under certain conditions of training and monitoring that we will discuss, are clearly able to provide appropriate tutoring services.

In *classwide* tutoring programs, all students in a class can legitimately serve as tutor, and, in fact, can serve as both tutor and tutee in the course of a single tutoring session. For example, Delquadri, Greenwood, Stretton, and Hall (1983) reported a classwide program in which tutor/tutee pairs were formed randomly each week. Students formed partnerships simply by drawing names from a box. In this program, each student served as the tutor for half the session and then switched roles in the second half of the session. Using answer sheets and assistance from the teacher, all students were able to present task trials and to make adequate corrections when in the tutor's role.

Arrangements: Pairs, Triads, and Teams

Integration is supported by the opportunity to have working interactions with tutors in the regular classroom and to participate directly in a team effort. Although pairs are the typical tutoring unit, some tutoring programs accommodate triads (i.e., one tutor and two tutees), and team arrangements (Greenwood, Dinwiddie, et al., 1987; Pigott, Fantuzzo, & Clement, 1986). Either by design or on those occasions when an uneven number of students with educational deficits are present in a class, one tutor can teach two tutees simultaneously (e.g., Greenwood, Dinwiddie et al., 1987). Other programs may employ teams composed of small student groups in which any team member may tutor any other member. For example, in team-assisted individualization (TAI), a form of cooperative learning, four or five teams consisting of four, five, or six students of heterogeneous ability, are formed in a classroom (Slavin, 1984). By design, each team is composed of students representing highest-, medium-, and lowest-ability students. Heterogeneous team composition procedures ensure access of lower-ability students to higher-skilled peers and to help when needed (Maheady, Sacca, & Harper, 1988; Slavin, Madden, & Leavey, 1984).

Other programs (e.g., Heward, Heron and their colleagues) employ both pairs and teams within a classwide peer tutoring program (Heward, Heron, Ellis, & Cooke, 1986). As in TAI, tutor/tutee pairs are assigned to heterogeneous teams. Teams meet together before and after tutoring sessions to introduce new material and correct completed work. The teams or "tutor huddles" are supervised by the higher-skilled students who introduce new material, clarify instructions, supervise, and correct. During tutoring sessions, the tutoring pairs work independently through the material to be learned (Heron et al., 1983).

Contingencies and Consequences

Integration is supported by tutoring programs that employ reinforcement contingencies. Because of their motivational properties, contingencies may be employed to improve each student's performance as a tutor and as a tutee, and to maintain enthusiasm and participation (Greenwood & Hops, 1981). However, tutoring procedures vary in the extent to which contingencies of reinforcement are employed and their beneficial effects are fully exploited.

In naturalistic applications of tutoring, individual contingencies of social reinforcement and punishment operate naturally in the context of the moment-to-moment interactions between tutor and tutee. Also in naturalistic applications, these contingencies are determined by the tutor and tutee as they work together. In the process of tutoring, tutors and tutees may or may not provide one another prompts for responses, feedback, and forms of approval or disapproval as they work together.

In most structured tutoring programs, however, a tutor's use of prompts, feedback, and approval are designed according to principles of effective teaching and monitored for occurrence by the classroom teacher. These interactions often take the form of the presentation of task trials by the tutor and task responses by the tutee (e.g., Kohler, Richardson, Mina, Dinwiddie, & Greenwood, 1985). For example, the tutor may be taught to award points and approval for correct tutee responses and/or to remove points based on off-task or slow responding.

In contrast with individual contingencies that exist within the tutor and tutee interaction, group-oriented contingencies are focused on the collective performance of *all* tutee and tutor pairs in the classroom. These contingencies increase the amount of reinforcement any single student can receive. For example, the classwide program developed by Delquadri and his colleagues employs a point system implemented by the tutors that is the basis for both individual and group reinforcement. At the individual level, tutees earn points for responding to the tutor and/or the tutoring materials. Additionally, each tutor/tutee pair is a member of one of two teams that are competing for the highest point total. At the group reinforcement level, each pair contributes their individual point totals towards a winning team effort. At the end of each session, the individual points are summed for each team and the team with the highest point total is announced the winner.

Data-based Evaluation

Integration is most supported by programs that employ several forms of evaluation. These measures often reflect information on the quality of the tutoring program (implementation quality), the effects of tutoring from day to day (formative evaluation), and the effects on academic achievement over a semester or an entire school year (summative evaluation).

Tutoring programs vary in the extent to which data are collected and used to monitor and improve the quality of the program. Relatively few programs have conducted assessments to confirm that the teachers' and tutors' are implementing the program as it was designed and intended. For example, Maheady and Harper (1987) and Greenwood, Dinwiddie et al., 1987 employed observational checklists to assess the presence of the necessary materials, correct sequence of teacher behaviors, and students' tutoring behaviors. Similarly, Greenwood, Dinwiddie, et al. (1987) used implementation data to certify teachers as trained in a tutoring program and to monitor the quality of their continued use of it over time. Because of these assessments, it was ensured that the results of these studies truly represented the effects of the program as designed by the researchers and were not confounded by teacher-specific variations made in the program.

Programs that employ point systems to reinforce tutoring behaviors may use point earning data to track the extent of tutees' participation in the daily tutoring sessions (e.g., Maheady & Harper, 1987). If participation is low (i.e., a low number of points earned relative to the number earned the day before or compared to peers' scores), adaptations in the program are made to improve students' work pace (e.g., the number of spelling words attempted or sentences read by the tutee).

Other programs have collected and graphed information concerning the errors made during tutoring sessions, or fluency on reading rate checks assessed sometime after tutoring sessions (e.g., Delquadri, Greenwood, Whorton, Carta, & Hall, 1986). The information is used to assess the daily or weekly impact of the program (e.g., Deno, 1985; Deno & Fuchs, 1987). Other programs have employed curriculum-based achievement measures, teacher-developed tests (e.g., pretest and posttest measures of material taught), or publishers' unit tests to assess the effects of tutoring activities. Because of their direct relationship to what is taught in the tutoring program, each measure just discussed is highly sensitive to daily and weekly instructional efforts.

In conjunction with these measures of program implementation, many peer tutoring programs also have assessed academic achievement indirectly through use of students' grades, individualized educational plan (IEP) objectives mastered, or standardized, norm-referenced achievement tests. These measures, however, are considerably less sensitive to daily and weekly instructional efforts but do reflect attainment of instructional goals over significant periods of time (e.g., Greenwood, Delquadri, & Hall, 1989).

Administrative Support

Integration is facilitated most when

clearly identifiable administrative supports exist for tutoring programs and resources are provided routinely by school personnel other than the classroom teacher. Tutoring programs vary in the extent to which they are implemented through individual teachers' classroom procedures rather than formally adopted classroom and school curriculum, in the context of the district's administrative structure.

One form of evidence of the formal adoption of tutoring procedures can be found in a district's published curriculum guide for teachers or as a procedure in the IEPs of special education students. Another form of evidence is formal descriptions of tutoring procedures and standards for their implementation. Another is formal training experiences provided teachers and district staff in these procedures.

Another indication of administrative support is the extent to which professionals other than the regular classroom teacher (e.g., special education teachers, school psychologists, school principals, grade-level curriculum coordinators, and district executive officers) have been informed of the rationale for tutoring and its particular procedures. More significantly, if both administrative and program personnel have a role to play in a specific tutoring program a greater impact can be expected.

For example, in buildings where the curriculum coordinators and lead teachers serve as trainers and coaches for a tutoring program, sustained use of tutoring programs is likely to occur. In buildings where the principal plays a role in objectively evaluating a teacher's implementation of a tutoring program or posts in the office weekly summaries of data produced in all classrooms where tutoring is occurring, tutoring programs likely will be implemented broadly and will be maintained over time (Delquadri, personal communication, 1989). In contrast, where teachers are allowed to employ peer tutoring at their own discretion and the principal plays no direct role, the program probably will not be employed schoolwide nor will it persist from year to year.

Up to this point, we have examined a number of basic components and issues concerning tutoring programs and support for integration. We now turn to a description of a specific peer tutoring program, classwide peer tutoring (CWPT) (Greenwood, Delquadri, & Carta, 1988), that has been widely evaluated in a number of experimental studies, independently replicated, and widely disseminated.

CLASS PEER TUTORING

CWPT is a result of our original goal of developing an effective instructional procedure for use in urban classrooms with students of heterogeneous ability levels. It is a program that has been employed extensively at the elementary level with a number of recent applications at the secondary level (see reviews by Delquadri et al., 1986 and Greenwood, Carta, & Hall, 1988). Before describing it, however, we first present a classroom illustration of the program's use.

A Typical CWPT Scenario

Compared to what I had been doing in spelling, CWPT called for some dramatic changes in classroom organization. Rather than working independently or in small groups, students now work together in pairs and each pair belongs to one of two teams. In spelling, I introduce new words to be learned on Mondays, rather than as I used to at the end of each unit. I continue to pull the words from my scope and sequence chart and the basal text I was using in reading. As per the manual, I put 15 words on each weekly list. Rather than assigning seatwork and homework as a means of practicing the spelling words like I used to do, in CWPT I now have the students tutor each other for 20 minutes each day, Monday through Thursday.

After tutoring for 10 minutes, the tutor and tutee trade responsibilities and a second 10 minute tutoring session begins. Thus, all students are asked to spell each word on the list orally and in writing. Tutors give their tutees points for correct spelling and for practicing the correct spelling of any word(s) they miss. After the two spelling periods, I tally up the points earned by each student on each team. I also tally up the points that I gave intermittently to the tutors as a reinforcer for using the correct tutoring behaviors.

What I like most about the program is that it gives me a positive way to supervise the responding of all my students at the same time. My lowest achievers and my mainstreamed LD students all participate. Because there is no grouping, my teaching during tutoring is more focused. Compared to my prior approach to spelling instruction, I now have time to check the practice of each pair of students, to give them praise, and to answer their questions immediately about words they can't read or understand. They all like having the opportunity to be the tutor and you should see how excited they are each week when we draw for partners and teams for the next week. I appreciate how much more positive my interactions are now with my class and they with me.

I followed the manual in implementing it so that before using the program we had practiced all parts of it before putting it all together. Thus, even on the first full tutoring day, things went quite smoothly.

The program has had a rapid impact on the accuracy of their Friday spelling tests and has most noticeably reduced down time and the behavior problems I had before tutoring when I assigned them spelling seatwork. It seems now that because the students are so busy giving words as tutors or writing words as tutees that they don't have time for behavior problems. Even my lowest students are reliably scoring above 70% correct and the class average for the last two weeks has been 88%. Most student are now spelling between 13 to 15 words correctly each week.

As soon as spelling tutoring was running smoothly, I incorporated it into my reading program. I decreased the time I spent in reading groups from four times to two times per week. I then scheduled the students to tutor each other three times per week on passages from the stories we were working on in the basal text. In the first reading group time each week, I introduce new vocab-

ulary, drill the students on the reading of these words in isolation, and then make the passage assignments for the week. Most stories can be divided into three 100-word passages that even my mainstreamed students could read through twice in ten minutes. During the last reading group on Fridays now, I have the students read to me from their last tutored passage. Based on these checks, I assess each student's reading rate and comprehension.

The reading rate checks which I learned to use to assess progress in the tutoring program were a real eye opener. Each student's chart indicated that they had increased their fluency; that is, they read faster with fewer errors after having tutored on the material. So my Friday reading group now is a time that I honestly enjoy listening to my students read. In the past I really dreaded listening to them read. The hesitations and outright pronunciation errors so frequent before are now gone. Because of CWPT, I now know for sure that the students have practiced the material in advance of reading it to me. I am now seeing my lowest readers for the first time interested in reading and really being successful with it. (Greenwood, Delquadri, & Carta, 1988)

Evident within this scenario are a number of issues that relate to the implementation of classwide peer tutoring. These include (a) the initial decision to employ CWPT, (b) the teacher's role, (c) the students' roles, and (c) the component procedures. We now discuss these in some detail.

When to Use CWPT

CWPT is appropriate for use in a number of situations. CWPT is a means of providing additional opportunities to respond and to practice tasks in a particular subject matter. It is also an efficient means of increasing students' academic engagement, providing feedback on their performance, reducing "down time" during direct instruction or independent seatwork, and reducing off-task and acting-out behavior problems. Consequently, it is an appropriate means for increasing the achievement of all students in a classroom. Because it may be used by all students at the same time and is only moderately constrained by heterogeneous academic ability levels, it is also a means of involving students with mild handicaps directly and simultaneously in instruction with their nonhandicapped peers. CWPT is particularly effective in building fluency in basic skills initially acquired in other instructional situations, enhancing students' acquisition of factual information in content area studies, and in increasing students' correct response rates.

Teacher's Role

The teacher's role in CWPT is spread across several levels. Clearly, the teacher's role is directed toward specific program tasks. As in conventional instruction, the teacher plans what will be taught, designs the materials, and trains the students to implement the program. Uniquely to CWPT sessions, however, the teacher serves as a *monitor of student responding* rather than as the direct conveyer of the lesson. During CWPT sessions, the teacher's first responsibility is to reinforce correct tutoring behaviors consistently. This is done by pinpointing tutoring behaviors that are to be used (e.g., presenting items, correcting errors) while observing tutoring pairs, and providing consequences in the form of praise and bonus points.

A second role of the teacher is that of providing clarification and correction when necessary. For example, tutors occasionally need help either in pronouncing or reading words or in understanding the assignment. Teachers limit the need for help by introducing new material prior to tutoring sessions, and thereafter by providing assistance directly when tutors signal the need for help.

A third role, performed by the teacher before and after tutoring sessions, involves the general operation of the tutoring sessions, including selecting partners and forming teams; starting, ending and timing sessions; and summarizing the points earned by individuals and their teams.

Students' Roles

Compared to traditional tutoring procedures, in which tutor and tutee roles are fixed, students in CWPT perform *both* tutor and tutee roles during each CWPT session. In the tutor role, students monitor the responding of their tutees. Depending on the accuracy of the tutees' responses, the tutors provide points and/or error correction trials. In passage reading, for example, the instructional task is the reading of sentences from a text. As the tutees read their passages, tutors provide points for each correctly read sentence and correction trials for hesitations, omissions, mispronunciations, and substitutions (for more detail see Greenwood, Delquadri, & Carta, 1988).

In math and spelling, tutors are also responsible for presenting their tutees with opportunities to respond. For example, reading from a list of spelling words, a tutor would state: "Spell forget." The tutee would spell it aloud and write it at the same time. If the tutee should misspell the word, the tutor would provide the correct spelling. The tutee then would have the opportunity to practice spelling the word correctly three times.

In the tutee role, students earn points for their team by responding correctly to the items presented or by correctly practicing any errors identified by their tutor. A correct response earns two points. If an error is made, the tutor models the correct spelling, after which the tutee practices spelling the word three times. In reading, the tutee correctly rereads the sentence. Either correction effort earns the tutee one point. After half of a CWPT session (i.e., 10 minutes) roles are changed. All tutors become tutees and vice versa.

Procedures

Content development. Relatively simple procedures are employed to develop instructional content for CWPT. The content selected to be taught in CWPT is based directly on the curriculum currently employed in the school and classroom. CWPT is designed specifically to support the current curriculum. The goal of content preparation for CWPT is to define a set of materials appropriate for the class that have not yet been mastered. Determining content is accomplished by reviewing grade-level scope and sequence goals and/or student IEP goals, fixing a hierarchical sequence of material to be learned, and updating this sequence on the basis of students' weekly pretest and posttest data. Thus, each week all students are encountering some material they have not yet mastered.

The weekly tutoring content in spelling or math, is a set of item lists sequenced in the same order as material that would be taught by traditional means in the class. One list of 10-20 items is tutored each week. In reading, passages of text are used. This material is read out loud by the tutee to the tutor. It is also the basis for oral reading rate and comprehension checks made by the teacher after tutoring sessions.

The material employed in CWPT is individualized, but not completely so for all students. Students may be advanced to (a) more *difficult* or (b) *longer* sets of material, on the basis of pretest assessment information. To keep the program simple and reduce tutor and teacher demands, the unit of curriculum individuation in CWPT is the group rather than the individual. That is, some students in the class will have mastered some words on a list. Materials are considered appropriately difficult when pretest group averages are between 0% and 40% correct or when reading rates are below peer normative rates (e.g., Greenwood, Delquadri, & Carta, 1988; Lentz, 1988).

In CWPT, the length of the material to be used (i.e., number of items on a list or number of words in a reading passage) is determined so that sufficient practice occurs in each session. A functional rule of thumb is that the length of material must be set so that the lowest ability student can practice through the entire material at least twice in a single 10 minute tutoring session.

Curriculum-based and criterion-based assessment. In CWPT, curriculum-based and criterion-based assessments serve to monitor the academic effects of weekly CWPT. To assess progress, spelling and math CWPT teachers are trained to employ weekly pretest and posttest assessments covering the material to be tutored. The pretest data are used to confirm that the material is appropriately new and difficult for the next week's tutoring. If the class mean is above 40% correct on the pretest, the teacher is advised to delete the most frequently correct items and to replace them with more difficult items. The posttest data are used to assess the mastery of the material tutored that week. Mastery is demonstrated if the class mean is at least 80% on the posttest. Pre- and posttest data are charted each week.

In reading, 1-minute rate checks are employed. From these checks, the rates of correct and incorrect words per minute are computed and charted. A qualitative rating of students' responses to five comprehension questions asked by the teacher also is used.

Pre- and posttest data or weekly reading rate checks are used by the teacher (a) to make optimal adjustments in the difficulty of new material, and (b) to demonstrate that CWPT consistently improves mastery and/or fluency levels compared to those in evidence before CWPT was introduced. These data are displayed publicly in the classroom so that students have the opportunity to know how well they perform each week.

Peer pairing. To achieve the general goal of classwide participation in tutoring (i.e., of ensuring that any child can be a tutor for another child), relatively loose criteria for peer pairing criteria are used in CWPT. In spelling, math, and vocabulary, a random system of pairing is employed. On Mondays each week, students draw from a hat for assignment to partners and partners to teams. Random pairing is possible in these three content areas because error correction by the tutors is supported by answer lists against which they can compare the tutees' written responses for accuracy.

In CWPT applications that rely on the

tutors' unaided ability to identify errors (i.e., when the correct answers are not available), ability matching is employed. For example, in tutoring of oral reading students are paired according to their placement in the reading program; students are paired from within the same or adjacent levels of the basal reader (Greenwood, Delquadri, & Carta, 1988). Thus, students placed in level A reader (same level) or in a level A and B reader (adjacent levels) could be paired but not usually students in levels A and C. Only in the case of a very low skilled student, a student with a disability, or a student for whom English is a second language, would nonadjacent pairings be considered as a means of temporarily supporting this student's instruction.

Group and individual contingencies. Both group and individual contingencies (points awarded) are employed in CWPT to maintain motivation and the quality of peer tutoring. Tutees are awarded points for each correct first time response (2 points) and for correctly practicing the correct response following an error (1 point). Points are recorded on a laminated point sheet that can be erased and reused. Tutors receive bonus points from the teacher for instances of correct tutoring behaviors. At the end of a tutoring session, students report their total points earned. Individual points are summed for each of two teams and the winning team is determined. The winning team is applauded after each tutoring session and the weekly winner is allowed to post a *Team of the Week Certificate.* The losing team after each session is also applauded for making a good effort and it is challenged to work harder in the next session.

Teacher training. Teachers learn to use the program through a manual (Greenwood, Delquadri, & Carta, 1988) and structured interactions with a CWPT consultant. Typically, three consultant visits are required to assist teachers in selecting the specific content to be taught in tutoring, in preparing the necessary materials, and in answering specific questions about fitting the program to the class. Then the teacher is ready to train students to implement the tutoring procedures.

Students are taught by the classroom teacher to implement the tutoring procedures in four 30-minute lessons. The full program is implemented when all students have mastered each of the four steps. An implementation checklist is used by a consultant as a means of providing feedback to teachers on the accuracy of their implementation (see Greenwood, Delquadri, & Carta, 1988). The aspects of the program that need improvement (i.e., either teacher behavior or student tutoring behavior) are reviewed and plans are made to incorporate them into the next tutoring session. The teacher and students are fully trained when these assessments indicate that 90% of the items (i.e., materials, teacher behaviors, and student behaviors) are in evidence during a tutoring session.

In one recent investigation of the training requirements of peer tutoring, Maheady, Winstanley, Mallette, and Harper (in preparation) found that eight elementary school teachers reached a predetermined criterion (i.e., three consecutive sessions with fidelity ratings of 90% and above without consultant assistance) with an average training time of 178 minutes. Subsequent fidelity checks indicate that implementation accuracy remained high (above 90%) without further involvement of the consultant.

Frequently Made Implementation Errors and Problems in CWPT

Implementation errors in CWPT generally occur at two levels, the school and classroom. At the school level, a common error is omitting complete orientation of all personnel. Complete orientation of personnel ensures that the program will not be terminated by one of these persons on the basis of lack of information. We have observed several programs that were terminated because persons were oriented on a need-to-know basis and those not advised believed the program to be inconsistent with some aspects of district policy or their own personal teaching philosophies.

At the classroom level, errors related to training, planning, scheduling, deviations from standard implementation, and evaluation may arise. Teachers who attempt to implement CWPT without sufficient knowledge of, and training in, the program commit a basic error. Teachers must use the CWPT manual and follow it precisely to avoid failure. The manual provides CWPT lessons in which tutoring skills and "etiquette" (i.e., being a good sport) are introduced, and practiced first in isolation and then in sequence. These lessons must be completed before attempting the first "full" tutoring session. The program likely will fail in the absence of advanced planning and the preparation of content material to be used.

An often-encountered implementation issue relates to scheduling. We recommend that tutoring sessions in a given subject (e.g., spelling), occur at least four times per week. It is not appropriate to schedule tutoring during times when some of the students are attending "pullout programs" if CWPT is expected to affect all students' achievement. Many teachers find themselves wondering if CWPT is to replace something they are currently doing, or if it is to be used in addition to what they are doing. In our experience, the instructional day is so tightly defined that it is unrealistic to consider CWPT as an add on. Instead, we recommend using CWPT as an alternative practice activity preferably in place of independent seatwork.

Teachers must not adapt or omit particular components of the peer tutoring program freely and expect CWPT to work for them. For example, we observed students' progress drop dramatically when a teacher permitted the oral spelling of words but omitted the written component (Experiment III in Greenwood, Dinwiddie et al., 1984). Similar problems have occurred when teachers have decided not to employ team competition or daily points.

Another frequently occurring implementation error involves the teacher's failure to use bonus points. The fidelity of peer tutoring behaviors will diminish if the teacher does not use the bonus point procedures reliably for shaping and maintaining tutoring behaviors. This is because points ensure quality control over correct tutoring behaviors. Teachers intermittently give bonus points to tutors for correct item presentations, and for making correct and rapid corrections. Teachers must not take time away from this important task to grade papers or conduct other administrative work. Similarly, students will lose interest in the program if the teacher does not follow through by adding up the points and identifying the winning team. It is also important that determination of the winning team be accomplished *immediately* after the session so that the use of points as a reinforcer is not diminished.

If the program is implemented correctly, most tutoring problems can be prevented. However, in our experience with CWPT, we have encountered four routine problems that often require remediation (a) increased noise levels, (b) student cheating, (c) occasional bickering and disruptiveness, and (d) low point totals. Any of these problems, if allowed to persist, may jeopardize the effectiveness and efficiency of CWPT for the entire class. External consultants should be aware of such problems, apply the procedures discussed in the CWPT manual to prevent them, and be prepared to offer instructional alternatives. For example, low noise levels can be maintained effectively through the use of explicit rules (e.g., talk only during tutoring sessions, speak only to your tutoring partner, and use your "inside" voices) and the contingent use of consequences. Students can be awarded bonus points for following rules, or a brief time-out from the opportunity to earn points (i.e., all pencils down for 15–30 seconds) can be used when noise levels become excessive.

Cheating may take a number of forms. Students may deviate from prescribed procedures by simply providing answers to tutees, or they may not require tutees to use the error correction procedure. We have found that teacher monitoring and reinforcement for following procedures to be most effective in either pre-empting or reducing cheating of this type. Occasionally, one may also find "point inflation," students reporting more points than they actually earned. Random selection and rescoring of individual papers and the awarding of bonus points for reporting correct totals have been used effectively to reduce this type of cheating.

Other problems with tutoring such as student bickering and disruptiveness, are dealt with through warnings and brief time-outs from point earning, while differential reinforcement (i.e., attention and bonus points) is continuously provided for quiet cooperative dyads on competing teams. Finally, students who because of low response rates, evidenced by low point totals, often are moved into tutoring triads after tutoring procedures have been well established. Here, they receive double practice by serving as tutees twice and by earning double points for their teams.

Effectiveness

A number of experimental studies evaluating CWPT have appeared in the literature. These studies have ranged from small sample, single-subject studies to studies of large-sample, longitudinal, experimental/control group designs.

Single-subject studies. An early study in which CWPT was employed in a single, urban school classroom demonstrated that the weekly spelling test scores of the lowest performing students could be improved to a level of accuracy on weekly tests that was comparable to that of other students in the classroom (Delquadri et al., 1983; Hall et al., 1982). Additional single-subject studies in urban school classrooms indicated that students improved their spelling, vocabulary, and math fact skills when CWPT was employed in comparison with results when the conventional teacher-designed instruction was employed (Dinwiddie, 1986; Greenwood, Dinwiddie et al., 1987; Kohler, 1986).

Greenwood, Dinwiddie, et al. (1987) also demonstrated that during CWPT students were engaged more frequently in

academic behavior than during conventional teacher-mediated instruction. Observation measures in this study and others (Greenwood, Delquadri, & Hall, 1984) have also indicated the presence of tutoring in the classroom by way of differences in teachers' observed instructional behavior and increases in the time students spend using tutoring tasks (e.g., paper and pencil, readers). In another study spanning 2 years, 211 students in Chapter 1 schools were found to be significantly more accurate on their spelling tests in comparison to students under teacher-designed instruction (Greenwood, Dinwiddie, et al., 1987).

The powerful academic effects of CWPT have subsequently been replicated and extended by independent investigators. For example, Maheady and Harper (1987) replicated tutoring effects in spelling with low-income, minority youngsters, and these effects were later extended to content area courses (e.g., social studies) at the secondary level (Maheady, Harper & Sacca, 1988; Maheady, Sacca, & Harper, 1988). Each application substantially improved the performance of entire classrooms, often by as much as two letter grades (i.e., D to B averages).

Experimental-control group studies. Delquadri and his colleagues conducted two experimental/control group studies in urban schools in which students with learning disabilities were mainstreamed. In the first study (Greenwood, Delquadri, & Hall, 1984), reading CWPT was employed by teachers in an experimental group who were trained by the investigators. In comparisons with a normative peer group and a control group, the CWPT group students significantly decreased their mean error rates (e.g., substitutions, omissions, hesitations).

Delquadri et al. (1986) replicated this previous study but added an additional level of training and service. The primary question addressed in this study was whether school-based consultants (i.e., LD resource-room teachers) could be trained to identify and teach regular classroom teachers to implement CWPT during reading. The results replicated those noted previously. CWPT students, including mainstreamed target students with learning disabilities, increased their reading fluency in terms of words read correctly and reduction in errors. Additionally, teachers' ratings of students' comprehension of the tutored material were significantly improved compared with ratings of control and normative peer groups.

In a longitudinal project spanning Grades 1-4 (Greenwood, Delquadri, & Hall, 1989), students in urban schools whose teachers employed CWPT each year performed significantly better on the reading, mathematics, and language subtests of the Metropolitan Achievement Test than did an equivalent control group. Effect sizes were 0.38 in mathematics, 0.58 in reading and 0.60 in language. By the end of fourth grade, tutoring group students approached the national normative level in these three subject areas, whereas controls were nearly one standard deviation below this level. Direct observation data confirmed that tutoring group students, in comparison with controls, increased their academic engagement (i.e., oral and silent reading, writing, academic talk, etc.) and reduced their time spent in task management (e.g., hand raising, attention, looking for materials), and in competing, inappropriate behaviors (e.g., looking around, disrupting, inappropriate locale).

Satisfaction of participants. In several of the previous evaluations, both teacher and students have expressed moderate to high degrees of satisfaction. For example, we reported that satisfaction ratings returned by 16 teachers on a 20-item survey ranged from a mean of 3.9 to 4.6 in one year (1 = lowest, 5 = highest rating) and 3.3 to 4.3 in a second year (Greenwood, Dinwiddie et al., 1987). In the same study, 211 students' satisfaction ratings on a 14-item survey ranged from 2.4 to 3.0 on a 3.0 point scaling (1.0 = low, 3.0 = high). Another recent investigation (Maheady, Winstanley, Mallette, & Harper, 1989) indicated that over 80% of 200 elementary students preferred CWPT over traditional teacher-led instruction and independent seatwork.

Cost. At present, the costs of CWPT are very reasonable. The manual, charts, and consumable materials for one classroom cost approximately $30.00–$50.00. Because the program adapts to the current curricula, no additional costs are necessary in this area.

ROLES AND TRAINING REQUIRED OF THE SCHOOL PSYCHOLOGIST

CWPT is a new development in instructional technology that supports aspects of the NASP statement concerning integration of handicapped students. If school psychologists are to play a major part in the integration effort, substantial role changes will be necessary. Most significant will be the use of school psychologists as implementers, supervisors, and evaluators of CWPT use.

Implementation Entry Skills

A number of skills are necessary for consultants who intend to provide teachers training in practices such as CWPT. First, in addition to consultation skills, school psychologists must demonstrate an ability to establish classroom interventions that can be successfully implemented by others. This knowledge and skill is clearly different from making diagnostic recommendations and advising teachers on how to solve a particular, troublesome problem. Because CWPT is a specific practice, it must be established in a classroom with a high degree of fidelity for it to produce optimal benefits. Psychologists must be able to provide in-class assistance or, at least, prepare a cadre of peer tutoring coaches to assist new teachers through their first implementation. School psychologists also should be experienced in the use of criterion-referenced and curriculum-based assessment. This knowledge will be useful in demonstrating the effects of CWPT intervention and in understanding the direct relationship between the CWPT program, student engagement, and measures of curriculum-based achievement.

Consultant–Trainer Role

As previously described, CWPT is an instructional option for solving a particular set of problems for all students simultaneously. School psychologists are in a unique position to recommend CWPT as one among a number of alternatives that teachers should consider. From our perspective, CWPT can be used as either a preventive or remedial intervention. Introducing tutoring procedures early in the year is often a useful strategy for preventing subsequent academic or behavioral problems. To use CWPT as a preventive option, school psychologists must engage in systematic staff development efforts, preferably at the beginning of the school year. Short awareness sessions can be conducted to acquaint teachers with the major components and principles underlying the use of CWPT. Subsequent in-class assistance then can be provided for interested teachers.

Psychologists also can use CWPT as a remediation option after learning problems have developed. CWPT is a particularly attractive intervention option in that (a) its powerful effects are almost immediately obvious, (b) it is feasible to implement, and (c) teachers and students usually like to use it. Moreover, the intervention target can be the entire class instead of a particular student. A class-wide intervention may facilitate integration in that handicapped students need not be singled out as the recipients of intervention. It also would appear that CWPT is an excellent option for prereferral intervention teams to consider when attempting to improve a student's performance prior to diagnostic assessment.

School psychologists may be in a good position to serve as primary disseminators of CWPT throughout school buildings and districts. Systematic dissemination efforts may include a "pyramid training model" of system wide intervention plans (Delquadri, Flanagan, & Greenwood, 1987). In such a model, the school psychologist engages the principal, a faculty elected

building representative, and the classroom teacher in a process of training, monitoring, and maintaining the program.

School psychologists also may function as direct teacher trainers in CWPT. This role may include the training of related school personnel including principals and regular and special education teachers in the roles of CWPT users and CWPT support personnel.

In this role, school psychologists might find themselves responsible for using curriculum- and criterion-based measures in the CWPT classrooms and within schools to provide feedback on progress. The school psychologist can provide the designs for summarizing and correctly interpreting these results. They can assist teachers in solving problems in the program. The psychologist is also responsible for providing checks on teachers' implementation and the feedback necessary to maintain a high level of program fidelity (e.g., Engelmann, 1989).

DISCUSSION AND CONCLUSION

In this chapter, we have argued that peer tutoring procedures are a means of orchestrating the classroom processes that are responsible for academic learning. Tutoring procedures are a means of increasing the breadth of instructional environments available to students with academic skills deficits. Some tutoring variations also may represent prototypes of the educational technology that will be necessary to address the frequently encountered problems of instructionally diverse student populations. Peer tutoring provides the opportunity for sufficient practice, high levels of student engagement, immediate error correction with feedback, and the integration of students with heterogeneous abilities including handicaps.

As a general class of procedures, peer tutoring is consistent with the recent NASP (1987) position statement on the regular education initiative. Moreover, peer tutoring programs have been used effectively by regular classroom teacher with students in urban schools including mainstreamed students with learning disabilities. In the evaluation studies we have conducted and reviewed, these procedures have been demonstrated to be acceptable to teachers, sustainable over time, and cost efficient relative to alternate practices.

Classwide peer tutoring, in particular, appears to be an underutilized technology that may benefit the rather large numbers of students who have mild disabilities. However, additional research will be necessary to confirm the breadth of its applicability across students, teachers, settings, and particular instructional goals. Furthermore, under the rather specific conditions of training, time, effort, and standards of classroom implementation we have described, tutoring may be delivered effectively by the school psychologist.

FOOTNOTE

[1]An effect size is a value reflecting the extent to which an experimental group mean exceeded the control group mean in terms of control group standard deviation units. Thus, an effect size of 2.0 indicates that the experimental group mean fell 2 standard deviations above the control group mean.

REFERENCES

Allen, V. L. (1976). *Children as teachers: Theory and research on tutoring.* New York: Academic.

Becker, W. C. (1977). Teaching reading and language to the disadvantaged: What we have learned from field research. *Harvard Educational Review, 47,* 518-543.

Becker, W. C. (1986). *Twenty years of Direct Instruction.* Paper presented at the XVII Banff International Conference on Behavioral Science, Banff, Alberta, Canada.

Bennett, W. J. (1986). Tutoring. *What works: Research about teaching and learning* (p. 36). Washington, DC: U.S. Department of Education.

Bloom, B. S. (1984). The 2 sigma problem: The search for methods of group instruction as effective as one-to-one tutoring. *Educational Researcher, 13,* 4-16.

Brophy, J. E. (1986). Teacher influences on student achievement. *American Psychologist, 41,* 1069-1089.

Brown, L., Fenrick, N., & Klemme, H. (1971). Trainable pupils learn to teach each other. *Teaching Exceptional Children, 4,* 18-24.

Carta, J. J., & Greenwood, C. R. (1988). Reducing academic risks in inner-city classrooms. *Youth Policy, 10,* 16-18.

Carnine, D. W. (1976). Effects of two teacher-presentation rates of off-task behavior, answering correctly, and participation. *Journal of Applied Behavior Analysis, 9,* 199-206.

Cooke, N. L., Heron, T. E., & Heward, W. L. (1983). *Peer tutoring: Implementing classwide programs in the primary grades.* Columbus, OH: Special Press.

Custer, J. D., & Osguthorpe, R. T. (1983). Improving social acceptance by training handicapped students to tutor their non-handicapped peers. *Exceptional Children, 50,* 175.

Delquadri, J. (1978). *An analysis of the generalization effects of four tutoring procedures on the oral reading responses of eight learning disability children.* Unpublished doctoral dissertation. University of Kansas, Department of Human Development and Family Life.

Delquadri, J., Flanagan, P., & Greenwood, C. R. (1987). *The pyramid administrative model for classwide peer tutoring.* Kansas City, KS: The Juniper Gardens Children's Project.

Delquadri, J., Greenwood, C. R., Stretton, K., & Hall, R. V. (1983). The peer tutoring game: A classroom procedure for increasing opportunity to respond and spelling performance. *Education and Treatment of Children, 6,* 225-239.

Delquadri, J., Greenwood, C. R., Whorton, D., Carta, J. J., & Hall, R. V. (1986). Classwide peer tutoring. *Exceptional Children, 52,* 535-542.

Deno, S. L. (1985). Curriculum-based measurement: The emerging alternative. *Exceptional Children, 52,* 219-232.

Deno, S. L., & Fuchs, L. S. (1987). Developing curriculum-based measurement systems for data-based special education problem solving. *Focus on Exceptional Children, 19*(8), 1-16.

Dinwiddie, G. (1986). *An assessment of the functional relationship between classwide peer tutoring and students' academic performance.* Doctoral Dissertation. University of Kansas, Department of Human Development and Family Life.

Edmonds, R. R. (1979). Effective schools for the urban poor. *Educational Leadership, 37,* 15-28.

Ehly, S. W., & Larsen, S. C. (1980). *Peer tutoring for individualized instruction.* Boston: Allyn and Bacon.

Engelmann, S. (1989). The logic and facts of effective supervision. *Education and Treatment of Children, 11*, 328-340.

Gartner, A., & Lipsky, D. K. (1987). Beyond special education: Toward a quality system for all students. *Harvard Educational Review, 57*, 367-395.

Gerber, M., & Kauffman, J. M. (1981). Peer tutoring in academic settings. In P. Strain (Ed.), *The utilization of peers as behavior change agents* (pp. 155-188). New York: Plenum.

Greenwood, C. R. (1981). Peer-oriented behavioral technology and ethical issues. In P. Strain (Ed.), *The utilization of peers as behavior change agents* (pp. 327-360). New York: Plenum.

Greenwood, C. R. (in press). A longitudinal analysis of time to learn, engagement, and academic achievement in urban versus suburban schools. *Exceptional Children.*

Greenwood, C. R., Carta, J. J., & Hall, R. V. (1988a). The use of tutoring strategies in classroom management and educational instruction. *School Psychology Review*, 258-275.

Greenwood, C. R., Delquadri, J., & Carta, J. J. (1988). *Classwide peer tutoring.* Delray Beach, FL: Educational Achievement Systems.

Greenwood, C. R., Delquadri, J., & Hall, R. V. (1984). Opportunity to respond and student academic performance. In W. L. Heward, T. E. Heron, J. Trap-Porter, & D. S. Hill (Eds.), *Focus on behavior analysis in education* (pp. 58-88). Columbus, OH: Merrill.

Greenwood, C. R., Delquadri, J., & Hall, R. V. (1989). Longitudinal analysis of the effects of classwide peer tutoring. *Journal of Educational Psychology, 81*, 371-383.

Greenwood, C. R., Delquadri, J. C., Stanley, S. O., Sasso, G., Whorton, D., & Schulte, D. (1981). Allocating opportunity to learn as a basis for academic remediation: A developing model for teaching. *Monograph in Behavior Disorders*, Summer, 22-33.

Greenwood, C. R., Dinwiddie, G., Bailey, V., Carta, J. J., Dorsey, D., Kohler, F. W., Nelson, C., Rotholz, D., & Schulte, D. (1987). Field replication of classwide peer tutoring. *Journal of Applied Behavior Analysis, 20*, 151-160.

Greenwood, C. R., Dinwiddie, G., Terry, B., Wade, L., Thibadeau, S., & Delquadri, J. (1984). Teacher- vs. peer-mediated instruction. *Journal of Applied Behavior Analysis, 17*, 521-538.

Greenwood, C. R., & Hops, H. (1981). Group contingencies and peer behavior change. In P. Strain (Ed.), *The utilization of classroom peers as behavior change agents* (pp. 189-259). New York: Plenum.

Greenwood, C. R., Hops, H., Delquadri, J., & Guild, J. (1974). Group contingencies for group consequences: A further analysis. *Journal of Applied Behavior Analysis, 7*, 413-425.

Greenwood, C. R., Hops, H., & Walker, H. M. (1977). Program for academic survival skills (PASS): Effects on student behavior and achievement. *Journal of School Psychology, 15*, 25-35.

Greenwood, C. R., Hops, H., Walker, H. M., guild, J. J., Stokes, J., Young, K., Keleman, K. S., & Willardson, M. (1979). Standardized classroom management program: Social validation and replication studies in Utah and Oregon. *Journal of Applied Behavior Analysis, 12*, 235-253.

Greer, R. D., & Polirstok, S. R. (1982). Collateral gains and short-term maintenance in reading and on-task responses by some inner-city adolescents as a function of their use of social reinforcement while tutoring. *Journal of Applied Behavior Analysis, 15*, 123-139.

Hall, R. V., Copeland, R. E., & Clark, M. (1975). The responsive teaching model: Management strategies for teachers and parents. In N. G. Haring & R. L. Schiefelbusch (Eds.), *Teaching special children* (pp. 157-195). New York: McGraw-Hill.

Hall, R. V., Delquadri, J., Greenwood, C., & Thurston, L. (1982). The importance of opportunity to respond in children's academic success. In E. D. Edgar, N. Haring, J. R. Jenkins, & C. Pious (Eds.), *Serving young handicapped children: Issues and Research* (pp. 107-149). Austin, TX: Pro-Ed.

Hallahan, D. P., Kauffman, J. M., Lloyd, J. W., & McKinney, J. D. (1988). The regular education initiative (Special Series). *Journal of Learning Disabilities, 21*, 1-65.

Heron, T. E., Heward, W. L., Cooke, N. L., & Hill, D. S. (1983). Evaluation of classwide peer tutoring systems: First graders teach each other sight words. *Education and Treatment of Children, 6*, 137-152.

Heward, W. L., Heron, T. E., & Cooke, N. L. (1982). Tutor huddle: Key element in a classwide peer tutoring system. *Elementary Education Journal, 82*, 115-123.

Heward, W. L., Heron, T. E., Ellis, D. E., & Cooke, N. L. (1986). Teaching first grade peer tutors to use verbal praise on an intermittent schedule. *Education and Treatment of Children, 9*, 5-15.

Jenkins, J. R., & Jenkins, L. M. (1981). *Cross age and peer tutoring: Help for children with learning problems.* Reston, VA: Council for Exceptional Children.

Jenkins, J. R., & Jenkins, L. M. (1985). Peer tutoring in elementary and secondary programs. *Focus on Exceptional Children, 17*, 1-12.

Jenkins, J. R., Mayhall, W. F., Peschka, C. M., & Jenkins, L. M. (1974). Comparing small group instruction in resource rooms. *Exceptional Children, 40,* 245–250.

Johnson, M., & Bailey, J. S. (1974). Cross-age tutoring: Fifth graders as arithmetic tutors for kindergarten children. *Journal of Applied Behavior Analysis, 7,* 223–232.

Johnson, D. W., Johnson, R. T., Warring, D., & Maruyama, G. (1986). Different cooperative learning procedures and cross-handicap relationships. *Exceptional Children, 53,* 247–252.

Kalfus, G. R. (1984). Peer mediated intervention: A critical review. *Child and Family Behavior therapy, 6,* 17–43.

Keller, F. S. (1968). "Good-bye teacher . . ." *Journal of Applied Behavior Analysis, 1,* 79–89.

Kohler, F. W. (1986). *Classwide peer tutoring: Examining natural contingencies of peer reinforcement.* Unpublished Doctoral Dissertation. University of Kansas, Department of Human Development and Family Life.

Kohler, F. W. (Chair). (1987, May). *Peer-mediation in the integrated classroom: A presentation of research at the LEAP preschool.* Symposium presented at the 13th annual convention of the Association for Behavior Analysis, Nashville, TN.

Kohler, F. W., Richardson, T., Mina, C., Dinwiddie, G., & Greenwood, C. R. (1985). Establishing cooperative peer relations in the classroom. *The Pointer, 29,* 12–16.

Lentz, F. E. (1988). Direct observation and measurement of academic skills: A conceptual review. In E. S. Shapiro & T. R. Kratochwill (Eds.), *Behavioral assessment in schools* (pp. 76–120). New York: Guilford.

Levin, H., Glass, G., & Meister, G. (1984). *Cost-effectiveness of four educational interventions* (Report No. 84-A11). Stanford, CA: Institute for Research in Educational Finance and Governance, Stanford University.

Lloyd, J. W., Crowley, E. P., Kohler, F. W., & Strain, P. (1988). Redefining the applied research agenda: Cooperative learning, prereferral, teacher consultation, and peer-mediated interventions. *Journal of Learning Disabilities, 21,* 43–52.

Maheady, L., & Harper, G. (1987). A classwide peer tutoring program to improve the spelling test performance of low-income, third- and fourth-grade students. *Education and Treatment of Children, 10,* 120–133.

Maheady, L., Harper, G. F., & Sacca, M. K. (1988). Classwide peer tutoring programs in secondary self-contained programs for the mildly handicapped. *Journal of Research and Development in Education, 21*(3), 76–83.

Maheady, L., Sacca, M. K., & Harper, G. F. (1988). The effects of a classwide peer tutoring program on the academic performance of mildly handicapped students enrolled in 10th grade social studies classes. *Exceptional Children, 55,* 52–59.

Maheady, L., & Sainato, D. (1985). The effects of peer tutoring upon the social status and social interaction patterns of high and low status elementary students. *Education and Treatment of children, 8,* 51–65.

Maheady, L., Winstanley, N., Mallette, B., & Harper, G. F. (1989). *Training requirements in the use of classwide peer tutoring.* Michigan State University, East Lansing, MI: Department of Counseling, Educational Psychology, and Special Education, Michigan State University.

NASP (1987). Position statement.

Niedermeyer, F. C. (1970). Effects of training on the instructional behaviors of student tutors. *Journal of Educational Research, 64,* 119–123.

Osguthorpe, R. T., & Scruggs, T. E. (1986). Special education students as tutors: A review and analysis. *Remedial and Special Education, 7,* 15–26.

Pigott, H. E., Fantuzzo, J. W., & Clement, P. W. (196). The effects of reciprocal peer tutoring and group contingencies on the academic performance of elementary school children. *Journal of Applied Behavior Analysis, 19,* 93–98.

Polirstok, S. R., & Greer, R. D. (1986). A replication of collateral effects and a component analysis of a successful tutoring package for inner-city adolescents. *Education and Treatment of Children, 9,* 101–121.

Purkey, S. C., & Smith, M. S. (1983). Effective schools: A review. *Elementary School Journal, 83,* 427–452.

Reynolds, M. G., Wang, M. C., & Walberg, H. J. (1987). The necessary restructuring of special and regular education. *Exceptional Children, 53,* 391–398.

Rosenshine, B., & Stevens, R. (1986). Teaching functions. In M. C. Wittrock (Ed.), *Handbook of research on teaching* (pp. 376–391). New York: Macmillan.

Sharan, S. (1980). Cooperative learning in small groups: Recent methods and effects on achievement, attitudes and ethnic relations. *Review of Educational Research, 50,* 241–271.

Skrtic, T. (1988). The organizational context of special education. In E. L. Meyen & T. M. Skrtic (Eds.), *Exceptional children and youth: An introduction* (Vol. 3) (pp. 479-517). Denver, CO: Love Publishing Co.

Slavin, R. D. (1984). Team assisted individualization: Cooperative learning and individualized instruction in mainstream classrooms. *Remedial and Special Education, 5*, 33-42.

Slavin, R. E., Madden, N. A., & Leavey, M. (1984). Effects of team assisted individualization on the mathematics achievement of academically handicapped and nonhandicapped students. *Journal of Educational Psychology, 76*, 813-819.

Stainback, W., & Stainback, N. (1984). A rationale for the merger to special and regular education. *Exceptional Children, 51*, 109.

Stallings, J. (1977). How instructional processes relate to child outcomes. In G. D. Borich (Ed.), *The appraisal of teaching: Concepts and process* (pp. 104-113). Reading, MA: Addison-Wesley.

Stanley, S. O., & Greenwood, C. R. (1983). How much "opportunity to respond" does the minority disadvantaged student receive in school. *Exceptional Children, 49*(4), 370-373.

Tucker, J. (1980). Ethnic proportions in classes for the learning disabled: Issues in nonbiased assessment. *Journal of Special Education, 14*, 93-105.

Wang, M. C., Peverly, S., & Randolph, R. (1984). An investigation of the implementation and effects of a full-time mainstreaming program. *Remedial and Special Education, 5*, 21-32.

Whorton, D., Locke, P., Delquadri, J., & Hall, R. V. (1989). Increasing academic skills of students with autism using fifth grade peers as tutors. *Education and Treatment of Children, 12*, 38-51.

Whorton, D., Rotholz, D., Walker, D., McGrale, J., & Locke, P. (1987). *Alternative instructional strategies for students with autism and other developmental disabilities: Peer tutoring and group teaching procedures.* Austin, TX: Pro-Ed.

Will, M. C. (1986). Educating children with learning problems: A shared responsibility. *Exceptional Children, 52*, 411-415.

Young, C. C. (1981). Children as instructional agents for handicapped peers: A review and analysis. In P. Strain (Ed.), *The utilization of classroom peers as behavior change agents* (pp. 305-326). New York: Plenum.

Ysseldyke, J. E., Thurlow, M. L., Christenson, S. L., & Weiss, J. (1987). Time allocated to instruction of mentally retarded, learning disabled, emotionally disturbed, and nonhandicapped elementary students. *Journal of Special Education, 21*, 43-55.

Self-Monitoring Applications for Classroom Intervention

John Wills Lloyd
Timothy J. Landrum
Daniel P. Hallahan
University of Virginia

Educators often cite instillment of self-control as one of the primary goals of education, particularly education of atypical learners (e.g., Kneedler, 1980; Polsgrove, 1979; Rueda, 1981; Rueda, Rutherford, & Howell, 1980). For example, teachers rate pupils' demonstration of self-control as a highly desirable characteristic (Kauffman, Lloyd, & McGee, 1989; Walker & Rankin, 1983). In addition to believing that self-control, in and of itself, is a desirable goal, educators working with atypical learners look favorably upon self-control interventions for other reasons, as well: Teaching self-control may (a) increase the effectiveness of an intervention (e.g., Kazdin, 1984); (b) decrease the demand for direct intervention by teachers, saving their time (e.g., Rooney & Hallahan, 1988); (c) improve the maintenance of treatment effects (McLaughlin, 1976); and (d) increase the chances of transfer of treatment effects (e.g., Neilans & Israel, 1981).

Models of self-control differ along many dimensions (e.g., see explanations for reactivity in self-monitoring; Nelson & Hayes, 1981). For example, Kanfer's model (e.g., Kanfer, 1970) of self-control includes a self-monitoring stage (observation of one's own behavior), a self-evaluation stage (comparison of one's observations with a standard behavior), and a self-reinforcement stage. The self-monitoring component in most models has been

applied both as a means of data collection and of influencing behavior.

Self-monitoring was initially used as an assessment technique. Clinicians who were seeking data about their clients' behavior during times the clients were not in treatment or about client behavior not directly observable (e.g., thoughts or feelings) taught clients to observe their own behavior. But clinicians soon observed that requiring people to observe their own behavior had reactive effects: *It caused changes in the behavior.*

Many researchers and practitioners have taken advantage of the reactive effects of self-monitoring in order to change pupils' behavior in school settings (Gardner & Cole, 1988; Mace & Kratochwill, 1988). In the remainder of this chapter we describe the general methods of using self-monitoring in this way, procedures that school psychologists can follow when implementing self-monitoring programs, and applications of self-monitoring to school problems.

METHODS OF SELF-MONITORING

In general, self-monitoring requires that the individual act as the observer for his or her own behavior. This task has two basic components: (a) observation of the behavior and (b) recording of the observational data. Pupils learn to perform a routine in which they stop what they are doing, assess their own behavior, and (usually) make note of whether a specific target behavior has occurred or is occurring. Teachers and clinicians often combine self-monitoring with other self-control techniques, which we do not discuss in detail here. For example, after performing the self-monitoring routine for an entire session, pupils may graph their performance (e.g., Harris, 1986). The self-monitoring procedure we have used is illustrated in the accompanying scenario.

Training and Implementation of a Self-Monitoring Program

The following script for a teacher's introduction of self-monitoring and the implementation scenario illustrate the application of the model.

"Johnny, you know how paying attention to your work has been a problem for you. You've heard teachers tell you 'Pay attention,' 'Get to work,' 'What are you supposed to be doing?' and things like that. Well, today we're going to start something that will help you help yourself pay attention better. First we need to make sure that you know what paying attention means. This is what I mean by paying attention." (Teacher models immediate and sustained attention to task.) "And this is what I mean by not paying attention." (Teacher models inattentive behaviors such as glancing around and playing with objects.) "Now you tell me if I was paying attention." (Teacher models attentive and inattentive behaviors and requires the student to categorize them.) "Okay, now let me show you what we're going to do. While you're working, this tape recorder will be turned on. Every once in awhile, you'll hear a little sound like this:" (Teacher plays tone on tape.) "And when you hear that sound quietly ask yourself, 'Was I paying attention?' If you answer 'yes,' put a check in this box. If you answer 'no,' put a check in this box. Then go right back to work. When you hear the sound again, ask the question, answer it, mark your answer, and go back to work. Now, let me show you how it works." (Teacher models entire procedure.) "Now, Johnny, I bet you can do this. Tell me what you're going to do every time you hear a tone.

Let's try it. I'll start the tape and you work on these papers." (Teacher observes student's implementation of the entire procedure, praises its correct use, and gradually withdraws.)

THE NEXT DAY

SCENE: A classroom of students engaged in various activities. One teacher is walking about the room, preparing for her next activity. Some students are sitting in a semicircle facing another teacher and answering questions she poses. Other students are sitting at their desks and writing on papers or workbooks. Edwin is working at his own desk. The teacher picks up some workpages that have green strips of paper attached to their top.

TEACHER: (Walking up to Edwin's desk.) Edwin, here are your seatwork pages for today. I'm going to start the tape and I want you to self-record like you have been doing. What are you going to ask yourself when you hear the beep?

EDWIN: (Taking papers.) Was I paying attention?

TEACHER: Okay, that's it. (Turning away.) Bobby, Jackie, and Anne; it's time for spelling group. (Starts a tape recorder and walks toward front of room where three students are gathering.)

EDWIN: (Begins working on his assignments; he is continuing to work when a tone comes from the tape recorder. Edwin's lips barely move as he almost inaudibly whispers.) Was I paying attention? Yes. (He marks on the green strip of paper and returns to work. Later, another tone comes from the tape recorder. Edwin whispers.) Was I paying attention? Yes. (He marks on the green strip of paper and returns to work. Later as the students in one group laugh, Edwin looks up and watches them. While he is looking up a tone occurs.) Was I paying attention? No. (He marks the strip of paper and begins working again. He continues working, questioning himself when the tone occurs, and recording his answers.)

A self-monitoring routine may combine the components of observations and recording in many different ways. Four interdependent facets of self-monitoring determine the variations in the way it is implemented: (a) the presence of cuing, (b) the observational procedure followed, (c) the method of recording, and (d) the training in self-monitoring provided to the pupil.

Presence of Cuing

Although not true in all cases (e.g., Broden, Hall, & Mitts, 1971), most applications of self-monitoring have employed cuing, that is, some means of indicating to the pupils that they should initiate the self-monitoring routine. In the procedure that we and others (e.g., Hallahan, Lloyd, Kneedler, & Marshall, 1982; Harris, 1986; Osborne, Kosiewicz, Crumley, & Lee, 1987) have used, a tape recorder plays tones at relatively frequent, irregular intervals (mean intertone interval of 45 sec); each tone serves as a prompt for the participating pupils to assess and record their behavior. In another procedure (e.g., Rhode, Morgan, & Young, 1983), cues occur less frequently and at regular intervals (initially every 15 min; later, every hour); after each period, the pupils assess and record their behavior. Evidence indicates that the cues are important for the effectiveness of self-monitoring (Heins, Lloyd, & Hallahan, 1986), although the trainer can remove them once the target behavior has improved (Hallahan, Lloyd, Kosiewicz, Kauffman, & Graves, 1979).

Teachers often ask if it would be appropriate to provide pupils with the cues through earphones so that they would not be audible to other people in the classroom. Sabatos (1986) has tried this variation with moderate success. However, there is some limited evidence suggesting that when other students who are not the targets of the intervention hear the cues, their behavior improves as well (Kosiewicz, 1981). Should one decide to use earphones, the trainer will need to plan for the systematic removal of this feature as well as others when programming for maintenance and transfer.

Some self-monitoring procedures do not include overt cues; the occurrence of the behavior itself (e.g., raising one's hand to ask a question or request permission) or the end of a task (e.g., completing a workbook page) can signal the pupils to monitor their behavior. In the case of academic performance, pupils may initiate the self-monitoring routine at the completion of a task. For example, Jones, Trap, and Cooper (1977) taught pupils to evaluate the quality of their handwriting; when they had completed an assignment, they used plastic overlays to assess whether their work met a legibility standard and then recorded the number of appropriate letter strokes. Similarly, Rooney, Polloway, and Hallahan (1985) marked certain problems on pupils' arithmetic worksheets; these marked problems served as cues for the pupils to stop and assess the accuracy of their work.

Observation Procedures

Self-monitoring routines can differ according to the observation system that the students follow (cf. Kazdin, 1982). In one form, they record by following a *frequency count* procedure; that is they observe their own behavior for any occurrence of a specific response and record each occurrence (e.g., Schunk, 1982).

Rather than counting every occurrence of a target behavior, individuals may use a *momentary time-sampling* procedure. Periodically, individuals stop to assess and record their behavior at that particular point in time. Hallahan et al. (1979), for example, provided periodic cues (with an audio tape recorder) to a learning-disabled pupil. Every time he heard the cue, he stopped his work, assessed whether he was on-task at the time the cue occurred, and placed a check in the appropriate yes or no column. Another approach approximates a *summary rating* procedure. In this system, individuals are taught to make overall judgments about their behavior *after* a set period of time (e.g., at the end of a class session). For example, Rhode et al. (1983) trained pupils to rate their own behavior on a 0-5 scale (and to make their ratings correspond to their teachers' ratings).

Of course, other observation procedures are also possible and procedures can be combined. Schwartz (1977), for example, had tutors require that tutees collect *duration* data on their reading practice. And Lloyd, Bateman, Landrum, and Hallahan (1989) used a combination of frequency counts and momentary time sampling: Pupils counted the number of arithmetic problems completed during each of many brief time intervals.

Method of Recording

Although it is possible for pupils to use a self-monitoring routine in which they do not keep a physical record of their observations, it is more effective when students record overtly (Lloyd, Hallahan, Kosiewicz, & Kneedler, 1982). Many different techniques for recording have been used; they generally fit into two categories: *pencil-and-paper* systems or *counting devices.*

In pencil-and-paper systems, pupils may simply make a tally mark for each time the target behavior occurs. Or they may record their behavior on a prepared record sheet. Prepared recording sheets may make it easier for pupils to monitor their own behavior because they provide a structured and consistent format for their recordings. The sheet in Figure 1 has been used successfully with 8- to 12-year-old students. Psychologists or teachers might wish to modify this basic design according to their own needs. For example, they might exclude the drawing of the student when using self-monitoring with a teenager.

Pupils also may record their behavior by using a counting device. For example, the teacher may teach them to count sets of arithmetic problems completed by moving beads on a leather strap worn on their wrists (e.g., Holman & Baer, 1979). Or they may record whether they were performing a given behavior by incrementing a mechanical golf-score counter worn on the wrist (e.g., Hallahan, Marshall, & Lloyd, 1981).

Training

In most instances, a teacher or school psychologist can teach students to use the self-monitoring procedure in a single 15- to 20-minute session. It is important, however, that the trainer be as explicit as possible in explaining the process. For example, in order for the training to be successful it is important that the trainer (a) define the behavior that the students will be recording, (b) model the defined behavior, (c) check for the students' understanding of the defined behavior, and (d) observe the students while they practice the procedure for a few minutes. The case study we presented earlier provides an example of how to teach students to monitor their attention-to-task behavior. Hallahan, Lloyd, and Stoller (1982) and Workman (1982) provide more detailed accounts of training procedures.

There are many variations in training. The teacher or psychologist may choose any of the following courses.

1. Train individuals (e.g., Hallahan et al., 1979) or groups (Hallahan et al., 1981; Howell, Rueda, & Rutherford, 1983; McLaughlin, 1984).

2. Implement self-monitoring in conjunction with other intervention procedures (e.g., a token economy; Shapiro & Klein, 1980) or on its own (e.g., Hallahan, Lloyd, Kneedler, & Marshall, 1982).

3. Use videotapes so that pupils can practice observing and recording behavior without also performing the behavior at the same time.

4. Require students to match their judgments of behavior with the judgment of a teacher as was done by Marshall (1983) and Smith, Young, West, Morgan, and Rhode (1988); this generally requires a more extensive training period than the one described in the previous paragraphs.

5. Reward pupils for correctly applying the self-monitoring procedure (Rooney, Hallahan, & Lloyd, 1984) even though reinforcement for improving behavior may not be necessary.

One question in need of research is that of who should provide the training to students. Although no one has empirically assessed the relative merits of having teachers rather than school psychologists

DATE _____

Was I paying attention?

	yes	no
1		
2		
3		
4		
5		
6		
7		
8		
9		
10		

	yes	no
11		
12		
13		
14		
15		
16		
17		
18		
19		
20		

FIGURE 1. Example of a Self Recording Sheet.

engage students in training, we believe it logical to assume that having teachers do the training would be more effective because they are in more consistent contact with the students.

IMPLEMENTING SELF-MONITORING PROGRAMS

Three factors should be considered in designing and implementing a self-monitoring program: (a) planning a system for *evaluating treatment*, (b) planning for the *withdrawal* of treatment, and (c) programming for *maintenance and generalization*.

Evaluating Treatment

Because pupils must observe and record their own behavior, self-monitoring programs generate substantial data about the target behavior. However, these data cannot be used to evaluate the effects of the treatment because students are not always accurate in their assessment of their own behavior. In our experience (Hallahan et al., 1979; Lloyd et al., 1989), data generated by the pupils generally reveal an overestimation of the occurrence of the appropriate behavior. It is important to note, however, that completely accurate self-monitoring may not be essential to obtaining acceptable intervention effects. That is, even when students' assessments of their own behavior are found to be exaggerated in comparison with independent observational data, positive changes in the target behaviors have still been observed (e.g., Hallahan et al., 1979; Zegiob, Klukas, & Junginger, 1978). Therefore, it is important that those responsible for implementing self-monitoring programs collect data that will permit an independent evaluation of the effects of intervention.

School psychologists can collect evaluation data either by gathering it themselves or by training an aide to serve as an independent observer and then scheduling periodic observations in the setting(s) where pupils are to perform the self-recording routine. Although sophisticated research designs are not needed for evaluating intervention effects, the manager of the program should evaluate outcomes according to general guidelines that help to assure that the program itself has caused changes. Recommendations about observation procedures and basic single-case research design are available elsewhere (Lloyd & Loper, 1986; Repp & Lloyd, 1980).

Withdrawing Treatment

As discussed in previous sections, having pupils monitor their own behavior often involves the introduction of overt features of training. For example, a tape recorder or a programmable kitchen timer may cue the pupils to assess their behavior and record its occurrence or nonoccurrence on a self-recording sheet or a wrist counter. We have found that the cues and the recording device are important in teaching pupils to use a self-monitoring routine (Heins et al., 1986; Lloyd et al., 1982). However, these components do not continue to be necessary after pupils have become proficient with the self-monitoring routine. In four studies (Hallahan et al., 1979, 1981; Hallahan, Lloyd, Kneedler, & Marshall, 1982; Lloyd et al., 1989), we have removed these elements systematically, either withdrawing the cues first or withdrawing the recording component first, and pupils have continued to maintain the target behavior at improved levels. There is no straightforward formula for determining when to remove each of these external components; the teacher or psychologist needs to use clinical judgment to decide whether the desired behavioral change is great enough and stable enough to warrant removing one of the treatment components.

Maintenance and Transfer

Immediate withdrawal of the entire self-monitoring program may not result in maintenance of the treatment effects (e.g., Workman, Helton, & Watson, 1982). As indicated by our studies, however, after training and practice in using self-monitoring, change in the target behavior can be maintained in the absence of the overt aspects of the treatment program. Follow-up observations made as long as two and one-half months after the termination of treatment have revealed continued effects (Heins et al., 1986). There is no available research, however, to specify for what period of time pupils must engage in self-monitoring before it is possible to achieve maintenance. Practitioners should monitor the treatment data they are independently gathering in order to ascertain whether students are still maintaining desired levels and/or frequencies of the targeted behavior; this requires periodic observations (at least once per week) after termination of treatment. If treatment effects begin to wane, the practitioner can provide "boosters" (brief retraining sessions).

Investigators have examined two types of transfer of self-monitoring treatment effects: (a) transfer to untreated but related behaviors and (b) transfer to other settings. As an example of the former, Hallahan et al. (1979) found effects on a boy's academic productivity even though he was only taught to monitor his own attending behavior. As an example of the latter, Warrenfeltz et al. (1981) taught adolescents to use social skills in a training setting and then used self-monitoring to engender transfer of those skills to a vocational classroom. (Although Hallahan et al. and Warrenfeltz et al. were successful, it is important to point out that generalization has proven as elusive for researchers in the area of self-monitoring as it has for virtually all intervention techniques with disabled students.) There are, however, some guidelines practitioners can use to maximize their chances of achieving transfer of treatment effects (see, for example, Rhode et al., 1983).

APPLICATION OF SELF-MONITORING TO SCHOOL PROBLEMS

Researchers and practitioners have used self-monitoring procedures in schools with students of varying ages and abilities to modify a wide range of behaviors. Research has demonstrated, for example, that self-monitoring can produce positive behavior change in regular

class students (Broden et al., 1971; Glynn & Thomas, 1974; Glynn, Thomas, & Shee, 1973; Roberts & Nelson, 1981; Sagotsky, Patterson, & Lepper, 1978), as well as students labeled learning-disabled (Blick & Test, 1987; Hallahan et al., 1979; Hallahan, Lloyd, Kneedler, & Marshall, 1982; Harris, 1986), behaviorally disordered (McLaughlin, 1983, 1984; McLaughlin, Krappman, & Welsh, 1985), mentally retarded (Ridley, 1986; Robertson, Simon, Pachman, & Drabman, 1979; Sugai & Rowe, 1984; Zegiob et al., 1978), and multiply handicapped (Morrow, Burke, & Buell, 1985).

The bulk of classroom investigations have focused on both increasing rates of positive behavior (attention-to-task, academic productivity, academic accuracy, use of social skills) and decreasing rates of negative or disruptive behaviors. We shall now discuss the most salient findings related to the use of self-monitoring for each of these areas, starting with the area that has probably received the most study — attention-to-task.

Attention

Several studies have investigated the effects of self-monitoring procedures on on-task behaviors. Researchers have variously defined on-task as (a) in seat with eyes on work materials (Hallahan et al., 1979; Lloyd et al., 1982); (b) looking at the teacher, writing, or raising hand for assistance (McLaughlin, 1983); or (c) simply doing what one is supposed to be doing (Christie, Hiss, & Lozanoff, 1984). We began a series of studies with self-recording of attention in the late 1970s at the University of Virginia Learning Disabilities Research Institute (Hallahan et al., 1979; Hallahan, Lloyd, Kneedler, & Marshall, 1982; Heins et al., 1986; Lloyd et al., 1982; Rooney et al., 1984). We focused our research on attentional problems because of the vast literature indicating that learning-disabled youngsters exhibit problems in attention. We chose to investigate self-monitoring over other interventions because of its emphasis on student involvement in the intervention process. There is a substantial body of research that demonstrates that learning-disabled students have difficulty in seeing themselves as instrumental in their own learning.

We have used a time-sampling procedure in which students are to ask themselves upon hearing a tape-recorded tone whether they were paying attention and then to record their answer on prepared answer sheets. We found that self-recording of attention results in increased rates of on-task behavior and that the effects are maintained over time following fading of the overt aspects of the procedures.

An important point to make is that our impression is that our self-monitoring technique is user-friendly for the teacher, the target student, and the other pupils in the classroom. One can use the procedure with little disruption to other students and minimal investment of teachers' time (cf. Kneedler & Hallahan, 1981). In fact, Rooney and Hallahan (1988) reported that teaching pupils to monitor their own behavior resulted in lessened demands on their teachers' time. When asked to implement the procedures, many teachers question whether the tones will be disturbing to other students in the class. However, none of the 15–20 teachers we have had implement self-monitoring have found that it interferes with their teaching or with the work of the other students in the class. Should it be found that the procedure is disturbing, the tones might be administered to the pupil via earphones.

Time-sampling procedures similar to those we have employed with learning-disabled pupils have been used to effect positive change in rates of attention to task with both handicapped and regular class students (e.g., Broden et al., 1971; Blick & Test, 1987; McLaughlin, 1983, 1984; Morrow et al., 1985; Young, Birnbrauer, & Sanson-Fisher, 1977).

Although the most commonly targeted behavior for self-monitoring interventions has been attention to task, research suggests that increasing attending behavior may result in increased academic productivity as well (e.g., Hallahan et al., 1979). If the teacher or school psychologist feels that the rate of aca-

demic productivity itself is more problematic for a particular pupil, they may intervene more directly by having pupils monitor their own productivity. In the next section, we briefly describe several studies that have employed self-monitoring of productivity.

Productivity

Classroom investigations that examined the effects of self-monitoring of academic productivity have demonstrated positive changes in rate of responding through the use of a variety of self-recording procedures, including summary records (Harris, 1986; Piersal & Kratochwill, 1979; Schunk, 1982), frequency counts (Holman & Baer, 1979), momentary time-sampling procedures (Lloyd et al., 1989), and a procedure in which pupils were cued to monitor the accuracy of their answers when they came to specially marked problems on their arithmetic worksheets. (Rooney et al., 1985).

Researchers employing summary records, for example, generally have had students record, at the end of each experimental session, the number of spelling words practiced (Harris, 1986), or the number of pages or units completed during that session (Piersel & Kratochwill, 1979; Schunk, 1982). Holman and Baer (1979) had students move a bead on a wrist device each time they completed one workbook page; in that investigation, the behavior itself served as the prompt to self-record. In the Lloyd et al. (1989) and Rooney et al. (1985) studies, external cues were provided as part of the treatment. Lloyd et al. provided tape-recorded tones that prompted students to count and record the number of arithmetic problems they had completed since the previous cue, whereas Rooney et al. had students stop when they reached specially marked problems on their worksheets and compare their answer to that problem with an answer sheet.

Whether students are prompted to engage in the self-recording routine by external cues (e.g., tones, specially marked problems) or less obtrusive prompts (e.g., end of page or unit, end of time period or lesson, occurrence of the behavior itself), positive change in rates of productivity can be achieved. Decisions regarding whether and how to provide cues must take into account the nature and frequency of the target behavior and the potential distraction of certain overt cues. However, we have found that (a) cues are an essential component of the self-monitoring procedures, (b) overt cues can be faded once treatment effects are apparent and students have demonstrated the ability to perform the self-monitoring routine, and (c) even overt cues are generally not distracting to students not involved in the intervention.

Accuracy of Work

Although research suggests that self-recording interventions that target on-task behavior or productivity may also result in improved accuracy of student responding (e.g., Lloyd et al., 1989), the results of studies that have targeted accuracy itself have been inconclusive. Wall (1982) and Knapczyk and Livingston (1973), for example, found that self-recording of accuracy procedures alone did not result in increased accuracy. In Wall's study, students checked their work on tests constructed by the experimenter against an answer key after they had handed in their own answer sheet, and they then recorded the number correct on a cumulative record sheet. Although the self-recording procedure alone did not result in increased accuracy, self-recording combined with a self-reinforcement procedure produced gains in the students' accuracy. Knapczyk and Livingston obtained similar results by using a procedure in which students first converted their number correct scores on reading assignments to percentages and then recorded these figures in specially prepared work record books. These investigations involved summary ratings made by students upon completion of specified tasks; no external cues were provided.

Roberts and Nelson (1981) also found that accuracy was not enhanced by an intervention involving self-recording of accuracy and external cues. A cue (kitchen timer) presented at a variable interval (5 minute average) schedule prompted students to stop and mark the last arithmetic problem they had completed, and then check the accuracy of their work to that point against prepared answer sheets placed face down on their desks. This procedure resulted in increases in response rate and on-task behavior, but the accuracy of responding was not significantly affected.

Although self-monitoring procedures can be easily integrated into many instructional strategies to facilitate gains in the rate of on-task behavior or amount of work completed, such procedures have also proven effective as a means of promoting transfer of skills or behaviors learned in one setting to other settings. Particularly in the area of social skills training, self-recording procedures have been used more often in programming for maintenance or transfer than in the initial acquisition of these skills.

Social Skills

School psychologists might play a particularly important role in facilitating the transfer of skills students learn in one setting (e.g., resource rooms) to other settings (e.g., regular classrooms). For special education students who are mainstreamed into regular classes for part of the day, such transfer of learning is particularly important. Several investigations have found self-monitoring to be useful in promoting this maintenance and generalization.

Warrenfeltz et al. (1981), for instance, used a combined role-play and self-monitoring procedure to enhance the generalization of appropriate interaction with supervisors to vocational training settings. That is, students were trained in the use of appropriate interaction skills through didactic teaching procedures in a classroom and were then taught through role-play a self-monitoring method for evaluating their responses to supervisors. Increases in appropriate interactions, as well as decreases in inappropriate responses to supervisors, were noted when the students were instructed to use the self-monitoring routine in the generalization site.

Kiburz, Miller, and Morrow (1985) used similar procedures to enhance maintenance and transfer of social skills taught to a behaviorally disordered student through modeling, role-play, and systematic feedback. Although the skills were taught in a special education setting, transfer to other settings was achieved through the use of a simple paper-and-pencil self-recording procedure. Kiburz et al. taught the student to monitor his use of the social skills he had learned (e.g., greeting, thanking) by circling a number next to the skill on a form he carried with him to the generalization sites.

In similar applications, Rhode et al. (1983) and Smith et al. (1988) used self-monitoring procedures to promote generalization and transfer of appropriate classroom behavior. First, appropriate behavior by behaviorally handicapped elementary-age students was increased in a resource setting by using token reinforcement and systematic verbal feedback. Then, pupils learned to rate their own behavior by awarding themselves points and comparing their self-evaluations with a teacher's evaluations at the end of each experimental session. The students were rewarded for approximating the teacher's rating, and the matching component was gradually faded across successive phases. Thus, the students eventually were evaluating their own performance and administering points with no external evaluation. Researchers facilitated generalization to the regular class by introducing a less intrusive form of the intervention in the new setting — having the students carry with them to the mainstream classroom the cards on which they had been recording their points. Regular class teachers then instructed the students to engage in the same self-monitoring routine that they had learned in the resource setting. The results suggest that self-monitoring not only enhanced the acquisition of the appropriate behavior but promoted transfer to other settings as well.

Although self-monitoring interventions have shown particular promise in increasing rates of positive behavior, as well as in promoting maintenance and generalization of the desired behaviors, self-recording of negative or disruptive behaviors has also been effective in reducing rates of these behaviors.

Disruptive Behaviors

Several researchers have targeted negative or disruptive behaviors for self-monitoring interventions in the classroom. Zegiob et al. (1978), for example, used a self-recording procedure involving a simple frequency count to reduce the head-shaking behavior of a moderately retarded adolescent girl. The girl was asked to record on a card each occurrence of head shaking during the self-monitoring phases. Though the student was highly inaccurate in her self-recording in comparison with independent observers, the procedure resulted in decreases in the rate of the inappropriate behavior.

Using a system combining elements of time-sampling procedures and a summative evaluation, Robertson et al. (1979) reduced the disruptive behavior of mentally retarded students by teaching the students to evaluate their classroom behavior at the end of consecutive 10-minute intervals. The self-rating phase followed systematic feedback, token reinforcement, and teacher-matching phases such that the students became familiar with the rating system that would be used (no points for two or more disruptive behaviors in a given 10-minute session, one point for only one disruptive behavior, and two points for no disruptive behaviors during the session). Students received points exchangeable for tangible rewards not only for appropriate behavior but for accurately matching the teacher's assessment of their behavior as well.

Several variations of these procedures have also been effective in reducing the rate of students' disruptive behavior. Turkewitz, O'Leary, and Ironsmith (1975) reduced disruptive behavior by having students rate both academic performance and classroom behavior at the end of each interval. Bolstad and Johnson (1972) taught students a self-regulation procedure involving both evaluation of their own behavior (based on number of disruptive behaviors per interval) and self-administered reinforcers (points). Finally, Sugai and Rowe (1984) used an interval recording system in which a mildly mentally retarded student recorded his out-of-seat behavior across 10-minute blocks of time. The student was provided with a simple chart containing 20 blocks and was cued by a kitchen timer set for consecutive 10-minute intervals. The student marked an *O* in the box for a given interval if *any* out-of-seat behavior occurred during that interval, and recorded an *I* only if he remained in-seat for the entire interval. At the end of each day, the teacher helped the student calculate the percentage of intervals in which he had remained in-seat. Despite the lack of reinforcement for either accurate self-recording or increased in-seat behavior, except the feedback provided in determining a percentage score each day, self-recording resulted in dramatic decreases in the percentage of intervals scored out-of-seat by independent observers.

CONCLUSIONS

Self-monitoring is a powerful intervention procedure that can be easily implemented. Because procedural adaptations make it possible to use self-monitoring in a variety of settings with pupils displaying any of many different social or academic problems, it is particularly valuable to those charged with helping pupils in regular education settings. School psychologists can facilitate its application by helping teachers to select appropriate observing and recording procedures, develop cuing systems appropriate to classroom situations, and design training programs and programs for fading overt aspects of treatment. Perhaps most importantly, school psychologists can provide important technical assistance by designing and implementing systematic procedures for evaluating the effectiveness of self-monitoring programs.

REFERENCES

Blick, D. W., & Test, D. W. (1987). Effects of self-recording on high-school students' on-task behavior. *Learning Disability Quarterly, 10,* 203–213.

Bolstad, O. D., & Johnson, S. M. (1972). Self-regulation in the modification of disruptive classroom behavior. *Journal of Applied Behavior Analysis, 5,* 443–454.

Broden, M., Hall, R. V., & Mitts, B. (1971). The effects of self-recording on the classroom behavior of two eighth-grade students. *Journal of Applied Behavior Analysis, 4,* 191–199.

Christie, D. J., Hiss, M., & Lozanoff, B. (1984). Modification of inattentive classroom behavior: Hyperactive children's use of self-recording with teacher guidance. *Behavior Modification, 8,* 391–406.

Gardner, W. I., & Cole, C. L. (1988). Self-monitoring procedures. In E. S. Shapiro & T. R. Kratochwill (Eds.), *Behavioral assessment in schools: Conceptual foundations and practical applications* (pp. 206–246). New York: Guilford.

Glynn, E. L., & Thomas, J. D. (1974). Effect of cuing on self-control of classroom behavior. *Journal of Applied Behavior Analysis, 7,* 299–306.

Glynn, E. L., Thomas, J. D., & Shee, S. M. (1973). Behavioral self-control of on-task behavior in an elementary classroom. *Journal of Applied Behavior Analysis, 6,* 105–113.

Hallahan, D. P., Lloyd, J. W., Kneedler, R. D., & Marshall, K. J. (1982). A comparison of the effects of self- versus teacher-assessment of on-task behavior. *Behavior Therapy, 13,* 715–723.

Hallahan, D. P., Lloyd, J. W., Kosiewicz, M. M., Kauffman, J. M., & Graves, A. W. (1979). Self-monitoring of attention as a treatment for a learning-disabled boy's off-task behavior. *Learning Disability Quarterly, 2*(2), 24–32.

Hallahan, D. P., Lloyd, J. W., & Stoller, L. (1982). *Improving attention with self-monitoring: A manual for teachers.* Charlottesville: University of Virginia Learning Disabilities Research Institute.

Hallahan, D. P., Marshall, K. J., & Lloyd, J. W. (1981). Self-recording during group instruction: Effects on attention to task. *Learning Disability Quarterly, 4,* 407–413.

Harris, K. R. (1986). Self-monitoring of attentional behavior versus self-monitoring of productivity: Effects on on-task behavior and academic response rate among learning disabled children. *Journal of Applied Behavior Analysis 19,* 417–423.

Heins, E. D., Lloyd, J. W., & Hallahan, D. P. (1986). Cued and noncued self-recording of attention to task. *Behavior Modification, 10,* 235–254.

Holman, J., & Baer, D. M. (1979). Facilitating generalization of on-task behavior through self-monitoring of academic tasks. *Journal of Autism and Developmental Disabilities, 9,* 429–446.

Howell, K. W., Rueda, R., & Rutherford, R. B., Jr. (1983). A procedure for teaching self-recording to moderately retarded students. *Psychology in the Schools, 20,* 202-209.

Jones, J. C., Trap, J., & Cooper, J. O. (1977). Students' self-recording of manuscript letter strokes. *Journal of Applied Behavior Analysis, 10,* 509-514.

Kanfer, F. F. (1970). Self-monitoring: Methodological issues and clinical applications. *Journal of Consulting and Clinical Psychology, 35,* 143-152.

Kauffman, J. M., Lloyd, J. W., & McGee, K. A. (1989). Adaptive and maladaptive behavior: Teachers' attitudes and their technical assistance needs. *Journal of Special Education, 23,* 185-200.

Kazdin, A. E. (1982). *Single-case research designs.* New York: Oxford.

Kazdin, A. E. (1984). *Behavior modification in applied settings* (3rd ed.). Homewood, IL: Dorsey.

Kiburz, C. S., Miller, S. R., & Morrow, L. W. (1985). Structured learning using self-monitoring to promote maintenance and generalization of social skills across settings for a behaviorally disordered adolescent. *Behavioral Disorders, 11,* 47-55.

Knapczyk, D. R., & Livingston, G. (1973). Self-recording and student teacher supervision: Variables within a token economy structure. *Journal of Applied Behavior Analysis, 6,* 481-486.

Kneedler, R. D. (1980). The use of cognitive training to change social behaviors. *Exceptional Education Quarterly, 1,* (1), 65-73.

Kneedler, R. D., & Hallahan, D. P. (1981). Self-monitoring of on-task behavior with learning-disabled children: Current studies and directions. *Exceptional Education Quarterly, 2*(3), 73-82.

Kosiewicz, M. M. (1981). *Self-monitoring of attention in an LD classroom: Across subject generalization.* Unpublished doctoral dissertation, University of Virginia, Charlottesville.

Lloyd, J. W., Bateman, D. F., Landrum, T. J., & Hallahan, D. P. (1989). Self-recording of attention versus productivity. *Journal of Applied Behavior Analysis, 22,* 315-323.

Lloyd, J. W., Hallahan, D. P., Kosiewicz, M. M., & Kneedler, R. D. (1982). Reactive effects of self-assessment and self-recording on attention to task and academic productivity. *Learning Disability Quarterly, 5,* 216-227.

Lloyd, J. W., & Loper, A. B. (1986). Measurement and evaluation of task-related learning behaviors: Attention to task and metacognition. *School Psychology Review, 15,* 336-345.

Mace, F. C., & Kratochwill, T. R. (1988). Self-monitoring. In J. C. Witt, S. N. Elliott, & F. M. Gresham (Eds.), *Handbook of behavior therapy in education* (pp. 489-522). New York: Plenum.

Marshall, K. J. (1983). *The effects of training to increase self-monitoring accuracy on the attention-to-task of learning disabled children.* Unpublished doctoral dissertation, University of Virginia, Charlottesville.

McLaughlin, T. F. (1976). Self-control in the classroom. *Review of Educational Research, 46,* 631-663.

McLaughlin, T. F. (1983). Effects of self-recording for on-task and academic responding: A long term analysis. *Journal of Special Education Technology, 6,* 5-12.

McLaughlin, T. F. (1984). A comparison of self-recording and self-recording plus consequences for on-task and assignment completion. *Contemporary Educational Psychology, 9,* 185-192.

McLaughlin, T. F., Krappman, U. F., & Welsh, J. M. (1985). The effects of self-recording for on-task behavior of behaviorally disordered special education students. *Remedial and Special Education, 6*(4), 42-45.

Morrow, L. W., Burke, J. G., & Buell, B. J. (1985). Effects of a self-recording procedures on the attending to task behavior and academic productivity of adolescents with multiple handicaps. *Mental Retardation, 23,* 137-141.

Neilans, T. H., & Israel, A. C. (1981). Towards maintenance and generalization of behavior change: Teaching children self-regulation and self-instructional skills. *Cognitive Therapy and Research, 5,* 189-195.

Nelson, R. O., & Hayes, S. C. (1981). Theoretical explanations for reactivity in self-monitoring. *Behavior Modification, 5,* 3-14.

Osborne, S. S., Kosiewicz, M. M., Crumley, E. B., & Lee, C. (1987). Distractible students use self-monitoring. *Teaching Exceptional Children, 19*(2), 66-69.

Piersal, W. C., & Kratochwill, T. R. (1979). Self-observation and behavior change: Applications to academic and adjustment problems through behavior consultation. *Journal of School Psychology, 17,* 151-161.

Polsgrove, L. (1979). Self-control: Methods for child training. *Behavioral Disorders, 4*(2), 116-130.

Repp, A. C., & Lloyd, J. (1980). Evaluating educational changes with single-subject designs. In J. Gottlieb (Ed.), *Educating mentally retarded persons in the mainstream* (pp. 73-105). Baltimore: University Park Press.

Rhode, G., Morgan, D. P., & Young, K. R. (1983). Generalization and maintenance of treatment gains of behaviorally handicapped students from resource rooms to regular classrooms using self-evaluation procedures. *Journal of Applied Behavior Analysis, 16,* 171-188.

Ridley, L. L. (1986). Effects of self-recording on the maintenance of appropriate eating behaviors by a moderately retarded six-year-old boy. *Education and Treatment of Children, 9*, 232-238.

Roberts, R. N., & Nelson, R. O. (1981). The effects of self-monitoring on children's classroom behavior. *Child Behavior Therapy, 3*, 105-120.

Robertson, S. J., Simon, S. J., Pachman, J. S., & Drabman, R. S. (1979). Self-control and generalization procedures in a classroom of disruptive retarded children. *Child Behavior Therapy, 1*, 347-362.

Rooney, K. J., & Hallahan, D. P. (1988). The effects of self-monitoring on adult behavior and student performance. *Learning Disabilities Research, 3*, 88-93.

Rooney, K. J., Hallahan, D. P., & Lloyd, J. W. (1984). Self-recording of attention by learning-disabled students in the regular classroom. *Journal of Learning Disabilities, 17*, 360-364.

Rooney, K. J., Polloway, E., & Hallahan, D. P. (1985). The use of self-monitoring procedures with low IQ learning disabled students. *Journal of Learning Disabilities, 18*, 384-389.

Rueda, R. (1981). Future directions in self-control research. In R. B. Rutherford, A. G. Prieto, & J. E. McGlothlin (Eds.), *Severe behavior disorders of children and youth* (Vol. 4, pp. 16-21). Reston, VA: Council for Children With Behavior Disorders.

Rueda, R., Rutherford, R. B., & Howell, K. W. (1980). Review of self-control research with behaviorally disordered and mentally retarded children. In R. B. Rutherford, A. G. Prieto, & J. E. McGlothlin (Eds.), *Severe behavior disorders of children and youth* (Vol. 3, pp. 188-197). Reston, VA: Council for Children With Behavior disorders.

Sabatos, M. A. (1986). *Private cues in self-monitoring: Effects on learning-disabled students' on-task performance and reading productivity during sustained silent reading.* Unpublished dissertation, University of Pittsburgh, Pittsburgh.

Sagotsky, G., Patterson, C. J., & Lepper, M. R. (1978). Training children's self-control: A field experiment in self-monitoring and goal setting in the classroom. *Journal of Experimental Child Psychology, 25*, 242-253.

Schunk, D. H. (1982). Progress self-monitoring: Effects on children's self-efficacy and achievement. *Journal of Experimental Education, 51*, 89-93.

Schwartz, G. J. (1977). College students as contingency managers for adolescents in a program to develop reading skills. *Journal of Applied Behavior Analysis, 10*, 645-655.

Shapiro, E. S., & Klein, R. D. (1980). Self-management of classroom behavior with retarded/disturbed children. *Behavior Modification, 4*, 83-97.

Smith, D. J., Young, K. R., West, R. P., Morgan, D. P., & Rhode, G. (1988). Reducing disruptive behavior of junior high school students: A classroom self-management procedure. *Behavioral Disorders, 13*, 231-239.

Sugai, G., & Rowe, P. (1984). The effect of self-recording on out-of-seat behavior of an EMR student. *Education and Training of the Mentally Retarded, 19*, 23-28.

Turkewitz, H., O'Leary, K. D., & Ironsmith, M. (1975). Generalization and maintenance of appropriate behavior through self-control. *Journal of Consulting and Clinical Psychology, 43*, 577-583.

Walker, H. M., & Rankin, R. (1983). Assessing the behavioral expectations and demands of less restrictive settings. *School Psychology Review, 12*, 274-284.

Wall, S. M. (1982). Effects of systematic self-monitoring and self-reinforcement in children's management of test performances. *Journal of Psychology, 111*, 129-136.

Warrenfeltz, R. B., Kelly, W. J., Salzberg, C. L., Beegle, C. P., Levy, S. M., Adams, T. A., & Crouse, T. R. (1981). Social skills training of behavior disordered adolescents with self-monitoring to promote generalization to a vocational setting. *Behavioral Disorders, 7*, 18-27.

Workman, E. A. (1982). *Teaching behavioral self-control to students.* Austin, TX: Pro-Ed.

Workman, E. A., Helton, G. B., & Watson, P. J. (1982). Self-monitoring effects in a four-year-old child: An ecological behavior analysis. *Journal of School Psychology, 20*, 57-64.

Young, P., Birnbrauer, J. S., & Sanson-Fisher, R. W. (1977). The effects of self-recording on the study behavior of female juvenile delinquents. In B. C. Etzel, J. M. LeBlanc, & D. M. Baer (Eds.), *New developments in behavioral research: Theory, method, and application* (pp. 559-577). Hillsdale, NJ: Erlbaum.

Zegiob, L., Klukas, N., & Junginger, J. (1978). Reactivity of self-monitoring procedures with retarded adolescents. *American Journal of Mental Deficiency, 83*, 156-163.

Use of Computer-Assisted Instruction in the Regular Classroom

Herbert J. Rieth
Vanderbilt University

Melvyn I. Semmel
University of California at Santa Barbara

INTRODUCTION

The use of microcomputers to deliver instruction has increased dramatically during the past decade. The Office of Technology Assistance (OTA) (1988) reported that there are approximately 1.7 million computers in United States schools, which translates roughly to an average of 1 computer for every 30 students. Since 1981 the number of public schools with computers has increased by about 11% per year. This record of growth is impressive and clearly suggests a widespread willingness on the part of school districts to investigate applications of computer technology in schools.

In particular, many school districts appear intrigued with the promise of computer-assisted instruction (CAI) for improving instruction with difficult-to-teach students. This appeal stems from the belief that successful teacher-based instruction (TBI) techniques can be easily transferred to CAI applications. The instructional advantages of using CAI to instruct difficult-to-teach students include "individualization and self-pacing, immediate feedback regarding academic responses, consistent correction procedures, repetition without pressure, immediate reinforcement for correct responses, well-sequenced instruction, high frequency of student responses, repeated opportunities to demonstrate mastery of academic subject matter, peer response, motivation, improved motor skills and visual motor coordination, and minimization of disabilities" (Budoff, Thormann, & Gras, 1984). In addition computers can serve as tools for increasing students' motivation, managing social behavior, and collecting daily performance data that enables teachers to engage in data-based instructional decision making.

Despite the rapid increase in the number of machines and the instructional promise of CAI for difficult-to-teach students, the data on the efficacy of this innovation are somewhat equivocal (OTA, 1988). Indeed, there is a considerable body of research that suggests that CAI is effective in enhancing achievement by difficult-to-teach students (Malouf, MacArthur, & Radin, 1986; Schmidt, Weinstein, Niemic, & Walberg, 1986; Trifiletti, Frith, & Armstrong, 1984; Watkins & Webb, 1981). However, there is an equally substantial number of studies that report only occasional achievement gains associated with the use of CAI (Carman & Kosberg, 1982; Kleiman, Humphrey, & Lindsay, 1983; McDermott & Watkins, 1983). Overall, these results suggest that certain hardware and software configurations, used with particular populations of children and implemented under the supervision of competent teachers, will contribute to meeting specific instructional objectives. The OTA report (1988) concludes that by and large the research to date supports the continued use of instructional technologies in schools.

Researchers are now beginning to investigate the specific conditions under which CAI is an effective instructional tool with difficult-to-teach students. This effort also attempts to identify instructional, contextual, and personal variables that may impinge on the effectiveness of CAI in promoting achievement (Bahr, in press). More recent research efforts are aimed at identifying effective applications of CAI and developing methods for effectively integrating this tool into predominantly teacher-based instructional systems (Rieth, Bahr, & Okolo, 1986).

The purpose of this chapter is to review the literature regarding the application of CAI with difficult-to-teach students and to discuss its implications for educational practice generally and for the practice of school psychology in particular. CAI applications and their impact on both student and teacher behavior will be described. Finally, the implications for "best practices" and for training practitioners will be highlighted.

This chapter is divided into four sections. The first section will examine the impact of the microcomputer on overall classroom ecology and will review organizational and managerial variables that influence teachers' and students' behavior and are correlated with academic success. The second section will describe the role of the microcomputer in collecting and analyzing the student assessment information that is required to develop effective instructional programs. Specific assessment administration, test scoring, performance analysis and profiling programs, and continuous performance monitoring systems will be described. The third section will provide a description of the various types of CAI and analyze the efficacy of CAI in specific academic content areas. The final section will summarize the implications of this literature for the practice and training of school psychologists.

SECTION ONE: CLASSROOM ECOLOGICAL FEATURES

This section focuses on the classroom ecology, which, according to Rieth and Evertson (1988), sets the stage for academic success. Specific ecological features to be reviewed include teacher behavior, classroom organizational and management issues, and student behavior variables that have influenced the efficacy of CAI.

Teacher Behavior

Rieth and his colleagues (Rieth, Bahr, Okolo, Polsgrove, & Eckert, 1987a) conducted a series of studies, over a 3-year period, to investigate the impact of microcomputers on the instructional ecology in high school classrooms serving difficult-to-teach students. The initial studies were designed specifically to investigate the impact of the microcomputer on curricular content, curricular format, teacher behavior, teacher focus, and student behavior by comparing the results of observations conducted in classes in which the teachers used microcomputers for instruction with classes in which microcomputers were not used for instruction.

Rieth et al. (1987a) reported significant differences between computer-use and non-computer-use classes in only 4 of 11 categories of teachers' behavior. One category, which occurred significantly more often in classes where computers were used, was administrative record-keeping activities, which included taking attendance, recording grades, and so forth. Likewise, teachers in computer-use classes were observed to spend significantly more time preparing instructional materials than did the teachers in the non-computer-use classes. Teachers in computer-use classes also spent significantly more time structuring and directing student assignments than did teachers in non-computer-use classes. These results suggest that the computer-use teachers were required to allocate more preparation time to provide CAI, since they had to ensure that (a) equipment was operational, (b) software was available, and

(c) students understood the purpose and format of the CAI task. Overall, these preparatory activities required more time to organize for CAI than for teacher-based instruction. In part, this may have occurred because students were just acclimating to CAI and were confused by the procedures required to initiate and complete CAI assignments when the study was conducted. It is also plausible that teachers were just learning routines for organizing instructional materials and routines in order to deliver CAI. The finding also suggests that teachers allocate time to orient students to the operation of microcomputers and to the software that will be used. Failure to do so may result in additional intrusions on instructional time.

Teachers in non-computer-use classes were also observed to spend significantly more time on planned explanation (describing and explaining lesson content) than the teachers in computer-use classes. This behavior was observed most frequently in language arts activities, involving oral and silent reading, workbook, and discussion activities — activities that typically require more frequent and elaborate teacher explanations. On the other hand, math computation content dominated the computer use classes. Given the abundance of good CAI software and the frequent use of drill and practice activities in this instructional area, additional elaborative explanations may have been unnecessary. Many teachers perceive drill and practice software as self-instructional and, therefore, rarely monitor or interact with students engaged in CAI (Okolo, Rieth, & Bahr, 1989; Rieth et al., 1987a). This suggests that teachers are comfortable in transferring instructional responsibilities to the computer. This transfer assumes that teachers view these important instructional components as deliverable by the CAI software (Rieth & Polsgrove, 1983).

Rieth et al. (1987a) also reported high frequencies of explanations by teachers, in computer-use and non-computer-use classes, in response to student requests for clarification of lesson content or related assignments. This in turn suggests that students were unable to clearly understand the lesson content, assignment content, or assignment directions. It is unclear whether this lack of clarity occurred because the explanations were confusing or the students didn't possess the academic skills required to understand the information. The frequent occurrence of this behavior is alarming since it is negatively correlated with achievement (Fisher et al., 1978). This result indicates that teachers should select lesson content that is consonant with the students' skill repertoires and provide clear directions for completion of assignments. It also highlights the importance of accurately assessing students' skill repertoires, skillfully translating assessment information into instructional strategies, and monitoring performance. Failure to do so will negatively influence student achievement.

Both groups of teachers provided very little academic feedback (i.e., only 1% on average during 50-minute observation periods). The small amount of available teacher feedback appears counterproductive, since it is one of the strongest correlates of academic success and improved achievement for both difficult-to-teach children (Rieth & Frick, 1983) and secondary school students with reading problems (Stallings, Needels, & Stayrook, 1979). The research literature on teacher behavior suggests that teachers should continuously monitor students' performance and provide academic feedback in excess of 10% of the class period if difficult-to-teach students are to progress academically (Carnine & Silbert, 1979; Lovitt, 1967; Rieth, Polsgrove, & Semmel, 1981; Stallings & Kaskowitz, 1974).

Teachers have been encouraged to use microcomputers because they will reportedly provide individualized self-instruction and thereby enable teachers to engage in direct instructional activities by relieving them of time-consuming drill and practice, tutorial, and record management tasks. Rieth et al. (1987a) observed, however, that CAI primarily replaced teacher-directed rather than paper-and-pencil instruction (worksheets and workbooks). Teachers in computer-use classes spent nearly 40% of their time engaged in non-student-focused activities such as preparation activities, consultation, and non-school-related activities. In addition, these teachers spent very little time monitoring or interacting with students working at the computers. For the most part, the students were observed working on the computers without any interactions with teachers. In fact, attempts to encourage teachers to monitor the students' performance and/or provide feedback were unsuccessful (Kinzer, Rieth, & Bahr, 1989). Thus, teachers who used computers came to rely entirely on the computer to supply instruction and feedback. This is not an intended or desired result of the application of CAI.

The teachers in this study considered CAI to be self-instructional, leaving their students to work individually on CAI while they completed individual educational plans (IEPs), progress reports, and lesson plans. In addition, computer use was found to impose some additional time demands for preparing the computer to deliver instruction. The teachers were required to monitor machine operation, to load programs, and to align printer paper before students were allowed to begin working. Thus, the presumption of CAI that teachers will be able to reallocate time to student instruction appears unfulfilled. It appears, instead, that increased instructional time allocated to individual or small groups of students will occur only after the required time-consuming activities of IEP development, progress reports, and classroom plans are completed or reduced. Any change in teachers' behavior to result from the use of CAI will require a modification of the paperwork required for PL 94-142 compliance and activities focusing on strategies for increasing direct instruction.

When computers were used by participating teachers the curricular content was most often math (55.9%), whereas in classes in which computers where not used, the curricular content was primarily language arts (40.5%). This finding corroborates earlier studies reporting that computers are used most often with difficult-to-teach students for mathemat-

ics drill and practice (Becker, 1984; Budoff, Thormann, & Gras, 1984; MacArthur, Haynes, & Malouf, 1986; Semmel, Goldman, Gerber, Cosden, & Semmel, 1985). The dominance of computer use in mathematics is influenced by the availability of suitable software. Conversely, the absence of appropriate software in other academic areas for difficult-to-teach students has substantially curtailed the use of CAI with difficult-to-teach students (Okolo et al., 1989).

Microcomputer games constituted almost half of the observed computer use (42.7%). Games were defined as game-format activities that had no academic content and were unrelated to a student's academic goals. A large standard deviation (10.2%) suggested that while games were a prevalent activity, there was considerable variation in their implementation. It is unclear from the data whether students were able to use games after completing prescribed work or simply because it was their turn at the computer. When interviewed about the findings, teachers reported that they viewed the computer as a motivational device to promote task engagement, task completion, and appropriate social behavior. When they used games students were quiet and attending to the task; this suggested that the games served as behavior management devices. Unfortunately, the games did not include academic content and did not increase student achievement.

Overall, these findings suggest that the mere presence of computers in a classroom did not drastically alter the classroom ecology and that the teachers did not behave appreciably differently when computers were available. In fact, the presence of the machine reduced the frequency of teacher–student interactions and the amount of teacher-led instruction and increased the amount of administrative record keeping. Computer-assisted instruction did enable teachers to reallocate instructional time, but usually it was reinvested in compliance and record-keeping activities that teachers typically characterize as required but onerous. Typically CAI was provided in math rather than in language arts because of the greater availability of software. Overall, these results suggest that CAI has the potential to assist teachers in providing instruction, but they must be trained to develop routines to organize and manage CAI. In addition, since students are not monitored and do not receive feedback during CAI, it is essential that these features be included in the software.

The teachers appeared to be interested in obtaining instruction in procedures for integrating CAI and teacher-based instruction and in participating in the development of strategies for reallocating instructional time. In addition, the teachers reported that the absence of pedagogically sound software had prompted reductions in the use of CAI. Despite all of these liabilities, teachers remain optimistic regarding the promise of CAI in instructing difficult-to-teach students (Okolo et al., 1989).

Teacher attitudes and training. The efficacy of CAI for improving student achievement outcomes may depend, to some extent, on the characteristics of the teacher who chooses to use the technology. Some researchers have examined teacher attitudes toward computer use in an effort to determine the relationship between teacher attitudes and student learning. Available data suggest that many special education teachers hold very positive attitudes toward the technology, but have become frustrated by the lack of resources, training, and administrative support.

Okolo et al. (1989) asked teachers to describe problems which prevented them from using microcomputers as they would have liked. Many teachers reported that they had limited access to equipment and would like to have microcomputers in their classrooms. Others reported that scheduling difficulties, lack of appropriate software for their students, lack of time to learn about and experiment with technology, and lack of technical resource personnel to assist them were barriers to full implementation of CAI. At least one teacher believed that computers were a waste of time as she observed students

spending considerable amounts of time playing games.

Preservice and inservice training has been used to improve special education teachers' attitudes toward technology (Rieth et al., 1988). This approach assumes that teachers who know more about the capabilities of the technology, have more positive attitudes toward using the media for instruction.

Classroom Organization and Management Issues

Research on effective instruction for difficult-to-teach students has focused primarily on specific instructional strategies for teaching academic skills (Rieth & Evertson, 1988). Some research, however, has revealed the importance of preinstructional variables that can be employed successfully to increase the achievement of difficult-to-teach students (Brophy & Good, 1986; Rieth & Frick, 1983; Rieth, Polsgrove, & Semmel, 1981).

Preinstructional strategies including the elements of advance preparation and planning, are essential to effective instruction. CAI, like teacher-based instruction, requires attention to organization and management if it is to succeed. Teachers must first develop routines that give students access to computers; despite the proliferation of hardware, student access, continues to be a barrier in making the computer a central element of classroom instruction.

The following is a discussion of organizational strategies for maximizing students' access to hardware resources through scheduling and grouping strategies.

Scheduling. Given the current national average of one computer for every 30 students, teachers must make important decisions about how to allocate computer access time among their students. Cosden et al. (1986) reported that teachers' decisions to assign groups or individuals to work on the computer(s) appeared to be based more on hardware constraints than on sound instructional practices. They found that teachers designated three types of computer instructional groups: the whole class, small groups working as co-equals, and small groups working with peer tutors. Small groups averaged from 2.1 to 2.3 students in co-equal groups and from 2.0 to 2.7 in peer tutor groups. There was also some evidence that group configurations varied by instruction setting. Cosden and Semmel (1987) reported that students in special education programs primarily use computers individually, while students in mainstream classes worked nearly equal amounts of time individually and in groups.

It is estimated that students who use computers average a little more than 1 hour per week working on the computer, or about 4% of their available instructional time. Computer use also varies as a function of demographic characteristics. For example, disadvantaged elementary or middle school students have been found to have significantly less potential access to computers than peers in relatively rich schools. Black students have less access than do whites, particularly at the elementary school level. Mildly handicapped students tend to have less access than nonhandicapped students (Cosden & Semmel, 1987). Students with limited English proficiency have the lowest access of all. Low-achievement students are more likely to use computers for drill and practice than for problem solving or other activities. These inequalities should abate, however, as additional hardware and instructionally sound software programs become available and teachers become proficient in their use.

Access translates to allocated time and opportunities to respond, which in the research literature on teacher effectiveness are correlated with gains in student achievement (Carnine & Silbert, 1979; Denham & Lieberman, 1980; Fisher et al., 1978; Hall, Delquadri, & Harris, 1977; Rieth & Frick, 1983; Rieth, Polsgrove, & Semmel, 1979). Bahr, Rieth, Polsgrove, Okolo, and Eckert (1986) experimentally analyzed the effects of differential CAI time allocations on the subtraction performance of a group of difficult-to-teach students. The research questions included (a) How does the amount of time students spend

using pedagogically sound drill and practice software affect the rate and accuracy of their academic responses? (b) What is the effect of increasing the amount of computer-based instruction on the rate and accuracy of math responses? Specifically they analyzed the impact of 5-minute and 11-minute increases in CAI drill and practice on the accuracy of performance on subtraction.

These results indicated that the effects on achievement of simply increasing the amount of time students spent on computer-based drill and practice instruction varied. For some students, the increased length of time working with the computer had positive effects: The rate of correct responses increased and the rate of incorrect responses decreased. This pattern occurred slightly more frequently in the 5-minute than in the 11-minute sessions. But the error rates of six students increased during the study. Since all of the students had positive attitudes toward using computers, the negative effect may have arisen because of the content (i.e., all the target students had long histories of failure in learning subtraction skills). For other students, whose error rates accelerated as the study progressed regardless of conditions, the increase may be attributable to poor motivation. They simply were not interested by the task, and the lack of motivation was exacerbated by the passage of time. It is noteworthy that five of the seven students whose error rates increased as the study progressed markedly reduced the number of errors they made on the criterion-referenced posttest. These findings lend credibility to the hypothesis that some students simply were not interested or motivated by the task. This lack of interest may have been, in some sense, due to the continuously sustained task requirements of the computer programming, while the students working on paper-and-pencil tasks were able to control the pacing of the assignments, thus diminishing their sense of work requirements.

For another group of students, the time spent working on the computer did not appear to exert any noticeable impact on their performance: They had stable rates of responding throughout the study. Yet another group simply increased their rates of correct responses regardless of condition, which suggests a practice effect. That is, access to regularly scheduled practice enabled them to increase their performance.

Overall, the lack of clear-cut patterns of student responses may simply suggest that the intervention was not sufficiently powerful to influence students with different academic skills repertoires, who were enrolled in classes that included different instructional ecologies, and whose teachers used different instructional approaches. The relatively small amount of time that students spent working on CAI during the school day simply may not have been enough to counteract these powerful variables. Also, these results highlight the importance of regularly monitoring students' performance, since the treatment had deleterious effects on the performance of some students and its continued use might well have compounded the negative effects.

Overall, these results suggest that teachers faced with time allocation decisions must carefully weigh the following factors: (a) the instructional needs of the students, (b) the available instructional options, (c) the hardware available, (d) the quantity and quality of available software, (e) the integration of CAI and teacher-based instruction, (f) the instructional needs of the class, and (g) the general classroom organization and management strategies employed.

Grouping strategies. There is relatively little empirical research regarding the effects of group computer use on students' achievement. Although there is an extensive literature on group instruction procedures using non-computer-based media (i.e., cooperative learning, peer tutoring, the effects of group composition, etc.), Cosden and Lieber (1986) argue that conclusions drawn from this literature cannot be directly applied to decisions on group use of microcomputers, because (a) the number of subjects who can work comfortably at a computer is limited, (b) microcomputer tasks are more public than paper-and-pencil tasks, (c) students working alone at a microcomputer are not really "alone," given the interactive nature of some forms of CAI, and (d) the kind of help offered by a computer may be different from assistance offered by teachers or peers.

Cosden and English (1986) studied the effects of having 28 learning-handicapped students work on their math performance in two 10-minute sessions under each of three conditions: alone, with a learning-handicapped partner, and with a nonhandicapped partner. These researchers reported that the students were more productive while working with a partner than when working alone. However, the group configuration did not appear to affect the degree of problem difficulty sensed by the students on the accuracy of their performance. They concluded that group work did not have a significant impact on performance.

Some investigators have attempted to use grouping strategies to maximize access to microcomputers and to use peers as supportive tutors. Lieber and Semmel (1987) examined the effect of group size on the math performance of difficult-to-teach students. The study examined the relationship between group size and task engagement, and the relationship of task engagement to performance, for handicapped and nonhandicapped learners. The results indicated no differences in achievement between students working with a partner at the computer and students working alone. This was true even though dyads had half as much time per individual student at the computer as students working alone. This finding is important, since it suggests that the dyad arrangement allows teachers to enable more students access to the computer without adversely affecting achievement.

Amount of task engagement also was similar for children working in dyads in comparison with those working individually. Following each computer work session, students were administered paper-and-pencil tasks and no difference in the number of correct responses as a function of individual or dyad was found. Interestingly, at the most difficult task level, difficult-to-teach children solved more problems correctly following a computer session in which they worked with a partner. The authors concluded that, given a software program that requires students to apply mathematics skills to a new situation, it is effective to have two children working together at the computer.

Cox and Berger (1985) used computers to administer three problem-solving tasks to adolescents who worked alone, in pairs, in groups of three, and in groups of five. The major findings from their study suggest that participants who worked in groups improved their problem-solving skill over time by decreasing the time required to solve successive problems. Individuals did not make comparable improvements. Overall, individuals solved fewer problems than groups, but groups of two or three tended to solve more problems with greater consistency than did teams of five.

Kinzer, Rieth, and Bahr (1989) examined the effects of heterogeneous ability level in comparison with homogeneous ability level, grouping arrangements of difficult-to-teach students on (a) computer use and (b) performance on informal reading inventory (IRI) and reading comprehension measures. The results indicated that, in general, homogeneously grouped students showed greater gains than heterogeneously grouped students, outperforming them on three of four reading comprehension measures.

The advantages of homogeneous in contrast with heterogeneous groups was more obvious in the classrooms of teachers trained to engage students in questioning prior to the completion of a reading comprehension task. In fact, heterogeneously grouped students retrogressed on the IRI; pretest scores actually were higher than posttest scores. This may have been due to the lesser focus in the heterogeneous groups, where informal observation suggests that more off-task behavior and discussion took place. In fact, observational data indicated that the

heterogeneous groups may have split into internal groups along ability levels. This result, for heterogeneous groups, is consistent with research showing deferential behavior and less attention to task by self-perceived poorer readers when students are grouped in classrooms (Hawley & Rosenholtz, 1984).

Several interesting findings were noted. First, there appeared to be a relatively high degree of on-task discussion within the homogeneously grouped students. That is, students did spend time discussing potential answers and, in effect, "voting" before the answer was keyed in by the student controlling the keyboard. Second, students with low achievement levels, when allowed a measure of control through the keyboard, appeared to show relatively more interest and on-task behavior than when they were not controlling the keyboard. Both groups were observed to have positive attitudes toward reading passages and answering questions on the computer.

Overall, the literature supports the use of computer-use groups. The data suggest that students tend to gain more access to the computer without adversely affecting achievement. Dyads and triads appear to work successfully on computer tasks. Finally, it appears that when the computer groups include only difficult-to-teach students, homogeneously rather than heterogeneously grouped students appear to obtain greater benefits from the instruction.

Student Behavior

On-task behavior. Rieth, Bahr, Polsgrove, Okolo, and Eckert (1987b) studied the impact of computer use on the behavior of difficult-to-teach high school students. They reported that students in computer-use classes were actively engaged significantly more often than those in non-computer-use classes. Active engagement was defined as an overt interaction with an instructional task, such as making a verbal response, reading out loud, and writing an answer on paper. However, a substantial amount of computer time was allocated to nonacademic games in the computer-use classes, which may have contributed to the increased active attending among the computer-use students but a low correlation between engaged time and academic achievement. Conversely non-computer-use classes were engaged in more passive engagement, which was defined as orientation to the substance of an academic task but with no observable response (e.g., silent reading, listening to recitations, etc.). The increased active task engagement found in computer-use classes is encouraging since active task engagement is one of the strongest correlates of student achievement (Delquadri, Greenwood, Stretton, & Hall, 1983; Denham & Lieberman, 1980; Rieth, Polsgrove, & Semmel, 1981). This finding establishes the rationale for additional studies that explore the nature of active task engagement as well as the relationship of active computer use to student achievement.

The data also indicated that concerns about increased off-task behavior during computer use were unsupported. When working on the computer, students were off task only 3.7% of the class period, which is considerably less than the overall rates which were in excess of 16%. Thus computers provide an effective means for attaining high rates of engaged time which are incompatible with off-task and/or disruptive behavior. The findings suggest that computer use may serve to reduce off-task and disruptive behavior and increase task engagement.

Student characteristics. The variation in student outcomes in computer effectiveness studies may also be attributed to differences in student characteristics. Salomon and Gardner (1986) argue that individual differences and prior knowledge play a crucial role in determining how learners process or carry out a computer activity. They assert that motivation, perception of task, and preferred learning strategy impact on the learner's experience with the computer. Furthermore, Salomon and Gardner (1986) state that the assumption that CAI is uniformly effective for all learners is unfounded. Rather, there is the possibility that

technology-based instruction may benefit some learners while inhibiting others.

Locus of control. One of the often-mentioned benefits of computers is that they allow the user to take control of the learning experience. Research suggests that students with learning problems, in particular, often attribute their performance to external factors, such as luck or task difficulty, rather than to factors within their control (Hallahan, Gajar, Cohen, & Tarver, 1978; Pearl, Bryan, & Donahue, 1980). These attributions prevent students from taking responsibility for their actions and working to correct their mistakes. If these students are not able to attribute their successes and failures to their own efforts, they may tend to be extremely reliant on the computer or not perceive themselves as capable of contributing to computer-assisted group work.

Cosden and English (1986) examined the relationship between locus of control, self-esteem, and grouping patterns among 28 learning-handicapped students using a mathematics problem-solving program. They found that students with an internal orientation asked for less help from the computer than did those with an external orientation when working on easy problems by themselves. Furthermore, students with an internal locus of control obtained a higher score on easy problems alone without help than did students with an external orientation. While locus of control has some effect on help-seeking, it did not appear to affect overall performance accuracy of performance while working with a partner.

Motivation. Proponents of CAI often argue that computers motivate students to learn (Okolo et al., 1989). However, the level of motivation a student brings to a computer activity may, in turn, adversely affect his or her performance on the activity. While educators believe that most difficult-to-teach students enjoy using CAI, there are some students for whom technology-based media are not appealing. These students may be apprehensive about using the equipment and embarrassed to make errors that can be viewed publicly on the screen. Bahr (1989) argues the need for additional research to investigate the effects of motivation on learning by students using CAI.

Keyboard skills. Typically, CAI requires that students use a keyboard in order to make a response. Some researchers (Goldman & Pellegrino, 1987) suggest that the search component may demand additional effort and attention from handicapped students that can "radically alter" their performance on a computer task. Christensen and Gerber (1986) found that students without learning difficulties acquired keyboard skills faster than did students who were considered difficult-to-teach. The "hunt and peck" method of keyboarding may enable students to enter responses, albeit slowly; however, here is evidence that the additional cognitive processing devoted to keyboarding may inhibit the student's ability to attend to the content of the task.

Neuman and Morocco (1986) observed teachers using three approaches to keyboard skill instruction: (a) daily drill and practice with emphasis on hand placement and letter positions, (b) occasional use of computer typing games, and (c) no keyboard practice. They found that daily keyboard drill and practice yielded the most positive results, and they concluded that keyboarding is an important skill that affects success in computer-based tasks.

Attitudes. Students' attitudes toward using CAI can affect their performance. But, performance on a CAI task can produce attitudinal changes among students (Bahr, in press). Okolo et al. (1986) interviewed 27 difficult-to-teach students, of whom 90% maintained that computers help students to learn and expressed a desire to use computers more often and for a wider range of activities. Only 39% of the sample, however, viewed classes in which computers were used as more fun than classes without computers.

It is clear that not all difficult-to-teach students hold positive attitudes toward the use of technology. However, additional research is needed to (a) develop reliable and valid instruments for measuring student attitudes, (b) determine the impact of students' attitudes on subsequent achievement with CAI, and (c) determine the effects of CAI on change in students' attitudes.

In general, student characteristics appear to influence the efficacy of CAI, producing results that frequently are idiosyncratic to individual learners. Current research that examines specific student characteristics as they relate to performance on CAI tasks (Bahr, in press) suggests that some variables, such as locus of control, do not appear to affect performance on CAI drill and practice activities, while other variables, such as keyboarding skill, do appear to play a vital role in student learning with this medium.

ASSESSMENT APPLICATIONS

Selecting appropriate CAI strategies for difficult-to-teach students must be guided by the appropriate educational information obtained through an assessment process. Educational assessment is a multifaceted process of collecting test data and other forms of information "for the purpose of (1) specifying and verifying problems and (2) making decisions about students" (Salvia & Ysseldyke, 1988). This information is used to make five general types of decisions about students: referral, screening, classification, instructional planning, and pupil progress evaluation. Computers can make an important contribution to this process and have been demonstrated to assist in (a) test administration and recording of student responses; (b) scoring and interpreting test data; and (c) management of the test data and integration into assessment reports (Fifield, 1989).

Test Administration and Recording of Student Responses

Administration of assessment instruments generally consists of presenting test stimuli and recording the student's responses. Both are tasks ideally designed for the computer, and in fact Krug (1984) reportedly identified 190 test administration and scoring programs. Most were basic screening applications; only 20% are appropriate to obtain "cognitive" or "achievement" information needed to identify and develop programs for difficult-to-teach students (Fifield, 1989).

Other programs have been developed that present questions on the screen and prompt a teacher or other service providers for input at the keyboard to gather information about a student's adaptive behavior. Programs have also been developed to guide a structured clinical interview. Fifield (1988) developed a program that administers, scores, and interprets the Walker–McConnell Scale of Social Competence and School Adjustment, a rating scale that is completed by a student's teacher. Interestingly the author reports that it takes nearly as long to administer the test by computer as it does by paper and pencil, but the computer version can score and interpret the test nearly 10 times faster than a person. Furthermore, the computer-scored version eliminates scoring errors of verified input data.

Recent advances in microcomputer technology have also greatly increased the speed and efficiency with which classroom observational data can be measured, coded, entered, sorted, and analyzed. Recently, Rieth, Haus, and Bahr (1989) described three such applications, which were used with portable laptop microcomputers to collect, analyze, and summarize classroom observational data to facilitate the delivery of feedback to teachers and students. These data were used to assist individual teachers to expand their teaching behavioral repertoire, analyze the effectiveness of staff development programs, and provide feedback to students regarding their classroom behavior. Clearly this technology can be a powerful tool for teachers and school psychologists to use in obtaining information to improve instructional programs for difficult-to-teach students.

Scoring and Interpretation

The procedures for scoring commonly used assessment instruments vary in complexity and difficulty. Some instruments, such as curriculum-based measures, simply require summing the number of correct responses (Deno & Fuchs, 1988), while others, such as the Woodcock–Johnson Psycho-Education Battery, require more complex scoring procedures. Some programs provide information regarding the accuracy of student responses to individual items, others provide information weight, sum results, and transform raw scores into standard scores, grade equivalents, or percentiles. Fifield (1989) reported that software is available to assist in transforming raw scores into scaled scores, percentiles, and grade equivalents for instruments that assess several domains, including cognitive abilities, achievement, adaptive behavior, social skills, and language development. Programs that aid in scoring multiple-scale instruments increase not only the speed with which the test can be scored, but the accuracy of the scoring and score transformations (Vance & Hayden, 1982).

Software can increase the fidelity of administration and alternate-forms reliability. Because computers are able to repeatedly execute a set of instructions with virtually 100% accuracy, standardization of the presentation of questions, scoring of responses, and even interpreting of scores can be maintained at a much higher level than with conventionally administered instruments. Furthermore, the computer can easily accommodate increasingly complex questions and scoring criteria. Novel presentation of stimulus items that heretofore have been too difficult to execute are likely to emerge as assessment software is developed and becomes more widely available. In addition, new, more objective and naturalistic methods of recording responses will be developed as computer technology continues to improve.

Test interpretation software is often more complicated than simple scoring programs. Some interpretation programs produce predetermined conclusions and recommendations when scores for the instrument fall in a certain range. These "cookbook" approaches to test interpretation can be useful when the conclusions and recommendations generated by the program have been empirically validated. More sophisticated expert-system programs that aid in interpreting psychometric data use artificial intelligence programming techniques to capture the strategies and rules used by human experts to derive conclusions and recommendations from testing results (e.g., Fifield, 1987).

Translating the guidelines used by human experts in interpreting a student's test performance into rules that can be used in expert-system software is quite complicated. However, it has been shown that once the rules that govern an interpretation model have been identified and clarified, a computer can execute the decisions faster and more reliably than human experts (Krug, 1984; Lubke et al., 1985).

Data Management

Frequent assessment of academic skills requires the management of large amounts of information, including reports, record management, and monitoring of students' progress on IEP goals and objectives. In some cases, software programs have been custom-developed to meet educators' data management needs. More recently, commercial products such as database management systems have been marketed that can be applied to many professional endeavors. For example, database programs have been applied to the management of student information, the monitoring of due process time lines outlined by PL 94-142, and the development of IEP goals and objectives for individual students (Minnick & School, 1982). Psychologists and teachers have used personal computers to help write test reports since they first became available (Fifield, 1989). Generic word-processing programs are currently available that assist in expediting the writing, editing, and printing of testing reports.

As the school psychologist's workload increases, the market for tests that can be administered or scored on a personal computer will continue to grow. Fifield (1989) proposes four areas of new computer test development: (a) development of real-time data collection procedures by which computer-administered tests will facilitate the collection of data regarding response latency, and response duration, and development of more accurate measures of rate and frequency as they apply to cognitive tasks and skills in academic and social domains; (b) development of alternative models of testing such as the use of response–contingent testing or programmed tests; (c) development of alternative stimulus presentation techniques such as a videodisk operated by a computer to present static as well as dynamic stimuli, and (d) development of alternative answering techniques using a mouse, touch pad, or touch screen, and voice recognition as an alternative to the keyboard.

Curriculum-based Monitoring

One of the most promising computer-based assessment procedures is the curriculum-based monitoring (CBM) of students' progress toward specified goals. It is a method for formatively evaluating educational plans and for empirically developing effective instructional programs over time. With curriculum-based progress-monitoring procedures, teachers select long-term curricular goals, design measurement systems that correspond to those curricular goals, routinely monitor students' progress toward the goals by using those measurement systems, use the database to evaluate the effectiveness of the educational program, and modify instruction as needed to ensure goal attainment (Deno & Fuchs, 1988).

Research on the effectiveness of CBM procedures is promising. However, teachers are reluctant to use these procedures because they are time-consuming (Deno & Fuchs, 1988; Fuchs & Fuchs, 1986; Wesson, King, & Deno, 1984). Fuchs, Fuchs, Hamlett, and Hasselbring (1987) examined the effects of using computer software to store, graph, and analyze student performance data. The data reported indicated that computer assistance was associated with a decrease in efficiency but an increase in teacher satisfaction.

This finding is potentially important, since it supports the implementation of CBM systems. If computer use renders teachers' perceptions more positive, practitioners may be more likely to implement such systems over time and to realize their related pedagogical and student achievement benefits.

In a follow-up study, Fuchs, Hamlett, Fuchs, Stecker, and Ferguson (1988) compared the level of efficiency and teacher satisfaction with CBM under two levels of computer assistance: (a) Student performance data were collected automatically as student interacted with computers, and (b) scores were saved for teachers' use by a data-management program that graphed and analyzed the scores. Observational data indicated that teachers spent less time in measurement and evaluation when data were collected by computers; furthermore, consumer satisfaction data revealed that teachers who made use of computer data collection were more satisfied with the procedures. It should be noted, however, that students spent more time in measurement with computer data collection.

Fuchs et al. (1988) reported that the findings appeared to support the use of CBM data collection systems. They concluded that computer administrations of the CBM tests tended to free practitioners from the routine tasks of generating, administering, and scoring the tests.

CAI INSTRUCTIONAL APPLICATIONS

Types of CAI Applications

As noted earlier, CAI has been used extensively to instruct difficult-to-teach students. Among the CAI applications, five types frequently reported in the literature are: drill and practice, tutoring, simulations, problem solving, and writing. Each is described briefly below.

Drill and practice. Currently, drill and practice is the most commonly used form of CAI. It is designed to help integrate and consolidate previously learned material through computer-based practice. Good drill-and-practice software provides immediate feedback, appropriate individualization, repetition, immediate reinforcement, and self-pacing, and it serves as a supplement to other forms of instruction.

The initial studies that examined drill and practice applications focused on math content and consisted of comparisons of the efficacy of CAI and teacher-based instruction. Suppes, Fletcher, Zanotti, Lorton, and Searle (1973) studied the relationship between the number of CAI lessons completed and increases on standardized achievement scores. The results indicated that the more lessons students completed, the higher they scored on a math achievement test. Watkins and Webb (1981) compared the efficacy of computer-based instruction with teacher-based instruction. The results indicated that the students receiving computer-based instruction attained significantly higher posttest scores than those who received traditional math instruction. McDermott and Watkins (1983) compared the effects of computer-based and teacher-based instruction on math achievement test scores. They found no differences in the effectiveness of the instruction; however, these authors suggested that the academic outcome measures may have been too global to accurately measure the achievement gains.

Virtually all of the studies that have examined the use of math drill-and-practice software, regardless of the software used, have reported that these programs fail to develop generalized math fluency (Christensen & Gerber, 1986; Goldman & Pellegrino, 1987; Hasselbring, Goin, & Bransford, 1988; Howell & Garcia, 1985; McDermott & Watkins, 1983). Generally, the findings have shown that drill and practice with difficult-to-teach students leads to slight decreases in response latencies that can be attributed to the students becoming more efficient at counting and not to the development of automatic recall of facts from memory.

Hasselbring et al. (1988) suggest that when students are using counting strategies to solve basic math facts, typical CAI drill-and-practice activities do not enable students to develop the processes necessary to retrieve the answers from memory. They argue that when a student cannot retrieve an answer from memory before engaging in drill and practice, the time spent in drill and practice is essentially wasted. On the other hand, if a student can retrieve a fact from memory, even slowly, then drill and practice will lead quickly to the fluent recall of that fact. The data suggest that if drill and practice is to be effective for developing fluency, difficult-to-teach students should practice only problems that have answers that they are able to retrieve from memory.

Several studies have demonstrated that microcomputers can provide effective practice that increases mildly handicapped students' word analysis skills. Lally (1981) examined the efficacy of using the microcomputer to assist in teaching sight words to mildly handicapped students. The results indicated that students using computer-based instruction learned substantially more sight words than students who had access only to teacher-based instruction.

Jones and Torgesen (1985) evaluated *Hint and Hunt* (Roth & Beth, 1984), a program designed to provide practice in analyzing medial vowels and vowel combinations. The results demonstrated that the software can increase decoding fluency, and the increase in speed was accompanied by an increase in accuracy.

Roth and Beck (1984) evaluated the effects of a drill-and-practice program designed to increase decoding by giving the students practice at forming many different words from the same sets of beginning and ending word parts. They found that low-achieving fourth graders increased sentence reading speed substantially when they were provided practice with the CAI software. In contrast, the control group's sentence-reading speed increased only slightly.

Cohen and Torgesen (1985) evaluated the effectiveness of a software program designed to teach sight words. The software reduced the time required to learn new words. The practice also had a slight effect on students' spelling skills. The authors concluded that the program would be appropriate when used as a supplemental practice activity to teach sight words. Rashotte and Torgesen (1985) found that students could improve their sight word fluency with CAI. They reported that word recognition speed could be increased by repeated readings.

The results of these studies suggest that microcomputer-based instruction is beneficial for increasing the fluency of students' decoding skills. Evidence regarding the use of microcomputers to teach comprehension skills, however, is equivocal at the present time (Kinzer et al., 1989).

The spelling data are also inconclusive. For example, Fitzgerald, Fick, and Milich (1986) found no differences between computer-based and traditional forms of practice. However, as expected, both the computer and the traditional method were superior to a no-practice condition. The investigators concluded from this research that the computer practice was at least equal to the traditional method. Similar findings have been reported by McDermott and Watkins (1983) and by Haynes, Kapinus, Malouf, and MacArthur (1984). Rieth and McCarthy (1985) found that both CAI and distributed practice (Rieth, Axelrod, Anderson, Hathway, & Fitzgerald, 1974) substantially increased weekly spelling test scores over results for traditional spelling instruction. Overall, however, students scored higher during the distributed practice than the CAI treatment. The differences appeared to be due, largely, to difficulties students encountered in entering responses into the computer through the keyboard. Frequently, students reported that they forgot words while searching for keys.

Hasselbring (1982, 1984) reported that students' test scores on spelling lists rose to over 90% when computer-based instructional procedures were employed. Unfortunately, the absence of experimental controls compromised the results of these studies. McDermott and Watkins (1983) reported no differences between computer-based and conventional remedial spelling instruction for a group of students who were having difficulty learning spelling words. Finally, Fitzgerald,

Fick, and Milich (1986) found little difference between computer-based instruction and traditional spelling instruction. However, the authors did report that both forms of practice were superior to "no practice."

The data do not document any distinct advantages for computer-based instruction in spelling. However, it would appear that with pedagogically sound software, computer-based instructional programs can be developed and can be used for independently tutoring students. This modality successfully spurs achievement even as the use of the computer relieves the teacher of the responsibility of directly supervising the tutoring sessions.

Tutoring. A tutorial program differs from drill and practice because it places the computer in the role of teacher while introducing new skills. Material is presented and the computer interacts with the child by questioning her or him about the material and responding to the answers. Tutorial CAI programs offer four advantages for teaching difficult-to-teach students. First, tutorials can provide a number of task repetitions, which are often required by difficult-to-teach students for mastery of a task (Engelmann & Carnine, 1982). Second, tutorial CAI can be structured by basic teaching tactics. Third, the CAI program presents material in a precise instructional sequence (i.e., it does not forget important steps in the learning sequence). Fourth, the student receives immediate feedback for all responses given.

Budoff et al. (1984) suggest that a sound CAI tutorial program should include (a) set objectives sequenced by subskills or component parts; (b) rules that teach learning strategies that enable students to generalize the strategy to other situations; (c) a high response rate and constant feedback regarding the correctness of the response, and (d) teaching done in modules and clusters with periodic review of previously learned concepts (Carnine & Silbert, 1979).

When software includes tutorial plus drill-and-practice content, the available data suggest that gains in automaticity occur. Trifiletti, Frith, and Armstrong (1984) found that 40 minutes of computerized tutoring plus drill per day was more than twice as effective as an equivalent amount of teacher-based math instruction. The students' gains included the number of math skills mastered and the fluency of problem solving; experimental subjects made nearly twice the gains on standardized math achievement tests as control subjects. Howell, Sidorenk, and Jurica (1987) found a combination of computer-based instruction and teacher-based instruction to be more effective than computer-based instruction alone in increasing the acquisition of multiplication facts.

Hasselbring, Goin, and Bransford (1988) examined the effect of tutoring plus drill on development of retrieval strategies by handicapped students. They compared the performance of a computer-use and non-computer-use group. The computer group received daily instruction to develop recall of addition and subtraction facts. Following each session the students received a brief period of drill and practice over the facts that the student could retrieve from memory. The combined retrieval training and drill and practice averaged only 10 minutes per day but increased the number of facts recalled from memory by 73% over the pretest. During the same period, the learning-handicapped group that received teacher-based instruction showed no change in the number of facts that they could recall from memory and a group of nonhandicapped contrast students averaged only 8 additional facts. Thus, the learning-handicapped students were developing fluency of recall of facts at a rate twice that of their nonhandicapped peers.

Hasselbring et al. (1988) concluded that the combination of recall training plus drill is a powerful mechanism for developing fluency in children with learning handicaps. Furthermore, with sufficient training, difficult-to-teach students should be able to develop fluency at a level commensurate with their "normal" peers.

Simulations. According to Ellis (1986), one of the most exciting promises of the microcomputer is its ability to provide interactive instruction with simulations. However, until recently the relative effectiveness of simulations as an instructional technique has been unimpressive. Simulations are designed to model some reality. Many simulations approximate commonplace problems found in daily living and offer students a chance to make decisions about hypothetical problems. Students are motivated to use many academically related skills, such as mathematics, to develop strategies to solve a problem or series of problems presented in the simulation. A simulation also makes it possible for students to experience events or explore environments that are otherwise too expensive, dangerous, or time-consuming to explore in the classroom. Through computer simulations, students can fly an airplane, take a trip inside the human body, or go on a geological expedition. Over the years, computer-based simulations have been recommended for teaching problem solving to learning-handicapped students (Goldenberg, Russell, & Carter, 1984).

Many simulations are described as programs for developing decision making, which is unquestionably an important aspect of problem solving. For example, in one of the most frequently used simulations, *Oregon Trail*, students must decide whether to buy food at a fort or hunt for it. Bransford et al. (1988) believe that students can solve and master a simulation such as *Oregon Trail* without developing effective problem-solving skills. They argue that decisions made in many simulations can be made mainly on the basis of trial and error rather than on systematic analysis of the available information. Initially, the danger that simulations will encourage trial-and-error responding is increased because students have very little information about the simulations and hence are reduced to guessing. Bransford et al. (1988) argue that a more effective procedure involves teaching information-gathering skills by first helping students consult external sources of information that could assist them in making more rational decisions during the simulations.

Woodward, Carnine, and Collins (1986) compared a simulation group with a conventional instruction group and found that the simulation group was superior to the conventional group on measures of problem solving in the areas of diagnosing health problems, prioritizing them as to their effects on longevity, and prescribing appropriate remedies. Although the evidence is limited, it appears that simulations may produce improved problem solving when prior information is provided and can be used as part of the simulation. However, as Bransford et al. (1988) caution, people often fail to use appropriate concepts and strategies because they do not realize that this information is relevant. Teaching methods that associate relevant pieces of information must be used to increase the probability that appropriate information will be used in improving decision making and problem solving through computer simulations.

Problem solving. Problem-solving skills can be taught with the computer, and the computer can be used to help students apply these skills in novel situations. Many educators have advocated the use of simulations to promote problem-solving skills (Doob, 1972; Greenblat & Duke, 1975; Budoff et al., 1984), but research comparing simulation instruction with conventional methods has not yielded any results favoring the simulation instruction. Woodward, Carnine, and Collins (1986) hypothesized that a more effective way to teach problem solving is not to choose between these methods of instruction but, rather, to use both. Initially, direct instruction in problem-solving preskills and strategies can be provided and followed up by opportunities to practice the new skills while interacting with a simulation. Thus, the simulation activities are used to enhance rather than replace problem-solving instruction.

Woodward et al. (1988) tested this hypothesis by using a series of computer simulation activities involving problem solving in health-related areas. The results indicated significant effects on test items reinforced by the simulation, and nonsignificant effects for items not reinforced. Thus the simulation appeared to be an effective procedure for reviewing material that already had been taught. When the groups that had participated in the activities were compared, the simulation group was significantly superior in problem-solving skills.

The Woodward et al. (1988) study provides important information about how computer simulations can be effectively used to teach problem solving. Although tentative, these results suggest that use of a structured approach to computer simulations (outcomes are specified and controlled) when preceded by direct instruction in problem-solving strategies, can be a highly effective approach.

Writing. Writing is an important skill for which CAI instructional programs have been developed. Many authors have noted the promises associated with using word processors to promote writing ability (Goldenberg et al., 1984; Hagen, 1984; MacArthur, Graham, & Skarvold, 1986). The advantages include the production of a clean and readable text, a sense of authorship, and the ease of revision. Recently some research has been conducted to determine the effectiveness of using word processors to teach difficult-to-teach students.

Morocco and Neuman (1987), for example, observed teachers who were using word processing to teach difficult-to-teach students. Three basic approaches to writing instruction were observed: (a) Teachers collaborated directly with children in eliciting content for their writing (substantive instruction); (b) they provided students with procedures for generating ideas to write about (procedural instruction); and (c) they directly taught skills or knowledge about writing rules (direct instruction). The authors concluded that students were most successful when teachers used a procedural approach to writing instruction. Being provided with strategies for generating ideas during writing, the students could generalize these procedures to other writing situations. In all cases examined, teachers' use of substantive instruction was less effective than the use of procedural instruction for getting students to generate ideas and produce a first draft.

MacArthur et al. (1986) compared students' use of three modes of writing: handwriting, dictation, and word processing. Of the three, dictated stories proved to be the significantly superior mode on a number of dependent variables. For example, dictated stories were longer (150 words as compared to 80 words) and had fewer grammatical errors. No differences were found between the handwritten stories and those composed on the word processor in respect to length, quality, structure, vocabulary, mean t-unit length, and mechanical and grammatical errors. On measures of composing rate dictation again was found to be superior.

One frequently touted advantage of word processors is that they allow the writer to make quick, easy revisions on a document with a minimal amount of inconvenience. Neuman et al. (1985) and MacArthur et al. (1986) found that just the opposite tends to occur. Neuman et al. (1985) observed that students tended to focus more on the editing process and that the documents were "technically correct, but shallow in ideas, insight" (p. 11). MacArthur (1986) reported that learning-disabled students tended to spend more time correcting minor errors during the composing process. They concluded that using word processors does not necessarily result in greater sophistication of revision strategies, but the word processing may facilitate instruction in revision strategies (i.e., students are more willing to make changes when recopying).

In summary, while word processors possess promise for improving writing ability, the data have yet to support the promise. Preliminary studies in this area suggest that using this writing tool does not necessarily improve writing skills, but explorations into effective instruction with the medium have just begun. Although it is unclear whether the problems experienced by difficult-to-teach students while learning word-processing skills are any different from those of their normal-achieving counterparts, specific instruction clearly is needed with this population.

Software Considerations

According to the Office of Technology Assessment (1988), more than 10,000 software products intended for instructional or educational use with stand-alone computers in schools and at home are on the market. Of these products, drill and practice applications are most prevalent, with tutorial, educational games, tool programs, and simulations making up the vast majority of the applications.

Math programs still dominate the market. Generic programs for word processing and data management are also among the best sellers; many teachers seem to appreciate software that affords them flexible classroom applications. Database, spreadsheet, and word processing programs have become classroom tools and are being applied in exciting ways to traditional classroom activities. Teachers use these tools for instruction, record-keeping, performance analysis, and data summary (OTA, 1988).

The OTA (1988) reports that while many software titles receive favorable ratings from review agencies and professional computer magazines, there is a general consensus among educators that the quality of educational software could be much better. Though commercial software publishers are reluctant to take risks with innovative software, many of the available titles are attractive and fun to use, even if they are geared toward familiar objectives.

Educational software, like other educational resources, can be criticized or praised on many criteria. Initially one must distinguish between technical quality (Does it work? How often does the program crash? Are the screen displays clear?) and educational quality (Do students learn? Are they motivated to continue learning?). Rapid advances in programming experience have substantially raised the proportion of technically sound products on the market, but teachers continue to lament those intermittent bugs and crashes that disrupt children's learning. Although most educators are more concerned with program content and educational effects, the costs of technical failures should not be underestimated (OTA, 1988).

In evaluating educational software through loosely structured interviews with 12 "leading edge" teachers, OTA (1988) identified and described 115 "best" programs. Most were characterized as "open-ended," allowing students substantial range of choices and decisions, and/or allowing the teacher considerable latitude to adapt program content to the needs of their particular student population. The highest percentage of programs favored by teachers were in the "comprehensive" category (multipurpose tools rather than structured curriculum-specific software).

Okolo et al. (1989) interviewed 31 high school teachers about CAI applications. The teachers reported that math instruction was the most frequently selected CAI content area; teachers were influenced by the greater availability of quality math software. It was followed, in order of preference, by language arts applications. Drill and practice and games software were used most often to increase student motivation. Software was used less frequently to provide such options as individualized instruction, exposure to record-keeping, presentation of instruction, and exposure to technology and enrichment.

When asked to identify preferred and/or ideal microcomputer applications, the teachers listed the following curricular areas (in order of preference): language arts, mathematics, social studies, and science. The levels of preference were so nearly equivalent however as to suggest that teachers prefer to use CAI in more subject matter areas but are stymied because of the absence of software. When questioned about the impediments to the use of desired software two major barriers were identified. They were concerned about the unavailability or inappropriateness of software and the lack of access to suitable software. When the teachers were asked to describe the characteristics of good software, they stipulated ease of use as a primary concern, motivational aspects, adequate length and repetition, readability and variety, and feedback to students being lower-ranking concerns. Virtually all of the teachers interviewed requested in-service training in CAI applications. In particular, the areas of programming, exposure to more software, and instruction in ways to use software appropriately by featuring hands-on experience were high priorities for in-service training.

Budoff et al. (1984) suggested that in evaluating software one should evaluate the technical quality, content, instructional quality, and the theory base to identify important quality variables. They suggest attending to the following software features for special-needs students: the programming should provide flexibility; the student or teacher should have control of presentation of materials; the number of problems or length of lesson should maintain maximum student attention; and the rate and type of reinforcement should be under the control of the student or teacher. Directions should appear on the screen in simple English. The program should also maintain student records that can be printed.

Special Considerations

In addition to its contributions in specific academic areas, computers have been viewed as possessing a potential for facilitating the following: attainment of goal structures, integration into teacher-based instruction, provision of appropriate feedback, and advancement of contextual learning.

Goal structures. Some investigators have examined the effects of group goals and interactions during computer-based instructional activities. Research on cooperative learning suggests that when students are instructed to work together, they tend to perform better than when they work competitively or individually. Johnson, Johnson, and Stanne (1986) compared the efficacy of cooperative, competitive, and individualistic goal structures on a computer-assisted social studies simulation program. In the cooperative learning situation, students worked together on the computer task and individually completed daily worksheets and a final exam. In the competitive condition, students were instructed to compete to see who was best while working on the CAI task. Findings suggested that students in the CAI cooperative learning condition completed significantly more worksheet items after working on the computer and tended to score higher on the final exam than students in the competitive and individualistic conditions.

Other investigators (Fuchs, Bahr, & Rieth, 1989) compared the effects of goal setting on students' performance when using CAI. They compared the effects of assigned versus self-selected goals on students' achievement in a computer-assisted math program. The results indicated that students who selected their goals achieved significantly higher scores on a computer-based math computation test than students who were assigned goals. Overall performance for students in the self-selected group was higher than for students in the assigned condition.

The impact of this work underscores the importance of the computer's unique capacity to provide specific feedback regarding progress toward goals. The work also suggests the feasibility of incorporating a goal setting option in software to enhance student performance.

Integration of CAI and teacher-based instruction. Rieth and Polsgrove (1983) reported that one factor that influences the effectiveness of CAI with difficult-to-teach students is the extent to which it is integrated with the ongoing classroom instructional program. They reported case study data that demonstrated that CAI had negative effects on achievement when used to reinforce skills that students had already mastered. The needless practice served as time off-task and reduced opportunities to learn. Rieth and his colleagues noted the absence of integration throughout the entire duration of their 4-year study of the implementation of microcomputers in school systems. CAI activities were perceived as separate activities independent of the curriculum.

One approach to improving the integration of CAI that has been proposed by Rubin and Weisgerber (1985) is the development of software guides to assist teachers in using and integrating widely available commercial software. Unfortunately, this approach has not been empirically validated.

Feedback. Rieth, Bahr, and Okolo (1986) compared the behavior of teachers when a computer was in use to their behavior when no computer was used. They found that during computer periods teachers provided significantly less academic feedback to students than when a computer was not in use. Furthermore, when performance feedback was available from the computer, teachers often did not attend to the data, inform students of their progress, or use the data to make instructional decisions. Budoff et al. (1984) reported that teachers expect students to work independently at the computer with little supervision from the teacher. As one teacher stated: "Like with all students, our goal is to have them be individual learners" — that is, not require supervision and extensive feedback. These findings underscore the importance of having feedback built into the software, since feedback has been demonstrated to be an important instructional component for difficult-to-teach students (Rieth, Polsgrove, & Semmel, 1981).

LeBlanc, Hoko, Aangeebrug, and Etzel (1985) suggested that analyzing students' computer-generated errors led to valuable assessment of their task approach behavior. This information can be used to identify students who have problems learning complex discrimination tasks and to prescribe learning tasks that follow a specific task sequence. The authors noted that feedback for incorrect responses should not be more reinforcing than that provided for correct responses. Elaborated corrective feedback has been found to be more effective than feedback that merely indicates whether a response is correct or incorrect, or that provides only the correct answer following an incorrect response (Collins, Carnine, & Gersten, 1987). In addition, following an incorrect response, the student should be required to make the correct response. Rieth and Frick (1983) found that task engagement was increased sevenfold when students were provided feedback regarding their academic performance. The increased task engagement was related to observed increases in achievement. These studies highlight the impact of feedback and underscore its role as a key component of software.

SUMMARY AND IMPLICATIONS FOR SCHOOL PSYCHOLOGISTS

Summary

Computer-assisted instruction can be used, under proper conditions, as an effective tool in teaching difficult-to-teach students. It can assist teachers to individualize instruction, provide self-paced instruction, and give students additional opportunities to respond, more immediate and frequent feedback, well-sequenced instruction, and increased motivation. To date, the literature suggests that much of this potential is unfulfilled because of inadequate numbers of computers, inadequate software, and insufficient training for teachers to utilize the power of the technology. In fact, data reported by Rieth et al. (1987b) suggest that the mere presence of computers in the classroom does not drastically alter the classroom ecology and that in the absence of facilitative factors teachers do not behave differently when computers are present in the classroom.

The key factors that accompany the effective use of CAI include a facilitative general classroom organization and management structure, content and software features that are consonant with the students' instructional needs, pedagogically sound software, and the integration of CAI and teacher-based instruction.

The classroom organization and management structure provide the essential staging area from which effective instruction is launched. Teachers must develop routines that enable students to access computers if CAI is to produce achievement. In some cases teachers have effectively employed grouping strategies to increase students' access to computers. Studies of grouping strategies suggest that they enable students to gain additional access to the computer without adversely affecting their achievement. Dyads and triads appear to work successfully on computer tasks (Kinzer et al., 1989; Lieber & Semmel, 1987).

Differences in students' learning characteristics have been shown to influence the effectiveness of computer use (Salomon & Gardner, 1986). Computers can be very helpful in collecting assessment data regarding students' characteristics. In turn, these data can help teachers monitor students' academic progress, identify and verify academic problems, assist in making instructional decisions, and develop and evaluate individualized instructional programs for difficult-to-teach students. One of the most promising computer-based assessment procedures is curriculum-based monitoring. It enables teachers to select long-term curricular goals, design measurement systems that correspond to those curricular goals, routinely monitor students' progress, use a database to evaluate the effectiveness of the educational program, and modify instruction as needed to ensure goal attainment (Deno & Fuchs, 1988).

Individualized instructional programs for difficult-to-teach students contain many of the same characteristics as effective CAI programs. The features include flexibility to accommodate individual differences, immediate feedback regarding academic responses, consistent correction procedures, well-sequenced instruction, repeated opportunities to demonstrate mastery of subject matter, and student or teacher control of the presentation of materials including the number or length of problems that will maintain maximum student attention, and the rate and type of reinforcement. Directions should appear on the screen in simple English and the program should

also maintain student records that can be printed (Budoff et al., 1984).

Unfortunately the OTA (1988) reports that while many CAI software titles receive favorable ratings from review agencies and professional computer magazines, there is general consensus among educators that the quality of educational software could be much improved. Okolo et al. (1989) reported, however, that teachers are optimistic that more pedagogically sound software will be developed.

Finally, Rieth and Polsgrove (1983) reported that a major factor influencing the effectiveness of CAI with difficult-to-teach students is the extent to which it is integrated with the ongoing classroom instructional program. They reported that the likelihood of achievement gains are substantially greater when teacher-based and CAI instruction are integrated. The absence of integration was found to be correlated with continuing low achievement rates.

Implications for School Psychologists

The school psychologist is perceived as an instructional resource person who, with training, can be prepared to work cooperatively with teachers to develop classroom ecologies that integrate CAI and effective teacher-based instruction to enhance the achievement of difficult-to-teach students. In addition, they can help teachers assess student behavior, translate assessment information into instructional strategies, select appropriate instructional tasks, develop appropriate instructional strategies, and monitor the efficacy of instructional programs.

The school psychologist must work cooperatively with the classroom teacher to identify organizational routines that accommodate CAI systems in the classroom instructional program. Cooperative efforts to identify pedagogically sound software that incorporates response monitoring, report gathering, feedback, and monitoring functions are essential for difficult-to-teach students. Failure to do so will increase the students' error rates and require more time from the teacher.

The school psychologist can assist the teacher in developing strategies to integrate teacher-based and CAI programs, thereby enabling teachers to use the computer to increase the amount of direct instruction provided to the difficult-to-teach student.

The literature on direct instruction, classroom organization and management, grouping strategy arrangements, and cooperative learning provides theoretical rationales along with concrete suggestions to enable the school psychologist to help teachers develop and implement effective intervention strategies. The psychologist's role is to provide problem-solving assistance to teachers interested in using CAI and to evaluate and provide feedback and support to teachers regarding the efficacy of their interventions.

To fulfill these requirements the psychologist must be trained in certain specialties. First, to assist in instructional planning decisions, the school psychologist must be well trained in curriculum-based measurement and observational systems methodology. This training will enable the psychologist to collect data that will isolate specific academic strengths and weaknesses and help link the assessment information to an intervention. Second, training in instructional content, principles of effective teaching, and behavior management will enable the school psychologist to work cooperatively with teachers to develop, implement, and evaluate effective instructional interventions. These principles, plus coursework in the application of technology in the classroom, will enable psychologists to help teachers use the instructional strengths of the computer in instructing difficult-to-teach students.

REFERENCES

Bahr, C. (in press). Using computer assisted instruction effectively. In R. Gable & S. Warren (Eds.), *Advances in mental retardation and developmental disabilities* (Vol. 5). Greenwich, CT: JAI.

Bahr, C., Rieth, H. J., Polsgrove, L., Okolo, C., & Eckert, R. (1986). *An analysis of the effects of increasing the time spent on computer-based instruction* (Technical Report #201). Nashville, TN: Vanderbilt University, Project MICROS.

Becker, H. J. (1984). Computers in schools today: Some basic considerations. *American Journal of Education, 93*(1), 22–39.

Brophy, J., & Good, T. (1986). Teacher behavior and student achievement. In M. C. Wittrock (Ed.), *Handbook of research on teaching.* New York: Macmillan.

Budoff, M., Thormann, J., & Gras, A. (1984). *Microcomputers in special education.* Cambridge, MA: Brookline Books.

Carman, G. O., & Kosberg, B. (1982). Educational technology research: Computer technology and the education of emotionally handicapped children. *Educational Technology, 22*(2), 26–30.

Carnine, D., & Silbert, J. (1979). *Direct instruction: Reading.* Columbus, OH: Merrill.

Christensen, C. A., & Gerber, M. M. (1986). *The effects of game format in computerized drill and practice on development of automaticity in single digit addition for learning disabled students* (Technical Report No. 29). Santa Barbara, CA: University of California, Project TEECh.

Cohen, A., & Torgesen, J. (1985). *Comparison of two versions of a computer program for increasing sight word vocabulary in learning disabled children.* Unpublished manuscript, Florida State University.

Collins, M., Carnine, D., & Gersten, R. (1987). Elaborated corrective feedback and the acquisition of reasoning skills: A study of computer-assisted instruction. *Exceptional Children, 54*(3), 254–262.

Cosden, M. A., & English, J. P. (1986). *The effects of grouping, self-esteem and locus of control on microcomputer performance and help seeking by mildly handicapped students* (Technical Report No. 30). Santa Barbara, CA: University of California, Project TEECh.

Cosden, M. A., & Lieber, J. (1986). Grouping students on the microcomputer. *Academic Therapy, 22*(2), 165–172.

Cosden, M. A., & Semmel, M. I. (1987). Developmental changes in microeducational environments for learning handicapped and non-learning handicapped elementary school students. *Journal of Special Education Technology, 8*(4), 1–13.

Cox, D. A., & Berger, C. F. (1985). The importance of group size in the use of problem-solving skills on a microcomputer. *Journal of Educational Computing Research, 1*(4), 459–468.

Delquadri, J. C., Greenwood, C. R., Stretton, K., & Hall, R. V. (1983). The peer tutoring spelling game: A classroom procedure for increasing opportunity to respond and spelling performance. *Education and Treatment of Children, 6*(3), 225-239.

Denham, C., & Leiberman, A. (1980). *Time to learn.* Washington, DC: National Institute of Education.

Deno, S. L., & Fuchs, L. S. (1988). Developing curriculum-based measurement systems for data-based special education problem solving. In E. L. Meyen, G. V. Vergason, & R. J. Whelan (Eds.), *Effective instructional strategies for exceptional children.* Denver: Lover Publishing.

Doob, P. (1972). *Prospects for simulation gaming in health planning and consumer health education.* Reston, VA. (ERIC Document Reproduction Service No. ED 070 596)

Ellis, E. S. (1986). The role of motivation and pedagogy on the generalization of cognitive strategy training. *Journal of Learning Disabilities, 19,* 66-70.

Engelmann, S., & Carnine, D. (1982). *Theory of instruction.* New York: Irvington.

Fifield, M. B. (1988). *Analysis of the technical adequacy of a computer version of the Walker-McConnell Scale of Social Competence.* Unpublished doctoral dissertation. Eugene: University of Oregon.

Fifield, M. B. (1989). Psychoeducational testing and the personal computer. *Journal of Special Education Technology, 9*(3), 136-143.

Fisher, C. W., Filby, N. N., Marliave, R., Cahen, L. S., Dishaw, M. M., Moore, J. E., & Berliner, D. C. (1978). *Teaching and learning in the elementary school: A summary of the beginning teacher evaluation study.* San Francisco: Far West Labs.

Fitzgerald, G., Fick, L., & Milich, R. (1986). Computer-assisted instruction for students with attentional difficulties. *Journal of Learning Disabilities, 19*(6), 376-379.

Fuchs, L. S., Bahr, C., & Rieth, H. (1989). Effects of goal structures and performance of adolescents with learning disabilities. *Journal of Learning Disabilities, 22*(9), 554-560.

Fuchs, L. S., & Fuchs, D. (Eds.). (1986). Linking assessment to instructional intervention. *School Psychology Review, 15*(3).

Fuchs, L. S., Fuchs, D., Hamlett, C., & Hasselbring, T. S. (1987). Using computers with curriculum-based progress monitoring: Effects on teacher efficiency and satisfaction. *Journal of Special Education Technology, 8*(4), 14-27.

Goldenberg, E., Russell, S., & Carter, C. (1984). *Computers, education and special needs.* Reading, MA: Addison-Wesley.

Goldman, S., & Pellegrino, J. (1987). Information processing and educational microcomputer technology: Where do we go from here? *Journal of Learning Disabilities, 20*(3), 144-154.

Greenblat, C., & Duke, R. (1975). *Gaming simulation: Rationale, design and application.* New York: Halsted.

Hagen, D. (1984). *Microcomputer resource book for special education.* Reston, VA: Reston Publishing.

Hall, R. V., Delquadri, J., & Harris, J. (1977). *Opportunity to respond: A new focus in the field of applied behavior analysis.* Paper presented at the annual meeting of the Midwest Association for Applied Behavior Analysis, Chicago.

Hallahan, D. P., Gajar, A., Cohen, S., & Tarver, S. (1978). Selective attention and focus of control in learning disabled and normal children. *Journal of Learning Disabilities, 11*(4), 47-52.

Hasselbring, T. (1982). Remediating spelling problems in learning-handicapped students through the use of microcomputers. *Educational Technology, 22,* 31-32.

Hasselbring, T. (1984). Using a microcomputer for imitating student errors to improve spelling performance. *Computers, Reading and Language Arts, 1*(4), 12-14.

Hasselbring, T., Goin, L., & Bransford, J. (1987). *Assessing and developing math automaticity in learning-disabled students: The role of microcomputer technology.* Paper presented at the annual meeting of the American Educational Research Association, Washington, DC.

Hasselbring, T. S., Goin, L. I., & Bransford, J. D. (1988). Developing math automaticity in learning handicapped children: The role of computerized drill and practice. *Focus on Exceptional Children, 20*(6), 1-7.

Hawley, W. D., & Rosenholtz, S. J. (1984). Good schools: What research says about improving student achievement. *Peabody Journal of Education, 61*(4), 1-178.

Haynes, J., Kapinus, B., Malouf, D., & MacArthur, C. (1984). *Effect of computer assisted instruction on learning disabled readers' metacognition and learning of new words* (Research Report #101). College Park, MD: University of Maryland, Institute for the Study of Exceptional Children and Youth.

Howell, R., & Garcia, J. (1985). *The effects of computer use on the generalization of learning with a learning disabled student.* Paper presented at the Research Symposium on Special Education, Washington, DC.

Johnson, D. W., & Johnson, R. (1985). Mainstreaming hearing-impaired students: The effects of effort in communicating on cooperation. *Journal of Psychology, 119,* 31-44.

Johnson, R. T., Johnson, D. W., & Stanne, M. B. (1986). Comparison of computer-assisted cooperative, competitive, and individualistic learning. *American Educational Research Journal, 23*(3), 382-392.

Jones, K., & Torgesen, J. K. (1985). *An evaluation of the Hint and Hunt I program with learning disabled children.* Unpublished manuscript, Florida State University.

Kinzer, C., Rieth, H., & Bahr, C. (1989). *An analysis of the effects of teacher training and student grouping on reading comprehension skills among mildly handicapped high school students using computer-assisted instruction* (Technical Report No. 410). Nashville, TN: Peabody/Vanderbilt, Project MICROS.

Kleiman, G., Humphrey, M., & Lindsey, P. H. (1983). Microcomputers and hyperactive children. In D. O. Harper & J. H. Steward (Eds.), *RUN: Computer education* (1st ed.). Monterey, CA: Brooks/Cole.

Krug, S. E. (1984). *Psychware.* Kansas City, MO: Test Corporation of America.

LeBlanc, J. M., Hoko, J. A., Aangeebrug, M. H., & Etzel, B. C. (1985). Microcomputers and stimulus control: From the laboratory to the classroom. *Journal of Educational Technology, 7*(1), 23-30.

Lieber, J., & Semmel, M. I. (1987). The relationship between group size and performance on a microcomputer problem-solving task for learning handicapped and nonhandicapped students. *Journal of Educational Computing Research, 3*(2), 171-187.

Lovitt, T. C. (1967). Assessment of children with learning disabilities. *Exceptional Children, 34,* 233-239.

Lubke, M. M., Ferrara, J. M., & Parry, J. D. (1985). *Expert systems in the individual education program process.* Logan: Utah State University. (ERIC Document Reproduction Service No. ED 263 735)

MacArthur, C. A., Graham, S., & Skarvold, J. (1986). *Learning disabled students' composing with three methods: Handwriting, dictation and word processing* (Technical Report No. 109). College Park: University of Maryland, Institute for the Study of Exceptional Children and Youth.

MacArthur, C. A., Haynes, J. A., & Malouf, D. B. (1986). Learning disabled students' engaged time and classroom interactions: The impact of computer assisted instruction. *Journal of Educational Computing Research, 2*(2), 189-198.

Malouf, D. B., MacArthur, C. A., & Radin, S. (1986). Using interactive videotape-based instruction to teach on-the-job social skills to handicapped adolescents. *Journal of Computer-Based Instruction, 13*(4), 130-133.

McDermott, P. A., & Watkins, M. W. (1983). Computerized vs. conventional remedial instruction for learning-disabled pupils. *Journal of Special Education, 17,* 81-88.

Minnick, B. A., & School, B. A. (1982). The IEP process. Can computers help? *Academic Therapy, 18*(2), 141-148.

Morocco, C., & Neuman, S. (1987). *Teachers, children and the magical writing machine* (Final Report). Newton, MA: Education Development Center.

Neuman, S. B., & Morocco, C. C. (1986). *Two hands is hard for me: Keyboarding and learning disabled children.* Newton, MA: University of Lowell, Education Development Center.

Office of Technology Assessment. (1988). *Power on! New tools for teaching and learning* (OTA-SET-379). Washington, DC: U.S. Government Printing Office.

Okolo, C., Rieth, H. J., & Bahr, C. (1989). Microcomputer use in secondary special education: Special education teachers', administrators', and students' perspectives. *Journal of Special Education, 23*(1), 107-117.

Okolo, C., Rieth, H. J., Polsgrove, L., Bahr, C., & Yerkes, K. (1986). *An analysis of special education students' attitudes toward computer-based instruction* (Technical report #104). Nashville, TN: Vanderbilt University, Project MICROS.

Pearl, R., Bryan, T., & Donahue, M. (1980). Learning disabled children's attributions for success and failure. *Learning Disability Quarterly, 3,* 3-9.

Rashotte, C. A., & Torgesen, J. K. (1985). Repeated reading and reading fluency in learning disabled children. *Reading Research Quarterly, 20*(2), 180-188.

Rieth, H. J., Axelrod, S., Anderson, R., Hathway, F., & Fitzgerald, C. (1974). Influence of distributed practice and daily testing on weekly spelling tests. *Journal of Educational Research, 68,* 73-77.

Rieth, H., Bahr, C., & Okolo, C. (1986). *The effects of microcomputers on the secondary special education classroom ecology: Project MICROS year three report* (Technical Report No. 302). Nashville, TN: Peabody/Vanderbilt, Project MICROS.

Rieth, H., Bahr, C., Okolo, C., Polsgrove, L., & Eckert, R. (1987a). An analysis of the secondary special education classroom ecology with implications for teacher training. *Teacher Education and Special Education, 10*(3), 113-119.

Rieth, H., Bahr, C., Polsgrove, L., Okolo, C., & Eckert, R. (1978b). The effects of microcomputers on the secondary special education classroom ecology. *Journal of Special Education Technology, 8*(4), 36–45.

Rieth, H., & Evertson, C. (1988). Variables related to the effective instruction of difficult-to-teach children. *Focus on Exceptional Children, 20*(5), 1–8.

Rieth, H. J., & Frick, T. (1983). *Evaluating and providing feedback on the effectiveness of instruction for handicapped children integrated in inner-city schools* (Final Research Project; Grant No. NIE-G-80-00899). Bloomington: Indiana University, Center for Innovation in Teaching the Handicapped.

Rieth, H., Haus, F., & Bahr, C. (1989). The use of portable microcomputers to collect student and teacher behavior data. *Journal of Special Education Technology, 9*(4), 190–199.

Rieth, H., & McCarthy, T. (1985). Analysis of student spelling performance. (Technical Report #108). Nashville, TN: Vanderbilt University.

Rieth, H. J., & Polsgrove, J. L. (1983). *Evaluating and providing feedback on the effectiveness of instruction for handicapped children integrated in inner-city schools* (Final Research Report). Bloomington: Indiana University, Center for Innovation in Teaching the Handicapped.

Rieth, H. J., Polsgrove, L., & Semmel, M. I. (1979). Relationship between instructional time and academic achievement: Implications for research and practice. *Education Unlimited, 1*, 53–56.

Rieth, H. J., Polsgrove, L., & Semmel, M. I. (1981). Instruction in the regular classroom: Variables that make a difference. *Exceptional Education Quarterly, 2*, 61–82.

Roth, S., & Beck, I. (1984). *Research and instructional issues related to the enhancement of children's decoding skills through a microcomputer program.* Paper presented at the annual meeting of the American Educational Research Association, New Orleans.

Rubin, D. P., & Weisgerber, R. A. (1985). The center for research and evaluation in the application of technology to education. *T.H.E. Journal, 12*(6), 83–87.

Salomon, G., & Gardner, H. (1986). The computer as educator: Lessons from television research. *Educational Researcher, 15*(1), 13–19.

Salvia, J., & Ysseldyke, J. E. (1988). *Assessment in special and remedial education* (4th ed.). Boston: Houghton Mifflin.

Schmidt, M., Weinstein, T., Niemic, R., & Walberg, H. J. (1986). Computer-assisted instruction with exceptional children. *Journal of Special Education, 19*, 493–501.

Semmel, D. S., Goldman, S. R., Gerber, M. M., Cosden, M. A., & Semmel, M. I. (1985). *Survey of special education and mainstream teachers' access to and use of microcomputers with mildly handicapped students* (Technical Report No. 9). Santa Barbara, CA: University of California, Project TEECh.

Slavin, R. E. (1980). Cooperative learning. *Review of Educational Research, 50*(2), 315–342.

Stallings, J., & Kaskowitz, D. (1974). *Follow-through classroom observation evaluation 1972–1973* (SRI Project URU-7370). Stanford, CA: Stanford Research Institute.

Stallings, J., Needels, M., & Stayrook, N. (1979). *The teaching of basic reading skills in secondary schools, Phase II and Phase III.* Menlo Park, CA: SRI International.

Suppes, P., Fletcher, J. D., Zanotti, M., Lorton, P. V., & Searle, B. W. (1973). *Evaluation of computer-assisted instruction in elementary mathematics for hearing-impaired students* (Report No. 200). Palo Alto: California Institute for Mathematical Studies in Social Sciences. (ERIC Document Reproduction Service No. ED 084 722)

Trifiletti, J. J., Frith, G. H., & Armstrong, S. (1984). Microcomputers versus resource rooms for LD students: A preliminary investigation of the effects on math skills. *Learning Disability Quarterly, 7*, 69–76.

Vance, B., & Hayden, D. (1982). Use of microcomputer to manage assessment data. *Journal of Learning Disabilities, 15*(9), 496–498.

Watkins, M. W., & Webb, C. (1981). Computer assisted instruction with learning disabled students. *Educational Computer Magazine, 1*(3), 24–27.

Wesson, C., King, R. P., & Deno, S. (1984). Direct and frequent measurement of student performance: If it's good for us, why don't we do it? *Learning Disability Quarterly, 7*(1), 45–48.

Woodward, J., Carnine, D., & Collins, M. T. (1986). *Closing the performance gap in secondary education.* Unpublished manuscript, University of Oregon, Eugene.

Mainstream Assistance Teams: A Prereferral Intervention System for Difficult-to-Teach Students

Douglas Fuchs
George Peabody College of Vanderbilt University

Since the passage of Public Law 94-142, there has been a sharp increase in special education enrollment (e.g., U.S. Department of Education, 1988). It is likely that this increase partly reflects attempts to ensure that handicapped children receive an appropriate education. Nevertheless, there is growing suspicion that (a) too many students are being identified as handicapped and (b) this overidentification or misidentification exemplifies general education's failure to accommodate the heterogeneous nature of its mainstream population. In other words, many educators and policymakers view general education as depending more and more on special education to deal with its handicapped and nonhandicapped difficult-to-teach pupils, thereby becoming increasingly exclusive in terms of the students judged appropriate for mainstream education.

Two basic strategies are emerging to strengthen general education's capacity to deal more effectively with student diversity. The first is development of *large-scale, full-time mainstreaming* programs that attempt to reintegrate handicapped students into general education (see, for example, Johnson & Johnson, 1986; Slavin, Leavey, & Madden, 1984). The second approach is *prereferral intervention*, or prereferral consultation, which targets additional help for difficult-to-teach pupils who have not been identified for special education services. Such help presumably precludes the need for refer-ral to special education in many instances.

Although prereferral intervention has been proposed by Graden, Casey, and Bonstrom (1985) and others as a solution to the apparent overidentification of mildly handicapped pupils, there has been infrequent demonstration of in-class interventions that are described explicitly. As a result, few prereferral intervention efforts have been validated with respect to student behavior and academic performance outcomes. Curriculum-based measurement (CBM) seems well suited to help evaluate these outcomes of prereferral intervention because it appears to be sensitive to student improvement that results from relatively short-term treatments (Deno & Roettger, 1983). However, a set of pertinent dependent measures, or a sensitive measurement system, does not ensure effective prereferral intervention. There is need for basic groundwork in this area, including developing and validating effective and efficient classroom interventions. My colleagues and I currently are involved in a 3-year program of research, funded by the Office of Special Education in the U.S. Department of Education that aims to develop, implement, and validate a prereferral intervention model entitled the Mainstream Assistance Team (MAT) Project.

The primary purpose of this chapter is to review the rationale for prereferral intervention and suggest important features of this approach. Additionally, the chapter describes MAT research partly to illustrate problems and issues that often accompany development and implementation of effective, efficient prereferral interventions. Specifically, I will first delineate the major dimensions of the MAT such as our use of behavioral consultation and written scripts that assure fidelity of the consultation process. Second, I will outline the implementation process, including a description of how we involved schools, consultants, general educators, and students and how we evaluated the effectiveness of the project. Finally, I will present a summary of our evaluative data on the MATs, and discuss the implications of these data (a) for implementing and conducting research on prereferral intervention in the schools and (b) in demonstrating an important role for CBM.

RATIONALE

Increasing Numbers of Mildly Handicapped Students

Since the U.S. Department of Education's first child count in 1976–1977, the number of students enrolled in special education has grown each year, with an increase of 17% from 1976–1977 to 1985–1986 (Singer & Butler, 1987). Dramatic increases in identification of mildly and moderately handicapped pupils account for much of the reported growth (U.S. Department of Education, 1984). It is probable that to some degree this increase results from legal, legislative, and professional initiatives directed toward assuring handicapped youths a free and appropriate public education. However, there is growing suspicion, both within the federal government (see, for example, Annual Report to Congress, U.S. Department of Education, 1984) and among professionals (see, for example, Gerber & Semmel, 1984), that too many children are being placed in special education. There are numerous and obvious reasons for the undesirability of incorrect identification and placement. For example, it causes unnecessary separation and stigmatization of children (Jones, 1972; Reynolds & Balow, 1972), disruption and fragmentation of school programs (Will, 1986), and

additional costs to school districts (Singer, 1988).

These and other negative effects of misidentification argue that we attempt to understand the reasons for observed increases in the mildly and moderately handicapped population. There are at least two important explanations. First, classroom teachers are referring increasingly large numbers of children for special education evaluation (Ysseldyke & Thurlow, 1983; Ysseldyke, Thurlow, et al., 1983). Second, few handicapped students exit special education (e.g., Anderson-Inman, 1987; Weatherly & Lipsky, 1977; Ysseldyke & Thurlow, 1984). While each explanation appears to be essential to understanding why special education enrollments are expanding, considerable professional attention has been focused on the first one, increased numbers of teacher referrals (e.g., Gerber & Semmel, 1984).

Frequency of teacher referrals. It has been estimated that, from 1977–1978 to 1978–1979, the average number of referrals initiated by classroom teachers increased nearly 50%, from 2.2 to 3.0 students (Ysseldyke & Thurlow, 1983). Furthermore, evidence indicates that referral by a teacher often leads to identification of a pupil as handicapped. Algozzine and Ysseldyke (1981) reported that over a 3-year period 92% of referred students were evaluated and 73% of evaluated students were placed in special education. Similarly, Foster, Ysseldyke, Casey, and Thurlow (1984) found that 72% of students referred were placed in special education; most were placed in the special education category for which they had been referred. Additionally, Ysseldyke, Algozzine, Regan, and McGue (1981) reported that "expert" diagnosticians, when faced with psychometric profiles indicating normal student performance, labeled over 50% of the profiles as eligible for special education and cited teacher referral reasons as justification for their decision.

Arbitrariness and precipitousness of teacher referrals. Despite the apparent confidence that diagnosticians and special educators place in classroom teachers' referrals, empirical evidence indicates that their referrals often are arbitrary, if not biased (Lietz & Gregory, 1978; Tobias, Cole, Zibrin, & Bodlakova, 1982; Tucker, 1980; Ysseldyke & Thurlow, 1984). Investigations have found that minority pupils, boys, and siblings of children identified as learning disabled are overrepresented when referrals are initiated by teachers as compared with those otherwise initiated by objective measure (see Marston, Mirkin, & Deno, 1984). Additionally, in contrast with the reasons typically cited on referral forms, classroom teachers frequently refer students primarily because of disturbing behaviors (Algozzine, 1977), which (a) tend to be defined idiosyncratically (Gerber & Semmel, 1984) and (b) often represent situation-specific problems rather than enduring student characteristics (Rubin & Balow, 1971).

In addition to findings that teachers' referrals often are arbitrary, if not biased, evidence suggests that teachers frequently make referrals in a precipitous, rather than a deliberate, manner. It seems that classroom teachers typically make few, if any, substantial programmatic changes prior to initiating referral (Ysseldyke, Christenson, Pianta, Thurlow, & Algozzine, 1983; Ysseldyke & Thurlow, 1980). The frequent observed result is that a high percentage of teachers' referrals fail to meet local eligibility criteria (Marston et al., 1984; Shepard, Smith, & Vojir, 1983).

The findings of arbitrariness and precipitousness in referral-related decision making suggest that many classroom teachers do not attempt to accommodate difficult-to-teach students. This hypothesis is corroborated by a related research literature demonstrating that teachers deliver qualitatively and quantitatively different and inferior instruction to lower achieving than higher achieving pupils (Allington, 1980; Mosenthal, 1984).

Traditional Assessment Versus Prereferral Assessment

Analysis of the often arbitrary and precipitous nature of the process of referral to special education placement highlights the importance of modifying conventional practices in educational assessment to permit prereferral assessment and intervention in general education classrooms. Such activity aims to enhance general educators' capacity to instruct and manage difficult-to-teach pupils, thereby reducing the number of students referred for formal assessment and possible placement in special education programs.

Traditional educational assessment. According to Salvia and Ysseldyke (1985), the traditional purposes of educational assessment are to specify and verify students' problems and to formulate decisions about referral, classification, instructional planning, and program modification. The referral and classification phases constitute an identification process in which pupils' performance on nomothetic aptitude and/or achievement measures typically are compared to identify "outliers" who warrant placement in special programs. In contrast, the instructional planning and program modification phases together represent a process by which assessment is relatively idiographic and related to the content and methods of instruction.

Prereferral assessment. The concept of prereferral assessment requires that we reconceptualize the nature of educational assessment in at least two important ways. First, the concept of prereferral assessment explicitly refers to activity that is preliminary or preparatory to teacher referral, and that formalizes the decision whether to refer. Second, and in contrast to activity conventionally associated with referral and classification phases of assessment, prereferral assessment represents an opportunity to collect data helpful to the development and evaluation of classroom interventions. Toward this end, information is often necessary about (a) instructional and social dimensions of the classroom and (b) students' performance in classroom curricula and/or social behavior. In addition to its potential contribution to the creation of classroom interventions, prereferral assessment signals an effort to fine-tune or validate these interventions. Thus, prereferral assessment typically is conceptualized as intervention-oriented, thereby necessitating the collection of data that are *sensitive to ecology* and *curriculum-based.* Moreover, such data may be used formatively to fashion classroom-based modifications that permit general educators to accommodate greater student diversity.

Characteristics of Prereferral Intervention

Although there is an infinite number of specific interventions that could be designed and implemented in classrooms, prereferral intervention is usually described in terms of five basic characteristics two of which already have been discussed. First, it is consonant with the *least restrictive* doctrine set forth in PL 94-142, which requires educators to attempt to accommodate difficult-to-teach students' instructional and social needs in the most "normal" setting possible. A second characteristic, related to the preceding point, is that prereferral intervention is meant to be *preventive.* According to Graden, Casey, and Christenson (1985), it focuses on (a) obviating inappropriate referral and placement of students in special programs and (b) reducing the likelihood of future students' problems by enhancing general educators' capacity to intervene effectively with diverse groups of children.

Third, prereferral intervention typically is "brokered" by one or more special service personnel (e.g., school psychologists and special educators), acting as consultants. Usually working indirectly with targeted pupils through collaborative consultation with the classroom teacher. These consultants often employ a *problem solving* approach borrowed from behavioral consultation (BC) to design, implement, and evaluate interventions (Curtis, Zins, & Graden, 1987). Fourth, prereferral intervention represents *immediate* assistance to pupil and teacher, since support is provided at the point at which the teacher contemplates referral. Finally, prereferral intervention encourages use of an *ecological* perspective that identifies teacher, physical setting, and instruc-

tional variables as well as the individual learner's characteristics as possible causes of student difficulties. In other words, rather than assume the source of student problems resides within the child, the prereferral intervention approach challenges educators to investigate a larger context for the source(s) of and solution(s) to pupil difficulties.

There are many ways to implement a prereferral intervention program. Two alternate approaches involve special service personnel, working either alone or as part of a team, in assisting classroom teachers. Cantrell and Cantrell (1976), Graden, Casey, and Bonstrom (1985), and Ritter (1978) have described programs in which support personnel consult independently. In contrast, Chalfant, Pysh, and Moultrie (1979) and Maher (in press) have mobilized teams of various professionals to deliver prereferral intervention.

Mainstream Assistance Teams. During the past 2 years, I and my associates have experimented with a number of the salient dimensions of prereferral intervention. At various times we incorporated all of the aforementioned well-known characteristics of the approach, including an ecological perspective and a collaborative problem-solving version of consultation. We also borrowed important programmatic features developed by other investigators. Following the pioneering work of Cantrell and Cantrell (1976), for example, we constructed the MAT to reflect a behavioral approach to consultation and classroom intervention. Additionally, like the project of Chalfant et al. (1979), the MAT in Year 1 of the project involved teams of special support personnel providing assistance to general educators.

However, the MAT has not merely reiterated others' prereferral intervention programs. Our version is distinctive in at least three major ways. First, as indicated, we are involved in a 3-year programmatic effort, permitting us to subject the MAT to systematic and ongoing formative evaluation. In short, the program is dynamic and evolving. Second, our version of prereferral intervention aims to be both effective and practical. Practicality is pursued in three ways: (a) MAT members follow written scripts that presumably contribute to efficient and proper use of behavioral consultation, (b) we have conducted component analyses of three increasingly inclusive versions of behavioral consultation to identify a most effective and economical process of consultation, and (c) we currently are evaluating the appropriateness of classroom interventions that are managed almost entirely by students, thereby reducing teachers' involvement.

A third distinctive aspect of the MAT is that we have used a variety of outcome measures, including checklists, rating scales, open-ended interviews, several types of systematic observation procedures, and standardized achievement tests. These measures have addressed student academic performance, student and teacher classroom behavior, and teacher and consultant satisfaction with the consultation process. In contrast to several prior investigations of prereferral intervention, we have used dependent variables that are subjective, objective, and socially valid. Several of our measures also have been curriculum based, and they are described below, although we have yet to incorporate CBM into our prereferral procedures.

Following is a more detailed description of the components, implementation, and effects of our prereferral intervention approach. This, in turn, will lay necessary groundwork for presentation of important, if not essential, features of prereferral intervention, and discussion of how CBM may facilitate its use by practitioners.

MATs: BASIC DIMENSIONS

Behavioral Consultation

We have based much of our MAT activity on a model of behavioral consultation (BC) because the process appears straightforward and there is at least limited support for its effectiveness (e.g., Tombari & Davis, 1979).

Definition and characteristics. BC, like alternative well-known consultation models of mental health and organiza-

tional development, involves a triadic network of persons (i.e., consultant, teacher, and pupil) and indirect service. Unlike other models, BC has roots in the learning theory tradition of Watson, Skinner, and Bandura. Not surprisingly, it emphasizes the role of environmental factors in modifying behavior. That is, BC encourages exploration of antecedents and consequences of behavior in naturalistic settings to permit identification of variables influencing the frequency, rate, intensity, and/or duration of problem behavior. Behavioral consultants employ respondent, operant, and modeling procedures to change disturbing behavior.

Additionally, BC is conducted within four well-defined, interrelated stages: problem identification, problem analysis, plan implementation, and evaluation. It depicts the consultee, and often the student, as a problem solver who participates as a coequal with the consultant in designing intervention strategies. Also, the nature and implementation of these intervention strategies are based on empirically validated laws of behavioral change. Finally, evaluation of the success of these planned interventions must be data-based; effectiveness is judged in terms of whether student and/or teacher behavior has been modified sufficiently to meet previously set goals.

Evidence of effectiveness. The effectiveness of BC has been evaluated experimentally more often than the success of alternative consultation models (Alpert & Yammer, 1983). Although some of this efficacy research suffers from conceptual and methodological limitations (Alpert & Yammer, 1983; Meyers, Pitt, Gaughan, & Friedman, 1978), we are impressed with the steadily growing corpus of school-based investigations indicating BC's success in increasing pupils' attention, study behavior, completion of homework assignments, and mathematics and compositional response rates and in reducing lateness, out-of-seat behavior, general disruptiveness, stealing, chronic absences, and digit reversals (e.g., Tombari & Davis, 1979).

Identifying Essential Components of BC

Stages of BC. As mentioned, BC is conducted during a series of four interrelated stages: problem identification, problem analysis, plan implementation, and problem evaluation. The consultant, typically a school psychologist, guides the teacher through a majority of these stages in a succession of structured interviews in which specific objectives must be accomplished before consultation can proceed to subsequent stages. The major objectives of the first stage, problem identification, are to define the problem behavior in concrete, observable terms, obtain a reliable estimate of the frequency or intensity of the behavior, and tentatively identify the environmental events surrounding the problem behavior.

In the second stage, problem analysis, the goal is to validate the existence of a problem, discover classroom factors that may influence problem solution, and develop with the teacher an intervention plan that directly addresses the problem. During the third stage, plan implementation, the consultant makes certain the agreed upon intervention plan is implemented and is functioning properly. Although plan implementation is primarily the responsibility of the teacher, the consultant monitors details, including the degree, of implementation. The goal of the final stage, evaluation, is for the consultant and teacher to collaborate in evaluating the effectiveness of the implemented intervention and, if necessary, to determine how it should be modified.

Rationale for component analysis. An apparent basic and widespread presumption in the literature on BC is that all four stages of the model are important; none is indispensable (e.g., Gresham, 1982). Although Bergan and associates (e.g., Bergan & Tombari, 1976; Tombari & Davis, 1979) have indicated that the initial stage, problem identification, may be the most important to consultation outcomes, we are unaware of any systematic attempt to determine the relative value of the various stages or components of the BC model, or whether all are necessary.

The absence of component analyses (i.e., an effort to determine which parts are important/unimportant) seems to reflect a more general dearth of process-outcome research in the consultation literature (e.g., Alpert & Yammer, 1983; Medway, 1982; Meyers, et al., 1978; Witt & Elliott, 1983). This is unfortunate, since process-outcome research, including component analyses, can help identify dispensable elements of the consultation process and lead to processes that simultaneously are effective and efficient: effective in that they are responsible for meaningful desirable change; efficient in the sense that they require a minimum of time, effort, and resources. To this end, as well as to contribute to the pertinent research literature, we undertook component analysis of the BC model in Years 1 and 2 of the Mainstream Assistance Team project.

Description of component analysis. We decided to explore the importance of the various components of the BC model by creating three increasingly inclusive versions of it. In the least inclusive variation, the consultant and teacher worked collaboratively on problem identification and analysis. However, the consultant did not help the teacher implement the intervention developed during the problem analysis stage. Moreover, the consultant and teacher did not evaluate intervention effects in any formative fashion, precluding an opportunity to modify or fine-tune the intervention. In other words, our first version of the model incorporated only the first two of the model's four stages (i.e., problem identification and problem analysis).

The second variant of BC also included the first two stages. Additionally, it required the consultant to make a minimum of two classroom visits, during which the consultant (a) observed the teacher implementing the intervention and (b) provided corrective feedback to the teacher. However, like the first version, this second variation of the model did not include a formative evaluation stage. Thus, the second version comprised the first three stages of BC. Finally, our third and most inclusive version, by requiring consultant and teacher to formatively evaluate intervention effects, incorporated all four stages of the BC model.

Written Scripts and Fidelity of Treatment

Three of four BC stages (1, 2, 4) are implemented during the course of formal interviews or meetings. Stage 3, plan implementation, typically is conducted in the classroom. Gresham (1982) has provided one of the more comprehensive descriptions of the substance to be covered during these meetings. Since my colleagues and I believe that prereferral interventions should be embedded in a well-structured and time-efficient consultation process, we recast Gresham's materials into written scripts that guided much of our consultants' verbal behavior.

The scripts, based loosely on the Cantrell's Heuristic Report Form (Cantrell & Cantrell, 1977, 1980) provided consultants with an efficient means to (a) create rationales and overviews for the meetings; (b) establish structure and maintain a logical and quick-paced flow; (c) obtain succinct descriptions of the classroom environment, qualitative and quantitative evaluations of most difficult-to-teach students, and logistical information such as days and times when the target child could be observed and tested; and (d) to check, and systematically double-check, that key information such as descriptions of the target pupil's behavior was sufficiently elaborate and precise to permit easy identification during the consultant's classroom observations.

In addition to promoting efficiency, we believe scripts enhance fidelity of treatment. That is, assuming that (a) the scripts accurately reflected the BC model and (b) consultants faithfully followed them, we could be confident that the model was implemented as intended. This issue of fidelity to treatment has been especially important to us, since a majority of our consultants have lacked formal consultation training and experience. Finally in Years 1 and 2, each of our three versions of BC had its own script. (See Fuchs and Fuchs, 1989, for an unabridged copy of Meeting #1 [Problem Identification], which is the only meeting that is the same across the three treatments.)

YEAR 1: IMPLEMENTATION

Participants

Schools. We recruited four inner-city middle schools to serve as project schools. Next, five control schools were selected that match project schools in terms of (a) location (inner-city), (b) level (middle schools), (c) average SAT reading and math scores, (d) student enrollment, (e) proportion of black students enrolled, and (f) annual rate of referrals for psychological evaluations. In comparison with all schools in the district, the nine project and control schools demonstrated lower SAT reading and math scores, a higher percentage of black enrollment, and a greater annual rate of referrals for psychological evaluations.

Consultants. Associated with the four project schools were 10 school-based consultants. Five consultants were special education resource room teachers, two were school psychologists, and three were pupil personnel specialists (PPSs), a newly created position requiring the assessment skills of a psychologist, the advising capacity of a school counselor, and the family-work experience of a social worker. Among the PPSs, two were formally trained and experienced school psychologists. Additionally, two graduate students with special and general education experience served as consultants. Thus, there was a total of 12 consultants serving four project schools.

Teachers and pupils. The consultants in project schools helped recruit 24 fifth- and sixth-grade classroom teachers. In control schools, principals and project staff also recruited 24 fifth- and sixth-grade teachers. In each of the nine schools, classroom teachers were asked to identify their most difficult-to-teach, nonhandicapped pupil. These 48 most difficult-to-teach children were largely boys (71%), mostly black (65%), and approximately 1 grade below expectations in reading and math. Additionally, 58% of the subjects were described as most difficult-to-teach students primarily because of "off task" or "inattentive" behavior; 23% because of "poor academic work," despite capability to perform better; 4% because they "lacked academic skills"; 8% because of "poor interpersonal skills with adults"; 4% because of "poor interpersonal skills with peers"; and 2% because of "intrapersonal characteristics."

Training

We conducted in-service and on-the-job training to prepare our consultants for their MAT responsibilities. Two all-day training sessions were conducted at our university for the school-based and graduate student consultants. During 14 hours, consultants were trained in three areas. First, we discussed the problem-solving, collaborative, and data-based nature of BC. To improve understanding of these features, we asked consultants to role-play consultation in the context of several prepared vignettes. Corrective feedback accompanied this role playing. Second, we trained consultants to reliably employ a systematic interval recording procedure. Videotapes of various real incidents of classroom conflict were used to train consultants to criterion. Third, we reviewed how to implement a broad range of behavioral interventions, including token economics, contingency contracts, and self-management strategies. At the same time, we informed consultants that they were not bound to implement such interventions. This message was based on a desire that they develop strategies collaboratively with their classroom teachers.

Assignment of Teachers and Scripts to Consultants

Assigning teachers. On the second day of in-service training, the 10 school-based consultants were grouped by school affiliation and handed a list of teachers in their respective buildings who had volunteered for the MAT project. Within these groups each consultant chose an average of two general educators with whom to consult. The consultants also assigned participating teachers to the two graduate student consultants. We purposely did not randomly assign teachers to consultants because many of the consultants worked as members of discrete teacher teams; to have paired them with teachers not part of their team would have saddled them with difficult logistical problems.

Assigning scripts. Nevertheless, we did randomly assign the 24 project teachers to the three script types, with 8 teachers per script. This random assignment of teachers to scripts also meant that a majority of consultants used one form of BC with one teacher and a contrasting (more inclusive or less inclusive) variant with another teacher. We were above-board with the consultants about these scripts: We said we had no compelling *a priori* reason to believe that one script would be more effective than another and, as a consequence, we suggested it would be a mistake for them to guess which script was superior.

Additionally, we asked the school-based consultants to rate each participating teacher in their buildings as to the teacher's capacity to work effectively with difficult-to-teach nonhandicapped students. A subsequent analysis of these ratings indicated no reliable differences among teachers assigned to the three variations of BC.

Procedures

Sequences of consultants' activity. Table 1 displays sequences of salient consultation activity associated with our three versions of BC. In part, Table 1 graphically presents what already has been discussed. That is, Script 1 (least inclusive version) differs from Script 2 and from Script 3 (most inclusive version) in its omission of classroom visitation, whereas the uniqueness of Script 3 in relation to 2 is the more inclusive script's potential for a third classroom visit, fourth meeting, and fifth observation. Table 1 also indicates that Scripts 1 and 2 call for a

TABLE 1
Sequence of Consultation Activity in Scripts 1, 2, and 3

Week	Consultant's activity	Scripts[a]		
		1	2	3[b]
1	Meeting 1	X	X	X
	Observation 1	X	X	X
2	Observation 2	X	X	X
	Meeting 2	X	X	X
	Intervention begins	X	X	X
3	Classroom visit 1		X	X
4	Classroom visit 2		X	X
5	Observation 3	X	X	X
	Observation 4	X	X	X
	Intervention ends	X	X	X
6	Meeting 3	X	X	X
7	Modified intervention begins			?
	Classroom visit 3			?
8	Observation 5			?
	Modified intervention ends			?
	Meeting 4			?

[a]Scripts 1 and 3 represent our least and most inclusive versions of BC, respectively.

[b]Question marks in this column denote that consultants using Script 3 had an option to pursue the point.

6-week consultation period, whereas Script 3 requires 6 to 8 weeks of consultation activity.

Multidisciplinary teams. Another important distinctive feature of MAT activities in Year 1 is that, irrespective of script, a multidisciplinary team convened for every Meeting 2. The team comprised (a) the classroom teacher, (b) a school-based special educator, and (c) either the building-based school psychologist or PPS. The presence of such a group at Meeting 2 reflected our beliefs that (a) the objectives for this meeting, including problem validation and analysis as well as the formulation of a classroom intervention, are relatively difficult and important to achieve, and (b) many heads are better than one or two, especially when

they collectively represent diversity and richness in formal training and professional experience.

Target behaviors and types of interventions. Approximately 60% of project teachers directed consultants to help them with off-task or inattentive behavior; about 20% of teachers targeted poor quality of work for planned interventions; the remaining teachers wanted treatment plans to address poor relations with adults, poor relations with peers, and lack of academic skills.

A total of 22 of 24 planned interventions included presentation of some type of reinforcer contingent on display of desired behavior. In two cases, the nature of the classroom treatment was unclear. Among the 22 described interventions, 7 involved use of activity reinforcers, 4 included tangible reinforcement, and 3 made use of teachers' verbal praise. Type of reinforcement for 8 interventions was not specified. Additionally, 17 of these 22 interventions included some form of monitoring of pupil behavior; 5 did not. Among the monitored interventions, 5 teachers developed wall charts, 6 kept track of behavior on informally fashioned tally sheets, and 6 did not use a written record. Combining this last group with the 5 who did not monitor yields a total of 11 teachers (50% of those on whom we obtained intervention-related information) who we suspect had only vague knowledge of whether a student was deserving of a reward. Finally, teachers dispensed reinforcers in 17 of the 22 described interventions; an aide delivered reinforcement in one case; and 4 descriptions of interventions were unclear on this point.

In Meeting 3, teachers were systematically asked whether the classroom interventions were successful. If a teacher judged an intervention to be ineffective, it was modified, implemented, and evaluated for a second (and last) time. During Year 1 of the project, teachers' evaluations of intervention success were based on comparisons of pre- and post-intervention observations of students' classroom behavior. In contrast to Year 2 of the MAT project, these evaluations were made in the absence of previously stated goals for student behavior or academic performance.

YEAR 1: RESULTS AND DISCUSSION

Prior to reporting results, two brief comments are necessary. First, discussion of MAT outcomes is confined to a subset of dependent measures that is most pertinent to an evaluation of project effectiveness. This group of measures includes consultants' global evaluations of MAT success, teachers' pre- and post-MAT ratings of most difficult-to-teach pupils' targeted behavior, and consultants' pre- and post-MAT classroom observations of the same children and the same behavior. Second, discussion of these data will be

general; a more detailed, research-oriented exposition can be found elsewhere (e.g., Fuchs & Fuchs, 1986, 1987, 1988, 1989; Fuchs, Fuchs, Bahr, & Fernstrom, 1988; Fuchs, Fuchs, Bahr, Fernstrom, & Stecker, in press).

Consultants responded to a 4-point scale with the following descriptive anchor points: 1 = *MATs were an unqualified failure;* 2 = *MATs were a qualified failure;* 3 = *MATs were a qualified success;* and 4 = *MATs were an unqualified success.* Consultants awarded mean evaluations of 2.0, 2.8, and 2.9, respectively, to Script 1 (least inclusive version), Script 2 (more inclusive version), and Script 3 (most inclusive version). When taking the perspective of their consultees (that is, evaluating MAT success as they believed their teachers would), consultants assigned virtually identical mean scores to the scripts. Descriptively, such evaluations suggest that consultants and teachers were rather satisfied with the comparatively inclusive versions of BC, but were dissatisfied with the least inclusive variant. However, this difference in evaluations was not statistically significant.

Using 5-point scales (1 = desirable, 5 = undesirable), teachers rated the severity, manageability, and tolerability of their most difficult-to-teach pupils' target behavior on a pre- and post-MAT basis. We aggregated the three ratings to generate a single pre-MAT score and single post-MAT score for each student. Subtracting pre-MAT ratings from post-MAT ratings yielded the following average change scores for control students and project pupils involved with Script 1 through Script 3, respectively: minus .2, minus .5, minus .9, and minus 1.0.

In other words, descriptively, teachers claimed that control students' problematic behavior decreased least; targeted behaviors of students in the most inclusive version of BC decreased most. Moreover, statistical analyses indicated that the reported decreases in problem behavior associated with scripts 2 and 3 were reliably greater than the decreases evidenced by pupils in the control and Script 1 groups. Thus, teachers' ratings and the descriptive, rather than the inferential, interpretation of consultants' evaluations evidence a similar pattern. Relatively inclusive versions of BC seem to be regarded as effective and viewed with satisfaction, but the least inclusive variant of BC appears to be perceived as ineffective and viewed with dissatisfaction.

Observational data on difficult-to-teach pupils' problem behavior were in part consistent and in part inconsistent with the emerging pattern in our findings. As expected, control students did not display a pre- to post-MAT decrease in targeted troublesome behavior; rather this group's behavior increased by 9%. Predictably, too, Script 2 pupils demonstrated a modest 6% decrease in problem behavior. However, the greatest percentage decrease in troublesome behavior (8%) was associated with the least inclusive variant of BC, or Script 1, which was the script consultants and teachers viewed least effective and least satisfying. Students involved with Script 3 activity surprisingly displayed no change in problem behavior from pre- to post-MAT observations. Differences among the groups' pre-to-post behavior changes approached (2-tailed $p = .11$), but did not reach, the conventional threshold ($p = .05$) of statistical significance. Therefore, there was no reliable difference between the respective groups observed behavior change.

My colleagues and I are at a loss to explain with certitude the inconsistency between our observation data and teacher rating data (see Fuchs & Fuchs, 1989, for a discussion of possible reasons for this disparity). Regardless, we were not impressed with the conceptualization or execution of many classroom-based interventions. Our impressions were based on our own observations and MAT members' descriptions of these interventions. As already mentioned, among 22 of 24 prereferral interventions that included teacher reinforcement, one-half failed to incorporate a record of student behavior, which raises the question of how teachers knew whether to reward students for appropriate behavior.

Following numerous debriefings with consultants and teachers, I came to believe there are at least two important reasons why many interventions were ineffective during Year 1. First, despite our training and materials, many consultants (and teachers) appeared insufficiently skilled to formulate and operationalize meaningful interventions. Second, consultants seemed to waste valuable time trying to engage teachers in collaborative consultation, when many teachers simply wanted to be handed solutions to vexing problems. Not only was time lost, but consultants' efforts to convince teachers to become coequal partners ironically seemed to irritate many teachers, which in turn confused and frustrated the consultants. Such anecdotal findings strongly influenced the nature of our project in Year 2.

YEAR 2: IMPLEMENTATION

Participants

Schools. Five project schools participated, three of which had served as project schools during the first year. Two of five control schools in Year 1 also continued their involvement in the project. These seven schools were inner-city middle schools that were alike in terms of SAT reading and math achievement, student enrollment, proportion of black students enrolled, and yearly rate of student referrals for psychological evaluations.

Consultants. There were eight school-based consultants: five special educators, two school psychologists, and a school librarian. Four graduate students also served as consultants, bringing to 12 the number of consultants in the five project schools.

Teachers and pupils. The consultants in the project schools helped recruit 31 teachers in fifth and sixth grades. In the control schools, principals and project staff recruited another 12 fifth- and sixth-grade teachers. Each of the 43 teachers was requested to identify a most difficult-to-teach, nonhandicapped pupil. These students were 77% male, 40% black, and approximately 1 grade below expectations in reading and math. Additionally,

53% of the subjects were described as difficult-to-teach students primarily because of "off task" or "inattentive" behavior; 21% because of "poor interpersonal relations with adults"; 19% because of "poor academic work," despite capability to perform better; 2% because they "lacked academic skills"; 2% because of "poor motivation"; and 2% because of "intrapersonal characteristics."

Training

As in Year 1, my colleagues and I conducted in-service and on-the-job training to prepare our consultants for their MAT responsibilities. Also as in Year 1, in two days of in-service training, we presented the problem-solving, collaborative, and data-based nature of BC and provided opportunity for consultants to become familiar with a systematic observation procedure. In contrast with the Year 1 procedure, however, we did not review a broad range of behavioral interventions. Rather, we presented the details of a specific intervention and communicated an expectation that this procedure would be implemented, in one of several variations, in all participating teachers' classrooms. This prereferral intervention is described below.

Prereferral Intervention

In Year 2 we attempted to strengthen project-related interventions by requiring use of contingency contracts and data-based monitoring procedures.

Contracts. Contracts, involving teachers and their most difficult-to-teach nonhandicapped pupil, stipulated six dimensions of the intervention: (a) The type and degree of the desired change in behavior or academic performance; (b) the classroom activity (or activities) to which the contract applies; (c) how student behavior and academic performance will be monitored; (d) the nature of the reward; (e) when and by whom the reward will be delivered; and (f) whether the contract can be renegotiated. Blank contracts, an example of which appears

in Figure 1, were provided to project teachers.

Contracts were selected as an intervention strategy for two reasons. First, during Year 1 many of our consultants and teachers had independently chosen to implement them. Second, and relatedly, recent surveys (e.g., Martens, Peterson, Witt, & Cirone, 1986) indicate that contracts are viewed positively by a large proportion of general educators.

In regard to use of contracts, the teachers were told the following. First, many difficult-to-teach students need motivation to improve their attitude and behavior. Such motivation can take the form of positive reinforcement, which is the "presentation of a reinforcer, or reward, immediately following the demonstration of a desirable behavior that increases the future rate and/or probability of that desirable behavior." Second, to use positive reinforcement effectively, (a) choose reinforcers on the basis of a student's interests, (b) award reinforcers only after the student has performed the desired behavior, and (c) dispense reinforcers as soon as possible after a student's demonstration of appropriate behavior. Finally, teachers were reminded that there were three major types of positive reinforcers from which to chose: activity, material, and token reinforcers.

The project teachers were required to use the contracts for a minimum of three weeks. They were directed to reinforce students every day during the first week, and a minimum of two times during the second and third weeks. Therefore, the minimum number of days covered by a contract was nine.

Data-based monitoring. Our data-based monitoring procedures involved either *time interval recording* or *product inspection.* Interval recording was defined as "a monitoring technique used to record whether a social behavior occurs or does not occur during a predetermined period or interval." Consultants and teachers were directed to use interval recording when a student's behavior was viewed primarily as disruptive to the teacher's and/or classmates' work or well-being.

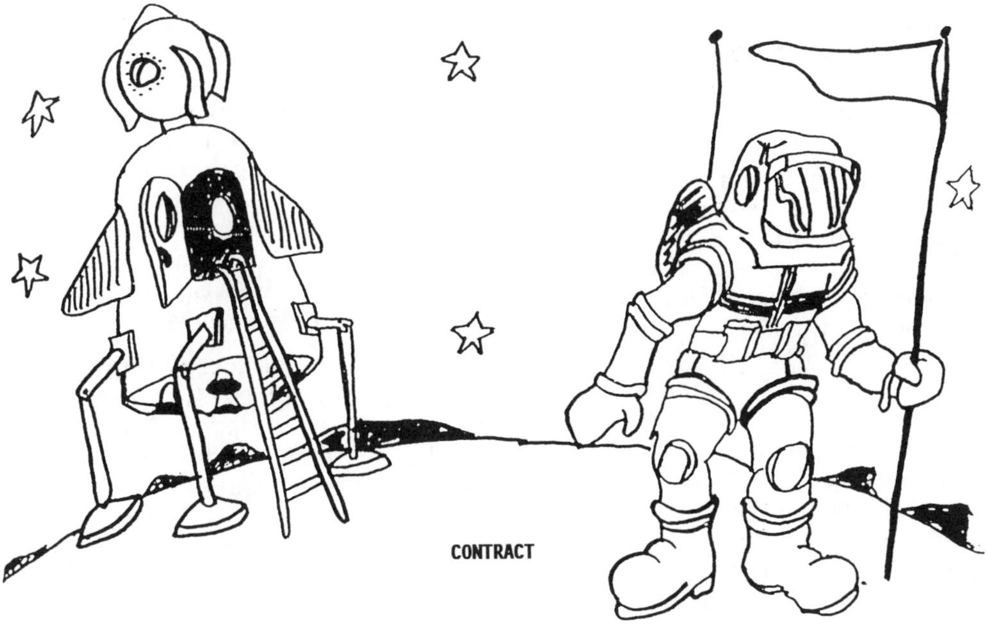

CONTRACT

This is an agreement between _____ and _____ .
                              (student)   (teacher)

If the student does _____ ,
                    (nature and amount/frequency of desired behavior)

or does NOT _____ during _____ ,
            (problem behavior)   (class/time/periods)

the student will earn _____ . The student
                      (rewards/privileges)

will receive the rewards/privileges as described above by _____

_____ . The teacher will monitor _____'s
  (method of delivery)   (student's)

behavior by _____ . The student's behavior will be
            (type of monitoring)

evaluated _____ . This agreement will begin
          (frequency of evaluation)

_____ , and will end _____ , at which time
       (date)   (date)

renegotiation may or may not be possible. I agree with the contract as specified:

_____   _____   _____   _____
   (student)   (date)   (teacher)   (date)

FIGURE 1. Example of the teacher-pupil contract used in Year 2.

Examples of such behavior are rudeness, teasing, and frequent talking to peers. Teachers were issued guides to the specific steps of interval recording (Figure 2) as well as an interval recording sheet (Figure 3).

Product inspection was defined as "the evaluation of academic work at the end of a predetermined duration." This form of monitoring was to be used for behaviors that primarily interfered with the student's own academic work. Examples of this type of behavior are daydreaming, being off-task or inattentive, and getting out of seat. By requiring the imposition of a time limit on academic activity specified by the contract, we were encouraging teachers to observe and record the amount and quality of work the student completed during the specified work interval. As with interval recording, teachers were required to adhere to specific guidelines in using product inspection. These are presented in Figure 4, along with a product inspection sheet (Figure 5).

Teacher versus student monitoring. Building on the work of Meichenbaum (1977) and Meichenbaum and Asarnow (1979), as well as Hallahan and associates (e.g., Hallahan, Lloyd, Kosiewicz, Kaufman, & Graves, 1979; Hallahan, Marshall, & Lloyd, 1981), we also explored experimentally the effectiveness and efficiency of teacher monitoring in comparison with student self-monitoring. That is, irrespective of use of interval recording or product inspection, 15 and 16 project teachers, respectively, were assigned to teacher- and student-monitoring conditions. As the name implies, pupils implementing self-monitoring evaluated their own social behavior (by interval recording) or academic performance (by product inspection), following a brief period in which their teacher modeled the monitoring procedures for them. Our student-monitoring procedures are presented in Figure 6 (Student Monitoring With an Interval Recording System) and Figure 7 (The Product Inspection Approach to Student Monitoring).

Procedure

Assigning teachers and scripts to consultants. The eight school-based and four graduate student consultants were matched to 31 participating teachers in a manner identical to that followed in Year 1. Also, during Year 2, one of our three scripts was randomly assigned to each teacher so that 10, 10, and 11 teachers were assigned to the least, more, and most inclusive scripts, respectively.

Sequences of consultants' activity. The sequences of consultants' activities associated with scripts 1, 2, and 3 were similar to those of the previous year. Scripts 1 and 2 required 8 and 9 weeks of consultation, respectively, whereas Script 3 involved a maximum of 10 weeks of consultation.

Multidisciplinary teams. In Year 2 we eliminated the multidisciplinary nature of Meeting 2. Instead of the obligatory three-member team, representing school psychology and special and general education, we required only the consultant and teacher to meet to review the prereferral intervention. Two factors argued for elimination of the multidisciplinary team. First, we now had a "packaged" classroom intervention, which reduced much of the need for a team's collaborative generation of interventions. Second, getting three school-based professionals together for an hour during Year 1 proved difficult; two-member teams were viewed by school personnel and ourselves as more feasible.

Dependent measures. Three of our more important dependent variables were (a) teachers' pre- and postintervention ratings of the severity, manageability, and tolerability of their difficult-to-teach pupils' most problematic behavior; (b) consultants' preintervention, postintervention, and follow-up observations of the frequency with which difficult-to-teach pupils, and randomly selected peers, displayed this problematic behavior; and (c) teachers' pre- and postintervention responses to the Revised Behavior Problem Checklist (Quay & Peterson, 1983).

TEACHER MONITORING WITH AN INTERVAL RECORDING SYSTEM

INTERVAL RECORDING

A monitoring technique used to record whether a social behavior occurs or does not occur during a predetermined period or interval.

HOW TO USE INTERVAL RECORDING:

1. Use the "Interval Recording" sheet attached to this cover page.

2. Determine how long the interval of recording will be. Use an interval of 3, 4, or 5 minutes in duration.

3. Determine how long the observation period will last. This period should be no less than 15 minutes and no more than 30 minutes.

4. Obtain an audiotape corresponding to the interval duration selected in Step 2.

5. Begin observing.

6. At the end of each interval, signaled by a beep, place a minus sign in the corresponding box if the target behavior occurred during that particular interval. Place a plus sign in the box if it did not occur. (The target behavior may occur more than once during an interval. Even if it does, place one and only one minus sign in the corresponding box for a given interval.)

7. Determine the frequency of the target behavior by following these four steps. First, at the end of the observation period, total the number of intervals in which the target behavior occurred (number of minus signs). Second, total the number of intervals during which the target behavior did not occur (total number of plus signs). Third, sum the number of minus signs and plus signs. This sum equals the total number of intervals recorded. Fourth, divide the number of minus signs by the sum of the minus and plus signs. This gives the frequency of the target behavior.

8. The teacher should use this system for a minimum of three weeks. During the first week, the teacher should monitor every day (total of 5 observations). During the second and third weeks, the teacher should monitor a minimum of two days, if not more, per week.

EXAMPLE:

If the target behavior occurred one or more times during an interval, place a minus sign in the corresponding space on the recording sheet.

If the target behavior did not occur at all during the interval, place a plus sign in the corresponding space.

Interval #1
Interval #2

FIGURE 2. Guide to the interval recording procedure provided to project teachers in Year 2.

INTERVAL RECORDING SHEET

Date: _____

Teacher Name: _____

Target Student: _____

Class Activity: _____

Target Behavior: _____

Length of Observation Period: _____ minutes

　　Minus Sign (–) = Target Behavior Occurs at Least Once
　　Plus Sign (+) = Target Behavior Does Not Occur

Interval #1	#2	#3	#4
#5	#6	#7	#8
#9	#10	#11	#12

STEP A:　Sum the number of intervals in which target behavior occurred (total number of minus signs):　　　　_____

STEP B:　Sum the number of intervals in which target behavior did not occur (total number of plus signs):　　　　_____

STEP C:　Sum the total number of minus signs and plus signs (add STEP A and STEP B):　　　　_____

STEP D:　Divide the number of minus signs (STEP A) by the sum of minus signs and plus signs (STEP C). This is the frequency of the target behavior.　　　　_____

* * PLEASE RETURN THIS SHEET TO THE CONSULTANT * *

FIGURE 3. Interval recording sheet provided to project teachers in Year 2.

THE PRODUCT INSPECTION APPROACH TO TEACHER MONITORING

PRODUCT INSPECTION

The evaluation of academic work at the end of a predetermined time period.

HOW TO USE PRODUCT INSPECTION:

1. Select an academic activity that results in an observable product such as a worksheet or essay.

2. Set a time limit for the student to work on the academic activity.

3. Clarify with the student the expectations for the amount and quality of work to be completed during the time period. For example, tell the student that, during a 30-minute time period, you expect him/her to complete half the math problems on a worksheet with at least 80% correct.

4. Be sure the student basically understands how to perform the activity before timing begins.

5. Tell the student to start.

6. Begin timing.

7. When the period is over, tell the student to stop work, and collect the academic product.

8. Evaluate the product using appropriate criteria such as number of problems attempted and number correct.

9. Use this system for a mininum of three weeks. During the first week, use product inspection every day (total of 5 observations). During the second and third weeks, use product inspection for a minimum of two days, if not more, per week. If the student's work improves at the end of the first week, use product inspection for the minimum of two days per week for the second and third weeks. If the student's work does not improve, use product inspection more than the minimum during the second and third weeks.

FIGURE 4. Guide to the product inspection procedure provided to project teachers in Year 2.

PRODUCT INSPECTION SHEET

Date: _____

Teacher Name: _____

Target Student: _____

Class Activity: _____

Product Inspected: _____

Beginning Time: _____

Ending Time: _____

Evaluation Criteria:

What is supposed to be completed? Example: One math worksheet with 20 items on it.

_____

What is the expected quality of the work to be completed?
Example: At least 80%, or 16 of 20 items.

_____

Evaluation Results:

How much of the work was completed? Example: 15 items.

_____

What was the quality of work completed?
Example: 10 out of 15 items correct, or 67%.

_____

Did the target student meet the criterion:

    (a) for the amount of the work completed?   _____ (Y/N)

    (b) for the quality of the work completed?   _____ (Y/N)

* * PLEASE RETURN THIS SHEET TO THE CONSULTANT * *

FIGURE 5. Product inspection sheet provided to project teachers in Year 2.

STUDENT MONITORING WITH AN INTERVAL RECORDING SYSTEM

INTERVAL SELF-MONITORING

A monitoring technique used to record whether a behavior occurs or does not occur during a predetermined period or interval.

Phase I: The Teacher Monitors

1. Using interval recording, monitor the student's behavior on the first two days for week one. This insures that you can instruct the student how to self-monitor.

2. Use the "Teacher Monitoring Sheet" attached to this cover sheet.

3. Determine how long each recording interval will be. Use an interval of 3, 4, or 5 minutes in duration.

4. Determine how long the observation period will last. This period should be no less than 15 minutes and no more than 30 minutes.

5. Obtain an audiotape corresponding to the interval duration selected in Step 3.

6. Begin observing.

7. At the end of each interval, signaled by a beep, place a minus sign in the corresponding box if the target behavior occurred during that particular interval. Place a plus sign in the box if it did not occur. (The target behavior may occur more than once during an interval. Even if it does, place one and only one minus sign in the corresponding box for a given interval.)

8. Determine the frequency of the target behavior by following these four steps. First, at the end of the observation period, total the number of intervals in which the target behavior occurred (number of minus signs). Second, total the number of intervals during which the target behavior did not occur (total number of plus signs). Third, sum the number of minus signs and plus signs. This sum equals the total number of intervals recorded. Fourth, divide the number of minus signs by the sum of the minus and plus signs. This gives the frequency of the target behavior.

9. Use this system for the first two days of week one.

EXAMPLE:

If the target behavior occurred one or more times during an interval, place a minus sign in the corresponding space on the recording sheet.

Interval #1
Interval #2

If the target behavior did not occur at all during the interval, place a plus sign in the corresponding space.

(Figure 6 continues on following page)

Phase II: The Student Self-Monitors

1. After conducting the two observation periods, explain how the student will use the interval recording system.

2. Give the student a "Student Self-Monitoring Sheet." Be sure you know how long each interval and observation period will be.

3. Give the student the same audiotape used in Phase I.

4. Have the student begin recording.

5. At the end of each interval, signaled by a beep, the student should place a minus sign in the corresponding box if the target behavior occurred during that particular interval. The student should place a plus sign in the box if it did not occur. (The target behavior may occur more than once during an interval. Even if it does, the student should place one and only one minus sign in the corresponding box for a given interval.)

6. The student should determine the frequency of the target behavior by following these four steps. First, at the end of the observation period, total the number of intervals in which the target behavior occurred (number of minus signs). Second, total the number of intervals during which the target behavior did not occur (total number of plus signs). Third, sum the number of minus signs and plus signs. This sum equals the total number of intervals recorded. Fourth, divide the number of minus signs by the sum of the minus and plus signs. This gives the frequency of the target behavior. (If the student finds this calculation difficult, the teacher should assist the student.)

7. Check the student's monitoring after each of the first two recording periods. Make sure that the student is conducting the interval self-recording properly and answer any questions that the student has.

8. The student should self-monitor for the remaining three days of the first week. During the second and third weeks, the student should monitor a minimum of two days, if not more, per week. If the student's behavior improves at the end of the first week, interval recording can be used for a minimum of two days per week. If the behavior does not improve, have the student continue to use the interval recording more than two days per week.

FIGURE 6. Guide to the interval recording procedure provided to project students in Year 2.

THE PRODUCT INSPECTION APPROACH TO STUDENT MONITORING

PRODUCT INSPECTION

The evaluation of academic work at the end of a predetermined time period.

Phase I: The Teacher Monitors

1. Select an academic activity that results in an observable product such as a worksheet or essay.

2. Set a time limit for the student to work on the academic activity.

3. Clarify with the student the expectations for the amount and quality of work to be completed during the time period. For example, tell the student that, during a 30-minute time period, you expect him/her to complete half the math problems on a worksheet with at least 80% correct.

4. Be sure the student basically understands how to perform the activity before timing begins.

5. Tell the student to start.

6. Begin timing.

7. When the period is over, tell the student to stop work, and collect the academic product.

8. Evaluate the product and record the results, using appropriate criteria such as number of problems attempted and number correct.

9. Use product inspection for the first two days of week one.

Phase II: The Student Self-Monitors

1. After conducting the first two product inspections on your own, explain to the student how to self-monitor using product inspection.

2. The academic activity used in Phase I should be used again during this phase.

3. Tell the student what the time limit is for completing the assigned activity.

4. Be sure the student basically understands how to perform the activity before timing begins.

5. Tell the student to begin timing and to start the assignment.

6. When the time limit is reached, the student should stop working.

7. Have the student inspect the product and record the results, using appropriate criteria such as number of problems attempted and number correct.

8. On the first few occasions when product inspection is used, check the student's self-monitoring to make sure that it is being conducted properly and answer any questions the student might have.

9. The student should use product inspection for the remaining three days of the first week. During the second and third weeks, the student should monitor a minimum of two days, if not more, per week. If the student's work improves at the end of the first week, product inspection can be used for a minimum of two days per week. If the student's work does not improve, have the student continue to use product inspection for more than two days per week.

FIGURE 7. Interval recording sheet provided to project students in Year 2.

YEAR 2: RESULTS AND DISCUSSION

Ratings, Checklists, and Observations

Teacher ratings. As in Year 1, teachers' ratings of difficult-to-teach pupils' most problematic behavior were aggregated across dimensions of severity, manageability, and tolerableness, generating a single pre- and postintervention score for each student (the higher a score the more positive a rating). Whereas control teachers' average ratings reflected virtually no change (preintervention = 5.8, postintervention = 6.0), teachers involved in each of the three MAT scripts expressed an impression of strong, positive pupil change. Mean ratings of teachers in least to most inclusive scripts, respectively, changed from 5.5 to 10.2, 5.8 to 10.1, and 6.6 to 11.3. Statistical analysis indicated that (a) the three groups of project teachers' ratings reflected reliably greater change than the controls' ratings, and (b) there was no significant difference among the project teachers.

Revised Behavior Problem Checklist. Teachers' responses to the Revised Behavior Problem Checklist (RBPC) were basically consistent with their severity, manageability, and tolerableness ratings. Total averaged RBPC scores for control teachers and for the teachers associated with least to most inclusive MAT scripts, respectively, changed from 53.8 to 56.0, 58.5 to 45.9, 60.8 to 40.3, and 42.6 to 28.0, respectively (where a lower score reflected a more positive rating). On the Conduct disorders subscale, one of four major dimensions of the RBPC, teachers involved with Scripts 2 and 3 noted a significantly greater improvement in their difficult-to-teach pupils than did Script 1 and control teachers. On the Attention Problems subscale, all three script groups indicated (a) significantly greater positive change among their students than did control teachers and (b) no reliable difference among themselves.

Student observations. Whereas difficult-to-teach pupils in nonproject schools displayed scant change in the observed frequency with which they displayed problematic classroom behavior (preintervention = 41%, postintervention = 37%), their counterparts in project schools evidenced dramatic improvement: 46% to 25% (Script 1), 53% to 24% (Script 2), and 42% to 17% (Script 3). Statistical analysis indicated that positive changes among Script 2 and Script 3 pupils were significantly greater than those of Script 1 and control pupils. Moreover, there was no statistically significant difference between behavior displayed at postintervention observation and at 2- to 3-week follow-up. This suggests that Script 2 and Script 3 pupils' positive behavior change was maintained, at least in the short term, beyond the intervention's time frame.

One more aspect of the Year 2 observation data is noteworthy. Not only did project pupils reduce their problem behavior in an *absolute* sense, they also lessened it *relative* to the frequency of peers' display of identical behavior. Difficult-to-teach pupils involved with Script 1, for example, demonstrated problem behavior 21% more often than peers at preintervention observation, but only 7% more frequently at postintervention observation. Script 2 students showed problem behavior 19% more often at preintervention observation, but reduced this figure to 1% *less* than peers at postintervention observation. Similarly, Script 3 students were 25% and 3% discrepant from peers at pre- and postintervention observation, respectively. Contrastingly, difficult-to-teach pupils in nonproject schools evidenced problem behavior 29% more often than peers at preintervention observation and 27% more frequently at postintervention observation.

Project pupils' positive change in Year 2 was greater than during the previous year, a fact clearly indexed by the observation data. As indicated, in Year 2 Script 1, 2, and 3 pupils evidenced pre-to-post reductions in problem behavior of 26%, 34%, and 28%, respectively. These decrements compare very favorably with reductions in similar behavior in Year 1 (i.e., Script 1 = 8%, Script 2 = 6%, and Script 3 = 0%). Additionally, unlike the project's first year, Year 2 observation data were supported by social validity data, and teachers' ratings and responses to the Behavior Problem Checklist.

Accounting for MAT Success

What accounts for project students' greater positive change in Year 2? I believe the answer is straightforward: Our intervention of contingency contracts and data-based monitoring was (a) understood by teachers and pupils, (b) implementing more or less as intended, and (c) sufficiently motivating for difficult-to-teach pupils. Moreover, in response to a questionnaire administered following completion of the project in Year 2, teachers indicated that our intervention strategy was unobtrusive (providing an average rating of 1.2 on a scale, where 1 = *"not at all obtrusive"* and 4 = *"most obtrusive"*). They also described the project as worthwhile (mean rating of 3.3 where 1 = *"not at all worth doing"* and 4 = *"definitely worth doing"*), and contributing to their professional development (average rating of 3.2 where 1 = *"contributing not at all"* and 4 = *"contributing very much"*). In short, my colleagues and I believe the evidence indicates that our prereferral intervention was effective and feasible (see Fuchs, Fuchs, Bahr, Fernstrom, & Stecker, in press, for Year 2 efficacy data).

Important Features of Prereferral Intervention

Following 2 years of experimentation as well as careful reading of the pertinent literature, my associates and I believe a number of salient features of prereferral intervention can be identified.

1. School systems interested in implementing prereferral intervention must build such activity into the job descriptions of support staff selected as consultants. School psychologists typically will *not* be capable of fulfilling such a role on top of a busy schedule of testing. Likewise, resource room teachers cannot be expected to provide direct service to a full caseload of students and also function as consultants.

2. A consultant, or team of consultants, should be responsible for the overall direction of the prereferral effort.

3. Consultants must receive adequate training, in the process of consultation, to understand completely the classroom intervention(s) to be used, and how to implement such interventions so as to cause the least disruption and burden to the teacher and classmates of the targeted pupil.

4. The consultation process must be efficient. Since school time is precious, the process must be carefully structured to include only activity that is essential to achieve desired outcomes, and the participants always should be time conscious.

5. As to the previous point, however, consultants cannot cut corners with the process. That is, lack of time may not be used as an excuse to eliminate essential aspects of consultation such as (a) defining problem behavior, (b) setting explicit goals for students and/or teachers, (c) collecting reliable and valid data on performance observed before, during, and after implementation of the intervention, and (d) conducting systematic formative evaluation of intervention effectiveness.

6. The classroom interventions must be acceptable to teachers, which, first and foremost, means they should be feasible. This very important characteristic cannot be defined in the absolute, since what is feasible to one teacher may not be feasible to another. Thus, the consultant must define and redefine "feasibility" with each teacher.

7. There must be provision for ensuring the "fidelity" of the classroom interventions. In other words, consultants must be certain that teachers and students implementing the interventions do so according to the manner in which they were instructed.

8. As indicated, data on student or teacher behavior should be collected at multiple points during the consultation process, and these data should be socially valid. One means of accomplishing this is

to obtain consumer satisfaction information; that is, teachers, students, and consultants should be encouraged to express their comprehension, thoughts, feelings, and overall evaluation of the process. They should also be asked to make recommendations for improving the effect.

Current and Future MAT Activity

Year 2 school-based consultants were less satisfied with the MAT project than were the teachers. Contributing to this dissatisfaction was a view that our directive approach preempted opportunity for them to exercise their professional knowledge, skill, and judgment. In the words of one consultant, "your prepackaged approach to intervention reduced us from clinicians to clerks."

School district adoption of the MATs. Central administration in the school district was as impressed by the salutary effects of the MAT project as by the resentment among our experienced consultants. Guided by both impressions, administration recently earmarked a newly created and inexperienced group of support staff, elementary guidance counselors, to implement MAT activity as a formal part of their job description. The explicit hope is that, *despite* the counselors' inexperience, our training will prepare them for their MAT role, and *because* of their inexperience, they will be more satisfied than previous support staff with our variant of consultation.

We are pleased with the school district's vote of confidence and "institutionalization" of MAT activity. Working with the elementary guidance counselors in Year 3, we intend to build on past efforts by determining how to transfer positive behavior change across school settings. The need for such generalization was presented poignantly to us when several pupil participants in Year 2, despite noticeable improvement in classrooms targeted by the project, were suspended from school for behavior displayed in nontargeted settings. Toward this end, we have developed a program for generalization that reflects Stokes and Baer's (1977) suggestions and we plan to implement it and the rest of our consultative activity in approximately 20 elementary schools.

Curriculum-based measurement and prereferral intervention. As for subsequent years, my colleagues and I plan to focus more on referral problems of an academic nature and to develop greater opportunity for decision making by consultants and their teacher clients. Toward this end, we will (a) create a larger set of valid, feasible, and academically oriented strategies, and (b) train consultants and teachers to implement them and use curriculum-based measurement to gauge their effectiveness. As discussed by Fuchs (1987), our training will emphasize an approach which teachers will experiment with alternative interventions on a regular, systematic basis. After every 7–10 days of data collection, representing 3–5 weeks of instruction, the targeted student's program will be modified. The teacher and consultant will evaluate the relative effectiveness of successive interventions, developing over time an optimally effective prereferral intervention. We believe that such a prereferral intervention approach to assure feasibility will require use of advanced computer technology, including so-called expert systems software with which we are now working (e.g., L. S. Fuchs & D. Fuchs, 1988).

ACKNOWLEDGMENTS

I wish to thank Mike Bahr, Pam Fernstrom, Bobbi Goodman, and Pam Stecker who helped implement Mainstream Assistance Teams in 1986–1987.

This chapter describes an Enhancing Instructional Program Options research project, supported by Grant No. G00853018 between the Office of Special Education in the U.S. Department of Education and Vanderbilt University. This chapter does not necessarily reflect the position or policy of the U.S. Department of Education and no official endorsement by it should be inferred.

REFERENCES

Algozzine, B. (1977). The emotionally disturbed child: Disturbed or disturbing? *Journal of Abnormal Child Psychology, 5,* 205–211.

Algozzine, B., & Ysseldyke, J. E. (1981). Special education services for normal children: Better safe than sorry. *Exceptional Children, 48,* 238-243.

Allington, R. (1980). Teacher interruption behavior during primary grade oral reading. *Journal of Educational Psychology, 72,* 371-377.

Alpert, J. L., & Yammer, D. M. (1983). Research in school consultation: A content analysis of selected journals. *Professional Psychology, 14,* 604-612.

Anderson-Inman, L. (1987). Consistency of performance across classrooms: Instructional materials versus setting as influencing variables. *The Journal of Special Education, 21,* 9-29.

Bergan, J. R., & Tombari, M. L. (1976). Consultant skill and efficiency and the implementation and outcomes of consultation. *Journal of School Psychology, 14,* 3-14.

Cantrell, R. P., & Cantrell, M. L. (1976). Preventive mainstreaming: Impact of a supportive services program on pupils. *Exceptional Children, 42,* 381-386.

Cantrell, R. P., & Cantrell, M. L. (1977). Evaluation of a heuristic approach to solving children's problems. *Peabody Journal of Education, 54,* 168-173.

Cantrell, R. P., & Cantrell, M. L. (1980). Ecological problem solving: A decision making heuristic for prevention-intervention education strategies. In J. Hogg & P. J. Mittler (Eds.), *Advances in mental handicap research* (Vol. 1). New York: Wiley.

Chalfant, J. C., Pysh, M. V., & Moultrie, R. (1979). Teacher assistance teams: A model for within-building problem solving. *Learning Disability Quarterly, 2,* 85-96.

Curtis, M. J., Zins, J. E., & Graden, J. L. (1987). Prereferral intervention programs: Enhancing student performance in regular education settings. In C. A. Maher & J. E. Zins (Eds.), *Psychoeducational interventions in schools: Methods and procedures for enhancing student competence.* Elmsford, NY: Pergamon.

Deno, S. L., & Roettger, A. (1983). *The effect of alternative data utilization rules on spelling achievement: An N of 1 study* (Research Report No. 120). Minneapolis: University of Minnesota Institute for Research on Learning Disabilities.

Foster, G. G., Ysseldyke, J. E., Casey, A., & Thurlow, M. L. (1984). The congruence between reason for referral and placement outcome. *Journal of Psychoeducational Assessment, 2,* 209-217.

Fuchs, D., & Fuchs, L. S. (1986, December). *Preliminary findings from the Mainstream Assistance Teams project.* Invited address presented at a colloquium sponsored by the Oregon School Psychology Association and the University of Oregon's Visiting Scholar's Fund, Eugene, Oregon.

Fuchs, D., & Fuchs, L. S. (1987, November). Mainstream Assistance Teams. In N. Safer (Chair), *Directive vs. nondirective approaches to prereferral intervention: Implications for school-based consultation.* Symposium presented at the annual meeting of the Teacher Education Division of the Council for Exceptional Children, Washington, DC.

Fuchs, D., & Fuchs, L. S. (1988). Mainstream assistance teams to accommodate difficult-to-teach students in general education. In J. E. Graden, J. E. Zins, & M. J. Curtis (Eds.), *Alternative educational delivery systems: Enhancing instructional options for all students* (pp. 49-70). Washington, DC: National Association of School Psychologists.

Fuchs, D., & Fuchs, L. S. (1989). Exploring effective and efficient prereferral interventions: A component analysis of behavioral consultation. *School Psychology Review, 18,* 260-281.

Fuchs, D., Fuchs, L. S., Bahr, M. W., & Fernstrom, P. (1988, April). *Mainstream Assistance Teams: Student–teacher contracts as prereferral intervention.* Paper presented at the annual meeting of the American Educational Research Association, New Orleans.

Fuchs, D., Fuchs, L. S., Bahr, M. W., Fernstrom, P., & Stecker, P. M. (in press). Preferral intervention: A prescriptive approach. *Exceptional Children.*

Fuchs, L. S., & Fuchs, D. (1988, April). *Effects of alternate goal structures within computerized formative evolution systems.* Paper presented at the annual meeting of The American Educational Research Association, New Orleans.

Gerber, M. M., & Semmel, M. I. (1984). Teacher as imperfect test: Reconceptualizing the referral process. *Educational Psychologist, 19,* 137-148.

Graden, J. L., Casey, A., & Bonstrom, O. (1985). Implementing a prereferral intervention system: Part II. The data. *Exceptional Children, 51,* 487-496.

Graden, J. L., Casey, A., & Christenson, S. L. (1985). Implementing a prereferral intervention system: Part I. The model. *Exceptional Children, 51,* 377-384.

Gresham, F. M. (1982, March). *Handbook for behavioral consultation.* Unpublished manuscript, Louisiana State University.

Hallahan, D. P., Lloyd, J., Kosiewicz, M. M., Kauffman, J. M., & Graves, A. W. (1979). Self-monitoring of attention as a treatment for a learning disabled boy's off-task behavior. *Learning Disability Quarterly, 2,* 24-32.

Hallahan, D. P., Marshall, K. J., & Lloyd, J. W. (1981). Self-recording during group instruction: Effects on attention to task. *Learning Disability Quarterly, 4,* 413.

Johnson, D. W., & Johnson, R. T. (1986). Mainstreaming and cooperative learning strategies. *Exceptional Children, 52*, 553-561.

Jones, R. L. (1972). Labels and stigma in special education. *Exceptional Children, 38*, 553-564.

Lietz, J. J., & Gregory, M. K. (1978). Pupil race and sex determinations of office and exceptional educational referrals. *Educational Research Quarterly, 3*, 61-66.

Marston, D., Mirkin, P. K., & Deno, S. L. (1984). Curriculum-based measurement of academic skills: An alternative to traditional screening, referral and identification. *The Journal of Special Education, 18*, 109-117.

Martens, B. K., Peterson, R. L., Witt, J. C., & Cirone, S. (1986). Teacher perceptions of school-based interventions. *Exceptional Children, 53*, 213-233.

Medway, F. J. (1982). School consultation research: Past trends and future directions. *Professional Psychology, 13*, 422-430.

Meichenbaum, D. (1977). *Cognitive behavior modification: An integrative approach.* New York: Plenum.

Meichenbaum, D., & Asarnow, J. (1979). Cognitive-behavioral modification and metacognitive development: Implications for the classroom. In P. C. Kendall & S. D. Hollon (Eds.), *Cognitive-behavioral interventions: Theory, research, and procedures.* New York: Academic.

Meyers, J., Pitt, N. W., Gaughan, E. J., & Friedman, M. P. (1978). A research model for consultation with teachers. *Journal of School Psychology, 16*, 137-145.

Mosenthal, P. (1984). The problem of partial specification in translating reading research into practice. *Elementary School Journal, 85*, 1-28.

Quay, H. C., & Peterson, D. R. (1983). *Revised Behavior Problem Checklist.* Coral Gables, FL: University of Miami.

Reynolds, M. C., & Balow, B. (1972). Categories and variables in special education. *Exceptional Children, 38*, 357-366.

Ritter, D. (1978). Effects of a school consultation program upon referral patterns of teachers. *Psychology in the Schools, 15*, 239-242.

Rubin, R. A., & Balow, B. (1971). Learning and behavior disorders: A longitudinal study. *Exceptional Children, 37*, 293-299.

Salvia, J., & Ysseldyke, J. E. (1985). *Assessment in special and remedial education* (3rd ed.). Boston: Houghton Mifflin.

Shepard, L., Smith, M. L., & Vojir, C. P. (1983). Characteristics of pupils identified as learning disabled. *American Educational Research Journal, 20*, 309-331.

Singer, J. D. (1988). Should special education embrace the Regular Education Initiative? Lessons to be learned from the implementation of PL 94-142. *Educational Policy, 2*, 409-424.

Singer, J. D., & Butler, J. A. (1987). The Education for All Handicapped Children Act: Schools as agents of social reform. *Harvard Educational Review, 57*, 125-152.

Slavin, R. E., Leavey, M. B., & Madden, N. A. (1984). Combining cooperative learning and individualized instruction: Effects on student mathematics achievement, attitudes, and behaviors. *Elementary School Journal, 84*, 410-422.

Stokes, T. F., & Baer, D. M. (1977). An implicit technology of generalization. *Journal of Applied Behavior Analysis, 10*, 349-367.

Tobias, S., Cole, C., Zibrin, M., & Bodlakova, V. (1982). Teacher-student ethnicity and recommendations for special education referrals. *Journal of Educational Psychology, 74*, 72-76.

Tombari, M., & Davis, R. A. (1979). Behavioral consultation. In G. D. Phye & D. J. Reschly (Eds.), *School psychology: Perspectives and issues* (pp. 281-307). New York: Academic.

Tucker, J. A. (1980). Ethnic proportions in classes for the learning disabled: Issues in nonbiased assessment. *The Journal of Special Education, 14*, 93-105.

U. S. Department of Education, Special Education Programs (1984). *Sixth annual report to congress on the implementation of Public Law 94-142: The Education for All Handicapped Children Act.* Washington, DC: Author.

U. S. Department of Education, Special Education Programs. (1984). *Tenth annual report to congress on the implementation of The Education of the Handicapped Act.* Washington, DC: Author.

Weatherly, R., & Lipsky, M. (1977). Street level bureaucrats and institutional innovation: Implementing special education reform. *Harvard Educational Review, 47*, 171-197.

Witt, J. C., & Elliott, S. N. (1983). Assessment in behavioral consultation: The initial interview. *School Psychology Review, 12*, 42-49.

Will, M. (1986). Educating children with learning problems: A shared responsibility. *Exceptional Children, 52*, 411-415.

Ysseldyke, J. E., Algozzine, B., Regan, R., & McGue, M. (1981). The influences of test scores and naturally-occurring pupil characteristics on psychoeducational decision making with children. *Journal of School Psychology, 19*, 167-177.

Ysseldyke, J. E., Christenson, S., Pianta, B., Thurlow, M. L., & Algozzine, B. (1983). An analysis of teachers' reasons and desired outcomes for students referred for psychoeducational assessment. *Journal of Psychoeducational Assessment, 1,* 73–83.

Ysseldyke, J. E., & Thurlow, M. L. (Eds.) (1980). *The special education assessment and decision making process: Seven case studies* (Research Report No. 44). Minneapolis: University of Minnesota Institute for Research on Learning Disabilities.

Ysseldyke, J. E., & Thurlow, M. L. (1983). *Integration of five years of research on referral* (Research Report No. 143). Minneapolis: University of Minnesota Institute for Research on Learning Disabilities.

Ysseldyke, J. E., & Thurlow, M. L. (1984). Assessment practice in special education: Adequacy and appropriateness. *Educational Psychologist, 19,* 123–136.

Ysseldyke, J. E., Thurlow, M. L., Graden, J., Wesson, C., Algozzine, B., & Deno, S. L. (1983). Generalizations from five years of research on assessment and decision making. *Exceptional Education Quarterly, 4,* 75–93.

Supporting Students with Severe Intellectual Disabilities and Severe Challenging Behaviors

Robert H. Horner
Richard W. Albin
Robert E. O'Neill
University of Oregon

In the years since passage of the Education for All Handicapped Children Act (Public Law 94-142), increasing emphasis has been placed on educating all students with disabilities in typical school settings (Brown et al., 1989; Gartner & Lipsky, 1987; McDonnell & Hardman, 1989; Stainback & Stainback, 1985). Students who present challenges that in the past might have resulted in their exclusion from regular schools are now more likely to gain entry to or be retained in regular school settings (Danielson & Bellamy, 1989). As a result, teachers, administrators, school psychologists, behavior specialists, and others involved in regular and special education face increasing opportunities to develop educational and behavioral support plans for students who present a compelling set of behavioral challenges.

With these increased opportunities has come controversy over the intervention strategies that should be used in those behavioral support plans. Several professional and advocacy organizations (e.g., the Autism Society of America [ASA], The Association for Persons with Severe Handicaps [TASH], the Association for Retarded Citizens, and the American Association on Mental Retardation) have issued position statements calling for the elimination of aversive procedures from behavioral interventions. The basis for

these resolutions rests both in arguments regarding the overall effectiveness of aversive procedures and in philosophical and ethical concerns regarding their use with people with severe disabilities (Guess, Helmstetter, Turnbull, & Knowlton, 1987; Turnbull et al., 1986). The National Association of School Psychologists' Position on Corporal Punishment calls for a ban on the use of corporal punishment in schools and other educational institutions, using arguments similar to those made in support for prohibition of all aversive procedures.

Opposition to the "nonaversive movement" tends to focus on the prohibition of aversive procedures (e.g., electric shock), arguing that such procedures are needed in some cases as a default technology (Iwata, 1988; Mulick, in press). Citing a right to effective behavioral treatment, organizations, such as the Association for Behavior Analysis and Division 33 (Mental Retardation and Developmental Disabilities) of the American Psychological Association argue against outright prohibition of any behavioral procedure that can be documented as effective, even if it is highly intrusive or aversive (American Psychological Association Division 33, 1988; Van Houten et al., 1988). However, those who oppose outright prohibition of behavioral procedures often do acknowledge the need for adherence to strict guidelines when highly intrusive procedures are used (Lovaas & Favell, 1987).

At present, the controversy over using highly intrusive or aversive procedures turns on whether there is ever a situation in which aversive stimuli should (or must) be used, and whether such procedures are consistent with the objectives of supporting a person in a typical school or community (Horner & Dunlap, 1988). This attention to the prohibition side of the issue overshadows developments in building a technology of positive behavioral support (Donnellan, LaVigna, Negri-Shoultz, & Fassbender, 1988; Horner, Dunlap et al., 1989; Meyer & Evans, 1989). These contributions toward a positive technology of behavioral support are what should characterize the nonaversive approaches to behavior management.

It is important to note that at this time no single spokesperson or approach captures the full range of procedural and theoretical efforts that have been identified with nonaversive behavior management. As with any developing clinical approach, there will be significant variety in interpretation for a number of years as critical issues are debated and examined. However, several important themes are emerging that have immediate and important implications for teachers, school psychologists, families, and researchers (Horner, Dunlap et al., 1989). This chapter introduces four themes and discusses their implications, both for a technology of positive behavioral programming and for the personnel in school systems whose task it is to support students with challenging behaviors.

COMMON THEMES IN POSITIVE APPROACHES TO BEHAVIORAL SUPPORT

Across the differing efforts to define nonaversive behavior management, we see four important themes that are emerging: (a) a focus on broad lifestyle outcomes, (b) expansion of the variables included in behavioral support plans, (c) addition of a "dignity" standard for determining the "acceptability" of behavioral interventions,

and (d) prohibition or regulation of specific procedures. These themes are detailed and discussed in turn.

Behavioral and Educational Support Should Yield Broad Lifestyle Results

Among the most important themes in the current aversive-nonaversive debate is the recognition of a new standard for evaluating our success as educators and community support personnel. The objective for schools, and for the adult service system as well, is more than simply teaching new skills and decreasing undesirable behavior. Schools should provide a person with the ability to live successfully in the community. Instruction on skills is valuable only if it results in changes in what the persons receiving support do, where they do it, with whom they do it, and the extent to which their behavior reflects personal choices (Bellamy, Newton, LeBaron, & Horner, in press). These are the same standards we use in assessing our own learning and experiences. Behavioral and educational support should result in a person's learning clusters of behaviors that are immediately useful (e.g., going shopping), produce socially and personally valued results, and change the social options available to the individual.

Similarly, behavioral programming should do more than decrease a particular behavior in a particular situation (e.g., school). Many actions of persons who exhibit challenging behavior, such as self-injury and aggression, present immediate dangers and are major barriers to social and physical integration. Our design of support systems should use a technical and theoretical knowledge of behavior to design and maintain environments that bring about a reduction of the challenging behaviors of such persons to near zero levels, across all settings they encounter during their daily activities, for a durable period of time. The reduction of these challenging behaviors also should be accompanied by development of adaptive behaviors. The combined effects of such behavioral support should expand the options these persons have for (a) performing different and desired activities, (b) interacting with more and preferred people, and (c) gaining access to an array of varied and enjoyed settings.

In many ways, the inclusion of indices of broad lifestyle outcomes is a call for a return to the standards proposed by Baer, Wolf, and Risley (1968) at the dawn of applied behavior analysis. It is a call, however, that must be met with more systematic and frequent assessment of issues related to activity patterns, social integration, physical integration, level of support by paid staff, and the degree of personal preference in a person's life (Bellamy et al., in press). Behavioral and educational support is a process by which we assist people to achieve reasonable and personal lifestyle goals.

Variables Included in Behavioral and Educational Support Plans Should Be Expanded

A second, prominent theme in the discussions surrounding positive behavioral support is the need for expanding the variables used to build a behavioral support plan. Applied behavior analysis has long been associated with manipulation of the events that immediately precede (antecedents) and follow (consequences) a targeted behavior (Alberto & Troutman, 1986; Cooper, Heron, & Heward, 1987). Positive approaches to behavioral support emphasize a broadened approach to behavioral programming that addresses ecological variables (Martens & Witt, 1988; Meyer & Evans, 1986, 1989) and broader setting events (Wahler & Fox, 1981). Attention to immediate antecedents and consequences has served us well, but it is not likely to be sufficient to attain the range of lifestyle outcomes noted above. Behavioral support plans must begin addressing much more basic issues in a person's life if fundamental changes in behavior are to be obtained and maintained. The following is an initial list of potential variables that should be considered for manipulation.

1. Activity patterns. The range and variety of activities a person performs can

have an impact on his or her target behaviors. For example, the extent to which aerobic exercise is part of a person's typical routine can have an effect on rates of problem behaviors such as self-injury, stereotypy, and inappropriate verbalizations (Bachman & Sluyter, 1988; Baumeister & MacLean, 1984; Kern, Koegel, & Dunlap, 1984).

2. Physical and social setting. Variables related to the physical structure (e.g., architecture and internal physical features) and the social structure (e.g., number and characteristics of classmates or co-residents) of living and educational settings affect behavior (Horner, 1980; Paine, Radicchi, Rosellini, Deutchman, & Darch, 1983). The relationships between these variables and severe challenging behaviors are just beginning to be addressed. Engineering positive, supportive environments is likely to be an important component of positive behavioral support plans.

3. Predictability. We believe that a major factor related to challenging behaviors for some individuals is the extent to which they can predict what activities are going to happen, when they will happen, how long they will last, and the consequences of performing the activity (Sprague & Horner, 1989). Although there is far too little empirical support for this hypothesis to warrant firm statements, predictability is a variable that is referenced with increasing frequency, especially with individuals labeled as autistic (Johnson & Koegel, 1982; Schreibman, 1988).

4. Self-management. Persons with challenging behaviors often live and learn in settings with extensive control and management by paid staff and/or their families. Efforts to build specific self-management systems, such as those related to self-monitoring of problem behaviors (Koegel, Parks, & Koegel, in press), self-selection of activities and reinforcers (Dyer, Dunlap, & Winterling, 1989), and self-control procedures for managing difficult situations (Groden, Baron, & Groden, 1984), hold significant

promise for a technology of positive behavioral support.

5. Diet and sleep cycles. An important set of variables that should be considered in behavioral support plans pertain to diet and sleep cycles. For example, interventions that manipulate variables related to food availability and intake have been shown to decrease dangerous rumination and pica behaviors (Favell, McGimsey, & Schell, 1982; Rast, Johnston, Ellinger-Allen, & Drum, 1985).

6. Medical status. A comprehensive technology of behavioral support must include an integration of behavioral and medical procedures. As a positive approach to behavioral support emerges, we anticipate companion advances in the physiological knowledge that can be brought to bear in supporting people with challenging behaviors (Schopler & Mesibov, 1987; Schroeder, Breese, & Mueller, in press). The concerns to be addressed in a behavioral support plan should include both assessment of potential physical, medical, and pharmacological variables related to problem behaviors, and the potential for inclusion of medical and pharmacological support strategies within a comprehensive support plan.

7. Staffing. The number, training, and management of professional staff in school, work, and community settings is a critical variable for any support plan (Favell & Reid, 1988; Reid, Parsons, & Green, 1989). Behavioral support plans that are outside the technical or logistical capacity of families or staff will have minimal impact. People who provide support need appropriate training, appropriate support, functional outcome measures and feedback to assess and improve their professional behavior, and adequate numbers of people and person-hours to perform the significant task of supporting people with severe challenging behaviors (Gilbert, 1978). The determination of what is adequate, however, is just beginning to emerge. As the technology of positive support takes shape, it will guide, and be guided by, the capacity of service systems to deliver, train, and support competent staff.

8. Social interaction. In general, people benefit from regular positive contact with other people (House, Landis, & Umberson, 1988). Persons whose behavior is characterized by severe aggression, self-injury, and resistance often live lives of significant isolation. As we learn more about the structure and functions of social networks, we believe increasing amounts of attention will be placed on building regular social interactions with a range of people as both an important lifestyle outcome *and* as an intervention variable.

These eight variables are offered, not as a comprehensive list, but as examples of the range of additional variables that are part of positive behavioral programming. The point is that as the standards for successful support change, there is an expansion of the range of variables that we must consider in building an effective plan of support. For example, we cannot limit ourselves to the manipulation of immediate antecedents and consequences to decrease severe self-injury with a person who lives in a barren, hostile setting that offers little option for control or anticipation of events in his or her life. The manipulation of the structural variables is an essential component of the support plan.

Similarly, we should not consider behavior modification and instruction to be separate and different technologies. Teaching new skills is among the most important positive strategies available for decreasing undesirable behavior (Carr & Durand, 1985a; Horner & Budd, 1985; Hunt, Alwell, & Goetz, 1988). As a more complete technology of support evolves, it will certainly be of a comprehensive nature with multiple components and strategies to address the complexities of severe challenging behaviors (Horner, Dunlap et al., 1989; LaVigna, Willis, & Donnellan, 1989; Meyer & Evans, 1986, 1989). The variables noted above will receive more attention, and the list will expand.

Addition of a Dignity Standard in Determining the Acceptability of Behavioral Interventions

A third major theme characterizing positive approaches to behavioral support is the addition of the subjective standard that any behavioral intervention must be designed *and implemented* in a manner that affords dignity and respect for the person receiving support. Behavioral interventions can entail active and pervasive intrusion into another person's life. In consequence, there is a long history of concern over how to determine the acceptability of a particular intervention for a particular person in a particular situation (Favell et al., 1982). How do we know when the level of intrusiveness is too great? This question is at the heart of the controversy surrounding the use of aversive stimuli.

There are many opinions on what features are critical for acceptable behavioral interventions. In our view, however, a major contribution of positive programming approaches is the addition of a "dignity standard" to two standards already applied in the field. The two existing standards stipulate the following.

1. The level of intrusiveness of an intervention must be balanced by the level of gain or benefit that the person will experience. Highly intrusive interventions should not be used to address minor problems.

2. An intervention (which may include an array of procedures) should be the least intrusive option that is expected to be effective. An important element of this standard is that the intervention must be expected to produce a clinically significant effect within a reasonable time period.

Note that these existing standards are themselves subjective. There are no a priori methods of assessing absolute levels for these standards. Personal (or group) judgment is involved in determining the balance between intrusiveness and benefit. Similarly, judgments are made regarding whether a particular intervention is the least intrusive that will be effective and

what constitutes a reasonable time period for an intervention to have an effect. Objective data can be collected to document the effectiveness of an intervention, but to a large extent the decisions made in designing and evaluating behavioral interventions reflect personal judgments.

Positive approaches add a third judgment to the list. The dignity standard requires that both the procedures within an intervention and the actual manner in which they are implemented treat the person with disabilities in a manner that is respectful and dignified. In essence, the concern is that interventions, and the manner in which they are implemented, may be so severe or unusual that they are outside the standards used to judge the acceptability of treatment of typical members of society. Such treatment stigmatizes persons with disabilities, placing them in a "different" category from other people and making the achievement of lifestyle outcomes even more difficult (Guess, 1988; Guess et al., 1987). An important feature of this standard is that it applies to all types of intervention strategies. Even very nonintrusive procedures can be implemented in a manner that would violate this standard.

The evaluation of behavioral interventions always will rely on standards of acceptability that are subjective. These standards are a major statement about the values that drive and control behavioral technology. Much of the current controversy is a conflict between those who are convinced that behavioral technology is running beyond acceptable limits of human values (Guess, 1988) and those who believe that our values are running ahead of available empirical evidence documenting the technology (Mulick, in press). Defining the process and standards for determining the acceptability of behavioral interventions is where these two viewpoints must be resolved.

Prohibition or Regulation of Specific Procedures

The single most controversial feature of the positive approach to behavioral support rests with the various calls for prohibition or regulation of certain procedures. No one is *for* aversive stimuli. The debate centers on whether we can afford to eliminate some procedures (even though they are intrusive and used only as a last resort) that have been documented as effective in some situations (Cataldo, 1988; Iwata, 1988; Mulick, in press). The response from those advocating a positive approach is that (a) even aversive procedures have not produced the level of lifestyle change we now hold as essential, and (b) we have alternative strategies that are as effective, although not all of these have been tested in traditional empirical studies (Lavigna & Donnellan, 1986; McGee, Menolascino, Hobbs, & Menousek, 1987). We anticipate that this debate will continue (and spur productive research and analysis) for an extended time.

Two issues growing out of the debate are of immediate relevance for teachers, school psychologists, and advocates.

1. It is important to understand the three types of interventions that are being identified for prohibition and regulation. The first is those procedures that include the administration of pain or physically noxious substances. The use of slaps, electric shock, loud noises, ammonia, lemon juice, and tabasco sauce are included in this category. The second type is intervention procedures that result in physical harm to the person. Behavioral support procedures should not produce cuts, burns, scrapes, bruises, broken bones, or the need for medical attention. The third type of procedures is those that do not meet the dignity standard described above. These three types of interventions are described in a variety of manners, associated in some cases with strong demands that they be totally prohibited, for example the ASA Resolution (Autism Society of America, 1988) and TASH Resolution (The Association for Persons with Severe Handicaps, 1981) and in other cases with complex procedures for regulation by state law and professional review boards (Goldblatt, 1988; Katz bill, 1988; Multnomah County Development Disabilities Office, 1987).

2. Although the debate over whether highly intrusive procedures are appropriate in some extremely difficult situations may continue for some time, it is clear that such procedures are *not* appropriate for use in typical school, work, residential, and community settings. The risks associated with the misuse of aversive stimuli (Guess et al., 1987), and the growing opportunities created by less intrusive (although perhaps more sophisticated) alternative interventions, make the use of aversive stimuli less and less tenable. Now is the time to change the approaches we teach and apply in community settings.

In this review of four themes that we believe best represent the positive approach to behavioral support we have not attempted to include all the variations of opinion and theory that are associated with the nonaversive movement. We present the themes as our best synthesis of existing efforts. We also look forward to continuing refinement and expansion of them as researchers, families, educators, service providers, and persons with severe challenging behaviors apply, verify, and test the limits of this emerging technology. While recognizing that work remains to be done in developing a technology of positive behavioral support, we believe that the strength of this approach lies in the documentation of alternative strategies.

TECHNICAL DEVELOPMENTS IN POSITIVE BEHAVIORAL SUPPORT

Recent technical developments in three areas related to positive behavioral support merit attention: (a) preventive behavior management, (b) functional analysis, and (c) comprehensive support plans.

Preventive Behavior Management

An important component of a positive approach to managing challenging behaviors is structuring living and learning environments in ways that promote positive, adaptive behaviors and minimize problem behaviors. The variables involved in this process fall into two categories: (a) basic principles of learning and behavior, and (b) broad ecological and setting variables that either directly influence behavior or that affect responses to other, more immediate environmental events and cues (i.e., variables labeled setting events by Wahler and Fox, 1981). Broad ecological variables and setting events will be discussed in more detail below as part of a comprehensive approach to behavioral support plans. The basic behavioral principles can be viewed as preventive behavior management procedures. These principles underlie guidelines that are important for ensuring that people with disabilities live and learn in environments that promote and support positive behaviors.

There is nothing new about the basic learning principles that underlie guidelines for preventive behavior management. In a classic work first published in 1911, Edward Thorndike presented his Law of Effect, which can be paraphrased as noting that responses closely followed by satisfying events are more likely to recur in the future, and responses followed by discomfort are less likely to recur (Thorndike, 1970). This basic law of learning serves as the foundation for the operant learning paradigm and the principles of reinforcement and punishment (Ferster & Skinner, 1957; Skinner, 1938). It stands as a cornerstone of applied behavior analysis. Unfortunately, practitioners in applied settings too frequently lose sight of this basic law of learning.

Five guidelines define basic procedures for preventive behavior management. The first three focus on promoting adaptive behaviors, the last two are directed toward minimizing problem behaviors.

1. Identify positive behaviors that you want to recur (e.g., communication, social interaction, self-initiation, on-task behavior, task completion, following requests).

2. Identify effective rewards. Many people take this for granted, but it is a critical and often difficult process in working with individuals with challenging behaviors (Green et al., 1988).

3. Ensure that rewards consistently are delivered when positive behaviors occur. The frequency of rewards should be relatively high for persons with challenging behaviors.

4. Minimize the rewards that occur for inappropriate or problem behaviors. In general, staff must create a balance in which two dangerous traps are avoided. The first trap is to inadvertently reward dangerous or problem behaviors by providing attention or positive consequences. Even reprimands can provide attention that rewards and maintains undesirable behaviors. At the same time, however, effective behavioral support does *not* mean that all undesirable behaviors should be ignored. In many instances, the message a person conveys by saying "No! I don't want to do this!" or hitting out, should be taken seriously and result in staff change even if the way the message is delivered is not socially acceptable.

5. Minimize environmental events and cues that trigger or promote challenging behaviors.

In evaluating environments to determine whether preventive procedures are in place, no fixed standards exist. Individual needs vary, so these needs must serve as the basis for determining whether preventive procedures are adequate. Common sense suggests that environments must provide positive contacts and rewards at a reasonable (though certainly individualized) rate. It seems likely that persons with challenging behaviors may need a higher rate of rewards for positive behavior than typical persons. One rule of thumb that has been proposed regarding rates of positive contacts is that they occur at a ratio of at least 4:1 in relation to negative interactions (Fredericks et al., 1977). In general the idea with preventive procedures is to provide plenty of opportunities to engage in positive behaviors and confer plenty of rewards for those positive behaviors. Neither a high percentage of negative interactions, nor the regular use of strong punishers is consistent with a positive environment.

Functional Analysis

Perhaps the most important technical development to occur in applied behavior analysis in recent years is in the area of assessment of challenging behaviors. Heavy emphasis now is being placed on determining the function(s) that negative actions may be serving for persons with challenging behaviors (Carr, 1988; Carr & Durand, 1985b; Donnellan et al., 1988; Donnellan, Mirenda, Mesaros, & Fassbender, 1984). This assessment process, typically referred to as functional analysis, is based on the behavioral principle that anyone who consistently performs a given behavior (including problem behaviors) must be securing some desired outcome from it. The outcome could be that the person obtains desired things (e.g., attention, access to favored objects or activities, internal "good feelings") or avoids or escapes undesired things (e.g., difficult tasks, demands, nonpreferred activities). Functional analysis is the process of determining the relationship between events in a person's environment and the occurrence of challenging behaviors. Through functional analysis, one looks to identify the consistent patterns of behavior that support conclusions regarding "causes" of challenging behavior(s) and predictions regarding when and where those behavior(s) will occur (O'Neill, Horner, Albin, Storey, & Sprague, 1989).

To date, functional analysis procedures most often have been carried out in the context of research studies that focus on particular procedures for managing challenging behaviors (Carr & Durand, 1985a; Horner, Day et al., 1989; Iwata, Dorsey, Slifer, Baumann, & Richman, 1982). However, increasing emphasis is being placed on making functional analysis a basic part of assessment and intervention procedures in typical applied settings (Axelrod, 1987; Donnellan et al., 1988; Durand, 1987; Meyer & Evans, 1986). Several methods for conducting a functional analysis have been described (Durand & Crimmins, 1988; O'Neill et al.,

1989; Wacker, 1989; Willis, LaVigna, & Donnellan, 1987).

The information gathered through functional analysis is critical to the planning of positive (nonaversive) behavioral support plans. One theme of positive approaches is the inclusion of a broader range of variables in behavioral support plans. Therefore, the information collected in a functional analysis must be comprehensive. At the least it should include the following:

1. Fully defining the problem both in terms of the topography, frequency, intensity, and duration of all targeted challenging behaviors, and determining whether topographically different behaviors actually form a class of responses.

2. Identifying setting events and broad ecological variables that affect challenging behaviors (e.g., medical conditions, sleep patterns, predictability of schedule, activity levels and variety, task/activity preference).

3. Identifying environmental events, conditions, and cues that serve as immediate antecedents for challenging behaviors (e.g., teacher request, difficult task, harsh voice, interruption, "no").

4. Determining the function(s) of challenging behaviors and the efficiency with which they serve that function (e.g., quick, consistent results from tantrums to get attention).

5. Identifying the person's current methods of communication, and existing skills and adaptive behaviors that could serve the same function(s) as the challenging behaviors.

6. Identifying effective rewards for the person.

7. Determining the person's history of previous interventions for challenging behaviors.

O'Neill et al. (1989) describe a process for conducting a functional analysis that includes three strategies for collecting the information noted above: (a) interview, (b) direct observation, and (c) environmental manipulations. Because it is logistically the easiest, interviewing persons who are familiar with the person with challenging behavior (e.g., parents, teachers, residential program staff) is typically the first step in conducting a functional analysis. The interview method alone may provide sufficient information to direct development of an intervention or support plan. If not, the next step in a functional analysis would be direct observation of the person with challenging behaviors. Interview information could be used to set up observation forms and direct the actual observations by identifying (a) the behaviors of concern, (b) the setting and antecedent events that are potentially related to those behaviors, and (c) the possible functions and maintaining consequences for those behaviors. Logistics such as the number of direct observations, where they occur, and the length of observation periods would be influenced by the nature of the problem and the nature of the information being collected (e.g., is it providing the necessary answers to our questions?).

Depending on the clarity of the information and data patterns obtained by direct observations, the people involved would decide whether sufficient information exists to develop a support plan, or whether additional controlled environmental manipulations are needed to clarify or confirm relationships between the challenging behavior(s) and the potentially relevant variables. This process of environmental manipulation typically involves presenting and withdrawing variables that are thought to be related to the occurrence of challenging behaviors and looking for concomitant changes in those behaviors. Examples of the variables that have been assessed in functional analysis manipulations include task difficulty (Carr & Durand, 1985b; Durand & Carr, 1987), level of attention (Durand & Carr, 1987), and demands (Carr, Newsom, & Binkoff, 1980).

More specific details on the methods of collecting functional analysis information, including examples of interview and direct observation forms, are provided by Durand and Crimmins (1988). Evans and Meyer (1985), Meyer and Evans (1989), O'Neill et al. (1989), Touchette, MacDonald, and Langer (1985), and Willis et al. (1987).

Comprehensive Behavioral Support Plans

Concern with expanding the range of variables considered in building behavioral support plans for persons with challenging behaviors has resulted in behavioral interventions that are more comprehensive, with multiple components and strategies included in a single plan. Whereas traditional behavior modification programs often have focused on manipulating only the consequences that follow appropriate and/or inappropriate behavior, the emphasis in the nonaversive approach is on the inclusion of procedures that address or manipulate additional programming variables (Donnellan et al., 1988; Evans & Meyer, 1985; LaVigna & Donnellan, 1986; Meyer & Evans, 1986; 1989). There are five major classes of programming variables from which specific intervention manipulations can be drawn: (a) ecological and setting event manipulations; (b) immediate antecedent event manipulations; (c) response and skill training manipulations; (d) consequence manipulations; and (e) emergency and crisis intervention procedures.

In the remainder of this section we describe a variety of intervention strategies and specific procedures from each of these areas.

Ecological and Setting Event Manipulations

This category is concerned with manipulating variables that may be considered to have a broader or more pervasive influence on behavior across time and/or settings, and thus may have an ongoing impact on more specific and immediate antecedent-behavior interactions (Wahler & Fox, 1981).

Overall environmental changes. Moving someone to a new or different physical environmental, such as a new residential or vocational setting, is one example of an overall environmental manipulation. A change of this type might result in differences in the typical number or "density" of people; ambient levels of heat, light, and noise; the presence of other persons exhibiting various problem behaviors; and the type of physical space or structure available to a person. Such variables may be implicated as problematic on the basis of the functional analysis procedures described above.

General activity patterns. The type and variety of general activities in which a candidate for a behavioral support plan participates may be in need of attention and change. Programming for ongoing engagement in functional, age-appropriate activities is the primary goal. In addition, such programming should include regular access to preferred objects/events/activities (i.e., functional reinforcers). The issue of incorporating expression of choice and preference for activities has begun to receive greater attention in recent years (Guess, Benson, & Siegel-Causey, 1985; Dattilo & Rusch, 1985). Recent data indicate that facilitating such choice can be helpful in increasing adaptive responding and reducing the occurrence of problem behaviors (Dattilo & Rusch, 1985; Dyer, Dunlap, & Winterling, 1989; Peck, 1985). Allowing maximum opportunities for such expression can be an important part of any overall program.

Social contact. Along with more general activities, the frequency and type of a person's social contacts may need to be assessed and changed. Recent years have seen an increasing focus by applied researchers and service providers on developing more normalized social networks for persons with handicaps, and on increasing their interactions with other persons with and without disabilities (Bellamy et al., in press; Lakin & Bruininks, 1985; Snell, 1987).

Schedule predictability and control. A programming aspect related to the choice and preference issues discussed above concerns the level to which persons can predict or understand the sequence of events in which they will be involved, and whether they have the power to control some or all aspects of that sequence. Such programming requires consistently trying to make it clear to a person what activities are planned and in what order. This concern may require the use of more concrete symbolic stimuli (e.g., picture schedules), depending on a person's receptive communicative abilities. Use of such schedules also allows for incorporating opportunities for making choices among different activities.

Medical/physical status. Both transient and more ongoing medical and physical problems or conditions may influence behavior patterns. These would include such things as allergies, ear and sinus problems, motor and orthopedic problems, skin rashes, and levels and types of medications. Monitoring such conditions and providing appropriate treatment or manipulations (e.g., adjusting medication levels) on an ongoing basis is an important component of a comprehensive support plan.

Immediate Antecedent Event Manipulations

Along with broad or pervasive variables, attention to the occurrence of more specific and immediate antecedent events also is required in developing comprehensive support plans.

Make discriminations and task requirements easier. For students who consistently display problem behavior when asked to complete particular tasks or activities, it may be important to look at the response requirements and discriminations they are being asked to make. It may be useful to break tasks down into smaller, easier steps or to change the cueing and prompting procedures that are being used, to facilitate successful performance. Such programming might require the use of various types of prosthetic devices and arrangements to facilitate completion of the tasks.

Reduce the presence of stimuli for problem behavior. One strategy that might be implemented, at least initially, is to reduce or eliminate the stimuli that appear to reliably occasion the problem behaviors. It might be possible to curtail or stop particular tasks or activities; moving to certain settings, or working with certain staff members. Specific plans would then be developed to reintroduce such stimuli, in different contexts or situations, in order to try to change the problematic stimulus control that has been developed.

Use varied and interspersed requests. One method for presenting problematic stimuli or requests is to embed the requests in the context of other requests that have a strong history of successful completion. This strategy has been shown to be successful in promoting successful responding and reducing the occurrence of problem behaviors (Dunlap, 1984; Horner, Day et al., 1989; Mace et al., 1988; Singer, Singer, & Horner, 1987; Winterling, Dunlap, & O'Neill, 1987). Typically, a person is asked to make two or three brief responses that have a high probability of correct performance, after which the problematic or difficult response is elicited. This strategy can be employed with a variety of situations and responses.

Response/Skill Manipulations

An area that has received major emphasis in recent years is teaching appropriate alternative responses that can serve the same function as problem behaviors. This approach has most often been applied in training appropriate communicative responses to achieve socially mediated functions (e.g., get attention/assistance, request a break or termination of activity, etc.). However, the types of alternative responses to be trained depends on the problem behavior functions that have been identified during the functional analysis process.

A diagram of the potential functions of behavior is presented in Figure 1. The two main categories of goals, obtaining desirable objects or events and avoiding undesirable objects or events, are further broken down into categories defined by internal stimulation or external and socially mediated stimuli (e.g., access to or avoidance of attention, objects/activities, etc.). This organization results in the six major categories of functions noted in Figure 1.

Consequence Manipulations

While there has been increased emphasis on antecedent variables and strategies in recent years, the appropriate application of contingency management procedures continues to be very important. Ongoing access to positive, preferred objects, events, and activities that is contingent on adaptive behaviors is an integral part of any programming efforts.

Identifying personalized reinforcers. Selecting reinforcing stimuli for persons with challenging behaviors is something that typically receives a good deal of lip service and not enough systematic attention. Investigations in recent years have shown that reinforcers chosen on the basis of more systematic assessment and observation procedures are more effective than those chosen through more typical expressions of staff opinion or consultation (Dyer, 1987; Green et al., 1988).

Minimizing or eliminating reinforcers for problem behaviors. Along with providing positive consequences for adaptive behaviors, it may also be important or necessary to block or prevent the usual consequences for problem behaviors in order to reduce their occurrence. For example, a child might be prevented from leaving an instructional situation during an episode of escape-motivated problem behavior, in order to block the typical reinforcer that would occur for such behavior. Similarly, peers, teachers, or staff persons might be instructed to ignore particular behaviors that have been identified as attention-motivated. Of course, whether and how such manipulations might be carried out will depend on the severity of the behaviors and their potential danger to staff or students. Also,

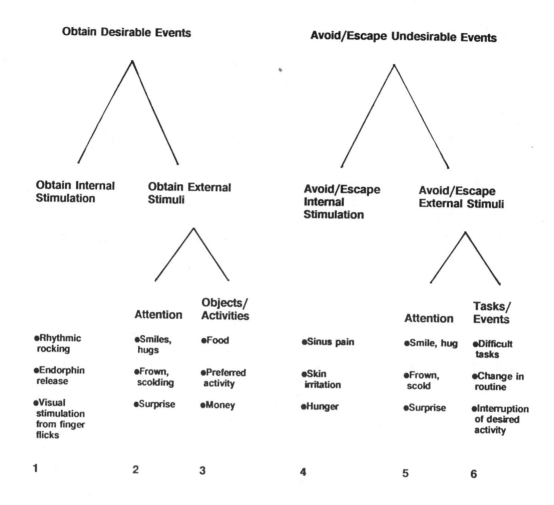

FIGURE 1. Six functions of behavior.

such manipulations should be implemented in the context of a comprehensive plan.

Such manipulations of reinforcers are relevant to the competing behavior framework described by Horner and Billingsley (1988). For example, in a study by Billingsley and Neel (1985), students who engaged in inappropriate food grabbing were taught requesting responses. However, the rate of appropriate requesting remained low and variable until staff persons began to block and prevent the grabbing attempts from being successful. Billingsley and Neel concluded that blocking the reinforcement of undesirable behavior may be a key component of effective programming.

Emergency Procedures

Even with the most carefully implemented programming procedures, incidents may occur that place a student, or others, at severe physical risk. It is important that there be a very clear set of procedures established for teachers or staff to follow in the case of such behavioral emergencies. Such procedures should include ways to protect the student and staff persons involved (e.g., blocking or brief restraint), a list of appropriate persons to notify, and the process for documenting the occurrence of the escalation. Most school districts or agencies will have a policy and related procedures with regard to such incidents. However, teachers and staff persons may also require more detailed guidelines on how to respond to specific types of problem behavior.

It is important to keep in mind that such emergency response procedures are *not* meant to provide adaptive programming opportunities. Rather, they are a means to protect the persons involved, and to end the incident as soon as possible. It typically will not be possible to engage in any meaningful instruction or interaction in such out-of-control situations. Teachers and staff should first bring the situation under control, and then attempt to reimplement adaptive programming procedures.

In this section we have presented introductions to three technical components of a positive approach to behavioral support: preventive behavior management, functional analysis, and comprehensive behavioral support plans. Many of the specific guidelines and procedures described have been documented, not only in research studies, but also in clinical applications in typical community settings (Berkman & Meyer, 1988; Donnellan, LaVigna, Zambito, & Thvedt, 1985; Durand & Kishi, 1987). However, there remains a need for continued empirical analysis of variables related to the implementation and utilization of positive support technologies in typical school and community settings.

IMPLICATIONS OF POSITIVE BEHAVIORAL SUPPORT FOR EDUCATORS

Utilization of positive behavioral support techniques may necessitate some changes in the ways that schools and education personnel address issues related to students with severe challenging behaviors. Positive approaches, with their emphasis on lifestyle outcomes, structuring positive environments, and comprehensive support plans, have important implications for school support systems. These include general issues in developing systems to support students with severe challenging behaviors in typical schools,

and specific aspects of the role school psychologists can play in those systems.

Teacher Support Systems

Students with severe challenging behaviors can be and are being given behavioral support allowing them to attend typical schools in their communities (Horner, Diemer, & Brazeau, 1989). However, in order to provide this support, there is usually a mechanism by which teachers of those students themselves receive special support, which may come in the form of added classroom assistants, time from a behavior specialist, special in-service training, or a variety of other mechanisms.

A formalized teacher support system is likely to be essential to successfully educating students with severe challenges in typical schools. The overall mission of such a support system should be to provide the consultation and support services to classroom staff that are necessary to enable them to maintain students with severe challenging behaviors in typical classrooms. A teacher support system is grounded on three basic commitments: (a) a commitment to keeping students with challenging behaviors in typical classrooms (i.e., those they would be in if they did not have challenging behaviors), (b) a commitment to providing the long-term support likely to be needed by these students, and (c) a commitment to producing the real lifestyle outcomes (e.g., physical and social integration, participation in a variety of activities) desired for these students. We believe that achieving these lifestyle outcomes is simply not as likely in a special "problem behavior" school or classroom as in the typical school classroom.

Given the commitments noted, the accomplishments and tasks that a successful teacher support system would need to complete fit into seven basic areas:

1. A referral and screening process that ensures identification of all students who need the support provided by a teacher support system.

2. Comprehensive assessment and program development procedures that ensure appropriate comprehensive support plans for all students supported by the system.

3. Implementation, evaluation, and modification of comprehensive behavioral support plans so that student behavior patterns will change in a manner that allows ongoing participation in school and community activities.

4. Transfer of responsibility for continued implementation and monitoring of the support plan to regular classroom staff, so that added support from the system can be faded to the minimum level needed to maintain the student in the classroom.

5. Regular supervision and monitoring in the classroom and other school settings with particular attention to the variables that are related to structuring positive, supportive environments (e.g., what is taught, how it is taught, nature of staff-student interactions, classroom organization, scheduling).

6. Provision of appropriate emergency support and respite to classroom staff.

7. Evaluation of the support system itself.

In reviewing these seven basic areas, the types of expertise and skills that a teacher support system must be able to provide are apparent. One obvious personnel need is a professional to fill the role of expert in behavioral assessment and program development. Teachers and usual classroom staff cannot be expected to be behavior specialists with all the skills needed to work with very challenging students. A second role is ongoing supervision and monitoring of classrooms and classroom staff. This requires that someone in the support system have the expertise and administrative ranking necessary to supervise teachers and staff and, if necessary, effect change in their behavior. A third role within a teacher support system requires people who can provide direct intervention assistance, to supplement regular classroom staff, respond in crisis situations, or provide

periods of respite to regular staff. This role can be filled by various personnel, including master teachers, itinerant teachers or support staff, and specially trained assistants or paraprofessionals. Other roles that would fit into a support system are personnel to provide in-service and specialized training to regular staff, and someone to oversee and evaluate the performance of the support system.

Implications for School Psychologists

School psychologists are one resource to which school districts can look to fill several of the roles required by a teacher support system. Two obvious areas for contribution are assessment of problem behaviors and development of comprehensive support plans. School psychologists also can play monitoring and supervision roles, both in structuring positive environments and in implementing and evaluating support plans, and they can provide specialized training to other staff. The possibility of assuming these roles has important implications for the training that school psychologists receive and the skills that they possess, particularly in the areas of assessment and comprehensive program development.

Assessment. Traditionally, school psychologists' assessment skills have been focused on administering standardized tests and instruments to provide information related to determination of eligibility for special services, diagnostic categorization, and appropriate placement. Supporting students with severe challenging behaviors in typical schools calls for additional assessment skills. Foremost among these is the ability to conduct a comprehensive functional analysis of challenging behaviors, one that provides information in each of the areas noted above in the Functional Analysis section. Subsumed within a functional analysis are a variety of more specific types of assessments (e.g., assessing a student's receptive and expressive communication abilities, determining effective rewards for an individual student, analyzing environments to determine whether they promote positive behaviors). Because functional analysis does not have quite the formalized protocol of more traditional assessment instruments, it relies on the individual observation, analysis, and summarization skills of the person(s) conducting the functional analysis. These are skills that develop through training and experience. We believe that one focus of training for school psychologists should involve practical experience in the assessment of severe challenging behaviors.

Comprehensive program development. Much of the traditional training provided in basic behavior management texts and courses focuses on the manipulation of consequences (rewards and punishers) in behavioral programs (Alberto & Troutman, 1986; Foxx, 1982a, 1982b; Walker & Shea, 1988). The broadened approach that underlies positive behavioral support strategies calls for more comprehensive, multicomponent support plans. As noted above, these comprehensive plans may include interventions that change ecological and setting variables, interventions that manipulate immediate antecedent events and variables, and interventions that provide response and skills training, in addition to the traditional consequence interventions. School psychologists working on program development must be able to draw from knowledge of how behavior may be affected by variables in each of these classes of interventions. This will require knowledge of "best practices" in a variety of areas, including curriculum, instructional procedures, classroom organization and management, augmentative communication, and teaching alternative or "functionally equivalent" (Carr, 1988) behaviors. When consequence interventions are considered as part of the support plan, knowledge of positive reinforcement strategies, such as differential schedules of reinforcement, is emphasized in positive programming approaches. Thus, school psychologists involved in positive behavioral support planning should receive training that allows them to draw from this variety of variables, with particular emphasis on practical experience with students who have challenging behaviors.

SUMMARY

This chapter has outlined four basic themes of positive approaches to behavioral support, described technical developments in three areas, and discussed the implications of positive approaches for schools and educators. The basic message is that strategies for supporting persons with challenging behaviors are changing. That change can be best described as a shift from reliance on a small number of "behavior management tricks" to a more comprehensive effort to design adaptive environments. Comprehensive behavioral support plans build from careful analysis of a broad set of factors that may be contributing to particular patterns of behavior. The results are multicomponent plans that attend to social, physical, and medical issues and extend well beyond traditional consequence-based behavior management programs.

Schools can, and in our view must, provide support to students with challenging behaviors in typical, integrated school settings. One important challenge to achieving this goal is the need to increase the technical support and assistance that teachers and classroom personnel receive. School psychologists can be an important resource in a formal support system for classroom staff. For example, we believe that school psychologists can play major roles in the assessment of problem behaviors and in the development and implementation of comprehensive support plans. Filling these roles will require training and supervised practical experience directly related to supporting students with severe challenging behaviors in the schools.

ACKNOWLEDGMENTS

Preparation of this chapter was supported by Cooperative Agreement #G0087C0234 from the National Institute on Disability and Rehabilitation Research. However, the opinions expressed herein do not necessarily reflect the position or policy of the U.S. Department of Education, and no official endorsement should be inferred.

REFERENCES

Alberto, P. A., & Troutman, A. C. (1986). *Applied behavior analysis for teachers* (2nd ed.). Columbus, OH: Merrill.

American Psychological Associaton Division 33 (1988, August). *Guidelines on effective behavioral treatment for persons with mental retardation and developmental disabilities.* Resolution by Executive Committee and Behavior Modification Special Interest Group of Division 33 (Mental Retardation and Developmental Disabilities) of the American Psychological Association adopted in principle by the Executive Committee.

Autism Society of America. (1988). Autism Society of America: Resolution on abusive treatment and neglect. *The Advocate, 20*(3), 17.

Axelrod, S. (1987). Functional and structural analyses of behavior: Approaches leading to reduced use of punishment procedures. *Research in Developmental Disabilities, 8,* 165-178.

Bachman, J. E., & Sluyter, D. (1988). Reducing inappropriate behaviors of developmentally disabled adults using antecedent aerobic dance exercises. *Research in Developmental Disabilities, 9*(1), 73-83.

Baer, D. M., Wolf, M. M., & Risley, T. R. (1968). Some current dimensions of applied behavior analysis. *Journal of Applied Behavior Analysis, 1,* 91-97.

Baumeister, A. A., & MacLean, W. E. (1984). Deceleration of self-injurious and stereotypic responding by exercise. *Applied Research in Mental Retardation, 5,* 385-393.

Bellamy, G. T., Newton, J. S., LeBaron, N. M., & Horner, R. H. (in press). Quality of life and lifestyle outcomes: A challenge for residential programs. In B. Schalock (Ed.), *Quality of life: Perspectives and issues* (Monograph of the American Association on Mental Retardation).

Berkman, K. A., & Meyer, L. H. (1988). Alternative strategies and multiple outcomes in the remediation of severe self-injury: Going "all out" nonaversively. *Journal of the Association for Persons With Severe Handicaps, 13,* 76-86.

Billingsley, F. F., & Neel, R. S. (1985). Competing behaviors and their effects on skill generalization and maintenance. *Analysis and Intervention in Developmental Disabilities, 5,* 357-372.

Brown, L., Long, E., Udvari-Solner, A., Davis, L., VanDeventer, P., Ahlgren, C., Johnson, F., Gruenewald, L., & Jorgensen, J. (1989). The home school: Why students with severe intellectual disabilities must attend the schools of their brothers, sisters, friends, and neighbors. *Journal of the Association for Persons With Severe Handicaps, 14,* 1-7.

Carr, E. G. (1988). Functional equivalence as a mechanism of response generalization. In R. H. Horner, G. Dunlap, & R. L. Koegel (Eds.), *Generalization and maintenance: Life-style changes in applied settings* (pp. 221-241). Baltimore: Paul H. Brookes.

Carr, E. G., & Durand, V. M. (1985a). Reducing behavior problems through functional communications training. *Journal of Applied Behavior Analysis, 18,* 111-126.

Carr, E. G., & Durand, V. M. (1985b). The social-communicative basis of severe behavior problems in children. In S. Reiss & R. Bootzin (Eds.), *Theoretical issues in behavior therapy* (pp. 219-254). New York: Academic Press.

Carr, E. G., Newsom, C. D., & Binkoff, J. A. (1980). Escape as a factor in the aggressive behavior of two retarded children. *Journal of Applied Behavior Analysis, 13,* 101-117.

Cataldo, M. F. (1988). Knowledge based approaches toward assisting the developmentally disabled and other considerations. In R. H. Horner & G. Dunlap (Eds.), *Behavior management and community integration for individuals with developmental disabilities and severe behavior problems.* Monograph from a symposium sponsored by the Office of Special Education and Rehabilitative Services and the Research and Training Center on Community-Referenced Behavior Management, Washington, DC.

Cooper, J. O., Heron, T. E., & Heward, W. L. (1987). *Applied behavior analysis.* Columbus, OH: Merrill.

Danielson, L. C., & Bellamy, G. T. (1989). State variation in placement of children with handicaps in segregated environments. *Exceptional Children, 55,* 448-455.

Dattilo, J., & Rusch, F. R. (1985). Effects of choice on leisure participation for persons with severe handicaps. *Journal of the Association for Persons With Severe Handicaps, 10,* 194-199.

Donnellan, A. M., LaVigna, G. W., Negri-Shoultz, N., & Fassbender, L. L. (1988). *Progress without punishment: Effective approaches for learners with behavior problems.* New York: Teachers College Press, Columbia University.

Donnellan, A. M., LaVigna, G. W., Zambito, J., & Thvedt, J. (1985). A time limited intensive intervention program model to support community placement for persons with severe behavior problems. *Journal of the Association for Persons With Severe Handicaps, 10,* 123-131.

Donnellan, A. M., Mirenda, P. L., Mesaros, R. A., & Fassbender, L. L. (1984). Analyzing the communicative functions of aberrant behavior. *Journal of the Association for Persons With Severe Handicaps, 9,* 201-212.

Dunlap, G. (1984). The influence of task variation and maintenance tasks on the learning and affect of autistic children. *Journal of Experimental Child Psychology, 37,* 41-64.

Durand, V. M. (1987). Look homeward angel: A call to return to our (functional) roots. *The Behavior Analyst, 10,* 299-302.

Durand, V. M., & Carr, E. G. (1987). Social influences on "self-stimulatory" behavior: Analysis and treatment application. *Journal of Applied Behavior Analysis, 20,* 119-132.

Durand, V. M., & Crimmins, D. M. (1988). *The motivation assessment scale: An administration manual.* Unpublished manuscript. State University of New York, Albany.

Durand, V. M., & Kishi, G. (1987). Reducing severe behavior problems among persons with dual sensory impairments: An evaluation of a technical assistance model. *Journal of the Association for Persons With Severe Handicaps, 12,* 2-10.

Dyer, K. (1987). The competition of autistic stereotyped behavior with usual and specially assessed reinforcers. *Research in Developmental Disabilities, 8,* 607-626.

Dyer, K., Dunlap, G., & Winterling, V. (1989). *The effects of choice-making on the problem behaviors of students with severe handicaps.* Manuscript submitted for publication.

Evans, I. M., & Meyer, L. H. (1985). *An educative approach to behavior problems.* Baltimore: Paul H. Brookes.

Favell, J. E., McGimsey, J. F., & Schell, R. M. (1982). Treatment of self-injury by providing alternate sensory activities. *Analysis and Intervention in Developmental Disabilities, 2,* 83-104.

Favell, J. E., & Reid, D. H. (1988). Generalizing and maintaining improvement in problem behavior. In R. H. Horner, G. Dunlap, & R. L. Koegel (Eds.), *Generalization and maintenance: Life-style changes in applied settings* (pp. 171-196). Baltimore: Paul H. Brookes.

Ferster, C. B., & Skinner, B. F. (1957). *Schedules of reinforcement.* New York: Appleton-Century-Crofts.

Foxx, R. M. (1982a). *Increasing behaviors of severely retarded and autistic persons.* Champaign, IL: Research Press.

Foxx, R. M. (1982b). *Decreasing behaviors of severely retarded and autistic persons.* Champaign, IL: Research Press.

Fredericks, H. D., Baldwin, V. L., Moore, W., Furey, V., Grove, D., Riggs, C., Moore, B., Gage, M. A., Levak, L., Alrick, G., Wadlow, M., Fruin, C., Bunse, C., Makohon, L., Lyons, B., Samples, B., Jordan, E.,

Moses, C., & Rogers, G. (1977). *A data based classroom for the moderately and severely handicapped* (2nd ed.). Monmouth, OR: Instructional Development Corporation.

Gartner, A., & Lipsky, D. K. (1987). Beyond special education: Toward a quality system for all students. *Harvard Educational Review, 57*(4), 367-395.

Gilbert, T. F. (1978). *Human competence: Engineering worthy performance.* New York: McGraw-Hill.

Green, C. W., Reid, D. H., White, L. K., Halford, R. C., Brittain, D. P., & Gardner, S. M. (1988). Identifying reinforcers for persons with profound handicaps: Staff opinion versus systematic assessment of preferences. *Journal of Applied Behavior Analysis, 21,* 31-43.

Goldblatt, E. S. (1988, May). *Controlling the use of behavioral aversives.* Presentation to the Ninth National Institute on Legal Problems of Educating the Handicapped, May 10-13.

Groden, J., Baron, G., & Groden, G. (1984, July). *The need for the development of self-control procedures with the autistic population.* Paper presented at the meeting of the National Society for Children and Adults with Autism, San Antonio.

Guess, D. (1988). Problems and issues pertaining to the transmission of behavior management technologies from researchers to practitioners. In R. H. Horner & G. Dunlap (Eds.), *Behavior management and community integration for individuals with developmental disabilities and severe behavior problems.* Monograph from a symposium sponsored by the Office of Special Education and Rehabilitative Services and the Research and Training Center on Community-Referenced Behavior Management. Washington, DC.

Guess, D., Benson, H. A., & Siegel-Causey, E. (1985). Concepts and issues related to choice-making and autonomy among persons with severe disabilities. *Journal of the Association for Persons With Severe Handicaps, 10,* 79-86.

Guess, D., Helmstetter, E., Turnbull, H. R., & Knowlton, S. (1987). *Use of aversive procedures with persons who are disabled: A historical review and critical analysis, (TASH Monograph Series, No. 2).* Seattle: TASH.

Horner, R. D. (1980). The effects of an environmental "enrichment" program on the behavior of institutionalized profoundly retarded children. *Journal of Applied Behavior Analysis, 13,* 473-491.

Horner, R. H., & Billingsley, F. F. (1988). The effect of competing behavior on the generalization and maintenance of adaptive behavior in applied settings. In R. H. Horner, G. Dunlap, & R. L. Koegel (Eds.), *Generalization and maintenance: Life-style changes in applied settings* (pp. 197-220). Baltimore: Paul H. Brookes.

Horner, R. H., & Budd, C. M. (1985). Teaching manual sign language to a nonverbal student; Generalization of sign use and collateral reduction of maladaptive behavior. *Education and Training of the Mentally Retarded, 20,* 39-47.

Horner, R. H., Diemer, S., & Brazeau, K. (1989). *Systems for supporting students with challenging behavior: Oregon's approach to teacher support.* Unpublished manuscript. University of Oregon, Specialized Training Program, Eugene OR.

Horner, R. H., Day, M., Sprague, J., O'Brien, M., & Tuesday Heathfield, L. (1989). *Interspersed requests: A nonaversive procedure for decreasing aggression and self-injury during instruction.* Manuscript submitted for publication.

Horner, R. H., & Dunlap, G. (Eds.). (1988, June). *Behavior management and community integration for individuals with developmental disabilities and severe behavior problems.* Monograph from a symposium sponsored by the Office of Special Education and Rehabilitative Services and the Research and Training Center on Community-Referenced, Nonaversive Behavior Management, Washington, DC.

Horner, R. H., Dunlap, G., Koegel, R. L., Carr, E. G., Sailor, W., Anderson, J. A., Albin, R. W., & O'Neill, R. E. (1989). *Toward a technology of nonaversive behavioral support.* Manuscript submitted for publication.

House, J. S., Landis, K. R., & Umberson, D. (1988). Social relationships and health. *Science, 241,* 540-544.

Hunt, P., Alwell, M., & Goetz, L. (1988). Acquisition of conversation skills and the reduction of inappropriate social interaction behaviors. *Journal of the Association for Persons With Severe Handicaps, 13,* 20-27.

Iwata, B. A. (1988). The development and adoption of controversial default technologies. *The Behavior Analyst, 11,* 149-157.

Iwata, B. A., Dorsey, M. F., Slifer, K. J., Bauman, K. E., & Richman, G. S. (1982). Toward a functional analysis of self-injury. *Analysis and Intervention in Developmental Disabilities, 2,* 3-20.

Johnson, J., & Koegel, R. L. (1982). Behavioral assessment and curriculum development. In R. L. Koegel, A. Rincover, & A. L. Egel (Eds.), *Educating and understanding autistic children* (pp. 1-32). San Diego: College Hill.

Katz bill, California Proposed Legislation, AB520, 1988.

Kern, L., Koegel, R. L., & Dunlap, G. (1984). The influence of vigorous vs. mild exercise on autistic stereotyped behaviors. *Journal of Autism and Developmental Disorders, 14,* 57-67.

Koegel, R. L., Parks, D. R., & Koegel, L. K. (in press). Extended reductions in stereotypic behavior through a self-management treatment program. *Journal of Applied Behavior Anslysis.*

Lakin, K., & Bruininks, R. H. (1985). Social integration of developmentally disabled persons. In K. C. Lakin & R. H. Bruininks (Eds.), *Strategies for achieving community integration of developmentally disabled citizens* (pp. 3-25). Baltimore: Paul H. Brookes.

LaVigna, G. D., & Donnellan, A. (1986). *Alternatives to punishment: Solving behavior problems with non-aversive strategies.* New York: Irvington.

LaVigna, G. W., Willis, T. J., & Donnellan, A. M. (1989). The role of positive programming in behavioral treatment. In E. Cipani (Ed.), *The treatment of severe behavior disorders: Behavior analysis approaches* (pp. 59-83). (Monographs of American Association on Mental Retardation, 12.) Washington, DC: AAMR.

Lovaas, O. I., & Favell, J. E. (1987). Protection for clients undergoing aversive/restrictive interventions. *Education and Treatment of Children, 10,* 311-325.

Mace, F. C., Hock, M. L., Lalli, J. S., West, B. J., Belfiore, P., Pinter, E., & Brown, D. K. (1988). Behavioral momentum in the treatment of noncompliance. *Journal of Applied Behavior Analysis, 21,* 123-141.

Martens, B. K., & Witt, J. C. (1988). Ecological behavior analysis. In M. Hersen, R. M. Eisler, & P. M. Miller (Eds.). (1988). *Progress in behavior modification* (Vol. 22, pp. 115-140). Newbury Park, CA: Sage.

McDonnell, A. P., & Hardman, M. L. (1989). The desegregation of America's special schools: Strategies for change. *Journal of the Association for Persons With Severe Handicaps, 14*(1), 68-74.

McGee, J. J., Menolascino, F. J., Hobbs, D. C., & Menousek, P. E. (1987). *Gentle teaching: A non-aversive approach to helping persons with mental retardation.* New York: Human Sciences Press.

Meyer, L. H., & Evans, I. M. (1986). Modifying excess behavior: An adaptive and functional approach for educational and community contexts. In R. H. Horner, L. H. Meyer, & H. D. Fredericks (Eds.), *Education of learners with severe handicaps: Exemplary service strategies.* Baltimore: Paul H. Brookes.

Meyer, L. H., & Evans, I. M. (1989). *Nonaversive intervention for behavior problems: A manual for home and community.* Baltimore: Paul H. Brookes.

Mulick, J. A. (in press). The ideology and science of punishment in mental retardation. *American Journal on Mental Retardation.*

Multnomah County Developmental Disabilities Office. Multnomah County Behavior Intervention Policy, (1987, August). Behavior Management. *Multnomah County Developmental Disabilities Program Policy and Procedure Manual.* Portland, OR: Author.

O'Neill, R. E., Horner, R. H., Albin, R. W., Storey, K., & Sprague, J. (1989). *Functional analysis: A practical assessment guide.* Eugene, OR: University of Oregon, Specialized Training Program.

Paine, S. C., Radicchi, J., Rosellini, L. C., Deutchman, L., & Darch, C. B. (1983). *Structuring your classroom for academic success.* Champaign, IL: Research Press.

Peck, C. A. (1985). Increasing opportunities for social control by children with autism and severe handicaps: Effects on student behavior and perceived classroom climate. *Journal of the Association for Persons With Severe Handicaps, 10*, 183-193.

Rast, J., Johnston, J. M., Ellinger-Allen, J. A., & Drum, C. (1985). Effects of nutritional and mechanical properties of food on ruminative behavior. *Journal of the Experimental Analysis of Behavior, 44*, 195-206.

Reid, D. H., Parsons, M. B., & Green, C. W. (1989). Treating aberrant behavior through effective staff management: A developing technology. In E. Cipani (Ed.), *The treatment of severe behavior disorders: Behavior analysis approaches* (pp. 175-190). (Monographs of the American Association on Mental Retardation, 12.) Washington, DC: AAMR.

Schopler, E., & Mesibov, G. (1987). *Neurobiological issues in autism.* New York: Plenum.

Schreibman, L. (1988). *Autism.* Beverly Hills, CA: Sage.

Schroeder, S. R., Breese, G. R., & Mueller, R. A. (in press). Dopaminargic mechanisms in self-injurious behavior. In D. K. Routh & M. Wolraich (Eds.), *Advances in developmental and behavioral pediatrics.* Greenwich, CT: JAI.

Singer, G. H. S., Singer, J., & Horner, R. H. (1987). Using pretask requests to increase the probability of compliance for students with severe disabilities. *Journal of the Association for Persons With Severe Handicaps, 12*(4), 287-291.

Skinner, B. F. (1938). *The behavior of organisms.* New York: Appleton-Century-Crofts.

Snell, M. (1987). *Systematic instruction of persons with severe handicaps* (3rd ed.). Columbus, OH: Merrill.

Sprague, J., & Horner, R. H. (1989). *Providing behavioral support for persons with low frequency, high intensity challenging behaviors.* Unpublished manuscript, University of Oregon, Specialized Training Program, Eugene, OR.

Stainback, S., & Stainback, W. (1985). *Integration of students with severe handicaps into regular schools.* Reston, VA: Council for Exceptional Children.

The Association for Persons With Severe Handicaps. (1981). *Resolution on intrusive interventions.* Seattle: Author.

Thorndike, E. L. (1970). *Animal intelligence: Experimental studies.* Darien, CT: Hafner.

Touchette, P., MacDonald, R., & Langer, S. (1985). A scatter plot for identifying stimulus control of problem behavior. *Journal of Applied Behavior Analysis, 18*, 343-351.

Turnbull, H. R., Guess, D., Backus, L. H., Barber, P. A., Fiedler, C. R., Helmstetter, E., & Summers, J. A. (1986). A model for analyzing the moral aspects of special education and behavioral interventions. In P. R. Dokecki & R. M. Zaner (Eds.), *Ethics of dealing with persons with severe handicaps* (pp. 167-210). Baltimore: Paul H. Brookes.

Van Houten, R., Axelrod, S., Bailey, J. S., Favell, J. E., Foxx, R. M., Iwata, B. A., & Lovaas, O. I. (1988). The right to effective behavioral treatment. *The Behavior Analyst, 11*(2), 111-114.

Wacker, D. P. (1989). *Functional analysis of severe behavior problems: Recent applications and novel approaches.* Paper presented to a symposium at the annual meeting of the Association for Behavior Analysis, Milwaukee.

Wahler, R. G., & Fox, J. J. (1981). Setting events in applied behavior analysis: Toward a conceptual and methodological expansion. *Journal of Applied Behavior Analysis, 14*, 327-338.

Walker, J. E., & Shea, T. M. (1988). *Behavior management: A practical approach for educators* (4th ed.). Columbus, OH: Merrill.

Willis, T. J., LaVigna, G. W. & Donnellan, A. M. (1987). *Behavior assessment guide.* Los Angeles: Institute for Applied Behavior Analysis.

Winterling, V., Dunlap, G., & O'Neill, R. (1987). The influence of task variation on the aberrant behavior of autistic students. *Education and Treatment of Children, 10*, 105-119.

Promoting Communication Competence in Preschool-Age Children

Kathleen D. Paget
University of South Carolina

Kimberly Galant
United Cerebral Palsy of Tampa Bay, Inc.

The limitations of developmental psychology can be attributed to its tendency to permit itself to become the science of the strange behavior of children in strange situations with strange adults for the briefest possible period of time.

– Bronfenbrenner (1979, p. 19)

The above passage, written by a psychologist versed in young children's development in ecological contexts, is a clear reflection of the spirit behind the regular education initiative (REI) and the contributions to this volume. For all children in general, and for preschool-age children in particular, our aim as psychologists should be to understand children's interactions with familiar adults in *natural* settings over the longest periods of time possible. With specific reference to intervention with very young children, Dunst (1986) asserted that one measure of a successful preschool program is the extent to which it employs naturalistic strategies that use the "least intrusive method feasible . . . and use these strategies wherever the opportunity occurs to teach a child" (p. 4).

As school systems address issues related to program development for preschool-age children in response to recent federal legislation (Public Law 99-457), increased attention is focused on how best to create frequent opportunities for teaching children who are so young. Although the preschool portion of the new law echoes the earlier provisions of PL 94-142 with respect to least restrictive environment (LRE), free and appropriate public education, multidisciplinary and nondiscriminatory assessment, and due process, a major departure from PL 94-142 is that traditional diagnostic labels do not have to be applied for a child to receive services (House of Representatives, 1986). Thus, the law helps to set the stage for avoiding negative consequences associated with labeling and special education placement. Other positive changes in the legislation for preschool-age children are that instruction of parents is written into the new law as an allowable cost, and variations in length of day and service model (home-based, center-based, combinations thereof) are more explicit. Thus, the new law clearly emphasizes the importance of family influences on young children's development during the preschool years and the need for flexibility when developing service delivery options.

Language and communication skills are an important focus of program development for preschool children and their families. Difficulties with the acquisition and use of language are associated with most types of developmental disabilities, including autism, cerebral palsy, hearing impairment, and mental retardation (Roberts & Crais, 1989), and theoretical notions underscore the mutual influences of social, motor, and cognitive development on young children's efforts to communicate (McLean & Snyder-McLean, 1978). In addition, prevalence data from the U.S. Department of Education (1986) indicate that of the 183,021 children aged 3-5 years who received services under PL 94-142 in 1984-1985, 70% were classified as having a speech or language impairment as their primary handicapping condition (cited in Roberts & Crais, 1989, p. 340). Thus, because language develops concurrently with other types of learning, is the basis for other learning, and is an area of deficit associated with numerous developmental disabilities, children served in compliance with PL 99-457 likely will have language and communication needs.

Perusal of the school psychology literature indicates growing recognition of the importance of communication disorders and the complexity of issues associated with their etiology, assessment, and treatment (Telzrow, 1989). We have taken a circumscribed focus for the present discussion, guided by strongly supported affirmations that the development of preschool programs should be based on principles of (a) normalization and (b) regular education (Biklen, 1988; Dunst, 1986; Fenrick, Pearson, & Peplenjak, 1984; Fine & Asch, 1988). Too often in the public schools, however, a need for language intervention is translated into a referral for "speech difficulties" that is responded to within a traditional "refer-test–place" paradigm. The use of such a paradigm with very young children is not only inefficient, but highly inappropriate, because natural opportunities for pragmatic language development abound in these children's daily environments, and extensive empirical support exists for teaching language to young children in natural communication environments (Halle, Alpert, & Anderson, 1984; Rogers-Warren & Warren, 1984; Warren & Kaiser, 1988).

With language intervention as a mechanism for conceptualizing the REI at the preschool level, the primary purpose of this chapter is to provide an empirical and practical rationale for naturalistic instruction in communication skills within preschool classroom settings. To achieve this goal, the chapter is divided into three major sections. First, evidence is presented that supports the movement toward increased use of naturalistic strategies for teaching oral language to children in general and preschool-age children in particular. This section is followed by a discussion of the essential components of naturalistic methods of oral language instruction and how these components can be implemented. Finally, implications of the information are derived for the practice of school psychology at the preschool level.

We introduce the term *communication competence* in addition to *language skills* to emphasize (a) the importance of communication as the desired outcome of intervention, with language skills serving as the mechanism for attaining that outcome (Holdgrafer & Dunst, 1986; Warren & Kaiser, 1988) and (b) the importance of enhancing children's sense of control in their daily experiences in the classroom. The chapter is guided strongly by the concept of competence, defined by Friedman and Vietze (1972) as "the ability to effect change in the environment and to learn that certain aspects of the environment are controllable" (p. 318). The chapter does not encompass guidelines for in-depth assessment of communication skills, although the importance of such assessments is recognized explicitly at the outset: See Kaiser, Alpert, and Warren (1988), Roberts and Crais (1989), Telzrow (1989), and Witt, Elliott, Gresham, and Kramer (1989) for more detail on this topic.

THE MOVEMENT TOWARD INTERVENTIONS IN NATURAL ENVIRONMENTS

Most efforts to teach language behaviors have used operant technology or diagnostic/prescriptive techniques focused primarily on the form and structure of language (Warren & Kaiser, 1988).

Efforts at applying operant technology have been described as "didactic" or "directive" in format, the primary features being the use of massed training trials; one-to-one structured, adult-controlled training sessions; emphasis on precision and specificity of procedures; and incorporation of a high degree of differential reinforcement. Training typically occurs in a therapy room outside the child's classroom and is directed at teaching articulation (e.g., *r* sound), vocabulary (e.g., *rabbit*), or syntax (e.g., "the rabbit is running").

The findings from studies employing an operant approach have had promising results, although there are inherent problems that make attainment and generalization of communicative competence difficult to achieve (Warren & Kaiser, 1988). To meet these difficulties it is necessary to (a) avoid overemphasis on structure that produces a corresponding lack of emphasis on normal function (Spradlin & Siegel, 1982), (b) create and maintain a high degree of attention and interest on the part of the students (Bricker & Carlson, 1981), (c) maintain a communicative match with the children (Warren & Kaiser, 1988), (d) teach the children to initiate language expression independently of specific adult cues (Charlop, Schreibman, & Thibodeau, 1985; Hale, 1987), and (e) avoid training that bears little resemblance to conditions in the natural environment (Fey, 1986). These problems also exist in traditional, diagnostic/prescriptive approaches that do not necessarily utilize the principles of applied behavioral analysis.

Despite the limitations of directed and diagnostic/prescriptive approaches to language instruction, there are specific situations in which they are most appropriate (Duchan, 1986). Directed training may be necessary, for example, for establishing initial language skills in children who require numerous training trials, for rapid training in motor and vocal imitation, and for establishing primary linguistic rules such as those for pluralization and verb tenses. Nevertheless, the features of didactic training that encourage acquisition of the above skills (e.g., stimulus control) actually may stand in the way of generalized, functional language development (Warren & Kaiser, 1988).

In an attempt to promote generalization and practical use of language, researchers have begun to investigate more "interactive" or "natural" methods for teaching language, including transactional teaching (McLean & Snyder-McLean, 1978), milieu teaching (Hart & Rogers-Warren, 1978), conversational teaching (MacDonald, 1985), child-oriented teaching (Fey, 1986), pragmatic intervention (Duchan, 1986), the developmental interactive approach (Bricker & Carlson, 1981), and unobtrusive training (Wulz, Meyers, Klein, Hall, & Waldo, 1982). These teaching approaches are characterized by the use of (a) dispersed training trials, (b) attempts to follow the children's attentional leads while teaching through normal conversational interchanges, and (c) an orientation toward teaching the form and content of language in the context of normal use (Warren & Kaiser, 1988). More specific techniques include *incidental teaching* (Hart & Risley, 1980), by which children's initiations of language create incidences for teaching; *time delay* (Halle, Marshall, & Spradlin, 1979), by which delays in the schedule or the granting of requests are introduced to encourage language; and *mand-model* (Rogers-Warren & Warren, 1984), which uses focused requests and modeling strategies. To illustrate important differences among diagnostic/prescriptive, directed operant/behavioral, and naturalistic teaching strategies, summary information is presented in Table 1.

Appropriateness of Naturalistic Teaching with Young Children

Similarities among various naturalistic approaches reflect considerable convergence of behavioral and developmental theory and research. Behaviorists have had an interest in naturalistic approaches because of their attempts to obtain generalization; and developmentalists increasingly have been applying recent theory and research with normal children to disordered children. Thus, the use of

TABLE 1
Differences Among Diagnostic/Prescriptive, Directed Operant/Behavioral, and Naturalistic Teaching Approaches

Dimension	Diagnostic/ Prescriptive	Directed Operant/ Behavioral	Naturalistic
Site of instruction	Outside regular classroom	Outside regular classroom	In regular classroom
Instructor	Speech and language teacher	Speech and language teacher	Regular classroom teacher
Teaching materials	Pictures and objects	Pictures and objects	Objects in use
Consequences for language use	Praise, correctness Attention from adults	Praise, correctness Attention from adults	Attention from adults and peers; obtaining needed materials; participation in social-verbal interactions
Focus	Acquisition of form, correct structures	Acquisition of form, correct structures	Acquisition, maintenance, and generalization of communicative function; form is secondary
Opportunities for language usage	Many to respond but few to initiate	Many to respond but few to initiate	Many to initiate and respond, although child may need to be prompted

Note. The site of instruction for diagnostic/prescriptive and directed operant/behavioral approaches may also be the regular classroom, although training often takes place outside the classroom.

naturalistic promotion of communicative competence is consistent with Paget's (1988) call for more interplay between applied behavioral analysis and developmental psychology when developing early intervention programs.

From a behavioral vantage point, naturalistic teaching incorporates shaping, prompting, differential reinforcement, and imitation procedures. It also utilizes approaches shown to be effective in facilitating generalization, such as "programming common stimuli" and "multiple exemplars" (Stokes & Baer, 1977; Stremel-Campbell & Campbell, 1985), and instruction in the contexts in which cues are similar or identical to those in typical conversations (Hart, 1985). From a developmental viewpoint, several elements that are assumed to be critical for language learning are implicit in naturalistic teaching. The trainer follows the children's leads and teaches to their interest and intentions (Schachter, 1979), establishes contiguity between the children's attention to an event and its linguistic representation (Hoff-Ginsberg & Shatz, 1982), and selects appropriate targets slightly in advance of the children's productive competence, thus applying the Piagetian principle of "moderate novelty" (Piaget & Inhelder, 1969). Given this match with important developmental principles, it comes as no surprise that this type of teaching has been characterized as resembling the teaching that occurs naturally in prelinguistic and linguistic interactions between mothers and their infants or toddlers (Fey, 1986; Martlew, 1988).

Effectiveness of Naturalistic Teaching with Young Children

Warren and Kaiser (1988) provide a cogent analysis of the effectiveness of naturalistic teaching methods. First, the effects on specific language responses have been consistently strong and immediate across a range of *subject populations* (e.g., preschool disadvantaged, language-delayed, mentally retarded, and adolescent autistic); *experimenter populations* (e.g., teachers, parents, and institutional staff); and *language responses* (e.g., labels, adjectives, general requests, one- and two-word utterances, yes/no responses, compound sentences, specific requests). Second, most studies have reported increases in both frequency of initiation and responsiveness, as well as linguistic aspects of language use, such as complexity and vocabulary size. Third, there is evidence of generalization across settings in each study in which this type of generalization was assessed. Research with young children with autism has not shown the same degree of generalizability as has occurred with other populations, although efficacy data with these populations are accumulating (Holdgrafer & Dunst, 1986). For the most part, however, the effects of naturalistic teaching of language appear to be most effectively generalized with children who have had limited language opportunities and with children with language delays.

An understanding of the range of outcome variables employed in effectiveness studies provides additional empirical support for naturalistic teaching strategies. Gains in language functions have included requesting (Hart & Risley, 1968), imitating and responding to questions (Rogers-Warren & Warren, 1984), affirming and negating (Neef, Walters, & Egel, 1984), and commenting/directing (Hart & Risley, 1982). Moreover, maintenance data reported by Hart and Risley (1974), Rogers-Warren and Warren (1984), and Warren, McQuarter, and Rogers-Warren (1984) indicate an ability on the part of the subjects to continue applying strategies after training is discontinued.

Since early studies conducted by Hart and Risley (1968, 1974, 1975, 1980), in which individual teaching strategies produced substantial gains in the language of inner-city preschoolers, incidental teaching has been modified in various ways for application with children who are low initiators of language. The mand-model technique has been used with socially isolated, language-delayed preschool children (Rogers-Warren & Warren, 1984; Warren et al., 1984); and Halle, Baer, and Spradlin (1981) used the time delay procedure to teach specific requesting strategies to six developmentally delayed preschool children. In addition, prekindergarten teachers with limited training in language intervention have demonstrated successful use of sample, mand, and delay techniques to enhance the skills of children with language delays in group settings (Pearson, Pearson, Fenrick, & Greene, 1988). These results followed provocative findings indicating that the language used by children with developmental delays was essentially the same in mainstream and segregated classrooms (Fenrick, Pearson, & Peplenjak, 1984). Because segregated settings did not elicit more mature language than did mainstream settings, the Fenrick et al. (1984) findings raise questions about the effectiveness of segregated environments for language instruction and lend substantial support to the need to ensure that language learning and use occur while children with delays are in mainstream settings.

IMPLEMENTATION OF NATURALISTIC TEACHING STRATEGIES

The collective evidence supporting the effectiveness of naturalistic teaching holds implications for the implementation of these teaching techniques in public school classrooms for preschool-age children. Following is a discussion of the major components of naturalistic teaching, an illustration of how to implement them in a preschool classroom, and limitations of these teaching strategies.

Components of Naturalistic Teaching

By examining four components of naturalistic teaching identified by Hart (1985), it becomes clear that naturalistic teaching illustrates what Prutting (1983) termed a flexible yet systematic arrangement of stimuli within an ongoing stream of environment–behavior interactions. Generally speaking, the four component activities involve (a) *arranging the environment* to increase the likelihood that the children will initiate speech to the adult and will thus provide incidences for teaching; (b) *selecting language targets* appropriate to the children's skill levels and interests and to the environment; (c) *responding to the children's initiations* with requests for elaborate language resembling the targeted forms; and (d) *reinforcing* the children's attempts at communication and use of specific forms with attention and access to the objects, actions, or events in which the child has expressed an interest.

Naturalistic teaching episodes are brief, positive, and oriented toward communication rather than toward language teaching per se. Communication or language targets are preselected for teaching, and a sequence of increasingly specific prompts is employed to ensure the children's use of the targets. Most importantly, the consequences for children's talking are functional ones and include control of the environment, continued interaction with the adult, and the realization of their communicative intentions (Warren & Kaiser, 1988).

A Model to Promote Communication Competence

A model described by Holdgrafer (1987) for promoting communication competence in young children provides a framework for conceptualizing the essential components of naturalistic teaching. The model is based on three basic premises:

1. Communication *competence* and *conversation* in the course of everyday events provide the context in which children learn language skills.

2. Children can be active participants in the language-learning process.

3. An interaction of adult teaching and child learning strategies is important for language growth.

Holdgrafer's model is comprised of two major components: *Initiation strategies* and *participation strategies*. Initiation strategies are aimed toward increasing the probability that the children will be motivated to take some action that can be responded to by the teacher as an attempt to initiate a conversation. Participation strategies are aimed at increasing the length of an interaction beyond a simple one-turn sequence and are based on the premise that children need to stay in conversations so as to learn and to use language.

Initiation strategies. Holdgrafer described three specific initiation strategies. The first strategy, providing an *engaging environment*, simply means that the environment is arranged to provide a variety of materials and activities with which a young child can become involved in a playful way. The remaining strategies, *creating disorder* in the child's normal routines and *creating change* in the normal routines, suggest that requests and comments initiated by a child are likely to occur when there are deviations in and changes from familiar routines. Such deviations may take the form of disorder (i.e., problems for the child to solve through communicative means such as taped-together scissors, dried-up pens, lack of utensils at mealtime) or *change* (i.e., unexpected events that provide new information, such as a novel food or drink at snack time or a surprise object in the child's coat pocket) (Holdgrafer, 1987).

Participation strategies. Two methods for encouraging participation in communication exchanges described by Holdgrafer (1987) are *elaborated repetitions* and *requests for elaboration*. When providing an elaborated repetition, the teacher (or peer) attaches words to a child's actions; expands what the child has said while providing more descriptive, grammatically well-formed language; or extends some aspect of the child's meaning by contributing new, but relevant information. When requesting more elaborate language, the teacher provides an explicit prompt for the child to elaborate on the original initiation behavior. These prompts may be verbal questions, comments, or nonverbal cues from facial expressions and gestures. McLean and Snyder-McLean (1978) suggest that expansions and extensions are most useful when (a) the child is already producing at least two-word utterances that afford grammatical expanding, (b) the expansion includes structures that the child is ready to begin producing, and (c) the expansion remains within the child's receptive competence. In addition, a technique termed a *recast sentence* is useful when teaching the structure of verb forms. Thus, a statement such as "The dog ran" might be recast as "The dog did run, didn't he?" (Nelson, 1977).

An Illustration of Naturalistic Teaching Methods

To illustrate the four components of naturalisic teaching described earlier and the procedures put forth by Holdgrafer (1987), samples of teacher–pupil interaction strategies are illustrated in the case below. The context for teaching is described, followed by a brief series of communication exchanges in the classroom and a summary of evaluation data.

Gabriel ("Gabe") is a 3½-year-old boy who recently has enrolled in a preschool program in the public school system. His family has participated in an early-intervention program from the time Gabe was 10 months of age and began having seizures. The seizure disorder has been controlled with medication for the past 2 years.

Gabe and his family participated in an evaluation and program-planning day prior to enrollment in a public school classroom. His parents and members of the multidisciplinary team discussed Gabe's strengths and need areas. Gabe was described by his parents as an independent child who enjoyed playing by himself or beside other children, completed tasks

well, and took pride in doing things by himself. Furthermore, his motor and self-care skills were areas of strength. The parents' concerns were focused on Gabe's communication skills, because he was communicating with one-word utterances and only in response to adult-initiated questions or comments. The assessment team, parents, and teacher developed a plan to increase Gabe's communication skills in the context of social interactions. The speech therapist served in a consultative role to the parents, psychologist, and the classroom staff to emphasize how Gabe could learn to communicate in familiar social exchanges and routines (rather than in the therapy room), with a variety of partners (e.g., peers, teachers' aide, parents), about familiar activities, in connection with the least intrusive teaching strategies possible.

An educational plan was developed from three broad communication goals: to increase the linguistic complexity of utterances, the frequency of initiations of interactions with peers and adults, and the length of participation (number of turns) in conversational exchanges.

Communication intervention with Gabe began with arrangement of the environment to maximize his active participation in language learning by encouraging his engagement with people and materials and promoting spontaneous communication. The environment included the following features:

1. A classroom of 12 3- to 5-year-old children, half of whom were nonhandicapped peers. This arrangement provided peer models for language and other social skills.

2. Duplicate materials and toys available to encourage parallel play and imitation.

3. A class schedule that allowed opportunities during the day for children to play in kitchen/housekeeping areas, where the content and function of language were readily apparent (putting baby to bed, cooking dinner, etc.).

4. Opportunities for choices (activities, partners, snacks) given to the children.

5. Small deviations made in daily routines to create a need or desire for Gabe to comment or request.

Three children, including Gabe, have chosen the kitchen area in which to play. Kitchen materials are available to the children to encourage them to become engaged in the activity. The silverware is placed in a clear container on a shelf, visible, but just out of reach. Gabe's favorite kitchen item, the pitcher, is placed on the refrigerator, where only the taller children can reach it. Thus, the teacher has created some "disorder" in the environment to increase the probability of speech. The three children come in and immediately become involved in some activity. One child (Jenny) places a doll in a highchair and begins giving it a bottle. Another (Sarah) plays with pots, pans, and spoons at the stove. Gabe takes the stacks of dishes and begins to set the table.

Aide: (Sitting at table with Jenny, who is feeding the doll) "It must be time to eat." (SD or prompt to Sarah)

Sarah: (At stove) "I'm cooking dinner. What do you want?"
(SD or prompt to Gabe)

Gabe: (To Sarah) "French fries."

Aide: (To Gabe) "Tell Sarah, I want french fries."
(A request for elaboration and SR for response from Gabe)

Gabe: (To Sarah) "Want french fries."

Sarah: (Pretending to put french fries on a plate) "O.K. Here they are."
(SR for response from Gabe)

Gabe: Passes out cups, then looks for pitcher. He tries to reach it, goes and taps the teacher, and points to the pitcher.

Aide: Looks in direction of his point, then using delay technique, holds pitcher in front of Gabe with an expectant look (raised eyebrows, eye contact).
SD or prompt for Gabe

Gabe: (To aide) "Pitcher."

Aide: (To Gabe) "Do you want the pitcher?"
(a request for elaboration and SD or prompt to Gabe)

Gabe: (To Aide) "Want pitcher."

Aide: Gives pitcher to Gabe.

Sarah: (To Gabe) "Gabe, I want milk to drink."
(SD or prompt to Gabe)

Gabe: (While pouring) "Milk."

Aide: (Modeling for Gabe, as he pours) "Pour milk in the cup."
(An elaborated repetition)

Gabe: "Milk in cup."

Jenny: (To Gabe) "Baby needs more milk."
(SD or prompt to Gabe)

Gabe: (To Jenny) "Open."

Aide: (As Jenny opens bottle) "Open the bottle."
(An elaborated repetition and SR for response from Gabe)

Gabe: (As he pours milk in bottle) "Milk in bottle."

Aide: (To Gabe) "You're pouring milk in the bottle."
(An elaborated repetition and SR for response from Gabe)

This sequence continues as the aide expands Gabe's utterances with additional syntactic or semantic information; encourages topic maintenance; contributes new information to extend his meaning; provides nonverbal, visual prompts (i.e., delay techniques); and uses peers to assist in communicative exchanges. Similar exchanges take place in the context of other activities in the classroom. Gabe's mother and father visit the classroom to contribute information regarding interaction strategies used at home and to learn strategies used in the classroom. The focus of parent involvement is threefold: first, learning to provide multiple exemplars of language productions (Stokes & Baer, 1977) in the context of everyday routines (e.g., eating, getting dressed, riding in the car); second, learning to create "disorder" and change in the home environment; and third, prompting more elaborate language with delay techniques.

Evaluation data from a 15-minute observation during free play the following week revealed substantial progress toward attainment of the three communication goals desired for Gabe. Frequency counts indicated an increase in the complexity of utterances (still in response to adult prompts) from one to three words; an increase in the frequency of initiations (still using one-word utterances) from 0 to 3; and an increase in the number of turns taken (with prompts provided) from one to five turns. From this information, it was determined that appropriate goals would be (a) to maintain the complexity of his self-initiated utterances with fewer adult prompts and (b) to increase the complexity of self-initiated utterances with peer prompts. Thus, a schedule was established to fade the prompts provided by the teacher's aide and begin training one of Gabe's peers to increase the number of prompts.

Guidelines for Implementation, Maintenance, and Generalization

To supplement the concepts discussed and illustrated above, additional guidelines or heuristics for implementing intervention plans must be considered. Although reviewed briefly for purposes of this discussion, these guidelines are discussed in more detail by Roberts and Crais (1989).

Intervening at appropriate levels. It is important to meet children at their levels of functioning and shape responses to the next higher skill level. Rather than prompt children who only produce nonverbal vocalizations to use entire words, for example, a teacher would use the concept of shaping to guide them to make increasingly closer approximations of the word and reinforce them for any attempts at communication. In addition, vocalization may be paired with gestures (e.g., head nod, hand signal) and encouraged across communication intents (e.g., re-

questing an object and protesting not getting it).

Choosing appropriate communication goals. The selection of appropriate goals is essential to effective implementation of naturalistic teaching strategies. Frequently occurring behaviors that need modification, and desired but nonexisting behaviors that have opportunities for practice and reinforcement, are appropriate targets. In addition, the selection of communication goals should be determined by factors such as (a) which goal will have the largest effect on other skills; (b) what goal will be most motivating for the child; (c) what skills are being targeted by other professionals; (d) what goals are most important to the caregivers; and (e) what goals are most important, given the social contexts in which the child functions. Selection of goals is a multicomponent process that sets the stage for success (or failure) of naturalistic teaching methods with young children.

Following the child's interests. A major tenet of naturalistic teaching is following the child's interest in selecting communication targets. An essential component of this process is the ability of the teacher to recognize and respond to individual children's specific ways of initiating communication. Prior to vocalizations, for example, some children who have multiple impairments may simply move their heads or direct their eye gaze in a certain direction to indicate interest. Learning *not* to preempt children's initiations requires training for educators who may be conditioned to anticipate children's needs and meet them noncontingently (Dunst, 1981). An illustration of the need for training is provided by Halle, Baer, and Spradlin (1981), who list nine requisite conditions for implementing a delay procedure, none of which are difficult to learn as single behaviors (e.g., visual prompting, raising eyebrows, kneeling close to child). The challenge arises when combining the nine steps into an appropriate tempo and rhythm to provide a conversational exchange while *following the lead* of a child with a language impairment.

Arranging environmental contingencies. A major tenet of naturalistic teaching is that the environment should facilitate a child's participation in activities. With this tenet, naturalistic teaching shifts the responsibility for failures of generalization from the child to the adults in caregiving roles, who must arrange environmental contingencies in such a way that antecedent conditions encourage children's initiation of language and consequent conditions increase the likelihood of continued responding. Halle (1985) describes several antecedent procedures as (a) withholding desired objects or events until requested, (b) strategically locating needed materials in sight but out of reach, (c) delaying upcoming steps in a schedule, waiting for the child to request it verbally, and (d) asking the child to name events or materials relevant in the current context. Other antecedent procedures from the applied behavior analysis literature are important to consider when generalization across settings, time, people, or tasks is desired. With the planned use of common antecedent stimuli (Stokes & Baer, 1977), for example the antecedent stimuli used during classroom interactions can be matched systematically with contingencies in the home environment (and other classrooms).

Although the antecedent procedures previously described facilitate maintenance, continued performance by children is mostly a function of the consequences delivered for behavior. Naturalistic teaching methods capitalize on what Stokes and Baer (1977) term "natural maintaining contingencies" (e.g., attention, participation in conversations, obtaining needed materials). Nevertheless, teachers and school psychologists should bear in mind that naturally occurring schedules of reinforcement may need to be changed from continuous to intermittent to implement the principle of "indiscriminable contingencies" (Stokes & Baer, 1977) and promote maintenance. In addition to maintenance of intervention effects, naturalistic teaching strategies provide a good mechanism for what Wacker and Berg (1988) term "spread of effects," that is, the reinforcement of behaviors other than those directly treated. Language intervention that takes place in the context of naturally occurring interactions and communication, for example, maximizes the reinforcement of important nonverbal communicative behaviors such as eye contact and turn taking.

LIMITATIONS OF NATURALISTIC TEACHING

Despite substantial evidence regarding its effectiveness, naturalistic teaching is not without limitations as an instructional strategy. Some very specific linguistic forms, such as grammatical morphemes (e.g., verb copulas, plurals, tense markers) may be difficult and inefficient to train naturalistically. Warren and Kaiser (1988) suggest these forms may best be taught didactically first, with naturalistic teaching used to facilitate maintenance and generalization. Furthermore, children with severe impairments with limited response repertoires and passive learning and interaction styles may exhibit too little behavior, language or otherwise. Such a set of circumstances may provide too few opportunities for teaching and learning to occur (Baer, 1981; Bricker & Carlson, 1981; Carr & Kologinsky, 1983; Duchan, 1986). Nevertheless, Conant, Budoff, Hecht, and Morse (1984) caution teachers and other professionals not to drop back to the use of didactic instruction because they simply cannnot wait for sufficient teaching incidents to occur naturally. In the same vein, Dunst (1986) asserts that most children, including those with severe, multiple impairments, frequently attempt to communicate, albeit nonverbally. He encourages professionals to "read" children's behavior carefully so as to anticipate and respond to their current ways of communicating. Practical illustrations of the manner in which communicative intentions are expressed in multiply impaired children are presented in Goldberg (1977), Dunst (1981), and Dunst and Wortman-Lowe (1986). Readers are encouraged to supplement this chapter with such readings.

The limitations of naturalistic teaching suggest the need to develop models for combining naturalistic teaching of language with more directive instructional strategies. On the basis of a comparison between naturalistic and directive approaches, Cole and Dale (1986) suggest that a combined approach may prove superior to either approach used separately. Conant et al. (1984) endorse a combination of adult-directed games, in which adult-directed approaches are used to instruct specific language skills (e.g., vocabulary and syntax), and a focus on the functional uses of these skills. Computer-assisted instruction also holds considerable promise for operationalizing creative combinations of adult- and child-directed teaching methods in the classroom (Fazio & Rieth, 1986; Robinson, 1986). Empirical investigations are needed to evaluate the efficacy of these combined approaches and to assess the effectiveness of multiple-component models that encompass what Warren and Kaiser (1988) term "language acquisition, generalization, and competence within a sequential learning paradigm" (p. 99).

IMPLICATIONS FOR SCHOOL PSYCHOLOGY PRACTICE

Numerous implications for the provision of services by school psychologists at the preschool level can be drawn from the information in this chapter.

1. The delivery of services to young children with language impairments offers school psychologists an opportunity to expand their consultation role through the provision of systematic consultative services to teachers in preschool classrooms. A flexible and responsive consultation role serves both direct and indirect functions by assisting teachers in interacting comfortably and effectively with children with language delays and reducing the number of children referred for ancillary services. Before implementing naturalistic teaching strategies, however, it is important to evaluate teachers' beliefs concerning these approaches (Witt, Martens, & Elliott, 1984). Wacker and Berg (1988) point out that establishing the acceptability of intervention is as important at the beginning of the treatment process as the use of normally available materials and staff are to its continuation.

2. The concept of competence extends beyond a focus on the child to encompass a focus on the adult. With a sense of competence associated with a belief that certain aspects of the environment are controllable (Friedman & Vietze, 1972), competent professionals are those who understand that classroom contingencies governing behavior in preschool-age children can be established in such a way that functional skills in communication are taught and reinforced.

3. Caregivers in the home are valuable and necessary resources for children in acquiring and maintaining communications skills and in generalizing their skills across settings. Visits to the home by school psychologists, discussions with parents about parent–child interactions, and visits to the classroom by parents and other caregivers are vital to the exchange of information regarding interaction strategies and setting variables that promote communication competence for specific children. Because of the risks associated with intrusiveness from professionals into family life (Dunst, Trivette, & Deal, 1988), steps must be taken to communicate with parents and other family members in a way that is respectful of their routines (Rainforth & Salisbury, 1988) and consistent with the principle of "least intrusive parent involvement" recently put forward by Simeonsson and Bailey (in press). School psychologists who are versed in instructional strategies designed to be unobtrusive in the classroom will be of the "right mind" to assist parents in the design of such strategies at home.

4. Systematic efforts need to be directed toward the empirical validation of pragmatic language interventions in public school-based preschool classrooms and training of family members (including siblings) in these interventions. The model

put forward in this chapter helps to provide a context for intervention focused on the pragmatic intentions underlying a child's acts and utterances. Moreover, a recent investigation into the utility of participant observation methodology as a means of assessing social-communication competence (Salisbury, Britzman, & Kang, 1989) provides preliminary validation of qualitative research methods in public school-based preschool classrooms. With a sound theoretical foundation and the beginnings of a workable methodology, research into the pragmatics of young children's language provides an arena for the use of innovative assessment and consultative methodologies useful to researchers and practitioners.

5. Knowledge of typical language development in preschool children and the deviations that occur with some children constitute an essential component of school psychologists' knowledge for functioning effectively at the preschool level.

6. Skills in combining naturalistic approaches with more directive methods are necessary for promoting communication competence in children who represent a wide array of articulation, vocabulary, and syntactical difficulties.

7. Strategies for training classroom peers in the skills of naturalistic communication exchanges are vital to the maintenance of communication skills in children who experience language deficits. School psychologists are in a good position to assist preschool teachers in developing workable peer-training strategies in their classrooms.

8. The interactive influence of language, cognitive, social, and motor development in children creates the need for exchange of information and application of skills in an interdisciplinary context. Such a context of communication across disciplines is another dimension to the notion of ecological service delivery (Bailey, 1989), and it challenges professionals not only to value collaborative working relationships but to take the necessary actions to operationalize them.

9. A specific and organized training agenda is needed to provide school psychologists opportunities to obtain skills in child-directed communication when interacting with young exceptional children who experience language or communication difficulties. Participation in preservice and inservice activities and experience in preschool classrooms are necessary steps toward operationalizing such a training agenda.

SUMMARY AND CONCLUSIONS

In this chapter, an empirical and practical rationale was provided for the use of naturalistic instruction of language and communication with very young children. The appropriateness and effectiveness of such instruction with young children were described, followed by conceptual and methodological issues relative to implementation strategies and implications for the practice of school psychology. The need to investigate the efficacy of models that combine child- and adult-directed strategies also was put forward.

In addition to these proximate goals, a more distal goal of the chapter was to utilize the focus on naturalistic teaching of communication skills as a catalyst for preschool program development in general. The growing empirical base supporting naturalistic strategies to promote communication competence with preschool-age children should encourage research investigations into the efficacy of such strategies for promoting cognitive, motor, and self-care skills. Whether preschool services are offered in public schools or through contractual arrangements with Head Start and day-care centers (Bagnato, Kontos, & Neisworth, 1987), school psychologists and other school personnel must be mindful of current developments and attend to the creation of new models of service delivery. As asserted by Dunst (1988), the appropriate direction for policy development is "bottom up" rather than "top down"; that is, traditional models used with school-age children must not be extended downward to preschool-age children. Thus, what we know from developmental and behavioral theory and research with young children is not only consistent with, but could serve as a *guide* to, implementation of the regular education initiative in public school systems. As stated approximately 5 years ago (Paget, 1985),

> preschool services provide fertile ground for a dramatic recasting of professional roles in the schools. Indeed, movement at the preschool level toward successful implementation of ecological services could have constructive reverberations at other levels of service delivery in schools (pp. 21-22).

REFERENCES

Baer, D. M. (1981). The nature of intervention research. In R. L. Schiefelbusch & D. D. Bricker (Eds.), *Early language: Acquisition and intervention* (pp. 559-574). Baltimore: University Park Press.

Bagnato, S. J., Kontos, S., & Neisworth, J. T. (1987). Integrated day care as special education: Profiles of programs and children. *Topics in Early Childhood Special Education, 7*, 28-39.

Bailey, D. B. (1989, March). *Personnel preparation needs in early intervention*. Invited presentation to the Leadership Conference in Early Intervention, Columbia, SC.

Biklen, D. (1988). The myth of clinical judgment. *Journal of Social Issues, 44*, 127-140.

Bricker, D., & Carlson, L. (1981). Issues in early language intervention. In R. L. Schiefelbusch & D. D. Bricker (Eds.), *Early language: Acquisition and intervention* (pp. 477-516). Baltimore: University Park Press.

Bronfenbrenner, U. (1979). *The ecology of human development: Experiments by nature and design.* Cambridge, MA: Harvard University Press.

Carr, E. G., & Kologinsky, E. (1983). Acquisition of sign language by autistic children: Spontaneity and generalization effects. *Journal of Applied Behavior Analysis, 16*, 297-314.

Charlop, M. H., Schreibman, L., & Thibodeau, M. G. (1985). Increasing spontaneous verbal responding in autistic children using a time delay procedure. *Journal of Applied Behavior Analysis, 18*, 153-166.

Cole, K., & Dale, P. (1986). Direct language instruction and interactive language instruction with language delayed preschool children: A comparison study. *Journal of Speech and Hearing Research, 28*, 205-217.

Conant, S., Budoff, M., Hecht, D., & Morse, R. (1984). Language intervention: A pragmatic approach. *Journal of Autism and Developmental Disorders, 14*, 301-317.

Duchan, J. F. (1986). Language intervention through sensemaking and fine tuning. In R. L. Schiefelbusch (Ed.), *Language competence: Assessment and intervention* (pp. 187-212). San Diego: College Hill.

Dunst, C. J. (1981). *Infant learning.* Hingham, MA: Teaching Resources.

Dunst, C. J. (1986, March). *The qualities of high quality preschool programs.* Keynote presentation at the First Annual Oregon Early Intervention Conference, Salem, OR,

Dunst, C. J. (1988, August). *Providing support to families in early intervention programs.* Keynote address. Summer Preschool Institute sponsored by Northern Arizona University, Arizona State Department of Education, and Arizona Association of School Psychologists, Flagstaff.

Dunst, C. J., Trivette, C. M., & Deal, A. (1988). *Enabling and empowering families.* Cambridge, MA: Brookline Books.

Dunst, C. J., & Wortman-Lowe, L. (1986). From reflex to symbol: Describing, explaining, and fostering communicative competence. *Augmentative and Alternative Communication, 2*, 11-16.

Fazio, B. B., & Rieth, H. J. (1986). Characteristics of preschool handicapped children's microcomputer use during free-choice periods. *Journal of the Division for Early Childhood, 10*, 247-254.

Fenrick, N., Pearson, A., & Peplenjak, J. (1984). The play, attending, and language of young handicapped children in integrated and segregated settings. *Journal of the Division for Early Childhood, 8*, 56-67.

Fey, M. (1986). *Language intervention with young children.* San Diego: College Hill.

Fine, M., & Asch, A. (1988). Disability beyond stigma: Social interaction, discrimination, and activism. *Journal of Social Issues, 44*, 3-21.

Friedman, S., & Vietze, P. (1972). The competent infant. *Peabody Journal of Education, 49*, 314-323.

Goldberg, S. (1977). Social competence in infancy: A model of parent-infant interaction. *Merrill-Palmer Quarterly, 23*, 163-177.

Halle, J. (1985). Enhancing social competence through language: An experimental analysis of a practical procedure for teachers. *Topics in Early Childhood Special Education, 4*, 77-92.

Halle, J. (1987). Teaching language in the natural environment to individuals with severe handicaps: An analysis of spontaneity. *Journal of the Association for Persons with Severe Handicaps, 12*, 28-37.

Halle, J., Alpert, C., & Anderson, S. (1984). Natural environment language assessment and intervention with severely impaired preschoolers. *Topics in Early Childhood Special Education, 4*, 36-56.

Halle, J. W., Baer, D. M., & Spradlin, J. E. (1981). Teachers' generalized use of delay as a stimulus control procedure to increase language in handicapped children. *Journal of Applied Behavior Analysis, 14*, 387-400.

Halle, J. W., Marshall, A. M., & Spradlin, J. E. (1979). Time delay: A technique to increase language use and facilitate generalization in retarded children. *Journal of Applied Behavior Analysis, 12*, 431-440.

Hart, B. (1985). Naturalistic language training strategies. In S. F. Warren & A. Rogers-Warren (Eds.), *Teaching functional language* (pp. 63-88). Austin, TX: Pro-Ed.

Hart, B., & Risley, T. R. (1968). Establishing the use of descriptive adjectives in the spontaneous speech of disadvantaged preschool children. *Journal of Applied Behavior Analysis, 1*, 109-120.

Hart, B., & Risley, T. R. (1974). Using preschool materials to modify the language of disadvantaged children. *Journal of Applied Behavior Analysis, 7*, 243-256.

Hart, B., & Risley, T. R. (1975). Incidental teaching of language in the preschool. *Journal of Applied Behavior Analysis, 8*, 411-420.

Hart, B., & Risley, T. R. (1980). In vivo language training: Unanticipated and general effects. *Journal of Applied Behavior Analysis, 12*, 407-432.

Hart, B., & Risley, T. R. (1982). *How to use incidental teaching for elaborating language.* Lawrence, KS: H & H Enterprises.

Hart, B., & Rogers-Warren, A. K. (1978). A milieu approach to teaching language. In R. L. Schiefelbusch (Ed.), *Language intervention strategies* (pp. 193-236). Baltimore: University Park Press.

Hoff-Ginsberg, E., & Shatz, M. N. (1982). Linguistic input and the child's acquisition of language: A critical review. *Psychological Bulletin, 92*, 3-26.

Holdgrafer, G. (1987). Getting children to talk: A model of natural adult teaching/child learning strategies for language. *Canadian Journal of Exceptional Children, 3*, 71-76.

Holdgrafer, G., & Dunst, C. (1986). Communicative competence: From research to practice. *Topics in Early Childhood Special Education, 6*, 1-22.

House of Representatives. (1986, September). *Report 99-860: Education of Handicapped Act Amendments of 1986.*

Kaiser, A. P., Alpert, C. L., & Warren, S. (1988). Language and communication disorders. In V. B. Van Hasselt, P. S. Strain, & M. Hersen (Eds.), *Handbook of developmental and physical disabilities* (pp. 395-422). Elmsford, NY: Pergamon.

Martlew, M. (1988). Children's oral and written language. In A. D. Pellegrini (Ed.), *Psychological bases for early education* (pp. 77-122). New York: Wiley.

MacDonald, J. D. (1985). Language through conversation: A model for intervention with language delayed persons. In S. F. Warren & A. K. Rogers-Warren (Eds.), *Teaching functional language* (pp. 89-122). Austin, TX: Pro-Ed.

McLean, J. E., & Snyder-McLean, L. (1978). *A transactional approach to early language training.* Columbus, OH: Merrill.

Neef, N. A., Walters, J., & Egel, A. L. (1984). Establishing generative yes/no responses in developmentally disabled children. *Journal of Applied Behavior Analysis, 17*, 453-460.

Nelson, K. E. (1977). Facilitating children's syntax acquisition. *Developmental Psychology, 13*, 101-107.

Paget, K. D. (1985). Preschool services in the schools: Issues and implications. *Special Services in the Schools, 1*, 3-25.

Paget, K. D. (1988). Early intervention: Infants, preschool children, and families. In J. C. Witt, S. N. Elliott, & F. Gresham (Eds.), *Handbook of behavior therapy in education* (pp. 569-600). New York: Plenum.

Pearson, M. F., Pearson, A., Fenrick, N., & Greene, D. (1988). The implementation of sample, mand, and delay techniques to enhance the language of delayed children in group settings. *Journal of the Division for Early Childhood, 12*, 342-348.

Piaget, J., & Inhelder, I. (1969). *The psychology of the child.* New York: Basic Books.

Prutting, C. (1983). Scientific inquiry and communicative disorders: An emerging paradigm across six decades. In T. Gallagher & C. Prutting (Eds.), *Pragmatic assessment and intervention issues in language* (pp. 247-266). San Diego: College Hill.

Rainforth, B., & Salisbury, C. L. (1988). Functional home programs: A model for therapists. *Topics in Early Childhood Special Education, 1*, 33-45.

Roberts, J. E., & Crais, E. R. (1989). Assessing communication skills. In D. B. Bailey & M. Wolery (Eds.), *Assessing infants and preschoolers with handicaps* (pp. 339-389). Columbus, OH: Merrill.

Robinson, L. (1986). Designing computer intervention for very young handicapped children. *Journal of the Division for Early Childhood, 10,* 209-215.

Rogers-Warren, A. K., & Warren, S. F. (1984). The social bases of language and communication in severely handicapped preschoolers. *Topics in Early Childhood Special Education, 4,* 57-73.

Salisbury, C. L., Britzman, D., & Kang, J. (1989). Using qualitative methods to assess the social communicative competence of young handicapped children. *Journal of Early Intervention, 13,* 153-164.

Schachter, F. F. (1979). *Everyday mother talk to toddlers: Early intervention.* New York: Academic.

Simeonsson, R. J., & Bailey, D. B. (in press). Family dimensions in early intervention. In S. J. Meisels & J. P. Shonkoff (Eds.), *Handbook of early childhood intervention.* Cambridge, MA: Cambridge University Press.

Spradlin, J., & Siegel, G. (1982). Language training in natural and clinical environments. *Journal of Speech and Hearing Disorders, 47,* 2-6.

Stokes, T. F., & Baer, D. M. (1977). An implicit technology of generalization. *Journal of Applied Behavior Analysis, 10,* 349-367.

Stremel-Campbell, K., & Campbell, C. R. (1985). Training techniques that may facilitate generalization. In S. F. Warren & A. K. Rogers-Warren (Eds.), *Teaching functional language* (pp. 251-288). Austin, TX: Pro-Ed.

Telzrow, C. (1989). Mini-series on communication disorders. *School Psychology Review, 18,* 440-441.

U.S. Department of Education, Office of Special Education and Rehabilitation Services. (1986). *Report submitted to the Subcommittee on Select Education of the U.S. House of Representatives.*

Wacker, D. P., & Berg, W. K. (1988). Behavioral habilitation of students with severe handicaps. In S. N. Elliott & F. M. Gresham (Eds.), *Handbook of behavior therapy in education* (pp. 719-737). New York: Plenum.

Warren, S., & Kaiser, A. P. (1988). Research in early language intervention. In S. L. Odom & M. B. Karnes (Eds.), *Early intervention for infants and children with handicaps* (pp. 89-108). Baltimore: Paul H. Brooks.

Warren, S. F., McQuarter, R. J., & Rogers-Warren, A. K. (1984). The effects of mands and models on the speech of unresponsive socially isolate children. *Journal of Speech and Hearing Disorders, 47,* 42-52.

Witt, J. C., Elliott, S. N., Gresham, F. M., & Kramer, J. J. (1989). *Assessment of special children.* Glenview, IL: Scott, Foresman.

Witt, J. C., Martens, B. K., & Elliott, S. N. (1984). Factors affecting teachers' judgement of the acceptability of behavioral interventions: Time involvement, behavior problem severity, and type of intervention. *Behavior Therapy, 15,* 204-209.

Wulz, S. V., Meyers, S. P., Klein, M. D., Hall, M. K., & Waldo, L. J. (1982). Unobtrusive training: A home-centered model for communication training. *Journal of the Association for the Severely Handicapped, 7,* 36-48.

Strategies to Promote Physical, Social, and Academic Integration in Mainstream Kindergarten Programs

Lynette K. Chandler
Southern Illinois University
at Carbondale

Education of children with handicaps in integrated or mainstream environments has received great impetus from Federal Legislation such as the Education for All Handicapped Children Act of 1975, the Rehabilitation Act of 1973, and the Education of the Handicapped Act Amendments of 1986. Integration presents a challenge to parents, educators, administrators, and school psychologists, as they must decide how best to meet the needs both of children with handicaps and normally developing children within an integrated educational setting (Spodek, Saracho, & Lee, 1984). This challenge is especially evident for practitioners who work with preschool-age children and children entering kindergarten programs. Few models are available to help practitioners develop and achieve integrated programs for young children (Odom & McEvoy, 1988; Safford & Rosen, 1981; Snell, 1987).

The purpose of this chapter is to provide information to help practitioners integrate young children with handicaps and developmental delays into regular education programs. The first section provides a historical overview concerning integration and the legislative decisions that form the foundation for this practice. This overview is followed by a discussion of the need to program for integration, supported by a brief review of research related to integration with kindergarten and preschool-age children. The next section describes the responsibilities associated with integration; it is followed by a discussion of strategies to facilitate integration. The chapter ends with a discussion of the changing roles and responsibilities of school psychologists who will work with young children in mainstream programs.

HISTORICAL OVERVIEW

Section 504 of the Rehabilitation Act of 1973 legislates federal commitment to persons with handicaps in the form of a civil rights statute. It was enacted to protect the rights of handicapped persons and to end discrimination on the basis of handicapping condition. In 1977 a final Section 504 regulation was issued for recipients of funds from the Department of Health, Education, and Welfare (HEW) including elementary schools and social service agencies (Department of Health, Education, and Welfare, 1978).

Several of the fundamental requirements of Section 504 relate to integration. These requirements specify that (a) no handicapped child will be excluded from public education because of a handicapping condition, (b) every handicapped child is entitled to a free and appropriate education, and (c) handicapped children must not be segregated in public schools; they must be educated with nonhandicapped students to the maximum extent appropriate while meeting their needs

(Department of Health, Education, and Welfare, 1978).

In 1975 President Ford signed Public Law 94-142, the Education for All Handicapped Children Act. This landmark legislation gave states the responsibility, and authorized funding, to provide a free and appropriate education to children with handicaps from ages 3 through 21 years. At the time this act was signed, it was estimated that the needs of more than 8 million children and youths with handicaps were not being met; more than half of these children were not receiving appropriate educational services, and more than 1 million children with special needs were excluded from education in the public school system (Neisworth, Willoughby-Herb, Bagnato, Cartwright, & Laub, 1980).

Basically PL 94-142 guarantees a free and appropriate education for all children, provided in the least restrictive environment. Although PL 94-142 provides for children 3-21 years old, there were several disclaimers that allowed the exclusion of children 3-5 years of age. For example, states that did not provide educational services to nonhandicapped children 3-5 years old were not required to provide education to handicapped children in this age group. As a result, some children within this age group continued to be excluded from educational services.

In 1986 President Reagan signed the Education of the Handicapped Act Amendments, PL 99-457. This law amends several sections of PL 94-142. Significantly, the rights and protections regarding free and appropriate educational services specified in PL 94-142 are extended to handicapped children 3-5 years old by the 1990-1991 school year. To promote this effort, PL 99-457 increases the amount of funding available to states to develop and provide these educational services (Ballard, Ramirez, Zantal-Wiener, 1987). While states are not required to serve these children, failure to do so will result in loss of Preschool Incentive Grant dollars, PL 94-142 funds for this age group, and the opportunity to apply for federal grants and contracts related to special education

with preschool-age children. At the time this law was passed, the Department of Education estimated that states were providing services to about 75% of the handicapped children 3-5 years old, although many of these programs were not integrated (Odom & McEvoy, 1988; Snell, 1987). It is hoped that through these enhanced incentives all eligible 3- to 5-year-olds will be served by the 1990-1991 school year.

PL 99-457 expands the role of families in their child's education by including instruction for parents in the child's individual educational program (IEP), whenever appropriate and to the extent desired by parents. In addition, states are not required to provide children within this age group with a diagnostic or categorical label as a requisite to special education service.

PL 99-457 provides discretionary funds and sets requirements concerning the establishment of comprehensive services for children from birth through 2 years of age who are experiencing developmental delays, have conditions that may result in delay, or who are at risk of developmental delay, and for their families. Early intervention services must include an individualized family service plan that recognizes the developmental functioning of the child as well as the strengths and needs of the family related to meeting the needs of the child, the provision of case management, and plans for transition into preschool services.

PROGRAMMING FOR INTEGRATION INTO THE MAINSTREAM

The basic rationale for integration was established in Section 504 and PL 94-142 and reinforced in PL 99-457. These laws require that handicapped children receive a free and appropriate education in the least restrictive environment (LRE). The imperative to educate in the LRE is not a provision for mainstreaming or integration (Neisworth et al., 1980). Federal laws do not mandate that handicapped children be educated in regular education classrooms. In fact, LRE is not defined and the terms *integration* and *mainstreaming* are not included in the acts (Odom & McEvoy, 1988). However, the intent of the laws is that children receive services in a manner and in settings that are as close to normal as possible, following the principal of normalization (Wolfensberger, 1972). Education with nondisabled children should be the primary objective, to the extent that it is appropriate to meet the educational and social needs of the handicapped child (Vincent, Brown, & Getz-Sheftel, 1981; Vincent et al., 1980). Placement in segregated classes or schools may occur only when the severity of a child's handicap is such that his or her needs cannot be met within the regular class environment (Neisworth et al., 1980; Winton, Turnbull, & Blacher, 1984).

Mainstream settings often are considered the LRE for many children, especially children with mild to moderate handicaps or developmental delays (Snell, 1987; Spodek et al., 1984; Walter & Vincent, 1982). Mainstream or integrated settings have been identified as the optimal educational milieu because they may provide a more stimulating, demanding, responsive, and normalizing environment for handicapped children than segregated settings typically containing children with similar behavior repertoires (Peterson, 1987). An integrated classroom provides a handicapped child with the opportunity to observe, imitate, and interact with typical peers (Safford & Rosen, 1981). Education in a mainstream setting emphasizes the similarities among children and encourages recognition of and programming to reinforce a child's strengths and normally developing skills, in addition to providing for remediation of the delayed areas of functioning (Bricker, 1978; Vincent et al., 1981). Other expected benefits of mainstreaming include improved self-concept for the child with handicaps, the development of positive attitudes (or improvement of attitudes) regarding the handicapped by regular education personnel and typical children and their families (Safford & Rosen, 1981; Wood, 1984).

The benefits reported for children in integrated settings has varied across studies. Some studies have shown that both typical children and those with handicaps enrolled in integrated settings make gains, sometimes in excess of those that might be expected from normative developmental rates (Guralnick, 1981a; Hoyson, Jamieson, & Strain, 1984; Jenkins, Speltz, & Odom, 1985). Others have shown that handicapped and normally developing children do equally well academically or developmentally in mainstream and segregated settings (Esposito, 1987; Odom, DeKlyen, & Jenkins, 1984; Strain, Hoyson, & Jamieson, 1985). Children in mainstream settings may show gains in nonacademic areas such as social skills, behavior self-management, and play skills that are not evident for children in segregated settings (Vincent et al., 1981). For example, Guralnick and Groom (1988) reported that developmentally delayed preschool-age children engaged in more peer-directed social behavior and constructive toy play in integrated play groups than they did in segregated play groups. It is important to note that the laws do not require better outcomes for children with handicaps in mainstream programs than in segregated programs; rather children with handicaps must do as well in these settings as they would in a segregated program (Vincent et al., 1981). Thus, children who benefit equally from both settings must be placed in the least restrictive mainstream classroom.

Mainstreaming has been distinguished from integration. For example, Odom & McEvoy (1988) describe mainstreaming as the placement of children with handicaps in educational settings for and with normally developing children in which at least 50% of the children are normally developing. They define integration as the process of actively mixing two groups of children. This distinction is an important one. It acknowledges one of the major problems with mainstreaming. Simply placing handicapped and normally developing children in the same physical setting does not guarantee that they will interact or associate with one another (Guralnick, 1976, 1978; McLean & Odom, 1988; Peterson, 1982). In fact, in the absence of specific integration efforts, segregation may occur within a mainstream setting (e.g., Johnson & Johnson, 1980; Schultz, Williams, Iverson, & Duncan, 1984; Strain & Kerr, 1981), although overt rejection and aggressive interactions usually do not occur (Guralnick, 1981a, 1986).

Several studies have demonstrated that without specific programming normally developing children tend to interact with other normally developing children or with children who exhibit mild delays but not with children who exhibit moderate or severe delays (e.g., Beckman, 1983; Guralnick, 1980, 1986; Peterson & Haralick, 1977; Strain, 1984; van den Pol, Crow, Rider, & Offner, 1985). When interaction does occur between normally developing children and their handicapped peers, often the form and function of interaction differs from that of normally developing peer groups (Guralnick, 1981a, 1986; Guralnick & Paul-Brown, 1977, 1984; Odom & McEvoy, 1988). One series of studies reported that children with advanced developmental skills often adjusted the sophistication of their speech during interactions with less advanced peers (Guralnick & Paul-Brown, 1984), assumed a directive or tutorial role during interactions (Guralnick & Paul-Brown, 1980; Guralnick, 1986), and provided numerous instructions during interactions (Guralnick & Paul-Brown, 1986).

Mainstreaming is a necessary, but not a sufficient, condition to promote active involvement between children (Odom & McEvoy, 1988). Effective planning and programming usually is needed to encourage and support integration in a mainstream setting (Spodek et al., 1984; Stainback & Stainback, 1985). For example, Kugelmass (1989) reported that 4-year-old children in a mainstream classroom who initially avoided each other engaged in positive peer interactions when teachers introduced activities that were designed to promote child–child interaction.

RESPONSIBILITY FOR INTEGRATION

The responsibility for integration rests with several social agents, including administrators, school psychologists, therapists, resource teachers, special and regular education teachers, and parents. Some specific responsibilities will be noted in the following sections.

Administrator Responsibilities

The first line of responsibility lies with principals and administrators, who do much to determine the support and commitment of school personnel, parents, and community agencies for mainstream programming (Samuels, 1986). One important way they do this is to demonstrate their own commitment to mainstreaming by encouraging and recognizing staff efforts, providing funding for materials (i.e., adapted materials, space, curricula) and support personnel (i.e., resource teachers, aides, therapists), and by allocating staff time to plan for integration (Peterson, 1987). Administrators also can shape the attitudes and abilities of program staff by offering in-service training and extracurricular instruction and consultation regarding integrated programming (Brady & Gunter, 1985; Walter & Vincent, 1982).

Interagency agreements and cooperation among members of multidisciplinary teams are strongly advocated in PL 94-142 and PL 99-457. Administrators are largely responsible for developing interagency agreements, inter- and intraprogram procedures and timeliness related to integration and for establishing hierarchical and lateral lines of communication among program personnel (Hains, Fowler, & Chandler, 1988). Administrators also provide support and guidance through evaluation of the integration process and problem-solving efforts. Evaluation may focus on (a) academic and developmental changes, (b) teacher, child, and parent satisfaction with the integration program, (c) child placement, and (d) child success within a given program.

Regular Education Teacher Responsibilities

The success of mainstreaming is largely dependent on the regular education teacher and his or her design of the classroom environment including curriculum, materials, routines, rules, and activities (Carta, Sainato, & Greenwood, 1988; Odom & McEvoy, 1988; Walter & Vincent, 1982). Teachers' attitudes and expectations are critical to the success of mainstreaming (Hains et al., 1988; Stainback & Stainback, 1985; Walker & Rankin, 1983). Teachers' perspectives are reflected in their behavior in the classroom. In addition, these perspectives can influence the attitudes about mainstreaming on the part of children with handicaps, nondisabled children, and parents.

Integration presents many challenges for teachers in the regular education classroom. Teachers in an integrated classroom need to work with a wide range of personnel, function as a team member, provide and receive consultation about various children, assess children's strengths and needs through criterion- and norm-referenced tests and observational assessments, write and implement IEPs, adapt curricula and teaching styles to meet a variety of needs, learn about handicapping conditions and related needs, and implement methods of instruction and handling recommended by special education staff and therapists (e.g., occupational therapists) (Chandler, 1986; Hains et al., 1988). These teachers also are likely to have a different relationship with families of children who are mainstreamed than they have with families of normally developing children. However, this relationship may vary across families. Teachers may find that parents of mainstreamed children desire greater as well as lesser levels of participation than do parents of normally developing children. For example, as their child enters the mainstream elementary school program, some families may yield to the educator's responsibility for their child's education. These families may need a break from the responsibilities that often are assigned to parents in preschool programs. Alternatively, some families continue to desire frequent formal and informal contact with teachers and staff and request training in home activities (Fowler, Chandler, Johnson, & Stella,

1988; Johnson, Chandler, Kerns, & Fowler, 1986; Spodek et al., 1984).

Teachers' roles can be thought of as both preparation and reception functions. Each role constitutes unique and overlapping responsibilities. In a preparation role, teachers are responsible for preparing children with handicaps to enter the mainstream of the next environment or classroom, as when a child enters kindergarten from a preschool program (Fowler, 1982). Indeed, one of the identified goals of early intervention is to prepare children to function in the LRE (Hains et al., 1988; Vincent et al., 1980). Teachers must identify and teach the readiness skills that are necessary for mainstream programs. They also may need to work on skills required in specific classrooms or programs (e.g., some programs may require a child to have independent toileting skills before entry) (Hains, Fowler, Schwartz, Kottwitz, & Rosenkoetter, 1989).

The receiving role also includes efforts to promote integration and meet the developmental and behavioral needs of all children in the classroom. This responsibility will entail learning about the strengths and needs of the children entering the program. Additional responsibilities may include adjusting expectations, instructions, class routines, and teaching practices; revising curricula and training materials; and altering the physical layout of the classroom to build on a child's strengths and meet the child's needs. Receiving teachers also are responsible for preparing normally developing children for mainstreaming. For example, a receiving teacher might arrange for "the kids on the block" program to be presented during the first few days of class (this program utilizes puppets to describe handicapping conditions and emphasizes the similarities of normally developing children and children with handicaps).

Parent Responsibilities

Parents also are vital to the success of integration. Parents and other family members tend to be a valuable but underutilized resource and source of support, especially in elementary school programs. They can provide a unique, multienvironment view of their child's strengths and needs and a long-term perspective of their child's history and experiences. This information should be helpful when selecting IEP goals and developing methods for teaching goals. Family members also can provide emotional support (Ziegler, 1985) and work with the mainstreamed child at home to help strengthen and generalize skills (Johnson et al., 1986; Shearer & Shearer, 1977). Parents may be especially valuable during the transition period by preparing their child for the change in programs, identifying adjustment problems, and serving as a bridge between programs (Hains et al., 1988). It is important to recognize, however, that family involvement must be individualized to reflect each family's needs, abilities, and desire to participate (Chandler, Fowler, & Lubeck, 1986; Dunst, Trivette, & Deal, 1988). Active parent participation is not required by PL 94-142, Section 504, or PL 99-457. Not all families want to be or are able to be maximally involved in their child's program. The level of participation is likely to vary across families. For example, Fowler and her colleagues (Fowler et al., 1988) reported that for a group of 30 parents of children entering a mainstream kindergarten, 27 different skills were identified as home-training goals. In a related study families indicated diverse numbers of hours they would work with their child, ranging from 0.5 to 40 hours per week (Fowler et al., 1989). Universal requirements concerning family participation may increase family stress and guilt and reduce the family's level of support for their child's program (Umansky, 1982; Winton & Turnbull, 1981). Program staff can maximize family participation by helping families identify an optimal level of involvement and by working with families at that level (Chandler et al., 1986).

Parents of normally developing children also may be involved in and contribute to the success of integration. They can offer support for the integrated program and teaching staff and shape the attitudes of their children concerning interactions with handicapped children (Reichart, Lynch, Anderson, Svobodny, & Mercury, 1989). Parents of normally developing and handicapped children each may have concerns related to integration and mainstreaming that should be addressed by administrators and program staff. For example, parents of children with and of children without handicapping conditions have expressed concern about teachers' time and ability to plan for and meet the needs of all children within a mainstream classroom (Reichart et al., 1989; Turnbull, Winton, Blacher, & Salkind, 1982).

Related Service Personnel

School psychologists, therapists, resource teachers, and aides also are responsible for integration. PL 94-142 and PL 99-457 require schools to provide a range of related services necessary to help handicapped children benefit from special education. Each of these persons will be involved in evaluating a child's strengths and needs, adapting curricula and materials, and planning for and working with the child who is mainstreamed into a regular education class (Wood, 1984). Related service personnel can facilitate integration by working cooperatively to incorporate the specialized methods required for a child with handicaps into the context of the regular classroom (Safford & Rosen, 1981). Therapists and other related staff also can collaborate to develop joint activities for teachers to use in the classroom and for parents to use at home. For example, a speech therapist and a physical therapist may create together a communication system that is suitable for a speech-delayed, orthopedically impaired child, in lieu of developing separate systems. Or the classroom teacher and speech therapist might develop activities that emphasize communication (e.g., pointing) and problem-solving skills (e.g., making choices or identifying similarities). This collaboration reduces the likelihood of providing teachers and parents with too many goals and activities or inconsistent strategies for meeting goals.

Many persons are responsible for designing programs for and working with a child who is mainstreamed into a regular education classroom. The success of each person in meeting her or his responsibilities for individual children and in developing integrated classrooms is largely dependent on a willingness and ability to function as part of a multidisciplinary team. Integration requires planning and communication between all members of the team, as described in federal legislation. Working as a team can help clarify or identify each person's specific responsibilities, promote information sharing, establish lines of communication, and build confidence and cooperation among team members. Benefits commonly attributed to interagency cooperation also may accrue to integration teams, such as reduced duplication of efforts and improved consultation, social support, and cost-effective service delivery (Peterson, 1987; Project BEST, 1986).

STRATEGIES TO PROMOTE INTEGRATION

Placing normally developing children and children with handicaps and developmental delays in the same physical setting is the first step in the process of integration, but it usually is not sufficient to meet the goal of integration (Schultz et al., 1984). As Johnson and Johnson (1980) have pointed out, "placing handicapped students into the regular classroom is the beginning of an opportunity" (p. 90). However, this opportunity must be supported by specific programming and the systematic arrangement of classroom events and procedures (Guralnick, 1978; Peterson, 1982, 1987; Safford & Rosen, 1981).

Three types of integration should be programmed in a mainstream setting: physical or temporal integration (children spend time in close proximity in the same physical setting), social integration (children interact in a manner that suggests social acceptance or friendship), and academic integration (children share the instructional environment) (Donder & York, 1984; Odom & McEvoy, 1988; Peter-

son, 1987; Rostetter, Kowalski, & Hunter, 1984; Strain & Kerr, 1981; Walter & Vincent, 1982). Direct interventions and planning for integration can occur within the sending program, within the receiving program, and between programs during the period of transition. Strategies that may be used within these three components often are applicable across levels. They are separated in this chapter for ease of presentation and planning within programs.

Preparation within the Sending Program

One of the primary responsibilities of teachers and staff in the sending program is the preparation of children for the future educational environment (Vincent et al., 1980). The educational environment that should be targeted for preparation is the regular education mainstream classroom (Walter & Vincent, 1982).

Two types of skills are important to consider when preparing children for an integrated, regular education setting. These are academic/preacademic skills and survival skills. Academic/preacademic skills are those skills traditionally assessed on developmental and kindergarten screening tests such as identifying colors, naming body parts, and printing first and last name (e.g., Learning Accomplishments Profile, Sanford and Zelman, 1981). These skills constitute a major portion of traditional curricula and classroom goals. Survival skills consist of academic support skills (e.g., completing tasks on time), social skills (e.g., responding to peer initiations), and behaviors (e.g., following classroom rules) that a child will need to function well and cope with the demands of an integrated setting. These survival skills often are not assessed on developmental and kindergarten screening tests and are not included in traditional curricula or as classroom goals (Hains et al., 1988; Vincent et al., 1980). Table 1 presents a list of skills that have been identified, from a variety of resources, as necessary to successful academic and social integration in mainstream kindergarten settings.

TABLE 1
Survival and Academic Skills Identified as Important for Children to Exhibit Upon Entry Into Mainstream Kindergartens

Social Behaviors and Classroom Conduct

    Separates from parents and accepts school personnel
    Expresses emotions and feelings appropriately
    Understands role as part of a group
    Respects others and their property
    Plays cooperatively
    Shares and takes turns
    Initiates and maintains peer interactions
    Interacts without aggression
    Plays independently
    Imitates peer actions
    Lines up
    Waits appropriately
    Willing to try something new
    Defends self appropriately
    Controls voice in classroom
    Follows classroom rules
    Responds to warning words (e.g., No, Stop)
    Modifies behavior when given verbal feedback

Task-Related Behaviors

    Finds materials needed for task
    Holds and manipulates materials
    Does not disrupt peers during activities
    Stays in "own space" for activity
    Works on activity for appropriate time (e.g., 15 minutes) with minimal cues and supervision
        by teachers
    Asks peers or teacher for information or assistance
    Seeks teacher's attention appropriately (e.g., raises hand)
    Completes tasks on time
    Completes tasks of ability level near criteria
    Replaces materials and "cleans up" work space
    Follows routine in transition
    Complies quickly with teacher instructions
    Generalizes skills across tasks and situations
    Recalls and follows directions for tasks previously described
    Follows 2- to 3-part direction by teacher
    Follows group instructions
    Attends to teacher in a large-group activity
    Makes choices

Self-Help Behaviors

    Locates and cares for personal belongings
    Cares for own toileting needs without supervision
    Feeds self independently
    Gets on and off school bus with minimal supervision
    Avoids obvious dangers
    Puts on and removes outer clothing within a reasonable length of time
    Recognizes problems, tries strategies to solve the problem
    Communicates own needs and wants

Note. These skills were selected from the following references: Carden-Smith & Fowler (1983); Hains et al. (1989); Project BEST (1986); Thompson (1979); Walker & Rankin (1983); Walter (1979); Walter & Vincent (1982).

Survival skills and academic/preacademic skills are both important to integration; both will influence a child's success in the future program. Academic skills that approximate those of normally developing peers promote physical and academic integration as children with disabilities participate in small- and large-group instruction with peers. In addition, peers may serve as models for academic behavior and survival skills and provide assistance during academic and social activities.

Survival and academic support skills have received much attention from special educators (e.g., Fowler, 1982; Rowbury, 1982; Vincent et al., 1980). These skills are considered critical to mainstream programs because they often are necessary for the initiation and completion of academic tasks and are useful across numerous activities (Hops & Cobb, 1973). For example, skills such as attending to and engaging in a task, following directions, and appropriate classroom deportment are necessary during academic activities as well as free play, fine-motor, and art activities.

The lack of survival skills (e.g., lack of appropriate peer interactions and appropriate classroom deportment behaviors) has been identified as one of the primary causes for referral to segregated special education classrooms (Carden-Smith & Fowler, 1983). Children who do not exhibit survival skills tend to require inordinate amounts of their teachers' attention, may be judged as less competent by teachers, may be associated with negative or immature skills, and often experience social isolation from peers. For instance, Carden-Smith and Fowler (1983) reported that children who were referred from mainstream programs for treatment of learning and behavior problems engaged in aggressive, noncompliant, and rule infraction behavior more frequently and for longer durations than their normally developing peers. These children's inappropriate behavior required inordinate amounts of their teachers' attention to resolve. Carden-Smith and Fowler recommend that preschool preparation focus on teaching survival skills, reducing inappropriate behaviors, and teaching children to behave in ways that require acceptable or expected amounts of teacher attention or assistance.

Walter and Vincent (1982) reported that children considered by their teachers to be successfully integrated into mainstream kindergarten classrooms engaged in appropriate amounts of on-task behavior, evidenced appropriate initiation strategies, and required less instructional and behavioral attention from teachers than children considered poorly integrated into mainstream programs. These authors recommend that preschool preparation focus on these skills as well as on academic behaviors and that teachers work to reduce the children's inappropriate behaviors during the preschool years. Other skills that teachers may incorporate as goals for children include discriminating male/female restrooms, toileting independently, raising hand, lining up, waiting appropriately, and following one-through three-step directions.

Teaching academic and survival skills in the sending program can occur both at a general level, in which all children participate in preparation activities, and at child-specific levels, in which preparation activities focus on the needs of individual children. Teachers and other practitioners (e.g., school psychologists) can develop preparation activities for all children by identifying a general set of skills, such as those listed in Table 1, that are common to many receiving programs. These general skills then can be integrated with existing goals and classroom activities or routines. For example, teachers might teach imitative behavior during circle activities with games such as "Simon Says"; they might teach choice-making behavior during snack by offering more than one edible (e.g., cookies and popcorn). The Integrated Preschool Curriculum (Odom et al., 1988) provides an excellent example of this process of preparing for integration. It describes a general set of social skills that will help preschool-age children "survive" in an integrated setting and provides a curriculum that teachers can use to teach those skills during free-play sessions in a preschool classroom.

Preparation usually focuses on child-specific needs when future educational programs are selected for individual children. In such instances, teachers may identify and teach skills and behaviors required for success in specific programs. For example, one program may require children to seek assistance by raising their hands and asking the teacher for help; another may require children to seek assistance from peers. Teachers might then employ more direct or intensive methods than usual to teach these skills through individual or small-group instruction. In other instances teachers can incorporate goals identified for one child into the general programming curricula. For example, all children may be taught to use worksheets or blackboards even though these materials are not used in every future environment.

In designing methods for teaching academic and survival skills it is helpful to consider the number and type of settings or activities in which the skill may be useful or required, the level of proficiency required for the skill to be useful, and normative examples of the quality and quantity of behavior across settings or activities (Chandler, Lubeck, & Fowler, 1990). These considerations will help teachers select goal attainment criteria.

Strategies for determining general and child-specific skills necessary in future environments have been outlined by several researchers (Hains et al., 1988, 1989; Vincent et al., 1980; Walker & Rankin, 1983); they include (a) visits to future classrooms, (b) completion of teacher expectation surveys, (c) examination of readiness scales and developmental assessments, (d) information exchange between teachers and program staff, (e) direct observation of ongoing classes, and (f) exchanging curricula. There are few commercially available curricula to assist teachers in developing comprehensive programs to prepare children for a mainstream setting. However, there are numerous books, journal articles, and book chapters that may inform teachers and other professionals (Brady & Gunter, 1985;

Certo, Haring, & York, 1984; Fowler, 1982; Neisworth et al., 1980; Strain, Guralnick, & Walker, 1986; Strain & Kerr, 1981; Spodek et al., 1984; Vincent et al., 1981; Wood, 1984). Teachers also may contact other preschool and kindergarten programs to obtain information on preparing children for a mainstream kindergarten. Several model programs that may be of interest to sending and receiving program staff are described in Appendix A.

Transition Between Programs

During a child's final year in a sending program, decisions concerning the future program will be made by a multidisciplinary, multiprogram team consisting of staff from the sending and receiving program and parents. The child's transition team will define the least restrictive educational setting that is most appropriate for the child, select a specific classroom and method of entry into the classroom, and determine initial classroom goals for the child.

Several types of classroom arrangements can be considered when defining the least restrictive educational placement for a child. These educational placements provide varying degrees of support and services to meet the varying needs of children. Options for placement include the following:

1. Mainstream class with no support.

2. Mainstream class with minimal support (e.g., special equipment, materials, etc.) (Peterson, 1987).

3. Mainstream class with support services provided in class through an itinerant teacher or aide (Huefner, 1988).

4. Mainstream class with support services provided through resource room.

5. Shared placement in mainstream and special education classrooms. Children attend mainstream class during activities they can successfully complete or participate in (Walter & Vincent, 1982), the amount of time spent in each class being dependent on the child's needs.

6. Half-day placement in mainstream classroom and half-day placement in special education or transitional classroom (Allen, 1981).

7. Special education class with opportunity for integration during nonacademic, often schoolwide, activities such as lunch, gym, and music activities (Hamre-Nietupski, Nietupski, Stainback, & Stainback, 1984; Stainback & Stainback, 1985).

After selecting a program and classroom that provides the type of least restrictive environment selected by the team, methods of familiarization with the new program and entry into the class can be considered. Several procedures have been identified that may facilitate a child's transition between programs:

1. Children may visit the receiving program during their final year in the sending program. Visits may occur during specified activities such as snack or free-play sessions or for an entire day. These visits allow children to become familiar with the future classroom and teacher and to interact with normally developing peers, and they tend to promote communication among program staff (Vincent et al., 1980).

2. Children may enter the receiving program on a gradual basis. For example, during the first 2–3 weeks of school a child may attend the program for 1 hour, gradually increasing the amount of time spent in the classroom (Fowler, 1982). This allows children time to adjust to unfamiliar aspects of the program such as routines and rules, peers, and the length of the program day.

3. Children may enter the program with assistance. For example, siblings, a familiar adult, or volunteer aides (e.g., high school students) may accompany a child to the new program and assist him or her in the classroom during the first few days of enrollment. This tactic might provide emotional support to children during the initial transition to an unfamiliar setting.

4. Entrance into the receiving program may occur simultaneously with attendance in the sending program. During the first few weeks of school, children may attend both programs for a portion of the day. Gradually, the amount of time spent in the receiving program increases as the amount of time in the sending program decreases. This strategy allows children time to adjust to the separation from sending program staff and peers as they become familiar with staff and peers in the receiving program.

5. Children may enter the receiving program in the same manner as other children in the class — that is, without assistance and for the full day.

Another important activity of the transition team involves the exchange of information between programs. During transition planning, staff in the sending and receiving programs begin to share information through formal and informal meetings, phone calls, progress and summary reports, and IEPs. The sending program staff share information about general classroom curricula and preparation goals, and about the child of interest. Information about a child with handicaps who enters a mainstream program is most helpful if it describes academic, social, behavioral, and survival skills. In addition to information about a child's developmental status, IEP goals, and progress in the program, summary reports should include information about the child's (a) social skills, (b) preferred activities, toys, and other reinforcers, (c) problem behaviors, (d) response to methods of behavior management, (e) attention span, and (f) preacademic areas of strength. These types of information can help a receiving program prepare for a child's entry into the class. In addition, the receiving teacher shares information about curricula and expectations concerning academic and survival skills during the first few weeks of class.

Teachers also should discuss areas of difference between sending and receiving programs, in order to determine methods to minimize those differences when possible, and to prepare the student to negotiate the differences as the need arises. A problem commonly associated

TABLE 2
Potential Areas of Difference Between Special Education Preschool and
Mainstream Kindergarten Programs

Teacher/Child ratio
Number of children in setting
Social and play skills of peers
Transportation
Length of the program day
Expected level of independence during academic and play periods
Length of activity periods
Size of instructional groups
Amount and availability of teacher attention and assistance
Type of teacher instruction
Number of instructions given consecutively
Expectations for personal responsibility (e.g., care of possessions, transition between
    activities, self-help)
Location and identification of male/female restrooms
Location of school areas (e.g., resource rooms, cafeteria, gym)
Expected tool skills and type of materials used (e.g., worksheets, scissors,
    blackboards, size and type of writing utensil)
Classroom rules for behavior and seeking assistance
Reinforcement and discipline techniques
Seating arrangements
Focus of academic curricula
Separation and visibility of play and work areas
Parent involvement in class and at home

with transition is that children fail to generalize skills across programs (Fowler, 1982; Hains et al., 1988). Table 2 provides a list of potential differences across preschool and kindergarten programs, or segregated and mainstream settings.

Sending and receiving program staff can promote generalization across settings by approximating the conditions and requirements of previous or future settings. For example, teachers might gradually alter the environment of a preschool classroom to approximate a kindergarten class in terms of the amount of teacher attention and assistance, rate of reinforcement, size of academic and play groups, and type and number of directions provided during activities (Fowler, 1982; Hains et al., 1988; Johnson et al., 1986). Teachers and staff from the receiving program might use similar curricular materials or a child's favorite activities to promote generalization and adjustment in the new program.

A final task of the multidisciplinary, multiprogram team in transferring a child to a mainstream setting is to involve parents. Many parents experience stress associated with their child's transition between programs, one source of stress identified by families being a lack of information about the transition process and the child's new program (Johnson et al., 1986). A parent's participation as a transition team member can help alleviate some of the stress associated with transition. Through participation, parents learn about the transition process, assist in making decisions about transition goals and placement, meet the child's new teacher, and learn about the expectations, curricula, and routines in the new program. In addition to gaining information through participation, parents can help the transition process by bridging the gap between programs during summer breaks and by teaching skills that are not easily taught in the school (Chandler, 1986). For example, they can promote a child's familiarity with a new program by visiting the new classroom and talking to the child about the change in programs. Finally, parents can provide children with opportunities to interact with normally developing age-mate peers through daycare programs, church nursery groups, and so forth.

Parents also can provide valuable information about the child that may help staff in the receiving program prepare for the child. They often are able to identify when a child is experiencing problems during transition and may offer suggestions to alleviate those problems. For example, parents may alert teachers to a child's need for predictability, difficulties in interacting with peers, or preference for reinforcers.

Promoting Integration within the Receiving Program

Teachers and staff in the receiving program are responsible for preparing the classroom environment and curriculum to accommodate a child with disabilities and for helping the child with special needs become integrated physically, socially, and academically. They also are responsible for helping normally developing children (and their families) adjust to the mainstream setting and prepare to interact with children who are handicapped or developmentally delayed.

Preparing typical classmates for integration. Preparing classmates for the entrance of children with special needs into the classroom can do much to decrease the often noted low expectations or negative reactions that nondisabled children (and adults) exhibit toward disabled classmates (Johnson & Johnson, 1980; Johnson & Meyer, 1985). Many of these reactions may result from a lack of experience and knowledge about children who are handicapped. Research indicates that the preparation of elementary-age children in mainstream programs generally has produced benefits for all children in respect to physical and social integration (Odom & McEvoy, 1988). For example, McHale and Simeonsson (1980) reported that preparation activities in which normally developing kindergarten-age children and children with autism

played together in the autistic childrens' classroom served to promote integration in the mainstream kindergarten class. Further work conducted by Raab, Nordquist, Cunningham, and Bliem (1986) also reported benefits from preparation activities with preschool-age children. Children who participated in simulation activities, viewed instructive videotapes, and spoke to the mothers of children who would enter the program interacted more satisfactorily with their special education classmates and assigned them higher sociometric ratings than did a control group of children who had not participated in preparation activities.

Preparation activities might provide (a) information about different handicapping conditions while emphasizing the similarities between disabled and nondisabled children (Donder & York, 1984; Taylor, 1982); (b) information about children who will enter the class by emphasizing the strengths, abilities, and needs of these children (Hamre-Nietupski et al., 1984; Turnbull et al., 1982); and (c) simulated or direct experience working or playing with children who have disabilities (Johnson & Johnson, 1980).

Arranging the environment to promote integration. Preparation and teaching in the receiving program should focus on academic and survival skills, emphasizing skills considered to be critical to the success of the child's enrollment in the program. Hains and her colleagues (Hains et al., 1989) asked kindergarten teachers to prioritize children's skills and skill areas that are considered to be critical upon program entry. These teachers identified the following areas and behaviors: comes to adults when called by name, responds to warning words, toilets independently, classroom conduct, instruction following, self-care, social interaction, and communication. Curricular emphasis might initially focus on skills within these areas.

Teaching survival and academic skills in the receiving program also can occur at general (classwide) and child-specific levels. The first and often least effortful strategy for teaching at a general level is to arrange the classroom environment to promote integration. The environment strongly influences behavior, providing experiences and opportunities that can promote learning and integration. It also sets the occasion for learning when skills are specifically taught (Carta et al., 1988; Chandler, 1989; Gump, 1977; Rogers-Warren, 1984; Wahler & Fox, 1981). Environmental arrangement strategies require teachers and other staff to identify variables that exist, or could exist, in the classroom and to arrange these variables to promote the type of behavior desired. Several types of environmental variables can be arranged to promote integration in a kindergarten. These include adults, play and academic groupings, toys and materials, and the physical layout of the classroom.

Adults are an important environmental variable to consider when developing procedures to promote integration. Several researchers have reported that when adults are present and interact with children, social interaction between children frequently decreases (Carta et al., 1988; Chandler, 1989; Huston-Stein, Friederich-Cofer, & Sussman, 1977; Innocenti et al., 1986). However, for some children an adult's presence may be critical to peer interaction and social integration. For example, interactions between a hearing-impaired child who uses sign language and hearing peers may be dependent on teachers to interpret communication between children.

In determining the arrangement of adults in the classroom, staff should consider for a given activity whether adults will be present, how much they will interact with students, the nature of teacher–child interaction (e.g., the teacher may promote teacher–child communication or encourage children to talk to each other), and the teacher–child ratio.

Adults who serve as itinerant or consulting specialists or class aides also are important environmental supports that may allow a child to be maintained in the physical setting (Huefner, 1988). Itinerant or consulting specialists help the teacher design individualized programs and methods for teaching children in the mainstream setting. They may adapt or develop curricular materials and provide in-class services to supplement those provided by the regular education teacher (Peterson, 1987). Consultation may be provided by special education teachers, school psychologists, and therapists (e.g., occupational therapists).

Toys and materials influence the quality and quantity of social and academic integration. Toys that can be used in a variety of ways by children with different developmental levels tend to promote interaction (Stainback & Stainback, 1985). It is important to note that novel toys and materials may result in decreased levels of positive social integration and increase instances of aggression (Odom & Strain, 1984). In contrast, some toys and materials may promote cooperation and interaction (e.g., gross-motor equipment, sociodramatic toys, and cars), while others promote isolation (e.g., art materials, small manipulatives, books, and puzzles) (Quilitch & Risley, 1973; Roth & Clark, 1987; Rubin & Howe, 1985). For example, Beckman and Kohl (1984) found that interaction in segregated and integrated play groups occurred more frequently with social toys than with isolate toys or combinations of isolate and social toys.

Toys and materials that are limited in number and variety tend to facilitate social integration by promoting sharing and child–child conversation (Gump, 1978; Rubin & Howe, 1985). For example, two children may be more likely to interact when they share one puzzle than when they each have a puzzle, or when one child has a puzzle and the other child has building blocks. Materials also can be used to facilitate the acquisition of survival and academic skills. For instance, academic materials that are a bit beyond the child's ability can be used by teachers to promote problem solving, persistence, and asking for assistance. Or, teachers might use materials such as a timer to help children develop self-management skills and attending behaviors during academic activities (Strain & Kerr, 1981).

The composition and size of academic and play groups also has a strong influence on integration. Groups that contain same-sex and similar-age children promote social integration (Gump, 1978; Parten, 1933). For children with handicaps, groups that contain developmentally advanced peers often promote academic integration as children serve as models for behavior and provide assistance with activities (Guralnick, 1981a, 1986). Groups that contain socially skilled and unskilled peers also tend to promote peer-directed behavior (Odom & Strain, 1984). In addition, heterogeneous groups in which children are in close proximity to one another also promote social integration (Guralnick & Groom, 1988). Brinker (1985) reported that within mainstream settings, social interaction between normally developing children and children with handicaps usually occurred when they were near each other (proximity defined as within 2 m). Similar results for severely multiply handicapped students have been reported by Speigel-McGill, Bambara, Shores, and Fox (1984). Opportunities for physical integration in heterogeneous groups can be arranged in both mainstream and segregated classes. For instance, children in segregated classes should be physically integrated with normally developing peers during some portion of the day (e.g., lunch, playground, physical education) (Hamre-Nietupski et al., 1984).

The size of academic or play groups may facilitate or inhibit integration. Peer interaction occurs more often in small groups than it does in large groups (Speigel-McGill et al., 1984; Stainback & Stainback, 1985). In addition, teachers often find it easier to individualize for the diverse academic needs and survival skills of students in small groups (Wood, 1984).

The physical arrangement of the classroom also influences academic and survival skills and the success of integration (Guralnick, 1981b). Teachers might look for visual and auditory distractions that may interfere with a child's ability to stay on task. For example, some children find it difficult to work on academic activities when they can see their classmates in the free-play or art area. Potential distractions can be reduced or removed through (a) the phys-

ical and visual separation of work and play areas (e.g., bookshelves that separate speech therapy, play, and academic areas), (b) seating arrangements (e.g., children who are highly distractible may sit at different tables; children's desks may be turned away from distracting stimuli), or (c) placement of task materials (e.g., materials for academic tasks can be located in areas that are separate from play materials and the play area).

Salient cues that signal appropriate behavior can be helpful in teaching children critical survival skills. For example, Sainato, Strain, Lefebvre, and Rapp (1987) were able to increase the rate of independent movement and appropriate behaviors exhibited during activity transitions with the use of picture cues. Fowler (1986) used polaroid pictures of behaviors prescribed for children during classroom routines (e.g., staying in seat) to teach and then cue these survival skills. Other salient cues might consist of flicking the lights to signal transitions between activities or placing names on each child's desk or chair. Teachers also might use multiple environmental cues such as visual and auditory stimuli or repetitive cues to teach survival skills.

Other environmental arrangements in the classroom that can be designed to promote integration include seating arrangements, the size of the work or play area, and placement of materials. Group seating arrangements tend to promote social and academic integration more than individual seating arrangements. For example, children who work at tables may have more opportunity to provide assistance, engage in conversation, and share materials than children who sit at individual desks. Small spaces tend to promote interaction, although too small a space may result in aggression (Brown, Fox, & Brady, 1987; Smith & Connolly, 1980). Materials that are not readily available (i.e., in close proximity) can facilitate the development of survival skills such as seeking assistance and problem solving.

As a strategy to promote social integration, environmental arrangements present several advantages to teachers and other program staff. Adaptations are fairly easy to arrange when they take advantage of naturally existing variables and opportunities within the classroom; they can be applied on a classwide basis; and they often fit into the existing structure of the class (Sainato et al., 1987). Initially, teachers and program staff should consider the type of activities used throughout the day and the type of integration desired within each activity. Arrangement of environmental variables can then be planned to promote integration and acquisition of critical survival skills. For instance, Walter and Vincent (1982) reported that peer interaction among kindergarten children occurred most often during free-play activities. Yet free-play activities were scheduled for only 9-17% of the school day. Teachers who wish to promote social integration might consider scheduling free-play activities during a larger portion of the day, especially at the beginning of the school year.

Interventions to promote social integration. Explicit interventions may be necessary to facilitate social and academic integration within a mainstream class-room. As DeWert and Helsels (1985) pointed out, "Interactions of handicapped individuals and persons unaccustomed to being with them should not be left to chance" (p. 102). Five types of interventions have been useful for promoting social integration: (a) environmental arrangement strategies, (b) affection activities, (c) the use of preferred activities, (d) teacher-mediated strategies, and (e) peer-mediated strategies. These are discussed in turn.

The first intervention builds on environmental arrangement strategies by combining in unique ways several environmental variables: (a) composition of the peer group, (b) type and amount of adult interaction, (c) number and type of available materials, and (d) structure of the activity as arranged in the play setting. One combination of environmental events, entitled the PALS approach to peer interaction, has been quite effective in promoting social integration among young

children (Lubeck, 1986; Chandler, 1989). The PALS approach advances the following recommendations:

1. **P**air children who are handicapped with socially skilled, normally developing children during activities.

2. **A**rrange for adults to be absent from the activity or reduce their rate of interaction.

3. **L**imit the number and variety of materials available during activities.

4. **S**tructure the activity so that children work toward a cooperative goal and understand their role in achieving the goal.

In one study using the PALS strategy, Chandler (1989) found that during free-play sessions language-delayed, socially isolated children, children who were at risk for developmental and social delays, and their normally developing peers interacted more often when the PALS system was in effect than when a variant of the system was employed (e.g., the teacher was present during the activity and interacted with children at a high rate). The combination of variables employed in the PALS approach is useful for producing social integration; however, it may not be optimal for promoting other behaviors commonly associated with free-play activities, such as elaboration of expressive language and appropriate toy play. The goal of an activity should guide the arrangement of environmental variables in the classroom. Teachers might consider arranging a variety of play areas with different combinations of environmental variables to set the occasion for different child behaviors. Diverse play areas would increase the types of survival skills and experiences children might acquire through play.

A second intervention strategy, affection activities, has been very successful at promoting social integration and the generalization of peer interaction across activities (McEvoy et al., 1988; Twardosz, Nordquist, Simon, & Botkin, 1983). Affection training occurs during large-group activities in which the importance of friendship is discussed and the expression of affection is practiced. Many affection activities involve modification of games, stories, or songs that teachers commonly use in preschool and kindergarten programs. For example, the first stanza of the song "If you're happy and you know it" usually is followed with "Clap your hands" or "Stomp your feet." During an affection activity the stanza might be followed with "Give your neighbor a high five," "Shake your friend's hand," or "Give your friend a hug." Or, children may engage in affectionate behavior during games such as "The farmer in the dell" or "Duck, duck, goose." In these games, the farmer may hug or tickle the wife and the child who is chosen as the goose may be given a warm fuzzy or a pat on the shoulder. In a study conducted by McEvoy and her colleagues (McEvoy et al., 1988) affection activities were used to increase the social integration of autistic children during placement in a mainstream kindergarten setting. The results indicated that reciprocal peer interaction between autistic and nondisabled children increased during affection training and was maintained during a 20-day follow-up for all but one child.

Social integration also may be increased by associating children with handicaps or social delays with preferred activities and tasks or pairing these children with preferred or popular peers. For example, Sainato, Maheady, and Shook (1986) successfully increased the frequency and appropriateness of social interaction between withdrawn kindergarten students and their peers by assigning the withdrawn students to serve as managers of preferred activities (e.g., feeding the class pet, passing out snack, etc.).

A fourth type of intervention, teacher mediation, comprises the most common strategies employed to promote social integration. During teacher-mediated interventions, teachers may demonstrate social behavior and provide instruction, prompts, feedback, and reinforcement for appropriate social behavior. Teacher-mediated interventions may be applied to all children in a class or to individual children whose behavior is targeted for intervention. For example, Wolfe, Boyd, and Wolfe (1983) increased the frequency of cooperative play between three children who exhibited behavior problems and social delays and their classmates through the use of teachers' prompts, instructions, and token and social reinforcement. In another investigation, Bryant and Budd (1984) combined several teacher-mediated strategies to increase sharing and reciprocal interactions and reduce negative and aggressive interactions among six behaviorally and socially handicapped children with mild developmental delays. Teachers in this study modeled appropriate sharing and utilized discussion, rehearsal, prompts, corrective feedback, and reinforcement.

It is important to consider the timing and frequency of the teachers' prompts and reinforcers when designing these strategies as such prompts and reinforcement can disrupt peer interactions as children attend to teachers, rather than each other (Shores, Hester, & Strain, 1976; Walker, Greenwood, Hops, & Todd, 1979). Children also may become dependent on teacher prompts to initiate interactions, thereby reducing the frequency of spontaneous peer interaction and the ease with which prompts can be reduced (Odom, Hoyson, Jamieson, & Strain, 1985).

A final approach, peer-mediation strategies, utilizes children rather than teachers as intervention agents. Here, designated peers learn to instruct, prompt, model, and provide feedback and reinforcement to other children. Normally developing children and children with handicaps or social delays have been trained as peer mediators (e.g., Odom et al., 1985; Shafer, Egel & Neef, 1984). For example, Odom, Strain, Karger, and Smith (1986) trained nondisabled peers to direct initiation behaviors (organize the play, share, offer assistance, and affection) to children with behavior disorders during free-play activities. This peer-mediation strategy produced social integration by increasing the frequency with which the targeted children (those with behavior disorders) responded to peer initiations. In another example, Sasso and Rude (1987) trained high- and low-status nondisabled students to direct initiations to severely handicapped peers during recess activities. The severely handicapped peers attended a segregated program within the elementary school. It was reported that reciprocal interactions between the high- and low-status peers and handicapped students increased during training. In addition, the results indicated generalization across untrained normally developing students who increased their rate of initiating and responding to handicapped peers, especially when a high-status student was present.

Academic Integration

Specific interventions also are needed to promote and support integration during academic activities. Both Spodek and his colleagues (Spodek et al., 1984) and Peterson (1987) pointed out that while a handicapping condition may require teaching some skills or concepts in isolation, only through sharing the educational environment and learning opportunities with all children will the handicapped child truly be integrated. Teachers can use several strategies to design educational activities and arrange the educational environment to promote academic integration.

Learning centers constitute a type of environmental arrangement that has received considerable attention from educators (e.g., Peterson, 1987; Spodek et al., 1984). Learning centers consist of self-contained areas of the classroom developed for particular academic activities. For example, classrooms may have reading, numbers (math), art, and writing centers. Learning centers provide an opportunity for children to share the educational environment. They are especially useful for promoting academic integration for children at different academic or developmental levels. Children in a center area may work on similar activities, but at individualized rates and levels. Teachers can facilitate academic integration in learning centers by using similar formats or curricular materials. For example, all children in a learning center may use worksheets or puzzles even though they are working at different skill levels.

Learning centers allow teachers the freedom to move among centers and work with individuals or small groups of children (Wood, 1984). Learning centers are examples of environmental arrangements that would support peer-mediated or peer-tutored interventions in that children are physically close to one another and are working on similar tasks and with similar materials.

The goals of academic lessons also can be designed to promote integration. Within an academic group or learning center lessons can be designed to foster competitive, individually paced, or cooperative work behavior (Stainback & Stainback, 1985). Competitive and individually paced activities, which dominate classroom practice in most elementary school classrooms, tend to promote isolation rather than integration. Johnson and Johnson (1986) reported that cooperative arrangements were used for only 7–20% of academic activities, yet cooperative arrangements produce the highest levels of social and academic integration, as well as high levels of achievement and motivation. Johnson and Johnson (1986) recommend that cooperative groupings include the following:

1. Positive interdependence such that each child contributes to the group goal (e.g., each child has a puzzle piece).

2. Individual accountability so that each member understands his or her contribution to the process.

3. Collaborative skills (these may need to be taught) (e.g., turn taking).

4. Time for group processes to occur (e.g., problem solving).

5. A specified group goal and criteria for success.

Another intervention to promote academic and social integration pairs a child with poor academic or academic support skills and a "buddy" with appropriate skills. The buddy may serve as a model for appropriate behavior or as a peer-tutor who provides instructions, feedback, and reinforcement for appropriate behavior (Kalfus, 1984; Sainato et al., 1986). A buddy also can accompany a handicapped peer to the restroom, lunchroom, and other out-of-class areas and serve as a model during activity transitions (Spodek et al., 1984; Taylor, 1982).

Self-monitoring and group monitoring procedures also have been used to teach survival and academic skills necessary for academic integration. For example, Fowler (1986) reduced inappropriate and disruptive behaviors and nonparticipation behaviors during activity transitions in a kindergarten class by having children serve as team captains during these activities. As team captains, children monitored the behavior of their teammates and themselves. They awarded points for following instructions and completing activity routines in a nondisruptive manner. Fowler was able to maintain appropriate transition behavior by fading the group monitoring system to a self-monitoring system. In a related study, Carden-Smith and Fowler (1986) compared the effects of teacher monitoring and peer monitoring on behavior during activity transitions. They found that the two interventions were equally effective at reducing disruptive behavior and increasing participation of children enrolled in a remedial kindergarten program.

ROLE OF THE SCHOOL PSYCHOLOGIST

With the passage of PL 99-457, the rights and protections in respect to a free and appropriate education in the least restrictive environment were extended to handicapped 3- to 5-year-old children, to be accomplished by the 1990–1991 school year. This legislation may significantly increase the number of children entering mainstream preschool and kindergarten classrooms provided through elementary school programs. The potential impact of this legislation on the traditional roles and responsibilities of school psychologists is great, especially for psychologists who have little training or experience with young children.

School psychologists will be called upon to assess a young child's abilities and readiness for program entry, to assist in defining the least restrictive environment for a child, and to assist in selecting a least restrictive classroom placement. School psychologists also will assist teachers and parents in developing a child's IEP and methods for meeting IEP goals. Although many of these duties currently are completed by school psychologists, the tools and methods necessary for working with young children will differ from those utilized for older children. For example, an assessment of readiness must facilitate the development of an IEP by identifying survival skills, preacademic behaviors, and service needs (Brady & Gunter, 1985; Bricker, 1978; Neisworth et al., 1980). This type of information is most often obtained from criterion-referenced assessments, rather than the traditionally employed achievement tests. School psychologists may need to learn more about assessing survival skills and using criterion-referenced tests for young children and about including such information to augment that obtained from norm-referenced tests (Wood, 1984; Zigmond & Miller, 1986).

The evaluative reports completed by school psychologists also may differ from those developed for older children. Evaluative reports should emphasize a child's needs and abilities rather than test scores or diagnostic categories (i.e., they should be formative rather than summative). Evaluative reports also may contain the following information:

1. A description of a child's functional limitations that may require adaptations or planning within the classroom setting (Neisworth et al., 1980).

2. A list of recommendations for instructional activities or materials that may be useful in teaching a child.

3. A description of a child's preferred approaches to learning and problem solving, as well as functional limitations (e.g., visual, auditory, child's methods of seeking information, level of persistence).

4. A list of specific skills that are mastered, not mastered, and emerging (Zigmond & Miller, 1986).

5. A description of situations or tasks that have resulted in optimum performance and identification of a child's preference for particular tasks, materials, or modes of responding.

In addition, evaluative reports should contain information obtained from observations of the child in the classroom. Information from observational assessment may be used to expand and reinforce information obtained from formal assessment methods.

School psychologists also may be asked to fulfill new roles and responsibilities as young children with handicaps enter elementary school programs. For example, Hamre-Nietupski et al. (1984) recommend that one individual be assigned responsibility for mainstreaming on a program-wide basis. This person might be the school psychologist, who has access to and is familiar with many program personnel. The integration coordinator must prepare materials and provide training to staff concerning federal legislation, the philosophy underlying least restrictive placement and mainstreaming practices, and the need to program for integration (Stainback & Stainback, 1985). As integration coordinator, the psychologist also would be available for consultation throughout the year. He or she also would evaluate the success of mainstreaming efforts by documenting procedures that produced successful integration.

School psychologists also may help teachers adjust their standards and expectations and provide assistance in planning for children with handicaps. Many teachers are apprehensive about or resistant to the placement of children with handicaps in their regular classrooms (Kugelmass, 1989; Walker & Rankin, 1983). This resistance is largely due to faulty expectations, lack of training, and lack of support services. Resistance may be especially strong when children do not exhibit critical survival skills and require more attention and assistance than normally developing children. School psychologists will need to work closely with teachers to develop programs to reduce inappropriate behaviors and teach positive survival and academic support skills (Spodek et al., 1984). They also may assist teachers in the often difficult task of adapting curricula, teaching methods, and materials (Huefner, 1988; Strain & Kerr, 1981).

School systems with financial shortages may ask school psychologists to fulfill some of the duties of consulting or itinerant teachers. For example, they may help teachers (a) implement activities to prepare nondisabled children for integration, (b) implement behavior management procedures, (c) develop task analyses, and (d) identify existing resources and procure additional resources from the school and community (Wood, 1984).

A school psychologist also may function as the coordinator of transitions between programs. Transition coordinators implement and monitor the interagency transition plan, coordinate assessments, serve as a liaison between programs, and help parents prepare for transition (Project BEST, 1986). Transition coordinators must be familiar with the various programs that may transfer children to elementary school (e.g., day-care centers, early intervention programs, Montessori programs). They also must be aware of the options for placement within the public school system and be familiar with the various classrooms children may attend. On a child-specific level, transition coordinators must be familiar with individual children's strengths and needs, special considerations related to their handicapping condition, the type of specialty services provided in the sending program (e.g., physical therapy), and family strengths and needs related to transition.

Many school psychologists will not be prepared to fulfill the various roles and responsibilities described in this section, as these duties are not necessarily part of a traditional curriculum for a degree in school psychology. However, psychologists who find themselves working with increasing numbers of young children must assess their own abilities and identify areas of need for professional development related to mainstreaming and integration. They must then work with administrators to obtain time and resources to pursue this development and continuing education.

SUMMARY

A child's first placement during the first several years of elementary school is a good predictor of subsequent placement (Edgar, McNulty, & Gaetz, 1984; Spodek et al., 1984; Vincent et al., 1980). Therefore, it is important that placement decisions be made with care and that specific procedures by used to help a child become integrated into the selected placement. The success of integration is a function of many factors that include the skills, needs, and behavioral adjustment of nondisabled or handicapped children in the classroom (Carden-Smith & Fowler, 1983; Walter & Vincent, 1983), the child–teacher ratio, the teachers' training and preparation for mainstreaming, the children's preparation for mainstreaming, and the structural features and spatial layout of the setting (Guralnick, 1981b). Systematic arrangements of classroom routines and activities and specialized procedures are needed to promote and support physical, academic, and social integration in mainstreamed settings. Staff from sending and receiving programs will need to consider a child's unique needs and abilities, the physical environment, and the expectations of teachers and children within the receiving program as they develop methods to prepare the child for the new program and to accommodate the child after he or she enters the new program.

School psychologists may play a new role in mainstream programs serving young children. They may serve as transition coordinators, integration coordinators, and consultants to teachers and program staff. Future training for school psychologists should prepare them for these new roles. School systems that require psychologists to adopt new roles must be prepared to provide additional training (e.g., university courses, workshops), support (e.g., financial support, release time), and materials to assist in the preparation for these changing roles.

REFERENCES

Allen, K. E. (1981). Curriculum models for successful mainstreaming. *Topics in Early Childhood Special Education, 1*(1), 45-55.

Ballard, J., Ramirez, J., & Zantal-Wiener. (1987). *Public Law 94-142, Section 504, and Public Law 99-457: Understanding what they are and are not.* Washington, DC: Council for Exceptional Children.

Beckman, P. J. (1983). The relationship between behavioral characteristics of children and social interaction in an integrated setting. *Journal of the Division for Early Childhood, 7,* 69-77.

Beckman, P. J., & Kohl, F. L. (1984, October). The effects of social and isolate toys on the interactions and play of integrated and nonintegrated groups of preschoolers. *Education and Training of the Mentally Retarded, 25,* 169-174.

Brady, M. P., & Gunter, P. L. (1985). *Integrating moderately and severely handicapped learners: Strategies that work.* Springfield, IL: Thomas.

Bricker, D. D. (1978). A rationale for the integration of handicapped and nonhandicapped preschool children. In M. J. Guralnick (Ed.), *Early intervention and the integration of handicapped and nonhandicapped children* (pp. 3-26). London: University Park Press.

Brinker, R. P. (1985). Interactions between severely mentally retarded students and other students in integrated and segregated public school settings. *American Journal of Mental Deficiency, 89,* 589-594.

Brown, W. H., Fox, J. J., & Brady, M. P. (1987). Effects of spatial density on 3- and 4-year-old children's socially directed behavior during free play: An investigation of a setting factor. *Education and Treatment of Children, 10,* 247-258.

Bryant, L. E., & Budd, K. S. (1984). Teaching behaviorally handicapped preschool children to share. *Journal of Applied Behavior Analysis, 17,* 45-56.

Carden-Smith, L. K., & Fowler, S. A. (1983). An assessment of student and teacher behavior in treatment and mainstreamed classes for preschool and kindergarten. *Analysis and Intervention in Developmental Disabilities, 3,* 35-57.

Carden-Smith, L. K., & Fowler, S. A. (1986). Positive peer pressure: The effects of peer monitoring on children's disruptive behavior. *Journal of Applied Behavior Analysis, 17,* 213-228.

Carta, J. J., Sainato, D. M., & Greenwood, C. R. (1988). Advances in the ecological assessment of classroom instruction for young children with handicaps. In S. L. Odom & M. B. Karnes (Eds.), *Early intervention for infants and children with handicaps* (pp. 217-239). Baltimore: Brookes.

Certo, N., Haring, N., & York, R. (Eds.). (1984). *Public school integration of severely handicapped students.* Baltimore: Brookes.

Chandler, L. K. (1986). *Planning the transition between infant development programs and special education units' programs.* Bismark, ND: Resource Guide for the North Dakota Department of Public Instruction.

Chandler, L. K. (1989). *An ecobehavioral analysis of the influence of multiple setting events on preschool children's peer social interaction.* Unpublished doctoral dissertation, University of Kansas, Lawrence, KS.

Chandler, L. K., Fowler, S. A., & Lubeck, R. C. (1986). Assessing family needs: The first step in providing family-focused intervention. *Diagnostique, 11,* 233-245.

Chandler, L. K., Lubeck, R. C., & Fowler, S. A. (1990). *The generalization and maintenance of preschool children's social skills: A critical review and analysis.* Manuscript submitted for publication.

Department of Health, Education, and Welfare. (1978). *Section 504 of the Rehabilitation Act of 1973. Handicapped person rights under federal law.* Washington, DC: Office of the Secretary, Office for Civil Rights.

DeWert, M., & Helsels, E. (1985). The Helsels story of Robin. In H. R. Turnbull & A. P. Turnbull (Eds.), *Parents speak out: Then and now* (pp. 81-106). Columbus, OH: Merrill.

Donder, D. D., & York, R. (1984). Integration of students with severe handicaps. In N. Certo, N. Haring, & R. York (Eds.), *Public school integration of severely handicapped students* (pp. 1-14). Baltimore: Brookes.

Dunst, C. J., Trivette, C., & Deal, A. (1988). *Enabling and empowering families: Principles and guidelines for practice.* Cambridge, MA: Brookline Books.

Edgar, E., McNulty, B., & Gaetz, J. (1984). Educational placement of graduates of preschool programs for handicapped children. *Topics in Early Childhood Special Education, 4*(3), 19-29.

Esposito, B. G. (1987). The effects of preschool integration on the development of nonhandicapped children. *Journal of the Division for Early Childhood, 12,* 31-46.

Fowler, S. A. (1982). Transition from preschool to kindergarten for children with special needs. In K. E. Allen & E. M. Goetz (Eds.), *Early childhood education: Special problems, special solutions* (pp. 309-334). Germantown, MD: Aspen Systems.

Fowler, S. A. (1986). Peer-monitoring and self-monitoring: Alternatives to traditional teacher management. *Exceptional Children, 52,* 573-581.

Fowler, S. A. (1988). Transition planning. *Teaching Exceptional Children, 20*(4), 62-63.

Fowler, S. A., Chandler, L. K., Johnson, T. E., & Stella, E. (1988). Individualizing family involvement in school transitions: Gathering information and choosing the next program. *Journal of the Division for Early Childhood, 12,* 208-216.

Fowler, S. A., Chandler, L. K., Johnson, T. E., & Stella, E. (1989). *Communicating with a new program: Individualizing family involvement in school transitions.* Unpublished manuscript.

Gump, P. V. (1977). Ecological psychologist: Critics or contributors to behavior analysis? In A. Rogers-Warren & S. F. Warren (Eds.), *Ecological perspectives in behavior analysis* (pp. 133-148). Baltimore: University Park Press.

Gump, P. V. (1978). School environments. In I. Altman & J. F. Wohwill (Eds.), *Children and the environment* (pp. 131-169). New York: Plenum.

Guralnick, M. J. (1976). The value of integrating handicapped and nonhandicapped preschool children. *American Journal of Orthopsychiatry, 46,* 236-245.

Guralnick, M. J. (1978). Integrated preschool as educational and therapeutic environments: Concepts, designs, and analysis. In M. J. Guralnick (Ed.), *Early intervention and the integration of handicapped and nonhandicapped children* (pp. 115-145). London: University Park Press.

Guralnick, M. J. (1980). The social behavior of preschool children at different developmental levels: Effects of group composition. *Journal of Experimental Child Psychology, 31,* 115-130.

Guralnick, M. J. (1981a). The efficacy of integrating handicapped children in early education settings: Research implications. *Topics in Early Childhood Special Education, 1*(1), 57-71.

Guralnick, M. J. (1981b). Programmatic factors affecting child-child social interactions in mainstreamed preschool programs. *Exceptional Education Quarterly, 1*(4), 71-91.

Guralnick, M. J. (1986). The peer relations of young handicapped and nonhandicapped children. In P. S. Strain, M. J. Guralnick, & N. M. Walker (Eds.), *Children's social behavior: Development, assessment, and modification* (pp. 93-140). New York: Academic.

Guralnick, M. J., & Groom, J. M. (1988). Peer interaction in mainstreamed and specialized classrooms: A comparative analysis. *Exceptional Children, 54*(5), 415-425.

Guralnick, M. J., & Paul-Brown, D. (1977). The nature of verbal interaction among handicapped and nonhandicapped preschool children. *Child Development, 48,* 254-260.

Guralnick, M. J., & Paul-Brown, D. (1980). Functional and discourse analyses of nonhandicapped preschool children's speech to handicapped children. *American Journal of Mental Deficiency, 84,* 444-454.

Guralnick, M. J., & Paul-Brown, D. (1984). Communicative adjustments during behavior-request episodes among children at different developmental levels. *Child Development, 55,* 911-919.

Guralnick, M. J., & Paul-Brown, D. (1986). Communicative interactions of mildly delayed and normally developing preschool children: Effects of listener's developmental level. *Journal of Speech and Hearing Research, 29,* 2-29.

Hains, A. H., Fowler, S. A., & Chandler, L. K. (1988). Planning school transitions: Family and professional collaboration. *Journal of the Division for Early Childhood, 12,* 108-115.

Hains, A. H., Fowler, S. A., Schwartz, I. S., Kottwitz, E., & Rosenkoetter, S. (1989). A comparison of preschool and kindergarten teacher expectations for school readiness. *Early Childhood Research Quarterly, 4*(7), 75-88.

Hamre-Nietupski, S., Nietupski, J., Stainback, W., & Stainback, S. (1984). Preparing school systems for longitudinal integration efforts. In N. Certo, N. Haring, & R. York (Eds.), *Public school integration of severely handicapped students* (pp. 107-141). Baltimore: Brookes.

Hops, H., & Cobb, J. (1973). Survival behaviors in the educational setting: Their implications for research and intervention. In L. Hamerlynck, L. Haney, & E. Mash (Eds.), *Behavior change: Methodology, concepts, and practice.* Champaign, IL: Research Press.

Hoyson, M., Jamieson, B., & Strain, P. S. (1984). Individualized group instruction for normally developing and autistic-like children: The LEAP curriculum. *Journal of the Division for Early Childhood, 8,* 157-172.

Huefner, D. S. (1988). The consulting teacher model: Risks and opportunities. *Exceptional Children, 54,* 403-414.

Huston-Stein, A., Friedrich-Cofer, L., & Susman, E. J. (1977). The relation of classroom structure to social behavior, imaginative play, and self-regulation of economically disadvantaged preschool children. *Child Development, 48,* 908-916.

Innocenti, M. S., Stowitschek, J. J., Rule, S., Killoran, J., Striefel, S., & Boswell, C. (1986). A naturalistic study of the relation between preschool setting events and peer interaction in four activity contexts. *Early Childhood Research Quarterly, 1,* 141-153.

Jenkins, J. R., Speltz, M. L., & Odom, S. L. (1985). Integrating normal and handicapped preschoolers: Effects on child development and social interaction. *Exceptional Children, 52,* 7-18.

Johnson, T. E., Chandler, L. K., Kerns, G. M., & Fowler, S. A. (1986). What are parents saying about family involvement in school transitions? A retrospective transition interview. *Journal of the Division for Early Childhood, 11,* 10-17.

Johnson, D. W., & Johnson, R. T. (1980). Integrating handicapped students into the mainstream. *Exceptional Children, 47,* 90-99.

Johnson, D. W., & Johnson, R. T. (1986). Mainstreaming and cooperative learning strategies. *Exceptional Children, 52,* 553-561.

Johnson, R. T., & Meyer, L. (1985). Program design and research to normalize peer interactions. In M. P. Brady & P. L. Gunter (Eds.), *Integrating moderately and severely handicapped learners: Strategies that work* (pp. 79-101). Springfield, IL: Thomas.

Kalfus, G. R. (1984). Peer mediated intervention: A critical review. *Child and Family Behavior Therapy, 6*(1), 17-43.

Kugelmass, J. W. (1989). The "shared classroom": A case study of interactions between early childhood and special education staff and children. *Journal of Early Intervention, 13,* 36-44.

Lubeck, R. C. (1986). *Assessing and facilitating social skills in preschool children.* Workshop presented at the National Head Start Conference, Springfield, IL.

McEvoy, M. A., Nordquist, V. M., Twardosz, S., Heckaman, K. A., Wehby, J. H., & Denny, R. K. (1988). Promoting autistic children's peer interaction in an integrated early childhood setting using affection activities. *Journal of Applied Behavior Analysis, 21,* 193-200.

McHale, S., & Simeonsson, R. J. (1980). Effects of interaction on nonhandicapped children's attitudes toward autistic children. *American Journal of Mental Deficiency, 85,* 19-24.

McLean, M., & Odom, S. L. (1988). *LRE and social integration.* Washington, DC: Division for Early Childhood White Paper.

Neisworth, J. T., Willoughby-Herb, S. J., Bagnato, S. J., Cartwright, C. A., & Laub, K. W. (1980). *Individualized education for preschool exceptional children.* Germantown, MD: Aspen Systems.

Odom, S. L., Bender, M., Stein, M., Doran, L., Houden, P., McInnes, M., Gilbert, M., Deklyen, M., Speltz, P., & Jenkins, J. (1988). *Integrated preschool curriculum: Procedure for socially integrating handicapped and nonhandicapped preschool children.* Seattle: University of Washington Press.

Odom, S. L., DeKlyen, M., & Jenkins, J. R. (1984). Integrating handicapped and nonhandicapped preschoolers: Developmental impact on the nonhandicapped children. *Exceptional Children, 51*, 41-49.

Odom, S. L., Hoyson, M., Jamieson, B., & Strain, P. S. (1985). Increasing handicapped preschoolers' social interactions: Cross setting and component analysis. *Journal of Applied Behavior Analysis, 18*, 3-16.

Odom, S. L., & McEvoy, M. A. (1988). Integration of young children with handicaps and normally developing children. In S. L. Odom & M. B. Karnes (Eds.), *Early intervention for infants and children with handicaps* (pp. 241-267). Baltimore: Brookes.

Odom, S. L., & Strain, P. S. (1984). Classroom-based social skills instruction for severely handicapped preschool children. *Topics in Early Childhood Special Education, 4*(3), 97-116.

Odom, S. L., Strain, P. S., Karger, M. A., & Smith, J. D. (1986). Using single and multiple peers to promote social interaction among preschool children with severe handicaps. *Journal of the Division for Early Childhood, 18*, 53-64.

Parten, M. B. (1933). Social play among preschool children. *Journal of Abnormal Child Psychology, 28*, 136-147.

Peterson, N. L. (1982). Social integration of handicapped and nonhandicapped preschoolers: A study of playmate preferences. *Topics in Early Childhood Special Education, 2*(2), 56-69.

Peterson, N. L. (1987). *Early intervention for handicapped and at-risk children: An introduction to early childhood-special education.* Denver: Love.

Peterson, N. L., & Haralick, J. G. (1977). Integration of handicapped and nonhandicapped preschoolers: An analysis of play behavior and social interaction. *Education and Training of the Mentally Retarded, 12*, 235-245.

Project BEST: Building Effective School Transitions. (1986). Unpublished manuscript, University of Kansas, Lawrence, KS.

Quilitch, H. R., & Risley, T. R. (1973). The effects of play materials on social play. *Journal of Applied Behavior Analysis, 6*, 573-578.

Raab, M. M., Nordquist, V. M., Cunningham, J. L., & Bliem, C. D. (1986). Promoting peer regard of an autistic child in a mainstreamed preschool using pre-enrollment activities. *Child Study Journal, 16*(4), 265-284.

Reichart, D. C., Lynch, E. C., Anderson, B. C., Svobodny, L. A., & Mercury, M. G. (1989). Parental perspectives on integrated preschool opportunities for children with handicaps and children without handicaps. *Journal of Early Intervention, 13*, 6-13.

Rogers-Warren, A. K. (1984). Ecobehavioral analysis. *Education and Treatment of Children, 7*, 283-303.

Rostetter, D., Kowalski, R., & Hunter, D. (1984). Implementing the integration principle of PL 94-142. In N. Certo, N. Haring, & R. York (Eds.), *Public school integration of severely handicapped students* (pp. 293-320). Baltimore: Brookes.

Roth, F. P., & Clark, D. M. (1987). Symbolic play and social participation abilities of language-impaired and normally developing children. *Journal of Speech and Hearing Research, 52*(1), 17-29.

Rowbury, T. G. (1982). Preacademic skills for the reluctant learner. In K. E. Allen & E. M. Goetz (Eds.), *Early childhood education: Special problems, special solutions.* Rockville, MD: Aspen.

Rubin, K. H., & Howe, N. (1985). Toys and play behaviors: Overview. *Topics in Early Childhood Special Education, 5*(3), 1-9.

Safford, P. L., & Rosen, L. A. (1981). Mainstreaming: Application of a philosophical perspective in an integrated kindergarten program. *Topics in Early Childhood Special Education, 1*(1), 1-10.

Sainato, D. M., Maheady, L., & Shook, G. L. (1986). The effects of a classroom manager role on the social interaction patterns and social status of withdrawn kindergarten students. *Journal of Applied Behavior Analysis, 19*, 187-195.

Sainato, D. M., Strain, P. S., Lefebvre, D., & Rapp, N. (1987). Facilitating transition times with handicapped preschool children: A comparison between peer-mediation and antecedent prompt procedures. *Journal of Applied Behavior Analysis, 20*, 285-291.

Samuels, J. S. (1986). Why children fail to learn and what to do about it. *Exceptional Children, 53*, 7-16.

Sanford, A. R., & Zelman, J. G. (1981). *Learning accomplishments profile.* Chapel Hill Training-Outreach Program. Winston-Salem, NC: Kaplan.

Sasso, G. M., & Rude, H. A. (1987). Unprogrammed effects of training high-status peers to interact with severely handicapped children. *Journal of Applied Behavior Analysis, 20*, 35-44.

Schultz, R. P., Williams, W., Iverson, G. S., & Duncan, D. (1984). Social integration of severely handicapped students. In N. Certa, N. Haring, & R. York (Eds.), *Public school integration of severely handicapped students* (pp. 15-42). Baltimore: Brookes.

Shafer, M. S., Egel, A. L., & Neef, N. A. (1984). Training mildly handicapped peers to facilitate changes in the social interaction skills of autistic children. *Journal of Applied Behavior Analysis, 17,* 461-476.

Shearer, M. S., & Shearer, D. E. (1977). Parent involvement. In J. B. Jordan, A. H. Hayden, M. B. Karnes, & M. M. Wood (Eds.), *Early childhood education for exceptional children: A handbook of ideas and exemplary practices.* Reston, VA: Council for Exceptional Children.

Shores, R. E., Hester, P., & Strain, P. S. (1976). The effects of amount and type of teacher-child interaction on child-child interaction during free play. *Psychology in the Schools, 13*(2), 171-175.

Smith, P. K., & Connolly, K. J. (1980). *The ecology of preschool behavior.* Cambridge, MA: Cambridge University Press.

Snell, M. E. (1987). Serving young children with special needs and their families and PL 99-457. *Association for Persons with Severe Handicaps Newsletter, 13*(9), 1-2.

Speigel-McGill, P., Bambara, L. M., Shores, R. E., & Fox, J. J. (1984). The effects of proximity on socially oriented behaviors of severely multiply handicapped children. *Education and Treatment of Children, 7,* 365-378.

Spodek, B., Saracho, O. N., & Lee, R. C. (1984). *Mainstreaming young children.* Belmont, CA: Wadsworth.

Stainback, S., & Stainback, W. (1985). Examining and fostering integrated school experiences. In M. P. Brady & P. L. Gunter (Eds.), *Integrating moderately and severely handicapped learners: Strategies that work* (pp. 65-78). Springfield, IL: Thomas.

Strain, P. S. (1984). The social behavior patterns of nonhandicapped and developmentally disabled friend pairs in mainstreamed preschools. *Analysis and Intervention in Developmental Disabilities, 4,* 15-28.

Strain, P. S., Guralnick, M. J., & Walker, H. M. (Eds.). (1986). *Children's social behavior: Development, assessment, and modification.* New York: Academic.

Strain, P. S., Hoyson, M., & Jamieson, B. (1985). Normally developing preschoolers as intervention agents for autistic-like children: Effects on class deportment and social interaction. *Journal of the Division for Early Childhood, 9,* 105-115.

Strain, P. S., & Kerr, M. M. (1981). *Mainstreaming of children in schools: Research and programmatic issues.* New York: Academic.

Taylor, S. J. (1982). From segregation to integration: Strategies for integrating severely handicapped students in normal school and community settings. *Journal of the Association for the Severely Handicapped, 7*(3), 42-49.

Thompson, B. (1979). *Out of the nest: Instructional strategies to prepare young exceptional children for the mainstream.* The Wisconsin EC:EEN Project, Department of Public Instruction, 126 Langdon St., Madison, WI 53702.

Turnbull, R. H., Turnbull, A. P., & Wheat, M. J. (1982). Assumptions about parental participation: A legislative history. *Exceptional Education Quarterly, 3*(2), 1-8.

Turnbull, A. P., Winton, P. J., Blacher, J., & Salkind, N. (1982). Mainstreaming in the kindergarten classroom: Perspectives of parents of handicapped and nonhandicapped children. *Journal of the Division for Early Childhood, 6,* 14-20.

Twardosz, S. L., Nordquist, V. M., Simon, R., & Botkin, D. (1983). The effect of group affection activities on the interaction of socially isolate children. *Analysis and Intervention in Developmental Disabilities, 3,* 311-338.

Umansky, W. (1982). More than a teacher: An approach to meeting children's special needs. *Childhood Education, 58*(3), 155-158.

van den Pol, R., Crow, R. E., Rider, D. P., & Offner, R. B. (1985). Social interaction in an integrated preschool: Implications and applications. *Topics in Early Childhood Special Education, 4*(4), 59-76.

Vincent, L. J., Brown, L., & Getz-Sheftel, M. (1981). Integrating handicapped and typical children during the preschool years: The definition of best educational practice. *Topics in Early Childhood Special Education, 1*(1), 17-24.

Vincent, L. J., Salisbury, C., Walter, G., Brown, P., Gruenewald, L. J., & Powers, M. (1980). Program evaluation and curriculum development in early childhood/special education. In W. Sailor, B. Wilcox, & L. Brown (Eds.), *Methods of instruction for severely handicapped students* (pp. 303-328). Baltimore: Brookes.

Wahler, R. G., & Fox, J. J. (1981). Setting events in applied behavior analysis: Toward a conceptual and methodological expansion. *Journal of Applied Behavior Analysis, 14,* 327-338.

Walker, H. M., Greenwood, C. R., Hops, H., & Todd, N. M. (1979). Differential effects of reinforcing topographic components of social integration. *Behavior Modification, 3,* 291-321.

Walker, H. M., & Rankin, R. (1983). Assessing the behavioral expectations and demands of less restrictive settings. *School Psychology Review, 12,* 274-284.

Walter, G. (1979). *The "survival skills" displayed by kindergarteners and the structure of the regular classroom environment.* Unpublished master's thesis, University of Wisconsin, Madison, WI.

Walter, G., & Vincent, L. (1982). The handicapped child in the regular kindergarten program. *Journal of the Division for Early Childhood, 6,* 82-95.

Winton, P. J., & Turnbull, A. P. (1981). Parent involvement as viewed by parents of preschool handicapped children. *Topics in Early Childhood Special Education, 1*(1), 11-19.

Winton, P. J., Turnbull, A. P., & Blacher, J. (1984). *Selecting a preschool: A guide for parents of handicapped children.* Baltimore: University Park Press.

Wolfe, V. V., Boyd, L. A., & Wolfe, D. A. (1983). Teaching cooperative play to behavior-problem children. *Education and Treatment of Children, 6,* 343-362.

Wolfensberger, W. (1972). *The principles of normalization in human services.* Toronto: National Institute on Mental Retardation.

Wood, J. W. (1984). *Adapting instruction for the mainstream: A sequential approach to teaching.* Columbus, OH: Merrill.

Ziegler, P. (1985). Saying good-bye to preschool. *Young Children, 41,* 11-15.

Zigmond, N., & Miller, S. E. (1986). Assessment for instructional planning. *Exceptional Children, 52,* 501-509.

APPENDIX A:
MODEL PROGRAMS

Integration Preparation Programs

Special Education Early Intervention Program. This program sponsored by the Department of Education at the University of Kansas, prepares children for the next school setting. A key focus of the program is the integration of typical preschoolers in the classroom and a cooperative student exchange program with a Montessori preschool. This allows children with handicaps the opportunity to participate in mainstream settings and to interact with typical children. Contact: Barbara Thompson or Nancy Peterson, Department of Special Education, University of Kansas, Lawrence, KS 66045; (913) 86404945.

Learning Experience — An Alternative Program for Preschoolers and Parents. This program sponsored by the University of Pittsburgh and Pittsburgh Public Schools, integrates autistic and normally developing children in preschool classrooms in the public schools. A key focus of this program is the utilization of normally developing children as models and intervenors on the social and language skills and classroom behavior of their autistic classmates. Contact: Phil Strain, Western Psychiatric Institute and Clinic, 3811 O'Hara St., University of Pittsburgh, Pittsburgh, PA 15213; (402) 462-2903.

Peabody Least Restrictive Project. This program, sponsored by the Department of Special Education at Peabody College, Vanderbilt University, has developed model integrated classrooms for children with severe handicaps in elementary schools. Model classrooms address four issues: systematic programming for social integration, implementation of the Individualized Curriculum Sequencing model for instruction, a transdisciplinary approach to service, and environmental design for academic integration. Contact: Mary McEvoy or Cathy Alpert, Box 328, GPC, Vanderbilt University, Nashville, TN 37203; (615) 322-8185.

Tennessee Outreach Training Program. This program, sponsored by the Kennedy Center at Peabody College, Vanderbilt University, provides technical assistance and training to early childhood special education programs. This program provides information on "Best Practices" in early childhood special education, including functional curriculum programming and preparing children for the transition between programs. Contact: Steven Warren or Donna DeStafano, Box 328, GPC, Vanderbilt University, Nashville, TN 37203; (615) 322-2249.

Social Integration Program. This program, sponsored by the Developmental Center for Handicapped Persons at Utah State University, integrates preschool-age children with special needs into mainstream daycare centers as preparation for mainstream elementary school programs. A key focus of the program is special education training provided for children in daycare and transdisciplinary consultation provided for daycare staff. This program also provides transition programming to assist children, families, and staff as a child leaves the daycare program and enters elementary school. Contact: Sara Rule, DCHP, Utah State University, Logan, UT 84322-6805; (801) 750-1987.

Transition Preparation Programs

Four exemplary transition programs were reviewed in *Teaching Exceptional Children* (Fowler, 1988). Each of these programs emphasizes interagency cooperation, family involvement, and child preparation.

Building Effective School Transition Programs. Sponsored by the University of Kansas. Contact: Robin Hazel, Kansas Early Childhood Research Institute on Transitions, Bureau of Child Research, University of Kansas, Lawrence, KS 99045; (913) 864-3050.

Sequenced Transition to Education in the Public School Program. Sponsored by the Child Development Center of the Bluegrass. Contact: Peggy Stevens, Child Development Centers of the Bluegrass, 465 Springhill Dr., Lexington, KY 40503; (606) 278-0549.

Transitioning into the Elementary Education Mainstream Program. Sponsored by the Center for Developmental Disabilities. Contact: Michael Conn-Powers, Center for Developmental Disabilities, 499 Waterman Bldg., University of Vermont, Burlington, VT 05405; (802) 656-4031.

The Early Childhood Interagency Transition Model. Sponsored by the University of Washington. Contact: Pam Taziolo or Gene Edgar, Experimental Education Unit, WJ-10, CDMRC, University of Washington, Seattle, WA 98195; (206) 543-4011.

Strategies for Maximizing Reading Success in the Regular Classroom

Bonnie Grossen
Doug Carnine
University of Oregon

The National Commission on Excellence in Education reported in *A Nation at Risk* (1983) that 13% of the 17-year-olds who graduate from school in the United States are functionally illiterate. Recent reports estimate that approximately 25% of the population drops out of school before high school graduation (Thorndike, 1973). Too many achieve too little in school. There is reason to believe that the quality of reading instruction in the early grades significantly influences student achievement levels at high school and at college (Chall, 1983), and in turn whether students stay in school.

To gain meaning from text (i.e., comprehension) is the purpose of reading, but comprehension will not be adequate unless a reader can translate the printed words into the language they represent (i.e., decode). Comprehension instruction assumes decoding. The phenomenon of "bright" students who cannot decode frequently indicates students who would have little trouble with the comprehension component of reading, if they could only decode the print into language.

Instruction that teaches the decoding of print into language is different from instruction in comprehension skills. Solutions will be presented for major problems in each of these two crucial areas.

DECODING INSTRUCTION

Students with decoding problems misidentify so many words or read so slowly that comprehension is impaired. Students who score poorly on a reading task can be identified as having a decoding problem only by listening to them read orally. If a student misidentifies more than 5% of the words in a text, or if a second grader (or older) reads at a rate of less than 100 words per minute, the student has a decoding problem that is severe enough to impair comprehension.

For this all-too-common problem, the best solution is preventive: use of a phonic approach in the initial 2 years of reading instruction. A recent study comparing a phonic and a whole-word approach has once again found the phonic approach superior to the whole-word on transfer to phonemically regular words (Gettinger, 1986). Students who had received phonic instruction could read 54% of the untaught transfer words; students in receipt of the whole-word approach read only 3% of them correctly. This finding means that a child who is taught the word *mad*, for example, by a phonic approach, should also be able to read the words *am, adam, maam, dam*, having learned the sound for each of the three letters in *mad* and being able to read them in any combination. A child taught by a whole-word approach likely will read only the word *mad* correctly.

The only way a whole-word reader can become independent of the teacher in figuring out a new word is either (a) to make a guess based on the context of the passage, or (b) to develop a personal ------ strategy. Guessing based on context is not very efficient, as you may have determined when you had to guess the missing word above. This is how the reading task looks to a whole-word reader. The missing word is: --on-c. Now the presence of a few letters allows you, a fluent reader, to combine context clues with a few phonic clues. Yes, the word is *phonic*. Did you guess correctly? Children who have been taught by the whole-word approach and have developed some personal phonic skills have more clues to the word.

If a child learning by a whole-word approach cannot develop phonic skills on her own, every new word is the equivalent of a total blank, and the child is permanently condemned to the psycholinguistic guessing game recommended by many as the way to read (Goodman, 1976; Smith, 1978). Because knowledge of some sounds for letters greatly increases reading efficiency (Carnine, Silbert & Kameenui, 1990), it is important to provide students with this knowledge, which involves taking a phonic approach to teaching reading.

A phonic approach does not mean learning a sound for every letter that will ever be encountered. English is not a completely phonetic language. Therefore, a modern research-based phonic approach seeks to teach only the most frequent letter–sound correspondences. From computer studies of the English language, Burmeister (1975) found that many of the "traditional" phonics rules did not generalize well enough to justify teaching them. She identified a smaller set of useful generalizations of approximately 55 letter–sound correspondences that can be used to decode about 80% of the English language. (For a list of these, see Carnine, Silbert & Kameenui, 1990.) This small set represents the most reliable, frequent letter–sound correspondences. Thus, every word is not a "blank" to be figured out from context.

In spite of years of research indicating that a phonic approach is best, the majority of the reading programs used in schools today either do not teach phonics at all or do not apply the research properly. In addition, many professionals still take issue with a phonic approach and advocate a whole-word approach to initial reading instruction instead. Because we regard the use of a phonic approach as a critical step in preventing decoding failure, and because the instruction is so often lacking or done incorrectly, we believe the issue warrants detailed positive and negative examples to illustrate the type of phonics instruction that has been proven to be effective, and a brief response to the main criticisms of phonics made by advocates of whole-word approaches.

Step 1: Introduce Letter–Sound Correspondence in Isolation

Most basal readers include a phonics component. However, most basal readers recommend that sounds not be presented in isolation but instead that letter-sound correspondences be presented implicitly. The following instructions from such an implicit phonic approach published by Harcourt, Brace, Jovanovich, direct the teacher to introduce the sound for *s:*

> (Write the words *sun* and *soap* on the chalkboard. Point to each word, say it, and have the children repeat it.) "The words *sun* and *soap* begin with the same sound. They also begin with the same letter." (Point to the *s* in *sun*.) "What letter does the word *Sun* begin with?" (Students say the letter name, *s*.) "The letter *s* stands for the beginning sound in *sun*." (Point to the *s* in *soap*.) "What letter does the word *soap* begin with?" (Students say the letter name, *s*.) "The letter *s* also stands for the beginning sound in the word *soap*." (Point to the *s* in both words.) "The letters *s* stands for the beginning sound in the words *sun* and *soap*." (Early, Cooper, Santeusanio, 1983, p. 70).

As is typical of the implicit approach, the sound [sss] for the letter *s* is never stated directly by the teacher, nor does the letter *s* appear in isolation. In contrast, the following is an example of instructions that present the letter–sound correspondence for *s* explicitly, in isolation:

(Write *s* on the blackboard. Point to *s.*) "This sound is *sss*. What sound?" (Students say the sound, sss.)

Here the letter–sound correspondence is clearly and explicitly presented. To expect the child to isolate the sound on her own requires skill in phonemic segmentation, which has been shown to be very difficult for young children (Bruce, 1964; Rosner, 1973). The teacher can prevent reading failure by directly telling children the sounds for letters.

A reading program with reading passages that use a high percentage of words that conform to the phonic generalizations that have been taught is called *code-based*. Using code-based material in the first 2 years is critical to effective reading instruction, because the material typically is arranged so that new sounds are taught sequentially, and cumulative review is available in the word lists and in the reading passages, which contain the new sounds and sounds learned earlier.

A high proportion of the words in the earliest selections a child reads must conform to the phonics she has been taught (Anderson, Hiebert, Scott, & Wilkinson, 1985). Otherwise, there will be little opportunity to apply and practice the letter–sound relationships in actual reading tasks. Unfortunately, this opportunity for practice is most often lacking, because code-based readers are rarely used in schools. For example, a popular basal reader (American Book Company, 1980) provides for implicit instruction in the letter–sound relationships of *d, m, s, r,* and *f* as the first letters for which the children learn sounds. However, the first sentence that the children read is "The dog is up." In this sentence, the *d* is the only letter–sound correspondence the children have learned. The letter–sound correspondences that children learn will appear useless to them in a program with this kind of sequencing.

In contrast, another basal reader, published by Allyn & Bacon, also recommends an implicit approach to introducing the sounds for *a, n, s,* and *t* as the first four sounds the children are to learn. It presents the following as the first sentence for the children to read: "Big Ann sat on Sad Sal" (Ruddell, Adams, & Taylor, 1978). Eleven of the 17 letters in this sentence conform to the phonic generalizations that children have learned.

If implicit instruction is recommended in such a code-based program, it can be easily adapted to explicit phonics instruction, and the program generally can be used to effectively teach reading by a research-based phonic approach. Besides the Allyn and Bacon series mentioned above, the linguistic readers lend themselves well to a phonic approach. These programs are published by *Merrill, Open Court, Palo Alto, SRA, Scribner.* However, at the beginning level, the basal reader from Scribner tends to provide less practice than the others. One basal program that uses explicit phonics instruction and uses an extremely high percentage of words that conform to the phonic generalizations learned is *Reading Mastery*, published by Science Research Associates, (Engelmann & Bruner, 1985).

Many basal readers expose students to too many letter–sound relationships and teach nonessential verbal rules about phonics. For example, one basal reader, although not known for providing intensive phonics, tries to teach over 200 letter–sound correspondences (American Book Company, 1980). These include such low-frequency letter–sound correspondences as *ch* sounding like /k/ as in chorus and *sc* sounding like /s/ as in *scene*. Another misleading generalization taught in this program is that *q* sounds like /kw/. A pupil learning this rule would try to sound out *quick* as /kw-uuu-iii-k/. *Q* never appears in the language without a *u* following it, so the pair of letters *qu* should be taught as having the sound /kw/; so that *quick* is sounded out as /kw-iii-k/ and *quest* is sounded out as /kw-eee-sss-t/.

Step 2: Teach Students to Blend

Blending sounds together into words is a critical step in reading. The reader approximates the word by sounding out and then matches the approximation to a real word from her oral language that fits the context of the passage. Teachers who spend more time on blending produce greater gains on reading achievement tests of young readers (Haddock, 1976; Rosenshine & Stevens, 1984). Regrettably, Beck's analysis (1981) of eight popular reading programs revealed that in the most popular of these programs (*Bank Street, Ginn, Houghton Mifflin, Merrill, Open Highways*, and *Sullivan*) there were *no* procedures for teaching blending. *Palo Alto* provided some minimal opportunity for blending practice that used ill-defined procedures. Only *Reading Mastery* (Engelmann & Bruner, 1985) was found to have a definite and effective instructional strategy for teaching blending (Beck, 1981).

Step 3: Provide Immediate Feedback on Oral Reading Errors

Because of the many irregularities in the letter–sound correspondences in the English language, students need extensive practice to read words accurately and fluently. This requires oral reading practice. It is crucial that students receive corrective feedback during this practice, so that they do not practice reading inaccurately. Having children read silently when they are not proficient will only make errors and misrules more difficult to correct.

Feedback should be consistent with a child's knowledge of phonetic analysis. For example, if a first grader sounds out the word *said* as s-a (as in *fat*)-i (as in *it*)-d, the teacher should not tell the child, "That is wrong; the word is *said*," but instead should say, "Good sounding out that word. That's the way we sound it out, but this is how we say it — *said*." (If a third grader should say the same sounds, the teacher would say, "That is wrong; the word is *said*,." The third grader should not be using sounds for common words such as *said*.)

Every oral reading error should be corrected, not just the ones that alter the meaning. Pany and McCoy (1988) found that third-grade reading-disabled children, who made a large number of errors during reading (10–15 errors), significantly improved their word recognition and their comprehension scores when given immediate feedback on every single error. When corrective feedback was provided after every error, the children made significantly fewer overall errors, significantly fewer errors that changed the meaning during reading of the passage, significantly fewer errors on lists of error words presented on an immediate and delayed basis, and significantly fewer errors on passage comprehension questions. Simply receiving feedback on errors that altered the meaning of the passages had no effect.

Step 4: Provide Extensive Practice

After presenting a sound in isolation, immediately present it in the context of words (word lists), and then in the context of a reading passage incorporating cumulative review of earlier learned sounds. A common problem to guard against in using explicit phonics instruction is not providing enough practice and review. Practice and review are provided by the words and sentences pupils read in the reading passages. A new sound should be practiced in isolation every day for several days, then incorporated in word-reading activities. It should appear several times every day for the rest of the program.

Responses to Criticisms of a Phonic Approach

Phonics skills are not needed for good reading. Marie Carbo (1987), a frequent and strong critic of a phonics approach, maintains that good readers exist who have never mastered phonics. She presents the following example of a phonics task:

> Say the word in each shape. If you hear a vowel sound that you hear in *hard*, color the shape green. If you hear a vowel sound that you hear in *corn*, color the shape blue. If you hear a vowel sound that you hear in *first*, color the shape orange. (*Skylights*, Houghton-Mifflin, 1981, p. 21).

This example is taken from a program that uses essentially a whole-word approach to teach reading and only includes a token phonic component. This type of phonics task has no research base and is irrelevant to reading. Certainly there are readers who cannot perform this task. Phonics skills, however, are not irrelevant. A pupil must be able to represent the letters in a new word as sounds to be able to turn print into language, and thereby read.

Examples of other common learning activities that are *not* part of a research-based phonic approach and that are irrelevant to reading are (a) requiring pupils to label sounds as *long* or *short*, (b) requiring pupils to name the letters of the alphabet, and (c) generally requiring pupils to memorize any verbal rules, such as "when two vowels go walking the first one does the talking." A research-based phonic approach simply presents a small set of letters or letter groups in isolation and systematically has pupils orally respond with the most common sound for those letters. Any phonics task that requires a written response is probably not relevant to reading.

Code-based programs use uninteresting stories. Some authorities criticize code-based programs because the stories are not as interesting and the language is not as natural as in meaning-based programs. However, regardless of the approach used, only a limited set of words can be used in the initial reading selections, and there is really no need for a code-based program to be more stilted than a meaning-based program. Consider the following examples of segments from stories to be read early in first grade. The first is an excerpt from a meaning-based reading selection published by Ginn:

> Little Duck said, "I can't hop.
> I can swim, but I can't hop.
> I don't want to swim.
> I want to hop, Little Rabbit.
> You can hop fast.
> I want to hop like a rabbit." (Clymer, Venezky & Indrisano, 1984).

The following passage is from a code-based basal:

> He has no feet. He has no nose. He has no teeth. He is not a cow, and he is not a cat.
> Is he a rat? No, he is not a rat.
> (Engelmann & Bruner, 1985)

The story in the second example contains natural-sounding language, and all of the words in the passage conform to the phonic generalizations the students have learned. In order to use more interesting stories and maintain the conformity of the words with the phonic generalizations that have been taught, the program uses special orthography. For example, *no* is written as *nō*, so the *ō* sound can be discriminated from the *o* sound in *not*. Other code-based programs, which do not use special orthography, either have a lower proportion of words in the initial passages that conform to the phonic generalizations that have been taught or use very stilted language (e.g., Nan can fan Dan.).

Phonics teaches the wrong purpose for reading. One of the major criticisms of a phonic approach is that it approaches reading as a mindless activity and obscures the purpose of reading, because the pupils do not have to use context to decode (i.e., the children do not have to think about what they are reading). This conception of phonics is not true, because a phonic approach only results in an approximation for many words. Successful reading with a phonic approach requires the use of context in matching the phonic representation of some words with the word from the pupils' oral language that fits the meaning of the sentence. When a phonic approach is taught well, use of context develops naturally (Carnine, Carnine, & Gersten, 1984).

Phonics produces poor comprehension. Some authorities criticize phonic approaches because students who have been taught from these programs sometimes have been found to be weak comprehenders, even though they have good decoding skills. However, a child who cannot decode (i.e., cannot say the words when reading orally) has *no* hope of comprehending. Learning to decode does not ensure comprehension, but a child who can decode subsequently can be taught strategies for better comprehension. There is no reason to believe that a phonic approach has *caused* any weakness in comprehension. A child who has learned to decode from a phonic approach, but has weak comprehension, is probably a child who would have failed completely in the whole-word approach.

Phonics is out, whole-language is in. Currently there is much talk about the whole-language approach, an approach that "integrates" all the language skills of reading, writing, telling, and listening. The whole-language approach is said to be neither a phonic approach nor a traditional whole-word approach. In fact, no basal reader or controlled vocabulary is used in the initial reading instruction. Pupils begin by writing their own stories in the first 2 months, a "language-experience approach," and then move into reading "real" literature.

The state of California has now adopted the whole-language approach as the official state methodology for teaching reading, and publishers are hustling to change their basal readers to conform. California's decision was based on recent reports of the high literacy rate of New Zealand, which uses a whole-language approach. A phonic approach has been unfashionable in New Zealand since the 1940s and the whole-word basal readers were discarded in 1963 (Clay, 1976). Two international literacy studies in 1973 (Purves, 1973; Thorndike, 1973) found New Zealand to have the highest literacy rate in the world. From this it was concluded that the whole-language approach is better than the others.

We believe the trend from a whole-word approach to a whole-language approach is a trend from bad to worse. Several criticisms of the international literacy studies have been made. New Zealand only retains 13% of the 18-year-old population in school, whereas the United States, for example, retains 75% of this population in school (Guthrie, 1981). Guthrie (1981) found a high correlation between the performance of the 18-year-old group in each country with the percentages of retention in school. Comparing the cream of New Zealand's crop with the masses of the United States biases the results considerably.

However, the literacy studies also compared samples of 14-year-old pupils. The results for these samples were less dramatic. The sample of 14-year-olds from New Zealand was average in word knowledge and below the median in reading speed. They scored highest in their ability to answer difficult questions over prose passages, especially literature, where they scored only approximately one-quarter standard deviation above the U.S. 14-year-olds.

Even assuming the samples from the United States and New Zealand are comparable, studies by Guthrie (1981) and Purves (1979) have presented strong evidence that the fact that New Zealand is a "print-oriented" society, which reads 20% more than the United States, is the causal factor for the high literacy rate. Another study comparing the performance of various ethnic groups within New Zealand found that Maori children, who have much better control of the English language, at the early ages tested, than Samoan children who speak Samoan in the home, make much less progress in reading than Samoans (Clay, 1976). Clay speculated that the social status and aspirations of these ethnic groups may be the significant factor in accounting for this strange difference (Clay, 1976).

The goal of research is to describe successful ways to teach. The whole-language approach uses no text, has no specific guidelines, and therefore results in great variety in what teachers do and in what their students achieve. New Zealand pupils seem to learn letter names in school (Clay, 1976), so there must be some talk about letters in isolation. Teachers are reported to be familiar with the "strategies of sounding out and syllabifying" (Clay, 1976, p. 338). Whole-language in practice seems to be an undefined approach, which may or may not include some of the effective phonic strategies described above. Comparing it with other approaches gives little information about what teaching strategies are effective.

Finally, without a study comparing the whole-language approach with a modern phonic approach, which does integrate all the language skills (Baxter, 1988), there is no evidence that the whole-language approach produces better reading performance than a phonic approach. There has been no such study completed. A meta-analysis of the results of studies comparing the language-experience approach, a component of the whole-language approach, with the traditional basal whole-word approach found that language-experience can be more effective in an early "cognitive phase," in which children become aware of the tasks involved in reading (Stahl & Miller, 1988). Two studies comparing reading programs with a phonic approach, a whole-word approach, and a language-experience approach have found the phonic program better than both the whole-word and language-experience programs (Stallings, 1975; Abt Associates, 1977).

Conclusions for Decoding Instruction

The most important consideration in providing effective reading instruction is the selection of a code-based material for the initial 2-year period of instruction. Regrettably, in many of the best-selling basal reading series (*Houghton Mifflin, Ginn, Bank Street, Open Highways*), there is little connection between the phonics lessons and the reading selections in the primers (Beck, 1981). Without a high proportion of words that conform to the phonic generalizations being taught, letter–sound correspondences will be very difficult for many children to learn, regardless of whether an explicit or implicit phonics approach is used.

Research indicates that the best reading instruction involves systematically teaching children the most common sound for a select group of letters and letter combinations. These letter–sound correspondences should then be practiced immediately in the context of words and, as soon as possible, in the context of sentences. Initial reading instruction should incorporate extensive oral reading practice with immediate corrective feedback.

COMPREHENSION INSTRUCTION

Reading comprehension, which assumes proficiency in decoding, encompasses many skills, and there are many interventions that are effective. In spite of there being many interventions available, few seem to be used in classrooms. Durkin (1978-1979) found that a representative sample of teachers in Grades 3–6 spent less than 1% of the reading period on comprehension instruction. Instruction for phonics or decoding was also rare. Most of the reading period was spent on noninstructional activities. Furthermore, instructional activities centered on assessment. Durkin (1978-1979) also observed social studies classes and found that there was no comprehension instruction present here either, even though the reading ability of many children was so poor that they could not read the textbook.

The instructional activities that have been shown to improve comprehension skills are generally *prereading* activities, such as establishing a clear purpose for the reading, building necessary background knowledge of the subject, teaching difficult vocabulary from the passage, and so on. Activities that *follow* reading are generally assessment, which does not improve comprehension skills beyond holding students accountable for their reading in some way.

Effective strategies valuable for students' use *while* they read have been less well defined, but they have received more attention recently. Two strategies for students to use during reading are described below. Both strategies teach students to use the structure of the passage as an aid in comprehension. One, the story grammar strategy, is suitable for narrative literature; the other, a text structure strategy, is suitable for use in content classes such as social studies and science, when the purpose of reading is to gather information.

Story Grammar for Narrative Literature

Stories are generally structured similarly. Characters have goals that are either stated directly or can be inferred. The characters are placed in settings and make plans and undertake actions to achieve these goals. The actions unfold in an orderly sequence. There is an outcome, which constitutes success or failure in reaching their goals.

Recent research has shown that students can be taught to notice this story structure by answering a predictable, repeated pattern of questions that focus attention on the structure of the story. These studies have shown that asking a predetermined pattern of questions produces better comprehension than the traditional approach of asking unpredictable, uniquely relevant questions (Carnine & Kinder, 1985; Dimino, 1988; Gurney, 1987; Idol, 1987; Short & Ryan, 1984; Singer & Donlan, 1982). This pattern of questions is called *story grammar*. The following is an example of a very basic story grammar from Carnine and Kinder (1985):

1. Who is the story about?

   _____

2. What problem does he or she have?

   _____

3. How does he or she try to fix the problem? _____

4. What happens in the end?

   _____

More complex story grammars have also been effective. The important element of a proposed story grammar is that a pattern be used and that the instructional stories lend themselves to the pattern selected. Instruction proceeds in three steps: (a) teacher-directed presentation, (b) guided practice, (c) independent use of the internalized story grammar. More complex patterns require longer instruction for the first two steps before students can internalize the pattern.

Step 1: Teacher Presentation. In presenting the above story grammar for the first story or two, the teacher should say the following:

> "We are going to read an action story. In an action story we ask four questions: (1) Who is the story about," et cetera.

During the reading, the teacher should interrupt the reading to ask the four questions at appropriate points, and ask for a summary based on the four questions at the end. The teacher should respond to errors by telling the correct answer.

Step 2: Guided Practice. In the next phase of instruction, students are asked to use the story grammar while reading a story. The teacher doesn't ask the story grammar questions as reading proceeds. The teacher just gives the following instructions to students before they read the story:

> "Read this story. Ask yourself the four questions as you read. At the end of the story, say to yourself what happened in the story."

After the students have finished reading, the teacher should pose the story grammar questions. If pupils make errors, the teacher should have them read the relevant part of the story and then give the right answer. If pupils make frequent errors and much of the story is being reread, return to Step 1.

Step 3: Independent Use of Internalized Story Grammar. This step is really assessment rather than instruction. At this point the strategy should be mastered. Here students are held accountable for maintaining their use of the story grammar. Step 3 is much like Step 2, with the exception that the teacher can ask questions beyond the story grammar questions, requiring greater detail and asking other questions that do not come directly from the story grammar. The main thrust of the questioning, however, should focus on the ideas represented in the story grammar.

The following example illustrates a sequence of questions for the story "the boy who cried wolf," which varies from the story grammar, but still uses the story grammar ideas as the basis for additional questions:

Teacher	Pupil
Who is the story about?	It's about a boy.
What is the boy's job?	To watch the sheep.
What problem does he have?	He is bored with his job.
What does he do to stop being bored?	He cries "wolf."
What happens when he cries "wolf"?	The villagers come to help him.
Why do you think he cried "wolf"?	He wants people to see him.
Yes, he probably likes the attention he gets when people run to help him. It feels good when people run to help you because it shows they care.	
How many times did he cry "wolf"?	Three times.
How did villagers react the third time?	They said they wouldn't come anymore when he cried "wolf."
What happens in the end?	The wolf comes and eats some of the sheep.
Tell the whole ending part.	A real wolf came and he cried "wolf" and nobody came and the wolf ate him.
Why did no one come when the wolf came?	Because they thought there was no wolf.
Why did they think that?	Because they came three times before and there was no wolf.
Could the boy have done something differently to have caused a different ending?	Yes, if he didn't cry "wolf" until the real wolf came, the villagers would have saved him.
Why would they have saved him?	Because they would have believed him.
Yes, after hearing the little boy tell several lies, the villagers would not believe him when he told the truth. What would you have told the little boy at the beginning of the story to make the story have a happy ending?	Don't tell a lie or people won't believe you when you tell the truth.
Do you think that is a good rule for you to follow?	Yes.

Four Text Structure Patterns for Text Material

The ways that information can be organized into more important and less important ideas are called *text structure patterns*. Winograd (1984) found that good readers were consistently able to identify the text structure patterns of the material they read and to identify what the author considered to be important.

Most of the instruction on text structure to date has consisted of teaching students to notice "signal" words, which indicate certain text structure patterns (Armbruster, Anderson, & Ostertag, 1987; Marshall & Glock, 1978-1979; McGee, 1982; Meyer, 1975; Meyer, Brandt, & Bluth, 1980; Raphael, Englert, & Kirschner, 1986; Raphael & Kirschner, 1985; Slater, Graves, & Piche, 1985; Taylor & Beach, 1984). For example, the use of words such as "in contrast," "however," "similarly," "but," and "on the other hand" indicate a comparison/contrast pattern.

Sinatra, Stahl-Gemake, and Morgan (1986) and others (Sinatra, 1984; Raphael, Englert, & Kirschner, 1986) have applied research in the area of visual-spatial displays (Sinatra, Stahl-Gemake, & Berg,

DESCRIPTIVE OR THEMATIC MAP

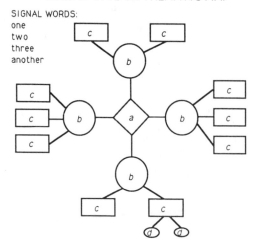

SEQUENTIAL EPISODIC MAP

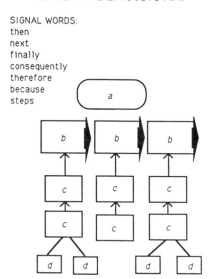

COMPARATIVE AND CONTRASTIVE MAP

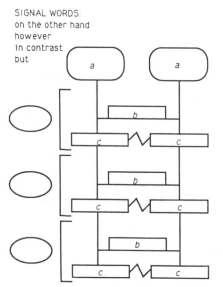

PROBLEM AND SOLUTION MAP

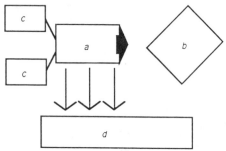

FIGURE 1. Four skeleton text maps.

1984) and advanced organizers (Ausubel, 1968) to instruction in text structure and have developed text structure maps that visually illustrate relationships between ideas. While no research has evaluated specifically the instructional importance of including the visual–spatial displays versus teaching students to note the relevant textual cues, the inclusion of the maps in the instruction would seem to enhance learning.

The work of Meyer and Rice (1984)

and of Sinatra, Stahl-Gemake, and Morgan (1986), and the results of research on signal words have been synthesized here into a model of four text structure maps (Figure 1) that may be useful in a variety of content areas. The maps illustrated here include the signal words, the presence of which can cue the reader to the particular pattern being used.

Pattern 1: Descriptive or Thematic Map.

This type of map has broad application in many subject areas in which ideas are subsumed by other superordinate ideas. For example, it can be used for describing systems (e.g., body systems) or for illustrating the relationship between ideas in persuasive essays, in which evidence is used to support each point. It is the pattern that is most comparable to the traditional outline pattern. Cell a would correspond to the main idea (e.g., body systems). At the next level, the b cells list the components of the main idea (e.g., nervous, circulatory, skeletal, and digestive systems). The c cells each contain a subordinate point (e.g., heart, veins, and arteries under circulatory system). Additional breakdown of points can be accommodated by adding additional subordinate levels of cells, as the d cells illustrate.

Pattern 2: Sequential Episodic Map.

The sequential episodic map can be particularly useful in a history class. Figure 2 illustrates a completed map of a history chapter dealing with the events that led Americans to organize at the First Continental Congress (labeled a in Figure 1). Arrow boxes (b in Figure 1) illustrate the relevant cause and effect relationships. The boxes below the arrow boxes (labeled c) indicate that a sequence of events contribute to a larger category of events. The student could also optionally describe important components of events in the Intolerable Acts, for example, by filling in the two boxes on the bottom (labeled d).

Pattern 3: Comparison and Contrast Map.

Comparison and contrast skills are important to clear concept formation. This map (Figure 1) becomes critical in any material when similar concepts are to be taught. The parallel structure is important to a comparison or contrast. Simply listing features of one item, then listing the features of the other item is a common error made in a comparison or contrast task. The top boxes (labeled a) display the concepts being compared and contrasted. The boxes below indicate either features that the concepts share (labeled b) or features unique to each concept (labeled c). The circles to the left name the dimensions along which the items are being compared. For example, a comparison between the North and the South before the Civil War might list the dimensions of economics, politics, and social order.

Pattern 4: Problem and Solution Map.

Text dealing with a problem may elaborate and describe the cause, then propose a solution that is developed from a clearer understanding of the causes. For example, discovering a cure for cancer requires identification of the cause. To illustrate the cause-and-effect relationship, the large arrow is used again here. The cause (labeled a) produces an effect, which is the problem (labeled b). Aspects of the descriptive map were also borrowed for the part of the map dealing with definition of the cause (boxes labeled c). This implies that analysis is required in the description of the cause of the problem. The small vertical arrows indicate that a description of the cause of a problem implies or leads to a solution map dealing with the problem of heart disease and the solution of modifying the diet.

In some content, the strategy for finding a solution may involve a careful description of the problem, rather than the cause. For example, in dealing with a personal problem, it may be too late or impossible to change the event that caused the problem. So the solution may result from a different strategy of analysis. The teacher should be aware of the strategy and develop a map that illustrates the strategy that commonly matches the given content area.

SIGNAL WORDS:
then
next
finally
consequently
therefore
because
steps

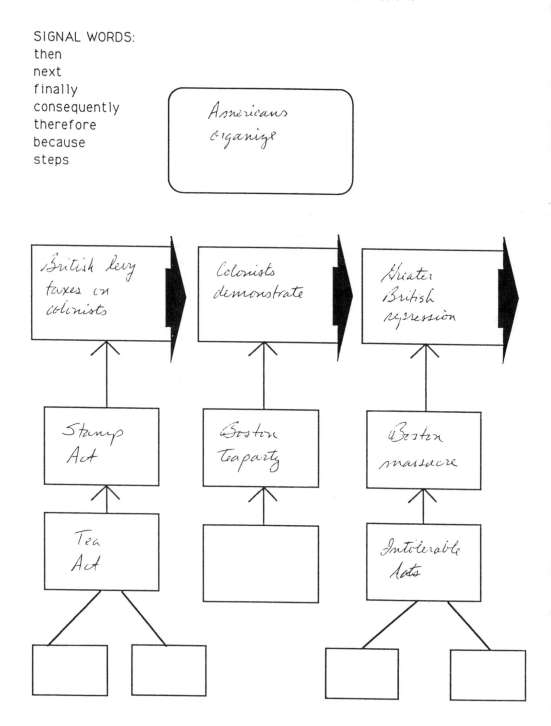

FIGURE 2. Completed sequential episodic map.

SIGNAL WORDS:
should
problem
solution
as a result
because
better

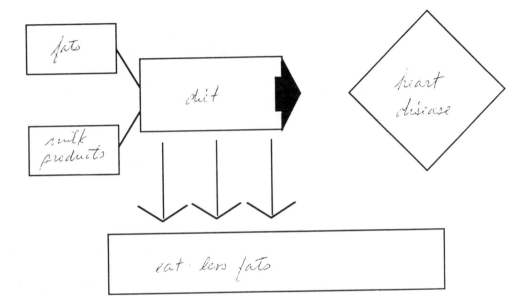

FIGURE 3. Completed problem/solution map.

Instruction in Use of Text Structured Maps

These four text structure maps can form a basis for teaching students to use text structure patterns to identify main points and relationships among them. However, the teacher may identify more specialized patterns that would be appropriate for particular content or text genres (e.g., newspaper articles, persuasive writing). The text structure patterns in Figure 1 are skeleton patterns; any mapped text may vary from the skeletal form in a number of ways.

Students could begin by using duplicated forms of each skeleton map in Figure 1 (with blank cells) to map single, brief examples that are similar in design to that of the skeleton map. Later, students can create their own forms with more varied designs. Finally they may be asked to do the forms in their heads when they read. The teacher can facilitate this mental activity by using tests and assignments that focus on main ideas and relationships among those ideas, rather than focusing on details of the students' reading.

For maximal effectiveness in improving reading comprehension, any instruction in text structure should be tightly integrated with instruction in other reading comprehension skills (e.g., differentiating fact and opinion, drawing inferences, etc.). Text structure instruction in reading integrated with an application of the same strategy in a process approach to writing has been found to produce impressive results in composition

(Raphael, Englert, & Kirschner, 1986).

Standard instructional sequencing principles can be applied to the design of instruction in the use of text maps. There are three dimensions to the sequencing of the learning tasks, namely, sequencing (a) the introduction of the various text structure patterns, (b) the nature of the text material pupils work with, and (c) the particular activities required to learn to use each text map.

Sequencing the introduction of the text maps. Not all text maps should be presented at once. One sequencing principle is to introduce the easiest map first. Raphael, Englert, and Kirschner (1986) found a sequential episodic pattern easier than a comparison and contrast pattern or a problem and solution pattern. Richgels, McGee, Lomax, and Sheard (1987) found that the cause–effect pattern was most difficult to identify. The patterns in these studies were not identical to the ones used here. Nevertheless, the above findings would imply that the descriptive/thematic map is probably the easiest; the cause–effect aspects of the sequential episodic map and of the problem and solution map would make them more difficult.

Another sequencing principle is to separate the introduction of highly similar items (Carnine, 1976). Of the four maps, the two most fundamental and most dissimilar text maps are the sequential episodic and the descriptive/thematic maps. The most fundamental map, the descriptive/thematic map, should be taught first, followed by the sequential episodic map. The comparison and contrast map and the problem and solution map would be presented last.

A third instructional sequencing principle is to teach the most frequently used items first. This implies that in a history class the sequential episodic map might be taught first. Science teachers may choose not to introduce the sequential episodic map at all but use the comparison and contrast map earlier, or they may adapt the sequential episodic map so that it better maps lab procedures. In most other content area classes the descriptive/thematic map would be the most useful.

Sequencing the reading material. The second instructional sequencing dimension turns on consideration of the difficulty of the textual material. Besides the complexity of the organization of ideas and the length of the text, a critical factor of difficulty is the presence of salient text features that cue the text pattern. Armbruster and Anderson (1985) have enumerated the text features that make for a "considerate," easy-to-read text that very clearly communicates its message through the use of all available text cues. These features include "signaling" (note the signal words listed on the maps in Figure 1), frequent use of headings and subheadings, frequent summary statements, and other cues that make the main points obvious.

Teachers should take care to select particularly "considerate" passages for initial learning tasks. The learning passages should make use of the particular text cues that are used well in the textbook: summary overviews, frequent enumeration of ideas, relevant headings, and so on. Gradually less "considerate" passages can be selected that approach the level of vagueness and the lack of explicit textual cues represented by the material used in the classroom. There is no need to go beyond the level of "inconsiderateness" represented by the text in use in the classroom.

Many textbooks contain some features that do not cue the main ideas; instructional passages need not incorporate the use of such features. For example, some history texts use headings that are designed to generate interest rather than to communicate concisely the content under the heading. Others include introductory anecdotes at the beginning of a chapter that do not necessarily reflect the main theme or organization of the chapter that follows. These types of interest-arousing textual cues, which do not inform the reader of the content or organization of the material that follows, are not helpful textual cues. Reader interest is a critical factor in comprehension, but developing this interest through text-based strategies has not yet been shown to help comprehension of material designed to communicate information (Hidi & Baird, 1988). Readers who are taught to use headings as an aid in filling out a text map will be frustrated when using them in a text that contains "interesting" headings, with little relation to the theme of the content that follows. In fact, readers should be taught to ignore "seductive details" that are systematically highlighted in some way. Garner, Gillingham, and White (in preparation), have found that such seductive details disrupt comprehension, even for expert readers.

The initial learning passages also should be very short, so that many examples can be presented in a shorter amount of time. Some longer passages used in the text may be subdivided for this learning task. Often various text structure patterns will be used in a single chapter, perhaps even under the same subheading. Teachers should be alert to these changes, so that appropriate passages can be selected as examples. No examples should be selected for initial learning that incorporate the use of more than one text structure pattern in a single passage.

Sequencing learning activities. The third dimension involves sequencing the particular learning activities from teacher-guided to independent domains, from receptive to expressive language (i.e., from reading to writing). The following teaching model illustrates these principles. The examples of textual material selected for this model would be appropriate for less sophisticated readers. A teacher with more sophisticated readers may choose to use more complex examples.

Step 1: Point out the wrong strategy. Poor comprehenders typically select the wrong information as important. Teachers often inaccurately consider poor readers to be unpredictable in their selection of wrong information. However, Winograd (1984) found that poor readers, as a group, are about as consistent in their judgments of the relative importance of

content as good readers; that is, poor readers consistently judge the same subordinate material to be important. They consistently identify rich, visual detail as important (Winograd, 1984). Winograd surmises that rich, visual detail better captures the poor reader's interest, but it is, of course, precisely the sentences that are full of such detail that are most frequently the examples or evidence used to support important points, rather than the rules or generalizations themselves.

Because poor readers consistently seem to use the same incorrect strategy of identifying vivid details as most important, an important first step, before teaching the use of text maps, is to teach students to discriminate between examples and "main ideas." This instruction should begin with a concise explanation of the difference. Suggested teacher wording for this explanation follows:

> "Good writers use examples to illustrate and prove their main ideas. A good reader tries to find out what the author's main ideas are and uses the examples to understand the main idea better."

Following this explanation, pupils should be asked to "find the main idea" in simple passages containing only one main idea that is illustrated by supportive examples. The following is an example of this exercise.

> "Find the author's main idea in this paragraph."
>
> Helicopters are very valuable. They are wonderful in rescue work. They can pick a person out of the sea, or off a high mountain top. However, helicopters have many other uses. They can carry passengers from the rooftops of city buildings to airports, avoiding city traffic. They can carry supplies to places that have no landing fields or roads. Helicopters are very useful.

If the pupils identify "picking a person out of the sea" or another example as the main idea, say "No, that is just one example of the main idea. It helps you understand the main idea." Ask them again to "find the author's main idea."

The teacher should present several

examples like this, so that students can practice discriminating the generalizations from specifics, until they can find the main idea on the first attempt. The teacher can also allow students to present their own examples, either written or oral. This expressive task should require pupils to decide on a main idea to advance and to select appropriate examples to illustrate it. In this way the skill is practiced and integrated into both receptive (reading and listening) and expressive (writing and speaking) language.

After students can successfully discriminate main ideas from examples in passages containing a single thesis, they are ready to learn to use text maps to help them conceptualize the relationships of several main ideas in more complex text structures.

In the model that follows pupils learn to identify the text structure of passages by selecting the appropriate map of the structure, rather than by applying a large, meaningless verbal label, such as "descriptive/thematic," which will not contribute to understanding the text organization and may be even detrimental by adding unnecessary complexity. Although use of the names is not necessary for developing proficiency in the use of the skill, the teacher may desire to attach names to the patterns. If so, familiar names like "wheel" pattern for the descriptive/thematic pattern and "steps" pattern for the sequential episodic would be preferable.

Step 2: Introduce the first map. The first map to be introduced in this model is the descriptive/thematic map. The following wording is suggested:

"Authors often have more than one main idea in their writing. Some ideas are more important than others. These ideas can be organized in different patterns. (Show first pattern in Figure 1.) This is one pattern. Here is an example of text that fits this pattern."

The beetle's body has three main parts. These parts are the head, the thorax, and the abdomen. The beetle's head has feelers (antennae) on it. The head may be long or short. The mouth has strong jaws used to grasp and chew food. The thorax is between the head and the abdomen and has one pair of legs on it. The abdomen has two pairs of legs. Attached to the abdomen is a pair of horny front wings used for protection. There is also a second pair of wings under the front wings. These are soft and fragile. The beetle uses these second wings to fly. The head, thorax, and abdomen are the major parts of the beetle's body.

"Let's map the ideas in this paragraph by using this pattern. Notice our map has four branches. We don't have to always use four branches. Sometimes we may only need two, and sometimes we may need many more. How many branches will we need for this paragraph?" (three)

As a group, the students can direct the teacher in mapping the passage using the descriptive/thematic pattern. In this process students will see that the specific number of branches and the level of detail depend on the passage.

After the teaching example is presented, additional short examples of considerate text should be presented for independent practice until students are able to map passages without any assistance or corrections. The following is an example of a text that could be used for independent practice at this point:

There are four common types of tents used by people who enjoy the outdoor life. The simplest tent looks like a bell and is called the bell tent. Its floor is shaped like a circle. One pole in the center holds up the rest of the tent in an Indian-teepee shape. Another simple tent is shaped like the letter A. It has two poles with a bar between. The tent is put over this simple frame and pegged to the ground. The umbrella tent has the frame on the inside also. It has a pole with arms that work like an umbrella frame to hold up the tent. A wall tent, the one with the most room, has four straight walls with an A as a roof. It usually has an outside frame to hold it up; this is made of poles and cross bars that go through loops in the tent cloth.

After students can map considerate text independently, they can begin to work with less considerate text, approaching the level of inconsiderateness displayed by the class materials. The next passage is

SIGNAL WORDS:
one
two
three
another

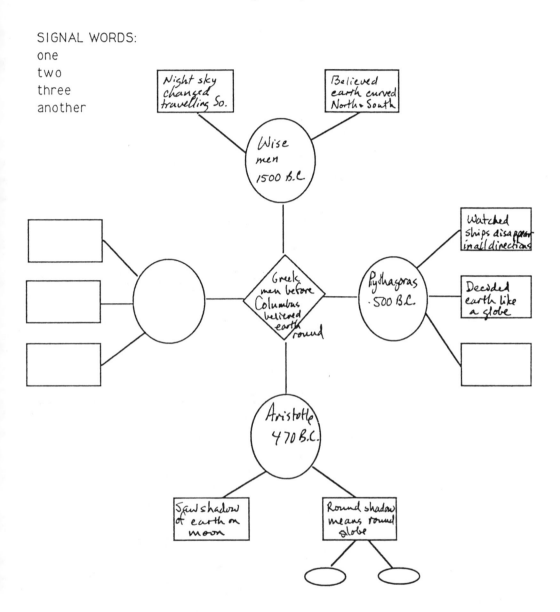

FIGURE 4. Solution map for an example of less considerate text.

an example of less considerate text that could be used (see Figure 4 for solution map):

Long before Columbus, a few wise Greek men believed the world was round. In ancient Greece, in around 1500 B.C. (1500 years before the birth of Christ), wise men studied the skies on clear nights. They noticed changes in the starry skies when they traveled south to Egypt. If the earth were flat, they thought, the night sky would always contain the same stars. However, they believed that the earth curved north-south only. Five hundred years before the birth of Christ, Pythagoras of Greece decided that the world was shaped like a globe. He watched ships disappear over the horizon. The hull (body of the ship) vanished

Recognizing text patterns

1. Decide which text map is used.

2. Map the passage on another piece of paper.

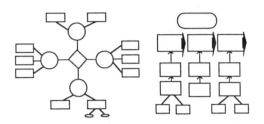

In early days, making butter in homes was a long process. The milk was "set" in jars or tin pans. When the cream came to the top, it was skimmed off. It was kept in a cream jar until there was enough to make butter. The rest of the milk was skim milk. When there was enough cream, it was churned with a wooden beater. After the butter was formed, a little cold water was put into the churn to harden the butter. This made it easier to scoop out with a spoon. It was put in a wooden bowl, washed with cold water, and pressed with a wooden spoon. It was salted and sometimes colored with carrot juice. To be sure tht all the buttermilk was out, it was pressed again. Then it was molded into pound pieces or stored in jars.

FIGURE 5. Example of a discrimination exercise.

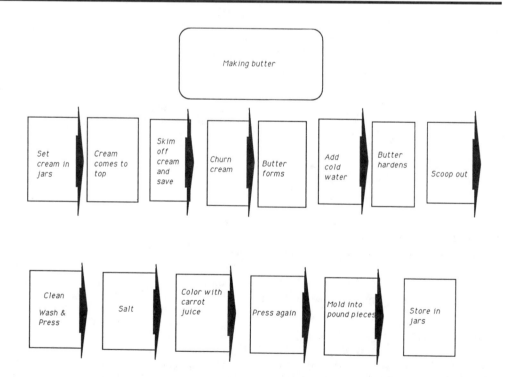

FIGURE 6. Solution for discrimination exercise.

Recognizing text patterns

1. Decide which text pattern is used.

2. Map the passage on another piece of paper.

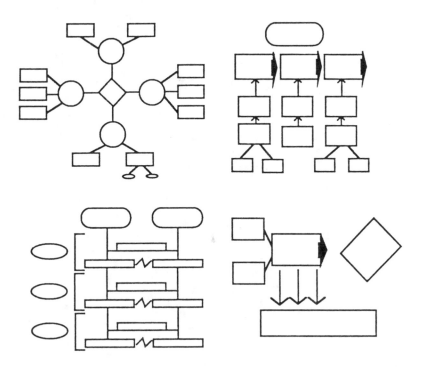

     In Antarctica live two very different Penguins, the Emperor and the Adelie. The Adelie penguin is tiny in comparison with the Emperor. He is only fifteen inches high and weighs from 6 to 15 pounds, compared to the four foot, eighty pound Emperor. The legs of the Adelie are much longer than those of the larger penguin and help him waddle around in a more lively fashion. He is bolder, much more curious, and more playful. The Emperor, on the other hand, has a dignified and serious waddle. An Emperor looks quite ashamed when he stumbles on ice, but an Adelie squawks and grumbles and rushes on his way. There are differences, too in breeding habits. The Adelie breeds in the summer, laying her eggs in a little nest of tiny stones. The Emperor breeds in winter and produces one egg per season. This egg is not put in a nest. Each parent takes turns holding it. Each places the egg on its feet with the point of the egg against a bare spot on the lower stomach. Although members of the same family, these antarctic inhabitants are different in appearance, actions, and habits.

FIGURE 7. Example of a final discrimination exercise.

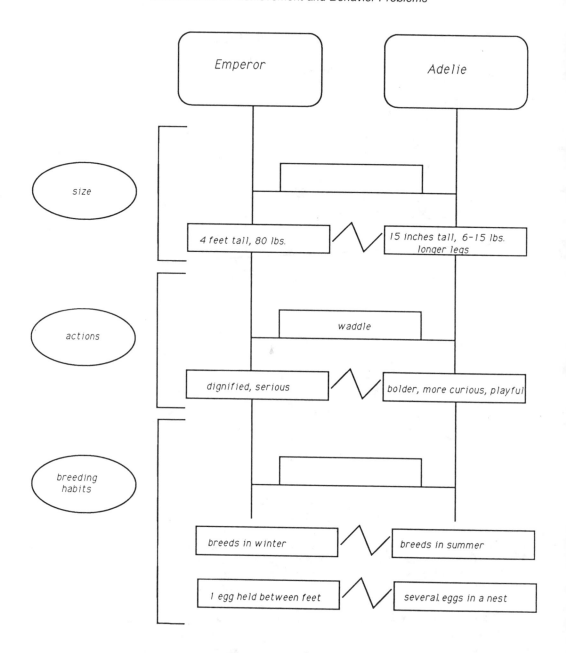

FIGURE 8. Solution for final discrimination exercise.

first, then the sail, then the top of the mast. When the ship returned, he saw the top of the mast first, then the sail, and then the hull. He pointed out that since ships traveled east–west as well as north–south, the earth must curve in all directions like a globe. Artistotle, in 470 B.C. Also thought the earth was a globe.

He saw the shadow of the earth on the moon during an eclipse. The shadow was curved like a globe. Other men besides Columbus knew that the world was not flat.

In addition to the above instruction, the teacher might ask for volunteers to present examples of information they know that could be organized by this pattern. These examples could be developed into a writing assignment.

Step 3: Introduce and integrate the second pattern. Do not introduce the second pattern until students can map text independently by the first pattern. The second pattern should be introduced in the same manner as the first. After students become proficient at working with the second pattern alone, discrimination practice should follow. Such discrimination practice is illustrated in Figure 5 (see Figure 6 for solution).

Assuming the second pattern introduced is the sequential episodic pattern, students are asked to first identify the type of pattern by selecting the appropriate pattern and then map the ideas. Again, practice on various examples is provided until the students become proficient at determining which of these two patterns is appropriate and at mapping the ideas accurately; then the third pattern can be introduced.

As students learn the remaining patterns, the discrimination exercise becomes more complex. A final discrimination exercise might look like Figure 7 (see Figure 8 for solution).

SUMMARY

Instruction in the use and recognition of text structure patterns can significantly improve reading comprehension scores. This instruction should be integrated with other reading comprehension activities taking place in the classroom. The teacher should select or develop patterns that reflect the typical patterns of idea organization in the relevant content. Instruction should explicitly model the way that the text maps should be used in reading and writing.

REFERENCES

Abt Associates. (1977). *Education as experimentations: A planned variation model: Vol. 4B Effects of follow through models.* Cambridge, MA: Abt Associates.

Alley, J. N., & Dohan, E. B. (1976). *Lessons in paragraphing.* North Billerica, MA: Curriculum Associates.

American Book Company. (1980). *American readers.* New York: Litton Educational Publishing.

Anderson, R., Hiebert, E., Scott, J., & Wilkinson, I. (1985). *Becoming a nation of readers: The report of the commission on reading.* Washington, DC: National Institute of Education.

Armbruster, B., & Anderson, T. H. (1985). Producing "considerate" expository text: Or easy reading is damned hard writing. *Journal of Curriculum Studies 17*(3), 247-274.

Armbruster, B., Anderson, T. H., & Ostertag, J. (1987). Does text structure/summarization instruction facilitate learning from expository text? *Reading Research Quarterly, 22*(3), 331-346.

Ausubel, D. (1968). *Educational psychology — A cognitive review.* New York: Holt, Rinehart & Winston.

Bank Street College of Education. (1973). *The Bank Street readers.* New York: Macmillan.

Baxter, C. (1988). Whole language and direct instruction: The battle of the day. *Association for Direct Instruction News, 7*(3), 1.

Beck, I. L. (1981). Reading problems and instructional practices. In G. E. MacKinnon & T. B. Waller (Eds.), *Reading research: Advances in theory and practice* (Vol. 2, pp. 53-95). New York: Academic.

Bruce, D. J. (1964). Analysis of word sounds by young children. *British Journal of Educational Psychology, 34*, 158-169.

Buchanan, C. D. (1973). *Programmed reading (3rd ed.): A Sullivan Associates program.* New York: McGraw-Hill.

Burmeister, L. (1975). *Words — From print to meaning.* Reading, MA: Addison-Wesley.

Carbo, M. (1987). Reading styles research: "What works" isn't always phonics. *Phi Delta Kappan, 68*, 431-435.

Carnine, D. W. (1976). Similar sound separation and cumulative introduction in learning letter–sound correspondences. *Journal of Education Research, 69*, 368-371.

Carnine, L., Carnine, D., & Gersten, R. (1984). Analysis of oral reading errors made by economically disadvantaged students taught with a synthetic-phonics approach. *Reading Research Quarterly, 19*(3), 343-356.

Carnine, D. W., & Kinder, D. (1985). Teaching low-performing students to apply generative and schema strategies to narrative and expository material. *Remedial and Special Education, 6*(1), 20-30.

Carnine, D., & Kameenui, E., & Silbert, J. (1990). *Direct instruction reading.* Columbus, Merrill.

Chall, J. S. (1983). Literacy: Trends and explanations, *Educational Researcher, 12,* 3-8.

Clay, M. M. (1976). Early childhood and cultural diversity in New Zealand. *Reading Teacher, 29,* 333-342.

Clymer, T., Venezky, R., & Indrisano, R. (1984). *Ginn reading program.* Lexington, MA: Ginn & Company.

Dimino, J. (1988). *The effects of a story grammar comprehension strategy on low-performing student's ability to comprehend short stories.* Unpublished doctoral dissertation, University of Oregon, Eugene, Oregon.

Durkin, D. (1978-1979). What classroom observations reveal about reading comprehension instruction. *Reading Research Quarterly, 14*(4), 481-533.

Durr, W., LePere, J., Pescosolido, J., Bean, R., & Glaser, N. (1983). *Houghton Mifflin Reading Program.* Boston: Houghton Mifflin.

Early, M., Cooper, E. K., & Santeusanio, N. (1983). *HBJ Bookmark reading program.* Orlando, FL: Harcourt Brace Jovanovich.

Engelmann, S., & Bruner, E. (1985). *Reading mastery: Distar Reading.* Chicago: Science Research Associates.

Garner, R., Gillingham, M., & White, J. (in preparation). Effects of "seductive details" on macroprocessing and microprocessing in adults and children. Manuscript in preparation.

Gettinger, M. (1986). Prereading skills and achievement under three approaches to teaching word recognition. *Journal of Research and Development in Education, 19*(2), 1-9.

Glim, T. E. (1973). *The Palo Alto reading program* (2nd ed.): *Sequential steps in reading.* New York: Harcourt.

Gurney, D. (1987). *Teaching mildly handicapped high school students to understand short stories using a story grammar comprehension strategy.* Unpublished doctoral dissertation, University of Oregon, Eugene, Oregon.

Guthrie, J. T. (1981). Reading in New Zealand: Achievement and volume. *Reading Research Quarterly, 17*(91), 6-27.

Haddock, M. (1976). The effects of an auditory and auditory-visual method of blending instruction on the ability of prereaders to decode synthetic words. *Journal of Educational Psychology, 68,* 825-831.

Hidi, S., & Baird, W. (1988). Strategies for increasing text-based interest and students' recall of expository texts. *Reading Research Quarterly, 23*(4), 465-483.

Idol, L. (1987). Group story mapping: A comprehension strategy for both skilled and unskilled readers. *Journal of Learning Disabilities, 20*(4), 196-205.

Marshall, N., & Glock, M. D. (1978-1979). Comprehension of connected discourse: A study into the relationships between the structure of text and information recalled. *Reading Research Quarterly, 14,* 10-56.

McGee, L. M. (1982). Awareness of text structure: Effects on children's recall of expository text. *Reading Research Quarterly, 17,* 581-590.

Meyer, B. J. F. (1975). *The organization of prose and its effects on memory.* Amsterdam: North-Holland.

Meyer, B., Brandt, D., & Bluth, G. (1980). Use of top-level structure in text: Key for reading comprehension of ninth-grade students. *Reading Research Quarterly, 1,* 72-102.

National Commission on Excellence in Education. (1983). *A nation at risk: The imperative for educational reform* (Stock No. 065-000-00177-2). Washington, DC: U. S. Government Printing Office.

Open Court Publishing. *Open Court readers.* LaSalle, IL: Author.

Otto, W., Rudolph, M., Smith, R., & Wilson, R. (1975). *The Merrill linguistic reading program* (2nd ed.). Columbus, OH: Merrill.

Pany, D., & McCoy, K. (1988). Effects of corrective feedback on word accuracy and reading comprehension of readers with learning disabilities. *Journal of Learning Disabilities, 21*(9), 546-550.

Purves, A. C. (1973). *Literature education in ten countries: An empirical study.* New York: Wiley.

Purves, A. C. (1979). *Achievement in reading and literature in the secondary schools: New Zealand in an international perspective.* Wellington: New Zealand Council for Educational Research.

Raphael, T. E., Englert, C. S., & Kirschner, B. W. (1986). *The impact of text structure instruction and social context on students' comprehension and production of expository text* (Research Series No. 177). East Lansing: Michigan State University, Institute for Research on Teaching.

Raphael, T. E., & Kirschner, B. W. (1985). *The effects of instruction in comparison/contrast text structure on sixth-grade students' reading comprehension and writing products* (Research Series No. 161). East Lansing: Michigan State University, Institute for Research on Teaching.

Richgels, D., McGee, L., Lomax, R., & Sheard, C. (1987). Awareness of four text structures: Effects on recall of expository text. *Reading Research Quarterly, 22*(2), 177-196.

Rosenshine, B., & Stevens, R. (1984). Classroom instruction in reading. In P. D. Pearson (Ed.), *Handbook of reading research* (pp. 754-798). New York: Longman.

Rosner, J. (1973). Language arts and arithmetic achievement and specifically related perceptual skills. *American Educational Research Journal, 10*, 59-8.

Ruddell, R., Adams, P., & Taylor, M. (1978). *Pathfinder.* Boston: Allyn & Bacon.

Science Research Associates (SRA). (1985). *The basic reading series.* Chicago: Author.

Scott, Foresman. (1974). *The new open highways* (2nd ed.). Glenview, IL: Author.

Short, E. J., & Ryan, E. B. (1984). Metacognitive differences between skilled and less skilled readers: Remediating deficits through story grammar and attribution training. *Journal of Educational Psychology, 76*(2), 225-235.

Sinatra, R. (1984). Visual/spatial strategies for writing and reading improvement. In A. Walker, R. Braden, & L. Dunker (Eds.), *Enhancing human potential* (pp. .....). Blacksburg, VA: Virginia Polytechnic Institute and State University.

Sinatra, R., Stahl-Gemake, J., & Berg, D. (1984). Improving reading comprehension of disabled readers through semantic mapping. *Reading Teacher, 38*, 22-29.

Sinatra, R., Stahl-Gemake, J., & Morgan, N. W. (1986, October). Using semantic mapping after reading to organize and write original discourse. *Journal of Reading, 30*, pp. 4-13.

Singer, H., & Donlan, D. (1982). Active comprehension: Problem solving schema with question generation for comprehension of complex short stories. *Reading Research Quarterly, 19*, 166-184.

Slater, W. H., Graves, M. R., & Piche, G. L. (1985). Effects of structural organizers on ninth grade students' comprehension and recall of four patterns of expository text. *Reading Research Quarterly, 20*(2), 189-201.

Smith, E. B., Goodman, K., & Meredith, R. (1976). The reading process: A psycholinguistic view. *Language and thinking in school* (2nd ed., pp. 265-283). New York: Holt, Rinehart & Winston.

Smith, F. (1978). *Understanding reading* (2nd ed.). New York: Holt, Rinehart & Winston.

Stahl, S., & Miller, P. (1988). Research on use of language experience in beginning reading. *Association for Direct Instruction News, 7*(2), 1.

Stallings, J. (1975). Implementation and child effects of teaching practices in Follow Through classrooms. *Monographs of the Society for Research in Child Development, 40*(7-8, Serial No. 163).

Taylor, B. M., & Beach, R. (1984). The effects of text structure instruction on middle grade students' comprehension and production of expository text. *Reading Research Quarterly, 19*, 134-146.

Thorndike, R. L. (1973). *Reading comprehension education in fifteen countries: An empirical study.* New York: Wiley.

Winograd, P. N. (1984). Strategic difficulties in summarizing texts. *Reading Research Quarterly, 19*, 404-425.

AUTHORS' NOTE

The passages used for exemplification in this chapter were adapted from Alley and Dohan (1976).

16

Teaching Reading to Mildly Disabled Students in Regular Classes

Paul T. Sindelar
University of Florida

Kim Stoddard
University of Louisville

INTRODUCTION

The ultimate purpose of reading instruction is to develop in children the ability to understand what they read, an ability that Anderson, Hiebert, Scott, and Wilkinson (1985) described as "a cornerstone for a child's success in school" (p. 1). Although comprehension is the primary purpose in reading, reading authorities recognize the importance of other related skills. For example, many regard reading fluency as an essential element of competent reading (Calfee & Drum, 1986). Indeed, Perfetti and Hogaboam (1975) demonstrated that good readers read more fluently than poor readers, and LaBerge and Samuels (1974) offered a useful theoretical account of how fluent reading can promote comprehension. Word knowledge, in addition to being a valued objective in its own right, also is related to reading comprehension. However, the evidence here is ambiguous (Mezynski, 1983), and only the strength of the underlying thesis — that comprehension is impaired when the meanings of words are unknown - has assured vocabulary instruction a place in our school curriculum.

In this chapter, it is our purpose to review research in which the effects of instructional strategies for promoting reading fluency, word knowledge, and reading comprehension of mildly disabled students are tested. We have organized our review into three sections — fluency, vocabulary, and comprehension — according to which skill each strategy is designed to promote. Furthermore, we have imposed three constraints upon ourselves in selecting studies. First, we have chosen to begin at a point at which children are considered transitional readers (Chall, 1983); they decode competently at the level of individual words but are not yet fluent in reading text. Our focus on these relatively advanced skills was an arbitrary decision on our part and is not intended to diminish the significance of such underlying skills as letter-sound correspondences, blending, and isolated word recognition. Second, we have not reviewed studies that evaluate the effects of curricula. The strategies included in the review share the attribute of being easily incorporated into a variety of curricula. Finally, we have attempted to concentrate on studies conducted in classrooms and to weigh more heavily those in which mildly disabled students are studied. As will be seen, this was not always possible to accomplish.

INSTRUCTIONAL APPROACHES FOR INCREASING READING FLUENCY

Teaching students to read faster and

more accurately is a common instructional goal in general and special programs alike. Many approaches have solid empirical bases, but some commonly used methods do not. We have chosen to include in our review certain approaches that lack a strong empirical basis but enjoy strong face validity and are used commonly in schools. For example, many teachers, particularly those who use basal reading series, teach new words to introduce a story. The logic underlying this approach is persuasive: Students will read more fluently and presumably with greater comprehension if they are able to read each of the words used in the story. However, the data do not strongly support this logic. Supplying words that students don't recognize is another widely used instructional tactic with stronger logical than empirical support. In this section, we will consider alternatives to these approaches among an array of strategies for increasing reading fluency.

Teaching Words and Phrases

Fleisher and Jenkins (1978) compared oral reading practice with and without preteaching new words. The six first-grade boys who participated in the study were labeled learning disabled (LD) and assigned to a special education resource program for reading instruction. The six boys worked with their reading tutors for 25 minutes daily. In the preteaching condition, this time was divided into a 7-minute period of isolated word practice and an 18-minute period of oral reading practice; in the other condition, all 25 minutes were devoted to oral reading practice. The boys read two books from the *Sullivan Series* in each condition, and were assessed daily on isolated word recognition and oral reading fluency.

Fleisher and Jenkins reported that the boys recognized a significantly greater percentage of isolated words with drill than without it; however, their improvement in oral reading fluency from the beginning to the end of books was no greater for word drill and practice than for practice alone. Confusing the interpretation of these results is the fact that in

word drill and practice, the boys read aloud to their tutors for 7 fewer minutes each lesson. Although Fleisher and Jenkins concluded that isolated word training did not enhance the effects of oral reading practice, their findings suggest that the combination of 7 minutes of word drill and 18 minutes of reading practice was the equivalent of 25 minutes of reading practice on a measure of fluency and superior to it on a measure of word recognition.

Subsequent studies (Dahl, 1979; Fleisher, Jenkins, & Pany, 1979; Sindelar, 1982) have clarified these findings. In every case, the effects of word drill have been limited, and in no case did they generalize to measures of reading fluency. The consistency of these findings supports Fleisher and Jenkins's assertion that reading fluency is unaffected by word drill. The various circumstances under which these results were obtained attest to the generality of the phenomenon. Dahl (1979), for example, studied flashed word recognition training over the course of an entire school year with 32 below-average second-grade readers. The participants in Fleisher et al. (1979) were fourth-, fifth-, and sixth-grade remedial reading students. Sindelar's second, third, and fourth graders received their reading instruction in resource programs; most were labeled LD. In the Sindelar study, word recognition training was admininstered by peer tutors.

By contrast, phrase training has proven to have positive and generalized effects on fluency and comprehension. Dahl (1979), for example, investigated the hypothesis/test (H/T) method, an approach to phrase training in which students are taught to read phrases rapidly by predicting the words that complete them. The H/T method involves training on these seven subskills.

1. Saying a word that begins with a particular sound.

2. Identifying (by stating) the beginning letter of a word said aloud.

3. Identifying (by pointing at) the beginning letter of a word said aloud.

4. Providing the last word of incomplete

spoken sentences. More technically, this skill was conceptualized as using auditory context to complete incomplete communications.

5. Providing the last word of incomplete sentences, given the word's first sound.

6. Predicting the final word of incomplete written sentences. This skill was conceptualized as using written context to complete incomplete communications.

7. Predicting the final word of incomplete written sentences, given the word's first letter (or consonant blend).

Once students master these seven skills, training focuses on the final step, and items such as "She cooked s——" or "The train climbed the h——" are used in training. The entire process may be understood as an effort to teach readers to use context (and minimum graphic information) to predict words. Competent readers are thought to develop hypotheses about words to come from their comprehension of text; these hypotheses allow competent readers to process words using less information than would be required if the same words were read out of context. H/T training allows teachers to teach this prediction and confirmation skill to readers who fail to develop it on their own.

Dahl reported that, as expected, H/T training produced significant effects on three measures of word recognition (words used in training, novel words, and words used in sentences). Unlike isolated word drill, however, H/T training also produced significant effects on measures of reading fluency and comprehension. In an extension of Dahl's work, Sindelar (1982) demonstrated that the H/T procedure could be implemented successfully by cross-age tutors. The generality of the effects of the H/T method and its ease of administration constitute a strong rationale for its use with disabled and other poor readers in mainstream classrooms. However, preparing materials would require considerable time, and training and supervising tutors might also prove time-consuming for teachers. Because H/T training requires individualized in-struction, it might by incorporated most easily into classrooms in which a peer or cross-age tutoring program already exists.

Repeated Readings

The method of repeated readings, introduced by Samuels (1979), was derived from a model of automatic information processing (LaBerge & Samuels, 1974). These authors believed that the comprehension of text requires the attention of the reader, and that proficient decoding frees attention for comprehending. To achieve proficient decoding, practice to automaticity is required. Once attained, automatic decoding requires little or no attention, so proficient readers direct their attention to understanding meaning. According to this model, strategies that promote automatic decoding should have concurrent effects on comprehension, as was true for H/T training.

The method of repeated readings requires only that readers read and reread passages, either a specified number of times (O'Shea, Sindelar, & O'Shea, 1985, 1987; Rashotte & Torgesen, 1985; Sindelar, Monda, & O'Shea, 1988) or until a criterion of performance is reached (Dahl, 1979; Dowhower, 1987; Herman, 1985; Samuels, 1979). The findings of O'Shea et al. (1985, 1987) suggest that the former may be more justified than the latter; they report diminishing improvements after three readings, for both LD and nondisabled readers. In either case, repeated readings produce significant effects on measures of within-passage fluency and comprehension (i.e., fluency and comprehension in the passages being read), and for many different groups of elementary-age students: average readers (Dowhower, 1987; O'Shea et al., 1985; Sindelar et al., 1988), below average readers (Dahl, 1979; Herman, 1985), and LD readers (O'Shea et al., 1987; Sindelar et al., 1988). Other researchers have replicated the effects of repeated readings on fluency. Rashotte and Torgesen (1985) asked only a single comprehension question after each passage reading, but reported improvements in fluency with LD readers. Samuels (1979) reported no comprehension data, but did find fluency gains for a mildly retarded reader. Finally, Sindelar et al. (1988) demonstrated that the effects of repeated readings were identical for LD and nondisabled readers functioning at the same reading levels.

These students constitute an impressive empirical foundation for the method of repeated readings. However, within-passage improvements seem predictable; a second, perhaps more critical question is whether the beneficial effects generalize across passages. Several studies (Dahl, 1979; Dowhower, 1987; Herman, 1985; Rashotte & Torgesen, 1985; Samuels, 1979) have addressed the question of whether rereading one passage improves reading in subsequent passages but have yielded mixed results. Rashotte and Torgesen (1985) concluded that generalization from one passage to another depends upon the number of words that occur in both passages. When only commonly occurring words were shared, four readings of the same passage produced no greater effect on subsequent performance than reading four different passages. These findings suggest that the passages used by Samuels (1979) overlapped considerably; his student's initial readings improved from passage to passage and the student took fewer and fewer readings to reach criterion.

Dahl (1979), on the other hand, reported significant effects on measures of word recognition, fluency, and comprehension that were attributable to the method of repeated reading. Her study extended over the course of a school year; by contrast, Rashotte and Torgesen's involved 21 sessions and may not have continued long enough for generalized effects to occur. However, both Dowhower (1987) and Herman (1985) reported generalized improvements in the short term. Both found that accuracy improved and fluency increased following rereading of five or six short stories to a preset fluency criterion. Both also reported evidence of improved comprehension.

The method of repeated readings requires neither the preparation of new materials nor the training of a cadre of sophisticated tutors, and for these reasons it may be easier to use than H/T training. However, repeated readings does require reading aloud and people to monitor oral reading. Because the effects of this treatment are similar for students of widely differing proficiency, it can be used as a whole-class activity. Pairs of students with similar abilities listen to each other read and, to the best of their abilities, they count errors, terminate hesitations, time readings, and the like. In several studies (O'Shea et al., 1985, 1987; Sindelar et al., in press), monitors ended hesitation and recorded errors but made no other effort to correct errors. It seems unnecessary, then, for tutors to know how and when to correct their partners' errors.

Previewing

Closely related to the method of repeated readings is the use of previewing to promote the fluency and comprehension with which a passage is read aloud. Two previewing approaches have been studied (Rose, 1984; Rose & Sherry, 1984; D. D. Smith, 1979): silent reading and listening. In the former, students read a passage silently before reading it aloud; in the latter, students listen as their teacher reads the passage. Although both methods proved superior to no previewing, listening (and requiring students to follow along in the text) had stronger effects on subsequent fluency than silent previewing, and the superiority of this treatment held for both elementary-age (Rose, 1984) and adolescent (Rose & Sherry, 1984) LD students. In testing a related strategy, D. D. Smith (1979) required students to listen to their teachers read the first 100 words of longer passages and then begin reading from that point. Improvement in oral reading fluency was reported after listening, even though the students had not listened to the same material they read themselves.

We would surmise that a listening procedure like the ones studied by Smith and by Rose and his colleagues is used commonly, particularly in the elementary classrooms. In addition to its face validity with teachers, it is easy to use and appropriate for all students reading the same story. However, although the research demonstrates that students will read more fluently after listening, no one has yet ascertained whether concurrent gains in comprehension are achieved. Furthermore, whether previewing and practice result in generalized gains to novel passages is not known either. Although these strike us as serious limitations, listening previewing may be recommended when the objective of the activity is to promote within-story fluency. When the focus of instruction is on comprehension, however, previewing should not be used as the primary instructional activity.

Error Correction During Oral Reading

When tutors or teachers listen to students read, what should they do about mistakes? The results of research on correction procedures for oral reading errors are not completely clear, but some consistency is emerging. Jenkins and Larsen (1979) were the first to report that end-of-lesson drill was an effective means for correcting errors. End-of-lesson drill is a simple procedure; during oral reading, tutors supplied words that students missed and, at the completion of the passage, required students to practice these words to a criterion of two consecutive correct readings. This type of drill proved superior, on measures of word recognition accuracy in context and in isolation, to (a) no correction, (b) sentence repeat, (c) end-of-page review (with no criterion), and (d) word meaning, a drill that requires students to define the words they have misread.

Word supply, the reading by teachers of words students have missed before they are allowed to continue, was an element of each of the four procedures studied by Jenkins and Larsen, and was studied in isolation as well. Used alone, word supply had no greater effect on accurate reading of isolated words than using no correction procedure at all, and it was significantly inferior to the other procedures. The weakness of word supply is particularly important, given the frequency with which it is used, alone, to correct oral reading errors. The findings of Jenkins and Larsen

suggest that word supply must be used in combination with more formal correction procedures, even though formal procedures are more difficult and time-consuming. For example, with end-of-lesson drill, tutors must prepare flash cards before drill can occur. Jenkins and Larsen also reported that drill itself required nearly 7 minutes per student per day, a considerable time for teachers in mainstream classrooms, particularly if they have no tutoring program in place.

Subsequent research has elaborated the effects of end-of-lesson drill. For example, O'Shea, Munson, and O'Shea (1984) found that end-of-lesson phrase drill, in which error words are presented in phrases from the text and not in isolation, was superior to isolated word drill on a measure of fluency in context for elementary-age readers. Rosenberg (1986) replicated the Jenkins and Larsen findings with adolescents.

In addition to simple end-of-lesson drill, Rosenberg also studied a correction procedure that combined end-of-lesson drill and phonetic analysis. In this procedure, the teacher first pronounced error words by sounding out their elements. Then the teacher and the student together sounded out the words, before the student did so alone. The final step in this correction procedure required students to sound out words silently, then read them aloud at normal speed. Rosenberg, like Pany, McCoy, and Peters (1981), found the phonetic approach inferior to simple end-of-lesson drill. Furthermore, Rose, McEntire, and Dowdy (1982) reported that their phonetic correction procedure was no different than word supply.

Apparently, the most commonly used correction procedures, word supply and sounding out, have little effect on subsequent reading accuracy or fluency. End-of-lesson drill strategies, with words presented in isolation or embedded in phrases, seems to be the method of choice, even though it extends the amount of time students must spend in individualized activities. Of course, placing students in material they can read with few errors will minimize the time required for any error correction procedure.

Antecedent and Consequent Events

Oral reading accuracy and fluency have been shown to be sensitive to contingencies of reinforcement (Lovitt, Eaton, Kirkwood, & Penalder, 1971). Teachers can increase oral reading performance, to a degree, by reinforcing students for making fewer errors or reading faster. Of course, over the short term, the effects of reinforcement are motivational, and reinforcement can be used in determining how well a student reads under optimal conditions. However, the use of edible or tangible reinforcers may reflect unfavorably on students in mainstream classrooms in which tangibles otherwise are not used. Many other reinforcers available to teachers are more common features of the typical classroom. Free time, time with the teacher, and privileges, to name a few, may be used to advantage without treating students with disabilities differently.

Also commonplace in mainstream classrooms are teachers' instructions, measures known to be sufficient for altering reading performance. For example, O'Shea et al. (1985) instructed average second graders to "read as fast and as accurately as you can". The students who received this instruction read significantly faster than others who did not. Also, students instructed to "remember as much as you can about this story" recalled more story content than others who were not. Although differentiated effects also were obtained with LD readers (O'Shea et al., 1987), they were not statistically significant. In short, instructing students to read for a particular purpose is likely to have an effect on their subsequent performance. It has the added advantage of being completely unobtrusive in mainstream classrooms.

Summary

On the basis of our review of the literature on increasing reading fluency, we have these recommendations for teachers and psychologists working together to promote the achievement of disabled students in regular classes.

1. Repeated practice will improve reading fluency and comprehension in a particular passage. To date, this finding has been established for oral reading only, so it is necessary for students to read to another person, perhaps to each other. Three readings seems to optimize the benefit of rereading. Repeated readings will promote more generalized skill development; accuracy and fluency in novel passages should improve, following rereading of as few as five or six short passages.

2. Isolated word drill should occur after oral reading practice, if at all, and should be based on errors that students make while reading. Practicing newly introduced words before reading a story is a less effective means of improving fluency. More commonly used error correction procedures, such as word supply and sounding out, are less effective than end-of-lesson drill.

3. Teaching students to use context to predict words, like repeated readings, will improve fluency and comprehension and in the long term will promote the generalization of reading skills. One well-established method for doing so is the hypothesis/test procedure. Also, end-of-lesson drill may be more effective when words are embedded in phrases than when they are presented in isolation.

INSTRUCTIONAL STRATEGIES FOR STRENGTHENING VOCABULARY

Some authorities (Davis, 1972; Spearitt, 1972; Stahl & Fairbanks, 1986) contend that there is a strong, positive relationship between word knowledge and reading comprehension, such that improved word knowledge increases understanding of text. However, not everyone agrees with this point of view, and there is even less agreement about the most effective methods for teaching vocabulary (Mezynski, 1983). Although some scholars have questioned the very necessity of teaching vocabulary, given the number of words that students learn in the early grades without direct instruction (Jenkins & Dixon, 1983), students with learning problems may not acquire information that others learn through simple exposure. This fact highlights the importance of vocabulary instruction for LD students. Perhaps the conclusion that Petty, Herold, and Stoll (1968) reached in their review of 80 vocabulary instruction studies still best summarizes the value of teaching vocabulary. These authors contended that although no single "best" method of instruction can be determined, several methods result in increased vocabulary and improved comprehension. Techniques that have been shown to produce reliable gains will be discussed in the following sections.

Estimates of the size of students' vocabularies range from 2,000 basic words in third grade to 51,000 words in seventh grade (Jenkins & Dixon, 1983). Jenkins and Dixon (1983) found that most basal reading series involve little vocabulary instruction and neglect such basic instructional components as review, multiple examples, and repetition. The following strategies for strengthening vocabulary may be used with any reading curriculum in providing practice on this often neglected skill.

Synonym Match With Practice

Most basal reading series suggest that teachers introduce new words before students read the stories in which the words first appear. Teachers typically introduce a word by stating its definition and reminding students that the word will appear in the story. Pany, Jenkins, and Schreck (1982) contrasted introducing words in this manner with a technique they referred to as "synonym match." Their procedure involved the following seven steps.

1. The student reads a word (printed on an index card), and the teacher states a synonym and a sentence using the target word.

2. The student then repeats the target word and the synonym.

3. After four words are presented, the teacher reviews the words and then shuffles the cards.

4. The teacher then presents all four cards, one at a time.

5. One student reads the words and attempts to state their synonyms.

6. The procedure continues until the student has given the correct synonym for all target words on three consecutive trials.

7. The teacher repeats the process with the next student.

Using synonym match requires the preparation of synonym cards, for which a thesaurus is essential. Otherwise, it is an easy technique to use. In Pany et al. (1982), synonym match was implemented under experimental conditions outside the classroom. However, it seems well suited for small-group instruction in regular classes. To expedite mastery, students may be required to respond as a group for one or two practice sessions. Synonym match lessons will require a great deal of teacher time to conduct and seems most feasible for use with peer tutors or parent volunteers.

In the Pany et al. (1982) study, synonym match was compared with two other approaches: providing meanings, as in traditional basal reading instruction, and deriving meanings from context. The meaning-from-context approach involved reading two-sentence paragraphs. The new word was used in the first sentence and defined in the second. In the first two of three experiments, the researchers demonstrated the superiority of synonym match with average fourth-grade and LD readers. All students learned and retained more words from synonym match instruction than from either providing meanings or deriving meanings from context. It is surprising that performance was poorest in deriving meanings. Furthermore, in the third study, mastery of vocabulary was shown to improve disabled readers' comprehension of sentences in which the words appeared. However, mastery of story vocabulary did not improve students' understanding of text as assessed by more general measures of comprehension.

Keywords

The fact that the effectiveness of synonym match was established for LD readers provides strong evidence that this technique can be used with success for mainstreamed students. The keyword method (Pressly, Levin, & Miller, 1981) is another potentially useful approach for teaching vocabulary words to mainstreamed students. The method comprises two stages of instruction.

Stage 1 of the keyword method comprises two steps.

1. The target words are written on 5″ × 8″ cards along with keywords that are acoustically similar to important parts of the vocabulary words (e.g., purse for persuade). The teacher presents the words in a random order to each student.

2. Students then are presented just the vocabulary word typed on one side of the card and are asked to supply the keyword. When students answer incorrectly or cannot respond, the teacher turns the card over and shows the student the correct keyword.

Stage 2 likewise is a two-step procedure.

1. Students are presented 12 vocabulary cards. Each card has an illustration in which the target word and keyword are used. (For example, two women engage in this exchange: "Oh, Martha, you should buy that PURSE!" "I think you can PERSUADE me to buy it.") In addition, the definitions of the target word and the keyword are typed at the bottom of the card.

2. The teacher presents the card, reading the description and pointing out the illustration of each card. The student is then given 15 seconds to study each picture.

The keyword method enables students to form links between familiar and unfamiliar words, and students are exposed to both written and pictorial cues in the process. The keyword and visual cue provide an image in which the newly learned word is linked its meaning; this link allows students to generate meanings. Students can be involved in developing the picture words; they may often have a creative association that a teacher may miss. Once developed, the cards can be used with other groups, reducing preparation time. Another advantage of keywords is that students can practice definitions independently in groups of two or more. On the other hand, the technique of using keywords is limited to those words for which links can be created between words, keywords, and pictorial representations of meaning. As teachers and students become more familiar with the keyword approach, their ability to develop new keywords increases. This activity also can be adapted for teaching the meanings of prefixes, suffixes, and other decodable word parts. For example, to teach "ow," a picture of a carpenter hitting his thumb with a hammer and shouting "OW!" would be useful.

In the past, the keyword method has been used with students studying foreign languages and has been shown to assist them in recalling significantly more vocabulary than other, more traditional approaches to foreign language instruction (Atkinson, 1975). More recently, the method has been used to teach vocabulary to elementary students. In one study (Levin, McCormick, Miller, Berry, & Pressly, 1981), 30 fourth-grade students were assigned randomly to receive either keyword vocabulary instruction or a more traditional approach. The latter group was given definition cards to study. The investigators reported that on a test of definitions, students receiving keyword training scored nearly 30% higher than the comparison group.

Gipe (1979) investigated a similar approach to teaching vocabulary by manipulating illustrations. In her study, one experimental group received illustrations using keywords and target words in dialogues between characters. The other experimental group's illustrations involved similar dialogue but not keywords.

Gipe reported that the keyword group scored significantly higher than the control group on a test of vocabulary. This investigation further supports the use of keywords and highlights the importance of establishing associations between target words and keywords, and between keywords and dialogues. It is important to note that the measures used in these two investigations tested only those words being taught. Thus, the keyword method seems to be an effective technique for increasing specific word knowledge, but its use as a method for increasing overall reading comprehension has not yet been examined. Although it has not been tested with poor readers in mainstream classrooms, its components suggest that the success achieved with regular education students could be replicated with disabled learners.

Category Grouping

The acquisition of vocabulary words can be enhanced by organizing them by conceptual categories (e.g., animals or names of utensils) and teaching the relationships among them. It is well known that lists of words are remembered better when the words can be organized into such conceptual groupings. The technique of category grouping exploits this phenomenon for vocabulary instruction. A typical instructional activity involves the following steps.

1. The teacher chooses a category and develops a list of words to be taught. For example, the category of people could involve the words accomplice, miser, philanthropist, novice, hermit, and tyrant. Although these words are relatively sophisticated, the category could be as simple as family and include only the words mother, father, brother, sister, and baby.

2. In the following practice sessions, students increase their understanding of words by examining their relationships to other words. The teacher presents the words to the students and models their use to increase students' understanding of the words and their relationships to other words in the same category. Practice progresses through the following steps: Day 1, words with definitions are presented on flash cards; Day 2, sentences that include the vocabulary words are pieced together; Day 3, students develop their own sentences and phrases containing the words; Day 4, a matching task is conducted and timed; students look at the words in a new way by comparing the words within categories (the teacher might ask how an accomplice and a tyrant are alike or could be alike); Day 5, a multiple choice test of the new words is administered; Review session, practice sessions of words already introduced are conducted.

3. Students are tested at the end of a 5-day cycle with a multiple-choice test.

4. Students earn points for proving they have heard, seen, or used the target words outside of class, in an activity called Word Wizard.

One advantage of category grouping for disabled readers is its provision for repeated practice. Furthermore, from a teacher's perspective grouping is appropriate for students at all skill levels, and it has been implemented classwide to students with reading difficulties. In addition, words from any reading curriculum or subject area text can be used. Although to implement the program teachers need to spend a considerable amount of time in planning and developing activities, they may find that, given the success of the program, preparation is time well spent. By teaching students through categories, new vocabulary takes on broad meaning, unattainable through the memorization of a series of definitions.

The effects of category grouping on comprehension have been examined with favorable results. Beck, Perfetti, and McKeown (1982) investigated a category grouping technique with a group of fourth graders of low socioeconomic (SES) background. Twenty-seven subjects from one class were matched with students from another class. The experimental group received category grouping and the control group received traditional language arts instruction. The investigators administered pre- and posttests in several areas, including vocabulary knowledge and speed in comprehension at the word, sentence, and passage levels. In addition, comprehension was assessed with a story recall procedure. Category grouping instruction was found to be superior to the traditional language arts approach in all areas assessed by the investigators. Further examination revealed that when the experimental group received "many" (26-40) explosures to a vocabulary category or word rather than "some" (10-18) exposures, comprehension and vocabulary knowledge increased further.

Preteaching Vocabulary

In traditional basal reading series, new words are introduced before students read stories. However, little time is spent on this activity, and "introducing" seldom means teaching in the sense of providing repeated practice. Actually preteaching students the meaning of new words has been found to be successful in strengthening recall and comprehension. In fact, Wixon (1986) argued that the actual preteaching of vocabulary is far more important than the method used; she compared one traditional and one novel approach to preteaching words. The dictionary method is familiar to all; students were required to look up definitions of words in the dictionary, copy the definitions, and write a sentence using each word. This method was contrasted to a concept method by which students learn words through group discussion. The concept method procedure is described below.

1. Words are presented on worksheets to students.

2. The teacher provides students with an example and a nonexample of each word. (The example provided by the author was "Dinosaurs are prehistoric animals. Lions are not prehistoric animals.")

3. Students then discuss what they know about the words and their characteristics.

4. Students are asked to complete an activity in which they indicate which characteristics and attributes listed on their worksheets are important to the meanings of the words. The students are instructed to "put an X by the words that describe prehistoric".

5. The teacher leads a second discussion, in which students review the salient characteristics of each word.

6. After the discussion, the students complete an independent exercise in which they determine examples and nonexamples for each word. (For example, they might be instructed: "Write yes if you agree. Stone hammers are prehistoric tools".)

7. Finally, the students are asked to write a definition of the words using previously presented information.

Instruction takes considerably more teaching time than having students look up and write down definitions, but it does allow them to use newly learned words in real situations and to develop an understanding of their full contextual meanings. Initially, teachers need time to create examples and nonexamples and to develop worksheets. Once completed, the worksheets can be used over again for other reading groups.

A comparison of these methods (Wixon, 1986) involved average and above-average fifth graders. The two methods of instruction described earlier, dictionary use and concept development, were compared, along with teaching central and noncentral vocabulary for a given story. By central vocabulary Wixon meant words essential to an understanding of the text. Noncentral words appear in the story, but knowing their meanings is not essential for understanding the stories.

Each student participated in two 45-minute group sessions. Four different measures — two vocabulary measures based on definitions and completion of examples and two measures of comprehension, assessed by story recall and question answering – were administered a day after the last session. Students scored higher on all four measures when assessed on the words, both central and noncentral, that they had been taught. Although no significant difference between the two methods of instruction was found, Wixon did conclude that preteaching, regardless of how it is conducted, will increase comprehension.

Reconciled Reading Lessons

Preteaching vocabulary was also stressed in Thames and Readence's (1988) investigation of the reconciled reading lesson, or RRL. The authors contended that typical basal reading programs have students read first and then complete enrichment and extension activities. By withholding such activities until after the passages are read, students may draw upon only their own experiences to provide context for comprehending a passage. In RRL, students complete these activities *before* reading a story. In this way, concepts are activated and vocabulary is practiced before stories are read. These activities provide all students the context necessary to comprehend the passage. Because experience often is lacking in disabled readers, this technique promises to be highly beneficial in increasing poor readers' comprehension.

One major advantage of using RRL is that it requires no extra work for the teacher. The only requirement is for the teacher to implement the enrichment activities recommended in the teacher's guide before, rather than after, reading a story. The advantage for the disabled reader is that they acquire the background knowledge and vocabulary necessary for comprehending the story.

An investigation of RRL (Thames & Readence, 1988) involved 75 average and above-average second graders. Three approaches were compared: a basal series lesson, list-group-label approach (LGL), and RRL. In the LGL group, students were given a topic word by the instructor and asked to create new words that related

to it. Once the list was generated, teams of students were asked to make small groups of words from the larger list and then label each list. In these ways, there are similarities between category grouping and the LGL method (although category grouping is a more involved activity). Comprehension measures were taken on three stories both before and after each 75-minute lesson. A question-and-answer format similar to the basal series used in the classroom was used to measure comprehension. All three groups increased their comprehension scores significantly from pre- to posttest, but the RRL group scored higher on the comprehension measures than the students in the other two treatment groups.

Summary

Vocabulary development may be a key component for successful reading comprehension (Beck, Perfetti, & McKeown, 1982). It is unfortunate that most basal reading series suggest little more than quick introductions for teaching new words (Jenkins & Dixon, 1983), because the lack of systematic instruction in developing vocabulary may cause poor readers to fall farther and farther behind their more proficient peers. By using one or more of the techniques we have reviewed, teachers can meet the needs of both disabled and nondisabled readers at the same time. On the basis of available empirical evidence, the use of the following strategies can be recommended.

1. In most basal reading series, teachers are instructed to introduce briefly the words found in a story. Yet if students truly do not know the meanings of words, introducing them in this fashion will have limited value, especially for students with limited abilities. More formal and systematic approaches are necessary when the goal of instruction is for students to write or state definitions, or for them to use words correctly in their own writing.

2. Synonym match provides repeated practice for disabled students, and still benefits able readers. Because synonym cards must be prepared, teachers will

need time to initiate this approach. However, once the cards are ready, the activity can be implemented effectively by peer tutors or parent volunteers.

3. Although the effectiveness of the keyword method has not been firmly established with disabled readers, the technique offers promise of being as successful with them as it has been shown to be with competent readers. Keyword training enables students to form links between known and unknown words. Additionally, students may be motivated by their involvement in creating the keyword associations and dialogues. This technique was applied originally to foreign language instruction, and only recently have investigators reported success with it in teaching vocabulary.

4. Category grouping has been demonstrated to be effective with poorer readers. Its individualized nature makes it ideal for whole-class instruction; students needing to practice more extensively can do so as part of their daily routine with little disruption to the regular class curriculum. Another advantage for teachers is that this activity can be used with vocabulary from any reading curriculum.

5. The reconciled reading lesson may be the easiest technique to use, because the teachers need only reverse the order in which activities in their lessons are normally conducted. In addition, teachers may use the enrichment and extension activities with students who ordinarily read slowly and seldom have time to undertake them. The importance of giving disabled readers background knowledge cannot be overestimated. The overlap between students' experiences and story content determines in large part the amount of information they will comprehend. By strengthening vocabulary, one prerequisite for full comprehension is met.

INSTRUCTIONAL APPROACHES FOR PROMOTING READING COMPREHENSION

Although the purpose of reading is to draw meaning from text, teachers of poor readers often spend more time on letter and word recognition activities and on building fluency than on activities to develop comprehension (Allington, 1983; Smith, 1979). As a result, poor readers may fail to understand that the words they decode also convey meaning. In fact, Paris, Oka, and Debutto (1983) found that younger and less skilled readers do equate reading with decoding and that they were unaware of any text structure in passages. Comprehension is a critical area of academic instruction (Bormuth, 1969; Duffy & Roehler, 1982; Durkin, 1979; Johnston, 1985), perhaps because no single teachable behavior adequately embodies comprehension. Nevertheless, the skills that constitute comprehension must be identified and time must be set aside to teach them if children are to improve their ability to understand written material. The strategies we review in the following paragraphs have been found to strengthen comprehension and to be feasible to implement in the classroom.

The difficulty that disabled readers experience in comprehending text may relate to their failure to use the kinds of cognitive strategies used by competent readers (Bos & Filip, 1982; Miller, Giovenco, & Rentiers, 1987; Wagoner, 1983). For competent reading, readers must have available various strategies, *and* they must be aware of how well they're understanding what they read. Competent readers realize when they're reading without comprehension, then select a suitable strategy to correct the problem (Miller, Giovenco, & Rentiers, 1987). The strategies discussed in this section are designed to enhance students' awareness of their own comprehension through self-monitoring and to enable them to correct comprehension problems through self-selection and self-instruction.

In most of the strategies students are taught to use self-statements to set the occasion for self-checking, self-evaluation, and self-reinforcement (Miller, Giovenco, & Rentiers, 1987). These steps are usually demonstrated by the teacher, then elicited from students with prompts, and ultimately performed covertly. The techniques we review are based on particular conceptualizations of reading comprehension. In *story mapping*, for example, students are taught to ask themselves questions that together make up a representation (or grammar or mapping) of the meaning of a story. In *reciprocal teaching*, teachers and students work together to gather meaning from text. Students learn a four-step process of summarizing, question gathering, clarifying, and predicting to aid them in comprehension. As they become more confident in their ability to complete the process, their teacher allows them to take over the primary responsibility for doing so.

Inference training also places primary responsibility for learning on the student. In this procedure, the background knowledge of the student is woven with the new knowledge gained from the text. In *paragraph restatement*, the students use keywords to assist them in comprehending text. For most competent readers, this procedure is thought to occur automatically; however, disabled readers must be taught to use this simple but critical skill. An easily implemented strategy that encourages independent functioning is *story retell*. Once students are assigned to pairs, the practice of story retell can occur on a daily basis with very little teacher involvement. Students can improve their comprehension by reviewing with their partner what they have just completed reading. These strategies are presented in detail in the sections to follow.

Story Mapping

We have chosen to use the term *story mapping* to refer to a general methodology derived from the idea that comprehension results from the correspondence between text and the existing knowledge of the reader. Readers are taught predictable elements of narrative or expository text and strategies for identifying them while reading. Although other terms have been used to describe particular applications of story mapping and details differ from application to application, all have

in common instruction in asking questions. In fact, Singer and Donlan (1982) described the purpose of story mapping as "reading to answer self-posed questions" (p. 169). Applications differ in the questions students are taught to ask themselves.

Singer and Donlan (1982) worked with 11th-grade students in literature classes, and their approach reflects the relative sophistication of this population. Students were taught to ask questions about certain elements (e.g., character, goal, obstacles, outcome, and theme) of narrative texts. They were taught a set of generic questions and a strategy for generating story-specific questions from them. The generic questions corresponded to the story elements of character ("Who is the leading character?"), goal ("What is the leading character trying to accomplish?"), obstacles ("What obstacles does the character encounter enroute to a goal?"), outcome ("Does the character reach the goal?"), and theme ("Why did the author write the story? What does the author want to show us about life?") (Singer & Donlan, 1982, p. 177).

Lessons were structured so that students listened to tape-recorded stories and read along from a copy. The reading was interrupted once and students were asked to write three questions they wanted to answer when the story was continued. At the end of the story, they were required to write any additional questions that arose while listening to the story. The five story elements were introduced one at a time, over five lessons. The students were taught to ask themselves the generic question associated with each element, and to generate related story-specific questions.

Students who received this training were compared on tests of story knowledge to students who received more traditional instruction, identical in every way except for the activities that occurred during the interruption and at the end of the story. Instead of generating questions of their own, students in the traditional group answered story-specific questions posed by the teacher. Once two-story elements (e.g., character and goal) had been taught to the experimental training group, their performance on the story quizzes surpassed the performance of the students in the traditional group, although only once did the difference reach statistical significance. It is important to note that these effects were obtained in a short time. The entire experiment involved only six lessons and was completed in 3 weeks, suggesting that the story elements were easily understood and the self-questioning strategy was readily acquired. As a result, the technique might prove successful with students who lag behind their peers.

The effects of teaching story elements also was investigated by Short and Ryan (1984), who conducted a study with younger, less-skilled readers and developed questions more appropriate to the kind of narrative text read by their fourth-grade subjects. Students were taught to ask themselves five questions that together constitute a story grammar. The questions were "(a) Who is the main character? (b) Where and when did the story take place? (c) What did the main character do? (d) How did the story end? and (e) How did the main character feel?" (Short & Ryan, 1984). In addition, students were taught to underline information in stories and note in the margin which question the information addressed. The strategy was first modeled, then practiced in game format. The meanings of the story elements themselves were never taught to the students.

Training was conducted in small groups and comprised seven lessons. The less-skilled students successfully learned to use the story grammar strategy. Furthermore, training promoted their comprehension of new story information so that, on two separate measures of recall, they remembered no less than skilled, but untrained fourth-graders. Like Singer and Donlan (1982), Short and Ryan produced these effects in a relatively short period of time. The ease with which the strategy was acquired by these relatively young and less-skilled students suggests that a similar approach may be effective with students with more serious learning problems.

A third related strategy was described by Idol and Croll (1987) as story mapping, a technique by which students are required to complete a pictorial story map comprising five elements: setting, problem, goal, action, and outcome (i.e., characters, time, and place). Five second-, fourth-, and fifth-grade LD students were taught to complete the story map in a tutoring format. The tutors first modeled the use and completion of the story map. Then, while monitoring oral reading, the tutors interrupted the students when map information was read and asked them to identify the information and write it on the map in the appropriate component. In the final stage of instruction, the students independently completed the map with prompting from their tutors only as needed. When performance on daily comprehension probes stabilized at 80% correct or above, the students were no longer required to complete the story map, even though their performance continued to be monitored.

All five disabled students, including one who was permitted to answer orally because of writing difficulty, improved their understanding of stories as measured on daily comprehension probes. The multiple-baseline design allowed the investigators to demonstrate that improvement in comprehension was associated with the initiation of the story mapping procedure. Furthermore, improved performance was sustained for four of the five students after the use of story maps was discontinued. Instruction continued for extended periods, ranging from 13 to over 80 story mapping and maintenance sessions. The positive effects of this procedure were evidenced less quickly than in either of the two previous studies, however. Furthermore, the procedure required individualized tutoring and would be difficult to use in mainstream classrooms in which no tutoring program existed. In a subsequent study, however, Idol (1987b) adapted story mapping for group instruction and studied its effects in a classroom in which five low-achieving and LD students were mainstreamed.

Although the same story map was used in this second study, instruction on the use of the map was conducted on a whole-class basis. The teacher first demonstrated the completion of the story map, then completed the map with the assistance of students who volunteered information for the components. Finally, students independently completed the maps, and did so until adequate performance was sustained and maintenance was undertaken. All five LD and low-achieving students improved their performance on daily comprehension probes, and most of them were able to sustain their improved performance into the maintenance phase. Furthermore, in the author's words, "the progress of the normally achieving children was not impeded by including low achievers in the group instruction" (p. 203). In our opinion, this outcome is significant. Idol (1987b) demonstrated the effectiveness of a technique that can be used with whole classes of students, including low-achievers and LD students.

Idol (1987a) also adapted the story mapping technique for use with secondary students reading expository text. This story map comprised five elements: (a) important events, (b) main idea, (c) other viewpoints or opinions, (d) conclusions, and (e) relevance to today. *Other viewpoints* referred to the background information of the reader, and *conclusions* to the integration of new and existing knowledge. *Relevance to today* may be specific to social studies, the content area studied in this investigation. As was true in the first two studies, students were instructed in the use of story maps with a model-lead-test approach and maps were completed either during or after the passages were read.

All six high school sophomores and juniors answered a greater percentage of comprehension questions with story mapping than during baseline; four of these six students sustained their improved performance after the use of the maps was discontinued. Idol also reported some evidence that the use of the strategy generalized to other social studies texts and to other subject area texts. The Idol (1987a) article itself also includes a careful explication of the steps involved

in initiating and conducting this story mapping treatment.

In our opinion, story mapping holds considerable promise for use with mildly disabled students, whether they are in pullout or mainstream programs. Idol (Idol, 1987a and b; Idol & Croll, 1987) has demonstrated its effectiveness in both settings. Short and Ryan (1984) reported that less-skilled readers instructed to ask five questions about story elements could perform as well as their more-skilled classmates. The strategy can be used in any subject area, and once the map is prepared and the components taught, little additional time is required for preparing materials. Furthermore, the completion of the story map is an independent activity that can be assigned to one reading group while the teacher works with another. Our one reservation is the fact that the effects of story mapping, although consistent, have been small.

Reciprocal Teaching

Palincsar (1986) described reciprocal teaching, a group-instruction approach for improving comprehension skills. The goal of reciprocal teaching is to assist students to construct, jointly with the assistance of the teacher, the meaning of the text they read. In the initial stages, the teacher provides the direction and leads students step-by-step through the process. As students become more proficient with the procedure, the teacher provides less direction and students assume responsibility for more and more of the process. The entire process involves these four steps:

1. Summarizing: Students identify and restate the main idea of a passage.

2. Question Generating: Students generate comprehension and recall questions from the passage.

3. Clarifying: Students decide on a strategy to use when they are unsure of the meaning of what they have read. They may choose to ask for assistance, reread, or read ahead.

4. Predicting: Students hypothesize

about the content and structure of the text that will be presented next.

Each lesson begins with students reviewing these four steps. The teacher then presents the title of the passage the group will be reading for the day, and students predict what the passage will be about and what they would like to learn from it. The teacher then appoints "teachers" to take charge of groups of 5 classmates to direct the first segment of the lesson. After silently reading the text, the "teachers" ask questions that follow the four-step procedure. The goal of reciprocal teaching is to make students independent learners.

In the first of two investigations reported by Brown and Palincsar (1982), small groups of junior high school students were taught by the reciprocal teaching method. Their findings indicated that students involved in reciprocal teaching improved their overall reading comprehension. Twenty-seven middle school students met daily with one of the experimenters in small groups (2 or 3 students) for reciprocal teaching activities. At the end of 20 days of instruction, the students reached criterion of answering correctly 7 of 10 comprehension questions for 4 of 5 days. The authors also reported that students became more confident of their ability to implement the strategies.

In their second experiment (Brown & Palincsar, 1984), the training groups were larger (7-15 students per group) and more heterogeneous, and reciprocal teaching was conducted by the classroom teacher. In addition, a control group was used to establish whether effects could be attributed unambiguously to reciprocal teaching. Nineteen percent of the control group and 70% of the experimental group reached criterion of correctly answering comprehension questions. These positive results were attained in typical mainstream classrooms and held for readers with a wide range of abilities.

Inference Training

During traditional reading lessons,

students are exposed to five literal comprehension questions (answers to which appear in the text) for each inferential question (answers to which must be inferred from the text). Not surprisingly, children perform better on literal comprehension qeustions then inferential questions (Guszak, 1978). Hansen (1981) investigated the possibility of improving students' inferential comprehension through inference training, which is an adaptation of traditional reading lessons. The teacher implements inference training as a prereading activity and attempts to weave students' prior knowledge with new information through a graphic metaphor, as described in the following steps.

Students first receive 9" by 12" sheets of grey paper with lengthwise cuts to represent their brains. In addition, all students receive strips of brightly colored paper to represent new knowledge. The teacher asks a question related to the previous experience of the students. For example, a story might be introduced about a boy who did not want to do his chores. The teacher then asks if the students ever had the same problem: The students write their personal situation on the grey sheet of paper. The teacher then asks the students to hypothesize about what would happen to the boy in this story. The suggestions are written on colored strips of paper. The same procedure is repeated with two questions for each of the central ideas of the story. Finally, the class discusses the concept of relating old information to new information, and follows up by weaving the old information (grey brain) with the new information (brightly colored strips).

Hansen (1981) compared this inference training approach to a second experimental approach that focused on inferential questioning and a control treatment suggested in the teacher's manual. The 24 students involved in the study were second graders reading at or above grade level. Posttests administered at the end of each story included 10 comprehension questions, with a mix of inferential and literal questions. Following training, the students were asked to read and then recall as much as they could about a story, and they also completed the vocabulary and reading comprehension subtest of the Stanford Achievement Test. Hansen (1981) reported that on all measures the performance of the two treatment groups was superior to the performance of the control group. The inference training group outperformed the inferential questioning group, but the difference was not statistically significant.

Inference training requires little extra teacher or student time because the lessons require no more time to administer than lessons conducted according to instructions in the teacher's edition. However, this technique does require that students be able to write their experiences and hypotheses, a difficult task for many disabled readers. Possible adaptations of this method are for teachers to write the comments of students who are unable to write their own, or for students to draw pictures of their ideas. The fact that this method was implemented successfully with young readers suggests that it should prove useful with older readers functioning at the same skill level. However, the idea-weaving activity may be inappropriate for use with older students.

In an application of inference training in which the idea-weaving activity was dropped, Hansen and Pearson (1983) investigated its effects with fourth-grade good and poor readers. Otherwise, the training was identical to Hansen's earlier investigation. Both good and poor readers receiving inference training outscored the good and poor readers in the control group. In addition, with inference training, poor readers scored almost as well as the good readers in the control group. These two investigations emphasize the advantage of this instructional activity with both young readers and disabled readers.

Paragraph Restatement

The techniques reviewed thus far focus on intertwining students' past experiences with new experiences to foster comprehension. In paragraph restatement, students focus on determining the main idea of a passage with the assistance of a cue. Many basal reading programs suggest that students understand the main idea of an instructional passage, but few offer ideas about how to do so. However, Doctorow, Wittrock, and Marks (1978) developed a simple approach for identifying main ideas.

Students first read a paragraph, above which a two-word cue is written. The words are the first and second most common nouns that occur in the text. After reading the passage, students are asked to generate a sentence about what happened in the story in the blank provided above the story.

Doctorow et al. (1978) reported favorable results for this method in an investigation with 488 sixth graders of both low and high reading ability. They studied various ways to implement the technique. Separate groups received either one-word cues only, sentence-generating practice only, one-word cues and sentence-generating practice, two-word cues only, or two-word cues and sentence-generating practice. Control groups received either typical reading instruction with stories similar to those read by the experimental groups, training to focus on headings embedded in the text, or typical reading lessons with different stories.

Comprehension was measured immediately after and 1 week after training. Students receiving both two-word cues and sentence-generating practice scored highest on the multiple-choice comprehension measure and the follow-up cloze recall test. This pattern held true for both poor and good readers.

This technique would require extensive initial teacher preparation to determine the two-word cues for every paragraph. Once this task was completed, however, it could be used repeatedly. To provide a cue for every two paragraphs or every page would cut down on teacher preparation time, but the effects of such a change on students' performance are unknown. Like inference training, this technique also requires that students be able to write sentences. It would be possible to have students draw pictures or tell the teacher the main idea of the paragraph and have the teacher write it down. Teachers would need to be aware that some students could copy a sentence from the text and fail to understand the meaning of the paragraph. To circumvent this problem, teachers could require that only original sentences be written. Another adaptation is to let students determine the two word cues after reading the passage and before writing the sentence.

The practice of paragraph restatement also was investigated with LD readers (Jenkins, Heliotis, Stein, & Haynes, 1987). In this investigation, 32 LD readers in fourth, fifth, and sixth grade were instructed using the following three phases:

1. The students were instructed to write the most important person and the major event from each paragraph in spaces provided at the top of each paragraph. The cues were "Who?" and "What's happening?"

2. The students practiced this activity and were instructed to write only three- or four-word restatements. In addition, teachers checked students' comprehension by asking them for elaborations of their restatements.

3. The students were given paragraphs without blanks and were asked to write the information on a separate piece of paper.

Story retell and comprehension questions were administered after a reading passage. The restatement group scored higher on both measures than a control group that received traditional classroom instruction. The investigators also examined students' ability to apply these skills when they were not asked to do so. The students receiving the practice in paragraph restatement again scored higher on both comprehension measures. Paragraph restatement is a fairly easy technique to implement, regardless of grade level. The versatility of this technique makes it a promising one for teachers interested in improving students' comprehension.

Story Retell

One of the most critical day-to-day problems for teachers is finding time for the direct instruction that many students require. Story retell is one method that allows children to practice comprehension skills without direct supervision by teachers. Gambrell, Pfeiffer, and Wilson's (1985) story retell strategy is carried out in two steps.

1. The students silently read a story and then complete a blank outline with one heading labeled *important idea*, and two separate headings labeled *supporting idea*. The teacher directs the activity for the first three or four lessons and then the students independently complete the outline.

2. The students are assigned partners with whom they retell the story. The retell occurs after the students have read the story silently and completed Step 1.

An investigation by Gambrell, Pfeiffer, and Wilson (1985) of 93 fourth graders compared the effects on comprehension of story retell and story illustration. The students in the story retell group followed the steps outlined above. The story illustration group followed a similar program except that they drew pictures representing all the important ideas of the story. Measures of immediate and delayed story recall, and literal and inferential comprehension were administered. The story retell group scored significantly higher on all measures.

This technique involves little direction by the teacher after the initial guidance on completing outlines. Students must be either capable of working independently or highly motivated by the technique. Perhaps keeping a chart of the number of facts remembered or using some other motivational device would enhance the success of this activity over an extended period of time. Story retell seems very similar to paragraph restatement. An investigation to compare the effects of story retelling and outlining would add insight into the efficiency and effectiveness of techniques for improving reading comprehension. A complete description of story retell for primary children can be found in Morrow (1985) and a more detailed description of the activity for older elementary students in Koskinen, Gambrell, Kapinus, and Heathington (1988).

Summary

For many disabled readers, the goal of comprehending text is not easily achieved. Several techniques with proven effects are available to teachers, many involving some form of metacognition. These metacognitive skills include making self-statements about completing a task, self-checking progress, reinforcing effort, and evaluating performance (Miller, Giovenco, & Rentiers, 1987). In implementing the techniques, teachers demonstrate the skill, prompt students in their initial attempts to practice the strategy, and provide opportunities for practice. The ultimate goal is the internalization of a step-by-step procedure that allows students to become self-sufficient readers. Based upon our review of this literature, we offer the following recommendations for classroom practice.

1. Story mapping has been implemented successfully with mildly disabled and low-achieving mainstreamed students in whole-class instruction and for this reason can be strongly recommended. This strategy has two additional advantages. First, because the story map itself does not change from story to story, use of the technique requires little or no extra preparation time for teachers. Second, because the strategy is general, it may be applied to novel reading material and, indeed, the research has demonstrated that generalized effects may occur.

2. Because reciprocal teaching focuses on self-management, it is well suited for use with older students. In its initial stages, reciprocal teaching requires teachers and students to work as teams in summarizing, generating questions, clarifying, and predicting from each reading passage. The advantage for classroom teachers using this method is the fact that their students eventually assume the role of teacher. In addition, the skill can be applied to reading material that students encounter in content areas, such as science and social studies.

3. One approach specifically designed for younger readers is inference training. Students integrate their own experiences with new knowledge introduced in the story to generate understanding of text. The concrete nature of this activity can reduce relatively sophisticated concepts to the level of understanding of young children. Poor readers taught with the inference training approach may read with nearly the same degree of comprehension as good readers who are not.

4. Paragraph restatement provides students with cues for understanding the main idea of paragraphs or longer passages. Initially, teachers must take time to develop cues, but when this step is completed they can allow students to work independently. A useful adaptation for students who do not write fluently is to allow them to draw pictures that represent the main idea of the story. This technique can be used with all types of reading material. Furthermore, students instructed in paragraph restatement have been shown to apply the skill when reading novel material.

5. Although story retell is similar to paragraph restatement, it requires less time by teachers for implementation because students work with classmates. The technique seems to be an ideal independent practice activity in small-group instruction in that it permits teachers to concentrate on other groups. A drawback is that disabled readers are less self-directed than nondisabled readers (Torgesen, 1977), and teachers may need to structure an activity to ensure its completion. However, once students have internalized the process, management problems can be minimized. For all disabled readers, independent awareness of the skills available to assist them in comprehending must be established along with the ability to implement the strategies independently.

SUMMARY

By listing these successful approaches to reading instruction, we do not mean to suggest that the task of accommodating mildly disabled students in mainstream classes is simple. To the contrary, we believe that the task is difficult and challenging, and that success will not be easily achieved. Rather, the review describes options available to teachers and psychologists in their efforts to accommodate in mainstream classes more and more students from pullout programs. We believe that the number of strategies with demonstrated effects should be a source of encouragement for teachers, if not a guarantee of success.

We also wish to emphasize that a successful experiment is no guarantee that a technique will work for a particular teacher and class, in a particular school at any given time. For one thing, it is not always possible to create in a classroom the conditions under which experimental effects were obtained. Although most of the studies we reviewed were conducted in applied settings, many involved specially trained teacher/researchers who conducted the instructional activities, often with students grouped together for the purpose of the experiment only. These are realities of conducting applied research; nevertheless, they limit the confidence we feel in adopting experimental treatments. In fact, very few of our studies were conducted with natural groupings of students and regularly assigned teachers. Whether experimental effects can be replicated in actual classroom practice remains to be seen.

For another thing, no treatment will be successful with every student and no single treatment will prove to be a panacea for all instructional problems. That a treatment has produced a particular effect for a group tells us only about the probability of its producing such an effect for an individual child. Put differently, a group effect is no guarantee that a treatment will work for an individual. A look at the single-subject studies in this review will attest to this phenomenon; in none was the effect of a treatment consistent across all subjects. Psychologists and teachers must recognize that not all students learn best in the same way, and that failures will occur in even the most carefully conceptualized programs. Nevertheless, that options exists should be a source of optimism for all of us who on occasion suffer such disappointments.

REFERENCES

Allington, R. L. (1983). Fluency: The neglected goal. *Reading Teacher, 36,* 556-561.

Anderson, R. C., Hiebert, E. H., Scott, J. A., & Wilkinson, I. A. (1985). *Becoming a nation of readers: The report of the commission on reading.* Washington, DC: The National Institute of Education, U. S. Department of Education.

Atkinson, R. C. (1975). Mnemotechnics in second language learning. *American Psychologist, 30,* 821-828.

Beck, I. L., Perfetti, C. A., & McKeown, M. E. (1982). The effects of long-term vocabulary instruction on lexical access and reading comprehension. *Journal of Educational Psychology, 74,* 506-521.

Bormuth, J. R. (1969). An operational definition of comprehension instruction. In K. S. Goodman & J. F. Fleming (Eds.), *Psycholinguistics and the teaching of reading* (pp. 218-289). Newark, NJ: International Reading Association.

Bos, C., & Filip, D. (1982). Comprehension monitoring sills in learning disabled and average students. *Topics in Learning and Learning Disabilities, 2,* 79-85.

Brown, A. L., & Palincsar, A. S. (1982). Inducing strategic learning from texts by means of informed, self-control training. *Topics in Learning Disabilities, 2,* 1-17.

Calfee, R., & Drum, P. (1986). Research on teaching reading. In M. C. Wittrock (Ed.), *Handbook of research on teaching* (3rd ed., pp. 804-849). New York: Macmillan.

Chall, J. S. (1983). *Stages of reading development.* New York: McGraw-Hill.

Dahl, P. R. (1979). An experimental program for teaching high speed word recognition and comprehension skills. In J. E. Button, T. C. Lovitt, & T. D. Rowland (Eds.), *Communications research in learning disabilities and mental retardation* (pp. 33-65). Baltimore: University Park Press.

Davis, F. B. (1972). Psychometric research on comprehension in reading. *Reading Research Quarterly, 7,* 628-678.

Doctorow, M., Wittrock, M. C., & Marks, C. (1978). Generative processes in reading comprehension. *Journal of Educational Psychology, 70,* 109-118.

Dowhower, S. L. (1987). Effects of repeated rereading on second-grade transitional readers' fluency and comprehension. *Reading Research Quarterly, 22,* 389-406.

Duffy, G., & Roehler, L. (1982). The illusion of instruction. *Reading Research Quarterly, 22,* 389-406.

Durkin, D. (1979). What classroom observations reveal about reading comprehension instruction. *Reading Research Quarterly, 14,* 481-533.

Fleisher, L. S., & Jenkins, J. R. (1978). Effects of contextualized and decontextualized practice conditions on word recognition. *Learning Disability Quarterly, 1*(3), 39-47.

Fleisher, L. S., Jenkins, J. R., & Pany, D. (1979). Effects on poor readers' comprehension of training rapid decoding. *Reading Research Quarterly, 15,* 30-48.

Gambrell, L. B., Pfeiffer, W., & Wilson, R. (1985). The effects of retelling on reading comprehension and recall of text information. *Journal of Educational Research, 78,* 216-220.

Gipe, J. (1979). Investigating techniques for teaching word meanings. *Reading Research Quarterly, 14,* 624-645.

Guszak, F. J. (1978). *Diagnostic reading instruction in the elementary school* (2nd ed.). New York: Harper & Row.

Hansen, J. (1981). The effects of inference training and practice on young children's reading comprehension. *Reading Research Quarterly, 16,* 391-417.

Hansen, J., & Pearson, P. D. (1983). An instructional study: Improving the inferential comprehension of fourth-grade good and poor readers. *Journal of Educational Psychology, 75,* 821-829.

Herman, P. A. (1985). The effect of repeated readings on reading rate, speech pauses, and word recognition accuracy. *Reading Research Quarterly, 20,* 553-565.

Idol, L. (1987a). A critical thinking map to improve content area comprehension of poor readers. *Remedial and Special Education, 8*(4), 28-40.

Idol, L. (1987b). Group story mapping: A comprehension strategy for both skilled and unskilled readers. *Journal of Learning Disabilities, 20,* 196-205.

Idol, L., & Croll, V. J. (1987). Story-mapping training as a means of improving reading comprehension. *Learning Disability Quarterly, 10,* 214-229.

Jenkins, J. R., & Dixon, R. (1983). Vocabulary learning. *Contemporary Educational Psychology, 8,* 237-260.

Jenkins, J. R., Heliotis, J. D., Stein, M. L., & Haynes, M. C. (1987). Improving reading comprehension by using paragraph restatements. *Exceptional Children, 54,* 54-59.

Jenkins, J. R., & Larsen, K. (1979). Evaluating error-correction procedures for oral reading. *Journal of Special Education, 13,* 145-156.

Johnston, P. (1985). Teaching students to apply strategies that improve reading comprehension. *Elementary School Journal, 85,* 635-645.

Koskinen, P. S., Gambrell, L. B., Kapinus, B. A., & Heathington, B. S. (1988). Retellings: A strategy for enhancing students' reading comprehension. *Reading Teacher, 41,* 892-896.

LaBerge, D., & Samuels, S. J. (1974). Toward a theory of automatic information processing in reading. *Cognitive Psychology, 6,* 293-323.

Levin, J. R., McCormick, C. B., Miller, G. E., Berry, J. K., & Pressley, M. (1982). Mnemonic versus nonmnemonic vocabulary learning strategies for children. *American Educational Research Journal, 19,* 121-126.

Lovitt, T. C., Eaton, M. C., Kirkwood, M., & Penalder, J. (1971). Effects of various reinforcement contingencies on oral reading rate. In E. Ramp & B. Hopkins (Eds.), *A new direction for education: Behavior analysis* (pp. 54-71). Lawrence, KS: University of Kansas.

Mezynski, K. (1983). Issues concerning the acquisition of knowledge: Effects of vocabulary training on reading comprehension. *Review of Educational Research, 53,* 253-279.

Miller, G., Giovenco, A., & Rentiers, K. A. (1987). Fostering comprehension monitoring in below average readers through self-instruction training. *Journal of Reading Behavior, 19,* 379-394.

Morrow, L. M. (1985). Retelling stories: A strategy for improving young children's comprehension, concept of story structure, and oral language complexity. *Elementary School Journal, 85,* 647-661.

O'Shea, L. J., Munson, S. M., & O'Shea, D. J. (1984). Error correction in oral reading: Evaluating the effectiveness of three procedures. *Education and Treatment of Children, 7,* 203-214.

O'Shea, L. J., Sindelar, P. T., O'Shea, D. J. (1985). The effects of repeated readings and attentional cues on reading fluency and comprehension. *Journal of Reading Behavior, 17,* 129-142.

O'Shea, L. J., Sindelar, P. T., & O'Shea, D. J. (1987). The effects of repeated readings and attentional cues on the reading fluency and comprehension of learning disabled readers. *Learning Disabilities Research, 2*, 103-109.

Palincsar, A. S. (1986). Metacognitive strategy instruction. *Exceptional Children, 53*, 118-124.

Palincsar, A. S., & Brown, A. L. (1984). Reciprocal teaching of comprehension-fostering and comprehension-monitoring activities. *Cognition and Instruction, 1*, 117-175.

Pany, D., Jenkins, J. R., & Schreck, J. (1982). Vocabulary instruction: Effects on word knowledge and reading comprehension. *Learning Disability Quarterly, 5*, 202-214.

Pany, D., McCoy, K. M., & Peters, E. E. (1981). Effects of corrective feedback on comprehension skills of remedial students. *Journal of Reading Behavior*, 131-143.

Paris, S. G., Oka, E. R., & DeButto, A. M. (1983). Beyond decoding: Synthesis of research on reading comprehension. *Educational Leadership, 41*(2), 78-83.

Perfetti, C. A., & Hogaboam, T. (1975). Relationship between single word decoding and reading comprehension skill. *Journal of Educational Psychology, 67*, 471-479.

Petty, W. T., Herold, C. P., & Stoll, E. (1968). *The state of knowledge about the teaching of vocabulary.* Champaign, IL: National Council of Teachers of English.

Pressley, M., Levin, J. R., & Miller, G. E. (1981). How does the keyword method affect vocabulary comprehension and usage? *Reading Research Quarterly, 16*, 213-226.

Rashotte, C. A., & Torgesen, J. K. (1985). Repeated reading and reading fluency in learning disabled children. *Reading Research Quarterly, 20*, 180-188.

Rose, T. L. (1984). The effects of two prepractice procedures on oral reading. *Journal of Learning Disabilities, 17*, 544-548.

Rose, T. L., McEntire, E., & Dowdy, C. (1982). Effects of two error-correction procedures on oral reading. *Learning Disability Quarterly, 5*, 100-105.

Rose, T. L., & Sherry, L. (1984). Relative effects of two previewing procedures on LD adolescents' oral reading performance. *Learning Disability Quarterly, 7*, 39-44.

Rosenberg, M. S. (1986). Error correction during oral reading: A comparison of three techniques. *Learning Disability Quarterly, 9*, 182-192.

Samuels, S. J. (1979). The method of repeated readings. *Reading Teacher, 32*, 403-408.

Short, E. J., & Ryan, E. B. (1984). Metacognitive differences between skilled and less skilled readers: Remediating deficits through story grammar and attribution training. *Journal of Educational Psychology, 76*, 225-235.

Sindelar, P. T. (1982). The effects of cross-aged tutoring on the comprehension skills of remedial reading students. *Journal of Special Education, 16*, 199-206.

Sindelar, P. T., Monda, L. E., & O'Shea, L. J. (in press). The effects of repeated readings on instructional and mastery level readers. *Journal of Educational Research.*

Singer, H., & Donlan, D. (1982). Active comprehension: Problem-solving schema with question generation for comprehension of complex short stories. *Reading Research Quarterly, 17*, 166-185.

Smith, D. D. (1979). The improvement of children's oral reading through the use of teacher modeling. *Journal of Learning Disabilities, 12*, 172-175.

Smith, F. R. (1979). Alec in reading land: Some reactions to and implications of the Durkin findings. *Reading Research Quarterly, 14*, 534-538.

Spearitt, D. (1972). Identification of subskills of reading comprehension by maximum likelihood factor analysis. *Reading Research Quarterly, 8*, 92-111.

Stahl, S. A., & Fairbanks, M. M. (1986). The effects of vocabulary instruction: A model-based meta-analysis. *Review of Educational Research, 56*, 72-110.

Thames, D. G., & Readence, J. E. (1988). Effects of differential vocabulary instruction and lesson frameworks on the reading comprehension of primary children. *Reading Research and Instruction, 27*(2), 1-12.

Torgesen, J. K. (1977). The role of nonspecific factors in the task performance of learning disabled children. *Journal of Learning Disabilities, 10*, 27-34.

Wagoner, S. A. (1983). Comprehension monitoring: What it is and what we know about it. *Reading Research Quarterly, 18*, 328-346.

Wixon, K. K. (1986). Vocabulary instruction and children's comprehension of basal stories. *Reading Research Quarterly, 21*, 317-329.

17

Two Strategies for Improving Students' Writing Skills

William L. Heward
Timothy E. Heron
Ralph Gardner, III
The Ohio State University

Renee Prayzer
Upper Arlington (Ohio) School District

Writing is judged to be clear and effective by its effects on the audience. After reading a report, does the reader know something as fully as the writer? After reading a set of instructions, can the reader successfully execute a procedure as the writer intended? After reading a short story, does the reader feel the writer's joy or sadness? Unlike oral communication, in which ideas can be clarified through verbal exchanges between parties, in written communication the printed word must carry the entire information load (Hansen, 1978).

What is involved in the act of writing? Braddock, Lloyd-Jones, and Schoer (1963) attempted to answer this important question more than 25 years ago. Their review of 504 titles revealed very few studies with sufficient experimental control to provide clear direction on how to teach writing. Perhaps their major finding was that "the teaching of formal grammar has a negligible or, because it usually displaces some instruction and practice in actual composition, even a harmful effect on improvement in writing" (pp. 37-38). When instruction in writing is examined today, the observer is still likely to notice an emphasis on spelling, punctuation, and form (mechanics and usage), rather than organizational or contextual skills (Dillon & Searle, 1980; Lewis & Doorlag, 1987).

A recent book by Hillocks (1986), *Research on Written Composition: New Directions for Teaching*, provides a synthesis of research on the teaching of writing. This seminal work includes a meta-analysis of the findings derived from 60 experimental studies published between 1963 and 1982. Although not without its critics (e.g., Stotsky, 1988), the Hillocks report concludes that writing is a recursive process in which the author thinks, plans, writes, and rewrites at different levels. Reflecting on what has been written influences what is about to be written. Hillocks' book is widely regarded as the most comprehensive and up-to-date review of research on the teaching of writing (cf. Langer, 1988).

Of specific interest to practitioners are Hillocks' conclusions that sentence combining, inquiry strategies, and self-monitoring or peer monitoring often result in improved written expression. In contrast, activities such as studying "model" writing, holding nondirective peer discussion, and revising were found to have little or no effect on the overall product. Hillocks agreed with Braddock et al. (1963) in concluding that an emphasis on teaching grammar and mechanics does not improve students' overall writing skills; however, he does conclude that some instruction on grammar and mechanics is essential.

Teachers' comments do not seem to improve writing, apparently because they are nonspecific, diffuse, and general. Sommers (1982) makes the point succinctly:

> Most teachers' comments are not text-specific and could be interchanged, rubber-stamped, from text to text. The comments are not anchored in the particulars of students' texts, but rather are a series of vague directives that are not text-specific. (p. 152)

For comments to be specific and useful, Freedman (1984) suggested that the comments must (a) set the occasion for the students to identify and resolve their own composing problems, (b) stimulate practice and rewriting, and (c) help students transfer writing skills across subject areas.

TWO FUNDAMENTALS OF WRITING INSTRUCTION

A body of literature dating from the work of John Dewey (1916) suggests that students learn best when they (a) are given many opportunities to respond during instruction (Greenwood, Delquadri, & Hall, 1984), and (b) receive specific feedback on their efforts (Van Houten, 1980). Unfortunately, much writing instruction incorporates only small doses of these two fundamental ingredients of effective instruction.

Too Few Opportunities to Write

In 1977, Hall, Delquadri, and Harris formally introduced the concept of "opportunity to respond" and its correlation with students' academic achievement at a meeting of the Association for Behavior Analysis (then the Midwestern Association for Behavior Analysis). As part of the Juniper Gardens Children's Project, aimed at discovering methods to improve teaching effectiveness in inner-city schools, Hall and his colleagues had systematically observed the extent to which pupils were actively responding to the curriculum. Among their findings related to writing, they discovered that approximately 50% of the total time available for instruction during academic class periods was lost to transition and management activities, and that fourth graders produced less than one page of written composition per day. Other researchers also have reported distressingly low levels of academic responding in the classroom, despite data that show that the amount of time students spend actively engaged has a direct relationship on academic achievement (Greenwood et al., 1984).

Relative to what has been reported for other academic subjects, a page-per-day of written composition might seem a relatively good average. However, even though language arts activities may be scheduled daily, too few school children actually write every day. In classrooms where students do write four or five pages per week, those pages are more likely the result of one day's session than the product of daily writing practice.

Feedback for Writing: Too Little, Too Late, and Too Punishing; or How Am I Ever Going to Grade All of Those Papers?

Feedback is most effective when it is immediate, precise, positive, and frequent, and when it highlights small increments of improvement (Van Houten, 1980). Unfortunately, these five characteristics of effective feedback are seldom defining features of what most schoolchildren receive as feedback on their writing. Classroom teachers who are expert at giving feedback for student performance in math, reading, science, and other academic areas are often at a loss when it comes to providing feedback for students' compositions.

We believe that the problem of providing feedback is the major reason why classroom teachers do not provide their students daily opportunities to write. Here is an illustration of the magnitude of the challenge: When given the opportunity to write for just 15 minutes each day, eighth graders will produce some 250–300 words organized in about 15–25 sentences (Heward, Gardner, & Prayzer, 1988). Using the low-end figures, a class of 25 students will write an everyday total of 6,250 words in approximately 375 handwritten sentences. Just reading the 25 papers, without providing any written feedback, will require 1–2 hours. Whether you are a middle or senior high school English teacher with five or six composition classes or an elementary teacher responsible for the entire spectrum of academic subjects, such a daily time commitment is out of the question. Something has to give.

What usually gives is the opportunity for students to write daily, and the problem is exacerbated by the insufficient and ineffective feedback students receive on the small quantity of writing they do produce. We believe students write infrequently in school not because teachers find it unimportant, but because the time required to provide feedback exceeds the time available to do so.

This chapter does not offer techniques for improving any specific writing skill (e.g., thematic maturity, grammar, organization, fluency). Nor is it about ways to improve any of the three stages associated with the writing process: prewriting, writing, postwriting. These subjects have been discussed thoroughly in the literature (e.g., Bos, 1988; Graham & Harris, 1988; Hillocks, 1986; Wallace, Cohen, & Polloway, 1987). Instead, we describe two strategies for providing writing instruction that can be used to improve any or all of these areas, depending upon how teachers and/or parents design the program. Both strategies — selective grading and telephone-managed, home-based writing — are predicated on the belief that students should write every day and receive precise, positive, and frequent feedback for their writing.

SELECTIVE GRADING

While it is relatively easy to set the occasion for writing each day — paper, pencils, and a topic are all that's necessary — providing feedback to students on their compositions is a much more difficult proposition. One solution to this almost universal problem is an approach called *selective grading* (Heward, Narayan, & Clingo, 1987). The selective grading strategy provides a daily opportunity for students to compose without requiring an inordinate amount of teacher time for reading and evaluating the many pages of writing that are produced. Although selective grading can be implemented in many ways, its defining features are the following.

1. The teacher reads and evaluates only 20–25% of the papers written each day.
2. While all students receive their papers back at the beginning of the next writing session, only those papers that were evaluated by the teacher are marked with specific statements of praise and suggestions for improvements.
3. The teacher presents to the whole class portions of the evaluated papers as instructional examples.
4. Students spend the remainder of the period writing that day's paper (i.e., writing a new story, extending or editing a previous paper).
5. Each student who produces a specified quantity of writing during the period receives a point that counts toward his or her course grade and/or other types of rewards.
6. All students in the class receive additional bonus points if a predetermined number of papers scored by the teacher meet specified criteria for the targeted writing skill(s) being taught.

How to Implement a Selective Grading Writing Program

Writing topics. Imagine being required to write every day, even for only 15–20 minutes. Your teacher may read your work (maybe in front of the whole class) with the expectation that it will be interesting, persuasive, and technically correct. What would you write about? For many people, school-age children and adults alike, a good portion of the timed writing period might be consumed by staring at a blank sheet of paper desperately trying to think of something to say.

Offering students challenging, thought-provoking, and interesting topics is an important part of any writing program in which students are expected to produce original compositions on a daily basis. Five minutes before the timed writing period begins, students should be presented with several possible "story starters." Table 1 lists 50 different writing topics and story starters that were used in a selective grading program with middle school students (Heward, Gardner, & Prayzer, 1988).

Good writing topics or story starters help students write productively and have fun. They should not be used to limit a student's imagination or cause a student to write about something in which she or he has little interest. The following suggestions and guidelines will help ensure that each student finds something to write about each day.

- Provide students with 3-5 topics to choose from each day.
- Allow students to alter the day's topics if they wish.
- Allow students to write about topics from previous days.
- Allow students to continue a story begun on the previous day's topic.
- Keep a folder of additional writing topics on hand in case there are students who find none of the day's primary choices satisfactory.
- Mount pictures or project 35-mm slides or overhead transparencies as story starters.
- Limit the discussion and choice of topics to no more than 3 minutes.

Determine writing targets and performance criteria. We recommend that the writing skills to be developed by the selective grading program (e.g., number of action words, percentage of sentences with connecting transitions) be identified through direct examination of students' actual writing samples. Target skills chosen in this manner are more likely to be relevant to the students' current writing abilities.

Obtaining writing samples is relatively easy. Students should be provided with suggested writing topics/story starters and instructed to write for a specified length of time. Usually 10-15 minutes is sufficient. If students write for the same duration during baseline as they will during selective grading, valuable information for setting initial performance criteria for total output (a simple count of number of words written) will be obtained. (A considerable amount of teacher time can be saved by having students count and record the total number of words written at the top of their papers.) Alternatively, students might simply be asked to write enough each day to fill at least one or two sides of a standard piece of lined notebook paper.

Three to five writing samples collected within a week's time will provide ample information for choosing initial target skills and determining appropriate performance criteria. Examination of students' papers is likely to reveal many areas in need of improvement. The teacher must avoid the temptation of targeting too many skills at once. The initial writing skills targeted for selective grading should be judged easiest for students to improve. More difficult and sophisticated writing skills can be programmed after students have mastered several simpler facets of good writing and have been rewarded for doing so.

Getting started on the first day. After a week of writing with no specific instruction or feedback, students are eager to hear about the selective grading program. All that is needed to begin is a wall chart illustrating examples of the specific writing skills targeted for improvement and a list of clear rules describing how students can earn points toward their class grade and other rewards for their writing. Here is what students in several eighth-grade English classes were told on the first day of selective grading (Heward, Gardner, & Prayzer, 1988):

> Today we are going to start something new. I think you will find it fun, and I'm confident it will help each of you become better writers. Starting today,

TABLE 1
Fifty Writing Topics and Story Starters

Write a story about a day in your life.

Assume you are a rubber ball. Write a story about your life.

What would happen if everyone in the world were the same size?

There was no other thought in my head except escaping from this forsaken place.

Who would have guessed that such a disaster would occur from an innocent situation?

His/her last words to me on that fateful day were . . .

I prayed for a release from this prison.

We searched for hours and couldn't find . . .

All hopes of finding (   ) were lost when . . .

At the stroke of midnight . . .

In the stillness of that night . . .

Not a sound was heard as the bailiff read the verdict: The court finds you (   ), said the foreman.

"I've won, I've won," shouted . . .

Your plane has crashed and you have landed in the heart of a jungle. A tribe of natives has captured you and . . .

The scariest moment in my life was when . . .

The most unusual person I have ever known was . . .

You have just been transformed magically into a car (your choice of type). Describe your experience.

You have just witnessed a crime, and the criminal knows that you saw the offense. What do you do now?

You are a bird flying north after a winter break in the sunny south. Take us with you on your journey.

Assume that you are the shoes on your feet. Tell us about your experiences in a single day.

You are responsible for orienting an incoming student to school. What things would you share with him or her?

If I were . . .

If I could change school rules, home rules, or the rules of the country, I would change . . .

My favorite childhood memory . . .

When I get older, I want to . . .

My mom makes me mad when she says . . .

If I met with Tom Sawyer and Huck Finn, I would . . .

Doctors make me . . .

"Never again," said . . .

Imagine that you are in a very expensive restaurant and a cockroach gingerly walks across your table.

You are all alone on a deserted highway and you spot an Unidentified Flying Object. What happens next?

You wake up one morning and suddenly time has magically turned back to the year (   ). Describe your experiences in that year.

You are adrift on a life raft in the middle of the . . .

If I were running for President . . .

"I claim this island as mine," I said on that day . . .

There are a few things in this world that really "get to me." Describe your pet peeve and gripes.

If I could be any animal for a day, I'd be . . .

You have just walked into a convenience store and are caught in the middle of a robbery. Describe the incident and your feelings at the time.

If I were (name a person), I would try to . . .

Instead of being born "young" and growing "old," what would happen if the reverse were true?

You have just awakened from being cryogenically frozen for the past 100 years. Describe your experiences.

You have won a contest that allows you to be a member of Jacques Cousteau's diving expedition on the *Calypso*.

Create a story using the following items: a horn, a skate board, and a kite.

The biggest problem facing young people today is . . .

Create a new sport with your own rules.

Describe yourself as a hero.

Rewrite the fairy tale "Little Red Robin Hood" from the wolf's perspective.

If you had 24 hours left to live, what would you do?

Imagine that a UFO lands and invites you for a ride. What would you do?

I like to . . .

What could you do with a deflated basketball.

and each time that we write from now on, I am going to randomly select four of your papers to grade. [There were 20 students in each class.] You will never know if your paper will be chosen or not. For example, your paper might be selected on two days in a row, or you might go for several days without having your paper selected. I will make sure that no one goes too long without having his or her paper read and evaluated by me.

When I grade the four randomly selected papers, I am going to count the number of action words that you have included in your story. Based on the papers you have been writing, we will begin with a goal of 15 action words per paper. That is, if a paper that I am grading has 15 or more action words in it, that person will have helped earn bonus points for everyone in the class.

Here's how it will work. First of all, each of you will continue to earn 5 points toward your English grade for writing at least one page. [Students had written under this contingency during the previous week's baseline phase.] But here's the new twist: If three of the four papers I check have 15 or more action words, then everyone in the class will receive 3 more bonus points, making a total of 8 points each of you would earn for that day's paper. And, if all four of the papers checked have 15 or more action words, then everyone in the class will receive 5 additional bonus points, making a total of 10 points for that day's paper. The chart over here (teacher points to chart) explains what I've just said. Are there any questions?

With third and fourth graders in another school, the selective writing program was called "Writing Is for Beans" (Heward, Narayan, & Clingo, 1987). During baseline, each student was given a lima bean to put in a large glass jar that held all of the beans earned by the class. When the beans contributed by all of the students in the class reached premarked levels, the whole class enjoyed a reward of activity picked from a list previously generated by the children. When the selective grading procedure was begun, if

three of the four papers selected had met the performance criterion, every student in the class was given two beans. Three beans were given to each student if all four of the papers scored by the teacher displayed the required level of performance. When properly implemented, interdependent group-oriented reinforcement contingencies such as those described above can produce significant performance improvements in students operating at all levels in a classroom (Cooper, Heron, & Heward, 1987).

Direct instruction. About 10 minutes of direct instruction on the target skill(s) should immediately precede each day's timed writing period. Although the instructional activities can vary from day to day, having students make active responses to specific examples and non-examples of the target skill(s) should be a featured component of each session's teacher-led instruction. For example, after identifying and explaining why several model sentences do or do not include the target skill under instruction, the teacher might present a series of "Yes-No" and "How do we fix it?" questions over 10–15 similar practice sentences.

Both the model and practice sentences (or words, phrases, transitions, etc.) should be taken from the students' own writing whenever possible. Seeing their own and their peers' actual writing used for instruction serves to heighten student interest. More important, what could be more functional for either reinforcement or remediation purposes than the students' actual compositions?

Rather than calling on individual students to answer, the teacher can generate more active student involvement in the instruction (and probably more learning) if every student in the class responds to each teacher-posed question or example. Choral responding — all students responding orally in unison — can be a fun way to make group instruction more effective (Carnine, 1976; Heward, Courson, & Narayan, 1989), even for students in the upper grades. Using response cards that each student holds up on cue to indicate his or her best answer (Narayan, Heward, Gardner, Courson, & Omness, in press) and brief dittoed worksheets are two other methods for enabling each student in the class to make numerous responses during the instructional period.

Timed writing period. A timed writing period of 10-20 minutes will be sufficient for students of most age and skill levels. A longer writing period does not necessarily provide a higher-quality experience, especially when students are writing every day. It is better to have students actively writing at the end of the timed period than watching the clock and feeling frustrated about being unable to write for the entire period. Use a kitchen timer or similar device to time each day's writing. Allowing students to continue a paper or story during the next day's session is a simple way to let students develop longer pieces.

Selecting and grading student papers. About 20-30% of the class should have their papers evaluated by the teacher each day. Depending upon class size, the teacher will carefully read and mark comments on four to eight papers per day. A schedule of whose papers are to be selected each day can be created by using a random numbers table or drawing names from a hat. To ensure equal distribution of the teacher's feedback, a student probably should not have her or his paper graded on more than two consecutive days and every student's paper should be selected at least once each week. The teacher may wish to deviate from the predetermined schedule if a particular student warrants additional attention.

The teacher should indicate all instances of a student's correct use of the target skill(s) with colored markers and/or highlighters. Either a number or percentage, depending on how the objective performance criterion was presented to the students, should be written at the top of each selected paper. A student's paper that meets or exceeds the required criterion should have a comment such as this written on it: "Wow, 19 different action words! That's great Tony! Do it again

tomorrow." On a paper that did not meet the criterion, the teacher might write: "These 8 action words are excellent, Sharon. Try hard to include at least 15 in tomorrow's story." The teacher should also write qualitative feedback comments regarding the student's use of the target skill (e.g., "Having the pitcher 'grab the ball' from his coach — instead of just getting or taking it — really conveyed his intense determination to get into the game. Good choice of verbs!")

Marking editorial suggestions and changes relevant to the target skill(s) can also be helpful. For example, indicating how several passive or nonactive words or phrases can be changed to the active voice. Better yet, the teacher might change or correct only one or two instances of a given type of error or problem along with a written prompt that the student improve or correct the remaining instances. Positive comments regarding other non-targeted aspects of a student's paper can be noted also (e.g., "Jill, you expressed your main character's feelings very well. I felt as frightened as she must have been!")

Because the teacher is evaluating only 4-8 papers each day, instead of 20-30, extra care should be taken to provide the specific and positive feedback that is so often missing in writing instruction. However, marking punctuation, grammatical, and stylistic errors not currently targeted for instruction should be avoided. A teacher who wishes to influence a student's progress positively along the difficult path to better writing should not return papers littered with corrections and x-outs (Hillocks, 1986).

Although most educators would agree that correct spelling is an important dimension of good writing, we generally do not recommend marking spelling errors on students' written compositions. When students are being encouraged to extend their current repertoires of written expression, they should not be deterred by the worry that every spelling error will be cited. Specific, recurrent spelling errors, especially of the type many teachers would call "careless" mistakes, can be addressed within a selective grading program. For example, papers free of certain spelling errors might earn bonus points for their authors. But caution is advised. Teachers must be careful not to build in contingencies that, while noble in purpose and positive in appearance, operate to discourage students from experimenting with and expanding their written vocabularies.

After the selected papers are marked, several paragraphs, sentences, and/or phrases from each paper should be selected for use as the next session's teaching examples. One paper might also be chosen for reading aloud to the class. Finally, the teacher should record the score obtained by each student on the objectively measured target skill(s) and how many points the group earned based on the scores of the papers graded.

Sharing feedback with the whole class. From the second day of selective grading onward, each session follows this basic sequence, though many variations are both possible and appropriate.

1. The teacher hands back the previous day's papers and announces how many met the performance criterion and how many points students have earned.
2. The teacher gives feedback to the entire class based on what was noted in the selected papers.
3. Direct instruction on the target skill(s) is provided.
4. Writing topics for the day are presented.
5. Students write for the timed period.

Students are eager to find out whether the selected papers have met the performance criterion. Their performance can be announced as the papers are returned or be recorded on a chart for students to see as they enter the classroom. The teacher never announces whose papers were scored, only whether the criterion was met. After all students have had their papers returned, the teacher discusses positive aspects that were found in the selected papers as well as common errors relevant to the target skills.

In classrooms in which we have evaluated the selective grading system,

most students have reported that they enjoyed having parts of their papers used as instructional illustrations. Even though the instructional examples are usually presented without identification of the authors, most students point out with pride whenever any of their writing is displayed. Nevertheless, teachers should be sensitive to any signs that a student does not like having his or her work presented to the class.

Reading aloud one of the graded papers and making both objective and qualitative remarks about its structure, content, and style can be an effective way to share feedback with the whole class (Freedman, 1984). The teacher should always check to determine that a student will not be uncomfortable having his or her work read to the class.

Variations. There are countless adaptations and modifications that can be added to the basic selective grading system as we have described it. Some of the variations presented here have been incorporated into selective grading programs that we have implemented in elementary and junior high school classrooms. Others have yet to be tried and evaluated systematically, but they are included because of their logical and practical appeal.

Proofreading/editing time. Students can be given an additional 5 minutes for proofreading and editing their papers after the timed writing period is over. Each student should have a dictionary and thesaurus.

Peer editing. Students can spend 5 minutes proofreading and editing a peer's paper after the timed writing period.

Individualize target skills and/or performance criteria. Each student's baseline stories can be analyzed to determine the writing skills most in need of improvement and the levels of performance criteria likely to be attainable (Heward, 1980). Both targeted writing skills and performance criteria then can be changed as a function of improvements in each student's writing. Teachers must be careful, however, not to individualize so many aspects of the program that group feedback is relevant to only a few students.

Change target skills regularly. Even though many students in the class still show a need for improvement on the current target skill(s), it is unrealistic to expect students to sustain interest in writing stories day after day in which they must include or concentrate on a particular aspect of writing (e.g., dialogue with quotations). One approach is to work on a different target skill each week. The teacher might still provide feedback, or even occasional bonus points, for students' correct usage of previous target skills.

Add secondary "focus" skills. If it is necessary to work on one or more target skills for several weeks because of their fundamental role in improving students' writing, secondary "focus" skills can be added and changed on a regular basis. For example, several students' papers may contain recurrent errors in use of commas in a series. If the teacher believes that one or two days of direct instruction, practice, and feedback might remediate the problem, using commas correctly in a series could serve as a focus skill. Selected papers still would be scored on the primary target skill(s), but students could earn additional bonus points for themselves and for the class by incorporating into their papers the correct use of commas in a series to some specified criterion.

Allow students to select focus skills. Students could be given the opportunity to identify focus skills by random selection or they could earn the privilege by meeting specified performance criteria.

Longer stories. From time to time, several consecutive days or an entire week might be devoted to writing longer pieces. Papers still would be selected and evaluated on a daily basis, but students would be able to develop extended stories.

Trading stories. This is a variation of the longer-stories procedure, except that students continue the story begun by a peer on the previous session.

Find and correct yesterday's errors. As the teacher provides feedback comments to the class that are based on specific errors found in the selected papers, students whose papers were not graded could locate and correct or improve those features in their papers.

Rewrite a previous story for publication. Every 2 weeks a day can be designated as "rewrite day." Students pick a favorite story to rewrite and submit to the teacher for publication in a book of class papers.

One-to-one teacher consultation. During the timed writing period, the teacher can meet with individual students to discuss how their writing has improved, give specific help, and jointly set individual performance objectives.

Students choose unselected papers for evaluation. Occasionally, each student in the class selects any one of her or his previously written, but ungraded, stories for evaluation and scoring by the teacher. The usual writing time could be used by students to select and edit the paper to be evaluated.

Combine with literature study. A selective grading program can be combined with the study of published literature. Instead of writing about story starters or other topics, students could write reviews, character studies, analyses, and so forth, based on their reading of classic or contemporary literature.

Public posting and the "good writing game." The daily and cumulative number of points earned by the class can be posted publicly on a classroom chart. Numerous studies have demonstrated the positive effects of publicly posting student performance data (Van Houten, 1980). A version of the good behavior game (Barrish, Saunders, & Wolf, 1969) can be incorporated by having different period classes compete with one another in meeting their daily performance criteria on the selected papers. See Cooper et al. (1987) for guidelines on setting up group-oriented reinforcement contingencies that promote positive peer support.

Evaluation

Over the past 2 years, we have conducted systematic evaluations of selective grading with students in three classrooms at three different schools. So far our preliminary analysis of student writing performance has been encouraging: Objective improvement has been noted on the skills targeted for selective grading. Furthermore, students and teachers have enjoyed selective grading and have offered numerous suggestions for improvements and adaptations, many of which have been included in this chapter.

TELEPHONE-MANAGED, HOME-BASED WRITING PROGRAM

Many instructional programs are more effective when extended into the home (Heron & Harris, 1987). Given the ever increasing complexities of the U.S. family (i.e., an increased number of single-parent families, higher percentage of families in which both parents work), any home-based strategy that hopes to improve writing should (a) be powerful enough to warrant the start-up costs, (b) be able to operate flexibly on a daily basis, and (c) be maintained easily over time.

One promising method for extending a writing program into the home is to use the telephone as the medium for instructional delivery. Not only do most U.S. families have access to a telephone, but programmatically it represents a minimally intrusive method for communicating with students and parents. Using the telephone to hear a taped story starter on a daily basis during the school year provides students with the opportunity to practice learned skills in a generalized setting. Also, a telephone-managed, home-based program can provide systematic writing practice over the summer months, a time when many exceptional students' skills regress (Larsen, Goodman, & Glean, 1981).

Description of the Basic System[1]

A telephone-managed, home-based writing program is defined here as any system by which teachers and parents use a telephone-answering device as the medium through which information relative to the writing process — topics, skills to be developed, and evaluation data — can be relayed. Such a system has the advantages of being accessible, dependable, flexible, and relatively inexpensive. One of its more distinctive features is that it provides another avenue to improve writing that can be used during the school year or the summer months (Heron & Harris, 1987; Weiss et al., 1984).

Whether the system is used during the school year or as a way to stimulate creative writing during the summer, the program can be conceptualized as occurring across four stages: (a) baseline (the student's current writing performance is assessed), (b) parent training (parents learn the operational aspects and the overall goals for the program), (c) daily practice (students actually use the system each day), and (d) evaluation (the effects of the program are determined).

Stage 1: Baseline. The program begins when a student calls a school phone number each day to hear a story starter recorded by a teacher. The student then writes on the daily topic for at least 10 minutes or until a production criterion is met (e.g., two pages of writing). Then the student brings (or mails, if the program is being conducted during the summer) his or her stories to the teacher. The teacher counts and records the number of target responses (e.g., action verbs, adjectives), in order to establish baseline levels for the student. Of course, the student's written language production also can be used to calculate a type-token ratio (the number of different words in relation to total words), a grammatical correctness ratio (an index of the number of grammatical errors), an index of diversification (the degree to which the student varies words within sentences and paragraphs), or T-units (an index of meaningful thought units of expression) (Mercer & Mercer, 1989).

Stage 2: Parent training. After collecting baseline data for 1–2 weeks, the teacher conducts a parent conference-workshop. The purpose of the meeting is to teach parents how to identify the targeted writing skills on which their children will be working and how to report this information to the teacher by using the message capacity of the phone-answering machine. Also, parents are instructed in ways to reinforce their children's writing at home. For instance, in addition to reminding parents to praise effort and accomplishment, rudimentary instruction in how to manage a simple token economy is provided. Specifically, the teacher explains how a lottery can be initiated that schedules reinforcement at specific intervals for improved writing on targeted skills. Students earn coupons if they increase their performance on the target skill from the previous day's effort. Bonus coupons are awarded each time a student beats her or his best daily or weekly score. Coupons can be exchanged for free or inexpensive school supplies or back-up reinforcers.

Parents also learn during the workshop how to identify and reward increases in a second target response when stable increases in the first writing skill are evident. Since parents are by then familiar with the program, we have found that mailing a self-instruction booklet with guidelines helps them recognize the next writing skill for intervention. This method saves both parents and teacher from having to participate in another workshop.

The basic orientation of the training workshop follows a direct instruction format: model, lead, and test (Engelmann & Carnine, 1982). After explaining the overall purpose of the program, the teacher models for the parents how to (a) set the occasion for the child to listen to the tape, (b) monitor the child's 10-minute writing session, (c) score each writing sample, (d) reinforce the child's writing behavior, and (e) communicate with the teacher by using the message side of the answering machine. Then, the teacher leads the parents through each stage, providing prompts as necessary. Ample practice is built into the workshop session to ensure the parents are competent with the steps. Finally, parents review all of the system's principles and procedures with the teacher to clarify any further questions.

Stage 3: Daily practice. During the daily practice stage, the period when the system is fully operational, the student calls each day to listen to the tape and writes for 10 minutes, and the parent monitors, scores, and reinforces writing. All of the skills demonstrated and practiced during the workshop are employed during these daily practice sessions.

The teacher, on the other hand, generates and encodes the story starters on the audiotape, responds to questions that may have been raised by parents, scores stories, including the calculation of interobserver agreement measures, and provides feedback to the student on the quality of his or her written language.

Stage 4: Evaluation. At least three sources of evaluative data are produced by the home-based, telephone-managed program. First, the number of students who call each day is tallied on a counter, an accessory available on most telephone-answering devices. Second, specific information relative to each student's progress can be obtained. That is, daily and weekly data can be gathered that show the total number of words produced and the number and/or percentage of target skills actually used. Finally, consumer satisfaction information can be obtained to provide the practitioner with a qualitative assessment of teacher, parent, and student preferences for the system.

Supporting Research

Several studies using home-based, telephone-managed instruction have been reported in the literature. Bittle (1975) showed that a telephone-answering device could be used to establish and maintain parent-teacher communication and also to improve students' performance on in-school daily spelling tests. Each day second graders took lists of spelling words home with them and were tested on these words the next day. During the intervention phases of the experiment, parents called to hear teacher-recorded phone messages. Each nightly message told something about what their child did that day in school and included the list of spelling words for the next day's test. The data clearly showed the functional effects of the phone messages: students' spelling performance improved when the phone messages were available and it deteriorated when the messages were not in effect. Heward and Chapman (1981) replicated these results with primary grade learning-disabled (LD) students.

The hard-won gains in academic skills of many special education students deteriorate during the summer. In response to this all-too-common phenomenon, Hassett et al. (1984) evaluated a home-based, telephone-managed program to improve the written language expression of three junior high school students with learning disabilities during the summer. Each weekday the students called a school number to hear a short prerecorded story starter. They then wrote for 10 minutes on the topic. After being trained during a 2-hour workshop, parents provided praise and feedback on the number of action words included in each story — a target skill identified by the teacher — and later, on the number of adjectives. Each student earned coupons awarded by their parents for each story depending on individualized criteria determined according to his or her baseline performance. The students exchanged the coupons at the end of the summer program for various low-cost rewards.

Although the effects were variable across subjects, all three students increased their use of action words and adjectives during the summer program. The results also showed that the parents were able to participate in the program by providing feedback to their child, and that they scored their children's work with reasonable accuracy (interobserver agreement scores ranged from 69% to 93%). Figures 1 and 2 show data and story samples for James, a 13-year-old student

whose writing improved the most over the course of the 9-week program.

Alessi (1985) demonstrated an interesting variation of the telephone-managed program. Her study involved six parents of third- and fourth-grade special education students enrolled in self-contained and mainstream classes. After learning how to identify nouns, adjectives, and verbs, the students were given a story starter and asked to write for 10 minutes on that topic. Each student tried to meet an individualized target criterion for each writing behavior. Each time students met one of their individualized criteria, they recorded a message on the answering machine that their parents could hear when they called that night. An example of a child's tape was "Hi, Dad. This is Ron. I wrote 5 nouns, 4 adjectives, and 4 verbs today. I met my goal." After hearing their child's message, parents recorded a brief message that their child could hear the next day in school (e.g., "That's great! Keep up the good writing, Ron."). The results of Alessi's 75-day study showed that (a) the students' writing improved, (b) the students and parents enjoyed the program, (c) the program could be sustained for over 3.5 months of school, and (d) it was convenient for the teacher to manage.

Weiss (1984) conducted a study using the home–school communication program combined with home tutoring to improve the academic performance of 11 students with learning disabilities who attended a private elementary school. During baseline, the students were pretested by the teacher on three academic skills: sight words, spelling words, and math facts. During training, parents learned the program's procedures, such as accessing words and facts by the telephone, tutoring their child, and reinforcing learning. Each day parents tutored their children on the facts and skills they had obtained from the teacher's prerecorded telephone tape. Then they used the message-receiving tape to report the results of their tutoring to the teacher. The results showed that the students' performance on daily and weekly in-class tests increased as a result of the telephone-managed, home-based system (see

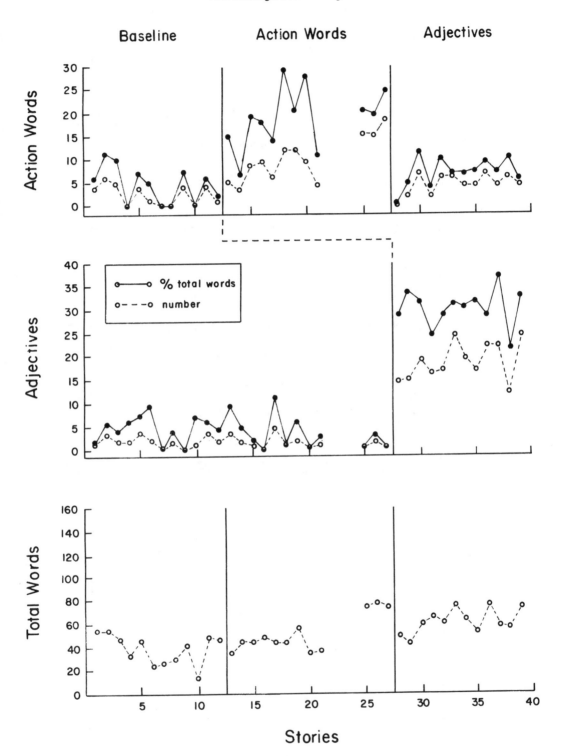

FIGURE 1. Action words, adjectives, and total words written by James during daily 10-minute writing periods during baseline, intervention on action words, and intervention on adjectives.

8

July 7, 1982   James D

First I would go to candy, allways thinking of myself. Later I would go to the meat deportment. After the meat deportment I would go to wine deportment

---

Aug 12 #33 Talking with a Star   James D

I look up from my salad, thick chocolate milk shake, hot golden crisp french fries, and delicious Big Mac with extra pickles.

I glance through shiney, clear glass and see a small, brown creature with a glowing red chest, short legs, long arms, and a large head with big greenish-blue eyes and a smashed-in nose.

I grab a white napkin and rush up to him. With the tip of his glowing right index finger he writes...

FIGURE 2. Two stories written by James, a 13-year-old student with learning disabilities. Story #8 was written during baseline ("What would you do if you won $6,000,000 in the lottery?"); Story #33 was written during the phase when adjectives were targeted ("Describe your reaction to meeting someone famous").

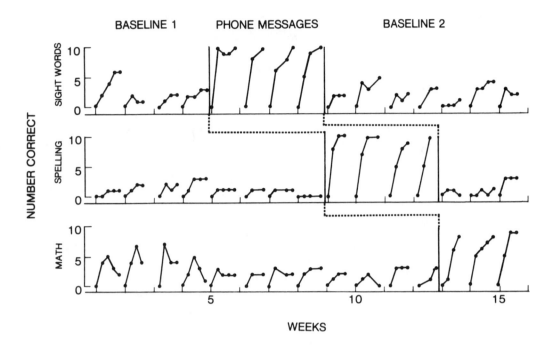

FIGURE 3. Number of items correctly answered on daily in-class assessments during baseline and phone messages. From "The effects of a telephone-managed home-school program using parents as home-based educators on the academic achievement of learning disabled students" by A. B. Weiss (1984). Unpublished doctoral dissertation, The Ohio State University, Columbus. Reprinted by permission.

Figures 3 and 4). Furthermore, the results confirmed again that parents can function successfully as home tutors for their children and enjoy the process at the same time.

In a follow-up study, Lazarus (1986) also merged the home–school communication program and tutoring at home, using preschool students as the target population and word parts and sight vocabulary development as the prime dependent measures. During the orientation-training workshop, parents learned how to access information by telephone-answering device, tutor and test their child at home, and report the results through the answering device. After calling a designated phone number to receive their child's word parts, practice words, and bonus words for the week, parents conducted tutoring in a three-part sequence. During "Practice: Get Ready," parents presented certain word parts (e.g., *ab*) and words containing those

word parts (e.g., *absent*). The parents would say, "This is *ab* as in absent," while simultaneously flipping the *ab* flashcard over to expose the word *absent*. The child imitated the parent's vocalization. During "Practice: Sequential Order," the word parts were again presented, except that the parents' verbal modeling was omitted. Praise was issued when the child said the word part and corresponding word correctly. If an incorrect response was made, the parent said, "Try again." If the child made another incorrect response or no response at all, the parent repeated "This is *ab* as in *absent.*"

During "Practice: Random Order," the parent shuffled the cards and presented them again to the child. Testing of the practice word consisted of having the parent present practice words without prompts, scoring each response as correct or incorrect by placing a 0 (correct) or X (incorrect) on the back of the card. Testing of bonus words was conducted in

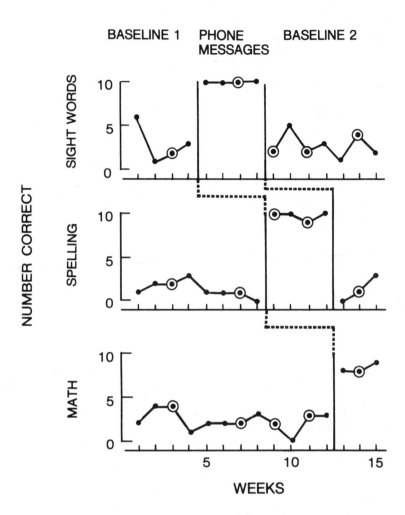

FIGURE 4. Number of items correctly answered on weekly in-class posttests during baseline and phone messagess (open circles represent scores obtained by second observer). From "The effects of a telephone-managed home-school program using parents as home-based educators on the academic achievement of learning disabled students" by A. B. Weiss (1984). Unpublished doctoral dissertation, The Ohio State University, Columbus. Reprinted by permission.

a similar fashion, only these words were not exposed to the child previously and served as a measure of response generalization. Finally, the parent used the telephone answering device to report the results of each night's testing. The results indicated that during the parent tutoring/home-school communication phase, each of the seven students who participated in the study improved significantly her or his recognition of word parts and words. Parents consistently reported their child's performance accurately, made use of the message to leave comments to the teacher, and found the system to be a convenient and efficient means to maintain home-school communication.

Planning and Implementing a Telephone-Managed, Home-Based Program

Before a telephone-managed, home-based writing program can be implemented, two fundamental obstacles need to be addressed. One is logistical: Who will run the program? The second is programmatic: How will the system operate?

As the previous studies have shown, during the school year many teachers are willing and able to carry out the tasks associated with the telephone-managed, home-based system: Preparing story starters for the announcement tape, conducting the workshop, grading papers, tracking results, and so forth. Such might not be the case, however, during the summer months when schools are closed. Hence, a teacher considering using the system over the summer might (a) apply for an extended contract, (b) link the program to a university-based research effort in which graduate student assistants or faculty could help collect data, and/or (c) apply for a funded project to earn "release" time dollars for summer employment.

Programmatically, designers should aim for generality of behavior change. That is, the written products that are generated at home during the school year or over the summer should become an integral part of the student's written language program. The guidelines that follow support that perspective.

Choosing the writing targets or skills. The written language skills targeted for instruction should be based on an assessment of the individual student's current writing ability. Using either norm- or criterion-referenced instruments and samples of the student's written language, teachers can design programs to improve any of the four basic written language skills areas: vocabulary, content, form, and organization (Mercer & Mercer, 1989; Wallace, Cohen, & Polloway, 1987). If exceptional students are integrated into the classroom, the individualized education program (IEP) should be a principal referent for selecting the target skills. Typically, after review of either the long-range goals or the short-range objectives, written language target skills will be evident.

Individualizing the program. To individualize the writing program, teachers or parents could ask students to select from or generate a "menu" of topical story starters to be recorded on the telephone-answering device. In this way, the students would not have to write a story based on someone else's notions of interest areas — the teacher's or parents' — but more specifically on their own interests and experiences.

The program could be individualized further by targeting skill development for specific students. Student 1, for example, might have a goal of writing 10 sentences, each of which begins with a capital letter and ends with a period. The goal for Student 2 might be to produce 10 sentences, each of which contains an action verb and an adjective.

Finally, the program could be individualized at the proofreading stage of writing by having the students use the COPS (capitalization, overall appearance, punctuation, and spelling) procedure before submitting their final drafts (Schumaker, Nolan, & Deshler, 1985). Depending upon each student's skill level, the time allocated for in-class writing, and the student's rate of learning, successive units of instruction can be delivered across vocabulary, content, form, and organization skills by using the written language generated by the telephone-managed program as the basis.

Providing feedback and follow-up exercises at school. The telephone-managed program is not a complete program for teaching written language, although the compositions generated by the students can be used in a more complete program. For example, using Giordano's (1982) CATS (copy, alter, transform, and supply) procedure with the telephone-managed, home-based program can be an excellent way to work on sentence structure, spelling, and grammar. Table 2 shows how the CATS procedure would work. The boldface sentences show what the student might write at home. The underlined sentences show what the student might produce in class.

Classroom feedback charts can be generated that show individual or group

TABLE 2
Hypothetical Examples of Sentences Produced in a Telephone-Managed, Home-Based Program That Were Rewritten at School Using the CATS Procedure (Giordano, 1982)

Copy	Home-based:	**I like to fish with my dad.**
	Class-based:	I like to fish with my dad.
Alter	Home-based:	**If I won the lottery, I would be rich.**
	Class-based:	If you won the lottery, you could give me some bucks.
Transform	Home-based:	**Concord was the scene of a famous battle.**
	Class-based:	Was Concord the scene of a famous battle?
Supply	Home-based:	**Do you like to go to the zoo?**
	Class-based:	Yes, I do like to go to the zoo.

performance across any of the target skills identified by the teacher or parent (Van Houten, 1980). For instance, contingent on improved sentence structure, spelling, or organization, students could earn extra privileges at school or home.

Recording messages from parents. Telephone-answering devices have the capability to allow callers to leave messages. Thus, parents can report directly and regularly to the teacher about the success of the home program. If parents have comments or questions (e.g., What do I do if my child does not write as directed? What should I do if the story my child writes does not make sense? How can I find out what stories my child enjoys writing about?), the message capability of the answering service can be of great assistance. The parents' concerns with respect to these questions can be communicated to the teacher, and appropriate action taken.

SUMMARY

Virtually everyone — researchers, teachers, parents, and, most of all, students — agrees that learning to write should be made more effective and enjoyable for all involved. Most people who have ever tried to teach or to learn functional writing skills have found it to be one of the most difficult and challenging of curriculum areas. Beyond these two points of agreement, however, the theoretical constructs and instructional methods concerning writing are as divergent as any domain of educational theory and practice.

Writing, like all other aspects of human performance tackled by the schools, is best viewed as learned behavior. That is, good writers have learned through their experiences to do certain things (e.g., use varying sentence patterns) that are different from the things writers of lesser talent have learned (e.g., writing exclusively in the passive voice). We use the term *experience* in this context in its broadest sense. Many events in addition to classroom instruction contribute to a person's repertoire of written expression. Instructional activities designed for the primary purpose of improving students' writing skills do, however, constitute a significant portion of that experience. Those experiences must be made more effective.

Two major reasons students do not develop better writing skills are that (a) they do not have regular opportunities to write, and (b) when they do write, the feedback they receive is usually too delayed, unspecific, and punishing (i.e., a previously written passage by a student might be returned with the comment, "Try to improve your writing style"). We agree with Graves (1985), who stated that students should write at least 4 days per week and perhaps more, depending on their skill level.

However, we must state an important limitation concerning selective grading and the telephone-managed, home-based systems — a qualification that might be overlooked by educators in their understandable eagerness to find something that works. Both strategies outlined in this chapter should be considered to be in early stages of development in that only a few promising demonstrations of effectiveness have been conducted to date. Nevertheless, the strengths of each approach are well grounded in the extensive literatures showing the powerful effects of increasing active student response, providing effective feedback, and involving parents in instructional activities. Furthermore, other procedures for improving writing can easily be incorporated into selective grading or a telephone-managed, home-based programs. For example, story mapping (Idol & Croll, 1987), contingency management (Ballard & Glynn, 1975), sentence-guided instruction (Phelps-Teraski & Phelps, 1980), sentence combination (Strong, 1983), the COPS procedure (Schumaker et al., 1981) and computer activities (Morocco & Neuman, 1986) can only serve to improve the environmental arrangements for writing and the outcome of writing sessions.

We are encouraged by the empirical results obtained from initial efforts to evaluate these two strategies for teaching students to write more effectively, and we are excited about the many adaptations, extensions, and improvements of selective grading and telephone-managed, home-based writing instruction that are still to come.

FOOTNOTE

[1]For a booklet describing the telephone-managed, home-based instructional program and how it can be adapted to other subject areas, write the first author at Department of Educational Services and Research, The Ohio State University, 1945 N. High Street, Columbus, OH 43210.

REFERENCES

Alessi, C. (1985). *Effects of a home–school communication system on the writing performance of learning disabled students.* Unpublished masters thesis, The Ohio State University, Columbus.

Ballard, K. D., & Glynn, T. (1975). Behavioral self-management in story writing with elementary school children. *Journal of Applied Behavior Analysis, 8,* 387-398.

Barrish, H. H., Saunders, M., & Wolf, M. M. (1969). Good behavior game: Effects of individual contingencies for group consequences on disruptive behavior in a classroom. *Journal of Applied Behavior Analysis, 2,* 199-224.

Bittle, R. G. (1975). Improving parent-teacher communication through recorded telephone messages. *Journal of Educational Research, 69,* 87-95.

Bos, C. S. (1988). Process-oriented writing: Instructional implications for mildly handicapped students. *Exceptional Children, 54,* 521-527.

Braddock, R. R., Lloyd-Jones, R., & Schoer, L. (1963). *Research in written composition.* Champaign, IL: National Council of Teachers of English.

Carnine, D. W. (1976). Effects of two teachers' presentation rates on off-task behavior, answering correctly, and participation. *Journal of Applied Behavior Analysis, 14,* 71-80.

Cooper, J. O., Heron, T. E., & Heward, W. L. (1987). *Applied behavior analysis.* Columbus, OH: Merrill.

Dewey, J. (1916). *Democracy in education.* New York: Macmillan.

Dillon, D., & Searle, D. (1980). The message of marking: Teacher-written responses to student writing at intermediate grade levels. *Research in the Teaching of English, 14,* 233-242.

Engelmann, S., & Carnine, D. (1982). *Theory of instruction. Principles and applications.* New York: Irvington.

Freedman, S. W. (1984, April). *The evaluation of, and response to, student writing. A review.* Paper presented at the annual meeting of the American Educational Research Association, New Orleans.

Giordano, G. (1982). CATS exercises: Teaching disabled writers to communicate. *Academic Therapy, 18,* 233-237.

Graham, S., & Harris, K. R. (1988). Instructional recommendations for teaching writing to exceptional students. *Exceptional Children, 54,* 506-512.

Graves, D. H. (1985). All children can write. *Learning Disabilities Focus, 1,* 36-43.

Greenwood, C. R., Delquadri, J. C., & Hall, R. V. (1984). Opportunity to respond and student academic performance. In W. L. Heward, T. E. Heron, D. S. Hill, & J. Trap-Porter (Eds.), *Focus on behavior analysis in education* (pp. 58-88). Columbus, OH: Merrill.

Hall, R. V., Delquadri, J. C., & Harris, J. (1977, May). *Opportunity to respond: A new focus in the field of applied behavior analysis.* Paper presented at the Midwest Association for Applied Behavior Analysis, Chicago.

Hansen, C. L. (1978). Writing skills. In N. G. Haring, T. C. Lovitt, M. D. Eaton, & C. L. Hansen (Eds.), *The fourth R: Research in the classroom* (pp. 93-126). Columbus, OH: Merrill.

Hassett, M. E., Engler, C., Cooke, N. L., Test, D. W., Weiss, A. B., Heward, W. L., & Heron, T. E. (1984). A telephone-managed, home-based summer writing program for LD adolescents. In W. L. Heward, T. E. Heron, D. S. Hill, & J. Trap-Porter (Eds.), *Focus on behavior analysis in education* (pp. 89-103). Columbus, OH: Merrill.

Heron, T. E., & Harris, K. C. (1987). *The educational consultant: Helping professionals, parents, and mainstreamed students* (2nd ed.). Austin, TX: Pro-Ed.

Heward, W. L. (1980). A formula for individualizing initial criteria for reinforcement. *Exceptional Teacher, 1,* 7, 9.

Heward, W. L., & Chapman, J. (1981). Improving parent-teacher communication through recorded telephone messages: Systematic replication in a special education setting. *Journal of Special Education Technology, 4,* 11-19.

Heward, W. L., Courson, F. H., & Narayan, J. S. (1989). Using choral responding to increase active student response during group instruction. *Teaching Exceptional Children, 21,* 72-75.

Heward, W. L., Gardner III, R., & Prayzer, R. (1988). [Providing feedback on students' writing with a selective grading procedure: Evaluation in three middle-school English classes]. Unpublished raw data.

Heward, W. L., Narayan, J. S., & Clingo, J. (1987). [Effects of a selective grading procedure on the written expression of elementary students]. Unpublished raw data.

Hillocks, G. (1986). *Research on written composition: New directions for teaching.* Urbana, IL: National Conference for Research in English.

Idol, L., & Croll, V. J. (1987). Story-mapping training as a means of improving reading comprehension. *Learning Disability Quarterly, 10,* 214-229.

Langer, J. A. (1988). Research on written composition: A response to Hillocks' report. *Research in the Teaching of English, 22,* 89-116.

Larsen, L., Goodman, L., & Glean, R. (1981). Issues in the implementation of extended school year programs for handicapped students. *Exceptional Children, 47,* 256-263.

Lazarus, B. (1986). *Effects of home-based parent tutoring managed by an automatic telephone answering machine on word recognition of kindergarten children.* Unpublished doctoral dissertation. The Ohio State University, Columbus.

Lewis, R. B., & Doorlag, D. H. (1987). *Teaching special students in the mainstream* (2nd ed.). Columbus, OH: Merrill.

Mercer, C. D., & Mercer, A. R. (1989). *Teaching students with learning problems* (3rd ed.). Columbus, OH: Merrill.

Morocco, C. C., & Neuman, S. B. (1986). Word processors and the acquisition of writing strategies. *Journal of Learning Disabilities, 19,* 243-247.

Narayan, J. S., Heward, W. L., Gardner III, R., Courson, F. H., & Omness, C. (in press). Using response cards to increase active student response and academic performance in an elementary social studies class. *Journal of Applied Behavior Analysis..*

Phelps-Teraski, D., & Phelps, T. (1980). *Teaching written expression: The Phelps Sentence Guide Program.* Novato, CA: Academic Therapy.

Schumaker, J. B., Deshler, D. D., Denton, P. H., Alley, G. R., Clark, F. L., & Warner, M. M. (1981). *Multipass: A learning strategy for improving reading comprehension.* (Research report No. 33). Lawrence, KS: University of Kansas, Institute on Research in Learning Disabilities.

Schumaker, J. B., Nolan, S. M., Deshler, D. D. (1985). *Learning strategies curriculum: The error-monitoring strategy.* Lawrence: University of Kansas.

Sommers, N. (1982). Responding to student writing. *College Composition and Communication, 33,* 148-156.

Stotsky, S. (1988). In J. A. Langer, (Ed.), Research on written composition: A response to Hillocks' report (pp. 89-99). *Research in the Teaching of English, 22,* 89-116.

Strong, W. (1983). *Sentence combining: A composition book* (2nd ed.). New York: Random House.

Van Houten, R. (1980). *Learning through feedback.* New York: Human Science Press.

Wallace, G., Cohen, S., & Polloway, E. (1987). *Language arts.* Austin, TX: Pro-Ed.

Weiss, A. B. (1984). *The effects of a telephone-managed, home-school program using parents as tutors on the academic achievement of learning disabled students.* Unpublished doctoral dissertation, The Ohio State University, Columbus.

Weiss, A. B., Cooke, N. L., Grossman, M. A., Ryno-Vrabel, M., Hassett, M. E., Heward, W. L., & Heron, T. E. (1984). *Home-school communication: Setting up a telephone-managed program.* Columbus, OH: Special Press.

18

Use of Self-Correction to Improve Spelling in Regular Education Classrooms

Beatrice A. Okyere
The Ohio State University

Timothy E. Heron
The Ohio State University

Spelling is an essential component of a total language arts curriculum. Graham and Miller (1979) made this point succinctly: "While spelling is neither the most important nor the least important aspect of writing, it is a crucial ingredient. Good spellers are able to express their thoughts on paper without unnecessary interruptions. Poor spellers are hampered in their ability to communicate freely through the written word" (p. 1). Furthermore, persons who spell correctly are perceived to be "educated," while those who do not spell accurately are not viewed so favorably (DeStefano, 1978). So, from both a personal and a societal perspective, those who are able to spell accurately and efficiently have an advantage over those who do not. That is, minimum effort (i.e., checking the dictionary, proofreading) is required to express thoughts clearly and concisely, and peers hold the individual in high regard for being able to do so.

Still, people are not born accurate spellers. They progress through a series of developmental stages (i.e., preliterate, prephonetic, phonetic, transitional) that end with correct spelling (Gearheart, DeRuiter, & Sileo, 1986; Gentry, 1984; Wallace, Cohen, & Polloway, 1987). The length of time that students remain at any one stage can be affected by such factors as previous direct language experiences (i.e., talking, reading, writing, spelling),

quality and duration of spelling instruction, amount of reinforcement and feedback, and short- and long-term memory capability. As spellers become more fluent at each stage, it appears that they become better able to combine several skills including visualization of letters, recall of letter sequences (referred to as *orthography*), and knowledge of phonology, morphology, semantics, and word generalizations.

This chapter is written with a threefold purpose. First, a taxonomy of spelling approaches will be presented as a way to orient the school psychologist to the overall methodologies associated with spelling instruction. This classification scheme, which includes the traditional approach, remedial approaches, and specialized strategies and tactics, captures the essence of the major alternatives that are available to teach spelling.[1] We concur with the findings of the larger body of educational studies, which to date report that no single method seems to be any more effective than another (Gearheart et al., 1986). Even so, practitioners faced with students with spelling deficiencies need functional alternatives to meet daily needs. Hence, the second purpose of our paper: We will describe how to use self-correction to enhance spelling ability. We believe that self-correction meets the criteria of being flexible, manageable, transportable, and effective and that it has several advantages over many of the remedial and other specialized programs. Our description of this system will be supplemented with findings from two recent studies (McNeish, 1985; Okyere 1989) that show that self-correction can be effective in promoting maintenance and generality of performance and that it has the added benefit of being preferred by students. Finally, implications for practitioners who use self-correction will be addressed.

A TAXONOMY OF SPELLING APPROACHES

Teachers, and the school psychologists who serve them, have a dizzying array of commercial programs, remedial approaches, and specialized strategies and tactics at their command to improve spelling performance (see Figure 1). The taxonomy is designed to provide a conceptual framework for classifying the numerous alternatives available to practitioners.

Traditional Approach

Most students learn to spell by using one or more of the traditional basic series of spelling textbooks. These commercially available texts generally employ a linguistic approach that emphasizes phonology, morphology, and syntactic rules or word patterns (Hammill & Bartel, 1978). Words for these commercial texts are selected from lists of words derived from child or adult written language, or common words in written vocabulary. A fundamental tenet of this approach is that students eventually learn basic word patterns, spelling similarities with respect to sound sequence, and generalization patterns.

Methodologically, a traditional approach varies the instructional format daily. For instance, on Mondays the students might receive a list of 10–20 words from the text; they might be required to write the words three times. On Tuesdays, the words would be written in sentences. On Wednesdays, the students would alphabetize the words, and Thursdays might be reserved for writing a story using the words. An end-of-the-week test would be administered on Fridays (McNeish, 1985). This cycle is repeated the next week with a new list of words, regardless of the student's performance on the weekly test.

There are a significant number of students who do not learn, or at least who do not learn efficiently, using the traditional commercial programs. For these students, the week-by-week cycle of receiving new word lists without having mastered previous spelling vocabulary is extremely counterproductive and frustrating. Stevens and Schuster (1987) state: "It is neither sensible nor satisfactory to recycle these students through a more individualized or slower-paced regular classroom curriculum using the same instructional methods that have already proven unsuccessful" (p. 9). When the commercial program has been shown to be ineffective, practitioners should consider one of the remedial or specialized approaches.

Remedial Approaches

There are five major remedial approaches that school psychologists could recommend, depending upon the unique needs of the student. Before deciding on a course of action, practitioners should review all pertinent assessment information to determine if (a) a match can be made between the student's spelling behavior (e.g., the rules the student applies to spell unknown words or variants), (b) the instructional strengths of a given program, and (c) the teacher's familiarity and competence with the potential remedial approach. Specifically, the school psychologist should attempt to answer the question: Does this student need a multisensory approach, more emphasis on sound–symbol relationships only, or merely more repetition and practice?

Fernald and Gillingham-Stillman approaches. If the student has a severe *reading* and *spelling* deficit, the Fernald

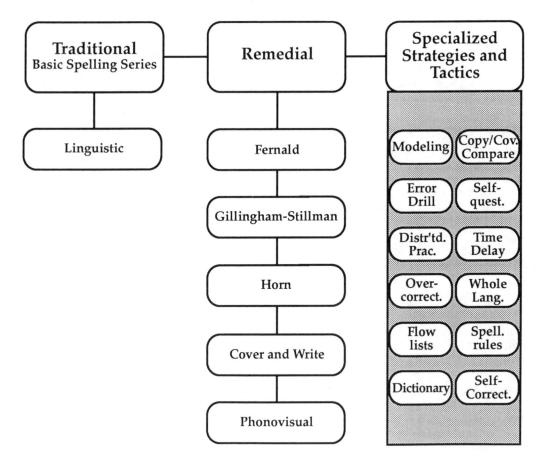

FIGURE 1. A taxonomy of spelling approaches showing the major orientations and subdivions to teach spelling.

(1943) approach or the Gillingham and Stillman (1970) method might be employed because these approaches integrate reading and spelling directly. For example, the Fernald method stresses whole-word learning in that words are selected from stories the student dictates, and the words are taught as a whole without phonic instruction. In effect, Fernald's method employs a language experience and tracing techniques. The Gillingham–Stillman method uses an alphabetic system and emphasizes sound blending, repetition, and drill (Mercer & Mercer, 1989). Furthermore, both of these approaches are based on the premise that building vocabulary (reading and spelling) must proceed systematically from words

that the student knows to words that the student needs to learn.

Horn method. E. Horn's (1954) multistep method combines elements of word pronunciation, visualization, spelling recall, written orthography, and proofreading. Students proceed through each of these steps sequentially. If an error is made at any step, the entire process is repeated until the student spells the word correctly without a mistake. For instance, if a student were directed to spell the word *middle*, he or she would pronounce each part of the word, "mid-dle." Next, the student would look at each part of the word and say it again. At the third step, the word is spelled orally letter by letter, visualized, and respelled orally. Finally, the student writes the word and checks it for accuracy. If an error is made when the word is spelled letter by letter [m-i-d-l-e] (step 3), the student returns to the first step (i.e., pronunciation) and begins the process over.

Cover-and-write technique. If the student has good short-term memory, but weak long-term memory, a cover-and-write approach, which capitalizes on short-term memory skills, might be used. In this approach, the student looks at the word and says it, writes the word twice while looking at it, covers the word and writes it again, and finally rechecks the spelling visually (Graham & Miller, 1979). An emphasis is placed on practicing, proofing, and correcting errors quickly.

Phonovisual approach. The phonovisual approach emphasizes visual and auditory discrimination of letter sounds. Students are introduced to consonant and vowel sounds by means of pictures of familiar images (e.g., *a* for *a*pple). This method is a phonetically based approach that stresses the association between the visual image and the letter sound (Schoolfield & Timberlake, 1960).

Specialized Strategies and Tactics

At least 12 specialized strategies and tactics can be employed to assist students in learning to spell (see Figure 1). To date, no clear guidelines exist as to which of these strategies would be a preferred first choice for a student who has difficulty learning to spell by using one of the traditional or remedial approaches. The decision to use one of these specialized approaches often depends on (a) the magnitude of the spelling difficulty (i.e., how deficient the student is compared to peers), (b) the time the teacher has to devote to spelling instruction (15 minutes/day; 35 minutes/day), or (c) whether a teacher-directed, peer-mediated, or semi-independent approach is desired. For instance, if the student possesses several spelling skills and can follow directions, and the teacher prefers a teacher-directed approach, then modeling, time-

delay, spelling rules, or whole language might be employed (Cooper, Heron, & Heward, 1987; Smith, 1989). Conversely, if the teacher wants to integrate peers into the spelling program, then error drills, distributed practice, positive practice overcorrection, and flow lists can be arranged through tutoring formats. Finally, if the teacher prefers the student to work semi-independently, copy–cover–compare, dictionary, self-questioning, or self-correction tactics could be instituted.

We recommend a self-correction procedure for several reasons. First, it has the best chance of maximizing success within a given instructional unit of time. We concur wholeheartedly with a number of educators who suggest that self-correction is the *single* most important instructional variable in learning to spell (Allred, 1977; Christine & Hollingsworth, 1966; Ganschow, 1983; Horn, 1947; Schoephoerster, 1962; Wallace et al., 1987). Second, self-correction can be integrated into a total language arts curriculum, including written expression, reading, and spelling. Programming common instructional features across subject areas is an important component of generality training (Cooper et al., 1987; Stokes & Baer, 1977). If self-correction can be used as part of a spelling improvement program, it also can be used for reading and/or written expression (Schumaker et al., 1981). Third, self-correction has been shown to be preferred by a wide range of students, including adolescents (McNeish, 1985; Okyere, 1989). Finally, self-correction is derived from a research base that demonstrates that this procedure is effective (Smith, 1989).

THE SELF-CORRECTION STRATEGY

Self-Correction Research Base

Self-correction for spelling is a teaching procedure in which students learn to spell by (a) comparing their misspelled words to a model (match-to-sample), (b) identifying specific types of spelling mistakes (e.g., omissions, repetitions, transpositions), (c) correcting their mistakes by themselves using proofreading marks, and (d) writing the correct sequence of letters for the word. Unlike other spelling approaches which consume instructional time when the teacher directs students to alphabetize lists of words, search the dictionary for a correct spelling, or associate pictorial images with sounds (tasks that are unrelated to practicing the specific orthography of the target words), self-correction enables students to focus specifically on letter sequence. Consequently, students have a lot of opportunities to respond (Greenwood, Delquadri, & Hall, 1984), since they make their own corrections and have immediate feedback on their spelling efforts by comparing their word to the model (Van Houten, 1980). Opportunity to respond and feedback have been shown to be effective in improving a wide range of behaviors, and both could easily be adapted to chart self-correction trials during spelling instruction (Figure 2).

One of the first demonstrations of self-correction to improve spelling was conducted by T. Horn (1947). He used a population of 268 sixth-grade students divided into three groups. Group 1 (N = 85) took a test over words in their regular spelling series, then corrected their work, and immediately retook the test. Students engaged in this sequence three times per week. Students in Group 2 (N = 87) also took a test over words of comparable difficulty, but they did not correct their work until the next session. The third group (N = 96) was administered the same procedures as Group 1, except that a pronunciation exercise was included during the first session of each week.

The results of the study showed that the students in Group 1, the immediate self-correction group, outperformed the members of the other groups on both weekly and delayed spelling tests. Horn recommended that "since the corrected test has been shown to be such a potent factor in learning to spell, it should be utilized during the spelling period in such ways as to insure its maximum effect" (1947, p. 285).

Ganschow (1983) described a self-correction format to improve spelling performance. Students used three proof-reading marks as the primary method by which to compare their spelling with the correct spelling of a word. Students were presented with the target words orally or from a language master. The correct spellings of the words were recorded in the first column of a five-column page. Students folded under Column 1, hiding the correct spellings while the language master or tape dictated the words to them. Then, they unfolded Column 1 to expose the words and self-correct. Ganschow (1983) suggested that the self-correction procedure set the occasion for students to work independently in the regular classroom while simultaneously improving their performance.

In an experimental test of Ganschow's self-correction format, McNeish (1985) conducted a study with five learning-disabled, seventh-grade students in a rural middle school. In an alternating treatment design, students used either a traditional or a self-correction approach for 20-minute periods of instruction 4 days per week. During traditional instruction, students wrote their spelling list of words three times each on Mondays, wrote each word in a sentence on Tuesdays, wrote the words in alphabetical order as many times as possible within 20 minutes on Wednesdays, and generated a story using as many words as possible on Thursdays. Fridays were reserved for posttesting.

During the self-correction procedure, students received a sheet of paper with five columns that contained their spelling words written in the first column. They folded this column under so that they could not see the words. Then they listened to a dictation of their spelling words from an older student. Once dictation was completed, they unfolded their paper, exposing the previously written spelling words, and used a series of four proofreading marks ($\wedge$, 0, /, ~) to self-correct each of their responses in the second column of the sheet. For instance, if for stimulus word *occasion* they had written *ocasion*, the caret mark would be inserted between the *c* and the *a* (oc$\wedge$asion) to indicate that the letter *c* had to be added. The student would write the letter to be added above the caret

Students	Week 1 Number of self-correction trials per list of 5 words					Week 2 Number of self-correction trials per list of 5 words					Consecutive Days @ Criterion.
	M	T	W	Th	F	M	T	W	Th	F	
MIKE	3	2	3	4	2	2	5	6	4	6	4
PETER	3	2	3	3	0	2	2	4	5	5	3
AMBER	3	2	2	4	2	2	5	6	6	6	4
JASON	3	2	3	4	3	2	5	6	6	6	4
CHRISTIN	2	2	2	1	0	1	5	6	5	6	4
MELISSA	3	2	3	4	3	2	4	4	5	6	4
JEREMY	3	2	3	5	3	2	5	6	6	6	4
CHRISTOPHER	3	2	3	5	3	2	5	6	6	6	4
KATHY	2	2	3	5	3	2	5	6	6	6	4
CHRISTINE	2	2	2	4	3	2	2	6	6	6	3
DEVIN	2	2	3	5	3	2	2	6	5	5	3
CLASS TOTAL	29	22	30	44	25	21	45	62	60	64	
POSS. TOTAL	33	22	33	55	33	22	55	66	66	66	

FIGURE 2. **Performance feedback chart showing student self-correction trials over a 2-week period. Criterion was achieved when four or more trials occurred in a day.**

mark, and then rewrite the complete word in the third column. This "proof plus write" strategy, proofing and then writing the complete letter sequence, was repeated for all of the words on the list. Students who spelled the word correctly on the first trial would simply place a checkmark in the second column. Students who completed the word list before the end of the 20-minute session were directed to repeat the process, using columns four and five, until time ran out.

McNeish's results indicated that students learned more words under the self-correction procedure than they did under the traditional approach. When the self-correction procedure was in effect, students learned an average of 24 more words each 5 weeks of instruction (4.8 words/week) than under the traditional approach. Figure 3 shows the data for weekly posttests aggregated for all students in each condition. The data show that self-correction was clearly superior to the traditional method in as much as the average percentage correct during the traditional approach was 65.6%, whereas during self-correction it was 86.2%. All students performed better under the self-correction procedure. Extrapolating these results over a 36-week school year, McNeish speculated that students had the potential to learn 173 more words per year with this approach.

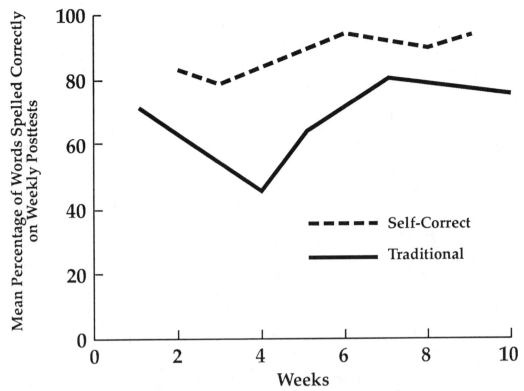

FIGURE 3. Mean percentage of words spelled correctly on weekly posttests per condition for each student. Adapted from McNeish (1985). Used with permission.

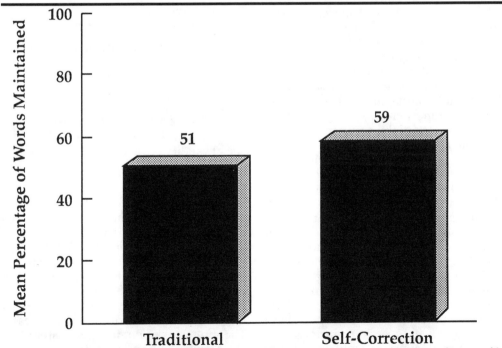

FIGURE 4. Mean percentage of words per condition maintained 10-15 days after weekly posttest. Adapted from McNeish (1985). Used with permission.

On delayed posttests designed to measure maintenance of learned words, four of the five students maintained an average of 2.8 more words during self-correction than the traditional approach, with no increase in time allocation for the lesson. Figure 4 shows the data for maintenance posttests conducted 10–15 days after the weekly test and aggregated for all students in each condition. The data show that self-correction was superior to the traditional method. During the traditional approach students maintained an average of 51% of their words, whereas during self-correction they maintained an average of 59% of their words. With the exception of one student, all pupils maintained more words under self-correction than they did during the traditional approach.

When generality of behavior was evaluated, all five students improved, averaging correct spellings for 5.2 more words in generalized settings (science, social studies, reading, and language arts) under the self-correction method than under the traditional approach (Figure 5). Aggregating and converting the data to percentages for all students shows that they generalized 41% of their words during traditional spelling, but 59% of their words during self-correction.

Finally, all five students indicated that they preferred the self-correction procedure to the traditional approach. In their view, "the time went faster when we did it [self-correction] this way," and "it wasn't as boring."

An experimental replication of McNeish's (1985) study was conducted by Okyere (1989), using a clinical population of six elementary-school-age students attending an after-school tutoring program. The students ranged in age from 7 to 13 years old, and each student had significant problems with spelling. Students participated in self-correction spelling activity for 30 minutes three times per week for 4 months, using essentially the same procedures as McNeish (1985), with the exception that parents also administered a pretest and posttest to their children at home as an initial and generalization measure.

The results indicated that students learned to spell their target words on weekly posttests with at least 93% accuracy when using the self-correction procedure. Furthermore, the results showed that students maintained at least 80% of their learned words 2 weeks after the initial posttest. With respect to generalization, five students (a) achieved at least 80% correct or more on the posttest administered by parents, (b) were able to write the learned words in sentences, and (c) were able to write variations for at least 80% or more of the words (e.g., *receive*/receiving; *attain*/attainment, *attend*/attendance).

Okyere (1989) also reported that the classroom teachers indicated subjectively that the students' written expression in school improved over the course of the study, and they were better able to work independently. Finally, parents noticed a change in their children's "attitude" toward spelling. That is, performing spelling homework did not seem to be as aversive as it had been in the past.

How to Implement a Self-Correction Spelling Program

To implement a self-correction procedure, the practitioner must assess students and provide them with the word list for practice, train them to use proofreading marks, orient them to the sequence of self-correction tasks, conduct daily sessions, and evaluate generality and social validity behaviors.

Identify appropriate words. Before using self-correction, the teacher has to be sure that the students do not already know how to spell the words on a given list. Otherwise, the process will be a waste of time. Students will be self-correcting words they already know how to spell, and the effectiveness of the program will not be realized. Therefore, the first step is to administer a written pretest of the weekly words the students are supposed to learn. The pretest should be administered at least twice within a 2-day period to confirm that words that students initially misspelled are, in fact, unlearned words.

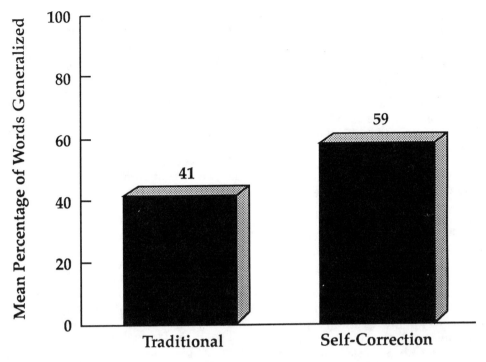

FIGURE 5. Mean percentage of words generalized per condition. Data obtained in science, social studies, reading and language arts. Adapted from McNeish (1985). Used with permission.

When administering the pretest, we recommend using a standard format. Assessors should say the word, use the word in a sentence, then say the word again. Using the word in context avoids any confusion that might originate from homonyms.

Word lists can come from a number of sources. For example, sight word vocabulary from a reading series might be used initially, or students might be asked what words they would like to learn (McLoughlin & Lewis, 1981). Graded word lists might also be considered, and in the case of students with chronic spelling problems, specialized lists might be consulted. For instance, E. Horn (1926) identified 100 words that account for 65% of all words written by adults. Hillerich (1981) and Horn (1960) indicated that eight words account for about 20% of words used in children's written language, whereas 100, 1,000, and 4,000 words account for 50%, 89%, and 97%, respec-

tively, of words used. In sum, selecting words from high-frequency lists or lists of common misspelled words might be a functional strategy for many practitioners (Horn, 1960; Kuska, Webster, & Elford, 1964).

Determine performance criteria. Having identified the words to be learned, the next step is to determine the performance criteria (i.e., the number of times a word must be written correctly on a test before it is considered learned). Typically, a criterion of two to three consecutive correct responses is sufficient in most applied settings, with the proviso that a maintenance check be administered 1–2 weeks after initial acquisition. If the word is spelled correctly at that point, additional practice would not be required (Cooke, Heron, & Heward, 1983; McNeish, 1985).

Train students to use proofreading marks. Asking students to correct their own mistakes without giving them adequate guidelines may confuse and discourage them. Therefore, before students begin to use the self-correction procedure, it is necessary to teach them how to use the four basic proofreading marks (Figure 6) to correct their mistakes.

We recommend using a model, lead, and test format to teach the students how to use the proofreading marks illustrated in Figure 6. In a model, lead, test format, the teacher shows the students the skill (editing their words) using the stage of an overhead projector. Examples of when to use and when not to use each mark are illustrated. Next, the teacher models the procedure with an individual student while other students look on. Students imitate the teacher's response. Teams carry out role-playing to ensure that each student understands how and when to use the marks. Finally, students practice individually, and the teacher provides feedback on the accuracy of their responses (Cooke et al., 1983). Generally, students learn these four basic marks in one 30-minute session, although periodic booster instruction might be required.

There are several advantages to using these proofreading marks. First, students have the opportunity to learn the types of mistakes they make in their spelling (e.g., adding too many letters [bettter]). Second, the proofreading marks enable the students to change their original response while simultaneously practicing the correct orthography for the word. Finally, attending to the types of mistakes they make in their spelling and correcting those mistakes enables them to learn the correct spellings easily and quickly.

Train students to use the self-correction form. The second part of the training procedure is devoted to showing students how the self-correction form is used, again by means of a model, lead, test format.

The form has five columns (Figure 7). Column 1 contains the unlearned words, typically 5–20 words depending upon the student. The other four columns, Column A-1 (labeled Self-Correct), A-2 (Write it right), and B-1 (Self-Correct), B-2 (Write it right) are initially blank. Column 1 is folded under so that the student cannot see the previously written words. Then the words are dictated directly or by an audiotape in the format "say the word, use the word in a sentence, say the word again." The students write their responses in Column A-1.

After writing responses to all the words, the students expose Column 1 and self-correct each word individually, using the proofreading marks. They write each word correctly in Column A-2 while looking at Column A-1. The teacher checks the students' papers to note the appropriate correction procedure. The first three columns then are folded back again in order for the students to write the words as they are dictated a second time in Column B-1 (the fourth column). Following the second dictation, the self-correction procedure is carried out again. When a word is spelled correctly, a check mark is placed in Column B-2 as before. The whole activity should last 20 minutes each session, depending upon the total number of students participating.

Conduct daily sessions. Self-correction sessions can be carried out 4 days per week. During the first few days, practitioners should review the proofreading marks procedure to ensure that students remember their function. At the end of the 20-minute self-correction session, the teacher can give a posttest as he or she would do normally with any other approach.

If students learn the words before the end of the week, as determined by spelling the words correctly three times without mistakes, they should be encouraged to continue the self-correction procedure using variants of the target words (e.g., live/lively). The more opportunities to practice the target words the students have, the more likely they will retain the words and become better spellers. Pretesting for the selection of the word list for the following week then can be administered before the end of the last session.

Program for generality of effects. The main purpose of teaching is to change the pupils' behavior in such a way as to

^ = insert a letter(s): the letter to be inserted is written above.

◯ = to omit a letter(s): the circled letters must be left out.

/ = wrong letter (correct letter is marked above).

~ = reverse the two letters.

FIGURE 6. The four proofreading marks for the self-correction procedure. From McNeish (1985). Used with permission.

enable them to function in an acceptable manner in the environment. Therefore, to ensure that the effect of the self-correction on the spelling words has generalized to other situations, practitioners can employ two basic tactics. First, encouraging and directing parents to administer posttests once every week can be an effective way of programming for stimulus generalization.

Response generalization, defined as the student's ability to (a) spell untrained words or variants, or (b) use the words in sentences, can be programmed by having students write out word variations or produce sentences containing their spelling words. Specifically, students can be given "story starters" and encouraged to write passages that incorporate each of their words at least once. Words previously learned by the students then can be located by the teacher. Words spelled correctly and those spelled incorrectly can be recorded and graphed for each student.

Assess for social validity. Any treatment procedure that is not valid and effective is probably questionable to use in applied settings. Self-correction is no exception. To assess for social validity, two methods can be employed. First, questionnaires can be prepared asking partici-

pants their views on the effectiveness of the program. Second, personal interviews can be conducted that permit more in-depth questioning of procedures, effects, or side-effects. Students, teachers, and parents can be assessed by one or both of these methods. As stated previously, findings indicate that students and teachers view self-correction positively and prefer it to traditional methods of spelling instruction (McNeish, 1985; Okyere, 1989).

Implications for Practitioners

The self-correction method of teaching spelling is a procedure that can be used with large groups, small clusters, or individuals. From the teacher's or parent's perspective, self-correction has a number of implications.

Student mastery is linked to specific words, not the passage of time. Unlike traditional approaches to spelling, in which students receive a new set of words each week regardless of their performance with former words, in a self-correction approach students practice each word until it is mastered. Further, they practice the *specific orthography* for spelling the word, and not tasks presumed to be related to spelling (e.g., visualization,

SELF-CORRECTION FORM

NAME: ——————————————

DATE: ——————————————

Word List	Column A-1 Self-Correct	Column A-2 Write it right	Column B-1 Self-Correct	Column B-2 Write it right

FIGURE 7. Self-correction form with 5-column format. Column 1 would contain the stimulus words and would be folded back. Column A-1 is reserved for the student's response and his or her proofreading marks. Column A-2 shows where the correct orthography would be spelled. The function of Columns B-1 and B-2 are identical to Columns A-1 and A-2. Adapted from McNeish (1985). Used with permission.

writing the words in alphabetical order). Providing direct instruction on specific words, coupled with programming for generality of behavior change, is a powerful tool for improving spelling performance (Smith, 1989).

Students receive immediate feedback. Van Houten (1980) provides convincing evidence that when students receive immediate, precise, and differential feedback on their responses, performance improves. Methodologically, self-correction is designed to incorporate each of these essential components of feedback. In self-correction, students correct their spelling immediately, not the next day; they deliver precise consequences to themselves with respect to letters that are omitted, substituted, or transposed; and they receive praise for appropriate spelling.

The strategy is easy to use. Self-correction is a manageable and flexible spelling procedure to use in the classroom. Most teachers are willing to spend 20 minutes per day on spelling, especially when they recognize that the program can be integrated into the larger language arts curriculum. Furthermore, teachers who use a learning center approach, in which students rotate from station to station, easily could adapt the self-correction procedures by placing the words on audiotape for the students. The spelling center would have the tape and player, the recording form, and the directions for use. Students would access the materials independently and proceed through the station in a manner consistent with other established stations in the classroom. Likewise, teachers could employ this procedure in the contexts of an open or traditional arrangement by reserving the procedure for those students who need supplemental assistance with spelling. While the majority of students might work from the traditional spelling series, small groups or individual students would practice spelling by using the self-correction approach.

Combine with other subject or skill areas or other approaches. As stated earlier, self-correction can be combined with other subject or skill areas or other tactics. For instance, having taught students the process of self-correcting their spelling words by using proofreading marks, the capitalization, overall appearance, punctuation, spelling (COPS) procedure (Schumaker et al., 1981) might be used to reduce spelling errors in written language. Furthermore, self-correction could be implemented in home-based programs that would allow parents to serve as monitors for spelling performance. The consensus of most educators is that well-designed home-based education programs increase the probability of school success for students (Heron & Harris, 1987; Heward, Dardig, & Rossett, 1979).

Finally, self-correction might be incorporated into the methodology of other specialized strategies or tactics without sacrificing the integrity of the approach. For example, self-correction might be integrated with a self-questioning tactic (Wong, 1986), directed spelling tactic (Frank, 1987), cognitive-behavioral training (Gerber & Hall, 1989), strategy training (Graham & Freeman, 1986), or a whole-language approach (Norris, 1989).

Students prefer self-correction. When students prefer to engage in academic tasks, the likelihood of success is increased. Given that self-correction is a strategy that many students enjoy (McNeish, 1985; Okyere, 1989), it is to the advantage of educators to consider it carefully. We recommend self-correction especially for those students in the regular classroom who have not profited from spelling instruction using traditional approaches, and for whom the whole idea of producing written language is aversive because of their perceived poor spelling. Giving these students successful experiences with spelling can be the building block for producing sentences, paragraphs, and stories at a later stage.

SUMMARY

The school psychologist's role as psychometrician has evolved steadily to that of an educational consultant to general and special teachers and parents. Hence, there is an increased need for them to be skilled with providing technical assistance with all aspects of the curriculum, including spelling instruction.

Even though a traditional approach to spelling is the most popular method for teaching this academic skill, psychologists should be aware that a significant number of students do not learn effectively with this approach. Consequently, the psychologist must be prepared to offer other alternatives to teachers.

Self-correction is one specialized strategy that offers numerous advantages for teachers and parents, including the fact that it produces demonstrable, generalized, and lasting gains in performance. Finally, students seem to prefer this method to others that they have experienced in the past.

We are encouraged by the empirical findings that have been reported in the literature, and we are impressed with the flexibility that this strategy has to offer practitioners and parents. We believe that school psychologists who design, implement, and evaluate programs using self-correction will be equally satisfied with the results.

REFERENCES

Allred, R. (1977). *Spelling: The application of research findings*. Washington, DC: National Education Association.

Christine, R., & Hollingsworth, P. (1966). An experiment in spelling. *Education, 86*, 565-567.

Cooke, N. L., Heron, T. E., & Heward, W. L. (1983). *Peer tutoring: Implementing classwide programs in the primary grades*. Columbus, OH: Special Press.

Cooper, J. O., Heron, T. E., & Heward, W. L. (1987). *Applied behavior analysis*. Columbus, OH: Merrill.

DeStefano, J. S. (1978). *Language, the learner, and the school*. New York: Wiley.

Fernald, G. (1943). *Remedial techniques in basic school subjects*. New York: McGraw-Hill.

Frank, A. R. (1987). Directed spelling instruction. *Teaching Exceptional Children, 20*(1), 10-13.

Ganschow, L. (1983). Teaching strategies for spelling success. *Academic Therapy, 19*, 185-193.

Gearheart, W., DeRuiter, J., & Sileo, T. (1986). *Teaching mildly and moderately handicapped students*. Englewood Cliffs, NJ: Prentice-Hall.

Gentry, J. R. (1984). Developmental aspects of learning to spell. *Academic Therapy, 20*(1), 11-19.

Gerber, M. M., & Hall, R. J. (1989). Cognitive-behavioral training in spelling for learning handicapped students. *Learning Disability Quarterly, 12*, 159-171.

Gillingham, A., & Stillman, B. (1970). *Remedial training for children with specific difficulty in reading, spelling, and penmanship* (7th ed.). Cambridge, MA: Educators Publishing Service.

Graham, S., & Freeman, S. (1986). Strategy training and teacher- vs. student-controlled study conditions: Effects on LD students' spelling performance. *Learning Disability Quarterly, 9*, 15-22.

Graham, S., & Miller, L. (1979). Spelling research and practice: A unified approach. *Focus on Exceptional Children, 12*(2), 1-16.

Greenwood, J. C., Delquadri, J., & Hall, R. V. (1984). Opportunity to respond and student academic achievement. In W. L. Heward, T. E. Heron, D. S. Hill, & J. Trap-Porter (Eds.), *Focus on behavior analysis in education* (pp. 58-88). Columbus, OH: Merrill.

Hammill, D. D., & Bartel, N. R. (1978). *Teaching children with learning and behavior problems* (2nd ed.). Boston, MA: Allyn and Bacon.

Heron, T. E., & Harris, K. C. (1987). *The educational consultant. Helping professionals, parents, and mainstreamed students* (2nd ed.). Austin, TX: Pro-Ed.

Heward, W. L., Dardig, J. C., & Rossett, A. (1979). *Working with parents of handicapped children*. Columbus, OH: Merrill.

Hillerich, R. (1981). *Spelling: An element in written expression*. Columbus, OH: Merrill.

Horn, E. (1954). *Teaching spelling*. Washington, DC: American Research Association.

Horn, E. (1960). *Spelling: Encyclopedia of educational research*. New York: Macmillan.

Horn, E. A. (1926). *A basic writing vocabulary. The 10,000 most commonly used in writing. University of Iowa Monographs in Education, First Series*, No. 4. Iowa City: University of Iowa.

Horn, T. D. (1947). The effects of the corrected test on learning to spell. *Elementary School Journal, 47*, 277-285.

Kuska, A., Webster, E. J. D., & Elford, G. (1964). *Spelling in language arts 6*. Ontario, Canada: Thomas Nelson & Sons (Canada).

McLoughlin, J., & Lewis, R. (1981). *Assessing special students*. Columbus, OH: Merrill.

McNeish, J. (1985). *Effects of self-correction on acquisition, maintenance, and generalization of spelling words with learning disabled students*. Unpublished masters thesis, The Ohio State University, Columbus.

Mercer, D. C., & Mercer, A. R. (1989). *Teaching students with learning problems* (3rd ed.). Columbus, OH: Merrill.

Norris, J. (1989). Facilitating developmental changes in spelling. *Academic Therapy, 25*(1), 97-108.

Okyere, B. A. (1989). *Effects of self-correction on the acquisition, maintenance, and generalization of the written spelling of elementary school children*. Unpublished doctoral dissertation, The Ohio State University, Columbus.

Schoephoerster, H. (1962). Research into variations of the test-study plan of teaching spelling. *Elementary English, 39*, 460-462.

Schoolfield, L., & Timberlake, J. (1960). *The phonovisual method*. Washington, DC: Phonovisual Products.

Schumaker, J. B., Deshler, D. D., Nolan, S., Clark, F. L., Alley, G. R., & Warner, M. M. (1981). *Error monitoring: A learning strategy for improving academic performance of LD adolescents* (Report No. 32). Lawrence: The University of Kansas, Institute of Research on Learning Disabilities.

Smith, D. D. (1989). *Teaching students with learning and behavior problems* (2nd ed.). Englewood Cliffs, NJ: Prentice-Hall.

Stevens, K. B., & Schuster, J. W. (1987). Effects of a constant time delay procedure on the written spelling performance of a learning disabled student. *Learning Disability Quarterly, 10*, 9-16.

Stokes, T. F., & Baer, D. M. (1977). An implicit technology of generalization. *Journal of Applied Behavior Analysis, 10*, 349-367.

Van Houten, R. (1980). *Learning through feedback*. New York: Human Sciences Press.

Wallace, G., Cohen, S. B., & Polloway, E. A. (1987). *Language arts*. Austin, TX: Pro-Ed.

Wong, B. Y. L. (1986). A cognitive approach to teaching spelling. *Exceptional Children, 53*(2), 169-173.

FOOTNOTE

[1]A synopsis of selected articles on spelling instruction can be obtained from Professor Timothy E. Heron, The Ohio State University, 356 Arps Hall, 1945 N. High St., Columbus, OH 43210.

19

Maximizing Mathematics Success in the Regular Classroom

John F. Cawley
Rene S. Parmar
Department of Learning and Instruction,
State University of New York at Buffalo

INTRODUCTION

Maximizing mathematics success for the mildly handicapped in the regular classroom requires an initial distinction between the processes of being educated *in* the regular class and being educated *with* the regular class.

Choosing a Goal

When the goal is to educate the mildly handicapped child *with* the regular class it is necessary that we establish a level of expectancy equivalent to the curriculum expectancies of the regular class. For example, suppose the regular class is doing division and the present level of functioning for one of the students is two-digit subtraction with renaming. Should we decide to teach this student *with* the regular class, we have to utilize effective instructional techniques to teach division in spite of the lack of traditional prerequisites. It is also necessary to convince school personnel of the validity of such a decision. Having made the decision to educate this child *with* the regular class, the curriculum decision is to teach division with an alternative sequence and with alternative algorithms. The subsequent modifications are instructional.

When the purpose is to educate a mildly handicapped child *in* the regular class, it is acceptable for the child to deviate substantially from grade expectancy proficiency. It is also acceptable and appropriate for the teacher to make assignments that acknowledge these differences. For example, assume a child is assigned to a regular sixth-grade class. Assume further that the performance level of the child indicates proficiency in both single-digit addition and single-digit subtraction at high percentages of correct results. In this instance, it would be quite proper, after extensive work with place value to the 10s place, to move on to double-digit combinations in addition and subtraction. These addition and subtraction assignments would be proper for the child even though other members of the class might be doing four-digit multiplication and three- or four-digit division.

Educating the child *in* the regular class or in connection with a special education setting (e.g., the resource room) involves modifications in both curriculum and instruction. The curriculum decision to assign the child to subtraction and addition and to select an instructional approach for these topics is appropriate.

Instruction in the Regular Class

Beginning with a form of curriculum-based assessment and incorporating a variety of other procedures as deemed appropriate, the school psychologist determines stages of proficiency for the skills and concepts of the basic operations on whole numbers and the stages of proficiency for problem solving. The emphasis on both the arithmetic operations (e.g., $2 + 3 = 5$) and problem solving (e.g., determining that 3 ducks and 2 ducks are 5 ducks) should be equivalent, for it may be determined that computation should come through problem solving.

The school psychologist should first report areas of strength or weakness directly and with illustrations such as the following.

> Given eight 2-digit-by-2-digit subtraction items of this type [$24 - 16 = 8$], the child completed the 8 items accurately within 4 minutes.

> Given three word problems of this type [If a boy has 4 apples left after giving 2 apples to a friend, how many apples did the boy start with?], the child erred on all 3 problems by interpreting the word "left" to mean subtraction.

The appraisal should include an interpretation of error patterns, making certain that the errors attributed to one operation (e.g., division) are not the result of errors in another operation (e.g., subtraction errors in division) (Miller & Milam, 1987). The school psychologist's primary responsibility is to convince the school of the appropriateness of the subtraction and addition assignments when others in the class are performing multiplication and division. A secondary responsibility is to convince the school of the need to provide quality instruction in these topics. That is, the child should be able to perform these operations with manipulatives and with expanded notation to demonstrate an understanding of the operation. It is important to avoid the Pygmalion view of the child as "one of those special ed kids who can't do this or that."

Instruction with the Regular Class

The job of the school psychologist is less straightforward when it has been decided to educate a child *with* the regular class. The appraisal specialist has to demonstrate that the child might profit from such a decision and also must be able to demonstrate procedures that will convince both the child and the teacher that this is an appropriate choice. If the appraisal specialist is not familiar with curriculum and instructional procedures in these areas, assistance can be obtained from math specialists in the school system. Even if the child is ordinarily held to the traditional prerequisites of column subtraction and basic multiplication (Silbert, Carnine, & Stein, 1981), it may be desirable to take this child to division because it is age-appropriate and this is what his or her classmates are doing.

Two elements are required in the appraisal. First, it must be determined that the child is an effective counter and both knows and can conserve place value (i.e., can prove that four 10s and three 1s are 43 and can also prove that when one of the 10s is changed to 1s [now thirteen 1s] the 43 is intact) in both manipulative and symbolic representations. Second, the appraisal must include teaching the child to divide without the involvement of multiplication or subtraction, for unless the child is taught to divide in this manner, he/she will not be able to participate with the rest of the class in a mathematics lesson (see Cawley, 1984, for a description of such an algorithm).

Relative Achievement

The overall achievement of mildly handicapped children shows mean scores for secondary school students that approximate fourth- to sixth-grade equivalent levels (Cawley & Goodman, 1968; Cawley & Miller, 1989; Warner, Alley, Schumaker, Deshler, & Clark, 1980). When viewed in a cross-sectional format, these data indicate that samples of learning-disabled (LD) children progress one or fewer years of grade equivalent growth for every two or three years in school. It is also reported that the typical performance of LD students is below the 10th percentile and that by the time they reach 10th grade their mastery of basic skills approximates the fourth-grade level (Schumaker, as cited by O'Neil, 1988).

One set of data on some 850 LD

children showed that those at 12 years of age had mean scores of only 51% correct on a test of 81 mathematics concepts ordinarily found in third and fourth grades (Cawley, Fitzmaurice, Shaw, Kahn, & Bates, 1979). In a sample of approximately 500 LD students with mean levels of achievement approximating the 5th- to 6th-grade equivalent, some 60% of the school marks in regular-class secondary school mathematics were Ds and Fs (Cawley, Kahn, & Tedesco, 1989). Finally, it has been noted that some 30–50% of the learning-disabled drop out of school (O'Neil, 1988). The data have implications for appraisal and the role of appraisal in making instructional and curriculum decisions.

We disagree with the suggestion that the needs of mildly handicapped children can be met solely by good, straightforward, direct instruction independent of the need for curriculum modifications (O'Neil, 1988). In fact, one of the more serious limitations of special education is its inefficiency. This inefficiency is manifested when the child spends an inordinate amount of time mastering a given skill. What the school psychologist needs to do is determine when a child is ready to be introduced to and master a specific rule, concept, or process. A determination of the *when* will enable teachers to teach something to a child precisely when the child becomes ready to master it. This *when* is a curriculum decision, not an instructional decision. Every decision to spend additional time on arithmetic computation, in place of time spent on arithmetic problem solving, is a curriculum decision; every decision to provide experiences in computation before problem solving is a curriculum decision. There simply is no instance when an instructional decision is made without being guided by or accompanied by a curriculum decision. The school psychologist is essential to the effective integration of curriculum and instruction and for guiding the interpretation of the child's needs in respect to either or both. To be effective, the school psychologist must combine data across samples of children and utilize these data to assist other personnel to make decisions and design programs.

CONTENT AND SEQUENCES

Content

The selection of content for presentation to mildly handicapped children is derived as much from value judgments as from empirical sources. In a holistic scheme, it seems that all children should be presented with a broad range of mathematics competencies and skills. A decision to emphasize geometry and measurement and to reduce the emphasis on computation has considerable merit if one considers mathematics that is useful in everyday life. A decision to stress problem solving over computation would be consistent with the goals of the National Council of Teachers of Mathematics (NCTM, 1980). And a decision to stress applications in functional life experiences (e.g., grocery shopping) would seem to be consistent with the efforts of specialists in Everyday Cognition (e.g., Levine & Langress, 1985) and those who recognize the many benefits of learning in and out of school (e.g., Resnick, 1987; Saxe, 1988). It is incumbent on the school psychologist to be aware of the varying positions that affect the selection of content and to be able to discuss them with teachers and other school officials. A knowledge of the different positions could influence the manner in which pupil appraisals are designed, conducted, and interpreted in reference to curriculum and instructional decisions.

Sequences

The sequencing of content in mathematics instruction is firmly rooted in tradition. In mathematics, we generally use a spiral curriculum in which we teach some geometry, move on to some counting, go on to addition, do a bit of measurement, continue with subtraction, and so forth. In computation, we count, add, subtract, multiply, and divide. In problem solving, we learn to read, to add, and to do word problems that require reading and addition. Although these are traditional sequences, they are not the only sequences and they may not be the best sequences for mildly handicapped children.

A recent report on the international assessment of mathematics (McKnight et al., 1987) is critical of the spiral form of curriculum sequencing and of the instructional practices that accompany it. The report argues for an intensified approach to curriculum design in which there is a concentration on a single topic for a substantial period of time. A serviceable example might be the teaching of fractions, which are introduced and included in the curriculum only in the seventh grade. About half of the seventh grade is devoted to fractions and the remaining half is devoted to geometry. No other topics are covered.

In computation, it has been suggested that we might consider altering the sequence of addition to subtraction to multiplication to division to one that considers each skill independently of the other. This would offer an opportunity to experiment with the professional perception that the traditional sequence is invariant (Cawley, Miller, & Carr, 1988; Cawley, 1984).

Problem solving can be taught to handicapped children long before they learn to read or demonstrate proficiency with computation. In fact, problem solving can be used to provide a conceptual background and reason for computation. In an ongoing project (Cawley & Parmar, 1989) one of the problem-solving units provides for some 500 hands-on division activities prior to any instruction in computational division. If the ultimate goal of computation is its use in solving problems, it would seem that problem solving could come before computation in the instructional sequence.

The McKnight et al. (1987) report also argued for changes in instructional practices. To illustrate, it is common in Japanese classrooms to find the teacher providing only a few items and then spending considerable time discussing them. By contrast, teachers in the United States give many more items, but conduct much less discussion. Is it possible for the

school psychologist to play a role in the decision-making process relative to these choices by pointing out the merits of each from their foundations in cognitive and learning psychology?

APPRAISAL IN RELATION TO CURRICULUM

Successful performance in the mathematics of the regular class must be viewed at two levels, the elementary and the secondary school. These levels differ in that we have the generalized standards for the elementary school (e.g., a broad number of topics at each grade level with considerable repetition at subsequent grade levels) and the specific topical standards (e.g., algebra, geometry) at the secondary school.

The Elementary Level

Throughout the elementary level there is considerable attention directed toward proficiency in computation. This proficiency is sought in whole numbers, fractions, decimals, and percentages. Furthermore, this proficiency is sought in skills far beyond single-digit computation.

Figure 1 shows the first page from two different sixth-grade arithmetic texts. Note the similarity in each as they emphasize place value to the thousands and billions. The similarity between the two is evidence that regular education has reasonably consistent curriculum standards across its programs. Making a decision to educate a child *with* the regular sixth-grade class must be done with the understanding that the child will perform computations with figures having place values in the thousand and billions. In contrast a decision to educate a child *in* the sixth-grade might only require place value to levels consistent with his or her present level of functioning (e.g., tens column in two digit addition).

Figure 2 shows the sixth-grade scope and sequence for one of these texts. The initial tasks for addition and subtraction involve number combinations to 6 digits. Note that the initial task in multiplication involves 5-digit by 4-digit items and that

Thousands

■ Our numeration system is based on 10.
The value of each place is 10 times the
value of the place to its right.

$$
\begin{aligned}
10 \text{ ones} &= 1 \text{ ten} \\
10 \text{ tens} &= 1 \text{ hundred} \\
10 \text{ hundreds} &= 1 \text{ thousand} \\
10 \text{ thousands} &= 1 \text{ ten-thousand} \\
10 \text{ ten-thousands} &= 1 \text{ hundred-thousand}
\end{aligned}
$$

■ In naming large numbers, the digits are
grouped into periods. Each period is a
group of three digits. Commas separate
the periods.

In 1790, this was the population of Virginia.

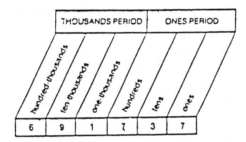

The digit 6 means 6 hundred-thousands, or 600,000.
The digit 9 means 9 ten-thousands, or 90,000.
The digit 1 means 1 thousand, or 1,000.
What does the digit 3 mean?

Write: 691,737
Read: six hundred ninety-one thousand, seven hundred thirty-seven

Another way to read large numbers
is to think about the periods: 691 thousand 737

■ In expanded form:

$$691{,}737 = 600{,}000 + 90{,}000 + 1{,}000 + 700 + 30 + 7$$

2   Chapter 1

FIGURE 1. Pages from two sixth-grade arithmetic texts.

PLACE VALUE TO BILLIONS

The telephone is used by millions of people throughout the world. Can you estimate the number of telephones in the world? In one particular year there were 472,136,700,020.

Billions			Millions			Thousands			Ones		
hundreds	tens	ones	hundreds	tens	ones	hundreds	tens	ones	hundreds	tens	ones
4	7	2	1	3	6	7	0	0	0	2	0

472 billion   136 million   700 thousand   20

The number above is read *four hundred seventy-two billion, one hundred thirty-six million, seven hundred thousand, twenty*. This is the word form. The standard form is 472,136,700,020.

The digit 6 is in the millions' place. Its value is 6,000,000. The expanded form of 472,136,700,020 is 400,000,000,000 + 70,000,000,000 + 2,000,000,000 + 100,000,000 + 30,000,000 + 6,000,000 + 700,000 + 20.

To help you read large numbers, commas are used between billions, millions, thousands, and ones. Often there are no commas in a calculator display. Think: What is the word form for 2563147?

CLASS EXERCISES

What is the word form for the number?

1. 1934

2. 297,654

3. 432,090

4. 27,000,018

5. 40,000,007,000

6. 142,000,000,000

What is the value of the underlined digit?

7. 352,482,7<u>9</u>6

8. 27,2<u>5</u>3,482

9. 9<u>9</u>8,999,999,999

2   LESSON 1-1

(Figure 1, continued)

CHAPTER OBJECTIVES

Chapter 1: Numeration, Addition and Subtraction

1a Write whole numbers through hundred billions in standard form.
1b Identify the value of a digit through hundred billions.
1c Compare and order whole numbers through hundred billions.
1d Round whole numbers to nearest billion.
1e Add and subtract whole numbers to 6 digits.
1f Estimate sums and differences.

Chapter 2: Multiplication

2a Multiply any number to 5 digits by any number to 4 digits.
2b Estimate products.
2c Write a product using an exponent; find a product when a number is written in exponential form.
2d Solve addition, subtraction, and multiplication problems including two-step problems.

Chapter 3: Division

3a Divide any number to 6 digits by any number to 3 digits.
3b Find an average.
3c Estimate quotients.
3d Solve problems by choosing the operation, including using information from a table, and problems with missing information.

Chapter 4: Decimals: Addition and Subtraction

4a Write a decimal through hundred thousands.
4b Identify the value of a digit through hundred-thousandths.
4c Compare and order decimals through ten-thousandths.
4d Round decimals to the nearest designated place.
4e Add and subtract decimals to ten-thousandths.
4f Estimate sums and differences of decimals.
4g Solve problems involving addition and subtraction of decimals.

Chapter 5: Decimals: Multiplication and Division

5a Multiply decimals.
5b Divide a decimal by a whole number or by a decimal; round the quotient to a given place.
5c Estimate products and quotients of decimals.
5d Solve problems involving decimals by choosing the operation, including using patterns and generalizing.

Chapter 6: Measurement

6a Determine equivalent units of time; calculate elapsed time.
6b Measure length to the nearest centimeter and millimeter, or inch, half-inch, quarter-inch, and eighth-inch.
6c Determine equivalent metric units of measurement.
6d Determine equivalent customary units of measurement.
6e Add and subtract customary units of measurement; add and subtract amounts of time.
6f Solve problems involving measurement, including using information from a double line graph, and problems with two steps.

Chapter 7: Number Relationships

7a Determine divisibility of a number.
7b Find the least common multiple of two numbers.
7c Find the greatest common factor of two numbers.
7d Solve problems including using information from a double bar graph.

Chapter 8: Fractions: Addition and Subtraction

8a Find equivalent fractions; write a fraction in lowest terms.
8b Write a fraction as a whole number or a mixed number.
8c Compare fractions and mixed numbers.
8d Add and subtract fractions and mixed numbers.
8e Solve problems involving addition and subtraction of fractions, including recognizing patterns and generalizing.

Chapter 9: Fractions: Multiplication and Division

9a Write a fraction as a mixed number or whole number; write a mixed number as a fraction.
9b Multiply and divide fractions and mixed numbers.
9c Write a fraction or mixed number as a decimal; write a decimal as a mixed number or fraction.
9d Solve problems involving fractions.

Chapter 10: Ratio and Percent

10a Write a ratio as a fraction; write an equal ratio.
10b Wolve proportions.
10c Find dimensions using a scale drawing.
10d Solve problems by using proportions, including making diagrams.

(Figure 2 continues on next page)

(Figure 2, continued)

Chapter 11: Geometry

11a Identify parallel and perpendicular lines; plane and space figures.
11b Measure angles; classify lines, angles, and figures.
11c Identify congruent lines, angles, and figures.
11d Identify similar figures.
11e Identify lines of symmetry.
11f Write and locate ordered pairs for lines on a graph.
11g Solve problems, including using information from a circle graph.

Chapter 12: Perimeter, Area, and Volume

12a Find the perimeer and area of polygons.
12b Find the circumference and area of circles.
12c Find the volume of rectangular prisms.
12d Solve problems involving perimeter, area, and volume, including multi-step problems.

Chapter 13: Statistics and Probability

13a Interpret frequency tables.
13b Find range, mean, median, and mode of a set of whole numbers.
13c Write a fraction for the probability of an event.
13d Solve problems involving statistics and probability.

Chapter 14: Integers

14a Write, compare, and order integers.
14b Add and subtract integers.
14c Locate ordered pairs of integers on a coordinate plane.
14d Solve problems involving addition and subtraction of integers, including using patterns and generalizing.

FIGURE 2. Sixth grade scope and sequence chart.

| (%) | Problem | | | | | | | | | | | | |
	$4/\overline{4}$	$4/\overline{40}$	$4/\overline{38}$	$6/\overline{38}$	$6/\overline{40}$	$4/\overline{400}$	$4/\overline{380}$	$4/\overline{4060}$	$6/\overline{4060}$	$6/\overline{380}$	$46/\overline{380}$	$46/\overline{406}$	$46/\overline{4060}$
Grade(N)														
3 (53)	51	25	4	–	4	4	4	4	2	–	2	4	2
4 (55)	20	13	–	–	–	–	–	–	–	–	–	2	–
5 (27)	85	78	59	59	56	59	44	37	37	37	26	26	15
6 (32)	91	88	81	81	78	66	75	69	59	72	44	25	16
7 (36)	97	89	83	81	78	75	86	81	67	86	75	67	64
8 (26)	100	96	85	81	73	77	73	92	77	62	73	65	54

FIGURE 3. Performance of mildly handicapped students on division items: Percentage passing.

the initial task in division involves 6 digits divided by 3 digits. The teacher's pacing chart indicates that all activities relative to the operations on whole numbers should be completed within the first 9 weeks of the school year. Note also that the scope and sequence chart shows no return to multiplication and division after the first few weeks of school. The curriculum developer and textbook authors of regular education anticipate that nonhandicapped children will demonstrate proficiency with these skills at the designated grade levels. Such may not be the case (Figure 3).[1]

Special educators (McLeod, 1985; McLeod & Armstrong, 1982) continue to find it necessary to direct attention to single-digit computation skills among children with learning disabilities in the upper elementary grades. Note, then, the discrepancy between the content focus of special educators who may be teaching single-digit operations to adolescents and that of regular educators who will have assumed their same-age students had mastered such skills long ago.

A scope and sequence chart provides a guide that can be used in determining the areas to be tested during appraisal in mathematics for special education students. By collating the scope and sequence charts from each level, the appraisal specialist can construct a curriculum-based assessment with considerable content validity. The appraisal should include a determination of (a) the child's skill and concepts in relation to the content of the grade contemplated for placement; (b) the rate at which the child can acquire new concepts and skills in relation to the progress expected of nonhandicapped children. Assume it has been found that the child undergoing appraisal is able to grasp the concepts of a particular operation, but not the skills. For example, assume the child can explain and demonstrate addition involving three columns and three rows, but cannot compute this efficiently or effectively. The child could be provided with a calculator to obviate the skill deficit, and the program emphasis could be redirected to problem solving and applications.

A child who is seriously discrepant in mathematics may experience difficulty in responding to the traditional curriculum and instructional demands of the classroom, particularly as the topics change every few weeks throughout the school year and may not be repeated. Appraisal of LD students should determine something about their learning characteristics — that is, the number of trials, days, and so forth that may be required for mastery and the extent to which this mastery is maintained when a new topic is introduced (Cawley, 1985). In effect, we raise a general question related to inhibition theory and the effects of proactive and retroactive sequences. That is, we feel it important to know something about the effects of prior learning on subsequent learning and about the effects of the new learning on the retention and transfer of the old learning. Does learning one set of addition facts on Monday, for example, interfere with or facilitate learning a new set of facts on Tuesday? Do the subsequent learnings on Wednesday and Thursday interfere with overall performance on the summative test on Friday?

Paired-associate learning activities accompanied by generalization requirements, as exemplified in Figure 4 can provide a base of knowledge about the effort a child is required to make to learn one set of facts (Miller & Carr, 1988).

For example, the top four problems in Figure 4 are presented to the child on a card. The eight remaining items are displayed on the reverse side of the card. The task first requires the child to memorize the items on the acquisition side of the card. Next, the card is turned over and the child is instructed to complete the response items. Two of the items cannot be done and it is predicted that the child will omit these. Other items can be completed only by the application of selected principles (e.g., commutative property). Thus, the paired-associate learning task is more than a measure of rote memorization. It provides an opportunity to evaluate the use of basic principles, tendency to overgeneralization (i.e., whether the child attempts those that cannot be done), and speed of acquisition.

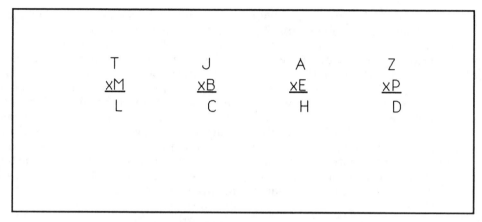

Acquisition side of card

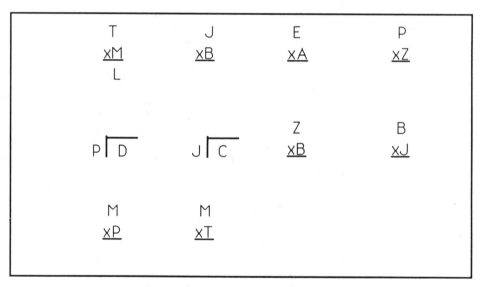

Response/test side of card

FIGURE 4. Paired-associate learning task.

Knowing these characteristics will enable the teacher to select a reasonable number of items to be learned at one time and to evaluate the extent to which the child knows some basic rules and principles.

The Secondary Level

Mathematics programs in secondary schools differ from those in elementary schools in a number of ways, two of which are considered here. First, as mentioned earlier, secondary schools are organized by topic (e.g., general math, algebra 1, etc.). Consequently, the teachers expect that the children enrolling in their courses have acquired the prerequisite background and skills. Second, secondary school teachers of math are trained specifically to teach students who have met and mastered the expected prerequisites. They frequently see little value in remedial courses and in adapting the regular courses to students who are substantially behind. These teachers need the assistance of school psychologists to differentiate between those mildly handicapped children who can achieve in regular secondary school math classes with instructional modifications (Shaw, 1985) and those students whose levels of functioning may be so discrepant that specialized curricula are needed. As to the former, the school psychologist needs to provide evidence that they have the "ability" to perform in these courses. This can be accomplished by combining measures of aptitude with measures of mathematics performance under modified conditions (e.g., reading is minimized). As to those students who are severely discrepant (e.g., doing work on single-digit and double-digit combinations), we see no value in continuing the remedial emphasis, with or without microcomputers. If technology is to be employed, it should be in the form of a hand-held calculator, and the curriculum emphasis should be on concepts and applications and not skills. A most compelling reason for minimizing the remedial effort is that these children simply do not have enough time left in school to master "facts" and routines that will not be used out of school. One comprehensive effort aimed at providing such an alternative curriculum for secondary students who are severely discrepant is Project MATH.

Project MATH. The upper grade levels of Project MATH (Cawley et al., 1976) contain 45 instructional units. One unit is directed to a traffic count in which data must be collected at specific times (e.g., 8:00 a.m.) and for specific time periods (e.g., 15 minutes). These units include a focus on social-behavioral needs and utilize mathematics and simulated applications to address these needs. For example, one might want to address the fact that a target child does not initiate his or her work on time, nor complete it in a timely manner.

The target child is given the responsibility of collecting certain data (e.g., the number of red automobiles that pass in a certain time period), without which the remainder of the group cannot complete its tasks. In completing the traffic count unit, a group of children may complete 2,000 calculations. In spite of this enormous number of calculations, walls covered with histograms, and numerous oral reports on the data, the youngsters consistently have reported that they "did not do any math" for they fail to recognize math as anything other than a ditto master or a page in a book. These examples show that the needs of a variety of mildly handicapped children can be addressed at the secondary level. The appraisal specialist needs to acquire data that will support the decision of the school to attend to the different options.

THE PROCESS OF APPRAISAL

A major purpose of appraisal of the math competencies of an LD child is to provide a data base and its accompanying qualitative descriptions of the performance of the child. An effective appraisal will enable the programming team to make the appropriate decisions on behalf of the child and to convince the regular class teacher and the parents or guardian that the recommended modifications are going to prove fruitful.

Computation

The appraisal specialist must be capable of conducting specially designed appraisals that, as defined for purposes of this chapter, access and describe performance on target variables (e.g., division) independent of any obstacles (e.g., inability to subtract or multiply) presented by other variables. Let us illustrate the specially designed approach with an example of a child who lacks even the most fundamental knowledge of the basic multiplication "facts" and let us show that this child could participate at another level of multiplication. To conserve space, the illustration will be relatively simple, but nonetheless beyond that which most people would teach the child.

The task is to multiply 324 × 2

The child gathers a set of manipulatives in the form of sets of toothpicks, and arranges them in the following array:

$$\# = 100s$$

** ′′′′   * = 10s

** ′′′′   ′ = 1s

and then proceeds through the array by counting the ′s (8), the *s (4) and the #s (6) and by stating this as "three hundred and forty eight."

This can be represented at a second stage with expanded notation to show:

100,100,100   10,10   1111

100,100,100   10,10   1111

The child counts her or his way through the array and informs us that 324 × 2 is 648.

Note that a counting algorithm was applied that did not require any knowledge of "basic facts." Although some might argue that this is not multiplication, it certainly solves the multiplication problem.

A child who can do this with renaming is a child for whom we would recommend a calculator until such time as the facts and other prerequisites are mastered. But we do not delay multiplication simply because the "facts" have not been mastered.

Specially designed appraisals also will lead to descriptions of individual strengths and weaknesses in the concepts and skills of mathematics in such a manner that a focus on enrichment and production will suppress the attention to routines and response levels of performance. The child will be challenged rather than drilled. The following examples are illustrative:

1. Give a child two items such as

$$\begin{array}{cc} 6 & 4 \\ \times 3 & \times 2 \\ \hline 18 & 8 \end{array}$$

and ask the child to make as many similar items (e.g., 5 × 3; 7 × 2, etc.) as possible

within the given time limits. Score the child for number produced, number correct, and number of different items that are not duplicates.

2. Show the child the following:

$$\begin{array}{r} {\scriptstyle 1} \\ 2\ 3\ 6 \\ \times\qquad 2 \\ \hline 4\ 7\ 2 \end{array}$$

Ask the child to take a set of manipulatives and prove that the 7 is correct and in the correct place.

3. Show the child the following picture. Ask the child to write as many word problems as possible for the picture.

A sample of some of the items generated by a class of children in the third grade is shown in Figure 5.

The items are shown as they were written by the children. Notice the quality and variability of the problems independently of matters such as spelling, punctuation, and so forth. The teacher could score performance by counting the number of different types of problems created by a child or by a group of children. The ultimate level of performance might be obtained when a child can be given 8 pictures and write a different type problem (e.g., addition, subtraction, etc.) for each picture.

Appraising Word Problem Proficiency

Appraising performance in solving word problems requires control over all factors that create obstacles to the problem itself. From our perspective, this means that one must exert control over variables such as reading level and

There were 9 sailboats,
3 rowboats, and 2 cars. How
more sailboats than cars?

There were 5 sailboats, 3
rowboats & 2 cars & 4 sailboats.
How many altogether?

There were 9 sailboats,
3 rowboats and two cars.
A girl bought 5 sailboats
How many sailboats were
there then?

one girl had 3 sailboats anorter
girl had two sailboats
One boy had 3 rowboats another
boy had for sailboats one
more boy 2 cars how many
cars in all?

One girl had 2 sailboats
and other girl had 3 sailboats
How many more
does one girl have

There are 5 children there are
9 sailboats there are 3 cars and 2
cars. They added 2 more of everything
How many things are there?

Two girl has five sailboat
and one boy has four
sailboat and a ohter boy
had three rowboats and a
other boy has two cars.

Five children had
14 toys 3 toys got
lost howmeny toys
left

5 chilers 14 toys they
lost 6 of there. How many
are left?

Two girls had 5 sailboats
+ three boys had 3 rowboats,
4 sailboats + 2 cars how
many more sailboats did
the girls have?

FIGURE 5. Stories created for one picture by a third grade class.

computation. If the child is unable to read the problem, the problem itself is not accessed and no data on actual problem solving are obtained. Similarly, if the computation requirements are too difficult, an incorrect answer might be due to a computational error and not a problem-solving error.

Ballew and Cunningham (1982) studied the ability of sixth-grade children to read a problem, their ability to set up the problem, their ability to perform the computation for the problem, and their ability to combine the three previous elements into a whole to solve the problems. Only 19 of 217 children had profiles showing they were able to perform all four tasks at the same high level.

One approach to appraisal for problem solving is the use of schemes built around matrices (e.g., Cawley, Fitzmaurice-Hayes, & Shaw, 1988; Cawley et al., 1979). Matrices are simple rows by columns arrangements in which the components of both are defined. The diagnostician or curriculum developer sets forth the standards upon which a matrix will be developed. These may include reading level, computational complexity, language characteristics, or any number of factors that may affect the appraisal (Cawley, 1985). One prominent concern emerging from the National Assessment of Educational Progress is two-step problems (Carpenter et al., 1988). Yet the literature does not offer a schema for the creation of two-step problems so that their characteristics can be controlled. Figure 6, which is taken from our present work, offers such a schema. The matrix provides for 16 combinations of two-step problems. The problem for cell 1 involves two addition steps. The first step of the problem in cell 2 requires subtraction and the second step requires addition. These problems are written to a common theme, clowns and their balloons, and they require only single-digit computation. Matrices of any characteristics can be developed.

MOVING TO SUCCESS

Maximizing the possibilities for success in the regular classroom for the mildly

	Addition	Subtraction	Multiplication	Division
Addition	1	2	3	4
Subtraction	5	6	7	8
Multiplication	9	10	11	12
Division	13	14	15	16

1. Dick the clown has 3 red balloons.
   Bill the clown has 2 red balloons.
   Sally the clown has 4 more blue balloons
   than all the red balloons.
   How many balloons does Sally have?

2. Dick the clown had 3 red balloons and
   2 of them popped.
   Bill the clown had 4 red balloons and
   1 of them popped.
   Sally the clown has 3 more blue balloons
   than all the red balloons left after some
   had popped.
   How many blue balloons does Sally have?

FIGURE 6. Matrix for construction of two-step word problems.

handicapped child involves a two-step procedure. The first step is to conduct a comprehensive appraisal that is directed at both concepts and skills. In effect, we want to determine the child's intuitive understanding of as many topics as possible (Figure 7). Here we see the measurement of the concept of parallel planes without specific vocabulary. Items such as this allow us to work to involve the child at the conceptual rather than the routine level. The child can be assisted to develop the meanings and understandings of many mathematics topics long before, or in place of, the computation routines or vocabulary lessons on these same topics.

The second step is to determine the extent to which the child can master alternative algorithms or procedures and solve problems in ways that will permit the highest possible level of performance by circumventing obstacles posed by traditional mechanics of computation. For example, assume the child is inordinately bogged down with "borrowing" in subtraction, but that it is possible for this child to learn to subtract by using an algorithm that does not require borrowing. Should the appraisal specialist actually teach the

child to master this alternative algorithm, the child could proceed to other topics (the traditional algorithm being presented later).

Four Steps on the Path to Success

Four steps can be implemented that will help to assure success in mathematics in *and* with the regular classroom.

1. Do not be misguided or misdirected by information obtained from existing tests.
2. Prevent the child from habituating incorrect routines and inappropriate understandings.
3. Assure the child a standard of progress that guarantees there will be more correct than incorrect responses.
4. Offer the child alternative ways to acquire and to demonstrate proficiency with the skills, concepts, and problem-solving components of mathematics.

On Being Misguided

Many sorts of misguided appraisal are common place in math assessment. For example, in the *Inventory of Basic Arith-*

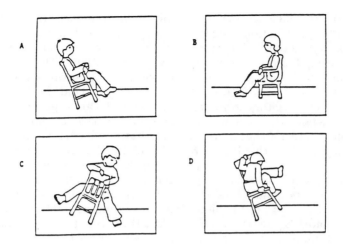

31. Look at all the pictures.
     Point to the one that shows safety in sitting.

     Geometry
     Parallel Planes

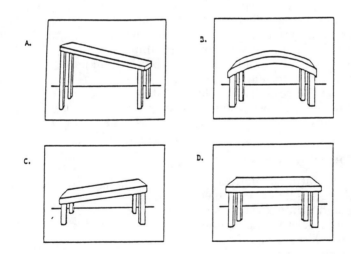

32. Here are pictures of different tables.
     Point to the one where it would be best to place a glass of
     milk.

     Geometry
     Parallel Planes

FIGURE 7. Assessment of the concept of parallel planes.

metic Skills (Enright, 1983) an example of error analysis for subtraction suggests that left-to-right subtraction is incorrect. Such is not the case, for the use of the left-to-right algorithm is perfectly legitimate. In fact, the use of left-to-right algorithms is perfectly legitimate for all the operations on whole numbers, particularly for division, where it is the standard approach (Cawley, Fitzmaurice-Hayes, & Shaw, 1988).

Another example of misguided appraisal is found in the original *Key MATH Diagnostic Test*, where two problem-solving items, J–6 and J–8, are both poorly constructed and misleading (Cawley, Fitzmaurice-Hayes, & Shaw, 1988). The items contradict each other. J–6 is described as containing extraneous information. Historically (Cruickshank, 1948), extraneous information has been employed as a foil and if the student includes it, the answer is incorrect. However, J–6 allows the child to get the correct answer by using the extraneous information. This, of course, renders the extraneous information useless for diagnostic purposes. J–8 contains a most appropriate illustration of the use of extraneous information, but it is not described as containing extraneous information. Should the child incorporate the extraneous information into her or his response, the response would be incorrect. However, no attention is given to this possibility.

Habituating Incorrect Routines

The available literature in mathematics shows that some mildly handicapped children develop and habituate seemingly bizarre approaches to arithmetic computation (e.g., Lepore, 1979; Pelosi, 1977) and that they have been known to make the same kinds of errors in problem solving for nearly 40 years (e.g., Cawley, Miller, & School, 1987; Cruickshank, 1948).

It would appear that the habituation of inappropriate computation algorithms and procedures can be linked to a practice by instructors scoring tests rather than analyzing test performance. Figure 8 shows examples of the performance of a mildly handicapped child. Performance on

all similar items was the same. How does one explain such a consistent pattern of distorted performance? There are at least two explanations. The first is that not enough attention was given to immediate intervention. That is, as soon as one instance of this type of performance is spotted, it should be immediately pointed out that it is incorrect and unacceptable. The child should be immediately challenged to replicate the item using manipulatives. It will be found that he or she cannot reproduce the incorrect algorithm. At this impasse, show the child a correct algorithm with the manipulatives, introducing the least possible correction. That is, if the child is adding left-to-right, help him or her to use the left-to-right algorithm correctly and then change to another algorithm at some convenient time. In over 20 years of teaching and research in mathematics with handicapped children, we have never encountered a single instance in which a child could reconstruct an inappropriate algorithm with manipulatives. All the distortions occur with paper–pencil formats. Maximizing success in the regular classroom can be facilitated by the use of manipulatives before and during the introduction of paper–pencil formats.

A second reason the child might habituate to inappropriate habits is that sometimes they work. Using an example from Pelosi (1977), we see that for the division problem

$$6/\overline{4\,2\,6}$$

if the child says, "Six into six is one" and writes

$$6/\overline{4\,2\,6}^{1}$$

and then goes on to say, "Six into 42 is seven" and writes

$$6/\overline{4\,2\,6}^{7\,1}$$

the correct answer results. Unfortunately, the algorithm lacks generalizability.

As seen below, the response would be incorrect if the child used the same approach to

$$6/\overline{4\,3\,6}\qquad\text{or}\qquad 6/\overline{4\,2\,7}.$$

1. When the multiplier had two digits, the following pattern was used:

A B C	E × C	300
× D E	E × B	× 82
	D × A	2382

Note that zero times any number was set equal to that number:
$2 \times 0 = 2; \quad 8 \times 0 = 8$

2. With a three-digit multiplier the following pattern was used:

A B C	F × C	527
× D E F	E × B	× 200
	D × A	1027

For both problems the student said, "you can't do it with zero, so I act like it's not there."

FIGURE 8. Incorrect algorithms for arithmetic problems demonstrated by one student.

Standards of Progress Based on High Percentages Correct

Successful integration with the regular class can be viewed from two perspectives. First, success can be associated with a quality of performance in which more correct than incorrect responses are produced on every mathematics assignment. This includes performance on worksheet drills, homework, quizzes, and examinations. This aspect of success is unrelated to age-in-grade progress or to school marks. Here, we are directing attention solely to the notion that effective school learning in mathematics requires that a child practice *right* more than *wrong*. This also will prevent the habituation to inappropriate habits. Applying this standard requires that the classroom teacher not give one assignment to all the children and then describe the children by their different levels of performance, but give different assignments to different children to guarantee a stipulated ratio of correct to incorrect responses for all. The teacher might say, "In this class you will generally score at or above 70% correct on each assignment. I will adjust your assignments until this happens." For example, one child might be given an assignment consisting of one-step word problems involving addition and subtraction. Another child might be given an assignment consisting of two-step problems involving addition and subtraction. Both are doing word problems at levels consistent with their levels of proficiency. Such an approach essentially will guarantee that each child's performance will be positively reinforced and that the teacher truly can praise the child for a job well done.

A second approach to achieving high percentages of correct responses can be implemented by allowing the children to acquire and to demonstrate their proficiency in mathematics in formats other than paper–pencil. Once the high levels of percentage correct are obtained, speed should be stressed, both with paper–pencil and manipulatives.

From the very beginning, word problems, for example, might be done by having the teacher read from a script and by having the children create the information set for the problem with objects or pictures (Cawley & Miller, 1986). Such an approach will assure that the children have access to the information or concepts and that they have a means of response that eliminates the effects of disabilities such as reading.

Alternative Representations

When we began our research and program development in mathematics over 20 years ago, we searched for a process that would provide a systematic, yet flexible approach to instruction and classroom management procedures. It also was necessary that this procedure be capable of guiding instruction across a range of mathematics topics and problem solving. We evolved a device referred to as the Interactive Unit (IU) (Cawley et al., 1976), which is demonstrated in Figure 9. The IU provides 16 combinations of instructional interactions that can be utilized in instruction in mathematics and most other school subjects. Beyond this, it was found (Cawley, 1985) that nearly every subtest of present-day appraisal instruments (e.g., WISC–R: Vocabulary is Say/Say; Block Design is Display/Manipulate) can be coded and patterned into the IU. It was also found that the IU can guide the development of materials and test items for any subject matter.

The IU is described as a system of equivalent representations of mathematics concepts and skills. It is not a system of preferred representations. In the IU, a manipulative representation of a mathematics concept or skill is valued at a level that is equivalent to a paper–pencil representation of the same concept. The use of the IU is compatible with forms of Data-Based-Instruction (e.g., Blankenship, 1985) in that data can be collected and compiled or charted for accuracy and time in any one of the 16 combinations.

All 16 combinations can be utilized to create problems settings and instructional activities in arithmetic problem solving. And they can be used to involve children as productive and creative participants in the problem-solving experience.

WORD PROBLEMS

Word problems are set in words so that one must first analyze and interpret the words in their specific setting. One then must make decisions as to the actions conveyed by these words and then perform the operations that provide a solution to the problem. It is the words and the manner in which they are structured that convey the message of the problem. Informally, one could create word problems by utilizing any combination of words in any form of setting. As stated earlier (Figure 6), one can arrange the words to appraise specific facets of problem solving. Examine the following:

1. A boy has 3 apples
   Another boy has 2 apples.
   How many apples do the boys have?

2. A biologist illuminated 3 microscopes.
   Another biologist illuminated 2 microscopes.
   How many microscopes did the biologists illuminate?

These examples are essentially the same. Although one is written with more difficult words, it does not require any more interpretive or analytic ability than the other.

Now, look at these:

1. One boy planned to buy 3 apples.
   Another boy planned to buy 2 apples.
   How many apples did the boys plan to buy.

2. One boy is buying 3 apples.
   Another boy is buying 2 apples.
   How many apples are the boys buying?

3. One boy bought 3 apples.
   Another boy bought 2 apples.
   How many apples did the boys buy?

Although similar in appearance, the three items are created each in a different tense. The school psychologist could first request a child to do each problem. In the above, it is not the arithmetic that is important. What is important is that the child recognize the different tenses in which the items are constructed. Once the items have been completed, the child could be asked to describe the similarities and differences among them. If the process of problem solving is our target, then it seems important to create problems in which the words and their arrangements have to be interpreted. These steps would provide further details

Manipulate...............Manipulation of objects (piling, arranging and moving)
Display......................(Instructor Interaction) Presentation of displays
(pictures, arrangements of materials)
Say............................ Oral discussion
Write........................ Written materials (letters, numerals, words, signs of
operation) and marking of these types of materials
Identify..................... (Learner Interaction) Selection from multiple choices
of nonwritten materials (pictures, objects)

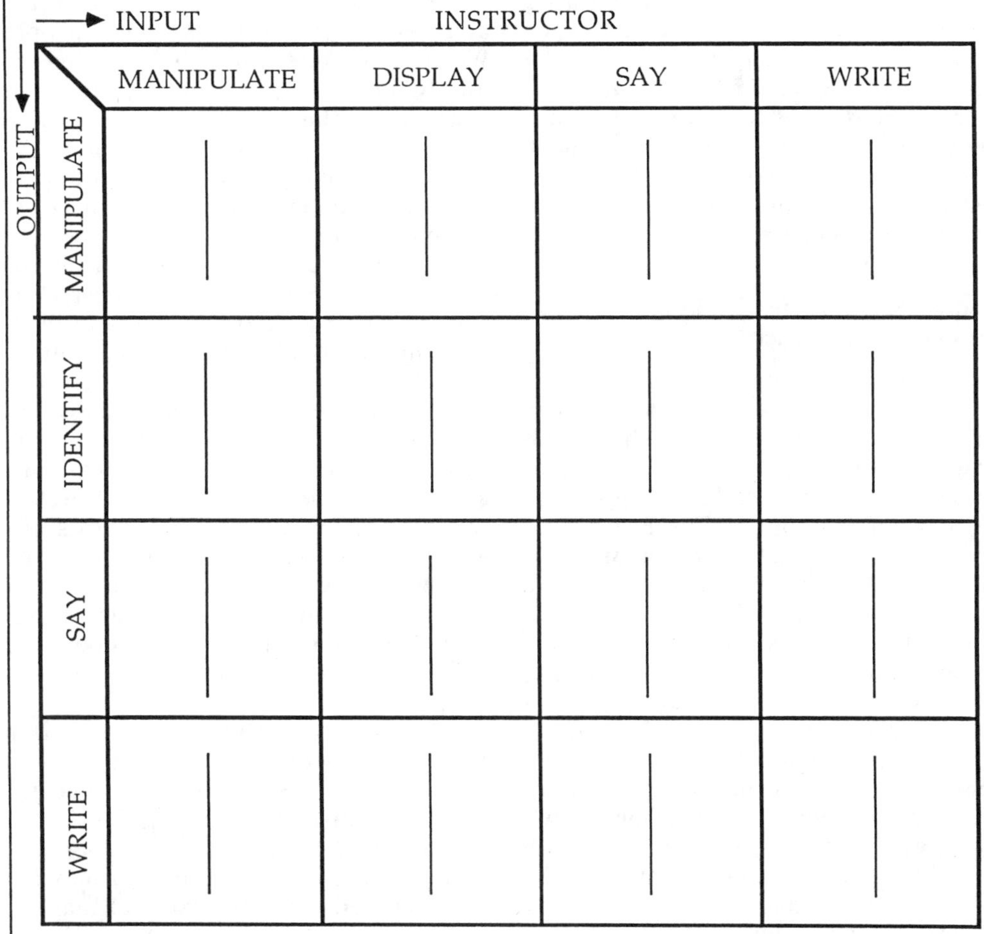

INPUT ⟶ INSTRUCTOR

	MANIPULATE	DISPLAY	SAY	WRITE
MANIPULATE				
IDENTIFY				
SAY				
WRITE				

OUTPUT

FIGURE 9. The interactive unit.

about the child's analysis and assist in the identification of language difficulties.

The primary limitation of most forms of word problem instruction is the dependency on cue words. Children are taught to look for words such as *left, gave,* and *remaining* as signals to subtract. We recommend teaching approaches that direct the child to analyze and interpret the information and encourage the child to activate the metacognitive processes of planning, strategy utilization, monitoring, and evaluation. Cueing strategies teach children to do the very thing we do not want them to do (Cawley, Fitzmaurice-Hayes, & Shaw, 1988). At the very most, the outcome of this form of approach provides success in the form of the correct answer without any understanding of what the problem is all about.

Promoting Strategic Thinking through Mathematics

Think-aloud protocol analyses (Peterson, 1988) have revealed that low-achieving students in mathematics show little strategic thinking. Low-achieving and mildly handicapped children appear to guess about appropriate procedures to solve problems and to obtain answers. They are satisfied with answers that are clearly inappropriate. Effective intervention in this case consists of providing students with specific cognitional strategies to enhance learning during mathematics instruction.

Students should learn to (a) verify answers, (b) redo problems, (c) reread directions, (d) incorporate prior knowledge, (e) ask for assistance, (f) utilize aides, (g) employ memory strategies, (h) try to understand a lesson, (i) use specific operations for problems, and (j) validate answers against external criteria (Carpenter, Fennema, & Peterson, 1987; Peterson, 1988; Peterson, Fennema, Carpenter, & Loef, 1988). Students' cognitional knowledge must be evaluated as part of a comprehensive appraisal so that effective interactions between students and material can be promoted.

Maximizing success in problem solving is a long-term process that requires both systematic and frequent experiences. It is precisely in the realm of problem solving that one encounters considerable difficulty in meeting the needs of mildly handicapped children.

Time and Resources of the Teacher

School psychologists who seek to intervene on behalf of mildly handicapped children need to be alert to the fact that regular class teachers at the elementary and secondary levels are busy people. When called upon to meet the needs of mildly handicapped children in their classrooms, they generally have to find time within their existing schedule.

A basic question exists as to how to define regular class and as to when a class can no longer be considered a regular class. *Most regular classrooms are curriculum-defined entities.* Their overriding feature is that they are expected to cover a defined curriculum, usually laid out in a textbook.

Teachers of fourth-grade classes, for example, know quite well what they are expected to cover during the year and, given the textbook as a guide and the thought of year end competency tests, just what the children are expected to master. They are expected to provide educational services to some 25 heterogeneously assembled children for some 6 hours per day and to cover five or more subjects in the process.

Teachers of ninth-grade general math also have a good idea of what is to be covered. They also know that teaching general math in the ninth grade is less desirable than teaching algebra 1. Strangely, these teachers may or may not be concerned with standards of mastery because ninth-grade general math classes are frequently composed of children who are covering work ordinarily mastered in the elementary grades. These teachers are likely to be teaching five sections of different mathematics classes in any given day to some 125–150 children.

Although these teachers may attempt to individualize instruction, reality suggests that they are already overburdened and that they are capable of only modest efforts to meet the needs of the mildly handicapped. The teachers can be assisted in two ways.

1. Provide them with planning and execution time at the initial level of concern. Provide them with an opportunity to work with the school psychologist and other specialists. When a teacher first identifies a problem and expresses concern for a child, the teacher should be provided with the time and the resources to invoke classroom interventions. By this we mean real time. Someone, possibly a special educator, could take over some segment of the teaching schedule and allow the teacher to work with the child.

2. Provide these teachers with individual or small-group instruction time after it has been determined that a child is eligible for special education and some or all of the child's time will be spent in the regular class. Again, this must be real time and it could be provided by special education personnel. This time can be devoted to direct instruction or it can be devoted to indirect instructional planning. An example of the latter is providing the teacher with the time and the resources to prepare instructional activities and materials that will assure the successful participation of the mildly handicapped children in the full spectrum of curricula and instructional experiences.

SOCIAL ASPECTS

No intervention can be entirely successful unless it addresses the affective domain that influences learning. Two aspects are to be considered: the child's perception that learning is possible and relevant and the teacher's perception that a skill is necessary and that it can be learned. Children who experience a feeling of control over their environment and are oriented toward learning until they have mastered a skill demonstrate the greatest success in the classroom (Kavale & Forness, 1985; Torgensen, 1977).

Teaching methods not oriented toward active student participation and maximization of success will tend to generate the maladaptive characteristics

of "learned helplessness" in children (McKinney, McClure, & Feagans, 1982; Meichenbaum, 1981; Ryan, Ledger, Short, & Weed, 1982). That is, inactive or helpless learners approach tasks in a passive and disorganized manner. They fail to apply monitoring and planning activities such as identifying goals, selecting appropriate courses of action, revising action plans when experiencing failure, and evaluating ultimate attainment of goals (Ryan et al., 1982).

Another consideration of importance in respect to interventions with the mildly handicapped is the children's feelings of self-worth. Positive correlations between high self-concept ratings and achievement have been documented over decades of research (Black, 1974; Gorlow, Butler, & Guthrie, 1961; Zeitz, 1976). Furthermore, Black (1974) found that estimates of self-concept showed a direct relation to the amount of achievement, children at the lowest levels of achievement indicating the lowest self-concept.

Research indicates that learning-disabled students expect to fail and feel there is nothing they can do about it. They tend to attribute success to luck and failure to lack of ability (Pearl, 1985; Pearl, Bryan, & Herzog, 1983) rather than lack of effort (Butkowsky & Willows, 1980). Diagnosticians and teachers need to be more aware of the import of these self-defeating attributions and their disruptive effects. Strategies to maximize achievement must include content that facilitates decision making by children, provides many opportunities for success, provides children with a feeling of achievement and thus, increases self-worth.

Enhancing Successful Learning

Classroom procedures that cause a child to experience repeated failure do not develop feelings of control or positive self-regard. For example, making children attempt a test at which they are likely to score over 70% incorrect merely gives them the occasion to practice appropriate math procedures in only 30% of the work. Increasing the amount of time they perform incorrectly encourages the habituation to incorrect or bizarre algorithms (Lepore, 1979; Pelosi, 1977). Simply changing the test so that they will achieve a success rate greater than 70% would go a long way toward promoting positive participation and increasing their motivation to learn, by demonstrating that learning is possible.

Making Learning Relevant

An important point to consider in maximizing success is the perceived relevance of the learning task to the student's long-term goals. For example, in the teaching of rounding of numbers, a task could be presented as a worksheet activity and the students instructed to convert final digits according to specified rules. Alternatively, the teacher could engage the students in a discussion of the use of rounding (telling time, comparative calculations in a grocery store, figuring out restaurant tips) and have students work on these examples from meaningful contexts. We believe that the latter approach would go a long way towards presenting mathematics to students as a skill that affects their everyday lives rather than an isolated classroom task.

The appraisal specialist must have an understanding that frequently poor performance on math tasks is not related to lack of conceptual understanding on the part of the child. Inconsistencies in rates of success could indicate that children have the ability in the area of interest but are unable to apply strategies for problem solving when the task is presented in certain unfamiliar contexts.

SUMMARY

Success in mathematics for the mildly handicapped child is predicated on an understanding of the differences between those children who can perform *with* the regular class when meaningful instructional adjustments are made and those children who are severely discrepant in mathematics and need both curricula and instructional adjustments.

Success is not defined in terms of scores on a standardized test or grades in class. Success is to be seen as the attainment of sets of skills and concepts that can be utilized to solve problems and to make decisions that are guided by quantitative information.

Such success can be maximized by appraisals that provide full and meaningful descriptions of the mildly handicapped child in such a way that teachers and other school specialists can make appropriate instructional and curricular decisions. These decisions must consider that success is a gradual and long-term process and that a variety of specialists must work together for its attainment.

FOOTNOTE

[1]Data in Figure 3 from Magwili (1987). Fē Magwili managed and processed all data for the computation study from which these data are derived as a result of her involvement in a research project undertaken as an undergraduate student.

ACKNOWLEDGMENTS

Preparation of this chapter was aided by a grant (No. H023C70500; Verbal Problem Solving for the Mildly Handicapped) from the Division of Innovation and Development, Office of Special Education and Rehabilitative Services, U.S. Department of Education. The views are those of the authors.

REFERENCES

Ballew, H., & Cunningham, J. (1982). Diagnosing strengths and weaknesses of sixth-grade students in solving word problems. *Journal of Research in Mathematics Education, 13*, 202-210.

Black, W. F. (1974). Self-concept as related to achievement and age in learning-disabled children. *Child Development, 35*, 1137-1140.

Blankenship, C. S. (1985). Linking assessment to instruction. In J. F. Cawley (Ed.), *Practical mathematics appraisal of the learning disabled* (pp. 59-80). Rockville, MD: Aspen.

Butkowsky, I. S., & Willows, D. M. (1980). Cognitive-motivation characteristics of children varying in reading ability: Evidence for learned helplessness in poor readers. *Journal of Educational Psychology, 72*, 408-422.

Carpenter, T. P., Fennema, E., & Peterson, P. L. (1987). *Teachers' pedagogical content knowledge in mathematics.* Paper presented at the annual meeting of the American Educational Research Association. New Orleans, LA.

Carpenter, T. P., Lindquist, M., Brown, C., Kouba, V., Silber, E., & Swafford, J. (1988). Results of the fourth NAEP assessment of mathematics: Trends and conclusions. *Arithmetic Teacher, 36*(4), 38-41.

Cawley, J. F. (1984). Selection, adaptation, and development of curricula and instructional materials. In J. F. Cawley (Ed.), *Developmental teaching of mathematics to the learning disabled* (pp. 222-252). Rockville, MD: Aspen.

Cawley, J. F. (1985). Nonmathematics appraisal. In J. F. Cawley (Ed.), *Practical mathematics appraisal of the learning disabled* (pp. 147-176). Rockville, MD: Aspen.

Cawley, J. F., Fitzmaurice, A. M., Goodstein, H. A., Lepore, A., Sedlak, R., & Althaus, V. (1976). *Project MATH.* Tulsa: Educational Progress Corp.

Cawley, J. F., Fitzmaurice, A., Shaw, R., Kahn, H., & Bates, H. (1979). LD youth and mathematics. A review of characteristics. *Learning Disabilities Quarterly, 2,* 25-41.

Cawley, J. F., Fitzmaurice-Hayes, A. M., & Shaw, R. (1988). *Mathematics for the mildly handicapped: A guide to curriculum and instruction.* Newton, MA: Allyn & Bacon.

Cawley, J. F., Fitzmaurice-Hayes, A. M., Shaw, R., Norlander, K., & Sayre, J. (1987). *Learner activity program: Mathematics.* Rockville, MD: Aspen.

Cawley, J. F., & Goodman, J. O. (1968). Interrelationships among mental abilities, language arts and arithmetic with the mentally handicapped. *Arithmetic Teacher, 15,* 631-636.

Cawley, J. F., Kahn, H., & Tedesco, A. (1989). An analysis of the school performance of learning disabled youth in vocational-technical schools. *Journal of Learning Disabilities, 22,* 630-634.

Cawley, J. F., & Miller, J. (1986). Selected views on metacognition, problem solving and learning disabilities. *Learning Disabilities Focus, 2,* 36-48.

Cawley, J. F., & Miller, J. (1989). Cross-sectional comparisons of the mathematical performance of children with learning disabilities: Are we on the right track toward comprehensive programming? *Journal of Learning Disabilities, 22*(4), 250-254.

Cawley, J. F., Miller, J., & Carr, S. (1988). Arithmetic. In G. G. Robinson, J. R. Patton, E. A. Polloway, & L. R. Sargent (Eds.), *Best practices in mental disabilities, Volume 2.* DesMoines, IA: State Department of Education.

Cawley, J. F., Miller, J., & School, B. (1987). A brief inquiry of arithmetic word problem-solving among learning disabled secondary students. *Learning Disabilities Focus, 2,* 87-93.

Cawley, J. F., & Parmar, R. S. (1989). Verbal problem-solving for the mildly handicapped: Year 1 report. Grant funded by the Office of Special Education and Rehabilitation Services, Washington, DC.

Cruickshank, W. (1948). Arithmetic ability of mentally retarded children. 1: Ability to differentiate extraneous materials from needed arithmetic facts. *Journal of Educational Research, 42,* 161-170.

Enright, B. (1983). *Inventory of basic arithmetic skills.* North Billerica, MA: Curriculum Associates.

Gorlow, L., Butler, A., & Guthrie, G. M. (1961). Correlates of self-attitudes of retardates. *American Journal of Mental Deficiency, 67,* 549-555.

Kavale, K., & Forness, S. (1985). *The science of learning disabilities.* San Diego: College Hill.

Lepore, A. (1979). A comparison of computational errors between educable mentally handicapped and learning disabled children. *Focus on Learning Problems in Mathematics, 1,* 12-33.

Levine, H., & Langress, L. (1985). Everyday cognition among mildly retarded adults: An ethnographic approach. *American Journal of Mental Deficiency, 90,* 18-26.

Magwili, F. (1987). *An investigation into the acquisition of mathematics proficiency in grades 3-8.* Unpublished manuscript. New Orleans: University of New Orleans.

McKinney, J. D., McClure, S., & Feagans, L. (1982). Classroom behavior of learning disabled children. *Learning Disability Quarterly, 5,* 45-52.

McKnight, C., Crosswhite, J., Dorsey, J., Kiper, E., Swafford, J., Travers, K., & Cooney, T. (1987). *The underachieving curriculum: Assessing U.S. school mathematics from an international perspective.* Champaign, IL: Stipes.

McLeod, T. (1985). Special education teachers and mathematics: Assessment, instruction, skill deficits, and teacher preparation. *Focus on Learning Problems in Mathematics, 7,* 4-17.

McLeod, T., & Armstrong, S. (1982). Learning disabilities in mathematics-skill deficits and remedial approaches at the intermediate and secondary level. *Learning Disability Quarterly, 5,* 305-311.

Meichenbaum, D. (1981). Cognitive behavior modification with exceptional children: A promise yet unfulfilled. *Exceptional Education Quarterly, 1,* 83-88.

Miller, J., & Carr, S. (1988). *Paired-associate learning and generalization.* Unpublished research paper. University of New Orleans, New Orleans.

Miller, J. H., & Milam, C. (1987). Multiplication and division errors committed by learning disabled students. *Learning Disabilities Research, 2,* 119-122.

National Council of Teachers of Mathematics. (1980). *Priorities in school mathematics.* Reston, VA: Author.

O'Neil, J. (1988). *How special should the special education curriculum be?* Curriculum Update. Washington, DC: Association for Supervision and Curriculum Development.

Pearl, R. (1985). Cognitive behavioral interventions for increasing motivation. *Journal of Abnormal Child Psychology, 13,* 443-454.

Pearl, R., Bryan, T., & Herzog, A. (1983). Learning-disabled and nondisabled children's strategy analysis under high and low success conditions. *Learning Disabilities Quarterly, 6,* 67-74.

Pelosi, P. (1977). *A report on computational variations among secondary school students.* Unpublished research report. Storrs, CT: University of Connecticut.

Peterson, P. L. (1988). Teachers' and students' cognitional knowledge for classroom teaching and learning. *Educational Researcher, 17*(5), 5-14.

Peterson, P. L., Fennema, E., Carpenter, T., & Loef, M. (1988). Teachers' pedagogical content beliefs in mathematics. *Cognition and Instruction, 5*(3), 1-40.

Resnick, L. (1987). Learning in school and out. *Educational Researcher, 16,* 13-30.

Ryan, E. B., Ledger, G. W., Short, E. J., & Weed, K. A. (1982). Promoting the use of active comprehension strategies by poor readers. *Topics in Learning and Learning Disabilities, 2*(1), 53-60.

Saxe, G. (1988). Candy selling and math learning. *Educational Researcher, 17,* 14-21.

Shaw, R. (1985). Adapting the college preparatory program for the learning disabled. In J. F. Cawley (Ed.), *Secondary school mathematics for the learning disabled* (pp. 271-290). Austin, TX: Pro-Ed.

Silbert, J., Carnine, D., & Stein, M. (1981). *Direct instruction mathematics.* Columbus, OH: Merrill.

Torgensen, J. K. (1977). The role of non-specific factors in the task performance of learning disabled children: A theoretical assessment. *Journal of Learning Disabilities, 10*(1), 27-35.

Warner, M., Alley, G., Schumaker, J., Deshler, D., & Clark, F. (1980). *An empidemiological study of learning disabled adolescents in secondary schools: Achievement and ability, socioeconomic and school experiences* (Research Report 13). Institute for Research in Learning Disabilities, University of Kansas, Lawrence, Kansas.

20

Adapting Textbooks for Mildly Handicapped Adolescents

Thomas C. Lovitt
Steven V. Horton
University of Washington

This chapter reviews selected approaches for adapting textbook passages for mildly handicapped and low-achieving students (i.e., those traditionally labeled learning disabled [LD] or remedial). More generally, the methods presented here focus on organizing content information to improve comprehension among low-achieving adolescents who are blended into regular education classes. We have restricted our interest to textbooks rather than other sources of information such as workbooks, lectures, and films, because textbooks represent the primary vehicle through which students are exposed to new information, beginning in the intermediate grades and continuing through secondary programs in the public schools. Many of the methods for adapting textbooks that will be discussed in this chapter, however, are applicable to other sources of information. Most of the research reviewed was conducted with students who were enrolled in secondary programs.

There are three primary reasons for adapting textbooks for mildly handicapped and low-achieving students. The first, and perhaps the most important, reason is that the majority of those students are unable to read their assigned textbooks with the proficiency required to gain information from them and to assimilate that information with previously learned material. In a study by Lovitt, Horton, and Bergerud (1987),

involving mildly handicapped and regular education students enrolled in social studies and science classes in middle school and high school, a significant correlation was found between the rate at which students read orally from their textbooks and scores on written tests based on textbook information. Specifically, of 72 students sampled, 27 (38%) who read at a rate of 135 words per minute or higher averaged 60% correct or higher on six written tests. Conversely, 24 students (33%) who read at a rate of less than 135 words per minute averaged less than 60% correct on the tests.

Not many mildly handicapped students are able to read orally at a rate of 135 words per minute or higher. In our textbook adaptation research at the University of Washington over the past 4 years, we have gathered data on the oral reading rates of 55 LD adolescents, of whom 20 were enrolled in social studies or science classes in middle school, and 35 were in high school social studies or health classes (Lovitt & Horton, 1988). The following oral reading rates are average scores of the 55 subjects derived from three assessments of each student, using three reading passages selected from the beginning, middle, and end of their content area textbooks: middle school, M = 99.95 words per minute; range = 28–166; high school, M = 103.62 words per minute; range = 40–160. At both the middle and high school levels, only 20% of the LD students had an average oral reading rate of at least 135 words per minute.

A second and related reason for adapting textbooks for mildly handicapped adolescents is that many of the books are poorly organized. They are not "user friendly," or as Kantor, Anderson, and Armbruster (1983) have put it, many textbooks are "inconsiderate." Those authors reported that when textbooks were evaluated on the basis of structure, coherence, unity, and audience appropriateness, many of them fell short. They estimated, in fact, that textbooks were appropriate for only the top 50% of the students.

The third reason for adapting textbooks for students is that scores of social studies and science teachers are poorly prepared in their specific instructional areas. In a study by Kaltsounis (1984) at the University of Washington, it was revealed that only 35% of social studies and 64% of science teachers had taken as many as 20 quarter credit hours in their discipline. This inadequate preparation of teachers is compounded in special education when resource teachers are the content teachers for students with mild handicaps (as is frequently the case); they offer instruction in U.S. history, biology, world history, and other subjects. Although many of these special education teachers know a great deal about behavior management and individualized instruction, they do not always have the backgrounds necessary to teach those content subjects.

We will comment below on two popular methods for adapting textbooks that we do *not* recommend — rewriting texts to reduce the difficulty and taping textual material — and on nine methods that we do recommend (see Figure 1). The nine methods we endorse are subsumed under three major categories: (a) verbal format (advance organizers, study guides, and vocabulary drills in a precision teaching model); (b) visual-verbal format (graphic organizers, visual-spatial displays, and mnemonic keywords involving thematic illustrations); and (c) computer-assisted instruction (vocabulary drills, graphic tutorials, and study guides). For each of the 11 methods of adapting textbooks, at least one empirically based investigation is summarized in some depth.

NONRECOMMENDATIONS

Rewriting Texts to Reduce Difficulty of Reading

The idea of reducing the level of difficulty of textbooks had its origin in the practice of comparing reading levels of textbooks (based on readability formulas) to reading levels of students (based on standardized achievement tests). A number of formulas such as the Fry Readability Formula (1968) and the McLaughlin SMOG Grading Formula (1969) are available for measuring the reading level of textbook passages.

Although the variables assessed by these formulas frequently differ, typically they include some weighted combination of sentence length or number of independent clauses, as well as measures of length and complexity of vocabulary. Two standardized tests that are commonly used to assess the reading level of students are the Metropolitan Achievement Test (Prescott, Balow, Hogan, & Farr, 1984) and the California Achievement Test (1985).

In matching students to textbooks some educators, when considering whether to modify textbooks for pupils, might determine that a text is written at the 12th-grade level and their students are reading at the seventh-grade level. Subtracting 7 from 12, they quickly discover that the text is 5 levels too high; therefore, they or someone else might set out to rewrite the book so that it more closely corresponds to the reading level of students.

Six steps have been recommended (e.g., Osterlag & Rambeau, 1982) for rewriting textbook passages to reduce the difficulty level:

1. Determine the readability level of the passage through the application of a readability formula. Decide on how much to reduce the level.

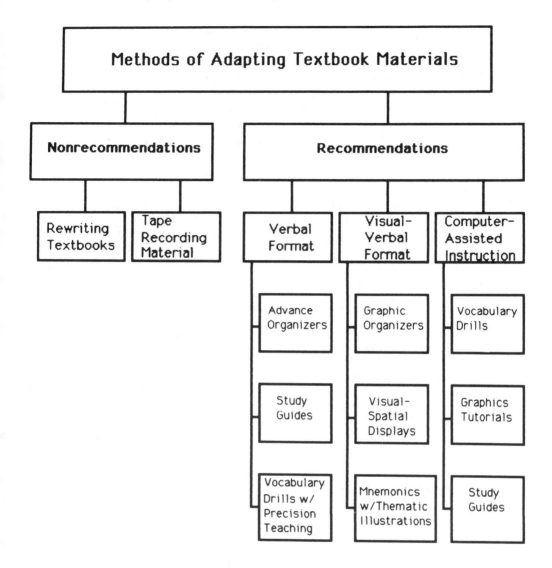

FIGURE 1. A graphic overview of recommended and nonrecommended methods of adapting textbook materials.

2. Eliminate extraneous facts and irrelevant information when rewriting a passage, but try not to alter the essential concepts.

3. Rely on shorter sentences when rewriting material. While doing so, consider the linguistic structure of the sentences.

4. Write sentences that flow smoothly; vary the length of sentences and paragraphs.

5. Reduce the difficulty of the vocabu-lary, depending on the type of material being modified. Include words with high imagery content that possibly enhance retention of the concepts.

6. Administer a second readability analysis once the passage has been rewritten to determine whether its reading level is closer to that of the target audience. If there is still not a proper match, make the necessary adjustments.

These procedures have been investi-gated empirically. For example, in an investigation with ninth- and tenth-grade biology students, Wright (1982) discovered that 67% of the participants could not understand the assigned textbook material satisfactorily. She therefore investigated the effects of reducing the difficulty of passages on students' comprehension and achievement. Wright found that the rewritten material produced significantly increased comprehension, as indicated by student performance on a cloze test. It did not, however, positively affect their achievement in biology, as measured by scores on an objective test given at the conclusion of the unit of study.

Results from research at the Center for the Study of Reading at the University of Illinois (e.g., Davison, 1984) strongly suggested that the practice of reducing the difficulty of content materials on the basis of readability formulas actually *may detract* from comprehension. That opinion was consistent with evidence that reducing sentence length may actually increase its difficulty (Pearson, 1975–1976). Davison also advised that altering content materials with respect to readability may seriously distort the logical relations between parts of the text, disrupt the presentation of ideas, and generally make it difficult to convey the meaning of the original text.

Beyond those reasons for not modifying text passages by reducing the level of difficulty, this practice is not recommended because of two other concerns. First, obtaining readability and achievement scores and determining the difference between the two is not a good practice for their is no close agreement across scores from different readability formulas on the same passage (Lovitt, Horton, & Bergerud, 1987), nor is there any near correspondence on a given pupil's scores on different achievement tests (Eaton, & Lovitt, 1972). Second, the considerable time involved in rewriting textbook passages to reduce the difficulty could be better spent providing direct service to students.

Tape Recording Passages from Textbooks

For some educators it appears reasonable that if mildly handicapped pupils are unable to read passages from their assigned textbooks and yet it is important for them to have the information contained in those passages, then one way to provide it would be to tape-record the material and have them listen to it. Rivers (1980), for example, maintained that tape-recorded materials would help students improve their skills in reading, writing, critical thinking, and listening. He suggested that students with reading difficulties should read along while listening to recorded textual materials and ask teachers for assistance when they do not understand a new concept or the meaning of a word.

With respect to taping content materials for mildly handicapped students, Deshler and Graham (1980) identified five elements that must be considered:

1. Instructional goals and objectives for the passage must be identified.

2. Specific portions of a passage based on the identified objectives should be considered.

3. Material that is not recorded verbatim should be paraphrased or outlined to provide students with the context in which the major concepts are presented.

4. The differentiation of important concepts from unimportant details, and emphasis on maps, tables, chapter titles, and headings, should be considered.

5. A marking system that coordinates text materials and recordings to prevent students from getting confused or lost should be developed. Such a system is especially important when several activities are dispersed throughout the tape, or when the text content is frequently paraphrased.

Limited research is available on the benefits of tape-recorded materials on mildly handicapped students' comprehension. It seems, however, that the form the recordings assume is a critical factor in the effectiveness. Schumaker, Deshler, and Denton (1982), for example, reported that text recorded verbatim did not facilitate comprehension of LD adolescents in mainstream classrooms. They claimed that those students actually performed more poorly on chapter tests when material was recorded than when they simply read the material themselves. When the recordings were organized to emphasize students' involvement, however, and were supplemented by direct instruction, significant achievement gains were observed.

In spite of the advice and success of Schumaker et al. (1982) the recording of text passages as an adaptation approach for mildly handicapped youngsters is not recommended. The primary reason for not endorsing this approach is that many texts are "inconsiderate," as noted earlier. It seems apparent that if a passage is disorganized and incoherent, it will continue to be disorganized and incoherent when taped. The only difference with respect to the consumer will be that initially it was "inconsiderate" to their eyes, and when recorded it will be "inconsiderate" to their ears.

RECOMMENDATIONS

Verbal Format

According to Torgesen (1977), children who actively organize and rehearse material perform better on memory tasks than children who do not. With respect to mildly handicapped individuals, he maintained that many of them are inactive, and one reason for this may be their lack of important prerequisite information. Wong (1980) has suggested that numbers of mildly handicapped persons do not generate constructive operations automatically as they encode information. A reason for this may be that they devote too much attention to lower levels of reading, such as decoding or syntactic analysis, and have less energy for higher levels (e.g., comprehending and integrating information from texts). Based on Torgesen's and Wong's hypotheses on

learning characteristics of learning disabled individuals, it appears that they might be aided in understanding content materials, and thus acquire broader conceptual bases for organizing new information, if they are assisted in recalling and applying pertinent background information. Advance organizers, specially prepared written passages containing background information that is used to introduce new material, may serve that purpose.

Advance organizers. Advance organizers (AOs) were developed by Ausubel (1960), who maintained that cognitive structures are arranged hierarchically and that "new meaningful material becomes incorporated into cognitive structure insofar as it is subsumable under relevant existing concepts" (p. 267). Accordingly, AOs act as a bridge between what students already know and the new concepts they are attempting to learn. As explained by Ausubel (1963), AOs are written at a higher level of abstraction, generality, and inclusiveness than the new material to be learned, and serve as an "ideational scaffolding" around which to organize more specific information.

The effectiveness of AOs was examined by Ausubel (1960) in a study involving 110 undergraduate students enrolled in an introductory educational psychology course. The students were assigned to experimental and control groups in matched pairs based on their performance on a multiple-choice pretest, which was given after they read an unfamiliar 1,800-word passage on endocrinology. Following a pretest, and before reading the new learning material (a specially prepared 2,500-word passage dealing with the metallurgical properties of plain carbon steel), the students in the experimental group were given an introductory passage (AO) that was written at a higher level of abstraction, generality, and inclusiveness than the 2,500-word passage. Although the AO provided relevant background concepts of a general nature, it did not contain any of the specific information found in the test material. By contrast, before reading the same 2,500-

word passage, the students in the control group read an introductory passage that did not contain ideational scaffolding, but rather consisted of historical information on methods used in processing iron and steel. Both groups were given 35 minutes to read the 2,500-word steel passage and took a 36-item test 3 days later. The results indicated that students in the experimental group, on the average, earned significantly higher scores.

While Ausubel's AOs involved specially prepared written passages for the purpose of facilitating acquisition of unfamiliar but meaningful verbal material, the term AO over time has been used more generally to denote an array of activities that teachers perform prior to teaching new material for the purpose of developing readiness. Today, the term AO is often used in a manner that focuses more on the temporal position of the activity than on its inherent organizational structure. In current terminology, AOs might be classroom activities as diverse as preparatory oral discussions conducted by a teacher prior to introducing new academic material, or teacher's presentation of new reading vocabulary by the use of various diagrammatic forms.

In one such variant, Lenz, Alley, and Shumaker (1987) conducted research on the effectiveness of AOs delivered orally by seven teachers in the following subjects: American history, English, physical science, general science, geography, and biology. There were seven LD pupils in the research, all of whom were served in resource rooms.

Student training sessions were held in a resource room during the students' regularly scheduled attendance period. On the basis of a review of the literature on AOs and on the difficulties LD adolescents have with organization, Lenz et al. (1987) identified the following 12 components of an effective AO and suggested that teachers incorporate them when AOs are developed.

1. Inform the learner of the purpose of the AO.

2. Clarify the task's physical parameters in terms of actions to be taken by the teacher.

3. Clarify the task's physical parameters in terms of actions to be taken by the student.

4. Identify the topic of the learning task.

5. Identify subtopics related to the task.

6. Provide background information.

7. State the concepts to be learned.

8. Clarify the concepts to be learned.

9. Motivate students through rationales for completing the task.

10. Introduce or repeat new terms or words.

11. Provide an organizational framework for the learning task.

12. State the desired outcomes from the learning activity.

During the baseline phase of their research, teachers were observed in order to determine the extent to which they incorporated any of the 12 AO components in their oral presentations. After the class period, students were interviewed for recall of information from the teacher's presentation that related to the AO categories. For the training phase, teachers were given a manual on how to develop AOs. Furthermore, they were instructed to develop organizers and shown data on how much they had used them throughout the baseline period. In a third phase, students were trained to identify and record in writing the information their teacher delivered in the AOs (e.g., the purpose of the AO). For this task, the students were provided worksheets on which they recorded information that related to the AOs.

A multiple-baseline-across-students design was implemented to evaluate the effects of teacher training in the use of the AO. The data indicated that before training, the teachers made about 12 informational statements about AOs. After training, they made an average of 37 statements. In the third phase, after student training, the average number of statements by teachers was 38. As for the students, the average number of statements they made about AOs in the baseline was about 17. In the second phase, after teacher training, their average was about 19, and in the third phase, about 29.

Although the authors of this study provided ample data to suggest that the components of AOs can be taught to LD students in resource rooms by special education teachers, they offered no data to indicate that that ability helped them acquire more information from social studies or science books.

From a more general perspective, Luiten, Ames, and Ackerman (1980) conducted a meta-analysis on 135 AO studies to determine their effects on learning and retention. They concluded that AOs facilitated both acquisition and retention of information and, furthermore, that the average effects were greater for special education pupils than for nonhandicapped junior or senior high school students. In addition, those researchers found that AOs aided learning in most subject areas, but were most efficient in the social studies.

Study guides. One textbook modification technique that has been successfully applied with academically handicapped and regular secondary students is the writing of study guides. Whereas AOs were conceived as specially designed written passages to be implemented prior to a lesson, study guides are questions or statements that appear on worksheets to help students learn content information during or after they have read a passage (Cheek & Cheek, 1983; Earle, 1969; Herber, 1970; Lovitt & Horton, 1987). Study guides abstract or isolate important pieces of information from larger contexts, thereby structuring and guiding the comprehension of textbook materials. According to Herber (1970), study guides can give direction to student reading of textual material at three levels of comprehension: applied, interpretive, and factual. In several studies researchers have demonstrated that study guides are effective in

guiding students through secondary textbooks, many of which contain numerous facts and details.

In one such study, Lovitt, Rudsit, Jenkins, Pious, and Benedetti (1985) significantly improved the academic performance of mainstreamed LD and regular seventh-grade science students by providing teacher-directed study guides that presented sequenced main ideas from a chapter. In another investigation, Bergerud, Lovitt, and Horton (1988) reported favorable effects resulting from student-directed study guides, in comparison with a self-study condition, among LD high school students who were taught science materials in a resource room. In a third study, Horton, Lovitt, Givens, and Nelson (1989) significantly increased the test performance of LD and remedial high school students by using computerized study guides to teach social studies material in a mainstream setting (see Computer-Assisted Instruction, below).

In the study guide research by Lovitt and colleagues, guide materials were presented as part of well-planned reading activities that consisted of reading textbook passages, completing a series of comprehension questions, and taking written tests. When presented in that manner, guide materials resemble adjunct postquestions that appear in text immediately after a passage. A written response to such questions in text has been shown to improve significantly the reading comprehension of nonhandicapped students, particularly when questions relate directly to criterion test items (Anderson & Biddle, 1975; Hamaker, 1986). Those results lend credence to the hypothesis that performance is enhanced by advance knowledge of the criterion task.

A two-experiment study by Horton and Lovitt (1989a) sought to answer three research questions regarding the applicability of study guides to heterogeneous groups in mainstream secondary classes; (a) Are study guides more effective than a self-study condition for three classifications of students – LD, remedial, and regular education? (b) Do study guides produce similar effects in middle school and high school, and in social studies and science? (c) Do study guides produce consistent effects when used for heterogeneous groups through teacher-directed and student-directed procedures? Several steps were taken to ensure the ecological validity of the study, including keeping intact such circumstances as the teachers, settings, textbooks, grouping arrangements, and the sequences of instruction that were normally used.

In that research, students in the experimental conditions were asked to read passages of approximately 1,500 words from their texts, and then were given study guides over the material. In the first experiment, teachers directed the activity as their classes studied from the guides. Specifically, teachers placed a transparency of the study guide questions without answers on an overhead projector and lectured from it. Study guides were made up of 15 short-answer questions based on the main ideas from the selected text passages. As the teachers directed the discussion by calling on students to read and answer questions, they wrote the answers on the study guide and instructed the pupils to do likewise (see Figure 2; example answers are shown in boldface type). Following that directed activity, the students studied their completed forms for a few minutes and then responded to a 15-item multiple-choice test that dealt with the material from their text and their study guides.

These students also were involved in an alternate condition. For this part of the first experiment they also read passages from their texts, but instead of being given study guides, they were provided self-study time in which they reread and took notes prior to taking the multiple-choice tests.

In the second experiment, Horton and Lovitt studied the effects of student-directed study guides with the same students in the same classes. The students were given study guides like those in the first study, but now they looked up the answers themselves. To help them do this, page numbers were printed alongside each study guide item to indicate where the missing information was located. The students were given the same amount of time for this activity as was scheduled when teachers directed the process in the first experiment. While the students searched through their books to find the answers and write them, teachers circulated throughout the rooms and assisted those who were having trouble with the exercise. Following this period, teachers placed a transparency of a completed study guide on the overhead and went over all the items. If pupils had written in incorrect information or were unable to answer a question, they were given time to complete their guides correctly.

As was the case in the first study, these pupils were involved in an alternate treatment — that of taking notes from their reading and studying those notes. Also like the first study, the dependent measures in this project were the pupils' scores on a multiple-choice test.

The results of the study guide investigation(s) led to an affirmative conclusion for all three research questions: Study guides were significantly more effective than self-study for secondary students of three types; study guides were superior to self-study in middle school and high school and in social studies and science; and teachers were able to successfully implement guide material to heterogeneous groups through teacher-directed and student-directed procedures.

Across the two studies, LD students averaged 73% correct with study guides and 46% correct with self-study, the corresponding scores were 83% and 61% for remedial students, and 91% and 76% for regular education students. In comparison to nonhandicapped students, the results indicated that LD students performed better on tests associated with study guides at the high school level than at the middle school level. One possible explanation for that finding might be that high school students benefit from increased maturity or that high school students are more experienced in abstracting information from textbooks than their middle school counterparts.

To assist school personnel in developing study guides, the following steps have been advanced by Earle (1969) and Tierney, Readence, and Dishner (1985):

1. Why did Washington's population grow slowly at first?
   Settlements were hard to get to because of a lack of a good transportation system (roads).

2. Who built the first road across the Cascades?
   Puget sound settlers.

3. What was the Mullan Road?
   It was a federally funded road that went from the Columbia river to the Missouri River.

4. Why did the federal government provide money to build the Mullan Road?
   It wanted to be able to move troops in and out of the territory, if necessary.

5. Why did so many people come to the Washington Territory in the 1850s–1860s?
   To find gold.

6. To what part of the Washington Territory did gold miners rush?
   Eastern Washington.

7. The treaty of 1846 set the boundary "at the channel that separates the continent from Vancouver Island." How many channels were there between the island and the mainland?
   Two.

8. What two countries sent troops to the San Juans?
   Great Britain and the United States.

9. Why didn't residents of Western Washington want to give up their capital to *any* eastern city?
   They did not want their government located near rowdy mining towns, and they did not want to lose their political power.

10. In addition to not wanting to lose their political power, why was the Idaho Territory created?
    People in Oregon wanted to continue trade with eastern territories without interference from Olympia.

FIGURE 2. A teacher's version of a study guide presenting the main ideas in a reading passage from a Washington State history textbook.

1. Analyze the material to be read for both subject matter and level of comprehension required.

2. Select the content to be emphasized during the lesson.

3. Decide on the processes that students must use in acquiring that content; for example, comprehending the material with respect to literal, interpretive, or applied responses.

4. Consider the students' abilities (i.e., reading, writing) in relation to the content and processes to be emphasized. Teachers should vary the structure of study guides (i.e., question type, format, method of implementation) so that the effects of the treatment might generalize.

5. Avoid overcrowding the print on the study guides, as too much information may overwhelm some students.

6. Write the guides so that they are interesting and will motivate students to deal with the information.

7. Make certain that the guides reflect the instructional decisions made with regard to content and process.

Vocabulary drill in a precision teaching model. This verbal technique for adapting textbook material consists of a series of timed drills (i.e., 1-minute assessments) in which students write terms that match definitions. For example, given a sheet of definitions from a reading passage that are placed on a worksheet and a list of terms at the top of the worksheet, students match vocabulary to their definitions by writing the terms on lines that precede their appropriate meanings. The rate data from these exercises are plotted on Standard Behavior Charts, affording evaluation according to the conventions of Precision Teaching (White & Haring, 1980).

The rationale for using this method to adapt textbook information is based on the idea that key vocabulary serves as a foundation on which facts and ideas are built. Even the most cursory inspection of secondary textbooks reveals that subject areas such as health, science, and geography are replete with idiosyncratic vocabulary. It follows that students who have command of a subject's vocabulary will stand a greater chance of mastering the ins and outs of that subject than will pupils who lack familiarity with the key terms.

A study by Lovitt, Horton, and Bergerud (1987) examined the extent to which knowledge of vocabulary is related to other measures of academic performance among nonhandicapped and LD students enrolled in social studies and science classes in middle school and high school. Correlations were conducted between vocabulary scores (based on 50 terms selected from their respective textbooks) and (a) measures of test performance on specific content following instruction, (b) oral reading rates, (c) oral comprehension, and (d) teachers' rankings of students' progress throughout the school year. The results indicated a significant correspondence between all variables for high-, average-, and low-achieving students, the variation of vocabulary performance accounting for over 43% of the variation in scores on tests of specific content following instruction.

The effects of vocabulary drills on comprehension of textbook information was investigated in a study by Lovitt, Rudsit, Jenkins, Pious, and Benedetti (1986), involving seventh-grade students enrolled in physical science. Among the participants were four classes of regular education students, as well as LD students mainstreamed into those classes, and two experienced science teachers.

For this study, the students in each class were rank-ordered according to their accumulated test scores on general coursework in the subject. From that listing, experimental groups were formed for the four classes. There were six students in each experimental group: two from the "high" third, two from the "middle" third, and two from the "low" third. The other students in the four classes were considered as the contrast group.

For 2 weeks, the second author of this study took the small groups from the regular classes into an adjoining room and administered the vocabulary drills. Those sessions ran about 30 minutes. During that time, the experimenter conducted a series of exercises with the vocabulary sheets included the scheduling of several 1-minute timings a day, and providing correction and feedback. Over the course of the 2-week period, the students did timings on two sheets, each of which contained eight vocabulary words. The contrast students were given instruction from their classroom teacher in the regular classrooms while the experimental students were in the other room. All the students were instructed on the same topic and for the same amount of time.

Prior to and following the 2-week period, the students in the experimental groups and the contrast pupils were given a 29-item multiple-choice test on science information from the section of the textbook from which the vocabulary items were drawn. Data revealed that the gain scores for the experimental pupils were significantly higher than those of the contrast students. This finding was true in all four classes, and for all ability levels.

The materials required for developing Precision Teaching pages consist of ordinary 8½″ × 11″ sheets of paper. The following are steps for constructing and utilizing those sheets:

1. Identify the important vocabulary in a passage.

2. Write the definitions to those terms.

3. Select about eight terms to place on a sheet.

4. Print, on Side 1 of the sheet (Figure

3), the eight vocabulary words on the top left corner, one word under the next.

5. Print below those words five rows and five columns to make up 25 squares.

6. Write the definition of one of the vocabulary words in each of those 25 squares; leave a blank for the vocabulary word. If a vocabulary word was "meter," then the definition with the blank might appear as "A---- is a SI unit of length."

7. Print the definitions randomly on the page, three or four times per vocabulary word.

8. Print the words again on Side 2 of the vocabulary sheet, on the top of the page, and write the definitions alongside the words. Below these, there are 25 squares from the five columns and five rows (Figure 4).

9. Print the vocabulary words in these boxes.

10. Give each student a manila folder with an acetate sheet attached to one flap (see Figure 5).

11. Ask students to place the vocabulary sheet beneath the acetate with Side 1 showing (the definitions without the words).

12. Give them special marking pens for filling in the vocabulary words.

13. Inform them to proceed from left to right on the top row, then move to the next row, and so forth. Tell them not to skip around as they fill in the words.

14. Inform the students, also, that if they can't remember a word, to look at the top of Side 1 and read the vocabulary words.

15. Tell them that if that doesn't help, they should turn the sheet over and look at the top of Side 2 where the words and definitions are printed. They are not to resort to either of these aids unless they have to.

16. Conduct a series of timings with these sheets. Ask students to fill in as many answers as they can in 1 minute.

17. Following those timings, request students to turn their sheets over and place them underneath the acetate sheet so that Side 2 is showing. When this is done, the answers on Side 2 match the squares in which the students wrote their answers; thus they are able to check their own work.

18. Tell students to circle the answers that are incorrect and write in the correct answers as they check their papers.

19. Inform them, finally, to count the number of correct and incorrect answers and to plot that number on a chart that is attached to their manila folder.

Verbal-Visual Format

The three verbal techniques that we have recommended for adapting textbook materials have been shown to facilitate the acquisition of new information among mildly handicapped and regular education students. Another approach to modifying textbook materials is to combine a verbal component with a visual component.

Graphic organizers. The term *graphic organizer* (GO) refers to both verbal and visual representation of key vocabulary or content information in which subordinate categories branch off from superordinate categories in the form of tree diagrams (Figure 6). Various terms have been used by researchers to describe the diagrammatic display of information, including graphic organizers, tree diagrams, structured overviews, semantic maps, semantic networks, concept maps, episodic maps, and flow charts, to name a few of the most familiar. The common feature underlying the various graphic terms is the visuospatial arrangement of information containing words or statements that are connected graphically in a meaningful way. Winn (1987) suggested that if words lie at one end of a continuum and realistic pictures at the other, the family of graphic forms is located in the middle.

Graphic organizers, originally called structured overviews, were first developed

UNIT 1, SHEET #1

buoyancy (buo)
displacement (dis)
SI (SI)
standard (stan)
hypothesis (hyp)
observing (ob)
inference (in)
scientific method (s.m.)

Chapter 1: Measuring and Experimenting

Student ________________

Date ________________

Teacher ________________

Period ________________

________ is an international system of units (Metric System).	________ is taking notice and gathering data; using senses to find out things.	A fixed quantity used in measuring is a ________.	________ is a way to determine the volume of an odd-shaped piece of matter.	________ is an international system of units (Metric System).
A ________ is a proposed answer to a question or tentative solution to a problem.	The upward push on an object placed in a liquid is called ________.	A conclusion based on observation is called an ________.	A ________ is a proposed answer to a question or tentative solution to a problem.	The ________ is a way to solve problems: observing, measuring, explaining, and testing.
________ is a way to determine the volume of an odd-shaped piece of matter.	A fixed quantity used in measuring is a ________.	The ________ is a way to solve problems: observing, measuring, explaining, and testing.	A conclusion based on observation is called an ________.	________ is a way to determine the volume of an odd-shaped piece of matter.
A conclusion based on observation is called an ________.	The ________ is a way to solve problems: observing, measuring, explaining, and testing.	________ is an international system of units (Metric System).	________ is taking notice and gathering data; using senses to find out things.	A ________ is a proposed answer to a question or tentative solution to a problem.
A fixed quantity used in measuring is a ________.	The upward push on an object placed in a liquid is called ________.	A fixed quantity used in measuring is a ________.	________ is taking notice and gathering data; using senses to find out things.	The upward push on an object placed in a liquid is called ________.

FIGURE 3. Side 1 of a Precision Teaching sheet containing textbook terms at the top left and their definitions below, printed randomly three or four times across five columns.

buoyancy
displacement
SI
standard
hypothesis
observing
inference
scientific method

= upward push on an object placed in a liquid
= way to determine the volume of an odd-shaped piece of matter
= international system of units (Metric System)
= fixed quantity used in measuring
= proposed answer to a question or tentative solution to a problem
= taking notice and gathering data; using senses to find out things
= conclusion based on observation
= orderly way to solve problems: observing, measuring, explaining, and testing

SI	observing (ob)	standard (stan)	displacement (dis)	SI
hypothesis (hyp)	buoyancy (buo)	inference (in)	hypothesis (hyp)	scientific method (s.m.)
displacement (dis)	standard (stan)	scientific method (s.m.)	inference (in)	displacement (dis)
inference (in)	scientific method (s.m.)	SI	observing (ob)	hypothesis (hyp)
standard (stan)	buoyancy (buo)	standard (stan)	observing (ob)	buoyancy (buo)

FIGURE 4. Side 2 of a Precision Teaching sheet containing textbook terms and their definitions at the top, and the terms that match the definitions presented on Side 1 (Figure 3).

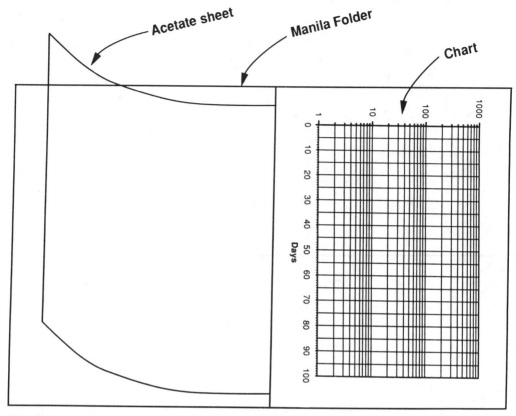

FIGURE 5. A Precision Teaching folder containing an acetate marking sheet and a Standard Behavior Chart for recording student performance.

to increase learner readiness by introducing new vocabulary prior to reading activities (Estes, Mills, & Barron, 1969), and they have their roots in Ausubel's theories and research (e.g., 1960, 1963, 1965) regarding advance organizers. A number of early and recent GO investigations have focused on stabilizing, clarifying, and organizing the prior content knowledge of pupils so that new information is assimilated efficiently. However, a series of such studies has produced inconsistent findings, with students showing improvement on some criterion variables but not on others (Alvermann, 1982; Alvermann & Boothby, 1983; Boothby & alvermann, 1984).

Other researchers have examined the effects of GOs used as introductory materials augmented with questions, study guides, or small-group discussions, or used after content area reading was completed as post organizers. In a meta-analysis of 21 GO studies involving non-handicapped students, Moore and Readence (1984) found GOs to be most beneficial when (a) completed as post organizers, (b) based on specific reading passages rather than on general course content, (c) applied with criterion variables that assessed vocabulary rather than with tests that measured overall comprehension, and (d) used with college-age students.

The theoretical construct underlying the effectiveness of GOs is that they provide a visual and verbal organizational structure that organizes information into a meaningful whole so that it appears to students that they are being taught a series of related terms, facts, or concepts. In essence, the diagrammatic aspect of a GO serves as a nonverbal, visuospatial referent that cues the learner to the

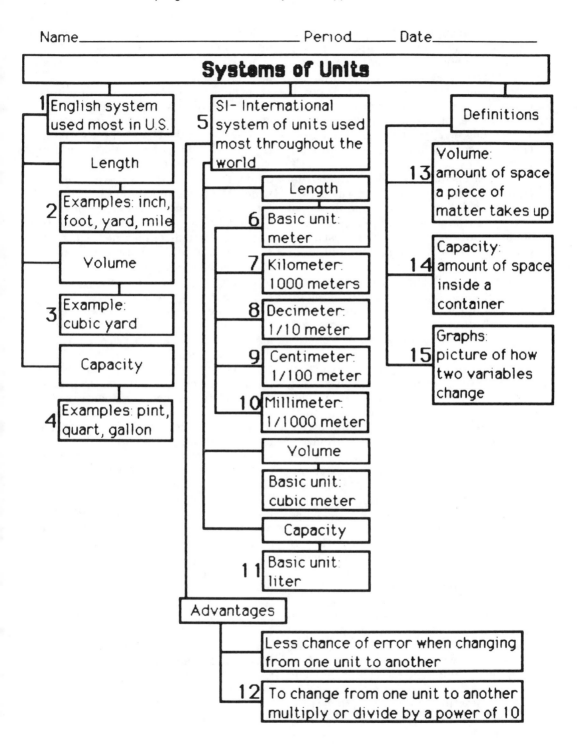

FIGURE 6. A graphic organizer for a reading passage in a middle school science textbook arranged in a hierarchial format.

interrelationships of ideas and to their logical connections to superordinate, equal, or subordinate pieces of information. Evidence exists that, in comparison with nonhandicapped learners, LD pupils experience difficulties in both recall and organization of verbal material (Bauer, 1977; Wong, 1978) but do not differ from them on nonverbal tasks (Vellutino, Harding, Stager, & Phillips, 1975).

Research on GOs was conducted by Horton, Lovitt, and Bergerud (in press), who studied their effects on middle school and high school students in science and social studies classes. Three studies comprised this investigation, and data were obtained on regular, remedial, and LD students. In the first study, the teacher directed most aspects of the treatment, whereas in the second and third studies the students were given more responsibility for developing and studying from the GOs.

There were two conditions in the first study. In one, students were given GOs after they had read a passage in their assigned textbook. For those GOs, all of the boxes and interconnecting lines were available, but much of the information that went in the subordinate categories was left out. The instructor placed an identical copy of the GO on the overhead projector, and conducted from it a lecture over material that had been read. While lecturing, the teacher called on pupils, and they filled in the missing information as a class. When the GOs were completed, the students were given a few minutes to study the material on their own and then were given a test. The format of the test was the incomplete version of the GO; there were 15 items to be filled in.

In the second condition of the study, the students were not given an organizer. They read a different passage from their text and were allowed time to study it by taking notes in a manner of their own choosing. They were encouraged to make an outline, write and answer questions, define terms, or use any other self-study strategy as long as they produced a written product. The students were given as much time for self-study as they had during the GO condition. Following these

sessions, the same type of test was administered that had followed GO sessions; students were given a blank GO and asked to fill it in.

The second and third studies in this series were like the first, except that the students were given more responsibility for developing the GOs. In Study 2, rather than being told which pieces of information belonged in the various spaces, the students were given a cover sheet on which the page and paragraph numbers for the answers in the textbook were printed. In Study 3, the students were simply given a sheet on which clues as to the facts and ideas required to complete the diagram were printed at the bottom of the page. (Figure 7 illustrates the "clues" for the GO in Figure 6.)

As the students filled in the missing information, their teacher circulated about the room and assisted those students who were having trouble. Following those periods of self-directed activity, the teacher placed a completed GO on the overhead and asked the students to check theirs and make the necessary adjustments. The students then were given a few minutes to study the organizers before taking the graphics tests. The alternate treatment in Studies 2 and 3 was the same as that described for the first study.

The results from the three GO studies indicated that this form of textbook modification was effective for LD, remedial, and regular secondary students. Across the three studies, students' average correct scores on tests were significantly higher when GO treatments were in effect than in self-study conditions (LD, 70% vs. 20%; remedial 74% vs. 42%; regular, 86% vs. 56%). Moreover, within each student classification the performances were comparable whether GOs were completed through teacher- or student-directed procedures.

The conclusions of Horton and colleagues regarding the effectiveness of GOs concur with and extend the findings of Moore and Readence (1984). Both groups of researchers found GOs to be effective when used as post organizers based on specific reading passages. Those researchers differed, however, with respect

<u>Worksheet Directions</u>: Study the graphic organizer, paying attention to how the boxes are arranged and connected by the lines. Then, beginning with number 1, (a) read the information in the box; (b) look for the answer on the list of "clues"; (c) check the answer with information in the book; and (d) write the answer in the box. If no information is given in a box, look at the information in connected boxes as a guide before locating the answer on the list of "clues," checking the answer with information in the book, and writing the answer in the box. Each of the 15 clues is an answer to be placed in one of the boxes.

<u>List of "Clues"</u>

- 1/1000 meter
- inch, foot, yard, mile
- amount of space a piece of matter takes up
- amount of space inside a container
- used most in U.S.
- 1/100 meter
- pint, quart, gallon
- liter
- meter
- used most throughout the world
- multiply or divide by a power of ten
- picture of how two variables change
- cubic yard
- 1/10 meter
- 1000 meters

FIGURE 7. Worksheet directions for a student-directed graphic organizer with clues.

to conclusions as to who benefited the most. Whereas Moore and Readence concluded that GOs were most effective with regular college students for learning vocabulary, Horton and co-workers concluded that GOs were most effective with low-achieving and regular secondary students for mastering general course content.

To assist teachers in constructing GOs from textbook materials and in offering them to heterogeneous groups, Horton and Lovitt (1989b) have suggested a four-step process:

1. Select and divide the chapters to be modified into reading passages of about 1,500 words. Begin by choosing material that has proven difficult for students or that is clearly lacking good organization.

2. Construct an outline of the main ideas in the reading passage.

3. Choose a GO format that matches the structure of the information, for example, a hierarchical (Figure 6) or compare-contrast (Figure 8) format.

4. Prepare a teacher's version of the GO that contains all of the information in the diagram, and a students' version for which some information from certain categories

(e.g., superordinate–subordinate, compare–contrast) is missing. Several excellent commercial software programs are available for developing graphics, such as Macpaint (Atkinson, 1985), Macdraw (Cutter, 1985), MORE (1986), and Superpaint (Snider, Zocher, & Jackson, 1986).

In implementing GOs, teachers may choose to present them before students read an instructional unit of text, or during or after the reading of a passage. We have presented examples of the use of GOs almost exclusively after students had read a unit of text. Graphic organizers can be completed as a teacher-directed activity, a student-directed activity with text references (page and/or paragraph numbers), or as a student-directed activity with a list of clues attached (answers that complete the diagram are provided on a cover sheet in random order).

Visual–spatial displays. Another way to adapt textbooks, or more generally to organize information, that has proven effective with low-achieving students is to prepare visual–spatial displays, which combine line drawings with words to convey facts and concepts or to express relationships between pieces of information. On an information continuum with words at one end and realistic pictures at the other, visual–spatial displays move from the midpoint, where graphic organizers are found, to a point closer to realistic pictures.

The contention that LD students may benefit more from graphically than from verbally presented information has been corroborated in studies investigating the use of visual–spatial displays. In research conducted by Bergerud, Lovitt, and Horton (1988), textbook passages were adapted in two ways for LD and remedial students in a ninth-grade science class. In one condition, students were required to read a passage from a science textbook and to complete a study guide made up of written questions from the passage. In another condition, the students read a different passage from the science text and completed visual displays (line drawings with words attached) of the human heart. On the tests for each condition, half of the items were presented in a verbal format as multiple-choice questions, and half of them were presented as visual displays.

The results indicated that the visual display treatment produced significantly higher performance on graphics test items than the study guide condition, but there was no significant difference between treatments on multiple-choice test items. In that study, 61% of students mastered the test material (i.e., scored > 80%) in the visual display condition, and 41% of them achieved mastery in the study guide treatment.

Visual–spatial displays have also been implemented through direct instruction and cooperative learning approaches, whereby students are taught content information through game formats. Following is a list of steps for developing and presenting visual–spatial displays as set forth by Engelmann and colleagues (Engelmann, Davis, & Davis, 1982):

1. Read the text passage carefully and identify the major theme of the unit. In Figure 9, for example, the major theme was "animals and vegetation at various levels."

2. Identify the key ideas that are most related to that theme. In the example, the key words were "vegetation," "animals," and "industries."

3. Place those key words on the top of the display: one on the left, one in the middle, and one on the right.

4. Identify the words or ideas that are subsumed by those subordinate words. In the example, note the graphic information about how vegetation changes as one goes up a mountain. Underneath "animals," several specific animals that live on mountains are pictured and labeled. Underneath "industries," there is a box for "mining," "lumber," and "tourism."

5. Divide the class into teams and give each student a copy of a completed visual–spatial display.

6. Discuss the theme, the subordinate topics, and the related items. Tie all the information together. Engage the students in a conversation about the theme.

Name_____ Period_____ Date_____

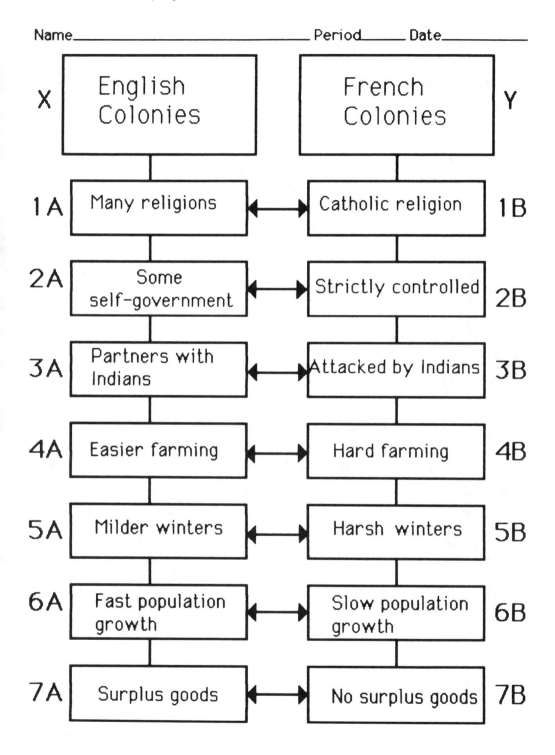

FIGURE 8. A graphic organizer for a reading passage in a middle school social studies text arranged in a compare-contrast format.

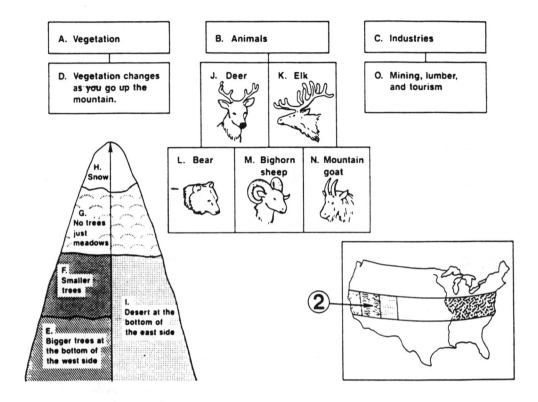

FIGURE 9. An example of a visual spatial display used to teach social studies and science information to elementary school students. *Note.* From "Teaching Content Area Material to Learning Disabled Students" by C. B. Darch and D. W. Carnine, 1986, *Exceptional Children,* 53(3), p. 243. Copyright 1986 by the Council for Exceptional Children. Reprinted by permission.

7. Ask the students to put away their completed diagrams; hand out a graphic to them on which none of the words or pictures are printed. On these, only letters are printed in the boxes.

8. Take turns with the groups of students. The first student rolls a pair of dice and says the word(s) that complete(s) the blank for the item on the graphic that corresponds to the number on the dice. If the answer is correct, that side is given a point. Then a student on the other team rolls the dice, provides an answer, and so forth.

The use of visual–spatial displays implemented through a game format was examined by Darch and Carnine (1986), who studied 24 fourth-, fifth-, and sixth-grade LD students, all of whom were in resource rooms. The youngsters were randomly assigned to one of two treatment groups. Half were in the visual–display group and half were in the textbook group. All the students were presented material over three units from their social studies or science textbooks.

The study took place over a 9-day period. The students in the visual–spatial group followed a regimen much like that described earlier. Initially, the graphic was presented to them on an overhead projector; the students followed along with their completed display while the teacher described the various cells in the display; the students were given displays with all the words deleted and divided into groups of three or four; then they took turns throwing the dice and naming the items on the display that corresponded to their dice roll.

The following procedures were in effect for the students in the text group: (a) The material was initially presented by the teacher, who led a discussion; (b) groups of students were formed; (c) the students first read the headings and subheadings; and (d) the students discussed the answers to those questions as a group.

On probe tests that were given after each unit, the visual–spatial group scored significantly higher than the text group. And on a posttest measure the visual–spatial group had a mean of 86% correct and the text group, a mean of 56% correct.

Mnemonic keywords involving thematic illustrations. Another technique for helping low-achieving students learn unfamiliar academic material, one that appears at approximately the same point on the verbal-graphics continuum as visual–spatial displays, is the mnemonic keywords approach when coupled with thematic illustrations. That procedure utilizes a combination of selected words and line drawings to facilitate direct recall of factual information.

Instruction in mnemonic (memory-facilitating) strategies designed to help low-achieving students learn factual information have appeared in the recent special education literature (Mastropieri, Scruggs, McLoone, & Levin, 1985). The rationale for mnemonics training rests on studies that suggest that many mildly handicapped students have deficiencies in short- and long-term memory and in the ability to produce memory strategies spontaneously (e.g., Torgesen & Kail, 1980).

Training in the use of keywords is often one component of a mnemonics approach. The use of keywords, presented in conjunction with thematic illustrations (line drawings), is an associative mnemonic technique that derives its strength from having a verbal and a visual component. That process has been described by Levin (1983) as consisting of three Rs: recoding, relating, and retrieving. To illustrate, according to Mastropieri, Scruggs, McLoone, and Levin (1985), if one were to teach the concept that Zeus was the king of the gods, the three R's of the keyword method using thematic illustrations would be implemented by having the learner follow these steps:

1. *Recode* the stimulus, Zeus, into a common, easily pictured, similar-sounding keyword. An appropriate keyword for Zeus is "zoo" because it is easily pictured and sounds much like the stimulus, Zeus.

2. *Relate* the transformed stimulus, *zoo*, to the to-be-associated response, *king*, by using an interactive picture or thematic illustration. For example, a king is pictured in a zoo (Figure 10).

3. *Retrieve* the information that Zeus was king of the gods, when asked about Zeus, by remembering the keyword "zoo" and associating it with the picture of the zoo containing a king.

The effectiveness of the mnemonic keyword approach with thematic illustrations was investigated in a study by Mastropieri, Scruggs, McLoone, and Levin (1985), that involved 36 seventh- and eighth-grade LD students. They were taught three dichotomous classifications for each of eight minerals: hardness level (hard–soft), color (pale–dark), and common use (home–industry). In that research, the students were placed randomly in one of three treatment groups — mnemonic instruction with key words and thematic illustrations, direct instruction, or free study — each group being presented the same list of eight minerals and their attributes.

For the mnemonics condition, each mineral and attribute combination was represented by a black-and-white line drawing that appeared on an 8½″ × 11″ sheet. Each thematic illustration contained a representation of the keyword interacting with a home or factory scene to show the use of the mineral; a baby or an old man to indicate whether the mineral was soft (baby) or hard (old man), and the keyword figure was either blackened (for dark color) or not blackened (for pale color). Students in that group were taught all of those symbols and relationships.

The students in the direct instruction condition were also given an 8½″ × 11″ sheet

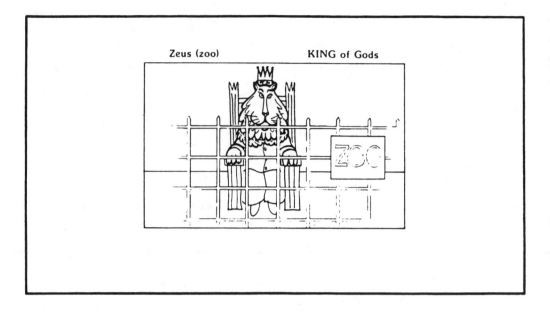

FIGURE 10. Mnemonic representation for Zeus (king of Gods) involving a thematic illustration. *Note.* **From "Facilitating Learning Disabled Students' Acquisition of Science Classifications" by M. A. Mastropieri, T. E. Scruggs, B. McLoone, and J. R. Levin, 1985,** *Learning Disability Quarterly, 8,* **p. 300. Copyright 1985 by the Council for Learning Disabiliites. Reprinted by permission.**

on which there were line drawings that represented the minerals themselves. For this condition, the experimenter showed the pictures to the students, explained each item, asked them to repeat what was said, took away the pictures, repeated the questions and prompts, and provided corrective feedback as necessary.

For the free-study condition, students were given a single 8½" × 11" sheet on which the mineral names and associated attributes were written. The experimenter explained the items on the list to the students and told them to read the list over and over, write down relevant information, cover up part of the list and test themselves, and use any other method they considered to be helpful.

The students in all groups were given the same amount of instruction time. Furthermore, they were told that they were to learn the information as well as they could, for a quiz would be given at the end of the session.

Data from the research were gathered with respect to three attributes: hardness level, color, and use. When the data were collapsed across the three attributes, the average total score of the students in the mnemonic group (95%) was significantly higher than the scores for students in both the free study (77%) and the direct instruction group (64%).

Computer-Assisted Instruction

Up to this point, we have discussed three verbal techniques for adapting textbook passages (advance organizers, vocabulary drills, and study guides), and three verbal-visual techniques (graphic organizers, visual-spatial displays, and mnemonics with thematic illustrations). The final category of techniques that we recommend for adapting or organizing textbook information for academically handicapped students is the use of computer-assisted instruction (CAI).

Using CAI to teach academic material to adolescents with learning handicaps would appear to be a common instructional technique, given present microcomputer technology and the availability of computers. As reported by Blaschke (1986), the number of microcomputers in classrooms for LD pupils in the United States has increased from 60,000 in 1983 to 200,000 in 1985. Unfortunately, teachers rarely rely on microcomputers to teach science, social studies, health, or other subjects other than math to students with learning handicaps in mainstream classes (Cosden, Gerber, Semmel, Goldman, & Semmel, 1987).

Three reasons have been advanced for the underutilization of microcomputers to teach content material to students with academic handicaps. First, a few efficacy studies have reported little difference between CAI and traditional instruction (Edwards, Norton, Taylor, Weiss, & Dusseldorp, 1975; McDermott & Watkins, 1983). Second, since the content to be taught varies from teacher to teacher, individual effort is involved in putting content into existing software shells, and some programming knowledge is required to write the necessary coursework. Third, some schools do not have sufficient numbers of computers to accommodate students, and in situations where hardware is abundant (e.g., computer labs), scheduling students from content classes can be difficult.

While there are conceptual and practical obstacles to incorporating CAI on a wide basis with academically handicapped students, progress has been made in isolating instructional and design variables that have proven effective in software construction and user interface (how the computer and user interact). Those variables include self-pacing, frequent responding, correction, feedback, and sequenced instruction (Budoff, Thormann, & Grass, 1984); the use of relatively small teaching sets, cumulative review, and computerized pretests (Johnson, Gersten, & Carnine, 1987); the use of mouse-controlled responding (Horton, Lovitt, & Slocum, 1988); and easy directions, with responses configured to focus student attention (Lee, 1987).

While teachers may use CAI to achieve a variety of objectives, including those considered academic, social, motivational, or recreational, we will discuss the use of that technology to impart content information normally presented by textbooks.

Our research on CAI at the University of Washington evolved from attempts to replicate on microcomputer some of the previous textbook modification research that we found to be effective when presented through pencil-and-paper activities. Specifically, we will discuss three types of computer-assisted programs that have been designed to teach low-performing and regular education students unfamiliar academic information: (a) a vocabulary exercise; (b) a graphics tutorial; and (c) two variants of a study guide.

Vocabulary exercise. Using an experimental computer program that incorporated the proven instructional design features noted previously, Horton, Lovitt, and Givens (1988) conducted a two-experiment study designed to investigate the effects of using CAI to teach textbook terminology to high school students. In Experiment 1, a pretest–posttest design was utilized involving 19 students enrolled in a ninth-grade world geography class. Six students were LD and 13 were classified as remedial by the school district (i.e., they scored at the 40th percentile or below on both the quantitative and the verbal subtests of the Metropolitan Achievement Test). The setting was a computer lab containing 24 Macintosh 512K enhanced computers.

From a 35-item pretest, 28 geography terms (e.g., geyser, atoll, wadi) were randomly selected for inclusion in a computer program, and seven terms were used as control items that appeared on the posttests but not in the computer program. The 28 terms in the computer program were presented in four sets of seven items.

The computerized vocabulary program was self-paced. In summary, the students: (a) completed as many seven-word sets as possible within a 30-minute period, working through a pretest-practice-posttest sequence by clicking on buttons containing vocabulary words that

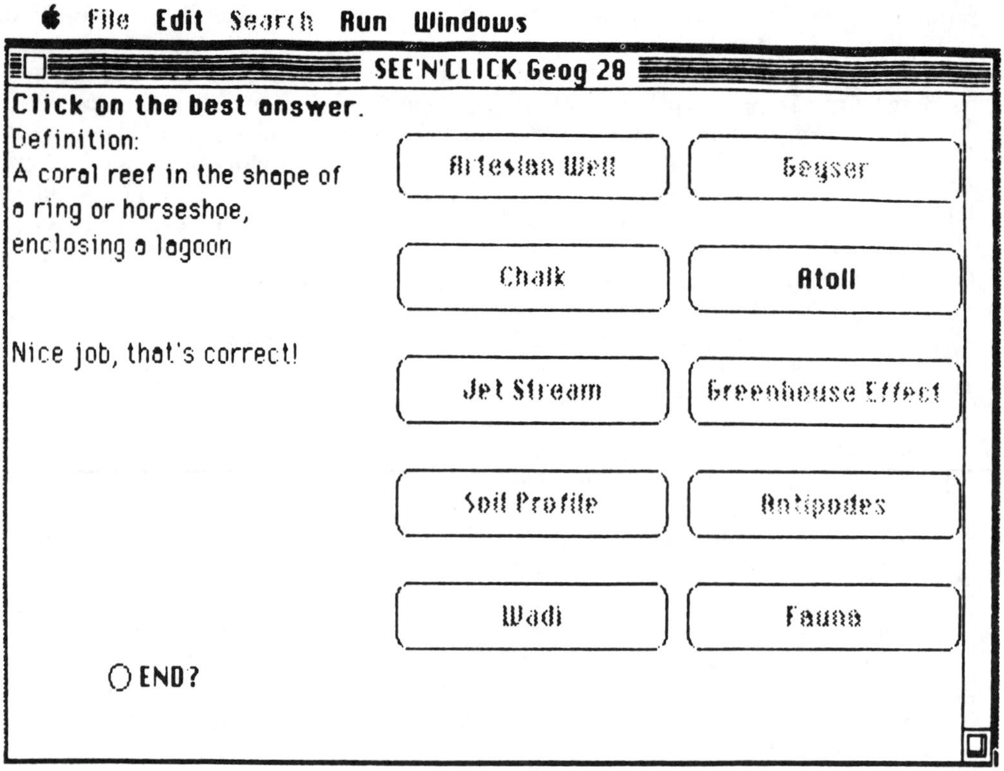

⌘ File Edit Search Run Windows

SEE'N'CLICK Geog 28

Click on the best answer.

Definition:
A coral reef in the shape of
a ring or horseshoe,
enclosing a lagoon

Nice job, that's correct!

Artesian Well	Geyser
Chalk	**Atoll**
Jet Stream	Greenhouse Effect
Soil Profile	Antipodes
Wadi	Fauna

○ END?

FIGURE 11. A screenful in the computerized vocabulary program containing the definition of a term in the upper left and ten terms presented in two columns on the right.

---

matched definitions that appeared in the upper left corner of the computer screen (Figure 11); and (b) took up to 20 minutes to complete a written posttest. They completed the written posttest at their individual work stations in the computer lab after the computers had been turned off. All students were provided three 30-minute computer sessions on consecutive school days.

The results of Experiment 1 indicated a significant gain on computer items after the second session for the LD students, and after the first session for remedial pupils. Performance on control items did not improve across measures for either group. On the final assessment, LD students averaged 68% correct on computer items and 29% correct on control items. The corresponding scores for the remedial pupils were 80% correct on computer items and 27% on control items.

In Experiment 2, a pretest–posttest control group design was arranged to investigate the effects of the same computer program when used to teach health terms (e.g., embryo, endometrium, hypoglycemia) to regular education high school students. The results were similar to the first experiment: On the average, students in the experimental group answered 75% of items correctly on the second posttest, whereas their counterparts in the control group selected 38% of the items correctly.

Graphics tutorial. In a study that blended both verbal and visual components with the proven design features of CAI, Horton, Lovitt, and Slocum (1988) examined the effectiveness of two treatments designed to teach the locations of major cities in Asia. Twenty-eight Asian cities were randomly assigned to two treatments in a repeated measures design. In one intervention, the students were presented the locations of 14 cities in Asia (e.g., Ulaan Baatar, Beijing, Bangkok) by completing a computerized map tutorial. In the other condition, the same students were asked to learn the locations of 14 different cities in Asia by referencing an atlas and transcribing that information to a workmap.

The participants consisted of 27 students, 12 of whom were LD and 15, remedial, who attended two ninth-grade world geography classes taught by the same teacher. The settings were the students' regular classroom (the same room was used in two different periods) and a computer lab located next to the classroom that contained 25 Macintosh computers.

The general procedure consisted of administering the two treatments to each class in a counterbalanced order. To summarize the steps that were followed to implement the atlas condition, students were allowed 30 minutes, using an atlas containing a map of the Far East, to transcribe and study the locations of 14 cities on a workmap; and 15 minutes to take a posttest that required the students to match numbers on an identical blank map to the names of the cities.

To implement the computerized map tutorial, students worked the map tutorial as many times as possible within a 30-minute period. During that time the locations of cities were taught by presenting a darkened arrow that pointed to the location of the city on an outline map of the Far East (Figure 12), followed by the program requiring them to locate the city when the arrow was removed by positioning the mouse on the correct location and clicking. Fourteen cities were presented in that manner involving repetitious loops that provided opportunity for overlearning. Then the students took up to 15 minutes to complete the posttest map at their work stations in the computer lab after the computers had been turned off.

For both LD and remedial students, treatment with the computer program produced significantly higher scores than treatment with the atlas. The LD students averaged 85% correct on posttests following the computer program and 19% correct on posttests following the atlas treatment. The figures for the remedial pupils were 86% correct in the computer treatment and 22% correct in the atlas condition. Within treatments, no significant difference was noted in the performance of the two groups.

Study guides. The purpose of a study by Horton, Lovitt, and Givens (1988) was to determine if the effects of a teacher-directed study guide (described above in the Verbal Format: Study Guides section) could be replicated on microcomputer. Again, the experimental groups consisted of two classes of ninth-grade students, 13 LD and 10 remedial, who were enrolled in a world geography class. The students in each experimental class received two treatments, self-study and a computerized study guide, the order of treatments being counterbalanced across classes. The settings were the students' regular classroom and the same computer lab, located next to the classroom.

In the self-study condition, students were required to read (and reread) a textbook passage of approximately 1,000 words on Canadian history for 15 minutes, to study the passage by taking notes in a manner of their own choosing for 15 minutes, and to take a 15-item multiple-choice test for up to 10 minutes. In summary, in the computer program students: (a) read a different passage of comparable length from the same textbook presented by computer for up to 15 minutes; (b) took 15 minutes to complete two times (mandatory) a computerized study guide that presented 15 study guide questions and, for each item, was required to read the question, respond silently, and push **Return** to check the answer; and (c) were given up to 10 minutes to complete a multiple-choice test on the computer.

The comparability of test difficulty between treatments was controlled by administering each assessment to a neutral group of LD and remedial stu-

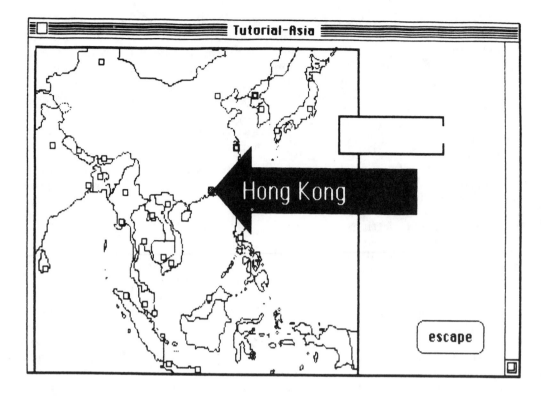

FIGURE 12. A screenful in the computerized map tutorial presenting the location of Hong Kong.

dents, and assigning the test thus found to be more difficult (and the accompanying passage), to the computer treatment, thus intentionally handicapping what was hypothesized to be the stronger of the two treatments. The results of the experiment significantly favored the computerized study guide over self-study for both LD students (76%, 42%) and remedial pupils (77%, 58%), providing a replication of the earlier study involving a teacher-directed study guide.

More recent research has addressed the effectiveness of computerized study guides developed in a *hypertext* format, a generic term for high-level software that allows users to explore information in a nonlinear and interactive fashion (Megarry, 1988). In a hypertext format, a study guide page might be thought of as several sheets of transparency film overlying each other. The surface layer not only provides the primary text to be read by the stu-

dents, but also serves as a menu for accessing additional information. This layering allows the students to access a variety of instructional concepts selectively. When the cursor is positioned on specific areas of the top layer, the appropriate layers beneath become accessible. Selecting a word with the cursor could provide the word's definition, its pronunciation (either phonetically or through voice simulation), or a graphic related to the word that would serve as a visual embellishment. Two hypertext authoring systems that are currently available for use with microcomputers are Guide (Dougan, 1986), and HyperCard (Atkinson, 1987).

Higgins (1988), while a doctoral student at the University of Washington, investigated the effects of hypertext study guide material in an experiment involving 40 students (LD, remedial, and regular) who studied Washington State history at the ninth grade level. The students were

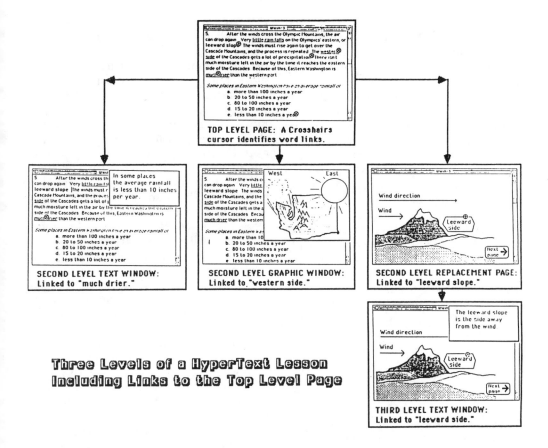

FIGURE 13. An example of three levels of a hypertext lesson, with word links between screenfuls shown by crosshairs in text. *Note.* From "Hypertext Computer-Assisted Instruction and the Social Studies Achievement of Learning Disabled, Remedial, and Regular Education Students" by A. K. Higgins, 1988. Unpublished doctoral dissertation. University of New Mexico. Reprinted by permission.

randomly assigned to one of three instructional groups: lecture only (LO), lecture/hypertext (LH), and hypertext only (HO). The settings were the student's regular classroom and a computer lab located next to the classroom.

In the LO group, the material was presented by the teacher in a lecture-discussion format. Students in the HO group received instruction by hypertext study guides on Macintosh 512K enhanced computers. The study guides were constructed so that students could access special enhancements regarding words, graphics, concepts, charts, or maps within the reading material. (In Figure 13, for example, a reading passage is shown at the top that contains crosshairs identifying links to special enhancements; by clicking on the crosshairs, students are provided additional explanations for the phrases *much drier, western side,* and *leeward slope* as illustrated.) The LH students received lecture instruction from the teacher and then worked with the hypertext study guides for the remainder of the instructional period. All students were presented exactly the same information for the same amount of time, only the instructional format being different.

The students in the three groups took a pretest, 10 daily quizzes, a posttest, and a retention test over the materials covered in the lessons. The results indicated that the HO treatment produced the highest average correct scores on the 10 daily quizzes for all types of students: LD, 68%; remedial, 81%; and regular, 84%. The superior average performance of the HO group was also evidenced on both the posttest and the retention test, while the average score was higher for the LO group than the LH group on the posttest, a pattern that was reversed on the retention test, the average of the LH group being higher than for the LO group.

A wider application of hypertext technology, beyond its use for study guides, would involve using computers to access huge data bases or stores of knowledge in much the same way that students might utilize the resources of a large library system containing many branches. Just as a student might begin an information search at a card catalogue in a library, a user in a hypertext system would begin by selecting from options provided on primary menus on the computer screen; those menus would be connected to other menus, producing a network of information accessible by positioning and clicking a cursor. Hypertext systems could allow users to interact with information by choosing text, graphics, or voice, depending on how the system was constructed and the type of information desired. While the vision of hypertext systems linking and making accessible most of the world's known knowledge may seem grandiose, when such technology is viewed as converging with innovations in information storage, such as compact disks, the possibilities are indeed enormous.

DISCUSSION

We have presented a number of methods for adapting materials for LD and other low-achieving students, many of which were also arranged to increase the academic performances of average and above-average students. We did not recommend rewriting textbooks to make them easier to read or taping textual material, because neither approach addresses the organization of the material, which is the central requirement of textbook modification. The methods we did recommend were subsumed under three categories: verbal, visual–verbal, and computer-assisted instruction. Furthermore, within each category we presented three techniques for adapting materials, each of which was supported by at least one empirical investigation that has been published in an educational journal. We now will address some practical considerations for each of the techniques that were promoted. Before doing that, however, we will briefly extend our earlier views on the necessity of adapting textbook materials for low-achieving students, and discuss several approaches that teachers might consider to accomplish the additional labor involved in such an undertaking.

In the past, one of the responsibilities of special education teachers who served mildly handicapped students in the public schools was to recommend the placement of those students, to the extent possible, in regular education classes. While the need for such advocacy still exists, problems of access have given way to issues of curriculum and instruction. A more common problem today is how to help Zach, an LD seventh grader, comprehend his social studies textbook. To the extent that school personnel can achieve such a task, the greater the likelihood that Zach will stay in school and feel good about it. According to Rumberger (1987), two of the prime reasons for dropping out of school are poor performance and disliking school, both of which are related to grades. It follows that if youngsters are encouraged to stay in school longer, they and society will benefit.

The biggest problem in adapting materials or modifying other instructional features is that many teachers, particularly those at the secondary level, where there is the greatest need for modifications, are not inclined to do so. There is a tendency among some secondary teachers to feel that they have been prepared to teach a subject area and not children. Unlike their counterparts at the elementary level, those secondary teachers are not generally as sensitive to individual differences. Hence, they are not as inclined to make adjustments in their materials and styles of teaching or grading for their pupils. Certainly, there is reason for secondary teachers to feel this way, as frequently they have heavy class loads and many subjects to prepare for.

The most common response that we receive in workshops designed to train secondary teachers in the various methods of adapting textbook materials is: "I can see that this would really help my students, particularly the slow ones, but when will I find the time for this?" This is indeed a thorny issue. The following, however, are some effective approaches for efficiently modifying materials: (a) Work with building or district personnel to develop small (15 or fewer pupils) "basic track" classes that contain LD and remedial-type students, thereby reducing student heterogeneity and affording a more uniform focus on materials; (b) Modify only textbook chapters or passages within chapters that have proven difficult for students or that are clearly lacking good organization; (c) Collaborate with other teachers who use the same text by dividing the materials modification load and sharing materials; (d) Use curriculum-based assessments prior to instruction to determine which students can interact with the text at an independent level and which students will need materials modifications; (e) Computerize the materials adaptation process by using commercial software, thereby developing a continuous and changing store of materials; (f) Encourage regular and special teachers to co-teach certain subjects and to modify the materials cooperatively; and (g) Urge teachers, through textbook adoption committees, to demand that publishing companies begin to offer study guides, graphic organizers, computer programs, or other condensations of material in addition to basic textbooks.

Perhaps the line of least resistance for increasing the performance of mildly handicapped students in regular education classrooms is to use modification techniques that are powerful enough to help all students. Each of the verbal techniques we endorsed — advance organizers, study guides, and vocabulary drills — have been shown to improve the academic performance of academically handicapped and regular education students.

Advance organizers, when viewed as any activity used to introduce new material, may take the form of a summary, graphic organizer, vocabulary exercise, oral discussion, or directed-reading activity that is applicable for all students. By choosing to use advance organizers, teachers focus on building effective links between the information students bring to a learning task and the parameters of the material to be learned.

If we could make only one recommendation among the many techniques we have espoused, we would suggest using *study guides* because of their versatility and ease of construction. To develop a study guide, the teacher selects the most critical information and places it on a worksheet in either a question or statement format and directs the student to learn it, either independently, as a cooperative effort, such as in a study by Meadows (1988), or as a teacher-directed activity. The key to using study guides effectively is for teachers to construct test items that relate directly to the guide material.

Vocabulary drills are fast-paced activities that teach the language of a subject, and are enjoyable for students when presented in a precision teaching format that involves students in charting their daily progress. Two oral variations of the vocabulary drill presented above that directs students to write responses on acetate sheets would be to use flash cards with terms written on one side and their definitions on the other, which could be studied individually or in groups, or "say fact" sheets, with which students study in pairs. To implement the say fact procedure, each member of a pair holds the same study sheet: One looks only at terms written along the left-hand fold of a sheet and "says" their corresponding definitions as fast as possible; the other conducts a

1-minute timing, assessing the accuracy of the oral responses by following the definitions printed along the right-hand fold. Then the partners switch roles. The resulting "say fact" rates are plotted on Standard Behavior Charts as part of an ongoing assessment procedure that uses the conventions of Precision Teaching.

Generally, modifying materials through visual–verbal techniques requires more labor than verbal methods, but they have the added benefit of student appeal. We have found that student interest in these types of materials is very high, possibly because they represent a welcome change from a steady diet of verbally oriented lessons. With practice, teachers develop a critical eye for which types of materials lend themselves to modification by a visual–verbal method. For example, textbooks in social studies, science, and health are filled with sections that can be neatly organized by *graphic organizers* of either a hierarchical (i.e., superordinate/subordinate arrangement) or compare-contrast format.

Most textbooks seem to use charts and tables, both of which are forms of graphic organizers, not as selected formats that clearly display information, but as embellishments to break up the monotony of several pages of verbal materials. We have found tabular formats to be extremely effective across subject areas and student classifications. To implement graphic organizers in a tabular format, some information is selectively removed on the students' copy, and they are directed to focus on the categorical relationships between pieces of information when completing the graphic using their textbooks. A few researchers (e.g., Meyer, Brandt, & Bluth, 1980) have provided evidence that students acquire more information of a higher level if taught from a compare-contrast format than from other text structures.

Visual–spatial displays have been shown to be quite effective with mildly handicapped students and have a great deal to recommend them in terms of flexibility in testing formats (i.e., graphic or verbal) and method of implementation (i.e., traditional instruction or direct instruction with cooperative learning). Students seem to particularly enjoy this technique when it is implemented through a game format.

Mnemonic keywords with thematic illustrations have the advantage of potentially offering the student a cognitive strategy that, if taught in a generic manner, may be applied by students to other learning tasks. Associative memory techniques of this type have wide application in higher education as students are faced with coursework requirements that entail heavy information loads.

While there are some limitations to *computer-assisted instruction*, including compatibility of hardware and software in the dissemination of materials, necessity for computer programming skills, and access to computers, we have found CAI to be an effective approach at an individual building level. Given the current interest in microcomputers in our society, it is not unusual to find competent hackers among the teaching ranks who would be interested in contributing to computerizing the teaching of content information. Each of the CAI programs that we developed at the University of Washington and studied experimentally (i.e., computerized vocabulary, map tutorials, and study guides) was developed by a computer buff, not a high-powered commercial programmer. We believe that the key to beginning such a process within a school is for staff members to discuss common needs and to look for ways to provide support for interested personnel by providing them both release time and stipends to utilize their talents.

Underlying the various methods for modifying textbooks that we have discussed, and the arguments that we have made for the necessity of such material adjustments for low-achieving students, is the premise that rarely, if ever, can all of the pertinent information in a textbook be successfully taught to heterogeneous groups in an unmodified state. To accept this premise is to elevate the organization of information to an equal status with its content.

REFERENCES

Alvermann, D. E. (1982). Restructuring text facilitates written recall of main ideas. *Journal of Reading, 25*(8), 754-758.

Alvermann, D. E., & Boothby, P. R. (1983). A preliminary investigation of the differences in children's retention of "inconsiderate" text. *Reading Psychology, 4,* 237-246.

Anderson, R. C., & Biddle, W. B. (1975). On asking people questions about what they are reading. In G. Bower (Ed.), *Psychology of learning and motivation* (Vol. 9, pp. 89-132). New York: Academic Press.

Atkinson, B. (1985). *MacPaint* [Computer program]. Cupertino, CA: Apple Computer.

Atkinson, B. (1987). *HyperCard* [Computer program]. Cupertino, CA: Apple Computer.

Ausubel, D. P. (1960). The use of advance organizers in the learning and retention of meaningful verbal material. *Journal of Educational Psychology, 63,* 267-272.

Ausubel, D. P. (1963). *The psychology of meaningful verbal learning.* New York: Grune & Stratton.

Ausubel, D. P., & Anderson, R. (1965). *Readings in the psychology of cognition.* New York: Holt, Rinehart, & Winston.

Bauer, R. (1977). Memory processes in children with learning disabilities: Evidence for deficient rehearsal. *Journal of Experimental Child Psychology, 24,* 415-430.

Bergerud, D., Lovitt, T. C., & Horton, S. V. (1988). The effectiveness of textbook adaptations in life science for high school students with learning disabilities. *Journal of Learning Disabilities, 21*(2), 70-76.

Blaschke, C. (1986). Technology for special education: A national strategy. *T.H.E. Journal, 13*(6), 77-82.

Boothby, P. R., & Alvermann, D. E. (1984). Classroom training study: The effects of graphic organizer instruction on fourth grader's comprehension. *Reading World, 23*(4), 325-329.

Budoff, M., Thormann, J., & Grass, A. (1984). *Microcomputers in special education.* Cambridge, MA: Brookline Books.

California Achievement Test. (1985). Monterey, CA: CTB/McGraw-Hill.

Cheek, E. H., & Cheek, M. C. (1983). *Reading instruction through content teaching.* Columbus, OH: Merrill.

Cosden, M. A., Gerber, M. M., Semmel, D. S., Goldman, S. R., & Semmel, M. I. (1987). Microcomputer use within micro-educational environments. *Exceptional Children, 53*(8), 399-409.

Cutter, M. (1985). *MacDraw* [Computer program]. Cupertino, CA: Apple Computer.

Darch, C., & Carnine, D. (1986). Teaching content area material to learning disabled students. *Exceptional Children, 53,* 240-246.

Davison, A. (1984). Readability — Appraising text difficulty. In R. C. Anderson, J. Osborn, & R. J. Tierney (Eds.), *Learning to read in American schools: Basal readers and content texts* (pp. 121-139). Hillsdale, NJ: Erlbaum.

Deshler, D. D., & Graham, S. (1980). Tape recording educational materials for secondary handicapped students. *Teaching Exceptional Children, 12,* 52-54.

Dougan, G. (1986). *Guide* [Computer program]. Bellevue, MA: Owl International.

Earle, R. A. (1969). Developing and using study guides. In H. L. Herber & P. L. Sanders (Eds.), *Research in reading in the content areas: First year report* (pp. 71-92). Syracuse, NY: University of Syracuse Reading and Languages Arts Center.

Eaton, M., & Lovitt, T. C. (1972). Achievement tests vs. direct and daily measurement. In G. Semb (Ed.), *Behavior analysis and education* (pp. 78-87). Lawrence, KS: University of Kansas, Department of Human Development.

Edwards, J., Norton, S., Taylor, S., Weiss, M., & Dusseldorp, R. (1975). How effective is CAI? A review of research. *Educational Leadership, 11,* 147-153.

Englemann, S., Davis, G., & Davis, K. (1982). *Your world of facts.* Portland, OR: C and C Publications.

Estes, T. H., Mills, D. C., & Barron, R. F. (1969). Three methods of introducing students to a reading-learning task in two content subjects. In H. L. Herber & P. L. Sanders (Eds.), *Research in reading in the content areas: First year report* (pp. 40-48). Syracuse, NY: University of Syracuse Reading and Language Arts Center.

Fry, E. (1968). A readability formula that saves time. *Journal of Reading, 11,* 513-516, 575-578.

Hamaker, C. (1986). The effects of adjunct questions on prose learning. *Review of Educational Research, 56*(2), 212-242.

Herber, H. L. (1970). *Teaching reading in content areas.* Englewood Cliffs, NJ: Prentice-Hall.

Higgins, A. K. (1988). *Hypertext computer-assisted instruction and the social studies achievement of learning disabled, remedial, and regular education students.* Unpublished doctoral dissertation, University of New Mexico, Albuquerque.

Horton, S. V., & Lovitt, T. C. (1989). Using study guides with three classifications of secondary students. *Journal of Special Education, 22*, 447-462.

Horton, S. V., & Lovitt, T. C. (1989a). Construction and implementation of graphic organizers for academically handicapped and regular secondary students. *Academic Therapy, 24*(5), 625-641.

Horton, S. V., Lovitt, T. C., & Bergerud, D. (in press). The effectiveness of graphic organizers for three classifications of secondary students in content-area classes. *Journal of Learning Disabilities.*

Horton, S. V., Lovitt, T. C., & Givens, A. (1988). A computer-based vocabulary program for three categories of students. *The British Journal of Educational Technology, 19*(2), 131-143.

Horton, S. V., Lovitt, T. C., Givens, A., & Nelson, R. (1989). Teaching social studies to high school students with academic handicaps in a mainstreamed setting: Effects of a computerized study guide. *Journal of Learning Disabilities, 22*(2), 102-107.

Horton, S. V., Lovitt, T. C., & Slocum, T. (1988). Teaching geography to high school students with academic deficits: Effects of a computerized map tutorial. *Learning Disability Quarterly, 11*(4), 371-379.

Johnson, G., Gersten, R., & Carnine, D. (1987). Effects of instructional design variables on vocabulary acquisition of LD students: A study of computer-assisted instruction. *Journal of Learning Disabilities, 20*(4), 206-213.

Kaltsounis, T. (1984). *Teacher assignment survey.* Unpublished manuscript. College of Education, University of Washington, Seattle.

Kantor, R. N., Anderson, T. H., & Armbruster, B. B. (1983). How inconsiderate are children's textbooks? *Journal of Curriculum Studies, 15*, 6-72.

Lee, W. W. (1987). Microcomputer courseware production and evaluation guidelines for students with learning disabilities. *Journal of Learning Disabilities, 20*(7), 436-438.

Lenz, B. K., Alley, G. R., & Schumaker, J. B. (1987). Activating the inactive learner: Advance organizers in the secondary content classroom. *Learning Disability Quarterly, 10*, 53-67.

Levin, J. R. (1983). Pictorial strategies for school learning: Practical illustrations. In M. Pressley & J. R. Levin (Eds.), *Cognitive strategy research: Educational applications* (pp. 213-237). New York: Springer-Verlag.

Lovitt, T. C., & Horton, S. V. (1987). How to develop study guides. *Journal of Reading, Writing and Learning Disabilities, 3*, 333-343.

Lovitt, T. C., & Horton, S. V. (1988). [Oral reading rates of learning-disabled adolescents]. Unpublished data.

Lovitt, T. C., Horton, S. V., & Bergerud, D. (1987). Matching students with textbooks: An alternative to readability formulas and standardized tests. *B. C. Journal of Special Education, 2*(1), 49-55.

Lovitt, T., Rudsit, J., Jenkins, J., Pious, C., & Benedetti, D. (1985). Two methods of adapting science materials for learning disabled and regular seventh graders. *Learning Disability Quarterly, 8*, 275-285.

Lovitt, T. C., Rudsit, J., Jenkins, J., Pious, C., & Benedetti, D. (1986). Adapting science materials for regular and learning disabled seventh graders. *Remedial and Special Education, 7*(1), 31-39.

Luiten, J., Ames, W., & Ackerman, G. (1980). A meta-analysis of the effects of advance organizers on learning and retention. *American Educational Research Journal, 17*, 211-218.

Mastropieri, M. A., Scruggs, T. E., McLoone, B., & Levin, J. R. (1985). Facilitating learning disabled students' acquisition of science classifications. *Learning Disability Quarterly, 8*, 299-309.

McDermott, P., & Watkins, M. (1983). Computerized vs. conventional remedial instruction for learning disabled students. *The Journal of Special Education, 17*(1), 81-88.

McLaughlin, G. H. (1969). SMOG grading — A new readability formula. *Journal of Reading, 12*, 639-646.

Meadows, N. (1988). *The effects of individual, teacher-directed and cooperative learning instructional methods on the comprehension of expository text.* Unpublished doctoral dissertation, University of Washington, Seattle.

Megarry, J. (1988). Hypertext and compact disks: The challenge of multi-media learning. *The British Journal of Educational Technology, 19*(3), 172-183.

Meyer, B. J. F., Brandt, D. M., & Bluth, G. J. (1980). Use of top-level structure in text: Key for reading comprehension of ninth-grade students. *Reading Research Quarterly, 16*, 72-103.

Moore, D. W., & Readence, J. F. (1984). A quantitative and qualitative review of graphic organizer research. *Journal of Educational Research, 78*, 11-17.

MORE. (1987). [Computer program]. Mountain View, CA: Living Videotext.

Osterlag, B. A., & Rambeau, J. (1982). Reading success through rewriting for secondary LD students. *Academic Therapy, 18*, 27-32.

Pearson, P. D. (1975-1976). The effects of grammatical complexity on children's comprehension, recall and conception of certain semantic relations. *Reading Research Quarterly, 10*, 155-192.

Prescott, G. A., Balow, I. H., Hogan, T. P., & Farr, R. C. (1984). *The Metropolitan Achievement Test.* New York: The Psychological Corporation, Harcourt, Brace, Jovanovich.

Rivers, L. E. (1980). Use a tape recorder to teach basic skills. *Social Studies, 71*(4), 171-174.

Rumberger, R. (1987). High school dropouts: A review of issues and evidence. *Review of Educational Research, 57*(2), 101-121.

Schumaker, J. B., Deshler, D. D., & Denton, P. H. (1982). *An integrated system for providing content to LD adolescents using an audio-taped format* (Research Report No. 66). Lawrence, KS: University of Kansas, Institute for Research in Learning Disabilities.

Snider, B., Zocher, E., & Jackson, C. (1986). *SuperPaint [Computer program].* San Diego, CA: Silicon Beach Software.

Tierney, R. J., Readence, J. E., & Dishner, E. K. (1985). *Reading strategies and practices: A compendium* (2nd ed.). Boston: Allyn & Bacon.

Torgesen, J. K. (1977). The role of nonspecific factors in the task performance of learning disabled children: A theoretical assessment. *Journal of Learning Disabilities, 10*, 27-34.

Torgesen, J., & Kail, R. J. (1985). Memory processes in exceptional children. In B. K. Keogh (Ed.), *Advances in special education: Basic constructs and theoretical orientations* (Vol. 1; pp. 55-99). Greenwich, CT: JAI Press.

Vellutino, F., Harding, C., Stager, J., & Phillips, F. (1975). Differential transfer in poor and normal readers. *Journal of Genetic Psychology, 126*, 3-18.

White, O. R., & Haring, N. G. (1980). *Exceptional teaching.* Columbus, OH: Merrill.

Winn, W. (1987). Charts, graphs, and diagrams in educational materials. In D. M. Williams & H. A. Houghton (Eds.), *Illustrations, graphs, and diagrams: Psychological theory an educational practice* (pp. 152-198). New York: Springer-Verlag.

Wong, B. (1978). The effects of directive cues on the organization of memory and recall in good and poor readers. *Journal of Educational Research, 72*, 32-38.

Wong, B. (1980). Activating the inactive trainer: Use of questions/prompts to enhance comprehension and retention of implied information in learning disabled children. *Learning Disability Quarterly, 3*, 29-37.

Wright, J. D. (1982). The effect of reduced readability text materials on comprehension and biology achievement. *Science Education, 66*, 3-13.

21

Teaching Routines for Content Areas at the Secondary Level

Jean B. Schumaker
Donald D. Deshler
Philip C. McKnight
University of Kansas

INTRODUCTION

Academic failure by adolescents with learning problems in secondary schools is well documented (e.g., Boyer, 1983; Deshler & Schumaker, 1988; Goodlad, 1984; Powell, Farrar, & Cohen, 1985). The reasons for this failure are often varied, exceedingly complex, and highly interrelated (Sinclair & Ghory, 1987). Recent research on low-achieving adolescents has indicated that these students' problems are related primarily to three major factors that appear singly or in combination: (a) learning inefficiencies or disabilities inherent in the student, (b) complex curricular and setting demands in secondary schools, and (c) ineffective teaching practices (Deshler, Schumaker, Lenz, & Ellis, 1984).

The first factor, the learning deficiencies evidenced by at-risk adolescents, has received significant attention from researchers, resulting in a profile of these youths that reflects a reduced probability of success for this population in mainstream secondary learning settings. First, these students' performance on reading, writing, and math achievement tests plateaus at approximately the fourth- or fifth-grade level when they reach the tenth grade in school (Warner, Schumaker, Alley, & Deshler, 1980). Thus, the "performance gap" between their skills levels and their grade level in school continues to

grow as they move from one high school grade level to the next and curricular demands escalate (Schumaker & Deshler, 1988). Second, these students often lack much of the prior knowledge of facts and concepts necessary for benefiting from the secondary curriculum (Bos & Anders, 1987). Third, they tend not to use effective strategies for coping with specific academic demands (Carlson, 1985) and often fail to invent strategies when approaching novel tasks (Ellis, Deshler, & Schumaker, 1989; Warner, Schumaker, Alley, & Deshler, in press). Fourth, these students often have difficulty in taking notes from lectures (Carlson & Alley, 1981), tending only to write what the teacher writes on the board (Bulgren, Schumaker, & Deshler, 1988). Fifth, when asked to write a paragraph or theme, these students generally write incomplete sentences or poorly structured complete sentences containing many spelling and grammatical errors; in addition, their written products suffer from lack of organization (Deshler, Kass, & Ferrell, 1978; Moran, Schumaker, & Vetter, 1981; Schmidt, 1983; Schumaker, Deshler, Alley, et al., 1982). Sixth, the majority of these students are concrete thinkers (Skrtic, 1980) and have difficulty making complex discriminations between main ideas and details as well as important versus unimportant information (Carlson & Alley, 1981; Lenz, 1984). Seventh, these students tend not to generalize newly learned skills across settings, conditions, and time unless they are specifically taught to do so (Ellis, Lenz, & Sabornie, 1987; Schmidt, 1983). Finally, they tend not to be motivated to learn (Seabaugh & Schumaker, 1981a, 1981b). In essence, research has shown that these students are severely deficient in the critical skills required for coping with the rigors of the secondary curriculum and associated higher-order learning tasks.

The second factor that often precipitates the failure of low-achieving adolescents relates to the complex curricular and setting demands in secondary schools. Putnam (1988), for example, found that success in secondary grades depends upon students' ability to gain information from textbooks that are often both poorly organized and written, typically with an eleventh-grade reading level. In addition, the classroom lectures and discussions from which they are expected to gain information (Schumaker, Wildgen, & Sherman, 1980) often are characterized as lacking: (a) advance organizers and postorganizers, (b) appropriate pacing to permit notetaking, (c) adequate instruction on prerequisite vocabulary, and (d) sufficient repetition of information (Lenz, Alley, & Schumaker, 1987; Moran, 1980). Grades in secondary content courses are largely dependent on students' ability to succeed on tests that contain primarily objective-type questions and require about 40 responses about factual information (Putnam, 1988). Grades on written products depend mainly on students' ability to write correctly spelled words and grammatically error-free, long sentences (Moran & DeLoach, 1982). In short, success in secondary schools is, in large measure, directly related to a student's ability to acquire, manipulate, store, and express or use large amounts of information that can be obtained only from sources that do not allow for learning inefficiencies in key areas.

A third factor that may contribute to student failure in secondary schools is the application of ineffective or inappropriate teaching practices by many teachers responsible for content instruction (e.g., chemistry, social studies, English litera-ture) (Cuban, 1984; Cusick, 1983). Secondary teachers often report that their primary role is to serve as "content experts" who have major responsibility for delivering accurate and current content information to students; in addition, they do not feel responsible for spoon-feeding students who are ill prepared to learn (Lieberman & Miller, 1978). Consequently, secondary teachers do not exhibit much variation in the pedagogical approaches they employ; the predominant instructional method used by these teachers is the lecture (Goodlad, 1984; Moran, 1980; Schumaker, et al., 1980). Although lecturing, per se, is not an ineffective format, Moran's (1980) and Lenz's (1984) research studies have underscored the failure of many secondary teachers to incorporate effective teaching skills within their lectures (e.g., organizing statements, clarifying questions).

Mainstream secondary teachers' reliance on the lecture may be the result of the fact that many preservice curricula offered by schools of education prepare secondary teachers to be primarily content rather than instructional experts. Specifically, the overwhelming majority of course hours taken by secondary trainees are in the content areas; relatively few deal with instructional methods (Scanlon, 1982). In short, many secondary teachers lack the technical teaching skills required to facilitate learning for all students, especially students with disabilities (McKnight, 1980).

Any combination of these three major factors in the learning situation can result in several potentially negative ramifications for student achievement and school adjustment. For example, suppose that one of the factors causes an increased number of students to be referred for special education services (Mellard & Deshler, 1984). Once students are placed in special education classes, much of the responsibility for their total educational program is shifted from regular class teachers to the special class teacher, including delivery of content information (Alley & Deshler, 1979). Allington (1984) strongly questioned the ability of special class teachers to teach appropriately all content subjects when they are not certified to do so. Furthermore, when the policy of readily referring students with learning problems to special education is followed over time within a given school building, it often becomes the accepted norm that the special class teacher carries the major responsibility for educating low-achieving students. Such a mind set might preclude the introduction of instructional changes in the regular classroom to accommodate students with learning problems. Additionally, unless the majority of teachers within a given school building assume some responsibility for low student achievement and modify their instructional practices accordingly, it becomes difficult if not impossible to reintegrate at-risk students who have been receiving services in the special classroom into the mainstream curriculum (Licopoli, 1984). Finally, the high dropout rate among high-risk populations is reported to be, in part, due to the existing environment in secondary schools that is predominantly unfriendly to learners with problems (Howe & Edelman, 1985).

The challenges related to educating at-risk students must be addressed. While the solution to these challenges will be multifaceted, a significant part of the solution will be found in designing instructional practices that will improve the technical teaching skills of secondary teachers as well as provide at-risk students the skills they need to succeed in mainstream learning environments. Improving the technical skills with which teachers teach content will go a long way toward enabling students with disabilities to benefit from the information taught in the content classroom. As the needs of low-achievers are better met in the regular classroom, there will be less need to refer large numbers of students for special services. Equally important, students who are referred to special classes can be taught specific strategies for enabling them to cope independently with regular class instruction instead of becoming dependent on tutoring from the special education teacher for content classes. In addition, the probability of mainstreaming

success after special instruction will be improved because of more accommodating learning environments in mainstream classes.

A NEW INSTRUCTIONAL MODEL FOR AT-RISK STUDENTS

Staff members of the University of Kansas Institute for Research in Learning Disabilities (KU-IRLD) have designed a new instructional model for at-risk secondary students that takes into account these students' need to learn techniques for independently succeeding in mainstream environments as well as their instructional needs within these environments (Deshler & Schumaker, 1988). In this model, hereafter referred to as the Strategies Intervention Model (SIM), special education teachers and mainstream teachers maintain different roles as they work cooperatively to improve the performance of low-achieving students in mainstream classes. In this model, the special education teacher's major role in the support class is that of the "learning specialist," one who teaches students how to learn and how to succeed in the mainstream. In turn, the major role of the teacher in the mainstream class is to deliver content to the students in such a way that students can understand and remember it. The partnership between the two teachers comes through their communication about: (a) the setting demands in the mainstream course of study, (b) the skills needed by particular students, (c) students' progress, and (d) techniques that can be used to help at-risk students.

Other persons also play critical roles in this model. The students must not only be willing and motivated participants, they must take major responsibility for their learning and performance. Administrators, school psychologists, other support staff, family members, and personnel in other community agencies also can play an important part in a SIM program.

How teachers, students, and others interact to promote successful participation of at-risk adolescents within the mainstream curriculum as well as facilitate their successful transition to post-secondary life has been the subject of a programmatic line of research for 8 years at the KU-IRLD. The products of this research have served as building blocks for the comprehensive SIM program. As the roles of participants in a SIM program are described in the following sections, the components of the model are clarified.

The Role of the Learning Specialist

The learning specialist's major responsibility in a SIM program is to teach students specific strategies by using a validated instructional methodology. Usually, this instruction takes place in a support class (e.g., a special education classroom, a strategies course, a remedial course). The strategies to be taught include: *learning strategies*, which enable students to learn and perform academic tasks; *social strategies*, which enable students to interact effectively with others; *motivational strategies*, which enable students to motivate themselves and exercise self-control; *transition strategies*, which enable students to solve their own problems and plan for the future; and *executive strategies*, which enable students to analyze a task, then select, adapt, or invent a strategy for use, and evaluate the results of applying the strategy (Schumaker, Deshler, & Ellis, 1986).

The instructional methodology used in teaching these strategies comprises eight major instructional steps to: (a) obtain a pretraining measure of the students' skills and gain the students' commitment for learning; (b) make the students aware of the strategy steps, where the strategy can be applied, and how the strategy will benefit them; (c) demonstrate for students how to use the strategy; (d) ensure that the students understand and can name the strategy steps; (e) ensure that the students master the use of the strategy in simplified materials/situations; (f) ensure that the students master the use of the strategy in materials and situations similar to those encountered in mainstream environ-

ments; (g) obtain a posttraining measure of the students' skills; and (h) ensure that the students generalize the use of the strategy to the mainstream (Deshler, Alley, Warner, & Schumaker, 1981). The materials and procedures to be used by the learning specialist in these undertakings have been empirically validated in a series of studies (e.g., Clark, Deshler, Schumaker, Alley, & Warner, 1984; Hughes, 1985; Robbins, 1982; Schmidt, 1983; Schumaker, Deshler, Alley, et al., 1982; Schumaker, Deshler, Denton, et al., 1982). Some of the materials have been published for teachers' use (e.g., Hazel, Schumaker, Sherman, & Sheldon-Wildgen, 1981; Hughes, Schumaker, Deshler, & Mercer, 1988; Lenz, Schumaker, Deshler, & Beals, 1984; Nagel, Schumaker, & Deshler, 1986; Schumaker, Denton, & Deshler, 1984; Schumaker, Hazel, & Pederson, 1988; Schumaker, Nolan, & Deshler, 1985; Schumaker & Sheldon, 1985; and Van Reusen, Bos, Schumaker, & Deshler, 1987)[1]; others currently are being prepared for publication.

In addition to fulfilling the major role of teaching strategies by means of intensive instruction, the learning specialist also must perform other functions that ultimately facilitate this major role. One function is to create a strategic environment within the support service setting. The strategic environment serves as the context in which specific strategies can be learned and generalized most effectively. In other words, if strategies are taught in an isolated fashion, unrelated to the solution of day-to-day problems within a broader context, students will have difficulty generalizing mastered strategies. Therefore, the learning specialist must model the use of strategic approaches to new problems and engage the students in strategic activities whenever possible in order to teach the students the generality of the approach to life situations.

Additionally, the learning specialist must promote students' independent functioning in academic and social realms. In partial fulfillment of this goal, the learning specialist must refrain from tutoring students in content subjects to avoid encouraging the dependence that typically results from such tutoring. Also, the learning specialist must deliberately involve students in planning their instructional programs, setting their own learning goals, and advocating for themselves in instructional planning sessions (Van Reusen et al., 1987). Finally, the learning specialist must require students to think and act on their own rather than performing tasks for the students. For example, when asked a question, the teacher should redirect the question in a way that students can answer it themselves. Materials and equipment should be accessible to students so that they can obtain needed resources and start work on their own. Academic work should never be done "for" students. They should be given the tools to complete the work independently.

In addition to these complex responsibilities within the support setting, the learning specialist also must perform a leadership role outside the support setting to promote a cooperative partnership with mainstream teachers. A set of "Teaming Strategies" have been developed and validated for use in this partnership. These strategies allow learning specialists and mainstream teachers to work together to identify mainstream setting demands, discuss and solve problems, negotiate conflict, and encourage the use of validated instructional techniques in mainstream classrooms (Knackendoffel, 1989). To summarize, the learning specialist must create a strategic environment in which a specialized set of curriculum materials is used in conjunction with a validated instructional methodology designed to promote students' independent functioning in mainstream classes. Additionally, this teacher must work cooperatively with mainstream teachers to ensure that the goal of independent student functioning is met.

The Role of the Mainstream Teacher

The major role of the mainstream content teacher is straightforward; it involves the delivery of content to students so as to promote: (a) their application of strategies learned in the support setting, (b) their understanding of the content information, and (c) their recall of that information. Occasionally (e.g., in the case of an English teacher who needs to teach students how to write complete sentences), the mainstream teacher also may be responsible for teaching a particular strategy — for example, the Sentence Writing Strategy (Schumaker & Sheldon, 1985).

To promote the use of strategies learned in the support setting, mainstream teachers can rely on a variety of cueing devices to remind students to use the strategies when appropriate; they can also structure their delivery of content so that strategies can be applied easily. For example, a teacher can organize a lecture into four major sections, orally cue students to use the Listening and Notetaking Strategy (Robinson, Deshler, Denton, & Schumaker, in preparation) before the lecture begins, and cue students when a transition is being made during the lecture to each of the four major sections.

To teach strategies in large classes, which are so prevalent in the mainstream at the secondary level, mainstream teachers can use a variety of instructional arrangements and techniques. To promote students' understanding and retention of the content of lectures and other lessons, mainstream teachers can use teaching routines or devices designed specifically to easily be integrated into the mainstream class routine while promoting gains in student performance. These routines and devices, as well as the cueing techniques and instructional arrangements that can be used by mainstream teachers, are described in detail later in the chapter.

The Role of Students

Two types of students have been served successfully in SIM programs: students who qualify for special services in support classes and other at-risk students. Normally, handicapped students have been served both in support classes and in mainstream classrooms. Other at-risk students (i.e., low-achievers, those at-risk for dropping out of school) traditionally have been served in mainstream classrooms, but some educators now are designing support-class settings (e.g., courses in learning strategies) for these students as well. Thus, students typically enrolled in a SIM program have roles to fulfill in both settings. In the support service setting, students are responsible for (a) planning their instructional programs, (b) specifying what they will learn and how fast they will learn it, (c) learning specific strategies to mastery, (d) recording their own progress, (e) evaluating their own progress, and (f) changing goals accordingly. In the mainstream setting, they are responsible for applying, adapting, and inventing strategies where they are needed and for monitoring and evaluating their own progress. Thus, students within a SIM program assume an active role in their learning; they are viewed by educators as persons who can learn to succeed independently instead of being dependent entities whose lives must be arranged for them.

The Role of Others

As the SIM has evolved, the roles that administrators, school psychologists, other support staff, family members and community agency personnel can play in promoting at-risk students' success within the mainstream curriculum have become clearer. School administrators, for example, can play a critical role in ensuring that the program operates as specified. Not only must they provide the necessary support, they must voice the necessary expectations so that learning specialists and mainstream teachers, in turn, can fulfill their roles and can work together productively. Support staff also can be helpful in promoting the program's success. School psychologists, for example, can help identify mainstream class demands (e.g., the readability level of textbooks, the types and length of assignments, the types of tests given) and ensure that all participants in educational planning meetings (including students and parents) have a voice in making decisions about students' learning. Like-

wise, scheduling officers can contribute by hand-scheduling (versus computer-scheduling) students' programs so that they can be grouped for appropriate instruction in the support setting as needed. Furthermore, parents can participate by offering support and encouragement in the home and by promoting the generalization of strategies to homework and other situations encountered in the home and community.

Finally, personnel in community agencies can aid the transition of graduates of SIM programs to adult life. For example, personnel in one community mental health center have been working for 4 years with school district staff to match each SIM student with a community volunteer who serves as the youth's mentor through the transition process. Agency staff recruit and train mentors, have regular contact with mentors, and monitor a youth's progress through a series of goal-setting and evaluation sessions with mentor–youth pairs. This type of program has proved very successful in getting youths involved in postsecondary education and training and employed in meaningful jobs (Moccia, Schumaker, Hazel, Vernon, & Deshler, in press; Schumaker, Hazel, & Deshler, 1985).

An Example of the Strategies Intervention Model

An example of how a SIM program might work for a student under certain circumstances illustrates some of the processes that have been activated in school districts across the nation. Suppose that in a school in which teachers, support staff, and administrators have worked together to promote a SIM program, the school psychologist has determined that students have to be able to memorize lists of items to succeed on a particular biology teacher's tests. A student enrolled in the learning specialist's support class also is enrolled in the targeted biology class. The learning specialist works with the student to determine whether he or she wants to learn a strategy that will help with this class demand. First, a pretest is given to determine how well the student can organize and memorize lists. Next, the results of the pretest are shared with the student, who decides whether to try to learn a strategy to help memorize lists. Upon deciding to learn the strategy, the student writes a goal to that effect. Then the learning specialist teaches the student (and others who have written a similar goal) the FIRST-Letter Mnemonic Strategy (Nagel et al., 1986), a strategy for (a) organizing information into list form, (b) memorizing the information, and (c) utilizing the information to answer test questions. After working hard over a period of about 3 weeks, the student masters the strategy so that it can be applied to the textbook used in the biology class and the notes taken in that class.

Meanwhile, the learning specialist and the biology teacher work together to ensure that the biology teacher understands the strategy the student (and other students in the class) is learning in order to be better able to facilitate the student's use of the strategy. Whenever possible, the biology teacher presents lecture information in list form and, in addition to writing lists on the board, cues students when lists must be memorized for tests. When time permits, students are helped in designing a mnemonic device for a given list or they are asked to work cooperatively to design the devices themselves. When the biology teacher reviews information the day before a test or when he or she gives students a study guide, the necessary information is provided in list form. The day before the test, the students who have learned the strategy are reminded to use the FIRST-Letter Mnemonic Strategy as they study for the test.

Throughout instruction on each new biology unit, the target student builds up a file of 3″ × 5″ cards containing important lists. The night before a test, in a study session supported by his parents, the student applies the FIRST-Letter Mnemonic Strategy to the lists taken from lectures as well as other lists derived from the assigned textbook chapter to ensure that he or she has memorized the necessary information. As he takes each test, the student recalls information through

use of the memory devices he has designed.

Our target student receives grades of As and Bs on his tests. After learning and integrating several strategies like this and applying them to several courses, the student graduates from high school. By working with a mentor, he or she later enrolls in junior college courses, taking biology and other courses at the local junior college and continuing to apply the strategies learned in high school. The support class student has become an independent learner and performer.

TEACHING ROUTINES FOR ENHANCING INSTRUCTION IN MAINSTREAM CLASSES

As described earlier, the role of the content teacher in a SIM program is not only to teach a prescribed body of subject matter to students but to do so in a way that facilitates students' understanding and recall of that content. It was argued further that mainstream teachers can rely on a variety of routines, devices, and instructional arrangements to promote performance gains by students with disabilities. The question then becomes "What form should these routines, devices, and instructional arrangements take?" This question is particularly pertinent in light of the increasingly heavy challenge that content teachers are expected to meet with respect to teaching not only more content but also more advanced and complex content (Powell et al., 1985). These increased pressures have surfaced in recent years as a result of the Excellence in Education movement (Spady & Marx, 1984).

In addressing the question of the form of instructional routines and devices that teachers should use and the need to increase the effectiveness of instruction in content classes, researchers at the KU-IRLD have applied five criteria when designing and researching instructional routines or devices. First, such routines and devices must be straightforward and easy to master in a relatively short time. Second, they must be perceived by teachers as practical and easy to use.

Third, they must be perceived by teachers as being effective for typical students as well as for the students with disabilities who are enrolled in mainstream classes. Similarly, typical students must perceive the teacher's use of the routines and devices as facilitative, not as "extra baggage" that gets in the way of learning. Fourth, the routines and devices must be sufficiently powerful to improve the performance of students with disabilities in mainstream classes in which heterogeneous groupings of students are enrolled. Finally, they must lend themselves to easy integration with current teaching practices. The following sections describe a variety of routines and devices that fulfill these criteria. All have been or are currently being validated experimentally.

Routines for Teaching Strategies in Mainstream Environments

In some instances, learning strategies can be appropriately taught in mainstream classes as well as in support classes, as detailed earlier. For example, learning strategies in the written expression strand of the Learning Strategies Curriculum — for example, the Sentence Writing Strategy (Schumaker & Sheldon, 1985), the Paragraph Writing Strategy (Schumaker & Lyerla, in preparation), the Theme Writing Strategy (Schumaker, in preparation) — can be taught in English and in language arts classes. Strategies that enable students to take notes (Robinson et al., in preparation) and study for tests (Hughes et al., 1988) can be taught in content classes such as history and science. Some school districts have adopted learning strategies classes or study skills classes as a standard part of their curriculum. Large numbers of students and heterogeneous groupings of students usually characterize these mainstream classes. Such characteristics create especially heavy demands on learning-strategies instructors because (a) students must practice using a strategy several times before mastering it, (b) they master the use of a strategy after varying numbers of practice attempts; and (c) they must receive specific, individual

feedback about each of their practice attempts to make progress toward mastery. Ensuring mastery and providing individual feedback in large classes is often problematic. Thus, teaching strategies to large numbers of students with a variety of learning characteristics requires special methods. Recently, a number of methods have been validated experimentally for accomplishing this type of instruction, including the use of special feedback systems, cooperative group instruction, and peer tutoring.

Special feedback systems. To determine whether a complex strategy like the Theme Writing Strategy (Schumaker, in preparation) could be taught in mainstream English classes, Howell (1986), an English teacher, taught the strategy to her five classes of high school students (a total of 150 students). She followed the instructions for teaching her students to acquire and generalize the strategy just as a resource teacher would, with one exception. Instead of giving feedback orally after each practice attempt (as a resource teacher might do with a small group of students), Howell provided specific written individual feedback to all 150 students after each attempt via a specially designed Feedback Sheet. The Feedback Sheet contained a list of descriptions of areas where students could do well and a list of descriptions of possible errors. After reading and scoring a theme, the teacher simply checked those items that had been done well and those that needed improvement. She also wrote brief comments on the sheet as needed. The Feedback Sheet allowed the teacher to give the majority of her feedback in written form so that class time could be spent on additional instructional activities, reviewing common trouble spots for the class, and providing oral feedback and help to students having major difficulties. Students were told to review their Feedback Sheets, ask the teacher for help with items that were unclear, and pay particular attention to the Feedback Sheets as they wrote their subsequent papers. Howell found that her students mastered the strategy at levels comparable to those students who had received individual instruction and individual feedback.

Cooperative group instruction. Another method for teaching strategies in the mainstream classroom that has been validated experimentally is cooperative group instruction. Beals (1983) conducted a study in which two strategies, the Sentence Writing Strategy (Schumaker & Sheldon, 1985) and the Paraphrasing Strategy (Schumaker et al., 1984), were taught in mainstream English classes. The students were divided into small heterogeneous groups, and assignments were given to the groups. At the end of a given lesson, one group member was selected randomly from each group to perform the target skill for the lesson. The group's grade for the day was contingent on that person's performance. Individual grades also were given for individual accomplishments. At the beginning of each subsequent lesson, group members were required to review and discuss the feedback received by each member on individual work and to help each other understand relevant concepts. Beals (1983) found that all the students (high-achievers, normal-achievers, low-achievers, and students with learning disabilities) showed improvement in their skills and mastered the use of the strategy. The students with learning disabilities achieved at levels comparable to levels attained when similar students were taught the strategies in resource room programs.

Peer tutoring. Peer tutoring also can be used when teaching strategies to large groups of students in mainstream classes. This method has been validated as effective in resource classes; thus, its use in mainstream classes seems to be a logical extension. Keimig (in preparation) developed a method by which learning disabled (LD) students who had mastered the Error Monitoring Strategy (Schumaker, Nolan, & Deshler, 1985) taught this strategy to other LD students in a resource room. Simple instructions were written on cards for the student tutors to follow as they taught each lesson. The student tutors were responsible for providing instruction, answering questions, scoring lessons according to answer keys, giving individual feedback after each practice attempt, and stating that mastery of the skills would be required. The tutors were taught how to perform these teaching tasks in 1½ hours of instruction. Keimig found that the LD students in his study learned to use the strategy at levels comparable to levels exhibited by LD students who had been taught the strategy by a teacher. They also mastered the strategy after comparable amounts of instruction. Keimig's study shows that, given some training, LD students who have mastered a learning strategy can serve as effective instructors of those strategies to other dysfunctional learners.

A logical extension of Keimig's work includes teaching learning strategies to small groups of students enrolled in mainstream classes by student tutors who have mastered these strategies and the necessary instructional procedures. Such an arrangement would allow students with disabilities to "shine" in their mainstream classes and conceivably could enhance their self-concept. Additionally, if supposed "dysfunctional" learners can be successful instructors of learning strategies, other, more functional, learners might be recruited as well to perform some of the teaching tasks that must be carried out in settings with large numbers of students. For example, they might lead verbal rehearsal exercises, check off verbal mastery of the concepts and steps of a strategy, and provide explanations and/or additional feedback on graded work.

Routines for Cueing Use of Strategies

When students with disabilities are taught strategies to mastery levels in support classes, they sometimes fail to generalize the use of those strategies to other classrooms. Several methods involving cueing (i.e., prompting the student to use strategies) in the mainstream classroom have been found to help ensure generalization.

Visual cueing methods. The first type of method involves visually cueing students to use a given strategy. One effective format for visual cueing (Schmidt, 1983) involves the use of cue cards. The student writes the steps of a strategy on a 3″ × 5″ or 4″ × 6″ card that is affixed to the appropriate textbook or notebook. For example, students who have learned a strategy for extracting important facts from textbook chapters make cue cards that list the steps of the strategy and attach them to the cover of each of their textbooks or use them as bookmarks. Students who have learned a strategy for taking notes during lectures make cue cards listing the steps of the strategy and affix them to each of their notebooks for classes in which notetaking is appropriate. The cards must be assigned a visually prominent place so that the students will see them as the textbook or notebook is opened. In the case of writing strategies, students make a set of cue cards of formulas and rules to which they can refer as they write.

Another type of visual cueing technique was built into one of the strategies, the Test Taking Strategy (Hughes et al., 1988). To perform the first step of the Test Taking Strategy, students must write a cue word on their test papers before they begin taking the test and applying the strategy. Each letter of the cue word represents something the students must do or attend to as they take the test. Thus, in effect by writing the cue word in a visually prominent place, the students cue themselves to use the strategy.

The mainstream teacher's role with respect to these visual cueing systems is to encourage their use; that is, mainstream teachers must be aware of the rationale for using these visual cueing devices and must allow their use. They also must be sensitive to adolescent students' need to "be like" other students and, therefore, avoid drawing attention to the fact that they are different because they use these visual cueing devices.

Verbal cueing methods. Another type of cueing that has been found effective in encouraging generalized use of a learning strategy is verbal cueing. For one verbal cueing technique, the mainstream teacher is designated as the person who supplies the cues. For example, if the student has mastered the Sentence Writing Strategy (called PENS by the students), the teacher surreptitiously says to the student, "Be sure to use 'PENS' on today's assignment" after giving the class an assignment to write a paragraph. Specifically, the mainstream teacher's role with verbal cueing consists of being aware of the strategies a student has mastered, matching those strategies appropriately to given assignments, and remembering to cue the student before she or he begins a task.

The other verbal cueing technique that has been found to be effective (Keimig, in preparation) involves student peers. Here, students who have learned a strategy in the special class also learn to cue each other to use the strategy in other classes and to help each other when needed. For example, two students who have learned the Error Monitoring Strategy (Schumaker, Nolan, & Deshler, 1985), a strategy for detecting and correcting errors in written work, can learn to become responsible for cueing each other to use the strategy any time written work is assigned in the classroom. That is, the students can be responsible for discriminating the conditions for which the use of the strategy is appropriate; in addition, they can be responsible for briefly communicating to each other about those conditions ("We should use the Error Monitoring Strategy on this assignment"). The mainstream teacher must allow the students to be seated close enough to each other that they can cue each other without disturbing others and let them briefly chat at the beginning of an assignment so that they can determine which strategies are most applicable and whether certain adjustments need to be made in the strategies.

Routines for Teaching Content

As emphasized earlier, the primary role of most secondary teachers is to convey information in such a way as to ensure that students understand it and remember it. When students with disabilities and other at-risk students are enrolled in content courses, the teacher's

TABLE 1
Routines for Teaching Content

	When used	Purpose	Teacher materials	Student materials
Survey routine	At the beginning of a unit of instruction	To provide an overview of the unit/chapter and the information to be learned	Textbook, "TRIMS" Planning Sheet	Textbook, student worksheet
Concept teaching routine	After the survey routine	To introduce the major concept in the unit	Completed concept diagram	Blank concept diagram
Advance organizer routine	At the beginning of a lesson	To provide an overview of the lesson	AO planning sheet	Paper and pencils
Verbal enhancement routine	At particular points during a lesson	To make abstract information more understandable and memorable	Understanding devices planning sheet	Paper and pencils
Visual enhancement routine	At particular points during a lesson	To make abstract information more understandable and memorable	Visual depictions (pictures, diagrams, tables, concept maps)	Paper and pencils

role becomes more complex. Thus, in classrooms where these types of students are being educated, effective techniques or teaching routines that correspond to their particular characteristics are needed. Recently, a number of specifically designed routines have been proved effective for helping at-risk students learn in mainstream environments (Table 1).

The advance organizer routine. One routine that has been shown to be effective in enhancing the performance of students with disabilities in mainstream classrooms entails the presentation of a prescribed set of information as an advance organizer for a lesson. An advance organizer has been defined as information that is delivered "in advance of and at a higher level of generality, inclusiveness, and abstraction than the learning task itself" (Ausubel & Robinson, 1969, p. 606). The purpose of the advance organizer is to strengthen a student's cognitive structures, which are defined by Ausubel (1963) as the student's knowledge of a

given subject matter at a given time with regard to its organization, clarity, and stability. For students with a paucity of background knowledge or an inability to organize information such that it can be easily retrieved, and for those with poor motivational and/or inactive learning styles, advance organizers take on special roles. They can serve as the vehicle for presenting background knowledge that is required for understanding a lesson, for highlighting organizational patterns about which the students should be aware, for motivating students to learn, and for communicating to students expectations about what they should be doing during the lesson.

Lenz et al. (1987) designed an advance organizer consisting of 12 components and evaluated its effectiveness in terms of student learning in mainstream classrooms. The 12 components can be used to inform the learner about: (a) the purpose of the advance organizer, (b) the actions to be taken by the teacher and the students, (c) the topic and subtopics to be covered in the lesson, (d) background knowledge, (e) concepts to be learned, (f) reasons for learning the information, (g) new vocabulary, (h) organizational frameworks, and (i) desired lesson outcomes.

Teachers were trained to design and deliver advance organizers containing the 12 components in their secondary content classes (e.g., history, English, physical science) at the beginning of each class period. Lenz et al. monitored the effects of the advance organizer on students' acquisition of the information presented in the class period by interviewing the students after each class. These researchers found that mainstream teachers who used few of the advance organizer components at the start of their lessons could be trained in less than an hour to use them at mastery levels in the classroom. When students with disabilities were specifically taught to attend to the advance organizer, the number of relevant statements they made about the content of the lesson increased substantially compared to the number of statements made when they had not been informed about how to attend to the advance organizer.

Lenz (1984) conducted another study to determine the effects of written advance organizers on students' acquisition of information. Basically, the same format was used for the advance organizer as described for the Lenz et al. (1987) study; a few adjustments were necessitated by the reading task as opposed to the lecture/discussion task. In addition, the usefulness of an advance organizer was explained specifically to the students, who were instructed to take advantage of the advance organizer before reading the assigned passage. Lenz found substantial differences between the recall performance of LD students when they received an advance organizer before reading a passage and their performance when they did not receive the advance organizer. LD students who had not received an advance organizer correctly answered more questions about unimportant information than questions about important informa-

tion in the passage. In contrast, LD students who had received an advance organizer answered more questions correctly about important information than about unimportant information. In fact, they correctly answered about the same number of questions correctly about important information (an average of 19 out of 30 questions) as a group of normal achievers who had not received an advance organizer (an average of 21 out of 30 questions). The use of the advance organizer only slightly improved the typical achievers' recall of important information (from an average of 21 to 22 answers correct), but it substantially improved the performance of the LD students (from an average of 13 to 19 answers correct).

These data indicate that advance organizers help students with disabilities discriminate important information from unimportant information. In addition, advance organizers help them store that information so that it can be recalled later for a test over the information. The result of this more efficient storage is that their performance on a test covering the important information is not substantially different from the performance of non-handicapped learners. These findings suggest that a teaching routine containing an advance organizer that precedes a classroom lesson or a reading assignment can be a beneficial tool for enhancing the performance of low-performing students. Although the research conducted to date has not identified the effects of advance organizers used on a daily basis on students' grades in mainstream courses, one logically might assume that the effects noted in the tests in Lenz's study (1984) would be reflected in higher scores on chapter tests. Since a large percentage of a student's grade is based on test scores in secondary classrooms (Putnam, 1988), one also might suppose that course grades would be improved.

The Concept Teaching Routine. Another routine that has had a positive effect on the performance of students with disabilities in mainstream courses at the secondary level is the Concept Teaching

Routine (Bulgren et al., 1988). The purpose of this routine is to deliver information about complex, abstract concepts (e.g., democracy) in such a way that students' understanding and memory of the information will be enhanced. The routine entails the use of a Concept Diagram, which serves to organize the information related to the concept into categories of information that: (a) name and define the concept; (b) are related to the characteristics that are always, sometimes, and never present in the concept; and (c) are related to examples and nonexamples of the concept. Symbols and shapes are used on the diagram to make the differences between information categories distinct and concrete for the students. The information on the Concept Diagram is prepared by the teacher before class and delivered in class through an interactive discussion process. Both teacher and students fill in blank diagrams during the discussion.

Bulgren et al. (1988) evaluated whether teachers could learn to use the Concept Teaching Routine and the subsequent effects of its use on students' performance in mainstream courses. These researchers found that content teachers readily learned to use the routine at mastery levels in less than 3 hours of instructional time.

When the teachers settled into a routine of presenting one major concept during each unit of study, students' performances were enhanced in a variety of ways. For example, both LD and typical students wrote three times more items of concept-related information in their notes than before the Concept Teaching Routine was used. When the students took a test over the concept information covered in a given unit, mean test scores also increased above baseline levels for all students. Test scores improved even further when the concept information was reviewed the day prior to the test along with other material in the regularly scheduled review session. Test scores on regularly scheduled unit tests also showed a significant improvement when the concept information was reviewed as a part of the regular review. During baseline,

only 57% of the students with learning disabilities were passing the regularly scheduled unit tests. During the concept training and review condition, however, 75% of the students with learning disabilities were passing the tests. Thus, the learning and retention of conceptual knowledge enhanced students' performance on unit tests, all of which were publisher-made tests designed to measure factual knowledge.

The Survey Routine. A third routine that has been used by mainstream teachers and appears to hold promise for enhancing the achievement of low-achieving students is the Survey Routine (Schumaker, Deshler, & McKnight, 1989). This routine was designed to enable mainstream teachers to provide an overview of a new textbook chapter to their students before initiating instruction in the unit. Low-achieving students frequently have difficulty reading textbooks written at grade level (Schumaker & Deshler, 1984), often demonstrate limited background knowledge for any lessons or assignments they might encounter (Graff, 1987), and have difficulty discriminating important from unimportant written information (Lenz, 1984). In addition, textbooks often are written in a way that is "inconsiderate" (Armbruster, 1984) for the reader. The Survey Routine was designed to help students compensate for these problems.

Like the Concept Teaching Routine, the Survey Routine was designed as an interactive routine in which the teacher leads students through a step-by-step process of analyzing the content of the new chapter. During this process, students are required to take notes on a specially constructed worksheet. There are places on the worksheet for the students to record information derived from each step of the survey process (e.g., a paraphrase of the title of the chapter). In the first step of the process, students read and paraphrase the chapter's title. Next, the relationship of the new chapter to previous and subsequent chapters is discussed by reference to the table of contents in the textbook. Third, the introduction of the chapter (or the first paragraph) is read aloud and paraphrased by the students. Fourth, the major sections of the chapter are delineated. Here, the teacher draws a diagram of the chapter on the board, using boxes to represent each part of the chapter. The title of a major section is paraphrased and written at the top of each box. The most important items to which the students should attend within each section (e.g., new vocabulary, a diagram, a map, an important explanation) then are listed within each box by the teacher. Finally, the summary of the chapter is read and paraphrased.

The results achieved through the use of this routine have been promising but inconsistent. For some teachers who used the routine, students' test scores on regularly scheduled chapter tests increased an average of 10 percentage points above baseline levels. All students including normally achieving students, realized some improvement, with the LD students achieving the largest gains; when the teachers stopped using the routine, all students' test scores returned to baseline levels. Other teachers did not achieve the same positive results. The reasons for these differences remain unclear. Perhaps the way in which the overall organization of the chapter is described and the ways in which important details are highlighted are factors. Perhaps the kinds of details that are highlighted or the enthusiasm with which the teacher delivers the information influence the results. Clearly, additional research is needed and will be forthcoming.

Factual enhancement routines. In studies sponsored under KU-IRLD auspices, additional routines currently are being developed for presenting factual information to LD students in mainstream classes to enhance the students' understanding and memory of the information. In one study, the use of a Verbal Enhancement Routine is being explored; in another, a Visual Enhancement Routine is being tested. Both routines have been compiled with the same purposes in mind.

Teachers need methods that enable them to make abstract information more concrete, to connect new knowledge with familiar knowledge, to enable students who cannot spell well to take useful notes, to highlight relationships and organizational structures in the information to be presented, and to draw unmotivated learners' attention to the information.

The Verbal Enhancement Routine (Schumaker et al., 1989) includes the oral presentation of instructional devices. One example of a verbal enhancement device is an analogy. Here, the teacher gives a familiar example from everyday life that makes an abstract concept more understandable. For instance, a science teacher might present an analogy of the camera and its working parts to help students understand how the eye works; a government teacher might present the analogy of a game, the players in the game, and the rules of the game to help students understand the "game" of politics. In another example of an verbal enhancement device, the teacher might use a story (e.g., a true story, a fictitious story, a personal story) to help the students understand information. For instance, a government teacher who is explaining the different governing styles of the various presidents of the United States might tell the story of Harry Truman and the sign on his desk that stated, "The Buck Stops Here."

These devices may be similar to those typically used by teachers, but their content is a critical feature of their construction. In order to qualify as a true factual enhancement device, a device must: (a) tie new information (information to be learned) to old information within the students' realm of experience, or (b) make an abstract concept more concrete. In addition, the routine that is used in employing the device is also critical. The Verbal Content Enhancement Routine involves three steps: Cue, Do, and Review. In the "Cue," the teacher must name the device for the students and link the device to the learning point (e.g., "I'm going to use a comparison to show you how the eye is like a camera"). Also, the teacher must provide a rationale for attending to the device (e.g., "If you learn how the eye is like a camera, you'll be better able to remember the parts of the eye and their functions. When an eye doctor talks to you about your cornea or your retina, you'll be able to understand what she's saying.") In the "Do" step, the teacher presents the device (e.g., "The pupil is like the shutter on a camera; it lets the light into the eye and it opens and closes according to how much light is present"). In the "Review" step, the teacher reminds the students about the device and its purpose at the end of the lesson or in a subsequent lesson (e.g., "Today, we used a comparison to help you remember the parts of the eye and its functions. Who remembers some similarities between the camera and the eye?").

Preliminary data on the effects of the use of the Verbal Enhancement Routine are promising. Specifically, the routine and associated devices appear to be integrated easily into teachers' presentations. For some teachers, the use of the devices enhances students' performance on regularly scheduled tests; however, the way in which the devices are put into use seems to be critical in producing these effects. The use of the preliminary cue that announces to the students that a device will be used and the review of the information linked with the device seem to be important ingredients in producing the enhanced learning effects. Additional research is required to determine the effects of regular use of these devices on students' learning.

A Visual Enhancement Routine also is being studied currently. This routine involves the presentation of visual depictions of information that relate to various categories of knowledge concerning regions and countries. A science teacher might draw a diagram of the heart on the board using red chalk for aerated blood and blue chalk for blood that carries wastes. A government teacher might draw a flow chart on the board to make the process of lawmaking more clearly understood. An English teacher might use a standard chart depicting headings for the setting, the characters, the plot, and symbols in the story lines to analyze a series of short stories.

The way in which these devices are constructed and utilized has been standardized through the use of the Visual Enhancement Routine, which has 10 steps. Initially, the teacher names the depiction and cues the students to attend to it and to take notes about it. Next, the teacher provides a rationale for why the students should learn the information. A conceptual bridge is built between the new information and previously presented information. As the information in the depiction is delivered, complete statements are made about particular parts of it and the depicted relationships. The teacher points to the parts as they are described and involves the students in the presentation by asking them questions and soliciting their comments. Finally, the teacher reviews and summarizes the use of the depiction at the end of the lecture or in subsequent lectures.

Preliminary results on the use of Visual Enhancement Routine indicate that teachers can learn the routine quickly and that students benefit from its use (Crank, Deshler, & Schumaker, in preparation). After a 2-hour training session, teachers improved from presenting about two major depictions per lesson to three depictions per lesson, and they improved the quality of their presentations from performing about 31% of the steps to performing about 72% of the steps of the routine. The quality of their depictions also improved from fulfilling 37% to fulfilling 91% of the specified characteristics of a good quality depiction.

In a separate study, the effects of this Visual Enhancement Routine were studied with regard to student performance on tests. Two groups of students with learning disabilities who had received lectures in which the routine was used scored an average of 11 percentage points and 15 percentage points higher than their respective control groups of LD students whose lectures did not include use of the routine. Nonhandicapped students also showed improved performance of similar magnitude.

Integration of routines. Certainly, additional research is required to study further the usefulness of the notion that mainstream teachers can enhance the understanding and recall of the information they present for students with disabilities and other low-achieving students. Some of the routines (e.g., the Survey Routine, the Factual Enhancement Routines) need further study in isolation to determine under what conditions they are most effective. Once several routines have been refined and found to be successful, the effects of their integration should be studied as well. For example, the Survey Routine might be used to introduce a new unit, the Concept Teaching Routine might be used to present information related to the major concept in the unit, the Advance Organizer Routine might be used to introduce each subsequent lesson, and the Factual Enhancement Routines might be used to highlight information as it is presented in each lesson. Conceivably, such an integrated sequence might have an even greater effect on students' performance than can be created when the routines or devices are used in isolation. Until further research has been conducted, one can only speculate about such possible effects. Another equally important issue is the acceptability by teachers of such an integrated sequence. If teachers find the routines and devices cumbersome or limiting, their usefulness will be diminished because teachers will be less likely to use them. Thus, ensuring that the routines and devices are acceptable to teachers is an additional goal for developers.

TRANSLATING RESEARCH INTO PRACTICE

The instructional devices and routines described in this chapter for use by regular class teachers in mainstream settings as well as those developed by other researchers (e.g., Brophy & Good, 1985; Weinstein, Goetz, & Alexander, 1988) provide reasons to be optimistic about being able to address effectively the learning and academic achievement problems of low-achieving adolescents in secondary schools. Regardless of the nature or magnitude of the results achieved through current research efforts, little change in school practices will occur unless appropriate steps are taken to ensure effective translation of these instructional procedures into usable teaching products and ongoing staff-development and teacher-training efforts.

The task of translating research prototypes into usable teaching products is a critical one if educational change is to occur. The literature is replete with research studies reporting that positive learning effects have been achieved as a result of using specific teaching procedures. Unfortunately, in the vast majority of cases, practitioners must extrapolate the procedures for implementing the instructional practice from the methodology section of a journal article. If they request additional information from the researcher, they often get a lengthy field-test protocol of the instructional procedures used during data collection, or receive an abbreviated synopsis of the procedure. In either case, the teacher still lacks the information needed to translate the instructional routine accurately, and with relative ease, into classroom practice. Researchers must rethink their responsibility to the educational community with regard to translating validated teaching routines into usable, teacher-friendly instructional packets or materials. The gap between research and practice that has existed historically in education may, in large part, be accounted for by the failure of researchers to view the research process as including the extra steps of translating field-test versions of innovative procedures into instructional materials conducive to use in the classroom.

When KU-IRLD staff members completed the first phases of intervention research on SIM, they thought that the magnitude of the reported improvement would be sufficiently powerful to encourage teachers to use the procedures. Only after discovering that classroom implementation rates were abysmally low did they realize that, as researchers, they needed to make a significant commitment to the translation process. Since then, KU-IRLD staff members have committed themselves to going the extra step of translating validated instructional routines or devices into teachers' manuals (and, where appropriate, student materials) that are published by a commercial vendor. To do so has required a significant investment of time and resources. In addition, staff members have had to make trade-offs between doing new research and translating completed research into usable products. In the process of making this translation, staff have found that working very closely with the ultimate consumers of the instructional packages is imperative to ensure that the packages are designed in a way that meets their instructional and classroom organization and management needs.

A second area to consider when attempting to optimize the transfer of research on instructional routines into practice has to do with staff development. Each year, school districts pour millions of dollars into efforts to upgrade the instructional effectiveness of their teachers though in-service training programs. The majority of these efforts tend to be one-shot programs (e.g., a 1- to 2-hour training session on a new teaching routine) with no follow-up included as a part of the overall training design. Research findings on the efficacy of such training efforts are clear: Very little, if any, permanent change in instructional practices results (Fullan, 1982; Hord, Rutherford, Huling-Austin, & Hall, 1987). As a profession, educators must stop ignoring documented principles of staff development and system change. Our current course of action will have little or no effect on bringing about significant changes in schools and will lead to inappropriate conclusions about the efficacy of new teaching procedures. In other words, teachers may conclude that the procedures lack power when the real reason for their failure may be that teachers were not given enough exposure to and practice with the procedure under controlled conditions to enable them to reach a sufficient level of comfort and fluency.

The following principles of effective staff development should be applied to facilitate translation of teaching routines into mainstream instructional practices. First, key stakeholders in a school district (e.g., administrators, teachers, and school psychologists) must be involved in deciding whether to adopt and receive training in a given procedure. In short, this step in a system's adoption of an educational innovation is evaluative. Questions as to whether the innovation is consistent with the district's philosophy and other on-line teaching practices must be addressed. Second, the issue of trade-offs must be resolved. That is, the incorporation of any innovation usually adds significantly to teachers' planning and/or instructional load initially; hence, decisions must be made regarding elimination or reduction of current programs or practices. Since such decisions are often difficult to make in education, educators often follow the course of least resistance and simply view the new procedure as an add-on. In turn, they often elect to keep using practices with which they feel most comfortable (the old practices); thus, the probability of adopting a new practice is greatly minimized. Strong administrative support and endorsement (including permission to make the necessary trade-offs) are very important.

Third, to ensure the adoption of complex educational innovations, training must be offered over a sustained period of time rather than as a one-shot event. Sustained training efforts allow time for modeling, practice, feedback, and questions. In addition, teachers need the opportunity to try out the new procedure (or portions of the new procedure if it consists of many steps or is complex) in their classroom and to debrief with the trainer(s) on problems encountered. Finally, following the formal training session(s), teachers must have the opportunity to receive ongoing support in their efforts to implement the new procedure. Initial support can be provided through the use of support teams (i.e., small groups of teachers who meet to discuss implementation problems and other issues) (Huberman & Miles, 1984) and peer coaching (Joyce & Showers, 1982).

Another area that must be considered in an effort to increase the likelihood of innovative adoptions is the role of pre-service teacher-training programs. The current teaching corps in the United States will be undergoing significant changes in the next decade (Darling-Hammond, 1988). There will be a large turnover in the nation's teaching staff owing to retirements and decisions to leave the teaching profession for another career (National Center for Education Statistics, 1985). Filling this void represents not only a tremendous challenge, but also a significant opportunity to affect the types of skills new teachers should possess in respect to the instruction of low-achieving students. The first step toward meeting this challenge requires careful review of the content of current teacher preparation programs. Especially in the preparation of secondary teachers, additional time is needed to train teacher trainees in specific procedures for effectively delivering their content. Prospective teachers not only need to be made aware of specific teaching routines and devices for enhancing the delivery of curriculum content but also need ample opportunities to practice such procedures to mastery in practicum and field experiences. Many who have written about the educational crisis confronting our nation's schools have argued that meaningful solutions will, in many cases, mean having to make dramatic departures from traditional practices (McKibbin, 1988). As dropout and low-achievement problems escalate in magnitude (700,000 students dropped out in 1988; another 700,000 were barely functionally literate), steps must be taken to equip teachers with skills that will enable them to organize and present content information more effectively to at-risk students. This process should begin most logically in the formative years of teacher preparation. The climate for such reform is right in light of current efforts to raise the quality of teacher preparation (e.g., the HOLMES Group, 1986).

Finally, the important role that school psychologists can play in effective translation and utilization of the teaching procedures discussed in this chapter must be underscored. To fulfill this role, school psychologists must expand the focus of their assessment efforts to include a profile of the different setting demands (e.g., the types of tests, the readability of the textbooks, the format of assignments) that students encounter in their regular classrooms. If teachers are informed about the setting demands that particular students will have difficulty in meeting, they will be better able to work with school psychologists and other personnel to adapt instruction to correspond with particular students' needs. Teachers will understand more fully how teaching practices and curriculum materials can precipitate failure as much as specific student deficits, and they will be more able to accommodate special learners in their classes.

Additionally, as contributors to IEP and other educational planning meetings, school psychologists must recognize the importance of having all members of the committee (teachers, parents, and students) actively participate in the decision-making process (Van Reusen, 1985; Van Reusen et al., 1987). Providing opportunities for participation in such meetings is central to obtaining the necessary commitment and support of key participants (mainstream and support service teachers, parents, and the student). The school psychologist should view his or her role in such meetings as a conveyor of information, problem solver, and advocate of change in teaching practices on the part of mainstream teachers as well as on the part of the student.

Also, the school psychologist can do much to promote cooperative planning and other interactions among teaching staff. Cooperative planning between special class teachers and mainstream teachers is particularly challenging because of the schedule conflicts that arise during a typical school day (e.g., planning periods or lunch periods that do not match). Because of school psychologists' relatively more flexible schedules, they can facilitate the efforts of different staff members in cooperative planning by being mediators or by encouraging a reluctant staff member to interact with other teachers on behalf of targeted students. Finally, school psychologists can play a valuable role by making staff aware of newly validated teaching routines and by modeling their use. They also can team with mainstream teachers in efforts to increase the effectiveness of their presentations of subject matter. This teaming relationship can be established, for example, in the form of a peer-coaching arrangement (Joyce & Showers, 1982). In brief, school psychologists can do a great deal to support and facilitate the processes that are critical to bringing about instructional improvements in school settings.

In summary, research has shown that to bring about a strong impact on the academic success and life adjustment of at-risk students requires the use of a broad array of instructional strategies and techniques in a coordinated fashion by several teaching and support personnel (Deshler & Schumaker, 1988). The major components of an innovative model for providing such services have been summarized in this chapter. A key element of that model is the effective use, by mainstream teachers, of a host of validated teaching routines and devices that can facilitate students' understandings and retention of content information presented in the mainstream setting.

It is our contention that in secondary schools, where so much emphasis is on the delivery and mastery of large amounts of content, mainstream teachers possess the means of significantly halting the decline in school achievement of many at-risk students as well as reducing the escalation of referral rates of these students to special education. Our data suggest that the most effective teachers are those who have the ability to manipulate, organize, and present their content information in such a way that it becomes easy to understand and to remember because it has been made learner-friendly by teachers who deliberately set out to do so.

FOOTNOTE

[1]Some of these materials (i.e., those associated with the Learning Strategies Curriculum) are available only through training sessions led by trainers associated with the KU-IRLD. For more information contact the Director of Training, KU-IRLD, 223 Carruth-O'Leary Hall, Lawrence, KS 66045.

REFERENCES

Alley, G. R., & Deshler, D. D. (1979). *Teaching the learning disabled adolescent.* Denver: Love.

Allington, R. L. (1984). So what is the problem? Whose problem is it? *Topics in Learning and Learning Disabilities, 3*(4), 91-99.

Armbruster, B. B. (1984). The problem of "inconsiderate text." In G. Duffy, L. Roehler, & J. Mason (Eds.), *Comprehension instruction: Perspectives and suggestions.* New York: Longman.

Ausubel, P. (1963). *The psychology of meaningful verbal learning.* New York: Grune & Stratton.

Ausubel, D. P., & Robinson, F. G. (1969). *School learning: An introduction to educational psychology.* New York: Holt, Rinehart & Winston.

Beals, V. L. (1983). *The effects of large group instruction on the acquisition of specific learning strategies by learning disabled adolescents.* Unpublished doctoral dissertation, University of Kansas, Lawrence.

Bos, C. S., & Anders, P. L. (1987). Semantic feature analysis: An interactive teaching strategy for facilitating learning from text. *Learning Disability Focus, 3*(1), 55-59.

Boyer, E. L. (1983). *High school: A report on secondary education in America.* New York: Harper & Row.

Brophy, J., & Good, T. L. (1985). Teacher behavior and student achievement. In M. Wittrock (Ed.), *Handbook of research on teaching.* New York: Longman.

Bulgren, J. A., Schumaker, J. B., & Deshler, D. D. (1988). Effectiveness of a concept teaching routine in enhancing the performance of LD students in secondary level mainstream classes. *Learning Disability Quarterly, 11*(1), 319-331.

Carlson, S. A. (1985). The ethical appropriateness of subject-matter tutoring of learning disabled adolescents. *Learning Disability Quarterly, 8,* 310-314.

Carlson, S. A., & Alley, G. R. (1981). *Performance and Competence of Learning Disabled and High Achieving High School Students on Essential Cognitive Skills* (Research Report #53). Lawrence, KS: University of Kansas Institute for Research in Learning Disabilities.

Clark, F. L., Deshler, D. D., Schumaker, J. B., Alley, G. R., & Warner, M. M. (1984). Visual imagery and self-questioning: Strategies to improve comprehension of written material. *Journal of Learning Disabilities, 17,* 145-149.

Crank, J. N., Deshler, D. D., & Schumaker, J. B. (in preparation). A visual enhancement routine for presenting content in secondary classrooms. Lawrence: KS: University of Kansas, Institute for Research in Learning Disabilities.

Cuban, L. (1984). *How teachers taught: Constancy and change in American classrooms, 1890–1980.* New York: Longman.

Cusick, P. A. (1983). *The equalitarian ideal and the American high school.* New York: Longman.

Darling-Hammond, L. (1988). The futures of teaching. *Educational Leadership, 46*(3), 4-10.

Deshler, D. D., Alley, G. R., Warner, M. M., & Schumaker, J. B. (1981). Instructional practices for promoting skill acquisition and generalization in severely learning disabled adolescents. *Learning Disability Quarterly, 4*(4), 415-421.

Deshler, D. D., & Schumaker, J. B. (1988). An instructional model for teaching students how to learn. In J. L. Graden, J. E. Zins, & M. J. Curtis, (Eds.), *Alternative education delivery systems: Enhancing instructional options for all students* (pp. 391-411). Washington, DC: National Association of School Psychologists.

Deshler, D. D., Schumaker, J. B., Lenz, B. K., & Ellis, E. S. (1984). Academic and cognitive interventions for LD adolescents: Part II. *Journal of Learning Disabilities, 17*(3), 170-187.

Deshler, D. D., Kass, C. E., & Ferrell, W. R. (1978). Monitoring of schoolwork errors by LD adolescents. *Journal of Learning Disabilities, 11*(7), 10-23.

Ellis, E. S., Deshler, D. D., & Schumaker, J. B. (1989). Teaching adolescents with learning disabilities to generate and use task-specific strategies. *Journal of Learning Disabilities, 22*(2), 108-119, 130.

Ellis, E. S., Lenz, B. K., & Sabornie, E. J. (1987). Generalization and adaptation of learning strategies to natural environments: Part I: Critical agents. *Remedial and Special Education, 8*(1), 6-20.

Fullan, M. (1982). *The meaning of educational change.* New York: Teachers College Press.

Goodlad, J. L. (1984). *A place called school.* New York: McGraw-Hill.

Graff, H. J. (1987). *The legacies of literacy: Continuities and contradictions in Western culture and society.* Bloomington, IN: Indiana University Press.

Hazel, J. S., Schumaker, J. B., Sherman, J. A., & Sheldon-Wildgen, J. (1981). ASSET: A social skills program for adolescents. Champaign, IL: Research Press.

Holmes Group. (1986). *Tomorrow's teachers: A report of the Holmes Group.* East Lansing, MI: Holmes Group.

Hord, S. M., Rutherford, W. L., Huling-Austin, L., & Hall, G. (1987). *Taking charge of change.* Alexandria, VA: Association of Supervision and Curriculum Development.

Howe, H., & Edelman, M. W. (1985). *Barriers to excellence: Our children at risk.* Boston: National Coalition of Advocates for Students.

Howell, S. B. (1986). *A study of the effectiveness of TOWER – A theme writing strategy.* Unpublished masters thesis, University of Kansas, Lawrence.

Huberman, A. M., & Miles, M. B. (1984). *Innovation up close: How school improvement works.* New York: Plenum.

Hughes, C. (1985). *A test taking strategy for learning disabled and emotionally handicapped adolescents.* Unpublished dissertation, University of Florida, Gainesville.

Hughes, C., Schumaker, J., Deshler, D. D., & Mercer, C. (1988). *The test taking strategy: Instructor's manual.* Lawrence, KS: Edge Enterprises.

Joyce, B. R., & Showers, B. (1982). The coaching of teaching. *Educational Leadership, 40,* 4-10.

Keimig, J. (in preparation). *The effects of peer tutoring on the acquisition and generalization of learning strategies* (Research Report). Lawrence: University of Kansas Institute for Research in Learning Disabilities.

Knackendoffel, A. (1989). *Development and validation of a set of teaming strategies for enhancing collaboration between secondary resource and content teachers.* Unpublished doctoral dissertation, University of Kansas, Lawrence.

Lenz, B. K. (1984). *The effect of advance organizers on the learning and retention of LD adolescents within the contexts of a cooperative planning model* (Final research report submitted to the U.S. Department of Education, Special Education Services).

Lenz, B. K., Alley, G. R., & Schumaker, J. B. (1987). Activating the inactive learner through the presentation of advance organizers. *Learning Disability Quarterly, 10*(1), 53-67.

Lenz, B. K., Schumaker, J. B., Deshler, D. D., & Beals, V. L. (1984). *The word identification strategy: Instructor's manual.* Lawrence, KS: University of Kansas Institute for Research in Learning Disabilities.

Licopoli, L. (1984). The resource room and mainstreaming secondary handicapped students: A case history. *Topics in Learning and Learning Disabilities, 3*(4), 1–16.

Lieberman, A., & Miller, L. (1978). The social realities of teaching. *Teachers College Record, 80,* 55–61.

McKibbin, M. D. (1988). Alternative teacher certification programs. *Educational Leadership, 46*(3), 32–35.

McKnight, P. C. (1980). Microteaching: Development 1968 to 1978. *British Journal of Teacher Education, 6*(3), 214–226.

Mellard, D. F., & Deshler, D. D. (1984). Modeling the condition of learning disabilities on post-secondary populations. *Educational Psychologist 19,* 188–197.

Moccia, R. E., Schumaker, J. B., Hazel, J. S., Vernon, D. S., & Deshler, D. D. (in press). A mentor program for facilitating the transitions of individuals with learning disabilities. *Journal of Reading, Writing, and Learning Disabilities, 5*(2).

Moran, M. R. (1980). *An investigation of the demands on oral language skills of learning disabled students in secondary classrooms* (Research Report #1). Lawrence, KS: University of Kansas Institute for Research in Learning Disabilities.

Moran, M. R., & DeLoach, T. F. (1982). *Mainstream teachers' responses to formal features of writing by secondary learning disabled students (Research Report #61).* Lawrence: University of Kansas Institute for Research in Learning Disabilities.

Moran, M. R., Schumaker, J. B., & Vetter, A. F. (1981). *Teaching a paragraph organization strategy to learning disabled adolescents* (Research Report #54). Lawrence, KS: University of Kansas Institute for Research in Learning Disabilities.

Nagel, D., Schumaker, J. B., & Deshler, D. D. (1986). *The FIRST-Letter Mnemonic Strategy: Instructor's manual.* Lawrence, KS: Edge Enterprises, Inc.

National Center for Education Statistics. (1985). *Projections of Education statistics to 1992.* Washington, DC: U.S. Department of Education.

Powell, A. G., Farrar, E., & Cohen, D. K. (1985). *The shopping mall high school: Winners and losers in the educational marketplace.* Boston: Houghton Mifflin.

Putnam, M. L. (1988). *An investigation of the curricular demands in secondary mainstream classrooms containing mildly handicapped students.* Unpublished doctoral dissertation, University of Kansas, Lawrence.

Robbins, D. (1982). *FIRST-Letter Mnemonic Strategy: A memorization technique for learning disabled high school students.* Unpublished master's thesis, University of Kansas, Lawrence.

Robinson, S., Deshler, D. D., Denton, P., & Schumaker, J. B. (in preparation). *The listening and notetaking strategy: Instructor's manual.* Lawrence, KS: University of Kansas Institute for Research in Learning Disabilities.

Scanlon, R. G. (1982). *Report of the Council of Chief State School Officers and Ad Hoc Committee on Teacher Certification Preparation and Accreditation.* Washington, DC: The Council.

Schmidt, J. (1983). *The effects of four generalizations conditions on learning disabled adolescents' written language performance in the regular classroom.* Unpublished doctoral dissertation, University of Kansas, Lawrence.

Schumaker, J. B. (in preparation). *The Theme Writing Strategy: Instructor's manual.* Lawrence: University of Kansas Institute for Research in Learning Disabilities.

Schumaker, J. B., Denton, P. H., & Deshler, D. D. (1984). *The Paraphrasing Strategy: Instructor's manual.* Lawrence, KS: University of Kansas Institute for Research in Learning Disabilities.

Schumaker, J. B., & Deshler, D. D. (1984). Setting demand variables: A major factor in program planning for LD adolescents. *Topics in Language Disorders, 4*(2), 22–40.

Schumaker, J. B., & Deshler, D. D. (1988). Implementing the regular education initiative in secondary schools: A different ball game. *Journal of Learning Disabilities, 21*(1), 36–42.

Schumaker, J. B., Deshler, D. D., Alley, G. R., Warner, M. M., Clark, F. L., & Nolan, S. (1982). Error monitoring: A learning strategy for improving adolescents' academic performance. In W. M. Cruickshank & J. W. Lerner (Eds.), *Coming of age: Vol. 3. The best of ACLD.* Syracuse, NY: Syracuse University Press.

Schumaker, J. B., Deshler, D. D., Denton, P. M., Alley, G. R., Clark, F. L., & Warner, M. M. (1982). Multipass: A learning strategy for improving reading comprehension. *Learning Disability Quarterly, 5,* 195–304.

Schumaker, J. B., Deshler, D. D., & Ellis, E. S. (1986). Intervention issues related to the education of LD adolescents. In J. K. Torgeson & B. L. Wong (Eds.), *Learning disabilities: Some new perspectives.* New York: Academic.

Schumaker, J. B., Deshler, D. D., & McKnight, P. (1989). *Teaching routines to enhance the mainstream performance of adolescents with learning disabilities* (Final Report submitted to the U.S. Department of Education, Special Education Services).

Schumaker, J. B., Hazel, J. S., & Deshler, D. D. (1985). A model for facilitating post-secondary transitions. *Techniques: A Journal for Remedial Education and Counseling, 1,* 437–446.

Schumaker, J. B., Hazel, J. S., & Pederson, C. (1988). *Social skills for daily living.* Circle Pines, MN: American Guidance Service.

Schumaker, J. B., & Lyerla, K. (in preparation). *The paragraph writing strategy: Instructor's manual.* Lawrence, KS: University of Kansas Institute for Research in Learning Disabilities.

Schumaker, J. B., Nolan, S. M., & Deshler, D. D. (1985). *The error monitoring strategy: Instructor's manual.* Lawrence, KS: University of Kansas Institute for Research in Learning Disabilities.

Schumaker, J. B., & Sheldon J. (1985). *The sentence writing strategy: Instructor's manual.* Lawrence, KS: University of Kansas Institute for Research in Learning Disabilities.

Schumaker, J. B., Wildgen, J., & Sherman, J. (1980). *An observational study of the academic and social behaviors of LD adolescents in the regular classroom.* (Research Report #22). Lawrence, KS: University of Kansas Institute for Research in Learning Disabilities.

Seabaugh, G. O., & Schumaker, J. B. (1981a). *The effects of three conferencing procedures on the academic productivity of LD and NLD adolescents* (Research Report #36). Lawrence, KS: University of Kansas Institute for Research in Learning Disabilities.

Seabaugh, G. O., & Schumaker, J. B. (1981b). *The effects of self-regulation training on the academic productivity of LD and NLD adolescents.* (Research Report #37). Lawrence, KS: University of Kansas Institute for Research in Learning Disabilities.

Sinclair, R. L., & Glory, W. J. (1987). *Reaching marginal students: A primary concern for school renewal.* Chicago: McCutchan.

Skrtic, T. (1980). *Formal reasoning abilities of learning disabilities adolescents* (Research Report #7). Lawrence, KS: University of Kansas Institute for Research in Learning Disabilities.

Spady, W. G., & Marx, G. (1984). *Excellence in our schools: Making it happen.* San Francisco: Far West Laboratory.

Van Reusen, A. K. (1985). *A study of the effects of training learning disabled adolescents in self-advocacy procedure for use in the IEP conference.* Unpublished doctoral dissertation. Lawrence: University of Kansas.

Van Reusen, A. K., Bos, C., Schumaker, J. B., & Deshler, D. D. (1987). *The educational planning strategy.* Lawrence, KS: Edge Enterprises.

Warner, M. M., Schumaker, J. B., Alley, G. R., & Deshler, D. D., (in press). An epidemiological study of school identified LD and low-achieving adolescents on a serial recall task: The role of executive control. *Learning Disabilities Research.*

Warner, M. M., Schumaker, J. B., Alley, G. R., & Deshler, D. D. (1980). Learning disabled adolescents in the public schools: Are they different from other low achievers? *Exceptional Education Quarterly, 1*(2), 27–36.

Weinstein, C. E., Goetz, E. T., & Alexandra, P. A. (1988). *Learning and study strategies: Issues in assessment, instruction, and evaluation.* New York: Harcourt Brace Jovanovich.

22

Mainstream Consultation Agreements in Secondary Schools

Gerald Tindal
University of Oregon

Gary Germann
Pine County (Minnesota) Special Education Cooperative

With implementation of the due process procedures outlined in Public Law 94-142, mainstreaming of students with handicapping conditions has become an important and prominent topic. Probably the most difficult mandate of this legislation is placement of students in the least restrictive environment (LRE). Providing definition to this phrase is problematic, operationalizing procedures for accomplishing it are questionable, and evaluating the success of such efforts is often lacking. Our purpose in this chapter is to provide a systematic strategy for placing middle and high school students with mild handicaps (MH) in the LRE. We assume that the mainstream content classes represent the LRE and only with data to indicate the lack of success with supplemental support should more invasive (i.e., special education) strategies be considered.

The law, both state and federal, is quite direct in its prescriptions: To the extent that there are no detrimental effects, children who are handicapped shall attend regular classes to be educated with children who do not have handicaps. A handicapped student shall be removed from a regular educational program only when the nature or severity of the handicap is such that education in a regular educational program cannot be accomplished satisfactorily. Furthermore, there must be an indication that the student will be served better outside of the regular program. The needs of the individual shall determine (a) the extent to which the student will be able to participate in mainstream regular educational programs, and (b) the type and amount of special education and related services provided to the student.

To date, educators have lacked a database to identify potentially successful or unsuccessful mainstreaming candidates. As a result, placement of handicapped students in regular education has been haphazard at best (U.S. Department of Education, 1989). For a mainstreaming program to be successful, the following conditions should be in place (Salend, 1984):

1. Criteria are used for assaying a student's readiness to be mainstreamed.

2. Handicapped students are prepared for entering mainstream environments.

3. Students in the mainstream environment are prepared to receive a handicapped student.

4. Communication among educators is planned and implemented.

5. Student progress is monitored regularly.

6. In-service staff development is provided.

Although special education teachers often believe their students should be spending more time in the mainstream classroom, students' lack of skills often prevent them from such participation (Halpern & Benz, 1987). Low achievement appears to be very characteristic of secondary learning-disabled (LD) students. In basic skills such as math (word problems, graph reading, geometry, and algebra), vocabulary (synonyms), reading (literal and inferential questions based on a short passage), and tests of pattern recognitions, these students are often significantly lower than their regular education cohorts (Gregory, Shanahan, & Walberg, 1986). They typically have attained mastery on few mathematics skills; large percentages of these students fail minimum competence examinations on skills that employers deem critical (Algozzine, O'Shea, Crews, & Stoddard, 1987).

Given MH students' lack of essential basic skills to maintain involvement in the content area class, instruction often is tutorial and is delivered by the special education (SE) teacher. Yet many SE teachers lack appropriate training to provide instruction in specific content area classes. It is presumed, therefore, that such programs are better provided by the content area specialists (e.g., regular education instructors in history, science, English).

In this chapter, we describe a program that attends to these issues in a systematic manner. The program, entitled mainstream consultation agreements (MCA) (Germann, 1986), is a procedure for general and special education teachers to work together in serving MH students in secondary mainstream content classes. MCAs are developed when special education students lack sufficient academic and/or behavior skills to succeed in the mainstream classroom without help. They define a system for identifying problems through a process of referral–assessment–placement and for developing programs by understanding and operationalizing teachers' expectations and ensuring the students' success. Outcomes are evaluated using student performance data to inform and make decisions, the responsibilities of everyone involved (students, parents, and teachers) being well delineated.

The MCA program incorporates the major tenets of behavior consultation:

1. It is premised upon the application of behavioral or social learning theory (Kratochwill & Bergan, 1978), in which the focus of consultation is more oriented toward problem solving than to the relationship between the consultant and consultee.

2. The goal of consultation is to increase desirable and decrease undesirable behaviors.

3. Four major phases are considered in the consultation process (problem identification, problem analysis, plan implementation, and program evaluation).

4. Reponsibilities are based upon the consultant as an expert, although mutual problem solving may be emphasized. MCAs also incorporate several features of the special education resource teacher (SERT) program developed by Deno and Mirkin (1977). In particular, an emphasis is placed on time-series evaluation to develop data-based instruction, which includes direct instruction in basic skills and indirect instruction in content areas.

AN OVERVIEW OF MAINSTREAM CONSULTATION AGREEMENTS

Mainstream consultation agreements are composed of three major components. First, minimum essential learner outcomes (MELO) are identified; second, responsibilities are allocated to all individuals implementing the agreement; third, measurement systems are established to document individual educational plan (IEP) goal attainment and provide frequent feedback. These three components are integrated into a communication and monitoring system that informs teachers of students' performance and helps determine appropriate interventions or support services in the mainstream classroom. Each of the components is defined carefully in the agreement so that when modifications are deemed necessary, a specified component of the original agreement can be readily identified and altered.

The six functions outlined by Salend (1984) are embedded in the major components of MCAs. First, teacher standards and expectations are considered in determining if students are ready for mainstreaming, and if so, the kinds of adaptations needed to ensure success. Second, preparation of handicapped students (and to a less extent, nonhandicapped students) for classroom integration is based upon specific roles and responsibilities set in the course of consultation. Furthermore, frequent contact between teachers and open, yet focused, communication is included in the established consultation relationship. Third, systematic measurement and evaluation of the students' progress is incorporated into the system. Although staff development is not an explicit part of the MCA while in operation, it does occur when general education teachers take part in materials development and curriculum adaptation in a summer work session, which we describe later.

MCAs provide very specific procedures for delivering specialized programs in mainstream classrooms, but they are clearly a service delivered through special education, specifically, special education resource room teachers or school psychologists who serve as case managers. MCA programs are provided to regular education teachers, the target for behavior change being the handicapped student. Individual education plans are the medium by which MCAs are developed; they emphasize the accommodations to be made in teaching the regular education curriculum. Such a system eventually is used to assist regular education teachers in implementing data-based program modifications in their classrooms to increase the probability of a handicapped student's success. Therefore, both the regular and special education teachers are the implementors of the IEP.

The Problem-Solving Focus

As noted by Ysseldyke et al. (1984), once students are referred for special education, there is a very high probability that they will be assessed and eventually placed. Most decision making in special education programs operates from a referral-to-placement perspective, rather than a referral-to-intervention perspective.

Presently, few contingencies exist for keeping students in mainstream classrooms. MCAs are procedures for maintaining the focus of decision-making on instruction rather than placement. For example, if an 11th-grade history teacher has a very low-performing student in class, a referral to special education is likely to result in placement. The assessment process does not focus on the teacher's accommodation of the student in the history class. Once a placement in special education is made, the student receives history on a tutorial basis. Again, no accommodation is made for delivering content instruction by the content expert, the general education teacher.

Using MCAs, however, we are rearranging the problem-solving system to better accommodate instruction in the mainstream class. We assert that this accommodation can succeed if we can better determine the student's performance and teacher's expectations for success, establish in very clear terms what has to be done and who has to do it, and finally, ensure that all decisions are data-based, using student progress as the key indicator of the need to maintain or change programs. The process is composed of three basic steps: (a) determining who should be served, (b) allocating roles and responsibilities, and (c) monitoring and evaluating student progress. All assistance is predicated upon accurate and functional student and classroom assessments and clear assignment of expectations and responsibilities among special and regular education staff.

Determining Eligible Candidates

The first step is to identify students for whom MCAs are a viable option. Conceivably, all handicapped students of secondary school age attending general education classes are eligible. At least part-time participation in general education is sufficient for an MCA to be considered. However, for special education students attending school and *not* enrolled in any general education classes, MCAs are not an option.

The second step is to determine whether the student is being evaluated in his or her mainstream classroom. If the IEP includes mainstream content classes that the student is required to attend *and* from which an evaluation will be made in the form of a report card grade, then MCAs are considered as an optional service. For students not receiving a grade on a report card, there is no need to develop an MCA. For example, students may attend classes during study hours or off-school hours, or audit classes, in which attendance is voluntary and they are not required to perform according to any standards. In such a case an MCA is not needed, as no standards or evaluations of performance are in use.

Designing Individual Education Plans

In the third step, IEPs are developed to be responsive to the student's curriculum and behavior needs. These IEPs may be for basic skills and/or content areas. The decision hinges on whether a student's lack of basic skills prevents the student from being successful in the mainstream classroom. If the basic skill deficit precludes success, an MCA is not needed and the IEP is designed for basic skills alone; the student is then served in a resource room by a special education teacher. For example, if a 10th-grade student cannot functionally read (i.e., oral reading fluency is less than 15 words per minute), the basic skill deficit is so severe that success in the mainstream classroom is very unlikely.

However, a basic skills deficit potentially can impede, but not preclude, the student's success in the mainstream classroom; then an MCA is necessary. In the case of mild skills deficits, a determination is made whether to develop an IEP goal for every regular education subject in which the student is enrolled. At this point, the MCA is developed using the IEP format. The three components of an IEP

(conditions of performance, relevant behavior exhibited, and levels of performance expected) should be established and formally written. Therefore, the student's skills must be documented and the teacher's expectations ascertained.

Assessing the Student Skill Level

The first task in writing an IEP is to adequately document student basic skills and current level of performance in the subject area. Although it is highly desirable to follow a competency-based approach, in which critical academic and social skills are identified and the student's proficiency is assessed (Hundert, 1982; Salend & Lutz, 1985), few measurement systems are currently available for documenting students' performance on content area mainstream classroom tasks. In elementary schools, curriculum-based measurement (CBM) has been well researched and utilized for making a range of educational decisions (Deno, 1985; Deno & Fuchs, 1987; Germann & Tindal, 1985; Tindal & Marston, 1986). Yet little parallel research has been completed with middle and high school students.

Ideally, academic assessments would help determine the degree to which a student's performance in the mainstream classroom is a function of basic skills deficits or behavioral/interactional deficits or excesses. The skills assessment would determine a special education student's relative standing vis a vis age- and grade-appropriate peers on curriculum-based assessments. To accomplish this type of assessment, norms from either the basic skills areas or the content area classroom would be established, and students appropriate for mainstreaming would be tested and compared against this level.

For example, in Pine County, a student had to demonstrate performance similar to that of students who were either 2 years younger (for 7th and 8th graders) or end-of-year 6th grade (for 9th through 12th graders). Alternatively, Tindal and Parker (1989) used a silent reading/written-retell procedure in content area material to document the range of performance exhibited by regular education middle and high school students. In either case, such data provided a reference to determine if special education students were eligible for special education and had the requisite skills to be mainstreamed in a content area class.

Ascertaining the Expectations of Mainstream Teachers

Not only must the magnitude of basic skills deficits of the student be determined, but the particular demands of the classroom for success must be considered. Teachers' expectations are an important part of the classroom environment, particularly in regard to the manner in which the classroom is organized and the strategies used in its management. As a consequence, successful mainstreaming of students implies an accurate description of these expectations.

Many of these expectations or requirements for success are quite universal, representing the minimal essentials for participation. For example, Kerr and Zigmond (1986) found that, generally, special and regular education high school teachers have similar expectations about the skills deemed critical for the students to succeed in their classrooms. They also agreed on the behaviors that are intolerable in the classroom. Regular educators were more rigorous in their expectations and standards for classroom behavior, "especially in the case of deportment. . . . A straightforward emphasis on self-control, good study habits, and teacher compliance comes through very clearly from the data on high-ranked items" (p. 247). Teachers from both groups emphasized the importance of a capacity at least to follow rules, listen to the teacher, and comply with teachers' requests and demands. The data from Kerr and Zigmond (1986) corroborate the findings of Walker and Rankin's (1983) survey of elementary school teachers. The findings from Salend and Salend (1986) are similar to those of Kerr and Zigmond (1986). In their survey of 334 secondary regular and special education teachers from New York and Pennsylvania, they

found three functions as critical for successful performance in secondary-level mainstream settings: exhibiting appropriate work habits, respecting others and their property, and following school rules.

Although most of the attention in the professional literature has been on behavioral and interactional skills of students (Gresham, 1982; Hundert, 1982; Salend & Salend, 1986), teachers' expectations also include academic concerns. In the list of teachers' expectations developed by Wilkes, Bireley, and Schultz (1979), many of the top 21 items dealt with academic performance. For example, teachers expected students to have the following skills, listed with their ranking in parentheses: recognition of similar phonic sounds (6), possession of a method for word attack (12), adequate sight vocabulary (8), capacity to follow written instructions (9), comprehension and use of speech (10), adequate reading level (18), and minimal math skills (21).

These expectations, once established, can be used to define student success (defined as receiving a passing grade) in the MCA model. This grading policy can be used later to establish minimum essential learner outcomes once MCAs are developed.

At this point in the problem-solving process, an important decision must be made. With knowledge of a grading policy and the minimum expectations for receiving a passing grade, teachers can decide whether to (a) accept help from special education in ensuring the success of handicapped students in their classroom or (b) assume sole responsibility for ensuring such success.

The former decision (*to develop an IEP for a particular class*) signifies that a special education consultation *is* necessary to ensure the student's success in that class. In this case, the classroom teacher and the case manager share the responsibility for the handicapped student's classroom performance by developing a MCA with a corresponding IEP. The decision by the classroom teacher and case manager to share the responsibility for a handicapped student's success *must* result in an IEP, including a specification of long-range goals and short-term objectives.

The decision *not to develop an IEP* for a particular class signifies that the classroom teacher does not require special education consultation to ensure the student's success in that class. In this case, the classroom teacher is assuming *sole* responsibility for the handicapped student's classroom performance. The IEP, then, is written to focus on basic skills instruction provided by special education alone.

If agreement between the general and special education teachers cannot be reached regarding the need for a MCA, the building principal makes the determination. Parent and student perspectives then need to be considered, in addition to the relationships among the educators in the building. In such cases, the consultation process needs to be mediated with an administrative decision, with primary consideration given to issues of due process and educational obligations for the handicapped student.

This entire decision-making process is depicted in Figure 1. Four different steps are considered, beginning with identifying an appropriate student population, proceeding to a determination of whether grading in mainstream classrooms occurs and whether a particular student's skill deficits preclude or impede success (receive a passing grade), and finally, culminating in a decision by the general education teacher about the need for help in ensuring this success.

COMPONENTS OF MAINSTREAM CONSULTATION AGREEMENTS

In this next section, we operationalize each of the three instrumental components that are embedded in the MCAs:

1. Defining teacher standards and expectations to develop MELOs.
2. Framing the mainstream agreement itself by delineating responsibilities and activities for operationalizing the program.

3. Establishing an evaluation and communication function by monitoring student performance.

Finally, we describe a summative evaluation system for ascertaining the effects of MCAs at the system level.

Defining Teacher Standards and Expectations and Developing MELOs

These two issues are essentially different sides of the same coin. While the former depicts requirements stated by teachers (ranging from critical to unimportant), the latter represents student behaviors (ranging from frequently to rarely). Teachers' expectations form the MELOs.

Defining teacher expectations. The findings on teachers' expectations discussed earlier in the chapter are helpful in describing the *general* expectations of teachers, yet, students eventually work with *individual* content area teachers. Although it may be assumed that certain common expectations are likely (e.g., attendance), variation across environments also may occur. Therefore, in developing an MCA, classroom expectations must be documented for *each* teacher for whom an MCA is developed.

Probably the most efficient strategy is to develop assessment instruments on the basis of the research discussed earlier. For example, in Figure 2, the 10 most salient issues identified by the teachers in the Kerr and Zigmond (1986) study are displayed. They are organized into rating scales (Social Behavior Standards; Walker & Rankin, 1983) to determine the salience accorded by each teacher (unimportant, desirable, or critical).

Developing MELOs (Minimum Essential Learner Outcomes). Both social and academic behaviors typically need to be targeted as important MELOs. It is obvious that deportment, compliant and orderly conduct within the classroom, is an important consideration for effective learning to occur and for successful mainstreaming. Although Nicholson (1967) found the preponderance of spe-

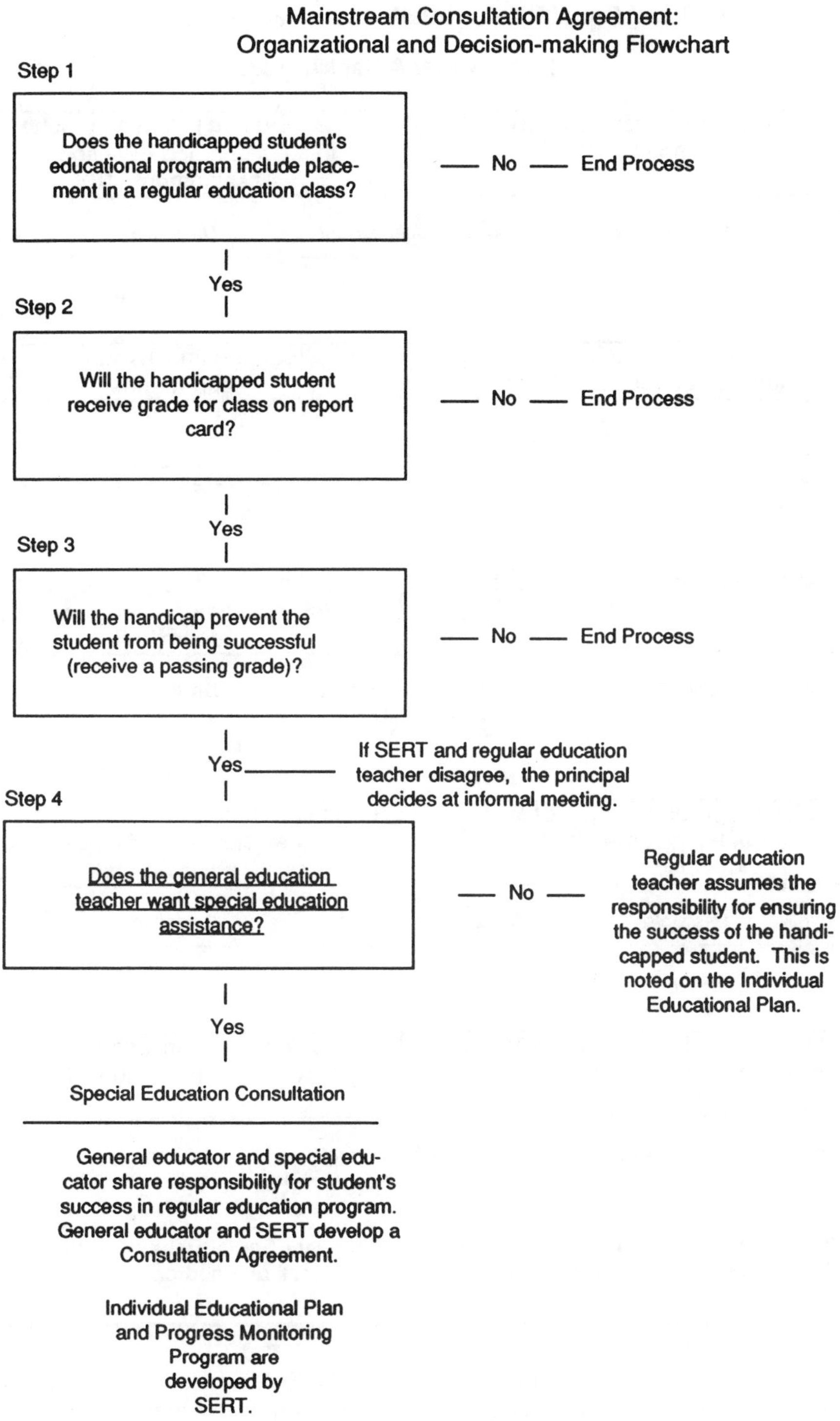

**Mainstream Consultation Agreement:
Organizational and Decision-making Flowchart**

Step 1

```
┌──────────────────────────────┐
│  Does the handicapped student's  │
│  educational program include place-  │ ── No ── End Process
│  ment in a regular education class?  │
└──────────────────────────────┘
```

|
Yes
|

Step 2

```
┌──────────────────────────────┐
│  Will the handicapped student    │
│  receive grade for class on report  │ ── No ── End Process
│           card?              │
└──────────────────────────────┘
```

|
Yes
|

Step 3

```
┌──────────────────────────────┐
│  Will the handicap prevent the   │
│  student from being successful   │ ── No ── End Process
│  (receive a passing grade)?      │
└──────────────────────────────┘
```

|
Yes_____   If SERT and regular education
| teacher disagree, the principal
               decides at informal meeting.

Step 4

```
┌──────────────────────────────┐
│  Does the general education      │           Regular education
│  teacher want special education  │ ── No ──  teacher assumes the
│           assistance?           │           responsibility for ensuring
└──────────────────────────────┘           the success of the handi-
                                            capped student.  This is
                                            noted on the Individual
                                            Educational Plan.
```

|
Yes
|

Special Education Consultation
_____

General educator and special educator share responsibility for student's
success in regular education program.
General educator and SERT develop a
Consultation Agreement.

Individual Educational Plan
and Progress Monitoring
Program are
developed by
SERT.

FIGURE 1. Special education flowchart for implementation of Mainstream Consultation Agreements.

Critical Behavioral Situations: Reaction Checklist

(From Walker & Rankin, 1983)

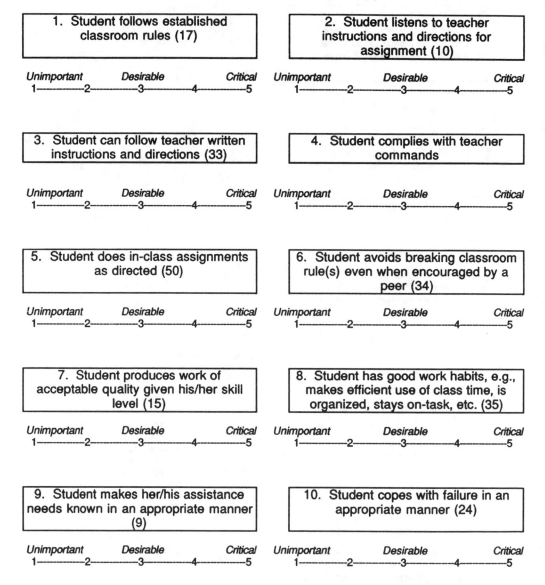

FIGURE 2. Walker and Rankin's (1983) Inventory of Teacher Social Behavior Standards and Expectations (SBS) for identifying situations and behaviors deemed critical for successful functioning.

cial education referrals to focus on academic difficulties, the presence of behavior problems is nevertheless a major consideration in teachers identifying students for specialized help. Thurlow, Christenson, and Ysseldyke (1983) and Ysseldyke and Thurlow (1983) have noted that learning problems alone are frequently insufficient to warrant referral and eventual placement into special education programs. The observation systems for these areas are often quite different from those used in measuring social interaction.

Teachers' expectations can be used to form minimum expected learner outcomes: The items that are deemed critical may become the areas in which more data are collected and/or programs are developed. MELOs represent the skill levels of individual handicapped students in a given classroom/content area in relation to other students in the classroom. A number of strategies can be used then to ascertain and operationalize MELOs. Teachers can be asked to simply state the rules and expectations of the classroom; alternatively observations can be made of the classroom, and the operational rules induced from the instructional practices.

Social–interaction behaviors. The first, and maybe most important, aspect of any data collection system is the definition of the behaviors to be evaluated. Either specific or practical behavior definitions can be used. If specific behavior definitions are used, the behavior is described precisely and all terms in the definition are addressed; as a consequence, great specificity is ensured (e.g., "Each day when the bell rings, the student will be seated in the second desk of the third row, 90% of the time"). Practical definitions, which are more general notations of groups of behaviors (e.g., "The student will arrive in class on time") may be less cumbersome and easier to measure consistently over time. For both systems, the conditions under which the behavior will occur should be included in the definition (e.g., work habits could be defined to include the following: "When given class time," "when presented homework," "in completing assignments with peers," etc.). Once a relevant behavior is defined with sufficient specificity, a data collection or assessment format and schedule needs to be developed that is sensitive to its (rate of) occurrence.

Two assessment strategies are available for documenting the level of social, interactional, or academic skills exhibited by students. Either observations or rated judgments can be useful. Both strategies are important, the former to generate low-inference information and the latter to provide qualified information or perceptions.

When direct observation procedures are used, student behaviors are defined objectively and measured systematically. A host of observation strategies have been employed in the last 20 years in the schools and in the professional literature. Many of these procedures are noninteractive; that is, observers watch students but do not participate in the instructional process in specific settings. The student is observed performing tasks within classroom or instructional episodes (Tawney & Gast, 1984). Most of these observation procedures employ some form of time-sampling system such as whole-interval, partial-interval, or momentary time sampling. Examples of such instruments include the Code for Instructional Structure and Academic Responding (CISSAR; Stanley & Greenwood, 1981), Ecobehavioral Interaction Analysis of Instruction (EIAI; Greenwood & Carta, 1987), and Activities Structures Observation Schedule (ASOS; Parker, Hasbrouck, & Tindal, 1989). These instruments provide specific classroom information on the instructional content (handwriting, language, math, reading, etc.), the medium for delivering instruction (lecture, worksheets, discussion, other media, etc.), and the student response (asking questions, talking academically, reading aloud, etc.).

In many instances, collection of direct observation data either is difficult to accomplish or provides an incomplete depiction of a student's performance. For example, a number of problems may prevent observational data from being useful:

1. Insufficient time is frequently available to observe more than one or two 20-minute periods.
2. Infrequently occurring behaviors are targeted for observation.
3. Reactivity to measurement may be present (i.e., the students know they are being observed).

In all of these instances, collection of judgmental information may be warranted, including teacher ratings to corroborate estimates of the student's performance.

When judgments of student performance are used, perceptions of specific behavior can be measured by rating scales. With behavioral ratings of students, teachers generally are presented a list of behaviors and asked to note how characteristic it is of the student by selecting the description that fits best. Rating scales can provide a useful and valid adjunct to other, more objective data collection procedures when they include adequate descriptions of (a) the behavior being rated, and (b) the anchors used to describe the person being rated.

An important component of MCAs is the use of rating scales. For example, in Figure 3, the 10 items ranked most important by subjects in the Kerr and Zigmond (1986) study can be reformatted so that the anchors reflect frequency (e.g., rarely, occasionally, frequently) rather than importance. The items then can be used to document teachers' perceptions of a student's performance or perceptions of their change over time. In Figure 3, the rating scale is used to collect some of the daily data that form the core MELOs.

Academic skills. A wide range of academic behaviors can be evaluated in the classroom from two major sources: (a) analysis of permanent products, and (b) performance on measures devised by the teacher. Most content classes require that students complete a number of activities to receive a passing grade, including reports, homework assignments, projects, and worksheets. Typically teachers grade student performance on these products according to accuracy, quality, and timeliness. In addition, many content area teachers administer tests they have prepared themselves at some time throughout the quarter, in the middle and end (examinations) or at regular intervals from week to week (quizzes). Both sources can be considered curriculum-based and an important part of the overall evaluation of success. Grades for the class typically are developed by evaluating the students' performance from both sources (activities and tests) and using a (weighted) sum to emphasize them equally or differentially.

Summary. We suggest that both types of student assessment data (social-behavior and academic) be utilized to develop and modify instructional programs and support services. The data collected on social-behavior performance, from either observation or rating scales, and academic performance, from curriculum-based assessments, become instrumental in judging program outcomes. As depicted in Figure 4, the MELO data collection form includes a range of behaviors, both social and academic, for frequent evaluation (daily, with weekly cumulative totals). Some of the behaviors have been defined from interviews with the teachers, some from direct observation, some from ratings of critical requirements of the classroom and teachers' perceptions of students, and some from the academic assessments conducted in the initial IEP development.

Framing the Agreement: Delineating Responsibilities for Program Operationalization

The second major component of MCAs is the delineation of *who* is responsible for *what* activities. As Lilly (1987) has noted, consultation-based programs have been described for over 20 years; yet, "consultation has been written about more than it has been practiced in special education" (p. 494). For the sake of clarity and efficiency, MCAs are premised upon a specific and well-delineated relationship between the consultant and the consultee (content area teacher).

The content of the agreement needs to establish clearly not only the responsibilities of all participants, particularly the mainstream teacher, the special education teacher, and the student, but as important, the process for working together. As noted earlier, this model of consultation presumes that the special educator will serve in a facilitative, rather than collaborative role. In the consultant/consultee relationship, the consultant's primary responsibility is to assist the

Teacher_____   Student_____   Date_____

10-Item Student Rating Form

1. Student follows established classroom rules

Rarely   Sometimes   Frequently
1------------2------------3------------4------------5

2. Student listens to teacher instructions and directions for assignment

Rarely   Sometimes   Frequently
1------------2------------3------------4------------5

3. Student can follow teacher written instructions and directions

Rarely   Sometimes   Frequently
1------------2------------3------------4------------5

4. Student complies with teacher commands

Rarely   Sometimes   Frequently
1------------2------------3------------4------------5

5. Student does in-class assignments as directed

Rarely   Sometimes   Frequently
1------------2------------3------------4------------5

6. Student avoids breaking classroom rule(s) even when encouraged by a peer

Rarely   Sometimes   Frequently
1------------2------------3------------4------------5

7. Student produces work of acceptable quality given his/her skill level

Rarely   Sometimes   Frequently
1------------2------------3------------4------------5

8. Student has good work habits, e.g., makes efficient use of class time, is organized, stays on-task, etc.

Rarely   Sometimes   Frequently
1------------2------------3------------4------------5

9. Student makes her/his assistance needs known in an appropriate manner

Rarely   Sometimes   Frequently
1------------2------------3------------4------------5

10. Student copes with failure in an appropriate manner

Rarely   Sometimes   Frequently
1------------2------------3------------4------------5

FIGURE 3. An adaptation of Walker and Rankin's (1983) Inventory of Teacher Social Behavior Standards and Expectations (SBS) for judging student performance on behaviors requisite for success in mainstream environments.

consultee, which is quite distinct from the collaborative and egalitarian relationship characterizing other models (Idol & West, 1987). Within a behavioral framework, then, relationships are established that focus on problem-solving, rather than process. Specifically, three individual's roles are considered.

Defining the consultant's responsibilities. The goal of the special education consultant is to help handicapped learners achieve success in mainstream classrooms, which often require inclusion of many specific objectives. Other than direct teaching in the content area, just about any activity can be included within

DAILY CLASSROOM PEFORMANCE TALLY SHEET

STUDENT: _____   CLASS: _____

TEACHER: _____   WEEK OF: _____/_____/_____

CONSULTANT: _____

Directions: The classroom teacher completes this form each day the student attends class. The teacher should put an 'X' in the appropriate point box.

	MONDAY		TUESDAY		WEDNESDAY		THURSDAY		FRIDAY	
Present or Excused	YES	1	YES	1	YES	1	YES	1	YES	1
	NO	0	NO	0	NO	0	NO	0	NO	0
Asks for Help	YES	1	YES	1	YES	1	YES	1	YES	1
	NO	0	NO	0	NO	0	NO	0	NO	0
Quality of Work Completed	GOOD	2	GOOD	2	GOOD	2	GOOD	2	GOOD	2
	AVERAGE	1	AVERAGE	1	AVERAGE	1	AVERAGE	1	AVERAGE	1
	POOR	0	POOR	0	POOR	0	POOR	0	POOR	0
Complies with Directions	GOOD	2	GOOD	2	GOOD	2	GOOD	2	GOOD	2
	AVERAGE	1	AVERAGE	1	AVERAGE	1	AVERAGE	1	AVERAGE	1
	POOR	0	POOR	0	POOR	0	POOR	0	POOR	0
Class Participation and Attentiveness	˙CONTRIB	2	CONTRIB	2	CONTRIB	2	CONTRIB	2	CONTRIB	2
	ATTEND	1	ATTEND	1	ATTEND	1	ATTEND	1	ATTEND	1
	NOT ATT.	0	NOT ATT.	0	NOT ATT.	0	NOT ATT.	0	NOT ATT.	0
Completes Assignments	YES	1	YES	1	YES	1	YES	1	YES	1
	NO	0	NO	0	NO	0	NO	0	NO	0
Follows Classroom Rules	FREQ	2	FREQ	2	FREQ	2	FREQ	2	FREQ	2
	OCCASION	1	OCCASION	1	OCCASION	1	OCCASION	1	OCCASION	1
	RARELY	0	RARELY	0	RARELY	0	RARELY	0	RARELY	0
Works Cooperatively with Others	FREQ	2	FREQ	2	FREQ	2	FREQ	2	FREQ	2
	OCCASION	1	OCCASION	1	OCCASION	1	OCCASION	1	OCCASION	1
	RARELY	0	RARELY	0	RARELY	0	RARELY	0	RARELY	0

TOTAL POINTS   ____   ____   ____   ____   ____

TOTAL WEEKLY POINTS   ____

FIGURE 4. Daily tally sheet for assessing performance on minimum essential learner outcomes (MELOs).

the consultant's responsibility. Three major activities include data collection and collation, intervention development, and program management.

As described above, a considerable amount of data typically need to be collected to help understand the problem and organize a program. Consultation is often quite labor-intensive in data collection (Tindal & Taylor-Pendergast, 1989), in which relevant information is collected, collated, summarized, and reported. With initial referrals, academic and behavioral assessments must be conducted, many persons must be interviewed, and a host of schedules must be coordinated.

In developing interventions, curricula often need to be adapted, requiring the consultant to help content area teachers incorporate principles of effective and explicit instruction (Brophy & Good, 1986). Later, of course, in actually adopting some of these modifications, more refinements may be necessary and/or training of others (parents, students, instructional assistants, etc.) may be needed.

Many support services require both management and vigilance while they are in operation. For example, a peer tutoring program requires monitoring; various self-monitoring programs require materials to be checked in and out; supplemental aids need to be incorporated into the mainstream content and sequence. This coordination of consultation services typically is assumed by the consultant, with two types of management: programs and evaluation systems. Since many programs are external to the classroom (incorporate people, materials, or procedures that are not part of the classroom), consultants involved in the MCA need to manage them. Since MCAs are data-based, a major responsibility of consultants is to manage the data so as to keep everyone involved (other teachers, administrators, parents, and students) up to date. This activity requires collecting data, summarizing them, and creating reports that provide graphic displays of change in performance over time. We present an example in the last section of this chapter.

Defining mainstream teacher's responsibilities. The mainstream content area teacher is the program implementor and is responsible for (a) providing daily classroom instruction, (b) collecting student performance daily or weekly, and (c) modifying instruction in the content area as needed, with the assistance of the consultant.

The modifications may use support services, altered instructional materials or interactive strategies, various motivational systems, and a range of physical or administrative arrangements. To date, the relatively scant research that has been completed in this area of instructional design reveals quite positive results (Bergerud, Lovitt, & Horton, 1988; Franklin, Little, & Teska, 1987).

In the MCAs operated in Pine County, Minnesota, general education content area teachers adapt materials for low-achieving students with the help of the consultant. Teachers define relevant and critical curriculum areas and consultants help initiate potentially effective adaptations. A number of different strategies are described in this volume by Lovitt and Horton, as well as by Deshler. The following are some examples of adaptations for a middle school curriculum:

1. The text is outlined, to highlight the main ideas.
2. Key vocabulary words are identified and listed with the meanings.
3. Diagrams and illustrations are developed to supplement the text.
4. Activities are developed for initiating active learning that moves beyond reading and writing.
5. The sequence of the material is modified.
6. Audio tapes are made that provide extended information.
7. Practice exercises are illustrated or graphic worksheets are devised for the student to practice problem solving.
8. A "cliff notes" version of the text is written.
9. Materials are developed for use by peers to teach students.

Finally, the content area teacher is responsible for communicating the student's progress to all involved persons (including daily/weekly tally sheets, progress reports to the home, and/or changes in the MCA) and for setting up conferences with the resource teacher, student, or parent.

Defining student's responsibilities. An increasing theme in secondary settings is student self-management through use of problem-solving strategies (Ally & Deshler, 1979). To capitalize on this theme, the MCA places major responsibility upon the student for establishing the content of the agreement and the process for monitoring outcomes. The student's primary responsibility is to engage in MELO behaviors as defined in the MCA, and request assistance or clarification of any aspect of the agreement.

Other issues regarding roles and responsibilities. Once the three major participants' responsibilities are clearly specified, several other components of the MCA need to be prepared prior to instituting the agreement, including (a) incorporation of parental involvement, (b) preparation of tally sheets, (c) agreement on the location and routing of the tally sheets (e.g., via teacher's mailbox or through the student), (d) identification of who will review progress and attend conferences, (e) consideration of proposed reinforcements or consequences for progress or lack of progress toward the goal, (f) organization of support services, and (g) establishment of evaluation period dates.

In summary, MCAs require content area teachers to accommodate students with learning or behavior problems with the help of special education teachers. A critical requirement for successful implementation is that the program be well articulated and the roles and responsibilities well delineated. In Figure 5, an MCA is displayed. The major components include identifying important target behaviors (using teacher expectations and MELOs), establishing specific accommodations, and finally, specifying the responsibilities of teachers, consultants, and students.

Establishing An Evaluation-Communication System: Monitoring Student Performance

The last major area needed to develop successful MCAs involves measurement and evaluation strategies for monitoring student performance and progress over time. A number of steps need to be followed to establish a daily evaluation system that reflects the individual student's program. First, as discussed earlier, the student's current level of performance on the MELO behaviors must be established prior to implementing the MCA. This information can serve as baseline data and provide a standard against which to compare the effects of interventions in the MCA when they are introduced. Second, IEPs must be established that provide both a long-range goal (LRG) and short-term objectives (STO). This IEP simply converts the information about the teacher's expectations, the student's target behaviors, and the interventions into an evaluation procedure. The IEP can then be used for making decisions about success — when is the student's progress sufficient to maintain programs and when is it insufficient, warranting modification of instructional programs. These three areas are presented as separate topics; in reality, they interact in the decision-making process.

Long-range goal. A long-range goal is a statement of the regular education teacher's expectations of a student at the end of a specified period of time, usually the end of the marking period. The LRG should have three components: (a) a description of the conditions under which the student is expected to behave, (b) a description of the specific task(s) or behavior(s) required of the student, and (c) specification of an evaluation or grading system, based on performance points assigned to the MELOs.

Two of these three components are standard for MCAs. Often, the conditions simply specify the class for which an agreement has been forged and the specific tasks required in the class. These tasks can be listed on a daily monitoring sheet and in the IEP itself, and they usually

Consultant	☐	Teacher ☐		Student Name ☐

IEP Goal Area ☐   Setting ☐

CONSULTATION AGREEMENT

Target Behavior(s)	Procedure for Implementation Plan	
Teacher's Responsibility	**Consultant's Responsibility**	**Student's Responsibility**

Signatures: _____ _____ _____

Position: _____ _____ _____

Attach Responsibilities for other persons involved in agreement

FIGURE 5. Mainstream Consultation Agreement, specifying responsibilities for consultants, teachers, and students.

are described as "earning points." For example, a long-range goal may specify that "*when attending Earth Science 101 on a daily basis and participating in the general class activities as well as using supplemental support services, the student will earn _____ points by exhibiting the following behaviors . . .*"

The third specification of an evaluation or grading system must be specifically established for *each* agreement, using the following procedures:

1. Together, the classroom teacher and consultant determine the number of points to be earned for each MELO behavior. These points are assigned on a weighted scale, with more points assigned to those MELO behaviors that most reflect the student's success in the classroom. For example, the student may be awarded more points for accurate and neat completion of weekly assignments or daily in-

volvement in classroom discussions than for working cooperatively with peers or asking for help. The number of points to be earned each day are multiplied by the total number of days in the marking period. This number serves as the criterion for the long-range goal.

2. The relationship between points and grades then is established. The evaluation standards are set with two major cut-offs identified: expectations of average student performance (C grade) and minimum expectations needed to pass the class (D grade). Both standards are set by estimating the level of performance of the peers in the classroom. Such grade cut-offs must be consistent with the district's marking system, (i.e., A, B, C, D, and F). An A or B grade is not usually negotiated, since this implies the student is above average and does not require a special education program modification for that

ANNUAL INDIVIDUAL EDUCATIONAL PLAN (19   - 19   )

Student

**Current
Level of
Performance**

	CONDITIONS	TASK	CRITERIA
Long Range Goal			
Short Term Objective			

Service Arrangement:

Type of Instruction		Time	Days per Week	Implementor	Place
Direct	Group	____ hours			Resource Room
Indirect	Individual	____ minutes			Classroom Other

FIGURE 6. Individual educational plans, specifying long-range goals (LRG) and short-term objectives (STO).

class. An alternative grading system also is not an option (P/N is D/F) unless it is available for nonhandicapped students.

Short Term Objectives (STO)

Once the points or weights assigned for each behavior are listed and the total points are summed, the short-term objective can be defined. The short-term objective breaks down the long-range goal into more limited time units to allow evaluation of progress (a week is usually a convenient unit). Like the long-range goal, a short-term objective contains a condition, a task, and a criterion for mastery or evaluation standard. The conditions and behavior typically remain the same as specified in the LRG (i.e., "*Each week, when attending Earth Science 101 on a daily basis . . .* "). The evaluation standard, however, changes from a focus on an *eventual* accomplishment to *successive* accomplishments (i.e., changes from the end of the quarter to the end of each week within the quarter). The short-term objective is established by simply dividing the number of points required in the long-range goal by the number of weeks in the marking period. This calculation provides the average weekly number of points for attaining a grade. Each IEP should have with it a corresponding graphic display that simply reflects all the information on the conditions, the task, and the evaluation standards.

In summary, the IEP translates the content of the mainstream consultation agreement into an evaluative document for determining its effects. While the MCA focuses on specific target behaviors and interventions, detailing individual responsibilities of all participants, the IEP establishes the general conditions of the classroom and provides a point system for evaluating whether the behavior is exhibited at an appropriate level and rate to achieve success (receive a passing grade in the class). The document includes both a long- and short-term focus, primarily to allow evaluation and modification concurrent with delivery of the program. The form used to write the IEP is displayed in Figure 6.

Evaluating progress. Decisions regarding a student's progress can be made daily or weekly, depending upon how frequently data are collected. However, in utilizing student performance data to evaluate the effects of MCAs, three conditions must be met.

First, the student's performance must be measured frequently to provide the necessary information for interpretation. Daily measurement is optimal; once weekly is the least amount possible for an evaluation system to be useful.

Second, administration of these measures must be as uniform as possible. Changes in the measurement procedures make it difficult to interpret program effects, as it is not clear whether the effect is due to interventions or changes in measurement. This issue becomes particularly important when the data used to measure performance are based on ratings or judgments.

Third, interventions need to occur in a systematic manner and should represent additions or deletions of support services, instructional materials, motivational techniques, and physical and administrative arrangements, or changes in the expectations of student performance.

If these three conditions are met, a goal-oriented decision guide (Fuchs, 1989) can be used to determine whether an intervention strategy is effective or if it should be changed. Throughout the course of consultation, the decision to change the program follows a set of circumscribed decision rules; they are based on *both* student performance/progress and the aim of the program. The student's current performance and trajectory is simply compared with the expected performance and trajectory (as specified in the long-range goal).

Data decision rules can be used to decide when to change a program that is not achieving an expected result. These rules attempt to improve the basis for making decisions by taking the guesswork out of deciding when to change. For example, the content area teacher and the consultant may establish ahead of time a decision guide that specifies a time

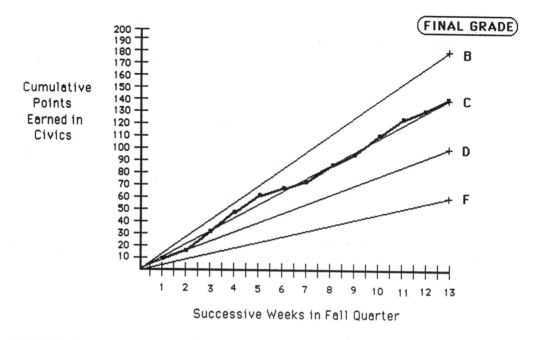

FIGURE 7. Daily progress/performance graph for evaluating program effectiveness.

period of 3 weeks for judging program effects. In this instance a program modification may be considered when student performance data are below the long-range goal on 3-5 consecutive weekly totals.

For maximum efficiency, the student's performance can be graphed on a computer through a progress monitoring program (PMP) (Jennen & Roddy, 1987). The PMP incorporates Apple II software that allows the user to define, collect, view, and analyze student progress toward the LTG and STO specified in the IEP. Changes in the agreement are made when the differences between the student's performance and the short-term objective becomes great, or when the student's cumulative point value is below the short-term objective or is approaching a failing level. In applying goal-oriented evaluation strategy, the consultant works with the teacher so that the student's performance reaches the IEP goal by a certain date. Changes in the MCA are indicated on the PMP graphs as a program change, thereby eliminating the necessity of writing a new MCA.

Ideally, consultation-based interventions represent substantial changes or interventions that have a high probability of improving student performance. Such changes also should be organized and systematic, since changing many parts of the plan at the same time would make it difficult to determine what produced the change in performance if, indeed, one occurs. To make certain this doesn't happen, instructional components need to be identified specifically and described so that the effectiveness of any one can be tested separately. This process of changing consultation strategies when performance is consistently below what is expected (represented by the short-term objective) should continue for the duration of the instruction/marking period.

In Figure 7, an idealized display of student performance is presented. The two important components of the graph are a plot of the student's weekly performance levels and a series of lines depicting levels of success (grades in the class). The vertical axis represents points earned on MELO behaviors and the horizontal axis represents successive weeks.

Summative Evaluation: Program Outcomes from MCAs

Special education consultation services are evaluated through the analysis of three data bases: (a) the degree to which MCA-based instructional procedures are implemented, (b) the degree to which handicapped students are successful in general education classrooms, and (c) consumer satisfaction with the consultation services — primarily mainstream education teachers, students, and parents.

Implementation review. As discussed thoroughly by Elliott, Witt, and Kratochwill earlier in this monograph, a very important question in evaluating any treatment program is whether the program was ever really implemented with integrity. Assessing treatment fidelity is an important component in the MCA process. The following questions are to be answered by the consultant during an implementation review conference, typically held within the first 3 weeks of the MCA:

1. Is the type of instruction the same as planned?
2. Is the time provided the same as planned?
3. Are the days provided the same as planned?
4. Is the program implementor the same as planned?
5. Is the place of instruction the same as planned?
6. Are mainstream consultation agreements in other content areas needed?
7. Is performance or behavior graphed?
8. Does the graph correspond with the IEP goal?
9. Are the data plotted the same as planned?

Any differences between the instructional plan that was proposed and the plan that was actually implemented can and should be corrected quickly.

Determining success in the mainstream. Assuming that the MCA-based program is delivered with integrity, the final issue is whether the program is working overall. To answer this question, all general education classes in which special education students are enrolled need to be summarized and analyzed as an aggregate. This program evaluation can be accomplished as follows.

1. Classes need to be organized into two groups, taking into account the type of student (MCA participation status) and class (academic focus): The most important group includes only those students who have *academic* classes with *and* without MCAs. Some students participate in MCAs and some students do not participate in MCAs in any given class. Furthermore, students take two types of classes: academic classes that use books and lectures as the primary mode of instructional delivery (Earth science, English, etc.), and nonacademic classes, which use projects and experiential learning as the primary mode of instructional delivery (art, woodworking, etc.). To evaluate MCAs, only academic (or nonacademic) classes must be selected within each student's course load, with some *utilizing* and some *not utilizing* the MCA process. If all classes utilize the MCA, no comparison is available. If MCAs are utilized only with academic classes and not the nonacademic classes, they are not comparable.

2. Student success must be operationalized for each of the two groups. Either the grade point average or a frequency count of the number of different grades can be tallied for the two groups.

In evaluating the program outcomes summatively, these two issues should be used to help validly organize the data and reports. For example, it is incorrect to simply compare the average GPA for all classes in which MCAs are involved with the classes in which special education students are attending without MCAs. Rather, the two groups of classes (with and without MCAs) can be analyzed only for students who have both. The reason for using this subset is that the difference between classes (those with and those without MCAs) may be a function of the type of student for whom MCAs are

	On MCAs		Not on MCAs	
	Academic	Non-academic	Academic	Non-academic
Students with both types of classes	Average GPA / Frequency Count of Grades			
Students with only one type of class				

FIGURE 8. Program evaluation for ascertaining unconfounded outcomes in implementing mainstream consultation agreements.

developed, which would distort the data. For example, MCAs may be developed only for extremely difficult students with very low academic skills, decreasing the likelihood of improvement. However, in classes for whom no MCAs were ever considered, the students may not have such extreme skill deficits. In addition, the nature of the class content may bias the interpretation of the data. It is possible for classes requiring more academic study to be overrepresented with MCAs (students need more help with these classes). As a result, when the data are aggregated, they dominate the effects.

By taking into account these two issues, a two-by-two table can be developed as depicted in Figure 8. One dimension is whether the class had an MCA or not; the other dimension is the type of class (academic or not academic). For each cell, either the frequency count of grades or the GPA can be computed.

To date, two program evaluations have been conducted on implementation of mainstream consultation agreements in the secondary schools in Pine County, Minnesota. Tindal, Shinn, Walz, and Germann (1987) found that, after a year of implementation, students performed as well in academic courses with MCAs as they did in academic courses without MCAs. Students receiving help in their academic content classes in the form of an MCA most frequently received a D grade, with the next most frequent grade being an F. Students who took content classes without MCAs also received a D grade most frequently; however, the next most frequent grade was a C. Nevertheless, when the GPA was calculated, no significant difference between these two groups (of classes, not students) was found. Tindal, Shinn, Walz, and Germann (1987) interpreted their data as supportive of MCAs, since the original contingencies to invoke such agreements was the virtual certainty of student failure in the class.

A follow-up study was completed by Tindal, Parker, and Germann (1990), in which students taking classes with and classes without MCAs were compared on two dimensions: the average GPA for a quarter and the change in GPA across two quarters (better, same, or worse). Again analyzing data for academic classes only, they found that students had the same GPA in classes with and in classes without MCAs. However, they also found that the stability of grades was more likely to change in classes with MCAs than those with no MCAs. Therefore, in each quarter students, teachers, and classes need to be carefully considered in designing subsequent MCAs: Previous success does not increase the likelihood of subsequent success.

Finally, program evaluation can and should include attention to process issues and to satisfaction of the consumers (parents, students, and teachers). They can be interviewed on a yearly basis to understand their perceptions of the entire MCA program. Since they must deliver most of the instructional programs, a considerable emphasis should be put on how well they feel supported: What is the quality of services from special education? How adequately are content area materials adapted and delivered? Is the consultation process appropriately supported through the scheduled meetings?

SUMMARY

We have described a consultation program that is designed to systematize the manner in which secondary students are mainstreamed into content area classes. The major components include a well-defined organizational flowchart for implementation of mainstream consultation agreements (MCAs). This structure is used to resolve two thorny issues that educators are faced with immediately upon entertaining any kind of a mainstreaming program: (a) who should be served, and (b) who should serve them. We described several issues that arise in targeting an appropriate group of students for whom MCAs are appropriate: analysis of situations and behaviors deemed critical for successful functioning, judgment of student performance on these behaviors, and development of curriculum-based and classroom-focused measures for assessing performance on minimum essential learner outcomes (MELOs). In defining who should serve these students, we described a system that actively incorporates the content area mainstream teacher in the decision-making process and service delivery. With students who receive special education

services, general education teachers have a *choice* of receiving help from special education to ensure the success of these students in their classroom. If this option is selected, consultants and teachers have accepted shared responsibility for ensuring such success. These contingencies are strong, yet they are likely responsible in some degree for success in implementation. Obviously, this form of intervention at the secondary level requires careful and systematic attention to and support from administrators, a variable that is often missing from most models of consultation (Tindal, Shinn, & Rodden-Nord, 1989).

Once students and teachers are identified for developing an MCA, the next step is a procedure for delineating responsibilities. This system should be considered the primary and most visible component of the process. A very specific form is used to help structure this step, the mainstream consultation agreement itself. An IEP is then completed that operationalizes a measurement and evaluation system using long-range goals and short-term objectives in respect to classroom behaviors. The most important part of this step is a daily progress or performance graph for evaluating program effectiveness. Finally, a procedure is carried out for evaluating MCAs summatively at the end of the year. The data collected in these last two steps are to be used to modify and improve programs for both students and teachers.

REFERENCES

Algozzine, B., O'Shea, D. J., Crews, W. B., & Stoddard, K. (1987). Analysis of mathematics competence of learning disabled adolescents. *Journal of Special Education, 21,* 97–107.

Ally, G., & Deshler, D. (1979). *Teaching the learning disabled adolescent: Strategies and methods.* Denver, CO: Love Publishing.

Bergerud, D., Lovitt, T. C., & Horton, S. (1988). The effectiveness of textbook adaptations in life science for high school students with learning disabilities. *Journal of Learning Disabilities, 21,* 70–76.

Brophy, J. E., & Good, T. L. (1986). Teacher behavior and student achievement. In M. Wittrock (Ed.), *Handbook of research on teaching* (pp. 328–375). New York: Macmillan.

Deno, S. L. (1985). Curriculum-based assessment: The emerging alternative. *Exceptional Children, 52,* 219-232.

Deno, S. L., & Fuchs, L. S. (1987). Developing curriculum-based measurement systems for data based special education problem solving. *Focus on Exceptional Children, 19*(8), 1-15.

Deno, S. L., & Mirkin, P. K. (1977). *Data-based program modification: A manual.* Reston, VA: Council for Exceptional Children.

Franklin, M. E., Little, E., & Teska, J. A. (1987). Effective teaching strategies used with the mildly handicapped in the mainstream. *Exceptional Children, 20,* 7-11.

Fuchs, L. S. (1989). Evaluating solutions: Monitoring progress and revising intervention plans. In M. R. Shinn (Ed.), *Curriculum-based measurement: Assessing special children* (pp. 153-181). New York: Guilford.

Germann, G. (1986). *Pine County Special Education Cooperative TSES Procedural Manual: Mainstream Consultation.* (Available from Gary Germann, Director of Special Education, Sandstone Public Schools, P.O. Box 228, Sandstone, MN.)

Germann, G., & Tindal, G. (1985). An application of curriculum-based assessment: The use of direct and repeated measurement. *Exceptional Children, 52,* 244-265.

Greenwood, C., & Carta, J. (1987). An ecobehavioral interaction analysis of instruction within special education. *Focus on Exceptional Children, 19,* 1-11.

Gregory, J. F., Shanahan, T., & Walberg, H. (1986). A profile of learning disabled twelfth-graders in regular classes. *Learning Disability Quarterly, 9,* 33-42.

Gresham, F. (1982). Misguided mainstreaming: The case for social skills training with handicapped children. *Exceptional Children, 48,* 422-433.

Halpern, A. S., & Benz, M. R. (1987). A state-wide examination of secondary special education for students with mild disabilities: Implications for the high school curriculum. *Exceptional Children, 54,* 122-129.

Hundert, J. (1982). Some considerations of planning the integration of handicapped children into the mainstream. *Journal of Learning Disabilities, 15,* 73-80.

Idol, L., & West, J. F. (1987). Consultation in special education (part II): Training and practice. *Journal of Learning Disabilities, 20,* 474-493.

Jennen, S., & Roddy, D. (1987). *Progress Monitoring Program, v 1, 1s.* Cambridge, MN: Performance Monitoring Systems.

Kerr, M. M., & Zigmond, N. (1986). What do high school teachers want? A study of expectations and standards. *Education and Treatment of Children, 9,* 239-249.

Kratochwill, T. R., & Bergan, J. R. (1978). Evaluating programs in applied settings through behavioral consultation. *Journal of School Psychology, 16,* 375-386.

Lilly, M. S. (1987). Response by M. Stephen Lilly, Washington State University. *Journal of Learning Disabilities, 20,* 494-495.

Nicholson, C. A. (1967). A survey of referral problems in 59 Ohio school districts. *Journal of School Psychology, 5,* 280-286.

Parker, R., Hasbrouck, J., & Tindal, G. (1989). *Activity structures observation system* (Training Module No. 1). Eugene, OR: University of Oregon Resource Consultant Training Program.

Salend, S. J. (1984). Factors contributing to the development of successful mainstreaming programs. *Exceptional Children, 50,* 409-416.

Salend, S. J., & Lutz, J. G. (1985). Mainstreaming or mainlining: A competency based approach to mainstreaming. *Journal of Learning Disabilities, 17,* 27-29.

Salend, S. J., & Salend, S. M. (1986). Competencies for mainstreaming secondary level learning disabled students. *Journal of Learning Disabilities, 19,* 91-94.

Stanley, S. O., & Greenwood, C. R. (1981). *CISSAR: Code for Instructional Structure and Student Academic Response: Observer's manual.* Kansas City, KS: University of Kansas, Bureau of Child Research, Juniper Garden's Children's Project.

Tawney, J. W., & Gast, D. L. (1984). *Single-subject research in special education.* Columbus, OH: Merrill.

Thurlow, M., Christenson, S., & Ysseldyke, J. (1983). *Referral research: An integrative summary of findings* (Research Report No. 141). Minneapolis, MN: University of Minnesota Institute for Research on Learning Disabilities.

Tindal, G., & Marston, D. (1986). Approaches to assessment. In J. Toregson & B. Wong (Eds.), *Psychological and educational perspectives on learning disabilities* (pp. 55-84). Boston: Academic.

Tindal, G., Parker, R. (1989). Development of written retell as a curriculum-based measurement in secondary programs. *School Psychology Review, 18*(3), 328-343.

Tindal, G., Parker, R., & Germann, G. (1990). An analysis of mainstream consultation outcomes for secondary students identified as learning disabled. *Journal of Learning Disabilities.*

Tindal, G., Shinn, M. R., & Rodden-Nord, K. (1989). Contextually-based school consultation: Influential variables. *Exceptional Children, 56*(4), 324–336.

Tindal, G., Shinn, M. R., Walz, L., & Germann, G. (1987). Mainstream consultation in secondary settings: The Pine County model. *Journal of Special Education, 21*, 94–106.

Tindal, G., & Taylor-Pendergast, S. (1989). A taxonomy for objectively analyzing the consultation process. *Remedial and Special Education, 10*, 6–16.

U.S. Department of Education. (1989). *Eleventh annual report to Congress on the implementation of the Education of the Handicapped Act.* Washington, DC: Author.

Walker, H. M., & Rankin, R. (1983). Assessing the behavioral expectations and demands of less restrictive settings. *School Psychology Review, 12*, 274–284.

Wilkes, H. H., Bireley, M. K., & Schultz, J. J. (1979). Criteria for mainstreaming the learning disabled child into the regular classroom. *Journal of Learning Disabilities, 12*(4), 46–51.

Ysseldyke, J., Graden, J., Thurlow, M., Algozzine, B., Wesson, C., & Deno, S. L. (1984). *Generalizations from five years of research* (Research Report No. 100). Minneapolis, MN: University of Minnesota Institute for Research on Learning Disabilities.

Ysseldyke, J., & Thurlow, M. (1983). *Identification/classification research: An integrative summary of findings* (Research Report No. 142). Minneapolis, MN: University of Minnesota Institute for Research on Learning Disabilities.

23

Prevention and Management of Secondary-Level Behavior Problems

Randall S. Sprick
Teaching Strategies, Eugene, Oregon

Victor Nolet
University of Oregon

INTRODUCTION

Secondary educators often express concerns about student discipline. Unfortunately, there is a paucity of empirically validated procedures for effective management of students' behavior in secondary classrooms. Disciplinary procedures employed at middle and high school levels seem to consist of more reactive administrative interventions (such as removal of problem students) than of proactive educational and behavioral procedures. We believe the use of effective instructional and classroom management practices can prevent many disciplinary problems that occur in secondary classrooms. This chapter reviews these management strategies, which can be employed by secondary classroom teachers. Some of the techniques described are documented in the research literature, some are extrapolations from research in the elementary grades, and some are based on the experiences of the authors.

There are many factors that may adversely affect a child's behavior in school, some of which are substance abuse, crisis situations, dysfunctional family life, physiological problems, and ineffective management practices by school personnel. Probably several of the above factors contribute to the inappropriate behavior of a child with chronic and severe behavior problems. However, since school personnel have more control over their own management practices than they do over the child's home life or physiology, it is our position that management of behavioral contingencies should always be one of the first interventions implemented to help a child improve his or her behavior. This chapter will examine those classroom procedures that have a high probability of improving student behavior in secondary settings.

Often, school psychologists do not become involved with behavior problems until a classroom teacher makes a referral to special education. Frequently, by the time the referral is made, the teacher's goal is to get a problem student out of the classroom. In these instances, the school psychologist is expected to confirm the teacher's perception that there is something wrong with the student and to validate the teacher's decision to seek removal of the student from the room. To further complicate this tenuous situation, in the absence of a concerted effort by school personnel to implement effective preventive behavior management practices, the problems may never really get solved but are often terminated administratively through disciplinary procedures (suspension, expulsion, etc.), or they are simply allowed to persist until the school year ends.

The procedures presented in this chapter are based on the premise that school psychologists can function (in a consultative role) as a resource to teachers to intervene with problems before a referral for special services becomes necessary. A major advantage that accrues when school psychologists assume a proactive role during prereferral interventions is that teachers may be more receptive to intervention suggestions if the problem has not been occurring over a long period of time. To be most effective, the school psychologist must cultivate a relationship with teachers in which he or she is viewed as a nonthreatening resource person rather than a gatekeeper whose primary role is to facilitate removal of problem students from the classroom.

In developing this collaborative relationship, the psychologist may be involved in classroom observations, student progress monitoring, intervention planning with staff, and in-service teacher training. Fundamental to the relationship is the establishment of the school psychologist's credibility as someone who has skills and expertise to offer teachers in the design of classroom interventions. To establish this credibility, school psychologists need to know about procedures that contribute to effective instruction and classroom management. The goal of this chapter is to provide school psychologists with precise information that will help them establish credibility as educational consultants who can help teachers manage student discipline in classrooms.

This chapter has three sections. The first part will present strategies for managing classrooms to prevent misbehavior. The second section will present strategies for reducing unacceptable behaviors and increasing desired behaviors. These first two sections consist of procedures that are to be implemented by the classroom teacher; it is assumed that the psychologist is serving as a consultant in helping a teacher implement these procedures. The final section presents a variety of strategies that can be implemented by either the teacher or the psychologist in working with individual students with chronic problems.

PREVENTING MISBEHAVIOR

A key to effective behavior management at the secondary level is preventing problems before they have a chance to start. The most effective management techniques involve "not merely responding effectively when problems occur but preventing problems from occurring frequently" (Brophy & Evertson, 1983, p. 263). Jones and Jones (1986) estimate proactive management techniques can prevent as much as 75% of disruptive student behavior. Effective managers know how they want each activity in the classroom to look, and they spend time teaching students to behave in appropriate ways. The teaching skills involved in this process are discussed below.

Rules and Behavioral Expectations

The expectations a teacher has regarding students' possibilities for success can have a significant effect on student learning. Good (1987) summarizes two types of teacher expectations. The first is *self-fulfilling prophecy:* A teacher's beliefs about students' performance in fact influence that performance in a direction consistent with the teacher's beliefs. The second type is referred to as *sustaining expectations:* A teacher fails to see some students' potential and thus does not respond to those students in ways that encourage them to fulfill their potential. Given these potential effects of teachers' expectations, teachers must strive to view every student as capable. More importantly, teachers must behave in a manner that clearly communicates expectations of good performance as well as behavior.

Classroom rules effectively communicate to students that teachers have specific expectations about student behavior. At least through ninth grade, rules should be posted in a prominent place for students to see. After ninth grade, the teacher may or may not choose to post the classroom rules (Emmer, Evertson, Sanford, Clements, & Worsham, 1988).

In general, positively stated rules have advantages over negatively stated rules. Positively stated rules communicate a positive expectation and let students know what is important to the teacher. When presented to students, a set of positively stated rules allows teachers to conduct an invitational optimistic discussion regarding classroom behavior. Negatively stated rules insinuate an expectation of inappropriate behavior, and may even invite some of the students to challenge the rules. Also, a long list of negatively stated rules may force the teacher to spend valuable instructional time policing all the misbehaviors listed in the rules.

In most cases, the teacher can get by with three to eight rules. It is possible that a few of these rules may be negatively stated for the sake of clarity. For example, the rule "No food or drink in the computer room" is clear and communicates important information.

Many people like to involve the students in the development of the rules, but this practice may be very difficult for the teacher who has six different classes of students. At secondary level, the best way to involve the students is to get them into a discussion of why the rules are important and how they relate to success in the subject of the class.

While positively stated rules are generally more desirable than negative ones, a disadvantage with the use of positive rules is that they are more broad and general than a list of "don'ts." For example, the positively stated rule "Students are expected to make appropriate contributions to class discussions" is more general than the negatively stated rule "No talking out during class." Consequently, the teachers need to spend time in the first week of a semester teaching students how the rules relate to the specific procedures and routines in the classroom.

To communicate how the rules relate to specific classroom procedures, teachers first must know exactly how they expect classes of students to behave during every activity and then successfully communicate this information to their students. Teachers who are unclear about their expectations for student behavior will be inconsistent in their interactions with students - for example, if they sometimes

expect students to raise hands and other times respond to call-outs; or if they sometimes let students talk in class and other times become angry with them for doing so. Secondary classroom teachers need to be unequivocal about (a) what students should do when they enter the room before the bell rings; (b) where students should go and what they should have with them at the beginning of class; (c) what students should be doing during the time the teacher is taking attendance or dealing with other administrative duties; (d) how students are expected to behave in lectures, discussions, independent work periods, films, and so on. A school psychologist working with a teacher who is experiencing difficulty managing student behavior could start by assisting the teacher in clarifying expectations for student behavior during each activity.

When teachers know how each activity and corresponding student behavior should look, they can communicate this information to students. A faulty assumption made by some teachers is that students in the secondary grades automatically know how to behave in every classroom setting. These teachers do not recognize that each teacher is slightly different in the way he or she conducts class and expects students to behave. In the absence of explicitly communicated expectations, students are forced to guess how each teacher wants them to act.

Teaching students to behave appropriately requires that the teacher discuss and clarify specific expectations throughout the entire first week of a new semester. Presenting all of this information only one time when going over the classroom rules on the first day may overwhelm some students. Thus, it is recommended that for the first five days of school, before beginning any new activity teachers should present information to the students on behavioral expectations for the upcoming activity. Students should be involved in discussions about how the expectations relate to the classroom rules and why the expectations are important for increasing every student's opportunity for success.

Also during the first week, at the conclusion of each activity, teachers should provide students with feedback about how well expectations were met. Here are examples of how this information can be communicated to students.

If behavior during the activity went well, the teacher might say: "During today's lecture, whenever anyone had anything to say you remembered to raise your hand, and all the questions and comments were very pertinent to the subject of the lecture. Hand raising is important if everyone in the room is to get an opportunity to participate when they wish to."

If an activity did not go well, the teacher might give feedback like this: "During our independent work period, there were three or four times that I had to say, 'It's too loud. Please quiet down.' Getting to work together on your assignments is useful because you can learn by working together. However, if I have to keep reminding you to keep the noise down and to talk only about the assignment, I may need to say that no talking will be allowed. Tomorrow, work a little harder on managing the noise level."

Introducing each activity with a reminder of expectations and concluding each activity with feedback about how well those expectations were met allows teachers to calmly and assertively communicate to students how they want the classroom to run. The goal for teachers is to create the impression that they are confident that each student will behave appropriately when given clear information about expectations.

Routines and Habits

Many classroom behavior problems can be prevented through use of established daily classroom routines and habits (for example, daily routines provide an efficient structure for keeping students actively engaged in academic tasks). Effective teachers have routines for beginning class, assigning and collecting homework and classwork, arranging for make-up work for students who are absent, taking roll, correcting papers in class, dealing with students who do not have necessary materials, dealing with late assignments, leaving the classroom, cleaning up after labs, and excusing the class at the end of the period. These routines create an efficient, businesslike atmosphere in the classroom, where student attention is focused on academic tasks.

A crucial time for employing routines is at the beginning of each class period. Without a routine for engaging students in academic tasks as soon as they enter the room, the teacher may be required to begin the period by quieting them down and getting them in their seats. An inefficient class beginning may result in two or three minutes wasted every day. If students are allowed to sit and do nothing for two minutes while the teacher completes administrative duties, some students will misbehave in order to have something to do.

Classroom routines should be established at the beginning of the school year or semester and reviewed or updated periodically, throughout the year. Here is an example of what a teacher could say to establish a routine for getting class started:

"Each day when you come into class, there will be a challenge problem on the overhead. Come into class, put your homework on your desk, and then get started on the challenge problem. You may work quietly with one or two other students on the problem. When the bell rings, continue to work on the problem, and I will take role and collect your homework. If you finish the problem, you may talk quietly to your neighbor, but only after you have worked out the solution to the problem.

"In my class if you are not in the room with all your materials by the time the bell rings, you are considered tardy. If you are late, sign your name on the clipboard by the door. If you have a blue slip from another staff member or the office giving you permission to be late, simply attach the slip to the clipboard when you sign in. When you are late, please do not disrupt class or interrupt me, just sign the clipboard."

Notice that the teacher in the example has students engaged in an academic task even while attendance is being taken. The teacher has outlined what students can do when they have finished the problem and has specified that until the problem is completed students are expected to continue working. In short, the teacher has (a) communicated the expectation that students will be on time to class and (b) provided clear information about what students should do when they are late.

Teachers also should establish and use routines during transitions between activities. A transition such as moving from a lecture/discussion format to working with students in the textbook requires that students get their books out and open. If this transition is handled poorly it can take too long and the attention of the class may be diverted. Teachers should try to conduct transitions quickly and efficiently so that students' attention is drawn to the next part of the task as soon as possible.

At the beginning of the school year, the teacher might introduce a transition in the following manner:

"Class, the next thing we are going to do is go over the assignment to answer the study questions at the end of the chapter. Before you get your books out, I want to let you know how I do things. First, I really dislike having to repeat instructions, so when I ask you to get your books open to a particular page, I will write the page number on the board, so there is no reason for anyone to ask, 'What page?' In addition, I do not like to waste time each day moving from the lecture to going over the assignment, so when I ask you to get your books out and open, please do so quickly and quietly. Open your books to page 42" (while writing the page number on the board).

Efficient routines and smooth transitions help to keep students actively engaged in instructional tasks. Keeping students involved in instruction reduces behavior problems and consistently is correlated positively with academic achievement (Brophy & Evertson, 1976).

Scanning

Another tool used by effective teachers to prevent misbehavior and increase student motivation is scanning. Scanning is the process of frequently glancing to all parts of the room where students are located. Almost all teachers are good at scanning during teacher-directed instruction, but scanning is also critical during activities such as independent seatwork or lab activities. One of the obvious purposes for scanning is to catch minor misbehavior before it becomes a severe problem. Another reason teachers should scan is to demonstrate that they observe and are aware of the students' efforts to meet classroom expectations. Teachers who neglect to scan tend to interact only with misbehavior; however, teachers who scan are aware of and can provide feedback on both desirable and undesirable behaviors. Scanning is an important strategy for developing what Kounin (1970) referred to as "withitness" — the ability of effective teachers to be so in touch with what is happening in the classroom that they almost seem to know what students are going to do before they have a chance to do it.

Scanning is an easily observable teacher behavior that can be increased through coaching and practice. School psychologists can help teachers become better scanners by observing teachers' rates of scanning and providing feedback and modeling as needed.

Scheduling

The way teachers arrange activities within a 50-minute class period can have a significant impact on student behavior. Teachers who expect students to spend the majority of each class period engaged in paper-and-pencil tasks or who always give students a long time at the end of the class period for independent work should expect behavior problems.

Look at the two schedules shown in Table 1.

Schedule A leaves lots of time for students to get off task. However, Schedule B, because it is so structured and teacher-

TABLE 1
Two Examples of 50-Minute Class Schedules

Time	Schedule A	Schedule B
8:00	Attendance/Challenge Problem	Attendance/Challenge Problem
8:03	Lecture/discussion	Teacher-directed review
8:08		Lecture/discussion
8:18	Independent work	
8:20		Guided practice on assignment
8:25		Independent work on part of assignment
8:30		Correct problems just completed
8:35	Independent work	
8:50		Questions/discussion of assignment
8:55	Class dismissed	Class dismissed

directed, does not allow as much opportunity for students to get off task. Intermixing teacher-directed instruction and student seatwork has a further advantage of giving students more guidance throughout their assigned tasks, thus reducing the chance that a student will make errors on an assignment. Some teachers are reticent about trying a sequence like Schedule B because of the number of transitions required. However, the teacher who establishes an active schedule from the beginning and runs the transitions efficiently as presented above can keep students focused on instructional tasks.

Student Involvement in the Lesson

Effective teachers do not simply lecture; they get students to participate in the lesson. By giving students frequent opportunities to respond and participate, the teacher can derive information on the degree to which students are mastering important concepts. On the basis of the correct and incorrect responses of students, the teacher can proceed with the lesson, or review and provide additional information and practice of key information. When giving a standard lecture without student participation, the teacher receives no information on the degree of student understanding or mastery.

One of the most obvious ways of facilitating student involvement in the lesson is for the teacher to ask questions frequently. However, care must be taken to involve all students, not just those who volunteer because students who tend to volunteer often are those who are highly motivated by the content of the presentation.

Effective questioning involves virtually every member of the class and there are three basic ways to accomplish this. One way to involve the class is to use whole-group choral responses. Choral responses are especially effective for the introduction of new vocabulary and for reviewing previously taught facts. However, choral responses are not feasible for responses that could be phrased in a variety of ways. So a second approach is used when asking questions that have numerous correct answers: Here, the teacher should ask the question, instruct everyone to get a answer ready, and then call on an individual student. By waiting to name the student who is assigned to answer the question, the teacher increases the likelihood that all students will be thinking about the question and trying to develop an answer.

A third way to involve students in lessons via question asking and answering is to give frequent ungraded quizzes. Having each student answer three or four questions on a quiz and then correct the answers allows every student to participate, practice, and receive feedback on correct and incorrect responses. Frequent ungraded quizzes are a common feature of most mastery learning models of effective instruction (Becker, 1986).

Structuring lessons in ways that require participation from students on a daily basis ensures that teachers receive ongoing feedback on whether students have achieved mastery on the material being taught. Teachers who rely primarily on lecturing and calling on volunteers receive insufficient feedback on mastery because students who do not understand rarely raise their hand to say "I don't know."

Effective Evaluation and Grading Policies

One of the key ways to increase student motivation is to demonstrate to students that if they participate in class, complete assignments, and try their best, it makes a difference in whether they will succeed in passing tests and getting decent grades. In many classes a low-performing student could do everything the teacher asks — follow the rules, attempt to participate in class, try to do assignments and tests — and still fail. A student who continually experiences failure after trying to comply with a teacher's expectations has no incentive for behaving the way the teacher asks.

This section will examine ways teachers can demonstrate to students that effort pays off with passing grades. First, the evaluation procedures used to determine mastery will be examined, and then other aspects of grading systems will be explored that can help improve a student's motivation for earning a passing grade.

An effective evaluation system can make a big difference in student motivation. Teachers can increase their students' success on tests and prevent behavior problems by following three relatively simple steps. (a) When preparing unit tests, write the test first. The test (or any other form of evaluation) should reflect the objectives the teacher has identified as being important. Thus, what is on a teacher's test should not be a surprise to students. (b) When introducing concepts in class that will be covered on the test, inform students that this information is important and they will be tested on it.

(c) Provide students the opportunities to practice on the concepts taught until they achieve mastery.

By following the above three steps, all students learn that if you pay attention in class, the lessons help prepare you for the test. Unfortunately in some classrooms the relationship between instruction and testing is not adequately clear to some students. Once students learn that passing tests is not a mysterious process, there is an increased chance that they will strive to achieve a passing grade. However, for students to be motivated toward grades, they must fully understand the teacher's grading system. The remainder of this section explores other aspects of grading systems that can affect student motivation.

Grades and their relationship to student behavior should function as a reinforcement system, not as a punishment tool. Many teachers expect students to be motivated to avoid getting bad grades. The problem with this assumption is that typically low-performing students may have become totally inured to receiving bad grades. An alternative approach is to construct grading systems so that a passing grade depends on student effort as well as mastery of material. When it is clear that effort and participation in class contribute to a student's grade, there is a good chance that the student will be more highly motivated to attend and behave in class.

Another factor affecting whether students are motivated by grades is the extent to which the grading system is understood. Grading policies should be clearly stated and simple enough to be summarized on a handout. At the beginning of each new semester, the teacher should distribute and discuss this handout with students and explain the system in 5-10 minutes. In essence, the teacher will teach students that if you play by the rules you can win the game — and winning the game means passing the course. If the system is so complex that students have trouble understanding it, some students will assume the rules are too complicated for them to possibly win the game — so why bother to play?

Another advantage in using an uncomplicated grading system is that simple and understandable policies allow students to monitor their own progress in class, and effective grading practices often involve students in keeping track of their own grades. Sophisticated students know where they stand at any point during the grading period. Ask high-performing students what their grades are and you get responses such as "In history I have a B but there are three more tests in the grading period so I know I can kick it up to an A if I study for those tests." Ask lower-performing students the same question and they look at you as if you are crazy. Many lower-performing students think that grades are something teachers do to them at the end of the semester. Students who do not know their current grade are unlikely to be motivated to want to get a better grade. Unless students are required to keep track of their grades, only the most motivated will do so. One way to help students track their own grades is to give them a form at the beginning of the semester that they can keep in their notebooks and that they are required to keep up to date. A sample of such a record sheet is shown in Table 2.

A sheet of this type makes it possible to have students total their points to date and determine their grades. Each week the teacher can put information on the board like that shown below:

Second Period — Grades as of
Monday, November 3.
325 points possible so far.

293 – 325 = A
260 – 292 = B
227 – 259 = C
195 – 226 = D
Less than 195, come and see me!

The procedure outlined above requires teachers to use a point system for determining grades. Unfortunately, some teachers will give letter grades on assignments without using a point system, making it very difficult to communicate to students the relative weight of different types of assignments. For example, a low-performing student who gets an A on a homework assignment may think that a D on a term paper has been offset. Through the use of points, the teacher can more readily communicate that the term paper is worth a possible 200 points and each homework assignment is worth 10 points. Therefore, it is expected that students should put far more time and effort into the term paper than into a homework assignment and it is clear that the term paper makes up a greater portion of a final grade than does a homework assignment.

Another point system grading technique that can increase student motivation involves establishing a percentage of the actual academic grade (and thus the total points earned) that is based on participation and effort. To incorporate this procedure the teacher must decide how many points students can earn each week for behavior and participation before the term begins. This number should be based on the approximate percentage input this behavior grade will have on the total grade. For example, in a ninth-grade science class the teacher estimates that there will be approximately 750 points for tests, labs, homework, and the final exam during the 12 week-trimester. If the teacher would like behavior and effort to have a 25% impact on the grade, the grading system should have approximately 1,000 total points possible. Assigning 20 points possible per week would result in 240 points for behavior during a 12-week trimester. Thus there would be a total possible of 990 points, 240 being approximately 25% of the 990 point total.

The recommended percentage of the grade to be based on behavior and participation can range from 0 to 80% depending on the class. Percentages generally will be higher in classes of middle and junior high school students than at the high school level. That is, in middle school and junior high, one of the major objectives should be to teach students how to behave in ways that will allow them to be successful in further academic pursuits. Consequently, a greater percentage of the grade can be based on the degree to which students exhibit these behaviors.

TABLE 2
Example of a Student Grading Record Form

Class Period _____

Student _____

TESTS:

    1 Score _____/100 points
    2 Score _____/100 points
    3 Score _____/100 points
    4 Score _____/100 points
    5 Score _____/100 points

                      Total _____/500 points

QUIZZES:

    1 Score _____/100 points
    2 Score _____/100 points
    3 Score _____/100 points
    4 Score _____/100 points
    5 Score _____/100 points

                      Total _____/500 points

TERM PAPER:

    Score _____200 points

                      Total _____/200 points

HOMEWORK:

    1 Score _____/10 points
    2 Score _____/10 points
    3 Score _____/10 points
    4 Score _____/10 points
    5 Score _____/10 points
    6 Score _____/10 points
    7 Score _____/10 points
    8 Score _____/10 points
    9 Score _____/10 points
    10 Score _____/10 points

                      Total _____/100 points

WEEKLY PARTICIPATION:

    1 Score _____/20 points
    2 Score _____/20 points
    3 Score _____/20 points
    4 Score _____/20 points
    5 Score _____/20 points
    6 Score _____/20 points
    7 Score _____/20 points
    8 Score _____/20 points
    9 Score _____/20 points
    10 Score _____/20 points

                      Total _____/180 points

                Final Score _____/1080 points

Once the number of participation points possible each week has been determined, the teacher must decide on a system for students to earn those points. The criteria for awarding points should be made as objective as possible, and students should be told in advance how their behavior will be evaluated. In the example of the science class above with 20 points possible each week, the teacher might present the plan to the class in the following manner.

"Each week, I will put a grade in the grade book based on your behavior and participation. There are 20 points possible, and each week you begin the week with 16 points. I will determine your points based on how well you use your class time and each of you will get a score between 0 and 20. Anytime I tell you that you are using your class time well, I will make a note next to your name on the class list attached to this clipboard, and that raises your score 1 point. Anytime you are wasting class time and I need to remind you to get back on target, you lose a point.

"Each Friday, I will post the scores on the bulletin board in the same way that I post the scores for tests. Look for your student number to find the points you earned for the week. Anytime during the week that you want to know where you are, come and look at my clipboard before or after class."

The teacher can extend this system to include consequences for tardies, late work, not having materials, and any other frequent but minor types of problems. However, the system should not be viewed as consisting predominantly of negative consequences. It is important to note that such a grading system carries with it the responsibility that the teacher must make a concerted effort to get to each student two to four times each week to acknowledge positive performance. The goal is for students to see that by using class time well they can improve their grade. Detailed information on establishing and implementing a system of this type is provided in Sprick (1985).

Teachers frequently are concerned about the legality of a system that bases a percentage of student grades on behavior. The most important consideration is that students be informed from the beginning of a course how behavior will affect their grades and how their points will be determined each week. Disputes with grading often involve a teacher who modifies a student grade at the end of the term because of misbehavior during the term.

It should be noted that some professionals have argued that a student's grade should entirely reflect the degree of mastery of course content and should not involve any aspect of student behavior (Gathercoal, 1987). However, the authors have found participation grading to be an effective tool for preventing and reducing minor misbehavior and for increasing the motivation of many students.

BEHAVIOR CHANGE

Many adolescents exhibit complex behavior patterns that have been maintained by a long history of attention from peers, teachers, or parents; escape from schoolwork; or even escape from school. Common sense suggests that if behavioral contingencies such as reprimands, time in the office, and detention or suspension were always effective, there would be few behavior problems in schools. Unfortunately these consequences often function as either positive or negative reinforcement procedures. To further complicate matters, by the time some students get to high school, they have learned a large repertoire of disruptive behaviors that can seem impervious to change.

Use of the strategies discussed thus far can prevent a significant amount of misbehavior in secondary classrooms. However, some misbehavior probably will occur regardless of the effectiveness of prevention strategies employed. This section will present procedures that teachers can use to increase desirable behaviors and address discipline problems that do occur. First, a review of some basic principles of behavior management will be presented. (Readers who desire a more in-depth treatment of application of behavior principles in classroom settings can consult such sources as Alberto and

Troutman [1986], Becker [1986], or Sulzer-Azaroff and Mayer [1977].)

1. Interventions with individual students who have discipline problems must be aimed at reducing undesirable behaviors, increasing desirable behaviors, and maintaining acceptable behaviors.

2. Behaviors that are positively reinforced are likely to occur more often in the future.

3. Behaviors that are not reinforced will tend to occur less often in the future. The process of extinction relies on this relationship.

4. Behaviors that are punished will tend to happen less often in the future.

5. Behaviors that terminate or remove an unpleasant (aversive) stimulus are likely to occur in the future whenever that aversive stimulus reoccurs. The principle of negative reinforcement is based on this relationship.

6. One person's meat is another's poison: Events that serve as positive reinforcers, punishers, or aversive stimuli differ from one person to the next.

7. Behaviors have a number of dimensions (White & Haring, 1980; Alberto & Troutman, 1986). The *topography* of a behavior is its shape, form, or style. The topography of a student's verbal responses to questions in class could be problematic if they are frequently preceded by the phrase "Call on me you dumb teacher." *Intensity* is the force or strength of a behavior. Talking too loudly and slamming books are examples of intensity problems. The *duration* of a behavior specifies how long it lasts. When students continue talking long after the bell rings, the duration of their behavior is a problem. *Latency* is the dimension that describes the amount of time that elapses between presentation of a stimulus and the occurrence of a behavior. Handing in homework late and taking too long to get a book out are examples of latency problems. *Rate* is the number of times a behavior occurs in a given period of time. A student who sharpens her pencil five times during a class period may be exhibiting too high a rate of the behavior. Finally, *locus* is the location of a behavior. If running is acceptable in the gym but not in the hallway, the locus of the behavior of a student who runs in the hall is problematic.

A thorough understanding of the above principles is important. However, the school psychologist should be careful not to alienate teachers with unfamiliar vocabulary. For example, to many teachers, the word punishment means something different than the classic behavioral definition (i.e., a stimulus that follows a behavior and reduces the future occurrence of that behavior). When some teachers hear the word punishment, they assume an angry, vengeful procedure implemented by the teacher. Given these potential differences in vocabulary, it is clear that communication between psychologists and teachers can be difficult, yet this communication must be precise. Throughout the remainder of this chapter, punishment procedures will be referred to as *punitive consequences.*

This section will first examine procedures for reducing misbehavior. Guidelines will be given for effectively implementing punitive consequences and then four specific consequences will be presented. An effective teacher must demonstrate an ability to act when misbehavior occurs. Thus, reprimands and sanctions are important procedures for teachers to be able to implement (Doyle, 1986). The remainder of this section will then present procedures for increasing student motivation.

Guidelines for Reducing Misbehavior with Punitive Consequences

Guideline 1: Stay calm. When working with secondary-level students, this is the most important guideline. Some students derive a great sense of power from their ability to make adults angry. In working with this type of student, an emotional response from the teacher serves as a powerful reinforcer of inappropriate behavior. As noted above, behaviors that are not positively reinforced will tend to happen less often in the future. When the teacher calmly informs the student of the consequence, it communicates that the misbehavior has no power to affect the teacher, and the student's misbehavior is essentially placed on an extinction program. A calm implementation also communicates that the teacher's feelings have nothing to do with the fact that the consequence is being implemented. The student has been previously informed that the behavior would lead to the consequence and now the teacher is calmly following through on that arrangement.

Guideline 2: Treat students with respect. During any implementation of a consequence students should be treated with dignity and respect. Humiliation, sarcasm, and ridicule should never be used as consequences. Respect for students is evidenced by use of adult vocabulary, offering students choices about events that affect them, use of realistic timelines, and use of age-appropriate consequences for desired as well as undesired behaviors.

Guideline 3: Develop a hierarchy of consequences. The most frequent misbehaviors in classrooms are minor infractions, and yet in many classrooms the teacher's only consequences are referral to the office. Office referral is appropriate for severe problems, but is inappropriate for behaviors such as talking in class, being off task, forgetting materials, handing assignments in late, and other minor disruptive behavior. If mild consequences are not used, the teacher must tolerate lots of these minor infractions, because office referral is too severe a consequence to reasonably fit the infraction. Each teacher needs a range of consequences to fit the range in severity of classroom rule infractions (Sprick, 1981).

For most behavior try soft reprimands and/or discussions as the first step. In many cases, simply informing the student that a behavior is unacceptable may be difficult to reduce the future occurrence of the behavior. A soft reprimand can be verbal or nonverbal, and can communicate to the student what behavior is expected.

Some advantages of reprimands are that they are quick, easy, and involve no record keeping on the part of the teacher. Also, reprimand has less probability of creating adversarial relationships between the teacher and the student than more intrusive consequences. An effective reprimand communicates that the teacher fully anticipates students will be successful in meeting the positive expectations.

Finally, reprimands are most useful for minor classroom infractions in the early stages of a semester while the teacher is still clarifying classroom expectations. However, if the misbehavior continues after the students know and understand the expectations, reprimands may not be sufficient and another consequence may need to be established.

Guideline 4: Plan ahead. For consequences to be most effective, students should know what behaviors will meet with a teacher response. If reprimands have not worked, inform the student that future infractions will no longer be reprimanded but will entail a specific consequence. After reviewing with the student what the specific consequence will be, the teacher should question the student to ensure understanding. When equipped with the information that misbehavior will result in a specific consequence, the student will thus understand that to choose to engage in the behavior is to also choose to receive the consequence.

Guideline 5: Establish a concurrent plan to reinforce success. When dealing with chronic misbehavior, a punitive consequence alone has a relatively low probability of changing student behavior. Many students with problem behavior have developed a "So what?" attitude toward being kept after school or sent to the vice-principal's office. If reprimands have not been effective and it becomes necessary to establish another consequence, the teacher needs also to think about how to motivate the student to cooperate. An intervention that applies consequences only for misbehavior is usually doomed to failure primarily because it does not teach students appropriate behavior.

The goal of the intervention is for the student to learn that inappropriate behavior results in aversive consequences, but appropriate behavior results in pleasant consequences. (How to accomplish this goal in ways that are not embarrassing to the student will be covered below.)

Guideline 6: Be as consistent as possible. Students must see that, once it is made clear that a behavior will lead to a specific consequence, the teacher follows through consistently. If some days the students "get away with it," the behavior can become part of a game the students play: "Let's see if I can do it again today and not get caught."

Guideline 7: Keep the interaction short. When an infraction occurs, the teacher should simply state the misbehavior and state the consequence and then resume instruction. If the teacher spends more than three seconds on the problem, the flow of the lesson is lost. All too often, misbehaving students can control the pace of the instruction through their misbehavior. Each time an infraction occurs, the teacher stops teaching and says things like: "Jason, I am getting very tired of this. We have discussed this before and you know that when this happens I keep you after school. I do not like keeping you after any more than you like being kept after, but you leave no choice. I now fully expect you to get your act together."

If the scenario above is happening several times a week, notice how much attention the student is receiving for the inappropriate behavior. Not only is the student getting attention from the teacher during the lecture, but every other student in the class is watching the interaction. When the teacher singles out an individual for a lecture on behavior, the student is put on display in front of peers. Some students like nothing better than being the center of attention for having been "bad."

When the chronic misbehavior occurs, the teacher should spend no more than three seconds with a student who has misbehaved. If the situation has previously been discussed with the student, at the time of the infraction the teacher can simply say, "Jason, that is disruptive; you owe me time after school. Now class look at Problem 3." Notice that the teacher immediately shifts the focus off the problem student and back to instruction.

Four Specific Classroom Consequences for Reducing Misbehavior

The most common consequence in the secondary schools seems to be office referral. Although office referral is a reasonable consequence for dangerous, illegal, or truly insubordinate behavior, it is not reasonable or terribly effective for typical classroom misbehavior. The teacher needs to understand that a mild consequence implemented calmly and consistently will tend to work better than a more severe consequence implemented emotionally or inconsistently. Below are four consequences that can be implemented for classroom misbehavior. They are presented in order of least to most intrusive. The first imploys the behavioral procedure we call response cost; which reduces the frequency of occurrence of a behavior through contingent removal of a previously earned reinforcer. In a general sense, the other three procedures could be thought of as forms of time-out, in which the student is denied the opportunity to receive reinforcement for a fixed period of time.

Reduction or loss of points earned for behavior and participation. This concept was briefly introduced earlier in this chapter. Students are informed that they start each week with a certain number of points and that they can lose or earn points for various types of behaviors. Each time the teacher reminds a student to get back to work, the teacher records the reprimand and the student loses one point. Please note that these points are not deducted from points earned from tests and assignments. The teacher actually gives each student a specific number of behavior points at the start of the week and then each student's number of points increase or decrease according to behavior.

For this to be effective, the students must be taught how the whole system works. Also, the teacher must keep the emphasis on awarding of points for positive behavior rather than simply taking away points for misbehavior.

Time owed. In essence time owed involves keeping a student after class for a short period of time. This consequence can be used only in schools that have passing periods long enough to keep a student after class for a short time and still give the student time to get to his next class. For example, if a school has 4-minute passing periods and in 3 minutes a student could get to the furthest room in the school, the teacher could keep a student after class for up to 1 minute without having to give the student an excuse to get into the next class.

The teacher informs students in advance that for certain infractions they may be kept after class for 30 seconds per infraction. This rule would allow the teacher to use this with any student for two infractions per class period. This consequence is very mild but it can be effective with some students, because it cuts into their time for socializing out in the school halls.

Although during instruction periods the goal is to have the student actively engaged in the lesson, assigned work should never be part of a consequence such as time owed, or the student may assume that assigned work is punishment. Furthermore, allowing academic work to be completed during this time can make the time go by very quickly and reduce the aversive nature of time owed. The student should sit and do nothing during the time owed.

Isolation area in class. Here, a desk and chair are set off to the side of the room and students are informed that for various infractions they will be sent to this area until they are ready to participate appropriately in class. Generally this procedure is used more frequently at the middle school and junior high levels than at the high school level. While in the isolation area, the students should have nothing to do. The goal of this procedure is to impress on the students that because of their misbehavior they are not being allowed to participate for a short time.

The length of time the students remain in the isolation area can either be a standard 5-minute period, or if the teacher prefers, they can be informed that they may rejoin the class whenever ready. However, if the isolated students are permitted to choose to come out on their own, the teacher should specify some criteria such as, "You may rejoin the group when you are ready to quietly work on your math at your seat." One of the major mistakes teachers make with this procedure is to isolate students for long periods of time; the time-out period should be relatively short.

After school detention. This is one of the most common consequences in use in secondary schools. All the students assigned to detention after school report to a particular room. In many schools there will be 20 or 30 students after school each day. The detention period is usually 30–60 minutes and students are usually required to do academic work during this time.

This consequence has more potential problems than any of the consequences previously described. The biggest problem is student transportation. Usually the infraction occurs on one day, the parents are notified that evening, the student stays after school the next day, and the student and/or the parents are responsible for arranging transportation. This means that there is a 24- to 31-hour delay between the infraction and the consequence. This time delay reduces the potential effectiveness of the consequence. Another problem with keeping students after school is getting the student to show up. If the student does not come to the assigned area, there need to be additional consequences imposed. A final problem is that the student is now in the same room with other students with problem behaviors and these students often reinforce one another's misbehavior.

If detention is being used, and the same students are being kept after school day after day, change the consequence.

Have the student pay the time after school with the teacher who assigned the time. In this way, the student is not in the room with other problem students and will probably find the after-school time to be more boring. Unfortunately, this procedure may be more punishing to the teacher than to the student. The teacher needs to evaluate if keeping the student after school would be effective in changing the behavior and if accomplishing this change is worth the time and effort required to keep the student after school.

Maintaining and Increasing Student Motivation

One useful way of thinking about motivation is the expectancy times value theory (Feather, 1982). According to this theory, student effort on a task will be a product of the degree to which the student values the rewards that accompany success. Note that the function described is multiplicative rather than additive, because if either expectancy or value is equal to zero, student effort will also be non-existent.

If the teacher does an effective job of organizing the classroom and running the first week, as was described in the first section of this chapter, students know exactly what is required to be successful. If the teacher does an exemplary job, every student believes it will be possible to be successful if they do the things the teacher asks them to do. If the teacher follows through and implements effective instructional practices, students will experience success in their daily learning activities. To put it another way, the teacher has built the expectancy that success will be possible, and the first half of the expectancy times value theory has been accomplished. The second half of the equation — value, will be addressed below.

The majority of students in the typical classroom already value good grades and the satisfaction associated with successful task completion. However, other students just don't seem to care. To motivate these students the teacher needs to do more than teach an interesting class and manage a reasonable grading system; the teacher needs to implement techniques that will increase student motivation in extrinsic ways. Although this can be accomplished with a variety of strategies, two major techniques will be discussed here: (a) using teacher and peer attention to reinforce desired behaviors and (b) using more structured rewards when necessary.

Differential Teacher and Peer Attention

Some students who do not seem to value success get far more attention for misbehavior than for positive behavior. It could be argued that the attention is in fact serving to reinforce the inappropriate behavior. One tool for increasing the motivation of these students is to change which categories of behaviors lead to attention and recognition from the teacher and from peers.

The first step in this behavior change process is to reduce the amount of attention the student receives for negative behavior. This can be accomplished by ignoring the majority of minor misbehavior and by implementing mild and quick consequences for the more severe misbehaviors. For example, the teacher may decide to ignore a student who neglects to raise her hand or gets out of her seat; but the teacher may institute consequences for the same student when she uses offensive language or is physically aggressive. As was previously described, when implementing consequences the teacher should be calm and should take no more than three seconds to state the consequence. By delivering consequences in this fashion, the teacher reduces the amount of time spent with the student following the severe misbehaviors. By ignoring the minor misbehaviors, the teacher reduces the number of times during each class period the student gets attention for misbehavior. In doing this, the teacher has also reduced the amount of peer attention the misbehaving student receives. By maintaining a focus on instruction, the teacher can keep the attention of the class focused on the task, rather than on the student who is trying to gain recognition through inappropriate behavior.

At the same time the teacher is working on reducing attention to misbehavior, effort must be put on giving time and attention to appropriate behavior. A teacher should attempt to interact with students while they are behaving appropriately three times more frequently than while they are behaving inappropriately. This can be accomplished in two ways. First, by simply interacting with a student while that student is behaving appropriately, and second by using effective praise.

Examples of interacting with a problem student while he is behaving appropriately include saying hello to him as he enters the classroom, calling on him when he appears to be listening, looking at his work while he is on task, talking with him in the hallway, smiling at the student when he hands in the assignment, sustained eye contact during a lecture, or asking the student to take a note to the office. Although none of the examples above involve overt praise, the interaction communicates that the student is of interest and value to the teacher, and that the student does not need to misbehave in order to be acknowledged or recognized.

Praise can be another useful technique for increasing student motivation. However to be effective, praise must be contingent, descriptive, and non-embarrassing. Contingent praise follows an appropriate behavior that is new or difficult for the student, or follows a behavior the individual is proud of. No one wants to be praised gratuitously.

Effective praise is descriptive rather than evaluative. In acknowledging a student's performance the teacher should state exactly what behavior the student exhibited that is important. The focus should be on what the student did, not on how much it pleases the teacher. Over time, descriptive praise will help students to learn to evaluate and reinforce their own behavior.

At the secondary level, the teacher should be careful not to put the student in the position of being embarrassed in front of peers for having done a good job. In general, praise will be less embarrassing if it is distributed so that every student gets positive feedback, if it is part of the flow of instruction, and if it focuses on the behavior rather than on the student. Another important factor is that the positive feedback be implemented in a manner that the teacher is comfortable with. If the teacher tends to be businesslike, then positive feedback to students can be given in a very businesslike manner. If the teacher is very energetic and friendly, then positive feedback can be given in a very energetic and friendly manner. If the businesslike teacher attempts to reinforce in an overly friendly manner, the students may feel that the interaction is insincere. For more details on effective praise see Sprick (1985) and Brophy (1981).

Structured Rewards

In addition to frequent attention to positive behavior, the teacher can increase student motivation through the use of more structured rewards. One systematic way to deliver feedback and rewards has already been presented — designing a portion of the grading system on student behavior. In this system, when praising a positive behavior or reprimanding an inappropriate behavior the teacher records the interaction. At the end of each week, every student is given a score for that week that is entered into the grade book based on the number of positive comments and negative comments. One of the goals of this procedure is for students to see that appropriate behavior can positively affect their grades.

Another way to reward appropriate performance is through a variety of intermittent rewards. Unlike structured reinforcement systems, where a contract is made that states, "If you do . . . , you get...," intermittent rewards are delivered sporadically at the discretion of the teacher. For example, when a student makes a really significant step toward success, the teacher may want to use a stronger reinforcer than praise. This is the time to provide a special reward. Intermittent rewards should give students the feeling that their behavior was truly special.

TABLE 3
Intermittent Rewards Suitable for Secondary Students

- Writing a note to the student's parents
- Writing a note to the student
- Calling the student's parents
- Calling the student
- Complimenting the student in front of another staff member
- Asking one of the administrators to reward the student's behavior
- Privately praising the student's classroom performance in a non classroom setting such as in the hall after school
- Give the student a responsibility
- Tokens for a video arcade
- Tickets to a school activity
- Food
- Coupon to rent a movie
- Let the student choose an activity for the class
- Check out a book the student might be interested in

If any specific reinforcer is used too much, there can be an inflationary phenomenon and the students may satiate on the reinforcer due to its overuse. This problem can be reduced if the teacher implements a variety of intermittent rewards. Table 3 shows a list of some potentially effective rewards that can be used intermittently at secondary level.

With the students who are not intrinsically motivated, effective praise, frequent attention, and occasional intermittent rewards will fill out the value portion of the motivation equation. The eventual goal is that every student will become intrinsically motivated; however, until that occurs the school staff must demonstrate that positive behaviors lead to positive consequences.

INTERVENTIONS INSTITUTED DIRECTLY BY THE PSYCHOLOGIST

The interventions presented thus far are procedures to be implemented by the classroom teacher. There are several effective interventions that can be facilitated through the direct involvement of the school psychologist.

Clarifying Rules and Expectations

With a student who is chronically misbehaving, the psychologist may observe in the classroom, review the teacher's rules with the student, and ask the student questions regarding the teacher's behavioral expectations. "What are you supposed to be doing during the time your teacher is taking attendance? If you have a question or something to say while the teacher is lecturing, how are you supposed to get the teacher to call on you?" By observing in the classroom and interviewing the student, the psychologist can determine if the student's misbehavior is a result of not understanding the teacher's expectations or a result of choosing to misbehave or break the rules.

If the student lacks a detailed understanding of the teacher's expectations, arrange a meeting with the teacher and the student so that these expectations can be discussed in a positive manner. As a third party at this meeting, ask questions of both the teacher and the student to help clarify the minute-by-minute expectations for that classroom. With some students it may also be helpful to practice and role-play classroom situations to be sure the student can meet the expectations.

Improving Students' Participation in Class

To help students who do not actively participate in class, meet with them and establish an expectation that they should be taking notes in class. Start by focusing on one class period. Tell them that they need to make at least three specific notes each day in their notebooks during fourth period. Give them some strategies for knowing what to write down. Meet with these students at least once a week to examine the notes. Reinforce their behavior if they are meeting the expectation of participating in class by taking notes.

Assisting Students in Understanding Grading Practices

Meet with students who are unsure about grading practices to discuss their grades. Ask them what their current grades are. If they do not know, have them go to each teacher and find out how many points they have currently, how many points are currently possible, any assignments that they have not turned in, and the teacher's grading scale (e.g., 90% for an A, and so on). Depending on the situation, it may be best to begin with focus on one class. After these students have gathered this information, teach them to track their own grades and monitor their own learning progress. Meet with them regularly to discuss current status, progress made, and plans for future work.

It may also be useful to help these students set realistic goals for improving performance. Goal setting has been demonstrated to be an effective procedure for improving student performance (Bandura & Schunk, 1981; Tollefson, Tracy, Johnsen, Farmer, & Buenning, 1984). The student may need assistance initially, because the goals should be specific and fairly immediate, and challenging but obtainable. Written contracts are also a useful tool for helping a student become more motivated to improve performance, and thus improve grades. For more

detailed information on goal setting and contracts see Sprick (1985).

Assessing Student Ability

Determine whether students who are having chronic problems are capable of reading their assigned texts. If they are unable to successfully read and understand their texts, misbehavior may be a result of their attempts to cover up the fact that they are unable to do the work. If a student is often frustrated in efforts to read academic material, assist the teacher to adapt assignments, set up a peer-tutoring arrangement (Greenwood et al., 1984), establish cooperative learning groups (Johnson, Johnson, Holubec, & Roy, 1984; Slavin, 1983), or apply some other method of helping the low-performing student master the instructional content through means other than primarily reading the text.

Mediating Consequences with Teachers and Students

In some situations, scheduling a meeting with the psychologist, the teacher, and the student can be useful in further clarifying expectations and in helping the teacher and the student negotiate the consequences for unacceptable behavior. During this meeting encourage the teacher to clarify exactly what behaviors are unacceptable and what the consequences will be for each infraction. The goal is to insure that the student understands which behaviors will lead to negative consequences and also understands which acceptable behaviors the teacher wishes to see. A meeting of this type not only helps clarify expectations for the student, it can also help the teacher be more consistent. When the teacher has explained his or her procedures to the student in front of a third party, there is an increased accountability for following through on what was stated.

Implementing a Reinforcement Program

In some cases teachers may be unwilling to establish a plan to reinforce success. In this situation, a plan can be established and implemented by the psychologist. One example would be a daily report card that the teacher signs if the student has behaved appropriately. The psychologist then meets with the student weekly to debrief the student's performance, awards points for good days, sets goals, and provides reinforcers as the student accumulates enough points.

Teaching Students to Interact with Teachers

If a student behaves in ways that result in frequent negative interactions with adults, try teaching the student to interact positively with the teacher. Train the student to say hello to the teacher. Teach when to go to the teacher and ask a question regarding the class. Teach the student to appropriately reinforce the teacher's behavior. When the student increases attempts at positive interactions with the teacher, it is often easier for the teacher to interact positively with the student.

CONCLUSIONS

Classroom management procedures implemented by the teacher play a major role in affecting the behavior of all students who are not intrinsically motivated. The effective teacher organizes the classroom and instruction in ways that communicate to students that they can be successful if they are willing to follow the rules and try. The effective teacher develops strategies for dealing with misbehavior that are efficient and consistent and that do not allow misbehavior to interrupt the flow of instruction. The effective teacher provides extrinsic motivation to the students who need it in the form of positive attention, praise, and intermittent rewards. Finally, the effective teacher uses a grading system that allows students to earn points for participation, completion of assignments, and tests, while providing frequent feedback to students regarding their performance.

The school psychologist can assist teachers and students to implement strategies such as clarification of expectations, goal setting, and training the student in how to interact with teachers. The goal of the psychologist should be to work with teachers and students before a problem has gone on so long that the teacher only wants the student removed from the room. The strategies presented in this chapter can counter many problems before they reach crisis proportions. Effective teaching and classroom management need to be proactive processes and the psychologist can play a significant role in helping teachers incorporate these practices into their teaching repertoire.

REFERENCES

Alberto, P. C., & Troutman, A. C. (1986). *Applied behavior analysis for teachers* (2nd ed.). Columbus, OH: Merrill.

Bandura, A., & Schunk, D. (1981). Cultivating competence, self-efficacy, and intrinsic interest through proximal self-motivation. *Journal of Personality and Social Psychology, 41,* 586–598.

Becker, W. C. (1986). *Applied psychology for teachers.* Chicago: Science Research Associates.

Brophy, J. E., & Evertson, C. M. (1976). *Learning from teaching: A developmental perspective.* Boston: Allyn & Bacon.

Brophy, J. E., & Evertson, C. M. (1983). Classroom organization and management. *Elementary School Journal, 83,* 265–285.

Doyle, W. (1986). Classroom organization and management. In M. C. Wittrock (Ed.), *Handbook of research on teaching* (3rd ed.; pp. 392–431). New York: Macmillan.

Emmer, E., Evertson, C., Sanford, J., Clements, B., & Worsham, M. (1988). *Classroom management for secondary teachers* (2nd ed.). Englewood Cliffs, NJ: Prentice-Hall.

Feather, N. T. (Ed.). (1982). *Expectations and actions.* Hillsdale, NJ: Erlbaum.

Gathercoal, F. (1987). *Judicious discipline.* Ann Arbor, MI: Prakken.

Good, T. L. (1987). Teacher expectations. In D. C. Berliner & B. V. Rosenshine (Eds.), *Talks to teachers,* (pp. 159–200). New York: Random House.

Greenwood, C. R., Dinwiddle, G., Terry, B., Wade, L., Stanley, S., Thibadeau, S., & Delquadri, J. (1984). Peer tutoring vs. teacher instruction: An eco-behavioral analysis. *Journal of Applied Behavior Analysis, 17,*(4).

Johnson, D., Johnson, R., Holubec, E., & Roy, P. (1984). *Circles of learning: Cooperation in the classroom.* Alexandria, VA: Association for Supervision and Curriculum Development.

Jones, V. F., & Jones, L. S. (1986). *Comprehensive classroom management: Creating positive learning environments* (2nd ed.). Boston: Allyn & Bacon.

Kounin, J. S. (1970). *Discipline and group management in classrooms.* New York: Holt, Rinehart and Winston.

Slavin, R. (1983). *Cooperative Learning.* New York: Longman.

Sprick, R. (1981). *The solution book: A guide to classroom discipline.* Chicago: Science Research Associates.

Sprick, R. (1985). *Discipline in the secondary classroom.* West Nyack, NY: Center for Applied Research in Education.

Sulzer-Azaroff, B., & Maye, G. R. (1977). *Applying behavior analysis procedures with children and youth.* New York: Holt, Rinehart and Winston.

Tollefson, N., Tracy, D., Johnsen, E., Farmer, W., & Buenning, M. (1984). Goal setting and personal responsibility for LD adolescents. *Psychology in the Schools, 21,* 224–233.

White, O. R., & Haring, N. G. (1980). *Exceptional Teaching* (2nd ed.). Columbus, OH: Merrill.

24

Prevention and Early Interventions for Addictive Behaviors: Health Promotion in the Schools

Herb Severson
Leslie Zoref
Oregon Research Institute

SCOPE OF THE PROBLEM

Drug use by adolescents is now seen as a major social problem. While there have been modest downward trends in the use of some illicit drugs, the overall rate of drug use by youths in the United States is still higher than that in any other industrialized country (Johnston, O'Malley, & Bachman, 1987). Sixty percent of high school seniors report using one or more illicit drugs. Forty percent of high school students have tried at least one non-cannabis illicit drug (Newcomb & Bentler, 1988). In a recent national survey of high school seniors, 19% reported daily use of cigarettes, 93% had experimented with alcohol, and 43% reported at least one episode of excessive alcohol use (five or more drinks on one occasion) in the previous 2-week period (Johnston, O'Malley, & Bachman, 1985). In addition, 18% of seniors reported weekly use of cannabis and 6% reported daily use of either alcohol or marijuana. Together these estimates are conservative because students who drop out of school before their senior year have been shown to have higher self-reported use of cigarettes and other drugs (Pirie, Murray, & Luepker, 1988). These figures show that teenagers' drug involvement is not merely a passing experimental phase; for many the use of drugs has become part of a daily life-style.

Surveys of drug use confirm that not only are drugs being used, but the age of initial use is at the elementary school level for most drugs. Studies of cigarette, chewing tobacco, and marijuana use report experimentation in fourth and fifth grades. This early experience with drug use is related to subsequent regular use and abuse (Severson, 1984).

While the public's highest interest is in illicit drug use, common popular drugs such as cigarettes and alcohol may pose a greater threat to public health. Today and every day of the year 2,000 adolescents in the United States will smoke their first cigarettes on their way to becoming regular smokers as adults (Glynn, 1989). During their lifetime, we predict that approximately 15 will be murdered, 20 will die in traffic accidents, and nearly 500 will be killed by smoking-related diseases (Dawson & Henderson, 1987). Given the ongoing experimentation noted above, and the fact that smoking has been linked to more deaths than all other life-style factors including the use of "hard" drugs, it is imperative that any efforts to prevent drug use target use of tobacco as a central theme. Prevention efforts should include the most prevalent drugs used by teens: tobacco (cigarettes and chew), alcohol, and marijuana.

In order for school-based prevention to be effective, the interventions or programs need to be introduced before the behavior has escalated into a regular use pattern. For example, in the case of smoking, over 90% of adult smokers report that they were regular users before leaving high school; and 62% report that they had at least tried cigarettes by ninth grade. Similarly, most students report that they have initiated the use of alcohol by the ninth grade. Our own research shows that on average seventh graders report that in the previous week 10% have used cigarettes, 14% of the boys have used chewing tobacco, and 23% have used alcohol. Of more serious concern is the fact that 11% of seventh graders report that in the previous week they have had five or more drinks of alcohol on a single occasion (a standard used to measure inebriation in place of asking the subjects whether they are drunk).

Early experience with a wide range of drugs can influence the lifelong pattern of drug use (Kandel & Raveis, 1989). It is clear that, if we want to change substance use patterns, we must identify users at the early stage of use and apply general prevention efforts to reduce the number of adolescents who go on to regular use. Early drug use has been shown to be related to a wide range of antisocial behaviors and subsequent school failure (Donovan & Jessor, 1978). Substance use by adolescents often occurs in the context of other problem behaviors, such as delinquency (Donovan & Jessor, 1978), school failure (Hundleby, Carpenter, Ross, & Mercer, 1982), high-risk sexual behavior (Biglan, Wendler, et al., in press), and low self-esteem (Bry, McKeon, & Padina, 1982). Indeed, the number of problems a youth experiences (e.g., poor relationship with parents of peers, psychopathology, low grade-point average) increases the risk of concurrent and later drug use (Newcomb, Maddahian, & Bentler, 1986). In addition, it has been fairly well documented that heavy use of one substance predicts involvement with other, hard substances. For example, abuse of alcohol precedes cannabis use, which in turn precedes use of hard drugs, including cocaine (Kandel, 1975; Newcomb & Bentler, 1988). Thus, one consequence of drug use is the increased probability of involvement with harder drugs (Donovan & Jessor, 1983). School personnel have the responsibility, as well as the opportunity, to intervene early in order to interrupt the cycle. While many factors, such as substance use by parents and substance accessibility, are beyond the scope of a school-based intervention, there is increasing evidence for the efficacy of early interventions to reduce drug use and abuse.

IMPORTANCE OF PREVENTION AND EARLY INTERVENTION

Prevention efforts can be viewed as either primary or secondary. In primary prevention, the intervention is designed to prevent a target person (or population) from engaging in a particular behavior, and it is implemented before the behavior occurs. In the case of smoking or drug prevention, this approach requires that the intervention be aimed at young students who have not yet begun either to smoke or to use other drugs. Secondary prevention is geared toward inhibiting the person (or the identified at-risk population) from continuing a behavior that has already been initiated. While we like to think that clear lines exist between primary and secondary prevention, the distinction is often blurred in the study of drug use. For example, if one were to intervene in the sixth grade and focus on the prevention of smoking, such an intervention could be considered primary prevention because most sixth-grade students are not smokers. Realistically, however, since some students of that age report that they have already experimented with cigarettes, the intervention must include secondary prevention components as well.

Most smoking prevention programs have been implemented in the public schools and aimed at middle school and high school students. The primary model target populations for these interventions have been sixth- or seventh-grade classrooms. Cross-sectional and longitudinal surveys suggest that the onset of smoking becomes significant at the seventh grade (Severson & Lichtenstein, 1986). It is postulated that the transition from elementary school to middle or junior high school is an important point of focus, as the new school environment exposes children to older classmates and peers, offering increased opportunity for experimentation with new behaviors, including drug use.

Clearly, the problem of drug use is shared by our general society, and some believe that widespread social changes are required before we will see a change in the demand for drugs. However, drug use by young people has made the schools the primary arena of hope for changing the pattern. While some social and attitudinal changes have already been achieved, as evidenced by the reduction of adult smoking and alcohol use, the most readily apparent vehicle for continued change is the education of our young people. Schools provide a cost-effective vehicle for interventions and provide the most reasonable option for exposing students to a specific set of materials or training. Although there has been a long history of using schools to educate our youth about the dangers of drug use, the efficacy of these programs has been questionable (Thompson, 1978). Smoking prevention programs have been experimentally evaluated for the past 10 years and provide the best empirical base for school-based prevention (Flay, 1985; Glynn, 1989). The program described here is intended as a model that can be adapted and implemented in any public school; it has been demonstrated to have a positive impact on reducing the use of cigarettes (Biglan et al., 1987). Before reviewing specific intervention programs, we will examine the conceptual basis for the proposed intervention.

CONCEPTUAL MODEL FOR PREVENTION

In order to develop effective prevention programs, it is critical to study the process by which the behavior develops. In the case of smoking, several studies have focused on understanding the variables that influence this process. Peer influence is the preeminent proximal factor in the initiation of smoking behavior (Mittelmark et al., 1983; Severson, 1984; Severson & Lichtenstein, 1986). (Most adolescents report obtaining their first

cigarette from a peer and being with same-age friends when initially experimenting with cigarettes [Biglan, Severson, Bavry, & McConnell, 1983; Friedman, Lichtenstein, & Biglan, 1985]).

The influence of peers on adolescent smoking is a direct one. Adolescents often smoke when they are with other adolescents who are smoking. Authors of cross-sectional studies have concluded that friends' smoking has a primary influence on an adolescent's smoking behavior (Allegrante, O'Rourke, & Tuncalp, 1977; Bewley & Bland, 1977). They have also concluded that, although both parents' smoking and peers' smoking are important factors in influencing an adolescent to smoke, peer influence appears to increase in importance with age, but parental influence decreases. In contrast, Krosnick and Judd (1982) found that parental influence did not decrease, but remained the same over time.

Longitudinal studies also point to the crucial influence of peer smoking. In one study, hierarchical multiple regression analysis of nonsmoking middle school students demonstrated that, at 1-year follow-up, the factors that predicted smoking were the number of offers to smoke, marijuana use, the number of smoking friends, and the level of smoking experience (Ary & Biglan, 1988). A parallel study of high school students found that the major predictors of an individual's smoking habits were the number of smoking friends and the level of smoking experience (Ary & Biglan, 1988). Other researchers (Biglan, Weissman, & Severson, 1985; Mittelmark et al., 1983) have also concluded that friends' smoking was the most important factor in predicting the onset of smoking. Thus, to deter smoking, it makes a good deal of sense for prevention programs to focus upon the peer influence process.

While there is still much to be learned about how peer influence works, it appears to be a critical variable in the onset of a number of drug use behaviors. A review of the initiation of marijuana and chewing tobacco use also found that peer use was the single most powerful variable in onset (Ary, Lichtenstein, & Severson,

1987). Although it is tempting to attribute the onset of smoking and drug use to one variable (i.e., peers smoking), recent studies have implicated a number of variables at work in concert, indicating that a multivariate model of initiation and use needs to be considered. For example, Newcomb et al. (1986) developed a 10-variable index-of-risk measure to predict use and abuse (heavy use) of cigarettes, alcohol, cannabis, cocaine, and hard drugs, and a composite score of substance use. These 10 variables accounted for over 50% of the variance in a measure of general drug use. Perceived approval of drug use by peers was the most powerful variable, but other variables such as early drug experiences, school absenteeism and failure, perception of adult drug use, sensation seeking, and poor relationship with parents all contributed to the variance. This study underscores the fact that no single cause can adequately explain drug use by adolescents; any model of prevention must be broad-based in its approach in order to affect the variables that may influence any single child.

The transition process from initial experimentation to regular cigarette use has been studied but is still not well understood. However, becoming a regular user of cigarettes appears to take some time. It is estimated that fully two-thirds of adolescents try at least one cigarette, but surveys of high school seniors report only 19% are regular daily users (Johnston, O'Malley, & Bachman, 1987). Keep in mind that this incidence is an underestimate, since high school dropouts have been shown to have a significantly higher smoking rate than nondropouts (Pirie, Murray, & Luepker, 1988). A high level of experimentation with alcohol, marijuana, and hard drugs also appears to occur; a small number of adolescents go on to regular use. The determinants that predict which experimenters go on to regular use are largely unknown. It is interesting, however, that when asked to predict the probability that they would become regular smokers, seventh-grade students can be remarkably accurate even if they

are not smoking at the time of assessment (Severson, 1984).

While no validated theory or model so far satisfactorily integrates the available data and provides guidelines for interventions, three alternative frameworks have been proposed for explaining smoking behavior. These frameworks reflect differing theoretical views of behavior and development.

First, the behavior analysis framework (Biglan & Lichtenstein, 1984) suggests five classes of variables that are important in understanding the onset of smoking: (a) the modeling effects of other persons' smoking; (b) the reinforcing practices of others; (c) the immediate physical and pharmacologic consequences of smoking cigarettes; (d) the teenager's repertoire of behaviors for refusing cigarettes; and (e) countervailing contingencies that reinforce nonsmoking. The emphasis is on specific, proximal variables; events that occur almost immediately prior to, or after, smoking or episodes of temptation.

Second, the cognitive-social perspective (Chassin, Presson, & Sherman, 1984; Sherman, Presson, Chassin, & Olshavsky, 1983), like the behavioral framework, emphasizes proximal variables, but these variables are of a cognitive nature. These variables include specific attitudes and beliefs about smokers, normative beliefs, and behavioral intentions (expected response of parents or peers to smoking). This perspective is based to a large extent on Ajzen and Fishbein's (1970) model of the relationship between attitudes, intentions, and behaviors. Attitudes and attributions concerning early smoking experiences are also of interest (Hirschman, Leventhal, & Glynn, 1984).

In contrast to the cognitive-social perspective, persons holding the behavior analysis view treat attitudes, beliefs, and intentions as products of adolescents' reinforcement history with peers, siblings, parents, and cigarettes. Intentions, for example, are seen as likely to be a function of prior exposure to discussions of others' smoking or one's own smoking experience. The verbal expression of an intention may itself increase the probability of the behavior, but this does not seem to be the sense in which intentions are typically said to cause particular behaviors (Biglan & Lichtenstein, 1984).

Finally, the problem behavior theory of Jessor and Jessor (1977) emphasizes variables more distant from the behavior of interest, including general personality traits and perceived environmental factors not specific to smoking. The variables are said to define a person's proneness to deviant behavior and to predict early or premature transition to a variety of adult activities in violation of age norms. Evidence to support this theory is the substantial covariation among risk behaviors for the same individuals. For example, adolescent smoking behavior is viewed as a part of a more general class of high-risk behaviors, including drug use, precocious sexual activity, aggression, and delinquency (Jessor, 1984). All three theoretical perspectives are likely to have heuristic value in prevention programs. We are aware of only one study that has directly compared the three approaches (Chassin et al., 1984). Variables from all three approaches were found to be significant predictors of smoking transitions over a 1-year period. Each framework independently contributed to predicting transition to regular smoking, so it is probably useful at this point to consider the implications of each and not to assume that one perspective alone is adequate for predicting behavior.

SMOKING PREVENTION AS A MODEL FOR ADDICTION PREVENTION

The notion of using smoking prevention as a model for the prevention of other drug use is not new (McAlister, 1983). This idea is strengthened by the recent Surgeon General's report on nicotine addiction: "The pharmacologic and behavioral processes that determine tobacco addiction are similar to those that determine addiction to drugs such as heroin and cocaine" (U.S. Department of Health and Human Services, 1988, p. 14). Nicotine clearly meets all the established criteria for drug dependence, primarily (a) highly controlled or compulsive use; (b) psy-

choactive effects; and (c) drug-reinforced behavior. Secondary criteria include stereotypical patterns of use, use despite harmful effects, relapse following abstinence, recurrent drug cravings, increased tolerance over time, physical dependence, and pleasant effects. The addictive properties of nicotine, along with the relatively high prevalence of tobacco use among youth (compared with other drug use), make tobacco prevention seem reasonable to use as a model for preventing use of other addictive drugs as well. Furthermore, the ample evidence that regular tobacco use is related to a wide range of health problems makes smoking and chewing tobacco excellent targets for educational programs.

Smoking prevention efforts provide several advantages as a model for other drug prevention strategies. First, a long history of empirical work on smoking prevention has produced a sizable database containing more information than is available for other drugs (Evans, 1976; Evans & Raines, 1982; Jessor & Jessor, 1977; Lichtenstein, 1982; Luepker, Johnson, Murray, & Pechacek, 1983; McAlister, Perry, & Maccoby, 1979; McCaul & Glasgow, 1985; Pentz, 1983; Snow, Gilchrist, & Schinke, 1985; Williams, 1971). Second, school-based programs that focus on tobacco prevention are widespread (see reviews by Flay, 1985, see also, Severson & Lichtenstein, 1986). Third, reliable, noninvasive biochemical measures for verification of use are available, for example, expired air and saliva (Bauman & Dent, 1983; Evans, Hansen, & Mittelmark, 1977; Grabowski & Bell, 1983). Fourth, outcome data for prevention programs are available across a variety of settings (Flay, 1985; Severson & Lichtenstein, 1986). As previously mentioned, early tobacco use is also a good predictor of other drug use.

There are some disadvantages to using a tobacco prevention model. Alternative approaches to prevention may be warranted if the variables affecting use differ across substances. For example, if peer pressure does not play a part in determining cocaine use, then refusal skills training to promote declining of offers from peers would have little impact on cocaine users. Another disadvantage is that tobacco use appears to parents and school personnel to be a less compelling concern than use of hard drugs. This is an interesting state of affairs: Tobacco use is much more widespread and, overall, causes more death and disease than alcohol and hard drugs combined (Johnston, O'Malley, & Bachman, 1988).

Perhaps this last fact points to the most convincing argument for using tobacco prevention as a model for other drug prevention: Smoking is the single most preventable cause of death in our society, and it is the premiere public health issue of our time (U.S. Department of Health and Human Services, 1982). The potential for engendering far-reaching health changes is highly probable if one can deter, or stop, tobacco use.

Recently, Flay (1985) reviewed 27 school-based studies of psychosocial approaches to smoking prevention that spanned four generations of research conducted over less than a 10-year period. The first generation began with Evans's (Evans, 1976; Evans et al., 1978) pioneer research at the University of Houston, where he applied social inoculation theory to deterring tobacco use. Students were "vaccinated" with various forms of anti-smoking information through films and peer leaders in order to combat social pressures to smoke. The second-generation work was conducted by researchers in Minnesota, New York, California, and Washington who built on Evans's work by refining the programs to be tested and by expanding their scope (Botvin & Eng, 1980; Gilchrist, Schinke, & Blythe, 1979; Hurd et al., 1980; McAlister et al., 1979, 1980). Third-generation studies were then directed by second-generation groups by adding improvements to their previous research designs such as increasing the number of classrooms per condition and some randomization. Fourth-generation research mainly focused on the enhancement of internal validity to establish the efficacy of previous prevention programs under more stringent conditions. Thus, these studies were much larger in scale and all used random assignment of either schools or classrooms to treatment conditions. However, this generation of research was not designed for component analyses. Identifying the segments of the programs that contributed to the positive treatment effects was impossible.

Flay (1985) categorized the prevention programs he reviewed as falling into one of two camps: "social influence" and "life/social skills." The social influence approach incorporates direct instruction about social pressures to smoke, teaching refusal skills as a means to resist those influences, and changing the adolescent view that most people smoke. The life/social skills approach embraces a broader arena by teaching skills intended to improve overall social competence. For example, students are taught decision-making skills and relaxation techniques. Flay reported that his analysis yielded consistent results across the studies; the programs appeared to reduce initial experimentation with cigarettes by about 50%, regardless of which approach was used. However, methodological limitations warranted that conclusions be drawn cautiously.

Other researchers (McCaul & Glasgow, 1985) agree with Flay in concluding that although these school-based programs showed positive effects, the research has yet to identify which program components are effective and why. Fortunately, studies are currently under way (Glynn, 1989) that have set out to rectify some of the methodological problems that beset previous efforts. We are hopeful that this fifth generation of research will serve to strengthen the positive results found in the past. The combination of a large empirical base and widespread current research makes smoking prevention a model for developing other school-based prevention programs for addictive behaviors.

SMOKING PREVENTION AS A MODEL: WHAT CAN WE DO AND HOW CAN WE DO IT?

Smoking prevention programs with students focus on both home and school environments. Initially, this section briefly discusses the components of a home-based program that address parent–child interactions around tobacco use, rules and expectations for children's use of tobacco, and parents' use of tobacco. Next, the components of a school-based program are examined in detail, including the evolution of smoking prevention programs, criteria for successful curricula, and issues of program adoption and implementation, including teacher training.

Components of a Home-Based Program

Parental involvement in tobacco and substance abuse prevention has not been thoroughly researched (Forman & Linney, 1987). However, the smoking status of parents, as well as a host of other family variables (e.g., rule setting, parent–child relationships, degree of independence from parents) have been examined with respect to their effect on children's smoking (Severson & Lichtenstein, 1986). Surprising as it may seem, parents' attitudes toward smoking, as well as parents' smoking behavior, appear to have little influence on the smoking habits of their children. For example, peer influence seems to be much more powerful than parental factors in predicting the future smoking status of adolescents (Ary & Biglan, 1988; Andrews, Hops, Ary, Lichtenstein, & Tildesley, in press). If parents are to help their children from using tobacco, they must understand how they can effectively do so. Thus, for starters, parents can be advised to set up clear rules and expectations for smoking in the home and elsewhere. At a more involved level, Forman and Linney (1987) have developed a training program for parents that was designed to complement the social skills being taught to children during school. Regardless of the extent of parental involvement, it is important to let parents who do smoke know that they can still be a positive influence on their children's smoking decisions.

Components of a School-Based Program

The traditional approach to smoking prevention in schools was to educate students in the long-term health effects of tobacco use. At best, this type of approach changed attitudes and knowledge, but did little to change actual smoking behavior (Thompson, 1978). One explanation for the lack of a deterrent effect is that long-term health consequences, no matter how serious, are less than persuasive to an audience of adolescents, who believe themselves to be invincible and immortal. Another explanation is that education around the long-term effects of tobacco use fails because too much time elapses between tobacco use and its health consequences for education to serve as a deterrent.

To overcome this weakness prevention programs that are currently in use were designed such that students can perceive their content as immediately relevant. The curricular changes incorporated into current prevention efforts grew out of a body of research that was funded first by the National Institute of Child Health and Human Development (NICHHD), and later by the National Cancer Institute (NCI). By 1983, the NCI staff, having concluded that tobacco-related research had amassed sufficient evidence around the carcinogenic properties of tobacco, shifted funding priorities toward disease prevention and health promotion. As a result of this altered course or emphasis, 15 school-based smoking prevention studies were funded. It is from these studies that the essential curricular components of present-day programs are derived. Glynn (1989) set out the critical program features, three of which have relevance here: (a) focus, (b) content, and (c) length.

Focus. With respect to focus, programs addressing only smoking appear equally effective in deterring use as those programs in which smoking is dealt with in the larger context of health promotion. However, it appears that if smoking prevention is to be promoted within a broader health curriculum, it is important that the smoking component receive sufficient attention. (This issue is discussed later under program length.)

Content. Program content should at the very minimum emphasize short-term consequences of tobacco use; how social influences affect use; and refusal skills training that incorporates modeling and skills practice. By stressing short-term effects of use, such as having bad breath, shortness of breath (for athletes), smelly hair and clothes, burn holes in one's clothes, and so forth, programs are capitalizing on students' desires to be socially acceptable. These immediate consequences of smoking have a greater probability of affecting behavior change in adolescent students than the distant threats of lung cancer and heart attacks.

Teaching students how to recognize the many ways in which people are influenced to behave is an important component in a prevention program. Adolescents commonly believe that they alone determine their own behavior (Seltzer, 1982). This, of course, is a normal stage of development in which adolescents try to assert their independence from their parents and adults in general. Curriculum activities are designed to make students aware of the subtle influences on their behavior by their peers, family, and the media. The goal is to help them identify when they are being influenced to do something they might not want to do, such as smoke or try drugs. An example of how such identification is achieved is to first show advertisements that are obviously attempting to sell cigarettes (for example, "Try Carltons") and then show more subtle advertising methods, in which the ads simply associate smoking with having fun, without a direct sales pitch. Examples include the majority for ads for Vantage cigarettes, which typically depict young people participating in a thrilling athletic activity. By increasing student awareness about such influences, they become better equipped to determine how they want to act.

Assuming that students do indeed prefer not to partake in certain activities, prevention programs provide behavioral rehearsal and practice in ways to refuse offers. Some programs go beyond refusal skills training and include lessons on decision making, problem solving, asser-

tiveness, positive thinking, and/or anxiety reduction (Biglan et al., 1987; Botvin & Eng, 1982; Gilchrist & Schinke, 1984; Murray, Swan, & Clarke, 1984). The intent of these lessons is to arm students with various strategies for overcoming pressures in such a way that peers do not become angry with them and their own integrity is maintained.

Length. The third critical program feature is length. An ideal program length of 10 sessions per year for Grades 6-9 has been recommended by Glynn (1989). However, this time allotment may be seen as too large for teachers and school districts to adopt. A more feasible commitment might be Glynn's minimal recommendation of two programs of five-sessions taught between Grades 6 and 9.

Other features. In-class curricula provide one avenue for reaching students. Another approach to prevention at school is to promote schoolwide activities, opportunities, and events such as quit-smoking contests and competitions to create antitobacco posters. In addition, drop-in resource centers can provide factual information, information about available services, and advice and support for students (and faculty) who want to quit using tobacco or to help someone who is trying to quit. Possible locations for housing such a center include the school library, the nurse's or counselor's office, or the main office.

Program Adoption and the Implementation Process

Adoption and implementation of prevention programs require steps parallel to those used when implementing new academic programs. First, administrative, staff, and community support must be garnered. Second, potential programs need to be identified; a list of recommended resources for tobacco and drug prevention curricula appears in Table 1. Regional and local school district offices are on most government mailing lists and are likely to have some of the resource guides we list. Third, documentation of

TABLE 1
Recommended Resources for Tobacco and Drug Prevention Programs

Resource/Author	Address
1. *School Programs to Prevent Smoking: NCI Guide to Strategies that Succeed.* (In press.) National Cancer Institute, 1989.	National Cancer Institute National Institutes of Health Bethesda, MD 20205
2. *Schools Without Drugs* U.S. Department of Education, 1986.	Schools Without Drugs Pueblo CO 81009 Phone: 1-800-624-0100 (In Washington, DC area: 1-800-659-4854)
3. *Drug Prevention Curricula — A Guide to Selection and Implementation.* U.S. Department of Education, 1988.	National Clearinghouse for Alcohol and Drug Information (NCADI) PO Box 2345 Rockville, MD 20852 Phone: 301-468-2600 *Note:* Calling is recommended; requests by mail take much longer.
4. NCADI Publications Catalog. NCADI, 1988.	Same address and phone number as above.

program efficacy should be presented. Establishing such evidence may be easier with prevention curricula than with other academic programs, as many were developed under federal grants and included evaluation components. Fourth, cost factors must be considered. For example, is staff training built into the price? Fifth, ease of adaptation into existing curricula must be examined.

Prevention programs need not be delivered by classroom teachers; school nurses and counselors are excellent candidates for this role. Some schools already employ drug counselors, the obvious choice for initiating a prevention unit. Regardless of who does the teaching, training in the implementation of smoking prevention programs is essential for outlining the goals of the program and emphasizing the importance of presenting the activities as designed. Training has two unique components. First, training should provide a compelling rationale for why smoking is a topic deserving of classroom time. Second, training should have teachers role-play participation in specific curricular activities in the same way that the students will experience them. An-other training objective might be to illustrate how to work with peer leaders, if peer leaders are to participate in the delivery of the program. Incorporating peer leaders into primary and secondary prevention programs has proven quite effective in reducing cigarette use. After conducting a meta-analysis of over 140 drug prevention programs, Tobler (1986) concluded that peer-led programs consistently showed positive effects on the use of alcohol, cigarettes, and soft and hard drugs.

THE ORI TOBACCO PREVENTION CURRICULA

Oregon Research Institute (ORI) has developed a set of tobacco prevention materials for Grades 6–12 (Biglan, James, et al., 1988) that incorporates the three critical program features just discussed. Project PATH (Programs to Advance Teen Health) is arranged by content area as well as by grade level. Levels A–D correspond with Grades 6–9, but the materials can be used effectively in immediately higher or lower grade levels. For example, Level A, though written for Grade 6, can be easily

TABLE 2
Scope and Sequence: Graded Programs for Health/Science/Social Studies

Level/Grade	Health Facts	Influence	Social Behavior
A/6	Short-term effects of cigarettes and long-term effects of chewing tobacco; review of the circulatory system.	Influences of parents and siblings to smoke, chew, use other substances; influencing parents and siblings to quit smoking and chewing	Introduction to refusal skills ("Six Ways to Say No")
B/7	Long-term effects of cigarettes, chewing tobacco, marijuana and alcohol	Influence of media to smoke, chew, and drink	Review and practice of refusal skills; using Think, Identify, and Practice (TIP)
C/8	Short-term and long-term effects of cigarettes and chewing tobacco	Three types of influence are presented: two-way peer influence and indirect sources	Supporting others' refusals; review of refusal skills
D/9	Long-term effects of cigarettes, chewing tobacco, marijuana, and alcohol; passive smoke	Peers are recognized as main group with whom to use refusal skills	Discussing how to deal with tough situations (these are primarily acquaintance situations); how thoughts affect behavior

Note: From *Project PATH (Programs to Advance Teen Health)* (p. 5) by Oregon Research Institute, 1899, Willamette Street, Eugene, OR. Copyright 1989 by ORI. Reprinted by permission.

adapted for use with fifth or seventh graders. Since most levels consist of only five sessions, they also can be combined within a grade level to form a multiple unit program.

Table 2 depicts the scope and sequence of Levels A–D. This table highlights the three major themes around which these levels of the curriculum were designed: health facts, influence, and social behavior.

Synopses for each level of Project PATH are given below.

Middle School/Junior High Programs for Health/Science/Social Studies

Level A includes the topics of refusal skills, decision making, helping parents to quit using tobacco, and health facts.

Students learn refusal skills ("Six Ways to Say No") through videotaped models of local teens who are shown saying no across a variety of typical social situations. Students then practice and review these skills in small groups and as a whole class, using situations that they have identified as personally relevant. Decision-making skills are presented by acknowledging that even though people are influenced in many ways, they all must make their own choices. A brief video discusses how informed decisions can be made after alternatives and consequences are considered. This video leads into a discussion about making decisions whether to use or not to use tobacco. Special emphasis is given to how students can help their parents stop using tobacco. A video shows what to do and what not to do in trying to get parents to quit and when they have already stopped. Students interview their parents to find out their tobacco-use histories and to determine what types of things were helpful if they have quit successfully. The short- and long-term effects of using cigarettes and chewing tobacco are interspersed throughout the program. Video is used for introducing these health facts; games serve to review them.

Level B, which uses same-age peer leaders, contains a review of refusal skills, additional ways to handle tough situations, advertising as a source of influence, and health facts. Students watch a video that reviews the "Six Ways to Say No" presented in the sixth grade. They then develop and perform skits that incorporate the refusal skills. Another video introduces the concept of thinking ahead about situations that might arise in which refusal skills could be used, and then talking to oneself in a positive way about success in handling these situations. The teacher presents information about the goals of advertising and how they are achieved, as well as about compelling facts about tobacco advertising. Students examine tobacco ads, then create anti-tobacco ads of their own to expose the misconceptions promoted in the real ads. A homework assignment to watch television is given to increase student awareness of how tobacco advertisers still manage to have cigarettes associated with attractive images, despite the television ad ban. The health effects of using tobacco, alcohol, and marijuana are taught by means of brainstorming activity, quizzes, and games.

Level C contains lessons on peer and media influences, helping friends to quit using tobacco, and health facts about cigarettes and chewing tobacco. Students watch a video that depicts the media and peers as two major sources of influence. Other influences are identified, and a discussion yields the conclusion that everyone is affected by influences. Subsequent activities build on this discussion to teach students that they are also a source of influence and can therefore affect the behavior of their friends. After viewing a video that models how to help out friends, students role-play "sticking up" for their friends who are using refusal skills, and helping prepare friends who anticipate situations in which refusals may be needed. Videos explaining the immediate effects of one cigarette and the social and health consequences of using smokeless tobacco remind students why it is important to counteract influences to use tobacco products. A game reinforces the skills and facts that have been taught.

Level D, which uses peer leaders, includes materials that address the deceptive nature of cigarette advertising, the tobacco industry's deliberate efforts to attract young smokers, passive smoke, strategies for dealing with peer pressure, and health facts. Students watch *Death in the West*, a film that exposes the reality of being a smoking cowboy. They then read an excerpt from the Federal Trade Commission's investigation of cigarette advertising, which reveals the industry's tactics for gaining more customers, notably young people. The regulatory role of the government with respect to cigarette advertising is discussed. Students interview people about passive smoke and their feelings about nonsmokers' rights; responses are pooled and students draw conclusions about whether smoking in public places should be restricted. By ninth grade, it is assumed that students have learned basic refusal skills; therefore attention is focused on ways to reduce anxiety in situations in which refusals might be used. Students identify the short- and long-term consequences of using cigarettes, chewing tobacco, marijuana, and alcohol and the positive aspects of substance use are short-lived, and that the negative consequences far outweigh the positive ones.

High School Programs

Five separate high school programs, spanning four content areas, were developed. Each is described below in respect to the content area(s) incorporated.

Health/Social Studies/English. This antitobacco program is an in-depth study of tobacco advertising. Students are informed of specific strategies used by tobacco companies to recruit more smokers. This information is juxtaposed to a presentation of the advertising code to which the tobacco industry supposedly adheres. Students work in pairs to develop their own antitobacco advertising campaign that includes TV/radio commercials, bumper stickers, and billboards/magazine ads. In addition, students read and react to a condensed version of the Surgeon General's speech for a "Smoke-Free Society by the Year 2000." Finally, through video and class discussion, passive smoking and quitting the smoking habit are addressed.

English. For use in English classes, three different expository writing assignments have been developed around the topic of tobacco use. The persuasive writing assignment (two class periods) has students rewrite a pamphlet about cigarettes into a pamphlet about chewing tobacco, with parents as the target audience. The argumentative writing assignment (two or three class periods) has students analyze the controversy surrounding the banning of cigarette advertisements. The editing assignment (five class periods) has students first respond to an editorial about the liability of tobacco companies, then write an editorial of their own.

Biology. This five-session biology program focuses on issues concerning passive smoke exposure. Students learn that passive smoke is actually more dangerous than the smoke drawn through the filter of a cigarette. This fact is dramatized by using a modified version of the Ames test, which shows the mutagenicity of cigarette smoke and chewing tobacco. In addition, a video is shown that debates passive smoke issues as they are encountered in daily living. Students learn about the health effects of carbon monoxide and have samples of their expired air read for its *CO* content. Ethical issues regarding the responsibility of scientists doing research on the health effects of using tobacco are presented and discussed.

Social Studies. In a three-day social studies program, the right to smoke is examined within the context of the First Amendment. Students discuss smoking bans, passive smoke, and their school's smoking policy. In addition to these lesson plans, a debate packet is also available. The debate packet includes the following four topics: Smoking in Public Places; Smoking in the Workplace; Banning Tobacco Ads; and Tobacco Products Liability. For each topic, articles have been collected and categorized as *pro*, *con*, or *mixed*. The three-day program and the debate packet can each stand alone, or they can be combined for expanded coverage of these First Amendment issues.

Health. This five-day program for health classes addresses a variety of issues related to tobacco use. Students watch the film *Death in the West* and discover what really happens to cowboys who smoke. They read and discuss an excerpt from the Federal Trade Commission's report on cigarette advertising. They interview people about their tobacco habits and feelings about nonsmokers' rights and watch a video that debates passive smoke issues as they affect daily living. Students themselves debate these same issues and draw conclusions about the rights of smokers/nonsmokers.

SMOKING ISSUES IN NONHEALTH CLASSES

Typically, school personnel have assumed that smoking prevention curricula belong in health classes. While it may be logistically appealing for schools to keep smoking programs in their health departments, it might be more effective to teach these programs in different subject areas. Our experience suggests that smoking prevention programs can easily be adapted to other subject areas, and that it is desirable to do so. Three reasons for considering implementation in nonhealth classes are discussed below.

First, health is generally not a required class for every year of school past the sixth grade. Thus, if you want to have students exposed to annual antitobacco themes, you must infiltrate other content areas. Fortunately, the potential for instruction about tobacco extends far beyond the domain of health concerns: Oregon Research Institute has developed curriculum materials for high school classes in English, Social Studies, U.S. Government, and Biology (Oregon Research Institute, 1989). These types of tobacco programs offer relevant content beyond health effects, and students can be exposed to tobacco issues on a yearly basis, once health classes are no longer seen as the only vehicle for addressing this topic. Yearly programs are preferred because they can provide continuity over time, allow review of previously introduced skills and information, and permit expansion of topics in an age-appropriate way.

Second, health classes by definition have an implicit health message: Smoking is bad for your health. In other classes, the teacher can focus on social issues without directly discussing the students' tobacco habits. Thus, non-health-directed programs take the onus off the students to examine their own health choices and shift it to the economic and social issues of the tobacco industry. For example, students can study the ethical issues of promoting a product that has known harmful effects. This type of curriculum provides opportunities for students to look at smoking as a social issue, rather than simply a health issue. But health issues cannot be ignored in this forum; it is hoped that incidental learning will occur because students must consider health concerns when examining economic and social costs.

The third reason for advocating non-health-oriented tobacco programs is that if the context is shifted away from health class, students may be more receptive to antitobacco messages. This alternate context can provide a range of relevant ways for getting the message across. For example, as noted above, during social studies or economics, older students can learn about the advertising strategies that tobacco companies use to attract people

their age to start smoking. Informing students that billions of dollars are spent to deliberately lure them to become paying, addicted customers sends a more compelling message than discussing the horrors of diseases, which adolescents perceive as remote events that affect other people. With the presentation of this type of information, students are given socially relevant reasons for studying tobacco use without directly being taught health.

WHAT CAN THE SCHOOL PSYCHOLOGIST DO?

Concerns about adolescent smoking and drug use will continue to confront schools and educators with the question, How can school psychologists help? Our answer is that the psychologist needs to be a resource to the school and should act to promote the school's role in carrying out primary and secondary prevention programs. Giving the school psychologists responsibility for carrying out health curricula or taking on the role of drug counselor or intervention specialist is unreasonable. The most realistic and useful role is promotion of the idea that the school *can* do something in a constructive way. The school psychologist can facilitate the schools' efforts by recommending programs that have proven effective.

Above all, the school psychologist needs to promote the idea of prevention. If the school psychologist adopts a public health perspective instead of a referral and remediation model, the prospect of mounting a school-based prevention program is easier to promote. There is a growing body of research that indicates that many serious disorders can be identified very early in the school career of a youngster and may be ameliorated by interventions at an early age (Zins, Wagner, & Maher, 1985). Other literature demonstrates the efficacy of efforts directed toward preventing problem behaviors and enhancing competence and well-being (Roberts & Peterson, 1984). Many organizations, including NASP, have called for increased emphasis on prevention in order to serve more students in mainstream settings and promote their mental health and welfare.

To take learning problems as an analogy, it is clear that more emphasis on identifying students who are failing to learn to read at an early age and intervening with appropriate instruction can ameliorate many learning problems. While many people have embraced the avowed value of prevention, most of our current activities and expenditures remain in the traditional "assess and intervene" mode, following a referral. It is clear that most school psychologists are able to spend only minimal time on prevention activities; such a shift in perspective will require a serious effort to change how you are perceived and how you define your role.

This chapter has attempted to sensitize the school psychologist to the issues involved in the prevention of smoking and drug use, as well as how a school-based program might work. A description of effective programs will assist the school psychologist in providing advice to school personnel and parents interested in this problem. Being a resource to the district is helpful, but being proactive in promoting the public health perspective of early identification and preventive intervention might be the most efficacious use of limited resources. Let the school know that you are aware of some effective programs that could be adopted and used. Provide empirical data from research that not only shows the efficacy of programs, but assists school personnel in understanding the importance of changing behavior patterns in children that can have serious health consequences in their future. Work with school personnel to help identify students who are early drug abusers. This identification can be done by schoolwide screening, assisting school personnel in being more sensitive to early signs of use, and providing referral for treatment when appropriate.

No program should be started prior to the development of a database of current drug use in the district against which to make informed decisions. This baseline survey can serve to motivate those involved as well as to increase public awareness. Set up a confidential, anony-

mous assessment procedure to gather data on the current use and abuse of drugs before starting on any program. Use questions and questionnaires previously used by other research groups, so that you have a basis for comparing your data to other districts or samples (Johnston, Bachman, & O'Malley, 1988; Severson, 1984). When evaluating a potential program, offer to examine its efficacy, thereby assisting the district in being a smart consumer. You can help avoid the scenario in which programs that have been rigorously evaluated are not given serious consideration because of competition by heavily promoted and slick, but not necessarily effective, programs. It is ironic that schools often purchase expensive programs but fail to evaluate their effectiveness.

The prevention of smoking or drug use is a very complex undertaking that involves the cooperation and involvement of many constituents. Table 3 shows some of the key components that we have identified; the school psychologist can be a significant player at any or all of these levels. The focus could be at a specific level, such as schoolwide, and could target a specific drug or group of drugs. The intervention can also vary within the context. This article has focused mainly on the school as the target setting of prevention efforts with interventions carried out in the classroom, but as the list in Table 3 illustrates, there is a wide range of choices. The school psychologist can assist in giving information, setting up or facilitating assessment of the problem, identifying the at-risk group, assisting the school to evaluate and implement an intervention, writing policy on identification and enforcement of school rules on substance use, and soliciting a public commitment from the school staff or administration on preventive efforts and health promotion. We could cite many examples that illustrate the foci and targets listed in Table 3, but suffice it to say that if school psychologists are committed to a public health perspective and recognize the importance of early identification and intervention, they can assist the school in instituting a school-

TABLE 3
Proposed Model for Comprehensive Drug Prevention Program by Intervention Modality*

1 Classroom Programs	2 Schoolwide	3 Family	4 Community
Smoking and drug prevention Refusal skills Health facts Media influences Peer group support Cessation plans Understanding peer influence	Drug use assessment[a] Drug Task Force Drop-in center Cessation groups[a] Free testing[a] Referral process[a] Student Assistance Program (SAP)[a] Social support for nonuse of drugs Social standards and norms School rules Administrative guidelines and discipline standards Contests	Social support Drug education Cessation of parental use[a] Alter expectations Reinforce behavior change Contingent rewards Contracting	Media programs Social group support Community education Contests/competitions Adopt health goals Worksite programs Community event, i.e., Great American Smokeout

*Adoption of health-enhancing behaviors; reduction of students' drug use; reduced community drug use; health promotion.
[a]Need protection of confidentiality.

based program aimed at preventing smoking and drug use. Any model or program can stand improvement; augmenting a program by involving parents, community groups, the media, and significant role models will enhance its likelihood of having a significant preventive effect (Ary et al., in press).

In general, this proactive approach will lead to new alliances between school psychologists, health educators, and health personnel such as nurses and community service providers (Zins, Wagner, & Maher, 1985). Community resources such as drug counselors, treatment facilities, hospitals, and voluntary organizations such as the American Cancer Society and American Lung Association often have materials and personnel ready to assist the school in implementing preventive interventions. The psychologist can be a valuable facilitator in bringing these resources to bear on this problem.

TRAINING IMPLICATIONS

The current training of school psychologists is probably inadequate in the area of promoting prevention of tobacco and drug use in the schools. A course covering preventive models and how prevention programs can be implemented would be a useful component of professional training when combined with the consultation and intervention skills already included. The most problematic issue encountered in our work with school psychologists is the absence of what we call the "public health perspective." This perspective involves the understanding and acceptance of the primary role of prevention in the amelioration of problems. Most psychologists have lots of practice in promoting and setting up interventions for students already identified as having a problem, in contrast to preventing the problem from arising. A prevention approach uses a psychologist's experience and practical knowledge about the process of early screening and identification in conjunction with putting preventive programs in place in the schools. A brief course in prevention might cover the behavioral epidemiology of problems most likely to confront psychologists in the schools, as well as what interventions have been tried and with what level of success.

There is evidence that this prevention perspective is finding roots in the school psychology literature. Recent issues of the *School Psychology Review* (Primary Prevention, No. 4, 1988; Behavioral Health, No. 2, 1984) and books by school psychologists on the topic (*Health Promotion in the Schools;* Zins, Wagner, & Maher, 1985) attest to this trend. This development is encouraging, but hardly a training revolution. School psychology training programs already put a heavy coursework demand on students to complete their certification, and it may not be realistic to require a specific course on prevention. However, we have tried to convey a "metamessage" in this chapter. There is a strong need and an empirical basis for conducting prevention activities in public schools. There is increasing evidence that we can identify early use of tobacco, alcohol, and other drugs, and that school-based preventive activities can reduce the subsequent use and abuse of these drugs. The school psychologist is in a unique role to advocate and coalesce these activities. With the clear mandate to promote mental health and the increasing awareness that physical and mental health are closely intertwined, school psychologists can no longer limit their attention to specific or more traditional referred problems. The education that would make prevention more comfortable for a school psychologist must include a focus on the importance of screening and early identification, as well as an awareness of the relationship of early drug experimentation and use to subsequent regular use and abuse.

Prevention is not easy work. In many ways it is frustrating, since it involves coordinating more persons and constituents than does the "diagnose and remediate" model. Screening, as well as intervention, must be done in the context of regular education. Working to educate teachers about what behaviors to look for and developing cost-effective ways to screen for the problem behaviors may put school psychologists in an uncomfortable or unfamiliar position. On the other hand, it puts the school psychologist in the mainstream of education and promotes participation in the education process. Our constituency is now general/regular education, not just special education. While this change may be uncomfortable new territory, the rewards are many. The likely impact of our work can be much broader than if we concentrate on a minority of students. This new role is not intended to replace those activities that require our skills in working with problems that require assessment and treatment, but it is a valuable adjunct to it. Training in prevention, screening, and early classroom intervention can promote our participation in all levels of school programming and, in the end, ensure a broader context for our role.

REFERENCES

Ajzen, I., & Fishbein, M. (1970). The prediction of behavior from attitudinal and normative variables. *Journal of Experimental Social Psychology, 6,* 466–487.

Allegrante, J. P., O'Rourke, T. W., & Tuncalp, S. (1977). A multivariate analysis of selected psychological variables on the development of subsequent youth smoking behavior. *Journal of Drug Education, 7*(3), 237–248.

Andrews, J., Hops, H., Ary, D., Lichtenstein, E., & Tildesley, E. (in press). The influence of parent attitude, encouragement, verbal behavior and use on adolescent substance use. *Journal of Drug Issues.*

Ary, D., & Biglan, A. (1988). Longitudinal changes in adolescent cigarette smoking behavior: Onset and cessation. *Journal of Behavioral Medicine, 11,* 361–382.

Ary, D., Biglan, A., Glasgow, R., Zoref, L., Black, C., Ochs, L., Severson, H. H., Kelly, R., Weisman, W., Lichtenstein, E., Brozovsky, P., & Wirt, R. (in press). The efficacy of social-influence prevention programs vs. "standard care"; Are new initiatives needed? *Journal of Behavioral Medicine.*

Ary, D., Lichtenstein, E., & Severson, H. H. (1987). Smokeless tobacco use among male adolescents: Patterns, correlates, predictors, and the use of other drugs. *Preventive Medicine, 16,* 385–401.

Bauman, K. E., & Dent, C. W. (1983). Influence of an objective measure on self-reports of behavior. *Journal of Applied Psychology, 67*(5), 623-628.

Bewley, B. R., & Bland, J. M. (1977). Academic performance and social factors related to cigarette smoking by school children. *British Journal of Preventive and Social Medicine, 31*, 18-24.

Biglan, A., James, L. E., LaChance, P., Zoref, L., & Joffe, J. (1988). Videotaped materials in a school-based smoking prevention program. *Preventive Medicine, 17*, 559-584.

Biglan, A., & Lichtenstein, E. (1984). A behavior-analytic approach to smoking acquisition: Some recent findings. *Journal of Applied Social Psychology, 14*(3), 207-223.

Biglan, A., Severson, H. H., Ary, D. V., Faller, C. L., Gallison, C., Thompson, R., Glasgow, R., & Lichtenstein, E. (1987). Do smoking prevention programs really work? Attrition and the internal and external validity of an evaluation of a refusal skills training program. *Journal of Behavioral Medicine, 10*, 159-171.

Biglan, A., Weissman, W., & Severson, H. H. (1985). Coping with social pressures to smoke. In T. Wills & S. Shiffman (Eds.), *Coping and substance use* (pp. 95-116). New York: Academic.

Biglan, A., Wendler, C., Wirt, R., Ary, D., Noell, J., Ochs, L., French, C. & Hood, D. (in press). Social and behavioral factors associated with high-risk sexual behavior among adolescents. *Journal of Behavioral Medicine.*

Botvin, G. J., & Eng, A. (1980). A comprehensive school-based smoking prevention program. *Journal of School Health*, Vol. 50, 209-213.

Botvin, G. J., & Eng, A. (1982). The efficacy of a multi-component smoking prevention program implemented by older peer leaders. *Preventive Medicine, 11*, 199-211.

Bry, B. H., McKeon, P., & Padina, R. J. (1982). Extent of drug use as a function of number of risk factors. *Journal of Abnormal Psychology, 91*, 237-279.

Chassin, L., Presson, C. C., & Sherman, S. J. (1984). Cognitive and social influence factors in adolescent smoking cessation. *Addictive Behaviors, 9*, 383-390.

Dawson, J., & Henderson, M. (1987). *Living with risk: A report of the British Medical Association.* Chichester, England: Wiley.

Donovan, J. E., & Jessor, R. (1978). Adolescent problem drinking: Psychosocial correlates in a national sample study. *Journal of Studies on Alcohol, 39*, 1506-1524.

Donovan, J. E., & Jessor, R. (1983). Problem drinking and the dimensions of involvement with drugs: A Guttman scalogram analysis of adolescent drug use. *American Journal of Public Health, 73*, 543-552.

Evans, R. I., (1976). Smoking in children: Developing a social psychological strategy of deterrence. *Journal of Preventive Medicine, 5*, 122-127.

Evans, R. I., Hansen, W. B., & Mittelmark, M. B. (1977). Increasing the validity of self-reports of smoking behavior in children. *Journal of Applied Psychology, 62*(4), 521-523.

Evans, R. I., & Raines, B. E. (1982). Control and prevention of smoking in adolescents: A psychological perspective. In T. J. Coates, A. C. Peterson, & C. Perry (Eds.), *Promoting adolescent health: A dialogue on research and practice* (pp. 101-136). New York: Academic.

Evans, R. I., Rozelle, R. M., Mittelmark, M. B., Hansen, W. B., Bane, A. L., & Havis, L. (1978). Deterring the onset of smoking in children: Knowledge of immediate physiological effects and coping with peer pressure, media pressure and parent modeling. *Journal of Applied Social Psychology, 8*, 126-135.

Flay, B. R. (1985). Psychosocial approaches to smoking prevention: A Review of findings. *Health Psychology, 4*(5), 449-488.

Forman, S. G., & Linney, J. A. (1987). Adolescent substance abuse prevention. In S. G. Forman (Chair), *Adolescents at risk: Innovations in school-based prevention.* Symposium conducted at the annual meeting of the American Psychological Association, New York.

Friedman, L. S., Lichtenstein, E., & Biglan, A. (1985). Smoking onset among teens: An empirical analysis of initial situations. *Addictive Behaviors, 10*, 1-13.

Gilchrist, L. D., Schinke, S. P., & Blythe, B. J. (1979). Primary prevention services for children and youth. *Children and Youth Services Review, 1*, 379-391.

Gilchrist, L. D., & Schinke, S. P. (1984). Self-control skills for smoking prevention. In P. F. Engstrom, P. N. Anderson, & L. E. Mortenson (Eds.), *Advances IN CANCER Control, 1983* (pp. 125-130). New York: Alan R. Liss.

Glynn, T. (1989). Essential elements of school-based smoking prevention programs. *Journal of School Health, 59*(5), 181-188.

Grabowski, J. & Bell, C. S. (1983). Measurement in the analysis and treatment of smoking behavior. *National Institute of Drug Abuse Research Monograph, 48.* (Department of Health and Human Services.) Washington, DC: U.S. Government Printing Office.

Hirschman, R. S., Leventhal, H., & Glynn, K. (1984). The development of smoking behavior: Conceptualization and supportive cross-sectional survey data. *Journal of Applied Society Psychology, 14*(3), 184–206.

Hundleby, J. D., Carpenter, R. A., Ross, R. A., & Mercer, G. W. (1982). Adolescent drug use and other behaviors. *Journal of Child Psychology and Psychiatry, 23,* 61–68.

Hurd, P. D., Johnson, C. A., Pechacek, T. F., Bast, L. P., Jacobs, D. R., & Luepker, R. V. (1980). Prevention of cigarette smoking in seventh grade students. *Journal of Behavioral Medicine, 3*(1), 15–28.

Jessor, R. (1984). Adolescent development and behavioral health. In J. D. Matarazzo, S. M. Weiss, J. A. Herd, N. E. Miller, & S. M. Weiss (Eds.), *Behavioral health: A handbook of health enhancement and disease prevention.* New York: Wiley.

Jessor, R., & Jessor, S. L. (1977). *Problem behavior and psychosocial development: A longitudinal study of youth.* New York: Academic.

Johnston, L. D., O'Malley, P. M., & Bachman, J. G. (1985). *Use of licit and illicit drugs by America's high school students, 1975–1984.* (DHHS Publication No. ADM 85-1394.) Washington, DC: U.S. Government Printing Office.

Johnston, L. D., O'Malley, P. M., & Bachman, J. G. (1988). *Illicit drug use, smoking, and drinking by America's high school students, college students, and young adults, 1975–1987.* (DHHS Publication No. ADM 89-1602.) Washington, DC: U.S. Government Printing Office.

Kandel, D. B. (1975). Stages in adolescent drug use. *Science, 190,* 912–914.

Kandel, D. B., & Raveis, V. H. (1989). Cessation of illicit drug use in young adulthood. *Archives of General Psychiatry, 46,* 109–116.

Krosnick, J. A., & Judd, C. M. (1982). Transitions in social influence at adolescence: Who induces cigarette smoking? *Developmental Psychology, 39*(1), 359–368.

Lichtenstein, E. (1982). The smoking problem: A behavioral perspective. *Journal of Consulting and Clinical Psychology, 50*(6), 804–819.

Luepker, R. V., Johnson, C. A., Murray, D. M., & Pechacek, T. F. (1983). Prevention of cigarette smoking: Three year follow-up of an educational program for youth. *Journal of Behavioral Medicine, 6*(1), 52–62.

McAlister, A. (1983). Social psychological approaches. In T. Glynn, C. Leukefeld, & J. Ludford (Eds.), *Preventing adolescent drug abuse: Intervention strategies* (pp. 36–50). NIDA Research Monograph No. 47 (DHHS Publication No. ADM 83-1280). Washington, DC: U.S. Government Printing Office.

McAlister, A., Perry, C., Killen, J., Slinkard, L. A., & Maccoby, N. (1980). Pilot study of smoking, alcohol, and drug abuse prevention. *American Journal of Public Health, 70* 719–721.

McAlister, A., Perry, C., & Maccoby, N. (1979). Adolescent smoking: Onset and prevention. *Pediatrics, 63,* 650–658.

McCaul, K. D., & Glasgow, R. E. (1985). Preventing adolescent smoking: What have we learned about treatment construct validity? *Health Psychology, 4*(4), 361–387.

Mittelmark, M. B., Murray, D. M., Luepker, R. V., Pechacek, T. F., Pirie, P. L., & Pallenon, U. (1983). *Adolescent smoking transition states over two years.* Presented as part of the symposium "Becoming a Cigarette Smoker: The Acquisition Process in Youth," at the annual meeting of the American Psychological Association, Anaheim, CA.

Murray, M., Swan, A. V., & Clarke, G. (1984). Long term effect of a school-based anti-smoking program. *Journal of Epidemiology and Community Health, 38*(3), 247–252.

Newcomb, M. D., & Bentler, P. M. (1988). *Consequences of adolescent drug use: Impact on the lives of young adults.* Newbury Park, CA: Sage.

Newcomb, M. D., Maddahian, E., & Bentler, P. M. (1986). Risk factors for drug use among adolescents: Concurrent and longitudinal analyses. *American Journal of Public Health, 76,* 525–531.

Oregon Research Institute (ORI) (1989). *Project PATH (Programs to Advance Teen Health).* Available from: ORI, 1899 Willamette, Eugene, OR 97401.

Pentz, M. A. (1983). Prevention of adolescent substance abuse through social skill development. In T. Glynn, C. G. Leukefeld, & J. Ludford (Eds.), *Preventing adolescent drug abuse: Intervention strategies* (pp. 195–225). Rockville, MD: National Institute on Drug Abuse.

Pirie, P. L., Murray, P. M., & Luepker, R. J. (1988). Smoking prevalence in a cohort of adolescents, including absentees, dropouts, and transfers. *American Journal of Public Health, 78,* 176–178.

Roberts, M. C., & Peterson, L. (Eds.). (1984). *Prevention of problems in childhood.* New York: Wiley.

Seltzer, V. C. (1982). *Adolescent social development: Dynamic functional interaction.* Lexington, MA: Heath.

Severson, H. H. (1984). Adolescent social drug use: School prevention programs. *School Psychology Review, 13*(2), 150–160.

Sherman, S. J., Presson, C. C., Chassin, L., & Olshavsky, R. (1983). *Becoming a cigarette smoker: A social psychological perspective.* Paper presented at the annual meeting of the American Psychological Association, Anaheim, CA.

Snow, W. H., Gilchrist, L. D., & Schinke, S. P. (1985). A critique of progress in adolescent smoking prevention. *Children and Youth Services Review, 7*, 1–19.

Thompson, E. L. (1978). Smoking education programs 1960–1976. *American Journal of Public Health, 68*(3), 250–257.

Tobler, N. S. (1986). Meta-analysis of 143 adolescent drug prevention programs: Quantitative outcome results of program participants compared to a control or comparison group. *Journal of Drug Issues, 16*, 537–567.

U.S. Department of Health and Human Services. (1982). *The health consequences of smoking: Cancer. A report of the Surgeon General* [DHHS (PHS) 82-50179.] Washington, DC: U.S. Government Printing Office.

U.S. Department of Health and Human Services. (1988). *The health consequences of smoking: Nicotine addiction. A report of the Surgeon General.* [DHHS Publication No. (CDC) 88-8406.] Washington, DC: U.S. Government Printing Office.

Williams, T. M. (1971). *Summary and implications of review of literature related to adolescent smoking.* U.S. Department of Health, Education, and Welfare: Health Services and Mental Health Administration: Center for Disease Control; National Clearinghouse for Smoking and Health. Bethesda, MD.

Zins, J. E., Wagner, D. I., & Maher, C. A. (1985). *Health promotion in the schools: Innovative approaches to facilitating physical and emotional well being.* New York: Hayworth.

25

Interventions for Vandalism

G. Roy Mayer
California State University, Los Angeles

Beth Sulzer-Azaroff
University of Massachusetts

School vandalism, a complex area of extreme social importance, is a continual problem affecting all areas of the United States and all socioeconomic levels. More than $600 million is spent annually on school property repair, security devices, insurance, and guards (Nicholson, 1981). Such costs can really add up. For example, during the 14 years up to and including 1986-1987, Los Angeles County Schools experienced a $52.3 million loss in property damage, $32.5 million as a result of arson and $25 million stemming from theft and burglary (Los Angeles County Office of Education, 1988).

FACTORS CONTRIBUTING TO VANDALISM

From the basic research on the behavior of organisms, we have learned that a few types of circumstances predictably set the stage for violence (including destruction of property by humans). One is *extinction*, another *punishment*. Another is receiving reinforcement for violent behavior or observing models who receive such reinforcement.

Extinction is defined as nondelivery of reinforcement following a previously reinforced response. Students who are accustomed to obtaining praise or attention and suddenly fail to receive them because their classroom assignments are too difficult may be incited to violence or vandalism (just as you are when the vending machine fails to deliver after consuming your coins).

Punishment, the presentation of an aversive stimulus that reduces the rate of a behavior, also can promote violence. Students who are reprimanded for failing to meet unusually demanding academic standards, or who feel demeaned or bored by overly simple ones, may react aggressively. That is why knowing and adjusting to students' repertoires of skills and abilities is so important.

Youngsters may receive reinforcement for being violent or destructive in the form of peer approval or may successfully use those tactics to attain positions of social leadership. Or they may see others obtain those enviable consequences. In those two cases every effort should be made, when possible, to remove such sources of reinforcement. Yet often this is beyond our capacities, so we must turn elsewhere: making vandalism less likely by using such strategies as *are* available and focusing on factors within the school that *are* under our control.

Factors within the school that contribute to vandalism have been difficult to identify because most are temporally remote from the acts of vandalism. However, by taking some of our research (Mayer & Butterworth, 1979, 1981; Mayer,

Butterworth, Nafpaktitis, & Sulzer-Aza-roff, 1983b; Mayer, Nafpaktitis, Butterworth, & Hollingsworth, 1987) as a point of departure, and by extrapolating from our knowledge of behavioral principles, we are beginning to identify some of the factors that appear to serve as *setting events* for vandalism. (Setting events are occurrences, or stimuli, that tend to be temporally remote, but may overlap with, and in any case influence current stimulus-response interactions.) Much evidence now points to a general setting event or factor, namely, an overly punitive school environment characterized by (a) an overuse of punitive methods of control; (b) a lack of clarity of both school and classroom rules and disciplinary policies; (c) weak or inconsistent administrative support and follow-through; and (d) few or no allowances made for individual differences in respect to the selection of academic materials, reinforcers and punishers.

Overuse of Punitive Methods of Control

Research indicates that schools too often emphasize punitive measures to manage student behavior. For example, results from a survey by the American Association of School Administrators (Brodinsky, 1980) indicated that school personnel spend more time and energy in implementing punitive than positive or preventive measures. Similarly, in some schools, teachers have been observed to use disapproval approximately three times more frequently than approval as a consequence of student behavior (Heller & White, 1975; Thomas, Presland, Grant, & Glynn, 1978; White, 1975). These findings are further substantiated by the fact that school districts have responded to the public outcry to address the problems of violence and vandalism with so-called hard measures (Reaves, 1981). For example, the Los Angeles Unified School District developed a security force of more than 325 agents, and various districts have implemented stringent student disciplinary programs (Reaves, 1981). In other schools, however, research has indicated that approving statements occurred more frequently than disapproving statements

(Nafpaktitis, Mayer, & Butterworth, 1985; Wyatt & Hawkins, 1987).

Greenberg (1969, 1974) has pointed out that reliance on heavy security arrangements and punitive discipline strategies appears to aggravate, not reduce, vandalism as well as aggression towards others. Similarly Mayer and his colleagues (1979, 1981, 1983b, 1987) have presented evidence suggesting that heavily relying on punishment as a schoolwide and classroom management procedure is a condition that can actually promote vandalism as well as other forms of disruptions. For example, the cost and frequency of vandalism were found to be higher in schools that emphasized punitive school disciplinary methods than those in which more positive methods were applied (Mayer et al., 1987). More compelling is the evidence that vandalism costs were found to decrease once teachers increased their ratios of approval to disapproval and implemented other positive changes in the school environment (Mayer & Butterworth, 1979, 1981; Mayer et al., 1983b). Others based on informal observation (Flaherty, 1987; Krause, 1985), have reported similar decreases in vandalism as a result of making the school environment less aversive and more reinforcing. Berkowitz (1983) also pointed to the "mounting evidence that aversive stimulation generates an instigation to aggression in our species as well as lower orders" (p. 1139). Such aggression can be against school facilities, teachers and other students. It seems reasonable to conclude from the above evidence, then, that at least some proportion of the aggression and destruction that takes place in our schools is tied to punitive school environments.

Lack of Clearly Stated Rules and Vague Discipline Policy

It is difficult for appropriate stimulus control, or rule-following, to be developed unless discipline policies and rules are clearly communicated (Sulzer-Azaroff & Mayer, 1986). Furthermore, student failure to follow rules tends to promote increased use of punishment because many youngsters simply do not know what behavior is expected of them.

When disciplinary policies are unclear to the staff or are inconsistently supported, both positive and negative consequences tend to be dispensed arbitrarily. Under such circumstances, youngsters have a difficult time knowing what to do because guessing the result of different behaviors becomes impossible. Anticipated reinforcement may fail to be received and punishment may be dispensed unexpectedly. Obviously, inappropriate student behaviors are much more likely to occur under such confusing conditions and result in increased uses of punishment by staff. It should come as no surprise, then, that Mayer et al. (1987) found this lack of clarity of rules and policies about conduct to be one factor that relates significantly to vandalism cost and frequency.

Weak or Inconsistent Administrative Support and Follow-Through

Weak or inconsistent administrative support tends to cause staff *not* to receive reinforcement for consistently and cooperatively implementing disciplinary programs (Mayer, Butterworth, Komoto, & Benoit, 1983a). A lack of support can also be aversive for staff, perhaps fostering aggression or a greater reliance on punitive methods of control in managing student behavior (Mayer et al., 1987). In any event, vandalism tends to be higher in schools where administrative support and follow-through is lacking or weak, rules are unclear, and insufficient allowances are made for individual differences (Mayer et al., 1987). Let us now look at the impact of the latter factor on vandalism.

Allowances Made for Individual Differences

It is hard to believe that in this age of enlightenment many educators fail to provide for individual differences. You can still walk into a high school history class and find the students required to read from a text that is at or beyond the 12th grade level in difficulty even though many of the students may only have about fourth-grade reading skills. As Mayer et al. (1983b) have pointed out,

> Many students, particularly those whose reading ability does not permit them to complete their assignments successfully, are more apt to experience defeat, reproach, ridicule, and other probable aversive consequences. This combination of extinction and punishment may also serve to imbue scholastic activities and materials with conditioned aversive properties. (p. 356)

Whether because of insufficient time for tailoring assignments to individual students' abilities, school policy, failure to detect the difficulty, inadequate instructional resources, or a combination of these factors, teachers often assign material that is either too difficult or too easy for their students. As Sulzer-Azaroff and Mayer (1986) have stated, "The result can be failure (i.e., punishment) or boredom (i.e., extinction). Many students respond to such situations by acting aggressively against their classmates, their teachers, or their physical surroundings" (p. 331). Similarly, Greenberg (1974) has shown a strong relation between delinquency and reading ability; Center, Deitz, and Kaufman (1982) have found that "failure level academic tasks resulted in significant increases in inappropriate behavior from some students" (p. 355); and Berkowitz (1983) has pointed out that even frustrations and failure to attain a desired goal "can produce aggressive inclinations because of their aversive nature" (p. 1143).

Leinhardt and Pallay (1982) report several features of effective instruction that can help reduce the likelihood that scholastic activities and materials are imbued with aversive properties. These include (a) incorporating mastery learning systems with clear goal statements and regular monitoring of progress; (b) high content overlap between teaching or learning activities and criterion tasks; (c) rapid pacing; (d) a formal management system that encourages working and successful completion; and (e) positive teacher affect to encourage learning.

Failure to individualize consequences, for example, by meting out common punishers and rewards, can result in an *increase*, rather than a decrease, of vandalism and other aggressive behavior (Mayer & Butterworth, 1979). This is because individuals have distinctive learning histories that cause particular consequences to be more or less effective for them. In our work, we have attempted to allow for individual differences by assigning reading materials appropriately matched to student performance levels and individualizing behavioral consequences. As a result, we have found that, compared to control schools and each school's previously used approaches, vandalism decreased, fewer discipline problems were reported, and cooperation and positive feeling among students and staff increased (Mayer & Butterworth, 1979, 1981; Mayer et al., 1983b). These findings are similar to those of Gold and Mann (1982), who concluded that "poor scholastic experiences are significant causes of delinquent and disruptive behavior" (p.313). They found that when curriculum was more closely tailored to the individual and the environment made more reinforcing, students' behavior and scholastic performance improved.

For the school psychologist who is concerned with the issue of vandalism, we recommend a formal program directed toward allaying the situation. The program consists of assessing the situation, designing and conducting the treatment program, maintaining it, and evaluating the program's effectiveness.

ASSESSING THE SITUATION

Assessing the Need and School Climate

To verify the need to undertake a program to reduce vandalism, an assessment should be undertaken. The costs and number of episodes of vandalism should be determined. Figure 1 displays a form used by Mayer et al. (1983b) to collect monthly vandalism data. The date of each incident and the cost of repairing and replacing vandalized property are recorded in the appropriate space. Note that

the form also helps to determine the location of the episodes. Data like these can help to determine if there is a need for a program throughout the school or only in a specific area. Also, the data gathered can constitute a baseline against which future change can be measured, should you subsequently decide to implement a program.

The relevant aspects of the school climate can be assessed by using the School Discipline Survey (SDS) (Mayer et al., 1987) as illustrated in Figure 2. The SDS attempts to measure how punitive the school environment is, particularly the discipline environment. The SDS is completed by the teaching staff. The higher the scores obtained on the SDS, the lower the vandalism cost and frequency tend to be and vice versa (Mayer et al., 1987). The survey is divided into the three major sections: clarity (items 1-2), administrative support (items 3-16), and individual differences (items 17-28). Maximum possible scores are the following: clarity, 32; administrative support, 56; individual differences, 48, for a total possible of 136 points. Such a score would indicate a highly reinforcing environment with clear discipline policies, good administrative support, and maximum allowance for individual differences (see Mayer et al., 1987, for scoring procedures).

Determining Environmental Support and Resources

To obtain the kind of ongoing support that is certain to be needed, considering the total system is critical. Examining the total system can help to identify organizational factors that may affect or determine the effectiveness of the program.

The school environmental analysis should be conducted at several levels, including supervisory, instructional, support staff, and students. As these people control many important contingencies and may possess important data that could be made available for the assessment, their cooperation is crucial. Similarly, at the district level, contact those in charge (e.g., the superintendent and

	CLASSROOM BUILDING		CAFETERIA		WASHROOM		OTHER (please specify, e.g., library, playground, administrative building, bus)	
	Date of Occurrence(s)	Cost*	Date of Occurrence(s)	Cost*	Date of Occurrence(s)	Cost*	Date of Occurrence(s)	Cost*
BROKEN GLASS								
EQUIPMENT THEFT								
FIRE DAMAGE								
PROPERTY DAMAGE (Graffitti, smashed furniture, fixtures torn off wall, carved desks, miscellaneous ruination)								

*Be sure to include labor cost. If precise dollar figures are not immediately available, estimate cost in pencil. When accurate figures are available, indicate in ink.

FIGURE 1. Recording sheet for occurrence and cost of vandalism.

whoever is in charge of security) to obtain their approval and support. Clarify their administrative roles, and determine how much help they will provide and what data they will make available, such as vandalism costs and incidence rates. Be sure to find out about programs and policies on vandalism the district may currently be operating, and if possible, try to work within those structures. Otherwise, try to collaboratively negotiate a mechanism for modifying those policies and procedures.

You will need to inform yourself about local and state laws governing acts of vandalism, and prevailing standards of administering such legislation among juveniles in your community. Contacting juvenile authorities is often helpful, as is soliciting the cooperation of parents and community leaders. Often these people are willing to help by supplying prizes, gift certificates, admission passes, funds, time, and other rewards. For example, in Burlington, Vermont, the operator of a video game arcade permitted children to earn tokens to operate his machines by accomplishing academic tasks (Barrera, 1984). When community leaders, busi-

nesses, and parents are informed about how they will all benefit when violence and vandalism diminish, they probably will become active supporters of your program.

Sulzer-Azaroff and Mayer (1986) have described an environmental analysis form that can be used as a guide to obtain most of the information described above (see Table 1). "If used appropriately, such an analysis of the system should provide information that will improve your chances of success, while an absence of such information and support can result in failure" (p. 333).

Measuring Vandalism and Its Setting Events

Measuring vandalism. Because acts of vandalism usually are impossible to observe directly, we must use indirect measures, such as the products or costs of vandalism, or count each day during which new damage was done as a separate instance. We have measured vandalism by using the monthly costs of repairing or replacing property (per 100 students to

DISCIPLINE SURVEY

The growing problems of school violence, vandalism, and absenteeism, are serious concerns of the Office of the Los Angeles County Superintendent of Schools. We are asking your help in a research project related to these problems. We need to know how student discipline is handled at your school. Most items in this survey pertain to what is actually being practiced in your school, except for specific questions that request your personal opinion.

Responses will be grouped to give an overall picture of your school, but your independent judgment is essential. The form should not take longer than fifteen minutes to complete.

Part I

Please read each item and place an "X" on the line corresponding to your answer.

	Yes	No
1. Our school has a written discipline policy. (If answered "no," proceed directly to item 2.)	___	___
a. I have read or referred to the school discipline policy within the past year.	___	___
b. A copy of the discipline policy is given at least on an annual basis to each student.	___	___
c. A copy of the discipline policy is given at least on an annual basis to the parents of each student.	___	___
2. I have a written set of standards for classroom discipline that I use. (If answered "no," proceed directly to Part II.)	___	___
a. I have read or referred to my written classroom standards within the past year.	___	___
b. A copy of my classroom standards is given at least on an annual basis to each student in my class.	___	___
c. A copy of my classroom standards is given at least on an annual basis to the parents of each student in my class.	___	___

Part II

Following is a series of statements describing student discipline and staff relationships. Place a check in the column below the word or phrase which best indicates how closely the statement describes your school or your opinion.

	Rarely	Sometimes	More Often Than Not	Consistently
3. Instructional materials to meet individual student differences are provided when I request them.	___	___	___	___
4. Action is taken promptly by school authorities when I make a disciplinary referral.	___	___	___	___
5. In my opinion, disciplinary action taken by school authorities is appropriate.	___	___	___	___
6. Good teaching is recognized and appreciated by the administration.	___	___	___	___
7. I confer with other teachers regarding instructional activities occurring in my classroom.	___	___	___	___
8. I confer with other teachers regarding how I maintain discipline in my classroom.	___	___	___	___
9. Faculty requests and suggestions regarding discipline policy are acted upon promptly.	___	___	___	___
10. When disciplining students, it is easy for me to follow the school-wide discipline policy.	___	___	___	___

	Rarely	Sometimes	More Often Than Not	Consistently
11. When I follow the discipline policy, I receive administrative support for my actions.				
12. When I follow my own judgment in administering discipline, I receive support for my actions.				
13. As far as I know, other teachers follow the school discipline policy.				
14. I am in agreement with the discipline practices of counselors and administrators.				

	Disagree	Somewhat Disagree	Somewhat Agree	Agree
15. In my opinion, the school discipline policy is effective.				
16. In my opinion, the school discipline policy is overly punitive.				
17. Every student who engages in a suspendable offense should be suspended.				
18. Every student who engages in an offense for which expulsion can be applied should be expelled.				

	Rarely	Sometimes	More Often Than Not	Consistently
19. I start to formulate an individual plan for improving a student's behavior when the usual methods of classroom discipline fail.				
20. An individual plan for improving a student's behavior is formulated when the usual methods of school discipline fail.				
21. Students who have not been attending school regularly are rewarded for improved attendance.				
22. Students receive school-wide recognition for behaving as they should.				
23. Students receive recognition in my classroom for behaving as they should.				
24. I consider using positive incentives to assist students who need to improve their behavior in my classroom.				
25. I consider using changes in assignments and materials to assist students who need to improve their behavior in my classroom.				
26. School authorities consider using positive incentives to assist students who need to improve their school behavior.				
27. School authorities consider using program or class changes to assist students who need to improve their school behavior.				
28. I make allowances for specific students when applying the school discipline policy.				

FIGURE 2. The school discipline survey.

TABLE 1
Suggested Activities for Assessing Environmental Support and Resources

I. District Level
  A. Inform and request support from each of the following.
    1. Superintendent.
    2. Person(s) with the major responsibility for overseeing data and programs in the area on which you plan to work (e.g., vandalism, attendance, discipline, etc.).
    3. Director of special services and/or others recommended by the superintendent.
  B. Locate supplemental resources such as the instructional materials center or other repository of extra books and materials.
  C. Familiarize yourself with any district-wide programs and policies that have been or are operating in your targeted area.

II. School Level
  A. Inform, request support, and discover information about each of the following:
    1. *Principal.* The principal's leadership role; his or her view of instructional and professional staff and school's strengths and weaknesses; programs supported; years in school; related background information; how principal is viewed by staff; degree to which he or she uses praise; behaviors; particular staff member he or she reinforces or recognizes more than others; availability to staff; and degree of rapport and interaction with students.
    2. *Vice-Principal* (when applicable). Obtain same information as for the principal, plus how that role differs from the principal's.
    3. *Secretary.* Attitude toward principal, instructional, and professional staff; years at school; attitude of staff toward secretary; strengths and weaknesses; interests; control over communications; and nature and degree of administrative responsibilities held.
    4. *Psychologist/Counselor.* Attitude toward staff and project; knowledge of behavioral approach; days per week at school; role; and background.
    5. *Custodian.* Role and attitude of staff and students toward custodian and vice versa.
    6. *School Staff.* Are there cliques? Views of psychologist, principal, and faculty leaders, gathering places for breaks, lunch, etc.; and current philosophical orientation.
    7. *Special Staff and Services.*
      a. *Remedial Reading Teachers.* Time spent at school; approach used in remediation; materials available; relation to staff; and willingness to cooperate.
      b. *Librarian.* Level of training; time available; relation to staff; and availability of high interest/low vocabulary materials.
      c. *Resource Specialist.* Level of training; number of days or time spent at school; relation to staff; any behavioral approaches used; and available materials.
      d. *Available Aids/Volunteers.* Degree of responsibility and training.
      e. *Student Council and Student Officers.* Degree of leadership and responsibility.
      f. *School Security Personnel.* Responsibilities; relation to students; number; and visibility.
      g. *School Nurse and Attendance Clerk.* Responsibilities and available information.
  B. Any school-wide programs and policies that have been or are operating in your targeted area.

III. Community Resources
  A. Inform, request support, and discover information about each of the following:
    1. *PTA.* Size; involvement; support funds; chairperson's telephone number; degree to which members are interested in supporting a project in your targeted area; and other leaders in the group.
    3. *Library.* Location and availability of films, records, tapes, etc.
    3. *Community Recreation.* Local programs; involvement; size; time; and location.
    4. *Description of Immediate Neighborhood.* Perception of school; socioeconomic status; and neighborhood service organizations that may be willing to help.
    5. *Local Educational Supply Stores.* Those available.
    6. *School Advisory Council.* Role.

This table is an adaptation of one developed by Mayer et al. (1983c) account for differences in school size) and the date of each occurrence derived from the Vandalism Cost and Occurrence form illustrated earlier in Figure 1 (Mayer & Butterworth, 1979; Mayer et al., 1983b; Mayer et al., 1987).

Measuring possible setting events. As previously noted, several temporally remote factors appear to be related to vandalism. These factors could be assessed not only by means of the *School Discipline Survey* (Mayer, et al., 1987), but also by collecting other data, such as tabulating positive notes sent to teachers by administrators, or directly observing many of the items listed in the school discipline survey. Collecting such observational data provides reasonably objective measures of factors that appear most relevant, but since such an activity does involve personnel time, consider the extent to which this information will contribute to the potential effectiveness of the program.

Whatever setting event or vandalism data are collected, it needs to be collected repeatedly over a period of several months in order to obtain a representative baseline.

Ecobehavioral assessment. In essence, we are recommending an ecobehavioral assessment, which is a type of assessment that examines behavior not only in relation to the social events that immediately precede and follow it, but also in terms of its general context of ongoing and prior events and elements of the physical environment. Its major purpose is to enable more effective planning, intervening, support, and evaluation over the long range (Hayes, Nelson, & Jarrett, 1987; Patterson, 1982; Rogers-Warren, 1984; Wahler, 1980).

DESIGNING AND CONDUCTING THE TREATMENT PROGRAM

Once the scope of the problem, the anticipated degree of support and cooperation, acceptable objectives, and the severity of the problem have been determined by means of a baseline measure, the stage is set for designing and implementing the treatment strategy. Recognize, though, at the onset, that no single treatment program has been totally effective in eradicating vandalism. Thus, we will discuss a variety of approaches for reducing and preventing this problem.

Selecting Deterrents and Punishment Strategies

Generally when faced with excessive violence and vandalism, administrators turn to deterrents or methods of detection or punishment as their first option (Brodinsky, 1980). Frequently, these methods are designed to inhibit or immediately suppress vandalism. They include hiring security personnel, installing alarm systems, posting punitive consequences, and involving community members in various school watch programs.

Security personnel. When hired, security personnel should be trained, and expected, to perform a role beyond that of just enforcers of the law. Because they serve not only to protect facilities but also to provide students and staff with a safe environment, security officers must be able to relate effectively with those people. Scrimger and Elder (1981) pointed out that the more successful security personnel programs provide a balance of security and educational functions. To accomplish this balance, security personnel need to receive training and supervision. Training should include not only technical preparation for the job but also a familiarity with local gangs, behavior management problems, skill in the use of reinforcement, and other interpersonal expertise.

Alarm systems. A wide variety of alarm systems have been used for the purpose of deterring vandalism. They range from a bell, horn, siren, or light activated by intruders to systems that notify protection or security agencies. Gamble, Sellers, and Bone (1987) have described a number of building security systems designed to prevent vandalism and provide some suggestions for their selection. However, because of the assortment of systems and the diversity of needs among schools, they suggest obtaining the help of an independent security consultant to design the best system for your school, instead of going to a commercial alarm manufacturer or distributor. It should be noted that some alarms limit access to the building by staff during nonschool hours, or require someone to be available on a 24 hour basis to allow legitimate access to the buildings.

Community watch programs. These programs are designed to alert local residents to the problems that the school is having with vandalism and solicit their support in reporting anything suspicious, such as the presence of vehicles on or near the school grounds during nonschool hours, people on roofs of buildings, unusual odors, lights, noises, smoke coming from the school, or individuals observed stealing or destroying school property. Local resident support has been obtained in several ways. Students have written and disseminated letters to residents that explained the problem and requested that they call the enclosed phone numbers if they should observe anything suspicious at the school. Teachers, uniformed peace officers from the school district's security department, and school administrators have all been involved in contacting persons living within view of the school. Regardless of who informs community members, Mullendore (1981) wisely suggests that the information distributed should describe useful items that the school could purchase with money saved by not needing to repair the effects of vandalism.

Another type of school watch program involves live-in "school sitters." In return for watching the school and reporting vandals to the police, school sitters receive a rent-free trailer site. Others have tried parent patrols, consisting of interested parents who patrol the school grounds whenever possible. For example, some parents may walk their dogs around a school building instead of around the block. Others may offer to drive by the school slowly on an evening out.

When the community shows concern about its schools, the climate becomes more conducive to reducing violence and vandalism. Also, such parental involvement may not only boost school morale but also foster more parental awareness and involvement in other aspects of school life.

Posting punitive consequences. Punitive deterrents, of course rely on the administration of aversive consequences. Typically a list of penalties is posted and one or more applied when a student has been caught vandalizing. These might include requiring students and their parents to pay for the damage (restitution), suspension, expulsion, or criminal charges.

Problems with deterrents and punishment. In addition to the obvious cost involved in hiring security agents and purchasing alarm systems, an overreliance on deterrent and punishment methods tends to result in several problems. First, the more these aversive control methods are used, the less effective they become, often requiring increasingly harsher methods to achieve similar results. Second, they do not address the factors that may be promoting vandalism, such as an overly punitive school environment. In fact, they contribute to the image of the punitive school. Perhaps this is why, according to Greenberg (1974) and Scrimger and Elder (1981), campus security forces often have appeared to aggravate rather than to deter violence and vandalism.

Sometimes a crisis situation mandates a crash program to deter vandalism and provide safety for students and staff. However, if the effects are to be enduring, these short-range deterrents must be combined with long-range preventive programs that will make the school a more reinforcing place for everyone. Deterrents like these must be viewed as temporary expedients to augment your long-term strategies of prevention.

Preventing Vandalism

Mayer and his colleagues (Mayer & Butterworth, 1979; Mayer et al., 1983b) have devised a model to prevent school violence and vandalism. One of the first steps is to implement a schoolwide vandalism prevention team. This is followed by implementing, maintaining, and evaluating various preventive programs.

Vandalism prevention team. Our research has indicated that the total school climate can be improved by collaborating initially with the most influential members of a school staff, including designated and natural leaders. We formed a team within each school that consisted of the principal, school counselor or psychologist, three or four teachers, and two or three students to lead in the selection and implementation of programs to reduce vandalism. The teachers on the team pilot tested the programs before recommending them to the entire staff, permitting us to observe and supervise closely and provide feedback frequently. Once programs were working effectively in their classes, the teachers on the team then served as models and resource persons for other staff interested in conducting similar programs. With teachers serving such a key modeling role, selecting the best candidates was of critical import. We chose participants who (a) demonstrated willingness to try and share new ideas; (b) were respected by their fellow staff members; and (c) consented to commit the time to work with administrators and others involved with the project, including having observers in their classrooms.

We have found that the membership of principals on the team is of critical importance, for without their support our efforts have failed (Mayer et al., 1983a). In particular, the extent of the principal's support of teachers and programs influenced the degree to which other teachers followed their colleagues in implementing similar programs. Clearly, the principal's support, encouragement, and participation is essential if the program is to succeed.

The counselors and psychologists provided valuable expertise in methods of modifying social behaviors. They consulted with team teachers and other staff members, helping them design and implement constructive discipline programs to meet the unique needs of individual students or classes.

Students were included on the team to represent their peers' perspectives, and because research (Fixsen, Phillips, & Wolf, 1973; Lovitt & Curtiss, 1969) has shown that programs tend to be better accepted, understood, supported, and enforced by students when they have been involved in the program planning. We selected students to serve on the team who were highly respected by their peers and committed to providing the time and energy required for team activities.

While forming a vandalism prevention team obviously takes organization and planning, the investment pays off in the form of broadened acceptance of and enthusiasm for the program and in its ultimate effectiveness. A well constituted team is in a position to assess the needs of the school, and collaborate toward solving vandalism problems by participating in designing and carrying out selected strategies.

Preventive programs. Once the team is operational, it begins to select and conduct various programs of intervention. When the situation is of crisis proportion, the team may begin by choosing a deterrent strategy to protect property and make conditions safer for students and staff as a *temporary expedient.* However, in the schools in which we have worked, deterrents were not implemented unless long-term preventive strategies also were initiated. Now let us look at some of the features of these preventive strategies.

If assessments have revealed the circumstances that tend to promote misconduct (e.g., assignment of inappropriate academic materials, failure to individualize consequences, and so on) try to alter or remove those circumstances (Touchette, MacDonald, & Langer, 1985). Academic materials need to be adjusted continually to students' level of functioning while still capturing their interests. Use of the materials also needs to be paired with considerable positive reinforcement if learning is to be encouraged (Leinhardt & Pallay, 1982) and if aggression and vandalism are to be reduced. Also, look carefully to see if a particular sequence of acts can be detected that culminate in serious misbehavior (O'Leary & Dubey, 1979). For example, students who are known to start by muttering and then swearing aloud, and subsequently to move on to pushing their own and then their neighbors' papers and books off the desk, may well start throwing large objects at the other children. Having observed this sequence several times, the experienced teacher will redirect such students to a preferred activity at the first mutter. Alternatively, redirecting toward the end of the sequence is *not* a good idea, as it can serve a reinforcing function. It's better to interrupt the sequence, if necessary with a simple sharp reprimand or some other punisher that is effective with the individual.

Our most successful preventive strategies have been based on what Goldiamond (1974) refers to as a *constructional approach* or what Sulzer-Azaroff and Mayer (1986) have called *constructive discipline*. The emphasis is on teaching or building rather than reducing or eliminating behavior, and involves (a) selecting behaviors to be established or strengthened, rather than those to be reduced or eliminated; (b) identifying academic and social repertoires upon which to build; (c) matching procedures of change to those repertoires; and (d) selecting reinforcing contingencies to increase and maintain the goal behaviors. Using reinforcers natural to the environment, such as those that previously reinforced the problem behavior, is emphasized.

Constructive discipline contrasts, then, with traditional discipline approaches, which have tended to rely much more heavily on punishment of misconduct, combined only to a minor extent with reinforcement of preferred alternatives. Such a heavy reliance on punishment produces an overly punitive school climate. Furthermore, when punishment is applied frequently over extended periods of time, its effectiveness begins to diminish. For example, when parents spank a child for every major and minor infraction, spanking begins to lose its reductive power, unless the blows become more intense (and the parent is on the road to physically abusing the child). Also, as we mentioned before, punitive consequences can provoke aggression and destruction of property. Therefore, *the use of punishment must be minimized. It should be delivered only for extremely serious or dangerous acts.* Sulzer-Azaroff and Mayer (1977, 1986, in press) extensively discuss punishment as a management procedure.

Overdependence upon punishment poses additional difficulties. We have already indicated that individuals may respond to the same consequences in different ways. For example, some students have been known to misbehave in order to be kept after school rather than return to an empty house or unpleasant home atmosphere. In other cases, teachers who rely heavily on punishment and use isolation as a management device actually may be teaching some of their students to misbehave by removing them from a classroom milieu that the students find unpleasant. For instance, a student who has a history of failure in math, might learn that he can avoid an onerous math session with a single sortie of spitwads, if such a misbehavior will lead to his being ejected from class. Though isolation may work to reduce the misbehavior of some, its influence upon behavior is particular to the individual student.

Built into the constructive discipline approach, then, is the recognition that uniform consequences, whether reinforcing or punitive, will not affect each student in the same way. Instead, to allow for individual differences, educators choose from a variety of jointly selected consequences. If a student should ask, "Why did you send me to the office for making a fire in the wastebasket, but you only fined Jim 5 points for doing the same thing?" the teacher should be honest and explain: "I didn't fine you 5 points because fines don't work for you, but they do work to stop Jim's misbehavior. Similarly, to reward you, I allowed you to work with Jane on that project, but I allowed Jim to work on his homework. Would you prefer to work on your homework rather than with Jane? You see, the point is that you and Jim are different people, so how can I treat you the same?"

Too heavy a reliance on punishment carries other disadvantages. Teachers who punish model the very class of behavior they are trying to reduce: use of aversive methods. Youngsters who are punished appear to learn by example to deliver punishment to others (Conger, 1982; Sulzer-Azaroff & Mayer, 1986). Additionally, when punishment is applied inconsistently as often is the case, students learn to risk misbehaving because they succeed in getting away with it sufficiently frequently. As mentioned earlier, punishment predictably promotes aggression, the acts we are hoping to eradicate. Effective punishment is intense, and is administered immediately, every single time the unwanted behavior occurs; these standards are difficult to meet in most schools and are questionable ethically when applied to minor infractions. So, as we can see, punishment is *not* the management strategy of choice in schools [Editor's note: For further discussion of these issues, also see the Horner et al., chapter on nonintrusive behavioral interventions in this Monograph].

An alternative and more effective method to apply is the triadic behavioral model illustrated in Figure 3. We have successfully used this constructional approach as a basis for designing our vandalism reduction programs. Reinforcing consequences, such as praise, privileges, and rewards are used to increase or maintain the occurrence of rule-following and other appropriate behaviors; punitive consequences, such as isolation, penalties, scolding, referral, suspension, restitution, and expulsion, are reserved for major or serious infractions. However, for the most commonly occurring minor infractions, constructive alternatives are selected.

Developing and communicating rules. Before specific consequences are selected and administered, rules of deportment need to be established and communicated clearly. Not only does this

step make sense, but it frequently is required by law. For example, Section 35291 of the California Education Code requires that the principal of each school "take steps to insure that all rules pertaining to the discipline of pupils are communicated to continuing students at the beginning of each school year, and to transfer students at the time of their enrollment in the school." Too often we assume that school discipline standards are understood or that students already know or should know how to behave. Furthermore, we frequently communicate standards indirectly, requiring that students learn the rules through trial and error, which necessarily entails using punishment.

Several steps will increase the likelihood that rules will be communicated clearly. First, *all relevant parties*, including students, *should be represented when schoolwide rules are being developed*. Rules tend to be better understood, accepted, supported, and enforced when all concerned parties, or their representatives, have been included in drawing up a conduct code. Once an initial draft of the rules and consequences has been developed, broadly based community input should be solicited. A draft, including formulated consequences, can be circulated to *all* staff, students, and parents for additional comments. A legal review of the document may be necessary before a final draft is drawn up for administrative approval.

As with the schoolwide rules, students should be involved in developing classroom rules. We suggest that the resultant classroom behavior code include no more than five or six rules, be simple and to the point, *stated positively*, and coordinated with schoolwide policies. Rather than stating, "Don't be late to class" or "Don't talk without raising your hand," you could say, "Be in your seat before the tardy bell rings" and "Raise your hand before asking questions." An illustrative set: (a) Bring books, pencil, and paper; (b) Be in your seat when tardy bell rings; (c) Listen carefully; (d) Follow directions; (e) Complete assignments; and (f) Show courtesy and respect to others. A positive

CONSTRUCTIVE DISCIPLINE

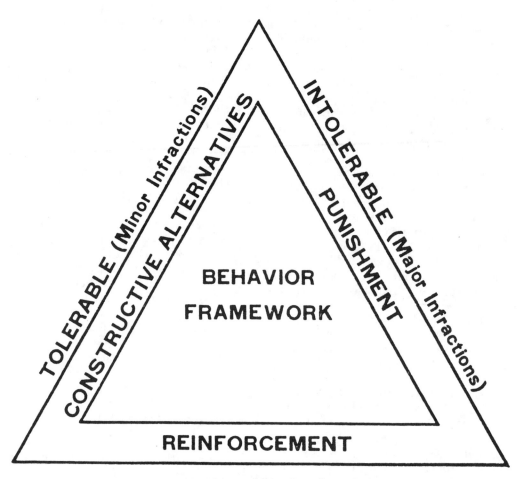

FIGURE 3. A triadic approach to discipline.

list will guide students in *how to* behave in preference to *how not to* behave, which will be more instructive and less suppressive. Once developed, the classroom rules, like the schoolwide rules, should be shared with and approved by the responsible administrator(s).

Once approval has been obtained, teach the behavior code to all involved parties, specifically, to staff and students. The rules can be presented to staff during meetings and workshops and follow-up consultation should be provided (Sulzer-Azaroff & Mayer, 1986). For students, presenting classroom and schoolwide rules both in writing and pictorially helps to assure understanding. Classroom rules can be displayed prominently on a poster, printed in handout form, and copied by students in their notebooks. For preschool and primary pupils, and for students with learning difficulties, role-playing each rule as part of the explanatory process is helpful. Schoolwide rules for older students can be printed in a student handbook and discussed in class. Both classroom and schoolwide rules should be reviewed orally at regular intervals and constructive changes made when necessary. In summary, students and staff must be helped to actively learn the code of conduct, not just presented with a paper or booklet and left to their own devices.

Ongoing parental support is important if classroom and schoolwide rules are to function successfully, so the code must be communicated to parents. This can be accomplished by sending a letter home with students. We have also found it helpful to request that the parents sign the letter to indicate that they agree to the rules and have discussed them with their youngsters. Using this form of communication gives evidence that parents have seen and support the code of conduct.

Selecting positive consequences for following rules. After the rules have been jointly established and posted, students must receive reinforcement for adhering to them, because *rules will only be followed when differential consequences are applied for compliance and noncompliance.*

People learn to behave differently in different contexts because they have experienced the distinctive consequences for acts that they have performed in those contexts. For example, students learn to raise their hands in Ms. Smith's classroom because she only recognizes students who have their hands up, but they learn to speak out freely in Ms. Freebee's classroom because she sometimes recognizes students who speak out. Discriminating how to behave often stems from students' experiences with their teachers. By reinforcing *rule following, the environment teaches students which behaviors are acceptable under what circumstances.*[1] However, if rule following is not

reinforced, it eventually will cease. If Ms. Freebee fails to call on those who raise their hands, hand raising will probably not occur in her classroom.

In the early stages of instruction in rule following, reinforcement needs to be delivered very frequently, perhaps daily or weekly for adherence to schoolwide rules, and possibly as often as every hour or following every period for classroom rules. The teacher might, for instance, plan to terminate instruction 5 minutes early for each class period in which the students, or those who complied with the code, are permitted a special event, such as a song, a dance, free time, or something similar. Later on, once adherence to rules reaches a high and steady rate for several weeks, praise and recognition can be substituted gradually for the special events, without eliminating them altogether.

Raising the general level of reinforcement. Beyond the differential reinforcement that teaches students to follow rules, schools that are seeking to reduce vandalism need to provide reinforcement in many other forms. High density reinforcement will imbue the school's atmosphere with positive properties and make it a place that students like and respect; vandalism should diminish as a result. We have accomplished reductions in vandalism by providing lots of praise and recognition, special rewards and activities as consequences of academic progress and also as noncontingent benefits by providing students access to many intrinsically reinforcing educational events, such as entertainment, arts, music, dance, handicrafts, trips, and audio-visual presentations. (See Sulzer-Azaroff & Mayer, 1986, in press, for reinforcing programs and lists of reinforcers for students. Also see Mayer et al., 1983c, for a variety of practical reinforcing programs that were used as part of an overall strategy to reduce vandalism.) As Nevin (1988) has demonstrated, dense reinforcement helps maintain prosocial behavior.

Selecting consequences for minor infractions. As we mentioned previously, individually effective punitive procedures are selected for major infractions, and reinforcement is withheld from minor infractions while constructive alternatives are selected and applied to diminish them. Constructive alternatives might include (a) providing reinforcement when target students engage in desirable alternatives to infractions, such as cleaning up messes on the campus and in the classroom, raising their hands, and acceptably completing assigned work (Alt-R: differential reinforcement of alternative responses); (b) reinforcing students' engagement in appropriate rule-following behavior to permit their actions to serve as models for those engaged in minor infractions (modeling); (c) providing reinforcement for reduced rates of the undesirable behavior, such as diminished rates of absenteeism, vandalism, littering, or blurting out (DRL: differential reinforcement of low rates); and (d) providing reinforcement when students stop engaging in specific misbehaviors for a period of time, such as fighting during break time, being tardy or committing vandalism for a month, or blurting out for a similar period (DRO: differential reinforcement of the zero-occurrence of a behavior). (We have elaborated and illustrated these strategies elsewhere: Mayer et al., 1983c; Sulzer-Azaroff & Mayer, 1986). Finally, assuming that rules are familiar to all and that punishment is called for, do not give warnings after observing a serious infraction, because such warnings can serve as an invitation to misbehavior. Instead, deliver the selected consequence immediately after the infraction occurs.

The triadic model appears especially effective for several reasons. First, by using constructive alternatives, instead of punishment for minor infractions, school and classroom climates become less punitive and more positive. In turn, this produces higher rates of reinforcement and a more positive learning climate, resulting in less vandalism and violence (Mayer & Butterworth, 1979; Mayer et al., 1983b). Also, on the rare occasions when we must use punishment, because it has not been overused, it is more likely to work effectively.

MAINTAINING PREVENTION PROGRAMS

Phasing Out Reminders and Consequences

Students soon will learn the rules if the conduct code is posted in a prominent place and reviewed periodically, and if consequences consistently are provided both for violating and for abiding by the rules. After students have been adhering consistently to the rules for a long time, the frequency of delivering the positive consequences can gradually be reduced, so that rule-following behavior will become more habitual and not overly dependent on rewards. This is particularly important if tangible incentives have been used because more natural reinforcers were not effective or meaningful to the youngster involved. These contrived reinforcers can be replaced gradually by the reinforcers indigenous to the situation or the learning activity. For example, if tickets, ice cream, certificates, or award assemblies are provided once a week initially, they should be paired with and slowly replaced by more natural reinforcers, such as praise and recognition, while the more intrusive reinforcers are phased back to twice a week for a couple of times, then to once a month several times, then perhaps to once every other month. *Do not stop the incentives abruptly*, because a sharp cutoff may cause the desired behavior to disintegrate. If adherence to the rules begins to fade, back up a bit and offer the incentives more frequently again; then phase them out more gradually than before.

Similarly, as students learn to abide by the rules, fewer reminders will be needed. Reviewing rules also can be phased out gradually. Rules may also be combined or made more general, perhaps as simple as "Bring supplies, pay attention, and behave according to the rules."

Fostering Continued Environmental Support

We have shown how vandalism can relate to the management strategies used by educators; thus, continuing environmental support of these strategies is essential. Beyond assurances, you need actively to promote continuation of effective behavior management strategies if change is to be sustained. What measures can you take?

Several. First realize that staff, like all of us, need to receive very frequent reinforcement for their initial efforts to make school more reinforcing and less punitive; as discussed previously in regard to students, this reinforcement of staff can become less frequent with time (MacDonald, Gallimore, & MacDonald, 1970; Holden & Sulzer-Azaroff, 1972). These efforts can take the form of specific feedback, recognition, praise or even special privileges or rewards. If abrupt termination of reinforcement occurs, changes or new programs are not likely to continue. Dustin (1974) stressed this point when he wrote:

> One reason that institutions change superficially has to do with ineffective behaviors on the part of the change agent. These proponents of change "burn out," or move on, before the change is fully implemented. It is necessary that a change agent possess tenacity to follow through and to return to the same tasks and the same individuals time and again. (pp. 423-424)

Often, reinforcing feedback is done in person, but we have found that adequate support can be attained by providing charts, telephone calls and notes (Fox & Sulzer-Azaroff, 1982; Hunt & Sulzer-Azaroff, 1974), and also by encouraging peers to provide positive recognition for the newly acquired skills. The advantage of involving peers in delivering reinforcement is that the natural social environment begins to assume discriminative control, to prompt and support the desired behaviors.

We strongly recommend that you not start your program until you are certain you (or someone reporting to you) can check with and provide the staff with reinforcement at least twice a week during the early phase of program implementation. This immediate and frequent reinforcement is necessary until the new

behaviors are well established; otherwise they are likely to disintegrate. The resultant failure will then punish attempts to implement the approach. Later on, the frequency of praise, phone calls, and so forth, can be reduced gradually. As Sulzer-Azaroff and Mayer (1986) noted, "this occasional intermittent reinforcement and the support provided by the consultees' peers, enables you to reduce the amount of time you need to devote to any one consultee while supporting the durability of change" (p. 92).

The importance of continued reinforcement must be stressed. This is especially true when attempting to implement preventive programs, because unlike the very discernible immediate reinforcement provided by deterrents and punishment, the reinforcing consequences for prevention are delayed and difficult to detect. Consequently, staff frequently require supplementary positive reinforcement (from one another, consultants, administrators, their students, and community members) if they are to continue conducting their preventive programs until the programs become embedded in the school's natural environment. Intermittent praise, though, may be sufficient. For example, Cossairt, Hall and Hopkins (1973) found that teachers use of praise was maintained and even increased when it was in turn praised intermittently by their principals. They concluded that

> This would seem to indicate that the excuse that principals and supportive staff do not have time for the social reinforcement of teacher behavior is invalid. Operant principles of reinforcement systematically applied would therefore seem to be functional in helping principals and consultants accomplish their primary goals, which should be improved instruction. It would also seem that this could be done with a minimal amount of time and effort. (p. 100)

Goal setting is another way to promote initial and enduring improvement in staff performance. This strategy, used in all types of organizations (Fellner & Sulzer-Azaroff, 1984) assists people to progress in increments towards their ultimate objectives (e.g., tailoring instruction to individual student skills and interests; developing and rehearsing classroom rules; planning and conducting reinforcing activities for students; suppressing reprimands, sarcasm, and other forms of punishment). After discovering their current levels of functioning by constructing a baseline composed of repeated measures of the performance of concern, the performer sets a level to be attained during the next few days or weeks that is challenging yet attainable. Achieving a level set as a goal becomes an occasion for feedback and reinforcement. Then a new goal is set, and so on until the ultimate objective is accomplished. Reinforcement and feedback are then continued as the newly acquired routine becomes habitual and incorporated into the staff members' daily routine (see Gillat, 1989, for an illustrative example).

EVALUATING THE PROGRAM'S EFFECTIVENESS

Every school is different, just as each student and staff member is unique. Consequently, the only way to determine whether a given program of vandalism prevention is successful is to conduct a formal evaluation.

As stated earlier, generally we have to rely on indirect measures of vandalism, such as the cost and frequency of damage, which can be misleading. For example, one frequently used method for evaluating the effectiveness of a vandalism program is to compare the cost and frequency of various types of vandalism (i.e., property damage, fire, theft) each month while the program is in effect against cost and frequency figures from previous years (Mayer & Butterworth, 1979). Another method is to use a multiple-baseline design across schools (Mayer et al., 1983b). This would involve collecting as accurate as possible baseline data in several schools on episodes and on severity of vandalism acts, and then implementing the selected treatment first in one, then in another, and perhaps later in yet another of the schools. If vandalism changes maximally in each school only after treatment is

applied, the evidence favors the treatment rather than some other influence.

We prefer the multiple baseline tactic (Sulzer-Azaroff & Mayer, 1977, in press) for evaluating the effectiveness of a vandalism reduction program. It is a natural way to approach the issue because you would first want to find out if the problem decreases in one school after the program has been carried out, but before proceeding to the next implementation. The most logical approach would be to replicate the presumably successful program in another school to see if similar positive results could be achieved.

One problem we have encountered following program implementation is that people involved tend to scrutinize the vandalism data more closely than previously, resulting in more accurate reporting (i.e., reporting more episodes of vandalism) than during baseline. Obviously, as this can obscure actual improvement to an unknown extent, you should try to obtain accurate data throughout baseline and treatment, enhancing the believability of the data by using two independent reporters (Mayer et al., 1983b). Disagreements can be discussed and resolved following observational recording sessions, and interreporter agreement indexes can be calculated. To help reduce errors in reporting school crimes like vandalism, California Assembly Bill 2583 (Chapter 78), which became law on January 1, 1989, stipulated that districts can be fined if a crime report is not submitted or contains intentionally misleading data.

Reducing rates of vandalism is the *outcome* (long range) objective. Intermediary (process) objectives can be evaluated similarly. For example, a small number of teachers can be involved initially in a program designed to increase their use of positive reinforcement, and other teachers added after longer baseline periods. Other evidence of change in performance can also be collected. For example, you might want to record and graph the number of positive notes sent to teachers by administrators, comparing baseline to program rates. Detailed descriptive data of staff training and disciplinary policy changes might also prove helpful in permitting later replication of the program.

IMPLICATIONS FOR THE ROLE AND TRAINING OF THE SCHOOL PSYCHOLOGIST

The factors contributing to vandalism obviously are complex and require a comprehensive approach to evaluation and to intervention and prevention. There are a variety of skills, then, that school psychologists need to possess if they are to work effectively in the area of school vandalism and discipline. These include skills in consulting, observing, recording, graphing, selecting and using behavioral strategies, ecobehavioral assessment, and leadership skills, such as being able to persuade, make decisions, take risks and amass support. The psychologist must be able to examine behavior both in the school and classrooms, not only in relation to its immediate antecedents and consequences, but also in relation to more temporally remote stimuli, such as setting events to vandalism, the general context of ongoing and prior events, and elements of the physical environment that might contribute to vandalism. The purpose of doing such an extensive ecobehavioral assessment is to help the psychologist to better plan, intervene and evaluate, and to provide more effective support services.

Not only do school psychologists need to assess ability, academic skills, learning styles, and interests, but they must be able to provide consultation with teachers, helping them to match assignments and curricula with students' skills, abilities, and interests. They need to be specialized in individual and group behavior management and goal setting strategies, and to consult, teach, and provide supervision and feedback regarding their use. They need to be educated in systems analyses, so that they can analyze the school as an organization within the community, and to be able to capitalize on potential support and detect and manage potential impediments to change. Finally, their skills must extend to consulting with and actively involving administrators and other specialists, as well as managing their own time, setting their own priorities, and devising a system to reinforce their own behavior.

SUMMARY

Vandalism is a major problem in many of our schools. Recent research, though, is beginning to give us some answers: Emphasize and implement prevention programs for dealing with some of the key direct and indirect factors related to promoting vandalism, such as punishment, extinction, and reinforcement.

Most school vandalism programs have relied on deterrents and punitive measures. The paradox is that such measures can sometimes inadvertently exacerbate the situation by making the environment more punitive, thereby setting the occasion for increased vandalism. Thus, deterrents and punitive measures should not be used unless implemented as a temporary expedient and combined with positive practices designed to prevent, reduce, or eliminate the factors that evoke acts of vandalism.

A constructive approach to school discipline has been described that is aimed at reducing the punitiveness and presumably, as a consequence, vandalism. Assignments are adjusted to promote individual success and sense of accomplishment, and school is made a more reinforcing place. Constructive discipline contrasts with traditional discipline approaches in several ways, namely, its reliance on primarily positive consequences, and its clarity and specificity. The first step involves determining a set of specific rules, using student input and administrative approval at the classroom level, and including student, staff, and parental input at the school level. Then these rules are to be stated positively, posted in a prominent place, and periodically reviewed. Students are most likely to follow the rules when consequences are applied immediately and consistently for adherence to and violation of them. Punitive consequences for rule violations, however, are kept to a minimum, because too many punitive consequences may cause the punishment to lose its effectiveness.

A triadic framework has been presented that categorized behaviors to be (a) reinforced, (b) dealt with by constructive alternatives to punishment, or (c) punished. This triadic model restricts the use of punishment to major infractions. As a result, punishment will be minimized, resulting in a more positive school environment, less vandalism, and aggression. Similarly, because constructive alternatives are used for minor infractions, *students are taught how to behave*, not just how *not* to behave, and student attitudes towards themselves and schools are likely to become more positive.

As with the specification of rules, selection of the actual consequences to be used in the classroom and at the school level should involve both student and teacher input and administrative approval. Educators must be able to choose from a variety of jointly selected reinforcing and punitive consequences *to allow for individual student differences*. Once a punishing consequence is selected for a student's major infraction, it should be applied immediately and consistently.

Any code of conduct should be viewed as a living document. Because of student, staff, and environmental changes, it needs to be reviewed, and revised as necessary, at least yearly. As the context of the school changes, the conduct code must adjust also, to allow for individual differences.

We now know that school psychologists and other educators can do more than just punish or design deterrents in response to vandalism, and we are in a good position to ensure that a more constructive approach to discipline is applied in our schools. Educators, pupil personnel specialists, students, and society all stand to benefit.

FOOTNOTE

[1]Rules as "contingency specifying stimuli" (Skinner, 1969) actually apply far more broadly to cover many classes of cognitive behavior (see Hineline & Wanchisen, in press), yet are developed essentially the same way.

REFERENCES

Barrera, R. D. (1984, August). *Programmed supplemental grammar instruction in the video arcade.* Paper presented at the annual Meeting of the American Psychological Association, Toronto.

Berkowitz, L. (1983). Aversively stimulated aggression: Some parallels and differences in research with animals and humans. *American Psychologist, 38,* 1135-1144.

Brodinsky, B. (1980). *AASA critical issues report: Student discipline, problems, and solutions* (Report No. 021-00334). Arlington, VA: American Association of School Administrators.

Butterworth, T., Mayer, G. R., Nafpaktitis, M., & Hollingsworth, P. (1982). *Constructive discipline: Improving attendance and reducing disruption and vandalism costs* (ESEA, Title IV-C end-of-year evaluation report). Downey, CA: Office of the Los Angeles County Superintendent of Schools.

Center, D. B., Deitz, S. M., & Kaufman, M. E. (1982). Student ability, task difficulty, and inappropriate classroom behavior: A study of children with behavior disorders. *Behavior Modification, 6,* 355-374.

Conger, R. D. (1982). Behavioral intervention for child abuse. *Behavior Therapist, 5,* 49-53.

Cossairt, A., Hall, R. V., & Hopkins, B. L. (1973). The effects of experimenter's instructions, feedback, and praise on teacher praise and student attending behavior. *Journal of Applied Behavior Analysis, 6,* 89-100.

Dustin, R. (1974). Training for instructional change. *Personnel and Guidance Journal, 52,* 422-427.

Fellner, D. J., & Sulzer-Azaroff, B. (1984). A behavioral analysis of goal setting. *Journal of Organizational Behavior Management, 6,* 33-51.

Flaherty, G. (1987). Reducing vandalism by changing the school community. *Thrust for Educational Leadership, 16*(5), 28-30.

Fixsen, D. L., Phillips, E. L., & Wolf, M. M. (1973). Achievement place: Experiments in self-government with pre-delinquents. *Journal of Applied Behavior Analysis, 6,* 31-47.

Fox, C. J., & Sulzer-Azaroff, B. (1982). *A program to supervise geographically dispersed foster parents' teaching of retarded youth.* Unpublished manuscript.

Gamble, L. R., Sellers, C. P., & Bone, C. E. (1987). School building intrusions: Prevention strategies. *School Business Affairs, 53*(6), 18-21.

Gillat, A. (1989). *The principal as an instructional leader.* Unpublished doctoral dissertation, University of Massachusetts, Amherst.

Gold, M., & Mann, D. W. (1982). Alternative schools for troublesome secondary students. *Urban Review, 14*, 305-316.

Goldiamond, I. (1974). Toward a constructional approach to social problems: Ethical and constitutional issues raised by applied behavior analysis. *Behaviorism, 2*, 1-85.

Greenberg, B. (1969, October). *School vandalism: A national dilemma*. Palo Alto, CA: Stanford Research Institute Research and Development Program.

Greenberg, B. (1974). School vandalism: Its effects and paradoxical solutions. *Crime Prevention Review, 1*, 105.

Hayes, S. C., Nelson, R. O., & Jarrett, R. P. (1987). The treatment utility of assessment: A functional approach to evaluating assessment quality. *American Psychologist, 42*, 963-974.

Heller, M. C., & White, M. A. (1975). Rates of teacher verbal approval and disapproval to higher and lower ability classes. *Journal of Educational Psychology, 67*, 796-800.

Hineline, P. N., & Wanchisen, B. A. (in press). Correlated hypothesizing, and the distinction between contingency shaped and rule governed behavior. In S. C. Hayes (Ed.). *Rule-governed behavior: Cognition, contingencies, and instructional control*. New York: Plenum.

Holden, B., & Sulzer-Azaroff, B. (1972). Schedules of follow-up and their effect upon the maintenance of a prescriptive teaching program. In G. Semb, D. R. Green, R. P. Hawkins, J. Michael, E. L. Phillips, J. A. Sherman, H. Sloane, & D. R. Thomas (Eds.), *Behavior analysis and education — 1972*. Lawrence: University of Kansas.

Hunt, S., & Sulzer-Azaroff, B. (1974, September). *Motivating parent participation in home training sessions with pretrainable retardates*. Paper presented at the American Psychological Association, New Orleans.

Krause, D. (1985). Our school C.A.R.E.S. for good behavior. *Principal, 65*, 44-45.

Leinhardt, G., & Pallay, A. (1982). Restrictive educational settings: Exile or haven? *Review of Educational Research, 52*, 557-578.

Los Angeles County Office of Education (1988). *1988 pupil services digest* (Publication No. 88-9-04R). Downey, CA: Author.

Lovitt, T. C., & Curtiss, K. (1969). Academic response rate as a function of teacher- and self-imposed contingencies. *Journal of Applied Behavior Analysis, 2*, 49-53.

MacDonald, W. S., Gallimore, R., & MacDonald, G. (1970). Contingency counseling by school personnel: An economical model of intervention. *Journal of Applied Behavior Analysis, 31*, 175-182.

Mayer, G. R., & Butterworth, T. (1979). A preventive approach to school violence and vandalism: An experimental study. *Personnel and Guidance Journal, 57*, 436-441.

Mayer, G. R., & Butterworth, T. (1981). Evaluating a preventive approach to reducing school vandalism. *Phi Delta Kappan, 62*, 498-499.

Mayer, G. R., Butterworth, T., Komoto, T., & Benoit, R. (1983a). The influence of the school principal on the consultant's effectiveness. *Elementary School Guidance & Counseling, 17*, 274-279.

Mayer, G. R., Butterworth, T., Nafpaktitis, M., & Sulzer-Azaroff, B. (1983b). Preventing school vandalism and improving discipline: A three-year study. *Journal of Applied Behavior Analysis, 16*, 355-369.

Mayer, G. R., Butterworth, T., Spaulding, H. L., Hollingsworth, P., Amorim, M., Caldwell-McElroy, C., Nafpaktitis, M., & Perez-Osorio, X. (1983c). *Constructive discipline: Building a climate for learning. A resource manual of programs and strategies*. Downey, CA: Office of the Los Angeles County Superintendent of Schools.

Mayer, G. R., Nafpaktitis, M., Butterworth, T., & Hollingsworth, P. (1987). A search for the elusive setting events of school vandalism: A correlational study. *Education and Treatment of Children, 10*, 259-270.

Mullendore, P. (1981). Program to divert dollars lost to crime. *Campus Strife, 2*, 4-5. (Available from School Safety Center, California Department of Justice.)

Nafpaktitis, M., Mayer, G. R., & Butterworth, T. (1985). Natural rates of teacher approval and disapproval and their relation to student behavior in intermediate school classrooms. *Journal of Educational Psychology, 77*, 362-367.

Nevin, J. A. (1988). Behavioral momentum and the partial reinforcement effect. *Psychological Bulletin, 103*, 44-56.

Nicholson, G. (1981). Pursuing school safety in the 80's: An opinion from the attorney general's office. *Thurst, 11*, 26-27.

O'Leary, S. G., & Dubey, D. R. (1979). Applications of self-control procedures by children: A review. *Journal of Applied Behavior Analysis, 12*, 449-465.

Patterson, G. R. (1982). *Coercive family process*. Eugene, OR: Castalia.

Reaves, A. (1981). We let it happen — We can change it. *Thurst, 11*, 8–10.

Rogers-Warren, A. K. (1984). Ecobehavioral analysis. *Education and Treatment of Children, 7*, 283–303.

Scrimger, G. C., & Elder, R. (1981). *Alternatives to vandalism: Cooperation or wreckreation*. Sacramento, CA: School Safety Center, California Department of Justice.

Skinner, B. F. (1969). *Contingencies of reinforcement: A theoretical analysis*. NY: Appleton-Century-Crofts.

Sulzer-Azaroff, B., & Mayer, G. R. (1977). *Applying behavior analysis procedures with children and youth*. New York: Holt, Rinehart and Winston.

Sulzer-Azaroff, B., & Mayer, G. R. (1986). *Achieving educational excellence with behavioral strategies*. New York: Holt, Rinehart and Winston.

Sulzer-Azaroff, B., & Mayer, G. R. (in press). *Behavioral analysis for lasting change*. New York: Holt, Rinehart and Winston.

Thomas, J. D., Presland, I. E., Grant, M. D., & Glynn, T. (1978). Natural rates of teacher approval and disapproval in grade-7 classrooms. *Journal of Applied Behavior Analysis, 11*, 91–94.

Touchette, P. E., MacDonald, R. F., & Langer, S. N. (1985). A scatter plot for identifying stimulus control of problem behavior. *Journal of Applied Behavior Analysis, 18*, 343–351.

Wahler, R. G. (1980). The insular mother: Her problems in parent–child treatment. *Journal of Applied Behavior Analysis, 13*, 207–219.

White, M. A. (1975). Natural rates of teacher approval and disapproval in the classroom. *Journal of Applied Behavior Analysis, 8*, 367–372.

Wyatt, W. J., & Hawkins, R. P. (1987). Rates of teachers verbal approval and disapproval: Relationship to grade level, classroom activity, student behavior, and teacher characteristics. *Behavior Modification, 11*, 27–51.

26

Truancy and School Absenteeism

David C. Guevremont
University of Massachusetts Medical Center

Persistent absence from school is a continuing concern among educators because of its social, educational, and legal implications. The most common reason for school absence in the United States is illness (Weitzman, Klerman, Lamb, Menary, & Alpert, 1982). Estimates of unjustifiable absence from school on any given day, however, have ranged from 1% to 22% of the school-age population (e.g., Nielsen & Gerber, 1979). In its legal context, a persistent and unjustifiable pattern of absence from school is referred to as truancy. The term *truant* has its roots in a French word meaning "an assemblage of beggars"; it was later applied to children who failed to attend school (Hersov & Berg, 1980). Although there is surprisingly little research on the long-term results of truancy, some studies have found persistent absence from school to be a reliable predictor of alcoholism, criminality, occupational difficulties, and other deviant behavior in adults (Robins & Ratcliffe, 1980).

Contemporary perspectives of truancy and school absenteeism distinguish two major types of school absence on the basis of psychological and social variables. Hersov and Berg (1980) have concluded that persistent school absenteeism is probably not a "true clinical entity" with a common etiology, course, or prognosis but is a heterogeneous set of behaviors. Nonetheless, a useful distinction between types of persistent school absence depends on whether the absence is a correlate of a larger class of antisocial and delinquent activity, or is associated with affective states (e.g., anxiety) without coexisting antisocial behavior. The former will be referred to in this paper as *truancy;* the latter will be called *school refusal* (Hersov, 1960).

TYPES OF SCHOOL ABSENCE

Truancy has routinely been identified by child, family, and social characteristics that closely resemble the attributes of conduct-disordered youth. School refusal, on the other hand, typically involves anxiety and/or phobic responses that interfere with school attendance. Children referred for school refusal, in comparison with those referred for truancy, are more likely to hold a high standard for schoolwork and classroom behavior while at the same time displaying overt signs of anxiety, panic, and somatic complaints (e.g., nausea, abdominal pain, headache) that are associated with their attendance at school (Hersov, 1960; Schmitt, 1971). These patterns of behavior are rarely reported in regard to truants.

In a study of 33 truants that incorporated structured interviews and school records, Nielsen and Gerber (1979) found a high prevalence of disruptive classroom behavior (81%), fighting (67%), stealing (55%), cruelty toward animals (7%), school vandalism (7%), running away (31%), firesetting (22%), and nonschool vandalism (7%). Moreover, regular use of alcohol

(39%) and marijuana (32%) were reported among the sample. With respect to family characteristics, 78% of the children in the sample had siblings who were also truant and 40% came from broken homes. Consistent with the above are the following findings: Truants are more likely than are school refusers to have academic problems, be unpopular with peers, drop out of school, dislike school, be absent without their parents' knowledge, come from disadvantaged social backgrounds, and spend their time, when absent, out of the home, for example with other truants (e.g., Fogelman, Tibbenham, & Lambert, 1980; Hersov, 1960; Nielsen & Gerber, 1979; Robins, 1966). School refusers, in contrast, are more likely to stay at home when absent, be satisfied with their teachers and schoolwork, show little associated antisocial behavior, and have parents who are aware of their absenteeism (e.g., Hersov, 1960; Hersov & Berg, 1980; Nielsen & Gerber, 1979).

A similar subtyping is provided by Kennedy (1965), who differentiates between Type I and Type II school refusers. Type I is characterized by acute onset, usually representing the first such episode during the early school years. Type II, in contrast, is characterized by gradual onset, a resulting history of school refusal, and referral for treatment in the upper grades. Like Hersov's (1960) distinction, Type II school refusers also are more likely to come from disorganized family environments and display additional antisocial behavior.

Finally, distinctions between school refusers have also been made between children who are primarily school-phobic and those who fear separation from their caregivers. In the former, anxiety may be related to a specific circumstance (e.g., school bully; harsh teacher) or to more general psychological or developmental variables (e.g., poor peer relations; concerns about physical development such as delayed puberty). In the latter, anxiety appears to be linked to fears associated with separation from primary caregivers rather than specific circumstances in the school. General correlates differentiating truancy and school refusal are presented in Table 1.

MULTIDIMENSIONAL ASSESSMENT

Because school absenteeism is an inherently complex problem, a multidimensional assessment of persistent school absenteeism is usually warranted. Although this chapter is not intended to provide a comprehensive or detailed account of assessment, at least four general areas of functioning should be routinely considered in assessing school absenteeism. First, the broader context of poor attendance is assessed with particular emphasis given to whether it is a circumscribed problem embedded in a larger context of antisocial behavior or psychiatric symptomology. Parent, child, and teacher interviews are often necessary to trace the onset of problems, precipitants, academic and social status, and family functioning. Completion of standardized child behavior rating scales by teachers and by parents (e.g., Child Behavior Checklist; Achenbach & Edelbrock, 1983) is a useful means of screening for general psychopathology and the development of deviant behavioral symptoms. A review of child behavior rating scales is found in Barkley (1988).

A second area of assessment addresses the child's possible need for additional or conjunctive treatments. Although a prompt return to school is desirable in most cases, assessment of school absenteeism may suggest the need for immediate interventions within the family (e.g., in cases of child abuse) or outside referrals to address significant psychiatric problems (e.g., depression, substance abuse) that may be causing or be related to absenteeism. In such cases, it may be determined that absenteeism is a secondary issue and greater priority is to be given to other areas that impinge upon the child's well-being and behavior.

Third, an overall assessment of academic and social skills and deficiencies should be conducted (if such information is not readily available or updated) to ascertain their contribution to school attendance problems. In line with this

TABLE 1
Correlates of Truancy and School Refusal

Truancy	School Refusal
Gradual onset	Early onset
Coexistence of antisocial behavior	Coexistence of separation/phobic anxiety
Academic deficiencies	Adequate academic performances
Poor classroom behavior	Adequate classroom behavior
Dissatisfaction with schoolwork and teachers	Satisfaction with schoolwork and teachers
Out-of-home activity during absences	In-home activity during absences
Parent unaware of absence	Parent aware of absence

recommended assessment is the need to carefully determine whether the child is placed in an appropriate classroom. Inappropriate classroom placement may result in pronounced academic underachievement and routine failure that, if overlooked, can seriously impede attempts to foster more consistent attendance. This concern is especially pertinent for children who display high levels of anxiety regarding academic performance or for youths with conduct problem, who may find out-of-school environments significantly more reinforcing than classrooms.

Fourth, a functional analysis of absenteeism is routinely conducted that includes assessment of common precipitants and causal antecedents (e.g., increased anxiety following a school vacation) as well as analyses of potential maintaining conditions (e.g., parents' reinforcement of avoidant behavior). Finally, the careful assessment of available resources and logistical issues surrounding individual cases is necessary prior to the formulation of treatment goals and strategies. In particular, the feasibility of procuring the cooperation and participation of the parent(s) in both the assessment and treatment process will, in part, dictate the nature of the treatments that can be attempted at the school level.

INTERVENTIONS FOR TRUANCY AND SCHOOL REFUSAL

Treatment of persistent absenteeism from school may include a single-treatment modality or a combination of various intervention strategies. Documented treatment approaches to date have included (a) brief supportive assistance, (b) behavioral therapies, (c) pharmacological treatment, (d) psychotherapy, and (e) community-based and legal interventions. Trained school personnel are usually capable of providing supportive services and developing behavior management programs to increase school attendance, but outside referral sources are generally required when medication or more intensive coordinated efforts involving other agencies are required. Although the choice of treatments is usually based upon the age of the child, severity of the problem, functional assessment of the problem, diagnostic status, and resources, most research indicates that quick intervention and rapid return to consistent attendance is pivotal to the success of the treatment.

Supportive Services

In cases involving transient school refusal, a variety of supportive intervention tactics are often used. These tactics may include advising the parent, providing firm reassurance regarding the anxiety-evoking event, and forced attendance supplemented with small rewards. In addition, teachers or other school personnel (e.g., guidance counselors) may be enlisted to assist the child during his or her arrival at school and to quickly get the child involved in a preferred activity. With mild, uncomplicated, and transient cases of school absence, supportive services alone are often sufficient in returning the child to school. In fact, these approaches may constitute the most common form of treatment of school refusal. Common precipitants of transient school refusal include a recent aversive experience at school (e.g., being chastised by the teacher), the end of a school vacation, absence secondary to an illness, or the recent illness of a family member.

When a child's refusal to attend school is related to a specific event or anxiety-inducing activity at school, environmental modifications may be indicated to alleviate the stressor. Kennedy's (1965) Type I school refusers were treated effectively with tactics primarily designed to rapidly return the child to school. Immediate return to school in such cases may prevent the development of secondary gains associated with staying home (e.g., parental attention) and tends to assure that the child will not fall behind on classroom work, which might intensify the reluctance to attend.

One should exercise caution, however, before concluding that supportive tactics alone are sufficient or optimal for improving school attendance. Most children cope adequately with the typical stress events associated with going to school without the need of outside assistance. The display of exaggerated emotional responses on the part of the child that are expressed in school refusal may be indicative of overanxious behavior that becomes apparent in the context of fairly typical school-related stress events. In such cases, it may be necessary to address the child's overanxious symptoms through further assessment. Finally, most experts agree that a child's stated reasons for not wanting to attend school should be taken seriously and carefully evaluated before being dismissed as unimportant to the resolution of the problem (Hersov & Berg, 1980).

Behavioral Approaches

Behavioral approaches to the treatment of persistent school absenteeism emphasize identifying and manipulating antecedents and consequences surrounding avoidance of school and are charac-terized by collection of objective data, testing of hypotheses, and careful evaluation of outcomes (Yule, 1977). There is substantial support for the behavioral treatment of school absenteeism (e.g., Bragg & Yule, 1984; Lazarus, Davison, & Polefka, 1965; Vaal, 1973). Behavioral treatments have primarily involved systematic reinforcement of school attendance, parent training, contingency contracting, and desensitization and in vivo exposure techniques. The two latter techniques are used when anxiety is related to school avoidance, the former in conjunction with desensitization procedures or when reasons other than anxiety are implicated.

Preventive approaches. Contingency management systems can be used to promote regular attendance in children who are considered to be at high risk for truancy or as a secondary prevention approach when truant behavior has been documented in the past. One form of contingency management involves the identified child earning points, tokens, or rewards for school attendance. When symbolic reinforcers (e.g., points) are used, they are later exchanged for more tangible rewards such as money, movie tickets, video arcade tokens, or special privileges at specified intervals (Kelley & Stokes, 1982). Additionally, a response cost tactic can be used, by which the child loses certain earned benefits for unjustifiable absences.

There is some evidence that preventive approaches can increase the consistent attendance of children who are at risk for truancy or for dropping out of school. Alexander, Corbett, and Smigel (1976) reported increased attendance of delinquent and truant adolescents by use of a token reinforcement program backed up by lunch money contingent upon attendance. Group contingencies (i.e., money was awarded only when all students in the class attended school on a given day) were found to be more effective than individual contingencies, presumably because of the powerful effects of peer pressure. Preventive approaches to school absenteeism have most often been employed with delinquent youth. Kelley and Stokes (1982) used monetary incentives for attendance and completion of schoolwork to prevent high-risk adolescents from dropping out of school. Furthermore, the use of monetary incentives, although not the only option, is often necessary because of the strong competing contingencies and secondary gains that may be associated with nonattendance. School- or community-based resources are often required to carry out such programs.

Parent training. Parent training interventions for school absenteeism may be employed when a functional analysis of the problem indicates that the child's avoidance of school is maintained, in part, by parental reinforcement of, and secondary gains for, nonattendance. Parent training interventions are appropriate when parents are willing and able to implement treatment procedures and when other conditions (e.g., severe phobic reaction to school) do not contraindicate its use. Typically, early protests by a child against going to school may be inadvertently reinforced by the parent and rapidly escalate into significant episodes of crying and temper displays. The extent of the child's apparent distress and/or the parent's inability to physically get the child to school may result in the child's staying home. Such instances are often complicated by secondary gains for nonattendance (e.g., parental attention, access to toys or television). The goals of parent training are (a) to educate the parent about the contingencies maintaining school refusal; (b) to assist the parent emotionally with the task of forcing the child to school and ignoring pleas and unjustified complaints of sickness; and (c) to teach the parent behavior management procedures to eliminate secondary gain and motivate cooperative attendance.

In effectively treating a 12-year-old boy who was absent for 30–60 days a term, Hersen (1970) involved the child's mother in a 10-session behavior management training program. The mother was taught to reinforce behavior consistent with school attendance and to not accommodate the child's avoidant behavior. More-

over, the secondary gains associated with nonattendance were removed. A 6-month follow-up indicated that the boy had continued to attend school on a routine basis. Similarly, Patterson (1965) involved the parents of a 7-year-old in treatment by teaching them to reinforce appropriate coping behavior that was incompatible with his separation anxiety.

Parent training interventions for school refusal generally involve the therapist or helping agent in devising a systematic plan for the parent to implement, with formal monitoring of progress and regular communication with the parent. When the parent is unable or unwilling to carry out the program, assistance from other family members, the therapist, or school personnel may be necessary (e.g., Blagg & Yule, 1984) or alternative treatments should be sought.

Contingency contracting. A contingency contract is a written agreement between two or more parties regarding both the specific behavior required to earn a positive consequence and the negative consequences that will follow a violation of the agreement. Five elements are used to ensure the effectiveness of contingency contracts: (a) The contract must be explicit in defining what the child will receive as a result of fulfilling the contract; (b) behaviors included in the contract must be susceptible to being monitored; (c) sanctions for breaking the contract should be explicitly defined; (d) "bonuses" for consistent compliance should be defined and awarded; and (e) a monitoring and record-keeping system should be established and regular feedback provided to the involved parties (Stuart, 1969; Stuart & Lott, 1971).

Contingency contracts have been successfully applied to treat school refusal (e.g., Cantrell, Cantrell, Huddleston, & Wooldrige, 1969). For example, Vaal (1973) used a contingency contract as the primary intervention with a 13-year-old boy who had been absent for 94% of the school days over a 6-month period. Reinforcers that were contracted for included activities and commodities that were previously available despite school absence. Access to reinforcers was made contingent upon school attendance, thus eliminating secondary gains for nonattendance. After introduction of the contract, the child immediately and voluntarily returned to school with perfect attendance for the remaining 3 months of the school year. This is especially impressive in light of the fact that the contract was in operation for only 6 weeks. Follow-up into the next school year indicated that regular attendance had been successfully maintained.

Desensitization and exposure therapies. Based on principles derived from classical conditioning and Wolpe's (1958) notion of reciprocal inhibition, desensitization and exposure therapies have been widely employed to treat school absenteeism, particularly when anxiety or phobic reactions are involved. In systematic desensitization, the child is gradually exposed to successively more anxiety-arousing situations while engaging in a behavior that is incompatible with anxiety. This substitution response (e.g., imagining a pleasant event, muscle relaxation) is intended to replace the anxiety through the process of conditioning.

The most common substitution response is deep muscle relaxation, which the child is taught prior to being exposed to anxiety-arousing scenes related to school avoidance. An anxiety hierarchy is then constructed and generally involves detailed and highly specific events that elicit anxiety, beginning with the least and progressing to the most anxiety-eliciting. Table 2 shows an example anxiety hierarchy pertaining to school refusal.

Through repeated therapy sessions, the child is instructed to imagine a scene from the anxiety hierarchy, beginning with the lowest items, and to use the substitution response whenever anxiety is experienced. As the child masters a scene from the hierarchy, a subsequent scene is paired with the substitution response until all hierarchy items can be experienced without significant discomfort. In the case of school refusal, for example, relaxation and feelings of well-being would

be substituted for intense anxiety related to specific school situations.

In vivo desensitization (Goldfried & Davison, 1976) is an extension of systematic desensitization that involves directly exposing the child to the actual anxiety-eliciting situation rather than having the child imagine the feared situation. With the assistance of a therapist, the child is gradually exposed to increasingly greater anxiety-eliciting situations while practicing a substitution response. Initially, the child and therapist might simply go to the school location during out-of-school hours. As treatment progresses, the child may be asked to attend one class period. As each progressive step is mastered (i.e., little anxiety is experienced), increasingly more participation in the normal school day is attempted. The school nurse or other helping personnel are often made ready for involvement should the child become overwhelmed. For example, "relaxation" breaks in the nurse's office may be arranged rather than allowing the child to return home.

There are several obvious advantages to in vivo desensitization in comparison with imaginal procedures in the treatment of school refusal. First, children may have difficulty vividly imaging scenes. Second, the therapist must rely exclusively on the child's self-report concerning the content of what is imagined and the degree of anxiety experienced. Third, the generalization or transfer of treatment effects are "built into" treatment when exposure occurs in the child's natural environment and involves the actual feared situations (Spiegler, 1983).

A final application of exposure therapies is flooding. With a flooding procedure, exposure to the anxiety-eliciting situation is "forced" without the opportunity for escape. An underlying assumption of flooding is that the avoidance of the feared situation maintains the fears. Thus, through exposure the individual should learn that the situation does not, in fact, result in harmful consequences. Blagg and Yule (1984) compared the relative effectiveness of flooding, hospitalization, and psychotherapy plus home tuition with 66 children and adolescents referred for

TABLE 2
Example Anxiety Hierarcy to Treat School Refusal Related to Separation Anxiety

Behavior Hierarchy	Rank-Ordering from Least to Most Anxiety-Evoking
Getting ready for bed the night before	1
Getting into bed	2
Hearing the alarm clock ring in the morning	3
Mother announces it is time to get up	4
Getting out of bed and dressed	5
Having breakfast	6
Leaving the house	7
Waiting for the school bus	8
Getting on the school bus	9
Riding to school	10
Approaching the school	11
Getting off the bus	12
Entering the school building	13
Sitting in homeroom	14
Beginning the first formal class of the day	15

school refusal. At follow-up more than 1 year later, 93.3% of those treated with flooding had reinitiated and maintained normal school attendance, whereas only 37.5% of those hospitalized and 10% of those receiving psychotherapy and home tuition showed similar improvement.

Summary of behavior therapies. Behavior therapies have been widely used in the treatment of school absenteeism. In cases involving high-risk groups (e.g., predelinquents) evidence suggests that monetary incentive systems can improve school attendance and participation. Such systems require financial backing and ample resources and have not been widespread. Contingency management and contracting approaches, both with and without parent training, appear to be useful when functional analyses suggest that secondary gains resulting from nonattendance compete with reinforcers available for school attendance.

School absenteeism related to separation anxiety or phobic reactions have been successfully treated with exposure therapies. Outcome research on the various exposure-based procedures has indicated that the critical process involved in successful treatment is the exposure to anxiety-eliciting situations in the absence of actual negative consequences (Bandura, 1969; Lang, 1969). Although not essential, gradual exposure and the teaching of substitution responses may function as facilitative components. Most applications of behavior therapy in treating school absenteeism involve a combination of techniques and procedures. For example, Phillips and Wolpe (1981) used a combination of deep muscle relaxation, systematic desensitization, in vivo desensitization, parent training, and positive reinforcement to treat the chronic absence of a 12-year-old boy with a history of severe separation anxiety. Treatment consisted of 88 total therapy sessions, following which the boy was able to attend school regularly without experiencing anxiety. A 2-year follow-up indicated that treatment gains had been maintained.

Behavior therapy for school absenteeism may be contraindicated as the sole or primary treatment mode when school absenteeism is related to other emotional or psychiatric disturbances such as depression or serious forms of substance abuse. In such cases, referrals for the treatment of these primary problems would generally be initiated prior to or in conjunction with behavioral treatment for absenteeism. Likewise, behavioral treatment of truancy that is embedded in a larger class of antisocial behavior may be ineffective because of powerful competing contingencies (e.g., drug use, contact with a deviant peer network) that undermine the potential reinforcers that behavior change agents can control. Significantly aggressive and defiant behavior that is unmanageable by parents or school personnel will also minimize the efficacy of behavioral treatment. For this reason, alternative approaches to school absenteeism will be briefly highlighted below.

Alternative Treatments

Supportive interventions and behavioral approaches generally represent the least intrusive and most efficient strategies for treating truancy and school refusal. The success of these procedures is related, in part, to the availability of resources necessary to carry out the interventions and to the characteristics of the child and family. For example, critical factors that may impede supportive or behavioral interventions include (a) no or limited cooperation of parents; (b) parents' inability to carry out procedures and effectively monitor the child's behavior; (c) limited access to and control of potent reinforcers by behavior change agents; (d) the availability of personnel to develop, carry out, and monitor the treatment; (e) parental psychopathology or family dysfunction; and (f) the child's psychopathology, such as depression or substance abuse.

Little systematic research has been conducted that adequately addresses the longer-term outcomes for children who either do not respond to, or are deemed appropriate for, supportive or behavioral treatments. Nonetheless, clinical and legal issues often warrant additional forms of intervention for children who are unresponsive to less intrusive traditional treatments. Several anecdotal accounts of alternative treatments are highlighted below.

Pharmacological treatment. When depressive symptoms or severe forms of separation anxiety or phobic responses impede successful return to school, antidepressant medications have sometimes been employed as treatment (e.g., Berney et al., 1981). Several controlled studies have used trials of imipramine when school refusal appeared to be secondary to severe separation anxiety (Gittelman-Klein & Klein, 1973; 1980). In these studies, children between the ages of 7 and 16 years underwent double-blind trials of imipramine after failed attempts to return the children to school. Medication was combined with supportive services and other forms of treatment, including desensitization procedures. After 6 weeks of treatment, 70% of those treated with imipramine were attending school, compared to 44% of those treated with placebo. Although medication treatment was more effective than placebo, a significantly large number of children were attending school after 6 weeks of treatment with the nonpharmacological services alone.

Other studies (e.g., Berney et al., 1981) have not found medication-based treatments to be superior to nonpharmacological forms of treatment. Thus, tentative findings about the effectiveness of medication treatments for school refusal suggest that antidepressants may complement other forms of treatment for severely anxious children or depressive disorders. The likelihood of success when medications are used alone or in the context of more serious family dysfunction appears to be limited (Hersov & Berg, 1980).

Psychotherapy. With the exception of anecdotal reports, very little research has addressed the relative effectiveness of psychotherapy as treatment for truancy and school refusal. Case studies have generally described various forms of psychodynamic and family systems approaches to therapy but with little consistency with respect to specific conceptualizations or procedures used (e.g., Epson, 1985). Consequently, clear guidelines on whether to refer truant/school refusing children for psychotherapy are currently unavailable.

Common sense suggests that individual or family-based psychotherapy may be warranted when (a) supportive or well-implemented behavioral treatments have failed; (b) family disorganization or dysfunction appears to be causing or maintaining school absence; (c) significant levels of emotional problems (e.g., depression) interact with school absence; or (d) conditions causing or maintaining school absence are largely unidentifiable or not understood. When psychotherapy is appropriate, other treatments may be added after or in conjunction with therapy, as necessary.

Community-based and legal interventions. The need to appeal to higher authority figures or agencies is often apparent in cases in which less intrusive treatments have failed to alter chronic school absence. This is most often true in cases involving a truant youth who displays associated antisocial behavior. Positive incentives for school attendance, which may be part of an initial treatment plan, are often undermined by powerful competing contingencies available for truant behavior (e.g., peer group activities). Likewise, the threat of a traditional punishment (e.g., removal of a privilege) may be inconsistently carried out or terminated because of significant forms of oppositional and aggressive behavior. When the school and family are unable to ensure regular school attendance by the child, alternative placements and/or the involvement of juvenile court officials is sometimes necessary.

Alternative placements have included classrooms with small student–teacher ratios and a modified academic curriculum to meet academic skills deficiencies (e.g., Stewart & Ray, 1984). Other possibilities include half-day school programs with behavioral management systems, such as token economies and contingency contracting, which can be supplemented with vocational or daily living skills programs (Waltzer, 1984). To ensure participation and regular attendance in alternative school programs, coordination of services with juvenile court personnel is often necessary. Stewart and Rose (1984), for example, evaluated a program that gave parents of truants the option of enrolling their child in a modified informal school program or attending a formal court hearing. Participants were referred to the program by the school principal. Probation officers informed parents and their children of their rights and discussed available options for treatment. In comparison with 159 children aged 13–15 years who did not attend the truancy intervention school program, there were significantly fewer subsequent court referrals for truancy among the 335 adolescents who had enrolled in the alternative program.

SUMMARY

Persistent absence among children and adolescents from school remains a concern among educators because of wide-ranging social, educational, and legal implications. Contemporary perspectives of school absence make distinctions between truancy and school refusal. Truancy is routinely embedded in a variety of other antisocial behaviors and is frequently associated with a gradual onset, academic deficiencies, unpopularity with peers, a strong dislike for school, disadvantaged home environments, out-of-home activities during school absences, and no knowledge by parents of the school absence. School refusal, in contrast, is frequently associated with an early onset, significant anxiety related to school or separation from parents, acceptable classroom behavior and performance, parents' knowledge of school absence, and the child's remaining at home during absences.

Interventions for school absence routinely involve strategies to promote a rapid return to school. Coordinated efforts between parents, school personnel, and sometimes outside agencies such as juvenile courts are often necessary, depending on the child's age, family conditions, severity of the problem, and available resources. Brief supportive services are often sufficient to insure a child's return to school. Behavioral therapies involving parent training, incentive approaches, contingency contracting, and exposure and desensitization procedures have been widely used to treat school absence. When less intrusive treatments are either ineffective or infeasible, alternative strategies will be necessary. Although little systematic research is available regarding their benefits, alternative approaches to interventions for school absence, such as pharmacological treatment, psychotherapy, and community-based programs with or without court involvement are sometimes warranted.

REFERENCES

Achenbach, T. M., & Edelbrock, C. S. (1983). *Manual for the Child Behavior Checklist and Revised Child Behavior Profile.* Burlington: University of Vermont.

Alexander, R. N., Corbett, T. F., & Smigel, J. (1976). The effects of individual and group consequences on school attendance and curfew violations with predelinquent adolescents. *Journal of Applied Behavior Analysis, 9,* 221-226.

Bandura, A. (1969). *Principles of behavior modification.* New York: Holt, Rinehart, & Winston.

Barkley, R. A. (1988). Child behavior rating scales and checklists. In M. Rutter, H. Tuma, & I. Lann (Eds.), *Assessment and diagnosis in child psychopathology* (pp. 113-155). New York: Guilford.

Berney, T., Kolvin, I., Bhate, S., Gardide, F., Jeans, B., Kay, B., & Scarth, L. (1981). School phobias: A therapeutic trial with climipramine and short-term outcome. *British Journal of Psychiatry, 138,* 110-118.

Blagg, N. R., & Yule, W. (1984). The behavioural treatment of school refusal — A comparative study. *Behavior Research and Therapy, 22,* 119-127.

Cantrell, R. P., Cantrell, M. L., Huddleston, C. M., & Wooldrige, R. L. (1969). Application of contingency contracts to four school attendance problems. *Journal of Applied Behavior Analysis, 2,* 215-220.

Epson, D. (1985). Short stories about school refusing. *Journal of Strategic and Systemic Therapies, 4,* 49-53.

Fogelman, K., Tibbenham, A., & Lambert, L. (1980). Absence from school: Findings from the National Child Developmental Study. In L. Hersov & I. Berg (Eds.), *Out of school: Modern perspectives in truancy and school refusal* (pp. 25-48). New York: Wiley.

Gittelman-Klein, R., & Klein, D. (1973). School phobia: Diagnostic considerations in the light of imipramine effects. *Journal of Nervous and Mental Disorders, 156,* 199-215.

Gittelman-Klein, R., & Gittelman, D. (1980). Separation anxiety in school refusal and its treatment with drugs. In L. Hersov & I. Berg (Eds.), *Out of school: Modern perspectives in truancy and school refusal.* New York: Wiley.

Goldfried, M. R., & Davison, G. C. (1976). *Clinical behavior therapy.* New York: Rinehart and Winston.

Hersen, M. (1970). Behavior modification approach to a school-phobia case. *Journal of Clinical Psychology, 26,* 128-132.

Hersov, L. (1960). Persistent non-attendance at school. *Journal of Child Psychology and Psychiatry, 1,* 314-319.

Hersov, L., & Berg, I. (1980). *Out of school: Modern perspectives in truancy and school refusal.* New York: Wiley.

Kelley, M. L., & Stokes, T. F. (1982). Contingency contracting with disadvantaged youths: Improving classroom performance. *Journal of Applied Behavior Analysis, 15,* 447-454.

Kennedy, W. A. (1965). School phobia: Rapid treatment of fifty cases. *Journal of Abnormal Psychology, 70,* 285-289.

Lang, P. J. (1969). The mechanics of desensitization and the laboratory study of fear. In C. M. Franks (Ed.), *Behavior therapy: Appraisal and status.* New York: McGraw-Hill.

Lazarus, A. A., Davison, G. C., & Polefka, D. A. (1965). Classical and operant factors in the treatment of a school phobia. *Journal of Abnormal Psychology, 70,* 225-229.

Nielsen, A., & Gerber, D. (1979). Psychosocial aspects of truancy in early adolescence. *Adolescence, 54,* 1-26.

Patterson, G. R. (1965). A learning theory approach to the treatment of the school phobic child. In L. P. Ullman & L. Krasnor (Eds.), *Case studies in behavior modification* (pp. 279-285). New York: Rinehart and Winston.

Phillips, D., & Wolpe, S. (1981). Multiple behavioral techniques in severe separation anxiety of a 12-year-old. *Journal of Behavior Therapy and Experimental Psychiatry, 12,* 329-332.

Robins, L. N. (1966). *Deviant children grown up: A sociological and psychiatric study of sociopathic personality.* Baltimore: Williams and Wilkins.

Robins, L. N., & Ratcliffe, L. (1980). The long-term outcome of truancy. In L. Hersov & I. Berg (Eds.), *Out of school: Modern perspectives in truancy and school refusal*. New York: Wiley.

Schmitt, B. D. (1971). School phobia — the great imitator: A pediatrician's viewpoint. *Pediatrics, 48,* 433-441.

Stewart, M. J., & Ray, R. E. (1984). Truants and the court: A diversionary program. *Social Work in Education, 6,* 179-192.

Stuart, R. B. (1969). Operant-interpersonal treatment for marital discord. *Journal of Consulting and Clinical Psychology, 33,* 675-682.

Stuart, R. B., & Lott, L. A. (1971). Behavioral contracting with delinquents: A cautionary note. *Journal of Behavior Therapy and Experimental Psychiatry, 3,* 161-169.

Spiegler, M. D. (1983). *Contemporary behavioral therapy.* Palo Alto: Mayfield.

Vaal, J. J. (1973). Applying contingency contracting to a school phobia: A case study. *Journal of Behavior Therapy and Experimental Psychiatry, 4,* 371-373.

Waltzer, F. (1984). Using a behavioral group approach with chronic truants. *Social Work in Education, 6,* 193-200.

Weitzman, M., Klerman, L., Menary, J., & Alpert, J. (1982). School absence: A problem for the pediatrician. *Pediatrics, 69,* 739-746.

Wolpe, J. (1958). *Psychotherapy by reciprocal inhibition.* Stanford: Stanford University Press.

Yule, W. (1977). Behavioural approaches. In M. Rutter and L. Hersov (Eds.), *Child psychiatry: Modern approaches* (pp. 923-948). Oxford: Blackwell.

27

Designing Interventions for Stealing

Gloria E. Miller
Ronald J. Prinz
University of South Carolina

Recent years have given rise to greater public and professional concern about the adverse impact of childhood stealing. There is a need for more research or effective assessment and treatment strategies for this common yet poorly understood antisocial behavior in childhood. This chapter is designed to provide an overview of the available empirical work concerning childhood stealing with an emphasis on issues critical to intervention and prevention in the schools.

NATURE AND SCOPE OF JUVENILE STEALING

Nonconfrontative stealing (i.e., taking personal objects, money, or property from buildings without direct contact with a victim) in children is one of the most difficult referral problems faced by educational and mental health professionals. Nonconfrontative property crimes that come to the attention of legal authorities are labeled theft or burglary, and are distinguished from assaultive theft (i.e., robbery). In the latest revision of the Diagnostic and Statistical Manual of Mental Disorders (DSM III–R), a single incident of nonconfrontative stealing within a 6-month period is the most discriminating diagnostic feature of childhood conduct disorder (American Psychiatric Association, 1987).

While most of the literature concerned with childhood conduct disorders has focused on overt problem behavior (e.g., aggression, noncompliance), scholars and clinicians have emphasized the need to make distinctions between overt and covert antisocial behavior (Kazdin, 1988). This trend is due in part to recent work indicating that childhood conduct disorder falls along an overt to covert continuum (Kazdin & Esveldt-Dawson, 1986; Loeber & Schmaling, 1985a, 1985b) and that covert and overt antisocial behaviors may have different symptom progression patterns (Kolko & Kazdin, 1986; Loeber, 1988; Patterson, 1982, 1986). Such work has given rise to research addressing key questions related to the etiology and treatment of nonconfrontative stealing in children.

Although nonconfrontative theft is considered the most pervasive class of juvenile crime (Belson, 1975; West & Farrington, 1973), it is difficult to assess the extent of the problem in our society. Few studies have specifically documented the prevalence or incidence of stealing behavior in the community or in the schools (Harris, Gray, Rees-McGee, Carroll, & Zaremba, 1987; Hutton, 1985). Not surprisingly, 40-70% of children referred to clinical settings evidence moderate to severe stealing behavior, which is identified more frequently in older than younger clinic children (Patterson, 1982). Other studies give some indication of the extent of the problem in the normal population. Estimates based on the "Isle of Wight" epidemiological study (Rutter, Tizard, & Whitmore, 1970) suggest that approximately 3% of teachers and 4% of parents of young children have concerns about serious childhood stealing. Other sources, however, have yielded results that suggest higher incidences of theft. On self-report surveys, a majority of adolescents admit to high levels of petty theft during childhood (Belson, 1975; Gold, 1970; Hood & Sparks, 1970). At the national level, 54% of all criminal arrests in 1987 of children aged 15 or under were for theft or burglary offenses (Uniform Crime Reports; U.S. Federal Bureau of Investigation, 1987). This figure reflected a substantial increase over the preceding 5 years. Finally, in a national survey of teachers' and students' perceptions of crime in schools (The Safe School Study), nonconfrontative theft of personal property was cited as the major crime occurring in our elementary and secondary schools (National Institute of Education, 1977). An average of 1 of 8 teachers and 1 of 9 students reported incidents of stealing within any given month.

These statistics probably underestimate the actual number of thefts committed by youth. Countless incidents are never reported in educational and community settings, particularly if the value of the stolen items is small. Nonetheless, there is a substantial body of literature concerning the dire consequences associated with excessive childhood stealing. The findings of both retrospective and prospective studies have shown that stealing persists across childhood and into adulthood (Anderson, 1984; Graham & Rutter, 1973; Mitchell & Rosa, 1981; Olweus, 1979; Robins & Radcliff, 1979). Moreover, a strong relationship has been found between stealing and long-term social maladjustment (Loeber, 1982; Robins, 1978; Robins & Radcliff, 1979; Rutter & Giller, 1983), delinquency, and adult criminality (Patterson, 1982, 1986; West & Farrington, 1973). Most alarming is the fact that young children who evidence stealing concomitantly with overt aggression are at significantly higher risk for later involvement with police than children referred for social aggression alone (Moore, Chamberlain, & Mukai,

1979; Patterson, 1982). The immediate repercussions of excessive stealing and other covert antisocial behavior (e.g., lying, firesetting) include academic skills deficits and peer rejection (Kolko, Kazdin, & Meyer, 1985; Patterson, 1986; Patterson & Dishion, 1985; Pink, 1982; Polk, Frease, & Richmond, 1974; Rutter et al., 1970; Stouthamer-Loeber, 1986).

Juvenile stealing behavior also has severe effects in the community. Theft committed by juveniles under age 15 results in billions of dollars of loss to victims each year (U.S. Federal Bureau of Investigation, 1987). Moreover, victims of theft experience significant psychological distress, similar in nature to that observed in victims of assault (Wirtz & Harrell, 1987). Beyond individual repercussions, high levels of juvenile antisocial behavior including theft in school and in the community negatively impact upon social climate variables such as staff morale, student respect for authority, student achievement, and student and staff affiliation (National Institute of Education, 1977; Olson, 1981; Rubel, 1980). Finally, a greater incidence of truancy, drug use, and vandalism is found in schools and communities characterized by high levels of theft, disruption, and vandalism (Baker, 1979; Mayer & Butterworth, 1979; Mott, 1986; Rubel, 1980).

ETIOLOGY OF STEALING

According to the *symptom progression model* of delinquency conceptualized by Patterson (1982, 1986), adolescent delinquency results from a breakdown of social learning processes within the family during childhood. Deficient family management practices produce an increase in low-intensity, high-frequency antisocial behavior in children in the home (noncompliance, defiance, aggression), and subsequent impairment in their social and academic development. The cumulative effects of these outcomes put these children at greater risk for academic failure, disengagement from the family, and future contact with a deviant peer group. These factors combined with continued ineffective parenting subsequently contribute to the emergence of high-intensity, low-frequency antisocial acts (stealing, truancy, firesetting).

Support for this model has been found in several studies specifically designed to assess interactional patterns in the families of stealers. In contrast to families of normal children or children referred solely for overt aggression, the parents of children referred for stealing have been characterized by detachment and a lack of involvement that results in substantially lower reinforcement for appropriate behavior and poorer monitoring of their children's whereabouts and activities (Loeber & Schmaling, 1985a; Reid & Hendricks, 1973). This detached parenting style has been posed as a major factor in the development of stealing (Loeber, Weissman, & Reid, 1983; Patterson, 1982; Reid & Patterson, 1976) and other antisocial behavior (Farrington, 1973; Patterson & Stouthamer-Loeber, 1984; Wilson, 1980). Wahler and Dumas (1987) have found that children who experience inconsistent and unpredictable adult monitoring may actually increase their level of misbehavior as a means of decreasing such unpredictability. This work is consistent with reports of higher levels of criminality in schools and communities characterized by inconsistent discipline and insufficient adult monitoring (Baker, 1979; Rubel, 1980).

Severe stressors in a family have also been associated with a greater persistence of antisocial behavior in children (Emery, 1982; Rutter & Giller, 1983). The *deviant vulnerability hypotheses* states that children with financial, home, or school problems have an increased susceptibility to antisocial behavior (Polk & Schafter, 1972). Similarly, severely stressful school or community environments are characterized by greater levels of disruption and criminal behavior (Baker, 1979). Goodyear, Kolvin, and Gatzanis (1985, 1987) recently reported that clinically referred conduct-disordered youths who exhibited high levels of theft had experienced a greater number of stressful events in the 12 months prior to referral than had children exhibiting other clinical symptoms. Stressful life events can significantly

affect personal relationships, alter interactional patterns, and lead to reductions in adult discipline and monitoring that may set the stage for increased antisocial behavior in children.

Finally, according to one sociological theory of juvenile delinquency, children may become involved in delinquent acts because of a weakening commitment to a conventional set of community values (Braithwaite & Braithwaite, 1981; Hirschi, 1969). Such environments often are characterized by an absence of clear and consistent rules that forbid moral transgressions. A child who frequently observes peers or significant adults enjoying the profits from theft without experiencing any negative consequences will be reinforced vicariously for stealing (Belson, 1975; Kniveton, 1986).

OBSTACLES TO THE ASSESSMENT OF STEALING

Problems with Common Assessment Procedures

Needless to say, the covert and sporadic characteristics of stealing create difficulty for most common assessment procedures (Miller & Moncher, 1988). Official records are unreliable estimates of stealing by young children because most offenses are diverted from the justice system and because arrest and subsequent conviction practices are biased by a child's age, family background, and other personal characteristics (Fisher & Mawby, 1982). For example, thefts by older black males are more likely to be recorded officially than those of other offender groups. Direct observation strategies are generally inefficient modes of assessment of stealing behavior because most childhood thievery is discovered after the fact and because observation might inhibit or at least delay the commission of theft (Buckle & Farrington, 1984). Alternatively, the legality of "detection methods" such as student searches or situations that "set up" a student to steal has been questioned as a means of identifying theft or other criminal behaviors in the schools

(Miller & Klungness, 1989; Sendor, 1987; Stevens, 1980).

Self- and third-party reports are the most common techniques for assessing theft behavior. Although self-report represents the most effective strategy for evaluating stealing and other covert antisocial behaviors, current self-report measures of problem behavior do not assess the severity or patterns of stealing and are of questionable reliability and validity with young children (Hardt & Peterson-Hardt, 1977; Miller & Moncher, 1988; Prout & Chizik, 1988). Reliance on third-party reports by adults or peers who hold central roles in a child's social system poses a problem, because many instances of stealing in young children are ignored. Moreover, neither parents nor teachers typically possess the knowledge to report on external cues (e.g., vulnerable shopping locations) or internal cues (e.g., need for approval) that are functionally related to stealing across many settings, and it is not always clear which or how many informants should be chosen to obtain the most valid information.

Unclear Guidelines

In preschoolers, isolated incidents of stealing are not necessarily cause for alarm, since very young children may not recognize that taking something belonging to someone else is wrong (Eisenberg, Shell, Pasternack, Lennon, & Mathy, 1987; Hartup, 1974). It is likely that stealing emerges and passes as part of many children's social development. There is ample evidence, however, that problematic stealing does exist in children as young as age 4 years (Achenbach & Edelbrock, 1978). Unfortunately, there are few established guidelines as to when stealing behavior becomes problematic. Even single incidents of stealing identified in a school may require careful attention to assess the likelihood of a serious stealing pattern. Frequency, severity, a variety of other conduct problems appearing in childhood, and the occurrence of stealing across various settings are significant factors in the continuation of antisocial behavior (Loeber, 1982, 1988;

Patterson, 1982; Rutter & Giller, 1983). More direct and immediate intervention efforts may be necessary when several of these features are uncovered during assessment.

Problems in Targeting the Behavior

Theft behavior is difficult to identify with consistency. Rarely is there consensus as to what constitutes a theft. Such behavior often is socially defined by a child's caretakers or by the victim of the offense. Adults often excuse stealing in young children because they attribute it to immaturity (Renshaw, 1979). Stealing also is likely to be ignored if the actual or perceived value of the stolen item is small. Children's alternative explanations of stealing (e.g., "I borrowed it"; "I found it"; "It was a gift") are accepted without a question, especially in situations where a theft is difficult to confirm (Reid, 1975). Reluctance to label taking others' possessions as stealing may be due to the fact that adults view stealing as a more deviant problem than other more socially accepted child misbehavior (Reid & Patterson, 1976; Vidoni, Fleming, & Mintz, 1983; Wilson, 1980). Professionals and parents may hesitate to label a theft as stealing because of ethical and legal concerns about the stigma attached to labeling a child as a thief (Miller & Klungness, 1989).

Reluctance to label stealing decreases somewhat after a child enters into a formal educational setting (Weger, 1987). However, it is a common practice for educators to relabel or ignore stealing to avoid police intervention and the possibility of a negative community image (Baker, 1979). Consequently, there is an underreporting of theft infractions in schools and an increased likelihood that referrals for problematic stealing will occur only after a prolonged and persistent stealing pattern has been confirmed. Unfortunately, school practices that allow incidents of stealing to go unnoticed promote the belief among children that stealing (as well as other antisocial acts) is readily tolerated in the school setting (Olson, 1981; Zakariya, 1987).

Limited Information on Factors that Promote Stealing

The assessment of stealing is hindered by our limited knowledge of personal characteristics or social domains that place a child at risk either for initial stealing or continued patterns of stealing. Researchers have begun to identify factors that increase a child's participation in stealing and more generalized types of delinquency over time (Kelson & Stewart, 1986; Loeber, 1988). For example, stealing is more likely to continue into adolescence when a child engages in other covert antisocial behaviors such as lying, drug use, truancy, and firesetting (Loeber & Schmaling, 1985a, 1985b). Different patterns of problem behavior exhibited during childhood relate to continued stealing (Kolko & Kazdin, 1986; Loeber, 1988; Loeber & Schmaling, 1985a, 1985b; Patterson, 1982, 1986). Stealing may emerge as one of the final links in a chain of antisocial problems that begin with overt aggression in early childhood. Children who exhibit early noncompliance and aggression and later covert antisocial behavior, such as stealing, may be most at risk for serious delinquency as adolescents (Patterson, 1982). Finally, children who have problems of aggression and stealing (or other covert antisocial behaviors such as firesetting) have been found to be less socially skilled (Kolko et al., 1985), to be less likely over the long-term to put an end to their antisocial behavior, and to exhibit more problematic family interaction patterns and less receptiveness to treatment than children who exhibit exclusively overt antisocial behavior (Loeber, 1988).

ASSESSMENT RECOMMENDATIONS

Employ an Ecobehavioral Approach

The assessment of a child's stealing behavior necessitates an ecobehavioral approach (Rogers-Warren, 1984) in which stealing is evaluated across home, school, and community settings to foster a comprehensive understanding of the factors that contribute to stealing. An ecobehavioral analysis goes beyond a typical child behavioral analysis by considering many settings and systems. A wide range of antecedent and consequent events are assessed across the child's major life domains, and attention is given to how these variables interact to influence the child's behavior (Martens & Witt, 1988; Wahler & Fox, 1981). Sensitivity to developmental expectations is required, because factors contributing to covert antisocial behavior at early ages may differ from influences at later ages (Kolko, 1987). For example, while parents' inattention may be an important promoter of stealing in young children, peer attitudes may become an important factor during adolescence.

Ecobehavioral assessment involves multiple methods. Biases associated with one assessment method are overcome when a variety of assessment techniques are employed across the child's home, school, and community environments. A comprehensive identification of specific patterns and functional aspects of stealing requires that information be gathered from parents, teachers, peers, and the target child through the use of interviews, standardized measures, and formal and informal ratings. Although interrater agreement is desirable, high agreement should not be expected with covert behaviors such as stealing (Cone, 1979). In fact, when two sources conflict, further examination should be made of the distinct contingencies operating in each environment (Kazdin & Esveldt-Dawson, 1986). When stealing is noted at home but not at school, it is important to assess, for example, whether parental attention is maintaining stealing at home while the child is receiving sufficient peer and adult attention at school without resorting to stealing.

Use Consistent Labels

An initial goal of assessment is the adoption of a consistent label for stealing behavior that addresses suspected stealing acts. We agree with the suggestions of Patterson, Reid, Jones, and Conger (1975) that stealing should be defined as the possession by the child of *anything* other than that which specifically belongs to him or her, regardless of the worth of the stolen item. Such a comprehensive and objective definition increases the probability that a behavior will be labeled consistently as stealing; but it also may heighten the chance of including nontheft acts. Therefore, considerable consultation and reassurance to parents and teachers will be necessary to alleviate concerns that employing such an overinclusive definition of stealing will subject a child to undue scrutiny. Adult resistance to the accurate labeling of stealing might be lowered and more accurate diagnostic information might be obtained by focusing the assessment initially on behavior problems viewed as less serious, such as noncompliance or verbal outbursts.

Determine the Severity of Stealing

Once a consistent definition for stealing is adopted, information should be gathered from all significant adults in the child's life to determine the severity of the stealing problem and to gather precise behavioral information regarding past and current antisocial and oppositional behaviors. Assessment should focus on how long the child has been stealing, how frequently, and whether there has been evidence of stealing in different settings. As stated earlier, because stealing has been shown to cluster with other antisocial behaviors (Loeber & Schmaling, 1985a, 1985b), inquiries should also assess other problem behaviors besides stealing. Histories should be obtained on all overt and covert behavioral problems that the child has exhibited (e.g., aggression, lying), since evidence about time of onset and sequencing of significant behavior problems can assist in determining the severity of the child's present stealing problem (Kazdin & Esveldt-Dawson, 1986; Loeber & Schmaling, 1985a, 1985b).

Conduct a Child-Focused Interview

The next step in the assessment process is a thorough interview of the child. In such interviews, children should be asked what typically occurs imme-

diately *before* and *after* an instance of stealing. It is important to assess their motoric, cognitive, and physiological responses (Cone, 1979). Children should be encouraged to describe a typical stealing incident. As a part of this description, they should be asked what they did, how they felt, and what they thought immediately before and after completing a theft. Comprehensive examination of such descriptions is useful for designing individualized interventions that focus on changing particular response patterns (Haug et al., 1987). A cognitive-behavioral intervention might be indicated for children who engage in stealing when angry with an adult or peer, whereas relaxation training may be more appropriate for children who report high levels of anxiety of arousal when engaged in stealing.

Children also should be asked specific questions about where, when, and with whom stealing occurs, as well as about the type of objects taken. In addition, perception of the reinforcement received from stealing should be clarified. Such information can be obtained through questions that address what happens to the stolen item, who typically discovers the thefts, and what usually happens once a theft is discovered. For example, adult attention, a potent reinforcer for many young children, may be a factor if adults often are lured into listening to a child's excuses and explanations for stealing. Peer acceptance is a secondary source of reinforcement for stealing, especially when peers receive tangible benefits from the thefts (e.g., the thief gives away stolen candy) or condone antisocial behavior. Analyses of factors that contribute to the stealing will help to isolate particular circumstances and conditions that influence and maintain stealing behavior.

A child's motives for stealing also should be evaluated. Kolko (1987) described motives for firesetting that are pertinent to stealing. Children may steal out of curiosity or because they desire peer acceptance and improved social status. Children also steal because they feel they need or deserve an unaffordable item either for themselves or as a gift for someone else. Finally, some children will engage in antisocial behavior because they intend to damage, to harm, to get retribution, or to get public attention. Unfortunately, there is little evidence that knowledge about a child's motives for stealing contributes meaningfully to effective intervention. However, adolescents' perceptions of mitigating circumstances have been found to affect their decisions to condone illegal acts (Brown & Lalljee, 1981). Such findings lend support to the idea that assessments of a child's reasons for stealing may uncover possible maintaining events or situations.

A final element of a child-focused interview should be evaluations of the child's ability to appraise and process social information effectively during conflict situations. Researchers have identified important deficiencies in antisocial in contrast with normal children's problem-solving abilities that have a direct impact upon their control of unacceptable behavior and expression of empathy toward victims (Dodge, 1980; Dodge & Frame, 1982; Milich & Dodge, 1984; Spivack & Shure, 1982). For example, when faced with a social conflict (e.g., another child breaks into the front of a line), antisocial children are more likely to attribute such behavior to hostile intent and are less likely to generate a variety of responses to such provocation. Cognitive-behavioral training programs have been used successfully in the remediation of such deficiencies (Kazdin, 1987; Lochman, 1985; Lochman, Nelson, & Sims, 1981; Shure, Spivack, & Jaeger, 1972). In light of this work, children's social-cognitive appraisals of theft incidents and the outcomes associated with their theft behavior should be assessed to identify possible avenues for cognitive-behavioral interventions. Vignettes describing another child's motives for and responses to theft could be read or theft situations could be role-played. These procedures could be used to obtain information about children's effective decision-making and problem-solving processes in social situations involving theft (Brown & Lalljee, 1981; Furnham & Jones, 1987; Kohlberg, 1976).

Assess a Child's Social Status

A comprehensive assessment of stealing also must focus on the child's social status especially in the school and the community. Observations and sociometric ratings can be employed to provide critical information regarding children's social status in these environments (Krehbiel & Milich, 1986). Knowledge of their social status provides important information about their ability to interact with adults and peers. Children with poor peer relations may engage in stealing to improve status within a peer group. In such cases, interaction may best focus on improved social skills in addition to the reduction of stealing.

It is important to note that a child's social status may be altered as a consequence of repeated stealing. One reason for this is that stealing typically is viewed by peers and adults as more deviant than other misbehavior (Alston, 1980; Loeber & Stouthamer-Loeber, 1986; Stouthamer-Loeber, 1986; Vidoni et al., 1983). Furthermore, the negative labeling of children as troublemakers in reaction to stealing has been shown to affect the amount of contingent adult and peer attention a child receives for both prosocial and antisocial behaviors (Reid, 1975). Such negative labeling has been associated with a deviant self-concept, poor self-esteem (Gibbs, 1974; Kulka, Klingel, & Mann, 1980; Pink, 1982), and increased involvement in criminal acts during adolescence (Farrington, 1977). Although it is not known if such effects generalize to children's stealing behavior in school settings, there is clearly a need for routine assessment of a child's reputation and relationships with adults and peers following even one stealing incident. Direct interventions to reduce the negative effects of a child's reputation as a thief will be necessary when a child's social status has been significantly affected.

Focus on Environmental Conditions

Given the factors named earlier that go into the etiology of stealing, it is critical that assessments of stealing routinely focus on environmental conditions in the child's home and community. Specific evaluations should be made of the quality of adult–child relationships, the consistency and frequency of adults' contingent attention for both prosocial and problem behavior, and the amount of unsupervised time a child experiences. This information can be obtained through parent interviews and observations of parent–child interaction. Additionally, a comprehensive evaluation must highlight the type, number, and timing of stressful events that may have occurred in the child's life. Information regarding the negative impact of such events is best obtained by asking children to give their personal appraisals of each stressful event (Goodyear, Kolvin, & Gratzanis, 1985, 1987). Two areas that must be assessed are the child's exposure to stealing (and other antisocial behavior) in the community or home, and possible involvement with delinquent peers (Dunford & Elliott, 1984; Klemke, 1982; Robins, 1978). Moreover, to identify circumstances in which stealing is implicitly reinforced, existing attitudes and social rules toward theft and dishonesty in the child's home and community must be documented as part of the assessment process (Kelson & Stewart, 1986; Miller & Klungness, 1989; Weger, 1985). Finally, differences in social conventions in regard to the use of personal property should be clarified across the child's school and home environments. While "borrowing a person's hairbrush without asking" might be a routine behavior at home, where all personal belongings are jointly owned, such behavior is often not tolerated at school. Intervention efforts in such cases would most likely include consultation to clarify acceptable behavioral norms across settings.

INTERVENTIONS FOR STEALING

In spite of the rising concern about stealing behavior in children and youths, there has been a paucity of well-controlled research evaluating interventions that focus directly on stealing. The multifaceted nature of covert antisocial behaviors and the obstacles encountered in assessment pose a considerable challenge for designing effective interventions. The majority of empirically evaluated interventions fall within a behavioral framework and include (a) contingency management techniques, (b) child-focused self-control procedures, and (c) parent training (Miller & Klungness, 1986).

Contingency Management Techniques

Disciplinary techniques such as scolding, lecturing, and physical punishment are among the most frequently reported procedures employed to eliminate stealing (and other misbehavior) in children. The usefulness and effectiveness of such procedures is questionable, however, since most assessments are based on anecdotal reports. In addition, numerous ethical questions arise regarding their use (Martin, 1975; Sulzer-Azaroff & Mayer, 1977). In contrast, empirical support has been demonstrated for behavioral contingency management techniques that utilize aversive procedures (i.e., covert sensitization, restitution or overcorrection, and time-out) or combine aversive and positive behavioral techniques (e.g., response cost and token or differential reinforcement) to eliminate stealing.

Covert sensitization. During covert sensitization, clients learn by imagination accurate aversive consequences with the stimuli that trigger stealing in order to foster avoidance of such undesirable behavior. Typically, they are asked to imagine an extremely noxious situation (e.g., intense embarrassment or gross vomiting) immediately after visualizing a sequence of events leading up to a stealing incident. This procedure has been applied most successfully in reducing the stealing behavior of adolescents and young adults (Cautela, 1973; Guidry, 1975). Guidry treated the stealing behavior of a young adult male by having him imagine a stealing sequence followed by a highly aversive imagined consequence. The client practiced these imaginal scenes at regular times during the day (e.g., getting in and out of his car). Stealing was successfully eliminated from an average rate of two times per month, and the client had maintained these changes at a 10-month follow-up. The advantage of a covert sensitization procedure rests with the fact that self-imposed aversive consequences can be applied immediately and consistently. However, the use of this procedure with young children is questionable, not only because of its exclusive focus on antisocial behavior and reliance on aversive procedures, but also because the effectiveness of covert sensitization depends upon a child's ability to employ cognitive imagery processes.

Time-out and restitutional procedures. During a time-out procedure, children are removed from a reinforcing environment upon the occurrence of an inappropriate behavior. In this procedure, they lose the chance to obtain positive reinforcement for a specified period of time. Time-out procedures may be especially effective when assessment data have revealed the possibility that stealing is being maintained by attention from adults or peers. Time-out was employed successfully to eliminate mealtime stealing by mentally retarded adults in one well-controlled study conducted in a residential setting (Barton, Guess, Garcia, & Baer, 1970). In that study, an offender was temporarily removed from the dinner table after each theft of food. Such an exclusionary time-out procedure was found to reduce overall stealing of food across all residents and led to increases in several other associated positive mealtime behaviors. However, in the absence of functional assessment data linking the occurrence of stealing with attention or some other reinforcer, this procedure may be more accurately termed removal from the environment than time-out.

Dramatic reductions in food theft by institutionalized mentally retarded adults also has been obtained from both simple restitutional (Azrin & Armstrong, 1973) and overcorrection restitutional procedures (Azrin & Wesolowski, 1974). In a simple restitutional procedure, an offender is required to replace or return to the victim the stolen item. In an overcorrection restitutional procedure, the offender is expected to return the stolen item and to compensate the victim further in some way. Although both restitutional procedures were effective in reducing the food theft behavior, Azrin and Wesolowski (1974) concluded that overcorrection procedures led to faster and more long-term changes than simple restitutional procedures.

There are problems in recommending the exclusive use of covert sensitization, time-out, and restitutional procedures to eliminate stealing in children. While the success of these behavioral procedures has been documented with older special populations, there are few data on their effectiveness with children in general educational settings. Moreover, few studies have demonstrated generalizable changes or long-term reductions in stealing. Many questions remain about the negative side-effects produced by these procedures. And legal and ethical challenges have consistently been raised regarding the application of aversive control procedures in school settings (Martin, 1975; Miller & Klungness, 1986). Finally, and most importantly, interventions that focus solely on the reduction of stealing may eliminate a major source of reinforcement for the child. Without adequate replacement of alternative sources of reinforcement, there is strong likelihood that stealing will reappear (Reid, 1975).

Combined positive and aversive approaches. The most appropriate behavioral contingency management interventions are those that focus on the development of prosocial in addition to the elimination of antisocial behaviors (Sulzer-Azaroff & Mayer, 1977). These combined interventions guard against a significant loss of reinforcement when stealing is eliminated from the child's repertoire. Typically, positive contingency management approaches (e.g., token programs, differential reinforcement) are combined with aversive procedures (e.g., time-out, restitution). For example, Kolko (1987) combined token reinforcers to increase a young child's receptivity to parental efforts with an overcorrection procedure to eliminate his serious firesetting behavior.

The most successful contingency management interventions for eliminating stealing in children have been those that combine differential reinforcement with response cost procedures. During the process of differential reinforcement of other behavior (DRO), a reinforcer is delivered that is contingent upon the occurrence of any presumably prosocial behavior other than stealing; whereas with a differential reinforcement of alternative behavior (DRA) procedure, a reinforcer is delivered upon the occurrence of any one of a specific set of behaviors assumed to be incompatible with stealing behavior. Response cost procedures involve the contingent removal of a specified amount of positive reinforcement after the occurrence of stealing. The combined use of response cost and positive reinforcement speeds up intervention effects, as Sulzer-Azaroff and Mayer (1977) have noted.

Rosen and Rosen (1983) obtained substantial reductions in the stealing behavior of a first-grade boy with a combined DRO and response cost procedure. All of the boy's possessions were marked with a green dot, and periodic checks were made of his possessions during the school day. Tokens, exchangeable for desirable activities and praise, served as the reinforcers and were administered when only marked items were found. Verbal reprimands and a one-token fine were administered for his possession of each unmarked item. Initial reductions in stealing were maintained during 31 days of follow-up. Similar reductions in stealing were reported for such a combined intervention by Wetzel (1966).

Combined response cost and differential reinforcement interventions were adapted for use in the classroom by Brooks and Snow (1972) in situations in which the thief was known, and by Switzer, Deal, and Bailey (1977) when the thief was not known. In the Brooks and Snow study, a DRA token reinforcement plan was combined with a response cost procedure to eliminate the stealing behavior of a 10-year-old boy. Several target behaviors incompatible with the stealing behavior (e.g., class participation, work completion) were chosen for reinforcement, and the identified thief earned or lost tokens for occurrence or nonoccurrence of these classroom behaviors. Any tokens remaining at the end of the class were then exchanged for an individual reward and extra free time for the entire class. In the Switzer et al. study, DRO and response cost procedures were combined and administered as a group contingency because the teachers were unable to determine which children were responsible for a series of classroom thefts. A number of desirable objects (e.g., pens, small toys) were randomly distributed throughout the classroom, and the presence of these items was checked systematically throughout the day. When all of the items remained intact, the class was rewarded with extra free time. Class free time was lost if items were determined to be missing and were not returned after one prompt by the teacher.

This limited research clearly supports the efficacy of a combined differential reinforcement and response cost intervention for reducing stealing in children of elementary school-age. The ease with which these procedures can be adapted for use in classrooms adds to their utility as effective school treatments. However, the generalizability to older children, the substantial investment of time by teachers or other adults, and the questionable acceptability and legality of these interventions (i.e., especially the use of student searches) may hinder their applicability in the schools (Miller & Klungness, 1986).

Self-control Procedures

Self-control interventions designed to alter internal stimulus events have been used to reduce stealing. These include (a) relaxation training (Goldfried, 1971), during which children are taught to progressively relax during events that stimulate stealing; (b) self-monitoring (Kanfer, 1970), during which children learn to record and evaluate their own performance in response to real (or imagined) situations that prompt stealing; and (c) self-instruction (Meichenbaum &

Goodman, 1971) during which children learn to employ a problem-solving self-verbalization strategy when faced with the temptation to steal. Such interventions emphasize change in the way the children typically think about and approach situations involving stealing behavior.

When combined with other behavioral procedures (e.g., response cost, token reinforcement), self-control treatments have led to substantial immediate and long-term reductions in theft (Haines, Jackson, & Davidson, 1983; Henderson, 1981, 1983; Stumphauzer, 1976). For example, Henderson (1981, 1983) combined relaxation, biofeedback, and self-monitoring techniques with a family-based token reinforcement procedure in which specific reinforcers were selected to substitute for the theft behavior. In a series of case reports, this multicomponent program was found to reduce the theft behaviors of students aged 8-15 years for follow-up periods ranging from 2½ to 5 years. In another multicomponent self-control intervention, Stumphauzer (1976) combined self-monitoring and self-instruction with consultation with parents and a home-based token program to reduce a 12-year-old girl's stealing. The child was taught to record instances of stealing and to employ self-verbalization to monitor, evaluate, and reinforce her performance when faced with real and imagined theft temptations. Significant reductions in stealing were reported after 15 individual sessions that were supplemented with consultations with her parents; these behavioral changes were maintained over an 18-month follow-up. Finally, Haines et al. (1983) taught fourth- and fifth-grade children to resist stealing by internalizing a series of problem solving statements that focused on the consideration of the owner's feelings. Significant improvements in children's resistance to stealing in hypothetical vignettes posing temptations were reported after several sessions of this self-instruction training, and these improvements were maintained over a 3-month period.

Clearly, the preliminary work with self-control procedures points to the efficacy of these approaches in facilitating improvement in children's cognitive and behavioral responses to stealing. The strength of self-control interventions rests with the fact that such procedures foster independent regulation, which in turn may improve chances of long-term and generalized reduction in stealing. Unfortunately, in all of the studies to date, because self-control interventions were employed simultaneously with other treatment approaches (e.g., parent consultation, token programs), the specific contribution of the self-control procedures in fostering changes in children's stealing behavior remains unknown.

Parent Training

Many researchers have stressed the need for family-based approaches to treat severe behavior problems in children effectively (Kazdin, 1985, 1987; Patterson, 1982). These approaches are based on the assumption noted earlier that children's antisocial behavior is sustained by dysfunctional interactions in their major life environments. The primary emphasis of these interventions is (a) to enhance parent–child communication, and (b) to improve adults' child management skills. Typically, parents are taught to employ effective conflict resolution and negotiation skills (e.g., how to express feelings, use of "I" statements, joint problem-solving), to observe and record their children's prosocial and antisocial behaviors, and to respond contingently and consistently to such behaviors through the application of social learning techniques (e.g., social and tangible reinforcement, extinction, time-out, response cost, and effective punishment procedures). Extensive discussion, modeling, role-playing, guided practice, and home practice are employed to teach these skills.

Although there is clear evidence in support of such comprehensive family interventions for a wide range of child problem behaviors (see reviews by Forehand & Atkenson, 1977; by Griest & Wells, 1983; and by Kazdin, 1985, 1987), modifications have been necessary to improve effectiveness for families with children who steal. The rationale for advocating modifications to family interventions rests on the significant differences observed in parent-child interactions and child management skills between the parents of typical or aggressive children and the parents of children who steal (Loeber & Dishion, 1983; Loeber, Weissman, & Reid, 1983; Miller, Ricker, Prinz, & Davenport, 1988; Patterson, 1982; Reid & Hendricks, 1973). Intervention modifications have included (a) the use of weekly payments to parents that are contingent on adequate participation (i.e., the parent receives money for attending scheduled appointments and bringing completed homework), (b) daily phone contacts (i.e., the therapist calls each day to get information about the child's behavior from the parent), and (c) the addition of preliminary sessions to improve parents' monitoring of their children's behavior (i.e., the first few sessions focus exclusively on the accurate labeling of stealing and how to track and record instances of particular behaviors) (Patterson et al., 1975; Reid & Patterson, 1976). Such treatment modifications have led to increased participation on the part of the parents and to better child and family results (Patterson & Reid, 1973; Reid & Hendricks, 1973; Reid & Patterson, 1976).

Further enhancement of treatment may be necessary when working with multiproblem families in which the children who steal display chronic patterns of overt and covert antisocial behavior, the parents report severe personal or marital maladjustment, or the family suffers extreme socioeconomic distress (Blechman, 1984; Dumas, 1984; Forehand & Brody, 1985; Kazdin, 1987; Wahler & Dumas, 1987; Wahler, 1980b; Webster-Stratton, 1985). Adjunctive treatments, such as personal, marital, and financial counseling, have been added to traditional social learning family interventions to promote greater initial and long-term gains (Blechman, 1981; Campbell, O'Brien, Bickett, & Lutzker, 1983; Dadds, Schwartz, & Sanders, 1987; Griest et al., 1982). Another adjunctive procedure, called mand review, or more recently *synthesis training*, has been offered as a potentially effective method for improving long-term

outcomes in multiproblem families (Wahler & Dumas, 1987, 1989). Parents are seen for traditional family intervention, but also participate in guided discussions designed to foster a recognition of the relationship between their exposure to "daily hassles" within family or in the community (e.g., having an argument with a husband, neighbor, or boss) and subsequent behavior toward their child. Mothers of severely distressed families who received such adjunctive sessions evidenced more consistent and positive parent–child interactions immediately after treatment and greater maintenance of treatment gains than mothers who received only a traditional social learning family intervention. Finally, researchers have suggested that an integration of behavioral and strategic (e.g., reframing, paradoxical intention) family intervention techniques may be needed to effectively serve multiproblem or resistive families (Spinks & Birchler, 1982; Szykula, Morris, Sudweeks, & Sayger, 1987; Teichman & Eliahu, 1986). Unfortunately, such comprehensive and multisystemic parent training procedures may be beyond the scope of school personnel because of practical constraints and limited skills.

Methodological Concerns with Past Research

Recommendations regarding behavioral management, self-control, and parent training interventions that are designed to eliminate childhood stealing must be tempered because of several general methodological concerns. The use of relatively small samples and uncontrolled case study designs in many studies make it difficult to draw specific causal connections between the administration of an intervention and the reduction of stealing. Moreover, little information typically is given about the characteristics of the referred children or the families employed in these studies, making it difficult to assess how individual characteristics of parents and children affect intervention outcomes, to decide which intervention to choose over another, or to compare effectiveness across interventions. Many questions remain regarding the social validity, generalizability, and long-term effectiveness of these interventions.

INTERVENTION RECOMMENDATIONS

Seven criteria are offered as essential considerations in designing interventions for childhood and adolescent stealing: definitional consensus, consistency and immediacy of aversive consequences, inclusion of reinforcement contingencies, consideration of individual differences, reputation enhancement, involvement of significant adults, and the adoption of a broad ecological perspective. In the following sections, each criterion is discussed in terms of rationale and application.

Definitional Consensus

As mentioned earlier in the chapter, the design of a stealing intervention program must be based on a consensus definition of stealing that targets *known* as well as *suspected* incidents of theft. All involved adults must agree to employ an inclusive definition that places the burden of proof of nonstealing on the child. This method does not require the adults to "prove" the child's guilt. The primary rationale for an inclusive definition is that it is more important to identify all stealing acts than it is to adjudicate every event. In addition, attention to explanations offered by the child, arguments with the child, or routine searches of the child should be avoided because such adult behavior can serve as a potent source of secondary reinforcement for stealing (Reid & Patterson, 1976). Routine searches may increase a child's hostility and may violate an individual's constitutional right to protection against unreasonable searches without probable cause (Stevens, 1980; Trosch, Williams, & Devore, 1982). Although a recent United States Supreme Court decision upheld public school officials' right to search students and lockers when "reasonable grounds" exist (*New Jersey vs. T.L.O.*, 53 USLW 4038–1985), alternative identification procedures are recommended that are less likely to constitute an invasion of privacy. For example, adults should increase their familiarity with a child's daily routine and improve the monitoring of secretive behavior, departures from routine, free-time activities, and personal belongings (Patterson, 1982; Williams, 1985). Finally, routine consultation with parents and teachers is necessary to ensure definitional consensus, especially when adults are hesitant to label stealing or when conventions regarding the use of personal property differ across settings.

Consistency and Immediacy of Aversive Consequences

When stealing is detected or suspected, the child immediately should be told in clear and simple language that the item in question has been stolen. Because stealing is reinforced by possession of the stolen item, it is essential that appropriate negative consequences be applied as soon after a theft as possible. One obstacle to immediate implementation of consequences is delayed detection of stealing; to offset this difficulty a child can be taught self-control procedures to increase the likelihood of consistent and immediate application of consequences (Henderson, 1981). To this end, Reid and Patterson (1976) recommend the careful selection of appropriate and practical consequences (e.g., the loss of one morning of free play rather than a whole week). Moreover, negative consequences should be selected that are based on adult (Martens, Witt, Elliott, & Darveaux, 1985) and child (Turco & Elliott, 1986) perceptions of effectiveness, acceptability, and compatibility with preexisting routines and resources (Witt, Martens, & Elliott, 1984). See Chapter 5 for more detail on these topics. There is a greater likelihood that interventions will be utilized and maintained when they are less intrusive, less aversive, and more in keeping with normal classroom or home routines (Witt, 1986). Another strategy to ensure accurate and consistent application of consequences for stealing is to target a more visible "keystone" problem behavior known to occur along with or "set the stage for" stealing (Voeltz & Evans, 1982; Wahler, 1975). For example, if a child's stealing typically occurs right after recess, when the child is freely roaming in the hallway, efforts should be directed to reducing opportunities to wander alone. In this case, a buddy system for entering the building could be instituted, adult monitors could be present, or a class or group contingency could be employed to reinforce children for returning quickly to their rooms.

Inclusion of Reinforcement Contingencies

Reinforcement procedures for the development of specific prosocial behaviors are critical in conjunction with contingencies to reduce stealing. Such dual-focus interventions are seen as more educative and have a greater likelihood of fostering durable behavioral changes of increased social validity (Kazdin, 1977; Wolf, 1978). Precise prosocial behavior should be selected for reinforcement rather than targeting the absence of stealing. Absence of stealing makes a poor target for reinforcement with individual children because the nonoccurrence of covert behavior is difficult to confirm (Reid, 1975). Targeted prosocial behavior should be selected on the basis of the child's stated motives for stealing and the type of reinforcement the child obtains by engaging in stealing. For example, adults and peers can be taught to increase their attention toward the target child during prosocial activities when a child reports that "it feels good when I get" peer attention as a consequence of sharing stolen items. Efforts to improve specific prosocial skills that may provide a foundation for future social and academic success are highly desirable (e.g., sharing, complimenting, turn-taking) (Bierman, 1986; LaGreca & Santogrossi, 1980), academic skills (e.g., math, reading) (Haberman & Quinn, 1986; Polk et al., 1974), social cognitive processes (e.g., situational attributions, retrieval of social cues) (Dodge, 1980; Dodge & Frame, 1982;

Milich & Dodge, 1984), and social problem-solving (e.g., problem definition, coping strategies) (Kendall & Willcox, 1980; Meichenbaum & Goodman, 1971). Such prosocial behaviors may have the greatest potential for enhancing a child's overall academic progress and social status and preventing later maladjustment. Although interventions designed to alleviate deficiencies in these skills have been successful in reducing impulsive responding and overt aggression in children and adolescents (Kendall & Braswell, 1985; Kennedy, 1982; Lochman & Curry, 1986; Lochman et al., 1981; Meichenbaum, 1977; Michelson, 1987; Yu, Harris, Solovitz, & Franklin, 1986), little is known regarding the impact of such interventions on the reduction of covert behavior problems such as stealing.

Consideration of Individual Differences

Individual differences must be analyzed carefully in the selection of target behaviors and intervention strategies. There is a need to focus on the specific behavioral characteristics (e.g., reports of anxiety or excitement, what happens to stolen items) of the identified child rather than on deficits or behaviors assumed to be universal for all children who steal. For example, a covert desensitization intervention may be more effective than a reinforcement or punishment intervention for children who report high levels of physiological arousal prior to or following a theft. Past and current patterns of behavior also must be analyzed individually. Children with an early onset of overt misbehavior who currently evidence more varied and severe misbehaviors require more comprehensive and immediate treatment than children exhibiting other individual problem behaviors (Kulik, Stein, & Sarbin, 1968; Loeber, 1988; Loeber & Dishion, 1984). Moreover, the success of an intervention may be constrained by a child's age or level of cognitive ability. For example, self-monitoring strategies that require the ability to match to a standard and to judge whether a particular action has been carried out are generally ineffective with children below 5 years of age (Ollendick & Hersen, 1984).

Reputation Enhancement

A child's reputation as a thief is often a continuing problem long after stealing has been successfully eliminated. Because of this problem, Patterson (1982) and Reid (1975) maintain that interventions for stealing must be designed to eliminate not only the stealing behavior but also the child's reputation as a thief. Procedures to enhance a child's prosocial image and adult and peer relationships are an integral part of a comprehensive treatment for stealing. The target child can be enlisted to watch or transport valued items (e.g., a teacher's purse, a set of small toys) and then publicly reinforced for the safe return of the items. Alternatively, the child can be paired with a trustworthy peer and given charge of a major responsibility (e.g., collecting lunch money) or can be taught how to monitor and avoid situations that can lead to accusations of theft (e.g., walking in the halls alone, staying in the classroom after others have left).

Involvement of Significant Adults

Interventions must be designed to involve all major adults in the child's life. At a minimum, parents and teachers must come to a consensus regarding the identification of an act of thievery, the consequences for such incidents, and the adoption of improved strategies to monitor the child's freetime activties. Routine discussions should be held with the child about proposed plans, and consistent checks should be made of the outcome of these plans. The use of aids to facilitate adult supervision are recommended. For example, a check-in system could be employed where children would be expected to sign in upon arrival at class, work, or other activities. Another idea to enhance monitoring is to provide clearly posted schedules that clarify who is to be where and when. Consultants also must be sensitive to circumstances in which adults in the child's life require direct interventions to improve child management skills. Such interventions can be conducted with individuals or groups of parents or teachers. The concepts and basic elements of such interventions should include strategies (a) to reduce antisocial behaviors, (b) to foster appropriate prosocial behavior, and (c) to enhance communication and problem-solving interactions between adults and children (Blechman, 1987; Dumas, 1989; Patterson et al., 1975).

Adoption of Broad Ecological Perspective

Finally, it is likely that an ecobehavioral systems perspective will be necessary in effecting long-term and generalized behavioral changes in children who exhibit severe antisocial behaviors (Dumas & Albin, 1986; Griest & Wells, 1983; Henggeler, 1982; Martens & Witt, 1988; Miller & Prinz, in press; Rogers-Warren, 1977). Interventions that adopt this perspective must focus on variables in the child's major life domains (e.g., home, school, community) as well as on variables that affect interrelationships between these systems. Such multilevel interventions will require a synthesis of environment-focused (i.e., parent training, marital counseling) and child-focused (i.e., academic or social skills training) contingencies (Dumas, 1984, 1989; Kazdin, 1987; Sallis, 1983).

PREVENTION RECOMMENDATIONS

In contrast to direct interventions to reduce theft behavior in children, strategies to prevent occurrences of theft also are recommended. Theft prevention strategies can be organized into approaches that focus (a) on internal or sociological factors related to crime, such as the role of vicarious processes; (b) on the impact of students' attitudes and moral reasoning; and (c) on the effects of social climate variables (e.g., perceptions of fairness) in promoting antisocial behavior. Alternatively, prevention strategies can be developed that are based on external or situational conditions that relate to criminal behavior in children. For example, analyses could be made of documented crime patterns in order to get ideas for deterrence procedures; then more effective and obvious methods of deterrence could be adopted. Finally, objective behavior codes or rule systems and strategies to publicize these rule systems could be developed.

Attention to Vicarious Processes

Clearly, modeling and vicarious processes play a critical role in the development and maintenance of interpersonal behavior (Bandura & Walters, 1963). Children are affected by their observation of others and by observation of the consequences others receive for engaging in a particular behavior. Minimizing children's exposure to models of misbehavior and maximizing exposure to prosocial role models in the school and the community have been posed as effective prevention strategies for reducing children's and adolescents' antisocial behavior (Belson, 1975; Kniveton, 1986; Mayer & Butterworth, 1978, 1979). Media coverage and public announcements of good deeds have been used in this regard (Olson, 1981). Children also benefit from discussions of instances in which adults have made a decision to act honestly (e.g., an adult backing into a parked car leaves a note with name and telephone number) (Dituri, 1977).

Attention to Attitudes and Moral Reasoning

Children should be given increased opportunities to express opinions and feelings about moral decisions and factors leading to antisocial behavior (Fischer, 1970; Furnham & Jones, 1987; Miller, 1987). LeCapitaine (1987) posed dilemmas of hypothetical temptation (including theft incidents) to groups of third- and fourth-grade children and directed discussion either about associated feelings or conflict resolution strategies, or a combination of the two. The combined discussion approach was most successful in improving the complexity and maturity of children's responses to a series of newly presented moral dilemmas. Self-report surveys of teachers' and students' attitudes toward crime provide valid information about sociocultural factors influencing dishonesty (Hardt & Peterson-Hardt, 1977) that can be utilized to plan and monitor the effectiveness of adopted prevention strategies.

Attention to Social Climate Variables

Routine assessments of general social climate variables also are recommended in developing crime prevention programs. Student ratings and perceptions of classroom and school environments have been correlated with a multitude of individual- and system-level changes (Houser, 1982; Trickett & Moos, 1973). For example, more favorable student affiliation ratings and lower levels of delinquent behavior have been found in schools that lay emphasis on individual versus competitive academic achievement, project more objective and consistent disciplinary policies, and maintain more predictable adult supervision (Figueira-McDonough, 1986; National Institute of Education, 1977; Pink, 1982; Walberg, 1968). Moreover, students' perceptions of control (e.g., opportunities to participate in decision making or opportunities for self-expression) are positively related to more favorable student attitudes, affect, and behavior in school and to greater levels of overall life satisfaction (Smith, Adelman, Nelson, Taylor, & Phares, 1987). In a study by Kulka, Klingel, and Mann (1980), level of student misconduct was related directly to a mismatch between what students expected from a school environment and what actually characterized the school's social climate. Such findings suggest that successful prevention efforts may need to focus on identifying means of reducing such discrepancies, possibly through direct discussions of the values and expectations held by both teachers and students or by parents and children (Colucci & Stevenson, 1989).

Analyses of Crime Patterns

Effective prevention strategies depend upon a thorough understanding of the circumstances and conditions that precipitate stealing and other misbehavior. Offense patterns (e.g., time of day, places where items are stolen) should be examined routinely to isolate children responsible for the majority of incidents and if possible to identify antecedent factors that affect children's decisions to steal (Clarke, 1984). The information gleaned from analysis of theft patterns also can be publicized directly as a prevention strategy. For example, significant reductions in retail theft have been obtained when the types and amounts of losses associated with theft are posted clearly and strategically. Carter, Hansson, Holmberg, and Melin (1979) used a multiple baseline across categories of items (e.g., candy, personal hygiene products, trinket jewelry) to assess the impact of graphs posted in an employees' lunchroom. Successive reductions in theft were obtained once graphs were introduced that clearly outlined the type and amount of loss associated with each item category. The success of this prevention strategy suggests that employees (or school and community members) play a critical role in theft prevention. Systematic feedback regarding patterns and outcomes of theft and other criminal incidents may heighten the threat of detection, encourage the use of consistent labels, and increase the vigilance of individuals in the work, school, or community environment.

Increased Use of Deterrent Strategies

When systematic patterns of theft (or other criminal behavior) are discovered, specific prevention procedures can be developed to deter such behavior on the part of individuals or groups (Bennett & Wright, 1983). For example, certain areas in schools (e.g., offices, locker halls) can be made off-limits, free-time schedules can be rearranged, and large signs that warn students to be watchful neighbors can be employed. In addition, deterrence efforts must focus on reducing opportunities for theft. Opportunities that openly invite theft (e.g., open lockers or windows) can prompt stealing by both the "seasoned" and the first-time offender (Clarke, 1984). Adult burglars report that a large portion of their thefts are a result of unanticipated opportunities rather than premeditated or planned actions (Bennett & Wright, 1983). Open opportunities to steal are provided by unmonitored areas, poor lighting, and easily accessible items. Curtailment efforts, such as increased adult monitoring of high-crime areas, increased use of lighting and locks, strategically posted signs that spell out the consequences to be associated with specific crimes, and telephone "hotlines" for anonymous calls about criminal behavior, have been effective in reducing student, consumer, and employee thefts (McNess, Egli, Marshall, Schnelle, & Risley, 1976; Olson, 1981; Taylor, 1986).

Adoption of Clear and Well-Publicized Rule Systems

A final critical recommendation for theft prevention is the establishment of a clear rule system that: (a) sets expected standards of acceptable and unacceptable behavior and (b) outlines explicit consequences for transgressions (Mayer & Butterworth, 1978; Zakariya, 1987). Strong rule systems are hypothesized to reduce the number of individuals who deviate from expected prosocial behavior (Allport, 1934). To be most effective, however, rule systems must be widely publicized, must be viewed as logical and fair, and must be applied in an atmosphere of respect and concern for students' rights and well-being (Gettinger, 1988; Hobson, 1986; Zakariya, 1987). Effective prevention strategies must include explicit instruction about personal ownership concepts so that children have a clear understanding of the difference between borrowing and taking personal property (Eisenberg, Haake, & Bartlett, 1981; Eisenberg et al., 1987). In particular, the definitional boundaries of what constitutes a theft and the rule systems for such violations across home and school environments should be addressed and differences in the application of rule systems across these environments must be clarified (Miller & Klungness, 1989).

CONCLUSIONS

Childhood stealing poses significant personal, family, community, and societal consequences. The early assessment of, and intervention to prevent, stealing is important for reducing the likelihood of continued misconduct and criminal behavior in a significant proportion of at-risk children. As the work described in this chapter clearly suggests, successful treatment of stealing is a difficult goal to obtain because of obstacles associated with peer influences, vicarious negative modeling, inconsistencies by adults, and ecological factors. Future work undoubtedly will result in more refined analyses of associated factors that contribute to the etiology and maintenance of stealing behavior. Such knowledge, in turn, will enhance our screening and identification efforts and ultimately will lead to the design of more effective intervention and prevention procedures for eliminating this detrimental childhood behavior.

ACKNOWLEDGMENTS

Preparation of this chapter was supported in part by grant MH38667 from the National Institute of Mental Health.

REFERENCES

Achenbach, T. M., & Edelbrock, C. S. (1978). The classification of child psychopathology: A review and analysis of empirical efforts. *Psychological Bulletin, 85,* 1275-1301.

Allport, F. H. (1934). The J-curve hypothesis of conforming behavior. *Journal of Social Psychology, 5,* 131-183.

Alston, L. (1980). Defining misconducts: Parents versus teachers in head start centers. *Child Care Quarterly, 9,* 203-205.

American Psychiatric Association. (1987). *Diagnostic and statistical manual of mental disorders* (3rd ed., rev.) Washington, DC: Author.

Anderson, D. R. (1984). Stability of behavioral and emotional disturbance in a sample of disadvantaged preschool-aged children. *Child Psychiatry and Human Development, 14,* 249-260.

Azrin, N. H., & Armstrong, P. M. (1973). The "mini-meal": A method for teaching eating skills to the profoundly retarded. *Mental Retardation, 11,* 9-13.

Azrin, N. H., & Wesolowski, M. D. (1974). Theft reversal: An overcorrection procedure for eliminating stealing by retarded persons. *Journal of Applied Behavior Analysis, 7,* 577-581.

Baker, K. (1979). Crime and violence in schools: A challenge to educators. In T. Kratochwill (Ed.), *Advances in school Psychology* (Vol. 5, pp. 57-85). Hillsdale, NJ: Erlbaum.

Bandura, A., & Walters, R. H. (1963). *Social learning and personality development.* New York: Holt, Rinehart & Winston.

Barton, E. S., Guess, E. G., Garcia, E., & Baer, D. M. (1970). Improvement of retardates' mealtime behavior by timeout procedures using multiple baseline techniques. *Journal of Applied Behavioral Analysis, 3,* 77-84.

Belson, W. A. (1975). *Juvenile theft: The causal factors.* London: Harper & Row.

Bennett, R., & Wright, R. (1983). *Constraints and inducements to crime: The property offender's perspective.* University of Cambridge, Institute of Criminology.

Bierman, K. L. (1986). The relationship between social aggression and peer rejection in middle childhood. In R. J. Prinz (Ed.), *Advances in behavioral assessment of children and families* (Vol. 2, pp. 151-178). Greenwich, CT: JAI.

Blechman, E. A. (1981). Toward comprehensive behavioral family interventions: An algorithm for matching families and interventions. *Behavior Modification, 5,* 221-236.

Blechman, E. A. (1984). Competent parents, competent children: Behavioral objectives of parent training. In R. F. Dangel & R. A. Polster (Eds.), *Parent training* (pp. 34-66). New York: Guilford.

Blechman, E. A. (1987). *Solving child behavior problems at home and at school.* Champaign, IL: Research Press.

Braithwaite, J., & Braithwaite, V. (1981). Delinquency and the question of values. *International Journal of Offender Therapy and Comparative Criminology, 25,* 273-289.

Brooks, R. B., & Snow, D. L. (1972). Two case illustrations of the use of behavior modification techniques in the school setting. *Behavior Therapy, 3,* 100-103.

Brown, L., & Lalljee, M. (1981). Young person's conceptions of criminal events. *Journal of Moral Education, 10*, 105–112.

Buckle, A., & Farrington, D. P. (1984). An observational study of shoplifting. *British Journal of Criminology, 24*, 63–73.

Campbell, R. V., O'Brien, S., Bickett, A. D., & Lutzker, J. R. (1983). In home parent training, treatment of migraine headaches, and marital counseling as an ecobehavioral approach to prevent child abuse. *Journal of Behavior Therapy and Experimental Psychiatry, 14*, 147–154.

Carter, N., Hansson, L., Holmberg, B., & Melin, L. (1979). Shoplifting reduction through the use of specific signs. *Journal of Organizational Behavior Management, 2*, 73–84.

Cautela, J. R. (1973). Covert sensitization. In J. S. Stumphauzer (Ed.), *Behavior therapy with delinquents* (pp. 302–314). Springfield, IL: Thomas.

Clarke, R. V. (1984). Opportunity-based crime rates. *British Journal of Criminology, 24*, 74–83.

Colucci, S., & Stevenson, J. F. (1989). *Discrepant school climate perceptions: Implications for school discipline.* Paper presented at the annual meeting of the National Association of School Psychologists, Boston.

Cone, J. D. (1979). Confounded comparisons in triple response mode assessment research. *Behavioral Assessment, 1*, 85–95.

Dadds, M. R., Schwartz, S., & Sanders, M. R. (1987). Marital discord and treatment outcome in behavioral treatment of child conduct disorders. *Journal of Consulting and Clinical Child Psychology, 16*, 192–203.

Dituri, J. (1977). Ten-year-olds' moral judgment of similar peer and adult behavior. *Graduate Research in Education and Related Disciplines, 9*, 5–21.

Dodge, K. A. (1980). Social cognition and children's aggressive behavior. *Child Development, 51*, 162–170.

Dodge, K. A., & Frame, C. C. (1982). Social cognitive biases and deficits in aggressive boys. *Child Development, 53*, 620–635.

Dumas, J. E. (1984). Child, adult-interactional, and socioeconomic setting events as predictors of parent training outcome. *Education and Treatment of Children, 7*, 351–364.

Dumas, J. E. (1989). Treating antisocial behavior in children: Child and family approaches. *Clinical Psychology Review, 9*, 197–222.

Dumas, J. E., & Albin, J. B. (1986). Parent training outcome: Does active parental involvement matter? *Behavior Research and Therapy, 24*, 227–230.

Dumas, J. E., & Wahler, R. G. (1985). Indiscriminate mothering as a contextual factor in aggressive-oppositional child behavior: "Damned if you do, damned if you don't." *Journal of Abnormal Child Psychology, 13*, 1–17.

Dunford, R. W., & Elliott, D. S. (1984). Identifying career offenders using self-reported data. *Journal of Research in Crime and Delinquency, 21*, 57–86.

Eisenberg, N., Haake, R. J., & Bartlett, K. (1981). The effects of possession and ownership on the sharing and proprietary behaviors of preschool children. *Merrill-Palmer Quarterly, 27*, 61–68.

Eisenberg, N., Shell, R., Pasternack, J., Lennon, R., & Mathy, R. M. (1987). Prosocial development in middle childhood: A longitudinal study. *Developmental Psychology, 23*, 712–718.

Emery, R. (1982). Interparental conflict and the children of discord and divorce. *Psychological Bulletin, 92*, 310–330.

Farrington, D. P. (1973). Self-reports of deviant behavior: Predictive and stable? *Journal of Criminal Law and Criminology, 64*, 99–110.

Farrington, D. P. (1977). The effects of public labeling. *British Journal of Criminology, 17*, 112–125.

Fiqueira-McDonough, J. (1986). School context, gender, and delinquency. *Journal of Youth and Adolescence, 15*, 79–98.

Fischer, C. T. (1970). Levels of cheating under conditions of informative appeal to honesty, public affirmation of value, and threats of punishment. *Journal of Educational Research, 64*, 12–16.

Fisher, C. J., & Mawby, R. I. (1982). Juvenile delinquency and police discretion in an inner-city area. *British Journal of Criminology, 22*, 63–75.

Forehand, R., & Atkeson, B. M. (1977). Generality of treatment effects with parents as therapists: A review of assessment and implementation procedures. *Behavior Therapy, 8*, 575–593.

Forehand, R., & Brody, B. (1985). The association between parental personal/marital adjustment and parent-child interactions in a clinic sample. *Behavior Research and Therapy, 23*, 211–212.

Furnham, A., & Jones, S. (1987). Children's views regarding possessions and their theft. *Journal of Moral Education, 16*, 18–30.

Gettinger, M. (1988). Methods of proactive classroom management. *School Psychology Review, 17*, 227–242.

Gibbs, L. E. (1974). The effects of juvenile legal procedures on juvenile offenders' self-attitudes. *Journal of Research in Crime and Delinquency, 11*, 51-55.

Gold, M. (1970). *Delinquent behavior in an American city.* Belmont, CA: Brooks/Cole.

Goldfried, M. R. (1971). Systematic desensitization as training in self-control. *Journal of Consulting and Clinical Psychology, 37*, 228-234.

Goodyear, I. M., Kolvin, I., & Gatzanis, S. (1985). Recent stressful life events in psychiatric disorder of childhood and adolescence. *British Journal of Psychiatry, 197*, 517-524.

Goodyear, I. M., Kolvin, I., & Gatzanis, S. (1987). The impact of recent undesirable life events on psychiatric disorders in childhood and adolescence. *British Journal of Psychiatry, 151*, 179-184.

Graham, P., & Rutter, M. (1981). Psychiatric disorder in the adolescent. A follow-up study. *Proceedings of the Royal Society of Medicine, 66*, 1226-1229.

Griest, D. L., Forehand, R., Rodgers, T., Breiner, J., Furey, W., & Williams, C. (1982). Effects of parent enhancement therapy on the treatment outcome and generalization of a parent training program. *Behavior Research and Therapy, 20*, 429-436.

Griest, D. L., & Wells, K. C. (1983). Behavioral family therapy with conduct disorders in children. *Behavior Therapy, 14*, 37-53.

Guidry, L. S. (1975). Use of covert punishing contingencies in compulsive stealing. *Journal of Behavior Therapy and Experimental Psychiatry, 6*, 169.

Haberman, M., & Quinn, L. M. (1986). Your schools can benefit from what we learned working with jailed delinquents. *American School Board Journal, 173*, 45-46.

Haines, A. T., Jackson, M. S., & Davidson, J. (1983). Children's resistance to the temptation to steal in real and hypothetical situations: A comparison of two treatment programs. *Australian Psychologist, 18*, 289-303.

Hardt, R. H., & Peterson-Hardt, S. P. (1977). On determining the quality of the delinquency self-report method. *Journal of Research in Crime and Delinquency, 14*, 247-261.

Harris, J. D., Gray, B. A., Rees-McGee, S. R., Carroll, J. L., & Zaremba, E. T. (1987). Referrals to school psychologists: A natural survey. *Journal of School Psychology, 25*, 343-354.

Hartup, W. W. (1974). Aggression in childhood: Development perspectives. *American Psychologist, 29*, 336-339.

Haug, T., Brenne, L., Johnson, B., Brentzen, D., Gotestamy, K., & Hugdahl, K. (1987). A 3-systems analysis of fear of flying: A comparison of a consonant versus a non-consonant treatment method. *Behavior Research and Therapy, 25*, 187-194.

Henderson, J. (1981). A behavioral approach to stealing: A proposal for treatment based on 10 cases. *Journal of Behavior Therapy and Experimental Psychiatry, 12*, 231-236.

Henderson, J. (1983). Follow-up of stealing behavior in 27 youths after a variety of treatment programs. *Journal of Behavior Therapy and Experimental Psychiatry, 14*, 331-337.

Henggeler, S. W. (Ed.). (1982). *Delinquency and adolescent psychopathology: A family ecological systems approach.* Littleton, MA: Wright-PSG.

Hirschi, T. (1969). *Causes of delinquency.* Berkeley, CA: University of California Press.

Hobson, P. (1986). The compatibility of punishment and moral education. *Journal of Moral Education, 15*, 221-227.

Hood, R., & Sparks, R. (1970). *Key issues in criminology.* New York: World University Library.

Houser, B. B. (1982). Student cheating and attitude: A function of classroom control technique. *Contemporary Educational Psychology, 7*, 113-123.

Hutton, J. B. (1985). What reasons are given by teachers who refer problem behavior students? *Psychology in the Schools, 22*, 79-82.

Kanfer, F. H. (1970). Self-monitoring: Methodological limitations and clinical applications. *Journal of Consulting and Clinical Psychology, 35*, 143-152.

Kazdin, A. E. (1977). Assessing the clinical or applied importance of behavior change through social validation. *Behavior Modification, 1*, 427-452.

Kazdin, A. E. (1985). *Treatment of antisocial behavior in children and adolescents.* Homewood, IL: Dorsey.

Kazdin, A. E. (1987). Treatment of antisocial behavior in children: Current status and future directions. *Psychological Bulletin, 102*, 187-203.

Kazdin, A. E. (1988). Conduct disorders in childhood and adolescence. Beverly Hills, CA: Sage.

Kazdin, A. E., & Esveldt-Dawson, K. (1986). The interview for antisocial behavior: Psychometric characteristics and concurrent validity with child psychiatric inpatients. *Journal of Psychopathology and Behavioral Assessment, 8*, 289-303.

Kelson, J., & Stewart, M. A. (1986). Factors which predict the persistence of aggressive conduct disorders. *Journal of Child Psychology and Psychiatry, 27*, 77-86.

Kendall, P. C., & Braswell, L. (1985). *Cognitive-behavioral therapy for impulsive children*. New York: Guilford.

Kendall, P. C., & Willcox, L. E. (1980). Cognitive-behavioral treatment for impulsivity: Concrete versus conceptual training in non-self-controlled problem children. *Journal of Consulting and Clinical Psychology, 48,* 80-91.

Kennedy, R. E. (1982). Cognitive-behavioral approaches to the modification of aggressive behavior in children. *School Psychology Review, 11,* 47-55.

Klemke, L. W. (1982). Exploring juvenile shoplifting. *Sociology and Social Research, 67,* 59-75.

Kniveton, B. H. (1986). Peer models and classroom violence: An experimental study. *Educational Research, 28,* 111-116.

Kohlberg, L. (1976). Moral states and moralization: The cognitive-development approach. In T. Lickona (Ed.), *Moral development and behavior: Therapy, research, and social issues* (pp. 31-53). New York: Holt, Rinehart, & Winston.

Kolko, D. J. (1987). Juvenile firesetting: A review and methodological critique. *Clinical Psychology Review, 5,* 345-476.

Kolko, D. J., & Kazdin, A. E. (1986). A conceptualization of firesetting in children. *Journal of Abnormal Child Psychology, 14,* 49-61.

Kolko, D. J., Kazdin, A. E., & Meyer, E. C. (1985). Aggression and psychopathology in child firesetters: Parent and child reports. *Journal of Consulting and Clinical Psychology, 53,* 377-385.

Krehbiel, G., & Milich, R. (1986). Issues in the assessment and treatment of socially rejected children. In R. J. Prinz (Ed.), *Advances in the behavioral assessment of children and families* (Vol. 2, pp. 249-270). Greenwich, CT: JAI.

Kulik, J. A., Stein, K. B., & Sarbin, T. R. (1968). Dimensions and patterns of adolescent antisocial behavior. *Journal of Consulting and Clinical Psychology, 32,* 375-382.

Kulka, R. A., Klingel, D. M., & Mann, D. W. (1980). School crime and disruption as a function of student-school fit: An empirical assessment. *Journal of Youth and Adolescence, 9,* 353-370.

LaGreca, A. M., & Santogrossi, D. A. (1980). Social skills training with elementary school students: A behavioral group approach. *Journal of Consulting and Clinical Psychology, 48,* 220-227.

LeCapitaine, J. E. (1987). The relationship between emotional development and moral development and the differential impact of three psychological interventions on children. *Psychology in the Schools, 24,* 372-378.

Lochman, J. E. (1985). Effects of different treatment lengths in cognitive behavioral interventions with aggressive boys. *Child Psychiatry and Human Development, 16,* 45-56.

Lochman, J. E., & Curry, J. F. (1986). Effects of social problem-solving training and self-instruction training with aggressive boys. *Journal of Clinical Child Psychology, 15,* 159-164.

Lochman, J. E., Nelson, W. M., & Sims, J. P. (1981). A cognitive behavioral program for use with aggressive children. *Journal of Clinical Child Psychology, 10,* 146-148.

Loeber, R. (1982). The stability of antisocial and delinquent child behavior: A review. *Child Development, 53,* 1431-1446.

Loeber, R. (1988). Natural histories of conduct problems, delinquency, and associated substance use: Evidence for development progressions. In B. Lahey & A. E. Kazdin (Eds.), *Advances in clinical child psychology* (Vol. 11, pp. 73-124). New York: Plenum.

Loeber, R., & Dishion, T. J. (1983). Early predictors of male delinquency: A review. *Psychological Bulletin, 94,* 68-99.

Loeber, R., & Dishion, T. J. (1984). Antisocial and delinquent youths: Methods for their early identification. In J. D. Burchard & S. N. Burchard (Eds.), *Prevention of delinquent behavior* (pp. 75-89). Beverly Hills, CA: Sage.

Loeber, R., & Schmaling, K. B. (1985a). Empirical evidence for overt and covert patterns of antisocial conduct problems: A meta-analysis. *Journal of Abnormal Psychology, 13,* 337-352.

Loeber, R., & Schmaling, K. B. (1985b). The utility of differentiating between mixed and pure forms of antisocial child behavior. *Journal of Abnormal Child Psychology, 13,* 315-335.

Loeber, R., & Stouthamer-Loeber, M. (1986). Family factors as correlates and predictors of juvenile conduct problems and delinquency. In M. Tonry & N. Morris (Eds.), *Crime and Justice* (Vol. 7, pp. 29-149). Chicago: University of Chicago Press.

Loeber, R., Weissman, W., & Reid, L. (1983). Family interactions of assaultive adolescents, stealers, and nondelinquents. *Journal of Abnormal Child Psychology, 11,* 1-14.

Martens, B. K., & Witt, J. C. (1988). Expanding the scope of behavioral consultation: A systems approach to classroom behavior change. *Professional School Psychology, 3,* 271-281.

Martens, B. K., Witt, J. C., Elliott, S. N., & Darveaux, D. (1985). Teacher judgements concerning the acceptability of school-based interventions. *Professional Psychology, 16,* 191-198.

Martin, R. (1975). *Legal challenges to behavior modification: Trends in schools, corrections and mental health*. Champaign, IL: Research Press.

Mayer, G. R., & Butterworth, T. (1978). Reducing school violence and vandalism. *Guidance Clinic, 6*, 11-15.

Mayer, G. R., & Butterworth, T. (1979). A preventive approach to school violence and vandalism: An experimental study. *Personnel and Guidance Journal, 57*, 436-441.

McNess, M. P., Egli, D. S., Marshall, R. S., Schnelle, J. F., & Risley, T. R. (1976). Shoplifting prevention: Providing information through signs. *Journal of Applied Behavior Analysis, 9*, 399-405.

Meichenbaum, D. H. (1977). *Cognitive-behavior modification: An integrative approach.* New York: Plenum.

Meichenbaum, D. H., & Goodman, J. (1971). Training impulsive children to talk to themselves: A means of developing self-control. *Journal of Abnormal Psychology, 77*, 115-126.

Michelson, L. (1987). Cognitive-behavioral strategies in prevention and treatment of antisocial disorders in children and adolescents. In J. D. Burchard & S. N. Burchard (Eds.), *Prevention of delinquent behavior* (pp. 190-219). Beverly Hills, CA: Sage.

Milich, R., & Dodge, K. A. (1984). Social information processing in child psychiatric populations. *Journal of Abnormal Child Psychology, 12*, 471-490.

Miller, G. E. (1987). School interventions for dishonest behavior. *Special Services in the Schools, ¾*, 21-36.

Miller, G. E., & Klungness, L. (1986). Treatment of nonconfrontative stealing in school-age children. *School Psychology Review, 15*, 24-35.

Miller, G. E., & Klungness, L. (1989). Childhood theft: A comprehensive review of assessment and treatment. *School Psychology Review, 18*, 80-95.

Miller, G. E., & Moncher, F. J. (1988). Critical issues in the assessment of childhood stealing behavior. In R. J. Prinz (Ed.), *Advances in behavioral assessment of children and families* (Vol. 4, pp. 73-96). Greenwich, CT: JAI.

Miller, G. E., & Prinz, R. J. (in press). The enhancement of social learning family interventions for child-hood conduct disorders. *Psychological Bulletin.*

Miller, G. E., Ricker, J. H., Prinz, R. J., & Davenport, H. S. (1988). *Mother–child interaction in stealer and nonstealer aggressive boys.* Paper presented at the 22nd annual meeting of the Association for Advancement of Behavior Therapy, New York.

Mitchell, S., & Rosa, P. (1981). Boyhood behavior problems as precursors to criminality: A 15-year follow-up study. *Journal of Child Psychology and Psychiatry, 22*, 19-33.

Moore, D. R., Chamberlain, P., & Mukai, L. H. (1979). Children at risk for delinquency: A follow-up comparison of aggressive children and children who steal. *Journal of Abnormal Child Psychology, 7*, 345-355.

Mott, J. (1986). Opioid use and burglary. *British Journal of Addiction, 81*, 671-678.

National Institute of Education, U.S. Dept. of Health, Education, & Welfare. (1977). *Violent schools — Safe schools. The safe school study report to the Congress* (Vol. 1). U.S. Government Printing Office.

Ollendick, T. H., & Hersen, M. (1984). An overview of child behavioral assessment. In T. H. Ollendick & M. Hersen (Eds.), *Child behavioral assessment: Principles and procedures* (pp. 3-21). New York: Pergamon.

Olson, J. R. (1981). Curbing vandalism and theft. *Educational Horizons, 59*, 195-197.

Olweus, D. (1979). Stability of aggressive reaction patterns in males: A review. *Psychological Bulletin, 86*, 852-857.

Patterson, G. R. (1982). *Coercive family processes.* Eugene, OR: Castalia.

Patterson, G. R. (1986). Performance models for antisocial boys. *American Psychologist, 41*, 432-444.

Patterson, G. R., & Dishion, T. J. (1985). Contributions of family and peers to delinquency. *Criminology, 23*, 63-79.

Patterson, G. R., & Reid, J. B. (1973). Intervention for families of aggressive boys: A replication study. *Behavior Research and Therapy, 11*, 383-394.

Patterson, G. R., Reid, J. B., Jones, R. R., & Conger, R. E. (1975). *A social learning intervention, Vol. 1: Families with aggressive children.* Eugene, OR: Castalia.

Patterson, G. R., & Stouthamer-Loeber, M. (1984). The correlation of family management practices and delinquency. *Child Development, 55*, 1299-1307.

Pink, W. T. (1982). Academic failure, student social conflict, and delinquent behavior. *Urban Review, 14*, 141-180.

Polk, K., Frease, D., & Richmond, F. L. (1974). Social class, school experience, and delinquency. *Criminology, 12*, 84-96.

Polk, K., & Schafter, W. (1972). *Schools and delinquency.* Englewood Cliffs, NJ: Prentice-Hall.

Prout, T., & Chizik, R. (1988). Readability of child and adolescent self-report measures. *Journal of Consulting and Clinical Psychology, 56*, 152-154.

Reid, J. B. (1975). The child who steals. In G. R. Patterson, J. B. Reid, R. R. Jones, & R. E. Conger (Eds.), *A social learning approach to family intervention: The socially aggressive child* (pp. 135-138). Eugene, OR: Castalia.

Reid, J. B., & Hendricks, A. F. (1973). A preliminary analysis of the effectiveness of direct home intervention for treatment of predelinquent boys who steal. In L. A. Hamerlynck, L. C. Hanky, & J. Mash (Eds.), *Behavior therapy: Methodology, concepts, and practice* (pp. 209-220). Champaign, IL: Research Press.

Reid, J. B., & Patterson, G. R. (1976). The modification of aggression and stealing behavior of boys in home setting. In E. Ribes-Inesta & A. Bandura (Eds.), *Analysis of delinquency and aggression* (pp. 123-145). Hillsdale, NJ: Erlbaum.

Renshaw, D. C. (1979). Stealing and school. *The Pointer, 21*, 91-113.

Robins, L. N. (1978). Sturdy childhood predictors of adult antisocial behavior: Replications from longitudinal studies. *Psychological Medicine, 8*, 611-622.

Robins, L. N., & Radcliff, K. S. (1979). Risk factors in the continuation of childhood antisocial behavior into adulthood. *International Journal of Mental Health, 7*, 96-111.

Rogers-Warren, A. K. (1977). Planned change: Ecobehaviorally based interventions. In A. Rogers-Warren, & S. F. Warren (Eds.), *Ecological perspective in behavior analysis* (pp. 197-210). Baltimore: University Park Press.

Rogers-Warren, A. K. (1984). Ecobehavioral analysis. *Education and Treatment of Children, 7*, 283-303.

Rosen, H. S., & Rosen, L. A. (1983). Eliminating stealing: Use of stimulus control with an elementary student. *Behavior Modification, 7*, 56-63.

Rubel, R. J. (1980). Extent, perspectives, and consequences of violence and vandalism in public schools. In K. Baker & R. J. Rubel (Eds.), *Violence and crime in the schools* (pp. 17-27). Lexington, MA: Lexington Books.

Rutter, M., & Giller, H. (1983). *Juvenile delinquency: Trends and perspectives*. Harmondsworth, England: Penquin Books.

Rutter, M., Tizard, J., & Whitmore, K. (Eds.). (1970). *Education, health, and behavior*. New York: Wiley.

Sallis, J. F. (1983). Aggressive behaviors of children: A review of behavioral interventions and future directions. *Education and Treatment of Children, 6*, 175-191.

Sendor, B. (1987). Your frustrating student search dilemma: Catching the guilty, but protecting the innocent. *American School Board Journal, 173*, 28, 41.

Shure, M. B., Spivack, G., & Jaeger, M. (1972). Problem-solving thinking and adjustment among disadvantaged preschool children. *Child Development, 42*, 1791-1803.

Smith, D. C., Adelman, H. S., Nelson, L. T., Taylor, L., & Phares, V. (1987). Students' perceptions of control at school and problem behavior and attitudes. *Journal of School Psychology, 25*, 167-176.

Spinks, S. H., & Birchler, G. R. (1982). Behavioral-systems marital therapy: Dealing with resistance. *Family Process, 21*, 169-185.

Spivack, G., & Shure, M. B. (1982). The cognition of social adjustment: Interpersonal cognitive problem solving thinking. In B. B. Lahey & A. E. Kazdin (Eds.), *Advances in clinical child psychology* (Vol. 5, pp. 323-372). New York: Plenum.

Stevens, G. E. (1980). Invasion of student privacy. *Journal of School Law and Education, 9*, 343-351.

Stouthamer-Loeber, M. (1986). Lying as a problem behavior in children: A review. *Clinical Psychology Review, 6*, 267-289.

Stumphauzer, J. S. (1976). Elimination of stealing by self-reinforcement of alternative behavior and family contracting. *Journal of Behavior Therapy and Experimental Psychiatry, 7*, 265-268.

Sulzer-Azaroff, B., & Mayer, G. R. (1977). Applying behavior-analysis procedures with children and youth. New York: Holt, Rinehart & Winston.

Switzer, E. B., Deal, J. E., & Bailey, J. S. (1977). The reduction of stealing in second graders using a group contingency. *Journal of Applied Behavioral Analysis, 10*, 267-272.

Szykula, S. A., Morris, J. B., Sudweeks, C., & Sayger, T. V. (1987). Child-focused behavior and strategic therapies: Outcome comparisons. *Psychotherapy with Families, 24*, 546-551.

Taylor, R. R. (1986). A positive guide to theft deterrence. *Personnel Journal, 65*, 36-40.

Teichman, Y., & Eliahu, D. (1986). A combination of structural family therapy and behavior techniques in treating a patient with two tics. *Journal of Clinical Child Psychology, 15*, 311-316.

Trickett, E. J., & Moos, R. H. (1973). Social environment of junior high and high school classrooms. *Journal of Educational Psychology, 65*, 93-102.

Trosch, L. A., Williams, R. G., & Devore, R. W. (1982). Public school searches and the fourth amendment. *Journal of School Law and Education, 11*, 41-63.

Turco, T. L., & Elliott, S. N. (1986). Assessment of students' acceptability ratings of teacher-initiated interventions for classroom misbehavior. *Journal of School Psychology, 24,* 277-283.

United States Federal Bureau of Investigation. (1987). *Uniform crime reports: Crime in the United States.* Washington, DC: U.S. Government Printing Office.

Vidoni, D. O., Fleming, N. J., & Mintz, S. (1983). Behavior problems as perceived by teachers, mental health professionals, and children. *Psychology in the Schools, 20,* 93-98.

Voeltz, L. M., & Evans, I. M. (1982). The assessment of behavioral interrelationships in child behavior therapy. *Behavior Assessment, 4,* 131-165.

Wahler, R. G. (1975). Some structural aspects of defiant child behavior. *Journal of Applied Behavior Analysis, 8,* 27-42.

Wahler, R. G. (1980a). The insular mother: Her problems in parent-child treatment. *Journal of Applied Behavior Analysis, 13,* 207-219.

Wahler, J. G. (1980b). The multiply entrapped parent: Obstacles to change in parent-child problems. In J. P. Vincent (Ed.), *Advances in family intervention, assessment and theory* (Vol. 1, pp. 146-170). Greenwich, CT: JAI‡

Wahler, R. G., & Dumas, J. (1987). Stimulus class determinants of mother-child coercive interchanges in multidistressed families: Assessment and intervention. In J. D. Burchard & N. Burchard (Eds.), *Prevention of delinquent behavior* (pp. 190-219). Beverly Hills, CA: Sage.

Wahler, R. G., & Dumas, J. E. (1989). Attentional problems in dysfunctional mother-child interactions: An interbehavioral model. *Psychological Bulletin, 105,* 116-130.

Wahler, R. G., & Fox, J. J. (1981). Setting events in applied behavior analysis: Toward a conceptual and methodological expansion. *Journal of Applied Behavior Analysis, 14,* 327-338.

Walberg, H. J. (1968). Structural and affective aspects of classroom climate. *Psychology in the Schools, 5,* 247-253.

Webster-Stratton, C. (1985). Predictors of treatment outcome in parent training for conduct disordered children. *Behavior Therapy, 16,* 223-243.

Weger, R. M. (1985). Stealing. In J. Grimes & Al Thomas (Eds.), *Psychological approaches: Problems in children and adolescents* (Vol. 2, pp. 83-134). Des Moines, IA: Iowa Department of Public Instruction.

Weger, R. M. (1987). Children and stealing. In A. Thomas & J. Grimes (Eds.), *Children's needs: Psychological perspectives* (pp. 571-578). Washington, DC: National Association of School Psychologists.

West, D. J., & Farrington, D. (1973). *Who becomes delinquent?* London: Heinemann.

Wetzel, R. (1966). Use of behavior techniques in a case of compulsive stealing. *Journal of Consulting and Clinical Psychology, 30,* 367-374.

Williams, R. L. (1985). Children's stealing: A review of theft-control procedures for parents and teachers. *Remedial and Special Education, 6,* 17-23.

Wilson, H. (1980). Parental supervision: A neglected aspect of delinquency. *British Journal of Criminology, 20,* 203-235.

Wirtz, P. W., & Harrell, A. U. (1987). Assaultive versus nonassaultive victimization: A profile analysis of psychological response. *Journal of Interpersonal Violence, 2,* 264-277.

Witt, J. C. (1986). Teachers' resistance to the use of school-based interventions. *Journal of School Psychology, 24,* 37-44.

Witt, J. C., Martens, B. K., & Elliott, S. N. (1984). Factors affecting teachers' judgements of the acceptability of behavioral interventions: Time involvement, behavior problem severity, and type of intervention. *Behavior Therapy, 15,* 204-209.

Wolf, M. M. (1978). Social validity: The case for subjective measurement of how applied behavior analysis is finding its heart. *Journal of Applied Behavior Analysis, 11,* 203-214.

Yu, P., Harris, G. E., Solovitz, B. L., & Franklin, J. L. (1986). A social problem-solving intervention for children at high risk for later psychopathology. *Journal of Clinical Child Psychology, 15,* 30-40.

Zakariya, S. B. (1987). Fair, unfailing discipline is the least schools owe to delinquent kids. *American School Board Journal, 174,* 23-29.

28

Honesty, Lying, and Cheating: Their Elaboration and Management

Trevor F. Stokes
Pamela G. Osnes
Florida Mental Health Institute,
University of South Florida

INTRODUCTION: HONESTY AND ITS MAINTENANCE

If only honesty worked as well as lying and cheating often does. It is not excessively pessimistic to note that the quickest and most likely reinforced way to a desired goal is frequently the shortest route with the least resistance. Therein lies the moral of a history of contingencies. All too often, a child or adolescent is taught that there are payoffs for lying and cheating, and some of those rewards are so powerful that the child may develop a history of reinforced deviance. This may not be a widespread repertoire of behavioral aberration. In fact, it will probably be well discriminated, subtle, and elusive from observation in the repertoire of the sophisticated deviant child.

In the innocence of young childhood, there are few shades of misrepresentation. Young children will frequently say or do whatever matches their inclination at the moment. They will report honestly without careful screening of information or concern about the effect of their actions or reports on others. Gradually, the differential consequences of such action lead to more functional behavior. They affect performance in such a way that an older child may avoid answering a direct question or may provide partial answers that supply acceptable content, with little or no elaboration. With more experience

in the wiles of the world, or with a history of contact with functional consequences, accuracy of reporting and answering may become a more elusive and subtle matter. By this time, various shades of performance may bring about a diversity of consequences for different reports, non-reports, or misrepresentation of reports.

The natural social environment tends to be accidental in the provision of functional contingencies. Its various reinforcements and punishments are not systematically planned and programmed by agents by means of carefully managed contingencies; instead, contingencies frequently appear to children to be the result of happenstance, occurring as if in random fashion. If by chance or neglect a child experiences positive consequences for appropriate and honest behavior, that reinforced activity is likely to be maintained and elaborated. Unfortunately, the opposite is true, also. That is, lying, cheating, and other maladaptive behaviors frequently are reinforced.

For teachers or school psychologists, there are few options available for encouraging honest behavior. One position to take is to answer that an environment is naturally better programmed to reinforce the behaviors generally valued in our society, in particular, honesty. A more skeptical position is to artificially engineer a more systematic, but still "natural," environment that consistently reinforces appropriate behavior and punishes or places on extinction the scourges of lying and cheating. Of course, as is well recognized by the cynics of the world, discriminating and reasonably frequent honesty may be the appropriate and realistic goal.

In regard to the development of lying and cheating, "morality" may not be the issue as much as are consequences and contingencies. Consequences have no ethics or morality in themselves; they simply exist and follow behaviors. Consequences have no valence; they simply are functional or not. The behaviors occur or fail to occur because of the function of the consequences. Children are not bad or good; it is their behavior that is regarded as good or bad by parents, teachers, and others. A child's "morality" reflects his or her functional history of interactions with the environment (Bijou & Baer, 1978). The behavior is the result of appropriate or inappropriate contingencies whether these consequences are deliberately programmed or not, whether entirely accidental or artificial.

SOURCES OF LYING AND CHEATING

Students' Reports

In the schools, there are various avenues of student performance that need to be monitored by teachers and psychologists, namely, various reports and permanent products that reflect past activity and future plans. Access to information available to students is also an area in need of consideration when considering lying and cheating.

Students' verbal reports of past activity. Teachers commonly inquire about students' activities that are not immediately observable by directly questioning the student and relying on the student's response. All is well if the answer (a) reflects accurately the student's actual observation of the activity in question, and (b) accurately characterizes the activity. Unfortunately, this may not always be the case. The student may well lack observational skill, may incline to incomplete reporting, or may simply report untruth-

fully. Such possibilities all need to be taken into account in evaluating reports of behaviors not independently observed. After all, the verbal report is subject to contingencies that may have no relationship to the contingencies operating on the behavior that originally was the focus of the report.

Students' verbal reports of future activity. Verbalizations can be related to a student's future activities, also, in a statement specifying what will be done at a certain time and place. Again, the task of a teacher or school psychologist will be to determine whether there has been a match between the verbalization and the actual behavior. It may be that the contingencies operating on the student's initial statement are different from those that operate when the occasion for performing the behavior arises.

Written reports of activity. Another potential source of lying and cheating is written reports. Essentially a written report of activity is the same as a verbal report except for the permanent product format. Written reports of unobserved activity are subject to the same momentary and situational contingency controls as are verbal reports.

Inappropriate Access to Restricted Information

When there are pressures to produce information or conclusions based on other sources of information or analyses, difficulty in producing the relevant information may lead to acquiring that information via alternative or unacceptable behaviors. Obviously a successful and likely reinforced avenue is to obtain the information through observation of materials in the possession of other persons. Even though this may be surreptitious or blatant, the outcome is the same: inappropriately obtained information is used for self-gain. Plagiarism and cheating are specific examples of inappropriate access to and/or use of material that does not conform to the requirements of the tasks for the student, for example, copying the answers of other students, or using concealed notes to assist in the completion of tests, and even allowing other students to have access to answers which facilitate use of information.

ASSESSMENT

Monitoring

The cornerstone of effective management of honest behavior is the monitoring of work in progress and its subsequent verbal and written products to accurately identify occurrences of lying and cheating. Miller (1987) has suggested that limited or inconsistent application of consequences, which essentially describes powerful schedules of intermittent reinforcement, may be a potent factor in the resilience and maintenance of dishonest behavior.

Matching

In order to determine whether there has been a problem with honesty, reports and other permanent products should be matched with other sources of the same information. Stouthamer-Loeber (1986) even suggested that persistent liars (and cheaters) may be made responsible for demonstrating that their reports or verbalizations are indeed accurate and correct presentations of their own work.

Note Inconsistencies and Implement Contingency Procedures

Inconsistency between self-reports and permanent products is an important sign of unacceptable variation that is possibly associated with lying and cheating. Inconsistency between student self-reports and the reports of others should be noted, also. Miller (1987) noted that ineffective or deficient detection of lying and cheating, as well as other forms of dishonest behavior, may be a significant factor in the repetition of such maladaptive behavior. Applying contingency management operations effectively is essential to the management of lying and cheating. Bushway and Nash (1977) concluded, after a review of published work on cheating, that when the chances of being caught increase, the likelihood of cheating by students diminishes. Thus, once problems have been noted, a plan for management and change of the behavior should be developed and implemented.

Continue Monitoring

Even if the immediate problems seem to diminish and the lying and cheating may be maintaining at a low level, occasional checking over time to ensure continued veracity of reports is advisable. It may be possible that the lying and cheating have become more devious and difficult to detect. Some continuing review may be necessary to demonstrate to the students that infractions are likely to be noted and that interventions will be implemented whenever warranted.

CONTINGENCY OPTIONS

When lying and cheating are noted, the issue becomes one of what to do next: how to react to and manage the maladaptive behaviors that have been identified. An accurate and thorough assessment of the circumstances of the lying and cheating, their history, and the current contingencies of gain, escape, and avoidance often will provide clues as to the best management strategies and options.

Miller (1987) and Stouthamer-Loeber (1986) noted that there have been few studies that have examined the effectiveness of interventions for dishonest behavior in the schools, and our knowledge is limited about such behaviors and their treatment. However, contingency management procedures have been demonstrated to be successful in this area.

A *contingency* is the relationship between a behavior and its controlling environmental stimuli (Stokes, 1985). An effective or *functional stimulus* is one that occurs prior to the performance of the behavior or one that has followed previous instances of the behavior and has resulted in a change in the frequency, duration, or magnitude of the behavior. Antecedent controlling stimuli are called *discriminative stimuli* because, when present, they reliably affect the occurrence of the behavior. Functional consequent stimuli are of two general classes: reinforcers and punishers. *Reinforcers* increase the frequency of the behavior they follow, whereas *punishers* decrease the frequency of the behavior they follow. Note that both reinforcers and punishers are defined by their effect upon the behavior: The operations of reinforcement and punishment are considered to have occurred only if the frequency of the behavior actually increases (reinforcement) or decreases (punishment). Relevant to issues of reinforcement and punishment are the circumstances surrounding the occurrence of a behavior, whether tightly related to a narrow range of conditions or whether the circumstances are broad and generalized.

Positive Reinforcement

The operation of positive reinforcement is demonstrated when implementation of a stimulus (consequence) following instances of a behavior result in an increase in the subsequent occurrence of the behavior. For example, if a teacher attends to honest reporting by a student by describing the accuracy and delivering recognition and praise and subsequently finds that the frequency of honest reporting increases and is maintained, veracity of reporting can be said to have been positively reinforced. Similarly, social and tangible consequences can be provided to reinforce correct use of materials and information. Positive consequences may best be used to reinforce behaviors considered to be alternative to or incompatible with the maladaptive behaviors of lying and cheating — for example, as part of a differential reinforcement of other behavior (DRO) procedures.

Negative Reinforcement

The operation of negative reinforcement is demonstrated when a stimulus (consequence) is removed following instances of a behavior with the result that the occurrence of the behavior subse-

quently increases. For example, if a teacher ceases to complain about cheating when honest test-taking occurs, and the honest test-taking increases and is maintained, then appropriate test-taking behavior can be said to have been negatively reinforced.

Punishment by Addition

The operation of punishment by addition is realized when, in response to the addition of a stimulus (consequence) following instances of a behavior, the occurrence of the behavior subsequently decreases. For example, if a child is caught lying and is then required to run 10 laps of the playing field as a sanction, after which the frequency of lying decreases and stays low, then lying can be regarded as having been punished by addition of consequences.

The operations of punishment should be employed carefully because punishing contingencies can have adverse side effects, such as aggression toward the person implementing the procedure or more sophisticated deviance as a result of more careful and successful concealment of the aberrant behavior. Miller (1987) noted that threats of punishment have typically been insufficient to modify dishonest behavior when the probability of detection is small and the outcome or payoff for the student is large.

Punishment by Cost

The operation of punishment by cost is realized when in response to the removal of a stimulus (consequence) following instances of a behavior, the occurrence of the behavior subsequently decreases. For example, if a child is caught cheating and the consequence implemented is that the student drops a grade or loses a classroom privilege such as an early release from the class or access to a special game-time activity, with the result that the frequency of cheating decreases and stays low, then cheating can be said to have been punished by cost.

Discrimination and Generalization of Behavior Changes

Discrimination and generalization are related concepts in that they refer to the conditions under which behavior occurs, whether under a regimen of tightly controlled and restricted circumstances related to the presence of particular stimuli (discrimination) or to the spread of effects to conditions extraneous to the initially targeted change (Stokes & Osnes, 1986, 1988, 1989). Ideally, honest behavior is to be admired in a wide variety of times, places, and circumstances that may or may not incorporate tightly controlled monitoring by teachers. Perhaps honesty is regarded as authentic only when it is a reasonably well generalized repertoire. On the other hand, well-discriminated cheating can be modified by an astute rearrangement by teachers of the discriminative stimuli of the classroom itself, such as separating the desks of two students who regularly share information during a test. These physical changes may be an appropriate initial and least intrusive intervention for some instances of cheating, but probably they should be carefully linked to other strategies such as a program of positive reinforcement.

EXAMPLES OF PROGRAMS FOR DIFFERENT AGE GROUPS

Preschool Programs

The correspondence between what children say they will do or have done and what they actually do or have done is a common source of problems related to honesty and accuracy of students' reports of their performance (Stokes, Osnes, & Guevremont, 1987; Guevremont, Osnes, & Stokes, in press). Some children display a reliable relationship between verbalization and action. Baer, Williams, Osnes, and Stokes (1985) studied the case of a preschool child whose once reliable verbal control over anticipated performance had declined with repeated measurement over time. This verbal regulation was recovered, however, by a brief training during which the child was provided positive consequences for doing what she said she would do. This research showed that in cases in which a child's reporting is not suitably reliable, accuracy may be restored through contingency manipulations. The study also showed that the relation between verbalization and performance may diminish over time unless some maintenance training is programmed.

The training histories of children provided programming designed to develop correspondence between verbalization and behavior may vary from child to child. Most documented research employs only positive contingency procedures, which are to be applauded for being also the least intrusive interventions. Sometimes, however, the typical positive procedures will not be sufficient. It may well be that procedures that combine a positive procedure with a mild sanction for noncorrespondence — probably the most typical procedures used naturally by teachers and parents — are the most effective ones for developing accurate reporting about a child's performance.

For example, Osnes, Guevremont, and Stokes (1986) demonstrated that peer interaction improved in young children through the use of correspondence training employing exclusively positive contingencies. In contrast, however, the results of another study (Osnes, Guevremont, & Stokes, 1987) indicated that when correspondence was followed by attention and brief activity consequences, interaction with peers, the targeted behavior, failed to improve. Therefore, this developmentally delayed child faced additional consequences for noncorrespondence, namely, a sit-out from play for 3 minutes. This combination of positive consequences for correspondence and negative consequences for noncorrespondence was sufficient to increase both frequency of interactions with peers and the amount of time spent in proximity to peers. In addition, the child's handraising and participation in large-group activities also increased when the combination of positive and mild negative procedures were introduced for interactions during play. The results of this study are depicted in Figure 1.

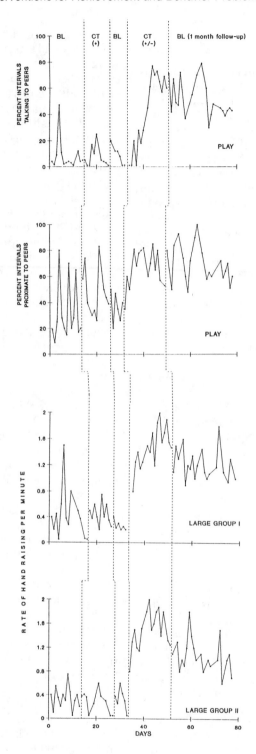

FIGURE 1. Percentage of intervals talking to and proximal to peers during play and rate per minute of hand raising during large-group instruction. BL = basline, and CT = correspondence training. Adapted from Osnes, Guevremont, and Stokes (1987).

Wherever possible, incorporating assessment of permanent products into programs is recommended so that performance can be compared with the child's verbalizations. In a study of verbal self-regulation, Guevremont, Osnes, and Stokes (1986) endeavored to control behavior at home by intervening with a specialized home program. These investigators examined behavior in four preschool settings and one home setting. Correspondence training procedures were introduced initially in the first large-group setting of the day that targeted behaviors such as sitting next to nonpreferred peers, participating in group activity, and clearing mats after the group. After this training, a setting and a behavior somewhat remote in time from the training were targeted: play with toys and initiation of social exchange with nonpreferred peers during play. After different behaviors had been targeted in settings more temporally remote from the correspondence training, verbalizations developed a controlling function such that they (i.e., the child's verbalizations) reliably predicted subsequent behavior in the preschool. Furthermore, although no interventions were instituted at home, a child's verbalization at the preschool at the end of the day was sufficient to control home behavior. Documentation of the changes at home were provided by permanent products brought from home to school, in much the same way as homework is returned, so as to allow assessment by the teacher. When the children returned with their cutting and writing tasks, the teachers politely took the materials and said OK. The significant outcome of these procedures was that even though there were only minimal consequences for bringing the homework to the preschool, the afternoon student statement regarding what homework would be completed was consistently related to the actual performance of the task.

Verbal regulation of the behavior of preschoolers is not always well developed and may need special training relevant to the guiding effect of the child's statements. An analysis of the function of guiding self-verbalizations and the development of such by preschoolers was documented in a recent study (Guevremont, Osnes, & Stokes, 1988). The results of this investigation are depicted in Figure 2. Here, preschoolers were taught to use the typical self-instructional strategies related to problem orientation, task statements, guiding self-verbalizations, and self-acknowledgement. In a training room, the children mastered the skills and showed that performance matched the use of the self-instructional procedures. There was no effect on the academic performance of the students in their regular classroom. In fact, the children did not show evidence of the use of the skills until the classroom teacher told them to use the instructions they had learned. Subsequent performance varied from child to child, but each child showed the same pattern of results: That is, when the self-instructions were used, performance improved; when the actual use of self-instructions decreased, performance also decreased. What had been developed was a straightforward relationship between verbalization and academic behavior. However, the behaviors of two children did not readily come under the control of the procedures, and an additional contingency was implemented: repetition of a work task if the use of self-instructions and performance were below the levels appropriate for the child. The noteworthy finding here is that even though these two children displayed a functional relationship between verbalizations and performance in one setting, that relationship was not evident in the classroom without the application of additional contingencies for the misuse of the self-instructions: Veracity did not automatically generalize across settings.

Elementary Programs

Maintaining a child's accurate reporting of activities and behavior continues to be an important issue for teachers into the elementary grades. Blount and Stokes (1984), in their examination of the literature on self-management and self-control, suggested that accurate reporting does not occur automatically, but in fact, some training frequently is necessary that

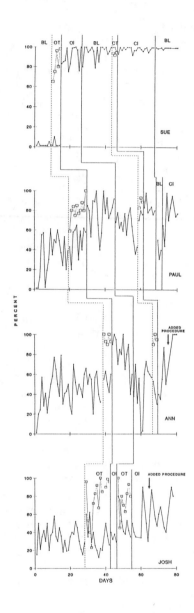

FIGURE 2. Percentage of correct items on worksheets and percentage of self-instructions daily across conditions. Open squares represent percentage correct on worksheets in the training setting, and solid dots represent the percentage correct on classroom sheets. The arrows indicate the point at which the additional classroom procedure was introduced. BL = baseline, OT = overt training, OI = overt instruction, CT = covert training, and CI = covert instruction. Adapted from Guevremont, Osnes, and Stokes (1988).

is focused on the development of correct evaluations and correct reporting by children. Comparison and matching of children's and teachers' evaluations of schoolwork is one way to develop correct evaluations, especially if there are positive consequences, hopefully reinforcers, for a close or appropriate match. For example, Drabman, Spitalnik, and O'Leary (1973) allowed elementary students to evaluate their own performance and determine the number of tokens they were to receive. Initially, for close matches the students earned the tokens and a bonus for the good match, whereas if there was a discrepancy between the teacher's and the student's allocation of points, no points were awarded. Accurate, appropriate, and "honest" evaluations and improved performance were observed.

In the absence of regular feedback, students may take the initiative to elicit such feedback. For example, Hrydowy, Stokes, and Martin (1984) trained elementary grade students to prompt evaluation and feedback from their teacher: Specifically, they were trained to work on an academic exercise, evaluate their own work quality, and prompt teachers for an evaluation. Typically, but not always, the teachers responded positively. The teachers were usually careful to be accurate in their feedback, responding positively where appropriate, but not for inaccurate or incomplete work, when correction and the provision of negative evaluative feedback was the appropriate course of action. In this study, the children showed they had considerable influence over the schedule of positive attention to their performance; positive attention from the teacher was successfully recruited by the students.

Accuracy of reporting may not always be the prime consideration when conducting programs of intervention, although monitoring of the accuracy of the information provided still may be essential. Consider the case, described by Stokes, Boggs, and Osnes (1989), of a 10-year-old with a diagnosis of separation anxiety disorder. This child, Barry, displayed excessive anxiety about separation from his parents even for brief periods of time;

his problem behaviors had been so extreme that his mother stayed at his school throughout the day because he "refused to allow her to leave." This arrangement allowed her to be available whenever Barry had problems. If the mother left the school unannounced for even brief periods of time, Barry would engage in manipulative crying which sometimes led to excessive shaking and tantrums if not responded to promptly. Barry had a history of avoiding classes and recruiting attention following inappropriate behavior in the classroom. Powerful positive and negative reinforcement contingencies operated to maintain his behavior.

A major part of the treatment designed for Barry was the provision of positive attention and inexpensive tangible rewards and activity consequences for increasingly larger periods of time of separation from his parents at both school and home. In order to facilitate active participation by Barry in setting treatment goals and tracking progress, he regularly negotiated performance and contingency goals with the psychologist, and maintained a record of his performance through self-recording. The combined provision of consequences by the therapist and parents was faded over time as behavior improvements were noted. First, the therapist reduced his control over the procedures and consequences so that the program operated through negotiated goals among the family members while the psychologist observed and provided occasional feedback. Later, the frequency of parentally recorded consequences was made more intermittent and unpredictable. In addition, the parents were provided other assistance in order to develop more effective general strategies for child management in this and other areas of concern.

As part of the treatment, Barry kept records on the performance of various behaviors and brought those records to the hospital when he and his family met with the psychologist. One record of significance was a measure of the amount of time spent away from his parents both in school and at home. Barry's records were routinely compared with the independent records of the parents; although there were occasional differences, the magnitude of the differences were small. Separate discussion with Barry and his parents attested to the independence and accuracy of the reports. Despite his confidence that the records were adequate as a measure of the program's success, the psychologist continued to monitor the veracity of the records, especially when additional contingencies were applied to increase the time away from parents.

Interestingly, when the time came for Barry to negotiate goals for improvement (i.e., goals for longer periods of time away from his parents), he consistently set goals that were below his current level of functioning, but were clear improvements over previous performance. Although such goal setting could have been considered an inaccurate reflection of current performance, the level of performance set was acceptable to the psychologist and appropriate for treatment progress. Therefore, the psychologist did not pressure Barry to change goals to more carefully match behavior outcomes. It should also be noted here that Barry enjoyed performing at a level far in excess of the goals he set. It appeared that the differential between goals set and actual performance was a factor of accomplishment that Barry pointed to with pride (he graphed them both while at his appointment). If the goals had been much higher, attainment of success in excess of the goals may not have had a similarly potent reinforcing function.

The program progressed well and the outcome was that Barry successfully separated from his parents at both school and home with little problem. These gains were maintained across the school year and subsequent years.

Adolescent Programs

When adolescent students are generally nonproductive in the face of potent contingencies for productivity, it is important to monitor performance and to set reasonable performance standards. For example, Kelley and Stokes (1982) used contingency contracting to improve the academic performance of adolescents who had returned to school after having dropped out for at least 6 months. As part of a government-funded incentive program to return students to educational and vocational training, these dropouts were paid for attendance at the program in a rural area. Unfortunately, students attended sufficiently to receive the monetary rewards, but their productivity in the classroom was not impressive. The students were not making adequate progress in preparation for examination for a general equivalency diploma (GED). They were essentially manipulating a system set up to help them. The error was that the procedural system had been poorly developed. The students were simply exploiting an operating contingency that called only for attendance, not for productivity. It may have been unethical, but it was certainly understandable, given the system, the students' prior histories, and their presumed sophisticated work avoidance repertoires. As a solution to these problems, a new procedure that emphasized the students' productivity was developed. The contingencies for the receipt of the reinforcer (the money) were changed to tie its delivery to attendance and completion of work. In acknowledgment of the developmental status of the students, arbitrary requirements were not imposed. Instead, the students negotiated contracts with their teacher about the amount of work that would be completed each day. The contracts were reasonable and fair, but once a week's contract was agreed upon, no changes were allowed. During negotiations, the teacher targeted a 10% change over baseline performance levels. The productivity on classroom self-paced workbooks in mathematics was carefully monitored by the teacher to ensure that the student did his or her own work to present for grading. In fact, all student workbooks had answer keys removed to prevent even unobtrusive referral for help. The students' productivity and attendance improved during the contracting procedures and both declined during an interim return to baseline assessment.

In a follow-up change of program, Kelley and Stokes (1984) made the procedures come more under the control of the students, while at the same time increasing monitoring and incorporating protections to safeguard the program from cheating. Student aides were used for routine grading of the mathematics, reading, science, social studies, and English self-paced workbooks because of the increased volume of work output anticipated. The graders sat at the front of the room next to the teacher and graded only objective answers that could be compared with answer keys; the teacher monitored the grading and work sequence of each student. In addition, students could bring only their completed worksheets to the desk to be graded.

In order to allow more student participation in these procedures, after a period in which the students had successfully negotiated a contractual performance level, they were allowed to set their own goals without input from the teacher. They simply presented the teacher with the written goals they had developed for the week. These goal-setting procedures were preferred by the students to the contracting procedures. Productivity under goal setting was superior to performance under the baseline conditions, which had neither contracting or goalsetting, but it was not as high as under contracting conditions. However, it was judged by the teacher to be satisfactory because the level was clearly above baseline (see Figure 3, which shows the numbers of work items correctly completed by the students).

Some question, though, remains regarding the maintenance of acceptable levels of performance. One student, Don, showed a clear downward trend in the number of correct items completed from the outset of goalsetting. Prior to day 76, he was instructed by the teacher that he had to set his work standards at a level more similar to performance during the contracting phase or the conditions of contracting with the teacher would be reinstated. This superordinate avoidance contingency was sufficient to quickly restore performance to more acceptable levels. However, there was a less precipitous downward trend in academic productivity. If there had been more time to document performance, Don might appropriately have been returned to contracting for a limited time prior to return to goalsetting. The implementation of these procedures again may have increased the salience of the negative reinforcement contingency that was being put in place to maintain some external control over the level of self-determined goals of the students.

The implication of these and the other data from the research of Kelley and Stokes (1984) is that there needs to be special monitoring of performance standards and of actual performance when students have extensive control in setting work standards and there are potent reinforcers for completing the work according to those standards

Seymour and Stokes (1976) also have demonstrated the need to monitor the veracity of reports and to modify procedures to assure accurate reporting and change in targeted behaviors. Female adolescent delinquents in various academic and vocational settings were taught to record their on-task activity with the goal of increasing their work productivity. They were then taught to prompt or cue their teachers to respond with (hopefully) positive comments regarding their performance. With three of the four students, self-recording with contingent tokens as the consequence resulted in increased work and the cues to the teachers resulted in an increased schedule of praise from the supervisors. The tokens were given by a counselor only for the amount of work noted by the students.

This procedure clearly presents the possibility for cheating by overestimating performance or deliberately reporting performance in excess of the work done. Such outcomes were tracked and efforts were made to manage the self-recording aberrations that did in fact occur. Figure 4 shows the data of one student, Yvonne. When self-recording began, improved work was noted in each setting. However, monitoring of Yvonne's records showed that on the fourth day of self-recording

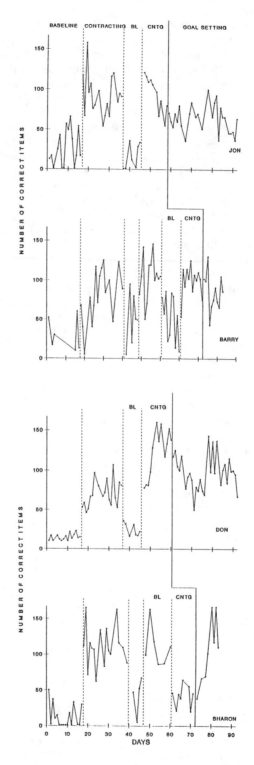

FIGURE 3. Jon/Barry graphs: Number of items completed correctly by Jon and Barry during each experimental condition. Don/Sharon graphs: Number of items completed correctly by Don and Sharon during each experimental condition. Adapted from Kelley and Stokes (1984).

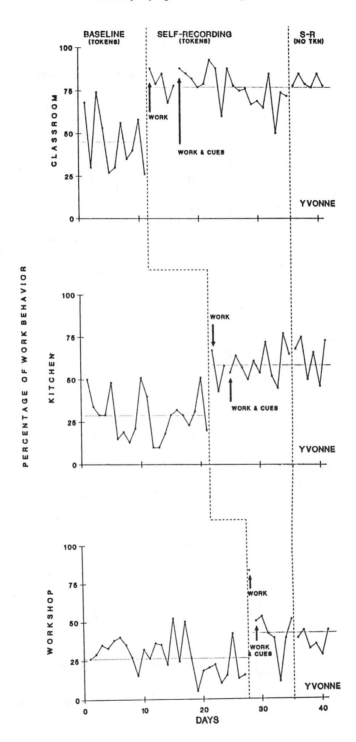

FIGURE 4. Observed work each day in each setting calculated as a percentage of the combined categories of work, interrupted work, and nonwork. The average percentage of work during baseline and the combined self-recording conditions is shown by the horizontal dotted line. Adapted from Seymour and Stokes (1976).

in the classroom, she recorded that she had worked more minutes than were actually available in the classroom that day. In order to provide consequences for such flagrant cheating, a 10-token response cost fine was imposed. No further instances of extreme cheating were noted. Occasional minor instances of cheating were noted but consequences were not levied because performance, for the most part, remained well above the baseline mean levels. Clearly, if Yvonne had been more sophisticated, she might have cheated more carefully. Under such circumstances, detection of the cheating would have been more difficult and she would have avoided the programmed negative consequences.

With a second student, it was determined that an initial problem was not blatant overscoring of work, but instead was inappropriate use of the self-recording intervention procedures. That is, she randomly marked her recording card, which consistently allowed her to earn tokens while her performance declined. Following this occurrence, her use of the self-recording procedures was discontinued for 6 days, which was essentially a time-out from the procedures. Reinstitution of the self-recording resulted both in correct use of the procedures and improved work performance. Blatant cheating on one day resulted in a 10-point fine; no further instances were noted.

A third student overscored consistently but by small amounts. No response cost correction procedures were implemented for that student because productivity remained high. Response cost procedures were implemented on three separate occasions with a fourth student but had no effect on her performance. All of these data emphasize the need to continue to monitor procedures and to provide reasonable positive or negative consequences for accurate use of the program procedures.

SUMMARY AND CONCLUSIONS

Honesty at school does not emerge naturally irrespective of management by school personnel. Naturally occurring consequences at school, home, and other important settings may encourage honest behavior, but the astute teacher or school psychologist will appreciate the fact that there exist supporting contingencies for the development of lying and cheating. That is, reinforced deviance may be as prevalent as reinforced honesty. The best course of action, therefore, is to maximize the detection of both honest and dishonest activity for children of all ages and to apply reasonable accelerative and decelerative consequences promptly. Monitoring students' verbal and written reports and their access to illegitimate sources of information is essential to any programmatic reaction to lying and cheating. This monitoring, which should occur repeatedly, should note inconsistencies among various sources of information so that appropriate conclusions can be drawn and consequences applied. This chapter has provided some examples from the published literature of management strategies that have been used to foster accurate and honest performance in the schools.

ACKNOWLEDGMENTS

Preparation of this chapter was supported in part by U.S. Department of Education grants #G008630340 and #HO24A80037 to the authors. The authors would like to acknowledge the assistance of Deb Odom in the preparation of this manuscript.

REFERENCES

Baer, R. A., Williams, J. A., Osnes, P. G., & Stokes, T. F. (1985). Generalized verbal control and correspondence training. *Behavior Modification, 9*, 477–489.

Bijou, S. W., & Baer, D. M. (1978). *Behavior analysis of child development.* Englewood Cliffs, NJ: Prentice-Hall.

Blount, R. L., & Stokes, T. F. (1984). Self-reinforcement by children. In M. Hersen, R. W. Eisler, & P. M. Miller (Eds.), *Progress in behavior modification* (Vol. 18; pp. 195–225). Orlando, FL: Academic.

Bushway, A., & Nash, W. R. (1977). School cheating behavior. *Review of Educational Research, 47,* 623–632.

Drabman, R. S., Spitalnik, R., & O'Leary, K. D. (1973). Teaching self-control to disruptive children. *Journal of Abnormal Child Psychology, 82,* 10–16.

Guevremont, D. C., Osnes, P. G., & Stokes, T. F. (1988). The functional role of preschoolers' verbalizations in the generalization of self-instructional training. *Journal of Applied Behavior Analysis, 21,* 45-55.

Guevremont, D. C., Osnes, P. G., & Stokes, T. F. (1986). Preparation for effective self-regulation: The development of generalized verbal control. *Journal of Applied Behavior Analysis, 19,* 99-104.

Guevremont, D. G., Osnes, P. G., & Stokes, T. F. (in press). Generalization and maintenance of verbal control using correspondence training. *Behavior Modification.*

Hrydowy, E. R., Stokes, T. F., & Martin, G. L. (1984). Training elementary students to prompt teacher praise. *Education and Treatment of Children, 7,* 99-108.

Kelley, M. L., & Stokes, T. F. (1982). Contingency contracting with disadvantaged youths: Improving classroom performance. *Journal of Applied Behavior Analysis, 15,* 447-454.

Kelley, M. L., & Stokes, T. F. (1984). Student-teacher contracting with goal-setting for maintenance. *Behavior Modification, 8,* 223-244.

Miller, G. (1987). School interventions for dishonest behavior. *Special Services in the Schools, 3,* 21-36.

Osnes, P. G., Guevremont, D. C., & Stokes, T. F. (1986). "If I say I'll talk more, then I will": Correspondence training to increase peer directed talk by socially withdrawn children. *Behavior Modification, 10,* 287-299.

Osnes, P. G., Guevremont, D. C., & Stokes, T. F. (1987). Increasing a child's prosocial behaviors: Positive and negative consequences in correspondence training. *Journal of Behavior Therapy and Experimental Psychiatry, 18,* 71-76.

Seymour, F. W., & Stokes, T. F. (1976). Self-recording in training girls to increase work and evoke staff praise in an institution for offenders. *Journal of Applied Behavior Analysis, 9,* 41-54.

Stokes, T. F. (1985). Contingency management. In A. S. Bellack & M. Hersen (Eds.), *Dictionary of behavior therapy techniques.*

Stokes, T. F., & Baer, D. M. (1977). An implicit technology of generalization. *Journal of Applied Behavior Analysis, 10,* 349-367.

Stokes, T. F., Boggs, S. B., & Osnes, P. G. (1989). Separation anxiety disorder and school phobia. In M. C. Roberts & C. E. Walker (Eds.), *Casebook in child and pediatric psychology.* New York: Guilford.

Stokes, T. F., & Osnes, P. G. (1986). Programming the generalization of children's social behavior. In P. S. Strain, M. J. Guralnick, & H. Walker (Eds.), *Children's social behavior: Development, assessment, and modification* (pp. 407-443). Orlando, FL: Academic.

Stokes, T. F., & Osnes, P. G. (1988). The developing applied technology of generalization and maintenance. In R. H. Horner, G. Dunlap, & R. L. Koegel (Eds.), *Generalization and maintenance: Lifestyle changes in applied settings* (pp. 5-19). Baltimore: Paul Brookes.

Stokes, T. F., & Osnes, P. G. (1989). An operant pursuit of generalization. *Behavior Therapy, 20,* 337-355.

Stokes, T. F., Osnes, P. G., & Guevremont, D. C. (1987). Saying and doing: A commentary on a contingency-space analysis. *Journal of Applied Behavior Analysis, 20,* 161-164.

Stouthamer-Loeber, M. (1986). Lying as a problem behavior in children: A review. *Clinical Psychology Review, 6,* 267-289.

29

Interventions for Swearing

James E. Gilliam
Laura Stough
Kathleen Fad
University of Texas at Austin

Swearing is a problem behavior that is occurring more frequently in schools. Behavioral interventions for swearing are necessary for several reasons. First, most teachers are not knowledgeable about techniques that are effective in reducing swearing, and the techniques that they naturally use are not effective. Second, swearing is often contagious. When one student begins to swear, other children are likely to join in. Third, swearing is a disruptive behavior; it distracts students and teachers from their work. Fourth, swearing frequently precedes or is accompanied by physical aggression. The fear of aggression causes teachers and students to be imtimidated and coerced by the swearer. Fifth, swearing by students is considered antisocial or deviant and is usually punished by persons in authority, either at school, at home, or in the community. Swearing in the presence of authority figures is considered antisocial or deviant and usually is consequated negatively. To summarize, interventions are needed that teachers can use to teach students how to control or reduce their swearing so that they do not get punished.

Research related to swearing has focused on adults and is esoteric. Relatively little research has been done on children's swearing in school. What literature is available describes operant techniques that are used to consequate swearing. The techniques presented in this chapter are based on the premise that students need to learn about their swearing and develop strategies for managing it.

WHY DO CHILDREN SWEAR?

Some children use swearing as a means of getting attention. It definitely gets them noticed by peers and adults even if it results in negative consequences. Some children swear for the shock value that most swearing produces. Most adults will respond to an 8-year-old's shout of "You motherfucker!" with alarm, anger, or even guilt. Adults tend to feel embarrassed and uncomfortable when children swear, and this often gives the child a feeling of importance over adults. Some children swear as an act of rebellion against their parents. In home environments where swearing is strictly taboo, using swearing is a way to defy parental authority.

Children tend to model adults. They hear adults use inappropriate language and assume that one way to be just like "grown-ups" is to talk like them. Children also use swearing as a means to win peer approval. Some may think it "tough" or "macho" to swear and in order to be an accepted member of one's peer group they must act tough and swear. Young children may swear if they become fascinated with body functions and enjoy talking about them. As children grow older, sexual awareness emerges and they turn to talking about the body organs and sex acts. For others, swearing acts as a release of anger, frustration, tension, even excitement (Schaefer & Millman, 1981). All of us at one time or another have let out a good "Damn it," or worse when we are frustrated.

WHAT IS SWEARING?

According to Cohen (1978), swearing can be classified into three major categories: (a) speech that involves disrespect for something that is considered sacred or holy, such as the name of God; (b) speech reflecting the wish to harm someone (e.g., "Damn you"); and (c) obscenity, which is disparaging reference to sexual organs or acts or to elimination topics (e.g., "Screw you"). For the purpose of this chapter, all language of the type described above will be referred to simply as swearing.

Most teachers will agree that swearing is one form of acting-out behavior. It not only disrupts the normal routine of the classroom; to a greater or lesser extent, an element of physical or personal assault is present in practically every form of swearing.

Most interventions teachers use in response to swearing have limited effectiveness. Some teachers attempt to ignore swearing in the hope that if it doesn't get any attention, it will not continue. This would be a sound strategy if swearing were maintained only by a teacher's attention. However, peers often provide excessive attention by way of approval of this type of behavior. Also, most teachers find that ignoring a disruptive behavior such as swearing usually results in escalation of the behavior, at least initially. Alternatively, reprimanding a child with a lecture on improper language is usually ineffective, or at best may produce a short-term reduction in the behavior. Often the attention received in the process of the reprimand will actually strengthen the swearing it was supposed to suppress (Walker, 1979). Consequently, the classroom routine becomes disrupted, the teacher finds it difficult to teach and becomes frustrated, and the child usually ends up in the principal's office; in short, everyone involved loses out in one way or another.

This chapter is intended to help teachers deal with swearing in the classroom, especially those who work with elementary-age populations in classrooms for children who are considered deviant, behavior problems, or emotionally disturbed. Some of the activities discussed can be modified for use with older students. Regular classroom teachers experiencing swearing problems with individual children or small groups rather than entire classes should find some of these activities useful also.

Recent literature has shown that the most successful classroom intervention strategies are those based upon systematic behavioral procedures. Presently the most widely used approaches in dealing with disruptive, acting-out behaviors such as swearing are those based on learning or behavior theory. This is primarily because intervention programs based on behavior theory have been shown to be effective through extensive research and practice. Also, such approaches emphasize the "teaching–learning" process by which children's acquisition of appropriate behaviors is a learning process guided by the teacher. And finally, behavior modification is easy to understand as well as practical for the classroom teacher (Alberto & Troutman, 1986).

Morgan and Jenson (1988) feel that most offenses attributed to children with behavior problems are normal behaviors — normal in that at one time or another all children lie, cheat, act aggressively, or use bad language. What makes these behaviors deviant is that they are exhibited in the wrong places, at the wrong times, in the presence of the wrong people and most importantly, to an inappropriate degree. These deviant or maladaptive behaviors have been learned in the same way that appropriate, prosocial behaviors are learned. Whether a child learns appropriate or inappropriate behavior depends largely on the type of consequences, either positive or negative, that are supplied contingently for each.

ACTIVITY NO. 1: Baseline Data

Objective: Teachers will determine which swearwords are used in the classroom, the frequency of their use, and the particular students who use them.

WORDS USED

Student's Name	Fuck you, Screw you	Shit, Turd	Mother Fucker	Damn, Goddamn	Ass, Asshole, Jackass	Bitch, Bastard	Piss, Pissed Off	Cock, Pussy

FIGURE 1. Log of particular swearwords used and frequencies by student. Construct a log to record each student's use of particular swearwords.

From several theoretical constructs of behavioral theory, Morgan and Jenson (1988) draw some pertinent conclusions: (a) Most inappropriate behavior is learned just like appropriate behavior. (b) A relationship exists between the behavior a child exhibits and the environment; this relationship can be described as well as predicted if various components of the environment are known. (c) Deviant behavior can be changed through the use of appropriate reinforcement techniques. (d) Looking for causes of deviant behavior is counterproductive, since the original cause of a given behavior is unlikely to be what is maintaining the behavior at the present time. Intervention based on behavior theory is primarily concerned with the "what" of behavior, rather than the "how" or "why." The underlying causal factors are largely ignored because the emphasis is on assisting a child in modifying his behavior to increase the probability of his success and acceptance in his environment.

Behavioral interventions start out by defining the behavior to be changed in an objective manner so that direct measurement of the behavior can be obtained. Measuring the behavior and obtaining baseline data are essential for three reasons. First, it helps the teacher to determine if a problem actually exists. Second, gathering baseline data aids the teacher in identifying any environmental stimuli that may be supporting or maintaining the inappropriate behavior (for example peer attention) and what environmental stimuli are likely to produce a desired change. Third, the baseline data provide a standard against which to evaluate treatment and measure future behavior or progress (Alberto & Troutman, 1986). The first three activities presented in this chapter describe techniques for obtaining baseline data. Activity 1 involves recording the frequency of certain swearwords (see Figure 1). Activities 2 and 3 encourage students to generate their most popular swearwords. NOTE: Teachers are cautioned that some of these activities may be controversial. Consent should be solicited and acquired from the students' parents before conducting some of the activities. Permission and consent should also be obtained from the appropriate school administrators.

ACTIVITY NO. 2:
"Cussing Up a Storm"

Objective

Students will become familiar with swearwords and terms commonly used by participating in a "brainstorming" session of swearing.

Procedure

1. Have children sit in a circle or semicircle facing the chalkboard. Teacher may want to use a posterboard instead of chalkboard to list words.

2. Start the discussion by calling attention to the fact that swearing is a common problem among students as well as adults. Point out that there are many words people use as swearwords, and what one person may consider a bad or dirty word another may not. So, in order that everyone will know what is a swearword and what isn't, students will have a "brainstorm" session to come up with as many words as possible that are known to be swearwords.

3. Tell students that everyone will have a chance to give at least one swearword or term. Ask them to think of words that they have used before or may have heard other people using. To keep things orderly so that everyone doesn't call out at the same time, have students raise their hands before speaking. The teacher may want to begin the session so that any students who feel uncomfortable swearing in front of the teacher will understand that it is quite acceptable in this activity.

4. As words and terms are called out, the teacher can list them on the board or poster. Encourage students to think of all different types of swearwords and their variations (ass, asshole, jackass, up your ass, etc.). Make sure that everyone gives their input and contributes something to the list.

5. When it is felt that most words and terms have been listed, the teacher can end the session by complimenting students for thinking very hard and coming up with so many words. The teacher needs to be prepared to deal with kids who are silly, agitated, etc. Some students may need to be removed if their behavior is too disruptive.

6. The teacher must remain calm, and nonchalant when the swearwords are said. The teacher *must* demonstrate that he or she is not affected by the students' swearing.

Evaluation

1. Ask students if there were any new swearwords they learned that they didn't know before.

2. Ask students to describe how they felt about swearing openly in front of the teacher.

3. Ask students why it is important to know which words are swearwords and which are not.

4. Ask if certain words bothered them or made them feel particularly uncomfortable.

Materials

Posterboard.

ACTIVITY NO. 3
"What's Number One?"

Objective

Students will determine the most "popular" swearwords by ranking choices in a class poll.

Procedures

1. Begin this activity with a review of some of the words on the list from Activity No. 2. Ask students if they think certain words are used more than other words. Ask for reasons why some words are used more than others.

2. Tell students that to find out which swearwords are used more often the class will take part in a poll to find the most "popular" swearwords.

3. Pass out 3 × 5 cards to students. Ask them to write down their two favorite "cuss" words or words they hear most often in order of preference. Collect all cards and tally the results.

4. Rank choices on the board according to class votes. For example if "shit" got the most votes, put a #1 by it, "damn" #2, etc. Ask those students who put "shit" as #1 to tell why it was their first choice. Ask questions such as:

   a. Do they use it themselves most often or hear others use it most often?
   b. Do they know what it means?

c. Under what circumstances do they use the word, etc.? Ask similar questions for some of the top choices in the poll.

Evaluation

1. The teacher can explain to students that she or her did a similar ranking on swearwords in the class a couple of weeks ago (Baseline Data, Activity #1) by marking down every time a swearword was used.

2. Using information obtained from baseline data, compare the teacher's ranking with that of students.

3. Discuss any discrepancies between the two ranks and reasons for the differences.

Note. Even though using data from Activity #1, there is no need to mention names of students and who "cussed" most frequently. Just use the frequency count of particular words.

Materials

3 × 5 index cards.
Data from Activity #1.

After gathering data, the next step in an intervention program is to identify potential reinforcers and arrange consequences. Reinforcers are defined by their effects on the behaviors they follow and not on the basis of how we think they should function. For example, positive reinforcement is any stimulus that acts to strengthen the behavior it follows; negative reinforcement is any stimulus that, by its removal, strengthens or increases the behavior it follows. Punishment, on the other hand, is any stimulus that decreases the behavior it follows. Different children as well as different adults do not find the same things reinforcing. For some children, a teacher's attention is a powerful reinforcer. Others find tangibles such as food, money, or tokens very reinforcing. Many children prefer activities or privileges as reinforcers such as extra free time or helping the teacher. Once reinforcers have been identified, they must be consistently applied to the desired behavior. Maintain-

ing a record of reinforcement will help to determine if the strength or frequency of the behavior has increased. And once inappropriate behavior is reduced and the desired behavior is achieved, fading reinforcement to natural levels can begin. Doing so allows the behavior to be exhibited at an appropriate level with a normal level of social reinforcement.

A variety of behavior management techniques have been used in dealing with acting-out behaviors such as swearing, and research shows positive results in decreasing such undesirable behaviors. A frequently used procedure is **time-out,** in which a child is temporarily removed from a *reinforcing situation* following the occurrence of an inappropriate behavior. Time-out is a form of punishment and its purpose is to decrease the occurrence of behaviors to which it is applied. In classrooms where it is used, the time-out period usually lasts from 5 to 15 minutes, although the shortest effective length of time is desirable. The most important aspect of time-out is removal from a reinforcing environment not the length of time. Lahey, McNees, and McNees (1973) used time-out procedures to reduce swearing in a 10-year-old retarded student. Josephs (1968) also obtained successful results by using time-out to control swearing and temper outbursts in the classroom.

Response cost is another strategy that can produce positive results in decreasing acting-out behaviors. Response cost involves the removal of previously awarded or earned reinforcers for the purpose of reducing problematic behavior. In the application of response cost, reinforcers are removed whenever instances of undesirable behavior occur. Iwata and Bailey (1974), McLaughlin and Malaby (1972) and Sulzbacher and Houser (1968) have demonstrated the effectiveness of response cost in reducing such behaviors as out-of-seat behavior and inappropriate language and gestures.

Token systems involve reinforcement in the form of tokens (points, chips, checks, etc.) for exhibiting appropriate behavior. Tokens are later exchanged for food, toys, activities, and privileges. In one classroom run on a token system Epstein, Repp, and Cullinan (1978) introduced a DRL schedule (differential reinforcement of low rates of responding) to reduce high rates of obscenity. A DRL schedule rewards children for making fewer than a specified number of undesirable responses within a given time limit. Advantages of DRL schedules are that they reward reduction of inappropriate behavior rather than punish its continued occurrence and can be used for a wide range of target behaviors.

Negative practice, sometimes called "instructed repetition," involves encouraging a person who exhibits an undesirable behavior to repeatedly perform the behavior, the intent being that the behavior should stop because the fatigue that accumulates by its repetition makes doing it painful or aversive (Blackman & Silberman, 1971). However, forcing a child to perform a behavior can produce unpleasant consequences for both teacher and student (Lahey, McNees, & McNees, 1973). Similar to negative practice is **satiation,** which involves presenting a reinforcing stimulus at such a high rate that its reinforcing properties are lost. Activity 4 illustrates this technique. Activity 4 is a "swear-down," during which students may swear so frequently that the swearwords lose their reinforcing quality. The intent of this activity is to remove the reinforcing properties of swearwords by causing the students to say them.

ACTIVITY NO. 4
"Get It Out of Your System" Swear-down

Objective

Students will become desensitized to the shock value of swearwords by repeatedly swearing with other classmates.

Procedure

1. Divide the class in half. Form two lines so that each student has a partner facing him across the line. Ask the students to think of their two favorite "cuss" words.

2. Tell them that for the next few minutes they are going to "cuss" the person across from them, using their first word and that word only. They can't use complete sentences such as "You are a . . ." When the signal to go is given, they must look the person directly across from them straight in the eye and start repeating their swearword. They should use a normal tone of voice, and no shouting, but they can't stop until the signal is given. A whistle or bell can be used to start and stop the activity.

3. Set up a tape recorder out of sight of the students and record the swearing.

4. After 5 minutes or so, blow the whistle to signal the students to stop. Now tell them to use another swearword and do exactly the same as before. Blow the whistle and begin.

5. After a few minutes you will find that the students will start to laugh because it sounds so ridiculous. After 10 minutes or so of this activity, the teacher can decide to stop it if the students are getting tired or too silly.

6. Lead a discussion on the activity. Ask questions such as the following:

a. Why did you start laughing?
b. Why do you think it sounded so funny to say the "cuss" word so often?
c. What did it sound like to hear everyone swearing at the same time?
d. Think about the word you used. Did you like the sound of the word?
e. Does the word you said still seem as strong, harsh, mean, and so forth?
f. Did the words used by others bother you or did they lose their power?

Evaluation

1. After discussion, play back the tape for the students.

2. Have each student make a list of feelings produced by the repetitive swearing (tired, angry, bored, silly, etc.).

3. List different things people felt on the chalkboard for all to see and compare.

Materials

Tape recorder.
Cassette tape.
Whistle.

WHY DO I SWEAR?

Circle YES or NO before each of the following statements:

Yes No   1.   Because everyone does.
Yes No   2.   Because my best friends do.
Yes No   3.   When I'm angry.
Yes No   4.   When I don't like someone.
Yes No   5.   When I can't do anything right.
Yes No   6.   Because it makes me feel important or grown-up.
Yes No   7.   Because my friends will think I'm "tough."
Yes No   8.   When I can't think of anything else to say.
Yes No   9.   When I don't want to do certain things.
Yes No   10.   I don't really know why.

FIGURE 2. "Why do I swear" activity questions.

If children are to learn that swearing is an inappropriate behavior, they must know which words most people consider inappropriate as well as how often they are used and what they sound like when they do swear. Once children are aware of the words, they need to know why people swear and the effect swearing has on others' feelings and emotions. Activity 5 identifies reasons and situations that cause people to swear and Activity 6 identifies and discusses feelings and emotions generated from swearwords.

ACTIVITY NO. 5
Why Do I Swear?

Objectives

Students will become aware of different reasons and situations that cause people to swear.

Procedures

1. Pass out the questionnaire in Figure 2. Instruct students to read each sentence, think about what it says, and answer Yes or No to each statement. For students who may have difficulty reading the sentences, the teacher can read each one aloud and have them circle Yes or No as it pertains to them.

2. After all students have had a chance to complete the questionnaire, begin a discussion by pointing out that we hear people swearing all the time, but just because two people use the same words it doesn't mean they are swearing for the same reasons. Give several examples such as "Bobby might swear when someone takes his pencil that he needs for math, but Kathy might swear because she wants Susan to think she's very grownup."

3. Write each statement on the board. Beginning with Statement No. 1, read each one and ask students to raise their hands if they circled Yes to that particular statement. Tally results on the board so that all can see which reasons are most often the cause for swearing.

4. Beginning with the reason most often cited for swearing, ask children to give examples or situations in which they ended up swearing. For example if No. 3. "When I'm angry" was cited by most students, ask several to tell about times when they got angry and "cussed" at someone ("when my sister took my skates"; "when I lost my lunch money"; etc.).

5. Read each statement and discuss why swearing is used in that situation. Examples: for No. 8, you might want to bring up the point that a person may swear if he doesn't know a better way to express his feelings or doesn't know the right words to say. For No. 5, point out that frustration is feeling that we can't do anything right. For Nos. 1, 2, and 7, you might want to talk about the importance of impressing friends, or doing things just because our friends do.

Evaluation

1. In their own words, have students write two or three statements different from those listed on the questionnaire that may be reasons people swear.

2. Read them aloud or list on the board.

Materials

Questionnaire.

ACTIVITY NO. 6
Dealing with Feelings

Objective

Students will identify and discuss feelings and emotions generated from swear words and their use.

Procedure

1. Begin the activity by asking students questions such as the following:

a. How do you feel when someone "cusses at you" ("angry"; "I feel like crying"; "It makes me want to hit them"; etc.)

b. How do you feel when you hear a "cuss" word? (embarrassed, silly, nervous, afraid, etc.)

c. Do you feel different when you call someone a name than you do when someone calls you a name?

d. Is it easier to call someone a bad name than to accept being called one?

e. Does it make you feel good to "tell someone off?"

2. Discuss with students how powerful words can be and how important it is to choose the right words when you want to convey a strong feeling to someone. Ask them, "What hurts people more, hitting someone in the stomach or calling them a dirty name?" Most students will say "hitting them in the stomach." Explain that swearing at someone and calling them bad names can hurt people very deeply. It can hurt someone just as much as a punch in the stomach. Then ask them again to think about times when people have called them names and whether or not they felt very hurt.

3. Ask students if they enjoy being "cussed at." If not, then remind them that swearwords produce a lot of emotions, some of which can be very painful. Tell them: "Remember, you shouldn't use them to call other people names if you don't like it yourself. After all, the person you swear at might get the same feelings you do."

Evaluation

Say several swearwords and ask students to write down the emotions they feel when they hear each one.

Peer attention and approval is a powerful reinforcer for most children. Using peers to bring about changes in students' behavior can be a powerful strategy in reducing undesirable behavior. It is a major factor in the maintenance of many deviant behaviors, and lack of it will often cause the rate of such behaviors to diminish. Studies by Mosier and Vaal (1970) and Lovitt, Lovitt, Eaton and Kirkwood (1973) have demonstrated the effects of using peer attention to decrease name-calling and other inappropriate language in elementary school children.

Modeling is a teaching technique that classroom teachers often use to teach certain skills and behaviors. A desired skill or behavior is demonstrated or modeled by the teacher, who then usually has the students practice it. Use of modeling procedures to strengthen desirable behaviors and inhibit undesirable ones has repeatedly been documented in research studies (Goldstein & Glick, 1987). Activities 7, 8, and 9 are innovative approaches to modeling. Activity 7 stresses the meanings of swearwords and suggests alternatives. Activities 8 and 9 identify times and places in which swearing is inappropriate and help make up nonsense words to replace swearwords.

ACTIVITY NO. 7
What Are You Really Trying to Say?

Objectives

1. Students will become aware of meanings and origins of swearwords.

2. Students will use more exact words when trying to convey a strong feeling.

Procedure

1. Ask a student to give you the definition of the word *bitch*. Most students will say it's a "cuss" word.

2. Ask the same student to look up the word in the dictionary. What does the dictionary say? (Definition: the female of the dog; an immoral woman; a spiteful, domineering woman; to complain, or a complaint.)

3. Begin a discussion on the meaning of swearwords by pointing out to students that in everyday conversation you wouldn't think of using a word if you didn't know what it meant, yet people use swearwords all the time without knowing what they mean. Also, explain that swearwords, like other words in our language, can have several meanings, some of which aren't considered "vulgar" or "bad." Sometimes it depends on how you use the word whether people consider it a "cuss" word.

4. Say: "Let's go back to the word *bitch*. What are you really trying to say when you call someone a bitch?" Are you calling that person a female dog? Lots of people have dogs for pets. They're lovable animals and they are our friends. If you call someone a bitch, are you telling her that she is your friend and she is nice like dogs? Or are you telling her that she is being mean and spiteful? That's why it's important to think about a word and what it means before you use it. Instead of calling her a bitch, tell her he is being mean or hateful. It's important to use exactly the right word so the person will know what you mean.

5. Another example to use: *ass*. Ask a student to look up the word *ass* (Definition: "a hardy gregarious mammal smaller than a horse with long ears: a donkey"; "a stupid, obstinate person"; "buttocks".) Ask: "When you call a person an ass, what are you really trying to tell him?" "Are you saying he's an animal, or a part of the body, or a stupid, stubborn person?" Continue with several examples.

6. Assign one word to each student and have them look up the definition or definitions of their word. Tell them to also look at the origin of the word if listed in the dictionary.

Evaluation

1. Ask each student to stand up and read all definitions listed of the words they looked up.

2. Then ask each student to name a word or words they could use in place of the swearword that conveys a more precise and exact meaning that they want to get across.

Materials

Dictionaries.

ACTIVITY NO. 8*
Don't Say That Here!

Objective

Students will be able to identify times, places, and situations in which swearing is considered inappropriate.

Procedures

1. Read the following to the students.

"Tony and Mark sat next to each other in class one day. Tony was working hard on his math when Mark turned to him and said, 'Let's stop all this work and go in the game corner to play checkers.' Tony didn't like being interrupted and said to Mark, 'Get away from me, you ass! I'm busy.' Mark didn't like being called an ass, so he called Tony a bastard. Back and forth they went until their name calling became so loud that their teacher heard them. 'We don't say things like that in class!' she said. 'You two go right to the principal's office.' Then Mark said to Tony, 'I guess we're really in trouble this time!' and off they went to the office."

2. Begin the discussion by asking students if school is an appropriate place to use swearwords. Continue with such question as the following:

a. Was math class the right time for Mark and Tony to start calling each other names?

b. What happened when they used inappropriate language?

c. Do you think they might have offended or disrupted other students in the class?

d. Did the boys have to use swear-words in this situation?

e. What could they have said to each other instead of swearing?

3. Next, read the following:

"One day after school, Bobby went out to the garage to fix the wheel on his bike. He had to work all by himself because no one was home that afternoon to help him. After an hour of hard work, Bobby was ready to put the fixed wheel back on but when he put it back in place, something was wrong. The wheel wouldn't turn. Bobby got mad because he felt like he had done all that work for nothing. 'Darn it,' he said, 'What's the matter with this wheel?' Then he took the hammer and struck the wheel very hard. The wheel became very bent and it made Bobby angrier to see what had happened. 'Shoot,' he said, 'Look what I've done now!' "

4. Discuss Bobby's reaction to the situation he was in. Ask questions such as the following:

a. What kinds of things did Bobby say and do when the wheel wouldn't turn?

b. Do you think the language he used was inappropriate? Why or why not?

c. Was anyone around to hear him? Did his language offend anyone?

d. What were the consequences of his anger when the wheel wouldn't turn?

e. In which situation, Mark or Tony in math class, or Bobby alone in the garage, was it the most inappropriate to swear? Why?

5. Point out to the students that there are certain times, places, and situations in which swearing would be considered very inappropriate. For example, at school, in the middle of class, in the cafeteria, and at gym would all be inappropriate times and places to swear. But there might be other times that swearing would not be considered so inappropriate depending on the reason. It would also depend on the particular

word you chose. Remind the students that some words convey stronger feelings than others.

6. Discuss with the students that in Bobby's situation he was alone with no one to help or hear him and got very frustrated with his problem. Swearing in that case may have let out some of that frustration. Also, Bobby's words were not strong ones and he wasn't disturbing or offending anyone else. So perhaps in his case, swearing would not be as inappropriate as it would in the classroom with Tony and Mark.

7. On the chalkboard make two columns, one for places and situations where swearing would be most inappropriate, and the other for places and situations where a little swearing might be allowed. Ask each student to name a place or situation in which someone swears and list it in the proper column to which it would apply. Prompt such responses as: church, library, at the dinner table, in front of my parents' friends (all very inappropriate) and others such as: in my backyard, in my room, when I stub my toe and yell "Darn" (not very inappropriate).

Evaluation

1. Divide the board and divide the class into two teams, having them stand in line at the front of the room.

2. Designate Team A to be the ones who will give situations and places where swearing is very inappropriate. Team B will give places and situations in which swearing is not considered to be as inappropriate.

3. The object of the game is to see who can get all its members seated first.

4. Begin by asking the first person on Team A to name the place or situation he's supposed to, and do the same with the first member of Team B. Continue down the line. Each person who answers correctly can sit down. If an incorrect answer is given, that person must go to the end of his team's line. The first team who gets all members sitting wins and may be rewarded with a privilege such as first to lunch or out to recess.

ACTIVITY NO. 9
"Dinglebuff and Smoodgeball"

Objective

Students will make up ten nonsense words to use as alternatives to swearing.

Procedure

1. Begin with a review of how strong emotions and situations can produce swearing. In particular, remind students that one reason people swear is that they can't think of other words to use.

2. Call attention to the fact that sometimes people say "shoot" or "shucks" instead of "shit" and they say "darn" for "damn." These are alternative words to use instead of swearwords and people usually don't consider them inappropriate.

3. Tell students, "If you get a strong urge to swear and you can't think of a better word to use, why not make up a word to use instead of that swearword. People might give you funny looks but you'll be the only one who knows what you really mean! For example, suppose someone cuts in front of you in the lunch line and you get so mad you want to call them a bastard, but instead, you call them a 'dinglebuff.' What do you think they will do or say?"

4. Discuss possible answers, such as "they'll laugh"; "they'll ask you to repeat what you said"; "they might give you your place in line back." Emphasize that because they didn't use a swearword they will be less likely to start a fight, or get in trouble with the teacher, or get themselves called a dirty name.

5. Ask each student to make up ten words that she or he would use instead of using a swearword.

Evaluation

Present a situation to each child and have them respond using one or two of their new "swear" words in the situation. Examples:

1. Someone tears several pages out of your notebook.
2. Someone tells a lie about you.
3. Someone trips you.
4. Someone breaks your last pencil.

5. Someone grabs the ball away from you at recess.

A final technique that seems to have a lot of potential for changing behavior is **role-playing.** Role-playing calls for students to step outside the accustomed "roles" they play in life, with their usual patterns of behavior and take on the role and patterns of another person. Since the students' own behavior is not at issue, they do not have to defend themselves or worry about appearing foolish. Role-playing allows students to see themselves as others see them and perhaps obtain a clearer understanding of how their behavior affects other people. With this awareness, they may be able to change their behavior and improve the nature of their social interactions and feelings about themselves. Activities 10 and 11 present role-play strategies.

ACTIVITY NO. 10:*
Marvin, the Problem Solver

Objective

Students will respond to name calling and swearing by ignoring, changing the subject, or using some other constructive means appropriate to the situation.

Procedures

1. Begin by telling the following short story:

Marvin, the Problem Solver

Everybody at _____ School liked Marvin. It was easy to see why. Marvin was kind to everyone and was very smart about staying out of trouble. In fact, Marvin was so smart about staying out of trouble that he was asked to be the "Problem-Solving Super" of the whole school. Marvin had his own office with purple carpeting, a big desk, and his own secretary! Anyone in the school could go to Marvin's office to talk about a problem and Marvin was always helpful.

One day John came running into Marvin's office with tears in his eyes. "Marvin," said John, "that big bully Billy just called me a name on the playground and I feel bad!"

"What did you do when Billy called you a name?" asked Marvin.

"Why, I started to cry and then came to your office," replied John.

"You were smart not to say anything back, John. Listen very carefully and I will tell you my magical secret that helps people stay out of trouble:

> If ever you are called a name
> Just keep this in mind —
> Ignore that name and walk away
> Or say something that is kind.

John thought about this poem for quite a while, then left Marvin's office to go back to the playground. There stood big bully Billy and when he saw John he called him another name. John remembered the poem:

> If ever you are called a name
> Just keep this in mind —
> Ignore that name and walk away
> Or say something that is kind.

Instead of crying, John said to Billy, "Billy, you are a good baseball player; would you like to show me how you bat so well?" Billy was so pleased with John's nice comment that he said, "Sure pal, let's go out to the baseball field."

2. Write the poem on the board and teach it to students. Have them practice several times to make sure everyone knows the words.

3. Discuss appropriate ways of responding to teasing. Prompt such responses as the following: One could ignore the teasing; one could walk away from the person doing the teasing; one could try to change the subject by talking about something else; one could show concern by something like, "Oh, I'm sorry you feel that way"; one could say something nice to the person.

4. Review steps to think about when responding to name calling such as (a) choosing an appropriate acceptable way of responding; (b) then doing what you have chosen.

Note: Teachers may want to teach certain children a specific way to respond rather than giving them alternatives to choose from. For example, the teacher could teach to respond to name calling by walking way or ignoring. This is recommended for young children and for older children with a strongly conditioned response to name calling.

Evaluation

1. Ask students to repeat the poem.

2. Instruct each student to select a specific way to respond to name calling. Call each student by name and say, "Pretend that I just called you _____ How would you respond appropriately?" See if students use the ways described above.

ACTIVITY NO. 11*
Role Playing

Objectives

Students will respond appropriately to conflict situations with nonaggressive words through the use of role-play.

Procedure

1. Begin by reading the following story:

"One morning, Engelbert brought 24 oatmeal cookies, his favorite kind, to school for his birthday treat. He put the cookies on the file cabinet as the teacher had told him to do. As he was about to return to his seat, he noticed a classmate, Corky, leaving the room. Engelbert knew that Corky would try to eat all of the oatmeal cookies, so he hid them in the file cabinet. Engelbert then left the room to go to the playground. When he left, Corky came back to the room and sniffed out the cookies. By the time Engelbert came back, Corky had eaten all 24 oatmeal cookies!

"Needless to say, Engelbert was very angry. But Engelbert knew how to handle his anger; he knew that hitting or calling Corky names would not get his cookies back and would get him in trouble with the teacher. So he said to Corky, 'Because you ate my oatmeal cookies, Corky, I have no dessert to serve for my birthday treat. This makes me angry.' "

"Then Corky felt very bad that he had eaten the oatmeal cookies. He said, 'I'm sorry, Engelbert. It was very selfish of me.'

Corky felt so bad that he went to the cafeteria and bought 24 cookies to give to Engelbert!"

2. Begin a discussion by asking: "How did Engelbert express his anger?" Continue with such questions as the following:

    a. Why do you think Engelbert's way of expressing anger was the best way?

    b. What are some things that make us angry?

    c. Sometimes when we get angry, we have to stop a minute and think clearly about the right way to express anger. Why should we stop to think about the right way to handle our anger?

3. Explain to students that when angry the best way to express anger is not by swearing but by telling the person how you feel, what he has done, and how what he has done affects you. Is this what Engelbert did in the story? What did he say? Review the story with students.

4. Tell the students, "Now it's time to act out Engelbert's story to help us understand how to respond to situations that make us angry." The teacher should play the part of Engelbert the first time to model the appropriate behavior. Choose a student to play Corky. Have another student read the narrative as "Engelbert" and "Corky" act out their parts.

5. Next, choose three other students to play the parts of Engelbert, Corky, and the narrator. Encourage students in the classroom to volunteer other appropriate responses that might be used in Engelbert's and Corky's story.

Evaluation

Set up role-playing situations to permit practice of appropriate behavior. Write each of the following on index cards and have pupils draw one card.

Examples:

    a. Student discovers that another has taken his or her crayons without asking.

    b. Student is interrupted by another during discussion.

    c. Student discovers that another student has lost his paint set.

    d. Student accidentally knocks another over during movement activity.

    e. Student sticks his foot into the aisle to trip another as he walks by.

    f. Student steals another's lunch money.

    g. Student cuts in line in front of another.

    h. Student takes a toy from another who had been playing with it.

    i. Student throws food at another during lunch.

Usually teachers use combinations of the above strategies in the classroom to deal with deviant behaviors. Positive social reinforcement or token reinforcement is often applied in conjunction with either time-out or cost contingency. Many teachers use teacher praise, tokens, and cost response to change the behavior of deviant children.

As a general rule, a combination of both positive reinforcement and mild punishment techniques will be required to effectively change the behavior of moderately to severely deviant and disruptive children (children who spend less than 50% of the time engaged in appropriate behavior). For children who exhibit mild to moderately deviant and disruptive behavior (children who engage in appropriate behavior more than 50% of the time) usually only positive reinforcement, either social or nonsocial, is required to bring about changes in behavior (Walker, 1979). However, these are only general guidelines. Each child's behavior will have to be considered individually for the purposes of designing different strategies. Teachers can also decide which behaviors are mild, moderate, or severe. Teachers can be powerful agents of social change, and the quality of their interactions with children and the kinds of feedback they provide regarding appropriate and inappropriate behavior are instrumental in shaping what is learned.

SUMMARY AND CONCLUSIONS

The major goal of the activities presented in this chapter is to decrease swearing in the classroom. The following objectives should also be accomplished:

1. Students will become aware of swearing as an antisocial behavior considered to be deviant and inappropriate to use as a means of expressing feelings.
2. Students will be able to identify cause and effect of swearing.
3. Students will learn definitions and origins of certain swearwords.
4. Students will learn to express feelings, frustration, and so forth with more appropriate words instead of swearing.
5. Students will increase interaction skills with peers and adults as a result of learning to express feelings more appropriately.
6. Students will increase self-control by learning to ignore, walk away from, and generally become less impulsive when others use swearwords.
7. Students will increase school performance owing to lessened disruption and keeping out of trouble as a result of a decrease in swearing.
8. Students will enhance self-concept as a result of an increase in self-control, interaction skills, and school performance.

Students participating in these activities will be developing prosocial behaviors and skills that will help them interact more effectively with people. These positive interactions, combined with a reduction of an antisocial behavior (swearing), should give students more positive feelings about themselves, their relationships with people, and their attitudes toward school. Swearing is a serious problem in many classrooms and current interventions have not been proven successful. These activities represent an innovative approach to decreasing a disruptive, antisocial behavior that may interfere with students' interpersonal relationships and acceptance in school.

* **Note:** Activities 8, 10, and 11 are reprinted with permission from Thomas M. Stephens, *Social Skills in the Classroom.* Columbus, OH: Cedars Press, 1978.

REFERENCES

Alberto, P. A., & Troutman, A. C. (1986). *Applied behavior analysis for teachers.* Columbus, OH: Merrill.

Blackham, G. J., & Silberman, A. (1971). *Modification of child behavior.* Belmont, CA: Wadsworth.

Cohen, S. S. (1978, June). Four letter words. *Westchester Magazine,* p. 65.

Epstein, M. H., Repp, A. C., & Cullinan, D. (1978). Decreasing obscene language of behaviorally disordered children through use of a DRL schedule. *Psychology in the Schools, 15*(3), 419-423.

Goldstein, A. P., & Glick, B. (1987). *Aggression replacement training.* Champaign, IL: Research Press.

Iwata, B. A., & Bailey, J. S. (1974). Reward vs. cost token systems: An analysis of the effects on students and teachers. *Journal of Applied Behavior Analysis, 7,* 567-576.

Josephs, E. (1968). Helping Billy control his temper. *Educational Technology Monographs, 1*(2), 9-10.

Lahey, B. B., McNees, M. P., & McNees, M. C. (1973). Control of an obscene "verbal-tic" through time-out in an elementary school classroom. *Journal of Applied Behavior Analysis, 6,* 101-104.

Lovitt, T. C., Lovitt, A. O., Eaton, M. D., & Kirkwood, M. (1973). The deceleration of inappropriate comments by a natural "consequence." *Journal of School Psychology, 1*(2), 148-150.

McLaughlin, T., & Malaby, J. (1972). Reducing and measuring inappropriate verbalizations in a token classroom. *Journal of Applied Behavioral Analysis, 5,* 329-333.

Morgan, D. P., & Jenson, W. R. (1988). *Teaching behaviorally disordered students.* Columbus, OH: Merrill.

Mosier, D., & Vaal, J. J., Jr. (1970). The manipulation of one child's behavior by another child in a school adjustment classroom. *School Applications of Learning Theory, 2,* 25-27.

Schaefer, C. E., & Millman, H. L. (1981). *How to help children with common problems.* New York: Van Nostrand Reinhold.

Stephens, T. M. (1978). *Social skills in the classroom.* Columbus, OH: Cedars Press.

Sulzbacher, S. I., & Houser, J. E. (1968). A tactic to eliminate disruptive behaviors in the classroom: Group contingent consequences. *American Journal of Mental Deficiencies, 1,* 182–187.

Walker, H. M. (1979). *The acting-out child: Coping with classroom disruption.* Boston: Allyn & Bacon.

30

Psychological Interventions for Depression in Children and Adolescents

William M. Reynolds
University of Wisconsin–Madison

INTRODUCTION

Internalizing disorders of childhood and adolescence, and in particular depression, are insidious problems. They present professionals with challenges regarding both identification and treatment. Historically, internalizing disorders either have gone unrecognized or have been considered aspects of externalizing behavior in the school-age population. Until the last decade, children who were characterized as sad, introverted, and melancholic, and adolescents viewed as brooding, detached, and lethargic, were thought to be going through a difficult, although relatively normal, stage of development. In extreme cases these behaviors may have been considered a reaction disorder of childhood according to old *Diagnostic and Statistical Manual of Mental Disorders* (American Psychiatric Association, 1968) nomenclature.

Depression is generally considered to be one of the nation's major mental health problems (Greist & Jefferson, 1984). Recent epidemiological surveys by the National Institute of Mental Health (NIMH) (Regier et al., 1988; Robins et al., 1984), suggest that depressive disorders are experienced by 6–10% of the adult population over the course of a lifetime, with one-month prevalence rates ranging from 2.2% to 3.3%. Silver (1988), citing recent but unpublished NIMH data, reports that 17.9% of all youngsters under the age of 18 years admitted to psychiatric settings and nonfederal hospitals had an intake diagnosis of an affective disorder. Depression therefore represents one of the most prevalent and pervasive forms of psychopathology, and it can be considered a significant problem in children as well as adults and adolescents.

Depression is more than just feeling sad, blue, or down in the dumps. Depression typically affects many areas of individual functioning, including behavioral, emotional, somatic, and cognitive domains. Depressive disorders are one of the more serious forms of psychopathology of childhood and adolescence, given that some depressive episodes may lead to potentially life-threatening outcomes if not identified and treated. Furthermore, depressive disorders experienced in childhood or adolescence may also be a precursor or risk factor for mental illness in adulthood (Kovacs, 1985).

Depression in Children and Adolescents

The past 15 years has witnessed a growing interest by clinicians and researchers in the examination and study of depression in children and adolescents. This interest has also been demonstrated by psychologists in schools, where depression in some youngsters is most likely to be first identified. The current attention to depressive disorders in youngsters is indeed fortunate, given that for many years depression in children was viewed as either nonexistent or masked, or was assumed to be expressed in symptomatology quite different from that of adults (Reynolds, 1985a). The latter perspective was primarily expressed via the construct of depressive equivalents (Cytryn & McKnew, 1972; Glaser, 1967; Hollon, 1970; Rie, 1966), in which depression in children was presumed to be demonstrated by overt negative behaviors such as acting-out, aggression, hyperactivity, and delinquency. On the basis of current investigations, it is now believed that there are many thousands of youngsters in this country who are experiencing clinical levels of depression and are in need of treatment (Reynolds, in press-a).

The current consensus is that depression in childhood is manifested by many of the same symptoms as it is in adulthood (American Psychiatric Association, 1980, 1987; Carlson & Cantwell, 1980, 1982; Cytryn, McKnew, & Bunney, 1980; Poznanski, Mokros, Grossman, & Freeman, 1985; Reynolds, 1984a, 1985a), with some minor differences that, for the most part, are due to developmental considerations (Carlson & Garber, 1986). As in adults, depression in children and adolescents is expressed not as a single symptom (e.g., manifest sad mood), but as a cluster of symptoms that may include anhedonia, lowered self-esteem, social withdrawal, fatigue, impaired school performance, crying spells or tearfulness, sleeping and eating disturbances, and self-destructive impulses (American Psychiatric Association, 1987; Carlson & Cantwell, 1982; Poznanski, 1982; Poznanski, Cook, & Carroll, 1979). Furthermore, as Shaw (1988) notes, depressive symptoms in children may also be expressed by a decreased ability to deal effectively with the demands of the classroom and to cope with family problems, and an inability to interact effectively with peers.

Depressed children demonstrate a wide range of symptoms associated with depression when assessed by formal clinical interviews (Poznanski et al., 1979; Puig-Antich, 1980; Puig-Antich, Chambers, & Tabrizi, 1983). Given the severity and constellations of symptoms experienced by youngsters, it is important not to view depressive symptomatology as a normal aspect of child or adolescent development (Costello, 1980). Depression in youngsters, if left untreated, may persist for months or years (Kovacs et al., 1984), and may have life-threatening consequences (Cohen-Sandler & Berman, 1980). A number of recent studies of depression and depressive symptomatology in children and adolescents support the need for school psychologists to be proficient in the assessment and treatment of depression in this population (e.g., Cantwell, 1983; Carlson & Cantwell, 1982; Kashani et al., 1983; McGee & Williams, 1988; Petti, 1983a; Reynolds, in press-b).

Depression in youngsters is most likely one of the most overlooked and undertreated psychological disorders of childhood and adolescence. General population estimates of prevalence of diagnosable cases of depression and individuals who demonstrate a "clinical" level of depressive symptomatology, range from roughly 6% to 12% of adolescents in regular schools (Kashani, Rosenberg, & Reid, 1989; Reynolds, 1987a), somewhat lower levels being found for children (Anderson, Williams, McGee, & Silva, 1987). As epidemiological estimates, these figures suggest a staggering number of youngsters in need of psychological attention and services.

A feature of depression in children and adolescents that is often overlooked is the relatively high degree of comorbidity with other psychiatric diagnoses. In particular, conduct disorders and anxiety disorders have been found to be relatively prevalent comorbid disorders with depression in youngsters (Alessi & Magen, 1988; Finch, Lipovsky, & Casat, 1989; Puig-Antich, 1982; Puig-Antich & Rabinovich, 1986; Strauss, Last, Hersen, & Kazdin, 1988). Furthermore, as Kovacs (1985, 1989) has suggested, the presence of other disorders along with depression in children and adolescents may increase the potential for long-term mental health problems.

Another important aspect of depression in children and adolescents is the relationship between depression and suicidal behaviors in youngsters. This is far from a perfect relationship; a large proportion of depressed youngsters can be considered not at risk for suicidal behaviors, a number of youngsters are depressed and suicidal, and a significant proportion of youngsters are at risk for suicidal behavior but are not depressed (Reynolds, 1988; in press-b). This underscores the need to conceptualize depression and suicidal behaviors as two related, but distinct forms of psychopathology. It is therefore recommended that psychologists examining depression in youngsters should not overlook the possibility that a nondepressed child or adolescent may be suicidal.

Treatment of Depression in Children and Adolescents

The treatment of depression in children and adolescents is an activity that should not be entered into without training, as well as extensive knowledge of affective disorders, psychological models of depression, and associated treatment modalities. There are many reasons for this caution. Foremost is the nature of depression with particular reference to the distress experienced by the youngster. Treating a disorder of childhood that is characterized by the youngster's experiencing intense subjective misery, along with numerous somatic disturbances such as sleep disturbance and appetite loss, as well as the potential for suicidal thoughts or intent, is a serious undertaking. Such a case represents a distinctly different task than the treatment of academic problems or behavioral problems such as aggression or acting-out. In the case of depression, failure to make significant, long-lasting treatment gains within a relatively short period of time may for some youngsters prolong a level of unbearable psychological distress. If treatment fails, the condition in some youngsters may be exacerbated by increased feelings of hopelessness and despondency.

Beginning in the late 1970s, a growing body of research on depression in youngsters has emerged, with investigations describing epidemiology; psychosocial, individual difference, and biological correlates; and classification, diagnosis,

and assessment (Reynolds, 1985a). Unfortunately, relatively little empirical work on psychological treatment of this disorder in youngsters has been conducted. Unlike the study of depression in adults, for which numerous experimental investigations of psychological intervention procedures, as well as studies comparing psychotherapy and pharmacotherapy outcomes, have been conducted, there have been few experimental studies of psychological treatments for depression in children and adolescents. It is interesting, however, that the majority of the controlled empirical treatment studies of depression in children and adolescents using psychological procedures have been conducted in school settings; as such they are of potential value to school psychologists (Reynolds, 1984b).

Scope of This Chapter

This chapter focuses on depression in youngsters and describes one set of strategies for the treatment of children and adolescents who demonstrate significant levels of depressive symptoms. Although the title of this monograph suggests interventions specific to academic and behavior problems in children and youths, it may be debated whether depression should be included under the rubric of behavior problems. Behavior problems in youngsters have typically been characterized by disorders of behavioral excesses, and as such are often viewed as externalizing problems. As will be discussed, depression is a disorder that is primarily internalizing in its phenomenological manifestation (Reynolds, in press-a). Thus, depression differs in many respects from more overt, externalizing problems which are characterized by behavioral excess or social inadequacy/inappropriateness. Depression also differs from most behavior disorders of children and adolescents in view of the comorbidity of suicidal tendencies associated with a significant number of depressed youngsters (Reynolds, in press-b).

A description of depression as a disorder in children and adolescent, including contemporary models, diagnostic criteria, assessment procedures, and a summary of intervention research, is presented below. Following this description is an illustration and discussion of a multicomponent therapy for the treatment of depression in children and adolescents. The therapy discussed is predicated in large part on tenets of cognitive and behavioral models of depression. A case presentation illustrates the application of the therapy with youngsters. Lastly, therapist requirements and the role of the school psychologist in the treatment of depression in children and adolescents is discussed.

THEORIES OF DEPRESSION

Models and theories of depression can be traced back to ancient times as seen in the notions of humors and melancholia (melancholia connoting black bile and a disease [Jackson, 1986]), and in more modern times to the psychoanalytic writings of Freud (1917) and Abraham (1911). Contemporary theories and models of depression, on which specific treatments used with children and adolescents are based, have been developed in the past two decades. For the most part, these models and theories of depression have been developed with adults in mind and do not take into account developmental differences or characteristics unique to youngsters.

Contemporary Theories

Given the focus of this chapter, only a cursory note of several contemporary theories of depression will be taken. One test of a theory is the outcome of its application to treatment procedures, their clinical efficacy providing limited evidence for the theory. An examination of the literature on the results of treatment of adults, with particular focus on therapies that are consistent with cognitive and behavioral theories, suggests relatively equivalent therapeutic efficacy across treatments (see Kovacs, 1980; Reynolds & Stark, 1983; and Williams, 1984 for reviews of representative treatment studies). Although beyond the scope of the present

discussion, Lewinsohn, Hoberman, Teri, and Hautzinger (1985) have recently presented an "integrative theory" of depression that subsumes cognitive, behavioral, and environmental components and their interaction. As a working model their conceptualization provides some interesting insights into the psychological mechanisms and etiology of depression. Although not yet applied to interventions for depression, future treatment programs may find components of this model useful.

Described below are several theories or models of depression. It should be noted that many of these theories conflate cognitive and behavioral orientations so that it becomes difficult to clearly place a dichotomous behavioral or cognitive label on the theory. Listed below are four theories of depression, presented in a rough order of primary focus from behavioral to cognitive.

Social learning theory. A social learning theory consistent with a behavioral model of depression was presented by Lewinsohn and colleagues (Lewinsohn, 1974, 1975; Lewinsohn & Arconad, 1981). Central to this theory is that depression is in part a function of a decrease in response-contingent reinforcement. This change results in reduced engagement in activities providing positive reinforcement, that is, pleasant activities. Depressed persons may actively avoid such reinforcing activities. Thus, treatment in this social learning approach emphasizes an increased engagement in pleasant activities and a decrease in negative activities.

Self-control theory. The self-control theory of depression was delineated by Rehm (1977, 1981) and by Fuchs and Rehm (1977). This theory of depression is, in part, predicated on the notion of self-regulation proposed by Kanfer (Kanfer, 1970; Kanfer & Karoly, 1972); it posits that depressed persons show specific deficits in self-control. These deficits include problems of self-monitoring, self-evaluation, and self-reinforcement. Depressed persons may selectively attend to (i.e., self-monitor) negative events and outcomes to the exclusion of positive events or outcomes. In addition, depressed persons typically attend to the immediate rather than the long-term or delayed consequences of events and outcomes. Depressed persons will demonstrate problems in self-evaluation by setting very high or excessively stringent criteria for performance success. In many cases, such standards may be unobtainable. Problems in self-reinforcement are demonstrated by a low level or rate of self-reward, typically in conjunction with a high rate of self-punishment.

Learned helplessness theory. The learned helplessness theory of depression was originally developed as a primarily behavioral theory by Seligman (1975). In the past decade the learned helplessness model has been reformulated to include significant cognitive features (e.g., cognitive attributions for success or failure) (Abramson, Seligman, & Teasdale, 1978); it has also been applied to childhood depression (Seligman & Peterson, 1986). The learned helplessness theory (as reformulated) proposes that depression is a result of belief that negative outcomes will occur, along with the expectation that the outcomes are beyond the individual's control. An insidious attributional style specific to the uncontrollability of these negative events results in lowered self-esteem and helplessness. Three categories of causal attributions are specified: internal versus external attributions, stable versus unstable attributions, and global versus specific attributions. Persons who make internal, stable, and global attributions for negative events are predisposed to become depressed when faced with such outcomes; they feel that nothing they can do will change the outcome or occurrence of the event, hence a feeling of helplessness.

Cognitive theory. A cognitive theory of depression, formulated by Beck (Beck, 1967; Beck, Rush, Shaw, & Emery, 1979), has had a major influence on the psychological treatment of depression (see Dobson, 1989, for reviews of studies). The cognitive model of depression specifies three distinct domains related to depres-

sogenic thinking patterns. These include the cognitive triad, in which negative cognitions are developed specific to the individual (self), current experiences (the world), and expectations for the future. A second basic element is schemas. In depressed persons, dysfunctional schemas are considered to be stable distorted thought patterns used by the individual to interpret information. Beck et al. (1979) consider this element as the "structural organization of depressive thinking." The third component consists of six formal types of cognitive errors made in the processing of information: it includes arbitrary inferences, selective abstraction, overgeneralization, magnification or minimization, personalization, and absolutist or dichotomous thinking. These depressogenic cognitive patterns are thought to be relatively stable, and according to Beck (1967), predispose an individual to depression.

DIAGNOSIS OF DEPRESSION IN CHILDREN AND ADOLESCENTS

Diagnosis is the application of specific criteria in identifying a disorder within an evaluation process. The outcome is typically a determination of whether a person meets the prespecified criteria. Thus, a dichotomous decision is made that is based on the symptoms presented as well as those not in evidence. In some instances of depression, diagnosis is important for the selection of the most appropriate therapy. Diagnosis, as I will discuss later, is a form of measurement. Thus, measurement error, or reliability, is a consideration when we make a diagnosis. As is the case for other forms of evaluation, there are numerous sources of measurement error possible in making a diagnosis, including the diagnostician and the diagnostic system. This section will describe a number of diagnostic systems that have been used to formulate a diagnosis of depression in children and adolescents. It should be understood that a diagnostic system is a procedure for the classification of psychiatric or other disorders. As we learn more about specific disorders, we revise our systems of classification to encompass new research and clinical information and, hopefully, increase the validity of these systems. Thus, classification systems should not be viewed as static or immutable in their listing of the inclusion and exclusion criteria for specific disorders.

Diagnostic Systems and Approaches

There are a number of diagnostic systems used by researchers and clinicians for the delineation of depression in children and adolescents. Several of the current classification systems utilize a taxonomic approach based on symptom clusters to differentiate sybtypes of depression. These employ both inclusion and exclusion criteria. At present, the primary system for the classification of mood disorders in children, adolescents, and adults is the *Diagnostic and Statistical Manual of Mental Disorders*-3rd Edition Revised (DSM-IIIR) (American Psychiatric Association, 1987). The current DSM-IIIR classification of mood disorders in children is similar to that of adults. The widespread professional acceptance of the DSM-IIIR taxonomy has provided common, formal criteria for the diagnosis of depression in children. The DSM-IIIR criteria for depression in children and adolescents will be described in greater depth.

Another classification system, the Research Diagnostic Criteria (RDC) was developed by Spitzer, Endicott, and Robins (1978). While the RDC is similar to DSM-IIIR criteria for depression, differences do exist. The RDC provide greater specificity of distinct subtypes of depression and were primarily designed for research purposes. The RDC psychopathologies are assessed by a formal diagnostic clinical interview, the Schedule for Affective Disorders and Schizophrenia (SADS; Endicott & Spitzer, 1978) for adults, and the Kiddie SADS for children (Puig-Antich & Chambers, 1978). Thus, these interview schedules are specific to the RDC in the diagnoses they provide.

One of the first of contemporary diagnostic descriptions of symptoms and criteria was that proposed by Weinberg, Rutman, Sullivan, Penick, and Dietz (1973). Although used less frequently today, the Weinberg Criteria are also noteworthy in that they comprise one of the first formal systems for classifying depressive disorders in children and adolescents. It may be suggested that the formulation of the Weinberg Criteria provided impetus toward the recognition of depression in children as a disorder phenomenologically similar to that found in adults. A systematic clinical interview for the evaluation of Weinberg-specified symptomatology in children, the Bellevue Index of Depression (BID), has been developed by Petti (1978; 1985). The Weinberg criteria are presented in Table 1. As shown in Table 1, many of the symptoms of depression in children and adolescents that are incorporated in currently used diagnostic criteria for depression (e.g., DSM-IIIR) were included in the Weinberg criteria.

Clinical symptomatology for depression in children has also been described by Poznanski and her colleagues (Poznanski, 1982; Poznanski, Mokros et al., 1985) who have also developed a clinical interview for the assessment of depression in children (Poznanski et al., 1979; Poznanski, Freeman, & Mokros, 1985; Poznanski, Grossman, et al., 1984). It should be noted that differences between these systems of criteria specifications are found between DSM-III and Weinberg (Carlson & Cantwell, 1982), as well as among RDC, DSM-III, Weinberg, and Poznanski (Poznanski, Mokros, et al., 1985).

DSM-IIIR

As was mentioned previously, the diagnostic system most often used for clinical purposes, as well as some research investigations, is the diagnostic criteria and classification presented in the current DSM-IIIR. In the DSM-IIIR classification, depressive disorders fall under the category of Mood Disorders. The forms of depressive disorders include Major Depression, Bipolar Disorders, Cyclothymia, and Dysthymia. Disorders are differentiated by specific clusters of symptoms,

TABLE 1
Weinberg Criteria for Childhood Depression

A. The presence of *both:*
   1. Dysphoric mood
   2. Self-deprecatory thoughts

B. Two or more of the following eight symptoms:
   1. Aggressive behavior
   2. Sleep disturbance
   3. A change in school performance
   4. Diminished socialization
   5. Change in attitude toward school
   6. Somatic complaints
   7. Loss of usual energy
   8. Unusual change in appetite and/or weight

C. Duration of symptoms:
   Symptoms need to be present for more than 1 month *and*
   represent a change in the child's usual behavior.

age of onset, and the duration of symptoms. Of interest to this review of depression in children and adolescents are Major Depression and Dysthymia, although Adjustment Disorder With Depressed Mood should also be considered diagnostically relevant for some youngsters (e.g., Kovacs, 1985). The depression disorders included in this domain of psychopathology (Mood Disorders) are illustrated in Table 2.

Major Depression is a diagnostic classification utilized in DSM–IIIR to denote a severe, acute form of depression. Major Depression is defined by the presence of either dysphoric mood (can be irritable mood in children and adolescents) or anhedonia (loss of interest or pleasure in all or almost all activities) and four of the following symptoms: sleep problems as indicated by insomnia or hypersomnia; complaints, or other evidence, of diminished ability to think, or difficulty in concentrating; loss of energy or general fatigue; eating problems as manifested by decreased or increased appetite or significant weight loss or gain (in young children failure to make expected weight gains is symptomatic); psychomotor retardation or agitation; suicidal or morbid ideation, death wishes, or suicide attempts; and feelings of self-reproach, worthlessness, or excessive or

inappropriate guilt (which may be delusional). Duration criteria specify that the symptoms need to be present nearly every day for a period of at least 2 weeks. In addition to the inclusion criteria noted above, a number of other pathologies, such as Organic Mental Disorder, are specifically excluded as concomitant problems in order to make a diagnosis of Major Depression.

Dysthymia is generally less severe in terms of symptom distress but typically is of greater duration than Major Depression. Dysthymia may be especially relevant to the study of depression in school populations of children and adolescents as Kovacs et al. (1984), in a longitudinal study, found that Dysthymia was an enduring problem for some children and adolescents, lasting 5 years or longer in some youngsters.

A diagnosis of Dysthymia in children and adolescents is based on depressed or irritable mood for most of the day, during the better part of a period of at least 1 year, although there may be periods of up to 2 months when symptoms are not present. In addition, at least two of the following symptoms must be present to sustain a diagnosis of depression: appetite loss or gain, insomnia or hypersomnia, fatigue or low energy level, low self-esteem, poor concentration or problems making

TABLE 2
DSM-IIIR[a] Diagnostic Classifications of Mood Disorders

Bipolar Disorder
    Mixed
    Manic
    Depressed

Cyclothymia

Bipolar Disorder Not Otherwise Specified

Major Depression [single episode, recurrent]
    Melancholic Type
    Seasonal Pattern

Dysthymia

Depressive Disorder Not Otherwise Specified

---

[a]*Diagnostic and Statistical Manual of Mental Disorders–3rd ed. revised.* American Psychiatric Association (1987).

decisions, and feelings of hopelessness. Exclusion criteria include no evidence of a Major Depressive Episode during the initial year of the disorder, no history of a Manic or Hypermanic Episode, no concomitant chronic psychosis, and no evidence that the condition is due to or maintained by an organic factor.

The criteria specified above are those delineated by DSM-IIIR for diagnosis of either Major Depression or Dysthymia. It should be noted that other symptoms of depression also are found in youngsters as well as adults, including crying, anxiety or worry, and social withdrawal, but they are not viewed as core symptoms specific to the diagnostic criteria for Major Depression or Dysthymia, according to the American Psychiatric Association. Table 3 presents a listing of symptoms of depression that includes both the core and secondary symptoms noted by the DSM-IIIR and modified for their expression in children and adolescents. As can be seen, the list includes a wide range of symptoms. It is recommended that psychologists be aware of these potential symptoms in children and adolescents.

ASSESSMENT OF DEPRESSION IN CHILDREN AND ADOLESCENTS

Assessment is a key element in the identification of depression in children and adolescents and in the determination of the efficacy of treatment. Adequate assessment measures are important features of any intervention study, being necessary in determining treatment outcome (Beutler & Hamblin, 1986; Kazdin, 1986, 1988; Reynolds & Stark, 1983). Assessment of depression is complicated by the availability of different measures, the presence of different sources of information (e.g., parent, child, teacher, peer), and use of different response formats (e.g., self-report versus clinical interview). What has emerged is a diverse set of procedures, the majority of research finding minimal concordance across sources (raters), but relatively high within-rater relationships. This section will describe four representative measures, two self-report and two clinical interviews, that have been used for the assessment of depression in children and adolescents. Prior to presentation of specific measures, a perspective on methods of evaluation of depression is presented to illustrate the relationship between diagnosis and assessment of depressive symptom severity.

Measurement Perspective

The evaluation and determination of depression as a clinical state in children and adolescents, as well as adults, is

TABLE 3
Depressive Symptomatology in Children and Adolescents

Major Depression	Dysthymia	Symptom
+	+	Dysphoria
+	+	Insomnia or hypersomnia
+	+	Change in appetite/weight or in expected weight gains
+	+	Fatigue — low energy
+		Psychomotor retardation/agitation
+		Suicidal ideation or attempt
+	+	Irritability or excessive anger (possible antisocial behavior)
+		Tearfulness or crying
+		Loss of interest in pleasurable activities
+		Pessimistic attitude toward the future — hopelessness
+	+	Decreased ability to think — poor concentration
+	+	Feelings of inadequacy, loss of self-esteem, or self-deprecation
+	+	Decreased effectiveness or productivity in school or school difficulties
+	+	Social withdrawal
+		Somatic complaints
+		Excessive guilt
+		Feelings of rejection
+		Anxiety
+		Desire to leave home
+		Mood congruent hallucinations

generally accomplished by one of two measurement perspectives: (a) the assessment of the severity or depth of a range of depressive symptoms to evaluate the "clinical level" of depression experienced by the subject, and (b) the formal diagnosis of depression manifested by the subject according to a specified set of rules or classification criteria. These two measurement perspectives typically utilize different assessment measures and provide different information on the nature of specific cases of depression. Although these approaches are not mutually exclusive, they are different in focus and outcome. Both approaches are valid, and they are to an extent complementary. Both have specific applications dictated by the type and level of information required in order to make a specific decision about a child or adolescent. This distinction can be conceptualized as a measurement continuum, with diagnosis at one end and assessment of severity at the opposite end, which is illustrated in Table 4.

The assessment of the depth or severity of depressive symptoms provides useful information as to the level of depressive symptomatology experienced by the youngster. This is usually accomplished by paper-and-pencil measures, but it may also involve a clinical interview such as the Children's Depression Rating Scale-Revised (CDRS-R) (Poznanski et al., 1984). In the depth or severity approach, a cutoff score is often used to delineate a clinically critical level of depressive symptomatology. A score at or above this level may result in a finding of depression. However, it is important to note that this cutoff score method is not the equivalent of providing a diagnosis of depression according to recognized classification systems. The formal diagnosis of depression can be competently made only when more extensive evaluation procedures, incorporating structured diagnostic interviews or other in-depth methodologies, are employed. Although there have been attempts to derive severity assessment information from diagnostic interview

TABLE 4
Measurement Perspective for the Evaluation of Depression

	Perspective	
	Diagnosis	**Severity**
Method:	A structured clinical interview or in-depth clinical evaluation.	A brief self-report measure of depression or semi-structured interview.
Outcome:	A specific diagnosis based on a formal classification system. With some interviews a severity score may be extracted.	A score indicating a level of symptom severity or depth of depressive symptomatology. A cutoff score, indicating a clinical level of depression may be obtained.

procedures (e.g., Endicott, Cohen, Nee, Fleiss, & Sarantakos, 1981), these two approaches have generally been mutually exclusive.

Assessment Methods

Four measures are described below that utilize the child or adolescent as the primary source of information regarding depressive symptomatology. These measures have been used extensively with youngsters, and three of the four have been used by the author as measures of treatment outcome in cognitive-behavioral treatment studies for depression in children and adolescents. These measures are presented here as examples of appropriate measures that can be used by psychologists in school settings. It should be noted that there also are other qualified measures for the assessment of depression in youngsters. A recent review of assessment measures by Kazdin (1987) is recommended for additional readings on this topic.

Reynolds Child Depression Scale. The Reynolds Child Depression Scale (RCDS) (Reynolds, 1989a), previously called the Child Depression Scale (e.g., Bartell & Reynolds, 1986; Reynolds, Anderson, & Bartell, 1985; Stark, Reynolds, & Kaslow, 1987) is a brief, 30-item self-report measure of depressive symptomatology in children aged 8–12 years. The RCDS is designed as a measure for the assessment of clinically relevant levels of depressive

symptomatology in children. It can be administered individually or in a group (e.g., in a classroom with a teacher as administrator). The RCDS consists of 29 items that utilize a four-point Likert-type response format and one item for which the response format is five smiley-type faces ranging from happy to sad. The general response format requires the child to record whether the symptom-related item has occurred almost never, sometimes, a lot of the time, or all the time, during the previous 2 weeks.

Normative information based on more than 1,600 children representing heterogeneous ethnic and socioeconomic backgrounds is reported in a detailed manual, along with procedures for administration, scoring, and interpretation, as well as extensive data on reliability and validity. Internal consistency reliability for the standardization sample was .90, which is high for a brief, self-report measure of children's depressive symptomatology. In a test–retest study of the RCDS reported by Reynolds and Graves (1989) with an ethnically diverse sample of 220 children from Grades 3–6, a 4-week test–retest time interval resulted in a test–retest reliability coefficient of .85. Validity data are presented in the form of high correlations with other self-report and clinical interview measures of childhood depression, as well as content validity, factor analysis, discriminant validity and clinical utility (Reynolds, 1989b). For example, the correlation between the RCDS and the

Children's Depression Rating Scale–Revised was .76 ($P < .001$), which can be considered high, especially given that the latter scale is an individually administered clinical interview for depression.

Children's Depression Rating Scale–Revised. The Children's Depression Rating Scale–Revised (Poznanski et al., 1984; Poznanski, Freeman, & Mokros, 1985) is an outcome measure frequently used in psychiatric studies of childhood depression. Contemporary, structured or semistructured clinical interviews are generally considered to be one of the most sensitive methodologies for the assessment of depression (Hamilton, 1982; Puig-Antich & Gittelman, 1982). Clinical interviews of depression allow for the clinical evaluation and probing of children's symptoms, the assessment of symptom severity, and the determination of whether symptom endorsement is a function of depression or extraneous factors. For example, a youngster who indicates sleep difficulty may be manifesting a symptom of depression or may be kept up at night by the crying of a newborn sibling. Thus, the interviewer has a better opportunity to determine the seriousness of symptom complaints, as well as their duration and intensity. Because the clinical interview is individualized for each child, this assessment format allows for the accommodation of developmental and cognitive restrictions in children (Kovacs, 1986).

The CDRS-R is a semistructured interview schedule, modeled after the Hamilton Depression Rating Scale (Hamilton, 1960, 1967), the latter having demonstrated utility for use with adolescents (Reynolds, 1987a). Designed for use with children aged 6-12 years, the CDRS-R requires about 20-30 minutes to administer to a child. The CDRS was revised in 1984; the revision includes 17 items, each rated on a 5- or 7-point scale. Items evaluate specific symptoms that are associated with depression in children. Items (symptoms) are scored from 1 (*no pathology*) to 5 or 7 (*severe* or *extreme pathology*). Poznanski and colleagues (Poznanski et al., 1979; Poznanski, Cook, Carroll, & Corzo, 1983; Poznanski et al.,

1984) report adequate test-retest and interrater reliability, and high correlations between the CDRS and psychiatrists' global ratings of depression, as well as accurate differentiation between RDC-diagnosed depressed and nondepressed children. Poznanski et al. (1984) recommend a cutoff score of 40 on the CDRS-R to describe a moderate to severe clinical level of depression in children.

Reynolds Adolescent Depression Scale. The Reynolds Adolescent Depression Scale (RADS) (Reynolds, 1986a, 1987a) is a 30-item, paper-and-pencil self-report measure of depression designed specifically for junior and senior high school adolescents aged 12-19 years. The RADS uses a four-point (almost never to most of the time) response format with item content reflecting symptomatology specified by the DSM-III for Major Depression and Dysthymic Disorder. Items are worded at a third-grade reading level so that reading is not a confounding variable for typical high school students. Items evaluate somatic, motivational, cognitive, mood, and vegetative components of depression.

Normative data on the RADS has been collected on over 11,000 adolescents from the midwestern, as well as southeastern and western areas of the country. Subjects were from senior and junior high schools (Grades 7-12; ages 12-19) in suburban/urban and suburban/rural communities. For screening and clinical applications, a cutoff score has been established to designate a clinically relevant level of symptom severity. This cutoff score has been validated in several studies, which used both Hamilton Depression Rating Scale scores and formal diagnosis based on the Schedule for Affective Disorders and Schizophrenia as criterion measures (Reynolds, 1987a; in press-b). Reliability of the RADS has been examined from the perspective of internal consistency and temporal stability. Internal consistency estimates have been uniformly high (ranging from .92 to .96) with different samples of normal and depressed adolescents ranging in size from 126 to 2,240 (Reynolds, 1985b, 1987a; Reynolds &

Miller, 1989). In a study of 26 mildly retarded adolescents reported by Reynolds and Miller (1985), the internal consistency reliability was .87. Test–retest reliability based on a sample of 104 adolescents who were tested with a 6-week interval between testings was .80, a value that is viewed as acceptable, given the nature of the construct assessed.

The validity of the RADS has been established in a number of studies using bivariate and multivariate procedures to examine relationships with other depression scales and measures of related constructs. The analyses encompassed by these investigations are too extensive to document here and are described in the RADS Manual (Reynolds, 1987a). To summarize, the RADS has been found to be highly correlated with other self-report measures of depression (r's ranging from .70 to .89). A correlation of .83 was found between the RADS and the HDRS with a sample of 111 adolescents.

Hamilton Depression Rating Scale. The Hamilton Depression Rating Scale is one of the most frequently used clinical interviews for the assessment of severity of depressive symptoms in adults. The HDRS has been found to demonstrate a high degree of clinical utility in distinguishing among adults with formal RDC diagnoses of Major Depression those with Minor Depression and nondepressed adult controls (Kobak, Reynolds, Rosenfeld, & Greist, in press). A modification of the adult form for use with adolescents has been developed by Reynolds (1982). This interview schedule, the Hamilton Depression Rating Scale–High School Adaptation (HDRS–HS) assesses the same 17 symptoms as evaluated on the adult version of the HDRS, with modification made for school-age-appropriate activities and developmental level. As with the CDRS–R, the 17 items of the HDRS–HS each measure specific symptoms of depression, although several items, such as those of hypocondriasis and loss of insight, may be somewhat questionable in light of contemporary diagnostic specifications of the disorder. The HDRS–HS typically requires 20–30 minutes to administer. In a longi-tudinal study of depression in adolescents, Reynolds and Bartell (1983) found high internal consistency reliability (r_α = .91), adequate test–retest reliability over 12 weeks (r_{tt} = .77), and interrater reliability (r_{rr} = .83) for the HDRS–HS.

School-Based Identification of Depressed Youngsters

The identification of depressed children and adolescents in school settings should be conceptualized as a proactive procedure. A major difficulty in the identification of depressed children and adolescents has been the lack of self-referral. In addition, there is a tendency by some parents to deny or reject information that their child may be suffering from an affective disorder. Likewise, the constellation of symptoms that make up the syndrome of depression makes difficult the identification of depressed children and adolescents by parents or teachers (Baker & Reynolds, 1988; Leon, Kendall, & Garber, 1980; Reynolds et al., 1985). Direct assessment may provide the best procedure for the initial identification of potentially depressed children. Given this situation, the school can be viewed as the optimal setting for the early identification of depressed children. Thus, school-based procedures to identify youngsters in need of treatment, referral, or observation is an important component of services to children and adolescents. A viable strategy to accomplish this is the use of a multiple-state screening procedure for the identification of depressed youngsters.

It is clear that the school is an important environment in a child's life. This is especially true in the case of youngsters who are depressed, given the high probability of dysfunctional or otherwise impaired family situations these youngsters may experience (Ammerman, Cassisi, Hersen, & Van Hasselt, 1986; Beardslee, 1986; Blumberg, 1981; Burbach & Borduin, 1986; Cytryn, McKnew, Zahn-Waxler, & Gershon, 1986; Kazdin, Moser, Colbus, & Bell, 1985; Philips, 1979). It is likely that if schools neither are aware of the mental health needs of children nor make the effort to become aware of these needs, it may be that no one else will assume this responsibility.

The identification of depressed youngsters requires a systematic evaluation of those potentially at risk. The screening procedure described here utilizes three assessment stages for identifying clinically depressed children and adolescents in the school. The screening procedure is illustrated in Figure 1 and has been elaborated in more detail by Reynolds (1986b). The use of a multistage procedure is important because of the number of false positives that may occur with a single administration of a self-report depression measure. In addition, a clinical interview for depression or a broad-bandwidth measure (i.e., one that assessed many types of psychopathology) for psychiatric disorders is a necessary step in making the final clinical determination.

Stage 1. The initial stage in the identification process is the large-group assessment (i.e., by classroom) with a self-report, paper-and-pencil measure of depression, such as the RCDS or RADS. An enhanced procedure for adolescents at this stage is the inclusion of a measure specific to the identification of youngsters at risk for suicidal behaviors, such as the Suicidal Ideation Questionnaire (Reynolds, 1987b, 1988). This assessment of an entire school or specific grade levels, including administration, directions, and distribution of the questionnaires, can be carried out in 15–20 minutes. Teachers are provided with adequate directions for administration of the questionnaires. Computerized scoring is available for the RADS, as is handscoring, although the latter will significantly increase the time involvement of school personnel.

A significant proportion of youngsters (8–15% depending on age level) are typically found to be at or above the clinical cutoff score of the depression measure on a single administration. To some extent, this is an overidentification of youngsters, overendorsement being due to such potential factors as acquiescence, poor metacognitive understanding of

symptom severity, noncompliance with directions, or in some students a rather transient mood disorder or a reaction to minor stressors. Conducting clinical interviews as a follow-up of a potentially large number of children can be costly in terms of time and resources. The overidentification at Stage 1 is considered appropriate since this will result in a decrease in false negatives (i.e., missing a youngster who is depressed).

Stage 2. To reduce both the occurrence of false positives in the identification of children and adolescents who endorse a depressed level of symptomatology and the costs that individual interviews would entail, the second stage of the screening consists of readministration of the self-report depression measure to previously identified youngsters. This can be accomplished by the assessment of small groups of 5–10 students at a time. Youngsters identified as reporting significant depressive symptoms on both assessments (Stages 1 and 2) should then be individually assessed by qualified school psychologists or mental health professionals with a structured or semistructured clinical interview, to make a final determination of level of depression and need and type of follow-up intervention procedures. This is elaborated in the Stage 3 processes described below.

Stage 3. For the systematic and clinical evaluation of depression in youngsters, an individual clinical interview for depression should be conducted by a school psychologist or other health professional knowledgeable about depression in youngsters and trained in the interview procedure used. This interview should be conducted with all students who meet the depression criteria at both Stage 1 and Stage 2, as well as youngsters who may have met criteria at only one stage but for other reasons may be viewed as potentially at risk.

Although paper-and-pencil self-report measures of depression provide reliable information at relatively little cost in time and effort, such information is best used for the initial evaluation of severity of depressive symptoms and not for formally classifying a youngster as depressed. A clinical interview with the youngster and possibly with parents is typically warranted to confirm a final diagnosis or clinical level of depression. A number of clinical interview measures for children are available, including measures of severity, such as the CDRS–R and the BID, both of which have been used in treatment outcome studies of depression in children and adolescents (Kahn, 1988; Reynolds & Coats, 1986; Stark et al., 1987), as well as other clinical interview measures used for diagnosis (i.e., Kovacs, 1978; Puig-Antich & Chambers, 1978).

Youngsters who meet the criteria for clinical levels of depression at all stages of the screening model should be referred for active treatment and intervention. Children who meet criteria at the first two, but not the third stage, should be considered nondepressed but in need of reevaluation at a later date. Because the first two screenings are group-administered, additional clinical information that may be known about a youngster should always be considered when decisions are made about a child's or adolescent's level of depression.

It should be noted that the majority of clinical interview measures for depression in children and adolescents, such as the CDRS-R, the Interview Schedule for Children (Kovacs, 1978), the HDRS, the BID, and the Schedule for Affective Disorders and Schizophrenia for School-Age Children (Puig-Antich & Chambers, 1978) require training and practice prior to their utilization in clinical or school settings.

TREATMENT OF DEPRESSION IN CHILDREN AND ADOLESCENTS: RESEARCH FINDINGS

To date, there have been few empirical demonstrations of the efficacy of psychological treatments designed for the amelioration of depressive symptoms in children and adolescents. This is an unfortunate situation given the potentially large number of youngsters who are in need of some form of intervention for depression. The relative lack of solid experimental research in this area is puzzling, given the large number of empirical studies on the treatment of depression in adults.

The formal, empirical demonstration that a psychological treatment is effective is of paramount importance, especially when dealing with as severe a psychological disorder as depression. Results of well-controlled, rigorous studies that show a treatment to be efficacious are necessary prior to widespread implementation and application. Unfortunately, many psychotherapies are used that have not been empirically tested, even though the need for such testing should be clear. Would we use a drug for a serious illness that our pharmacist has concocted in his office and who feels that it will help us? Obviously the answer is no, we would only take a drug that has been tested and that we know is proven effective with no or minimal side-effects. The same position should be taken when we consider the use of a psychological therapy for the treatment of depression in children and adolescents.

Psychological Intervention Research

Several single-case studies for the treatment of depression in children have been reported. One study, by Petti, Bornstein, Delamater, and Conners (1980), involved a multimodal treatment of depression in a 10-year-old girl. This program, which also included tricyclic antidepressant medication, did demonstrate efficacy in reducing depressive symptoms. Another case presentation, by Frame, Matson, Sonis, Fialkov, and Kazdin (1982), involved a behavioral intervention for depression in a 10-year-old boy. Reduction of symptoms was shown in four target behaviors (inappropriate body position, lack of eye contact, poor speech, and bland affect), although formal change across a range of depressive symptoms was not presented.

A pilot study presented by Petti, Kovacs, Feinberg, Paulauskas, and Finkelstein (1982) involved the use of cognitive therapy for the treatment of atypical

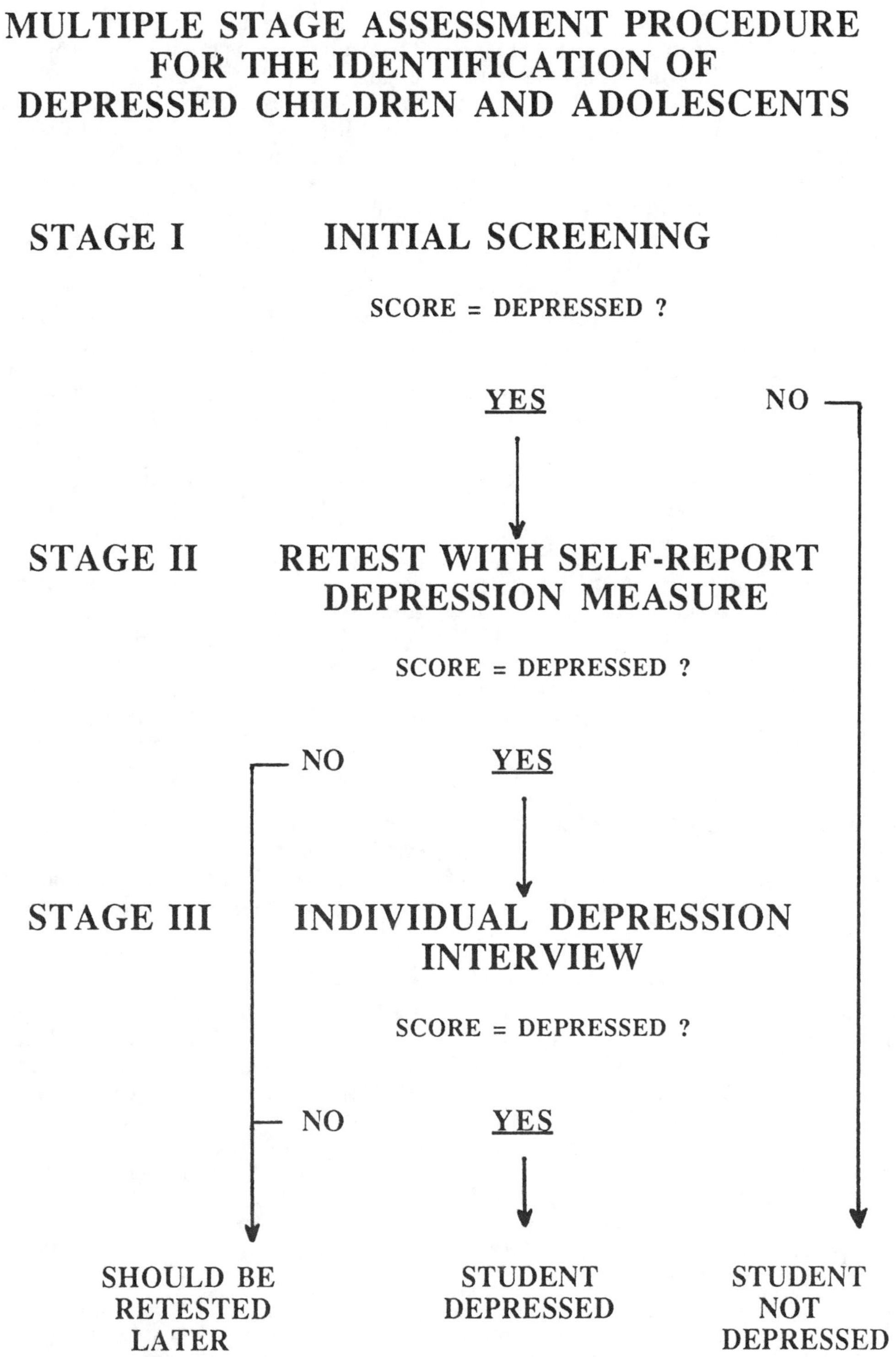

MULTIPLE STAGE ASSESSMENT PROCEDURE FOR THE IDENTIFICATION OF DEPRESSED CHILDREN AND ADOLESCENTS

STAGE I   **INITIAL SCREENING**

SCORE = DEPRESSED ?

YES   NO

STAGE II   **RETEST WITH SELF-REPORT DEPRESSION MEASURE**

SCORE = DEPRESSED ?

NO   YES

STAGE III   **INDIVIDUAL DEPRESSION INTERVIEW**

SCORE = DEPRESSED ?

NO   YES

SHOULD BE RETESTED LATER

STUDENT DEPRESSED

STUDENT NOT DEPRESSED

FIGURE 1. Multistage assessment procedure for the identification of depressed children and adolescents.

depression in a 12-year-old boy. Treatment included components of cognitive restructuring, self-monitoring, self-evaluation, attribution retaining, relaxation training, and parent training aimed at improving the home atmosphere. The results derived from administering the Interview Schedule for Children (ISC) (Kovacs, 1978) and the BID (Petti, 1978) to assess primary symptoms at referral, pretreatment, posttreatment, and follow-up suggested significant reduction of major symptoms of depression. On the BID, the subject's score (based on the mother's report of symptom severity) changed from a score of 39 at initial evaluation to a score of 4 at the 22-month follow-up evaluation.

A number of authors have presented illustrative case descriptions of interventions for depression or closely related problems in children. Although not a formal research study, Gotlib and Colby (1987) present a brief case description of a 10-year-old boy who underwent an "interpersonal systems treatment" for depression. As a case illustration, Meichenbaum, Bream, and Cohen (1985) discuss the application of a cognitive-behavioral therapy for the treatment of social withdrawal in an 11-year-old girl. Petti (1981) describes several treatment cases that entailed the use of a multimodal treatment approach that included antidepressant medication.

A number of controlled-group-treatment studies have been conducted that examined the efficacy of psychological treatments for depression in children and adolescents. In one of the first reported studies (Butler, Miezitis, Friedman, & Cole, 1980), which consisted of moderately depressed fifth- and sixth-grade children, one group who had received a social role-play treatment emphasizing social skills and social problem solving and another group who had received a cognitive restructuring treatment based in part on rational emotive therapy were compared with children in attention and waiting list control conditions. Subjects in the two active treatments and in the attention condition met for 10 1-hour sessions in small groups. A pretest–posttest design

was used, and unfortunately, no follow-up evaluation was made to determine the maintenance of treatment gains. Several outcome measures were used, including the Children's Depression Inventory (Kovacs, 1979, 1981, 1983). At the posttest, significant decreases in depression were evidenced for both of the active treatment conditions, as well as for the waiting list control condition. The attention group remained relatively little changed as to their level of self-reported depression. Overall, the results of this study were somewhat mixed. However, this study is noteworthy in that it was the first experimental group intervention with depressed children and because it was conducted in a school setting.

Stark et al. (1987) conducted a controlled group-treatment study that compared cognitive-behavioral (self-control) and behavioral problem-solving treatment conditions with a waiting list control group. The subjects were 20 moderately depressed children aged 9–12 years. Assessment measures included the RCDS, CDI, and individual clinical interviews with the CDRS-R. Treatment which took place in an elementary school, consisted of 12 sessions, each lasting approximately 50 minutes, and was administered in group format over a 5-week period. All three groups of children manifested a moderate level of depression at the pretest.

The cognitive-behavioral treatment relied to a large extent on the self-control methodology for the treatment of depression as developed by Rehm and colleagues (Fuchs & Rehm, 1977; Rehm, 1977). In addition, cognitive components consistent with Beck's (1976) cognitive therapy procedures and some attribution retraining were included. The behavioral problem-solving therapy included some training in self-monitoring as a precursor to the presentation of more behavioral components. A primary focus was on the teaching of procedures aligned with Lewinsohn's social learning theory (Lewinsohn, Munoz, Youngren, & Zeiss, 1978) that were designed to increase the children's involvement in pleasant activities. Additional components included modeling by the children of problem-solving skills demonstrated by the therapist, with an emphasis on increasing engagement in pleasant activities as well as improving social behavior.

The results of the Stark et al. (1987) study indicate that at posttest both active treatments produced significant improvement in depressive symptomatology whereas the difference for the waiting list control group was nonsignificant. An 8-week follow-up assessment showed a general maintenance of treatment effects, with some indication that children in the self-control condition continued to improve from posttest to follow-up. It should be noted that children in the control condition were treated after the posttest and thus were not included in the between-group comparisons at follow-up. The treatments were shown to be reasonably effective, 88% of the children in the self-control group and 67% of those in the behavioral group being assessed as nondepressed at the follow-up assessment.

The first published group treatment study of depression in adolescents was conducted by Reynolds and Coats (1986). This investigation contrasted a cognitive-behavioral treatment, a relaxation training group, and a waiting list control group. Assessments included a preliminary screening, pretest, posttest, and follow-up to evaluate treatment outcome. The subjects were 30 moderately to severely depressed high school students; treatment was administered in the high school. Treatments for both active conditions were administered in 10 1-hour sessions over a 5-week period. Assessment measures included the RADS and BID.

Both active therapies were presented in a structured format, with detailed treatment manuals established for each condition. The cognitive-behavioral therapy followed procedures used in the treatment of depression in adults, with modifications made for developmental and situational (e.g., home, school, peer group, etc.) differences of adolescents. The components of the cognitive-behavioral therapy included elements of self-control procedures (i.e., self-monitoring, self-evaluation, and self-reinforcement), cog-

nitive restructuring consistent with aspects of Beck's cognitive therapy, and procedures for increasing involvement in pleasant activities (Lewinsohn et al., 1978). The relaxation training condition included training in progressive relaxation procedures based on the tenets of Jacobsen (1938), with some guided imagery included. Treatments were matched for therapist time and amount of homework assignments.

Significant treatment effects were found for both active treatment conditions at the posttesting. In addition, these treatment gains were found to have been maintained at the 4-week follow-up evaluation. To illustrate the treatment outcome realized in this investigation, Table 4 provides RADS scores for the experimental and control groups at the pretest, posttest, and follow-up assessment points. As can be seen, significant decreases were reported by youngsters in the cognitive-behavioral and relaxation groups at posttest, and almost no change was reported by the waiting list youngsters. We can also see that without treatment, depressed adolescents did not show a significant reduction in their level of depressive symptoms.

In a recent study with moderately depressed youngsters in middle school (Grades 6-8) Kahn (1988) investigated the clinical efficacy of several active treatments, including cognitive-behavioral, relaxation training, and a self-modeling condition, along with a waiting list control group. The cognitive-behavioral treatment focused primarily on pleasant activity scheduling and other behavioral components consistent with the approach of Lewinsohn et al. (1978), with some cognitive, self-control, and social skills training added. The relaxation training group was similar to that of Reynolds and Coats (1986). The latter two treatments were group-administered, and consisted of 12 50-minute sessions. The self-modeling condition was unique in that it involved individually administered treatments in which youngsters initially were coached in the development of a 3-minute videotape in which they modeled behaviors inconsistent with depression,

TABLE 5
**Summary of Two Adolescent Depression Treatment Studies with
Reynolds Adolescent Depression Scale (RADS) as Outcome Measure**

Study	Groups	Pretest	Posttest[a]	Follow-up
Reynolds & Coats (1986)	Cognitive-behavioral	85.67	66.74	62.60
	Relaxation training	80.09	65.80	54.73
	Waiting list control	80.70	81.12	72.25
Kahn (1988)	Cognitive-behavioral	85.41	53.44	54.18
	Relaxation training	83.82	61.76	61.58
	Self-modeling	84.27	62.12	64.18
	Waiting list control	86.91	80.12	74.70

Note. In both studies reported above, a screening assessment was utilized prior to the pretesting.
[a]Posttest and follow-up RADS scores for the Reynolds and Coats study are adjusted means based on an analysis of covariance using pretest scores as the covariate.

such as smiling, positive verbalizations, and appropriate eye contact. Assessment measures included the RADS, CDI, and BID.

All therapeutic groups demonstrated significant treatment gains at posttesting and at a 4-week follow-up. Overall, the cognitive-behavioral and relaxation training conditions tended to show the greatest therapeutic benefits, especially when proportions of nondepressed cases within each condition were examined at posttesting and follow-up. The results of Kahn's study as to treatment outcome on the RADS are presented in Table 5. As shown, the results of this investigation are quite consistent with those of Reynolds and Coats (1986), and they suggest that the techniques applied had clinically meaningful utility in the psychological treatment of depression in youngsters.

Although they are not numerous, the above controlled treatment studies demonstrate the efficacy of psychological treatments for the amelioration of depressive symptoms in children and adolescents. One caveat in regard to the group treatments described above is the lack of formal diagnosis of a depressive disorder as a selection criterion. However, given the levels of depression demonstrated by subjects across several pretreatment evaluations, it is likely that a significant proportion of treated youngsters would have met diagnostic criteria for a depressive disorder.

Pharmacotherapy and Electroconvulsive Therapy for Depression in Children and Adolescents

By far, most of the empirical literature on the treatment of depression in children and adolescents has been specific to the application of psychopharmacological procedures. Pharmacological interventions and procedures for the treatment of depression in children and adolescents have been described by Petti (1983b), Puig-Antich, Ryan, and Rabinovich (1985), and Weller and Weller (1984, 1986). To a large extent, these investigations have demonstrated the clinical efficacy of several tricyclic antidepressants, although not all studies have utilized double-blind procedures. Although not a criticism of this research area, Puig-Antich et al. (1985) note that unlike the extant research with adults, psychopharmacological studies of depressed youngsters have not been as subtype-specific and have not delineated the psychotic subtype. In addition, at least one case study has been reported in which psychotherapy and a tricyclic antidepressant (imipramine) were used in combination (Petti et al., 1980).

Relatively few case studies of electroconvulsive therapy (ECT) with youngsters have been reported. In most instances, ECT was prescribed as a "last alternative" after numerous treatment trials with pharmacotherapy. For example, Berman and Wolpert (1987) report a case study of a 18-year-old adolescent girl with a history of many episodes of minor depression beginning at age 13, and a current diagnosis of rapid-cycling bipolar illness (manic–depressive psychosis) with suicidal ideation in the depressive stage. Over a 5-month period, across two hospital settings, pharmacotherapy that included, over various periods, the administration of thioridazine, fluphenazine, phenobarbital, lozapine, haloperidol, carbamazephine, chloridiazepoxide, lithium carbonate, chlorpromazine, desipramine, imipramine, diazepam, paraldehyde, clonaepam, and trifluoperazine proved relatively ineffective. Six ECT treatments administered over 2 weeks, and weekly supportive psychotherapy, resulted in a complete remission documented over a 14-month follow-up period. This case is presented here as an example of an intractable condition requiring relatively severe, invasive procedures well beyond the treatment scope of most school professionals. It should also be noted that this case of early-onset bipolar illness was preceded by a long period of minor depression beginning in early adolescence.

TREATMENT CASE PRESENTATION

Described below is an example of a cognitive-behavioral treatment for depression as presented in a prototypic case study of a 16-year-old youngster. This case study is predicated on an amalgamation of clinical cases drawn from experimental intervention studies of depression in children and adolescents conducted by the author and colleagues (Reynolds & Coats, 1986; Stark et al., 1987). The case presentation that follows is designed to illustrate the core therapeutic components used to treat depression in youngsters. Although not an actual case, in that the individual described below is a composite of a number of youngsters, the complaints, history, and treatment procedures are from actual clinical cases.

Treatment Orientation

The intervention procedures utilized here can be considered to fall under the general rubric of cognitive-behavioral therapy. For the most part these treatment components were based on contemporary cognitive and behavioral theories of depression and were adapted from treatment packages designed for use with adults. We have found that it is useful in clinical practice to go beyond the application of a treatment based solely on a single theoretical model, such as self-control therapy or cognitive therapy. A diversity of therapeutic components allows for the greatest broad-spectrum treatment of depressive symptoms and the modification of dysfunctional cognitive and behavioral mechanisms. In addition, by incorporating specific treatment components based on deficit or dysfunctional cognitions and behaviors hypothesized by formal models or theories of depression, this approach adopts multiple "targets" for clinical change (e.g., Kanfer, 1985; Kazdin, 1985).

Treatment Components

The general structure of the treatments for depression in children and adolescents presented here involves the systematic integration of therapeutic components derived from various contemporary models of depression (e.g., behavioral, cognitive, etc.), as well as the addition of ancillary procedures such as relaxation training. As in the experimental treatment studies described above, self-monitoring is an important therapeutic component in the treatment of depression. Self-monitoring as an active component is usually introduced early in treatment and involves training in the cognitive self-observation of one's own behavior. More specifically, self-monitoring typically focuses on the determination of the occurrence or nonoccurrence of one or more target behaviors, cognitions, or events, and is often operationalized with the use of recording forms. Barlow, Hayes, and Nelson (1984) provide a useful review and discussion of self-monitoring procedures and implementation strategies. As noted earlier, self-monitoring is the initial component within the self-control model of depression (Rehm, 1977). Subsequently, in conformation with this model of self-regulation, training in accurate self-evaluation and self-reinforcement are incorporated into therapy.

Cognitive restructuring is often included in therapy; it takes the form of a number of techniques designed to promote the identification and remediation of faulty or dysfunctional thought patterns. Variants of procedures developed by Ellis' (1980) rational emotive therapy (RET), Beck's (1967; 1976) cognitive therapy (CT) and Meichenbaum's (1977) self-instructional training (SIT) have been applied separately and in combination as components in child and adolescent depression treatment packages. Attribution retraining is also included in treatment, typically as a secondary, rather than primary, therapeutic component.

A significant behavioral component of therapy has been the use of activity scheduling to increase youngsters' engagement in pleasant or reinforcing activities. This is consistent with procedures developed by Lewinsohn et al. (1978) to overcome the reduced incidence of response-contingent reinforcement which is often experienced by depressed individuals. Along with this tactic, social skills training often is included to increase depressed youngsters' interaction with the environment, a major source of positive reinforcement.

This multimodal approach to treatment results in a broad-spectrum intervention program for treating depression in children and adolescents. The intervention described below is presented as a somewhat structured treatment package. However, it is important that the therapist utilize clinical observations and judgment as treatment progresses, noting specific cognitive or behavioral distortions or deficits that may be subsequently targeted for additional therapy and watching out particularly for the existence of suicidal ideation or intent, or recent history of a suicide attempt. In cases of depressed and actively suicidal youngsters, other components that specifically target suicidal behaviors and incorporate life-preserving adjuncts to therapy must be included.

Identification

The treatment case described is that of "Richard," a 16-year-old white male. Richard was identified by a schoolwide mental health screening as potentially at risk for depression. The multistage school screening procedure for depression in children and adolescents was similar to that described by Reynolds (1986b). In the case of Richard, this screening was conducted in his high school as an annual activity. Because of the difficulties of relying on self-referral and referral by others, the school identifies depressed students who are in need of treatment either within the school or through referral to mental health service providers.

In conformation with the original formulation by Reynolds (1986b), the depression screening procedure implemented by the school consisted of three assessment stages incorporating several methods of evaluation, as described in the previous section. The first stage was the schoolwide administration of the RADS to all students in the high school, which required approximately 10 minutes for most students. At this assessment stage approximately 12% of the youngsters in the school were identified as scoring at or above the critical cutoff score of 77 on the RADS. Approximately 2 weeks after the initial screening, these students were then reassessed with the RADS in small groups of 20–25. Youngsters who continued to demonstrate a clinical level of depressive symptoms on the RADS were then individually interviewed with the HDRS-HS.

On the initial and the Stage 2 assessment, Richard demonstrated a significant level of depressive symptomatology. Anecdotal reports from teachers lent additional support, the thrust of which suggested a decrease in his school performance and periodic observations of lethargy and an overt appearance of sadness in the classroom. Shortly after the second administration of the RADS, Richard was interviewed for depression with the HDRS-HS. On the basis of the evidence gathered by the school and in the clinical interview with the HDRS-HS, Richard was viewed as demonstrating a clinical level of depressive symptomatology. At the initiation of treatment, Richard was re-administered the RADS, on which he received a score of 82, which is at the 96th percentile for adolescent boys based on the RADS standardization sample of 1,223 boys in high schools. Because Richard had been interviewed within the previous week with the Hamilton, this measure was not readministered. His HDRS-HS score was 31, which is quite high, and significantly above the cutoff scores of 17 or 20 that are most typically used in clinical research on depression in adults (e.g., Kobak et al., in press). Richard was referred for participation in an experimental program conducted in the school for the treatment of depression.

Pretreatment Assessment and Case History

Prior to active treatment, a case history and pretreatment assessment of the depressed youngster is an important initial step, once permission for treatment has been granted by parents. It is also requisite that the youngster understand the general nature and intent of the treatment and consent to therapy. At Richard's intake meeting a current life history was obtained, focusing on his current family situation, the occurrence of major life events, pervasiveness of daily hassles (minor negative events), and the availability of social supports. In addition, the interviewer examined Richard's cognitive appraisal of events and situations. The evaluation of Richard's perceptions of the cause(s) of his problems, his perceived ability to deal with them, and his cognitions of responsibility or blame provided the therapist with an initial determination of Richard's ability to accurately self-monitor and self-evaluate events and his own behavior, as well as a partial examination of his attributional style and potential cognitive distortions and/or deficits.

Richard had a distinctly sad and downcast appearance. He seemed to have quite flat affect, showing very little facial response to questions. Richard's movements were slow, and he spoke in a low, slow monotone, suggestive of significant psychomotor retardation. After the therapist described the nature and intent of the forthcoming therapy sessions, Richard agreed to participate in the treatment.

The intake interview started with a brief evaluation of Richard's current family, school, and extracurricular functioning. It revealed that he lived with his mother, who was an alcoholic. He had a paper route after school to help support them, which required a significant amount of time and effort for him. Richard noted that he had few friends and engaged in few social activities. The therapist then asked if anything bad had happened to him in the past few months. In reply to this inquiry, Richard described how 6 weeks prior to the interview he had hit a hitchhiker with the family car when attempting to get onto the highway. Continuing in a slow, monotone voice with little affect, Richard explained that the hitchhiker was currently in a coma in the hospital: It was unknown at that time if he was going to live. This event was unknown to the school. Richard appeared to accept this mishap as another indication of the hopelessness of his life situation. It was established at the time of the Hamilton interview and at the intake evaluation that Richard was not suicidal, although he did admit to thoughts of death and morbid ideational themes which clearly were consistent with the automobile accident and hospitalization of the hitchhiker.

Overall, Richard felt that his life seemed quite worthless and his view of the future suggested a hopeless perspective. There was a significant amount of self-deprecation in his description of himself. Although he had no specific thoughts of taking his own life, he reported that a year previously he had been thinking about it and had been troubled by such thoughts.

A clinical picture of Richard's depression, based on an examination of specific symptoms and symptom clusters obtained on the Hamilton interview and the intake evaluation, indicated anhedonia, as illustrated by his lack of pleasure and enjoyment of his usual activities. His overtly sad appearance and depressed mood, suggested a pervasive dysphoric mood. Richard said that he had been very depressed for about 2 months, but that his mood had been low even before the automobile accident. He felt that things were pretty bad and would not get better and reported occasional tearfulness. Also evident were somatic complaints of general fatigue and difficulty concentrating in school. He had insomnia, reporting that three or four times a week he required 1-2 hours to fall asleep. Attending school required a significant amount of effort. Most of the symptoms noted were experienced nearly every day. In sum, Richard presented a clinical picture of a youngster with Major Depression, most likely subsequent to Dysthymia. No delusions or hallucinations of either a mood-congruent or mood-incongruent nature were noted.

Treatment Planning

The treatment plan used consisted primarily of cognitive-behavioral therapy, with additional therapeutic components that have shown some degree of treatment efficacy, such as relaxation training. The therapy for depression, as described here was brief and intense, administered in 10 sessions of 50 minutes twice a week, over a 5-week period. This short-term approach to psychotherapy is consistent with many contemporary cognitive psychotherapeutic procedures used with adults (e.g., Dobson, 1989). In youngsters, relatively brief, structured psychotherapies designed to be administered over a 5- to 10-week period are advisable because they quickly demonstrate to the youngster that a change in their affect can occur if they maintain compliance to the therapeutic regimen. The time and length of treatment is not a set requirement and

should be considered quite flexible in that it can be extended in duration of sessions and in the number of sessions. With younger children, it is advantageous to increase the number of sessions rather than the length of sessions: This allows for therapeutic components to be presented with greater specifications and examples, and it provides the youngster with more opportunities to practice the homework exercises and receive and act upon the therapist's feedback. Furthermore, younger children have short attention spans, and may experience interference caused by depressive symptoms of fatigue and difficulty with concentration. However, one drawback to this relatively short-term treatment is the potential for reoccurrence of depression. Although this phenomenon has not been studied in youngsters, routine booster sessions at intervals of several months following completion of successful treatment may provide a prophylaxis against further depressive episodes.

The presentation of therapeutic components involved the teaching of self-help skills, within what might be called a psychoeducational model. Like depression in adults, depression in children and adolescents is often characterized by behavioral and cognitive deficits and/or distortions. Therefore, a major emphasis of therapy was the modification of cognitive distortions and development of cognitive strategies where deficits were evidenced. In addition to the specific treatment components tied to models of depression, reinforcement was provided during and at the completion of the treatment program that was contingent on active involvement in the therapy (attending sessions, completing homework assignments, etc.).

Administration of Therapy

The treatment was relatively structured in presentation, and originally designed to be completed in a 5- to 6-week period. Richard's treatment was group-administered; four depressed youngsters including Richard were in the group. Group treatment works quite well as a therapeutic procedure and also assists some youngsters to see that their problems are not unique. The group format also provides a ready mechanism for developing social skills among participants and often results in a time-limited social support network. The administration of therapy and the structure of each session is described below, with a delineation of specific therapeutic goals and examples of treatment elements.

Session 1. The initial treatment session started with an introduction to the goals of therapy. This was followed by a discussion of some general problems faced by people who are depressed. A rationale for the treatment was presented with examples specific to depressed youngsters. The relationship between activity level and mood was introduced, and youngsters were told that it is necessary to understand the relationship between their own mood and activity level. It was explained how people who are depressed tend to focus on unpleasant events to the exclusion of positive events or outcomes. To illustrate this, the therapist would say, "For example, if you were complimented by a friend during the day or did well on a difficult exam, but later lost in a game of tennis or had to stay with your mother instead of going out with your friends, you might tend to focus on or think of the negative events rather than the compliment you received or the fact that you did well on the test."

In this session, youngsters were told that depressed persons attend to immediate rather than delayed outcomes, especially delayed rewards. These points were related to an explanation of self-monitoring and the importance of making accurate self-observations for influencing mood. Procedures for self-monitoring external events and one's own behavior were described. Richard was provided with a logbook for use in self-monitoring positive activities, as well as recording his mood at the end of each day. The logbook included a list of pleasant activities that had been generated to assist Richard by providing examples of pleasant events to self-monitor. Richard was instructed to use a new log sheet for each day, and to bring his logbook to each session. As a homework assignment, he was directed to record his daily mood and positive activities in the self-monitoring log.

Session 2. The second session focused on teaching the group members the relationship between mood and activity, and how mood can be changed by changing activity. The self-monitoring logs that Richard had completed for several days were examined to see how the number of pleasant activities he had engaged in related to his mood of that day. Richard was praised for completing the homework assignment, with an emphasis on the effort taken and a discussion of the aspects that were completed correctly. In this session, as in all others, the therapist devoted very little attention to participants' complaints or negative statements.

Richard and the other students in the therapy group were asked to graph the number of positive activities that they had engaged in along with the associated mood for each of the past 4 days. Using his self-monitoring logs, Richard graphed the number of positive activities along with his mood (on a 1–10 *low* to *positive* scale) on a specially prepared graph that the therapist provided. In this exercise, Richard was told, "Look at the 1 or 2 days on which your mood was the most positive and figure out the number of positive activities or pleasant events for those days. Now do the same for the days that your mood was the lowest. Is the number of activities higher for the days when your mood was good?" Further explanation on the connection between mood and activities was presented, and Richard was encouraged to identify those activities that were consistently associated with a positive mood. He was also told to try to increase activities related to positive mood and to continue to self-monitor both positive activities and daily mood.

Session 3. This session focused on the tendency of depressed persons to attend to immediate rather than long-term, delayed outcomes of their behavior and of events. Cognitive distortions and the tendency to view the world negatively were presented as ways in which depressed persons maintain their low affect. Training and examples were provided to illustrate how circumstances can be viewed as either positive or negative, and have immediate or delayed consequences. As an example, Richard was told that the activity of eating an ice cream sundae may be viewed as having the immediate positive effect afforded by its pleasing taste, and the delayed positive effect associated with getting more done if one takes a break every now and then. Conversely, it may be viewed as having the immediate negative effect of costing too much money, and the delayed negative effect of causing a gain in weight. With all of these potential outcomes brought to mind, Richard was asked: "Which is easier to think of, immediate or long-term effect? Positive or negative effects? Which are you more likely to think of when you are doing something?"

Using an "Immediate Versus Delayed Effects Worksheet," Richard filled in the effects of three activities selected from his self-monitoring logs. He was reminded of the tendency of the depressed to selectively attend to immediate negative events, and was told to attend more closely to the delayed positive outcomes of his behavior and events, and to fill in a positive delayed effect of at least one positive activity each day on his self-monitoring log.

Session 4. The primary goals of this session were the initial development of self-evaluation skills and attribution retraining. The therapist determined from an examination of his homework assignments that Richard was now able to accurately self-monitor his behavior and events; the next step was training to develop skills in making accurate self-evaluations for success and failure, and setting realistic, obtainable goals. A rationale was presented that depressed individuals often make inaccurate evaluations, particularly for their successes and failures. Specifically, depressed persons often hold faulty beliefs about their responsibility for events. This session explored the assumptions people make in assigning responsibility for events and the outcomes of their behavior, and how accurate self-evaluations of the outcomes of such events can assist in reducing depression. The second focus of this session, based upon the learned helplessness model of depression and the role of attributions in the maintenance of depression, was on teaching Richard to accurately evaluate the extent to which his own effort, skill, and ability (or lack of them) were responsible for the occurrence of positive and negative events, as well as the extent to which other people, chance, or luck were responsible. The goal was for Richard to make realistic and adaptive attributions (attribute failure to more external, unstable, and specific factors and success to internal, stable, global factors) for his behavior and events.

To demonstrate this depressogenic attributional style, an "attribution of responsibility" exercise was presented to illustrate the assumptions depressed persons make in assigning credit, blame, or responsibility for various events and outcomes. It was shown how the depressed often make faulty assumptions about responsibility for both positive and negative events. Richard was directed to show, using the self-monitoring logs to identify several fairly important events, how he has considerable responsibility for the positive events in his life, and how he is able to influence or increase the occurrence of these events. Likewise, examples of several minor unpleasant events were used to illustrate to Richard that he is not solely responsible for their occurrence, and that in most cases the latter events can be attributed to external factors such as other persons or chance. As a homework assignment, Richard was asked to continue self-monitoring in his daily log, and to record the percentage of responsibility he bore for each of the positive activities recorded.

Session 5. This session focused on procedures for developing a self-change plan. The underlying rationale for a self-change plan was presented as consisting of the following elements: (a) believing that you can change, (b) knowing that self-change, like self-control, is a skill that can be learned, and (c) recognizing the necessity of a plan for effective change. Most of the session had to do with teaching how to make a self-change plan. Richard was taught how to specify a problem and decide what to change; how to collect baseline information and keep track of progress; ways to discover antecedents (events or conditions such as social situations, own feelings or behaviors, physical settings, behavior of other people) related to the problem and how to control these antecedents; and how to discover the consequences of engaging in specific behaviors, with the understanding that we wish to increase behavior that is followed by positive consequences and decrease a behavior that is not.

Basic to this session was the notion that Richard was to overcome and deal with his problems and that he could have an active role in changing things for the better. The emphasis on skill building and positive change by means of his own actions, effort, and ability was designed to promote a sense of self-efficacy or self-mastery. Richard was told that the next session would involve instruction in setting goals and contracting. As a homework assignment, he was requested to identify a specific problem to work on and to begin to collect baseline information, using a tally sheet. In addition, he was instructed to attend to antecedents and consequences of his behavior and the events in his life.

Session 6. This session, which continued training in self-change skills, focused on setting realistic, obtainable goals and subgoals, on contracting, and on obtaining reinforcement. It was explained how depressed persons tend to set unrealistically high goals for themselves, how the depressed, by failing to reach these goals, set themselves up for failure and consequent negative self-evaluations. The therapist explained that goals should be modest and attainable and that they can be changed in response to continued monitoring. Furthermore, goals should be increased slowly, and only after a previous goal has been reached. Richard

was taught to select a realistic final goal that was within his control and to break this goal down into small subgoals. And he was instructed to make a contract to reward himself when he accomplished a subgoal. Specific rewards were determined in advance through the development of a "reward menu." It was also explained that the reward was to be awarded as close in time to the achievement of the goal as possible.

Richard was further informed that the reward (reinforcer) he selected should be one that (a) made him feel good, (b) was accessible, (c) matched the effort expended in reaching the goal, and (d) was reasonably under his control. Richard was given a Goal-Setting Worksheet to assist him in developing long-range goals and subgoals pertinent to the problem he had identified in the previous session, and he began collecting baseline information. The therapist provided feedback and praise for Richard's efforts to construct subgoals. Richard was instructed to continue to examine his goal and subgoals, making revisions to ensure that they are realistic, specific, and within his control.

This session also introduced training in progressive relaxation techniques. The relationship between stress-related problems and depression was discussed, and the rationale for using relaxation training to deal with stress was presented. Richard was informed that relaxation training reduces tension, which often results from stress. In addition, the reduction of tension allows for more accurate self-monitoring of mood, events, and the consequences of particular behaviors. Specific training in progressive muscle relaxation training was provided by the therapist, who led the group through some initial exercises. A program of muscle relaxation exercises was provided, along with relaxation homework assignment log sheets.

Session 7. After Richard had learned and implemented the procedures for goal setting presented in Session 6, the process of self-reinforcement was presented in greater detail in this session. It was explained how depressed persons do not self-reinforce sufficiently and may in fact punish themselves too much. The therapist described how systematic errors in thinking lead to negative interpretations of events and outcomes and result in poor self-evaluation and self-punishment. The emphasis in this session was on learning how to self-reward rather than self-punish by understanding the basics of self-reinforcement. To assist in the understanding and application of self-reinforcement, Richard was given further instructions in the development of a reward menu, which is a list of many enjoyable rewards, ranging from large to small. (A critical characteristic of the reward menu was that all rewards had to be relatively obtainable.)

Richard was instructed to develop a self-reward program to assist in increasing his goal-related activities. It was pointed out that self-reward is an effective way of producing desired long-range change, and that one goal should be replacing self-punishment with self-reward. A sheet for developing a Reward Menu was passed out with the directions that rewards should be truly enjoyable, vary from large to small, and be relatively available. Rewards could be material things such as clothes, things to play with (e.g., electronic games or puzzles), or activities such as going to a movie, taking a hike, eating out, and so on. Each reward on the menu was then assigned a point value from 1 to 10 depending on the magnitude of the reward. After he had developed a reasonable reward menu, Richard was instructed to assign points (1 to 10) to the subgoals he had established earlier. He was then told to consider the points earned in carrying out his subgoals as applicable toward spending on the rewards on the menu. At this stage he was instructed to use his self-monitoring logs to keep track of the points he earned by achieving his subgoals and goals, and the points he spent on rewards. He was again reminded that it was important to cash in points as soon as possible, so that the reward would be associated with performing and achieving the subgoal.

Session 8. The activities of the previous session had focused on the increase in self-reinforcement and the decrease in self-punishment. To a large extent, these procedures focused on overt activities, heavily dependent on active self-monitoring and self-evaluation. In session 8, Richard was taught procedures (similar in many respects to components of self-instruction training) for covert self-reinforcement. Rewards or punishment, it was explained, could be overt (having or denying oneself a piece of cake) or covert (praising oneself or thinking about one's failures). Depressed persons tend to engage in extensive and covert self-punishment, often to the exclusion of covert self-reward. To counteract this tendency, an exercise for increasing covert self-reinforcement was presented. Richard was first asked to make a list of positive self-statements that describe his best qualities, assets, and achievements. He was then instructed to repeat this list of positive attributes to himself for 30 seconds. It was noted how difficult it often is for people to talk well of themselves to themselves. Richard was told to say something positive about himself to himself (covertly) every time he accomplished one of his subgoals. For example, he might say to himself "That was good, I'm making progress," or "I finished this just like I had planned to. I must be doing well." Richard also was told that in addition to overt pleasant activities and events, such as going to a movie or to a party, pleasant thoughts also can be viewed as a positive activity and always available. These reinforcers also should be included in a reward menu. In addition to positive self-statements, Richard was instructed to use pleasant images and even pleasant feelings as covert self-reinforcers.

Session 9. This session was a check and review, and session of practice of many of the components presented in previous sessions. Richard's compliance with the treatment components and instructions was evaluated by determining through an examination of his self-monitoring logs, how well he had monitored and increased his performance of positive activities and engagement in pleasant activities.

In this session, the therapist also checked on Richard's selection and revision of goals and subgoals, and how well these goals met the criteria of controllability, attainability, and operationalization, providing praise and feedback for Richard's assignment of points to the subgoals and his development of a reward menu. In addition, Richard was complimented for his list of the positive self-statements that he had used as covert reinforcers for each subgoal achieved.

Session 10. The final treatment session was a review of the basic principles that had been presented about the reduction of depression and the associated activities for instituting self-change. The therapist provided extensive praise and encouragement for Richard's compliance and therapeutic gains. To ensure that Richard would have a clear understanding of what he had learned, and that these skills would be maintained and practiced after the conclusion of therapy, this session focused on generating a sense of hopefulness and optimism about Richard's current level of affective functioning and his ability to reduce his depression in the future. To the end of reinforcing a sense of self-efficacy it was emphasized that most of the positive change in Richard's affect and feelings was due to his own ability to actively help himself.

To assist in the evaluation of treatment efficacy, Richard completed a self-report depression questionnaire as well as a semistructured clinical interview at the beginning of this final session. On the RADS, Richard had a score of 61, which indicated some very mild symptoms but was clearly within a normal range for adolescents. On the HDRS–HS, he obtained a score of 5, which is very low and demonstrates the greater sensitivity of clinical interviews to true pathology.

At the time of the last session, Richard exhibited very few symptoms of depression. Upon recalling his previous response to the questions on the HDRS–HS, he realized the level and magnitude of change

and was able to accurately see the progress he had made. Richard no longer experienced difficulty in falling asleep and did not show symptoms of fatigue. He indicated that he enjoyed engaging in activities, and showed an interest in school and being with his friends. Although his mother's alcoholism was still a problem, Richard felt capable of dealing with it, and did not dwell on or internalize the somewhat negative circumstances in his life.

Follow-up and Summary

The treatment program described above may be considered a brief psychotherapeutic procedure that is structured to be time-limited. At the beginning of therapy, the program was described to Richard and a contract was drawn, specifying the reinforcement to be received contingent upon attendance and completion of homework assignments. At the completion of the primary treatment program, Richard was provided with additional therapeutic exercise forms and told to continue to self-monitor and engage in the therapy activities that were used as homework assignments. He also was allowed to select a major reward from a list prepared by the therapist (together with his mother).

Richard was reevaluated at a 4-week follow-up that included a self-report depression measure, a clinical interview, and discussion with the therapist. At this time, Richard reported no significant depressive symptoms and seemed reasonably positive about the future. He was told to continue to follow the procedures learned in therapy and, most important, to be watchful for any reoccurrence of depressive symptoms, especially those that might persist for several weeks or more. Finally he was instructed that should he become depressed and unable to deal effectively with his situation, he should seek out the school psychologist and work out a plan of therapy.

One year after the conclusion of the initial treatment Richard was once again reevaluated as part of the school's annual mental health screening. At this time, he scored in the nondepressed range on the screening measure and was viewed as well-adjusted. In addition, his performance in school showed significant improvement over that of the previous year.

TRAINING REQUIREMENTS, ISSUES, AND ROLE OF THE SCHOOL PSYCHOLOGIST IN TREATING DEPRESSED CHILDREN AND ADOLESCENTS

The treatment of the clinically depressed child or adolescent by school psychologists must be a cautious and carefully considered undertaking (Reynolds & Stark, 1987). As noted above, in addition to being knowledgeable and experienced in the provision of therapy for depression, there are a number of considerations that the therapist should note prior to beginning treatment. Foremost among these is to determine the youngster's suicide potential. It is also advisable to ascertain whether the depression is concomitant with other pathology, such as conduct or anxiety disorders, that may create a less than optimal therapeutic situation or suggest alternative treatment approaches.

A major concern in the treatment of depressed youngsters, as well as adults, is treatment compliance. A number of depressive symptoms, such as fatigue, withdrawal, feeling of worthlessness, and generalized anhedonia, may contribute to the difficulty that is often experienced by the therapist in treating depressed youngsters. Many of the cognitions of depressed children and adolescents may lead them to the generalization that nothing they do helps and that the future is hopeless. These factors, combined with the tendency to focus on immediate versus delayed reinforcement, and the developmentally normal perspective of children and some adolescents that curing a hurt means making it go away quickly, supports the application of brief psychotherapies. Unless the therapist can produce relatively quickly some therapeutic relief and demonstrate that positive change is possible, a number of negative, dysfunctional cognitions, such as hopelessness,

may become even more entrenched. Children especially seem to need proof that therapeutic relief will be forthcoming if they do as the therapist asks. Furthermore, this relatively quick, observable link between therapy and reduced distress will in all likelihood assist in the youngster's development of the feelings of self-efficacy that are specific to the therapy. Much of the cognitive and behavioral treatment literature suggests that development of self-efficacy is a critical component in these therapeutic processes (Bandura, 1977; Reynolds & Coats, 1986; Zeiss, Lewinsohn & Munoz, 1979).

In conducting therapy for depression with children, it is advisable to incorporate enjoyable, "fun" activities into the therapy sessions, and whenever possible utilize such activities in the teaching of skills and concepts. Incorporating enjoyable activities, such as role-playing, in a friendly, relaxed, "fun" therapeutic atmosphere will assist in engaging the youngster in the therapy and in complying with treatment requirements. Such activities, used in conjunction with reinforcement applied contingently upon treatment compliance and involvement, assists in the youngster's acceptance of therapy.

SUMMARY AND CONCLUSIONS

Depression is a major psychological problem that, to judge from rough estimates, is experienced by hundreds of thousands of youngsters. Consequently, there is a very great need for the development and application of treatment strategies for the amelioration of these problems in youngsters. Furthermore, as Kovacs (1989) notes, the early identification and treatment of depression in youngsters may be of critical importance in the prevention of more severe, and potentially long-lasting, negative consequences.

The cognitive-behavioral approach to the treatment of depression described above has been shown to be effective in treating children and adolescents, at least in experimental investigations. To date, our knowledge of the treatment of depression in children and adolescents is based in large part on modifications of treatment approaches and programs designed for use with adults. However, we have incorporated therapeutic techniques, such as self-instructional training, that have been developed for use as components in the treatment of other childhood disorders, particularly those amenable to cognitive-behavioral intervention such as impulsivity and problems of self-control. The author and colleagues have found that these cognitive-behavioral interventions work quite well with children and adolescents when administered in a small-group format, with groups consisting of three to five youngsters who are reasonably matched with regard to maturity level.

Although not presented in this chapter, modifications in the treatment package illustrated above should be made for younger children. In the treatment case described here, the depressed youngster was an adolescent. When treating children, it is advisable to increase the number of therapy sessions, and incorporate greater parental participation during treatment. This is especially important for increasing the opportunity for the child to engage in pleasant activities, as well as in operationalizing a reinforcement schedule. As to the latter, parents typically need to be involved to assist in carrying out activities, providing transportation, and taking care of monetary costs. We have found that when treating children, role-play and social problem-solving activities are useful mechanisms for the presentation of various components of the therapy. In some cases, family involvement may go beyond assistance in the application of therapy. When necessary, family therapy or parent training is recommended as an active component of a broad-based intervention for depression in children as well as adolescents.

The school psychologist should be aware that it is not unusual to find affective disorders in parents of children who are depressed (e.g., Morrison, 1983; Reid & Morrison, 1983). In such cases, it is possible that biological, psychosocial, environmental, and social learning conditions have a causal role in the mainte-nance of the disorder. In any case, depression (as well as many other psychopathologies) in one or both parents is a complicating factor in the treatment of depression as well as other psychological problems in children and adolescents: A depressed parent may reinforce depressive cognitions and behaviors in the youngster. Hence, the child treatment program may be compromised unless an effective therapeutic situation can be devised for both the parent and the child. For the school psychologist, the determination of depression in parents is difficult, given that the primary client is the youngster. However, a brief talk or interview with both parents, individually and together, may provide an opportunity to determine the parents' affective status.

In many cases of depression in children and adolescents, in fact, the youngster's depression may be a direct reaction to parental behavior. Bowlby (1985) suggests three classes of family experiences that may lead to cognitive disturbance in children: "a. those that parents wish their children not to know about b. those in which parents have treated children in ways the children find too unbearable to think about. c. those in which children have done, or perhaps thought, things about which they feel unbearably guilty or ashamed" (p. 183). In our research, we have found that family problems are the largest category of sources of depression endorsed by adolescents and that these youngsters tend to be more depressed than those who indicate academic, boyfriend/girlfriend, peer, or other problems as the cause of their depression (Reynolds & Coats, 1982). In addition, we find that marital discord is related to depression in youngsters, especially in girls (Reynolds & Coats, 1982). It is important to inform parents who are in conflict situations that any constructive actions that they may take toward resolving their own conflict in an amicable manner will be helpful to the mental well-being of their youngster. A recommendation of marital or family therapy is a useful suggestion, although not always effective with resistant families.

The focus of this chapter has been on the psychological treatment of depression in children and adolescents. However, pharmacological interventions also have been used with success for the treatment of this psychopathology in youngsters, and for some depressed youngsters, the utilization of pharmacotherapy in conjunction with psychotherapy may be recommended.

The distinction between cases that should be treated primarily with psychotherapy from those for which pharmacotherapy is recommended is unclear, and potentially debatable, but in general youngsters with depressions that are of the endogenous, melancholic subtype, or are unresponsive to psychotherapy, are probably good candidates for pharmacotherapy. In particular, youngsters with bipolar depression should be referred for psychiatric treatment. In any case, the use of antidepressant medications is a procedure that is clearly beyond the domain of school psychologists, requiring intervention by a psychiatrist or other medical professional (e.g., pediatric neurologist). However, antidepressants also may be useful as an adjunct for producing a receptive mood for the learning and development of skills and procedures taught in the course of psychotherapy. Such treatment may be particularly useful when dealing with extremely despondent youngsters who are unresponsive to engagement in therapy.

The case study presented here is an illustration of the application of cognitive-behavioral therapy for the treatment of depression in youngsters. The treatment was predicated on our early experiences with therapies for depression in children and adolescents that are based on psychological theory. It should be understood that this treatment technology is in its early evolution and hopefully will be a precursor to more sophisticated and efficacious procedures. It is anticipated that the technology specific to the treatment of depression in children and adolescents will advance from these beginnings.

ACKNOWLEDGMENTS

The author wishes to thank Jean A. Baker for her helpful comments on an earlier draft of this chapter.

REFERENCES

Abraham, K. (1911/1960). Notes on the psychoanalytic investigations and treatment of manic-depressive insanity and applied conditions. In *Selected papers on psychoanalysis* (pp. 137-156). New York: Basic Books.

Abramson, L. Y., Seligman, M. E. P., & Teasdale, J. D. (1978). Learned helplessness in humans: Critique and reformulation. *Journal of Abnormal Psychology, 87,* 49-74.

Alessi, N. E., & Magen, J. (1988). Comorbidity of other psychiatric disturbances in depressed psychiatrically hospitalized children. *American Journal of Psychiatry, 145,* 1582-1584.

American Psychiatric Association. (1968). *Diagnostic and statistical manual of mental disorders* (2nd ed.). Washington, DC: Author.

American Psychiatric Association. (1980). *Diagnostic and statistical manual of mental disorders* (3rd ed.). Washington, DC: Author.

American Psychiatric Association. (1987). *Diagnostic and statistical manual of mental disorders* (3rd rev. ed.). Washington, DC: Author.

Ammerman, R. T., Cassisi, J. E., Hersen, M., & Van Hasselt, V. B. (1986). Consequences of physical abuse and neglect in children. *Clinical Psychology Review, 6,* 291-310.

Anderson, J. C., Williams, S., McGee, R., & Silva, P. A. (1987). DSM-III disorders in preadolescent children. Prevalence in a large sample from the general population. *Archives of General Psychiatry, 44,* 69-76.

Baker, J. A., & Reynolds, W. M. (1988, August). *Training teachers to identify depressed students in their classroom.* Paper presented at the annual meeting of the American Psychological Association, Atlanta.

Bandura, A. (1977). Self-efficacy: Toward a unifying theory of behavior change. *Psychological Review, 84,* 191-215.

Barlow, D. H., Hayes, S. C., & Nelson, R. O. (1984). *The scientist practitioner: Research and accountability in clinical and educational settings.* New York: Pergamon.

Bartell, N. P., & Reynolds, W. M. (1986). Depression and self-esteem in academically gifted and nongifted children: A comparison study. *Journal of School Psychology, 24,* 55-61.

Beardslee, W. R. (1986). The need for the study of adaptation in the children of parents with affective disorders. In M. Rutter, C. E. Izard, & P. B. Read (Eds.), *Depression in young people: Developmental and clinical perspectives* (pp. 189-204). New York: Guilford.

Beck, A. T. (1967). *Depression: Clinical, experimental and theoretical aspects.* New York: Harper & Row.

Beck, A. T. (1976). *Cognitive therapy and the emotional disorders.* New York: International Universities Press.

Beck, A. T., Rush, A. J., Shaw, B. F., & Emery, G. (1979). *Cognitive therapy of depression.* New York: Guilford.

Berman, E., & Wolpert, E. (1987). Intractable manic-depressive psychosis with rapid cycling in an 18-year-old woman successfully treated with electroconvulsive therapy. *Journal of Nervous and Mental Disease, 175,* 236-239.

Beutler, L. E., & Hamblin, D. L. (1986). Individual outcome measures of internal change: Methodological considerations. *Journal of Consulting and Clinical Psychology, 54,* 48-53.

Blumberg, M. L. (1981). Depression in abused and neglected children. *American Journal of Psychotherapy, 35,* 342-355.

Bowlby, J. (1985). The role of childhood experience in cognitive disturbance. In M. J. Mahoney & A. Freeman (Eds.), *Cognition and psychotherapy* (pp. 181-200). New York: Plenum.

Burbach, D. J., & Borduin, C. M. (1986). Parent-child relations and the etiology of depression: A review of methods and findings. *Clinical Psychology Review, 6,* 133-153.

Butler, L., Miezitis, S., Friedman, R., & Cole, E. (1980). The effect of two school-based intervention programs on depressive symptoms in preadolescents. *American Educational Research Journal, 17,* 111-119.

Cantwell, D. P. (1983). Assessment of childhood depression: An overview. In D. P. Cantwell & G. A. Carlson (Eds.), *Affective disorders in childhood and adolescents — an update* (pp. 146-156). Jamaica, NY: Spectrum Publications.

Carlson, G. A., & Cantwell, D. P. (1980). Unmasking masked depression in children and adolescents. *American Journal of Psychiatry, 137,* 445-449.

Carlson, G. A., & Cantwell, D. P. (1982). Diagnosis of childhood depression: A comparison of the Weinberg and DSM-III criteria. *Journal of the American Academy of Child Psychiatry, 21,* 247-250.

Carlson, G. A., & Garber, J. (1986). Developmental issues in the classification of depression in children. In M. Rutter, C. E. Izard, & P. B. Read (Eds.), *Depression in young people: Developmental and clinical perspectives* (pp. 399-434). New York: Guilford.

Cohen-Sandler, R., & Berman, A. L. (1980). Diagnosis and treatment of childhood depression and self-destructive behavior. *Journal of Family Practice, 11,* 51-58.

Costello, C. G. (1980). Childhood depression: Three basic but questionable assumptions in the Lefkowitz and Burton critique. *Psychological Bulletin, 87,* 484-490.

Cytryn, L., & McKnew, D. H. (1972). Proposed classification of childhood depression. *American Journal of Psychiatry, 129,* 149-155.

Cytryn, L., McKnew, D. H., & Bunney, W. E. (1980). Diagnosis of depression in children: A reassessment. *American Journal of Psychiatry, 137,* 22-25.

Cytryn, L., McKnew, D. H., Zahn-Waxler, C., & Gershon, E. S. (1986). Developmental issues in risk research: The offspring of affectively ill parents. In M. Rutter, C. E. Izard, & P. B. Read (Eds.), *Depression in young people: Developmental and clinical perspectives* (pp. 163-188). New York: Guilford.

Dobson, K. S. (1989). A meta-analysis of the efficacy of cognitive therapy for depression. *Journal of Consulting and Clinical Psychology, 57,* 414-419.

Ellis, A. (1980). Rational-emotive therapy and cognitive behavior therapy: Similarities and differences. *Cognitive Therapy and Research, 4,* 325-340.

Endicott, J., Cohen, J., Nee, J., Fleiss, J., & Sarantakos, S. (1981). Hamilton Depression Rating Scale extracted from regular and change versions of the Schedule for Affective Disorders and Schizophrenia. *Archives of General Psychiatry, 38,* 98-103.

Endicott, J., & Spitzer, R. L. (1978). A diagnostic interview: The Schedule for Affective Disorders and Schizophrenia. *Archives of General Psychiatry, 35,* 837-844.

Finch, A. J., Lipovsky, J. A., & Casat, C. D. (1989). Anxiety and depression in children and adolescents: Negative affectivity or separate constructs? In P. C. Kendall & D. Watson (Eds.), *Anxiety and depression: Distinctive and overlapping features* (pp. 171-202). Orlando, FL: Academic Press.

Frame, C., Matson, J. L., Sonis, W. A., Fialkov, M. J., & Kazdin, A. E. (1982). Behavioral treatment of depression in a prepubertal child. *Journal of Behavior Therapy and Experimental Psychiatry, 13,* 239-243.

Freud, S. (1917/1946). Mourning and melancholia. In J. Srachey (Ed. and Trans.), *The standard edition of the complete psychological works of Sigmund Freud* (Vol. 14, pp. 243-258). London: Hogarth Press.

Fuchs, C. Z., & Rehm, L. P. (1977). A self-control behavior therapy program for depression. *Journal of Consulting and Clinical Psychology, 45,* 206-215.

Glaser, K. (1967). Masked depression in children and adolescents. *American Journal of Psychotherapy, 21,* 565-574.

Gotlib, I. H., & Colby, C. A. (1987). *Treatment of depression: An interpersonal systems approach.* New York: Pergamon.

Greist, J. H., & Jefferson, J. W. (1984). *Depression and its treatment: Help for the Nation's #1 mental problem.* Washington, DC: American Psychiatric Press.

Hamilton, M. (1960). A rating scale for depression. *Journal of Neurology, Neurosurgery, and Psychiatry, 23,* 56-62.

Hamilton, M. (1967). Development of a rating scale for primary depressive illness. *British Journal of Social and Clinical Psychology, 6,* 278-296.

Hamilton, M. (1982). Symptoms and assessment of depression. In E. S. Paykel (Ed.), *Handbook of affective disorders* (pp. 3-11). New York: Guilford.

Hollon, T. H. (1970). Poor school performance as a symptom of masked depression in children and adolescents. *American Journal of Psychotherapy, 24,* 258-263.

Jackson, S. W. (1986). *Melancholia and depression: From Hippocratic times to modern times.* New Haven, CT: Yale University Press.

Jacobsen, E. (1938). *Progressive relaxation.* Chicago: University of Chicago Press.

Kahn, J. (1988). *Assessment and treatment of depression among early adolescents.* Unpublished doctoral dissertation, University of Utah, Salt Lake City.

Kanfer, F. H. (1970). Self-regulation: Research, issues, and speculations. In C. Neuringer & J. L. Michael (Eds.), *Behavior modification in clinical psychology* (pp. 178-220). New York: Appleton-Century-Crofts.

Kanfer, F. H. (1985). Target selection for clinical change program. *Behavioral Assessment, 7,* 7-20.

Kanfer, F. H., & Karoly, P. (1972). Self-control: A behavioristic excursion into the lion's den. *Behavior Therapy, 3,* 398-419.

Kashani, J. H., McGee, R. O., Clarkson, S. E., Anderson, J. C., Walton, L. A., Williams, S., Silva, P. A., Robins,

A. J., Cytryn, L., & McKnew, D. H. (1983). Depression in a sample of 9-year-old children: Prevalence and associated characteristics. *Archives of General Psychiatry, 40,* 1217-1223.

Kashani, J. H., Rosenberg, T. K., & Reid, J. D. (1989). Developmental perspectives in child and adolescent depressive symptoms in a community sample. *American Journal of Psychiatry, 146,* 871-875.

Kazdin, A. E. (1985). Selection of target behaviors: The relationship of the treatment focus to clinical dysfunction. *Behavioral Assessment, 7,* 33-47.

Kazdin, A. E. (1986). Comparative outcome studies of psychotherapy: Methodological issues and strategies. *Journal of Consulting and Clinical Psychology, 54,* 95-105.

Kazdin, A. E. (1987). Assessment of childhood depression: Current issues and strategies. *Behavioral Assessment, 9,* 291-319.

Kazdin, A. E. (1988). *Child psychotherapy: Developing and identifying effective treatment.* New York: Pergamon.

Kazdin, A. E., Moser, J., Colbus, D., & Bell, R. (1985). Depressive symptoms among physically abused and psychiatrically disturbed children. *Journal of Abnormal Psychology, 94,* 298-307.

Kobak, K., Reynolds, W. M., Rosenfeld, R., & Greist, J. H. (in press). Development and validation of a computer administered version of the Hamilton Depression Rating Scale. *Psychological Assessment: A Journal of Consulting and Clinical Psychology.*

Kovacs, M. (1978). *The Interview Schedule for Children* (ISC-Form C). Unpublished manuscript. University of Pittsburgh.

Kovacs, M. (1979). *Children's Depression Inventory.* University of Pittsburgh School of Medicine.

Kovacs, M. (1980). The efficacy of cognitive and behavior therapies for depression. *American Journal of Psychiatry, 137,* 1495-1501.

Kovacs, M. (1981). Rating scales to assess depression in school-aged children. *Acta Paedopsychiatrica, 46,* 305-315.

Kovacs, M. (1983). *The Children's Depression Inventory: A self-rating scale for school-aged youngsters.* Unpublished manuscript.

Kovacs, M. (1985). The natural history and course of depressive disorders in childhood. *Psychiatric Annals, 15,* 387-389.

Kovacs, M. (1986). A developmental perspective on methods and measures in the assessment of depressive disorders: The clinical interview. In M. Rutter, C. E. Izard, & P. B. Read (Eds.), *Depression in young people: Developmental and clinical perspectives* (pp. 435-465). New York; Guilford.

Kovacs, M. (1989). Affective disorders in children and adolescents. *American Psychologist, 44,* 209-215.

Kovacs, M., Feinberg, T. L., Crouse-Novak, M., Paulauskas, S. L., Pollock, M., & Finkelstein, R. (1984). Depressive disorders in childhood: II. A longitudinal study of the risk for a subsequent major depression. *Archives of General Psychiatry, 41,* 229-237.

Leon, G. R., Kendall, P. C., & Garber, J. (1980). Depression in children: Parent, teacher, and child perspectives. *Journal of Abnormal Child Psychology, 8,* 221-235.

Lewinsohn, P. M. (1974). Clinical and theoretical aspects of depression. In K. S. Calhoun, H. E. Adams, & K. M. Mitchell (Eds.), *Innovative treatment methods in psychopathology* (pp. 63-120). New York: Wiley.

Lewinsohn, P. M. (1975). The behavioral study and treatment of depression. In M. Hersen, R. M. Eisler, & P. M. Miller (Eds.), *Progress in behavior modification* (pp. 19-64). New York: Academic.

Lewinsohn, P. M., & Arconad, M. (1981). Behavioral treatment of depression: A social learning approach. In J. F. Clarkin & A. I. Glazer (Eds.), *Depression: Behavioral and directive intervention strategies* (pp. 33-67). New York: Garland STPM Press.

Lewinsohn, P. M., Hoberman, H., Teri, L., & Hautzinger, M. (1985). An integrative theory of depression. In S. Reiss & R. R. Bootzin (Eds.), *Theoretical issues in behavior therapy* (pp. 331-359). New York: Academic.

Lewinsohn, P. M., Munoz, R. F., Youngren, M. A., & Zeiss, A. M. (1978). *Control your depression.* Englewood Cliffs, NJ: Prentice-Hall.

McGee, R., & Williams, S. M. (1988). A longitudinal study of depression in 9-year-old children. *Journal of the American Academy of Child and Adolescent Psychiatry, 27,* 342-348.

Meichenbaum, D. H. (1977). *Cognitive behavior modification.* New York: Plenum.

Meichenbaum, D. H., Bream, L. A., & Cohen, J. C. (1985). A cognitive-behavioral perspective of child psychopathology: Implications for assessment and training. In R. J. McMahon & R. DeV. Peters (Eds.), *Childhood disorders: Behavioral-developmental approaches* (pp. 36-52). New York: Brunner/Mazel.

Morrison, H. L. (Ed.). (1983). *Children of depressed parents: Risk, identification, and intervention.* New York: Grune & Stratton.

Petti, T. A. (1978). Depression in hospitalized child psychiatry patients: Approaches to measuring depression. *Journal of the American Academy of Child Psychiatry, 17,* 49-59.

Petti, T. A. (1981). Active treatment of childhood depression. In J. F. Clarkin & A. I. Glazer (Eds.), *Depression: Behavioral and directive intervention strategies* (pp. 311-343). New York: Garland STPM Press.

Petti, T. A. (1983a). The assessment of depression in young children. *Journal of Children in Contemporary Society, 15,* 19-28.

Petti, T. A. (1983b). Imipramine in the treatment of depressed children. In D. P. Cantwell & G. A. Carlson (Eds.), *Affective disorders in childhood and adolescents — an update* (pp. 375-415). Jamaica, NY: Spectrum Publications.

Petti, T. A. (1985). Scales of potential use in the psychopharmacologic treatment of depressed children and adolescents. *Psychopharmacology Bulletin, 21,* 951-977.

Petti, T. A., Bornstein, M., Dalamater, A., & Conners, C. K. (1980). Evaluation and multimodality treatment of a depressed prepubertal girl. *Journal of the American Academy of Child Psychiatry, 19,* 690-702.

Petti, T. A., Kovacs, M., Feinberg, T., Paulauskas, S., & Finklestein, R. (1982, October). *Cognitive therapy of a 12-year-old boy with atypical depression: A pilot study.* Paper presented at the annual meeting of the American Academy of Child Psychiatry, Washington, DC.

Philips, I. (1979). Childhood depression: Interpersonal interactions and depressive phenomena. *American Journal of Psychiatry, 136,* 511-515.

Poznanski, E. O. (1982). The clinical phenomenology of childhood depression. *American Journal of Orthopsychiatry, 52,* 308-313.

Poznanski, E. O., Cook, S. C., & Carroll, B. J. (1979). A depression rating scale for children. *Pediatrics, 64,* 442-450.

Poznanski, E. O., Cook, S. C., Carroll, B. J., & Corzo, H. (1983). Use of the Children's Depression Rating Scale in an inpatient psychiatric population. *Journal of Clinical Psychiatry, 44,* 200-203.

Poznanski, E. O., Freeman, L. N., & Markros, H. B. (1985). Children's Depression Rating Scale-Revised. *Psychopharmacology Bulletin, 21,* 979-989.

Poznanski, E. O., Grossman, J. A., Buchsbaum, Y., Banegas, M., Freeman, L., & Gibbons, R. (1984). Preliminary studies of the reliability and validity of the Children's Depression Rating Scale. *Journal of the American Academy of Child Psychiatry, 23,* 191-197.

Poznanski, E., Mokros, H. B., Grossman, J., & Freeman, L. N. (1985). Diagnostic criteria in childhood depression. *American Journal of Psychiatry, 142,* 1168-1173.

Puig-Antich, J. (1980). Affective disorders in childhood: A review and perspective. *Psychiatric Clinics of North America, 3,* 403-424.

Puig-Antich, J. (1982). Major depression and conduct disorder in prepuberty. *Journal of the American Academy of Child Psychiatry, 21,* 118-128.

Puig-Antich, J., & Chambers, W. (1978). *The Schedule for Affective Disorders and Schizophrenia for School-Age Children (Kiddie-SADS).* New York: New York State Psychiatric Institute.

Puig-Antich, J., Chambers, W. J., & Tabrizi, M. A. (1983). The clinical assessment of current depressive episodes in children and adolescents: Interviews with parents and children. In D. P. Cantwell & G. A. Carlson (Eds.), *Affective disorders in childhood and adolescents — An update* (pp. 157-179). Jamaica, NY: Spectrum Publications.

Puig-Antich, J., & Gittelman, R. (1982). Depression in childhood and adolescence. In E. S. Paykel (Ed.), *Handbook of affective disorders* (pp. 379-392). New York: Guilford.

Puig-Antich, J., & Rabinovich, H. (1986). Relationship between affective and anxiety disorders in childhood. In R. Gittelman (Ed.), *Anxiety disorders of childhood* (pp. 136-156). New York: Guilford.

Puig-Antich, J., Ryan, N. D., & Rabinovich, H. (1985). Affective disorders in childhood and adolescence. In J. M. Wiener (Ed.), *Diagnosis and psychopharmacology of childhood and adolescent disorders* (pp. 151-178). New York: Wiley.

Regier, D. A., Boyd, J. H., Burke, J. D., Rae, D. S., Meyers, J. K., Kramer, M., Robins, L. N., George, L. K., Karno, M., & Locke, B. Z. (1988). One-month prevalence of mental disorders in the United States. *Archives of General Psychiatry, 45,* 977-986.

Rehm, L. P. (1977). A self-control model of depression. *Behavior Therapy, 8,* 787-804.

Rehm, L. P. (1981). A self-control therapy program for treatment of depression. In J. F. Clarkin & A. I. Glazer (Eds.), *Depression: Behavioral and directive intervention strategies* (pp. 68-109). New York: Garland STPM Press.

Reid, W. H., & Morrison, H. L. (1983). Risk factors in children of depressed parents. In H. L. Morrison (Ed.), *Children of depressed parents: Risk, identification, and intervention* (pp. 33-46). New York: Grune & Stratton.

Reynolds, W. M. (1982). *Hamilton Depression Rating Scale: High School Adaptation.* Unpublished manuscript, University of Wisconsin–Madison.

Reynolds, W. M. (1984a). Depression in children and adolescents: Phenomenology, evaluation and treatment. *School Psychology Review, 13,* 171-182.

Reynolds, W. M. (1984b, August). *Controlling childhood depression in school settings: Clinical perspectives for school psychologists.* Paper presented at the annual meeting of the American Psychological Association, Montreal.

Reynolds, W. M. (1985a). Depression in childhood and adolescence: Diagnosis, assessment, intervention strategies and research. In T. R. Kratochwill (Ed.), *Advances in school psychology* (Vol. 4; pp. 133-189). Hillsdale, NJ: Erlbaum.

Reynolds, W. M. (1985b, March). *Development and validation of a scale to measure depression in adolescents.* Paper presented at the annual meeting of the Society for Personality Assessment, Berkeley, CA.

Reynolds, W. M. (1986a). *Reynolds Adolescent Depression Scale.* Odessa, FL: Psychological Assessment Resources.

Reynolds, W. M. (1986b). A model for the screening and identification of depressed children and adolescents in school settings. *Professional School Psychology, 1,* 117-129.

Reynolds, W. M. (1987a). *Reynolds Adolescent Depression Scale: Professional Manual.* Odessa, FL: Psychological Assessment Resources.

Reynolds, W. M. (1987b). *Suicidal Ideation Questionnaire.* Odessa, FL: Psychological Assessment Resources.

Reynolds, W. M. (1988). *Suicidal Ideation Questionnaire: Professional Manual.* Odessa, FL: Psychological Assessment Resources.

Reynolds, W. M. (1989a). *Reynolds Child Depression Scale.* Odessa, FL: Psychological Assessment Resources.

Reynolds, W. M. (1989b). *Reynolds Child Depression Scale: Professional Manual.* Odessa, FL: Psychological Assessment Resources.

Reynolds, W. M. (in press-a). Depressive disorders in children and adolescents. In W. M. Reynolds (Ed.), *Internalizing disorders in children and adolescents.* New York: Wiley.

Reynolds, W. M. (in press-b). Suicidal ideation and depression in adolescents: Assessment and research. In P. F. Lovibond & P. Wilson (Eds.), *Proceedings of the 24th International Congress of Psychology: Clinical volume.* Amsterdam: Elsevier.

Reynolds, W. M., Anderson, G., & Bartell, N. (1985). Measuring depression in children: A multimethod assessment investigation. *Journal of Abnormal Child Psychology, 13,* 513-526.

Reynolds, W. M., & Bartell, N. P. (1983). Stability of depressive symptomatology in adolescents. Unpublished data.

Reynolds, W. M., & Coats, K. I. (1982, July). *Depression in adolescents: Incidence, depth and correlates.* Paper presented at the 10th International Congress of the International Association for Child and Adolescent Psychiatry, Dublin, Ireland.

Reynolds, W. M., & Coats, K. I. (1986). A comparison of cognitive-behavioral therapy and relaxation training for the treatment of depression in adolescents. *Journal of Consulting and Clinical Psychology, 54,* 653-660.

Reynolds, W. M., & Graves, A. (1989). Reliability of children's reports of depressive symptomatology. *Journal of Abnormal Child Psychology, 17,* 647-655.

Reynolds, W. M., & Miller, K. L. (1985). Depression and learned helplessness in mentally retarded and nonretarded adolescents: An initial investigation. *Applied Research in Mental Retardation, 6,* 295-307.

Reynolds, W. M., & Miller, K. L. (1989). Assessment of adolescents' learned helplessness in achievement situations. *Journal of Personality Assessment, 53,* 211-228.

Reynolds, W. M., & Stark, K. D. (1983). Cognitive behavior modification: The clinical application of cognitive strategies. In M. Pressley & J. R. Levin (Eds.), *Cognitive strategy research: Psychological foundations* (pp. 221-266). New York: Springer-Verlag.

Reynolds, W. M., & Stark, K. D. (1987). School-based intervention strategies for the treatment of depression in children and adolescents. In S. G. Forman (Ed.), *School-based affective and social interventions* (pp. 69-88). New York: Haworth.

Rie, H. E. (1966). Depression in childhood: A survey of some pertinent contributions. *Journal of the American Academy of Child Psychiatry, 5,* 553-583.

Robins, L. N., Helzer, J. E., Weissman, M. M., Orvaschel, H., Gruenberg, E., Burke, J. D., & Regier, D. (1984). Lifetime prevalence of specific psychiatric disorders in three sites. *Archives of General Psychiatry, 41,* 949-958.

Seligman, M. E. P. (1975). *Helplessness: On depression, development, and death.* San Francisco: Freeman.

Seligman, M. E. P., & Peterson, C. (1986). A learned helplessness perspective on childhood depression: Theory and research. In M. Rutter, C. E. Izard, & P. B. Read (Eds.), *Depression in young people: Developmental and clinical perspectives* (pp. 223-249). New York: Guilford.

Shaw, J. A. (1988). Childhood depression. *Medical Clinics of North America, 72,* 831-845.

Silver, L. B. (1988). The scope of the problem in children and adolescents. In J. G. Looney (Ed.), *Chronic mental illness in children and adolescents* (pp. 39-51). Washington, DC: American Psychiatric Press.

Spitzer, R. L., Endicott, J., & Robins, E. (1978). Research diagnostic criteria: Rationale and reliability. *Archives of General Psychiatry, 35,* 773-782.

Stark, K. D., Reynolds, W. M., & Kaslow, N. J. (1987). A comparison of the relative efficacy of self-control therapy and behavioral problem-solving therapy for depression in children. *Journal of Abnormal Child Psychology, 15,* 91-113.

Strauss, C. C., Last, C. G., Hersen, M., & Kazdin, A. E. (1988). Association between anxiety and depression in children and adolescents with anxiety disorders. *Journal of Abnormal Child Psychology, 16,* 57-68.

Weinberg, W. A., Rutman, J., Sullivan, L., Penick, E. C., & Dietz, S. G. (1973). Depression in children referred to an educational diagnostic center: Diagnosis and treatment. *Journal of Pediatrics, 83,* 1065-1072.

Weller, R. A., & Weller, E. B. (1984). Use of tricyclic antidepressants in prepubertal depressed children. In E. B. Weller & R. A. Weller (Eds.), *Current perspectives on major depressive disorders in children* (pp. 50-63). Washington, DC: American Psychiatric Press.

Weller, R. A., & Weller, E. B. (1986). Tricyclic antidepressants in prepubertal depressed children: Review of the literature. *Hillside Journal of Clinical Psychiatry, 8,* 46-55.

Williams, J. M. G. (1984). *The psychological treatment of depression.* New York: Free Press.

Zeiss, A. M., Lewinsohn, P. M., & Munoz, R. F. (1979). Nonspecific improvement effects in depression using interpersonal skills training, pleasant activity schedules, or cognitive training. *Journal of Consulting and Clinical Psychology, 47,* 427-439.

31

Interventions for Attention Problems

George J. DuPaul
University of Massachusetts Medical Center

**Gary Stoner, W. David Tilly III,
and David Putnam, Jr.**
University of Oregon

Attention problems displayed by children are commonly reported by parents and teachers as interfering with peer relationships, parent–child interactions, and academic performance. The goal of this chapter is to provide an introductory guide to data-based interventions for children with attention problems and to discuss current issues regarding treatment implementation. We begin with a brief review of historical and current perspectives regarding the definition and etiology of attentional disorders and then move on to a delineation of several school-based treatment strategies for children who traditionally have been referred to as "hyperactive." In addition, case illustrations are presented to exemplify specific treatment strategies. This chapter is not intended to be an exhaustive review of all possible treatment approaches for ameliorating attentional difficulties (see Ross & Ross, 1982, for a comprehensive review) but rather to familiarize school psychologists with the most effective intervention procedures.

OVERVIEW OF ATTENTION-DEFICIT HYPERACTIVITY DISORDER

Historical Perspective: Diagnostic Criteria and Assessment

Children displaying concurrent problems of inattention, impulsivity, and hyperactivity (e.g., high rates of non-goal-directed activity) are frequently referred to pediatricians, mental health clinics, and school psychologists, and these children are often diagnosed as having Attention-Deficit Hyperactivity Disorder (ADHD) (Barkley, 1981, 1987a). The term *hyperactivity* has been used extensively in the past 50 years to describe a syndrome of behavior that is diagnosed primarily in children. Few diagnostic labels have generated more controversy or caused greater confusion in the areas of etiology and prognosis. One factor contributing to this lack of clarity is that the term is used in two primary ways with reference to children: (a) as a *descriptor* of child behavior, and (b) to signify a *syndrome* of behavioral characteristics (Gadow, 1986). The two uses of the term confuses communication both among and between parents and professionals. For example, a mother might describe her child's excessive motor behavior as "hyperactive," whereas physicians or educators might assert that a child's behavior is symptomatic of a syndrome of problem behavior and "meets diagnostic criteria for hyperactivity" based on information obtained from child behavior rating scales, direct observations, and other assessment procedures. Similar confusion currently exists regarding such terms as *attention; problems paying attention;* and *Attention-*

Deficit Hyperactivity Disorder (American Psychiatric Association, 1987).

The psychiatric classification of children presenting with attention and activity-level problems has undergone slow but steady change over the years (Aman, 1984). Germane to traditional conceptualizations of "hyperactivity" is the notion that an underlying dysfunction or abnormality exists within those persons diagnosed. Professionals historically have argued that "hyperactivity" is attributable to a wide range of physiological characteristics and have assigned different names to the syndrome accordingly. Suggested causes and/or labels have included deficits in moral control (Still, 1902), minimal brain damage (Smith, 1926), minimal brain dysfunction (Bax & McKeith, 1963), hyperkinetic reaction of childhood (American Psychiatric Association, 1968), and hyperkinetic syndrome (Rutter et al., 1969).

Within the last 20 years, however, diagnostic attention has shifted from targeting within-person variables to examining observable behaviors. In addition, recognition of the covariation of hyperactivity with attentional and impulsivity problems has evolved, primarily from the work of Virginia Douglas and her colleagues (see Douglas, 1984, for a review). This constellation of characteristics (i.e., inattention, impulsivity, and excessive motor activity) was subsequently defined, described, and adopted by the American Psychiatric Association (APA) in its most recent diagnostic manuals as Attention Deficit Disorder with Hyperactivity (APA, 1980) and Attention-Deficit Hyperactivity Disorder (APA, 1987). Thus, diagnoses no longer are aimed at identifying suspected physiological causes and correlates of behavior (e.g., minimal brain dysfunction) but instead are concerned with the frequency and intensity of specific observable behaviors as compared to a child's peers.

The current psychiatric diagnosis for children with significant attentional problems is Attention-Deficit Hyperactivity Disorder (APA, 1987)[1]. Current best practices in the assessment of ADHD requires a multimethod, multi-informant diagnostic assessment approach (see Barkley, 1988, and Rapport, 1987a). Such assessments are conducted across both home and school environments, with the parents, teachers, and child asked to provide information regarding behaviors of concern. The defining behaviors and characteristics of ADHD are presented in Table 1. While certainly typical of any child at one time or another, the behaviors noted become clinically significant when their frequency or intensity become widely discrepant from peer behavior or a significant adult's expectations.

Prevalence, Developmental Course, and Associated Deficits

Although exact prevalence figures are unavailable, recent estimates suggest that between 3% and 10% of school-age children (Wender, 1987) or roughly 1 to 3 children in *each* elementary school classroom could be diagnosed with ADHD. These figures provide a strong rationale for promoting informed, responsible assessment practices and intervention efforts for this problem in the schools.

ADHD is diagnosed approximately six times as often in boys as it is in girls (Ross & Ross, 1982), although epidemiological studies suggest a ratio of 3:1 among community samples (Trites, Dugas, Lynch, & Ferguson, 1979). The incidence of ADHD is relatively uniform across socioeconomic strata (Barkley, 1988), yet has been shown to differ across cultures (e.g., O'Leary, Vivian, & Nisi, 1985). Despite a wealth of epidemiological data, the causes of the disorder are yet to be fully understood (see Etiology, below). In addition to the core characteristics of ADHD, numerous studies have reported associated behavioral characteristics including poor tolerance of frustration (Rapport, Tucker, DuPaul, Merlo, & Stoner, 1986), problematic family interactions (Tallmadge & Barkley, 1983), noncompliance with commands of authority figures (Barkley, 1985; Whalen, Henker, & Dotemoto, 1980), and difficult peer relationships (Pelham & Bender, 1982).

Regardless of causes and correlates, behavioral scientists are becoming in-

TABLE 1
Diagnostic Criteria for Attention-Deficit Hyperactivity Disorder

Note: Consider a criterion met only if the behavior is considerably more frequent than that of most people of the same mental age.

A. A disturbance of at least 6 months during which at least eight of the following are present.

1. Often fidgets with hands or feet or squirms in seat (in adolescents, may be limited to subjective feelings of restlessness).
2. Has difficulty remaining seated when required to do so.
3. Is easily distracted by extraneous stimuli.
4. Has difficulty awaiting turn in games or group situations.
5. Often blurts out answers to questions before they have been completed.
6. Has difficulty following through on instructions from others (not due to oppositional behavior or failure of comprehension), e.g., fails to finish chores.
7. Has difficulty sustaining attention in tasks or play activities.
8. Often shifts from one uncompleted activity to another.
9. Has difficulty playing quietly.
10. Often talks excessively.
11. Often interrupts or intrudes on others, e.g., butts into other children's games.
12. Often does not seem to listen to what is being said to him or her.
13. Often loses things necessary for tasks or activities at school or at home (e.g., toys, pencils, books, assignments).
14. Often engages in physically dangerous activities without considering possible consequences (not for the purpose of thrill-seeking), e.g., runs into street without looking.

Note: The above items are listed in descending order of discriminating power based on data from a national field trial of the DSM-III-R criteria for Disruptive Behavior Disorders.

B. Onset before the age of seven.

C. Does not meet the criteria for a Pervasive Developmental Disorder.

Criteria for severity of Attention-Deficit Hyperactivity Disorder:

Mild: Few, if any symptoms in excess of those required to make the diagnosis and only minimal or no impairment in school and social functioning.

Moderate: Symptoms or functional impairment intermediate between "mild" and "severe."

Severe: Many symptoms in excess of those required to make the diagnosis and significant and pervasive impairment in functioning at home and school and with peers.

Note. From *American Psychiatric Association: Diagnostic and Statistical Manual of Mental Disorders, Third Edition, Revised* (pp. 52–53), by American Psychiatric Association, 1981, Washington, DC. Copyright 1987 by American Psychiatric Association. Reprinted by permission.

creasingly aware of both important long-term implications for persons diagnosed with ADHD, and several variables related to predicted outcomes for them. First, early investigators considered hyperactivity to be a disorder limited to childhood, with symptoms that diminished and disappeared over time. This conceptualization has been seriously challenged by a large body of recent research indicating that children do not grow out of ADHD as was once presumed (Weiss & Hechtman, 1986). Second, current evidence suggests that children with ADHD are at risk for developing antisocial and delinquent behavior in adolescence (Gittelman, Mannuzza, Shenker, & Bonagura, 1985; Satterfield, Hoppe, & Schell, 1982; Weiss & Hechtman, 1986), psychopathology as adults (Weiss & Hechtman, 1986), poor peer relationships and low self-esteem as adolescents and adults (Minde, Weiss, & Mendelson, 1972), and underachievement in school and work (Lambert & Sandoval, 1980; Weiss, Hechtman, Milroy, & Perlman, 1985). Finally, individual outcomes appear to be related to several factors, including intelligence, frequency of aggressiveness or noncompliance, peer acceptance and relationships, extent of parental psychopathology, and socioeconomic status (Hechtman, Weiss, Perlman, & Amsel, 1984; Loney, Whaley-Klahn, Kosier, & Conboy, 1981; Paternite & Loney, 1980).

Etiology

Many variables have been proposed as leading to ADHD; however, no single one has been identified that can account for all cases of the disorder. The variables that have been studied most often include neurological substrates, environmental toxins, genetic linkages, and environmental consequences (see Anastopoulos & Barkley, 1988, for a more detailed review). While each of these factors is discussed below, current empirical data suggest that ADHD is a syndrome of behaviors that may result from a complex interaction of several possible etiological events (Barkley, 1988).

Early formulations of ADHD identified neurological damage resulting from head trauma or illness as its primary cause (Strauss & Lehtinen, 1947). Consequently, all children presenting with ADHD symptomatology were presumed to have some level of structural insult (even in the absence of overt evidence), resulting in the use of the term *minimal brain dysfunction* as a diagnostic label. This assumption has been refuted, however, as *most* brain-injured children do not display ADHD symptoms (Rutter, Chadwick, & Shaffer, 1983) and the majority of children diagnosed with ADHD do not exhibit clear evidence of structural damage. More recently, investigations into the etiological role of neurotransmitter imbalances (Shaywitz, Shaywitz, Cohen, & Young, 1983) and lower than expected levels of cerebral blood flow to certain regions of the brain (Lou, Henriksen, & Bruhn, 1984) have produced produced promising results. These findings have led to speculation that children with ADHD have decreased activity or stimulation in the frontal white matter and frontal-midbrain tracts of the brain. However, more thor-

ough investigations are needed to confirm this hypothesis empirically.

Environmental toxins or allergens such as food additives, sugar, and lead also have been proposed as causal factors in ADHD (e.g., Feingold, 1975). Many well-controlled investigations have studied the role of each of these substances, but minimal evidence resulted to attest to their etiological significance. In general, the empirical data with regard to food additives (Conners, 1980), sugar (Milich, Wolraich, & Lingren, 1986), and lead (Gittelman & Eskanazi, 1983) clearly indicate that their causal influences on ADHD are quite weak.

One of the more promising areas of current inquiry on etiology is research into genetic or hereditary correlates of ADHD. One study has shown that the incidence of psychiatric disorders (e.g., depression) among biological relatives of children with ADHD is significantly greater than that found in the general population (Biederman et al., 1987). Furthermore, there is an increased incidence of ADHD among the biological parents and siblings of children with ADHD (Deutsch, 1987). It would appear that two factors may be operating interactively in this context: the natural variation of biological characteristics (Blaw, Rapin, & Kinsbourne, 1977) and some, as yet, unspecified mode of inheritance of psychopathological symptomatology (Anastopoulos & Barkley, 1988).

Although the etiological role of behavioral factors (e.g., situational antecedents and consequences) in ADHD has not been studied extensively, available data indicate that such variables play a negligible role in the onset of the disorder (Anastopoulos & Barkley, 1988). For example, negative mother–child interactions and a low frequency of parental reinforcement of child behaviors are frequently found in conjunction with ADHD. Rather than functioning as causative agents, however, these interactions can be characterized as maintaining variables. Additionally, these parental responses appear to be a reaction to the child's poor behavioral control and have been found to be ameliorated following successful treatment with stimulant medication (e.g., Barkley, Karlsson, Strze-lecki, & Murphy, 1984). Alternatively, situational antecedents and consequences play a vital role in modulating the *severity* of the child's behavioral control difficulties. The success of behavioral interventions, as discussed below, is based partially upon this premise.

In summary, the operation of biological factors (e.g., neurological and genetic), whether in isolation of in combination, appear to be the primary cause of ADHD in the majority of children diagnosed. Environmental toxins play a minimal role in this disorder. The situational antecedents and consequences of the behavioral correlates of ADHD, while not important etiologically, have a direct bearing on the severity of the child's adjustment difficulties. Thus, ADHD appears to result from the complex interactions of a number of differing etiological variables (Anastopoulos & Barkley, 1988).

AN OVERVIEW OF INTERVENTION METHODS

A variety of adjustment problems are frequently associated with ADHD including learning difficulties (Lambert & Sandoval, 1980), noncompliance with commands of authority figures (Barkley, 1988), physical aggressiveness and/or conduct disturbance (Prinz, Connor, & Wilson, 1981), and poor peer relationships (Pelham & Bender, 1982). Given these associated difficulties and the protracted nature of the disorder, a variety of long-term treatments provided by different professionals and implemented in the home and the school is often necessary to optimize the chances for a successful outcome. Furthermore, not only is there no known cure for the disorder, but no single intervention method (e.g., stimulant medication) is sufficient in providing short- or long-term relief to ADHD children (Barkley, 1989; Pelham & Murphy, 1986). Thus, a multimodal intervention program must be developed that will comprehensively address symptoms of ADHD and associated problems. The overriding goal of this program should be to aid the child and his or her caretakers

in coping with the ramifications of the disorder throughout the child's development.

While many professionals (e.g., physician, mental health professional) may be involved in the treatment of an individual child with ADHD, the school psychologist is in a unique position to fill a variety of therapeutic roles in an educational context. Certainly, the school psychologist's ability to directly assess and intervene in one of the more problematic environments (e.g., the classroom) for these children is highly advantageous. Furthermore, the school psychologist can serve as a consultant to related professionals in regard to the design, implementation, or ongoing monitoring of various interventions. In that capacity, school psychologists need not only a thorough understanding of interventions that are to be implemented under their direct supervision (e.g., behavior change programs), but also of therapeutic modalities (e.g., psychotropic medication) for which they are not directly responsible, but which can impact on the children's classroom status.

The primary interventions that have documented effectiveness in enhancing the classroom performance of children with ADHD include psychotropic medications (e.g., central nervous system stimulants), contingency management procedures, and their combination. A variety of contingency management procedures will be detailed next, with specific recommendations for promoting the generalization of achieved effects across time, caretakers, and settings. In addition to a review of the research literature pertinent to stimulant medication effects, suggestions will be made for aiding physicians in monitoring a child's response to medication. Adjunctive interventions (e.g., parent training in behavior management skills) that typically are necessary to promote further success within the classroom or other environments will be discussed briefly, as well. Since many fad therapies (e.g., an additive-free diet) have been proposed for ADHD over the years, their limitations will be identified so that valuable professional time is not allocated to interventions with minimal proven efficacy. This chapter is not intended to be an exhaustive review of the treatment literature; hence references to more thorough discussions of intervention strategies will be provided throughout.

SPECIFIC INTERVENTION METHODS

Behaviorally-Based Interventions

Intervention procedures based on operant learning principles have a long history of documented use in ameliorating the behavioral problems of children (Kazdin, 1984). These behavior change strategies have been successful in reducing the disruptive, off-task behavior of ADHD children and in increasing their academic productivity (e.g., Rapport, Murphy, & Bailey, 1982). Given the difficulties hypothesized to underlie ADHD symptomatology (e.g., motivation deficits, lack of internalized rules), this finding is not surprising. It is hypothesized that behavioral interventions increase the overall level of appropriate classroom behavior by "capturing" children's attention through enhancement of the stimulation or motivational value of the task at hand. The most widely studied specific intervention techniques will be discussed below under the broad rubrics of school-based contingency management procedures (e.g., token economy) and systems that involve home-based delivery of contingencies. Case examples will be used to illustrate the application of specific procedures with the ADHD child.

Several general guidelines should be kept in mind prior to designing a specific intervention program for ADHD:

1. A functional analysis of the specific presenting problems should be conducted to guide the design and selection of intervention components.

2. Children with ADHD require more frequent and specific feedback than their classmates to optimize their performance. Thus, the initial stages of any ADHD intervention should incorporate relatively continuous contingencies. Leaner schedules of reinforcement should be introduced cautiously and gradually, as some laboratory-based evidence indicates that ADHD children have more difficulty maintaining their behavior under intermittent reinforcement schedules than do their peers (Douglas, 1984).

3. While contingent positive reinforcement should be the primary component of a behaviorally-based intervention program for ADHD, an exclusive reliance on reinforcement may distract the child from the task at hand and thus necessitate the use of prudent negative consequences (e.g., brief reprimands) to maintain appropriate on-task behavior (Rosen, O'Leary, Joyce, Conway, & Pfiffner, 1984). Verbal reprimands should be delivered in a specific, consistent fashion immediately following the occurrence of disruptive behavior. Furthermore, these are most effective when given so as to be audible only to the child committing the transgression.

4. If student behavior during independent work periods is targeted for change, initial task instructions should not involve more than a few steps and the child should be requested to repeat the directives to ensure that they are understood. Academic assignments should be delivered one at a time, lengthier tasks being broken into smaller units to minimize overburdening the child's attentional abilities. The length of these subtasks should be gradually increased as the child demonstrates successful independent completion. Repetitive material (e.g., reassigning erroneously completed worksheets) should be avoided. Alternatively, an assignment that taps the same skill or concept area can be substituted to avoid boredom and exacerbating attentional problems.

5. Concrete results of appropriate behaviors (e.g., tasks completion and accuracy) should be used as goals of intervention rather than specific task-related behaviors (e.g., attention to task or staying in one's seat). This focus allows easier monitoring by teachers, increases the frequency of the components of behavior chains (e.g., working with the appropriate materials for an assignment, soliciting formative feedback on initial task performance) that lead to the

selected goals, entails responding that is incompatible with inattentive, disruptive behavior, and facilitates evaluation of treatment outcomes.

6. In general, preferred activities (e.g., recess time, access to classroom computer) should be used as reinforcers rather than concrete rewards (e.g., candy). This may include consequating completion of an assignment in a less-preferred subject area with an assignment in a more-preferred academic area (e.g., completion of math worksheet leads to access to reading activities). Furthermore, the specific rewards employed should be varied or rotated quite frequently to prevent boredom with the program (i.e., reinforcer satiation). Finally, rather than assuming that specific activities will be reinforcing for the child, develop reward "menus" by directly asking the child what she or he wants to earn or by observing her or his preferred activities.

7. Employ a "priming" procedure with the child prior to academic assignment periods (Rapport, 1987b), to enhance the positive incentive value of classroom privileges. Priming is a procedure for review by teachers and students of a list of possible classroom privileges *prior* to beginning an academic work period in which the students choose which activity they would like to participate in following the work period.

Contingency Management Procedures

A variety of behaviorally-based interventions are available that incorporate frequent, immediate feedback to children following the performance of specifically defined academic or social responses. Although most of these procedures include contingent social praise from the teacher (e.g., O'Leary, Pelham, Rosenbaum, & Price, 1976), children with ADHD often do not exhibit consistent behavioral change in the absence of additional contingencies. Thus, a formal classroom behavior change program would include one or more of the following components: token reinforcement, contingency contracting, response cost, and time-out from positive reinforcement. Each of these

techniques will be described in detail below, with additional discussion focusing on factors to consider when training teachers in their use.

Token reinforcement programs. While contingent social praise and positive attention can be effective in producing behavioral change in many children, it is typically insufficient to bring about consistent improvement in the ADHD child's classroom performance. Behavioral strategies that incorporate secondary generalized reinforcers (i.e., token economies) provide immediate, specific, and potent rewards that are often required for children with ADHD. Behavior management systems with these components are usually highly successful in enhancing the academic productivity and appropriate behavior of inattentive children (e.g., Ayllon, Layman, & Kandel, 1975; Robinson, Newby, & Ganzell, 1981).

Designing a school-based token reinforcement system involves several steps:

1. One or more classroom situations are identified as problematic for the child and are targeted for intervention. These situations can be determined by a teacher interview and/or use of an objective rating scale such as the School Situations Questionnaire (Barkley, 1981); the determination should be validated further through direct observation in the classroom. Typically, children with ADHD exhibit their greatest behavioral control difficulties during assigned independent work periods.

2. Target behaviors are selected, and typically include behavioral products (e.g., number of math problems completed in a given amount of time) or specific actions (e.g., appropriate interactions with peers during recess). In general, products are preferred because as noted, they incorporate ease of monitoring and usually involve responding that is incompatible with inattentive, disruptive behavior (see Robinson, Newby, & Ganzell, 1981).

3. Types of secondary reinforcers (i.e., tokens) must be selected, and may include multicolored poker chips, check marks on a card, or points on a card stand. Younger children (e.g., up to 9 years old) generally

prefer tangible rewards (e.g., poker chips); older youngsters respond more positively to points or check marks. Typically, token economy systems are not recommended for children under 5 years of age and primary reinforcers (e.g., food) may need to be supplied contingent upon the occurrence of appropriate behavior.

4. The teacher and student should jointly develop a list of privileges or rewarding activities within the school for which tokens can be exchanged. In some cases, the parents may be asked to collaborate on this list and make available additional home privileges in exchange for tokens. The amount of tokens or points necessary to "purchase" each privilege can be determined collaboratively between those individuals involved in the program. As a rough guide, one might estimate the total number of tokens that can be earned on a daily basis and divide this sum among available reinforcers.

5. The targeted goal behaviors are broken down into their component parts (e.g., "successful completion of work" can be defined as completing a certain number of items within a specified time period, attaining a certain level of accuracy, and reviewing the work before requesting the teacher's feedback). Thus, a task analysis is necessary to explicitly delineate expected behaviors. The number of tokens earned by completing each target behavior or its subcomponents is determined by task difficulty. Difficult or time-consuming tasks for the child should lead to more tokens than less involved assignments.

6. Tokens are exchanged for classroom privileges on at least a daily basis. As a rule, the longer the delay between receiving tokens and exchanging them for back-up reinforcers, the less effective the program will be. Although tokens can serve as immediate reinforcers of an interim nature, they quickly lose their reward value for ADHD children if they cannot be "cashed in" until a long period of time has elapsed.

7. The efficacy of the intervention program should be evaluated on a regular basis (see case study) through the use of multiple assessment procedures. On the basis of the results of this ongoing evaluation, new behavioral targets may be added, old ones deleted or modified, and privileges rotated or varied. Response cost procedures (as discussed below) may also be incorporated into the system once a degree of success has been achieved in changing behavior.

8. The consideration of several additional procedures is necessary to ensure the generalization of obtained effects across settings and time. First, any additional problematic situations must be identified and targeted for change by implementing the above strategies. It is erroneous to assume that one need only obtain performance in one situation for such behavior to spontaneously generalize to other settings. Secondly, the use of tokens and back-up reinforcers must be faded in a gradual fashion. For example, rather than continuing to provide tokens following successful completion of each step in an academic task, reinforcement would be provided contingent upon completion of several steps first, and then following completion of the entire assignment. Eventually, the system would evolve into a contingency contract as discussed below. Numerous other strategies are available in the professional literature for enhancing both generalization and maintenance of treatment gains (c.f., Horner, Dunlap, & Koegel, 1988).

Contingency contracting. This behavior management technique involves the negotiation of a contractual agreement between the teacher and student that stipulates the desired classroom behaviors and consequences available contingent upon their performance. As with a token economy program, specific academic and behavioral goals are identified that the child must meet in order to gain access to preferred activities or other rewards. Contracting typically involves a direct connection between target behaviors and primary contingencies, rather than the use of secondary reinforcers (e.g., token delivery). Thus, there may be a longer delay between completion of an objective and receipt of reinforcement than with a token economy program. A sample contract appears in Table 2

TABLE 2
Sample Behavior Contract

I, John T. Jones, agree to do the following:

1. Complete all of my written math and language arts assignments with at least 75% accuracy, before lunchtime.

2. Pay attention to my teacher when (s)he is speaking to the entire class or my reading group.

3. Remain quiet when lining up for recess, lunch, and art class.

4. Follow all playground rules (no fighting or loud yelling) during recess.

If I do these things, then I will get to choose **one** of the following:

1. Time at the end of the school day to play a game with a classmate of my choosing.

2. Play or work quietly on the classroom computer for twenty minutes.

3. Complete some errands for my teacher.

If I have a successful week, I will be able to purchase a paperback book of my choosing.

If I do **not** do these things as I promised, then I will lose:

1. Daily recess time.

2. The opportunity to participate in daily free-time activities.

I agree to fulfill this contract to the best of my abilities.

      Signed:

_____   _____
(Student's signature)   (Teacher's siignature)

      Date: _____

Although such contracting is relatively straightforward, there are a number of factors that directly affect its efficacy with ADHD children. First, the age of the child is an important consideration; contracting procedures are typically unsuccessful with children under the age of 6. This may be due to several factors, including a lack of sufficient verbal skills and an inability to defer reinforcement for longer time periods. A second consideration is the length of the time between performance of the requisite behavior and provision of reinforcement. For example, a procedure requiring 8-year-old children with ADHD to correctly complete 80% of their math problems each day for a 1-week period before earning a reward is doomed to failure. Since immediacy of reinforcement is crucial with ADHD children, it would be more effective to provide access to preferred activities at the conclusion of the successful work period or school day.

Definition of target behaviors and the manner of their incorporation into an intervention program are important determinants of a behavioral contract's success. For example, during the initial stage of a contract a large number of goals, extremely high standards of quality, or completion of complex (e.g., multistep) tasks might be expected. Such features could present the ADHD child with insurmountable tasks and quite likely lead to failure. A preferable approach would be to delineate a few, simple behaviors or products so that the child can achieve success right from the start. More difficult or complex goals can be gradually incorporated such that terminal objectives are reached with minimal chances of failure along the way.

A final consideration that is important in designing a behavioral contract is the identification of appropriate reinforcers. Unfortunately, identified "rewards" all too often take the form of activities or items which are assumed by school personnel to be motivating for all children, without regard for personal preferences. Two alternatives to this practice are suggested. First, it is advisable, especially with older children, to negotiate directly with the student regarding possible privileges. This not only assures identification of potent reinforcers, but also enlists the student's cooperation in the contractual process. A second procedure is to observe the child's preferred off-task behaviors (e.g., drawing, playing with objects at seat) and employ these as reinforcers. This tactic is especially helpful when a child is unable or unwilling to provide suggestions for possible rewards.

Response cost. An exclusive reliance upon positive reinforcement procedures is rarely effective in maintaining appropriate levels of academic and social behavior among children with ADHD. In fact, several recent studies have identified the need for concurrent application of mild punishment contingencies following inappropriate (i.e., off-task) behavior to bring about consistent behavioral change (Pfiffner & O'Leary, 1987; Pfiffner, O'Leary, Rosen, & Sanderson, 1985; Rosen et al., 1984). For example, in addition to prudent reprimands (as discussed previously), the loss or removal of privileges, points, or tokens (i.e., response cost) contingent upon inattentive, disruptive behavior has proven quite useful in combination with positive procedures.

The concurrent use of rewards of tokens or points and of response cost has been found to increase the levels of on-task behavior, seatwork productivity, and academic accuracy of children with ADHD, in many cases to a degree equivalent to that obtained with stimulant medication (Rapport, Murphy, & Bailey, 1980, 1982). For example, Rapport (1987b) describes a token delivery system that incorporates response cost. The student and teacher are each supplied with a card stand or an electronic apparatus[2] that serves to display point totals earned by the child. Points are earned for on-task behavior on a fixed-interval schedule and are deducted following incidents of off-task behavior. The teacher awards or deducts points by flipping the cards on his or her cardstand (or by pressing a button on a remote control device). The children change their cards to match the teacher's or automatically receive or lose points on the electronic apparatus. Thus, "token" delivery and deduction are accomplished on a remote basis, allowing the teacher to simultaneously engage in activities with other students. As with other token systems, at the conclusion of an academic work period a child's accumulated points are totaled and "cashed in" for various back-up reinforcers (e.g., free-time activity).

It is important to consider several factors prior to using response cost procedures. First, since response cost is a form of punishment, the whole token system could potentially be viewed by the child as a negative experience. Thus, it becomes important to preface its implementation by emphasizing the program's positive aspects to the student and teacher (e.g., the student will have a chance to earn points and rewards for completing work accurately). Second, many children with ADHD will initially "test the system" by deliberately engaging in off-task behavior to see if they will lose points. It is important that teachers not get caught up in a "point reduction game" of this sort. Accordingly, point reductions should not occur more than once per minute regardless of the frequency of off-task behavior, and the teacher should be instructed to look away from the child immediately following point reductions (Rapport, 1987b). Finally, a child's point total should never fall below zero; when a point total is zero, all disruptive, off-task behavior should be ignored. If zero point totals are a common occurrence, the criteria for point reductions may need to be revised so that point reductions do not occur for minor infractions. Once the child begins to experience success and is "hooked" into the system, the criteria for point reductions can become more stringent.

Time-out from positive reinforcement. Another category of mild punishment methods for classroom use consists of various forms of time-out from positive reinforcement. An adaptation of Barkley's (1987b) procedures for use within the home may be most applicable. To be effective, time-out procedures should be (a) implemented only when there is a reinforcing environment to be removed from; (b) implemented swiftly following a rule infraction; (c) applied with consistency; and (d) for the smallest amount of time (e.g., 1–5 minutes) that proves effective (i.e., removal from a reinforcing environment is the most salient variable here, *not* amount of time spent in time-out). The time-out area should be located in a relatively dull corner of the classroom rather than a separate room, closet, cloakroom, or hallway (to allow monitoring of the child's activities). Criteria for terminating the time-out period should include (a) a time-out period sufficiently long enough to be effective; (b) a short period of calm, nondisruptive behavior prior to its termination; and (c) the child's expressed willingness to correct, amend, or compensate for the misbehavior that led to the time-out contingency (or a rule that stipulates this condition as part of the management procedure). Finally, children who leave the time-out area without permission should have their time lengthened by a fixed amount for each violation, or lose points or tokens if a token economy system is being used. A further option is to remove the child from the classroom, perhaps involving an in-school or at-home suspension from the classroom.

As with response cost, it is imperative that restrictive procedures such as time-out be employed only in the context of ongoing positive reinforcement procedures (e.g., token economy). Furthermore, time-out contingencies should be the intervention of last resort following implementation of a hierarchy of both positive and less punitive procedures. For example, inappropriate behavior would initially lead to brief, prudent reprimands, followed by response cost, followed by time-out with head down at desk, followed by time-out in a corner of the room, and finally, by removal from the classroom as necessary if the transgression were to continue. More severe disruptive behaviors (e.g., physical aggression) should lead to immediate application of the more restrictive, time-out procedures and/or time-limited suspension. It is also important to point out that the use of time-out needs to be monitored very carefully, and it should not be considered a management strategy to be used in an ongoing fashion but rather as a short-term behavior reduction technique.

Case study. Jason was a 7-year-old boy referred to his school psychologist for severe attention problems, impulsivity (i.e., careless completion of work), and excessive motor restlessness. A psychological evaluation indicated the presence of an Attention-Deficit Hyperactivity Disorder (see Barkley, 1988, or Rapport, 1987a, for assessment guidelines). Consideration was being given to special education placement and/or a referral to his pediatrician for a trial of psychostimulant medication. Before implementing these interventions, his psychologist and classroom teacher designed a behavior management system incorporating a token system as described above. Baseline data were collected on a number of variables in independent work situations (which were targeted for intervention) as well as large- and small-group instruction periods (e.g., reading group). These included direct observations of his on-task behavior, teacher ratings of attention and behavior, and behavioral products (i.e., work completion and accuracy). Percentages of the latter variables are presented in Figure 1 across treatment phases. Work completion percentages were calculated

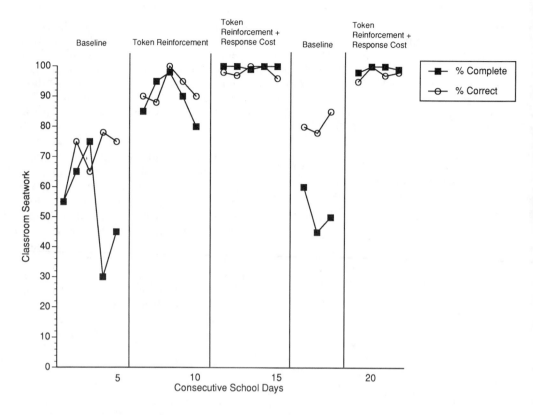

FIGURE 1. Classroom performance data during behavior change program.

relative to the average number of items completed by Jason's class. Interobserver reliability checks on all observational and behavioral product data were conducted during 20% of the treatment sessions by the psychologist and were consistently above 85%. Prior to treatment, Jason's academic performance was highly variable, and he completed an average of 54% of his work at less than a 70% accuracy level (see Figure 1). Furthermore, teacher ratings of his attention and self-control were in the abnormal range and he was observed to be on-task approximately 65% of the time.

The introduction of a token economy program resulted in abrupt, consistent gains in Jason's academic behavior. He was observed to be on-task over 80% of the time while completing nearly 90% of his work at a 93% accuracy level. Teacher ratings of his behavior during independent task periods were improved and were

approximately one standard deviation above the mean for his age. Since further behavioral improvements were possible, his teacher and psychologist decided to implement response cost contingencies (i.e., loss of tokens) following the occurrence of off-task behavior. The combination of token reinforcement and response cost procedures resulted in further improvements in Jason's academic performance (see Sessions 11–15 in Figure 1). His on-task behavior increased to an average of 90% while he completed close to 100% of his work at a 98% accuracy level. Not surprisingly, teacher ratings of his behavior and attention were within the expected range for independent task situations.

A brief return-to-baseline condition was conducted (see Sessions 16–18 in Figure 1) to determine whether changes in Jason's behavior were directly related to the intervention. All contingencies were withdrawn and the teacher returned to her preintervention strategies for dealing with Jason's behavior. As expected, his behavior returned quickly to baseline levels as he was observed to be on-task less than 60% of the time while completing 52% of his work at an 81% accuracy level. Teacher ratings were consistently within the abnormal range. Both token reinforcement and response cost contingencies were reinstated beginning with Session 19, which resulted in high percentages of on-task behavior, work completion, and task accuracy. Teacher ratings of Jason's behavior returned to their prior, positive levels.

The results of this case study demonstrate several important points beyond the specific effectiveness of the contingency management procedures used. First, the causal properties of any classroom procedure should be established within the context of an acceptable research design (e.g., an A-B-A-B single-subject design as above). Second, multiple measures (e.g., teacher ratings, direct observations, behavioral products) should be collected across situations and treatment conditions to allow a comprehensive assessment of outcomes. Third, programming for generalization and maintenance is typically necessary to promote cross-situational and cross-time treatment effects. For instance, while Jason's behavior significantly improved during independent task situations, he continued to be disruptive and inattentive during other classroom activities (based on teacher ratings and direct observations). Thus, it was necessary to implement contingency management procedures during these time periods as well. Furthermore, as the school year progressed, formal behavior modification techniques (i.e., token reinforcement and response cost) were gradually faded to less time-consuming strategies such as behavioral contracting and a home reinforcement program. Finally, a number of interventions (i.e., parent training in behavior modification techniques, psychostimulant medication) were necessary to promote the maintenance and generalization of obtained gains in Jason's behavioral and academic performance.

Home-based contingencies. Home-based reinforcement programs involve the management of contingencies at home that are based upon the child's performance at school, and can be used as an effective supplement to classroom behavior change systems (see Atkinson & Forehand, 1979, for a review). One example of a home reinforcement program has been proposed (Barkley, 1983) and employs a daily report card similar to that displayed in Figure 2. Several behavioral goals are identified, such as participation in class activities, completion of assigned work, following rules, and interaction with classmates. The specific goals may vary with the presenting problems of the individual student (e.g., accuracy on classwork can be targeted if the child is prone to completing work in a careless fashion). The columns of the card correspond to different subject areas or periods of the school day. Thus, if the child has more than one teacher, they may all participate. The teacher enters ratings (in ink to prevent their alteration) of the child's performance in the appropriate area of the card, initials the bottom of the card, and provides comments where necessary. The student is responsible for giving the card to each teacher and returning it home on a daily basis.

The teacher's ratings will vary from 1 to 5, the former representing excellent performance and the latter poor performance. When the card is brought home, the parent(s) briefly discusses the positive and negative ratings with the child. Then, specified point values are assigned to the numbers on the card (e.g., each 1 earns +25 points, a 2 earns +15 points, and so on down to a loss of 25 points for each 5) and they are summed to yield the net total points earned for the day. To produce behavior change, a home token reinforcement program must be arranged such that these points can lead to the "purchase" of back-up reinforcers (e.g., household privileges, television time, spending a night at a friend's home). As with other token programs, this system's effectiveness is

DAILY REPORT CARD

Name _____   Date _____

Please rate this child in each of the behavioral areas listed below as to how (s)he performed in school today using ratings of "1" to "5". "1" = excellent, "2" = good, "3" = fair, "4" = poor, "5" = very poor or did not work.

CLASS PERIODS/SUBJECTS

BEHAVIOR	1	2	3	4	5	6	7	8

FIGURE 2. An example of a daily report card designed to facilitate communication between teachers and parents about a child's classroom behavior.

dependent upon its motivational value and the availability of a variety of back-up reinforcers.

Home-based contingency programs (keyed to school behavior) have several benefits. First, children receive direct feedback from their teachers as to performance in several areas of classroom functioning on a daily basis. Second, parents receive information about their children's classroom performance on a regular basis, thereby providing a forum for teacher–parent communication rather than waiting for a parent–teacher conference or end-of-the-term report card. Finally, the system circumvents some of the practical limitations (e.g., restricted range of possible reinforcing activities) to classroom-based contingency management systems since the parents provide reinforcement for performance at school.

However, several factors may limit the effectiveness of home-based reinforcement programs (Rapport, 1987a). One of the greatest drawbacks of such a system is that, by definition, it involves a delay in the provision of reinforcement. Since children with ADHD have difficulty in responding appropriately to delayed reinforcement (Rapport, Tucker, DuPaul, Merlo, & Stoner, 1986), home-based contingencies may be less successful than classroom-based systems during initial stages of intervention (i.e., in promoting acquisition of behavior). This is particularly the case when working with children younger than 6 years. Secondly, school personnel have limited means to assess parental compliance with the procedures. Finally, parents must be discouraged from relying solely on material rewards, which can lose some of their potency as back-up reinforcers through overuse. Overall, however, home-based contingency systems can be effective in improving school performance, especially as a supplement to classroom behavior change procedures (e.g., to cover periods of the school day when the latter procedures are not in effect).

Training Teachers in Behavior Management Procedures

Although several excellent texts are available (Becker, 1986; Sulzer-Azaroff & Mayer, 1986; Wolery, Bailey, & Sugai, 1988) on training teachers in the use of behavior change principles, several important considerations will be reviewed in the context of working with ADHD children. It is helpful to provide teachers with a detailed explanation of what ADHD is, its presumed causes, developmental course, and implications for education and management. This will serve to establish ADHD as a behavioral handicap that can be partially ameliorated through the use of structured, behavior management programs. Provision of such information is a crucial step, particularly when the educator objects to the use of tangible rewards for promoting academic performance in fear of reducing the child's intrinsic motivation. Since many children with ADHD do not appear to be sufficiently motivated by the natural contingencies associated with completion of work, the use of external consequences becomes necessary. Another common reaction of teachers to token economy systems, in particular, is that the child's classmates will become envious or come to view the child in a negative light. When envy reactions do occur, they typically are temporary and do not lead to the deterioration of other students' performances. Furthermore, since these management systems primarily employ positive reinforcement procedures, they may be more likely to engender positive rather than negative perceptions of the identified student. Finally, group-dependent contingencies can be considered, whereby earned rewards are shared equally with classmates.

Psychostimulant Medication

The most frequent intervention for ADHD is the prescription by physicians of stimulant medication, typically methylphenidate (MPH) (Safer & Krager, 1983). While recent estimates in the popular press have indicated that as many as 4 million children in the United States receive stimulant medication for the treatment of ADHD, a more conservative and data-based report (Gadow, 1986) indicates that between 300,000 and 600,000 school-age children are currently prescribed stimulants. By any account, the use of stimulant medication in the treatment of problems of inattention and impulsivity is widespread, and it affects the lives of a significant number of school-age children.

Stimulant medication treatment needs to be undertaken with caution, although beneficial short-term effects (i.e., decreases in impulsivity and non-goal-directed activity levels, with improved ability to sustain attention) have been demonstrated for approximately 70–80% of ADHD children, the remainder experience either adverse effects or no effects (Barkley, 1977). Care in the use of such drugs is warranted owing to the potential occurrence of adverse side effects such as appetite suppression, nausea, headaches, and insomnia. While salutary effects of stimulants have been documented for children's academic performance (Rapport, Stoner, DuPaul, Birmingham, & Tucker, 1985; Rapport, Stoner, DuPaul, Kelly, Tucker, & Schoeler, 1988), social interactions (Whalen, Henker, Collins, Finck, & Dotemoto, 1979; Whalen, Henker, & Dotemoto, 1980), and performance on a variety of clinic-based cognitive tasks (Brown & Sleator, 1979; Rapport, DuPaul, Stoner, Birmingham, & Masse, 1985; Sprague & Sleator, 1977; Swanson & Kinsbourne, 1975), many of these same studies have shown that response to MPH varies from child to child (even those of the same body weight; Rapport, DuPaul,

& Kelly, 1989), and from target behavior to target behavior for any given child.

Undoubtedly, most readers are aware that stimulant treatment for children with ADHD has been controversial for more than a decade (Bacon, 1988; Toufexis, 1989), and recent court cases have charged prescribing physicians and school personnel with malpractice. It is curious that more often than not these controversies appear to be based on emotional rather than data-based concerns. However, given both legal concerns and the individualized manner in which children respond to MPH, it is recommended that all stimulant medication trials include a systematic evaluation of effects on a child's behavior across targeted areas of concern. A relevant question is, then, which data are appropriate for evaluating stimulant medication effects in children with ADHD?

The answer to this critical question no doubt depends on who is being asked. From an educational perspective, it is deemed essential to conduct a comprehensive evaluation including monitoring of the child's progress in academic skill areas, work completion, classroom behavior, and social relations, as well as assessing possible adverse side-effects. However, this same perspective may not be shared by other professionals. For example, pediatricians may focus on parents' and teachers' reports and physiological measures of a child's response to medication. It is equally likely that physicians value comprehensive classroom indicators of children's response to medication, but simply have limited access to classroom performance and behavior data. In contrast, education or mental health practitioners have limited access to and knowledge about medical information and issues. Coordinated consideration of all of these measures of response to medication could optimize results; thus, it appears that collaboration in data collection and decision making between educational and medical professionals are critical.

The following discussion is intended to describe (a) the current practices of medical professionals in evaluating stimulant medication effects; (b) what presently is considered best practice in the assessment of treatment with stimulant medication; and (c) future research trends in this area.

Current practices in medical settings. The effects of stimulant medication on attentional and related behavior problems often are evaluated with little direct information regarding a child's behavior. Typically, determinations by physicians regarding the efficacy of treatment are based on contacts with parents and teachers that are infrequent at best (Barkley, 1981; Gadow, 1981). For example, Gadow (1981) surveyed parents and teachers to gather information regarding the administration and monitoring of drugs prescribed for behavior disorders with a group of special education students. On the basis of typical practice, the researchers set a criterion of three office visits per year by the medicated child as a minimum level of monitoring. The results indicated that this criterion was met in only 58% of the cases. Even more disheartening was the finding that in only 9 of the 118 cases examined were teachers contacted directly, and in only three of these cases were behavior rating scales used.

Behavior rating scales have been endorsed in the medical literature as a means of monitoring the effects of stimulant medication on student behavior. For example, the use of the ADD-H Comprehensive Teacher Rating Scale (ACTeRS) (Ullman, Sleator, & Sprague, 1985) has been developed as a means for pediatricians to access teachers' perceptions of students' performance in the classroom. While such attempts to gather information from teachers or others having direct contact with the children are laudable, the use of a single rating scale for monitoring treatment effects has its shortcomings.

Since rating scales quantify an individual's perceptions of the behavior of a child instead of directly measuring the behavior itself, these may not always provide reliable, accurate results. Second, the ACTeRS, like most other rating scales, includes items describing overt classroom behavior while excluding direct reports or estimates of academic performance. Moreover, the items included in most rating scales tend to focus on maladaptive behaviors rather than prosocial behaviors (the ACTeRS is a notable exception to this criticism). Thus, while well-constructed rating scales can provide valuable information regarding teachers' perceptions of a child's response to medication, it is important to note that the information represents primarily the social validity of perceived treatment effects. Therefore, it is unlikely that a single rating scale used in isolation will provide sufficiently detailed information with which to make reliable and valid treatment evaluation decisions.

Assessing stimulant effects in school settings. The following measures and behaviors have been reported in the literature to be useful in monitoring the effects of stimulant medication with ADHD children.

Academic performance. Gadow (1986) reviewed the literature regarding the effects of stimulant medication on the academic performance of students with behavior and related academic problems. He cites a series of research studies, dating back some 50 years, that demonstrate positive effects of stimulant medication on academic performance in many cases. Interestingly, this body of literature is consistent with current findings that indicate that stimulant effects vary from child to child, with documentation of impaired performance in some cases. Recent reviews, however, have raised questions regarding the direct enhancement of academic performance by stimulant medication treatment (Barkley, 1981; Gadow, 1986).

Further research in the area of stimulant medication and academic performance conducted in the 1980s changed the tide of opinion once again. Researchers found that students demonstrated enhanced academic output and, in some cases, an increase in accuracy that was mediated by increased attention to tasks (Pelham, Bender, Caddell, Booth, & Moorer, 1985; Rapport, DuPaul, Stoner, &

Jones, 1986). For example, Rapport, DuPaul, Stoner, and Jones (1986) measured both the amount and accuracy of regularly assigned seatwork that students completed. Assignments had to be quantifiable in terms of number as well as percentage correct in order to be used as measures of performance. While individual responses to MPH clearly were idiosyncratic, average group performance increased along both dimensions as the dosage of medication increased from placebo to 20 mg of MPH. Thus, monitoring academic performance, both in terms of quantity and quality of work completed, can provide valuable information regarding medication effects on a student's classroom functioning. Unfortunately, the collection of such data may be hampered by programmatic factors (e.g., limited time or availability of staff to collect data). The use of curriculum-based measurement (as discussed below) or teacher ratings of academic performance may circumvent these difficulties.

Classroom behavior. Children with ADHD may exhibit a variety of maladaptive behaviors in the classroom that interfere with the classroom performance of themselves and their peers. These may include excesses in motor activity (e.g., leaving their seat), conduct problems (e.g., defiance of commands, aggressiveness towards peers), and noncompletion of work. The research literature has demonstrated consistently that stimulant medication can be helpful in altering these behaviors in a desirable direction, particularly in structured situations. Once again, behavior rating scales have typically been used to document changes in these domains. One of the most frequently used rating scales is the Conners Teacher Rating Scale (CTRS) (Conners, 1969) and an abbreviated version consisting of ten items (ACTRS) (Goyette, Conners, & Ulrich, 1978). The ACTRS has been shown to be sensitive to treatment effects at both individual and group levels (Rapport et al., 1988). Another rating scale that may prove useful in evaluating changes in attention-related classroom behavior is the Edelbrock Child Attention/Activity

Profile (CAP) (Barkley, 1987a). The CAP is composed of 15 items taken directly from the Child Behavior Checklist–Teacher Rating Form (Achenbach & Edelbrock, 1983) that pertain to attention and overactivity, and for which separate normative data have been developed (Barkley, 1987a).

Direct observation systems for analyzing student classroom behavior also have been employed to assess response to medication (Rapport, Stoner, DuPaul, Kelly, Tucker, & Schoeler, 1988). When used in conjunction with direct measures of academic performance, such observations can help to document a range of behavioral effects of medication.

Social interactions. Positive effects of stimulant medication on child social interactions with significant adults have been well documented (Whalen, Henker, & Dotemoto, 1980). Parents and teachers tend to deal with children with ADHD more negatively because of the difficulty in managing these children's behaviors. When stimulant medication contributes to reduction in undesirable behavior, the demands placed on a parent or teacher to respond to negative behavior are reduced. This response may lead to improved interactions between the child and the adult (Barkley, Karlsson, Pollard, & Murphy, 1985; Barkley, Karlsson, Strzelecki, & Murphy, 1984).

A small but growing literature suggests that stimulants may affect the social interactions of ADHD children with their peers. For example, Pelham and Bender (1982) obtained mixed results regarding the effects of stimulant medication on social interactions. Their findings suggested that stimulant medication may have little effect on a child's peer relations per se, except for reducing high levels of aggression. However, recent studies indicate that MPH may lead to more positive peer interactions for ADHD children beyond reductions in aggressive behavior (Pelham & Hoza, 1987; Pelham, Sturges et al., 1987). Specifically, MPH has been associated with significant reductions in problematic social responses while not diminishing approach behaviors (Wal-

lander, Schroeder, Michelli, & Gualtieri, 1987).

A variety of direct observation coding systems can be used to assess children's peer relations both in the classroom and on the playground. For example, Pelham et al. (1987) utilized a modified version of the RECESS code (Walker, Garrett, Crossen, Hops, & Greenwood, 1978). This direct observation code facilitates the gathering of information regarding positive and negative peer interactions by a time sampling method of observation.

Adverse side-effects. As with most medications, treatment with stimulants can result in adverse physical side-effects. These include nausea, loss of appetite, headaches, irritability, overfocused behavior, restlessness, sleeplessness, and in some cases motor or vocal tics. Although these are found most often at relatively high doses of medication, they also may occur at low doses. Thus, it is important to monitor the incidence of side-effects carefully and to obtain information from various informants, as adverse responses may not be apparent across settings and time. One approach is to have a child's parent and teacher independently complete rating scales documenting frequency and severity of side-effects (see Barkley, 1981, for one such scale). Collecting baseline side-effects data is also necessary, as identified children may in fact demonstrate difficulties typically attributed to medication (e.g., problems sleeping, eating, complaints of physical ailments) prior to medication treatment (Barkley, McMurray, Edelbrock, & Robbins, in press).

Case study. Robert was an 8-year-old, third grader referred by his teacher to the school psychologist regarding classroom attentional problems, noncompletion and poor quality of classroom work, and high levels of motor activity compared with others in the class. A psychological evaluation indicated that Robert met criteria for Attention-Deficit Hyperactivity Disorder (see Barkley, 1988, or Rapport, 1987a, for assessment guidelines). A discussion between parents, the teacher, and the school psychologist yielded a decision to make a referral to his pediatrician for consideration of a psychostimulant medication trial. The pediatrician agreed that a medication trial was a reasonable option. Furthermore, to facilitate systematic evaluation of the trial it was agreed that Ritalin® would be prescribed at doses of 5 mg, 10 mg, and 15 mg, 1 week at each dose, mornings only, Monday through Saturday, for 3 weeks, following 1 week of baseline data collection.

Prior to the trial's start, the school psychologist and classroom teacher designed a data collection system to be used daily throughout the medication trial. The system focused on the time period of 10 a.m. to 10:30 a.m. each day. This time period was selected for two reasons: First, Robert was to take medication at 8:15 a.m. each day, and the time selected falls within 45 minutes to 3 hours after ingestion and thus is within the "window" of peak effects. Second, the time period selected is one during which students typically work independently on academic assignments (in this case language arts) and independent seatwork was an identified problem area. Baseline data were collected on a number of variables including direct observations of on-task behavior (by the teacher, using a 1-minute momentary time sampling system), teacher ratings of attention and behavior (using the CAP), and classroom performance products (work completion and accuracy). Measures of each of these variables are presented in Figure 3 across treatment phases. Work completion percentages were calculated relative to the average number of items assigned to Robert. Interobserver agreement checks on all observational and behavioral product data were conducted during 20% of the baseline and treatment observations by the school psychologist and were consistently at 90% agreement or above.

During baseline, Robert's academic performance was highly variable as he completed an average of 60% of his work at less than a 65% accuracy level. Furthermore, teacher ratings of his classroom behavior were in the atypical range and he was observed to be on-task approximately 50% of the time. The data across treatment conditions from each of these measures, as well as from a side-effects rating scale, are presented in Figure 3.

The results of this medication trial indicated that Robert's academic performance was optimally enhanced by 10 mg MPH in comparison with no medication, 5 mg MPH, and 15 mg MPH. During the 10 mg MPH phase of treatment, Robert was observed to be on-task during approximately 90% of the intervals while completing 90% of his work at an 85% accuracy level. Teacher ratings of his behavior across morning activities were significantly improved. Furthermore, no increases in adverse side-effects were observed with the 10 mg MPH treatment. It is important to note that with the 15 mg MPH treatment, Robert's rates of on-task behavior, work completion, and work accuracy were improved in comparison with baseline conditions, but not with the 10 mg dose. However, while teacher ratings of daily behavior with 15 mg MPH were comparable with the ratings for the 10 mg MPH condition, Robert's and the teacher's reports of adverse side-effects increased dramatically at the 15 mg dose. Thus, the pediatrician, parents, and education professionals all agreed that a continuation of the 10-mg MPH treatment was warranted, and they planned for short- and long-term monitoring activities to assess the continued need for treatment. This case study demonstrates the importance of interdisciplinary cooperation and the use of multiple measures (e.g., teacher ratings, direct observations, behavioral products) collected across baseline and treatment conditions to allow a comprehensive assessment of outcomes.

Future Directions for Evaluation of Stimulant Medication Effects

The procedures summarized above can be useful in detecting changes in a student's behavior as a result of medication treatment; however, their value may be limited by several factors. First, some of the dependent measures may lack sensitivity to change and/or accuracy in reflecting behavior. Moreover, potentially

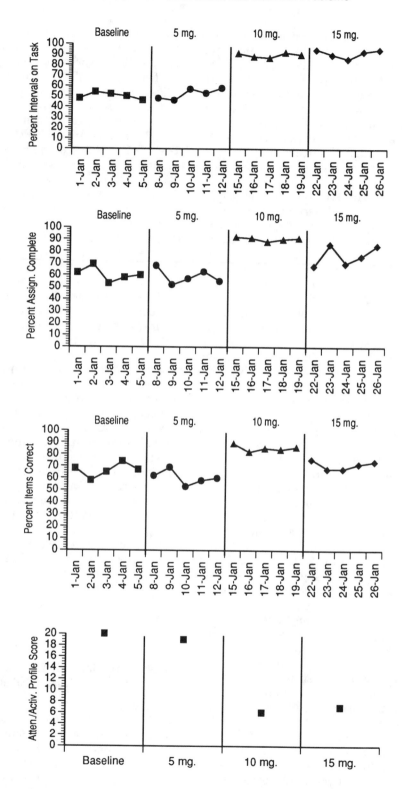

FIGURE 3. Outcome data on four dependent measures as a function of medication dose.

useful measurement procedures may not be utilized in making treatment decisions, because of a lack of professional collaboration between educators and medical personnel and physicians' limited access to direct observation of important child behavior. Thus, increasing the technical adequacy of the procedures used to monitor medication effects, and improving communication between medical and educational professionals around the monitoring of treatment effects, are two important directions for future research and practice.

Academic measures. To date, academic measures of responses to stimulant medication have involved either achievement tests or quantification of daily seatwork assignments. While these measures have been useful in documenting changes in student performance at different levels of medication, neither is without problems when used as a direct, repeated measurement of academic performance. The limitations of achievement tests include (a) their lack of sensitivity to small increments of change; (b) the unavailability of alternate forms; (c) extensive time demands to administer and score; and (d) their scores are inappropriate metrics for evaluating change. Using scores from daily seatwork assignments is inherently problematic as well since it is difficult to determine that assignment and setting conditions remain constant from one day to another. Thus, the reliability and validity of these procedures across repeated probes should be questioned.

Curriculum-based Measurement (CBM) may provide a viable alternative to the strategies noted previously. CBM is a system of measurement that addresses the shortcomings of daily assignment monitoring by sampling material directly from a student's curriculum while providing educators with discrete measurements of the student's performance on an ongoing basis. CBM in reading, spelling, written expression, and, to a lesser extent, math, has been demonstrated to be a reliable and valid system for measuring the academic performance of both regular and special education students over time (see Shinn, 1989 for an overview of CBM). Although the research to date has not focused on ADHD children specifically, CBM could be applied directly to the measurement of stimulant medication effects on the academic performance of ADHD children.

Finally, it is important to note that previous research on stimulant medication effects upon academic performance typically has focused on measuring changes in the *level* of a child's performance. For example, one might count the number of math problems completed in a 10-minute period across a series of different doses of medication. Computing and comparing the average number of correct problems at each dose results in examination of the child's level of performance between doses. Alternatively, with CBM, it is possible to compare changes in a student's *rate* of learning (with a concomitant focus on *trend* of performance) and in a standardized fashion. To do this, an assessor would sample the child's performance repeatedly during each treatment phase (i.e., dosage of medication) and then plot the resultant data in graph form. The obtained trend line or slope of data points represents a child's rate of performance for that time period (see Kazdin, 1982, and Shinn, Good, & Stein, 1989, for details about summarizing level and trend data). Thus, CBM could be used to evaluate MPH-related changes in a child's rate of performance or learning.

Increasing Collaboration Among Professionals

The information presented herein indicates that more communication between school professionals and physicians is necessary to improve the evaluation of medication treatment. Currently, school involvement in medication assessment typically consists of sharing anecdotal information with parents and physicians. However, it may well be that the most useful and critical information for evaluating and monitoring stimulant medication effects are academic performance data, since ADHD children are referred for treatment primarily because of a lack of academic progress that results from behavioral excesses and deficits. Unfortunately, direct measures of academic performance are rarely included in evaluations conducted outside of research settings. This situation suggests that education professionals could be increasingly involved in the collection of classroom performance data to aid in the objective assessment of stimulant effects, and to improve treatment services to ADHD children. Specific suggestions for school involvement and collaboration with prescribing physicians have been made previously (Gadow, 1982; Johnston, Kenney, & Davis, 1976), and include (a) establishing district-wide or schoolwide policy and communication systems for collaboration with community physicians, (b) establishing a systemwide outcome measurement system for use with children being treated with stimulant medications, and (c) delineating the specific roles of school system personnel in the implementation and monitoring of medication trials and insuring that all staff are appropriately trained to fulfill their responsibilities. School psychologists should be qualified to facilitate the coordination and implementation of each of these suggestions within their districts.

ADJUNCTIVE INTERVENTIONS

Given the myriad difficulties associated with ADHD and the chronicity of the disorder, a variety of long-term treatments provided by a number of professionals and implemented across home and school settings are often necessary to optimize the results of intervention. No single intervention method discussed above typically is sufficient to produce either short- or long-term behavioral change. Thus, the above interventions are frequently augmented by individualized academic instruction or special education placement, social skills training (Pelham & Bender, 1982), cognitive-behavioral strategies (Hinshaw, Henker, & Whalen, 1984; Kendall & Braswell, 1985), and/or parent training in behavior management skills (Barkley,

1981). The advantages and limitations of several of these interventions will be discussed below.

Social skills training procedures have been successfully implemented with a variety of child populations (see the chapter by Sabornie in this volume). While social skills training appears to be a viable approach for ameliorating the interpersonal difficulties of ADHD children, surprisingly little research has been conducted regarding the efficacy of these specific procedures with these youngsters. The studies that have been conducted to date have focused on reducing aggressive behavior or enhancing anger control in peer group situations (Hinshaw et al., 1984). A major limitation of these procedures is that highly structured motivational strategies must be employed to promote generalization of obtained effects to "real world" settings. A question that must be examined is whether targeting social responding with ongoing behavior change programs is necessary or sufficient to produce acceptable outcomes (i.e., are social skills training sessions necessary?). This is an important question as it may be that children with ADHD do not lack social skills per se, but rather do not exhibit them at an acceptable level in the absence of external contingencies to support their use.

In addition, various forms of cognitive-behavior change interventions have been devised to ameliorate the attentional difficulties and poor impulse control of children with ADHD (see Abikoff, 1985, for a review). These approaches to treatment typically have combined cognitive procedures such as self-instructional strategies (Brown et al., 1986) or self-evaluation procedures (Hinshaw et al., 1984) with behavioral techniques (e.g., contingent positive reinforcement, response cost). Target behaviors have ranged from performance on laboratory or academic tasks to interpersonal skills. While these techniques appear to have therapeutic potential, the results of recent investigations indicate that they suffer from several shortcomings that may limit their clinical efficacy. With rare exceptions (e.g., Hinshaw at al., 1984), the combination of cognitive-behavior modification and psychostimulant medication is no more effective at ameliorating attentional or behavioral control difficulties than is medication alone (Abikoff, 1985; Whalen, Henker, & Hinshaw, 1985). Furthermore, these interventions have produced neither long-term nor generalizable behavioral change beyond the therapeutic environment. As with social skills training, for generalization and maintenance to occur, they must be directly included in programming by the implementation of motivational strategies across time, caretakers, and settings. Thus, future research must document whether cognitive procedures are superfluous or represent integral components of treatment beyond behaviorally-based interventions.

Parent counseling and/or training in the use of behavior change procedures at home has been found to be a highly effective intervention with ADHD children (Barkley, 1981). Although this intervention does not directly target school performance, it may include behavioral goals related to classroom adjustment (e.g., increase frequency of homework completion). Intervention with the family generally includes several components: (a) information regarding the nature, etiology, and prognosis of ADHD; (b) training in general behavior management principles; (c) instruction in the use of effective command-giving, contingent positive attention, token reinforcement, response cost, and time-out from positive reinforcement; (d) strategies for improving compliance in public places; and (e) programming for generalization and maintenance (see DuPaul, Guevremont, & Barkley, in press, for a more detailed discussion). To the extent that similar procedures are implemented at home and school and that there is consistent parent–teacher communication (e.g., daily report card), the child's overall adjustment can be optimally affected. Since this is a fairly involved, time-consuming program, its effectiveness is limited by such factors as poor parental adherence to programmed procedures, disciplinary inconsistency between parents, and the level of parental or family stress. Overall, however, these procedures, if implemented correctly, are effective supplements to stimulant medications and classroom interventions.

TREATMENTS WITH LIMITED EFFICACY

In addition to treatments with demonstrated beneficial effects on the behavior of children with ADHD, several interventions commonly used or proposed have demonstrated few, if any, positive results in empirical investigations. Some of the more commonly proposed interventions include restricted diets, the ingestion of caffeine, and psychological counseling. In general, support for the use of these treatments is derived from theory, "expert judgment," and face validity (i.e., the approaches appear to make great intuitive sense and consequently have tremendous consumer appeal). However, research findings do not support the efficacy of these treatment modalities in attenuating the behavioral excesses and deficits of ADHD children.

Dietary Control

Probably the most well known dietary approach to the treatment of ADHD children is the Kaiser-Permanente diet prescribed by Feingold (1975). Stated simply, Feingold's hypothesis is that ADHD and other childhood disorders are often caused by ingestion of foods containing food additives and salicylates by children who are physiologically intolerant of these chemicals. He believed that these children have a natural toxic reaction to salicylates and additives that results in or exacerbates the occurrence of hyperactivity. Thus, the Kaiser-Permanente diet treatment regimen consists primarily of eliminating certain chemicals and food additives from a child's diet in order to reduce hyperactive behavior.

Initial results supporting the veracity of Feingold's theory came from his own clinical case studies, in which he claimed that "dramatic change in the behavioral pattern was observed within 1 to 4 weeks after instituting the diet" (Feingold, 1975). It was argued that the ability to turn the symptoms of ADHD on and off at will using this diet demonstrated a causal relationship between the variable being manipulated (i.e., the diet) and the children's observed behavior pattern (Conners, 1980). These claims, coupled with a perceived lack of methodological control, however, led other researchers to engage in programs of research aimed at validating his assertions. While a few studies provided support for the hypothesis that food additives exacerbated the behavior of some ADHD children (e.g., Ross, 1978; Swanson & Kinsbourne, 1980), the majority of investigations found few, if any, positive effects of the Feingold diet on hyperactive behavior (e.g., Harley, Matthews, & Eichman, 1978; Weiss et al., 1980).

Another dietary agent suggested as a treatment for ADHD children's overactive behavior is caffeine. Reasoning that central nervous system stimulants attenuate certain behavioral excesses, the hypothesis that caffeine might have similar effects was explored. Research findings suggest that while caffeine may exert some behavioral effects on children (Elkins et al., 1981), which behaviors are affected and to what degree remains uncertain (Reichard & Elder, 1977; Baer, 1987).

A final treatment sometimes recommended for ADHD children is individual counseling or psychotherapy. Research on the effectiveness of individual psychotherapy for ADHD, however, has been universally unsupportive (O'Malley & Eisenberg, 1973; Weiss, Minde, Werry, Douglas, & Nemeth, 1971; Wender, 1971). These results are not surprising when examined from current etiological perspectives. ADHD is not considered to be specifically an emotional disturbance and as such one might not expect counseling to alleviate core symptoms. Existing data should not be interpreted, however, as disparaging the use of counseling as an adjunctive treatment with ADHD children. In fact, individual counseling may be useful to help children deal with associated emotional difficulties accompanying ADHD (e.g., low self-esteem, low self-image, discouragement) and could serve an important role in an overall treatment program (Barkley, 1981; Safer & Allen, 1976).

ROLES AND FUNCTIONS OF THE SCHOOL PSYCHOLOGIST

School psychologists are in a unique position relative to other mental health professionals in that they have greater control over the choice and implementation of classroom interventions. In consequence they may serve effectively in a variety of roles and functions, including the following:

1. Coordinating prereferral and assessment processes and collection of baseline data (e.g., classroom observations of academic engaged time).

2. Communication with medical or mental health professionals involved with the identified student. This may include gathering data (e.g., direct observations, teacher rating scales, curriculum-based measurement) for the assessment of medication response(s) and adverse side-effects.

3. Design, implementation, and evaluation of classroom-based behavior change systems that would include ongoing consultation with other school personnel.

4. Provision of adjunctive interventions such as parent training in behavior modification or direct instruction of the student in self-control strategies.

5. Design, implementation, and evaluation of in-service workshops for school personnel and/or parents regarding the identification issues, educational implications, and effective interventions for children with ADHD.

SUMMARY

Attentional difficulties, and more specifically ADHD, are among the most common school-related problems that children experience. Since these difficulties are often chronic and associated with other behavior and learning problems, long-term multimodal intervention strategies are frequently necessary. This chapter has reviewed the major treatment modalities (i.e., behavior modification and stimulant medication) that have proved effective with this population. Adjunctive interventions to promote generalization across time and settings (e.g., parent training in behavior management skills) were also briefly discussed. In addition, the limitations of untested or ineffective treatments (e.g., dietary regimens) were delineated. The school psychologist is in an ideal position to consult with other education professionals with regard to the implementation and evaluation of treatment interventions in the classroom. School-based consultation is especially crucial given that the school is typically the most problematic environment for youngsters with ADHD. Thus, it behooves the school psychologist to be cognizant of both the empirically sound and the less efficacious interventions with these children in order to more effectively manage their current problems and reduce the risk for later academic and behavioral difficulties.

FOOTNOTES

[1]The designation ADHD will be used throughout this chapter to represent the previous classifications of "Attention deficit disorder with hyperactivity," "hyperactivity," and "hyperkinesis."

[2]For more information about this technology, contact: Gordon Systems, Inc., P.O. Box 746, DeWitt, NY 13214.

ACKNOWLEDGMENTS

Preparation of this chapter was supported in part by National Association of School Psychologists Research Grants to the first and second authors, and by personnel preparation grants #8029D80051-90 and #008715710 from the United States Department of Education, Office of Special Education and Rehabilitative Services to the University of Oregon.

REFERENCES

Abikoff, H. (1985). Efficacy of cognitive training interventions in hyperactive children: A critical review. *Clinical Psychology Review, 5*, 479-512.

Achenbach, T. M., & Edelbrock, C. (1983). Manual for the Child Behavior Checklist and the Revised Child Behavior Profile. Burlington, VT: Thomas Achenbach.

Aman, M. G. (1984). Hyperactivity: Nature of the syndrome and its natural history. *Journal of Autism and Developmental Disorders, 14*, 39-56.

American Psychiatric Association. (1968). *Diagnostic and statistical manual of mental disorders* (2nd ed.). Washington, DC: Author.

American Psychiatric Association. (1980). *Diagnostic and statistical manual of mental disorders* (3rd ed.). Washington, DC: Author.

American Psychiatric Association. (1987). *Diagnostic and statistical manual of mental disorders* (3rd ed., revised). Washington, DC: Author.

Anastopoulos, A. D., & Barkley, R. A. (1988). Biological factors in Attention Deficit-Hyperactivity Disorder. *The Behavior Therapist, 11*, 47-53.

Atkinson, B. M., & Forehand, R. (1979). Home-based reinforcement programs designed to modify classroom behavior: A review and methodological evaluation. *Psychological Bulletin, 86*, 1298-1308.

Ayllon, T., Layman, D., & Kandel, H. (1975). A behavioral-educational alternative to drug control of hyperactive children. *Journal of Applied Behavior Analysis, 8*, 137-146.

Bacon, J. (1988, February 17). What's the best medicine for hyper kids? *USA Today*, p. 4D.

Baer, R. A. (1987). Effects of caffeine on classroom behavior, sustained attention, and a memory task in preschool children. *Journal of Applied Behavior Analysis, 20*, 225-234.

Barkley, R. A. (1977). The effects of methylphenidate on various measures of activity level and attention in hyperkinetic children. *Journal of Abnormal Child Psychology, 5*, 351-369.

Barkley, R. A. (1981). *Hyperactive children: A handbook for diagnosis and treatment.* New York: Guilford.

Barkley, R. A. (1983). Hyperactivity. In R. J. Morris & T. R. Kratochwill (Eds.), *The practice of child therapy* (pp. 87-112). New York: Pergamon.

Barkley, R. A. (1985). The social interactions of hyperactive children: Developmental changes, drug effects, and situational variation. In R. McMahon & R. Peters (Eds.), *Childhood disorders: Behavioral-developmental approaches* (pp. 218-243). New York: Brunner/Mazel.

Barkley, R. A. (1987a). The assessment of attention deficit-hyperactivity disorder. *Behavioral Assessment, 9*, 207-234.

Barkley, R. A. (1987b). *Defiant children: A clinician's manual for parent training.* New York: Guilford.

Barkley, R. A. (1988). Attention Deficit–Hyperactivity Disorder. In E. J. Mash & L. G. Terdal (Eds.), *Behavioral assessment of childhood disorders* (pp. 69–104). New York: Guilford.

Barkley, R. A., & Cunningham, C. E. (1980). The parent–child interactions of hyperactive children and their modification by stimulant drugs. In R. Knights & D. Bakker (Eds.), *Treatment of hyperactive and learning disordered children* (pp. 219–236). Baltimore, MD: University Park Press.

Barkley, R. A., Karlsson, J., Pollard, S., & Murphy, J. (1985). Developmental changes in the mother-child interactions of hyperactive boys: Effects of two dose levels of Ritalin. *Journal of Child Psychology and Psychiatry, 26*, 705–715.

Barkley, R. A., Karlsson, J., Strzelecki, E., & Murphy, J. (1984). Effects of age and Ritalin dosage on the mother-child interactions of hyperactive children. *Journal of Consulting and Clinical Psychology, 52*, 750–758.

Barkley, R. A., McMurray, M. B., Edelbrock, C. S., & Robbins, K. (in press). The side effects of Ritalin in ADHD children: A systematic placebo-controlled evaluation of two doses. *Pediatrics.*

Bax, M., & McKeith, R. (1963). *Minimal cerebral dysfunction.* London: Heineman.

Becker, W. C. (1986). *Applied psychology for teachers: A behavioral cognitive approach.* Chicago: SRA.

Biederman, J., Munir, K., Knee, D., Armentano, M., Autor, S., Waternaux, C., & Tsuang, M. (1987). High rate of affective disorders in probands with attention deficit disorders and in their relatives: A controlled family study. *American Journal of Psychiatry, 144*, 330–333.

Blaw, M., Rapin, I., & Kinsbourne, M. (Eds.). (1977). *Topics in child neurology.* New York: Spectrum.

Brown, R. T., & Sleator, E. K. (1979). Methylphenidate in hyperkinetic children: Differences in dose effects on impulsive behavior. *Pediatrics, 64*, 408–411.

Brown, R. T., Wynne, M. E., Borden, K. A., Clingerman, S. R., Geniesse, R., & Spunt, A. L. (1986). Methylphenidate and cognitive therapy in children with Attention Deficit Disorder: A double-blind trial. *Developmental and Behavioral Pediatrics, 7*, 163–170.

Conners, C. K. (1969). A teacher rating scale for use in drug studies with children. *American Journal of Psychiatry, 126*, 884.

Conners, C. K. (1980). *Food additives and hyperactive children.* New York: Plenum.

Deutsch, C. K. (1987). *Genetic factors in Attention Deficit Disorders.* Paper presented at symposium on Disorders of Brain and Development and Cognition, Boston, MA.

Douglas, V. A. (1984). The psychological processes implicated in ADD. In L. M. Bloomingdale (Ed.), *Attention deficit disorder: Diagnostic, cognitive, and therapeutic understanding* (pp. 147–161). New York: Spectrum.

DuPaul, G. J., Guevremont, D. C., & Barkley, R. A. (in press). Attention Deficit–Hyperactivity Disorder. In R. J. Morris & T. R. Kratochwill (Eds.), *The practice of child therapy* (2nd ed.). New York: Pergamon.

Elkins, R. N., Rapoport, J., Zahn, T., Buchsbaum, M., Weingartner, H., Kopin, I., Langer, D., & Johnson, C. (1981). Acute effects of caffeine in normal prepubertal boys. *American Journal of Psychiatry, 138*, 178–183.

Feingold, B. (1975). *Why your child is hyperactive.* New York: Random House.

Gadow, K. D. (1981). Drug therapy for hyperactivity: Treatment procedures in natural settings. In K. D. Gadow & J. Loney (Eds.), *Psychosocial aspects of drug treatment for hyperactivity* (pp. 325–378). Boulder, CO: Westview Press.

Gadow, K. D. (1982). School involvement in pharmacotherapy for behavior disorders. *Journal of Special Education, 16*, 385–399.

Gadow, K. D. (1986). *Children on Medication: Vol. 1. Hyperactivity, learning disabilities, and mental retardation.* San Diego: College Hill.

Gittelman, R., & Eskinazi, B. (1983). Lead and hyperactivity revisited. *Archives of General Psychiatry, 40*, 827–833.

Gittelman, R., Mannuzza, S., Shenker, R., & Bonagura, N. (1985). Hyperactive boys almost grown up. *Archives of General Psychiatry, 42*, 937–947.

Goyette, C., Conners, C. K., & Ulrich, R. (1978). Normative data on revised Conners parent and teacher rating scales. *Journal of Abnormal Child Psychology, 6*, 221–236.

Harley, J. P., Matthews, C. G., & Eichman, P. L. (1978). Synthetic food colors and hyperactivity in children: A double-blind challenge experiment. *Pediatrics, 62*, 975–983.

Hechtman, L., Weiss, G., Perlman, R., & Amsel, R. (1984). Hyperactives as young adults: Initial predictors of outcome. *Journal of the American Academy of Child Psychiatry, 23*, 250–260.

Hinshaw, S. P., Henker, B., & Whalen, C. K. (1984). Self-control in hyperactive boys in anger-inducing situations: Effects of cognitive-behavioral training and of methylphenidate. *Journal of Abnormal Child Psychology, 12*, 55–77.

Horner, R. H., Dunlap, G., & Koegel, R. L. (1988). *Generalization and maintenance: Lifestyle changes in applied settings.* Baltimore: Brookes.

Johnson, R. A., Kenney, J. B., & Davis, J. B. (1976, November). Developing school policy for use of stimulant drugs for hyperactive children. *School Review*, 78-96.

Kazdin, A. E. (1982). *Single-case research designs: Methods for clinical and applied settings*. New York: Oxford University Press.

Kazdin, A. E. (1984). *Behavior modification in applied settings* (3rd ed.). Homewood, IL: Dorsey.

Kendall, P. C., & Braswell, L. (1985). *Cognitive-behavioral therapy for impulsive children*. New York: Guilford.

Lambert, N. M., & Sandoval, J. (1980). The prevalence of learning disabilities in a sample of children considered hyperactive. *Journal of Abnormal Child Psychology, 8*, 33-50.

Lapouse, R., & Monk, M. (1958). An epidemiological study of behavior. *American Journal of Public Health, 48*, 1134-1144.

Loney, J., Whaley-Klahn, M. A., Kosier, T., & Conboy, J. (1981, November). *Hyperactive boys and their brothers at 21: Predictors of aggressive and antisocial outcomes*. Paper presented at the meeting of the Society of Life History Research, Monterey, CA.

Lou, H. C., Henriksen, L., & Bruhn, P. (1984). Focal cerebral hypoperfusion in children with dysphasia and/or attention deficit disorder. *Archives of Neurology, 41*, 825-829.

Milich, R., Wolraich, M., & Lindgren, S. (1986). Sugar and hyperactivity: A critical review of empirical findings. *Clinical Psychology Review, 6*, 493-513.

Minde, K., Weiss, G., & Mendelson, N. (1972). A five-year follow-up study of 91 hyperactive school children. *Journal of the American Academy of Child Psychiatry, 11*, 595-610.

O'Leary, K. D., Pelham, W. E., Rosenbaum, A., & Price, G. H. (1976). Behavioral treatment of hyperkinetic children: An experimental evaluation of its usefulness. *Clinical Pediatrics, 15*, 510-515.

O'Leary, K. D., Vivian, D., & Nisi, A. (1985). Hyperactivity in Italy. *Journal of Abnormal Child Psychology, 13*, 485-500.

O'Malley, J. E., & Eisenberg, L. (1973). The hyperkinetic syndrome. *Seminars in Psychiatry, 5*, 95-103.

Paternite, C., & Loney, J. (1980). Childhood hyperkinesis: Relationships between symptomatology and home environment. In C. K. Whalen & B. Henker (Eds.), *Hyperactive children: The social ecology of identification and treatment* (pp. 105-141). New York: Academic.

Pelham, W. E., & Bender, M. E. (1982). Peer relationships in hyperactive children: Description and treatment. In K. Gadow & E. Bialer (Eds.), *Advances in learning and behavioral disabilities* (Vol. 1, pp. 365-436). Greenwich, CT: JAI.

Pelham, W. E., Bender, M. E., Caddell, J., Booth, S., & Moorer, S. H. (1985). Methylphenidate and children with attention deficit disorder. *Archives of General Psychiatry, 42*, 948-952.

Pelham, W. E., & Hoza, J. (1987). Behavioral assessment of psychostimulant effects on ADD children in a summer day treatment program. *Advances in Behavioral Assessment of Children and Families, 3*, 3-34.

Pelham, W. E., & Murphy, H. A. (1986). Attention deficit and conduct disorders. In M. Hersen (Ed.), *Pharmacological and behavioral treatment: An integrative approach* (pp. 108-148). New York: Wiley.

Pelham, W. E., Sturges, J., Hoza, J., Schmidt, C., Bijjlsma, J. J., Milich, R., & Moorer, S. (1987). Sustained release and standard methylphenidate effects on cognitive and social behavior in children with Attention Deficit Disorder. *Pediatrics, 80*(4), 491-501.

Pfiffner, L. J., & O'Leary, S. G. (1987). The efficacy of all-positive management as a function of the prior use of negative consequences. *Journal of Applied Behavior Analysis, 20*, 265-271.

Pfiffner, L. J., O'Leary, S. G., Rosen, L. A., & Sanderson, Jr., W. C. (1985). A comparison of the effects of continuous and intermittent response cost and reprimands in the classroom. *Journal of Clinical Child Psychology, 14*, 348-352.

Prinz, R. J., Connor, P. A., & Wilson, C. C. (1981). Hyperactive and aggressive behaviors in childhood: Intertwined dimensions. *Journal of Abnormal Child Psychology, 9*, 191-202.

Rapport, M. D. (1987a). Attention Deficit Disorder with Hyperactivity. In M. Hersen & V. B. Van Hasselt (Eds.), *Behavior therapy with children and adolescents: A clinical approach* (pp. 325-361). New York: Wiley.

Rapport, M. D. (1987b). *The Attention Training System: User's Manual*. DeWitt, NY: Gordon Systems.

Rapport, M. D., DuPaul, G. J., & Kelly, K. L. (1989). Attention-Deficit Hyperactivity Disorder and methylphenidate: The relationship between gross body weight and drug response in children. *Psychopharmacology Bulletin, 25*, 285-290.

Rapport, M. D., DuPaul, G. J., Stoner, G., Birmingham, B. K., & Masse, G. (1985). Attention Deficit Disorder with Hyperactivity: Differential effects of methylphenidate on impulsivity. *Pediatrics, 76*(6), 938-943.

Rapport, M. D., DuPaul, G. J., Stoner, G., & Jones, J. T. (1986). Comparing classroom and clinic measures of attention deficit disorder: Differential, idiosyncratic, and dose-response effects of methylphenidate. *Journal of Consulting and Clinical Psychology, 54*, 334-341.

Rapport, M. D., Murphy, A., & Bailey, J. S. (1980). The effects of a response cost treatment tactic on hyperactive children. *Journal of School Psychology, 18*, 98-111.

Rapport, M. D., Murphy, A., & Bailey, J. S. (1982). Ritalin vs. response cost in the control of hyperactive children: A within-subject comparison. *Journal of Applied Behavior Analysis, 15*, 205-216.

Rapport, M. D., Stoner, G., DuPaul, G. J., Birmingham, B. K., & Tucker, S. (1985). Methylphenidate in hyperactive children: Differential effects of dose on academic, learning, and social behavior. *Journal of Abnormal Child Psychology, 13*, 227-244.

Rapport, M. D., Stoner, G., DuPaul, G. J., Kelly, K. L., Tucker, S. B., & Schoeler, T. (1988). Attention deficit disorder and methylphenidate: A multilevel analysis of dose-response effects on children's impulsivity across settings. *Journal of the American Academy of Child and Adolescent Psychiatry, 27*, 60-69.

Rapport, M. D., Tucker, S. B., DuPaul, G. J., Merlo, M., & Stoner, G. (1986). Hyperactivity and frustration: The influence of size and control over rewards in delaying gratification. *Journal of Abnormal Child Psychology, 14*, 191-204.

Reichard, C. C., & Elder, S. T. (1977). The effects of caffeine on reaction time in hyperkinetic and normal children. *American Journal of Psychiatry, 134*, 144-148.

Robinson, P. W., Newby, T. J., & Ganzall, S. L. (1981). A token system for a class of underachieving hyperactive children. *Journal of Applied Behavior Analysis, 14*, 307-315.

Rose, T. L. (1980). The functional relationship between artificial food colors and hyperactivity. *Journal of Applied Behavior Analysis, 11*, 439-446.

Rosen, L. A., O'Leary, S. G., Joyce, S. A., Conway, G., & Pfiffner, L. J. (1984). The importance of prudent negative consequences for maintaining the appropriate behavior of hyperactive students. *Journal of Abnormal Child Psychology, 12*, 581-604.

Ross, D. M., & Ross, S. A. (1982). *Hyperactivity: Current issues, research, and theory* (2nd ed.). New York: Wiley.

Rutter, M., Chadwick, O., & Schaffer, D. (1983). Head injury. In M. Rutter (Ed.), *Developmental neuropsychiatry* (pp. 83-111). New York: Guilford.

Rutter, M., Lebovici, S., Eisenberg, L., Sneznevskij, A. V., Sadoun, R., Brooke, E., & Lin, T. Y. (1969). A tri-axial classification of mental disorders in childhood. *Journal of Child Psychology and Psychiatry, 10*, 41-61.

Safer, D. J., & Allen, R. P. (1976). *Hyperactive children: Diagnosis and management.* Baltimore: University Park Press.

Safer, D. J., & Krager, J. M. (1983). Trends in medication treatment of hyperactive school children. *Clinical Pediatrics, 22*, 500-504.

Satterfield, J. H., Hoppe, C. M., & Schell, A. M. (1982). A prospective study of delinquency in 110 adolescent boys with attention deficit disorder and 88 normal adolescent boys. *American Journal of Psychiatry, 139*, 795-798.

Shaywitz, S. E., Shaywitz, B. A., Cohen, D. J., & Young, J. G. (1983). Mono-aminergic mechanisms in hyperactivity. In M. Rutter (Ed.), *Developmental neuropsychiatry* (pp. 330-347). New York: Guilford.

Shinn, M. R. (Ed.). (1989). *Curriculum-based measurement: Assessing special children.* New York: Guilford.

Shinn, M. R., Good, R. H., & Stein, S. (1989). Summarizing trend in student achievement: A comparison of methods. *School Psychology Review, 18*, 356-370.

Smith, G. B. (1926). Cerebral accidents of childhood and their relationships to mental deficiency. *Welfare Magazine*, 18-33.

Sprague, R. K., & Sleator, E. K. (1977). Methylphenidate in hyperkinetic children: Differences in dose effects on learning and social behavior. *Science, 198*, 1274-1276.

Strauss, A. A., & Lehtinen, L. E. (1947). *Psychopathology and education of the brain-injured child.* New York: Grune & Stratton.

Still, G. F. (1902). Some abnormal physical conditions in children. *Lancet, 1*, 1077-1082.

Swanson, J., & Kinsbourne, M. (1975). Stimulant-related state-dependent learning in hyperactive children. *Science, 192*, 1354-1357.

Swanson, J., & Kinsbourne, M. (1980). Food dyes impair performance of hyperactive children on a laboratory learning test. *Science, 207*, 1485-1486.

Tallmadge, J., & Barkley, R. A. (1983). The interactions of hyperactive and normal boys with their mothers and fathers. *Journal of Abnormal Child Psychology, 11*, 565-579.

Toufexis, A. (1989, January 16). Worries about overactive kids: Are too many youngsters being misdiagnosed and medicated? *Time*, p. 65.

Trites, R. L., Dugas, F., Lynch, G., & Ferguson, B. (1979). Incidence of hyperactivity. *Journal of Pediatric Psychology, 4,* 179-188.

Ullmann, R. K., Sleator, E. K., & Sprague, R. L. (1985). Introduction to the use of ACTeRS. *Psychopharmacology Bulletin, 21,* 915-920.

Walker, H. M., Garrett, B., Crossen, J., Hops, H., & Greenwood, C. (1978). *Reprogramming environmental contingencies for effective social skills: Recess.* Eugene, OH: University of Oregon, Center at Oregon for Research in the Behavioral Education of the Handicapped.

Wallander, J. L., Schroeder, S. R., Michelli, J. A., & Gaultieri, C. T. (1987). Classroom social interactions of attention deficit disorder with hyperactivity children as a function of stimulant medication. *Journal of Pediatric Psychology, 12,* 61-76.

Weiss, B., Williams, J. H., Margen, S., Abrams, B., Caan, B., Citron, L., Cox, C., McKibben, J., Ogar, D., & Schultz, S. (1980). Behavioral responses to artificial food colors. *Science, 207,* 1487-1488.

Weiss, G., & Hechtman, L. (1986). *Hyperactive children grown up.* New York: Guilford.

Weiss, G., Hechtman, L., Milroy, T., & Perlman, T. (1985). Psychiatric status of hyperactives as adults: A controlled prospective 15-year follow-up of 63 hyperactive children. *Journal of the American Academy of Child Psychiatry, 24,* 211-220.

Weiss, G., Minde, K., Werry, J. S., Douglas, V., & Nemeth, E. (1971). Studies on the hyperactive child. VII: Five year follow-up. *Archives of General Psychiatry, 24,* 409-414.

Wender, P. H. (1971). *Minimal brain dysfunction in children.* New York: Wiley.

Wender, P. H. (1987). *The hyperactive child, adolescent, and adult.* New York: Oxford University Press.

Whalen, C. K., Henker, B., Collins, B. E., Finck, D., & Dotemoto, S. (1979). A social ecology of hyperactive boys: Medication effects in structured classroom environments. *Journal of Applied Behavior Analysis, 12,* 65-81.

Whalen, C. K., Henker, B., & Dotemoto, S. (1980). Methylphenidate and hyperactivity: Effects on teacher behaviors. *Science, 208,* 1280-1282.

Whalen, C. K., Henker, B., & Hinshaw, S. P. (1985). Cognitive-behavioral therapies for hyperactive children: Premises, problems, and prospects. *Journal of Abnormal Child Psychology, 13,* 391-410.

Wolery, M., Bailey, D. M., & Sugai, G. M. (1988). *Effective teaching: Principles and procedures of applied behavior analysis with exceptional students.* Boston: Allyn & Bacon.

32

Early Prevention and Intervention with Conduct Problems: A Social Interactional Model for the Integration of Research and Practice

John B. Reid
G. R. Patterson
Oregon Social Learning Center

THE DEVELOPMENTAL STABILITY AND EARLY BEGINNINGS OF AGGRESSION AND ANTISOCIAL BEHAVIOR

Over the last two decades, it has become increasingly clear that enduring patterns of conduct problems and antisocial behavior have their roots in early social development. In her benchmark study, Robins (1966) concluded that almost all adult sociopaths had histories of conduct problems that began at 10 years of age or younger. Although the investigation was retrospective in design, her conclusions have been consistently supported by a large number of prospective longitudinal studies. In his review of 16 independent longitudinal studies, Olweus (1979) found that the stability of aggressive behavior over development was similar in magnitude to that observed for measures of intellectual performance. The age of first assessment of the subjects in those studies varied from 2 to 18 years, and the retest intervals varied from 6 months to 21 years. In relating length of retest interval to magnitude of stability, he found the mean stability coefficient was .76 for intervals of a year or less, and .69 for intervals of 5 years (Olweus, 1980). This extremely high developmental stability may still be an underestimate, because most measures of antisocial behavior and aggressiveness may well be unidimensional constructs (i.e., scores tend to be most interpretable at the high end). If true, it would mean that these strong stability coefficients may be driven primarily by extreme stability of the most antisocial individuals. Patterson (1982), for example, conducted a reanalysis of data from a longitudinal study conducted by Eron and his associates (Eron, Walder, Huesmann, & Lefkowitz, 1978), who reported a stability coefficient of .38 for peer ratings of aggression over a 10-year interval. Patterson found that *all* students who were rated at the 95th percentile or higher in Grades 3 were rated above the sample mean 10 years later. Taken together, these data clearly show that aggressiveness and antisocial behavior are extremely stable over time, particularly for the most troublesome youths.

More recent studies indicate that this behavior pattern becomes salient and developmentally predictable even earlier for both boys and girls. Using the Behavior Screening Questionnaire (Richman & Graham, 1971), Stevenson, Richman, and Graham (1983) examined the stability of problem behaviors in children from 3 to 8 years. The boys' BSQ ratings at age 3 were moderately predictive of teacher report scores at age 8. Fagot (1984), using observational data collected in toddler and preschool classrooms, found high behavioral stability for aggressive behaviors in *both* boys and girls over a period of 1 year, and for boys over a period of 2 years. There is good evidence that children who are aggressive and noncompliant at age 3 continue to have similar problems when entering school and that over half the hard-to-manage preschoolers continue to demonstrate similar problems when followed up at age 6 (Campbell, Ewing, Breaux, & Szumowski, 1986). This longitudinal research, together with epidemiological findings (e.g., Earls, 1981; Fischer, Rolf, Hasazi, & Cummings, 1984), indicates that serious behavior problems are present in a significant subset of children by Grade 1, and will be stable thereafter.

PREDICTABLE OUTCOMES FOR TROUBLESOME AND ANTISOCIAL CHILDREN

Children who continue aggressive and noncompliant behaviors, particularly those youngsters officially diagnosed as having oppositional or conduct disorders, are at high risk for developing persistent psychiatric, academic, and social impairment (Graham & Rutter, 1973; Robins, 1978). The most common reason for clinical referral of young children is noncompliant, unmanageable behavior (Bentovin, 1973). Failure because of the child's inability to comply with school rules is the leading cause of children's falling behind their age groups in school — and this problem is particularly prevalent among boys (Eme, 1979). Children who do not comply with adult requests are extremely disruptive in the classroom, and such children are at high risk for developing later conduct disorders and delinquency, and for dropping out of school (Kazdin, 1987). Robins (1986) found that girls with conduct problems in childhood were at increased risk for both externalizing and internalizing disorders later on; and the risk for developing later psychiatric disorders was about equal for boys and girls. In other studies, Robins (1966, 1978, 1984) found consistent patterns of reduced attainment and competence in persons with early diagnoses of conduct disorder.

Children with conduct problems are not only at risk for later personality disorders, but for a myriad of other problems such as substance abuse, chronic unemployment, divorce, a range of physical disorders, motor vehicle accidents, and dependence on welfare services (Caspi, Elder, & Bem, 1987; Kazdin, 1987; Robins, 1966; Robins & Ratcliff, 1979; Roff, 1972; Walker, Shinn, O'Neill, & Ramsey, 1987; Wilson & Herrnstein, 1985). Aggressive children are also at extreme risk for early and decisive rejection by large segments of their peers, leaving only similar groups of aggressive children to accept them and nurture their development into delinquent careers (Coie & Kupersmidt, 1983; Dishion, in press; Dodge, 1983).

Perhaps of most interest to society is the relationship of early conduct problems and later delinquency, particularly chronic delinquency. The behaviors that characterize the oppositional, defiant, and aggressive child are powerful predictors of subsequent criminal offenses and recidivism (Loeber & Dishion, 1983). About 25% of boys in any given cohort will be arrested at least once by the time they are 19 years old; about half go on to a second offense, and about a quarter (i.e., 6% to 7%) show patterns of chronic arrests (e.g., Farrington, 1983; Wolfgang, Figlio, & Sellin, 1972). In 1986, nearly 2.3 million youngsters were arrested (FBI, 1987) and this statistic may reveal only the very tip of the iceberg, because official offense rates may account for only about 2% of actual criminal activity (Dunford & Elliott, 1982; Williams & Gold, 1972). Most relevant to this chapter, about 50% to 70% of juvenile crime is committed by about 5% to 7% of the adolescent population who are chronically antisocial (West & Farrington, 1977).

The costs to society of antisocial behavior and juvenile delinquency are enormous, even if one limits consideration to the costs of maintaining correctional facilities and programs for seriously emotionally disturbed (SED) youngsters in our educational system. Over $1 billion was spent to maintain public juvenile correction facilities in 1985 (U.S. Department of Justice, 1986), and over 350,000 students were receiving SED services in 1985 (U.S. Department of Education,

1986), at an average per student educational cost of over $4,500 per year, which is about three times the cost of regular educational services (Kauffman, 1985). Most experts agree that only a small fraction of the 6% to 10% of school children who need SED services receive them (Kauffman, 1985).

NEED FOR A DEVELOPMENTAL MODEL OF ANTISOCIAL BEHAVIOR

The data presented above show that the development of serious antisocial behavior begins early in childhood and is quite stable thereafter. Because of this developmental stability and the large number of studies documenting its antecedents and correlates, it should be possible to employ passive and experimental longitudinal research designs to develop models to clarify key and *malleable* variables involved in the development of antisocial behavior. To be useful for the systematic development of prevention and intervention strategies, such theoretical models must be composed in significant part of variables that can actually or potentially be targets of effective intervention. Although presently no treatment or prevention model has been proven consistently effective for application to antisocial behavior, a great deal of research has identified promising strategies and targets of change (Kazdin, 1985, 1987). The development of integrated theoretical models for prevention and intervention of antisocial behavior should be guided and informed by this body of literature, as well. Our work on one such set of models is described in the rest of this chapter.

There are literally hundreds of studies in the literature that report significant relationships between a myriad of demographic, social, educational, familial, and psychological variables and the development of antisocial behavior (Elliott, Huizinga, & Ageton, 1985; Kazdin, 1985; Patterson, 1982; Robins & Ratcliff, 1979).

Kazdin (1987) reviewed the research on significant antecedents and risk factors for conduct disorders and delinquency, and the list is formidable, including such major factors as grandparent and parent psychopathology, particularly involving antisocial behavior, substance abuse, and depression; family stress, including size, marital discord, bereavement, and divorce; child temperament, including intellectual and academic deficits and early oppositional behavior; and parenting variables, in particular ineffective discipline, supervision, and involvement. Molar variables — such as social and economic disadvantage defined by such factors as living in high-crime neighborhoods, attending disorganized schools, and exposure to delinquent peers — have also been shown to be intimately related to the development of antisocial behavior patterns (e.g., Elliott et al., 1985; Farrington, 1987).

On the one hand, this extensive literature tells us a great deal about the development of antisocial behavior; on the other hand, such a wide array of antecedents makes the search for mechanisms that *mediate* these relationships absolutely essential if we are ever to develop a useful model of prevention and intervention. If each antecedent identified in the empirical literature exerted an independent and direct effect on the development of antisocial behavior, then the task of prevention and intervention would be impossible from a practical perspective. Empirically guided and comprehensive universal prevention strategies would essentially require a nearly total restructuring of our society. Intervention strategies designed to alter the early trajectories of aggressive and oppositional children would require effective strategies to treat such antecedent involved in each individual case. We simply do not have effective treatment strategies to deal with even a fraction of the known antecedents of antisocial behavior. And even if they did exist, we would not have the time or resources to deal with them all.

It is not surprising that Kazdin (1985, 1987) concluded that although there are certainly *promising* strategies for treating and preventing conduct disorders, there is no approach that has been demonstrated to be consistently or persistently effective. Each "promising" approach described by Kazdin emphasizes or targets a subset of variables associated with the development of antisocial behavior. Parent training strategies basically focus on changing ongoing family interactional processes (e.g., Patterson, Chamberlain, & Reid, 1982; Prinz & Miller, 1988; Webster-Stratton, Kolpacoff, & Hollingsworth, 1988); cognitive and social skills training emphasize cognitive and interpersonal sensitivity problems of the youngsters (e.g., Kendall & Braswell, 1985; Spivak, Platt, & Shure, 1976); community-based programs often target peer group relations and involvement in prosocial activities (e.g., Feldman, Caplinger, & Wodarski, 1983); and classroom-based programs focus on social and academic difficulties at school (e.g., Walker et al., 1983).

The present writers believe that research on the development of prevention and intervention strategies for antisocial behavior will be enhanced if guided and informed by developmental or longitudinal models of antisocial behavior. The goal of such models should be to tie together the diverse antecedents, mapping them out in terms of their general importance and the developmental level at which they exert most influence. Useful models should emphasize variables that are potentially malleable, so that they provide the basis for theory-driven intervention and prevention studies that are, in turn, experimental tests of those models.

A SOCIAL INTERACTIONAL MODEL

Loeber and Dishion (1983) carried out an analysis of longitudinal studies of antisocial behavior. Comparing a large number of early antecedents, they found that parenting variables — specifically those relating to harsh and inconsistent discipline, poor supervision, and low involvement — were the best predictors of later delinquency and criminality. They consistently outperformed other important variables such as parental antisocial behavior, social and economic disadvantage, and even earlier conduct problems demonstrated by the child. Similar conclusions have been reached by other reviewers (e.g., Farrington, 1978; McCord, McCord, & Howard, 1961; Olweus, 1980; Wadsworth, 1979; West & Farrington, 1973). In the next two sections, social interactional models for the development of antisocial behavior during early and middle childhood will be described.

Early Development of Antisocial Behavior

Given that conduct problems begin to stabilize in early childhood and that parental discipline and supervision are strong predictors of later antisocial behavior, the family seems a good place to start in the search for a developmental model that has straightforward implications for prevention and intervention. As described elsewhere (e.g., Patterson, 1982; Reid & Patterson, 1989), our attempts to create models of the early development of antisocial behavior give primary importance to early patterns of socialization. An overview of the model for early development of antisocial behavior patterns will be presented, followed by a description of its components, supporting data, and current gaps in our research.

All the models to be presented here are constructed around the core hypothesis that the development of antisocial behavior is a social-interactional or bidirectional process (Patterson, 1982). Specifically, we argue that aggressive behavior patterns are initially developed and maintained through the daily interaction between the child and the parents, and perhaps siblings, as well. Although most of a young child's interactions with his or her parents are affectionate, positive, or neutral, even nondisturbed preschool boys demonstrate an aversive act about once every two minutes when interacting with their families in the home (Patterson, 1982). These rates of aversive child behavior are consistently correlated with the rates of both mothers' and fathers' aversive behavior (r_{xy} = .50 and .59, respectively), and even in the case of nondistressed mothers, their rates of generally aversive behavior are strongly related to the rates at which they hit and threaten their children (r_{xy} = .61 and .66, respectively) (Reid, Patterson, & Loeber, 1982). These data indicate that antisocial behavior does not develop in a vacuum, but is embedded in a microsocial system of family coerciveness. The relationships are similar for preschool children referred for treatment because of conduct problems, but the rates of aversive behavior are approximately twice as high (Patterson, 1982).

As children reach elementary school age, an interesting pattern emerges. The rates of aversive behavior demonstrated in the home by nonreferred boys drop by about half (i.e., from an average of .6 to .3 per minute). The mean rate shown by referred children does not drop at all; it remains at about 1.2 per minute (Patterson, 1982). Thus, during the preschool years, referred children show about twice the rates of nonreferred controls; as they enter school, they show four times the rates! This has powerful implications. Recent work by Coie and Dodge and their colleagues (Coie & Kupersmidt, 1983; Dodge, Coie, & Brakke, 1982) indicates that highly aggressive children are quickly shunned and rejected by normal peers they meet for the first time, and social status among such children is stable and difficult to change (Bierman, in press). Thus, children who are aggressive when they enter school will be likely to start their education on the wrong foot. This second phase of the development of antisocial behavior patterns will be further explored later in the next section.

Our goal in creating models for the early development of antisocial behavior is to understand why antisocial children and their parents continue to show highly coercive interactional patterns into the elementary school years, whereas their normal counterparts show increasingly positive socialization patterns. The assumption guiding our work is that the ways parents deal with children's aversive behavior in general, and discipline confrontations in particular, are a key determinant of the development of antisocial behavior. To the extent that parents are ineffective, noncontingent, and irritable in their attempts to manage aggressive and noncompliant children's behavior on

a moment-by-moment basis, that behavior will become stronger over time. And as the children's aggressive patterns increase in frequency and intensity, the parents' attempts to deal with the children become even less effective, which further exacerbates the childrens' aggressiveness, and so on. It is a truly interactive, bidirectional, and coercive process. Not only do parents of oppositional youngsters show higher rates of aversive and irritable reactions to their children's misbehavior than do parents of nonproblem children (Patterson, 1982), but they are less likely to elicit compliance upon confrontation (Reid, Taplin, & Lorber, 1981). This lack of skill or ability extends to their sensitivity in observing their children's behavior. In a study by Holleran, Littman, Freund, and Schmaling (1982), parents of antisocial children were less able than parents of normals to differentiate positive and aversive behaviors of children. It is not surprising that Patterson (1982) found that parents of antisocial children, compared with nondistressed controls, were about twice as likely to react aversively to their childrens' prosocial behavior. He labeled these related patterns of interaction *coercive family process*. Using home observation data, Patterson and his colleagues (see reviews by Patterson, 1982 and by Patterson, Reid, & Dishion, in press) have conducted a large number of sequential analyses to explicate the coercion process. Basically, families of young antisocial children rely heavily on coercion and "pain control" in their daily interactions. Compared with controls, members of these families exchange high rates of aversive initiations, maintain longer durations of negative interaction, and use more negative reinforcement strategies and less positive reinforcement. Patterson and Forgatch (1987) concluded that such interwoven reinforcement patterns keep the parent and child in a coercive rut that prevents the positive socialization of the child.

It is our position that this microsocial coercive family process is the most proximal determinant underlying the early development of antisocial behavior. Given the high rates of aversive interchanges that occur even with "normal" children and their families (i.e., about once every two minutes), extraordinary opportunities exist for children and their parents to develop the strong and stable aggressive patterns of interaction that lay the groundwork for future conduct disorders. But these *patterns* can be changed by training parents to systematically pay attention to the specific behaviors of their children, to consistently reinforce positive behaviors, and to use mild but very specific, contingent, and consistent punishment for a child's coercive behaviors (Taplin & Reid, 1977). Furthermore, many studies indicate that such intervention strategies reliably effect at least temporary reductions in children's aggressive behavior (see review by Kazdin, 1987).

Though our model specifies that irritable and inconsistent parent discipline is the most direct and proximal "cause" of aggression and coercion in young children, it also specifies that many variables can and do affect the development of antisocial behavior by undermining the effectiveness of parent discipline. More specifically, our model predicts that such factors as maternal depression, social and economic disadvantage, parents' drug use, and parents' criminality will account for variance in a child's antisocial behavior only to the extent that they disrupt day-to-day parent–child interaction, and parental discipline in particular. Conceptually, the model is shown in Figure 1.

Although each of the extradyadic[1] factors shown in Figure 1 has been shown to increase the risk for subsequent antisocial behavior and delinquency, *most* families experiencing each type of problem do not raise children with conduct problems. Such problems serve to make the job of socialization more difficult and risky. We believe that parents with a wide variety of handicaps and problems can help their children develop positive and productive social adjustments even if their children have difficult temperaments or learning difficulties. If this conceptualization is accurate, then parent–child interaction could be a key variable that serves as a sort of "junction box," tying a wide variety of clinical and social risk factors

together in their relation to the development of antisocial child behavior. It also has clear implications for early prevention and clinical intervention. To the extent that we can develop cost-effective and reliably consistent strategies for teaching parents to improve their skills when dealing with their children's coercive behaviors, we may be able to short-circuit the negative effects of the more distal variables shown in Figure 1 without having to intervene directly on those diverse and difficult-to-change risk factors.

This is obviously an idealistic picture of the situation. Although parent training with multiproblem families of antisocial children has been repeatedly demonstrated to produce significant reductions in problem behavior (Patterson et al., 1982), posttreatment persistence effects have been inconsistent (Kazdin, 1985). A noteworthy example is a study by Wahler (1980), who worked with extremely distressed families of oppositional children. The consistent treatment effects observed immediately after intervention had almost totally disappeared a year later. If extradyadic risk variables disrupted child-management skills in the first place, it would not be surprising if they eroded the benefits of intervention after the supportive aspects of the treatment relationship were terminated, particularly among families experiencing chronic and severe stress. For such families, the use of adjunctive intervention strategies may be required to help them deal with the specific factors that are disrupting their daily interactions with the child.

The conceptualization in Figure 1 does not imply that all aggressive children can be successfully treated, even in the short run, with a sole focus on day-to-day parenting skills. Certainly, individual families have extradyadic problems that prevent them from learning, improving, or even practicing effective parenting strategies. Some parents experience marital distress that makes their participation in treatment impossible; others are so depressed that they simply cannot carry out the procedures or keep up with their children; others are usually intoxicated to the extent that no progress can be made.

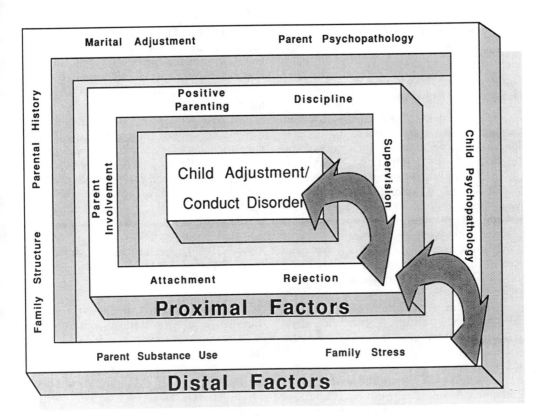

FIGURE 1. The concept model.

The implication of the conceptualization is that one begins intervening with the proximal parenting variables first, regardless of other risk factors that might be present. One deals with extradyadic factors only when they interfere with the parents' progress in learning or practicing the skills, or when follow-up assessments indicate that a given risk variable is highly related to a deterioration of gains after intervention. The model indicates the starting point of initial strategy. In our conceptualization, the hypothesized causal relationship between parent–child interaction and many distal risk variables goes both ways. It may be, for example, that having an oppositional child exacerbates parental depression, substance use, or marital dissatisfaction. For some subset of families, improving parenting skills may improve parental adjustment.

Because coercive parent–child interactions tend to be maintained and strengthened by interlocking reinforcement patterns, we assume that the detrimental effects of extradyadic disruptors will be maintained even if the disruptors are subsequently eliminated. For example, a young parent experiencing a divorce may become temporarily depressed, socially isolated, and economically disadvantaged. This could initiate or amplify a coercive family process. After the young parent adjusts to the stress of the divorce, his or her problems with the child could continue to worsen because they are now driven by reinforcement processes internal to the dyadic interaction. A *history* of factors that are no longer present, such as parental antisocial behavior or substance abuse, depression, or economic stress may actually bode well for the short- and long-term effects of parent training.

Phase 2 in the Development of Antisocial Behavior

As indicated above, there are two parenting practices that are highly predictive of later antisocial behavior and delinquency: discipline and supervision. Up to this point, we have examined the role of discipline. As children grow older, they spend increasing amounts of time outside the direct supervision of their parents. They visit the homes of friends, parents leave them unattended for minutes, rather than seconds, and they begin school. Once they begin school, a similar process unfolds. In the early elementary years, they are often in one classroom and catch the first bus home from school, often to be met at the bus by their parents, who walk them home. As they grow older, both parents and teachers leave them increasingly on their own. By middle school, most kids move from classroom to classroom throughout the day and are increasingly given schoolwork to be done at home. By fourth grade, parents are not sure of their children's whereabouts for an average of nearly one hour per day (Patterson & Stouthamer-Loeber, 1984). It is now that parental supervision and monitoring become increasingly relevant to the development of antisocial behavior.

Aggressive, noncompliant children are at serious risk for the exacerbation and expansion of their problems at the transition to elementary school. Not only is it likely that they will continue in a coercive and increasingly hostile relationship with their parents, but their aggressive behavior patterns make it likely that they will engage in similar patterns with teachers and classmates. In an unpublished analysis of longitudinal data by B. Fagot (personal communication, 1989), the level of directly observed coercive-negative interaction between parents and their 18-month-old toddlers accounted for 40% of the variance in their rates of aggression toward peers when they began kindergarten. Ramsey, Patterson, & Walker (in press) conducted a multimea-sure analysis of home and school behavior for a sample of fourth-grade boys. They found that antisocial behavior in the home accounted for approximately 50% of the variance in measures of antisocial behavior at school.

If elementary-school children are aggressive toward their peers, they are at very high risk for immediate and lasting rejection (Coie & Kupersmidt, 1983; Dodge, 1983). Peer rejection has consistently been shown to be a powerful precursor of a wide variety of mental health and adjustment difficulties, in addition to later delinquency (Parker & Asher, 1987). Similar relationships have been reported for the ties between early coercive behavior patterns in the home and academic engagement, academic performance, conduct problems, and poor homework completion at school (e.g., Patterson et al., in press; Walker et al., 1987).

Most children do not experience significant problems in adjusting to the demands of the classroom and peer group. They have mastered the rudimentary social skills necessary for successful relationships with peers, their aggression has declined significantly between the ages of 3–5, and they have learned to comply with demands made by adults. In short, they are ready to learn new and more complex survival skills in the potentially rich learning environments of the playground and classroom. For most children, their continued social development will be handled in those settings. For the better-socialized children, a phone call from the teacher or school counselor will be effective when and if additional intervention is required.

In fact, most parents do very little monitoring of their children's activities at school. In a dissertation by Schoen (1989), it was reported that well-educated and affluent parents of 150 kindergarten children spent an average of only about 30 minutes, over the entire year, in discussion with teachers. Even though the average rate is low, the parents of children who are most at risk monitor their children's activities least both in the school and in peer group settings outside the school (Ladd & Golter, 1988; Stevenson & Baker, 1987). Data are accumulating to show that parents' monitoring and involvement in children's homework, at least as early as Grade 4, become powerful determinants of subsequent academic achievement (Hill Walker, personal communication, 1989).

On the basis of such findings, our model of the development of antisocial behavior places heavy emphasis on parental monitoring as the child enters the school system. There is consistent evidence that any major transition in the life of a child is a time of serious risk (e.g., Coddington, 1972; Felner, Farber, & Primavera, 1983; Felner, Primavera, & Cauce, 1981; Patterson & Capaldi, in press). For young antisocial children, the transition to school is a particularly risky period. Because of their early experience and training in aggressive relationships at home, we hypothesize that they will start the same relationships with peers and teachers, that these socialization agents will tend to react in kind, and that mutually maintaining coercive processes will be developed in each new setting and relationship these children enter. To the extent that coercive behavior patterns are developed across settings, the risks of later antisocial behavior increase dramatically (Loeber, 1982). Teachers well know that the social and classroom behaviors of all children must be carefully monitored as they enter school so that corrective action can be taken as necessary. If aggressive children are to have a chance to change their trajectory, we believe it is essential to teach their parents to play a heavy monitoring and support role in out-of-home settings.

To the extent that parents fail to keep track of their children's out-of-home activity, they are simply unable to encourage the acquisition of positive social skills or to provide corrective feedback for antisocial behavior. This increases the odds of successful lying, stealing, and truancy; parents will be unable to intervene when their children act up in school, fail to complete homework, or get in trouble with peers. Rather than being proactive in the child's socialization

during middle childhood and adolescence, they will become reactive, becoming involved and informed only when neighbors, teachers, or police demand their attention.

A central assumption in our models is that poor parental monitoring has its main roots in earlier failures of parents to deal successfully with the face-to-face aggressive, coercive, and noncompliant behaviors of their children. Recall that Holleran et al. (1982) found that parents of oppositional children did not discriminate positive from antisocial behaviors as well as control parents. We assume that if parents are consistently defeated when they try to deal with aggressive behavior, they become less careful in specifically tracking or noticing it. At one level, if they don't "notice" an obnoxious behavior, they save themselves the embarrassment and pain involved in their ineffectual attempts to correct it. When the child is out of their direct view, it is even easier not to notice signs of misbehavior. If the parents of antisocial children ask them about their day, they are likely to lie; when confronted, these children are also likely to lie, leading to an argument the parents typically lose (Reid & Patterson, 1976). If parents try to discipline the child for an infraction reported by others, they will probably be even less likely to succeed than they are in trying to correct aggressive behaviors that they directly witness. If young aggressive children are inclined to behave badly when they go to school or to the house of a friend, simply because they are well practiced in that sort of behavior, poor parental monitoring should increase their risk of continued development of antisocial behavior patterns even further.

As this process continues to unfold over the elementary and middle school years, one can expect the child to become increasingly rejected by parents, teachers, and well-adjusted children; to become increasingly aggressive, noncompliant, and obnoxious, and to fall further behind in school; to associate with other aggressive youngsters and become truant; and to become at extremely high risk for delinquent behavior, substance abuse, and so on.

If this overall conceptualization of the development of antisocial behavior is reasonably accurate, it has clear implications for systematic assessment, prevention, and intervention activities, focused first on the families of young-at-risk children, and second on the parents and teachers during the elementary and middle school years.

PUTTING THE MODEL TOGETHER

We have presented evidence to show the overall relationships of poor parental discipline and monitoring to subsequent antisocial behavior and school failure, as well as to support many of the specific relationships among individual components of the hypothesized model. The next step is to provide evidence that these individual findings and relationships fit together at various points along the preadolescent life course and that the predicted relationships at earlier points also predict relevant outcomes and relationships among variables later in development. First, comprehensive studies are required that measure all the main constructs within the same studies. Second, multivariate statistical strategies are required to assess simultaneously the relative contributions of each of the constructs to antisocial behavior and its correlates. Such strategies have the potential to elucidate the relationships of those constructs to each other. Third, longitudinal studies are required to demonstrate the predicted temporal relationships. Finally, experimental studies are required to demonstrate that altering a key variable (e.g., discipline or monitoring) actually changes subsequent levels of antisocial behavior. Our work to date on these tasks will be described in this section. In the final section of this chapter, specific recommendations for prevention and intervention strategies will be outlined, as well as studies that need to be completed.

The Data Base

Most of our modeling analyses were conducted with data from a longitudinal study that began in 1984 (Patterson, 1984). The sample consists of two cohorts, totaling 206 boys and their families. The boys under study were in the fourth grade (ages 9–10) when the study began. The sample is considered moderately at risk, since it was drawn from the elementary schools in our community that serve the areas with the highest rates of juvenile crime and substance use, as determined by police arrest data. All fourth-grade boys and their parents in each target school were asked to participate in the study. Of those families who met eligibility requirements (i.e., fluent in English, no immediate plans to move from the area), 78% agreed to participate. Analyses of demographic data and data from teachers' reports on adjustment indicated that the boys who participated were slightly more at risk than those who refused. The project began with a 3-year feasibility/pilot study during which the measures, subject recruitment, and retention procedures were tested and refined. In 1984, we began data collection on the 9–10 year old boys for the main study and have assessed the subjects each year since. The Cohort 1 boys are now 15–16 years, and the Cohort 2 boys are 14–15 years. We have lost only 1% of the subject families who originally agreed to participate.

During odd years, the subjects and their families participate in about 25 hours of assessment; during even years, they participate in an abbreviated assessment lasting about 15 hours. The major types of data collected are demographics; questionnaires about family circumstances and stress; some data on grandparents; psychometric data on parents and child for several types of adjustment, antisocial behavior, substance use, and other mental health problems; home and laboratory observations and global reports by interviewers and observers; school, police, and motor vehicle file data; and teacher and peer questionnaires and sociometrics. Where possible, commonly used procedures and instruments were employed. The goal of the assessment strategy was to collect data using several methods, agents, and settings for the measurement of each major construct in the models. In some cases, it was possible to use standard measures to measure constructs; more often, it was necessary to create and refine scales from the large data set.

Before we address the specific measurement strategy employed in this study, it should be noted that we have other longitudinal data sets that employed very similar measure for somewhat different populations (e.g., children of recently divorced mothers, preschool children, and very aggressive children and their families participating in an intervention study). The overall strategy has been to develop and cross-validate models on the two cohorts from the main longitudinal data set, and to replicate them on the other sets. When the major longitudinal study was designed in the late 1970s and early 1980s, the available research literature indicated that antisocial behavior began to stabilize at about the fourth grade (e.g., Olweus, 1979; Robins & Ratcliff, 1979). As described in the preceding sections of this chapter, we know that the process begins much earlier, and we are now evaluating the downward generalizability of the models to be presented in this chapter.

To date, we have developed over a dozen constructs that are currently used in our analyses. They are described in detail elsewhere (Capaldi & Patterson, 1989). Although space does not permit the complete description of each measure, the antisocial behavior construct will be outlined in some detail to elucidate the process.

General antisocial behavior has been the most important dependent variable in our work so far. The central purpose of our modeling analyses is to relate the proximal and distal variables and processes (described earlier) to current and future antisocial behavior. It is important to us that this construct be generalizable across agents, settings, and methods of assessment. Based on work reviewed earlier, we wanted to develop a number of indicators of this construct, using data across the home, the classroom, and peer group settings, by means of questionnaires, interviews, observation, global ratings, and file data. The first step was to develop scales for each indicator, then to use both exploratory and confirmatory factor analyses to ensure the convergence on other constructs. We developed more indicators for this construct than would be needed for a test of any single structural equation model. Because the observed relationship between constructs can be due in part to shared method variance, we choose specific indicators for each construct in a given analysis so that the same measures and agents are not used to define different constructs. The antisocial construct for fourth-grade boys and its primary indicators are shown in Figure 2. As can be seen, the construct is made up of a variety of indicators, including various modes of measurement, different agents, and different settings.

The Core Model: Contribution of Two Family Process Variables to Children's Antisocial Behavior

As noted early in this chapter, we think that the earliest and most proximal determinants of generalized antisocial behavior are to be found in the daily interaction between parent and child. Specifically, it was argued that, to the extent that a child's *coercive behavior* in the home is dealt with by ineffectual and irritable discipline, both sets of behavioral patterns will persist and become exacerbated because of interlocking sets of negative reinforcement processes. To the extent that this pattern characterizes the parent–child interaction concerning socialization and discipline, the parent will be unable and disinclined to *monitor* the child's out-of-home activity. To the extent that the child is coercive and poorly monitored, he or she will drift into a generalized pattern or trait of *antisocial behavior* across settings. First, we tested the overall conceptualization to show that this pattern could be demonstrated at the fourth grade.

In order to test this model, constructs for irritable parental discipline, the child's irritable exchanges with other family members, parental monitoring, and affiliation with deviant peers were developed. The *Discipline* construct was defined by

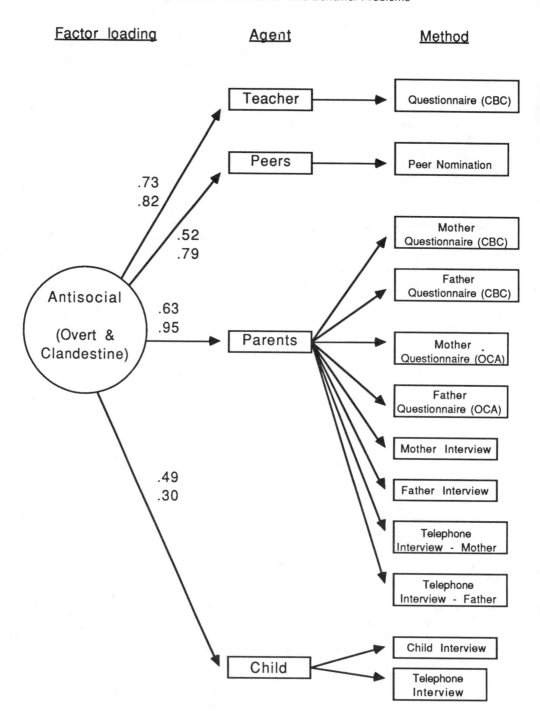

FIGURE 2. The Antisocial construct. Factor loadings based on Patterson, Reid, and Dishion (in press), Cohorts I and II.

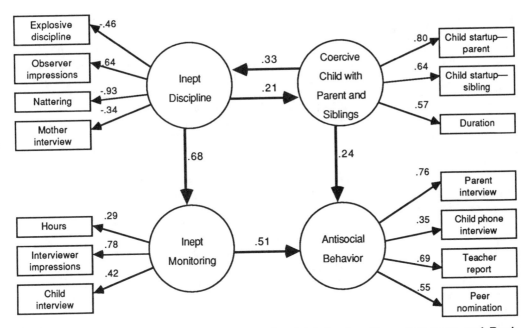

FIGURE 3. Basic training in the home for antisocial behavior. From Patterson and Bank (1986). Reprinted by permission.

(a) two home observational measures (Nattering, parental rates of low-intensity negative initiations to the child; and Explosive Punishment, observed parental rates of hitting, yelling, and threatening); (b) the home observers' global ratings of ineffective, irritable, and abusive discipline; and (c) self-reports of the mothers' use of ineffective discipline. The *Coercive Child* construct was completely defined by variables from the home observation data (the rate at which the child initiated aversive interactions with the parents and with siblings; and the mean durations of these aversive interactions). The *Monitoring* construct was defined on the basis of global ratings by interviewers on the quality of parental supervision, interview data from the parent on amount of time spent with the child, and interview data from the child on the amount and quality of parental supervision. In this model, the *Antisocial Trait* was defined by questionnaire and interview measures from parents and teachers. The structural equation model (Patterson & Bank, 1986) is depicted in Figure 3.

Each of the predicted relationships is supported by the model. All predicted path coefficients between constructs are significant at least at the .05 level; no unpredicted paths were significant. On the basis of our past work (e.g., Reid et al., 1981), the relationships between irritable discipline and a child's aggression in the home were not surprising. The link between irritable discipline and poor monitoring is extremely important to our conceptualization, and received strong support. As predicted, poor monitoring was strongly related to generalized antisocial behavior. Note that there was a significant and direct path between the child's aggression in the home and the generalized antisocial construct. The model provided an acceptable fit to the data, and accounted for 40% of the variance in antisocial behavior. The concurrent structural relationships among discipline, monitoring, and antisocial behavior have been replicated on two other data sets at our center: a sample of 150 recently divorced mothers and their 6- to 12-year-old children, and a sample of 70 6- to 12-year-old children referred because of severe behavior problems and their parents (Forgatch, in press). In those analyses, the model tested was the same as that shown in Figure 3. Both models accounted for about 40% of the variance in antisocial child behavior.

These modeling studies provided strong and consistent support for the core model, relating ineffectual and irritable discipline to coercive child behavior in the home and showing a powerful relationship of discipline and monitoring to antisocial behavior across settings. Taken together, the data discussed to this point provided empirical support for the parent training strategies that have been used with moderate success for treating preadolescent aggressive and oppositional children (Kazdin, 1987). On the basis of these modeling studies, we believe that the effectiveness of parent training can be improved if more emphasis is placed on teaching parents to better supervise the out-of-home activities of their children.

Relationship of Contextual Factors to Family Process and to the Development of Antisocial Behavior

As noted earlier, a large number of variables other than those describing the interactional processes between parent and child are importantly related to the development of antisocial careers; among them are characteristics of the child, such as poor verbal reasoning (Rutter, Maugham, Mortimore, & Outson, 1979) and early troublesomeness (Craig & Glick, 1963); characteristics of the parents, such as maternal depression (Patterson & Forgatch, in press) and parents' criminality (Farrington, 1978); social and economic disadvantage (May, 1981); and family size, loss of parents, and parents' divorce (Wadsworth, 1979).

The developmental model of antisocial behavior proposed here assumes that the effects of these *contextual* factors on child antisocial behavior is *indirect*. That is, we hypothesize that their effects are mediated to a large extent through their disruptive effects on day-to-day parental discipline and monitoring. The other side

of the coin is that parents and families who suffer a wide variety of social, behavioral, and psychological handicaps can be, and usually are, effective in raising well-socialized children. To the extent that they can maintain effective family management skills in the face of adversity, the risk that the children will develop antisocial behavior patterns can be minimized.

If this general model is correct, the implication for prevention and early intervention are extremely important. By teaching and supporting high-risk families to strengthen their discipline and supervision practices, it may be possible to reduce the risk of delinquency and antisocial behavior without having to try to fix the long and impossible list of risk factors that characterize the families most in need of help. The technology for providing families with affordable and reasonably effective training in the basic parenting skills of discipline and supervision is within our grasp (e.g., Patterson et al., 1982; Webster-Stratton, 1989). Such help for parents could be given universally as children begin elementary or middle school, and the training could be expanded to include teaching parents to better monitor and facilitate their children's transition from home to the demands of the classroom and peer group.

For multiproblem families whose children have already gotten out of control, the present conceptualization would suggest a sequential intervention strategy. Regardless of the personal, social, or psychological problems presented by a family, first try to teach them the parenting strategies. For some families, this might be sufficient; for others, their response to intervention might indicate a subset of one or more contextual variables that must also be addressed. For example, if marital conflict makes it impossible for parents to agree on consistent discipline or supervision strategies, then marital therapy might be indicated; if depression or a drug problem makes effective parental monitoring impossible, then the parent should be referred for appropriate treatment. The key would be to keep the focus on family management, intervening on contextual factors only as necessary to keep them from blocking progress in the development of parenting skills.

The proposed model does not suggest ignoring contextual factors; in fact, their importance was highlighted in Figure 1. The model specifies that the day-to-day parenting practices of the family constitute the most proximal and direct determinants of early child antisocial behavior, and that the contextual factors are distal determinants that operate through those proximal determinants. The development of social, economic, educational, and clinical strategies to deal with those distal factors will be critical if we are ever to mount a comprehensive program to deal with children's conduct problems.

To begin testing the conceptual model shown in Figure 1, it was necessary to use a data set that included measures of the dependent variable (antisocial behavior) and measures of *both* proximal and distal variables. This was critical in order to assess simultaneously the direct and indirect effects of both classes of factors. In our research projects at the Oregon Social Learning Center, we have collected enough data on selected distal factors to allow a number of tests of the contextual model shown in Figure 1. In Forgatch's ongoing study of recently divorced mothers (Forgatch, in press), a structural equation model was presented showing that maternal stress, defined by daily hassles, negative life events, and financial and health problems, was significantly related to inept discipline, which was in turn significantly related to the level of children's antisocial behavior. Using data from Patterson's longitudinal study, Capaldi (1989) developed a construct measuring "poor child adjustment." Its indicators influenced antisocial behavior, trying out drugs, associations with deviant peers, peer rejection, poor academic skills, low self-esteem, and depression. In one analysis, she showed a linear relationship between the number of family transitions experienced by fourth-grade boys and the level of poor adjustment. Number of transitions was scored 0 if the child was living with two biological families; 1 if the child was living with a single parent, once divorced; 2 if with a biological and first

step-parent; 3 if with a single parent twice divorced; and so on. She showed a parallel set of relationships between number of transitions and poor discipline and monitoring. Finally, she conducted a structural equation model that tested the predicted indirect relationships between contextual factors (transitions, family income, and socioeconomic status), family management variables (monitoring and discipline), and child adjustment. The model and the correlations among latent constructs are shown in Figure 4.

As can be seen, parents' transitions were found to have a significant effect on child adjustment mediated through monitoring, as did sociometric status mediated through discipline. Income was found to have a direct effect on child adjustment. The mediated model fit the data (χ^2, df = 67, p = .12) and accounted for 38% of the variance in child adjustment.

In a recent analysis of data from Patterson's longitudinal study (Dishion, Reid, & Patterson, 1988), parents' drug use was found to be a correlate of poor monitoring and discipline, as well as of drug use by their sons. In a multiple regression analysis, however, poor monitoring and association with deviant peers both contributed significantly to the variance in marijuana and alcohol use by the boys. Parents' drug use did not account for any *unique* variance in the boys' substance use, other than that mediated by its disruption of parental supervision. Finally, using data from three generations in the same study, Patterson and Dishion (1988) found that parent-reported explosiveness by grandparents was related to antisocial behavior of the parents, and that the effect of antisocial parental patterns on child antisocial behavior was mediated through poor discipline practices.

Taken together, these analyses provide strong and consistent support for a mediated model relating contextual factors to child antisocial behavior. If the effects of family stress, disadvantage, and parental problems on the development of antisocial behavior are funneled through parenting practices, we should definitely consider testing the efficacy of lowcost

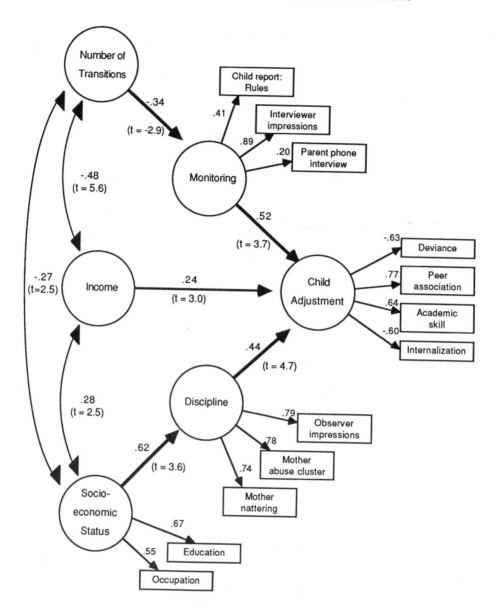

	#Trans	Income	SES	Monitoring	Discipline	Child Adj.
#Transitions	—					
Income	-.48	—				
SES	-.19	.17	—			
Monitoring	-.30	.11	.18	—		
Discipline	-.23	.28	.54	.24	—	
Child Adjustment	-.45	.41	.49	.57	.58	—

R's Between Latent Constructs from Measurement Model

FIGURE 4. Relation of social and economic disadvantage to child adjustment. From Capaldi & Patterson (1989).

parent training in universal prevention studies of conduct disorder.

Some Products of Child Antisocial Behavior

In the present conceptualization, given its high developmental stability, we argue that one clear outcome of early antisocial child behavior is antisocial and delinquent behavior during adolescence. Furthermore, we argue that early antisocial behavior patterns place children at risk for other problems that further increase the risk of delinquency. Specifically, data were presented earlier to indicate that poor academic performance, rejection by peers, and erosion of the relationship between parent and child all increase the risk of later, broader-band maladjustment. If the child's own antisocial behavior is a major determinant of peer rejection, academic failure, and alienation with parents, then intervening on these "products" should not significantly lessen a child's risk for delinquency unless his or her basic antisocial behavior patterns are addressed as well. And this is apparently the case. The majority of studies examining the efficacy of problem-solving skills training (PSST), for example, have demonstrated gains on cognitive measures and laboratory task performance and have shown effectiveness with "impulsive" rather than clearly aggressive children (Kazdin, 1987). The PSST approaches appear to work best on the least aggressive children (Kendall & Braswell, 1985).

Patterson et al. (in press) tested a mediated model relating parent discipline, child antisocial behavior, and three hypothesized products — peer relations, academic skills, and parent–child relationship. The model was tested on Patterson's sample of fourth-grade boys and is shown in Figure 5.

Figure 5 shows that each of the predicted paths is significant, indicating the powerful role played by antisocial child behavior in each of the dependent variables. The fit of the model was improved by adding a direct path between parental discipline and academic skills,

underscoring the important role of the parent in the child's overall early adjustment. In an analysis of Patterson's data, Hill Walker (personal communication) showed correlations in the .6 to .8 range between parental monitoring at fourth grade and scores on a range of academic skills at seventh grade. Although more research and analyses are badly needed on this issue, these analyses strongly support the central role of early parenting practices and child antisocial behavior on the development of a wide range of children's problems. Our position is that prevention and intervention strategies for any of these problems must incorporate procedures to directly reduce antisocial child behavior, and that comprehensive programs must involve work with the parents.

Longitudinal Analyses

Up to this point, most of the analyses presented have assessed the concurrent or cross-sectional relationships among constructs in our model at the fourth grade. The next step is to demonstrate that the concurrent models have predictive utility (e.g., that contextual, family management, or early antisocial constructs are systematically related to *subsequent* behavior problems and delinquency). If longitudinal relationships can be shown that implicate potentially *malleable* factors such as parenting skills in the development of antisocial behavior, then the scientific groundwork can be laid for the systematic design of randomized prevention or intervention trials. Such trials could employ the same assessment strategies as those used in the longitudinal work, and intervention strategies would be designed specifically to alter those potentially malleable factors. Using appropriate control groups, such experimental studies would not only test the efficacy of the interventions, but would serve as *experimental* tests of the longitudinal models.

Although our analyses are far from complete, the longitudinal models tested to date are quite promising. In a study recently completed by Larzelere & Patter-

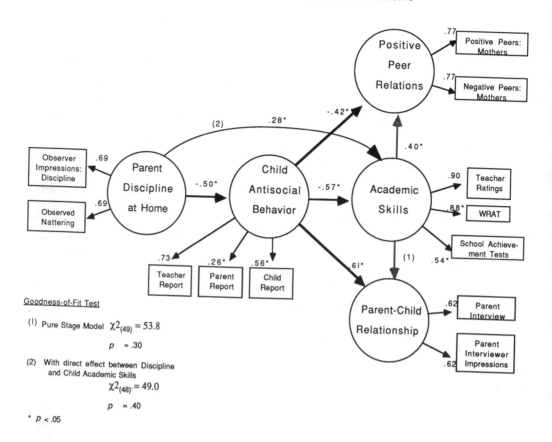

FIGURE 5. Relation of parent discipline and child antisocial behavior to peer relations, the parent–child relationship, and academic skills in Grade 4. From *Antisocial Boys* by G. R. Patterson, J. G. Reid, and T. J. Dishion, 1990. Eugene, OR: Castalia. Copyright 1990 by Castalia Publishing Co. Reprinted by permission.

son (1990), the relationships among socioeconomic status of the families assessed at the fourth grade, parental management practices (discipline and monitoring) assessed at the sixth grade, and delinquency assessed at the seventh grade were modeled. In line with the present conceptualization, it was predicted that social advantage at Time 1 should have a significant and positive relationship to good discipline and monitoring by parents at Time 2, and that good parenting practices at Time 2 should have a significant and negative relationship with delinquency at Time 3. The structural equation model is shown in Figure 6.

As shown, socioeconomic status (SES) is defined by parent education and occupation; Parental Management is a second-order construct, defined by discipline and monitoring; Delinquency is defined by a self-report measure and number of police-recorded offenses. The predicted paths between the three constructs are both significant, and the model accounts for 46% of the variance in delinquency. Note that the direct path between SES and delinquency was weak and not significant, indicating that its effect on delinquency is mediated by parenting practices. Given that many antisocial youngsters do not engage in significant delinquency as early as seventh grade, it is possible that the model will account for even more variance as the sample gets older.

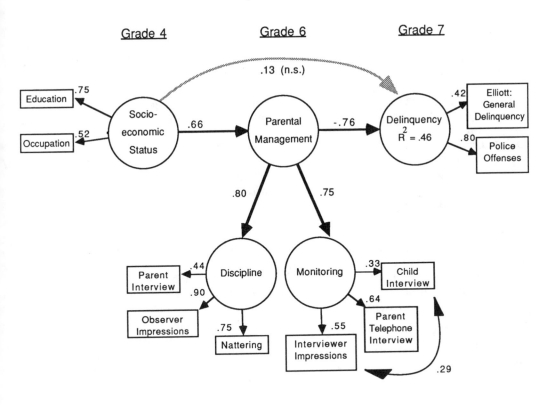

FIGURE 6. Effects of socioeconomic status and parental management skills on early delinquency (N = 180). From Larzelere & Patterson (1990).

Patterson, Capaldi, and Bank (in press) tested a model relating parental monitoring, child antisocial behavior, and academic achievement at fourth grade, association with deviant peers at sixth grade, and delinquency at seventh grade. They reported strong and significant relationships among monitoring, antisocial behavior, and academic achievement at fourth grade. Those three constructs accounted for 68% of the variance in association with deviant peers at sixth grade; and association with deviant peers at sixth grade accounted for 50% of the variance in delinquency at seventh grade. This model is interesting in at least three

ways. First, it shows a clear relationship between parental supervision and both antisocial behavior and academic achievement in elementary school, suggesting strongly that parent training may be a viable strategy to affect school performance as well as to deal with problems of aggression. Second, it highlights the role of parenting (particularly supervision) in the antisocial child's drift to the deviant peer group, which in turn further increases the child's risk of delinquency. Third, the strong relationship between association with deviant peers in sixth grade and delinquency in seventh grade suggests that intervention must begin early (i.e., in the primary grades). Parent management variables play an extremely powerful role in the early development of antisocial behavior. Once consistent patterns of antisocial behavior are developed, the child is likely to fall behind in school, be rejected by nonagressive peers, and associate with other aggressive youngsters. If parental supervision has deteriorated, the main socializing influence is provided by a delinquent peer group, and the family may become a minimal force in the child's development.

Many other longitudinal models will be tested with our longitudinal data sets, but the two presented here clearly support the conceptualization that day-to-day parenting practices are powerful and proximal determinants in the development of antisocial and delinquent behavior patterns.

We are currently conducting an intervention study with families of antisocial youngsters that is designed to systematically assess the effectiveness of training parents to practice monitoring and discipline skills. We are assessing the children and families using the same measures that have been employed in the longitudinal studies. This study is an experimental test of the model and should tell us much about the actual causal status of parenting variables in the development of delinquent behavior patterns.

IMPLICATIONS FOR
PREVENTION AND INTERVENTION

We have attempted to present evidence for a conceptualization of antisocial behavior based on the premise that the most proximal determinants of its development are found in the social interactional fabric in which it is embedded. The process begins early, when interactions between parent and child become dysfunctional around discipline issues. Specifically, the dysfunction involves the parent's inability to effectively and consistently deal with the child's oppositional behavior. The ineffective discipline becomes increasingly irritable and coercive, further increasing the child's aggressive and oppositional behavior. The behavior

of parent and that of the child become progressively more coercive through the action of the interlocking positive and negative reinforcement processes that have been described by Patterson (1982). During this preschool phase of development, parent training should be an effective and reasonably comprehensive intervention strategy for families with aggressive children (Kazdin, 1985, 1987). In addition to clinical strategies for use with children who demonstrate severe problems (e.g., Patterson et al., 1982), the feasibility and effectiveness of low-cost videotape formats for teaching parenting skills has been demonstrated (Webster-Stratton et al., 1988) and holds great promise for early prevention in the home.

The transition to kindergarten or first grade is an important milestone in the development and prevention of antisocial or conduct problems. As the research presented indicates, children who have developed aggressive and coercive behavior patterns at home are at significant risk for displaying similar problems in school for at least three reasons. First, since these children have developed strong oppositional and aggressive patterns with their parents and siblings in the home, they are primed to demonstrate those patterns when confronted by teachers and peers. Past behavior is a powerful and straightforward predictor of future behavior. Second, if the child is immersed in a coercive family process while attending school, continuing reinforcement of aggressive behavior in the home will be likely to compete with, rather than support, attempts at socialization at school. Third, and most importantly, the child's coerciveness and noncompliance at school are neither inert nor internally maintained. The child's aggressive behavior will induce microsocial interactional coercive patterns with the teachers and peers with whom she or he interacts. That is, the coercive process will probably be recreated with each person who must deal with the child on a daily basis. Therefore, the same negative and positive reinforcement processes that gave birth to coercive behavior in the home will continue to nurture its further development in the school. Studies reviewed earlier indicate that these coercive processes will put the child at extreme risk for rejection by peers and teachers, poor academic and social adjustment, and delinquency.

A crucial implication of the present conceptualization of antisocial child behavior for prevention and intervention during *the school years* is that it must be considered across settings. For example, a first grader's oppositional and aggressive behavior can probably be understood by knowing that it was learned or developed previously within the family (and even that it is still being aggravated in that setting). This does not mean, however, that correcting the situation at home will significantly alter ongoing aggressive behavior in the classroom or playground. Based on the model and supporting data previously described, the at-risk child will be likely to engage new interactants in coercive interchanges, and they will be likely to set up powerful contingencies to maintain the antisocial behavior. Without direct intervention in each setting, previously unfamiliar peers will quickly reject an antisocial child, particularly one who also has social skills deficits, thereby further increasing the probability of coercive interchanges that lead to the interlocking negative reinforcement contingencies that will support and maintain aggressive behavior. Needless to say, the aggressive behavior will lead to reciprocal coerciveness from teachers, as well.

We suggest that three major domains are relevant to intervention with, and prevention of, antisocial behavior during the school years: interaction with parents, teachers, and peers. We further suggest that the most proximal (or immediately critical) determinants of aggression in each setting involve the daily microsocial interchanges between the child and others in each domain. Unless the social contingencies for aggressive behavior are altered in a given setting, it will not be efficiently corrected or prevented. At a more distal or systemic level, the models presented indicate that problems of aggression and noncompliance in any one setting are related to similar problems in the other settings.

Neither teachers nor parents can reasonably assume that successful prevention or intervention can be carried out in only one setting. It must be a cooperative venture that integrates intervention in both school and home. As argued previously, the extent to which the parents monitor the behavior of their children is highly correlated with antisocial behavior *across* settings, and most parents spend depressingly little time tracking their children's activity at school. A first step in prevention and intervention during the school years is to promote a cooperative rather than adversary relationship between parents and school personnel. When the child begins school, every attempt should be made to induct the parents into the educational process, to explain the educational and behavioral goals and strategies, to enlist their assistance in achieving those goals, and to set up mechanisms to keep parents informed of their children's progress and problems. For children who demonstrate noncompliance and aggression, this liaison is critical. The communication must be more frequent than periodic parent–teacher conferences or crisis meetings that are occasioned by the child's extreme misbehavior. A number of straightforward and uncomplicated procedures for drawing parents into active involvement with the teacher and with the daily educational and social aspects of their children's school experience have been recently developed, and initial outcome evaluations indicate that such techniques will be quite promising in attaining these goals (e.g., Epstein, in press). Simple procedures for keeping parents informed about their child's daily progress and problems in academic and social behavior are readily available (e.g., Blechman, 1985; Patterson, Reid, Jones, & Conger, 1975).

As argued repeatedly in this chapter, the core of our model of antisocial behavior is that its most proximal and powerful determinants are to be found in the social interactional situation in which it occurs (Patterson & Reid, 1984; Reid & Patterson, 1989). Therefore, the first consideration of the interventionist in any out-of-home setting such as the school must be to deal directly with the problem (or its prevention) in that setting. It is our position that the primary locus for prevention of and intervention in aggressive and antisocial behavior in school is in the classroom and on the playground. Strategies and procedures for achieving these goals are described in other chapters in this volume. The next challenge in the creation of a comprehensive approach for intervening in the development of antisocial behavior patterns is to find ways of molding integrated partnerships between parents and teachers in this task.

ACKNOWLEDGMENTS

The following grants provided support for the work represented in this manuscript: MH 37940, MH 38730, and MH 38318 from National Institute of Mental Health, U.S. Public Health Service. The research reported here could not have been completed without the continuous support and cooperation of the Lane County Juvenile Court and the Bethel, Eugene 4-J, and Springfield school districts.

REFERENCES

Bentovin, A. (1973). Disturbed and under vie. *Special Education, 62*, 31–35.

Bierman, K. L. (in press). Improving the peer relationships of rejected children. In B. B. Lahey & A. E. Kazdin (Eds.), *Advances in clinical child psychology*. New York: Plenum.

Blechman, E. A. (1985). *Solving child behavior problems at home and at school.* Champaign: Research Press.

Campbell, S. B., Ewing, L. J., Breaux, A. M., & Szumowski, E. K. (1986). Parent-referred problem three-year-olds: Follow-up at school entry. *Journal of Child Psychology and Psychiatry, 27*(4), 473–488.

Capaldi, D. M. (1989, April). *The relation of family transitions and disruptions to boys' adjustment problems.* Paper presented at the biennial meeting of the Society for Research in Child Development, Kansas City, MO.

Capaldi, D., & Patterson, G. R. (1989). *Psychometric properties of fourteen latent constructs from the Oregon Youth Study.* New York: Springer-Verlag.

Caspi, A., Elder, G. H., & Bem, D. J. (1987). Moving against the world: Life course patterns of explosive children. *Developmental Psychology, 23*, 308–313.

Coddington, R. (1972). The significance of life events as etiological factors in the disease of children: The study of the normal population. *Journal of Psychosomatic Research, 16*, 205–213.

Coie, J. D., & Kupersmidt, J. B. (1983). A behavioral analysis of emerging social status in boys' groups. *Child Development, 54*, 1400–1416.

Craig, M. M., & Glick, S. J. (1963). Ten years experience with the Glueck Social Prediction Table. *Crime and Delinquency, 9*, 249–261.

Dishion, T. J. (in press). The peer context of troublesome child and adolescent behavior. In I. Leone (Ed.), *Understanding the troubled and troublesome child.* Beverly Hills, CA: Sage.

Dishion, T. J., Reid, J. B., & Patterson, G. R. (1988). Empirical guidelines for a family intervention for adolescent drug use. *Journal of Chemical Dependency Treatment, 1*(2), 189–214.

Dodge, K. A. (1983). Promoting social competence in school children. *Schools and Teaching, 1*(2), 67–76.

Dodge, K. A., Coie, J. D., & Brakke, N. P. (1982). Behavior patterns of socially rejected and neglected preadolescents: The roles of social approach and aggression. *Journal of Abnormal Child Psychology, 10*, 389–410.

Dunford, F. W., & Elliott, D. S. (1982). *Identifying career offenders with self-reported data.* Rockville, MD: National Institute of Mental Health.

Earls, F. (1981). Epidemiological child psychiatry: An American perspective. In E. F. Purcell (Ed.), *Psychopathology of children and youth: A cross cultural perspective* (pp. 3–28). New York: Josial Macy, Jr. Foundation.

Elliott, D. S., Huizinga, D., & Ageton, S. S. (1985). *Explaining delinquency and drug use.* Beverly Hills: Sage.

Eme, R. J. (1979). Sex differences in childhood psychopathology: A review. *Psychological Bulletin, 86*, 574–595.

Epstein, J. L. (in press). Effects of teacher practices of parent involvement on student achievement in reading and math. In S. Silvern (Ed.), *Literacy through family, community, and school interaction.* Greenwich, CT: JAI.

Eron, L. D., Walder, L. O., Huesmann, L. R., & Lefkowitz, M. M. (1978). The convergence of laboratory and field studies of the development of aggression. In W. W. Hartup & J. Dewitt (Eds.), *Origins of aggression.* The Hague: Morton.

Fagot, B. I. (1984). The consequences of problems behaviors in toddler children. *Journal of Abnormal Child Psychology, 12*, 385–395.

Farrington, D. P. (1978). The family backgrounds of aggressive youths. In L. A. Hersov, M. Berger, & D. Shaffer (Eds.), *Aggression and antisocial behaviour in childhood and adolescence* (pp. 73-93). Oxford: Pergamon.

Farrington, D. P. (1983). Offending from 10 to 25 years of age. In K. T. Van Dusen & S. A. Mednick (Eds.), *Prospective studies of crime and delinquency* (pp. 17-37). Boston: Kluwer-Nijhoff.

FBI. (1987). *Crime in the United States: Uniform Crime Reports, 1986.* Washington, DC: U.S. Government Printing Office.

Feldman, R. A., Caplinger, T. E., & Wodarski, J. S. (1983). *The St. Louis conundrum: The effective treatment of antisocial youths.* Englewood Cliffs, NJ: Prentice-Hall.

Felner, R., Farber, S., & Primavera, J. (1983). In R. D. Felner, L. A. Jason, J. N. Moritsugu, & S. Farber (Eds.), *Preventive psychology: Theory, research, and practice* (pp. 199-215). New York: Pergamon.

Felner, R., Primavera, J., & Cauce, A. (1981). The impact of school transitions: A focus for preventive efforts. *American Journal of Community Psychology, 9,* 449-459.

Fischer, M., Rolf, J. E., Hasazi, J. E., & Cummings, L. (1984). Follow-up of a preschool epidemiological sample: Cross-age continuities and predictions of later adjustment with internalizing and externalizing dimensions of behavior. *Child Development, 53,* 137-150.

Forgatch, M. S. (1990). The clinical science vortex: Developing a theory for antisocial behavior. In D. Pepler (Ed.), *The development and treatment of childhood aggression.* Hillsdale, NJ: Erlbaum.

Forgatch, M. S., Patterson, G. R., & Skinner, M. L. (in press). A mediational model for the effect of divorce on antisocial behavior in boys. In E. M. Hetherington & J. D. Arasteh (Eds.), *Impact of divorce, single parenting, and stepparenting in children.* Hillsdale, NJ: Erlbaum.

Graham, P., & Rutter, M. (1973). Psychiatric disorder in the young adolescent: A follow-up study. *Proceedings of the Royal Society of Medicine, 66,* 1226-1229.

Holleran, P. A., Littman, D. C., Freund, R., & Schmaling, K. B. (1982). A signal detection approach to social perception: Identification of negative and positive behaviors by parents of normal and problem children. *Journal of Abnormal Child Psychology, 10,* 547-557.

Kauffman, J. M. (1985). *Characteristics of children's behavior disorders* (3rd ed.). Columbus, OH: Merrill.

Kazdin, A. E. (1985). *Treatment of antisocial behavior in children and adolescents.* Homewood, IL: Dorsey.

Kazdin, A. E. (Ed.). (1987). *Conduct disorders in childhood and adolescence* (Vol. 9). Beverly Hills, CA: Sage.

Kendall, P. C., & Braswell, L. (1985). *Cognitive-behavioral therapy for impulsive children.* New York: Guilford.

Ladd, G. W., & Golter, B. S. (1988). Parents management of preschooler's peer relations: Is it related to children's social competence? *Developmental Psychology, 24,* 109-117.

Larzelere, R. E., & Patterson, G. R. (1990). *Parental management: Mediator of the effect of socioeconomic status on early delinquency.* Manuscript submitted for publication. (Available from R. E. Larzelere, PhD, Rosemead School of Psychology, Biola University, 13800 Biola Ave., La Mirada, CA 90639.)

Loeber, R. (1982). The stability of antisocial and delinquent child behavior: A review. *Child Development, 53,* 1431-1446.

Loeber, R., & Dishion, T. J. (1983). Early predictors of male delinquency: A review. *Psychological Bulletin, 94,* 68-99.

May, R. D. (1981). The Aberdeen delinquency study. In S. A. Mednick, A. E. Baert, & B. P. Bachmann (Eds.), *Prospective longitudinal research.* Oxford: Oxford University Press.

McCord, W., McCord, J., & Howard, A. (1961). Familial correlates of aggression in nondelinquent male children. *Journal of Abnormal and Social Psychology, 62,* 79-93.

Olweus, D. (1979). Stability of aggressive reaction patterns in males: A review. *Psychological Bulletin, 86*(4), 852-875.

Olweus, D. (1980). Familial and temperamental determinants of aggressive behavior in adolescent boys: A causal analysis. *Developmental Psychology, 16,* 644-660.

Parker, J. G., & Asher, S. R. (1987). Peer relations and later personal adjustment: Are low-accepted children at risk? *Psychological Bulletin, 102*(3), 357-389.

Patterson, G. R. (1982). *Coercive family process.* Eugene, OR: Castalia Publishing Co.

Patterson, G. R. (1984). *Understanding and prediction of delinquent behavior.* Grant No. MH 37940. Public Health Service, National Institute for Mental Health, Center for Studies of Antisocial and Violent Behavior.

Patterson, G. R., & Bank, L. (1986). Bootstrapping your way in the nomological thicket. *Behavioral Assessment, 8,* 49-73.

Patterson, G. R., & Capaldi, D. (in press). Antisocial parents: Unskilled and vulnerable. In P. Cowan & E. M. Hetherington (Eds.), *The effect of transitions on families.* Hillsdale, NJ: Erlbaum.

Patterson, G. R., Capaldi, D., & Bank, L. (in press). An early starter model for predicting delinquency. In D. Pepler & K. M. Rubins (Eds.), *The development and treatment of childhood aggression.* Hillsdale, NJ: Erlbaum.

Patterson, G. R., Chamberlain, P., & Reid, J. B. (1982). A comparative evaluation of a parent training program. *Behavior Therapy, 13,* 638-650.

Patterson, G. R., & Dishion, T. J. (1988). Multi-level family process models: Traits, interactions, and relationships. In R. Hinde & J. Stevenson-Hinde (Eds.), *Relationships within families: Mutual influences* (pp. 283-310). Oxford: Clarendon.

Patterson, G. R., & Forgatch, M. S. (1987). *Parents and adolescents: I. Living together.* Eugene, OR: Castalia.

Patterson, G. R., & Forgatch, M. S. (in press). Initiation and maintenance of processes disrupting single-mother families. In G. R. Patterson (Ed.), *Depression and aggression in family interaction.* Hillsdale, NJ: Erlbaum.

Patterson, G. R., & Reid, J. B. (1984). Social interactional processes within the family: The study of the moment-by-moment family transactions in which human social behavior is embedded. *Journal of Applied Developmental Psychology, 5,* 237-262.

Patterson, G. R., Reid, J. B., & Dishion, T. J. (in press). *Antisocial boys.* Eugene, OR: Castalia.

Patterson, G. R., Reid, J. B., Jones, R. R., & Conger, R. E. (1975). *A social learning approach to family intervention: Families with aggressive children* (Vol. 1). Eugene, OR: Castalia.

Patterson, G. R., & Stouthamer-Loeber, M. (1984). The correlation of family management practices and delinquency. *Child Development, 55,* 1299-1307.

Prinz, R. J., & Miller, G. E. (1988). *Behavioral family treatment of conduct disorders: Learning from the dropouts.* In R. Prinz (Chair), *Advances in Behavioral Family Treatment.* Symposium conducted at the meeting of the Association for the Advancement of Behavior Therapy, New York City.

Ramsey, E., Patterson, G. R., & Walker, H. M. (in press). Generalization of the antisocial trait from home to school settings. *Journal of Applied Developmental Psychology.*

Reid, J. B., & Patterson, G. R. (1976). The modification of aggression and stealing behavior of boys in the home setting. In E. Ribes-Inesta & A. Bandura (Eds.), *Behavior modification: Experimental analyses of aggression and delinquency* (pp. 123-145). Hillsdale, NJ: Erlbaum.

Reid, J. B., & Patterson, G. R. (1989). The development of antisocial behavior patterns in childhood and adolescence. *European Journal of Personality, 3,* 107-119.

Reid, J. B., Patterson, G. R., & Loeber, R. (1982). The abused child: Victim, instigator, or innocent bystander? In D. J. Bernstein (Ed.), *Response structure and organization* (pp. 47-68). Lincoln: University of Nebraska Press.

Reid, J. B., Taplin, P. S., & Lorber, R. (1981). A social interactional approach to the treatment of abusive families. In R. Stuart (Ed.), *Violent behavior: Social learning approaches to prediction, management, and treatment* (pp. 83-101). New York: Brunner/Mazel.

Richman, N., & Graham, P. (1971). A behavioral screening questionnaire for use with three-year-old children: Preliminary findings. *Journal of Child Psychology and Psychiatry, 12,* 5-33.

Robins, L. N. (1966). *Deviant children grow up: A sociological and psychiatric study of sociopathic personality.* Baltimore: Williams and Wilkins.

Robins, L. N. (1978). Study of childhood predictors of adult antisocial behavior: Replications from longitudinal studies. *Psychological Medicine, 8,* 611-622.

Robins, L. N. (1984). *Conduct disorder and adult psychiatric diagnosis.* Unpublished manuscript.

Robins, L. N. (1986). The consequences of conduct disorder in girls. In D. Olweus, J. Block, & M. Radke-Yarrow (Eds.), *Development of antisocial and prosocial behavior: Research, theories, and issues* (pp. 385-414). San Diego: Academic.

Robins, L. N., & Ratcliff, K. S. (1979). Risk factors in the continuation of childhood antisocial behavior into adulthood. *International Journal of Mental Health, 7*(3-4), 06-116.

Roff, M. (1972). A two-factor approach to juvenile delinquency and the later histories of juvenile delinquency. In M. Roff, L. N. Robins, & M. Pollack (Eds.), *Life history research in psychopathology* (Vol. 2, pp. 77-101). Minneapolis: University of Minnesota Press.

Rutter, M., Maughan, B., Mortimore, P., & Ouston, J. (1979). *Fifteen thousand hours: Secondary schools and their effects on children.* Cambridge, MA: Harvard University Press.

Schoen, D. (1989). *Early child temperament and achievement in kindergarten children.* Unpublished doctoral dissertation, University of South Carolina.

Spivack, G., Platt, J. J., & Shure, M. B. (1976). *The problem solving approach to adjustment.* San Francisco: Jossey-Bass.

Stevenson, D., & Baker, D. P. (1987). The family-school relation and the child's school performance. *Child Development, 58,* 1348-1357.

Stevenson, J., Richman, N., & Graham, P. (1983). Behavior problems and language abilities at three years and behavioral deviance at eight years. *Journal of Child Psychology and Psychiatry, 24,* 215-230.

Taplin, P. S., & Reid, J. B. (1977). Changes in parent consequation as a function of family intervention. *Journal of Consulting and Clinical Psychology, 4,* 973-981.

U.S. Department of Justice. (1986). Sourcebook of criminal justice statistics — 1985 (NCJ-100899). Washington, DC: U.S. Government Printing Office.

U.S. Department of Education. (1986). *Annual evaluation report: Fiscal year 1984.* Washington, DC: Office of Planning, Budget, and Evaluation.

Wadsworth, M. E. J. (1979). *Roots of delinquency: Infancy, adolescence, and crime.* Oxford, England: Robertson.

Wahler, R. G. (1980). The insular mother: Her problems in parent–child treatment. *Journal of Applied Behavior Analysis, 13,* 207-219.

Walker, H. M., McConnell, S., Holmes, D., Todis, B., Walker, J., & Golden, N. (1983). *The Walker social skills curriculum: The ACCEPTS program.* Austin, TX: Pro-Ed.

Walker, H. M., Shinn, M. R., O'Neill, R. E., & Ramsey, E. (1987). A longitudinal assessment of the development of antisocial behavior in boys: Rationale, methodology, and first year results. *Remedial and Special Education, 8*(4), 7-16.

Webster-Stratton, C. (1989). Systematic comparison of consumer satisfaction of three cost-effective parent training programs for conduct problem children. *Behavior Therapy, 20*(1), 103-116.

Webster-Stratton, C., Kolpacoff, M., & Hollingsworth, T. (1988). Self-administered videotape therapy for families with conduct-problem children: Comparison with two cost-effective treatments and a control group. *Journal of Consulting and Clinical Psychology, 56*(4), 558-566.

West, D. J., & Farrington, D. T. (1973). *Who becomes delinquent?* London: Heinemann Educational Books.

West, D. J., & Farrington, D. T. (1977). *The delinquent way of life.* New York: Crane, Russak.

Williams, J. R., & Gold, M. (1972). From delinquent behavior to official delinquency. *Social Problems, 20,* 209-229.

Wilson, J. Q., & Herrnstein, R. J. (1985). *Crime and human nature.* New York: Simon & Schuster.

Wolfgang, M. E., Figlio, R. M., & Sellin, T. (1972). *Delinquency in a birth cohort.* Chicago: University of Chicago Press.

FOOTNOTE

[1]In this chapter, *extra-dyadic* refers to any variable that is not defined within the observed parent-child interaction (e.g., child temperament, parent psychopathology, marital dysfunction, social or economic disadvantage).

33

Instructional Problems and Interventions: Training Needs for School Psychologists

Scott R. McConnell
Michelle Hecht
University of Minnesota

INTRODUCTION

This chapter addresses the training of school psychologists to provide consultation and direct intervention assistance for children and youths experiencing problems of academic performance. Our goals are (a) to describe one view of best practices in school psychology training for instructional intervention and consultation, (b) to describe current practices for teaching instructional intervention in a sample of university-based school psychology programs, and (c) to offer some measured observations and suggestions for further development of this critical part of training for future school psychologists.

Before turning to a discussion of specific competencies and procedures, however, it seems appropriate to describe the instructional problems and interventions this training is designed to address. Problems that children experience in school can be subdivided in a broad and somewhat arbitrary way into two general categories: problems of social behavior or classroom deportment, and problems of academic achievement or related performance. This arbitrary categorization of child behavior is typical to many of the current models of school adjustment (e.g., Green, Forehand, Beck, & Vosk, 1980; McConnell et al., 1984), and serves as basis for the organization of topical chapters in the current volume.

What, then, are "problems of academic achievement or related performance?" For the purposes of this chapter, we define this domain as the complex array of child behaviors necessary to produce correct, age- or grade-appropriate academic responses in the classroom. This domain can be subdivided further into two closely related areas. First, children may evidence problems of academic achievement; for example, given an opportunity to respond to an academic question (e.g., "What is the square root of 100?" or "Please read the following passage") and optimal motivation (e.g., discriminative stimuli that signal likely reinforcement for responding), children fail to produce a response desired by the classroom teacher. Academic performance problems may be the result of a student's learning history (e.g., failure to master necessary prerequisites, lack of necessary background information), a teacher's presentation of the academic task (e.g., not specifying a desired response form, using unfamiliar instructional prompts), or characteristics of a curriculum's design (e.g., improper sequencing of skills introduction, insufficient practice opportunities) (Becker, Engelmann, & Thomas, 1975). Whatever the reason, academic achievement problems are said to occur when a student fails to produce a correct or desired response in an academic or other criterion setting.

Second, students may exhibit problems in performance of academic survival skills. Academic survival skills are the aspects of a child's in-class performance that promote or facilitate academic achievement but are not academic responses per se. Academic survival skills include attention to the teacher or task, appropriate interaction with instructional materials, requesting assistance, or volunteering information (see Cobb & Hops, 1973; or Paine, Radicchi, Rosellini, Deutchmann, & Darch, 1983, for more complete information and descriptions of academic survival skills). Problems in the performance of academic survival skills may be the result of a child's learning history and experience (e.g., students in special education may not have learned to attend to large-group lectures or to request information by raising one's hand), the organization of the classroom (e.g., materials may be hard to obtain or students may face a number of distracting stimuli during teachers' presentations), or the presentation of the instruction (e.g., students may attend less during relatively slow-paced lessons in which teachers present a great amount of information and ask relatively few questions). Academic survival skills problems usually are identified when a child produces academic responses more often in a carefully structured situation such as one-to-one testing than in typical classroom activities.

School Psychologists and Instructional Problems

Although philosophies of instructional intervention vary widely, there is general consensus that a population of children who have difficulty in school due to poor academic performance need some type of specialized education. Traditionally, and especially since the rapid expansion of special educational programs beginning in the early 1970s, school psychologists have played a central role in psychoeducational diagnosis and remediation planning for students with academic performance problems. In this educational service delivery model, psychologists are responsible for completing general measures of cognitive functioning

and academic achievement, quite often along with more detailed diagnostic testing of a child's specific skills and deficits (or "strengths and weaknesses") in a given academic domain. This information is then considered by a multidisciplinary team (which frequently includes the school psychologist) in deciding a child's eligibility for special education, developing an Individualized Educational Plan (IEP), and selecting an educational placement where appropriate remediation can occur.

In recent years, the effectiveness and efficiency of this traditional psychoeducational model of school psychology services has come under increasing scrutiny. Researchers in special education and school psychology have amassed substantial evidence that "traditional" diagnosis and placement decisions lack reliability (Ysseldyke et al., 1981) and validity (Algozzine et al., 1982), are expensive, and may be at counter purposes to the intent of federal and state laws governing special education (Gallagan, 1985). In addition, self-contained settings and special curricula have not always been successful in meeting children's educational needs (Wang, Reynolds, & Walberg, 1987–1988); rather, there is an equal or greater likelihood that most children will be best educated in regular education settings, using instructional methods that have been demonstrated to be effective for most student populations (Finn & Resnick, 1984; Messick, 1984).

Simultaneously with these disclosures of flaws or weaknesses in traditional practice, substantial advances have been made in the development of assessment and intervention techniques to identify and serve more effectively children who exhibit academic problems. Researchers have developed more efficient and curriculum-specific procedures for identifying children with academic problems (Deno, Marston, & Mirkin, 1982; Deno, Mirkin, & Chiang, 1982; Shinn, Tindal, & Stein, 1988), have described the components of effective instructional design (Engelmann & Carnine, 1982) and intervention (Carnine & Silbert, 1979), and have described school psychologists' possible roles in planning and evaluating instructional interventions provided in a wide array of classroom settings (Deno, 1986; Rosenfield, 1987).

School Psychology and Instructional Consultation

The disconcerting absence of support for the traditional, yet prevalent assessment–classification–placement model (Ysseldyke et al., 1983), and the increasing sophistication of direct assessment, intervention planning, and consultation practices, have led to the development of new types of school psychology services (Graden, Zins, & Curtis, 1988). These newer approaches are based on several assumptions. First, regular education must be strengthened to meet the needs of all students in the mainstream in accordance with the spirit of Public Law 94-142 (Giangreco & Meyer, 1988; Zins, Curtis, Graden, & Ponti, 1988). Second, the integration of teachers, support staff, and other personnel, as well as material resources, is critical for strengthening regular education services (Stainback & Stainback, 1988). Finally, indirect service is a most efficient means for school psychologists and other professionals to meet the heterogeneous educational needs of students in the mainstream (Bardon, 1988); in other words, while school psychologists are directly concerned about a child's school performance, the focus of psychologists' work is with teachers and parents.

Instructional consultation is perhaps one of the most important of these alternative models. As described by Rosenfield (1987), instructional consultation represents a combination of knowledge and practice from the fields of instructional psychology and school consultation, and rests on an assumption of academic performance as a *transaction:*

> Taking this transactional perspective forces us to shift the focus from the defective learner to viewing the learner as part of the instructional system. The major components of the system include three sets of variables: the task, or what is to be learned; the learner, in terms of

his or her readiness to undertake the learning task; and the treatment, or the instructional and management strategies. (Rosenfield, 1987, p. 10)

This model of instructional consultation (Meyers, 1980; Rosenfield, 1987) casts the instructional interventionist in a role of indirect service provider. The consultant and teacher review current interventions and their effects and, if necessary, generate revised plans. It is the classroom teacher who actually implements an intervention; the consultant remains somewhat apart from the actual intervention program. However, the school psychologist's role in this transaction assumes mastery of both the knowledge base and skill to implement interventions of proven effectiveness as well as expertise in imparting that content to the individual providing direct intervention. Without demonstrated mastery of both the content and the implementation skills for academic interventions, the school psychologist is not likely to contribute substantially to the remediation of academic problems.

School psychologists may be uniquely qualified for the role of instructional interventionist (Berliner, 1988). Given that an intervention is only as good as the assessment information on which it is based, school psychologists' strong background in assessment prepares them for an obvious and important role in the development of programs for children with academic achievement problems. In addition, training in assessment "primes" the school psychologist with a *problem-solving set,* a complex array of attitudes and skills that produce a constructive, creative approach to instructional intervention in today's heterogeneous classrooms (Meyers, 1980). Furthermore, school psychologists may know and be able to apply procedures drawn from the effective teaching literature. This component should be (but still is not) elemental to most educational training programs (i.e., regular education, special education, school psychology). Finally, school psychologists also can provide information on classroom learning. Psychologists are assumed to have, in addition to their knowledge of assessment, a solid grasp of information regarding behavior and the mechanisms that foster adaptive versus maladaptive development.

Furthermore, school psychology has a long tradition of serving other professionals in school programs. Unlike most professionals in schools, psychologists provide relatively little direct service. Rather, psychology is offered as an ancillary service, one that facilitates the work of other disciplines. Expertise in consultation increases the likelihood of success in communicating information about effective intervention strategies. In addition, the school psychologist, as a skilled indirect service provider, can be more successful in facilitating the professional development of teachers by strengthening their knowledge and skills in solving problems and accessing resources (Berliner, 1988; Witt & Martens, 1988). In sum, with a preparatory background in assessment, knowledge of literature on effective teaching, and experience providing indirect service in the schools, the school psychologist is a most likely and well-qualified candidate for filling the role of instructional interventionist.

School Psychologists as Instructional Interventionists

Our conception of the school psychologist as an instructional interventionist is based on the functioning of a uniquely qualified professional within the transactional, indirect model described previously, and it extends the roles and responsibilities typically assigned to instructional consultation. As an instructional interventionist, the school psychologist works in active collaboration *with* the classroom teacher, rather than acting as an expert who is consultant *to* the teacher. Together, the psychologist and teacher (a) assess the need for intervention, (b) select short- and long-term goals, (c) design an intervention plan likely to produce the desired effects, given available instructional resources, and (d) implement and evaluate the intervention

effort. In this way, the school psychologist should be integrated fully into the design, implementation, and evaluation of an instructional intervention.

School psychologists working as instructional interventionists experience benefits beyond those available from "instructional consultation" alone. First, the collaborative nature of this model is likely to produce *role release* (Lyon & Lyon, 1980), the active transfer of skills and perspectives of one discipline (here, school psychology) to professionals from another discipline (e.g., classroom teaching) in ways that promote professional development and quality of services for both groups of professionals. Second, personal responsibility for an intervention outcome is shared more equitably by those who developed the original plan. By actively involving themselves in ongoing instructional interventions, school psychologists increase the likelihood that they will detect variables (e.g., integrity of implementation, peer attention) associated with success or failure of their intervention plans. In this way, school psychologists will begin to benefit more directly from the fruits of their own efforts, thus improving job satisfaction and performance over time. Finally, when school psychologists collaborate with teachers in intervention planning and implementation, both groups of professionals are responsible for the increased effectiveness of intervention and therefore can share professional and personal satisfaction.

Increasing heterogeneity in the educational mainstream, and the simultaneously expanding mandate for increased effectiveness in education (Berliner, 1988; Stainback & Stainback, 1988), only highlight the need for school psychologists to participate more actively in the remediation of instructional problems. Classroom teachers, and the administrators who supervise their work, are under increasing pressure to produce and document solid gains in academic achievement for *all* children. At the same time, teachers in general education are providing increased service to special education or other low-achieving students in their classes. Classroom teachers may find few colleagues in their buildings or districts who have expertise to help them respond to the growing, and seemingly contradictory, demands of improving academic achievement for increasingly heterogeneous groups. School psychologists, perhaps more than any other group of professionals, are uniquely qualified to serve as colleagues and resources to teachers who find themselves in this position.

The purpose of this chapter is to review current models for training school psychologists as instructional interventionists. This review will include a description of the assumptions on which training in instructional intervention is based, the core competencies necessary for school psychologists to serve as instructional interventionists, the extent to which these competencies are included in a sample of preservice school psychology programs, and the ways in which these competencies are taught. This review of assumptions, competencies, and training methods will serve as a basis for analysis of the current status of this field, and for modest proposals for its continued development.

CURRENT MODELS FOR TRAINING SCHOOL PSYCHOLOGISTS AS INSTRUCTIONAL INTERVENTIONISTS

The training of school psychologists as instructional interventionists, like any other instructional program, requires specification of (a) content, or critical skills and competencies, to be mastered; (b) methods for providing instruction; and (c) evaluation standards and procedures for assessing instructional outcomes. Ideally, persons interested in training any set of complex skills should have an empirical literature to guide their work in each of these steps. However, this type of research is too seldom available for *many* instructional domains, including the training of school psychologists as instructional interventionists. As a result, developers of instructional programs for school psychologists must rely on logical analyses or expert evaluations of content areas and post hoc assessments of training

effectiveness to guide their development and evaluation efforts.

Critical Skills for Instructional Intervention

Several documents have been developed by national organizations and panels of experts to describe core skills or competencies in school psychology (e.g., *NASP Standards for Training and Credentialing in School Psychology*, 1986; National School Psychology Inservice Training Network, 1984). Unfortunately, these documents describe competencies for instructional intervention only in the most general terms. For instance, a national panel of experts in school psychology collaborated on the development of *School Psychology: A blueprint for training and practice* (National School Psychology Inservice Training Network, 1984). This document recommends that school psychologists develop specific proficiency regarding instruction in "basic academic skills."

[t]he school psychologist should be knowledgeable about and prepared to offer consultation on major theories of learning, research on teaching basic skills, research on study skills and practices, and research on factors related to metacognitive aspects of basic skills. The school psychologist can be expected to know the types of family behaviors, teaching behaviors, and administrative practices that are related to mastery of basic skills. School psychologists should be able to help teachers master basic skills in reading, writing, mathematics, speaking, and listening. (p. 10)

Similarly, one of the *Standards for the Provision of School Psychological Services* developed by the National Association of School Psychologists (NASP, 1984) pertains to competencies for instructional intervention:

3.5.5 Educational Programming and Follow-Through. School psychologists are involved in determining options and revisions of educational programs to ensure that they are adaptive to the needs of children. The contributions of diverse cultural backgrounds should be emphasized in educational programs. School psychologists follow up on the efficacy of their recommendations. Student needs are given priority in determining educational programs. Specific educational prescriptions result from the assessment team's actions. Where a clear determination of the student's needs does not result from initial assessment, a diagnostic teaching program is offered as part of additional procedures. Regular, systematic review of the students' program is conducted and includes program modifications as necessary. (Thomas & Grimes, 1985, p. 512-513)

Along with these recommendations a small but strong collection of journal articles and textbooks is used as foundation in training school psychologists to conduct instructional interventions (e.g., Bergan & Schnaps, 1983; Deshler & Schumaker, 1988; Engelmann, Granzin, & Severson, 1979; Rosenfield, 1987). Either implicitly or explicitly, many of these documents address the identification of core skills and competencies for designing and conducting instructional interventions. For instance, Rosenfield's (1987) text, *Instructional Consultation*, is designed specifically "to present a synthesis of consultation techniques with the knowledge base about instruction to enable school psychologists to improve their effectiveness in working with teachers in the classroom around instructional issues" (p. 10). While Rosenfield does not state a set of core skills or competencies explicitly for consultants interested in instructional consultation, her list perhaps can be inferred from chapter topics and other information presented in her text. She suggests that school psychologists interested in instructional interventions must be able to (a) conduct effective problem-identification interviews; (b) conduct thorough observational and curriculum-based assessments (including an analysis of learner errors); (c) communicate effectively with and work with the classroom teacher to specify an intervention plan, and (d) evaluate existing interventions and identify possible modifications. Rosenfield

particularly emphasizes practices that reflect current research in classroom management, arrangement of consequences for academic performance, adaptation of curricular materials, and instructional presentation and management.

Professional standards and professional publications generally are helpful to persons interested in training school psychologists, but they lack the specificity necessary to design preservice or in-service training programs. Ideally, school psychology trainers would benefit from clear specification of target skills, and information on the sequencing of these skills for instruction.

For the purpose of this chapter, and in the absence of any clear empirical guidance regarding essential skills, we have conducted a logical analysis of core competencies for instructional intervention in school psychology. This logical analysis is based on general guidelines offered by professional groups and the authors of basic texts and references discussed previously. Additionally, it is based on our analysis of best practices in the assessment, planning, and implementation of instructional interventions (Fuchs & Fuchs, 1986; Meyen, Vergason, & Whelan, 1988; Ysseldyke & Marston, in press), and our own experiences conducting assessments, planning interventions, and implementing and evaluating those interventions over long periods of time. Our list of the core competencies necessary for school psychologists to serve as instructional interventionists is presented in Table 1.

We assume that the list of skills in Table 1 represents a "union set" of competencies for instructional intervention, and that all *essential* skills are included in this list. Given our assumption of the inclusive nature of this list, we presume that school psychology training programs concerned with instructional intervention will include some, if not all, of these competencies in their programs for preservice students. It is possible, however, that only subsets of these competencies will be included in some training programs. This limitation may be due to a somewhat reduced focus on

TABLE 1
Core Competencies for Instructional Interventionists in School Psychology

Psychometric Competencies	Teaching Competencies	Consultation Competencies	Intervention Competencies	Research and Evaluation Competencies
Conduct norm-referenced tests and educational diagnosis	Classroom organization	Knowledge of school systems, classroom activities, and consultation process	Identifying acceptable, effective interventions	Knowledge of basic principles of learning
Analyze published curricula	Academic presentation	Building rapport	Planning intervention	Knowledge of research on effective instruction
Assess for treatment planning	Behavior management	Defining role as instructional interventionist	Implementing intervention	Design and implementation of idiographic treatment outcome evaluations
Assess intervention effects (continuous progress monitoring)		Communication skills	Monitoring and revising intervention	
Assess for exit from special education			Termination	

instructional interventions as compared to other aspects of school psychology, or to different analyses of core competencies in this area of work.

We also assume that this list of competencies is exhaustive, and that school psychology programs will include few competencies specifically for instructional intervention that are not contained, in some way or to some degree, in Table 1. As a result of our assumptions of inclusiveness and exhaustiveness for our logical analysis, we posit that our list of core competencies is an adequate basis for comparing the focus and directions of training in instructional intervention among different university programs.

Psychometric competencies. Psychometric competencies are those associated with assessment and analysis for instructional intervention. Skills for *conducting norm-referenced testing and making educational diagnoses* are a familiar part of many school psychologists' repertoires. In this instance, *diagnosis* means the identification of children who meet administrative eligibility criteria for special programs or would otherwise benefit from additional educational assistance (Hawkins, 1979). Norm-referenced

tests are used to identify students with the greatest need for instructional intervention; in some instances, these students will be identified by traditional nosological categories (e.g., *learning disability* or *educable mental retardation*), but in other instances more functional criteria may be used (e.g., Germann & Tindal, 1985). In either case, school psychologists will be called upon often to identify children who meet administrative criteria for the provision of special interventions.

Instructional interventionists also must be able to *analyze published curricula* to identify target skills and the order in which they are to be introduced (Stein, Jenkins, & Arter, 1983; Vargas, 1984). This detailed analysis of a student's academic curriculum provides an absolute standard for planning instructional interventions and evaluating their effect for individual learners. Instructional interventionists can use the results of this analysis to *assess for treatment planning*. This level of assessment differs significantly from that conducted for determining eligibility for special interventions (Hawkins, 1979; Ysseldyke & Marston, in press) in that the interventionist must identify the skills a child has already mastered (or under what conditions such mastery is demonstrated), and identify the skills for which additional instruction is needed. Not surprisingly, this information forms the core of all intervention planning efforts.

Once a new program is implemented, the instructional interventionist must be able to *assess intervention effects and conduct continuous progress monitoring.* The instructional interventionist directly and frequently measures a pupil's performance and evaluates this information against a standard of progress (Deno, 1986; Deno & Espin, this volume). Ongoing evaluation helps interventionists and consumers decide if intervention is producing desired results or if some change in intervention is necessary.

Finally, instructional interventionists must be able to *assess for exit from special education* or reduction in special services. One of the primary assumptions of instructional intervention is that specialized services will produce gains such that a student's future need for such services is reduced or eliminated. Continuous progress monitoring should document accelerations in an individual child's academic achievement and should prompt reduction or revision in the specialized nature of intervention in response to these changes. As academic achievement in response to instructional intervention begins to approximate standard expectations, the instructional interventionist must have reliable, valid data to document the appropriateness of typical instructional programs in the absence of specialized services.

Teaching competencies. Teaching, or the organization and provision of educational activities, is a central feature of instructional intervention. School psychologists working as instructional interventionists must be able to assess different aspects of teaching to understand current problems and plan necessary revisions (Engelmann et al., 1979). Additionally, instructional interventionists must be able to conduct or implement various aspects of teaching. Actual implementation of teaching procedures is necessary when the consultant pilots new interventions, including demonstrates their use to others, or actively participates in continued intervention.

Classroom organization is a necessary precondition for effective instruction (Paine et al., 1983). A well-organized classroom has explicitly stated rules and expectations, is physically arranged for efficient use of space, and runs in an orderly and predictable fashion. As part of any intervention, a school psychologist must be able to evaluate the efficiency and effectiveness of a given classroom, and develop a plan for improving (if necessary) the organizational arrangement. The school psychologist may also help the teacher implement this new organizational plan, especially during the earliest part of intervention.

Behavior management complements classroom organization variables, helping establish and maintain behaviors that increase the likelihood that students will benefit from academic instruction (Cobb & Hops, 1973; Paine et al., 1983). Whereas classroom management variables (e.g., classroom rules, arrangement of desks and play areas) typically are molar and function as antecedents to child behavior, behavior management procedures often are highly specific and are provided as consequences for adaptive and maladaptive responses (e.g., teacher praise, response cost, or time out from reinforcement). In instructional intervention, behavior management may be designed for groups (e.g., Cobb, & Hops, 1973) or individuals (e.g., Sprick, 1981), and it may be implemented to prevent problems (e.g., Paine et al., 1983) or to remediate problems once they occur.

Academic presentation encompasses the broad array of variables necessary to present information, elicit responses, and provide feedback in any instructional content area (Berliner, 1988). Effective academic presentations include statements of instructional objectives, presentation of examples that lead learners to one and only one interpretation, frequent opportunities to respond, and high rates of both teacher praise and corrective feedback following learner responses.

Consultation competencies. As noted earlier, school psychologists typically provide indirect services to classroom teachers, who are responsible for providing actual instructional intervention. School psychologists need specific competencies to ensure positive, effective, and efficient interactions when consulting with classroom teachers.

The school psychologist functioning as an instructional interventionist must have a foundation store of *knowledge of school systems, classroom activities, and the consultation process.* This knowledge serves to frame children's and teachers' need for instructional intervention. This foundation provides a basis for estimating the social validity or acceptability of different interventions in various settings. It is presumed that interventions teachers judge to be more acceptable are more likely to be implemented, and thus are more likely to be effective (Elliott, Kratochwill, & Witt, this volume).

A school psychologist's skill at *building rapport* may directly influence the likelihood of success of an instructional intervention. As noted earlier, teachers often will expend the greatest degree of energy, and assume the greatest degree of responsibility, for implementing instructional interventions. Conventional wisdom suggests that teachers are more likely to implement new procedures or to adapt established practices if they have a personal history of positive interaction with the consultant (Caplan, 1970). Furthermore, building- and district-level identification and support of the school psychologist as instructional interventionist will enhance teachers' confidence in, and collaboration with, this outside consultant (Caplan, 1970; Meyers, Parsons, & Martin, 1979).

Communication skills are another set of competencies that are central to effective consultation (Bergan, 1977). Without the ability to communicate interest and support clearly, to understand and identify teachers' concerns or problems, and to work collaboratively to generate possible solutions, even the most creative psychologist is unlikely to succeed as an effective agent for instructional intervention.

A subset of consultation competencies relates to the design of specific instructional interventions. First, the school psychologist must be able to *identify efficient, effective interventions* for use in classroom settings. This requires knowledge of the empirical literature on instructional intervention and detailed analysis of the feasibility of any possible intervention (McConnell & Odom, 1989). This feasibility analysis must include attention to the resources available for intervention in addition to the overall acceptability of a given procedure.

Intervention competencies. The instructional interventionist must be skilled in *planning intervention.* The school psychologist, in collaboration with the teacher, must consider and synthesize information from several earlier stages of assessment and consultation, including analysis of curricula or other instructional programs (e.g., Engelmann et al., 1979); assessment of children's performance in these programs (Ysseldyke & Marston, in press); the current arrangement of school, classroom, and instructional resources for the targeted academic area (Lentz & Shapiro, 1986); and the range of interventions that can be implemented and are likely to produce significant effects in the children's classrooms. The plans must specify what is to be taught, when it is to be taught, what materials will be needed, who will provide the intervention, and how this intervention will operate. The last part, the how-to of instructional intervention, is key. Here, the consulting instructional interventionist must describe the presentation of instructional information, the types and frequencies of responses expected from the students, praise and correction procedures for possible student responses, and plans for practice, review, and assessment of introduced skills. Often, plans are presented to teachers in the form of a script, in which general procedures (e.g., correction strategies) are presented and each individual lesson is fully detailed (see Carnine & Silbert, 1979, or Walker et al.,

1983, or Paine et al., 1983, for examples). In all cases, however, the plans for implementation should be comprehensive, complete, and detailed, so that teachers or other direct intervention agents know exactly what needs to be done.

Once a plan is complete, the consultant must help teachers or others *implement the intervention*. At this level, the consultant may carry out a pilot test of the actual intervention, gaining both an opportunity to fine-tune instructional procedures and also a chance to model implementation for others. Conversely, the consultant may relieve the teacher temporarily from other responsibilities, so that more attention can be devoted to establishing a new program in the classroom. Finally, the consultant may actually provide the bulk of intervention. Although this may be logistically difficult, given the nature of many consultants' schedules, a school psychologist's participation as direct interventionist may go a long way toward establishing the importance of individualized academic programs, and the school psychologist's commitment to supporting teachers to make those interventions work.

Once intervention is initiated, the consultant will assist teachers in *monitoring and revising the intervention*, including ongoing assessment of students' performance and progress. Typically interventions require adaptations, from minor adjustments to major revisions, before desired effects are obtained. To do this, the consultant might meet periodically (e.g., biweekly or weekly) with the teacher to discuss actual implementation of intervention procedures and review student progress data to evaluate performance. Any changes should be made deliberately and systematically (Deno, 1986; Deno & Mirkin, 1977), and should be based on information like that considered in the original design of intervention.

Finally, the consultant should be prepared to *terminate* his or her involvement in an intervention program. For example, the consultant might terminate involvement when all intervention goals have been achieved and specialized programming ends. Or the consultant

might terminate involvement when the teacher no longer requires assistance to operate the intervention effectively. Since the acquisition of intervention skills by the consultee is an ideal among consultation goals, the consultant should gradually increase the degree to which the classroom teacher makes all decisions regarding the design, implementation, evaluation, and revision of intervention programs.

Research and evaluation competencies. Research and evaluation is perhaps one of the most overlooked groups of core competencies for school psychologists interested in instructional intervention. In all likelihood, school psychologists are the sole professionals at the local building level who have direct training in reviewing, designing, and implementing educational research. As a result, school psychologists can increase the impact of empirical knowledge on the day-to-day practice of classroom education, and can provide the most direct resource for designing and implementing systematic research, development, and evaluation efforts (McConnell, 1990).

Knowledge of *basic principles of learning* serves as foundation for this set of competencies. This body of knowledge includes information on basic behavioral development (Bijou & Baer, 1961), educational psychology (Becker, 1986), and the applications of basic laws of learning to the design and implementation of instructional programs (Engelmann & Carnine, 1982; Heward, Heron, Hill, & Trap-Porter, 1984; Meyen, Vergason, & Whelan, 1988). This foundational knowledge also might include some familiarity with the models of normal cognitive development inspired primarily by Jean Piaget (Flavell, 1985), as well as post-Piagetian treatments of this topic (Carey, 1985); it should be noted, however, that the direct links between this base knowledge and school learning (especially for students at risk for instructional problems and those with educational handicaps) are only recently being investigated. *Knowledge of research on effective instruction* (Berliner, 1988; Wittrock, 1986) provides the specific content necessary for instructional intervention. Taken together, knowledge of established principles of learning along with information on recent research on effective instruction provides a basic framework for analyzing students' current performance and for designing program adaptations or improvements. Thus, facility with these concepts can be seen as key to effective instructional intervention.

This basic knowledge of empirical research becomes operational when the school psychologist masters design and implementation techniques for *idiographic evaluation of treatment outcomes*. While a host of evaluation approaches exist for use in the schools (McConnell, in press), school psychologists generally will find single-case research and evaluation methods most useful (Tawney & Gast, 1984; Deno, 1986). These evaluation designs enable interventions to study in careful detail the process of instruction and to systematically evaluate any modifications to an initial treatment plan. Furthermore, these procedures are adapted easily for use in classroom settings and thus represent an essential component of school-based evaluation of instructional and other intervention programs (McConnell, in press).

Core competencies and current training practice. As noted earlier, the competencies presented in Table 1 are the result of our logical analysis of available literature and accepted best practices in instructional intervention. While logical analysis appears necessary, given the current dearth of empirical guidance, this approach may be limited by several factors. First, while "competencies" identified in this manner may have face validity, they may lack any functional utility for achieving the goal at hand. That is, competencies described here may sound good, but may not *truly* be necessary for a school psychologist to function competently as an instructional interventionist. Second, these competencies may not be distinct; instead, several of the "core competencies" presented here may covary to the extent that they form a single

response class for effective instructional intervention. Third, competencies that are indeed critical may not be included. These missing competencies may be identified by another logical analysis or by empirical research, but may fail to appear on our current list. As a result of these three possible limitations, the current analysis of core competencies should be seen as descriptive but not empirical and should be used primarily for heuristic purposes.

Methods of Training for Core Competencies

Like our assumption that school psychology training programs can be compared as to the extent to which they include core competencies for instructional intervention in their preservice training program, we similarly assume that programs can be compared by the procedures used to teach these competencies to students. Specifically, school psychology programs can differ in the extent to which competencies are taught *directly* through structured activities (i.e., coursework or supervised practica) or taught *indirectly* through less formal experiences. Furthermore, programs can differ in the extent to which they require conceptual versus behavioral mastery of core competencies.

Direct instruction or training is distinguished by a systematic, scheduled, and sequenced introduction of information to a learner or group of learners. It may include didactic presentation and/or behavioral rehearsal, and may take place in classes, clinics, or practicum placements. In any instance, however, this instruction is fully integrated into a regularly scheduled plan of study. Indirect instruction lacks any systematic plan for the introduction, sequencing, or practice of core competencies. Instead, the student is presumed to master a given competency and demonstrate proficiency *outside* of formally scheduled training activities. Like direct instruction, this learning may take place in classrooms or clinics, but indirect instruction in school psychology is generally presumed to occur primarily in practicum and internship placements and similar settings.

Programs can be differentiated by the ways in which mastery of core competencies is demonstrated by learners (Walker, Hops, & Greenwood, 1984). Conceptual mastery is demonstrated in instructional intervention when a student can describe and/or discriminate essential features of a treatment procedure but has not necessarily demonstrated proficiency in the application of a given skill. Conceptual mastery is assessed through performance on verbal or paper-and-pencil tests, or through labeling and describing ongoing interventions. Behavioral mastery, on the other hand, is demonstrated when a student applies an essential feature of intervention in an analogue or criterion setting. This demonstration may be performed across a variety of settings, time periods, and perhaps even content domains. Behavioral mastery usually is assessed through some form of direct observation, including role-play tests, supervisor observations, consumer rating forms, or self-monitoring and self-report.

Few school psychology training programs will represent "pure types" of methods for teaching competencies or demonstrating mastery in instructional intervention; instead, it is more likely that instruction will vary along continua of behavioral-to-conceptual mastery and direct-to-indirect instruction. As with our list of core competencies, however, we believe these distinctions have heuristic value for describing current practices in school psychology training and for planning direct research in this area in the future.

SURVEY OF CURRENT PRACTICES FOR TRAINING INSTRUCTIONAL INTERVENTIONS

Survey Procedures

As noted earlier, there is little empirical guidance for persons interested in training school psychologists as instructional interventionists. As a result, we can reasonably expect variations in the ways

this training is currently provided. To assess and describe these variations we surveyed a group of leading school psychology training programs.

Eight APA-approved school psychology programs were selected for this survey. The schools represented a range of training and psychological service approaches, as reflected in their respective reputations, research, and training practices. A telephone interview was conducted for each program with a faculty member or senior graduate student who was familiar with the program's training requirements. We requested that respondents identify the instructional intervention competencies required for each graduate of their entry-level program, how these competencies were taught, and how mastery was demonstrated. For comparison, all responses were referenced against competencies listed in Table 1.

The survey design was based on the assumption that instructional intervention competencies would indeed be specified as requirements for completion of each participating program. During our interviews, it became apparent that while many skills are described as "required," some of them are assumed to be mastered during field or practicum experiences. Thus, the survey results are likely to overestimate the degree to which school psychology training programs demand acquisition of some competencies, particularly behavioral mastery in consultation and in teaching techniques. This assumption that students master skills in practicum and internship has implications for the quality of training being provided and will be addressed in the Discussion section.

Survey Results

A summary of survey results is presented in Table 2, with responses from each of the participating programs tallied for each core competency. Programs that reported no direct instruction in a given competency area, but assumed that the students mastered this area in practica or other informal situations, were considered to offer "indirect instruction only." Programs that presented information in courses and assessed students' mastery through written or oral examinations were assumed to provide instruction for "conceptual mastery." Programs that extended coursework or practicum experiences to test specifically the students' application in a given competency area were assumed to teach to "behavioral mastery."

Analysis of these data suggests that school psychology training programs require students to gain competence in several areas that are central to instructional intervention. All programs require some demonstrated competency in each of five skill areas: psychometrics, consultation, teaching techniques, intervention, and research and evaluation. In the areas of consultation and intervention, all programs require conceptual and/or behavioral mastery of each identified core competency. The requirements for the three remaining skill areas vary to a larger extent across schools. For example, in the psychometric skills area, conceptual (if not behavioral) mastery of some types of norm-referenced testing and educational diagnosis are required by all schools. However, one program does not require skill in assessment for monitoring of treatment effects, and only five of the remaining schools demand behavioral as well as conceptual mastery of this skill.

In addition, there is some degree of variability in requirements across competency areas. For example, while all schools require mastery of competencies in norm-referenced testing and educational diagnosis, fewer schools specify mastery of teaching techniques in academic presentation, classroom organization, and behavior management. In fact, only two schools require high degrees of mastery for teaching effectiveness and classroom management.

Variability is also noted at the level of individual schools as well. While School #3 does not require competence in assessment for monitoring of treatment effects, it does specify consultative competencies in the monitoring and revision of treatment, research and evaluation of the design and implementation of idiographic treatment evaluation, and design and

implementation of treatment outcome studies. In contrast, School #4 requires psychometric and consultative competencies in treatment monitoring, but does not require research and evaluation skills in conducting treatment outcome studies.

Schools also vary across skill areas in the degree to which they require behavioral versus conceptual mastery of individual competencies. A large majority of schools require both conceptual and behavioral mastery of all listed competencies in the area of consultation. However, these results suggest that some training programs require lower levels of mastery for the rest of the skill areas. For example, while six of the schools require training in the identification of critical variables for effective academic presentation (e.g., pacing, providing correction), four of these programs require mastery of didactic material only, two require that students demonstrate behavioral mastery of assessment, and only one program expects students to actually perform academic presentations. Similarly, whereas six schools require competence in assessment for exit from special education or reduction in special services (reevaluation and/or continuous progress monitoring), only two of these programs require that students actually demonstrate this skill. The four remaining programs specify that only conceptual mastery of this skill is needed.

The omission of several issues in our survey may have affected our understanding of these results. First, the questionnaire solicited yes/no responses to the question "Are the following competencies specified requirements for students in your training program"; it is likely that schools responded positively for optional courses or competencies. Thus, our results may describe what students *can* learn, rather than what they *must* learn. Similarly, our survey was not limited to masters or doctoral level training programs, and our questions did not elicit a distinction between requirements for these two degrees. Furthermore, the survey did not gather information on the extent to which skills are actually taught and mastered. Thus, it is possible that

TABLE 2
Percentage of Doctoral School Psychology Programs
Requiring Mastery of Core Competencies

Competency	Instruction Provided			
	None	Indirect Only	Conceptual Mastery	Behavioral Mastery
Psychometric Competencies				
Conduct norm-referenced tests and educational diagnosis	0	0	12.5	87.5
Analyze published curricula	37.5	0	50	12.5
Assess for treatment planning	0	12.5	25	65.2
Assess intervention effects (continuous progress monitoring)	12.5	0	25	62.5
Assess for program exit	25	0	50	25
Teaching Competencies				
Classroom organization				
Assessing	12.5	0	62.5	25
Conducting	25	25	25	25
Academic presentation				
Assessing	25	0	50	25
Conducting	50	0	37.5	12.5
Behavior management				
Assessing	0	12.5	50	37.5
Conducting	25	25	12.5	37.5
Consultation Competencies				
Knowledge of school systems, classroom activities, and consultation process	0	0	12.5	87.5
Building rapport	0	12.5	0	87.5
Defining role as instructional interventionist	0	12.5	25	67.5
Communication skills	0	12.5	0	87.5
Intervention Competencies				
Identifying acceptable, effective interventions	0	0	12.5	87.5
Planning intervention	0	12.5	12.5	75
Implementing intervention	0	25	0	75
Monitoring and revising intervention	0	12.5	0	87.5
Termination	0	37.5	12.5	50

(Table 2, continued)

Competency	Instruction Provided			
	None	Indirect Only	Conceptual Mastery	Behavioral Mastery
Research and Evaluation Competencies				
Basic principles of learning	0	0	75	25
Research on effective instruction	0	0	75	25
Design and implementation of idio-graphic treatment outcome evaluations	0	0	25	75
Design and implementation of group or program outcome evaluations	37.5	0	25	37.5

respondents for two schools may respond that they require conceptual mastery of the analysis of published curricula, but differ greatly in the extent to which they teach this skill: One school may require attendance at a single lecture on analyzing published curricula, while the other may require a course with numerous readings or a term paper on the subject. Finally, it is difficult to assess the state of flux for participating school psychology training programs. Although some training programs may be on the cutting edge of research and practice in our field, others may serve as the enduring core of an area of fading importance. We interpret our findings in light of traditions and recent developments in the field of school psychology; however, our survey was designed to describe the present state of practice for training in instructional interventions. We presume that responses for individual programs may change in the months and years ahead.

In sum, the results of the survey show much variability in program requirements within all skill areas except consultation, as well as variability in the levels of mastery required within individual programs. In addition, all schools specify only conceptual mastery for some competencies. These results raise numerous important questions about training content, process, and evaluation in instructional

intervention education in school psychology programs.

Implications of Survey Results

The results of this small survey raise several questions and issues regarding current and future practice in training school psychologists as instructional interventionists. First, competencies required by a large fraction of the surveyed schools can be assumed to have wide, almost universal, support for their importance in instructional intervention. For instance, all schools require competence in some type of norm-referenced testing and educational diagnosis; in all but one case, training programs require that students demonstrate *behavioral* mastery in this area. Psychometric evaluation has long served as the core of school psychology practice, and these results seem to reflect some continued support for this professional function. Our results also indicate some movement in this area: Several respondents indicated that innovative alternative methods of educational assessment and diagnosis (e.g., curriculum-based measurement) are being introduced into their programs while some focus is maintained on "traditional" psychometric methods in educational decision making. For instance, one school described a recent effort to reorganize core assessment courses to de-emphasize, but not eliminate, intelligence testing as one part of educational assessment. Time previously devoted to training in intelligence testing now will be devoted to instruction in observational and curriculum-based assessment for determining special education eligibility and planning instructional programs. In this way, training programs are integrating newer procedures into a general area of competence that is well accepted as a core element of school psychology practice.

Additionally, all responding programs require some level of competence in consultation, apparently reflecting a recent and flourishing trend toward increased indirect provision of services in school psychology (Graden et al., 1988). As can be seen, however, there is still some variability in the specific consultation skills required and in the methods with which these skills are taught. This suggests continued need for identification of core skills in consultation and increased specification of best practices for training preservice students in these skills.

While widescale adoption of certain competencies may indicate almost universal support for them in the practice of school psychology, alternative explanations can also be advanced. Rather than reflecting the importance of these competencies to practice, it may be that training programs give relatively more attention to those skills that can be most effectively taught or most directly evaluated. Consider, for example, training in individualized achievement testing using commercially published tests as one component of preparation for providing instructional intervention. Although some would argue that these types of norm-referenced evaluations are relatively unimportant for planning or evaluating instructional programs (e.g., Carver, 1974; Fuchs & Fuchs, 1986), school psychology trainers have identified specific behavioral standards for standardized test administration, scoring, and interpretation (e.g., Sattler, 1988). Other, more innovative approaches to educational diagnosis and assessment, such as observational assessment (Alessi, 1988) or educational error analysis (Vargas, 1984), may present more complex instructional and evaluative challenges for school psychology trainers. In fact, critical skills or competencies in these areas are being identified only now.

Competencies that are less frequently included in school psychology training programs may be viewed similarly in terms of their historical position in school psychology. For instance, relatively few of the programs sampled here expected their students to demonstrate mastery in the analysis of published curricula or the application of specific teaching competencies. These omissions may be due to the historical practice of requiring teaching experience prior to entry into school psychology training and to a presumption that skills of this sort were covered in earlier teacher training programs. Similarly, training in these two areas may raise "turf issues" between school psychologists and teachers. In this circumstance, whether students have completed teacher training or not, instructional competencies may be seen as outside of a school psychology program's appropriate domain.

It also is possible that competencies included by relatively few programs in our survey are not in fact prerequisite for effective practice as an instructional interventionist in school psychology. This may explain in part why few programs require students to analyze published curricula or to master specific teaching skills. We included these competencies in our evaluation primarily for two reasons: First, it was assumed that the design and implementation of effective instructional interventions require that school psychologists be able to participate fully in all phases of intervention and that this involvement might vary from simple demonstration of procedures for participating teachers to actual collaboration in the implementation of in-class programs. Second, we assumed that prior mastery of these competencies might increase the probability that school psychologists will design and recommend interventions that classroom teachers will find feasible and acceptable and will be more likely to implement (cf. McConnell & Odom, 1989).

However, some empirical research is still needed to establish the relative importance of these skill areas, as well as many others included in our analysis. We expect, however, that such research will identify positive contributions from competence in these areas, and we encourage educators and trainers to consider these goals in their design and evaluation of training programs and research activities.

Variability *across* skill areas also raises questions related to the comprehensive nature of training for individual programs. For example, not all schools require psychometric, consultative, and research/evaluation competencies in treatment monitoring. Common wisdom would suggest, however, that treatment monitoring will be most effective when psychologists design or select appropriate assessment tools (i.e., psychometric competence), select an appropriate design for evaluating students' progress (i.e., research and evaluation competencies), and analyze and synthesize data in a way that helps the classroom teacher make solid, data-based decisions regarding a child's programs (i.e., consultation skills). While each of these skill areas may be important in isolation, instructional interventions benefit most when competencies across these areas are integrated. Again, however, more empirical research is needed to identify how much these more complex skill repertoires contribute to effective instructional intervention.

Finally, considerable variation was noted in the type of mastery required for individual competencies. In all content areas (but especially assessment, teaching, and research/evaluation), a number of programs require only conceptual mastery of at least some competencies. Some critical aspects of instructional intervention (e.g., assessment to plan instructional interventions or to exit children from special education; designing behavior management and classroom organization programs) are being covered by many school psychology programs in classes only; students are expected to participate in discussions, write papers, or answer test questions in these content areas, but they are not required to demonstrate that they can *apply* the knowledge acquired in college courses to situations in preschool, elementary, or secondary classrooms. It often is assumed that adults, especially those with the skills needed to be admitted to graduate school, will transfer skills learned verbally in a classroom easily (perhaps "automatically") to application in a much broader range of situations. However, it appears that adults, like our young clients, are more likely to transfer skills and knowledge to new situations when training programs are specifically designed to promote generalization and maintenance of performance (Stokes & Ossnes, 1986).

Explicit programming for generalization requires a much tighter link between didactic presentation, demonstration of conceptual mastery, and standards for behavioral mastery of the core competencies in school psychology training programs. For instance, one responding program submitted the following description of its procedures for providing students with a wide range of situations for instruction and practice in instructional intervention. First, information on intervention planning is described and tested in class; at this level, conceptual mastery is demonstrated. Next, the students work with university faculty and more experienced students to conduct treatment planning evaluations in an on-campus psychoeducational clinic; at this level, behavioral mastery is first demonstrated. Repeated practice across cases and content areas is provided as the students continue their involvement in the clinic. Finally, the students complete practica in applied settings, where supervisors are asked to provide explicit evaluation of treatment planning activities. Across this range of activities, students demonstrate their mastery of the application of a given competency while being given a wide range of opportunities for practice with feedback. This combination would be expected to produce a well-generalized set of skills for the new school psychologist, and provides some assurance that the students are well prepared for their professional roles.

**Future Directions in
Preservice and Inservice Training**

The survey results presented here highlight several future directions that might be considered in expanding and improving current training in instructional intervention for school psychologists. First, it is clear that more research is needed to identify those skills or competencies that are essential for instructional interventionists who work primarily in consultative roles. As noted earlier, there is a broad and well-developed literature that describes key features of instructional interventions. However, there has been relatively little attention to the ways in which these individual features fit together to form a comprehensive approach to consultation for instructional intervention. Some well-considered descriptions exist to guide this practice (e.g., Bergan & Schnaps, 1983; Rosenfield, 1987), and indeed a small amount of research has been conducted to evaluate the efficacy of different approaches to instructional intervention (e.g., Graden, Casey, & Bonstrom, 1985). To date, however, practitioners and trainers must rely on personal experiences, expert opinions, and tradition to guide much of the design and implementation of instructional interventions in school psychology.

In a related vein, more research is needed to establish the social validity of different approaches to instructional intervention employed by school psychologists. Empirical evaluations of the necessary features of instructional intervention can be expected to identify a wide range of skills or behaviors that make it *possible* for school psychologists to produce changes in classroom programs to improve the academic achievement and classroom deportment of handicapped and high-risk students. However, it may be that these "necessary" features vary as to how acceptable they are judged by classroom teachers, or how likely they are to lead to more effective interactions between teacher and psychologist in the future. When two or more procedures are likely to achieve similar effects, but differ in their acceptance by teachers, we assume that the preferred intervention should be implemented. To accommodate teachers' preferences, both preservice and in-service school psychologists will need information on the relative acceptance or social validity of different components of instructional intervention (Elliott, Kratochwill, & Witt, this volume), as well as the degree to which acceptance influences the implementation and overall impact of any given intervention (McConnell & Odom, 1989).

The results of this survey also suggest a need to evaluate critically the methods we use to train school psychologists in instructional intervention. While a small amount of research has been conducted on training effectiveness in instructional intervention (e.g., Brown, Kratochwill, & Bergan, 1982; Veltum & Miltenberger, 1989), most evaluations of graduate programs in school psychology consist of surveys and internal or external evaluations written for accreditation or other administrative reviews. This general dearth of empirical evaluation of preservice training programs is true for many fields of education (McCollum & McCartan, 1988). In school psychology, a discipline that prides itself on careful attention to empirical evaluation (Stoner, Shinn, & McConnell, 1989), it seems essential that trainers increase their attention to empirical evaluation and the identification of best practices for education in preservice and in-service programs.

In the absence of empirical guidance, one step that trainers might consider in program design is the closer integration of didactic instruction, analogue practice, and practicum/internship experiences. Given the weak evidence for a "hope and train" approach to generalization of behavior change (Stokes & Osnes, 1986) and the uncontrolled and sometimes undesired effects of practicum placements in education (McCollum & McCartan, 1988), one simply cannot assume that students will master skills as intended except when acquisition and practice are carefully planned to move from information to application to practice with feedback under a wide range of conditions.

In summary, school psychologists have firmly established their intent to contribute to the design and implementation of interventions that improve instructional outcomes for a wide range of students in U.S. schools. Furthermore, our discipline has moved toward the development of a variety of both direct and indirect service delivery models for including school psychologists in instructional interventions. In this chapter, we have described a model in which school psychologists assume a consultative yet active role in the design, implementation, and evaluation of instructional interventions, and we have presented a logical analysis of necessary skills for this type of intervention. Eight school psychology programs with national reputations of excellence were surveyed regarding the extent to which these critical skills were included in their training, and the ways in which instruction was provided. The results of this survey indicated some commonalities across programs in standards of performance for competence in psychometric evaluation and consultation, but more variability across programs in the areas of teaching, intervention, and research competencies for instructional intervention.

Instructional intervention holds a central place in the expanding definition of school psychology, and training programs are responding to this change by increasing their attention to preservice preparation in related areas. Yet it is clear that much of this training must proceed at present without the benefit of close empirical guidance. School psychology has a long and rich tradition of systematically studying and developing more effective educational programs; it may now be time to turn that tradition to the task of training our future colleagues.

REFERENCES

Alessi, G. (1988). Direct observation methods for emotional/behavioral problems. In E. S. Shapiro and T. R. Kratochwill (Eds.), *Behavioral assessment in schools: Conceptual foundations and practical applications* (pp. 14-75). New York: Guilford.

Algozzine, B., Christenson, S., & Ysseldyke, J. (1982). Probabilities associated with the referral to placement process. *Teacher Education and Special Education, 4,* 19-23.

Bardon, J. (1988). Alternative educational delivery approaches: Implications for school psychology. In J. Graden, J. Zins, & M. Curtis (Eds.), *Alternative educational delivery systems: Enhancing instructional options for all students* (pp. 563-571). Washington, DC: NASP.

Becker, W. C. (1986). *Applied psychology for teachers: A behavioral-cognitive approach.* Chicago: Science Research Associates.

Becker, W. C., Engelmann, S., & Thomas, D. R. (1975). *Teaching 2: Cognitive learning and instruction.* Chicago: Science Research Associates.

Bergan, J. R. (1977). *Behavioral consultation.* Columbus, OH: Merrill.

Bergan, J. R., & Schnaps, A. (1983). A model for instructional consultation. In J. Alpert & J. Meyers (Eds.), *Training in consultation* (pp. 104-119). Springfield, IL: Thomas.

Berliner, D. (1988). Effective classroom management and instruction: A knowledge base for consultation. In J. Graden, J. Zins, & M. Curtis (Eds.), *Alternative educational delivery systems: Enhancing instructional options for all students* (pp. 309-325). Washington, DC: NASP.

Bijou, S. W., & Baer, D. M. (1961). *Child development I: A systematic and empirical theory.* New York: Appleton-Century-Crofts.

Brown, D. K., Kratochwill, T. R., & Bergan, J. R. (1982). Teaching interview skills for problem identification: An analogue study. *Behavioral Assessment, 4,* 63-73.

Caplan, G. (1970). *The theory and practice of mental health consultation.* New York: Basic Books.

Carey, S. (1985). *Conceptual change in childhood.* Cambridge, MA: MIT Press.

Carnine, D., & Silbert, J. (1979). *Direct instruction reading.* Columbus, OH: Merrill.

Carver, R. P. (1974). Two dimensions of tests: Psychometric vs. edumetric. *American Psychologist, 29,* 512-518.

Cobb, J. A., & Hops, H. (1973). Effects of academic survival skill training on low achieving first graders. *Journal of Educational Research, 67,* 108-113.

Deno, S. L. (1986). Formative evaluation of individual student programs: A new role for school psychologists. *School Psychology Review, 15,* 358-374.

Deno, S. L., Marston, D., & Mirkin, P. (1982). Valid measurement procedures for continuous revaluation of written expression. *Exceptional Children, 48,* 368-371.

Deno, S. L., & Mirkin, P. K. (1977). *Data-based program modification: A manual.* Reston, VA: Council for Exceptional Children.

Deno, S. L., Mirkin, P. K., & Chiang, B. (1982). Identifying valid measures of reading. *Exceptional Children, 49,* 36-45.

Deschler, D. D., & Schumaker, J. B. (1988). An instructional model for teaching students how to learn. In J. L. Graden, J. E. Zins, & M. J. Curtis (Eds.), *Alternative educational delivery systems: Enhancing instructional options for all students* (pp. 391-411). Washington, DC: National Association of School Psychologists.

Engelmann, E., & Carnine, D. (1982). *Theory of instruction.* New York: Irvington.

Engelmann, S., Granzin, A., & Severson, H. (1979). Diagnosing instruction. *Journal of Special Education, 13,* 355-363.

Finn, J., & Resnick, L. (1984). Issues in the instruction of mildly mentally retarded children. *Educational Researcher,* 9-11.

Flavel, J. H. (1985). *Cognitive development* (2nd ed.). Englewood Cliffs, NJ: Prentice-Hall.

Fuchs, L., & Fuchs, D. (1986). Linking assessment to intervention: An introduction. *School Psychology Review, 15,* 318-324.

Gallagan, J. (1985). Psychological educational testing: Turn out the lights, the party's over. *Exceptional Children, 52,* 288-299.

Germann, G., & Tindal, G. (1985). An application of curriculum-based assessment: The use of direct and repeated measurement. *Exceptional Children, 52,* 244-265.

Giangreco, M., & Meyer, L. (1988). Expanding service delivery options in regular schools and classrooms for students with severe disabilities.

Graden, J., Casey, A., & Bonstrom, O. (1985). Implementing a prereferral intervention system: Part II: The data. *Exceptional Children, 51,* 487-496.

Graden, J., Zins, J., & Curtis, M. (Eds.). (1988). *Alternative educational delivery systems: Enhancing instructional options for all students.* Washington, DC: NASP.

Graden, J., Zins, J., Curtis, M., & Cobb, C. (1988). The need for alternatives in educational services. In J. Graden, J. Zins, & M. Curtis (Eds.), *Alternative educational delivery systems: Enhancing instructional options for all students* (pp. 3-16). Washington, DC: NASP.

Green, K. D., Forehand, R., Beck, S. J., & Vosk, B. (1980). An assessment of the relationship among measures of children's social competence and children's academic achievement. *Child Development, 51,* 1149-1156.

Hawkins, R. P. (1979). The functions of assessment: Implications for selection and development of devices for assessing repertoires in clinical, educational, and other settings. *Journal of Applied Behavior Analysis, 12,* 501-516.

Heward, W. L., Heron, T. E., Hill, D. S., & Trap-Porter, J. (1984). *Focus on behavior analysis in education.* Columbus, OH: Merrill.

Lentz, E., & Shapiro, E. S. (1986). Functional assessment of the academic environment. *School Psychology Review, 15,* 346-357.

Lyon, S., & Lyon, G. (1980). Team functioning and staff development: A role release approach to providing integrated educational services for severely handicapped students. *Journal of the Association for the Severely Handicapped, 5,* 250-263.

McCollum, J., & McCartan, K. (1988). Research in teacher education: Issues and future directions in early childhood special education. In S. L. Odom & M. G. Karnes (Eds.), *Early intervention for infants and children with handicaps: An empirical base* (pp. 269-286). Baltimore: Brookes.

McConnell, S. R. (1990). Best practices in evaluating educational programs. In A. Thomas & J. Grimes (Eds.), *Best practices in school psychology* (2nd ed.). Washington, DC: NASP.

McConnell, S. R., & Odom, S. L. (1989). *Factors affecting the implementation of social interaction skill interventions in early childhood special educational settings.* Unpublished manuscript, University of Minnesota, Vanderbilt-Minnesota Social Interaction Project.

McConnell, S. R., Strain, P. S., Kerr, M. M., Stagg, V., Lenkner, D., & Lambert, D. (1984). An empirical definition of school adjustment: Selection of target behaviors for a comprehensive treatment program. *Behavior Modification, 8,* 451-473.

Messick S. (1984). Placing children in special education: Findings of the National Academy of Sciences Panel. *Educational Researcher,* 3-8.

Meyen, E. L., Vergason, G. A., & Whelan, R. J. (1988). *Effective instructional strategies for exceptional children.* Denver: Love.

Meyers, J. (1980). *Consultation skills: How teachers can maximize help from specialists in schools.* Washington, DC: American Association of Colleges for Teacher Education.

Meyers, J., Parsons, R. D., & Martin, R. (1979). *Mental health consultation in the schools.* San Francisco: Jossey-Bass.

National Association of School Psychologists. (1986). *Standards for training and credentialing in school psychology.* Washington, DC: NASP.

Paine, S., Radicchi, J., Rosellini, L., Deutchman, L., & Derch, C. (1983). *Structuring your classroom for academic success.* Champaign, IL: Research Press.

Rosenfield, S. (1987). *Instructional consultation.* Hillsdale, NJ: Erlbaum.

Sattler, J. M. (1988). *Assessment of children* (3rd ed.). San Diego: Jerome M. Sattler.

Shinn, M., Tindal, G., & Stein, S. (1988). Curriculum-based assessment and the identification of mildly handicapped students: A research review. *Professional School Psychology, 3* 69-85.

Sprick, R. (1981). *The solution book.* Chicago: Science Research Associates.

Stainback, S., & Stainback, W. (1988). Changes needed to strengthen regular education. In J. Graden, J. Zins, & M. Curtis (Eds.), *Alternative educational delivery systems: Enhancing instructional options for all students* (pp. 17-32). Washington, DC: NASP.

Stein, M., Jenkins, J., & Arter, J. (1983). Designing successful mathematics instruction for low-performing students. *Focus on Learning Problems in Mathematics, 5,* 79-99.

Stokes, T., & Osnes, P. (1986). Programming the generalization of children's social behavior. In P. Strain, M. Guralnick, & H. Walker (Eds.), *Children's social behavior: Development, assessment and modification* (pp. 407-443). New York: Academic.

Stoner, G., Shinn, M., & McConnell, S. (1989). *Applied behavior analysis and school psychology: Current relationships, future directions, and implications for research, practices, and training in school psychology.* Paper presented at the Fifteenth Annual Convention, Association for Behavior Analysis, Milwaukee, WI.

Tawney, J., & Gast, D. (1984). *Single-subject research in special education.* Columbus, OH: Merrill.

Thomas, A., & Grimes, J. (1985). *Best practices in school psychology.* Washington, DC: NASP.

Vargas, J. S. (1984). What are your exercises teaching? An analysis of stimulus control in instructional materials. In W. L. Heward, T. E. Heron, D. S. Hill, & J. Trap-Porter (Eds.), *Focus on behavior analysis in education* (pp. 126-141). Columbus, OH: Merrill.

Veltum, L. G., & Miltenberger, R. G. (1989). Evaluation of a self-instructional package for training assessment interviewing skills. *Behavioral Assessment, 11,* 165-177.

Walker, H. M., Hops, H., & Greenwood, C. R. (1984). The CORBEH research and development model: Programmatic issues and strategies. In S. Paine, G. T. Bellamy, & B. L. Wilcox (Eds.), *Human services that work: From innovation to standard practice* (pp. 57-78). Baltimore, MD: Brookes.

Walker, H., McConnell, S., Holmes, D., Walker, J., Todis, B., & Golden, N. (1983). *The Walker Social Skills Curriculum: ACCEPTS.* Austin, TX: Pro-Ed.

Wang, M., Reynolds, M., & Walberg, H. (Eds.). (1987-1988). *Handbook for special education: Research and practice* (Vols. 1-3). London: Pergamon.

Witt, J., & Martens, B. (1988). Problems with problem solving consultation: A re-analysis of assumptions, methods and goals. *School Psychology Review, 17,* 211-226.

Wittrock, M. C. (1986). *Handbook of research on teaching* (3rd ed.). New York: Macmillan.

Ysseldyke, J. E., & Marston, D. (in press). The use of assessment information to plan instructional interventions. In C. R. Reynolds & T. Gutkin (Eds.), *The handbook of school psychology* (2nd ed.). New York: Wiley.

Ysseldyke, J., Algozzine, B., Regan, R., & McGue, M. (1981). The influence of test scores and naturally occurring pupil characteristics on psychological decision making with children. *Journal of School Psychology, 19,* 167-177.

Ysseldyke, J., Thurlow, M., Graden, J., Wesson, C., Algozzine, B., & Deno, S. (1983). Generalizations from five years of research on assessment and decision making: The University of Minnesota Institute. *Exceptional Children Quarterly, 41,* 75-93.

Zins, J., Curtis, M., Graden, J., & Ponti, C. (1988). *Helping students succeed in the regular classroom.* San Francisco: Jossey-Bass.

34

Behavior Disorders: Training Needs for School Psychologists

William R. Jenson
University of Utah

Hill M. Walker
University of Oregon

Elaine Clark
University of Utah

Thomas Kehle
University of Connecticut

INTRODUCTION

This chapter focuses on the training of school psychologists to work effectively with behaviorally disordered students. Behaviorally disordered students will be described as basically those children who engage in behavioral excesses such as aggression and noncompliance. Withdrawn, anxious, or phobic students who show primary internalizing problems will not be included or covered here because they are less frequently referred for services and have fundamentally different problems. Withdrawn students are in need of services, but these services are qualitatively different from those appropriate for aggressive, acting-out students.

The children most frequently referred to mental health services, psychiatric hospitals, and special education fall into the behaviorally disordered category (as reviewed by Morgan & Jenson, 1988). Kauffman (1985) has estimated that 6–10% of all school-age children need some type of special education services because they are behaviorally disordered. The table of contents of this volume reads like the priority special education services list of many school districts: truancy, stealing, swearing, aggression, lying and cheating, attention problems, oppositional behav-

ior, and vandalism. These areas are also considered serious problems by teachers. For example, not following classroom rules, aggression, disrupting the class, and defying the teacher are only a few problems associated with behaviorally disordered students that are ranked as serious problems by teachers (Nicholsen, 1989; Walker, 1983; Walker & Fabre, 1987; Walker, Severson, & Haring, 1987). Table 1 provides a listing of adaptive behaviors that behaviorally disordered children engage in too infrequently and maladaptive behaviors they engage in too frequently (Walker & Fabre, 1987). In addition, Walker and Fabre (1987) also cite a list of teacher-rated critical behaviors that regardless of frequency have serious developmental implications (Table 2). These behaviors, even if they occur once, will usually result in a referral.

The relative stability and long-term negative developmental outcomes associated with these behavior problems are also of concern. Problems such as aggression, arguing, and tantrums appear to remain stable over many years unless effective interventions are applied systematically (Achenbach & Edelbrock, 1981; Kazdin, 1985; Olweus, 1979). Likewise, the general outcome for many behaviorally disordered students who

TABLE 1
Adaptive and Maladaptive Classroom Behaviors in Order of Frequency of Referrals

• Follows classroom rules	• Talks out of turn
• Complies with teachers' demands	• Gets out of seat
• Takes turns	• Whines
• Listens to teacher instructions	• Disturbs others
• Makes assistance needs known	• Defies the teacher
• Produces work of acceptable quality	• Disrupts the class
• Attends to assigned tasks	• Does not complete assignments
• Volunteers	

tend to exhibit these behaviors is poor. Behaviorally disordered children who are aggressive and noncompliant typically continue to have major problems throughout their school-age lives and into adulthood (Walker et al., 1986; Robins, 1974, 1979). Estimates vary, but 70–80% of aggressive, antisocial children are thought to experience extremely poor adjustment to adult life, with problems such as frequent changes in employment, divorce, substance abuse, psychiatric problems, and incarceration (Morris, Escoll, & Wexler, 1956; Robins, 1974, 1979).

Ample evidence exists to suggest that the problems associated with behaviorally disordered children are manifested frequently, are serious, and have significant long-term consequences for the child and society at large. School psychologists who can effectively intervene to attenuate these problems are in demand. Some program models exist in the special education area for the management of behaviorally disordered children, and these models have generally been associated with university training programs (Hewett & Taylor, 1980; Hewett & Forness, 1977; Jenson, Reavis, & Rhode, 1987; Walker, Reavis, Rhode, & Jenson, 1985; Walker & Buckley, 1974). However, these are special education programs and are generally designed to train teachers and other special education professionals. There are few such model programs designed to prepare school psychologists to be specialists with behaviorally disordered children. Numerous problems or "road blocks" exist in training school psychologists to be behavior disorders specialists. Some of these obstacles are surmountable with planning

and a well-specified training model. Others, however, are more intractable and will perhaps take years to change.

OBSTACLES TO EFFECTIVE PROFESSIONAL TRAINING IN SCHOOL PSYCHOLOGY

The Definition of Behavior Disorder as a Conceptual Obstacle to Professional Training

The definition of *behavior disorder* used by professionals in the United States is problematic to training. On the federal level, the term is not a part of the legislation dealing with a population involved. Instead the term *seriously emotionally disturbed* (SED) is used in the regulations for Public Law 94-142 to define this handicapping condition:

The term (SED) means a condition exhibiting one or more of the following characteristics over a long period of time and to a marked degree, which adversely affects educational performance:

(a) An inability to learn which cannot be explained by intellectual, sensory, or other health factors;

(b) An inability to build or maintain satisfactory interpersonal relationships with peers and teachers;

(c) Inappropriate types of behavior or feelings under normal circumstances;

(d) A general pervasive mood of unhappiness or depression;

(e) A tendency to develop physical symptoms or fears associated with personal or school problems;

TABLE 2
Walker and Fabre's Critical Index Behaviors

- Child masturbates in public
- Child assaults an adult
- Child attempts to seriously physically injure another
- Child engages in self-mutilation, e.g., head banging, biting, or cutting him/herself
- Child's verbal behavior is irrational and/or incomprehensible
- Child is not in contact with reality
- Child sexually molests another child
- Child threatens suicide
- Child shows evidence of physical abuse
- Child shows evidence of drug use

(f) The term includes children who are schizophrenic. The term does not include children who are socially maladjusted unless it is determined that they are also seriously emotionally disturbed.

The SED definition is a clear obstacle to professional training in that it does not address or describe the basic externalizing behaviors that most frequently give rise to referrals for special education services (Jenson, Kehle, & Robinson-Awana, 1989). Instead the SED definition emphasizes the internalizing child who may be unhappy, depressed, or fearful. In fact, it excludes most behaviorally disordered students with conduct disorders who may be viewed as "socially maladjusted."

The 98th U.S. Congress requested a study to determine if there should be a label and terminology change from seriously emotionally disturbed to behaviorally disordered (SRA Technologies, 1985). The investigators concluded that a decision to change the term was not warranted, since existing service patterns, social integration, and stigma would not be substantially altered. However, a leading national organization in the field of behavior disorders, the Council for Children with Behavioral Disorders (CCBD), issued a statement strongly in support of the proposed change in terminology (Huntze, 1985).

Graduate level training programs are adversely affected by this definitional confusion. For example, should school psychologists receive specialized training in a behavior disorder that is of urgent concern to regular school personnel but is not officially recognized by the most important federal legislation designed to protect and serve handicapped children? The currently used definition and certification process identifies as handicapped those students who have primarily emotional, internalizing types of disorders that call for clinical interventions. This contradiction poses an interesting problem for school psychology training programs. That is, should such programs focus on clinical interventions that may have only limited relevance to the broad range of social-behavioral adjustment problems occurring in schools? Or should trainees be required to master the complex technical skills necessary to intervene effectively with conduct disorders and socially maladjusted students who are of great concern but do not meet certification criteria?

Traditional Training Models as an Obstacle

The discipline of school psychology is well represented by national training models that are designed by its two national professional organizations, the National Association of School Psychologists (NASP) and the American Psychological Association (APA). Both associations are involved in the accreditation of school psychology programs. The accreditation is important to universities interested in attracting quality students to their school psychology training programs. Both the NASP and APA models emphasize the need to produce scientist-practitioners. The basic differences between the training models of APA and NASP have been well summarized (Engin & Johnson, 1983; Pryzwansky, 1982). Essentially, the differences are based on entry-level status into the profession (doctoral or masters level) and whether a school psychologist is purely a psychologist or a hybrid of a psychologist and educator. These differences may be strategically important to association accreditation, but they are less critical to development of specialized skills in the area of behavior disorders. What is important is the type of school psychologist that is produced by these models, and whether the models sufficiently allow for the development of subspecialization in the assessment of and intervention for behavior disorders.

According to the NASP training model, the content of a school psychology program should include the broad areas of psychological foundations, educational foundations, assessment, interventions, statistics and research design, and professional school psychology (National Association of Psychologists, 1986). Through this model, entry into the profession is at the specialist level, with a minimum of 60 semester hours, although doctoral programs are also defined. The areas of a graduate program (according to the NASP model) most relevant to behavior disorders are the assessment, interventions, and research components. The intervention component includes consultation, counseling, and behavior management. The assessment component is less detailed as to the exact areas required. Even in *School Psychology: A Blueprint for Training and Practice* (National School Psychology Inservice Training Network, 1984) the domains that are suggested to be most relevant for be-

havior disorders include class management, basic academic skills, and affective/social skills. When the overall structure of the NASP training model is reviewed, it becomes clear that the end product is essentially a generalist who has been trained across several areas and has limited specialization.

Similar to the NASP program, the APA training model describes a generic core in doctoral training that includes biological bases of behavior, cognitive-affective bases of behavior, social bases of behavior, and individual behavior. In addition, the accreditation standards emphasize psychological measurement and assessment, research, history and systems, and ethics (American Psychological Association, 1986). These are essentially generic standards for all psychologists in training in APA-approved programs. The standards, however, also allow for course requirements in particular specialty areas. These areas are school, clinical, counseling, and industrial psychology. Little emphasis is placed on specific skills in the area of behavior disorders, especially for school psychologists. As with the NASP model, under the APA model, the training program's primary goal is to train a general psychologist. Secondarily, the training program allows specialization in one of the broad fields of school, clinical, counseling, or industrial psychology. The product is the same, a generalist with a subspecialty in school psychology.

These general models produce coursework that reflects the generic accreditation standards. Students are required to spend most of their training hours in courses ranging from historical and multicultural issues through projective testing. Little room is left for producing an experienced school psychologist with specialized skills to manage behaviorally disordered students. Currently, in most programs, a student interested in the behavior disorders area has to develop the skills either on his/her own or through professional development activities following graduation.

The Scientist–Practitioner Gap as an Obstacle

The scientist–practitioner model is a lofty ideal for the practice of scientifically based psychology. Its development comes out of the Boulder Conference, which set a standard for training psychologists as practicing researchers and consumers of research (Raimy, 1950). This model has been adopted as a standard by many school psychology programs (Edwards, 1987; Martens & Keller, 1987). In essence, a scientist–practitioner is trained in the first instance to conduct and evaluate research in order to improve clinical practices in applied settings. Second, a scientist–practitioner should be able to evaluate published research on practices and techniques to determine their effectiveness. The results of these efforts should lead to improved program practices. But many clinical practices represent ingrained habits.

Old habits die slowly, particularly if they are clinical practices. Skinner (1984) quotes Fredrick Mosteller's comment on scurvy as an example. The cure for Scurvy was discovered in 1601, but more than 190 years passed before the British Navy used it regularly to stop the disease. The rest of Skinner's article, "The Shame of American Education," is a review of the failure of educators to implement research-proven educational practices. School psychology is no exception despite the fact that many training programs espouse the scientist–practitioner model. Numerous instances of the teaching and implementation by school psychologists of nonvalidated assessment and treatment techniques with behaviorally disordered children can be found in a majority of training programs and school districts.

A breakdown in the scientist–practitioner function can be found in some of the most popular assessment techniques currently used by school psychologists. Projective techniques are still preferred as decision-making tools by many school psychologists. In a recent survey of graduate training programs in school psychology, projective tests were found to be the most popular assessment technique taught in personality assessment courses (Knoff, 1986). Of all the programs surveyed 70% taught thematic apperception techniques and 57% taught projective drawing techniques. However, these measures are largely without scientific merit in assessing children with behavioral difficulties (Gittelman-Klein, 1978, 1980). In a review, Gittelman-Klein (1978) stated (concerning projective techniques) that "sometimes they tell us poorly something we already know" (p. 160). Projective tests do not stand the test of the scientist–practitioner model; however, they continue to be used extensively by school psychologists.

Similarly, current intervention practices in school psychology should be brought more into line with the scientist–practitioner model. Traditional relationship-based psychotherapy for children with antisocial behavior problems is usually ineffective or less effective than behavioral interventions (Kazdin, Esveldt-Dawson, French, & Unis, 1987; Kazdin, 1987; Weisz, Alicke, & Klotz, 1987). Play therapy, nondirective relationship-based counseling, and catharsis techniques are not only expensive, but they may be ineffective with behaviorally disordered children (Bandura, 1973; Kazdin, 1985, 1987; Kazdin et al., 1987). However, 30% of surveyed school psychology training programs included counseling and psychotherapeutic intervention strategies in their course content (Knoff, 1986). Although general behavioral intervention strategies were the most popularly identified strategy in this survey (60%), specific techniques such as social skills training, stress management, or assertiveness training made up only 10% of the actual course content.

To be educationally effective with behaviorally disordered students, school psychology students have to be taught scientifically based assessment and intervention procedures. Preference and popularity have to give way to research-validated best practices. School psychology students need to be trained in research skills that allow them to evaluate published techniques and to conduct clinically relevant research in their own settings. The implementation of a scientist–practitioner training program with a specific emphasis on behavior disorders is suggested as a model to fill this gap in school psychology training programs.

SPECIAL EDUCATION REFORM: A SCHOOL PSYCHOLOGY REVOLUTION

A recent article (Reschly, 1988) has pointed to a revolution in school psychology services that is the result of the special education reform movement. This reform movement is an outgrowth of federal and state priorities to serve mildly handicapped students (particularly, learning-disabled and behaviorally disordered students) in regular education with research-validated practices for both assessment and intervention. A strong endorsement has been made to combine regular and special education services, especially in providing remediation services in the regular classroom (Will, 1988). Reschly has pointed out that 90% of students classified as handicapped are mildly handicapped, and that at least two-thirds of a school psychologist's time is devoted to this group. However, with this clinical demand and the demands of the national reform movement, school psychologists still provide services that are outdated.

For example, in a recent survey, Reschly, Wang, and Walberg (1987) found that the three assessment instruments most widely used by school psychologists are the Wechsler scales, the Wide Range Achievement Test-Revised (WRAT-R), and the Bender. The technical adequacy of two of these measures is limited and all three of these instruments have practically no direct intervention value for mildly handicapped students. Reschly (1988) calls for more practical assessment techniques such as curriculum-based assessment and observation in natural settings that have utility in "measuring target behaviors, monitoring progress and assessing outcomes" (p. 471). In addition, school psychologists will have to be trained to provide prereferral interventions, behavioral classroom interventions,

and instructional interventions. Graduate programs will need to make a training shift, and continuing education programs will have to provide relevant training opportunities. The call is for *less* special education services rather than more, and the services provided will have to be more effective, particularly for behaviorally disordered students. If we do not respond, the reform movement will bypass traditional school psychology; "there will not be a traditional role of that nature [school psychology services that focus on classification/placement] for very many of us, not if the changes described here occur on a widespread basis" (p. 472) (Reschly, 1988).

Survey Results: How School Psychologists Should Be Trained to Effectively Manage Behaviorally Disordered Students

A questionnaire was sent by the authors to 211 school psychology training programs in the United States that were listed in the NASP *Directory of School Psychology Training Programs* (1984), of which 78 returned the questionnaire. The questionnaire asked training directors specific questions pertaining to the training of school psychologists to effectively work with behaviorally disordered students. The results of the questionnaire indicated that only 11% of the 78 responding programs had any type of subspecialization training in behavior disorders. The course offerings in the programs that related to the behavior disorders area included an applied behavior analysis, behavior modification, or behavior therapy course (87% offered this type of course), a course specifically in behavior disorders (69%), an interventions course (69%), and a behavioral assessment course (53%). The questionnaire also included an item on forced ranking of the importance of six predetermined training areas for behaviorally disordered students. The rankings in order of importance were (a) classroom behavioral interventions; (b) prereferral/consultation skills; (c) behavioral assessment; (d) generalization/integration skills; (e) social skills training;

TABLE 3
Ten Important Competencies to Deal Effectively with Behaviorally Disordered
Students as Ranked by Graduate Program Trainers

Rank	Competency	N
1.	Behavior Management Skills	52
2.	Behavioral Assessment	46
3.	Behavioral Consultation	37
4.	Classroom Behavioral Intervention	35
5.	Understanding Childhood Psychopathology	19
6.	Counseling Skills	19
7.	Social Skills Training	13
8.	Counselor's Personal Skills	7
9.	Understanding Human Development	4
tie | 10.	Academic Intervention Skills	3
10.	Parenting Skills	3

Rank ordering is based on ratings of 78 respondents to a questionnaire.

and (f) academic interventions. An open-ended question asking the responder to list the basic competencies needed by a school psychologist to work with behaviorally disordered students also was included. The results of the open-ended question are listed in Table 3.

The results of the survey yielded several interesting findings. First, the area of subspecialization training in dealing with behavior disorders is clearly underrepresented in school psychology training programs. That only 11% of the responding programs offered any type of subspecialization training for one of the most frequently referred childhood disorders is analogous to training general practice physicians without subspecialization in cardiac disorders (the leading cause of death in the United States). Clearly, classroom interventions, consultation skills, and behavioral assessment were rated as the most important competencies that school psychologists require to manage behaviorally disordered children. The basic skills of generalization/integration, social skills training, and academic interventions were less valued. However, these very skills (i.e., the skills called for by the reform discussed above) are the ones needed to insure the long-term adjustment of behaviorally disordered students in regular education.

Recommended Steps for Training School Psychologists in a Behavior Disorders Specialty

There is no absolute model of training school psychologists to effectively manage behaviorally disordered children in school. The federal definition that educationally protects handicapped children excludes most externalized behavioral disorders as social maladjustment and places a strong emphasis on internalizing personality disorders of children. The national organizations such as NASP and APA promote standards that tend to produce generalists rather than specialists as school psychologists. Many graduate training programs tend to cling to practices that are outmoded and nonvalidated. If new, effective models are to be developed, they will need to be based on a practical definition of behavior disorder that leads to the identification and teaching of effective practices to manage and educate children with these problems. A proposed model for achieving these goals is described below.

A working definition for behaviorally disordered students. Most behaviorally disordered students are referred to school psychologists because of behavioral excesses that teachers and school administrators find intolerable. These excesses have been referred to as externalizing behaviors by several researchers (Achenbach & Edelbrock, 1981; Walker, 1983; Walker & Fabre, 1987). The term *externalizer* is used because the problem behavior is directed towards other people and the external social environment (Gelfand, Jenson, & Drew, 1988). Tantrums, arguing, aggression, noncompliance, and property destruction are all examples of externalizing problem behaviors. The behaviorally disordered externalizer is qualitatively different in a behavioral sense, from the personality-disordered, *internalizing* child. For the internalizer, the problems tend to be directed inwardly, away from the social environment. Examples of internalizing problems are depression, fears, anxiety, and social withdrawal.

Behaviorally disordered students are most directly characterized by behavior excesses that adversely affect others. Many of the behavioral attributes that constitute this disorder can be found in populations of nonhandicapped children. However, the *frequency* and *intensity* of these externalizing behaviors separate behaviorally disordered children, as a rule, from their normal peers (Morgan & Jenson, 1988). These excesses also have another effect. They substantially interfere with the developmental and educational progress of the child who exhibits them. This interference handicaps the child over time by causing severe deficits in academic, social, and self-control skills. In fact, a majority of behaviorally disordered children display academic deficits (Dishion, Loeber, Stouthamer-Loeber, & Patterson, 1984; Rutter & Yule, 1973). Similarly, many behaviorally disordered children also have difficulty with peer relations, are socially deficient, and experience self-control problems (Loeber & Patterson, 1981; Morgan & Jenson, 1988; Gresham & Reschly, 1988). Patterson (1976) has characterized aggressive behaviorally disordered children as seriously delayed "in the development of many basic social skills" (p. 289).

One of the most frustrating characteristics of behaviorally disordered children is their absence of empathy for and basic lack of respect for the rights of others. These children often violate the rights of others in exchange for immediate or short-term gains (Achenbach & Edelbrock, 1981; Goldstein, Glick, Reiner, Zimmerman, & Coultry, 1987; Jurkovic & Prentice, 1977). This attribute has been characterized as a deficit in rule-governed or self-control behavior (Barkley, 1985). That is, such children are often controlled by the available immediate rewards or social contingencies and show relatively poor ability to display self-control, delay of gratification, or rule-governed behavior.

A basic definition of behaviorally disordered children with accompanying characteristics of behavioral excesses and deficits is given in Table 4 (Gelfand, Jenson, & Drew, 1988). Successful programs that educate behaviorally disordered children must first manage the behavioral excesses that regular education teachers find so intolerable. Once the coercive excesses have been successfully addressed, remediation of behavioral deficits in academics, social skills, and self-control behaviors can follow. The last step in this process of behavioral change is to develop a systematic generalization and maintenance program (Jenson, Reavis, & Rhode, 1987).

A training program for school psychologists with a specialization in behavior disorders can follow naturally from the definitional approach presented in Table 4. That is, accurate and practical assessment of behavioral excesses and deficits, which, in turn, leads to recommendations for interventions, is a necessary and very important first step. Second, direct intervention and consultation skills in the management of disruptive behavioral excesses (i.e., aggression, arguing, and noncompliance) is an essential program component. Third, a systematic plan of teaching social skills, self-control, and problem-solving skills to children is of critical importance. Fourth, school psychologists should also become skilled in basic academic enhancement strategies, effective curricula, and curriculum-based assessment procedures. Finally, school psychologists need skills in essential generalization techniques so that behav-

TABLE 4
Definition of a Behaviorally Disordered Student

Type Disorder	Specific Behaviors
	Behavioral Excesses
Aggression	Physically attacks others
	Verbally abusive
	Tantrums
	Sets fires
	Destroys property
	Vandalizes
	Cruel to animals
	Revengeful
Noncompliance	Breaks established rules
	Argues
	Does not follow commands
	Does the opposite of what is requested
	Behavioral Deficits
Rule-governed behavior	Cannot delay reinforcement
	Impulsive
	Lack of conscience
	Lack of concern for others
	Shows little remorse
Social behavior	Has few friends
	Lacks affection or bonding
	Has few problem-solving skills
	Lacks cooperation skills
	Constantly seeks attention
	Poor conversation skills
	Does not know how to reward others
Academics and school	Generally behind in academic basics, particulary reading
	Has difficulty acquiring new academic information
	Off task
	Truant

Note. Adapted from *Understanding Child Behavor Disorders,* by D. M. Gelfand, W. R. Jenson, and C. J. Drew, 1988, New York: Holt, Rinehart, and Winston. Copyright 1988. Adapted by permission.

iorally disordered children can be successfully reintegrated into mainstream settings.

Practical assessment skills for behaviorally disordered children. Vast professional resources are often wasted in the nonproductive assessment of behaviorally disordered children. Behavioral assessment should be a structured information-gathering process that leads to identification and decisions for place-

ment and intervention (Coulter & Morrow, 1978; Cronbach, 1960; Gelfand, Jenson, & Drew, 1988). The information produced should both diagnose and prescribe interventions. Several investigators have noted that much of current assessment is diagnostic with few implications for treatment and intervention (Fuchs & Fuchs, 1986; Hobbs, 1975; Reschly, 1988). Assessment information that merely identifies problems and is diagnostic but devoid of treatment implications is unproductive for behaviorally disordered children.

Assessment practices that have poor standardization may be difficult to use clinically and to defend legally. Unstructured assessment approaches such as nonsystematic interviews, anecdotal observations, and projective techniques usually have poor to nonexistent standardization and inadequate reliability and validity. For example, Anastasi (1982) classifies projective assessment methods as "clinical tools" rather than tests, because they do not measure up to acceptable psychometric standards of basic reliability and validity. Similarly, the practical intervention information derived from an assessment method must be balanced against the cost of collecting the information (Hartmann, Roper, & Bradford, 1979). Information that is too costly to collect or suggests unrealistic intervention practices does not meet the basic criterion of utility in connection with behaviorally disordered students (Morgan & Jenson, 1988).

Innovative assessment practices for behaviorally disordered students should include identification systems, assessment of social skills, academic assessment, and assessment of generalization and maintenance outcomes. New models of screening and identification of behaviorally disordered children have been developed in recent years (Achenbach & Edelbrock, 1983; Walker et al., 1987). These assessment methods form a system rather than a single assessment technique or test for the identification of behaviorally disordered children. For example, the Achenbach and Edelbrock (1983) Child Behavior Checklist system includes a 118-item behavior checklist for parents, teachers, and the student, plus a classroom observation system. The checklist is well standardized with a Social Competency Profile and a Child Behavior Profile. These profiles can be used to pinpoint specific behavioral excesses and deficits, and the various derived factors can be used for diagnostic purposes. Similarly, the teacher and youth report forms parallel the parent form questions. The classroom observation form also uses many of the questions from the checklist and adds a sample of on-task behavior. Since the measures are well standardized and have solid psychometric properties, they can be used normatively (through the use of standardized T-scores) to indicate the severity of a problem by comparison with the standardization group. Most important, the individually scored items (e.g., argues a lot, lying and cheating, gets in many fights) can be used as the target behaviors for interventions. The routine use of the Achenbach and Edelbrock system (1983) in schools has been shown to be highly efficient, reliable, and valid (McConaughy, 1985).

A system similar to the Child Behavior Checklist that is currently under production is the multigating approach developed by Walker et al. (1987). A multigating approach has several steps of assessment that increase in cost and detail (Loeber, Dishion, & Peterson, 1984; Walker, Hops, & Greenwood, 1981). If a child is identified as possibly behaviorally disordered at the first step or gate then the next more precise step is taken until the child has been accurately identified through the last step of the system. The Walker et al. (1987) multigating system is designed specifically for identifying behaviorally disordered children. At the first step, a classroom teacher merely ranks the children in the classroom who may be at risk for externalizing or internalizing problems (two lists). Gate 2 also relies on the teacher's judgment: Children who were ranked highest at Gate 1 on the externalizing and internalizing behavioral dimensions are now compared on common adaptive and maladaptive behaviors. The specific behaviors (e.g., physically assaults an adult) are identified and the frequencies are estimated. Rated students who exceed the normative criteria on Gate 2 are independently assessed at Gate 3. At Gate 3 the children are observed in natural settings (i.e., classroom and playground) by a school psychologist or other school professional. Academic engagement time and social interaction data are collected and compared to age- and sex-appropriate normative levels to determine if a child qualifies. The major advantage of the Walker et al. (1987) multiple gating system is that large populations of children can be screened at relatively little cost. The children most likely to exhibit severe externalizing and internalizing behavior problems are initially assessed by teachers who are most familiar with their behavior. The most severe children are then observed in natural and meaningful educational settings by school psychologists. The problems identified by this system are easily converted to behaviors targeted for an intervention.

In addition to applying practical screening systems that identify behaviorally disordered students and pinpoint specific behavioral excesses, school psychologists should be trained to directly assess academic and social deficits in children. Traditional academic achievement tests have been used for years to identify academically delayed students. However, these measures have been criticized because they yield a composite or average score but do not give information about specific subskills (Shapiro & Lentz, 1985, 1986); it is difficult to design specific academic interventions for behaviorally disordered students from average or composite scores. Similarly, many norm-referenced achievement tests have also been criticized because they represent a bias that favors one specific curriculum (Good & Salvia, 1988; Jenkins & Pany, 1978). A more practical approach for school psychologists is a direct assessment of academic skills that includes several related approaches such as curriculum-based assessment (Deno, 1985; Shinn, Tindal, & Stein, 1988; Tucker, 1985), direct assessment of the academic environment (Howell, 1986; Lentz & Shapiro, 1985), and a functional assessment of the learning environment (Lentz & Shapiro, 1986). All of these approaches emphasize practical identification and remediation of deficiencies in specific skills; they use the child's classroom academic materials in the assessment process; and they use the child's actual learning environment to assess motivation and learning problems.

Difficulty in interacting with peers and adults is another serious deficit experienced by many behaviorally disordered children. Assessing social skills so that appropriate interventions can be designed and used is an important skill of school psychologists. The basic assessment of social skills can include naturalistic observation, teachers' ratings with a checklist, and sociometric measures involving peer nominations or ratings (Morgan & Jenson, 1988). The naturalistic observation of social skills should involve systematic observation systems that have been designed for this purpose (Gresham, 1983). There are several good social skills checklists that can be used by school psychologists for screening, prescription, placement, and program evaluation purposes (Brown, Black, & Downs, 1984; Gresham & Elliott, in preparation; Walker & McConnell, 1988). Sociometric and peer nomination assessment procedures can also be used to screen effectively for children who are socially deficient and unpopular (McConnell & Odom, 1986).

Other measurement skills that are useful for school psychologists are assessment strategies for the generalization and maintenance of behavioral and academic gains, social integration strategies, and a knowledge of single-subject research design. Assessment for generalization and maintenance is important because of PL 94-142, the mandate to educate handicapped children in the least restrictive environment, and because of the importance of producing durable gains in student performance. Assessment skills such as identifying controlling antecedent events and common stimuli in regular classrooms and the determination of critical survival skill behaviors can be essential for training behaviorally disordered children to adjust to the demands of regular classrooms (Epps, Thomas, & Lane, 1985; Walker & Rankin, 1983). A knowledge of single-subject research designs is most useful in evaluating the effectiveness of prescribed interventions (Kazdin, 1981; Kratochwill, 1985; Shapiro, 1987). Their sensitivity to environmental events and changes make them especially suitable for this purpose.

It seems clear that implementation of practical behavioral approaches in the assessment of behaviorally disordered students requires a different training model than many school psychologists are currently receiving. Traditionally used assessment approaches are often lacking in their ability to identify and practically pinpoint many of the behavioral excesses and deficits experienced by behaviorally disordered children (Gresham, 1985a). The more promising assessment approaches emphasize socially valid, low-cost assessments of children in natural settings that use common educational materials. These approaches include multigating systems, behavior checklists, observational procedures, structured interviewing, curriculum-based assessment techniques, and sociometric measures. Many of these techniques are included in behavioral and educational assessment courses and should be offered to school psychology trainees.

Practical intervention skills for school psychologists. There are several models and types of interventions that can be used by school psychologists for a multitude of children's behavior problems (as reviewed by Witt & Elliott, 1985; by Maher & Zins, 1987; and by Thomas & Grimes, 1985, 1987). Many of these models include direct forms of classroom intervention, crisis intervention, school counseling, prereferral intervention, and consultation. This section will focus on four basic intervention areas for behaviorally disordered students: prereferral interventions, direct classroom interventions, consultation, and generalization interventions.

At the outset, however, development of skilled intervention requires a set of general courses that should serve as the core of school psychology training programs. For example, an essential knowledge of learning theory and applied behavior analysis is required before many of the research-based classroom interventions can be applied skillfully. Similarly, a background in basic counseling techniques and group process skills can greatly aid a psychologist who plans to conduct a social skills training group or negotiate a behavioral contract with an adolescent.

After a student has acquired the essential knowledge, then specific intervention skills can be taught in courses with practical applications implemented in practicum and internship. For the treatment and education of behaviorally disordered students, these skills form a related set of competencies for managing behavioral excesses and deficits. Each of these types of intervention is described below.

Direct interventions. The school psychologist's mastery of direct interventions provides the standard by which their competencies often are judged by teachers. If school psychologists are not directly effective with behaviorally disordered students, their prereferral and consultation skills will likely be viewed as suspect by school personnel who work directly with the children. The management of behavioral excesses such as aggression, arguing, tantrums, and property destruction usually call for the systematic application of direct interventions. In particular, noncompliance is the "kingpin" event that is central to many behavioral excesses (Jenson et al., 1987). Numerous other behavioral excesses also covary with noncompliance: If noncompliance can be decreased or prevented, other behavioral excesses such as arguing and aggression will frequently decrease or not occur (Russo, Cataldo, & Cushing, 1981). Some of the most widely used approaches to reducing children's noncompliance in the family and the school have been developed at the University of Oregon (Patterson, 1974, 1976, 1982) and the University of Georgia (Forehand, 1977; Forehand & McMahon, 1981). Essentially these approaches focus on effectively reducing coercive interactions through the use of planned consequences (i.e., both positive and mildly aversive) and maximizing precision in request making (i.e., the antecedents that often trigger noncompliance). Models for applying planned consequences and maximizing precision request making across educational settings have been developed and tested (Morgan & Jenson, 1988; Walker et al., 1985). A more thorough discussion of these techniques is given in this volume in the chapters on interventions for antisocial children and oppositional behavior.

Once behavioral excesses have been remediated by these techniques, expectations can be established to remediate the two most commonly encountered related deficits of behaviorally disordered students, *social skills* and *academics*. Loeber and Patterson (1981) reported that 72% of all behaviorally disordered children referred to the Oregon Social Learning Center had poor peer relations. Several excellent social skills training programs currently exist that can be used to successfully improve behaviorally disordered students' competency level (Table 5). These packages are research-validated, can be implemented in most schools, and are readily taught in a graduate level interventions class with specific practice opportunities arranged in a practicum or internship. Several investigators have elaborated on the utility of social skills assessment and training activities and their value to school psychologists (Carr & Elliott, 1984; Gresham, 1985b; Rathjen, 1984). It is important to stress that whenever possible these packages should be introduced by the school psychologist as a direct intervention procedure.

One of the strongest correlates of antisocial behavior in adolescents is basic academic skills deficits (Dishion et al., 1984). These skills are essential to successful adjustment when a student reenters a regular classroom from special education. Few academic curricula have been validated specifically for behaviorally disordered students. However, several excellent direct instruction curricula for reading, mathematics, and spelling are available (Engelmann & Carnine, 1980, as reviewed by Morgan & Jenson, 1988). Some research (Kesler, 1985) has shown that behaviorally disordered students make exceptional progress when exposed to a direct instruction reading program. The school psychologist should be familiar with the program instructional format and placement tests of these programs.

School psychologists should also be capable of designing an academic reme-diation program based on the regular classroom curriculum. This skill is particularly important when behaviorally disordered students are integrated into regular education settings that use a standard curriculum. Curriculum-based assessment probes can be implemented to identify a student's weak areas, and can then be used to design skills-building interventions from a particular curriculum (Rosenfield, 1987; Shapiro & Lentz, 1985, 1986). In addition, the school psychologist can help design programs that enhance general academic motivation (Shapiro, 1988) such as classroom incentive systems (Becker, 1986; Paine, Radicchi, Rosellini, Deutchman, & Darch, 1983; Walker & Buckley, 1974), public posting and feedback systems (Van Houten, 1980), level systems (Jenson, Reavis, & Rhode, 1987; Morgan & Jenson, 1988), cooperative learning environments (Slavin, 1983), programs to maintain on-task behavior (Hendersen, Jenson, & Erken, 1986; Lentz, 1988), peer tutoring and grading programs (Ehly, 1986; Greenwood, Carta, & Hall, 1988; Paine et al., 1983), parent tutoring programs (Gang & Poche, 1982), home-based contingency systems (Kelly & Carper, 1988), homework programs (Anesko & O'Leary, 1982), and others.

School psychologists perform a very important role as direct intervention specialists with behaviorally disordered students in the school. To capitalize on the overall effectiveness of proven interventions, however, school psychologists should also function as consultants to teachers and as members of schoolwide technical assistance teams.

Consultation and service of technical assistance teams. A great deal has been written about school psychologists as consultants, and several teacher consultation models have been suggested (Bergan, 1977; Bergan, Kratochwill, & Luiten, 1980; Curtis & Zins, 1981; Gresham & Kendall, 1987; Gutkin & Curtis, 1982). There are numerous problems, however, with current consultation models. Some research indicates that practicing school psychologists assign consultation a low

TABLE 5
Social Skills Training Programs Available to School Psychologists

Getting along with others: Teaching social effectiveness to children (Jackson, Jackson, & Monroe, 1983)

ACCEPTS: Social skills curriculum (Walker, McConnell, Holmes, Todis, Walker, & Golden, 1983)

ACCESS: Adolescent curriculum for communication and effective social skills (Walker, Todis, Holmes, & Horton, 1988)

Teaching social skills to handicapped children and youth: Programs and materials (Morgan, Young, Likins, Cheney, & Peterson, 1983)

Skillstreaming the elementary school child: A guide for teaching prosocial skills (McGinnis & Goldstein, 1984)

ASSET (Hazel, Schumaker, Sherman, & Sheldon-Wildgen, 1981)

PEERS: Program for establishing effective relationship skills (Hops, Fleishman, Guild, Paine, Street, Walker, & Greenwood, 1978)

ART: Aggression replacement training (Goldstein, Glick, Reiner, Zimmerman, & Coultry, 1987))

School social skills rating scale (Brown, Black, & Downs, 1984)

Walker-McConnell scale of social competence and school adjustment: A social skills rating scale for teachers (Walker & McConnell, 1988)

practical priority in their repertoire of professional activities (Stewart, 1986). Furthermore, many of the articles published on school consultation are largely polemic and nonempirical: A review of this area revealed that only 26% of the published consultation articles had an empirical data base (Pryzwansky, 1986). However, there are too many behaviorally disordered children for school psychologists to be directly involved in every case.

All school psychology training programs should include a theory and practicum course in consultation. These courses should highlight empirically validated techniques that can be used effectively with behaviorally disordered children (Gresham & Kendell, 1987). Practicum and internships should allow exposure to, and practice of these empirically based techniques. In addition, school psychology students should understand the relationship between teachers' preferences for a range of intervention tech-

niques that might be recommended and the likelihood of implementation (Martens, Peterson, Witt, & Cirone, 1986; Reimers, Wacker, & Koeppl, 1987; Witt & Elliott, 1985; Witt, Martens, & Elliott, 1984). In particular, school psychology students should thoroughly understand teachers' resistance to offered suggestions and the dynamics of professional relationships in schools that affect consultation practices (Piersel & Gutkin, 1983; Witt & Martens, 1988; Witt, 1986).

Many requests for consultation in relation to behaviorally disordered children are motivated by the child's inappropriate behavioral excesses such as aggression and noncompliance. As a general rule, consultation for behaviorally disordered students requires not only the reduction of behavioral excesses, but the strengthening of appropriate behavior through the teaching of more adaptive behaviors and skills. Some behavioral intervention programs currently available to school psychologists that can be used in the consultation process and that meet these general requirements are the CORBEH packages (i.e., CLASS, PASS, RECESS, and PEERS) from the University of Oregon. Three of these packages are designed for behaviorally disordered students — these are CLASS, PASS, and RECESS. The CLASS program is an in-class program that is used to manage an acting-out child who is noncompliant and destructive and disrupts the class (Hops, Beickel, & Walker, 1976). The school psychologist works directly with the classroom teacher and the child and gradually fades as a consultant. Similarly, the RECESS program is designed for the aggressive child who is primarily socially inept and behaves inappropriately on the playground (Walker, Street, Garrett, Crossen, Hops, & Greenwood, 1978). The PASS program is used to improve academic behaviors and skills of mildly behaviorally disordered children who are inattentive, unmotivated, and hyperactive (Greenwood, Guild, & Hops, 1977). The major advantages of these research-based programs are that they are self-instructional and have all the needed materials, data collection systems, intervention guidelines, and forms necessary for their implementation in either regular or special education settings.

Another approach to consultation is the use of school psychologists as part of school-based multidisciplinary teams (Maher & Yoshida, 1985; Pryzwansky & Rzepski, 1983). These technical assistance teams (TATs) are designed for the case consultation process in which a teacher brings a problem to a team for suggestions that can be used in the classroom. The teams are generally made up of experienced teachers, a school psychologist, and other school personnel. Such teams can be very cost-effective and particularly useful to new or inexperienced teachers at the beginning of their careers. A TAT-based program that is especially useful for consultation is the RIDE Project (Beck, 1986). Project RIDE is a complete package designed to aid TATs in offering practical solutions for academic and social problems referred by teachers. With RIDE a problem description can be entered into a personal Apple computer, which will then print five or six empirically validated interventions with implementation instructions for the teacher. The types of problems for which solutions are included in the RIDE data bank are talking out in class, fighting, daydreaming, noncompliance, stealing, sexual behavior, cheating, swearing, and others. In addition, RIDE also provides a series of videotapes that demonstrate many of the recommended techniques in realistic classroom settings. The major advantage of a package like RIDE is that, when it is used in conjunction with a technical assistance team, it brings a multidisciplinary approach to case consultation with empirically validated procedures. Social validity outcomes for RIDE are very positive as well.

Individual or team-based case consultation systems are not the only models that are useful to school psychologists when dealing with behaviorally disordered students. Proactive or preventive classroom consultation is important (Gettinger, 1988). With a proactive approach, the school psychologist helps design the classroom setting and implements procedures that help prevent behavior problems. The school psychologist acts in advance to avoid reactive, crisis-oriented consultation (Gettinger, 1988). For example, school psychologists can help teachers properly design the physical layout of classrooms, start effective management practices early in the year, post rules, implement effectively paced curricula, start a classroom management system, and improve the information flow in classrooms (Gettinger, 1988; Paine et al., 1983). This type of consultation can be offered as in-service presentations or helping new or troubled teachers establish effective proactive procedures.

Generalization interventions. Without engineered generalization practices, many of the gains achieved with behaviorally disordered students will not be transferred to regular education settings. *Generalization* is defined as an extension of newly acquired skills or behaviors into settings in which treatment procedures have not been implemented (Wahler, Berland, & Coe, 1979). Failure to plan for generalization is one of the basic reasons that behaviorally disordered students fail when they are reintegrated into least restrictive educational settings. For school psychology students, efficient generalization skills require a theoretical knowledge of both the types of generalization that can occur and practical generalization enhancement techniques (Morgan & Jenson, 1988).

Effective planning for generalization requires several components, namely, practical assessment, direct intervention, and consultation skills. Generalization assessment should include a thorough evaluation of the academic and behavioral requirements of target regular classes (Epps et al., 1985). For example, the expected length of time allotted for individual seatwork and other classroom activities and the nature of classroom rules should be assessed. School psychology students must be trained in the direct intervention skills required to develop in their student clients those competencies that will be necessary to survive in a regular class, such as working with a new curriculum, staying on task, and following a teacher's directions. To help prevent a placement failure, consultation will often involve problem solving with the receiving teacher once a child is reintegrated into a mainstream classroom.

A useful model for generalization interventions for behaviorally disordered students who are returned to regular education is the generalization project of the Children's Behavior Therapy Unit (CBTU) in Salt Lake City (Zimmerman, Christopolis, Jenson, Nicholas, & Reavis, 1989). This program is funded by the Utah State Office of Education and involves school psychology students and special education teachers. CBTU is a separate, special school that specializes in the education of severely behavior disordered students. The CBTU generalization project focuses on the transfer of behavioral, academic, and social skills from a special school environment (CBTU) to regular school settings (regular public schools).

When a student is ready to be returned to a regular neighborhood school from CBTU, several generalization steps are taken. First, a common stimuli assessment is conducted by means of classroom observations and teacher interviews for the prospective school. This assessment pinpoints the basic classroom structure, curriculum, classroom rules, and teacher's expectations. This generalization information is then used to formulate an individualized generalization plan. For example, the behaviorally disordered student is taken out of his or her sessions of direct academic instruction and placed in an academic group that uses the prospective classroom's curriculum. The student is also taught to spend extended periods of time doing independent seatwork with the new classroom's academic materials. In addition, after having mastered a basic social skills curriculum such as ACCEPTS (Walker et al., 1983), the student is taught a series of "teacher-pleaser" skills. Teacher-pleasers are skills that are particularly valued by teachers: volunteering to help the teacher at recess; asking "How did I do?" (prompting for reinforcement); smiling and nodding while the teacher talks; or simply thanking the teacher for help. Teacher-pleaser skills are designed to help the behaviorally disordered students overcome poor reputations, particularly during the first 2 weeks of their placements back into regular classrooms.

Once students have been taught the specific expectations of the new teacher, have been exposed to the regular classroom curriculum, and have mastered the teacher-pleaser skills, they are placed in the regular classroom. However, they are each given a generalization folder (book) to take with them. This folder contains several generalization tools to help them. The folder contains a "lucky charm" — simply a picture of their CBTU teacher and class — to serve as a visual generalization stimulus or link back to their old classroom. Lucky charms have been shown to be effective in helping generalize academic skills from resource rooms to regular classrooms (Ayllon, Kuhlman, & Warzak, 1983).

Poor		OK		Good
1	2	3	4	5

FIGURE 1. Self-rating cartoon of a boy on task from the CBTU generalization project.

The folder also contains five to ten behaviors selected as particularly difficult for each given student, but also by the receiving regular classroom teacher as important. These behaviors are depicted in the folder in cartoon form. For example, Figure 1 is a sample of a cartoon depicting a boy working quietly and independently. Each day the student records a progress rating on each of the target behaviors on a 1-to-5 scale. Independently, the teacher also randomly rates the student's behavior on some of the days. On the comparison days, if there is a match between the student and the teacher, the student is rewarded in accordance with a special contract (Rhode, Morgan, & Young, 1983). If there is not a match, the student receives no reward.

In addition to the lucky charms and the matching program, the folder contains a list of problem-solving skills for difficult situations, a section on monitoring teacher-pleasers, a list of the new classroom rules, and a reinforcement contract for doing well. School psychology students and staff monitor a student's progress for 90 days through telephone contacts and classroom visits. Slowly, the contacts are faded over a 90-day period. At the time of this writing, 17 students have been integrated from CBTU with reasonable success. Although this program is new, an approach of this type is important for the success of behaviorally disordered students, and school psychologists are an integral factor in making the program succeed.

Model school psychology training programs. There are a limited number of school psychology programs that have a strong record in training school psychologists to effectively manage and educate behaviorally disordered students. The reasons for the relative lack of such programs despite such a high demand for them have already been reviewed. However, some current school psychology programs have outstanding training components. Lehigh University's school psychology program, for example, has a unique training program for behavioral school psychologists with particular skills in curriculum-based assessment and behavioral interventions. Similarly, the University of Oregon has excellent curriculum-based assessment, direct instruction, and social skills training program components that are available for school psychologists. Louisiana State University also has an excellent classroom consultation and social skills training component. The University of Wisconsin has developed over several years a superb record in direct instruction, consultation, and proactive classroom strategies.

The University of Utah's School Psychology Program has been particularly fortunate in the past several years in obtaining external funding to help establish an interventions-oriented program. Currently this program holds a Personnel Preparation Grant from the U.S. Office of Education to train school psychologists to be intervention-oriented practitioners. This grant enables four students each year to select two mentors (i.e., recognized local experts) to teach them specific intervention skills. For example, students have selected the mentoring areas of parent training, social skills training, generalization skills (e.g., the CBTU program), compliance training, classroom skills for attention-deficit children, and others. Each student studies with a mentor for 4 months to learn the practical and academic aspects of a skill.

The basic curriculum of the school psychology program at Utah is also intervention-oriented. All students are required to take courses in applied behavior analysis, school interventions, consultation, and an intervention-based childhood psychopathology course. The program is also establishing an intervention subtrack within the general school psychology curriculum. The subtrack is designed to guide students through elective courses that will give them specific skills to manage behaviorally disordered students. The course outline is given in Table 6.

Elective courses that students will be offered include single-subject design, an interventions seminar, behavioral assessment, prevention strategies with children, child behavior change methods, curriculum development, advanced applied behavior analysis, and others. In addition to these courses, students that opt for the interventions subtrack will be given special practicum and internship experiences that include skill-building experiences in practical intervention. For doctoral students, a substantial part of their preliminary examination will be on the effective use of interventions and they will be encouraged to do their dissertation research in the area of behavior disorders.

The interventions subtrack allows a program such as Utah's to meet the general requirements of APA and NASP but also offers students an option to become experts in the interventions area. It is one way that school psychologists can move from a generalist orientation to a specific interventions orientation to serve behaviorally disordered students. Specific skills development, scientist–practitioner interventions, practical assessment that relates to interventions, and a workable definition of behaviorally disordered students are central to this program.

SUMMARY

This chapter outlined the need for the formal preparation of graduate level psychologists to work effectively with behaviorally disordered students. Three primary blocks to developing effective training programs were discussed: (a) the "definition" problem posed by the reference in federal legislation to behaviorally disordered children as "seriously emotionally disturbed," implying incorrectly a central internalized reason for maladjustment; (b) NASP's and APA's traditional training models, which function to encourage programs that essentially prepare generalist school psychologists rather than specialists who are well educated in scientifically based interventions designed for behaviorally disordered children; and (c) the scientist–practitioner gap — the continued teaching in graduate programs,

TABLE 6
Intervention Subtrack at the University of Utah's School Psychology Program

Master's Program Options

Learning and Behavior
Child and Adolescent Psychopathology
Applied Behavior Analysis and Social Skills with Exceptional Children
Individual Child Assessment
Behavioral Assessment
Interventions for Schools
Applications of Behavior Theory
Intervention Strategies for Elementary Students with Learning Disabilities
Psychological and Educational Consultation
Child Behavior Change Methods
Prevention Strategies with Children
Seminar in School Psychology
Practicum
Internship

Additional Doctoral Program Course Options

Single-Subject Research Methods
Curriculum Development I & II
Child Counseling and Psychotherapy
Group Counseling

Note. These courses are taught between the Edudational Psychology, Special Education, and Psychology Departments at the University of Utah.

and subsequent use by students in later practice, of unproven, or even disproven, invalid, and unreliable, techniques of assessment and therapies.

Training suggestions based on the research literature and a survey of several school psychology training programs were presented for designing a training program to prepare school psychologists to work effectively with behaviorally disordered children. Fundamental to this effort is the development of a working definition of the behaviorally disordered student. Suggested emphasis was placed on developing, in graduate course instruction, practicum, and internship experiences, a core of intervention-based competencies. These competencies are required to make accurate practical assessments of children's behavioral excesses and deficits and to design and implement scientifically based, direct and indirect interventions that promote the behaviorally disordered student's academic and social functioning. To accomplish the above, the training

program also needs to ensure that school psychology students possess the expertise to teach behaviorally disturbed students social skills, self-control, and problem-solving skills. In addition, if such children are to be successfully reintegrated into regular educational settings, the school psychologist must be well versed in generalization techniques.

The viability of school psychology as a profession will ultimately rest not on legislation, which to a large degree currently supports school psychologists, but on the ability of individual school psychologists to employ scientifically based interventions that positively promote children's academic and social development. Obviously, the most salient, frustrating, and difficult classroom problem facing teachers is the challenge of behavior disordered students. To teach psychology students to effectively deal with difficult behaviorally disordered students should be an essential component of graduate training programs. This expertise is effective not only with behaviorally disordered children, but also with several handicapping conditions, across age, and across educational and home environments.

ACKNOWLEDGMENT

Part of this project was supported by the U.S. Office of Education, Personnel Preparation Grants for Related Services Grant # G0008730047, Project #029FH70066, Training School Psychologists to be Intervention Experts.

REFERENCES

Achenbach, T. M., & Edelbrock, C. S. (1981). Behavioral problems and competencies reported by parents of normal and disturbed children ages 4 through 16. *Monograph of the Society for Research and Development, 46* (Serial No. 188).

Achenbach, T. M., & Edelbrock, C. S. (1983). *Manual for the Child Behavior Checklist and Revised Child Behavior Profile.* Burlington: University of Vermont, Department of Psychiatry.

American Psychological Association. (1986). *Accreditation handbook.* Washington, DC: American Psychological Association.

Anastasi, A. (1982). *Psychological testing* (5th ed.). New York: Macmillan.

Anesko, K. M., & O'Leary, K. D. (1982). The effectiveness of brief parent training for the management of children's homework problems. *Child and Family Behavior Therapy, 4,* 113-127.

Ayllon, T., Kuhlman, C., & Warzak, W. J. (1983). Programming resource room generalization using lucky charms. *Child and Family Therapy, 4,* 61-67.

Bandura, A. (1973). *Aggression: A social learning analysis.* Englewood Cliffs, NJ: Prentice-Hall.

Barkley, R. A. (1985). Attention deficit disorders. In P. H. Bornstein & A. E. Kazdin (Eds.), *Handbook of clinical behavior therapy with children* (pp. 158-217). Homewood, IL: Dorsey.

Beck, R. (1986). *Responding to individual differences in education: Project RIDE.* Great Falls, MT: Great Falls School District.

Becker, W. D. (1986). *Applied psychology for teachers: A behavioral cognitive approach.* Chicago: SRA.

Bergan, J. (1977). *Behavioral consultation.* Columbus, OH: Merrill.

Bergan, J., Kratochwill, T., & Luiten, J. (1980). Competency based training in behavioral consultation. *Journal of School Psychology, 18,* 91-97.

Brown, L. J., Black, D. D., & Down, J. C. (1984). *School Social Skills Rating Scale.* East Aurora, NY: Slosson Educational Publications.

Carnine, D. (1979). *Direct instruction reading.* Columbus, OH: Merrill.

Carroll, J. L., & Elliott, S. N. (1984). Social competence and social skills: Development, assessment, and intervention. *School Psychology Review, 13,* 265.

Cronbach, L. J. (1960). *Essentials of psychological testing.* New York: Harper & Row.

Coulter, W. A., & Morrow, H. W. (Eds.). (1978). *Adaptive behavior concepts and measurements.* New York: Grune and Stratton.

Curtis, M. J., & Zins, J. E. (Eds.). (1981). *The theory and practice of school consultation.* Springfield, IL: Thomas.

Deno, S. L. (1985). Curriculum-based assessment: The emerging alternative. *Exceptional Children, 52,* 219-232.

Dishion, T. J., Loeber, R., Stouthamer-Loeber, M., & Patterson, G. R. (1984). Skills deficits and male adolescent delinquency. *Journal of Abnormal Child Psychology, 12,* 37-54.

Edwards, R. (1987). Implementing the scientist-practitioner model: The school psychologist as data-based problem solver. *Professional School Psychology, 2,* 155-161.

Ehly, S. (1986). *Peer tutoring: A guide for school psychologists.* Washington, DC: National Association of School Psychologists.

Engelmann, S., & Carnine, D. (1980). *Theory of instruction: Principles and applications.* New York: Irvington.

Engin, A. W., & Johnson, R. (1983). School psychology training and practice: The NADP perspective. In T. R. Kratochwill (Ed.), *Advances in school psychology* (Vol. 3, pp. 21-44). Hillsdale, NJ: Erlbaum.

Epps, S., Thomas, B. J., & Lane, M. P. (1985). *Procedures for incorporating generalization and maintenance programming into interventions for special education.* Des Moines: Iowa Department of Public Instruction.

Forehand, R. (1977). Child compliance to parental requests: Behavior analysis and treatment. In H. Hersen, R. M. Eisler, & P. M. Miller (Eds.), *Progress in behavior modification* (Vol. 5, pp. 111-145). New York: Academic.

Forehand, R., & McMahon, R. J. (1981). *Helping the noncompliant child: A clinician's guide to parent training.* New York: Guilford.

Fuchs, L. S., & Fuchs, D. (1986). Linking assessment to instructional interventions: An overview. *School Psychology Review, 15,* 318-323.

Gang, D., & Poche, C. E. (1982). An effective program to train parents as reading tutors for their children. *Education and Treatment of Children, 5,* 211-232.

Gelfand, D. M., Jenson, W. R., & Drew, C. (1988). *Understanding childhood behavior disorders.* New York: Holt, Rinehart, and Winston.

Gettinger, M. (1988). Methods of proactive classroom management. *School Psychology Review, 17,* 227-242.

Gettelman-Klein, R. (1978). Validity of projective tests for the psychodiagnosis of children. In R. L. Spitzer & D. F. Klein (Eds.), *Critical issues in psychiatric diagnosis* (pp. 413-438). New York: Raven.

Gittelman-Klein, R. (1980). The role of tests for differential diagnosis in child psychiatry. *Journal of the American Academy of Child Psychiatry, 19,* 413-438.

Goldstein, A. P., & Glick, B. (1987). *Aggression replacement training: A comprehenisve intervention for aggressive youth.* Champaign, IL: Research Press.

Goldstein, A. P., Glick, B., Reiner, S., Zimmerman, D., & Coultry, T. M. (1987). *Aggression replacement training: A comprehensive intervention for aggressive youth.* Champaign, IL: Research Press.

Good, R. H., & Salvia, J. (1988). Curriculum bias in published, norm referenced reading tests: Demonstrable effects. *School Psychology Review, 17,* 51-50.

Greenwood, C. R., Carta, J. J., & Hall, R. V. (1988). The use of peer tutoring strategies in classroom management and educational instruction. *School Psychology Review, 17,* 258-275.

Greenwood, C. R., Guild, J. J., & Hops, H. (1977). *Programming for academic survival skills: PASS.* Eugene, OR: University of Oregon, Center at Oregon for Research in the Behavioral Education of the Handicapped.

Gresham, F. M. (1983). Social validity in the assessment of children's social skills: Establishing standards for competency. *Journal of Psychoeducational Assessment, 1,* 199-207.

Gresham, F. M. (1985a). Behavior disordered assessment: Conceptual, definitional, and practical considerations. *School Psychology Review, 14,* 495-509.

Gresham, F. M. (1985b). Best practices in social skills training. In A. Thomas & J. Grimes (Eds.), *Best practices in school psychology* (pp. 181-192). Kent, OH: National Association of School Psychologists.

Gresham, F. M., & Elliott, S. N. (1989). *Social Skills Rating Scales.* Circle Pines, MN: American Guidance Service.

Gresham, F. M., & Kendell, G. K. (1987). School consultation research: Methodological critique and future research directions. *School Psychology Review, 16,* 306-316.

Gresham, F. M., & Reschly, D. J. (1988). Issues in the conceptualization, classification, and assessment of social skills in the mildly handicapped. In T. R. Kratochwill (Ed.), *Advances in school psychology* (Vol. 6, pp. 203-247). Hillsdale, NJ: Erlbaum.

Gutkin, T., & Curtis, M. (1982). School based consultation: Theory and techniques. In C. R. Reynolds & T. B. Gutkin (Eds.), *The handbook of school psychology* (pp. 796-828). New York: Wiley.

Hartmann, D. P., Roper, B. L., & Bradford, D. C. (1979). Some relationships between behavioral and traditional assessment. *Journal of Behavioral Assessment, 1,* 3-21.

Hazel, J. S., Schumaker, J. B., Sherman, J. A., & Sheldon-Wildgen, J. (1981). *ASSET.* Champaign, IL: Research Press.

Hendersen, H. S., Jenson, W. R., & Erken, N. (1986). Focus article: Variable interval reinforcement for increasing on task behavior in classrooms. *Education and Treatment of Children, 9,* 250-263.

Hewett, F. M., & Forness, S. R. (1977). *Education of exceptional learners* (2nd ed.). Boston: Allyn & Bacon.

Hewett, F. M., & Taylor, F. D. (1980). *The emotionally disturbed child in the classroom: The orchestration of success* (2nd ed.). Boston: Allyn & Bacon.

Hobbs, N. (Ed.). (1975). *Issues in the classification of children.* San Francisco: Jossey-Bass.

Hops, H., Beickel, S. L., & Walker, H. M. (1976). *Contingencies for learning academic social skills program for acting out children: CLASS.* Eugene, OR: University of Oregon, Center at Oregon for Research in the Behavioral Education of the Handicapped.

Hops, H., Fleischman, D. H., Guild, J., Paine, S., Street, A., Walker, H. M., & Greenwood, C. R. (1978). *Program for establishing effective relationship skills (PEERS): Consultant Manual.* Eugene, OR: University of Oregon, Center for Research in the Behavioral Education of the Handicapped.

Howell, K. W. (1986). Direct assessment of academic performance. *School Psychology Review, 15,* 324–335.

Huntze, S. L. (1985). A position paper of the Council for Children With Behavior Disorders. *Behavior Disorders, 10,* 167–174.

Jackson, N. F., Jackson, D. A., & Monroe, C. (1983). *Getting along with others: Teaching social skill effectiveness to children.* Champaign, IL: Research Press.

Jenkins, R. J., & Pany, D. (1978). Standardized achievement tests: How useful for special education? *Exceptional Children, 44,* 448–453.

Jenson, W. R., Kehle, T. J., & Robinson-Awana, P. (1989). Seriously emotionally disturbed versus behavior disordered: Consideration of a label change. In J. E. Gilliam, K. S. Fad, & Boston, J. A. (Eds.), *Education of the behaviorally disordered* (pp. 1–6). Austin, TX: Behavior Learning Center.

Jenson, W. R., Reavis, K., & Rhode, G. (1987). A conceptual analysis of childhood behavior disorders: A practical educational approach. In B. K. Scott & J. E. Gilliam (Eds.), *Topics in behavioral disorders* (pp. 27–38). Austin, TX: Behavior Learning Center.

Jurkovic, G. J., & Prentice, N. M. (1977). Relation of moral and cognitive development to dimensions of juvenile delinquency. *Journal of Abnormal Psychology, 86,* 414–420.

Kauffman, J. M. (1985). *Characteristics of children's behavior disorders* (3rd ed.). Columbus, OH: Merrill.

Kazdin, A. E. (1981). Drawing valid inferences from case studies. *Journal of Consulting and Clinical Psychology, 49,* 183–192.

Kazdin, A. E. (1985). *Treatment of antisocial behavior in children and adolescents.* Homewood, IL: Dorsey.

Kazdin, A. E. (1987). Treatment of antisocial behavior in children: Current status and future directions. *Psychological Bulletin, 102,* 187–203.

Kazdin, A. E., Esveldt-Dawson, K., French, N. H., & Unis, A. S. (1987). Problem solving skills training and relationship therapy in the treatment of antisocial child behavior. *Journal of Clinical and Consulting Psychology, 55,* 76–85.

Kelley, M. L., & Carper, L. B. (1988). Home based reinforcement procedures. In J. C. Witt, S. N. Elliott, & F. M. Gresham (Eds.), *Handbook of behavior therapy in education* (pp. 419–437). New York: Plenum.

Kesler, J. (1985). *The use of direct instruction techniques with behaviorally disordered students.* Unpublished masters thesis, University of Utah, Salt Lake City.

Knoff, H. M. (1986). *Graduate training in school psychology: A national survey of professional coursework.* Washington, DC: National Association of School Psychologists.

Kratochwill, T. R. (1985). Case study research in school psychology. *School Psychology Review, 14,* 204–215.

Lentz, F. E. (1988). On-task behavior, academic performance, and classroom disruptions: Untangling the target selection problem in classroom interventions. *School Psychology Review, 17,* 243–258.

Lentz, F. E., & Shapiro, E. (1985). Behavioral school psychology: A conceptual model for the delivery of psychological services. In T. R. Kratochwill (Ed.), *Advances in school psychology* (Vol. 5, pp. 191–221). Hillsdale, NJ: Erlbaum.

Lentz, F. E., & Shapiro, E. (1986). Functional assessment of the academic environment. *School Psychology Review, 15,* 346–357.

Loeber, R., Dishion, T. J., & Patterson, G. R. (1984). Multiple gating: A multiple stage assessment procedure for identifying youths at risk for delinquency. *Journal of Research in Crime and Delinquency, 21,* 7–32.

Loeber, R., & Patterson, G. R. (1981). The aggressive child: A concomitant of a coercive system. *Advances in Family Intervention, Assessment and Theory, 2,* 47–87.

Maher, C. A., & Yoshida, R. K. (1985). Multidisciplinary teams in the schools: Current status and future possibilities. In T. R. Kratochwill (Ed.), *Advances in school psychology* (Vol. 4, pp. 13–44). Hillsdale, NJ: Erlbaum.

Maher, C. A., & Zins, J. E. (Eds.). (1987). *Psychoeducational interventions in the schools.* New York: Pergamon.

Martens, B. K., & Keller, H. R. (1987). Training school psychologists in the scientific tradition. *School Psychology Review, 16,* 329–337.

Martens, B. K., Peterson, R. L., Witt, J. C., & Cirone, S. (1986). Teacher perceptions of school-based interventions. *Exceptional Children, 53,* 213–223.

McConaughy, S. H. (1985). Using the Child Behavior Checklist and related instruments in school-based assessment of children. *School Psychology Review, 14,* 479–494.

McConnell, S., & Odom, S. L. (1986). Sociometrics: Peer-referenced measures and the assessment of social competence. In P. S. Strain, M. J. Guralnick, & H. M. Walker (Eds.), *Children's social behavior: Development, assessment, and modification* (pp. 215–286). New York: Academic.

McGinnis, E., & Goldstein, A. P. (1984). *Skillstreaming the elementary school child.* Champaign, IL: Research Press.

Morgan, D. P., & Jenson, W. R. (1988). *Teaching behaviorally disordered students: Preferred practices.* Columbus, OH: Merrill.

Morgan, D. P., Young, K. R., Likins, M., Cheney, D., & Peterson, T. J. (1983). *Teaching social skills to handicapped children and youth: Programs and materials.* Logan, UT: Utah State University, Special Education Department.

Morris, H. H., Escoll, P. J., & Wexler, R. (1956). Aggressive behavior disorders of childhood: A follow-up study. *American Journal of Psychiatry, 112,* 991–997.

National Association of School Psychologists. (1984). *Directory of school psychology training programs.* Washington, DC: National Association of School Psychologists.

National Association of School Psychologists. (1986a). *Standards: Training programs, field placements programs, credentialing standards.* Washington, DC: National Association of School Psychologists.

National Association of School Psychologists. (1986b). *Intervention assistance teams: A model for building level instructional problem solving.* Washington, DC: National Association of School Psychologists.

National School Psychology Inservice Training Network. (1984). *School psychology: A blueprint for training and practice.* Minneapolis, MN: National School Psychology Inservice Training Network.

Nicholsen, F. (1989). *Evaluation of a three state multiple gate standardized procedure for the screening and identification of behavior disordered elementary school students.* Unpublished doctoral dissertation, University of Utah, Salt Lake City.

Olweus, D. (1979). Stability of aggressive reaction patterns in males: A review. *Psychological Bulletin, 86,* 852–875.

Paine, S. C., Radicchi, J. A., rosellini, L. C., Deutchman, L., & Darch, C. B. (1983). *Structuring your classroom for academic success.* Champaign, IL: Research Press.

Patterson, G. R. (1974). Interventions for boys with conduct problems. Multiple settings, treatments, and criteria. *Journal of Clinical and Consulting Psychology, 42,* 471–481.

Patterson, G. R. (1976). The aggressive child: Victim and architect of a coercive system. In E. J. Mash, L. A. Hamerlynck, & L. C. Handy (Eds.), *Behavior modification and families* (pp. 267–316). New York: Brunner/Mazel.

Patterson, G. R. (1982). *Coercive family processes.* Eugene, OR: Castilia.

Piersel, W. C., & Gutkin, T. B. (1983). Resistance to school-based consultation: A behavioral analysis of the problem. *Psychology in the Schools, 20,* 311–326.

Pryzwansky, W. B. (1982). School psychology training and practice: The APA perspective. In T. R. Kratochwill (Ed.), *Advances in school psychology* (Vol. 2, pp. 19–39). Hillsdale, NJ: Erlbaum.

Pryzwansky, W. B. (1983). School based teams: An untapped resource for consultation and technical assistance. *School Psychology Review, 12,* 174–179.

Pryzwansky, W. (1986). Indirect service delivery: Consideration for future research in consultation. *School Psychology Review, 15,* 479–488.

Raimy, V. C. (Ed.). (1950). *Training in clinical psychology: Boulder Conference.* New York: Prentice-Hall.

Rathjen, D. P. (1984). Social skills training for children: Innovations and consumer guidelines. *School Psychology Review, 13,* 302–310.

Reimers, T. J., Wacker, D. P., & Koeppl, G. (1987). Acceptability of behavioral interventions: A review of the literature. *School Psychology Review, 6,* 212–227.

Reschly, D. J. (1988). Special education reform: School psychology revolution. *School Psychology Review, 17,* 459–475.

Reschly, D. J., Wang, M. C., & Walberg, H. J. (1987). The necessary restructuring of special education and regular education. *Exceptional Children, 53,* 391–398.

Robins, L. N. (1974). *Deviant children grown up.* Huntington, NY: Krieger.

Robins, L. N. (1979). Follow-up studies. H. C. Quay & J. S. Werry (Eds.), *Psychopathological disorders of childhood* (3rd ed., pp. 483–513). New York: Wiley.

Rhode, G., Morgan, D. P., & Young, K. R. (1983). Generalization and maintenance of treatment gains of behaviorally handicapped students from resource rooms to regular classrooms using self-evaluation procedures. *Journal of Applied Behavior Analysis, 16,* 171–188.

Rosenfield, S. A. (1987). *Instructional consultation.* Hillsdale, NJ: Erlbaum.

Russo, D. C., Cataldo, M. F., & Cushing, P. J. (1981). Compliance training and behavioral covariation in the treatment of multiple problems. *Journal of Applied Behavior Analysis, 14,* 209-222.

Rutter, M., & Yule, W. (1973). Specific reading retardation. In L. Mann & D. Sabatino (Eds.), *The first review of special education* (pp. 127-145). Philadelphia: Buttonwood Farms.

Shapiro, E. S. (1987). Intervention research methodology in school psychology. *School Psychology Review, 16,* 290-305.

Shapiro, E. S. (1988). Preventing academic failure. *School Psychology Review, 17,* 601-613.

Shapiro, E. S., & Lentz, F. E. (1985). Assessing academic behavior: A behavioral approach. *School Psychology Review, 14,* 325-338.

Shapiro, E. S., & Lentz, F. E. (1986). Behavioral assessment of academic skills. In T. R. Kratochwill (Ed.), *Advances in school psychology* (Vol. 5, pp. 87-140). Hillsdale, NJ: Erlbaum.

Shinn, M. R., Tindal, G. A., & Stein, S. (1988). Curriculum-based measurement and the identification of mildly handicapped students: A research review. *Professional School Psychology, 3,* 69-86.

Skinner, B. F. (1984). The shame of American education. *American Psychologist, 39,* 947-954.

Slavin, E. E. (1983). *Cooperative learning.* New York: Longman.

SRA Technologies. (1985). *Special study on terminology: Comprehensive review and evaluation report* (Contract No. 300-84-0144, Report No. MV-85-01). Mountain View, CA: Author.

Stewart, K. J. (1986). Innovative practice and indirect service delivery: Realities and idealities. *School Psychology Review, 15,* 466-478.

Thomas, A., & Grimes, J. (Eds.). (1985). *Best practices in school psychology.* Kent, OH: National Association of School Psychologists.

Thomas, A., & Grimes, J. (Eds.). (1987). *Children's needs: Psychological perspectives.* Washington, DC: National Association of School Psychologists.

Tucker, J. A. (1985). Curriculum-based assessment: An introduction. *Exceptional Children, 52,* 199-204.

Van Houten, R. (1980). *Learning through feedback: A systematic approach for improving academic performance.* New York: Human Sciences Press.

Wahler, R. G., Berland, R. M., & Coe, T. D. (1979). Generalization processes in child behavior change. In B. Lahey & A. E. Kazdin (Eds.), *Advances in clinical child psychology* (Vol. 2, pp. 36-69). New York: Plenum.

Walker, H. M. (1983). *Walker Problem Behavior Identification Checklist-Revised.* Los Angeles: Western Psychological Services.

Walker, H. M., & Buckley, N. K. (1974). *Token reinforcement techniques.* Eugene, OR: E-B Press.

Walker, H. M., & Fabre, T. R. (1987). Assessment of behavior disorders in the school setting: Issues, problems, and strategies revisited. In N. G. Haring (Ed.), *Assessing and managing behavior disabilities.* Seattle, WA: University of Washington Press.

Walker, H. M., Garrett, B., Crossen, J., Hops, H., & Greenwood, C. (1978). *Reprogramming environmental contingencies for effective social skills: RECESS.* Eugene, OR: University of Oregon, Center at Oregon for Research in the Behavioral Education of the Handicapped.

Walker, H. M., Hops, H., & Greenwood, C. R. (1981). RECESS: Research and development of a behavior management package for remediating social aggression in the school setting. In P. Strain (Ed.), *The utilization of classroom peers as behavior change agents* (pp. 261-303). New York: Plenum.

Walker, H. M., & McConnell, S. R. (1988). *The Walker-McConnell Scale of Social Competence and School Adjustment: A social skills rating scale for teachers.* Austin, TX: Pro-Ed.

Walker, H. M., McConnell, S., Holmes, D., Todis, B., Walker, J., & Golden, N. (1983). *ACCEPTS: The Walker social skills curriculum.* Austin, TX: Pro-Ed.

Walker, H. M., O'Neill, R., Shinn, M., Ramsey, B., Reid, J., & Capaldi, D. (1986). *Longitudinal assessment and long term follow-up of antisocial fourth grade boys: Rationale, methodology, measures, and results.* Eugene, OR: University of Oregon, Social Learning Center.

Walker, H. M., & Rankin, R. (1983). Assessing the behavioral expectations and demands of less restrictive settings. *School Psychology Review, 12,* 274-284.

Walker, H. M., Reavis, K., Rhode, G., & Jenson, W. R. (1985). A conceptual model for delivery of behavioral services to behavior disordered children in educational settings. In P. Bornstein & A. Kazdin (Eds.), *Handbook of clinical behavior therapy with children* (pp. 700-741). Homewood, IL: Dorsey.

Walker, H. M., Severson, H., & Haring, N. (1987). *Standardized screening and identification of behavior disordered pupils in the elementary age range: Rationale, procedures, and guidelines* (pp. 198-243). Eugene, OR: University of Oregon.